GALE
ENCYCLOPEDIA
OF AMERICAN
LAW

3RD EDITION

GALE ENCYCLOPEDIA OF AMERICAN LAW

3RD EDITION

VOLUME 5

FRI TO I

 GALE
CENGAGE Learning™

Detroit • New York • San Francisco • New Haven, Conn • Waterville, Maine • London

GALE
CENGAGE Learning™

Gale Encyclopedia of American Law, 3rd Edition

Project Editor: Donna Batten

Editorial: Laurie J. Fundukian, Kristin Key, Jacqueline Longe, Kristin Mallegg, Jennifer Mossman, Brigham Narins, Andrew Specht, Jeffrey Wilson

Product Manager: Stephen Wasserstein

Rights Acquisition and Management: Dean Dauphinais, Leitha Ethridge-Sims, Barbara McNeil, Kelly Quin, Susan Rudolph

Editorial and Production Technology Support Services: Charles Beaumont, Luann Brennan, Grant Eldridge

Composition: Evi Abou-El-Seoud, Mary Beth Trimper

Product Design: Pamela A.E. Galbreath

Imaging: John Watkins

© 2011 Gale, Cengage Learning

For product information and technology assistance, contact us at
Gale Customer Support, 1-800-877-4253.
For permission to use material from this text or product,
submit all requests online at **www.cengage.com/permissions.**
Further permissions questions can be emailed to
permissionrequest@cengage.com

While every effort has been made to ensure the reliability of the information presented in this publication, Gale, a part of Cengage Learning, does not guarantee the accuracy of the data contained herein. Gale accepts no payment for listing; and inclusion in the publication of any organization, agency, institution, publication, service, or individual does not imply endorsement of the editors or publisher. Errors brought to the attention of the publisher and verified to the satisfaction of the publisher will be corrected in future editions.

EDITORIAL DATA PRIVACY POLICY: Does this product contain information about you as an individual? If so, for more information about our editorial data privacy policies, please see our Privacy Statement at www.gale.cengage.com.

LIBRARY OF CONGRESS CATALOGING-IN-PUBLICATION DATA

Gale encyclopedia of American law. -- 3rd ed.
    p. ; cm.
    Rev. ed. of: West's encyclopedia of American law. 2nd ed. 2005.
    Includes bibliographical references and index.
    ISBN-13: 978-1-4144-3684-5 (set)
    ISBN-10: 1-4144-3684-X (set)
    ISBN-13: 978-1-4144-3685-2 (vol. 1)
    ISBN-10: 1-4144-3685-8 (vol. 1) [etc.]
    1. Law--United States--Encyclopedias. 2. Law--United States--Popular works.
I. West's encyclopedia of American law. II. Title: Encyclopedia of American law.

KF154.W47 2011
349.7303--dc22   2010045527

Gale
27500 Drake Rd.
Farmington Hills, MI, 48331-3535

ISBN-13: 978-1-4144-3684-5   ISBN-10: 1-4144-3684-X   (14 vol. set)
ISBN-13: 978-1-4144-3685-2   ISBN-10: 1-4144-3685-8   (vol. 1)
ISBN-13: 978-1-4144-3686-9   ISBN-10: 1-4144-3686-6   (vol. 2)
ISBN-13: 978-1-4144-3687-6   ISBN-10: 1-4144-3687-4   (vol. 3)
ISBN-13: 978-1-4144-3688-3   ISBN-10: 1-4144-3688-2   (vol. 4)
ISBN-13: 978-1-4144-3689-0   ISBN-10: 1-4144-3689-0   (vol. 5)
ISBN-13: 978-1-4144-3690-6   ISBN-10: 1-4144-3690-4   (vol. 6)
ISBN-13: 978-1-4144-3691-3   ISBN-10: 1-4144-3691-2   (vol. 7)
ISBN-13: 978-1-4144-3692-0   ISBN-10: 1-4144-3692-0   (vol. 8)
ISBN-13: 978-1-4144-3693-7   ISBN-10: 1-4144-3693-9   (vol. 9)
ISBN-13: 978-1-4144-3694-4   ISBN-10: 1-4144-3694-7   (vol. 10)
ISBN-13: 978-1-4144-3695-1   ISBN-10: 1-4144-3695-5   (vol. 11)
ISBN-13: 978-1-4144-3696-8   ISBN-10: 1-4144-3696-3   (vol. 12)
ISBN-13: 978-1-4144-3697-5   ISBN-10: 1-4144-3697-1   (vol. 13)
ISBN-13: 978-1-4144-3698-2   ISBN-10: 1-4144-3698-X   (vol. 14)

This title is also available as an e-book.
ISBN-13: 978-1-4144-4302-7   ISBN-10: 1-4144-4302-1
Contact your Gale, Cengage Learning, sales representative for ordering information.

Printed in Mexico
1 2 3 4 5 6 7 15 14 13 12 11

DEDICATION

Gale Encyclopedia of American Law (GEAL) is dedicated to librarians and library patrons throughout the United States and beyond. Your interest in the American legal system helps to expand and fuel the framework of our Republic.

—ɯ—

CONTENTS

The U.S. legal system is admired around the world for the freedoms it allows the individual and the fairness with which it attempts to treat all persons. On the surface, it may seem simple, yet those who have delved into it know that this system of federal and state constitutions, statutes, regulations, and common-law decisions is elaborate and complex. It derives from the English common law, but includes principles older than England, along with some principles from other lands. The U.S. legal system, like many others, has a language all its own, but too often it is an unfamiliar language: many concepts are still phrased in Latin. The third edition of *Gale Encyclopedia of American Law (GEAL)*, formerly *West's Encyclopedia of American Law*, explains legal terms and concepts in everyday language. It covers a wide variety of persons, entities, and events that have shaped the U.S. legal system and influenced public perceptions of it.

MAIN FEATURES OF THIS SET

Entries

This *Encyclopedia* contains nearly 5,000 entries devoted to terms, concepts, events, movements, cases, and persons significant to U.S. law. Entries on legal terms contain a definition of the term, followed by explanatory text if necessary. Entries are arranged alphabetically in standard encyclopedia format for ease of use. A wide variety of additional features provide interesting background and supplemental information.

Definitions

Every entry on a legal term is followed by a definition, which appears at the beginning of

the entry and is italicized. The Dictionary of Legal Terms volume is a glossary containing all the definitions from *GEAL*.

Further Readings

To facilitate further research, a list of Further Readings is included at the end of a majority of the main entries.

Cross-References

GEAL provides two types of cross-references, within and following entries. Within the entries, terms are set in small capital letters—for example, LIEN—to indicate that they have their own entry in the *Encyclopedia*. At the end of the entries, related entries the reader may wish to explore are listed alphabetically by title.

Blind cross-reference entries are also included to direct the user to other entries throughout the set.

In Focus Essays

In Focus essays accompany related entries and provide additional facts, details, and arguments on particularly interesting, important, or controversial issues raised by those entries. The subjects covered include hotly contested issues, such as abortion, capital punishment, and gay rights; detailed processes, such as the Food and Drug Administration's approval process for new drugs; and important historical or social issues, such as debates over the formation of the U.S. Constitution.

Sidebars

Sidebars provide brief highlights of some interesting facet of accompanying entries. They complement regular entries and In Focus essays by adding informative details. Sidebar topics include trying juveniles as adults, the Tea Party Movement, and the branches of the U.S. armed services. Sidebars appear at the top of a text page and are set in a box.

Biographies

GEAL profiles a wide variety of interesting and influential people—including lawyers, judges, government and civic leaders, and historical and modern figures—who have played a part in creating or shaping U.S. law. Each biography includes a timeline, which shows important moments in the subject's life as well as important historical events of the period. Biographies appear alphabetically by the subject's last name.

ADDITIONAL FEATURES OF THIS SET

Enhancements Throughout *GEAL*, readers will find a broad array of photographs, charts, graphs, manuscripts, legal forms, and other visual aids enhancing the ideas presented in the text.

Appendixes

Four appendix volumes are included with *GEAL*, containing hundreds of pages of documents, laws, manuscripts, and forms fundamental to and characteristic of U.S. law.

Milestone Cases in the Law

Special Appendix volumes entitled Milestones in the Law, allows readers to take a close look at landmark cases in U.S. law. Readers can explore the reasoning of the judges and the arguments of the attorneys that produced major decisions on important legal and social issues. Included in each Milestone are the opinions of the lower courts; the briefs presented by the parties to the U.S. Supreme Court; and the decision of the Supreme Court, including the majority opinion and all concurring and dissenting opinions for each case.

Primary Documents

There is also an Appendix volume containing more than 60 primary documents, such as the English Bill of Rights, Martin Luther King Jr.'s Letter from Birmingham Jail, and several presidential speeches.

Citations

Wherever possible, *GEAL* entries include citations for cases and statutes mentioned in the text. These allow readers wishing to do additional research to find the opinions and statutes cited. Two sample citations, with explanations of common citation terms, can be seen below and opposite.

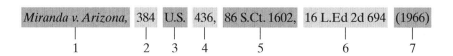

1. *Case title.* The title of the case is set in italics and indicates the names of the parties. The suit in this sample citation was between Ernesto A. Miranda and the state of Arizona.

2. *Reporter volume number.* The number preceding the reporter name indicates the reporter volume containing the case. (The volume number appears on the spine of the reporter, along with the reporter name).

3. *Reporter name.* The reporter name is abbreviated. The suit in the sample citation is from the reporter, or series of books, called *U.S. Reports*, which contains cases from the U.S. Supreme Court. (Numerous reporters publish cases from the federal and state courts.)

4. *Reporter page.* The number following the reporter name indicates the reporter page on which the case begins.

5. *Additional reporter page.* Many cases may be found in more than one reporter. The suit in the sample citation also appears in volume 86 of the *Supreme Court Reporter*, beginning on page 1602.

6. *Additional reporter citation.* The suit in the sample citation is also reported in volume 16 of the *Lawyer's Edition*, second series, beginning on page 694.

7. *Year of decision.* The year the court issued its decision in the case appears in parentheses at the end of the citation.

Brady Handgun Violence Prevention Act, Pub. L. No. 103–159, 107 Stat. 1536 (18 U.S.C.A. §§ 921–925A)

| | | | | | | | |
|1| |2|3|4|5|6|7|8|

1. *Statute title.*

2. *Public law number.* In the sample citation, the number 103 indicates this law was passed by the 103d Congress, and the number 159 indicates it was the 159th law passed by that Congress.

3. *Reporter volume number.* The number preceding the reporter abbreviation indicates the reporter volume containing the statute.

4. *Reporter name.* The reporter name is abbreviated. The statute in the sample citation is from *Statutes at Large.*

5. *Reporter page.* The number following the reporter abbreviation indicates the reporter page on which the statute begins.

6. *Title number.* Federal laws are divided into major sections with specific titles. The number preceding a reference to the U.S. Code stands for the section called Crimes and Criminal Procedure.

7. *Additional reporter.* The statute in the sample citation may also be found in the *U.S. Code Annotated.*

8. *Section numbers.* The section numbers following a reference to the *U.S. Code Annotated* indicate where the statute appears in that reporter.

How to Use This Book

■ 1 ■   Article Title

■ 2 ■   Definition in italics with Latin translation provided

■ 3 ■   First-level subhead

■ 4 ■   Sidebar expands upon an issue addressed briefly in the article

■ 5 ■   Quotation from subject of biography

■ 6 ■   Biography of contributor to American law

■ 7 ■   Timeline for subject of biography, including general historical events and life events

■ 8 ■   In Focus article examines a controversial or complex aspect of the article topic

■ 9 ■   Further readings to facilitate research

■ 10 ■   Cross references at end of article

■ 11 ■   See reference

■ 12 ■   Full cite for case

■ 13 ■   Internal cross-reference to entry within GEAL

---

than $100,000. During the war, Catron continued to support the Union by broadly interpreting the federal government's war powers. In one case, he wrote an opinion refusing to release a prisoner if evidence showed that he was a Confederate sympathizer. After 1862, Catron also worked hard to keep order in the states forming his new circuit: Tennessee, Arkansas, Louisiana, Texas, and Kentucky. He stayed in close touch with President ABRAHAM LINCOLN and worked hard to keep the federal judiciary effective during the war.

On May 30, 1865, Catron, one of the last embodiments of Jacksonian democracy to leave the national scene, died in his adopted city of Nashville.

FURTHER READINGS

Anderson, Burnet. 1996. "John Catron." In The Supreme Court Justices Illustrated Biographies, 1789–1995, 2d ed. Claire Cushman. Washington, D.C.: Congressional Quarterly.

Gatell, Frank O. 1995. "John Catron." In The Justices of the United States Supreme Court 1789–1969: Their Lives and Major Opinions, Volumes I–V. New York: Chelsea House.

Tennessee Dept. of State. "Catron, John (1786–1865) Papers 1822–[1833–1862]–1918." Nashville, TN: Tennessee State Library and Archives.

CROSS REFERENCES

Judicial Review; Native American Rights.

CAUSA MORTIS

[Latin, In contemplation of approaching death.] *A phrase sometimes used in reference to a deathbed gift, or a gift causa mortis, since the giving of the gift is made in expectation of approaching death. A gift causa mortis is distinguishable from a gift inter vivos, which is a gift made during the donor's (the giver's) lifetime.*

The donor of the gift of PERSONAL PROPERTY must expect to die imminently from a particular ailment or event. This has important consequences in terms of the donor's ability to revoke the gift.

For example, an elderly man is suffering from pneumonia and believes he is going to die as a result of the sickness. He tells his grandson that if he dies, he will give the grandson his pocket watch. If the man recovers and wants to retain his watch, he will be able to do so, because a gift *causa mortis* is effective only if made in CONTEMPLATION OF DEATH due to a

known condition and the donor actually dies as a result of that condition.

A gift *causa mortis* is taxed under federal estate tax law in the same way as a gift bequeathed by a will.

CAUSE

A suit, litigation, or action. Any question, civil or criminal, litigated or contested before a court of justice.

Cause and Causality in American Law

If an individual is fired from a job at the bank for embezzlement, he or she is fired *for cause*—as distinguished from decisions or actions considered to be arbitrary or capricious.

In CRIMINAL PROCEDURE, PROBABLE CAUSE is the reasonable basis for the belief that someone has committed a particular crime. Before someone may be arrested or searched by a police officer without a warrant, probable cause must exist. This requirement is imposed to protect people from unreasonable or unrestricted invasions or intrusions by the government.

In the law of torts, the concept of *causality* is essential to a person's ability to successfully bring an action for injury against another person. The injured party must establish that the other person brought about the alleged harm. A defendant's liability is contingent upon the connection between his or her conduct and the injury to the PLAINTIFF. The plaintiff must prove that his or her injury would not have occurred but for the defendant's NEGLIGENCE or intentional conduct.

Actual, Concurrent, and Intervening Cause

The *actual cause* is the event directly responsible for an injury. If one person shoves another, thereby knocking the other person out an open window and he or she breaks a leg as a result of the fall, the shove is the actual cause of the injury. The IMMEDIATE CAUSE of the injury in this case would be the fall, since it is the cause that came right before the injury, with no intermediate causes. In some cases the actual cause and the immediate cause of an injury may be the same.

Concurrent causes are events occurring simultaneously to produce a given result. They are contemporaneous, but either event alone would bring about the effect that occurs. If one

---

The First Payments of Social Security

After the enactment of the Social Security Act of 1935 (42 U.S.C.A. § 301 et seq.) and the creation of the Social Security Administration (SSA), the federal government had a short time to establish the program before beginning to pay benefits. Monthly benefits were to begin in 1940. The period from 1937 to 1940 was to be used both to build up the trust funds and to provide a minimum period for participation for persons to qualify for monthly benefits.

From 1937 until 1940, however, Social Security paid benefits in the form of a single, lump-sum payment. The purpose of these one-time payments was to provide some compensation to people who contributed to the program but would not participate long enough to be vested for monthly benefits.

The first applicant for a lump-sum benefit was Ernest Ackerman, a Cleveland motorman who retired one day after the Social Security Program began. During his one day of participation in the program, five cents was withheld from Ackerman's pay for Social Security, and upon retiring, he received a lump-sum payment of seventeen cents.

Payments of monthly benefits began in January 1940. On January 31, 1940, the first monthly retirement check was issued to Ida May Fuller of Ludlow, Vermont, in the amount of $22.54. Fuller died in January 1975 at the age of one hundred. During her thirty-five years as a beneficiary, she received more than $20,000 in benefits.

pay into the Social Security system should be allowed to pay the funds into personal retirement accounts. Under this proposal, employees would have the option of converting these funds into other investments, such as stock. Bush did not push the issue hard during his first term, but in his second term he attempted to move it forward. However, the idea of privatizing Social Security went nowhere, and the precipitous decline in STOCK MARKET beginning in the fall of 2007 provided fresh ammunition to the critics of the idea.

In 2009, the Social Security Administration predicted that the OASDI tax income would fall short of outlays by 2016, and the OASDI trust fund was predicted to be exhausted by 2037 if no adjustments were made to the program. The total combined OASDI assets in 2008 amounted to $2.4 trillion.

FURTHER READINGS

Béland, Daniel. 2007. Social Security: History and Politics from the New Deal to the Privatization Debate. Lawrence, Kans.: Univ. Press of Kansas.

Mitchell, Daniel J. B. 2000. Pensions, Politics, and the Elderly: Historic Social Movements and Their Lessons for Our Aging Society. Armonk, N.Y.: M.E. Sharpe.

Sass, Steven A. 1997. The Promise of Private Pensions: The First Hundred Years. Cambridge, Mass: Harvard Univ. Press.

Schieber, Sylvester J. 1999. The Real Deal: The History and Future of Social Security. New Haven, Conn.: Yale Univ. Press.

CROSS REFERENCES

Disability Discrimination; Elder Law; Health Care Law; Old Age, Survivors and Disability Insurance; Senior Citizens.

SOCIAL SECURITY ACT OF 1935

The Social Security Act (42 U.S.C.A. § 301 et seq.), designed to assist in the maintenance of the financial well-being of eligible persons, was enacted in 1935 as part of President FRANKLIN D. ROOSEVELT's NEW DEAL.

In the United States, SOCIAL SECURITY did not exist on the federal level until the passage of the Social Security Act of 1935. This statute provided for a federal program of old-age retirement benefits and a joint federal-state venture of UNEMPLOYMENT COMPENSATION. In addition, it dispensed federal funds to aid the development at the state level of such programs as vocational rehabilitation, public health services, and child welfare services, along with

240 ALITO, SAMUEL ANTHONY, JR.

5

IF SOMEONE HAS BEEN THE SUBJECT OF ILLEGAL LAW ENFORCEMENT ACTIVITIES, THEY SHOULD HAVE A DAY IN COURT. AND THAT'S WHAT THE COURTS ARE THERE FOR, TO PROTECT THE RIGHTS OF INDIVIDUALS AGAINST THE GOVERNMENT OR ANYONE ELSE WHO VIOLATES THEIR RIGHTS.

—SAMUEL ALITO

Additionally, critics assailed the absence of alimony provisions in Texas family law as being unduly harsh. In a large number of divorces where neither spouse had acquired substantial assets during the marriage, Texas courts were powerless to compensate spouses who had sacrificed educational and career opportunities, since in such situations there were essentially no assets to divide in the first place. As a result, spouses who successfully pursued educational or career opportunities at the expense of their partner were allowed to walk away from the marriage "scot-free."

Despite the late twentieth-century universality of alimony laws in the all 50 states, lawmakers in some jurisdictions continued to propose legislation that would abolish it. In 1999 several Iowa legislators proposed a bill to abolish alimony, arguing that alimony laws provide incentive to get divorced. The bill never passed.

Because alimony is an award for support and maintenance that one spouse may be compelled to pay to another after dissolution of the marriage, it would seem to follow that no alimony could be awarded to a spouse following an annulment, which treats the marriage relationship as if it had never existed. In fact, alimony is not awarded to spouses under any conditions following the annulment of a marriage in most jurisdictions. However, in some jurisdictions the enforcement of a flat prohibition of alimony awards to spouses whose marriages have been annulled has sometimes been found to impose unnecessary hardship on a spouse, usually the wife, especially where the parties have lived together for a considerable period of time. Consequently, judicial and legislative exceptions have been created to the basic rule of treating an annulled marriage as if it had never existed, for the purposes of determining whether an alimony award is appropriate. Under these exceptions, temporary as well as permanent alimony have been awarded.

FURTHER READINGS

"Alimony Strategies" 2003. *Family Advocate* 25, vol. 4 (spring).
American Law Institute. 2002. *Principles of the Law of Family Dissolution: Analysis and Recommendations.* Newark, NJ: Bender.
Sheldon, John C., and Nancy Diesel Mills. 1993. *In Search of a Theory of Alimony.* Orono, ME.: Univ. of Maine School of Law 45.
Storey, Brenda L. 2003. "Surveying the Alimony Landscape: Origin, Evolution and Extinction." *Family Advocate* 25 (spring).

CROSS REFERENCES

A Mensa Et Thoro; Child Support; Damages; Divorce; Family Law; Husband and Wife; Marriage; No Fault Divorce; Sex Discrimination.

◆ **ALITO, SAMUEL ANTHONY, JR.** 6

Samuel Alito is a conservative justice appointed to the U.S. Supreme Court in 2006. Upon his confirmation, he became the 110th associate justice in the Court's history and only the second Italian-American. He replaced Sandra Day O'Connor on the Court.

Alito was born on April 1, 1950, in Trenton, New Jersey. His father emigrated from Italy as a boy and became a high school teacher. His father later changed careers in the 1950s to work as the research director of a nonpartisan agency that analyzed legislation for state legislators. Alito's mother was an elementary school principal. Alito excelled as a student, deciding on a legal career after discovering a special affinity for in-depth research and finely honed argument on the high school debate team. He graduated as valedictorian of his class and headed off to Princeton University in 1968.

After receiving his undergraduate degree in 1972, Alito pursued a law degree at Yale Law School, where he graduated in 1975. At Yale he served as an editor of the *Yale Law Journal* and quickly became known as a traditionalist with a quick intellect. It was a reputation that he was to carry with him throughout his working life. In 1976 Alito was hired as a law clerk by Third Circuit Court of Appeals Judge Leonard I. Garth (who eventually became a colleague when Alito was named to the same bench). After clerking for Garth, Alito spent 1977 to 1981 as an assistant U.S. attorney in New Jersey. He then went to Washington, D.C., to work for the Department of Justice, first as an assistant to the solicitor general from 1981 to 1985 and then as a deputy assistant attorney general from 1985 to 1987. In the former position, he argued several cases before the U.S. Supreme Court. By 1987 Alito returned to New Jersey as U.S. attorney, in which role he handled cases from organized crime to child pornography.

Alito took a seat on the U.S. Court of Appeals for the Third Circuit in 1990. While his time there undisputedly marked him as a solidly conservative jurist, it also showed a man unwilling to express his political views openly. He was widely respected by Democrats and

GALE ENCYCLOPEDIA OF AMERICAN LAW, 3RD EDITION

ALITO, SAMUEL ANTHONY, JR. 241

Republicans alike, and few saw him as either rigid or an ideologue. Still, one of Alito's controversial opinions was his lone dissent in a 1991 case that struck down a Pennsylvania law requiring married women seeking abortions to inform their husbands *Planned Parenthood of Southeastern Pennsylvania v. Casey*, 947 F. 2d 682). He also concluded in a 1998 opinion that a holiday display that included secular symbols along with religious ones did not violate the First Amendment. By contrast, Alito voted with the majority to find a ban on late-term abortions unconstitutional where there is no exception considering the health of the mother. These, and the broad array of other published opinions stemming from 15 years on the bench, were to come under intense scrutiny when Alito was nominated to replace retiring U.S. Supreme Court Justice O'Connor in October 2005.

Alito's nomination came in the wake of the withdrawal of previous nominee Harriet E. Miers, whom many believed was unqualified for the position. It also came at a time when President George W. Bush was lagging in the polls and there was increasing acrimony between parties in the Senate. The situation was further sharpened by O'Connor's pivotal role as a centrist justice on a fairly divided Court, thus making the stakes particularly high for both parties in finding a suitable replacement. In short, there was little doubt that Alito's confirmation hearings were destined to be difficult and time-consuming, with conservative and liberal agendas likely to take precedence.

Several groups, including the American Civil Liberties Union, strongly opposed Alito's nomination. According to the ACLU, Alito had

Samuel Alito.
STEVE PETTEWAY, COLLECTION OF THE SUPREME COURT OF THE UNITED STATES

displayed a "willingness to support government actions that abridge individual freedoms." In reviewing Alito's professional qualifications, though, a committee of the American Bar Association concluded that Alito was "well-qualified" to serve on the Court.

As expected, the ideological battle between the parties caused great friction and talk of filibustering the Alito nomination. Despite Democratic attempts to block a vote on the nomination by filibustering, a Senate closure motion ended debate by a 72-25 vote. The closure motion forced a vote on the nomination, and the Senate confirmed Alito by a 58-42 vote, the smallest margin since Clarence Thomas

7

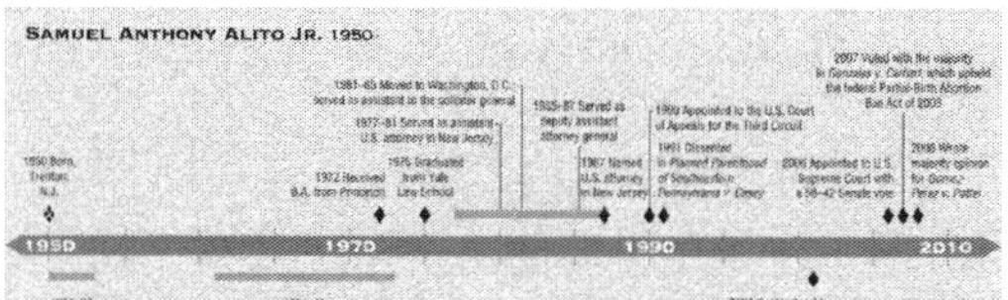

GALE ENCYCLOPEDIA OF AMERICAN LAW, 3RD EDITION

272 SOCIAL SECURITY

8

IN FOCUS

THE FUTURE OF SOCIAL SECURITY

The payment of old-age, survivors, and disability insurance (OASDI) benefits has been a cornerstone of U.S. social welfare policy since the establishment of the Social Security Administration (SSA) in 1935. At the same time, the long-term financial stability of OASDI has been a constant worry. In the early 2000s, concerns about Social Security mounted as policy makers assessed the impact of the retirement of the "Baby Boom" generation. Many younger people raised the issue of "generation equity." They express doubt that Social Security benefits will be available when they retire and anger that they will be forced to pay, through payroll taxes, for the baby boomers' retirement benefits.

Reform of the Social Security system has always been a politically charged subject. Retirees and those approaching retirement form a strong lobbying force, and they zealously protect their benefits. Employers and employees are equally vocal in their opposition to higher payroll taxes to fund OASDI. Thus, changes in Social Security required bipartisan support, which materialized in the face of an impending Social Security crisis. The 1982–1983 National Commission on Social Security Reform successfully secured from Congress the short-term financing of OASDI. As a result, Congress passed a series of laws meant to accumulate surpluses as a hedge against future burdens. The Social Security surplus is the amount by which revenue from the federal payroll tax exceeds the amount of Social Security benefits paid out.

Shortly after these new laws went into effect, Social Security began running a surplus. Surplus Social Security revenue can be used to fund other government programs and to help retire the national debt. During the favorable economic climate of the late 1990s, Congress began to use the surplus to pay down the federal debt, hoping to better position the government to meet its obligations to future retirees. Also, in 2000, the federal government generated enough revenue so that the entire Social Security surplus was available for paying off debt.

The state of Social Security became a major campaign issue in the 2000 elections, with both Republicans and Democrats attempting to appear as though they were guardians of Social Security assets. Candidates from both parties promised to create a "lockbox," meaning that the Social Security surplus would be spent entirely on debt retirement. With the advent of fiscally lean years in the early 2000s, the lockbox approach was largely disregarded by politicians who advanced other ideas about what to do with Social Security surpluses. These ideas included using the surplus to help offset decreases in revenues brought about by tax cuts and using the surplus to fund new or expanded spending initiatives.

Analysts argue that the real issue often is clouded. It is not how to spend the surplus now, but how to maintain the long-term solvency of the Social Security trust fund. Planners estimate that the income from the trust fund will exceed expenses each year until 2017. The trust fund balances will then start to decline as investments are redeemed to meet the increased expenses from a swelling retired workforce. The SSA estimates that beginning in 2041, payroll taxes would have to rise to 28 percent to cover the projected deficit.

In its 1996 report, the Social Security Administration's Advisory Council looked at various long-term financing options for OASDI. The council could not reach consensus on a specific long-term plan, but it did suggest several types of financing that represent a marked departure from previous efforts to fund Social Security. The council noted that past efforts have generally featured cutting benefits and raising tax rates on a "pay-as-you-go" basis. The council agreed that this approach must be changed and offered three ways of restoring financial solvency.

One approach, called Maintenance of Benefits (MB), calls for an increase in income taxes on OASDI benefits, a redirection of some revenue from other trust funds, and, most importantly, the adoption of a plan allowing the federal government to invest a portion of the trust fund assets directly in common stocks. Rates of returns on stocks have historically exceeded those on federal government bonds, where all Social Security funds are invested. If the returns

legislative changes. The final bill, signed into law in 1983 (Pub. L. 98-21, 97 Stat. 65), made numerous changes in the Social Security and Medicare Programs; these changes included taxing Social Security benefits, extending Social Security coverage to federal employees, and increasing the retirement age in the twenty-first century.

By the 1990s, however, concerns were again raised about the long-term financial viability of Social Security and Medicare. Various ideas and plans to ensure the financial stability of these programs were put forward. The budget committees in both the House of Representatives and the Senate established task forces to investigate proposals for Social Security reform. Other

GALE ENCYCLOPEDIA OF AMERICAN LAW, 3RD EDITION

114 NLRB V. JONES & LAUGHLIN STEEL CORP.

The Supreme Court, in a unanimous decision (Justice William H. Rehnquist recused himself because he had served in the Nixon administration), recognized for the first time the general legitimacy of executive privilege. Nevertheless, Chief Justice Warren E. Burger, writing for the Court, rejected Nixon's claim of "an absolute, unqualified Presidential privilege of immunity from judicial process under all circumstances." Burger found that [a]bsent a claim of need to protect military, diplomatic, or sensitive national security secrets," the need to protect the confidentiality of presidential communications must give way to a legitimate request by the courts for information vital to a criminal prosecution. Burger noted that the judge would review the subpoenaed tapes in private to determine what portions should be released to the prosecutors. This confidential review would prevent sensitive, but irrelevant, information from being disclosed.

Nixon obeyed the order and turned the tapes over to the district court. When relevant portions were released, they revealed that the president had been intimately involved with the attempt to cover up White House involvement in the Watergate burglary. Less than three weeks after the Court announced its decision, Nixon resigned the presidency, thereby avoiding impeachment by Congress.

9 FURTHER READINGS

Gray, L. Patrick, and Gray, Ed. 2009 *In Nixon's Wake A Year in the Crosshairs of Watergate.* New York: Holt.
Jaworski, Leon. 1976. *The Right and the Power: The Prosecution of Watergate.* New York: Reader's Digest.
Johnsen, Dawn. 1999. Executive Privilege Since *United States v. Nixon*: Issues of Motivation and Accommodation." *Minnesota Law Review* 83 (May).
Rozell, Mark J. 1999. "Executive Privilege and the Modern Presidents: In Nixon's Shadow." *Minnesota Law Review* 83 (May).

10 CROSS REFERENCES

Nixon, Richard Milhous; Watergate.

11 **NLRB**

See National Labor Relations Board.

NLRB V. JONES & LAUGHLIN STEEL CORP.

From the 1870s through the mid-1930s the U.S. Supreme Court was generally hostile to federal legislation that sought to regulate business through the use of the Constitution's Commerce Clause. A conservative judiciary believed that the free market should govern economic activities; consequently laws that attempted to regulate labor relations were overturned. The Great Depression of the 1930s led to the presidential election in 1932 of Franklin D. Roosevelt, who advocated an aggressive role for the federal government in national economic affairs. Congress consistently turned Roosevelt's legislative agenda into law yet the Supreme Court ruled these new laws unconstitutional. However, in the landmark case of *NLRB v. Jones & Laughlin Steel Corp.*, 301 U.S. 1, 57 S. Ct. 615, 81 L. Ed. 893 (1937), the Court reversed course, paving the way for New Deal legislation and a new judicial attitude toward the Commerce Clause. 12

For generations labor unions had confronted a business community that was hostile to the concept of collective bargaining. Therefore, the passage of the National Labor Relations Act (NLRA or Wagner Act) of 1935 (29 U.S.C.A. § 151 et seq.) was a dramatic recognition of workers' rights. The law gave workers the right to organize unions and to require employers to negotiate with a certified union. An elaborate administrative process was also established, headed by the National Labor Relations Board (NLRB). The NLRB was create to review complaints about alleged violations of the law and issue administrative sanctions against employers for retaliatory discharges based on union membership or organization activities. Employers vowed to test the constitutionality of the NLRA and the actions of the NLRB.

In July 1935, 13 employees of the Jones and Laughlin Steel Corporation plant in Aliquippa, Pennsylvania, were discharged for minor infractions of company rules. Most of these workers had been actively involved in a union. The union filed with the NLRB a charge of unfair labor practices against the steel company, claiming that the discharges were because of union membership. At a subsequent NLRB hearing, Jones & Laughlin argued that the NLRA was unconstitutional because it regulated labor relations and not interstate commerce. Therefore, Congress had no authority to regulate labor relations. The NLRB rejected the argument and found that the company was the fourth largest steel producer in the United States and was clearly involved in interstate commerce. It ordered the workers reinstated and directed Jones & Laughlin to cease and 13

GALE ENCYCLOPEDIA OF AMERICAN LAW, 3RD EDITION

CONTRIBUTORS

Editorial Reviewers
Patricia B. Brecht
Matthew C. Cordon
Frederick K. Grittner
Halle Butler Hara
Scott D. Slick

Contributing Authors
Richard Abowitz
Paul Bard
Joanne Bergum
Michael Bernard
Gregory A. Borchard
Susan Buie
James Cahoy
Terry Carter
Stacey Chamberlin
Sally Chatelaine
Joanne Smestad Claussen
Matthew C. Cordon
Richard J. Cretan
Lynne Crist
Paul D. Daggett
Susan L. Dalhed
Lisa M. DelFiacco
Suzanne Paul Dell'Oro
Heidi Denler
Dan DeVoe
Joanne Engelking
Mark D. Engsberg
Karl Finley

Sharon Fischlowitz
Jonathan Flanders
Lisa Florey
Robert A. Frame
John E. Gisselquist
Russell L. Gray III
Frederick K. Grittner
Victoria L. Handler
Halle Butler Hara
Lauri R. Harding
Heidi L. Headlee
James Heidberg
Clifford P. Hooker
Marianne Ashley Jerpbak
David R. Johnstone
Andrew Kass
Margaret Anderson Kelliher
Christopher J. Kennedy
Anne E. Kevlin
John K. Krol
Lauren Kushkin
Ann T. Laughlin
Laura Ledsworth-Wang
Linda Lincoln
Theresa J. Lippert
Gregory Luce
David Luiken
Frances T. Lynch
Jennifer Marsh
George A. Milite
Melodie Monahan

Sandra M. Olson
Anne Larsen Olstad
William Ostrem
Lauren Pacelli
Randolph C. Park
Gary Peter
Michele A. Potts
Reinhard Priester
Christy Rain
Brian Roberts
Debra J. Rosenthal
Mary Lahr Schier
Mary Scarbrough
Stephanie Schmitt
Theresa L. Schulz
John Scobey
Kelle Sisung
James Slavicek
Scott D. Slick
David Strom
Linda Tashbook
Wendy Tien
M. Uri Toch
Douglas Tueting
Richard F. Tyson
Christine Ver Ploeg
George E. Warner
Anne Welsbacher
Eric P. Wind
Lindy T. Yokanovich

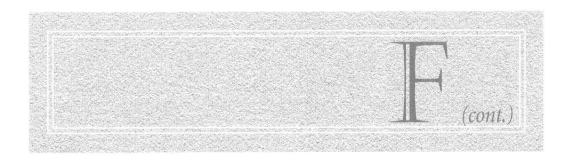

F (cont.)

⬧ FRIEDAN, BETTY NAOMI GOLDSTEIN

In 1963 author Betty Naomi Goldstein Friedan's first book, *The Feminine Mystique,* launched the feminist movement, which eventually expanded the lifestyle choices for U.S. women. By the 1990s, she had also become a spokesperson for older and economically disadvantaged people and was recognized and honored by women outside the United States for her global leadership and influence on women's issues.

She was born Elizabeth Naomi Goldstein on February 4, 1921, in Peoria, Illinois. Her father, Harry Goldstein, was a successful storeowner who emigrated from Russia. Her mother, Miriam Horowitz Goldstein, graduated from Bradley Polytechnic INSTITUTE and wrote society news as a Peoria newspaper journalist. Friedan entered Smith College in 1939, majored in psychology, and served as editor of the college newspaper. After graduating summa cum laude in 1942, she interviewed for the only type of job available to women journalists at the time: researcher for a major U.S. news magazine. But the position of researcher amounted to doing all the work while someone else received the byline, and Friedan was not interested in that. Instead, she wrote for a Greenwich Village news agency, covering the labor movement.

When WORLD WAR II ended, Friedan lost her job to a returning veteran. (Returning veterans were guaranteed their pre-war jobs.) Friedan then thought of going to medical school, a choice very few women could pursue. But instead, she followed the traditional path, marrying returning veteran Carl Friedan in 1947 and starting a family. After her first child was born, she worked for another newspaper, but was fired when she became pregnant with her second child. She protested to the newspaper guild, as no one had ever questioned her ability to perform her job, but was told that losing her job was "her fault" because she was pregnant. At that time, the term *sex* DISCRIMINATION did not exist.

While she was a mother and housewife living in suburban New York, Friedan wrote articles for women's magazines such as *McCall's* and *Ladies' Home Journal* on a freelance basis. Tapped by *McCall's* to report on the state of the alumnae of the Smith class of 1942 as they returned for their fifteenth reunion in 1957, Friedan visited the campus and was struck by the students' lack of interest in careers after graduation. This disinterest in intellectual pursuits contrasted greatly with Friedan's perception of her Smith classmates of the 1930s and 1940s.

Extensive research over the next several years brought Friedan to the conclusion that women's magazines were at FAULT because they defined women solely in relationship to their husbands and children. This had not always been the case; the magazines had evolved in the postwar years from promoters of women's INDEPENDENCE into paeans to consumerism, bent on keeping

MEN WEREN'T REALLY THE ENEMY— THEY WERE FELLOW VICTIMS SUFFERING FROM AN OUTMODED MASCULINE MYSTIQUE THAT MADE THEM FEEL UNNECESSARILY INADEQUATE WHEN THERE WERE NO BEARS TO KILL.
—BETTY FRIEDAN

Betty Friedan.

U.S. housewives in the home by selling them more and more household products.

Not surprisingly, Friedan was unable to get her work on this issue published in an acceptable format by the women's magazines she was criticizing. Her report was published in book form in 1963 as *The Feminine Mystique,* in which she chronicled the dissatisfaction of suburban housewives, dubbing it "the problem with no name." The book struck a common chord among U.S. women, who recognized themselves in the women she described in its

pages. For the first time since the women's SUFFRAGE movement ended successfully with the passage of the NINETEENTH AMENDMENT granting women the right to vote, women gathered together on a large scale to work for equal rights with men, a concept that at the time was nothing less than revolutionary.

In 1966, with Kathryn Clarenbach, Friedan cofounded the NATIONAL ORGANIZATION FOR WOMEN (NOW). NOW's original statement of purpose was written by Friedan: "Women want feminism to take the actions needed to bring women into the mainstream of American society, now; full equality for women, in fully equal partnership with men." Friedan served as NOW's president until 1970. Under her leadership, NOW propelled the women's movement from middle-class suburbia to nationwide activism. Friedan also helped organize the National ABORTION Rights Action League (now NARAL PRO-CHOICE AMERICA) in 1969, and the National Women's Political Caucus in 1971. All three organizations were still active participants in U.S. politics and culture into the 2000s.

On August 26, 1970, the fiftieth anniversary of the RATIFICATION of the Nineteenth Amendment, the Women's Strike for Equality took place. Friedan's brainchild, this women's rights demonstration was the largest that had ever occurred in the United States. Thousands of U.S. women marched in the streets for a day rather than working as housewives, secretaries, and waitresses, to show how poorly society would fare without women's labor and to demand three things for women: equal opportunity in employment and education, 24-hour CHILD CARE centers, and legalized abortion. Although the media at

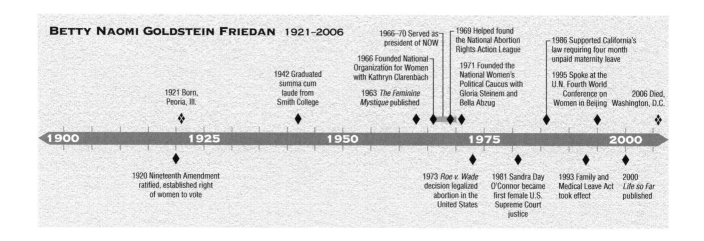

BETTY NAOMI GOLDSTEIN FRIEDAN 1921–2006

1966–70 Served as president of NOW

1969 Helped found the National Abortion Rights Action League

1986 Supported California's law requiring four month unpaid maternity leave

1966 Founded National Organization for Women with Kathryn Clarenbach

1942 Graduated summa cum laude from Smith College

1971 Founded the National Women's Political Caucus with Gloria Steinem and Bella Abzug

1995 Spoke at the U.N. Fourth World Conference on Women in Beijing

1921 Born, Peoria, Ill.

1963 *The Feminine Mystique* published

2006 Died, Washington, D.C.

1900   1925   1950   1975   2000

1920 Nineteenth Amendment ratified, established right of women to vote

1973 *Roe v. Wade* decision legalized abortion in the United States

1981 Sandra Day O'Connor became first female U.S. Supreme Court justice

1993 Family and Medical Leave Act took effect

2000 *Life so Far* published

the time portrayed the strike as FRIVOLOUS or a result of female hysteria, their compulsion to pay the event any attention at all was a step forward for the women's movement.

By the 1980s it was apparent that Friedan's feminism differed from that of other U.S. feminists such as GLORIA STEINEM and Kate Millett. When other feminist leaders were saying women could "have it all," meaning a successful career, fulfilling MARRIAGE, and happy children, Friedan, who had been divorced from her husband since 1969, wrote articles such as "Being 'Superwoman' Is Not the Way to Go" (*Woman's Day,* Oct. 1981) and "Feminism's Next Step" (*New York Times Magazine,* July 1981). Rather than focusing on sexual violence and abortion rights, Friedan's writings emphasized the necessity of working with other groups to improve the plight of children, members of minorities, and economically disadvantaged people.

In her 1981 book *The Second Stage,* Friedan called for an open discussion of traditional feminism's denial of the importance of family and of women's needs to nurture and be nurtured. She predicted that the women's movement would die out if feminists did not take the issues of children and men more seriously. It was not surprising that this position was roundly criticized as antifeminist by many of Friedan's contemporaries.

Another position that was at odds with NOW surfaced in 1986 when she declared her support for a California law requiring employers to grant up to four months of unpaid leave for women who were disabled by pregnancy or childbirth. The 1980 law (West's Ann. Cal. Gov. Code § 12945) was the subject of a U.S. Supreme Court case, *California FEDERAL Savings and Loan Ass'n v. Guerra,* 479 U.S. 272, 107 S. Ct. 683, 93 L. Ed. 2d 613 (1987). NOW opposed the law as a dangerous singling out of women for special treatment; Friedan called it outrageous that feminists would side with employers who were trying to evade offering women important and needed benefits. These opinions, among other things, caused Friedan to lose support within the women's movement as well as an audience in the media.

Another reason for Friedan's fall from media attention was her style, which, like her philosophy, also differed from that of other feminist spokespersons, most notably Steinem. Whereas Steinem was a favorite of the media and actively courted their attention, Friedan did not seek out media attention and often railed against what she saw as the stereotyping of women. Her stormy relationship with the media contributed to an image of her as old, unattractive, and out of touch with modern feminism.

By 1990, although Friedan was moving away from what was considered mainstream feminism, she had earned a permanent place in history. That year, *Life* magazine named her one of the 100 most important people of the twentieth century.

In September 1995, a new generation of journalists seemed surprised at Friedan's extensive international influence, which was demonstrated at the Non-Governmental Organization Forum on Women, an unofficial gathering at the U.N. Fourth World Conference on Women. Friedan attended the forum as one of only a few women who had participated in all four U.N. women's conferences since the first one was held in Mexico City in 1975. Women of all nationalities and ages sought her out, listened to her speeches, and attended her workshops.

Friedan's focus was to move the women's movement away from conflict with men and toward economic policies that benefited both sexes, such as shorter workweeks and higher minimum wages. As she saw it, policies that were pro-women alone were portrayed in the media and by opponents as anti-family and anti-men. Poor economic conditions and shrinking job opportunities often resulted in the treatment of women's developing economic power as a scapegoat for difficulties suffered by men or families. In Friedan's opinion, this unnecessary tension between men and women diverted attention from the issues that really threatened the well-being of women and families: poverty, unemployment, lack of education and health care, and crime. To combat these problems, she supported a proposal put forth by distinguished academics and public policy researchers that would provide low-income parents, not just women on WELFARE, with HEALTH INSURANCE and child care.

Friedan's focus on more gender-neutral policies was an outgrowth of her research into gerontology and the issues facing aging people. The 1993 publication of *The Fountain of Age* had put Friedan back in the media spotlight as the spokesperson of her generation, an advocate for freeing older people from damaging stereotypes, just as she had previously done for women. Friedan brought to her advocacy for older people her philosophy of cooperation, developed during her decades of work in the women's movement. A DELEGATE to the Fourth White House Conference on Aging in 1995, she fought against the polarization of young and older U.S. citizens that some politicians encouraged in order to increase their political power. She eschewed the idea of forced retirement, instead arguing for older workers to voluntarily and gradually cut down their work schedules and to explore job sharing and consultant work. At the same time, Friedan vowed to save programs such as SOCIAL SECURITY, MEDICARE, and MEDICAID, which were under attack by FISCAL conservatives. With that full plate of issues, it was clear that she was not ready to stop her advocacy work.

In the late 1990s, Friedan continued to speak at schools and other forums around the country and throughout the world. She wrote for a number of publications and taught at several schools, including the University of California, New York University, and Mount Vernon College in Washington, D.C, where she was the Distinguished Professor of Social Evolution. She has also served as an adjunct scholar at the Smithsonian Institution's Wilson International Center for Scholars. In 1993 she was inducted into the National Women's Hall of Fame. In 2000 she published her autobiography, *Life So Far*. Friedan died of congestive heart failure at her home in Washington, D.C., on February 4, 2006, her 85th birthday.

FURTHER READINGS

Evans, Sara. 1980. *Personal Politics: The Roots of Women's Liberation in the Civil Rights Movement and the New Left.* New York: Random House.

Horowtiz, Daniel. 2000. *Betty Friedan and the Making of "The Feminine Mystique": The American Left, the Cold War, and Modern Feminism.* Boston: Univ of Massachusetts Press.

CROSS REFERENCES

Age Discrimination; Ireland, Patricia; Sex Discrimination.

FRIEND OF THE COURT

A person who has a strong interest in a matter that is the subject of a lawsuit in which he or she is not a party.

A FRIEND OF THE COURT may be given permission by the court to file a written statement of his or her views on the subject, ostensibly to bolster the case of one party but even more to persuade the court to adopt the party's views. The Latin translation, AMICUS CURIAE, is used most often for a friend of the court; the written argument that he or she files may be called an amicus curiae BRIEF.

FRIENDLY FIRE

Fire burning in a place where it was intended to burn, although damages may result. In a military conflict, the discharge of weapons against one's own troops.

A fire burning in a fireplace is regarded as a friendly fire, in spite of the fact that extensive smoke damage might result therefrom. Ordinarily, when an individual purchases fire insurance, the coverage does not extend to damages resulting from a friendly fire but only to loss resulting from an uncontrollable hostile fire.

❖ FRIENDLY, HENRY JACOB

Henry Jacob Friendly served for 27 years on the U.S. Court of Appeals for the Second Circuit, where he won a wide reputation for his scholarly, well-crafted opinions.

Friendly was born July 3, 1903, in Elmira, New York. He graduated summa cum laude from Harvard College in 1923 and from Harvard Law School in 1927. In law school he studied under Professor FELIX FRANKFURTER, later a U.S. Supreme Court Justice, who recommended Friendly for a clerkship with Supreme Court Justice LOUIS D. BRANDEIS. After his clerkship Friendly entered private practice where he specialized in railroad reorganizations and corporate law. He later became a VICE PRESIDENT and general counsel for Pan American Airways.

In 1959 President DWIGHT D. EISENHOWER appointed Friendly to the U.S. Court of Appeals for the Second Circuit, where he remained until his death. Although Friendly was a semi-retired senior judge during his last years on the court, he remained an active participant and was involved in more than one hundred cases each year. He served as chief judge of the court from 1971 to 1973. In 1974 Friendly took on the additional duties of the presiding judge of the Special Railroad Court, which was established to deal with the reorganization of rail service in the Northeast and the Midwest that resulted from

Pat Tillman

Even though friendly fire is a recognized hazard of modern warfare, particular incidents garner public attention. One example is that of Pat Tillman, a star collegiate and National Football League player who gave up a multi-million dollar pro football contract to join the U.S. Army after September 11, 2001. Tillman became an Army Ranger and a member of an infantry regiment that was deployed to Afghanistan, where he was killed on April 22, 2004. The circumstances of his death were first portrayed as the result of a firefight with Taliban fighters, leading to Corporal Tillman's elevation as a special American hero. However, three weeks later, the Army revealed that he had died of friendly fire, and Tillman's mother and his brother Kevin, also a Ranger, expressed concerns over two fact-finding investigations by his regiment, believing there was a conspiracy to conceal the true facts of his death.

The revelation in May 2004 that Tillman had been shot by his comrades took the public by surprise. His commanding general had quickly awarded Tillman the Silver Star, the Purple Heart, and a posthumous promotion, knowing he had died of friendly. Lt. Gen. Stanley McChrystal approved the Silver Star citation six days after Tillman's death, which included a narrative regarding Tillman's death that included the phrase "in the line of devastating enemy fire." However, the next day he sent a memo to senior government officials that warned of the possibility Tillman might have been killed by friendly fire. Nevertheless, these officials allowed a nationally televised memorial service to go forward, in which a false account of his death was given. There were later reports that members of Tillman's unit were told to lie to the family about his death.

Troubling details began to emerged that suggested his unit attempted to cover up his death by friendly fire. His body armor and uniform, along with his personal journal were burned, which violated Army rules. Though several members of his unit were discharged from the Army or disciplined, Tillman's family was not convinced it had heard the true story. They feared that Tillman might have been killed because he had become disenchanted with the war. Their complaints led the Army inspector general to open an investigation in August 2005.

In March 2006 the Defense Department inspector general directed the Army to open a criminal investigation into Tillman's death, which resulted in a report, filed in March 2007, that provided no new information. It concluded that the death was accidental and that the initial reports that he died of hostile fire were based on confusion the day of the fire fight. The House of Representatives Committee on Oversight and Government Reform conducted its own investigation and released a report in July 2008 that criticized "the pervasive lack of recollection and absence of specific information" that made it impossible for it to assign responsibility for the misinformation in Tillman's death.

FURTHER READINGS

Krakauer, John. 2009. *Where Men Win Glory: The Odyssey of Pat Tillman.* New York: Doubleday.

Tillman, Mary. 2008 *Boots on the Ground: My Tribute to Pat Tillman.* New York: Modern Times.

---

the BANKRUPTCY of the Penn Central Railroad and the former Conrail.

Friendly wrote nearly a thousand judicial opinions as well as a number of notes and articles on a wide range of issues, but he is probably best known for his work in the areas of diversity JURISDICTION, CRIMINAL PROCEDURE, and SECURITIES law. Diversity jurisdiction refers to the jurisdiction that federal courts have over lawsuits in which the plaintiff and the DEFENDANT are residents of different states. Friendly first became interested in the subject when he was in law school, and one of his first articles was "The Historic Basis of Diversity Jurisdiction," 41 *Harvard Law Review* 1928. Later, after the U.S. Supreme Court had established a new precedent for cases involving diversity jurisdiction (*Erie Railroad co. V. Tompkins*, 304 U.S. 64, 58 S. Ct. 817 82 L. Ed. 1188 [1938]). Friendly wrote, "In Praise of *Erie*—and of the New FEDERAL Common Law," 39 *New York University Law Review*, 1964. A few years later he provided an overview of federal jurisdiction in *Federal Jurisdiction: A General View* (1973).

During the 1960s Friendly became involved in the debate over changes in criminal procedure that were occurring as the U.S. Supreme Court, in a series of decisions, held that many of the rights guaranteed in the BILL OF RIGHTS applied to the states. In "The Bill of Rights as a Code of Criminal Procedure," *Benchmarks* (1967), Friendly expressed doubts about some of the Court's decisions and worried that they would cut off debate in Congress and the state legislatures that might have proved fruitful in developing new solutions to the problems of criminal procedure. He also criticized the decision in MIRANDA V. ARIZONA, 384 U.S. 436, 86 S. Ct. 1602, 16 L. Ed. 2d 694 (1966), on the ground that it was predicated on the unfounded ASSUMPTION that all custodial interrogations are inherently coercive.

In the area of securities law, Friendly wrote more than one hundred opinions, several of them in the relatively new field of TRANSNATIONAL LAW, which deals with corporations that have activities in several countries. He was also notably unsympathetic toward white-collar criminals who perpetrated financial frauds; in *United States v. Benjamin,* 328 F.2d 854 (1954), he observed that "[i]n our complex society the accountant's certificate and the lawyer's opinion can be instruments for inflicting pecuniary loss more potent than the chisel or the crowbar."

Friendly's colleagues respected him for his scholarship, his reasoning, and his self-restraint. In 1977 he received the Presidential Medal of Freedom from President GERALD R. FORD for having brought "a brilliance and a sense of precision to American JURISPRUDENCE, sharpening its focus and strengthening its commitment

to the high goal of equal and exact justice for every American citizen." As another federal JURIST, JOHN MINOR WISDOM, put it, Friendly was "unsurpassed as a judge—in the power of his reasoning, the depth of his knowledge of the law, and his balanced judgment in decision-making."

In 1985, Sophie Stern, Friendly's wife of 55 years, died. Despondent over her death and plagued by failing eyesight, Friendly took his own life in his New York City apartment on March 11, 1986.

FURTHER READINGS

Boudin, Michael. 2007. "Judge Henry Friendly and the Mirror of Constitutional Law." *New York Univ. Law Review* (October) 82. Available online at http://www.law.nyu.edu/ecm_dlv/groups/public/@nyu_law_website__journals__law_review/documents/documents/ecm_dlv_015190.pdf; website home page: http://www.law.nyu.edu (accessed September 3, 2009).

"Henry Jacob Friendly." Judges of the United States. *Federal Judicial Center* Web site. Available online at http://www.fjc.gov/servlet/tGetInfo?jid=802; http://www.fjc.gov (accessed September 3, 2009).

Norman, Michael. "Henry J. Friendly, Federal Judge in Court of Appeals, Is Dead at 82." *The New York Times* (March 12, 1986).

FRIENDLY SUIT

A lawsuit brought by an executor or administrator of the estate of a deceased person in the name of a creditor as if that creditor had initiated the action. The executor or administrator brings the suit against himself or herself in order to compel the creditors to take an equal distribution of the assets of the estate. An action brought by parties who agree to submit some doubtful question to the court in order to obtain an opinion on that issue.

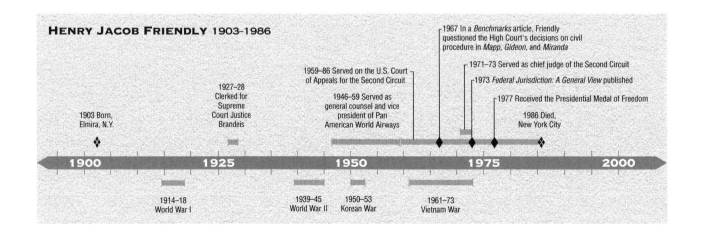

HENRY JACOB FRIENDLY 1903–1986

1903 Born, Elmira, N.Y.

1927–28 Clerked for Supreme Court Justice Brandeis

1946–59 Served as general counsel and vice president of Pan American World Airways

1959–86 Served on the U.S. Court of Appeals for the Second Circuit

1967 In a *Benchmarks* article, Friendly questioned the High Court's decisions on civil procedure in *Mapp, Gideon,* and *Miranda*

1971–73 Served as chief judge of the Second Circuit

1973 *Federal Jurisdiction: A General View* published

1977 Received the Presidential Medal of Freedom

1986 Died, New York City

1900　1925　1950　1975　2000

1914–18 World War I

1939–45 World War II

1950–53 Korean War

1961–73 Vietnam War

FRIES'S REBELLION

John Fries was an auctioneer from rural Pennsylvania who led a small group of tax protesters in what came to be known as Fries's Rebellion. He was tried and convicted of TREASON but was eventually pardoned.

Fries served as a captain in the Continental Army during the WHISKEY REBELLION of 1794. He then returned to Pennsylvania to resume his life there. In 1798, Congress authorized the collection of property taxes to replenish funds depleted by the Whiskey Rebellion and to finance an anticipated war with France. Revenue officers were sent to all parts of the United States to assess the value of homes, land, and slaves for TAXATION. The tax assessment was well publicized and understood in urban areas, where most residents paid little attention to the assessors' activities. However, in the rural regions of northeastern Pennsylvania, where many residents spoke and read only German, many people were unaware of Congress's action and were resentful and fearful of the inquisitive assessors. They responded by attacking the revenue officers, both verbally and physically. Their treatment of the assessors was dubbed the Hot Water War, after an incident in which a woman dumped a bucket of hot water on a revenue agent.

The Pennsylvanians' protests escalated until a group of residents took several revenue officers captive and held them until they had satisfactorily explained their actions. Upon their release, the officers arrested twenty-three men for INSURRECTION. Fries and a group of men who believed that the property tax was a deprivation of liberty took up arms and liberated their detained comrades. When the group resisted orders from President JOHN ADAMS to disperse and to allow the FEDERAL officers to carry out their duties, Fries and its other leaders were arrested for treason.

Fries was brought to trial in 1799, before Judge Richard Peters, of the Pennsylvania district court, and Justice JAMES IREDELL, of the Supreme Court. Fries's DEFENSE counsel argued that their client's offense was a simple protest that perhaps could be characterized as sedition, but certainly did not rise to the level of treason, a capital crime. They contended that, in a free republic, the treason charge should be reserved for the most extreme cases of armed attempt to overthrow the government.

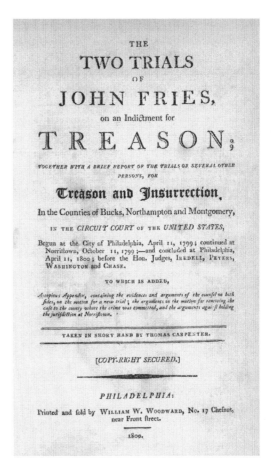

THE
TWO TRIALS
OF
JOHN FRIES,
on an Indictment for
TREASON;
TOGETHER WITH A BRIEF REPORT OF THE TRIALS OF SEVERAL OTHER PERSONS, FOR
Treason and Insurrection,
In the Counties of Bucks, Northampton and Montgomery,
IN THE CIRCUIT COURT OF THE UNITED STATES,
Begun at the City of Philadelphia, April 11, 1799; continued at Norristown, October 11, 1799;—and concluded at Philadelphia, April 11, 1800; before the Hon. Judges, IREDELL, PETERS, WASHINGTON and CHASE.
TO WHICH IS ADDED,
A copious Appendix, containing the evidence and arguments of the counsel on both sides, on the motion for a new trial; the arguments on the motion for removing the cause to the county where the crime was committed, and the arguments against holding the jurisdiction at Norristown.

TAKEN IN SHORT HAND BY THOMAS CARPENTER.

[COPY-RIGHT SECURED.]

PHILADELPHIA:
Printed and sold by WILLIAM W. WOODWARD, No. 17 Chesnut, near Front street.

1800.

In 1800, William W. Woodword, a Philadelphia publisher, used shorthand notes taken by Thomas Carpenter to produce a report of John Fries's two trials for treason.
LIBRARY COMPANY OF PHILADELPHIA

Defense counsel's pleas for freedom of expression of political sentiment did not convince members of the jury, who were probably influenced by Iredell's and Peters's INSTRUCTIONS. In those instructions, Peters equated opposing or preventing the implementation of a law with treason, and Iredell agreed with him. Fries was found GUILTY, but was granted a new trial when the court learned that before the trial began, one juror had expressed a belief in his guilt.

Fries's second trial took place in April 1800, before Justice Samuel Chase, of the Supreme Court, and Judge Peters. Determined to expedite the second trial, Chase took the unprecedented step of preparing an opinion on the LAW OF THE CASE. Before the trial began, he distributed copies of his summary to the defense attorneys, the DISTRICT ATTORNEY, and the jury. Chase made it clear that his opinion represented the court's view of the law of treason and that the defense would not be permitted to present lengthy arguments to the contrary, as it had in the first trial.

Outraged that the court had prejudged their client's case, Fries's attorneys withdrew from the case. Fries chose to proceed to trial without benefit of LEGAL REPRESENTATION. He was again found guilty and sentenced to death by hanging. However, after studying the case, President Adams pardoned him and the other insurgents. Soon after his pardon, Fries was promoted from captain to lieutenant colonel in the Montgomery County, Pennsylvania, militia.

Justice Chase's conduct in Fries's second trial was harshly criticized as indirectly depriving Fries of counsel. The justice's actions were used against him in 1805, in an unsuccessful IMPEACHMENT proceeding.

FURTHER READINGS

Adams, Charles. 1998. *Those Dirty Rotten Taxes: The Tax Revolts That Built America.* New York: Free Press.

Elsmere, Jane Shaffer. 1979. "The Trials of John Fries." *Pennsylvania Magazine of History and Biography* 103 (October).

Presser, Stephen. 1978. "A Tale of Two Judges...." *Northwestern Univ. Law Review* 73 (March/April).

CROSS REFERENCE

Whiskey Rebellion.

FRISK

A term used in criminal law to refer to the superficial running of the hands over the body of an individual by a law enforcement agent or official in order to determine whether such individual is holding an illegal object, such as a weapon or narcotics. A frisk is distinguishable from a search, which is a more extensive examination of an individual.

CROSS REFERENCE

Stop and Frisk.

FRIVOLOUS

Of minimal importance; legally worthless.

A *FRIVOLOUS suit* is one without any legal merit. In some cases, such an action might be brought in BAD FAITH for the purpose of harrassing the DEFENDANT. In such a case, the individual bringing the frivolous suit might be liable for DAMAGES for MALICIOUS PROSECUTION.

A *frivolous appeal* is one that is completely lacking merit, since no reviewable question has been raised therein.

FROLIC

Activities performed by an employee during working hours that are not considered to be in the course of his or her employment, because they are for the employee's personal purposes only.

The doctrine of RESPONDEAT SUPERIOR makes a principal liable for the torts of his or her agent occurring during the COURSE OF EMPLOYMENT. This is based on the concept that a principal has control over his or her agent's behavior. If an agent was hired to drive from point A to point B, and, through reckless driving, hit a pedestrian along the way, the principal would ordinarily be held liable. If, however, the agent was engaged in FROLIC, the principal would not be liable. This might occur, for example, if an employee were hired to transport goods from point A to point B and made several detours along the way for personal reasons. If the employee became involved in an accident while on a frolic, the employer would not be liable unless it could be established that he or she was negligent in the hiring or supervision of the employee.

FRONTIERO V. RICHARDSON

The fight to end gender DISCRIMINATION in the U.S. began in the nineteenth century with the women's SUFFRAGE movement and the enactment of laws that protected the property that women brought into marriages. By the 1960s the focus had shifted to ending pay and benefit discrimination based on gender. By the early 1970s, Congress had passed the EQUAL RIGHTS AMENDMENT (ERA) of the U.S. Constitution, which proclaimed equality between the genders. RATIFICATION appeared close by 1973, as 38 states had ratified the ERA. The court system also became an arena for the issue of gender discrimination. The U.S. Supreme Court began to consider cases of gender discrimination but hesitated to place gender in the same category as race or ethnicity as a SUSPECT CLASSIFICATION inviting the most rigorous CONSTITUTIONAL review. However, a plurality of the court endorsed gender as a suspect classification in *Frontiero v. Richardson*, 411 U.S. 677, 93 S. Ct. 1764, 36 L. Ed.2d 583 (1973). This important case pushed the Court, and society in general, to recognize the legal disabilities that women had lived with for centuries. Though not a LANDMARK decision, *Frontiero* signaled the willingness of the high court to take gender issues seriously.

The facts of the case illustrated the disparate treatment built into U.S. society concerning the role of women. Sharron Frontiero was a

U.S. Air Force officer who was married to Joseph Frontiero, a full-time student at a college near the Alabama base where Sharron was stationed. Congress had passed a law that provided fringe benefits to members of the armed forces in the hopes that they would re-enlist and pursue a military career. Under this law, a member of the armed forces with dependents was entitled to an increased housing allowance and comprehensive dependent medical and dental care. However, the law made a distinction between male and female members. A serviceman could claim his wife as a dependent simply by certifying that they were married. A servicewomen such as Frontiero, however, could not claim her husband as a dependent unless she proved that he was dependent upon her for more than one-half of his support. Joseph Frontiero's living expenses totaled $354 per month, but he received $250 per month in veteran's benefits. Therefore, he was not dependent on his wife for more than one-half of his support. Based on these calculations, the Air Force denied Sharron Fronteiro the additional benefits.

Frontiero sued the Air Force, alleging that the difference in treatment was unconstitutional discrimination under the Fifth Amendment's Due Process Clause. A three-judge panel from the U.S. Court for the Middle District of Alabama rejected this claim, with one judge dissenting. Frontiero, with the help of the AMERICAN CIVIL LIBERTIES UNION (ACLU) and its ATTORNEY, RUTH BADER GINSBURG, took the case to the U.S. Supreme Court.

The Court, in an 8–1 decision, overturned the lower RULING and held that the salary supplement law violated the Due Process Clause. However, the justices could not agree on the constitutional standard of review that should be applied to allegations of gender discrimination. In a plurality opinion for four justices, Justice William Brennan concluded that gender, like race, was a suspect classification. The suspect classification standard holds that laws which classify people according to race, ethnicity, or RELIGION are inherently suspect and that they are subject to the STRICT SCRUTINY test of JUDICIAL REVIEW. Strict scrutiny requires the state to provide a compelling interest for the challenged law and to demonstrate that the law has been narrowly tailored to achieve its purpose. If a suspect classification is not involved, the Court will apply the RATIONAL BASIS TEST, which requires the state to provide any type of reasonable ground for the legislation. Under strict scrutiny, the government has a difficult burden to meet, while under the rational basis test, most laws will be upheld.

In 1971, the Court, in *Reed v. Reed*, 404 U.S. 71, 92 S. Ct. 251, 30 L. Ed.2d 225, extended the application of the EQUAL PROTECTION clause of the FOURTEENTH AMENDMENT to gender-based discrimination. However, the Court had used the rational basis test. Nevertheless, Justice Brennan argued that *Reed* IMPLIED that gender was a suspect classification and that strict scrutiny should apply. There were four reasons in his view for making gender a suspect class. First, gender was, like race, an "immutable" accident of birth that was IRRELEVANT to the purpose of the FEDERAL law. Second, Brennan pointed to the long history in the U.S. of discrimination based on gender. He noted that statute books had been filled with "gross, stereotyped distinctions between the sexes." Although women had seen their lot improve in modern America, they still faced "pervasive, although at times more subtle, discrimination in our educational institutions, in the job market and, perhaps most conspicuously, in the political arena." In addition, gender, like race, was a highly visible trait. Finally, Brennan acknowledged the ERA, which made clear that gender classifications were "inherently invidious."

Based on these factors, Brennan had no trouble ruling the law unconstitutional. The government could not show a compelling interest for the benefit discrimination. It claimed that administrative efficiency justified the law, as most members of the armed forces were men. It would have cost more to process applications required from Frontiero and the small percentage of women in uniform. This was not a compelling interest for Brennan and the plurality.

Justice LEWIS POWELL, in a concurring opinion joined by Chief Justice WARREN BURGER and Justice HARRY BLACKMUN, agreed that the law was unconstitutional. Powell disagreed with the plurality's conclusion that strict scrutiny was warranted. He contended that the Court should not make that conclusion while the ratification of the ERA was pending. By declaring gender a suspect clarification, the judicial branch would, in effect, trump the ERA. In his view, it was better to allow the states to determine whether gender should be regarded as a suspect class. The seven-year ratification period had run for just one year, so the Court should refrain from ruling. Powell concluded that the rational basis test applied in *Reed* worked in this case as well. The government did not have a reasonable justification for unequal treatment of service members.

Justice WILLIAM REHNQUIST dissented, citing the reasoning of the lower court to show that the administrative savings from not requiring men to justify dependent benefit eligibility provided a rational basis for the law.

By failing to gain a majority, the court did not ESTABLISH gender as a suspect classification requiring strict scrutiny. By the end of the decade, the ERA was losing support. The time period for ratification was extended until 1982, but that deadline passed and the ERA died. The Court, in *Craig v. Boren*, 429 U.S. 190, 97 S. Ct. 451, 50 L. Ed.2d 397 (1976), settled on an "intermediate scrutiny" standard for gender discrimination. Therefore, classifications by gender must serve important governmental objectives and must be substantially related to the achievement of those objectives.

FURTHER READINGS

Cole, David 1984. "Strategies of Difference: Litigating for Women's Rights in a Man's World." *Law & Inequality* 2 (February).

Matthews, Donna Meredith. 1998. "Avoiding Gender Equality." *Women's Rights Law Reporter* 19 (winter).

Stephens, Otis H., Jr., and John M. Scheb II. 2002. *American Constitutional Law.* Belmont, CA: Wadsworth.

CROSS REFERENCE

Women's Rights.

FRUIT OF THE POISONOUS TREE

The fruit of the poisonous tree is a doctrine that prohibits the use of secondary evidence in trial that was culled directly from primary evidence derived from an illegal search and seizure.

The FRUIT OF THE POISONOUS TREE doctrine is an offspring of the EXCLUSIONARY RULE. The exclusionary rule mandates that EVIDENCE obtained as a direct result from an illegal arrest, an unreasonable search, or a coercive interrogation must be excluded from trial. Under the fruit of the poisonous tree doctrine, evidence that is derived as an indirect result from an illegal arrest, unreasonable search, or coercive interrogation may also be excluded from trial. Like the exclusionary rule, the fruit of the

poisonous tree doctrine was established primarily to deter law enforcement from violating rights against unreasonable searches and seizures.

The name *fruit of the poisonous tree* is thus a metaphor: the poisonous tree is evidence obtained during an illegal arrest, search, or interrogation by law enforcement. The fruit of this poisonous tree is evidence later discovered because of knowledge gained from the prior illegal search, arrest, or interrogation. The poisonous tree and the poisonous fruit are both excluded from a criminal trial.

Example

Assume that a police officer searches the automobile of a person stopped for a minor traffic violation. This violation is the only reason the officer conducts the search; nothing indicates that the driver is impaired by drugs or alcohol, and no other circumstances would lead a reasonable officer to believe that the car contains evidence of a crime. This is an unreasonable search under the FOURTH AMENDMENT to the U.S. Constitution.

Assume further that the officer finds a small amount of marijuana in the vehicle. The driver is subsequently charged with possession of a controlled substance and chooses to go to trial. The marijuana evidence culled from this search is excluded from trial under the exclusionary rule, and the criminal charges are dropped for lack of evidence.

Also suppose that before the original charges are dismissed, the police officers ask a magistrate or judge for a warrant to search the home of the driver. The only evidence used as a basis, or probable cause, for the warrant is the small amount of marijuana found in the vehicle search. The magistrate, unaware that the marijuana was uncovered in an illegal search, approves the warrant for the home search.

The officers search the driver's home and find a lawn mower stolen from a local park facility. Under the fruit of the poisonous tree doctrine, the lawn mower must be excluded from any trial on theft charges because the search of the house was based on evidence gathered in a previous illegal search.

History and Development of the Doctrine

Silverthorne Lumber Co. v. United States: **The Supreme Court Lays the Foundation for**

Later Development The Supreme Court first hinted at the fruit of the poisonous tree doctrine in *Silverthorne Lumber co. v. United States,* 251 U.S. 385, 40 S. Ct. 182, 64 L. Ed. 319 (1920). In *Silverthorne,* DEFENDANT Frederick W. Silverthorne was arrested on suspicion of FEDERAL violations in connection with his lumber business. Government agents then conducted a warrantless, illegal search of the Silverthorne offices. Based on the evidence discovered in the search, the prosecution requested more documents, and the court ordered Silverthorne to produce the documents. Silverthorne refused and was jailed for CONTEMPT of court.

On APPEAL, the Supreme Court reversed the contempt judgment. In its argument to the Court, the government conceded that the search was illegal and that the prosecution was not entitled to keep the documents obtained in it. However, the government held that it was entitled to copy the documents and use knowledge gained from the documents for future prosecution. The Court rejected this argument. According to the Court, "[T]he essence of forbidding the acquisition of evidence in a certain way is that ... it shall not be used at all." *Silverthorne* concerned only evidence gained in the first illegal search or seizure, but the wording of the opinion paved the way for the exclusion of evidence gained in subsequent searches and seizures.

Nardone v. United States: The Supreme Court First Invokes the Doctrine The term *fruit of the poisonous tree* was first used in *Nardone v. United States,* 308 U.S. 338, 60 S. Ct. 266, 84 L. Ed. 307 (1939). In *Nardone,* Frank C. Nardone appealed his convictions for smuggling and concealing alcohol and for CONSPIRACY to do the same. In an earlier decision, the Supreme Court had ruled that an interception of Nardone's telephone conversations by government agents violated the Communications Act of 1934 (47 U.S.C.A. § 605). The issue before the Court was whether the trial court erred in refusing to allow Nardone's lawyer to question the prosecution on whether, and in what way, it had used information obtained in the illegal wire tapping.

In reversing Nardone's convictions, the Court stated that once a defendant has established that evidence was illegally seized, the trial court "must give opportunity, however closely confined, to the ACCUSED to prove that a substantial portion of the case against him was a fruit of the poisonous tree." The *Nardone* opinion established that evidence obtained in violation of a statute was subject to exclusion if it was obtained in violation of a statutory right.

Wong Sun v. United States: The Doctrine Is Held Applicable to Fourth Amendment Violations The fruit of the poisonous tree doctrine was first held applicable to Fourth Amendment violations in the LANDMARK case *Wong Sun v. United States,* 371 U.S. 471, 83 S. Ct. 407, 9 L. Ed. 2d 441 (1963). The Court in *Wong Sun* also set forth the test for determining how closely DERIVATIVE EVIDENCE must be related to illegally obtained evidence to warrant exclusion.

In *Wong Sun,* a number of federal narcotics agents had arrested Hom Way in San Francisco at 2:00 a.m. on June 4, 1959, on suspicion of narcotics activity. Although the agents had been watching Way for six weeks, they did not have a warrant for his arrest. Way was searched, and the agents found heroin in his possession. After his arrest, Way stated that he had bought an ounce of heroin the night before from someone known to him as "Blackie Toy," the proprietor of Oye's Laundry on Leavenworth Street.

Though Way had never been an informant for the police, the agents cruised Leavenworth Street. At 6:00 a.m., they stopped at Oye's Laundry. The rest of the agents remained out of sight while Agent Alton Wong rang the bell. When James Wah Toy answered the door, Wong said he was there for laundry and dry cleaning. Toy answered that he did not open until 8:00 a.m. and started to close the door. Wong then identified himself as a federal narcotics agent. Toy slammed the door and began to run down the hallway, through the laundry, and to his bedroom, where his wife and child were sleeping. Again without a warrant, Wong and the other agents broke open the door, followed Toy, and arrested him. A search of the premises uncovered no illegal drugs.

While Toy was in handcuffs, one of the agents told him that Way had said Toy sold Way narcotics. Toy denied selling narcotics, but then said he knew someone who had. When asked who, Toy answered that he knew the man only as "Johnny." Toy told the officers that "Johnny" lived on Eleventh Avenue, and then he described the house. Toy also volunteered that "Johnny" kept about an ounce of heroin in his bedroom and that he and "Johnny" had smoked some heroin the night before.

The agents left and located the house on Eleventh Avenue. Without a search or an ARREST WARRANT, they entered the home, went to the bedroom, and found Johnny Yee. After a "discussion" with the agents, Yee surrendered a little less than one ounce of heroin.

The same morning, Yee and Toy were taken to the office of the Bureau of Narcotics. While in custody there, Yee stated that he had gotten the heroin about four days earlier from Toy and another person he knew as "Sea Dog." The agents then asked Toy about "Sea Dog," and Toy identified "Sea Dog" as Wong Sun. Some of the agents took Toy to Sun's neighborhood, where Toy pointed out Sun's house. The agents walked past Sun's wife and arrested Sun, who had been sleeping in his bedroom. A search of the premises turned up no illegal drugs.

Toy and Yee were arraigned in federal court on June 4, 1959, and Sun was arraigned the next day. All were released without BAIL. A few days later, Toy, Yee, and Sun were interrogated separately at the Narcotics Bureau by Agent William Wong. Sun and Toy made written statements but refused to sign them.

Sun and Toy were tried jointly on charges of transporting and concealing narcotics in violation of 21 U.S.C.A. § 174. Way did not testify at the trial. The government offered Yee as its principal witness, but Yee recanted his statement to Agent William Wong and invoked his FIFTH AMENDMENT right against SELF-INCRIMINATION. With only four items IN EVIDENCE, Sun and Toy were convicted by the court in a BENCH TRIAL. The Court of Appeals for the Ninth Circuit affirmed the convictions (*Wong Sun,* 288 F.2d 366 [9th Cir. 1961]). Sun and Toy appealed to the U.S. Supreme Court.

The Supreme Court accepted the case and reversed the convictions. The Court began its analysis by noting that the court of appeals had held that the arrests of both Sun and Toy were illegal. The question was whether the four items in evidence against Sun and Toy were ADMISSIBLE despite the illegality of the arrests. The four pieces of evidence were the oral statements made by Toy in his bedroom at the time of his arrest, the heroin surrendered to the agents by Yee, Toy's unsigned statement to Agent William Wong, and Sun's unsigned statement to Agent William Wong.

The government submitted several theories to support the proposition that the statements made by Toy in his bedroom were properly admitted at trial. The Court rejected all the arguments. According to the Court, the arrest was illegal because the agents had no evidence supporting it other than the word of Way, an arrestee who had never been an informer for law enforcement. The officers did not even know whether Toy was the person they were looking for. Furthermore, Toy's flight did not give the officers probable cause to arrest Toy: Agent Alton Wong had first posed as a customer, and this made Toy's flight ambiguous and not necessarily the product of a GUILTY mind. Thus, under the exclusionary rule, the oral statements made by Toy in his bedroom should not have been allowed at trial.

The Court then turned to the actual drug evidence seized from Yee. The Court, in deference to *Nardone,* stated, "We need not hold that all evidence is 'fruit of the poisonous tree.'" Instead, the question in such a situation was "'whether, granting establishment of the primary illegality, the evidence ... has been come at by exploitation of that illegality or instead by means sufficiently distinguishable to be purged of the primary taint.'"

According to the Court, the narcotics in *Wong Sun* were indeed "come at" by use of Toy's statements. Toy's statements were, in fact, the only evidence used to justify entrance to Yee's bedroom. Since the statements by Toy were INADMISSIBLE, the narcotics in Yee's possession were also inadmissible, as fruit of the poisonous tree. The Court went on to hold that Sun's written statements about Toy should also have been excluded as HEARSAY, and the Court ultimately overturned Toy's CONVICTION.

The Court did not reverse Sun's conviction. The heroin in Yee's possession was admissible at trial, as was Sun's own statement. According to the Court, "The exclusion of narcotics as to Toy was required solely by their tainted relationship to information unlawfully obtained from Toy, and not by any official impropriety connected with their surrender by Yee." The Court did, however, grant Sun a new trial, because it was unable to conclude that Toy's statements, erroneously admitted at trial as evidence against Sun, had not affected the verdict. The Court advised that on REMAND and in similar cases, "particular care ought to be taken ... when the crucial element of the accused's possession is proved solely by his own admissions."

Exceptions

There are three main exceptions to the fruit of the poisonous tree doctrine: (1) the independent source exception; (2) the inevitable discovery exception; and (3) the attenuation exception. Under the independent source exception, the prosecution may use evidence that was derived from an illegally tainted source, if the police could also have obtained the evidence from an untainted source. For example, a warrant to obtain a defendant's cellular telephone records was properly issued, notwithstanding that those records had already been examined PURSUANT to an improperly issued SUBPOENA, since the AFFIDAVIT of probable cause for the warrant was not based on any information obtained through the subpoena and there was a sufficient probability that the defendant's telephone records would reveal information useful to solving the crime at issue (*Commissioner v. McEnany*, 446 Pa. Super. 609, 667 A.2d 1143 [1995]).

The inevitable discovery exception to the fruit of the poisonous tree doctrine is a variation on the independent source exception. But it differs in that the question is not whether the police did in fact acquire certain evidence by reliance upon an untainted source but instead whether the illegally obtained evidence would have been inevitably discovered in a lawful manner. For example, suppose federal agents visit a suspect's house and interview the suspect's wife about his whereabouts. After the interview, the police conduct an illegal search of the house and seize some evidence. After completing the search, the police leave the defendant's premises only to catch the defendant outside his house with drug-making equipment in his possession. The defendant cannot exclude the drug-making equipment as a fruit of the illegal search of his home because the police would have inevitably discovered the defendant carrying the equipment outside his home anyway.

The attenuation exception to the fruit of the poisonous tree doctrine permits the introduction of incriminating evidence against the defendant when that evidence itself is seized lawfully and the seizure occurs after a significant passage of time and events from the time of an earlier police illegality. For example, evidence obtained from a defendant who is being illegally detained at his house may not be excluded as fruit of the poisonous tree when the defendant voluntarily gives the police an incriminating item almost an hour after the DETENTION begins, and the detention is congenial in nature and not marked by threats or violence.

In *Hudson v. Michigan,* 547 U.S. 586, 126 S. Ct. 2159, 165 L. Ed. 2d 56 (2006), the Supreme Court further clarified the attenuation exception to the fruit of the poisonous tree doctrine and the exclusionary rule as a whole. In *Hudson,* the state of Michigan admitted to violating the knock-and-announce rule governing the length of time police must wait after knocking on a suspect's door before breaking in to preserve incriminating evidence for trial. However, the state argued that the evidence seized after the illegal ENTRY should still be admissible at trial because the REMEDY of exclusion would not adequately balance the policy justification underlying the exclusionary rule, namely the DETERRENCE of police misconduct, with the interests of society in crime prevention and punishment.

In a 5–4 decision, the Court agreed. The Court first identified the interests protected by the knock-and-announce rule: (1) protection of human life and limb, because an unannounced entry may provoke violence in the form of self-defense by a surprised resident; (2) protection of property by AVOIDANCE of forcible entry; and (3) protection of the privacy and dignity of those inside the house. The Court next assumed that exclusion of the evidence seized following the illegal entry would advance the interests underlying the knock-and-announce rule. But "what the knock-and-announce rule has never protected," the Court said, "is one's interest in preventing the government from seeing or taking evidence described in a warrant, [and] since the interests that were violated in this case have nothing to do with the seizure of the evidence, the exclusionary rule is inapplicable."

But quite apart from the requirement of unattenuated causation, the Court continued, the exclusionary rule has never been applied except where its "deterrence benefits outweigh its substantial social costs." The costs of applying the exclusionary rule in *Hudson,* the Court said, were considerable. In addition to the grave adverse consequence that exclusion of relevant incriminating evidence always entails (i.e., the risk of releasing dangerous criminals into society), the Court opined, imposing such a

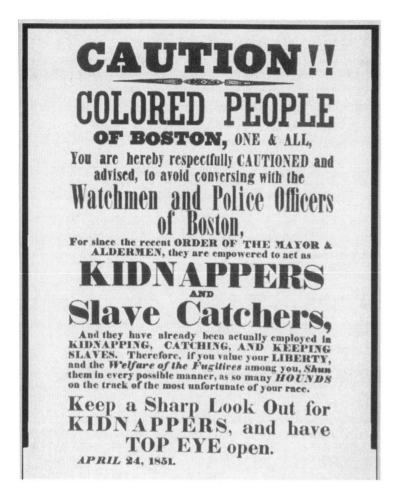

CAUTION!!

COLORED PEOPLE

OF BOSTON, ONE & ALL,

You are hereby respectfully CAUTIONED and advised, to avoid conversing with the

Watchmen and Police Officers of Boston,

For since the recent ORDER OF THE MAYOR & ALDERMEN, they are empowered to act as

KIDNAPPERS
AND
Slave Catchers,

And they have already been actually employed in KIDNAPPING, CATCHING, AND KEEPING SLAVES. Therefore, if you value your LIBERTY, and the *Welfare of the Fugitives* among you, *Shun* them in every possible manner, as so many *HOUNDS* on the track of the most unfortunate of your race.

Keep a Sharp Look Out for KIDNAPPERS, and have TOP EYE open.

APRIL 24, 1851.

The Compromise of 1850 included the Fugitive Slave Act, which mandated that citizens assist in the capture of runaway slaves. Pictured here is a handbill warning African Americans in Boston to avoid law enforcement agents empowered to enforce the act.

LIBRARY OF CONGRESS

massive remedy for knock-and-announce violations would generate a constant flood of litigation, with defendants claiming law enforcement failed to observe the rule. Allowing defendants to follow this path would overwhelm the criminal justice system with knock-and-announce complaints, the Court concluded, and result in a "get-out-of-jail-free card" for untold numbers of defendants. The Court refused to let this happen.

Legal scholars anticipated the Court to revisit the exclusionary rule, the fruit of the poisonous tree doctrine, and exceptions to that doctrine as the court's personnel continued to change in the following years.

FURTHER READINGS

Bloom, Robert M., and Mark S. Brodin. 2006. *Criminal Procedure: The Constitution and The Police.* 5th ed. New York, NY: Aspen Publishers.

Fauver, Deborah. 2003. "Evidence not Suppressed Despite Failure to Give Miranda Warning." *Daily Record (St. Louis, Mo./St. Louis Countian)* (October 14).

Hurley, Lawrence. 2003. "Reversal Leaves Federal Case Intact, Prosecutor Says." *Daily Record (Baltimore, MD)* (June 2).

McCrackin, Sidney M., 1985. "*New York v. Quarles:* The Public Safety Exception to Miranda." *Tulane Law Review* 59 (March).

CROSS REFERENCES

Criminal Law; Criminal Procedure.

FRUSTRATION

In the law of contracts, the destruction of the value of the performance that has been bargained for by the promisor as a result of a supervening event.

FRUSTRATION of purpose has the effect of discharging the promisor from his or her obligation to perform, in spite of the fact that performance by the promisee is possible, since the purpose for which the contract was entered into has been destroyed. For example, an individual reserves a hall for a wedding. In the event that the wedding is called off, the value of the agreement would be destroyed. Even though the promisee could still literally perform the obligation by reserving and providing the hall for the wedding, the purpose for which the contract was entered into was defeated. Apart from a nonrefundable deposit fee, the promisor is ordinarily discharged from any contractual duty to rent the hall.

In order for frustration to be used as a DEFENSE for nonperformance, the value of the anticipated counterperformance must have been substantially destroyed and the frustrating occurrence must have been beyond the contemplation of the parties at the time the agreement was made.

FUGITIVE FROM JUSTICE

An individual who, after having committed a criminal offense, leaves the jurisdiction of the court where such crime has taken place or hides within such jurisdiction to escape prosecution.

A FUGITIVE FROM JUSTICE who flees from one state to another may be subjected to EXTRADITION in the state to which he or she has fled.

FUGITIVE SLAVE ACT OF 1850

The FUGITIVE SLAVE ACT OF 1850 mandated that states to which escaped slaves fled were obligated to return them to their masters upon their discovery and subjected persons who helped runaway slaves to criminal sanctions. The first

Fugitive Slave Act was enacted by Congress in 1793 but as the northern states abolished SLAVERY, the act was rarely enforced. The southern states bitterly resented the northern attitude toward slavery, which was ultimately demonstrated by the existence of the Underground Railroad, an arrangement by which abolitionists helped runaway slaves obtain freedom.

To placate the South, the Fugitive Slave Act of 1850 (9 Stat. 462) was enacted by Congress as part of the COMPROMISE OF 1850. It imposed a duty on all citizens to assist FEDERAL marshals to enforce the law or be prosecuted for their failure to do so. The act also required that when a slave was captured, he or she was to be brought before a federal court or COMMISSIONER, but the slave would not be tried by a jury nor would his or her testimony be given much weight. The statements of the slave's alleged owner were the main EVIDENCE, and the alleged owner was not even required to appear in court.

Northern reaction against the Fugitive Slave Act was strong, and many states enacted laws that nullified its effect, making it worthless. In cases where the law was enforced, threats or acts of mob violence often required the dispatch of federal troops. Persons convicted of violating the act were often heavily fined, imprisoned, or both. The refusal of northern states to enforce the Fugitive Slave Act was alleged by South Carolina as one reason for its secession from the Union prior to the onset of the Civil War.

The acts of 1793 and 1850 remained legally operative until their REPEAL by Congress on June 28, 1864 (13 Stat. 200).

✧ FULBRIGHT, JAMES WILLIAM

James William Fulbright served as a U.S. senator from Arkansas from 1945 to 1974. Fulbright played an important role in shaping U.S. foreign policy as chairman of the Senate Foreign Relations Committee. His opposition to the VIETNAM WAR and to unbridled presidential power in foreign affairs contributed to major shifts in the conduct of U.S. foreign relations.

Fulbright was born in Sumner, Missouri, on April 9, 1905, the son of a prosperous Arkansas businessman. Fulbright was the youngest of four children born to Jay and Roberta Waugh Fulbright. His father was a banker, farmer, and businessman. His mother wrote a column for the family-owned Fayetteville newspaper. He

James W. Fulbright.
LIBRARY OF CONGRESS

entered the University of Arkansas at the age of 16, and graduated in 1925. From 1925 to 1928 Fulbright attended Oxford University, in England, as a Rhodes Scholar. This educational experience deepened his intellectual interests and provided a strong background for public life. He graduated from GEORGE WASHINGTON University Law School in 1934, and then taught at that school for two years. In 1936 he accepted a teaching position at the University of Arkansas. In 1939 he was appointed president of the University of Arkansas. At age 34 he was the youngest college president in the United States. His tenure was short, however, as a new governor dismissed him in 1941.

Fulbright then turned his focus to politics. As a Democrat he was elected to the U.S. House of Representatives in 1942. In 1945 he was elected to the U.S. Senate. His previous time as a Rhodes Scholar led him to sponsor the Fulbright Act of 1946, 22 U.S.C.A. § 245 et seq., which awards scholarships to U.S. citizens for study and research abroad and to citizens from other nations for study in the United States. The establishment of the Fulbright Scholarship exchange program has proved to be an enduring legacy.

Fulbright, although personally a moderate on matters of race, believed in the 1950s that he needed to move to the right on race issues to protect his political future in Arkansas. This led

POWER TENDS TO CONFUSE ITSELF WITH VIRTUE AND A GREAT NATION IS PECULIARLY SUSCEPTIBLE TO THE IDEA THAT ITS POWER IS A SIGN OF GOD'S FAVOR.
—JAMES W. FULBRIGHT

him to sign the Southern Manifesto, a 1956 DOCUMENT signed by southern senators and representatives that expressed their displeasure at the Supreme Court's decision in BROWN V. BOARD OF EDUCATION (Brown I), 347 U.S. 483, 74 S. Ct. 686, 98 L. Ed. 873 (1954), which struck down state-sponsored racially segregated public school systems, and *Brown v. Board of Education (Brown II),* 349 U.S. 294, 75 S. Ct. 753, 99 L. Ed. 1083 (1955), in which the Court directed that schools be desegregated with "all DELIBERATE speed." The manifesto condemned these decisions as abuses of judicial power and approved of Southern resistance, by all legal means, to the demand for desegregation. Fulbright doomed his national political prospects by signing the manifesto.

In the 1950s Fulbright became a close friend and colleague of Senate Majority Leader LYNDON B. JOHNSON, a Democrat from Texas. In 1959 Johnson engineered Fulbright's elevation to chairman of the Senate Foreign Relations Committee. Following the election of JOHN F. KENNEDY as president in 1960, Johnson, now VICE PRESIDENT, urged Kennedy to appoint Fulbright SECRETARY OF STATE. Johnson's efforts failed, in large part because Fulbright had supported the Southern Manifesto and racial segregation.

During the Kennedy administration, Fulbright opposed the United States's indirect involvement in the 1961 Bay of Pigs invasion, in which Cuban exiles made a futile attempt to overthrow the premier of Cuba, Fidel Castro. When the Vietnam War escalated under President Johnson, Fulbright became a consistent critic of presidential foreign policy. Fulbright had supported Johnson's Vietnam policy in the early part of the conflict, sponsoring the Gulf of Tonkin Resolution in 1964, Pub. L. No. 88-408, 78 Stat. 384, which allowed Johnson to wage war without seeking a congressional declaration. Within a year, however, Fulbright had become convinced that Johnson had misled him about events that had brought about the 1964 resolution.

Fulbright used the Foreign Relations Committee as a platform to criticize Vietnam policy. In January 1966, he held televised hearings on Vietnam. Leading opponents of the war testified that the conflict was going badly and that the United States did not have a legitimate role to play in Vietnam. Fulbright called Secretary of State Dean Rusk to appear three times during the hearings, repeatedly asking hard questions about U.S.-Asian policy. These hearings and additional ones in 1967 gave credibility to the antiwar movement and damaged the Johnson administration's credibility.

Skeptical about U.S. foreign policy and the attitudes of those who conduct it, Fulbright criticized policy makers in his books, *Old Myths and New Realities* (1964) and *The Arrogance of Power* (1967). His opposition continued during the Nixon administration.

In 1974 Fulbright was defeated by Dale L. Bumpers in the Democratic primary election. He served as a Washington lobbyist following his defeat and remained active in the Fulbright Scholarship program. In 1993 President BILL CLINTON awarded to Fulbright the Presidential Medal of Freedom, the highest award given to a

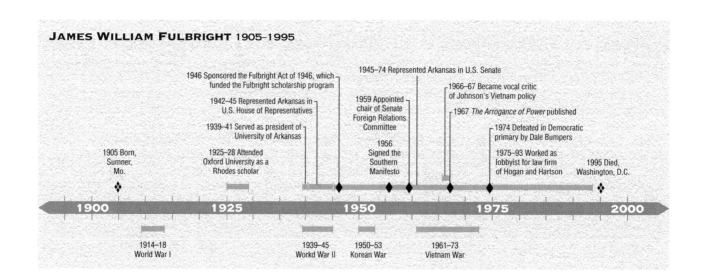

JAMES WILLIAM FULBRIGHT 1905–1995

1905 Born, Sumner, Mo.

1925–28 Attended Oxford University as a Rhodes scholar

1939–41 Served as president of University of Arkansas

1942–45 Represented Arkansas in U.S. House of Representatives

1946 Sponsored the Fulbright Act of 1946, which funded the Fulbright scholarship program

1956 Signed the Southern Manifesto

1959 Appointed chair of Senate Foreign Relations Committee

1945–74 Represented Arkansas in U.S. Senate

1966–67 Became vocal critic of Johnson's Vietnam policy

1967 *The Arrogance of Power* published

1974 Defeated in Democratic primary by Dale Bumpers

1975–93 Worked as lobbyist for law firm of Hogan and Hartson

1995 Died, Washington, D.C.

1900   1925   1950   1975   2000

1914–18 World War I

1939–45 Workd War II

1950–53 Korean War

1961–73 Vietnam War

civilian by the FEDERAL government, in honor of Fulbright's dedication to public service. Fulbright died of a stroke in Washington, D.C., on February 9, 1995.

FURTHER READINGS

Halberstam, David. 1993. *The Best and the Brightest.* New York: Ballantine.

O'Neill, William L. 2005. *Coming Apart: An Informal History of America in the 1960s.* Chicago: Dee.

Woods, Randall Bennett. 2006. *J. William Fulbright: A Biography.* Cambridge, MA: Cambridge Univ.

CROSS REFERENCES

Cuban Missile Crisis; Vietnam War.

FULL FAITH AND CREDIT CLAUSE

The Full Faith and Credit Clause—Article IV, Section 1, of the U.S. Constitution—provides that the various states must recognize LEGISLATIVE ACTS, public records, and judicial decisions of the other states within the United States. It states that "Full Faith and Credit shall be given in each State to the public Acts, Records, and judicial Proceedings of every other State." The statute that implements the clause, 28 U.S.C.A. § 1738, further specifies that "a state's preclusion rules should control matters originally litigated in that state." The FULL FAITH AND CREDIT CLAUSE ensures that judicial decisions rendered by the courts in one state are recognized and honored in every other state. It also prevents parties from moving to another state to escape enforcement of a judgment or to relitigate a controversy already decided elsewhere, a practice known as forum shopping.

In drafting the Full Faith and Credit Clause, the Framers of the Constitution were motivated by a desire to unify their new country while preserving the autonomy of the states. To that end, they sought to guarantee that judgments rendered by the courts of one state would not be ignored by the courts of other states. The Supreme Court reiterated the Framers' INTENT when it held that the Full Faith and Credit Clause precluded any further litigation of a question previously decided by an Illinois court in *Milwaukee County v. M. E. White Co.,* 296 U.S. 268, 56 S. Ct. 229, 80 L. Ed. 220 (1935). The Court held that by including the clause in the Constitution, the Framers intended to make the states "integral parts of a single nation throughout which a remedy upon a just obligation might be demanded as of right, irrespective of the state of its origin."

The Full Faith and Credit Clause is invoked primarily to enforce judgments. When a valid judgment is rendered by a court that has JURISDICTION over the parties, and the parties receive proper notice of the action and a reasonable opportunity to be heard, the Full Faith and Credit Clause requires that the judgment receive the same effect in other states as in the state where it is entered. A party who obtains a judgment in one state may petition the court in another state to enforce the judgment. When this is done, the parties do not relitigate the issues, and the court in the second state is obliged to fully recognize and honor the judgment of the first court in determining the enforceability of the judgment and the procedure for its execution.

The Full Faith and Credit Clause has also been invoked to recognize the validity of a MARRIAGE. Traditionally, every state honored a marriage legally contracted in any other state. However, in 1993, the Hawaii Supreme Court held that Hawaii's statute restricting legal marriage to parties of the opposite sex establishes a sex-based classification, which is subject to STRICT SCRUTINY if challenged on EQUAL PROTECTION grounds (*Baehr v. Lewin,* 852 P.2d 44, 74 Haw. 530). Although the court did not recognize a CONSTITUTIONAL right to same-sex marriage, it raised the possibility that a successful equal protection challenge to the state's marriage laws could eventually lead to state-sanctioned same-sex marriages. In response to the *Baehr* case, Congress in 1996 passed the DEFENSE of Marriage Act (110 Stat. § 2419), which defines marriage as a union of a man and a woman for FEDERAL purposes and expressly grants states the right to refuse to recognize a same-sex marriage performed in another state.

During the 1980s and 1990s, the Full Faith and Credit Clause was applied to new matters. CHILD CUSTODY determinations had historically fallen under the jurisdiction of state courts, and before the 1970s, other states did not accord them full faith and credit enforcement. As a result, a divorced parent who was unhappy with one state's custody decision could sometimes obtain a more favorable RULING from another state. This was an incentive for a dissatisfied parent to kidnap a child and move to another state in order to petition for custody. In response to this situation, the Uniform Child Custody Jurisdiction Act (UCCJA) was adopted by the National Conference of Commissioners on Uniform State Laws in 1968. By 1984 every state had adopted a version of the UCCJA. In 1980, Congress passed the Parental KIDNAPPING Prevention Act (28 U.S.C.A. § 1738A), which aids enforcement and promotes finality in child custody decisions by providing that valid custody decrees are entitled to full faith and credit enforcement in other states. The VIOLENCE AGAINST WOMEN ACT OF 1994 (Pub. L. No. 103-322 [codified in scattered sections of 8 U.S.C.A., 18 U.S.C.A., 42 U.S.C.A.]) extends full faith and credit to the enforcement of protective orders, which previously were not enforced except in the state where they were rendered. This gave a new measure of protection to victims who moved to a different state after obtaining a protective order in one state.

FURTHER READINGS

Cooke, Edward F. 2002. *A Detailed Analysis of the Constitution.* Lanham, MD: Rowman & Littlefield.

Demelis, Linda M. 1994. "Interstate Child Custody and the Parental Kidnapping Prevention Act: The Continuing Search for a National Standard." *Hastings Law Journal* 45.

Hamilton, Heather. 1998. "The Defense of Marriage Act: A Critical Analysis of Its Constitutionality under the Full Faith and Credit Clause." *DePaul Law Review* 47 (summer).

Hasegawa, Kaleen S. 1999. "Re-Evaluating the Limits of the Full Faith and Credit Clause after Baker v. General Motors Corporation." *Univ. of Hawaii Law Review* 21 (winter).

Olson, Thomas A. 1995. "Rethinking Montana's View of Interstate Custody Disputes." *Montana Lawyer* 20.

Shuki-Kunze, Jeennie R. 1998. "The 'Defenseless' Marriage Act: The Constitutionality of the Defense of Marriage Act as an Extension of Congressional Power under the Full Faith and Credit Clause." *Case Western Reserve Law Review* 48 (winter).

❖ FULLER, MELVILLE WESTON

Melville Weston Fuller served as chief justice of the U.S. Supreme Court from 1888 to 1910. Fuller's term as chief justice was marked by many decisions that protected big business from FEDERAL laws that sought to regulate interstate COMMERCE. In addition, the Fuller Court's restrictive reading of the FOURTEENTH AMENDMENT led it to render the infamous SEPARATE BUT EQUAL racial segregation decision in PLESSY V. FERGUSON, 163 U.S. 537, 16 S. Ct. 1138, 41 L. Ed. 256 (1896).

Fuller was born February 11, 1833, in Augusta, Maine. He grew up in the household of his maternal grandfather, the chief justice of the Maine Supreme Judicial Court. Following his graduation from Bowdoin College in 1853, he apprenticed in his uncles' law offices and briefly attended Harvard Law School. Even though he did not receive a law degree, he was the first chief justice of the U.S. Supreme Court to serve with significant academic legal preparation. Fuller moved to Chicago in 1856 and established a law practice. An active member of the DEMOCRATIC PARTY, he served in the Illinois CONSTITUTIONAL Convention of 1861 and for one term (1862–64) in the state house of representatives. He attended as a DELEGATE every national Democratic convention between 1864 and 1880.

Fuller withdrew from day-to-day politics after he married Mary Ellen Coolbaugh, the daughter of a prominent Chicago banker, in 1866. His law practice thrived because of this family connection, and with his new wealth, he invested in real estate. Fuller specialized in APPELLATE practice, appearing before the U.S. Supreme Court many times.

Fuller's appointment to the Court in 1888 was driven by presidential politics and his long service to the Democratic Party. President Grover Cleveland, a Democrat who believed that it would be essential to win the state of Illinois as part of his re-election bid, nominated Fuller as chief justice to replace MORRISON R. WAITE, who had died in March 1888. Fuller and Cleveland were friends and political colleagues. At the time, the press described Fuller as "the most obscure man ever appointed Chief Justice" (Baker 1991, 360). Others were more unkind, dubbing him "the fifth best lawyer from the City of Chicago" (review of *The Chief Justiceship of* MELVILLE W. FULLER 1996, 109).

Fuller's 22-year term as chief justice was distinguished by his skillful handling of often contentious Court conferences. Justice OLIVER WENDELL HOLMES, JR. thought highly of Fuller's ability to maintain collegiality. At the end of his own legal career, Holmes ranked Fuller as the best chief justice under whom he had served. Fuller was an energetic JURIST who also served on the Permanent Court of ARBITRATION, at The Hague, Netherlands. That international organization, comprising jurists from various countries, ruled on world disputes. In 1899 Fuller arbitrated a boundary dispute between Venezuela and British Guyana.

The U.S. economy grew rapidly while Fuller served as chief justice. This expansion led to the concentration of economic power in certain industries by a small number of individuals and corporations. The federal government's efforts to regulate interstate commerce and to curtail the power of monopolies and trusts met fierce opposition from both the affected businesses and those who believed in a restricted role for the national government. Opponents of national power argued for continued adherence to the doctrine of FEDERALISM. That doctrine has many facets, including a fundamental ASSUMPTION that the national government must not intrude on the power of the states to manage their affairs.

Fuller believed in federalism, and he demonstrated this belief in his votes with the conservative majority on the Court. Writing for the majority in *United States v. E. C. Knight co.,* 156 U.S. 1, 15 S. Ct. 249, 39 L. Ed. 325 (1895), Fuller took the teeth out of the SHERMAN ANTI-TRUST ACT of July 2, 1890, which had declared illegal "every contract, combination in the form of a trust, or CONSPIRACY in RESTRAINT OF TRADE and commerce among the several states" (26 Stat. 209, c. 647). finding in favor of the Sugar Trust, a corporation that controlled virtually all sugar refining, Fuller held that a monopoly of manufacturing was not a monopoly of trade or commerce prohibited by the Sherman Act, as the manufacture of a product for sale is not commerce. It was up to each state, not the federal government, to protect its citizens from monopolistic business practices. The mere fact that goods were transported in interstate commerce was not sufficient to give Congress, under the COMMERCE CLAUSE, the

Melville W. Fuller.
LIBRARY OF CONGRESS

authority to regulate business. The holding in *Knight* survived until the NEW DEAL era of the 1930s, when power shifted to the federal government.

Fuller's belief in a limited role for the federal government was also demonstrated in Pollock v. Farmers' Loan & Trust Co., 157 U.S. 429, 15 S. Ct. 673, 39 L. Ed. 759 (1895). In *Pollock,* Fuller ruled invalid a federal law that imposed a two-percent tax on incomes of more than $4,000. Article I of the Constitution requires that "direct taxes shall be apportioned among the

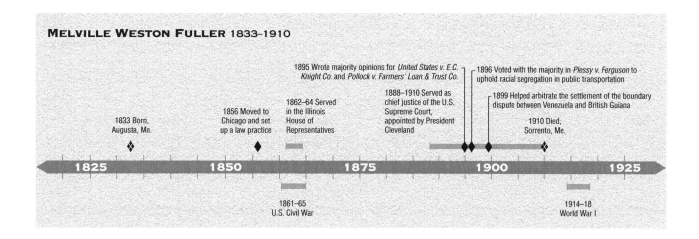

MELVILLE WESTON FULLER 1833–1910

1833 Born, Augusta, Me.

1856 Moved to Chicago and set up a law practice

1862–64 Served in the Illinois House of Representatives

1888–1910 Served as chief justice of the U.S. Supreme Court, appointed by President Cleveland

1895 Wrote majority opinions for *United States v. E.C. Knight Co.* and *Pollock v. Farmers' Loan & Trust Co.*

1896 Voted with the majority in *Plessy v. Ferguson* to uphold racial segregation in public transportation

1899 Helped arbitrate the settlement of the boundary dispute between Venezuela and British Guiana

1910 Died, Sorrento, Me.

1825   1850   1875   1900   1925

1861–65 U.S. Civil War

1914–18 World War I

several states ... according to their respective numbers." In a 5–4 vote, Fuller's Court held that the new INCOME TAX was a DIRECT TAX insofar as it was based on incomes derived from land and, as such, it had to be apportioned among the states. As the law did not provide for APPORTIONMENT, it was unconstitutional.

Decisions such as *Knight* and *Pollock* led critics to call Fuller and the conservative members of the Court the puppets of business interests and the protectors of wealth. In response to *Pollock,* the SIXTEENTH AMENDMENT was ratified by the states in 1913, authorizing the collection of a federal income tax.

Fuller's most dubious distinction is that he voted with the majority in *Plessy* to uphold racial segregation in public transportation. At issue in *Plessy* was an 1890 Louisiana law that required passenger trains that operated within the state to provide "separate but equal" accommodations for the "white and colored races." By a 7–1 vote, with one judge abstaining, the Court rejected the idea that the Fourteenth Amendment, enacted after the Civil War to preserve the CIVIL RIGHTS of newly freed slaves, "could have been intended to abolish distinctions based upon COLOR, or to enforce social, as distinguished from political, equality, or a COMMINGLING of the two races upon terms unsatisfactory to either."

With its focus on a limited national government and support of legally enforced racial segregation, the 22-year period of the Fuller Court has, in the words of legal historian Richard A. Epstein, "often been regarded as a black hole of American Constitutional law." With the conservative political and legal renaissance of the 1980s and 1990s, however, Fuller came back into favor, being regarded by some legal scholars as a jurist who was committed to economic development, market institutions, and limited government.

Fuller died July 4, 1910, in Sorrento, Maine.

FURTHER READINGS

Baker, Liva. 1991. *The Justice from Beacon Hill: The Life and Times of Oliver Wendell Holmes.* New York: HarperCollins.

Ely, James W., Jr. 1995. *The Chief Justiceship of Melville W. Fuller, 1888–1910.* Columbia, SC: Univ. of South Carolina Press.

Furer, Howard B., ed. 1986. *The Fuller Court, 1888–1910.* New York: Associated Faculty Press.

IF THE PROVISIONS OF THE CONSTITUTION CAN BE SET ASIDE BY AN ACT OF CONGRESS, WHERE IS THE COURSE OF USURPATION TO END?
—MELVILLE WESTON FULLER

FUND

A comprehensive term for any money that is set aside for a particular purpose or that is accessible for the satisfaction of debts or claims.

The term *public funds* is a colloquial label for the revenue of a government, state, or MUNICIPAL CORPORATION.

FUNDAMENTAL LAW

The constitution of a state or nation; the basic law and principles contained in federal and state constitutions that direct and regulate the manner in which government is exercised.

FUNDAMENTAL RIGHT

A fundamental right is a core individual constitutional right that is given the highest degree of judicial deference.

The Supreme Court has identified certain individual rights as fundamental CONSTITUTIONAL rights that must be protected from government restrictions. To accomplish this objective, the Court has established the STRICT SCRUTINY test, which is the most rigorous standard of JUDICIAL REVIEW. The Court will apply the scrutiny test only when a FUNDAMENTAL RIGHT or a SUSPECT CLASSIFICATION such as race is involved. The government must have a compelling interest to restrict a fundamental right. Even if the government has such an interest, it must show that the law or policy is the least restrictive means of achieving this goal.

The fountainhead of fundamental rights is the Constitution's BILL OF RIGHTS. The FIRST AMENDMENT identifies the right to FREEDOM OF SPEECH, the right to religious freedom, and the right to freedom of association as fundamental rights. The SECOND AMENDMENT protects the right to keep and bear arms, which is viewed as a core right. The FIFTH AMENDMENT protects the right to DUE PROCESS OF LAW and the right against SELF-INCRIMINATION. Over time the Supreme Court has acknowledged other fundamental rights that are not explicitly stated in the Constitution. These include the right to travel within the United States, the right to private property, the right to vote, the right to privacy, the right to procreation, and the right to marry.

The recognition of certain fundamental rights applied only to actions taken by the FEDERAL government until the enactment of the FOURTEENTH AMENDMENT following the Civil War. This amendment guaranteed individuals that state governments could not deny them due process of law, EQUAL PROTECTION of law, or all recognized PRIVILEGES AND IMMUNITIES of law. The Supreme Court, concerned that the amendment gave too much power to the federal courts, refused to read these three clauses broadly until the late 1930s. The Court slowly began to apply fundamental rights from the Constitution to the states, selectively incorporating them into the Fourteenth Amendment's due process clause.

Fundamental rights that are not specifically stated in the Constitution have been based on due process clauses of the Fifth and Fourteenth Amendments. The doctrine of SUBSTANTIVE DUE PROCESS bars the government from infringing on fundamental constitutional right. Unlike procedural process, where the administration of the law is examined, substantive due process deals with liberties that are not expressly listed in the Bill of Rights but which are found to be essential concepts of freedom and equality.

Using substantive due process, the Supreme Court has recognized the right to personal autonomy, bodily integrity, self-dignity, sexual identity, and SELF-DETERMINATION under the umbrella of an individual's right to privacy. In the 1960s, the Court used the right to privacy in *Griswold v. Connecticut* (381 U.S., 85 S. Ct. 1678, 14 L. Ed. 2d 510 [1965]) to strike down a law forbidding married adults from using BIRTH CONTROL. The right to privacy was extended in *Eisenstadt v. Baird* (405 U.S. 438, 92 S. Ct. 1029, 21 L. Ed. 2d 349 [1972]). The Court struck down a state law that prohibited unmarried persons from obtaining contraceptives. This decision paved the way for one of the most controversial decision in U.S. LEGAL HISTORY, which was based on substantive due process: *Roe v. Wade* (401 U.S. 113, 93 S. Ct. 705, 35 L. Ed. 2d 147 [1973]). The Court ruled that the due process clause gave women the right to have an ABORTION during the first trimester of pregnancy without state INTERFERENCE.

Critics of substantive due process point to the *Roe* decision as an example of the perils of using the doctrine. They contend that substantive due process gives judges the ability to inject their own values and prejudices into a controversial issue. Moreover, the use of this doctrine to identify fundamental rights discredits the judicial decision-making process and leads many to believe the decision was illegitimate.

In addition, critics note that later generations of justices have overturned substantive due process rulings, concluding that the right identified, such as liberty of contract, is not fundamental.

Despite these criticisms, the Court used substantive due process in 2003 to overturn a RULING on homosexuality. In *Lawrence v. Texas* (539 U.S. 558, 123 S. Ct. 2472, 156 L. Ed. 2d 508), the Court overturned a state law that made SODOMY between homosexuals a crime. Justice ANTHONY KENNEDY, writing for the majority, invoked *Roe* and the birth control decisions, stating that these cases made clear that the due process clause "has a substantive dimension of fundamental significance in defining the rights of the person." As a general rule, the state should not attempt to "define the meaning of the relationship or to set its BOUNDARIES absent INJURY to a person or abuse of an INSTITUTION the law protects." If homosexuals wish to express their sexuality in certain conduct the Constitution allows them "the right to make the choice." The Court's decision to declare a due process right to consensual, intimate conduct again angered social conservatives, who claimed that the Court was applying its own pro-homosexual views rather than following the commands of the Constitution.

The identification of fundamental rights is important. Once given this status and the strict scrutiny review standard that makes it difficult for the government to impose restrictions, the right becomes one more piece in the foundation of U.S. CONSTITUTIONAL LAW.

FURTHER READINGS

Flack, Horace Edgar. 2003. *The Adoption of the Fourteenth Amendment.* Birmingham, Ala.: Palladium Press.

Langran, Robert. 2003. *The Supreme Court: A Concise History.* New York: Peter Lang.

Tribe, Lawrence. 2008. *The Invisible Constitution.* New York: Oxford Univ. Press.

CROSS REFERENCES

Rational Basis Test; Strict Scrutiny; Suspect Classification.

FUNGIBLE

A description applied to items of which each unit is identical to every other unit, such as in the case of grain, oil, or flour.

FUNGIBLE goods are those that can readily be estimated and replaced according to weight, measure, and amount.

Elmer Branch, one of the plaintiffs in Furman v. Georgia, holds out a newspaper to another death row inmate after the Supreme Court held that the death penalty constituted cruel and unusual punishment.

AP IMAGES

FURMAN V. GEORGIA

In *Furman v. Georgia*, 408 U.S. 238, 92 S. Ct. 2726, 33 L. Ed. 2d 346 (1972), the U.S. Supreme Court struck down three death sentences, finding that they constituted CRUEL AND UNUSUAL PUNISHMENT in violation of the Eighth and Fourteenth Amendments to the U.S. Constitution. Hailed, at the time, as a victory for opponents of the death penalty, *Furman* actually helped states rewrite their death penalty laws to pass CONSTITUTIONAL muster.

The path to *Furman* began in 1962 with ROBINSON V. CALIFORNIA, 370 U.S. 660, 82 S. Ct. 1417, 8 L. Ed. 2d 758. In *Robinson*, the U.S. Supreme Court ruled that the Cruel and Unusual Punishments Clause could be applied to the states through the FOURTEENTH AMENDMENT. Opponents of the death penalty saw this RULING

as an opportunity to litigate the constitutionality of state death penalty cases in FEDERAL court.

Furman centered on the convictions and death sentences of three African American men: William Henry Furman was convicted in Georgia for murder, Lucious Jackson was convicted in Georgia for RAPE, and Elmer Branch was convicted in Texas for rape. The juries in each of the cases were not mandated by law to vote for the death penalty, nor were they given specific criteria to evaluate in making their penalty decisions.

The U.S. Supreme Court issued a PER CURIAM opinion, on a 5–4 vote to reverse the death sentences. The Court typically issues its decisions with a majority opinion written and signed by one the justices. On rare occasions the Court will issue a per curiam decision, which takes the form of a BRIEF, unsigned opinion. A per curiam decision signifies that the Court was deeply divided over the reasons that went into its ultimate decision to either affirm or reverse the lower court.

All nine justices wrote a separate opinion to articulate their reasoning. Although five justices voted to reverse the death sentences, their concurring opinions revealed that it was a shaky coalition. Justices WILLIAM O. DOUGLAS, William J. Brennan Jr., and THURGOOD MARSHALL doubted that any application of the death penalty could avoid being a cruel and unusual punishment.

Justice Douglas concluded that the death penalty was disproportionately applied to people who were poor and socially disadvantaged. This disproportion suggested that the EQUAL PROTECTION Clause of the Fourteenth Amendment must be applied to strike down the death penalty because any inequality of application was cruel and unusual punishment. Douglas's opinion raised the possibility that proportionate application would make CAPITAL PUNISHMENT constitutional.

Justices Brennan and Marshall staked out an absolutist position, finding the death penalty per se cruel and unusual punishment, given the "evolving standards of decency" they saw in contemporary U.S. society. This meant that no matter the FACT SITUATION, no matter the proper application of due process and equal protection, capital punishment was inherently unconstitutional.

The most influential opinion came from Justice POTTER STEWART:

> The penalty of death differs from all other forms of criminal punishment, not in degree

but IN KIND. It is unique in its rejection of rehabilitation of the CONVICT as a basic purpose of criminal justice. And it is unique, finally, in its ABSOLUTE renunciation of all that is embodied in our concept of humanity.

Stewart held that because death was different from any other punishment, it had to be administered rationally and fairly. He rejected the absolutist position of Brennan and Marshall, yet still voted to reverse the penalties of Furman, Jackson, and Branch because he believed their death sentences were imposed capriciously.

Stewart looked at the circumstances surrounding the imposition of the three death sentences. The juries in these cases had been given unbridled discretion to do what they wished in deciding whether to impose capital punishment. The result, in Stewart's view, was that the death penalty was "wantonly and ... freakishly imposed." These death sentences were "cruel and unusual in the same way that being struck by lightning is cruel and unusual."

Justice BYRON R. WHITE took a slightly different tack, concluding that the infrequency of execution prevented the penalty from serving as an effective deterrent and from consistently meeting legitimate social needs for retribution.

Chief Justice WARREN E. BURGER dissented, as did Justices HARRY A. BLACKMUN, Lewis F. Powell Jr., and WILLIAM H. REHNQUIST. The dissenters argued that the Court was straying into an area properly delegated to the judgment of state legislatures. The private opinions of justices about the morality of capital punishment, they opined, should not be presented as public policy in a court of law.

The *Furman* decision stopped all executions then pending in the 39 states that authorized the death penalty. More than six hundred persons were awaiting execution at the time. Faced with a splintered Supreme Court decision, states had three options: develop mandatory death sentences for crimes that were carefully defined by STATUTE, develop jury guidelines to reduce juror discretion, or abolish capital punishment.

The state of Georgia chose to develop guidelines for jurors. Once a person is convicted in a capital trial, the jury must determine, in the penalty phase, whether any unique aggravating and MITIGATING CIRCUMSTANCES should be considered before the court decides whether to impose a death sentence. In 1976, the U.S. Supreme Court upheld these jury guidelines in

GREGG V. GEORGIA, 428 U.S. 153, 96 S. Ct. 2909, 49 L. Ed. 2d 859. With the *Gregg* decision, the four-year moratorium on the death penalty ended and, according to some, launched the modern era of capital punishment.

FURTHER READINGS

Baldus, David C., et al. 1998. "Racial Discrimination and the Death Penalty in the Post-Furman Era: An Empirical and Legal Overview, with Recent Findings from Philadelphia." *Cornell Law Review* 83 (September).

Banner, Stuart. 2003. *The Death Penalty: An American History.* Cambridge, MA: Harvard Univ. Press.

Sarat, Austin. 1998. "Recapturing the Spirit of Furman: The American Bar Association and the New Abolitionist Politics." *Law and Contemporary Problems* 61 (autumn). Available online at http://www.law.duke.edu/shell/cite.pl?61+Law+&+Contemp.+Probs.+5+(Autumn+1998); website home page: http://www.law.duke.edu (accessed July 25, 2009).

CROSS REFERENCE

Incorporation Doctrine.

FUTURE ACQUIRED PROPERTY

Property that is received or obtained by a borrower subsequent to the date that he or she executes a loan agreement which offers property currently owned as collateral.

FUTURE ACQUIRED PROPERTY, which is also known as after-acquired property, encompasses both personal property and real property and provides additional COLLATERAL to ensure that a loan will be satisfied. There must, however, be a provision in the loan agreement between the borrower and the lender that gives the lender a right to the specific property of the borrower that he or she acquires subsequent to the execution of the agreement.

SECURED TRANSACTIONS frequently involve the treatment of personal property as future acquired property. For example, a debtor who owns a retail store might accept a future acquired property provision in a security agreement with a creditor in order to obtain funds to buy additional INVENTORY. The purchase of new inventory constitutes additional collateral that ensures the satisfaction of the loan. Language commonly used to phrase a future acquired property term in a contract is "any or all obligations covered by the security agreement are to be secured by all inventory now or HEREAFTER acquired by the debtor."

Mortgages, particularly those affecting commercial properties, involve the treatment of real property as future acquired property. The mortgagee (who is the lender) will include in the mortgage an AFTER-ACQUIRED PROPERTY CLAUSE which provides that the mortgagee will have an equitable lien, which is a right to have property used to repay a debt, in all the real property that the mortgagor (who is the borrower) obtains after the mortgage is executed. For example, ABC Co. owns BLACKACRE and borrows funds from XYZ Bank. ABC executes a note and mortgage on Blackacre to XYZ, which XYZ records. The mortgage also contains an after-acquired property clause. When ABC subsequently purchases WHITEACRE to serve as its warehouse, XYZ automatically obtains an equitable lien in Whiteacre. Because a mortgage with an after-acquired property clause cannot be traced through an examination of the CHAIN OF TITLE of the after-acquired property, anyone who subsequently buys or has a lien against the mortgagor's property has no notice of the equitable lien of the mortgagee. Such purchasers or lienors might, therefore, have greater rights to the property than the mortgagee if they took the property in GOOD FAITH and without notice. The mortgagee must take additional steps to protect the priority of his or her lien in future acquired property. It is a common practice for mortgage lenders to require that the mortgagor execute a recordable amendment to his or her mortgage describing in detail the future acquired property immediately after its acquisition.

The treatment of future acquired property varies, however, from JURISDICTION to jurisdiction.

FUTURE EARNINGS

Earnings that, if it had not been for an injury, could have been made in the future, but which were lost as result of the injury.

FUTURE INTEREST

A claim on property, real or personal, that will begin at some point in the future. A future interest allows the grantor to retain the right to use that property until the specified transfer date. Future interest agreements are often used by donors for tax purposes. For example, a person may grant a future interest in his or her home to a charity, with the stipulation that he will retain use of the home for the remainder of his life, also called a "life estate". Although the charity will not receive the property until the donor's death, the donor can claim a tax deduction the same year the future interest is granted. Also called future estate.

CROSS REFERENCES

Bequest; Will.

FUTURES

Contracts that promise to purchase or sell standard commodities at a forthcoming date and at a fixed price.

This type of contract is an extremely speculative transaction and ordinarily involves such standard goods as rice or soybeans. Profit and loss are based upon promises to deliver—as opposed to possession of—the actual commodities.

GAG ORDER

A court order to gag or bind an unruly defendant or remove her or him from the courtroom in order to prevent further interruptions in a trial. In a trial with a great deal of notoriety, a court order directed to attorneys and witnesses not to discuss the case with the media—such order being felt necessary to assure the defendant of a fair trial. A court order, directed to the media, not to report certain aspects of a crime or criminal investigation prior to trial.

Unruly defendants who disrupt trials are very rarely literally gagged in modern courts. However, the U.S. Supreme Court has upheld the constitutionality of the PRACTICE in cases where a DEFENDANT is particularly disruptive. In *Illinois v. Allen*, 397 U.S. 337, 90 S. Ct. 1057, 25 L. Ed. 2d 353 (1970), the Court affirmed that gagging or binding the defendant, or removing him or her from the courtroom, does not violate the Confrontation Clause of the SIXTH AMENDMENT to the U.S. Constitution, which holds, "In all criminal prosecutions, the ACCUSED shall enjoy the right ... to be confronted with the witnesses against him." According to ASSOCIATE JUSTICE Hugo L. Black, who wrote the Court's opinion,

> [A] defendant can lose his right to be present at trial if, after he has been warned by the judge that he will be removed if he continues his disruptive behavior, he nevertheless insists on conducting himself in a manner so disorderly, disruptive, and disrespectful of

the court that his trial cannot be carried on with him in the courtroom. Once lost, the right to be present can, of course, be reclaimed as soon as the defendant is willing to conduct himself consistently with the decorum and respect INHERENT in the concept of courts and judicial proceedings.

Of the three methods that the Court found available to a judge when faced with a disruptive defendant—gag and shackles, CITATION for CONTEMPT of court, and physical removal—the Court held that a gag and shackles should be considered the option of LAST RESORT. According to the Court,

> Not only is it possible that the sight of shackles and gags might have a significant effect on the jury's feelings about the defendant, but the use of this technique is itself something of an affront to the very dignity and decorum of judicial proceedings that the judge is seeking to uphold.

One of the few modern instances of literal gagging occurred in the 1968 CHICAGO EIGHT trial (sometimes called the Chicago Seven trial because one defendant was removed). In that trial, FEDERAL judge Julius J. Hoffman ordered Black Panthers leader Bobby Seale bound and gagged after Seale and Hoffman engaged in vociferous argument during the trial. Seale still managed to disrupt the proceedings. He was then removed from the trial and tried separately.

Courts may attempt to control prejudicial publicity by restricting the information that trial participants can give to the press both before and during a trial. This remains the type of GAG ORDER most frequently used by courts.

Another type of gag ORDER was for a while used by courts to restrict the press from reporting certain facts regarding a trial. This gag order became more common after the Supreme Court's 1966 decision in *Sheppard v. Maxwell*, 384 U.S. 333, 86 S. Ct. 1507, 16 L. Ed. 2d 600, in which it reversed a criminal CONVICTION on the grounds that PRETRIAL PUBLICITY had unfairly prejudiced the jury against the defendant and denied him his Sixth Amendment right to a fair trial. However, in a 1976 decision, *Nebraska Press Ass'n v. Stuart*, 427 U.S. 539, 96 S. Ct. 2791, 49 L. Ed. 2d 683, the Court held that pretrial gag orders on the press are unconstitutional. It ruled that such orders represent an unconstitutional PRIOR RESTRAINT and violate the FIRST AMENDMENT, which guarantees the FREEDOM OF THE PRESS.

FURTHER READINGS

"Challenges to Gag Orders End in Mixed Results." 2000. *News Media & the Law* 24 (spring).

Minnefor, Eileen A. 1995. "Looking for Fair Trials in the Information Age: The Need for More Stringent Gag Orders against Trial Participants." *Univ. of San Francisco Law Review* 30 (fall).

Weiss, Eric A., and Debra L. Slifkin. 1999. "Enforceability of Rule 26(c) Confidentiality Rrders and Agreements." Federation of Insurance & *Corporate Counsel Quarterly* 49 (winter).

CROSS REFERENCE

Sheppard, Samuel H.

GAG RULE

A rule, regulation, or law that prohibits debate or discussion of a particular issue.

Between 1836 and 1844, the U.S. House of Representatives adopted a series of resolutions and rules that banned petitions calling for the ABOLITION of SLAVERY. Known as gag rules, these measures effectively tabled antislavery petitions without submitting them to usual House procedures. Public outcry over the gag rules ultimately aided the antislavery cause, and the fierce House debate concerning their future anticipated later conflicts over slavery.

The submission of petitions to Congress has been a feature of the U.S. political system ever since its inception. The FIRST AMENDMENT to the U.S. Constitution guarantees "the right of the people ... to petition the Government for a redress of grievances." First used in England, petitions have been considered an important means for the people to communicate grievances to their representatives or other public officials.

When the first GAG RULE was instituted in 1836, House protocol required that the first thirty days of each session of Congress be devoted to the reading of petitions from constituents. After those 30 days, petitions were read in the House every other Monday. Each petition was read aloud, printed, and assigned to an appropriate committee, which could choose to address or ignore it. This traditional procedure had been interrupted in 1835, when the House began to receive a large number of petitions advocating the abolition of slavery. Many of the petitions were organized by the American Anti-Slavery Society, which had formed in 1833.

Southern representatives, many of whom were slave owners and entertained no thoughts of abolishing slavery, were outraged by the antislavery petitions. In December 1835, southerners, uniting with northern Democrats, won a vote to table a petition that called for the abolition of slavery in the DISTRICT OF COLUMBIA. Breaking established precedent, the pro-slavery faction also won a vote to deny the petition its usual discussion, printing, and referral to committee.

This procedure for the "gagging" of abolition petitions was made into a formal resolution by the House on May 26, 1836: "All petitions, memorials, resolutions, propositions, or papers, relating in any way, or to any extent whatsoever, to the subject of slavery or the abolition of slavery, shall, without being either printed or referred, be laid on the table and ... no further action whatever shall be had thereon." The resolution incited strong opposition from many northerners, who perceived it as a violation of their time-honored CIVIL RIGHTS. JOHN QUINCY ADAMS, a former president and now a representative from Massachusetts, emerged as the leader of an effort to revoke the new resolution. JOHN C. CALHOUN (D-S.C.), although a member of the Senate rather than the House, orchestrated the battle to preserve it.

The pro-slavery faction succeeded in renewing the gag resolution, which expired at the end of each session of Congress, in both sessions of the Twenty-fifth Congress (1837–39). On January 28, 1840, it succeeded again when it won a vote to turn the resolution into House Rule 21 (in later versions, Rules 23 and 25):

> No petition, memorial, resolution, or other paper praying the abolition of slavery in the District of Columbia, or any State or Territory, or the slave trade between the States or TERRITORIES OF THE UNITED STATES, in which it now exists, shall be received by this House, or entertained in any way whatever.

As a formal House rule rather than a resolution, the gag rule was now a permanent part of House procedure and did not have to be renewed by vote each session.

This new gag rule provoked even stronger opposition. Whereas the previous gag resolution tabled antislavery petitions after they were received, the new gag rule did not allow petitions to be received. It was also more extreme than the Senate's approach, which was to receive such petitions but answer them in the negative. As a result of these changes, northerners who had previously supported the gag now joined Adams in opposing it. Several years later, on December 3, 1844, those opposed to the gag rule finally succeeded in rescinding it.

The term *gag rule* has also been applied to presidential regulations banning ABORTION counseling by employees of family planning clinics that received a particular type of FEDERAL funding.

FURTHER READINGS

Holmes, Stephen. 1988. "Gag Rules, or the Politics of Omission." In John Elster and Rune Slagstad, eds. *Constitutionalism and Democracy.* Cambridge: Cambridge Univ. Press

Jenkins, Jeffrey A., and Charles Stewart III. 2003. "The Gag Rule, Congressional Politics, and the Growth of Anti-Slavery Popular Politics." Available online at http://th.myweb.uga.edu/gagrule.pdf; website home page: http://th.myweb.uga.edu (accessed September 3, 2009).

Miller, William Lee. 1996. *Arguing about Slavery: The Great Battle in the United States Congress.* New York: Knopf.

CROSS REFERENCE

Congress of the United States.

GAME

Wild birds and beasts. The word includes all game birds and game animals.

The state, in its sovereign power, owns game for the benefit of the general public. The only manner in which a private individual can acquire ownership in game is by possessing it

An Ohio hunter displays a trophy buck taken during deer hunting season. Game laws govern the killing or taking of birds and beasts.

AP IMAGES

lawfully such as by hunting and killing it under a license.

Generally, every individual has the right to hunt and take game in any public place where his or her presence is lawful, so long as the person neither violates statutory regulations nor injures or infringes upon the rights of others. A hunter does not acquire an ABSOLUTE right to a wild animal by mere pursuit alone, and the individual forfeits any potential ownership by abandoning the chase prior to capture. The exclusive right to hunt or take game on privately owned property vests in the owner or his or her grantees. This PROPERTY RIGHT of the owner is limited by the right of the state to regulate and preserve the game for public use. A suit for trespass may be brought against one who interferes with another's right to hunt.

A statute that proscribes the hunting of game without a license, and that requires the payment of a fee for such license, constitutes a proper exercise of the police power of the state.

Game laws govern the killing or taking of birds and beasts. Game wardens ordinarily can arrest violators, seize illegally taken game, bring actions for trespass, or INSTITUTE prosecutions for violations of the game laws.

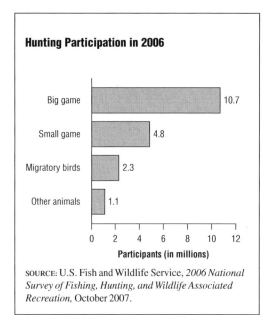

Hunting Participation in 2006

SOURCE: U.S. Fish and Wildlife Service, *2006 National Survey of Fishing, Hunting, and Wildlife Associated Recreation,* October 2007.

Under a number of game laws, it is a penal offense to kill or take certain types of game in certain seasons of the year or without a license. A hunter is required to exhibit a license when properly called on to do so, and it constitutes a legal violation if the person cannot do so.

In a situation where an individual has lawfully obtained possession of game—enclosing and caring for them as DOMESTIC animals—the person can kill one or more of them if necessary for care and management or for humane purposes. In addition, an individual might be justified in killing game in violation of the law if it were necessary for the protection of persons or property. It sometimes constitutes an offense to export game beyond the limits of the nation or state in which it was killed or captured, to ship it for sale in a certain manner, or to absent certain information upon the package.

The United States has entered into treaties with other countries, including Great Britain and Mexico, for the protection and preservation of migratory birds and game animals. It constitutes an offense to violate statutes that were enacted to implement such treaties. For example, a regulatory statute might limit the number of birds that can be killed by any individual each day, and it would be an offense to exceed such limit.

The FEDERAL government, subject to the CONSENT of the state, can establish a game refuge for the protection of game and migratory birds and proscribe all hunting in the vicinity. The U.S. Fish and Wildlife Service is administered by the INTERIOR DEPARTMENT, to conserve and preserve fish and game in wildlife refuges and game ranges.

CROSS REFERENCES

Endangered Species Act; Fish and Fishing.

GAMING

Gaming is the act or practice of gambling. It is an agreement between two or more individuals to play collectively at a game of chance for a stake or wager, which will become the property of the winner and to which all involved make a contribution.

Since the early 1990s, GAMING laws have been in a constant state of flux. Regulation of gaming is generally reserved to the states, but the U.S. Congress became involved in it in 1988 with the passage of the Indian Gaming Regulatory Act (Gaming Act) (Pub. Law. No. 100-497, 102 Stat. 2467 [25 U.S.C.A. § 2701 et seq.] [Oct. 17, 1988]), which brought tribal gaming under the regulation of state and FEDERAL governments.

Before the 1990s most gaming was illegal in a majority of states. Since the passage of the Gaming Act, many state legislatures have approved gaming in a variety of forms. Some states still outlaw all but charitable gambling, but most have expanded their definition of legal gaming operations to promote economic development.

The LEGAL HISTORY of gambling in the United States is marked by dramatic swings between PROHIBITION and popularity. In colonial times, games of chance were generally illegal except for state and private lotteries. Other gaming was considered a sin and not fit for discussion in polite society. In the early nineteenth century, the popular belief changed from seeing gaming as a sin to seeing it as a vice. Gamblers were no longer considered fallen in the eyes of God but were now seen as simply victims of their own weaknesses.

Gaming came under renewed attack during the presidency of ANDREW JACKSON (1829–1837). Part of the so-called Jacksonian morality of the period revived the view of gambling as sinful. By 1862, gaming was illegal in all states except Missouri and Kentucky, both of which retained state lotteries.

After the Civil War, legal gaming experienced a brief renaissance, only to fall out of favor again in the 1890s. At this point, it was outlawed even in the western territories, where card games such as poker and blackjack had become a regular DIVERSION in frontier life. By 1910, the United States was again virtually free of legalized gaming. Only Maryland and Kentucky allowed gambling, in the sole form of horse race betting.

In 1931 Nevada re-legalized casino gaming. Many states followed this lead in the 1930s by legalizing *pari-mutuel betting*, wherein all bets are pooled and then paid, less a management fee, to the holders of winning tickets. In 1963 New Hampshire formed the first STATE LOTTERY since the 1910s. By the 1990s gaming was the largest and fastest growing segment of the U.S. entertainment industry. In 1992, for example, U.S. citizens spent approximately four times more on gaming than on movies. Gaming is still illegal in some states, but most states have at least one form of legal gambling, most commonly a state-run lottery. In fact, instead of prohibiting gaming, many states now actively promote it by sponsoring lotteries and other games of chance.

Gaming laws vary from state to state. Idaho, for example, declares that "gambling is contrary to public policy and is strictly prohibited except for" pari-mutuel betting, bingo and raffle games for charity, and a state lottery (Idaho Const. art. III, § 20). Like lotteries in other states, the purpose of the one in Idaho is to generate revenue for the state. The lottery is run by the Idaho State Lottery Commission, which oversees all aspects of the game, including expenses and advertising. As of 2009, 43 states permit lotteries.

In addition to lotteries, some states with direct access to major river systems or lakes expanded their venues for gaming to include riverboats. On July 1, 1989, Iowa became the first state to authorize its Racing and Gaming Commission to grant a license to qualified organizations for the purpose of conducting gambling games on excursion boats in counties where referendums have been approved. Illinois quickly followed Iowa with its Riverboat Gambling Act (230 ILCS 10), which went into effect on February 7, 1990. Five more states passed legislation permitting licensing for riverboat casinos: Illinois,

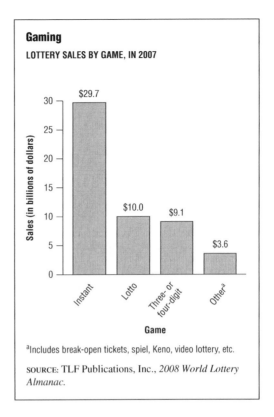

Gaming

LOTTERY SALES BY GAME, IN 2007

[Bar chart showing Sales (in billions of dollars) by Game:
Instant: $29.7
Lotto: $10.0
Three- or four-digit: $9.1
Other[a]: $3.6]

[a]Includes break-open tickets, spiel, Keno, video lottery, etc.

SOURCE: TLF Publications, Inc., *2008 World Lottery Almanac*.

ILLUSTRATION BY GGS CREATIVE RESOURCES. REPRODUCED BY PERMISSION OF GALE, A PART OF CENGAGE LEARNING.

Indiana, Louisiana, Mississippi, and Missouri. Some riverboat gambling vessels are permanently docked while others embark on brief cruises and return to their docks after several hours of gaming, dining, and entertainment for passengers.

Alabama is one of the few states that prohibit all gambling except for charitable gaming. Alabama maintains no state lottery and punishes gambling through criminal statutes. Under the Code of Alabama, sections 13A-12-24 and 13A-12-25 (1975), the possession of gambling records is a class A misdemeanor, which carries a penalty of not more than one year in JAIL or a $2,000 fine, or both.

Nevada is the most permissive state for gambling. Its public policy of gaming holds that "[t]he gaming industry is vitally important to the economy of the state and the GENERAL WELFARE of the inhabitants" (Nev. Rev. Stat. § 463.0129). Nevada statutes allow the broadest range of gaming activities, including pari-mutuel betting, betting on sports competitions and other events, and the full panoply of casino games. Gambling is heavily regulated by the Nevada Gaming Commission, and a wide range of criminal statutes are designed to ensure cooperation with the regulations of the commission.

Patrons of this South Dakota casino can play blackjack and slot machines. Regulation of gaming is generally reserved to the states.
DEADWOOD GULCH RESORT AND CASINO. DEADWOOD, SOUTH DAKOTA.

New Jersey is another active promoter of gaming. In 1976, New Jersey voters passed a REFERENDUM approving casino gaming, and that decision was codified in the Casino Control Act (N.J. Stat. Ann. § 5:12-1 et seq.). Gaming is limited to Atlantic City, and it does not include betting on sports events other than horse and dog races. However, like Nevada, New Jersey offers the full array of casino games.

The Gaming Act divides all gambling into three classes. Class I includes all traditional Indian games performed as a part of, or in connection with, tribal ceremonies or celebrations. Class II is limited to bingo, pull tabs, and card games not explicitly prohibited by the laws of the state. Class III encompasses all other forms of gambling, such as slot machines, poker, blackjack, dice games, off-track betting (where bets may be placed by persons not at the race track) and pari-mutuel betting on horses and dogs, and lotteries.

An Indian tribe may operate a class I game without restrictions. It may offer class II games with the oversight of the National Indian Gaming Commission, and class III games only if it reaches an agreement with the state in which it resides.

The Gaming Act provides that Native American tribes may operate high-stakes casinos only if they reach an agreement with the state in which they reside. Under the act, a state is required to enter into GOOD FAITH negotiations with a federally recognized tribe

to allow class III gaming that was legal in the state before the negotiations began. For example, if a state has legalized blackjack but not poker, blackjack is available for negotiations but not poker. Furthermore, when a state approves a new form of gambling, the state must make the new game available in negotiations with native tribes.

Native American groups have criticized the Gaming Act as interfering with tribal SOVER-EIGNTY. Indeed, a primary purpose of the act was to reconcile state interests in gaming with those of the tribe. Before the act, some Native American tribes ran sizable gambling operations on their land without regulation by the federal or state governments. Nevertheless, gaming has become a major source of income for many Native American tribes. As of 2009, there are approximately 400 Native American gaming establishments operated by about 220 federally recognized tribes.

The Gaming Act has also created opposition in some states that seeks to minimize gambling within their BOUNDARIES. Maine, for example, refused to give the Passamaquoddy tribe a license to conduct class III gaming operations on tribal land in Calais, near the Canadian border. The tribe sued the state for the right to conduct the high-stakes gaming. However, several years earlier, Maine had given land to the tribe in exchange for the tribe's agreement to submit to state JURISDIC-TION. In *Passamaquoddy Tribe v. Maine* (75 F. 3d 784 [1st Cir. 1996]), the First CIRCUIT COURT of Appeals ruled against the tribe. The court noted that Congress had been aware of Maine's agreement with the tribe and that Congress could have added to the Gaming Act, but chose not to, language making the act applicable to the state of Maine. According to the court, the gaming statute did not erase the 1980 agreement between the tribe and the state, and Maine had the right to refuse the tribe's request.

FURTHER READINGS

American Gaming Association. Available online at www.americangaming.org (accessed July 26, 2003).

Campion, Kristen M. 1995. "Riverboats: Floating Our Way to a Brighter Fiscal Future?" *Seton Hall Legislative Journal* 19.

Rose, I. Nelson. 1993. "Gambling and the Law—Update 1993." *Hastings Communications and Entertainment Law Journal* 15.

CROSS REFERENCES

Native American Rights; State Lottery.

❖ GANDHI, MOHANDAS KARAMCHAND

Widely known as Mahatma or "Great Soul", MOHANDAS KARAMCHAND GANDHI is considered one of history's great political pacifists. He is remembered nearly as much for his austere persona (frail, bespectacled, clad only in a draped loincloth) as his political achievements. Gandhi played a major role in leading India to INDEPENDENCE from British rule, in 1947, following WORLD WAR II.

The quintessential nonviolent activist, Gandhi dedicated his life to political and social reform. His teachings and example were to later influence such leaders as MARTIN LUTHER KING Jr. and Nelson Mandela, who also utilized passive resistance and conversion rather than confrontation to bring about social change. Gandhi's signature marks were what he called Satyagraha (the force of truth and love) and the ancient Hindu ideal of Ahisma, or nonviolence toward all living things.

Gandhi was born in western India in 1869. Just 11 years earlier (in 1858), Britain had declared India a loyal colony. The young Gandhi completed a British-style high school education and was greatly impressed with British manners, genteel culture, and Christian beliefs. He aspired to become a BARRISTER at law, but was prohibited from doing so by the local head of his Hindu caste in Bombay. His first act of public defiance was his decision to assume the role of an "outcaste" and leave for London to study law.

While studying in England, Gandhi first read (and was inspired by) the Bible and the Bhagavad Gita, a Hindu religious poem. The story of the Sermon on the Mount in the Christian New Testament stirred in him an interest in passive resistance, and he also became intrigued with the ethical basis of vegetarianism after befriending a few enthusiasts at a local restaurant. He would later use dietary fasting as a means to draw attention to social causes.

But it was an incident in 1893 that put into motion Gandhi's focused role in history. While on a legal assignment in South Africa, he was traveling on a train near Johannesburg when he was ordered to move from his first-class compartment to the "colored" car in the rear of the train. He refused. At the next station, he was thrown from the train and spent the night at the station. The experience triggered his

Mohandas Gandhi.
TIME LIFE PICTURES/
GETTY IMAGES

lifelong dedication to CIVIL RIGHTS and to the improvement of the lives of those with little political voice.

By 1906 he had taken on his first major political battle, confronting the South African government's move to fingerprint all Indians with publicized passive resistance. His efforts failed to provoke legal change, but he gained a wider following and influence.

Returning to India in 1915, Gandhi began a succession of political campaigns for independence in his homeland. He orchestrated widespread boycotts of British goods and services, and promoted peaceful noncooperation and nonviolent strikes. He is widely remembered for his 1930 defiance of the British law forbidding Indians to make their own salt. With 78 followers, he started on a march to the sea. Soon more than 60,000 supporters were arrested and jailed, but Britain was forced to negotiate with the gentle and powerful little man. Gandhi himself was arrested several times by the British, who considered him a troublemaker, and all total, spent about seven years of his life in JAIL.

Although his unrelenting efforts played a major role in India's independence in 1947, the victory was bittersweet for Gandhi. Britain announced not only the independence of India, but also the creation of the new Muslim state of Pakistan. With all his power and influence, Gandhi

AN UNJUST LAW IS ITSELF A SPECIES OF VIOLENCE. ARREST FOR ITS BREACH IS MORE SO.
—MOHANDAS GANDHI

could not undo the years of hatred between the Hindus and Muslims. On January 30, 1948, while arriving for evening prayers, he was gunned down by a Hindu fanatic who blamed the formation of Pakistan on Gandhi's tolerance for Muslims. Gandhi was 78 at his death.

The legacy of Ghandi, and his call for "conversion, not coercion," spread worldwide. Passive resistance, peace marches, sitdown strikes, and silent noncooperation became common means of nonviolent activism through much of the latter twentieth century, especially influencing demonstrators during the civil rights and VIETNAM WAR eras. Governmental entities accustomed to punishing violent protesters were forced to revamp their response to demonstrations in which the only violence was coming from police or guards. The U.S. Supreme Court was inundated with cases clarifying the limitations on FIRST AMENDMENT rights of speech and association. To this day, passive resistance remains a principal form of protestation for those seeking attention for their cause(s).

FURTHER READINGS

Hay, Stephen. 1989. "The Making of a Late-Victorian Hindu: M. K. Gandhi in London, 1888–1891." *Victorian Studies* (autumn).

McGeary, Johanna. 1999. "Mohandas Gandhi." *Time* (December 31).

Sudo, Phil. 1997. "The Legacy of Gandhi." *Scholastic Update* (April 11).

GANGS

A gang is sometimes difficult to define, especially in legal terms. Although gangs typically involve a congregation of individuals, primarily young males, certainly not all congregations or informal gatherings of young individuals constitute gangs. Definitions of gangs or street gangs vary among the laws governing them. Alabama law, for example, defines a "streetgang" as, "[A]ny combination, confederation, alliance, network, conspiracy, understanding, or similar arrangement in law or in fact, of three or more persons that, through its membership or through the agency of any member, engages in a course or pattern of criminal activity." Ala. Code § 13A-6-26 (2002).

The rise in gang violence since the 1980s caused lawmakers to seek a variety of methods to curb the formation and activities of these GANGS. According to statistics from the National Youth Gang Center, more than 24,500 gangs, consisting of more than 770,000 members, exist in about 3,330 cities in the United States. Congress spends as much as $20 billion per year in health care costs treating victims of gunshot wounds, and many of the incidents involving guns also involve street and other types of gangs.

Congress, state legislatures, and municipal governments have responded to the growing tide of gangs by considering a variety of bills addressing gang violence. Although efforts at the FEDERAL level have largely been unsuccessful, many states and municipalities have enacted laws designed to deter gang-related violence. Several of these statutes and ordinances have been fashioned as anti-loitering statutes, which often raise FIRST AMENDMENT concerns. The U.S. Supreme Court in 1999 made it more difficult for municipalities to draft gang loitering ordinances

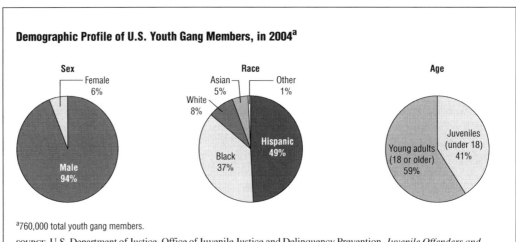

Demographic Profile of U.S. Youth Gang Members, in 2004[a]

Sex

Female 6%
Male 94%

Race

Asian 5%
White 8%
Other 1%
Hispanic 49%
Black 37%

Age

Young adults (18 or older) 59%
Juveniles (under 18) 41%

[a]760,000 total youth gang members.

SOURCE: U.S. Department of Justice, Office of Juvenile Justice and Delinquency Prevention, *Juvenile Offenders and Victims: 2006 National Report.*

when it found that an ordinance such as this in the city of Chicago was unconstitutional. *City of Chicago v. Morales*, 527 U.S. 41, 119 S. Ct. 1849, 144 L. Ed. 2d 67 (1999).

Background

Activities of gangs predate the formation of the United States, though the common perception of these gangs has changed over time. The level of violence among street gangs is a relatively new phenomenon. Because different organizations and individuals define the term gang differently, accurate statistics are often difficult to compile. Many of the crimes committed by gangs are violent crimes, including HOMICIDE. Moreover, many of the gang members are juveniles or young adults.

According to the 1999 *National Youth Gang Survey*, 90 percent of gang members are male. Seventy-one percent of these members are between the ages of 15 and 24, and 16 percent are age 14 or under. About 79 percent of the gang members, according to this survey, are Hispanic or black, while only 14 percent are white. Because of the large discrepancy in the number of minorities, some commentators have suggested that young minority males are unfairly stereotyped, leading to racial profiling of groups consisting of these young minority males.

Until the late 1980s, public and law enforcement agencies perceived gangs as racially and ethnically segregated, loosely organized fighting groups. However, a 1988 study of two major Los Angeles gangs, the Crips and the Bloods, showed that these gangs had become highly organized and entrepreneurial. These gangs had begun to engage in drug trafficking and had expanded their operations to multiple cities and states. As the gangs' interest in drug trade increased, so too did the level of violence perpetrated by their members. Between 1984 and 1993, the number of homicides committed by juveniles increased by 169 percent, representing a sharp increase in the number of gang-related crimes. Gang membership also increased markedly during this time. Between 1989 and 1995, the number of students reporting a gang presence at their school increased from 15 to 28 percent.

In response to the concerns caused by gang violence, several states and cities enacted statutes and ordinances designed to address street crime. In 1988 California enacted the Street TERRORISM Enforcement and Prevention Act (STEP Act), Cal. Pen. Code §§ 186.20–.33 (2001). Since that time, at least 28 other states have enacted similar legislation. Cities with traditional gang strongholds, such as Chicago and Los Angeles, enacted a series of ordinances that enabled law enforcement to take a more proactive approach in fighting street gangs in those cities.

Boston, which experienced the most number of homicides in its history in 1990 DUE in large part to gang violence, initiated a community-based strategy designed to target at-risk youth before they considered joining a gang. It also developed strategies for youth INTERVENTION and enforcement of GUN CONTROL laws. Due to this initiative, youth homicides dropped 80 percent from 1990 to 1995. Similarly, Salinas, California, experienced a 200 percent increase in the total number of homicides from 1984 to 1994. After receiving federal funding, the city improved it anti-gang task force and developed a series of additional programs. As a result of these programs, gang related assaults decreased by 23 percent, and the homicide rate fell by 62 percent.

Federal Law

In his 1997 state of the union address, President BILL CLINTON requested that Congress "mount a full-scale ASSAULT on juvenile crime, with legislation that declares war on gangs," including more prosecutions and tougher penalties. The same year, Congress considered two bills under the title Anti-Gang Youth Violence Act of 1997 (S. 362, H.R. 810, 105th Cong.). Despite initial support for this legislation, which would have provided $200 million in funding for local programs, neither bill passed through its respective committee.

Although Congress has been unable to enact comprehensive anti-gang legislation, other federal law and actions of federal authorities have been used in the effort to curb gang violence. Federal prosecutors have relied upon the Racketeer Influenced and Corrupt Organizations (RICO) statute to prosecute gang members. In the 1990s the number of RICO prosecutions against gang members more than doubled. Federal authorities have also assisted local law enforcement through a variety of funding programs. For example, in February 2003, the Los Angeles City/County Community Law Enforcement and Recovery (CLEAR)

DO ANTI-GANG LAWS VIOLATE THE CONSTITUTION?

The national aversion to GANGS has sparked debate over FIRST AMENDMENT rights of gang members versus citizens' safety at home and on the streets. Anti-gang injunctions and the enactment of anti-gang loitering ordinances are the two most prominent legal WEAPONS currently employed against gangs. Critics of these efforts, most notably the AMERICAN CIVIL LIBERTIES UNION (ACLU), contend that these initiatives violate the First Amendment's right of free association. Defenders of anti-gang initiatives reply that society's rights to peace and quiet and to be free from harm outweigh the gang members' First Amendment associational rights.

Critics reject the idea that public safety allows the government to tell citizens they may not associate with each other. As long as citizens are not committing a crime, the state cannot tell them not to stand on a street corner together or walk down the street. The Supreme Court has recognized that freedom of association is on par with FREEDOM OF SPEECH and FREEDOM OF THE PRESS.

The Court has allowed municipalities to require permits for parades, sound trucks, and demonstrations, in the interest of public order. However, the courts have been careful not to abridge the right of unpopular assemblies or protests. In 1977 the largely Jewish suburb of Skokie, Illinois, enacted three ordinances designed to prevent a march through the city by the American Nazi Party. The ACLU sued the city, and a FEDERAL court ruled that Skokie had violated the First Amendment by denying the Nazis a permit to march (*Collin v. Smith*, 578 F.2d 1197 (7th Cir. 1978)).

Critics of anti-gang laws also argue that just because gang members are unpopular to a large segment of society does not give society the right to restrict their right to association. Why, for example, should the KU KLUX KLAN be allowed to march through an African-American neighborhood while persons in that neighborhood cannot congregate on a playground to talk or play sports?

Critics believe there are better alternatives to controlling illegal gang activity than loitering laws and community injunctions. The ACLU contends that anti-gang injunctions do not work and may even make things worse. The resources of law enforcement are concentrated in one area, causing the shift of criminal activity into other neighborhoods. In addition, arresting a gang member for violating a loitering ordinance will not change the underlying dynamic of gang activity in urban areas. Critics argue that these anti-gang efforts are a cynical, political ploy that has more to do with creating a tough-on-crime appearance than with effective law enforcement.

anti-gang program received $2.5 million in federal funding for its efforts in reducing gang-related violence.

State Law

State legislatures have approached the problems related to gang violence through the enactment of a number of different statutes. Due to rulings by the courts within the various states, some legislatures are more restricted than others in enacting these types of legislation because of potential violations of state CONSTITUTIONAL provisions.

Gang Participation A number of states proscribe participation in criminal street gangs, though these statutes vary from state to state. In Georgia, for instance, it is unlawful "for any person employed by or associated with a criminal street gang to conduct or participate [in such a gang] through a pattern of criminal gang activity." Ga. Code Ann. § 16-15-4 (1998).

Likewise, in Texas, a person commits an offense "if, with an INTENT to establish, maintain, or participate in a combination of or in the profits of a combination of or as a member of a street gang, he commits or conspires to commit" one of several crimes, including violent crimes or distribution of controlled substances. Tex. Pen. Code Ann. § 71.02 (Vernon 1997).

Gang Recruitment Several states make it a crime for a person to recruit another to join a criminal gang. In Florida, an individual "who intentionally causes, encourages, solicits, or recruits another person to join a criminal street gang that requires as a condition of membership or continued membership the commission of any crime" commits a THIRD DEGREE FELONY. Fla. Stat. Ann. § 874.05 (1999). In Kentucky an individual who solicits or entices another person to join a criminal gang is GUILTY of the crime of criminal gang recruitment. Ky. Rev. Stat. Ann. § 506.140 (2000).

As an alternative, critics would emphasize community policing, increased resources for law enforcement, and efforts to improve the economic status of urban areas. They note that crime prevention and effective enforcement of criminal laws will do more to make a community safe than telling a suspected gang member to leave a street corner. In time, they believe, both the public and law enforcement will realize that solid, everyday police work produces better results.

Defenders of anti-gang initiatives contend that although First Amendment rights should be protected as much as possible, no CONSTITUTIONAL right is ABSOLUTE. In the case of gangs, the violence and criminal activity in certain parts of urban areas have reached a stage where normal law enforcement techniques do not work. Although the ACLU may say that individual rights must be protected, such a claim rings hollow when a gang can take over a neighborhood through violence and intimidation and yet evade law enforcement. In a crisis situation, additional steps must be taken to restore public confidence in the police and local government.

Restricting gang activity is not unconstitutional, argue defenders of the laws, because the Supreme Court has made it clear that no group of persons has the right to associate for wholly illegal aims. Moreover, associations engaging in both legal and illegal activities may still be regulated to the extent they engage in illegal activities. Defenders emphasize that the mere existence of an association is not sufficient to bring all that association's activities within scope of the First Amendment. Therefore, nonexpressive gang activities can be regulated.

Defenders also emphasize that injunctions and loitering ordinances are constitutional because they serve significant, and often compelling, government interests by reducing the threat to public health and safety caused by gang activities. They note that in the case of an INJUNCTION, gang members are free to conduct their expressive activities outside of the geographic area defined in the injunction. Thus, the injunction is likely to be upheld because it is narrowly tailored.

Though defenders believe these anti-gang initiatives will become important weapons for law enforcement, they acknowledge the danger of guilt by association. They believe, however, that this problem can be avoided if law enforcement officials adhere to constitutional standards in determining who should be subjected to anti-gang provisions. Judges must also carefully review EVIDENCE for each DEFENDANT to make sure the person has not been unfairly prosecuted.

Despite criticisms leveled by the ACLU and others, proponents of anti-gang laws adamantly support their use. While some of these initiatives may prove ineffective, law enforcement should be given the chance to test new ways of addressing destructive elements within their communities. Modifications can be made, and new initiatives plotted, but proponents insist that the law is necessary to protect the health and safety of citizens.

FURTHER READINGS

Perez, Silvia. 2001. "Alternatives in Fighting Street Gangs: Criminal Anti-Gang Ordinances v. Public Nuisance Laws." *St. Thomas Law Review* 13 (winter): 619–40.

Smith, Stephanie. 2000. "Civil Banishment of Gang Members: Circumventing Criminal Due Process Requirements?" *University of Chicago Law Review* 67 (fall): 1461–87.

Vertinsky, Liza. 1999. *A Law and Economics Approach to Criminal Gangs.* Aldershot, England; Brookfield, Vt.: Ashgate.

Gang-Related Apparel A number of states permit schools to prescribe a dress code, and several of these states specifically allow the schools to prevent gang members from wearing their gang apparel at the schools. For example, under New Jersey law, "a board of education may adopt a dress code policy to prohibit students from wearing, while on school property, any type of clothing, apparel, or accessory which indicates that the student has membership in, or affiliation with, any gang associated with criminal activities." N.J. Rev. Stat. § 18A:11-9 (1999). Tennessee law allows similar restrictions for students in grades six through twelve. Tenn. Code Ann. § 49-6-4215 (1998).

Enhanced Penalties for Gang-Related Activities Some states now allow courts, including juvenile courts, to enhance the sentences of individuals convicted of gang-related activities. In Illinois, if a juvenile age 15 or older commits an offense in furtherance of criminal activities by an organized gang, then a juvenile court is required to enter an order to try the juvenile as an adult under the criminal laws of the state. 705 Ill. Comp. Stat. § 405/5-805 (1999). An organized gang under the statute is defined as "an association of 5 or more persons, with an established HIERARCHY, that encourages members of the association to perpetrate crimes or provides support to members of the association who do commit crimes."

Local Ordinances

Municipalities have enacted a variety of measures designed to curb gang violence. Some ordinances contain provisions similar to state statutes. For example, the city of Albuquerque, New Mexico, enacted an anti-gang recruitment ordinance to protect its citizens from the fear, intimidation, and physical harm caused by the criminal activities of gangs. The ordinance provides a laundry list of offenses that are considered gang crimes and prohibits individuals from recruiting members to join criminal street gangs.

One of the most common forms of municipal ordinances aimed at reducing gang activities appears in the form of anti-loitering laws. The use of these laws to reduce unwanted elements within a city has a long history. Many cities have enacted such laws to allow police to arrest vagrants and others deemed to be menaces to society. Several cities adapted these laws to apply specifically to gang members. However, some courts have determined that these laws are unconstitutional either on their FACE or as applied to particular defendants.

Local governmental entities have also enacted public nuisance laws designed to allow local law enforcement to enjoin criminal activities. Like the anti-loitering ordinances, these laws have come under attack on a variety of constitutional grounds.

Constitutionality of Anti-Gang Laws

Laws aimed specifically at prosecuting members of gangs have come under attack due to a variety of constitutional theories. Anti-loitering laws have been challenged on some several grounds, including First Amendment prohibitions against vagueness and overbreadth, FOURTH AMENDMENT proscriptions of unreasonable searches and seizures, and constitutional provisions that prevent the government from punishing individuals merely because of their status.

Vagueness has been the primary reason why the Supreme Court has determined that anti-loitering statutes have been unconstitutional. In *Coates v. Cincinnati*, 402 U.S. 611, 91 S. Ct. 1686, 29 L. Ed. 2d 214 (1971), the Court determined that an ordinance prohibiting people from assembling on a sidewalk in such a way that it would be annoying to passersby was unconstitutionally vague because its application was based on sole discretion of police officers to determine what was "annoying." One year later, in *Papachristou v. City of Jacksonville*, 405 U.S. 156, 92 S. Ct. 839, 31 L. Ed. 2d 110 (1972), the Court held that an ordinance which encouraged arbitrary and erratic arrests was also unconstitutionally vague. Likewise, in *Kolender v. Lawson*, 461 U.S. 352, 103 S. Ct. 1855, 75 L. Ed. 2d 903 (1983), the Court held that a California statute that allowed police to arrest individuals who could not show credible and

reliable identification and account for their presence at a particular location was unconstitutional due to vagueness.

The Chicago City Council in 1992 enacted the Gang Congregation Ordinance that prohibited loitering among criminal street gang members at any public place. The ordinance allowed police officers to order any group of individuals who were congregated "with no apparent purpose" to disperse if the officer believed one of the group was a street gang member. In three years Chicago police issued more than 89,000 dispersal orders and made more than 42,000 arrests under the ordinance.

In *City of Chicago v. Morales*, the Supreme Court, per Justice JOHN PAUL STEVENS, determined that the ordinance was unconstitutional due to vagueness for two primary reasons. First, according to the Court, the ordinance failed to provide fair notice of prohibited conduct. Noted the Court, "It is difficult to imagine how any citizen of the city of Chicago standing in a public place with a group of people would know if he or she had an 'apparent purpose'" under the ordinance. Accordingly, citizens, even those who appeared in public with a gang member, were not provided fair notice of the type of conduct proscribed under the ordinance. Second, the ordinance failed to provide minimum guidelines for enforcement. The determination of whether individuals were standing around with no apparent purpose was based on the discretion of the officer.

After the 1992 gang ordinance was declared unconstitutional the city of Chicago enacted a second Gang Congregation Ordinance in 2000. The second ordinance authorizes police to command gang members to disperse when they are congregated on streets for the purpose of establishing control over certain areas of the city.

Other efforts to curb gang violence have been ruled constitutional. In *People ex rel. Gallo v. Acuna*, 929 P.2d 596 (Cal. 1997), the city of San Jose successfully requested an INJUNCTION against local gangs based on violations of state public nuisance laws. The gang members brought suit, challenging that both the statute and the injunction violated the First Amendment. The California Supreme Court determined that neither the injunction nor the statute violated the gang members' associational rights and that the gang members' conduct qualified as a public nuisance under the statute. Several cities in

California have sought and received temporary and permanent injunctions against local gangs preventing the gang members from congregating in public places.

FURTHER READINGS

Bureau of Justice Assistance. 1997. *Urban Street Gang Enforcement.* Washington D.C.: Justice Department, Bureau of Justice Assistance by the Institute for Law and Justice, Inc.

Huff, C. Ronald. 2001. *Gangs in America III.* Thousand Oaks, CA: Sage.

Strosnider, Kim. 2002. "Anti-Gang Ordinances after City of Chicago v. Morales: The Intersection of Race, Vagueness Doctrine, and Equal Protection in the Criminal Law." *American Criminal Law Review* 39 (winter).

CROSS REFERENCES

Racketeering; Vagrancy.

GAOL

The old English word for JAIL.

❖ GARFIELD, JAMES ABRAM

James Abram Garfield was a soldier and congressman who became the twentieth PRESIDENT OF THE UNITED STATES. His inability to perform the duties of office following an ASSASSINATION attempt on July 2, 1881, raised, for the second time in U.S. history, the question of presidential succession.

Garfield was born November 19, 1831, in a log cabin near the town of Orange in Cuyahoga County, Ohio. He was the fourth and final child of Abram Garfield and Eliza Ballou Garfield. Garfield's father's ancestors were among the original settlers of the Massachusetts Bay Colony. In 1827 the father carried their pioneering spirit to Ohio, where he worked on an Ohio Canal construction crew. By the time Garfield was born, his father was a struggling farmer and a founding member of the local Disciples of Christ church. In 1833, when Garfield was just two years old, his father died suddenly, leaving the family in poverty.

Garfield's mother, a descendant of an old Rhode Island family, was a remarkable woman. After her husband's death, she ran the small family farm on her own and saw to it that Garfield and his siblings worked hard, attended church, and finished school.

After completing his studies at the local school in Orange, Garfield enrolled at the Western Reserve Eclectic INSTITUTE (later Hiram College),

at Hiram, Ohio. He eventually went on to Williams College, in Massachusetts. After graduating from Williams with the class of 1856, he returned to the institute at Hiram and assumed the duties of teacher and later principal. On November 11, 1858, he married Lucretia Rudolph, his childhood friend, fellow student, and pupil.

In addition to teaching and tending to the administration of the institute, Garfield frequently served as a lay speaker in Disciples of Christ churches throughout northern Ohio. Like many members of his church, Garfield advocated free-soil principles and was a firm supporter of the newly organized REPUBLICAN PARTY. (Free-Soilers were opposed to the expansion of SLAVERY in the western states and territories.)

With his natural speaking ability, Garfield soon found himself in the political arena. In 1859 he was elected to the Ohio state senate. As the United States neared civil war, Garfield put his speaking abilities to work for the Union, recruiting men and raising troops for battle.

In the summer of 1861, he followed his own advice and recruited a group of volunteers from his former school. He assembled the Forty-second Ohio Volunteer Infantry, and served as the unit's lieutenant colonel and later colonel. Though he had no military experience, Garfield did have a voracious appetite for knowledge and access to books that could guide his command. He and his men fought at the Battle of Shiloh, in western Tennessee. Garfield left the field when he became ill. After recovering he returned as chief of staff under Major General William S. Rosencrans, with whom he fought at Chickamauga, Georgia.

After Chickamauga, Garfield was promoted to brigadier general of volunteers, and he was elected, in absentia, to a seat in the U.S. House of Representatives. It has been suggested that Garfield was reluctant to surrender his command and take the seat, but he acquiesced when President ABRAHAM LINCOLN pointed out that brigadier generals were in far greater supply than administration Republicans.

In December 1863 Garfield took his seat in the Thirty-eighth Congress as the Republican representative from the nineteenth congressional district of Ohio. When the Republicans became the minority party in the House after the election of 1864, Garfield and Congressman James G. Blaine, of Maine, emerged as minority party leaders. Garfield distinguished himself as

ALL FREE GOVERNMENTS ARE MANAGED BY THE COMBINED WISDOM AND FOLLY OF THE PEOPLE.
—JAMES GARFIELD

James A. Garfield.
LIBRARY OF CONGRESS

the administration of President Ulysses S. Grant—including the Cr|Aaedit Mobilier scandal. Crédit Mobilier of America was a construction company established to build the Union Pacific Railroad. It became known that Garfield was among a group of congressmen who had accepted stock in Crédit Mobilier, in exchange for legislative consideration. Garfield ultimately refused the stock, but it took him two years to do so. His critics maintained that he decided not to take the stock only because the issue had placed him in political hot water.

During the same period, Garfield accepted a RETAINER for legal services from a Washington, D.C., company seeking to supply paving materials in the nation's capital. He argued that because he had no direct connection to city government, there was no CONFLICT OF INTEREST. Not everyone shared his opinion.

Though many public servants of the day conducted personal business while in office, Garfield found it increasingly difficult to distinguish clients who wanted his legal advice from those who wanted his political influence. Garfield was reelected in 1874, despite the controversy, but to avoid future problems, he ceased taking outside legal clients. The incident also fueled Garfield's desire to eliminate political PATRONAGE in the CIVIL SERVICE system.

Garfield took an active role in the 1876 presidential election of RUTHERFORD B. HAYES. When Senator JOHN SHERMAN, of Ohio, was named to the Hayes CABINET, Garfield expressed an interest in filling his vacant Senate seat. Needing Garfield in the House, Hayes discouraged him from pursuing the matter. Near the close of Hayes's term, there was talk that Sherman would seek to regain his Senate seat, but he chose instead to seek his party's

chairman of the COMMITTEE on appropriations, and he established himself as an expert on the budget. He also focused his attention on legislation related to Reconstruction policies in the South, protective TARIFF issues, and the maintenance of a sound currency. When Blaine was elected to the Senate in 1876, Garfield became the House minority leader—a position he held for the remainder of his congressional service.

Garfield held his House office for eighteen years, for the most part easily winning the nomination of his party and the vote of the electorate as each term concluded. Only once during his time in the House was his reelection in question. In the early 1870s the Republican party was discredited by allegations of scandal in

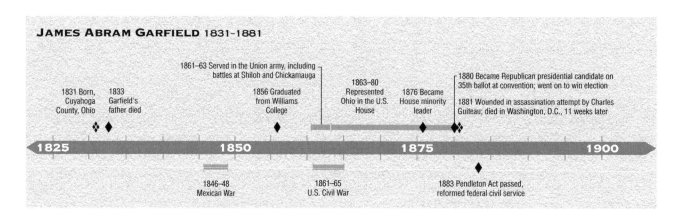

JAMES ABRAM GARFIELD 1831–1881

1861–63 Served in the Union army, including battles at Shiloh and Chickamauga

1880 Became Republican presidential candidate on 35th ballot at convention; went on to win election

1831 Born, Cuyahoga County, Ohio

1833 Garfield's father died

1856 Graduated from Williams College

1863–80 Represented Ohio in the U.S. House

1876 Became House minority leader

1881 Wounded in assassination attempt by Charles Guiteau; died in Washington, D.C., 11 weeks later

1825   1850   1875   1900

1846–48 Mexican War

1861–65 U.S. Civil War

1883 Pendleton Act passed, reformed federal civil service

nomination for the presidency. It was widely presumed that Sherman supported Garfield's election to the Senate in exchange for Garfield's support at the Republican convention, but no such deal was struck.

In due course the Ohio legislature elected Garfield to the U.S. Senate for a six-year term to begin in 1881, and he attended the 1880 Republican National Convention in Chicago as head of the Ohio DELEGATION. Because of home state support for Sherman, Garfield reluctantly agreed to act as Sherman's floor manager and to canvass for delegates on his behalf—even though Senator Blaine, Garfield's old friend and colleague, was also seeking the party's nomination.

Garfield was a formidable and well-known figure at the convention. His persuasive skill on the floor did not go unnoticed. He kept Sherman's chances alive by fighting for the delegates' freedom to vote their choice, and by opposing a unit rule that forced delegations to cast all their votes for the candidate holding the majority of votes within a state delegation. Former president Grant, who was also running for nomination, and his supporters, called the Stalwarts, supported the unit rule because Grant held the majority in many delegations.

Garfield managed to block the nominations of Blaine and Grant, but he could not secure a majority for Sherman. With the convention deadlocked, twenty Wisconsin delegates made a bold move on the thirty-fifth ballot and, in protest, cast twenty votes for Garfield.

On the next ballot, Garfield found himself the unanimous choice of the convention and the unwitting BENEFICIARY of his own floor maneuvering. CHESTER A. ARTHUR was named his running mate. Blaine followers supported the ticket, and most Sherman followers were willing to overlook the manner in which the nomination had been secured, but Grant's forces never forgave Garfield for his opposition.

Garfield pacified unhappy Sherman supporters by surrendering his new Senate seat, enabling Sherman to return to his old post. Throughout the summer of 1880, Garfield attempted to meet with the national committee and with Grant supporters, but he was never given an audience. In November Garfield returned to his farm in Mentor, Ohio, to wait them out.

Finally, on the eve of the election, Grant was persuaded to recognize Garfield as the party's choice. Grant and his followers were invited to the Garfield farm for a historic meeting, often called the Mentor Summit. What was said at the meeting—and what was promised—has been the subject of much debate. Grant thought he had extracted a personal promise from Garfield that, in exchange for Grant's support, the Stalwarts would be named to influential posts in the new administration.

With the help of Grant's supporters, Garfield won the election by a narrow margin over Democrat Winfield Scott Hancock. Between the election and the inauguration, Garfield busied himself with the selection of his cabinet. All factions of the party called on the president-elect to lobby for their preferred nominees, but Grant Stalwarts remained assured that Garfield would bow to their influence. Garfield's first known appointment, making Blaine SECRETARY OF STATE, caused an uproar among the Grant faction and was viewed as a breach of the promises made at Mentor. Garfield nevertheless remained committed to building a conciliation cabinet that would balance everyone's interests and eliminate political patronage jobs—and kept the rest of his choices well guarded until inauguration day, March 4, 1881.

The first months of his term continued to be plagued with appointment and confirmation battles. Grant supporters continued to believe that he should have been the party's presidential nominee and that in an election deal Garfield had agreed to consult Grant about appointments. Those in the Senate who supported Grant rallied to systematically reject undesirable appointments, but Garfield was equally stubborn. Of the Stalwarts' attempt to derail his nomination for collector of customs for the port of New York City, Garfield said, "They may take him out of the Senate head first or feet first, but I will never withdraw him."

Though confirmation battles consumed a majority of Garfield's time, he also carried out other presidential duties and commitments. On July 2, 1881, he was en route to a speaking engagement at his alma mater Williams College, when lawyer Charles J. Guiteau shot him at a Washington, D.C., railroad station. Described as an erratic character, Guiteau shouted to a crowd at the railroad station that he was a Stalwart.

Garfield lingered for eleven weeks. Daily reports from physicians showed that he was unable to carry out his responsibilities. By August the question of Garfield's succession was being discussed in the press and debated by CONSTITUTIONAL scholars. It was agreed that the VICE PRESIDENT was constitutionally allowed to assume the president's powers and duties, but it was not clear whether he should serve as acting president until Garfield recovered, or assume the office itself and displace Garfield altogether. The pertinent provision of the Constitution—Article II, Section 1, Clause 6—was ambiguous, and expert opinion was still divided over the precedent set by JOHN TYLER, who had taken the oath of office in 1841 after the death of President WILLIAM H. HARRISON, rather than merely assuming Harrison's duties until the next election.

Because Congress was not in session, the issue could not be debated there, but it was addressed by Garfield's cabinet members on September 2, 1881. They agreed that it was time for the vice president to assume Garfield's duties, but they too were divided as to the permanence of the vice president's role. The problem was never resolved because Garfield died September 19, 1881, before any action was taken by the cabinet or the vice president. Following the precedent set by Tyler, Arthur took the oath of office and assumed the presidency, following Garfield's death.

Garfield's unexpected nomination, bitter election, and tragic death often overshadow his previous accomplishments and his presidential agenda. His efforts to build a conciliation cabinet and to purge administrative agencies of old patronage jobs made him a strong advocate of civil service reforms. Ironically, the appointment battles preceding his murder probably caused Congress to pass civil service reforms in 1883 that were far broader in reach and scope than anything Garfield had envisioned.

FURTHER READINGS

Ackerman, Kenneth D. 2004. *Dark Horse: The Surprise Election and Political Murder of James A. Garfield.* Saddle Brook, NJ: Avalon.

Peskin, Allan. 2004. *Garfield: A Biography.* Jefferson City, MO: Easton.

Rutkow, Ira. 2006. *James A. Garfield: The American Presidents Series: The 20th President, 1881.* New York: Times.

❖ GARLAND, AUGUSTUS HILL

Augustus Hill Garland served as attorney general of the United States from 1885 to 1889 under President Grover Cleveland.

Garland was born June 11, 1832, in Tipton County, Tennessee. His parents, Rufus K. Garland and Barbara Hill Garland, settled in Hempstead County, Arkansas, when he was an infant. Garland was educated at local schools in Hempstead County, and at St. Joseph's College, in Bardstown, Kentucky. He graduated from St. Joseph's in 1851 and was admitted to the bar in 1853. Garland's first practice was established in Washington, Arkansas. He eventually moved to Little Rock, Arkansas, where he earned a reputation as one of the best lawyers in the South. He married Sarah Virginia Sanders in Little Rock. She died early in their MARRIAGE, and Garland's mother ran his household for most of his life.

At the outbreak of the Civil War, Garland opposed the secession of Arkansas, but he eventually supported his state when the

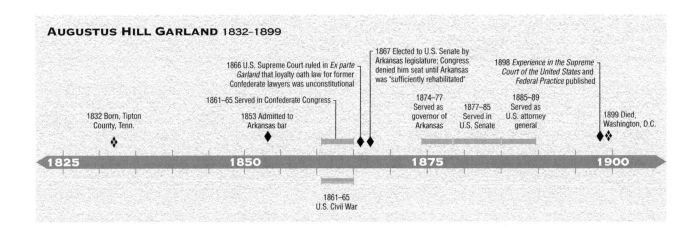

AUGUSTUS HILL GARLAND 1832–1899

1832 Born, Tipton County, Tenn.

1853 Admitted to Arkansas bar

1861–65 Served in Confederate Congress

1866 U.S. Supreme Court ruled in *Ex parte Garland* that loyalty oath law for former Confederate lawyers was unconstitutional

1867 Elected to U.S. Senate by Arkansas legislature; Congress denied him seat until Arkansas was "sufficiently rehabilitated"

1874–77 Served as governor of Arkansas

1877–85 Served in U.S. Senate

1885–89 Served as U.S. attorney general

1898 *Experience in the Supreme Court of the United States* and *Federal Practice* published

1899 Died, Washington, D.C.

1861–65 U.S. Civil War

1825   1850   1875   1900

ordinance of secession was passed. He was elected to the Confederate provisional congress, in Montgomery, Alabama, and to the first and second Confederate congresses, in Richmond.

In an effort to unify the North and South after the war, President ANDREW JOHNSON granted a full pardon to Garland (and others) for wartime service to the CONFEDERACY. The president's actions were not widely supported; Congress enacted a number of laws that continued to punish the pardoned Southerners for their wartime allegiances by restricting their ability to participate in their former businesses or professions. Two restrictions, enacted in 1865, required attorneys to swear a test (loyalty) oath affirming that they had not participated in the rebellion, as a condition for appearing before the U.S. Supreme Court, the district and circuit courts, and the COURT OF CLAIMS (13 Stat. 424). Attorneys who could not take the oath were denied the right to appear before the high courts—and thereby prevented from practicing law.

Garland challenged the law in 1867. He argued that the law was unconstitutional, and that even if the law were CONSTITUTIONAL, he would be released from compliance with its provisions by his presidential pardon. The Supreme Court found the law to be unconstitutional because it violated the president's power to pardon. "When a pardon is full," the majority opinion said, "it releases the punishment, and blots out of existence the guilt" (*Ex parte Garland,* 71 U.S. (4 Wall.) 333, 18 L. Ed. 366 [1866]). The case restored Garland's right to practice law before the nation's high courts and established him as a nationally recognized constitutional lawyer. It also reestablished him as a political force in the South.

In 1867 Garland was elected to the U.S. Senate by the legislature of Arkansas, only to be denied a seat because Congress found that his state had not been sufficiently rehabilitated. For the next few years, he used his abilities to return his state to favor. By 1874 he was elected governor of the state; his administration is credited with bringing order out of the chaos that permeated Arkansas during the Reconstruction era. In 1877 Garland was finally allowed to take his seat in the U.S. Senate. He was reelected in 1883 and became a ranking member of the Senate's JUDICIARY Committee.

Garland resigned his Senate seat on March 4, 1885, to accept the position of ATTORNEY general in President Cleveland's CABINET. As attorney general, he was frequently consulted on issues of CONSTITUTIONAL LAW. He was known as an advocate who insisted on the enforcement of constitutional freedoms for all citizens.

He also worked to earn the trust of those who condemned him for his Confederate service. As a U.S. senator and cabinet officer, Garland was wary of both individuals and institutions who sought to influence his opinions and actions. It is said that he steadfastly avoided society events and that he refused to read daily newspapers. Even so, he was once called back from a holiday by an angry President Cleveland to explain his ownership of stock in a company that would have been helped by a JUSTICE DEPARTMENT lawsuit. (The lawsuit was eventually withdrawn.)

In 1889 Garland returned to the PRACTICE OF LAW, and he maintained an active caseload until the end of his life. He also began to record his life's work for publication. His *Experience in the SUPREME COURT OF THE UNITED STATES* and *Federal Practice* were published in 1898.

Having fought so hard to retain his right to appear before the nation's high courts, Garland's final hour was fitting: he died while arguing a case before the Supreme Court of the United States on January 26, 1899.

FURTHER READINGS

Watkins, Beverly Nettles. 1985. *Augustus Hill Garland, 1832–1899: Arkansas Lawyer to United States Attorney-General.* Ph.D. diss. Auburn Univ.

GARNISHEE

An individual who holds money or property that belongs to a debtor subject to an attachment proceeding by a creditor.

For example, when an individual owes money but has for a source of income only a salary, a creditor might initiate GARNISHMENT proceedings. If the creditor is successful, a certain portion of the debtor's salary will be automatically sent to the creditor from each paycheck. In such case, the debtor's employer is the GARNISHEE.

GARNISHMENT

A legal procedure by which a creditor can collect what a debtor owes by reaching the debtor's

WE, AS ATTORNEYS, GET LITERALLY WRAPPED UP IN OUR CLIENT'S CAUSE ... AND SEE NOTHING BUT HIS SIDE OF THE CASE ... AND DECLARE THAT THE COURT CAN DECIDE IT ONLY OUR WAY.
—AUGUSTUS GARLAND

property when it is in the hands of someone other than the debtor.

GARNISHMENT is a drastic measure for collecting a debt. A court order of garnishment allows a creditor to take the property of a debtor when the debtor does not possess the property. A garnishment action is taken against the debtor as DEFENDANT and the property holder as GARNISHEE. Garnishment is regulated by statutes, and is usually reserved for the creditor who has obtained a judgment, or court order, against the debtor.

A debtor's property may be garnished before it ever reaches the debtor. For example, if a debtor's work earnings are garnished, a portion of the wages owed by the employer go directly to the JUDGMENT CREDITOR and is never seen by the debtor.

Some property is exempt from garnishment. Exemptions are created by statutes to avoid leaving a debtor with no means of support. For example, only a certain amount of work income may be garnished. Under 15 U.S.C.A. § 1673, a garnishment sought in FEDERAL court may not exceed 25 percent of the debtor's DISPOSABLE EARNINGS each week, or the amount by which the debtor's disposable earnings for the week exceed thirty times the federal minimum hourly wage in effect at the time the earnings are payable. In Alaska, exemptions include a burial plot; health aids necessary for work or health; benefits paid or payable for medical, surgical, or hospital care; awards to victims of violent crime; and assets received from a retirement plan (Alaska Stat. § 09.38.015, .017).

Because garnishment involves the taking of property, the procedure is subject to due process requirements. In *Sniadatch v. Family Finance Corp. of Bay View,* 395 U.S. 337, 89 S. Ct. 1820, 23 L. Ed. 2d 349 (1969), the U.S. Supreme Court struck down a Wisconsin statute that allowed pretrial garnishment of wages without an opportunity to be heard or to submit a DEFENSE. According to the Court, garnishment without prior notice and a prior HEARING violated fundamental principles of due process.

Garnishment may be used as a provisional remedy. This means that property may be garnished before a judgment against the debtor is entered. This serves to protect the creditor's interest in the debtor's property. Prejudgment garnishment is usually ordered by a court only when the creditor can show that the debtor is likely to lose or dispose of the property before the case is resolved. Property that is garnished before any judgment is rendered is held by the THIRD PARTY, and is not given to the creditor until the creditor prevails in the suit against the debtor.

Garnishment is similar to LIEN and to ATTACHMENT. Liens and attachments are court orders that give a creditor an interest in the property of the debtor. Garnishment is a continuing lien against nonexempt property of the debtor. Garnishment is not, however, an attachment. Attachment is the process of seizing property of the debtor that is in the debtor's possession, whereas garnishment is the process of seizing property of the debtor that is in the possession of a third party.

FURTHER READINGS

Fair Debt Collection.com Web site. 2009. Available online at http://www.fair-debt-collection.com/state-garnishment-laws.html; website home page: http://www.fair-debt-collection.com (accessed September 3, 2009).

Lee, Randy. 1994. "Twenty-Five Years after Goldberg v. Kelly: Traveling from the Right Spot on the Wrong Road to the Wrong Place." *Capital Univ. Law Review* 23.

"Wage Garnishment" 2003. Rules and Regulations. *Federal Register* 68.

❖ GARRISON, WILLIAM LLOYD

WILLIAM LLOYD GARRISON, publisher of the anti-slavery newspaper *The Liberator* and founder of the American Anti-Slavery Society, was one of the most fiery and outspoken abolitionists of the Civil War period.

Garrison was born in Newburyport, Massachusetts, on December 10, 1805. In 1808 Garrison's father abandoned his family, leaving them close to destitute. At age 13, after working at a number of jobs, Garrison became an APPRENTICE to Ephraim Allen, editor of the *Newburyport Herald.*

Garrison later moved to Boston where he became editor of the *National Philanthropist* in 1828. At that time, Garrison became acquainted with the prominent Quaker Benjamin Lundy, editor of the Baltimore-based antislavery newspaper, the *Genius of Universal* EMANCIPATION. In 1829 Garrison became co-editor of Lundy's publication and began his vigorous advocacy for abolishing SLAVERY. Shortly thereafter, Garrison was sued by a merchant engaged in the slave trade. He was convicted of libel and spent seven weeks in prison, an experience that strengthened his CONVICTION that all slaves should be set free.

After his release from JAIL in 1830, Garrison returned to Boston where he joined the American Colonization Society, an organization that promoted the idea that free blacks should emigrate to Africa. When it became clear that most members of the group did not support freeing slaves, but just wanted to reduce the number of free blacks in the United States, Garrison withdrew from membership.

In January 1831 Garrison founded *The Liberator,* which he published for 35 years and which became the most famous antislavery newspaper of its era. Although he was a pacifist, Garrison struck a formidable stance in the very first issue in which he proclaimed, "I do not wish to think, or speak, or write, with moderation . . . I will not retreat a single inch—AND I WILL BE HEARD." *The Liberator,* which never had a paid circulation greater than three thousand became one of the most widely disseminated, consistent, and dominating voices of the ABOLITION movement.

Antislavery advocates of the day, or abolitionists, were widely divergent in their views of how and when slavery should be ended and what should happen to freed slaves after emancipation. Garrison was part of a group that believed that abolition of slavery must happen as quickly as possible. Those who sought "immediatism," however were divided on how to achieve this goal. Garrison, though searing in his language and unyielding in his beliefs, believed only in CIVIL DISOBEDIENCE, and opposed any method of active resistance.

William Lloyd Garrison.
LIBRARY OF CONGRESS

In 1832 Garrison founded the country's first immediatist organization, the New England Anti-Slavery Society. The following year, in 1833, he helped organize the American Anti-Slavery Society. He wrote the society's constitution and became its first corresponding secretary. He befriended fellow abolitionist and writer FREDERICK DOUGLASS, and made him an agent of the Anti-Slavery Society. Over the next several years Garrison came to reject the teachings of established churches and the government of the United States,

I DO NOT WISH TO THINK, OR SPEAK, OR WRITE, WITH MODERATION. . . . I AM IN EARNEST— I WILL NOT EQUIVOCATE—I WILL NOT EXCUSE—I WILL NOT RETREAT A SINGLE INCH—AND I WILL BE HEARD.
—WILLIAM LLOYD GARRISON

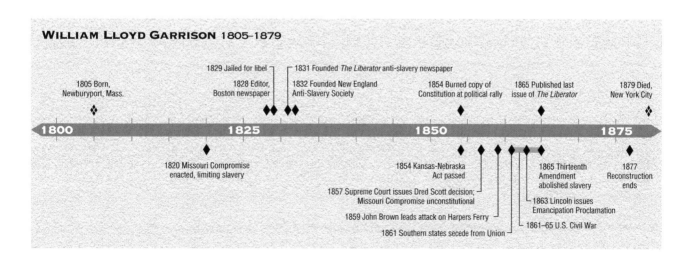

WILLIAM LLOYD GARRISON 1805–1879

1829 Jailed for libel — 1831 Founded *The Liberator* anti-slavery newspaper

1805 Born, Newburyport, Mass.

1828 Editor, Boston newspaper

1832 Founded New England Anti-Slavery Society

1854 Burned copy of Constitution at political rally

1865 Published last issue of *The Liberator*

1879 Died, New York City

1800   1825   1850   1875

1820 Missouri Compromise enacted, limiting slavery

1854 Kansas-Nebraska Act passed

1857 Supreme Court issues Dred Scott decision; Missouri Compromise unconstitutional

1859 John Brown leads attack on Harpers Ferry

1861 Southern states secede from Union

1865 Thirteenth Amendment abolished slavery

1863 Lincoln issues Emancipation Proclamation

1861–65 U.S. Civil War

1877 Reconstruction ends

which he viewed as supporting slavery. Increasingly hewing to a philosophy of moral absolutism, Garrison embraced not only the cause of nonviolent resistance, but temperance, women's rights, and Christian perfectionism.

In 1840 Garrison's views precipitated a split in the Anti-Slavery Society between the minority who supported his radical beliefs and the majority who disapproved of his views regarding RELIGION, government, and the participation of women in the struggle for emancipation. When Garrison's supporters voted to admit women, a group seceded from the society and formed the rival American and Foreign Anti-Slavery Society. Another group, interested in continuing to seek reform through political activity, later left to start the Liberty party.

Over the next two decades, Garrison's influence declined as his radicalism became more pronounced. In the 1850s *The Liberator* hailed John Brown's raid on Harpers FERRY while denouncing the COMPROMISE OF 1850, the KANSAS-NEBRASKA ACT, and the U.S. Supreme Court's decision in DRED SCOTT V. SANDFORD. He continued to support secession of the antislavery states and publicly burned a copy of the U.S. Constitution at an abolitionist rally in 1854.

After the Civil War began, Garrison put aside his pacifism to support President ABRAHAM LINCOLN and the Union Army. He welcomed the EMANCIPATION PROCLAMATION and the passing of the THIRTEENTH AMENDMENT, which outlawed slavery. In 1865 Garrison published the last issue of *The Liberator,* although he continued to advocate for women's rights, temperance, and pacifism. Garrison died on May 24, 1879, in New York City.

FURTHER READINGS

Cain, William E., ed. 1995. *William Lloyd Garrison and the Fight Against Slavery: Selections from the Liberator.* New York: St. Martin's.

Hagedorn, Ann. 2002. *Beyond the River: The Untold Story of the Heroes of the Underground Railroad.* New York: Simon & Schuster.

Mayer, Henry. 2008. *All on Fire: William Lloyd Garrison and the Abolition of Slavery.* New York: Norton.

"William Lloyd Garrison Papers, 1833–1882" *Massachusetts Historical Society.* Available online at http://www.masshist.org/findingaids/doc.cfm?fa=fa0278; website home page: http://www.masshist.org (accessed September 3, 2009).

CROSS REFERENCES

Brown, John; Temperance Movement.

❖ GARVEY, MARCUS MOZIAH

MARCUS GARVEY was a charismatic leader who preached black pride and economic self-sufficiency. He is internationally recognized as the organizer of the first significant movement of black nationalism in the United States.

MARCUS MOZIAH GARVEY was born on August 17, 1887, in St. Ann's Bay, Jamaica, to Marcus Moziah Garvey, a stonemason, and Sarah Jane Richards, a DOMESTIC and farmer. He and his sister Indiana were the only two of the eleven Garvey offspring to reach adulthood. As a child, he used his father's extensive library to educate himself. When Garvey was 14, he went to work as a printer's APPRENTICE. In 1908 he participated in the country's first Printers Union strike; when the strike failed, the union disbanded. Because he had been one of the strike leaders, Garvey found himself blacklisted. He began working at the GOVERNMENT PRINTING OFFICE and briefly published his own small journal, *Garvey's Watchman.* Garvey then traveled through Central America and lived in London from 1912 to 1914, where

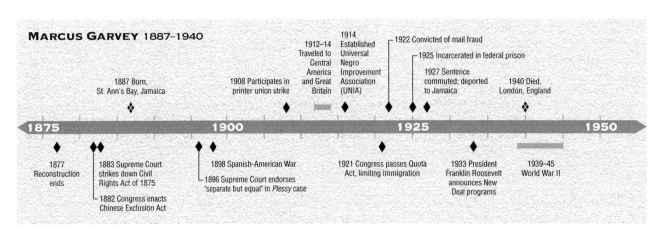

MARCUS GARVEY 1887–1940

1887 Born, St. Ann's Bay, Jamaica

1908 Participates in printer union strike

1912–14 Traveled to Central America and Great Britain

1914 Established Universal Negro Improvement Association (UNIA)

1922 Convicted of mail fraud

1925 Incarcerated in federal prison

1927 Sentence commuted; deported to Jamaica

1940 Died, London, England

1875 1900 1925 1950

1877 Reconstruction ends

1883 Supreme Court strikes down Civil Rights Act of 1875

1882 Congress enacts Chinese Exclusion Act

1898 Spanish-American War

1896 Supreme Court endorses "separate but equal" in *Plessy* case

1921 Congress passes Quota Act, limiting immigration

1933 President Franklin Roosevelt announces New Deal programs

1939–45 World War II

he attended Birkbeck College. During this period he was exposed to the problems engendered by racial DISCRIMINATION and first began to think about ways to help black persons become economically self-sufficient.

Garvey returned to Jamaica in 1914 and established the Universal Negro Improvement Association (UNIA). He cofounded the UNIA with Amy Ashwood, who was the association's first secretary, and who would later become Garvey's first wife. At the time, most of Africa's countries were colonies under the domination of European nations. The purpose of the UNIA, whose motto was "One God, One Aim, One Destiny," was to promote black nationalism throughout the world by establishing an African country where blacks would run their own government.

In 1916 Garvey moved to the United States and toured the country, espousing the Back-to-Africa movement. In 1917 he started a chapter of UNIA in New York City, setting up headquarters in Harlem. To build economic self-reliance, the UNIA started several businesses including the Negro Factories Corporation (NFC) and a steamship company called the Black Star Line. Garvey also began publishing the *Negro World,* in 1918, a journal that advocated his ideas for African nationalism and served as the voice of the UNIA.

Around this same time, the UNIA achieved one of its most ambitious goals—it reached an agreement with the African nation of Liberia to make land available for black people who would come to that country from the United States and the Caribbean, as well as from countries in Central and South America. In Garvey's view, Liberia would be a beacon of hope drawing new groups of settlers who would create their own culture and civilization.

In 1920 the UNIA held its first international convention at Madison Square Garden in New York City, during which Garvey laid out his plans for an African nation-state. The association adopted a constitution, a Declaration of Rights of the Negro Peoples of the World, as well as a national FLAG. The UNIA also elected officials for its provisional government, with Garvey serving as Provisional President of Africa.

By the early 1920s, the UNIA developed an ardent following, with 700 branches in 38 states and more than 2 million members. The association drew adherents not only from the United States, but also from Canada, Caribbean countries, and throughout the African continent. A consummate showman, Garvey loved to put on parades and street celebrations in Harlem where he and other members of the UNIA "nobility" appeared in elaborate military uniforms, along with banners and vividly decorated automobiles. From the outset, however, Garvey ran into opposition from both whites who were frightened at the idea of black solidarity and blacks who viewed INTEGRATION into the American mainstream as the key to progress.

Before the UNIA could move forward with its resettlement plans, problems began to mount. The Liberian government withdrew its approval for repatriating the new settlers. In 1922 Garvey was convicted for MAIL FRAUD concerning the Black Star Line, and in 1925 he was jailed in Atlanta, Georgia. In 1927 President CALVIN COOLIDGE commuted Garvey's five-year sentence. Garvey was labeled an undesirable alien and deported to Jamaica.

In 1929 Garvey toured Canada and Europe giving lectures. In 1930 he ran in the general election for a seat in Jamaica's legislature, but was defeated. Further attempts to launch a newspaper and a magazine met with failure as did his creation of an organization that was supposed to provide job opportunities for the poverty-stricken rural inhabitants of Jamaica.

In 1935 Garvey moved to England. He continued to hold UNIA conventions and to make speeches to dwindling numbers of people. Garvey died in London on June 10, 1940. Although Garvey was mostly ignored toward the end of his life, his dedication to black pride and self-sufficiency made him a national hero in Jamaica. Garvey and his movement were celebrated in the music of such reggae stars as Bob Marley and Burning Spear. Adherents of the BLACK POWER MOVEMENT of the 1960s acknowledged their debt to Garvey's nationalist crusade as did blacks fighting for INDEPENDENCE from colonial rule in Africa. As of 2009, the UNIA still functions. Garvey's son, Marcus Garvey Jr., served as president until 2004.

FURTHER READINGS

Cronon, Edmund, and John Hope Franklin. 1969. *Black Moses: The Story of Marcus Garvey and the Universal Negro Improvement Association.* 2d ed. Madison: Univ. of Wisconsin Press.

Jacques-Garvey, Amy, ed. 1992. *Philosophy and Opinions of Marcus Garvey.* New York: Atheneum.

DAY BY DAY WE HEAR THE CRY OF **AFRICA FOR THE AFRICANS.** THIS CRY HAS BECOME A POSITIVE, DETERMINED ONE. IT IS A CRY THAT IS RAISED SIMULTANEOUSLY THE WORLD OVER BECAUSE OF THE UNIVERSAL OPPRESSION THAT AFFECTS THE NEGRO.
—MARCUS GARVEY

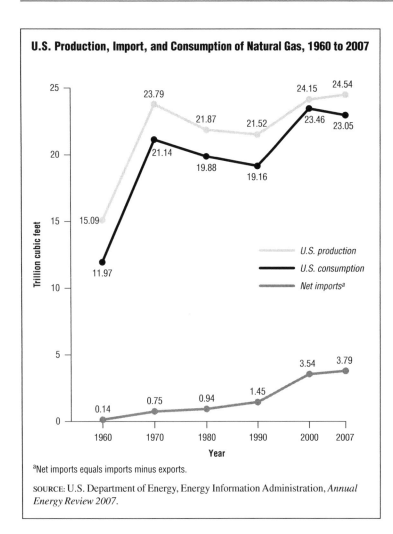

U.S. Production, Import, and Consumption of Natural Gas, 1960 to 2007

Trillion cubic feet

- U.S. production
- U.S. consumption
- Net imports[a]

Year

[a]Net imports equals imports minus exports.

SOURCE: U.S. Department of Energy, Energy Information Administration, *Annual Energy Review 2007*.

GAS

Various legal issues arise concerning the use and distribution of gas.

Supply

A MUNICIPAL CORPORATION does not have the duty to supply gas to its population. In the event that a city assumes the performance of such function, it is acting merely as a business corporation.

The CHARTER of a gas company is a FRANCHISE granted by the state. The manufacture of distribution of gas for light, fuel, or power is a business of a public character, and, therefore, a gas company is ordinarily considered to be a public or quasi-public corporation or a BUSINESS AFFECTED WITH A PUBLIC INTEREST. A state may regulate gas companies for the protection of the public and may DELEGATE its regulatory powers to municipal corporations in which gas companies operate. In a number of states, gas companies are subject to a public service commission or other such agency. The JURISDICTION of the commission ordinarily includes the power to establish rates and to set forth rules and regulations affecting the service, operation, management, and conduct of the business.

Consumer Supply

Upon obtaining a franchise to supply gas to a particular geographic area, a gas company is bound to fulfill its obligation; it cannot withdraw its service from an area merely because it is dissatisfied with the rates permitted there. Once the franchise of a company has expired, it may withdraw the service. A court may, in certain instances, enjoin the DISCONTINUANCE of service for a reasonable period—to circumvent undue hardship and inconvenience to the residents of the area.

A gas company has the duty to serve all those who are within the franchise area who desire service and subscribe to the reasonable rules that it may set forth. A municipality or corporation supplying gas may make reasonable rules and regulations to secure the payment of bills, such as eliminating service to the consumer. If there is a genuine controversy about the amount owed, a company is not permitted to discontinue service. A gas company may not require the owner or occupant of a building to pay overdue and unpaid bills by a former owner or occupant before it continues service to the building. Some statutes require that gas companies install a meter on the premises, in order to register the consumption of gas by each customer; and where a customer tampers with the meter and uses a significant amount of unmetered gas, the company can discontinue service and refuse to restore it until the customer pays the amount due for the unmetered gas taken.

A gas company that wrongfully refuses to supply a customer with gas is liable for DAMAGES. There are also statutory penalties in some states for such wrongful refusal.

Injuries

A gas company is under the obligation to EXERCISE ordinary care in the construction of its works and the conduct of its business in order to protect life and property.

Gas has a highly dangerous and volatile character and tends to ESCAPE. A gas company must, therefore, exercise care to avoid harm to others and is liable for its negligence that results in INJURY to others by reason of the escape or explosion of gas. It must exercise reasonable care in the INSPECTION of its pipes to ensure that leaks may be discovered promptly; and if leaks or defects in the pipes of the company occur due to faulty construction or maintenance, the company is liable for resulting injuries, even though it did not know about the leak.

In the event that the company has taken due care in the inspection of its pipes and a DEFECT or a break occurs through natural causes or by the act of a third person, the gas company must be given notice of the defect and reasonable time to repair it before liability accrues. A gas company subject to notice that gas is escaping is under an obligation to shut off the gas supply until the necessary repairs have been made.

A gas company has a PROPERTY RIGHT in the mains and pipes and other appliances, and where there is unauthorized INTERFERENCE with, or damage to, this property, the company is entitled to recover damages and an INJUNCTION if the circumstances so warrant.

Rates

A gas company has a legal obligation to charge reasonable rates. One of the main purposes of the regulation of gas companies is to prescribe fair and reasonable rates for the selling of gas to the public. Rate increases are permitted only following an IMPARTIAL and complete investigation—with the object of doing justice to the gas company as well as the public. Relief can be sought in the courts if gas rates are unreasonable—to determine whether the rate making body acted beyond the scope of its power or against the weight of the EVIDENCE. The courts, however, cannot decide what rates are reasonable, nor can they put those rates into effect.

CROSS REFERENCE

Public Utilities.

GAULT, IN RE

Originally, juvenile court was a place for the informal resolution of a broad range of matters concerning children. The hearings were not adversarial. Instead, they focused on the juvenile's best interests. A juvenile was brought to the juvenile court, the prosecution presented EVIDENCE, the juvenile and other witnesses gave testimony, and the juvenile court judge made a decision based on the perceived best interests of the juvenile.

In the same spirit of informality, juvenile courts provided fewer procedural protections than did adult courts. Juveniles did not have the right to a court-appointed ATTORNEY or to notice of charges of criminal behavior. They did not have the right to confront accusers and cross-examine witnesses. They did not have the right to a written record of the proceedings or to APPEAL the juvenile court judgment.

The problem with this lack of procedural protections was that a juvenile risked losing his or her liberty for several years. The best interests of the child usually involved placement in a secure reformatory or some other secure facility until the age of eighteen or, in some states, twenty-one. This amounted to a deprivation of liberty similar to that resulting from a prison sentence.

In 1967 the U.S. Supreme Court issued a decision that would change dramatically the character of juvenile courts. In IN RE Gault, 387 U.S. 1, 87 S. Ct. 1428, 18 L. Ed. 2d 527, fifteen-year-old Gerald Gault was committed to a reform school until age twenty-one for allegedly making an obscene phone call to a neighbor. Gault had been found delinquent without receiving notice of the charges or the assistance of an attorney. In addition, Gault had been interviewed by a probation officer without having an attorney present, and the statements made in this interview were submitted as proof that Gault had made the obscene phone call.

The U.S. Supreme Court ruled that Gault's commitment to the reformatory constituted a deprivation of liberty. This meant that Gault should have been provided with most of the procedural protections afforded to adults in criminal prosecutions. According to the Court in Gault, "[U]nbridled discretion, however benevolently motivated, is frequently a poor substitute for principle and procedure."

The purpose of the Gault decision was to make juvenile proceedings more fair to the juvenile. The decision accomplished this, but it also made juvenile proceedings more adversarial. With the increased procedural protections, juveniles became more capable of resisting commitment to secure REFORMATORIES, and it became more difficult for the juvenile courts summarily to obtain control over juveniles.

The adversarial tenor in contemporary juvenile courts is thus an unfortunate by-product of the decision in *Gault*. Prosecutors must now work harder to persuade the juvenile court to find in favor of the state so that the system may take control of the juvenile. They must shift the focus of juvenile court proceedings away from the needs of the juvenile and onto the offense. This shifted focus is similar to the focus of proceedings in adult criminal court, and it amounts to a reversal of the traditional emphasis in juvenile court.

FURTHER READINGS

Bernard, Thomas J. 1992. *The Cycle of Juvenile Justice.* New York: Oxford Univ. Press.

Buss, Emily. 2003. "The Missed Opportunity in Gault." *Univ. of Chicago Law Review* 70 (winter).

Cooper, N. Lee, Patricia Puritz, and Wendy Shang. 1998. "Fulfilling the Promise of In Re Gault: Advancing the Role of Lawyers for Children." *Wake Forest Law Review* 33 (fall).

CROSS REFERENCES

Adversary System; Children's Rights; Criminal Procedure; Juvenile Law.

GAY AND LESBIAN RIGHTS

Gay and lesbian rights seek to provide full legal and social equality for gay men and lesbians sought by the gay movement in the United States and other Western countries.

The term *gay* originally derived from slang, but it gained wide acceptance in the late twentieth century, and many people who are sexually attracted to others of the same sex prefer it to the older and more clinical term *homosexual.* The drive for legal and social equality represents one aspect of a broader gay and lesbian movement that, since the late 1960s, has worked to change attitudes toward homosexuality, develop gay community institutions, and improve the self-image of gay men and lesbians.

Although homosexuality has been recorded in every historical period and culture, the gay and lesbian rights movement developed only with the emergence of a self-conscious, gay-identified subculture that was willing to openly assert its demands for equality. Until the 1960s, many lesbians and gay men were secretive about their sexual orientation and frequently shared the attitude of the general society that homosexuality was a sickness or a sin, or both. The phrase "in the closet" refers to gay men and lesbians who hide their sexual orientation.

The first national gay organizations in the United States were the Mattachine Society (1951) and the Daughters of Bilitis (1956). The emergence of the CIVIL RIGHTS MOVEMENT of the 1960s energized gay and lesbian groups, and the development of the women's movement of the late 1960s made explicit the link between political activities and personal identity.

The watershed moment for gay men and lesbians occurred in 1969 when the patrons of the Stonewall Inn, a gay bar in New York City's Greenwich Village, forcefully resisted arrest by city police officers who had raided the bar. Stonewall became a symbol for a new set of attitudes on the part of younger gay men and lesbians who resisted DISCRIMINATION and negative stereotyping. As gay men and lesbians became more open and decided to "come out of the closet," U.S. society was challenged to question its assumptions about homosexuality.

Though most gay and lesbian rights activity remains local, national organizations such as the National Gay Task Force, the Lambda DEFENSE and Education Fund, and the HUMAN RIGHTS Campaign have played a significant role in challenging discriminatory treatment. For example, in 1974 the National Gay Task Force successfully lobbied the American Psychiatric Association to remove homosexuality from its list of mental disorders.

The recognition of gay and lesbian rights has been accomplished through both court challenges and legislative action. The ability of gay and lesbian organizations to make significant financial contributions to political candidates has helped lead to more sympathetic hearings in the legislative arena.

Criminal Prohibitions on Sexual Activity

Most gay men and lesbians remained in the closet until the modern movement for equality because homosexual behavior has been a crime throughout U.S. history. Homosexual activity includes anal sex and oral sex. SODOMY is defined as sexual acts against nature, either anal sex or BESTIALITY. Criminal laws against sodomy date from the colonial period, when a CONVICTION for a crime against nature could lead to a death sentence. Although few if any people have ever been executed for sodomy, the penalties for this crime remained heavy. By 2003, however, 36 states had repealed their sodomy statutes, usually as part of a general revision of the criminal code and with the recognition that heterosexuals as well as homosexuals engage in oral and anal sex. Of the remaining 14 states, the sodomy statute applied only to homosexual conduct in four states, including Texas.

In 1986 the Supreme Court ruled that state laws prohibiting homosexual sodomy were not unconstitutional. In *Bowers v. Hardwick,* 478 U.S. 186, 106 S. Ct. 2841, 92 L. Ed. 2d 140 (1986), the Court upheld the Georgia sodomy statute. It reasoned that there was a long legal and moral tradition against acts of sodomy and homosexuality. Therefore, homosexuals did not have a CONSTITUTIONAL right to commit sodomy. The decision was severely criticized by legal commentators and state supreme courts, which had overturned sodomy statutes based on state constitution due process clauses.

The Court reversed course in 2003, overruling *Bowers* in *Lawrence v. Texas,* 539 U.S. 558, 123 S. Ct. 2472, 156 L. Ed. 2d 508. The Court based its decision on a set of SUBSTANTIVE DUE PROCESS rulings dealing with BIRTH CONTROL and ABORTION, including the controversial decision in *Roe v. Wade,* 410 U.S. 113, 93 S. Ct. 705, 35 L. Ed. 2d 147 (1973). Under the FOURTEENTH AMENDMENT due process clause, the Court has found certain unwritten but fundamental liberty interests that the state cannot restrict. These cases made clear that the due process clause "has a substantive dimension of fundamental significance in defining the rights of the person." Therefore, women have a right to make decisions affecting their destiny, and married and unmarried couples may make decisions about birth control. This line of cases mandated that private sex acts between consenting adults deserves similar protection. To accomplish this objective, the Court had to discredit and reverse *Bowers.*

The Court, in a majority opinion written by Justice ANTHONY KENNEDY, found the reasoning used in *Bowers* to be flimsy and conjectural. The *Bowers* Court had framed the issue at stake as solely the right of homosexuals to commit acts of sodomy. Kennedy disagreed, concluding that the true issue had been the state's attempt to control personal relationships through the CRIMINAL LAW. He declared that as a general rule the state should not attempt to "define the meaning of the relationship or to set its BOUNDARIES absent INJURY to a person or abuse

of an INSTITUTION the law protects." If homosexuals wish to their express their sexuality in certain conduct the Constitution allows them "the right to make the choice." *Bowers* had also misread history. Sodomy laws directed at homosexuals had only been enacted since the 1970s and only nine states had done so. Moreover, sodomy laws in general had not been enforced against heterosexuals or homosexuals when the acts took place in private. Though traditional religious and cultural beliefs argued against the morality of homosexual conduct, these considerations had no bearing on the legal issue before the Court.

Having discredited prior precedent, the Court declared a due process right to consensual, intimate conduct. It rejected an alternate argument based on the EQUAL PROTECTION clause. That argument would have struck down the Texas law solely because it applied to acts committed by homosexual but not heterosexuals. The Court declined to go in that direction because it might lead to the redrafting of the law to ban sodomy by "same-sex and different-sex participants." This statement IMPLIED that all sodomy laws are unconstitutional.

Antidiscrimination Laws

Advocates of gay and lesbian rights have sought the passage of legislation that prohibits discrimination in employment, housing, public accommodations, or public service on the basis of sexual orientation. Many U.S. cities have passed gay rights ordinances that accomplish these objectives. In 1982 Wisconsin became the first state to pass gay rights legislation.

At the national level, gay men and lesbians fought legal battles in the 1980s and 1990s to allow them to serve in the ARMED SERVICES. A series of lawsuits were filed that sought to overturn military regulations that mandated DISCHARGE for disclosing a homosexual orientation.

In *Meinhold v. United States Department of Defense,* 34 F.3d 1469 (9th Cir. 1994), a three-judge panel ruled that Petty Officer Keith Meinhold, of the U.S. Navy, could not be discharged for stating on a national TELEVISION broadcast that he was gay. In the discharge proceedings, the Navy had taken the position that Meinhold should be discharged even though the Navy had not proved that Meinhold had committed any act of homosexual conduct.

The Ninth CIRCUIT COURT of Appeals concluded that a Navy policy against homosexual conduct was constitutional, as it was based on the Navy's professional judgment that homosexual conduct "seriously impairs the accomplishment of the military mission." However, the court of appeals ruled that Meinhold's statement that he was gay was not grounds for discharge. In the court's view, Meinhold had not demonstrated "a concrete, expressed desire to commit homosexual acts." Thus, the focus for the armed services must be on prohibited conduct and persons who are likely to engage in prohibited conduct.

The issue moved into the political arena following President Bill Clinton's election in November 1992. Clinton promised to honor his campaign pledge to exercise his authority as commander in chief of the armed forces and remove the military ban against gays. But the Joint Chiefs of Staff, headed by General Colin L. Powell, and many other senior Pentagon officers, strenuously objected to Clinton's plan, claiming that ending the ban would interfere with military order, discipline, and morale. Led by Senator Sam Nunn (D-GA), chairman of the powerful Armed Services Committee, Congress demanded an opportunity to comment on the policy.

Faced with increasing pressure at the beginning of his administration, Clinton agreed to a six-month delay in lifting the ban. He agreed to establish a temporary policy developed by Nunn and issued a directive ordering the military to stop asking new recruits about their sexual orientation; stop investigations to ferret out gays in uniform; and suspend current cases seeking to discharge gays, as long as those cases were based solely on homosexual status rather than on improper conduct. This policy, dubbed "don't ask, don't tell," became permanent when Congress wrote it into law in September 1993 (Pub. L. No. 103-160, 1993 H.R. 2401 § 571[a]). With this policy, gay men and lesbians were directed to keep their sexuality hidden if they intended to pursue a military career. After its implementation, the policy drew fierce criticism, as thousands of service members were discharged because of their sexual orientation. President BARACK OBAMA announced shortly after his inauguration that the DEFENSE DEPARTMENT would conduct a review of the policy. During his presidential campaign he indicated that he was in favor of equal

treatment for gays and lesbians in the military. However, at the beginning of 2010 the policy remained in place.

Congress has also considered laws that would include homosexuals as a protected class in some instances. However, these laws have met with strong resistance. In 2009, however, the House of Representatives passed an amendment to the FEDERAL hate crimes statute that would broaden the law to include attacks based on a victim's sexual orientation, gender identity, or mental or physical ability. As of May 2009, the Senate had not voted on the measure, but President Obama had indicated his intention to sign the measure if passed by Congress.

Legal Recognition of Gay and Lesbian Relationships

Gay and lesbian activists have pressed for legal recognition of homosexual relationships. Under current law in most states, a gay couple is treated differently than a married heterosexual couple. Thus, the benefits of probate and tax law are denied same-sex couples. For example, if a partner in a same-sex relationship dies, under law, the surviving partner is not entitled to any of the deceased's property, unless the deceased provided for such an ENTITLEMENT in a will.

With the appearance of ACQUIRED IMMUNE DEFICIENCY SYNDROME (AIDS), health benefits became particularly important to gay couples. Unless a company or government unit makes specific provisions for same-sex couples, an employee's same-sex partner who is not employed by the organization will not be allowed to join the employee's health plan.

Faced with these disparities, gay and lesbian activists first focused their attention on DOMESTIC partnership laws that would allow unmarried couples to register their relationship with a municipality. Attempts to implement domestic partnership failed in several cities, but New York City; Madison, Wisconsin; Takoma Park, Maryland; and Berkeley, San Francisco, Santa Cruz, and West Hollywood, California, enacted this type of ordinance. However, pressure on state governments led to the passage of civil union statutes that offer either all or most of the rights and responsibilities of heterosexual MARRIAGE. By 2009, eight states and the DISTRICT OF COLUMBIA had enacted such measures.

The fight for the legalization of same-sex marriage began in Hawaii in the early 1990s, when gay and lesbian couples filed a lawsuit when they were refused marriage licenses. The issue of same-sex marriage reached the Hawaii Supreme Court in *Baehr v. Lewin*, 74 Haw. 530, 852 P.2d 44 (1993). The court ruled that prohibiting same-sex couples from marrying was a violation of Hawaii's constitutional ban on SEX DISCRIMINATION. The voters of Hawaii derailed the RULING when they passed a REFEREN-DUM to amend the constitution to allow the state Legislature to restrict marriage to men and women only. As a result, the lawsuit was dismissed and the state restricted marriage solely to that of men and women.

Similar lawsuits were filed in other jurisdictions, and in Massachusetts, the state's highest court granted gays and lesbians the right to same-sex marriage in 2003. State supreme courts in California and Connecticut ruled in favor of same-sex marriage in 2008, and the Iowa Supreme Court did so as well in 2009. In California the voters passed Proposition 8 in November 2008, amending the state constitution to overturn the court decision. In May 2009 the California Supreme Court upheld the validity of the proposition. State legislatures in Vermont, New Hampshire, and Maine passed same-sex marriage statutes as well, but the voters in Maine rescinded its law in the November 2009 election.

The issue of same-sex marriage is of national interest because states traditionally ACCORD full faith and credit (full legal recognition) to marriages performed in other states. Faced with the prospect of gay and lesbian couples flying to Hawaii to marry and then demanding legal recognition of their union in their home states, several state legislatures passed laws that forbid recognition. Congress responded by enacting the DEFENSE OF MARRIAGE ACT OF 1996 (DOMA), 1 U.S.C.A. 7. The act denies certain federal benefits and entitlements to same-sex marriage partners by defining marriage as a legal union between a man and a woman. It also allows states to ban same-sex marriages within their borders and to not recognize such marriages performed in other states. With five states recognizing same-sex marriage, legal commentators believe it is only a matter of time before married same-sex couples challenge the constitutionality of DOMA.

In contrast to the national focus on issues such as same-sex marriage, local gay and lesbian

Two men are married at the Moose Meadow Lodge in Vermont, one of the six states legally recognizing gay marriage in 2009. Vermont's state legislature overrode the Vermont governor's veto of a bill conferring marriage rights to same-sex couples.

AP IMAGES

groups have spent their energies helping defend lesbian mothers and gay fathers faced with the loss of their children in custody cases. In the Virginia case of *Bottoms v. Bottoms*, 18 Va. App. 481, 444 S.E.2d 276 (1994), a trial judge awarded custody of Sharon Bottoms's son to her mother, solely because Bottoms is a lesbian. The Virginia Court of Appeals reversed the decision as an abuse of the court's discretion and returned custody to the mother. This case indicates the problems gay men and lesbians have in court. The National Center for Lesbian Rights estimates that only approximately 100 homosexuals gained parental rights through the courts between 1985 and 1994.

Despite the efforts of these local groups, several courts have continued to uphold legislation and judicial rulings that disfavor homosexuals as parents. For example, in 2001, the U.S. district court for the Southern District of Florida upheld a 1977 Florida law that prohibits homosexuals from adopting children (*Lofton v. Kearney*, 157 F. Supp. 2d 1327 [S.D. Fla. 2001]). Similarly, in 2002 the Alabama Supreme Court ruled unanimously to award custody of three teenagers to their father instead of to their lesbian mother (*Ex parte H.H.*, 830 So. 2d 21 [Ala. 2002]). The states of Arkansas, Nebraska, Utah, and Mississippi also have laws that either directly or indirectly prohibit adoptions by gays.

Backlash

As the same-sex marriage issue demonstrates, the efforts of gay men and lesbians to achieve social and legal equality have generated a backlash from those who oppose their agenda. Domestic partnership acts and gay rights ordinances have been rejected by voters in a number of cities and municipalities. At the state level, the voters of Oregon in 1988 approved a referendum that repealed an EXECUTIVE ORDER by former governor Neil Goldschmidt that had prohibited state agencies from discrimination based on sexual orientation. Measure 8, as the referendum was labeled, never went into effect, as the Oregon Court of Appeals ruled it unconstitutional (*Merrick v. Board of Higher Education,* 116 Or. App. 258, 841 P.2d 646 [1992]).

Undaunted by this court decision, the anti-gay Oregon Citizens Alliance placed a referendum on the 1992 Oregon ballot called Measure 9. Measure 9 was a strongly worded initiative that would have prohibited CIVIL RIGHTS protection based on sexual orientation and required state and local governments and school districts to discourage homosexuality. Proponents of the initiative believed that homosexuality is abnormal and perverse. The referendum was rejected on November 3, 1992, by a margin of 57 to 42 percent.

In contrast, voters in Colorado signaled a distinct displeasure with gay and lesbian rights. In November 1992 Colorado took the unprecedented step of amending the state constitution to prohibit state and local governments from enacting any law, regulation, or policy that would, in effect, protect the civil rights of gays, lesbians, and bisexuals. The amendment, known as Amendment 2, did not go into effect, as a lawsuit was filed challenging the constitutionality of the new provision.

This lawsuit, *Romer v. Evans,* 517 U.S.620, 116 S. Ct. 1620, 134 L. Ed. 2d 855 (1996), reached the U.S. Supreme Court. In a LANDMARK and controversial decision, the Supreme Court struck down the amendment as unconstitutional. Justice ANTHONY M. KENNEDY, writing for the majority, declared that the Colorado provision violated the equal protection clause of the Fourteenth Amendment. The Court found that the amendment did more than REPEAL state and municipal gay rights laws. The amendment prohibited "all legislative, executive or judicial action at any level of state or local government designed to protect ... gays and lesbians." Under this provision, the only way gay men and lesbians could secure their civil rights was through amendment of the state constitution.

This approach was too limited. Kennedy concluded that "[i]t is not within our constitutional tradition to enact laws of this sort." The Colorado amendment classified gay men and lesbians "not to further a proper legislative end but to make them unequal to everyone else. This Colorado cannot do."

The *Romer* decision was a major advance for gay and lesbian rights, as in it, the Supreme Court made clear that states cannot use a broad brush to limit civil rights. The political process cannot be changed to prevent gay men and lesbians from using the political and legal tools afforded all other citizens. The decision did suggest, however, that it is not unconstitutional to repeal specific legislation that favors gay rights.

Legislative and Judicial Responses after *Romer v. Evans*

State and local governments did not respond uniformly to *Romer.* A significant number of governmental entities expanded the legal rights of gays and lesbians. By the year 2000 ten states, the District of Columbia, 27 counties, and more than 150 cities had passed laws protecting gays and lesbians from discrimination. Most laws were limited to prohibiting discrimination against homosexuals in the workplace. A few laws went further, however, barring gay discrimination by public accommodations, credit institutions, healthcare providers, educational facilities, and landlords.

Conversely, other state and local governments enacted measures restricting homosexuals' civil rights. Unlike Amendment 2 in Colorado, these measures did not generally attempt to completely exclude gays and lesbians from seeking legal REDRESS for discrimination. Instead, some state and local governments tried to prevent gays and lesbians from exercising particular legal rights traditionally exercised only by heterosexuals. The right to marry and the right to adopt children continue to be the two most frequent targets of these anti-gay laws.

In 1993 voters in Cincinnati, Ohio, passed an initiative amending its city CHARTER to prohibit the city from adopting or enforcing any ordinance, regulation, rule, or policy that entitled gays, lesbians, or bisexuals the right to claim minority or protected status. Gay and lesbian groups challenged the constitutionality of the amendment in federal court, arguing that it denied them equal protection of the law.

In *Equality Foundation of Greater Cincinnati v. Cincinnati*, 860 F. Supp. 417 (S.D. Ohio 1994), the U.S. District Court for the Southern District of Ohio granted the plaintiffs a permanent INJUNCTION that precluded the charter amendment from going into effect. The District Court's decision was overturned on APPEAL in *Equality Foundation of Greater Cincinnati v. City of Cincinnati*, 128 F.3d 289 (6th Cir. 1997). The Sixth Circuit Court of Appeals stated that Cincinnati's charter amendment was different from Colorado's Amendment 2 because the charter amendment did not deprive gays and lesbians of all legal redress in the entire state.

The Sixth Circuit found that the charter amendment's scope was limited to the confines of the city and that homosexuals' FUNDAMENTAL RIGHT to participate in the state's political process was not affected by the local law. Thus, the court concluded that the charter amendment was rationally related to the city's valid interest in conserving public costs that are incurred from investigating and adjudicating sexual orientation discrimination complaints. The Supreme Court surprised many legal observers when it denied CERTIORARI to consider the Sixth Circuit's decision (*Equality Foundation of Greater Cincinnati, Inc. v. City of Cincinnati*, 525 U.S. 943, 119 S. Ct. 365, 142 L. Ed. 2d 302 [1998]).

Some plaintiffs have sought, though ultimately unsuccessfully, to challenge discrimination under a variety of state laws. The Boy Scouts of America, an organization that refuses to admit homosexuals, has been the subject of several of these lawsuits. In 1998 the California Supreme Court ruled that the state's human rights act did not apply to the Boy Scouts because the organization was not a business establishment (*Curran v. Mount Diablo Council of the Boy Scouts of America*, 952 P.2d 218 [Cal. 1998]).

The plaintiff in the case, Timothy Curran, was a Boy Scout from 1975 to 1979, when he was 14 to 18 years of age. He had a distinguished scout career, attaining the rank of Eagle Scout and earning numerous honors. After he had left the organization upon turning 18, he appeared in a series of articles in an Oakland newspaper about gay teenagers. When he later applied to become an assistant scoutmaster, scout officials denied his application due to his homosexual lifestyle. He first filed suit in 1982, but the original trial did not take place until 1990. Both the trial court and a California court of appeals

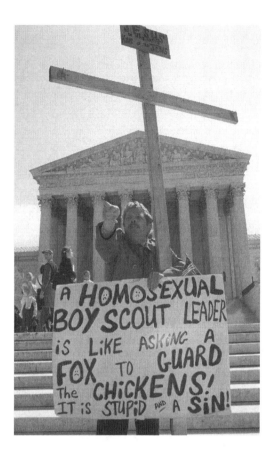

A man stands outside of the Supreme Court in protest of the case of James Dale, a homosexual who was kicked out of the Boy Scouts after becoming co-president of a gay and lesbian organization.
GETTY IMAGES

held, similar to the later ruling by the California Supreme Court, that because the Boy Scouts was not a business establishment, the human rights law did not apply to them.

The California Supreme Court decision was the opposite of decisions by courts in New Jersey. James Dale had been involved in the Boy Scouts from the age of eight. Like Timothy Curran, Dale was an exemplary member, earning the rank of Eagle Scout. Dale was later approved for adult membership. However, while he attended Rutgers University, he became the co-president of the university gay and lesbian campus organization and appeared in an article where he admitted to being a homosexual. The Boy Scouts then revoked his membership based on his homosexuality.

The New Jersey Superior Court's APPELLATE Division, in *Dale v. Boy Scouts of America*, 706 A.2d 270 (N.J. Super. 1998), determined that the Boy Scouts' policy violated the state's public accommodation law under New Jersey's Law Against Discrimination, N.J. Stat. Ann. § 10:5-1 et seq. The case was eventually appealed to the New Jersey Supreme Court, which agreed with

SAME-SEX MARRIAGE: A CIVIL RIGHT OR A MORAL WRONG?

Since the beginning of the U.S. GAY AND LESBIAN RIGHTS movement in the late 1960s, members of the movement have sought to attain CIVIL RIGHTS already granted to racial and ethnic minorities. These attempts at legal change have met with some success, yet a fundamental issue for many gay and lesbian couples, same-sex MARRIAGE, has found strong resistance, even from supporters of gay rights. Nevertheless, by 2009 the states of Massachusetts, Connecticut, New Hampshire, Vermont, and Iowa permitted same-sex marriage. California and Maine briefly permitted same-sex marriage, but voters overturned these measures in 2008 and 2009 respectively.

Same-sex marriage is controversial not only because it requires legal change but also because it raises a host of issues surrounding the definitions of marriage and family. The issue is packed with social and cultural beliefs and symbols that force parties in the debate to examine basic assumptions about how social life should be ordered. Though the overwhelming majority of opposition comes from heterosexuals, there are also some gays and lesbians who have doubts about the wisdom of same-sex marriage.

Advocates of same-sex marriage argue that many same-sex couples consider themselves married for all intents and purposes. The only thing lacking is legal recognition by the government—in this case, the state government—that such marriages exist. The denial of legal recognition constitutes sexual DISCRIMINATION, resulting in the loss of legal rights and benefits afforded to married individuals. Thus, unless a surviving member of a same-sex couple has been named in the deceased partner's will, the survivor has

no legal right to any portion of the deceased's probate estate, whereas in heterosexual marriages, a surviving spouse has a legal right to such assets. In addition, same-sex couples lose out on healthcare benefits extended to heterosexual married couples.

The legal arguments for same-sex marriage are grounded in the CONSTITUTIONAL concepts of EQUAL PROTECTION and due process. Proponents of same-sex marriage point to the U.S. Supreme Court's decision in *Loving v. Virginia* (388 U.S. 1, 87 S. Ct. 1817, 18 L. Ed. 2d 1010 [1967]), which ruled that state laws that prohibited interracial marriages (anti-miscegenation laws) were unconstitutional. The case established that it is a denial of DUE PROCESS OF LAW to forbid marriages on the basis of race and that the creation of such classifications denied couples equal protection of the law because the classifications had "no legitimate purpose independent of invidious racial discrimination."

For advocates of same-sex marriage, *Loving* is an example of the proper modern legal response to irrational racial prejudice. The Hawaii Supreme Court's decision in *Baehr v. Lewin* (74 Haw. 530, 852 P. 2d 44 [1993]), which held that the state must have a compelling STATE INTEREST in order to ban same-sex marriage, used *Loving* as a controlling legal precedent. The highest courts in Massachusetts, Connecticut, California, and Iowa all agreed that state laws banning same-sex marriage violated equal protection.

Opponents of same-sex marriage make three main arguments against it: the definition-of-marriage argument, the moral tradition argument, and the pragmatism argument.

The definition-of-marriage argument uses basic social and cultural assumptions. Opponents claim that marriage is necessarily the union of a man and a woman and, therefore, cannot include same-sex couples. Thus, any statute that describes marriage could have only contemplated heterosexual couples, even if the statute does not use the specific terms *husband* and *wife*. In *Jones v. Hallahan* (501 S.W.2d 588 [1973]), the Kentucky Court of Appeals used this line of reasoning to prohibit same-sex marriage, noting that "marriage has always been considered as the union of a man and a woman and we have been presented with no authority to the contrary."

Proponents of same-sex marriage argue that courts have not been presented with "authority to the contrary" because gays and lesbians have been ignored by historians. Major research on gay and lesbian history and anthropology has led some historians and legal scholars to conclude that Western and non-Western cultures have recognized same-sex relationships. In European history, stigmatizing and closeting of gays and lesbians started at the end of the medieval period and the beginning of the growth of nation-states. Thus, the North American continent was colonized at a time when same-sex relationships had lost their cultural and legal protection.

Opponents of same-sex marriage who make the moral tradition argument state that defining marriage to include only heterosexual couples is justified to preserve family values and traditional ethical notions. They point to passages in the Bible that either AFFIRM heterosexual

the superior court's decision (*Dale v. Boy Scouts of America*, 734 A.2d 1196 [N.J. 1999]). These decisions were initially considered major victories for gay and lesbian rights supporters.

However, the U.S. Supreme Court reversed the decisions of the New Jersey courts in *Boy Scouts of America v. Dale*, 530 U.S. 640, 120 S. Ct. 2446, 147 L. Ed. 2d 554 (2000). The Court,

marriages (Adam and Eve) or denounce homosexual practices (Sodom and Gomorrah). The Judeo-Christian moral tradition formed the basis of ENGLISH LAW; thus, it must be assumed that religious teachings against homosexual relationships informed the law. The U.S. Supreme Court echoed the moral tradition argument in its RULING that criminal SODOMY laws are not unconstitutional, suggesting that "millennia of moral teaching" supported a state's right to forbid homosexual acts (*Bowers v. Hardwick*, 478 U.S. 186, 106 S. Ct. 2841, 92 L. Ed. 2d 140 [1986]). This case was overruled by *Lawrence v. Texas* (539 U.S. 558, 123 S. Ct. 2472, 156 L. Ed. 2d 508 [2003]), with the Court overturning *Bowers*. It held that a Texas statute making it a crime for two persons of the same sex to engage in certain intimate sexual conduct was unconstitutional, as applied to adult males who had engaged in the consensual act of sodomy in the privacy of a home.

Another argument often raised with moral tradition is that heterosexual marriage is based on the need to procreate, something that same-sex couples cannot do. Proponents of same-sex marriage point out that heterosexual couples who cannot procreate are not denied a marriage license. Elderly, disabled, and infertile individuals may choose to marry for reasons other than procreation. In addition, both heterosexual and homosexual couples have taken advantage of advances in technologies such as ARTIFICIAL INSEMINATION and in vitro fertilization to overcome physical limitations on procreation.

Critics of the moral tradition argument contend that it is based on misguided readings of the Bible and history. They note that many religious leaders support same-sex marriage and that many same-sex couples solemnize their relationship in a religious ceremony performed by a minister or rabbi.

The pragmatism argument against same-sex marriage is typically made by those who support gay and lesbian rights generally but stop short of endorsing same-sex marriage. The call for marriage, they maintain, will create a backlash against the entire gay and lesbian rights movement. In addition, permitting same-sex marriage would be interpreted as legitimizing homosexuality. The pragmatic position is that gays and lesbians should be tolerated and protected; it does not extend to support the recognition of an alternative lifestyle or the expansion of the traditional concept of marriage.

Along with homosexual opponents who advance these arguments, some gays and lesbians are less than enthused with the prospect of same-sex marriage. This group believes that heterosexual marriage is not a good model for gays and lesbians, as it has traditionally established a hierarchical relationship that has produced the SUBORDINATION of women. The structure of marriage has fostered DOMESTIC abuse, economic disempowerment, and other forms of social dysfunction.

Another argument against same-sex marriage is that it will assimilate gays and lesbians into the DOMINANT culture and drain off the radicalism implicit in the gay and lesbian lifestyle. In lobbying for same-sex marriage, gay and lesbian leaders will put forward couples who most resemble their mainstream, heterosexual counterparts. This argument has been met with skepticism as romanticizing the movement. All gays and lesbians cannot be grouped as radicals, and it is to be expected that many gays and lesbians would enjoy the legal protection that same-sex marriage would bring.

When the debate has moved into the legal arena, reaction has been strong and swift. In the 1990s, proponents of same-sex marriage scored victories after courts ruled against state bans on such

marriages in both Hawaii in 1993 (*Baehr v. Lewin*, 852 P. 2d 44 [Hawaii 1993]) and Alaska in 1998 (*Brause v. Bureau of Vital Statistics* 21 P. 3d 357 [2001]). In both states, a backlash ensued. Hawaiian voters ratified a state CONSTITUTIONAL AMENDMENT authorizing lawmakers to define marriage only as a union between a man and a woman. Similarly, Alaskans voted by a 2-1 margin in favor of a similar amendment. California voters in 2008 overturned the state supreme court decision authorizing same-sex marriage, and Maine voters in 2009 voted to overturn a new state law that would have permitted same-sex marriage.

In 1996 Congress passed the DEFENSE of Marriage Act (DOMA) to give states the right to refuse to recognize same-sex marriages performed in other states. DOMA offered a strong rebuke to proponents by creating the first explicit FEDERAL definitions of "marriage" and "spouse" in strictly heterosexual terms, and its very name IMPLIED that the INSTITUTION of marriage needed protection from them. With legalization of same-sex marriage in five states, it was expected that DOMA would be challenged in the courts.

Perhaps unavoidably, the debate over same-sex marriage becomes heated because of the fundamental issues at stake. Proponents see marriage as socially constructed and, therefore, open to changes that society wishes to make. Opponents see less flexibility, citing tradition, morality, and the integrity of the family.

FURTHER READINGS

Sullivan, Andrew, ed. 1997. *Same-Sex Marriage, Pro and Con.* New York: Vintage Books.

Wardle, Lynn D., et al., eds. 2003. *Marriage and Same-Sex Unions: A Debate.* Westport, Conn.: Praeger.

CROSS REFERENCES

Civil Rights; Marriage; Privacy.

in a 5–4 decision, held that forcing the organization to accept gay troop leaders violates the Boy Scouts' right of free expression and free association under the FIRST AMENDMENT.

Prior decisions by the Court had reached similar holdings. In *Hurley v. Irish American Gay, Lesbian, and Bisexual Group of Boston*, 515 U.S. 557, 115 S. Ct. 2338, 132 L. Ed. 2d 487

(1995), the Court ruled that the sponsor of Boston's St. Patrick's Day parade could not be forced to allow a group of gays and lesbians to participate. The Court held that parades are a form of expression and that the sponsors could not be forced to include "a group imparting a message the organizers do not wish to convey."

In *Dale,* the Court, per Chief Justice WILLIAM H. REHNQUIST, found that the Boy Scouts similarly engage in expressive activity. More specifically, the Court recognized that the Boy Scout oath and creed, which include provisions admonishing scouts to be "morally straight" and "clean," were the types of expressive conduct protected by the First Amendment. The Boy Scouts in the case proclaimed that the organization did not wish to admit homosexuals because it did not want to "promote homosexual conduct as a legitimate form of behavior." Because the Boy Scouts could not be forced to convey a message contrary to one they did not want to convey, they could not be forced to allow homosexuals to become members.

Gay and lesbian rights groups, who decried the decision in *Dale,* have continued to strive for equality. These groups have sought to put pressure on such organizations as the Boy Scouts of America. For example, the Broward County School Board in Florida voted to ban the Boy Scouts from each of the 215 schools in the district due to the organization's discriminatory policies regarding homosexuals. In another form of protest, some Eagle Scouts, both gay and straight, returned their Eagle badges to the Boy Scouts' headquarters.

FURTHER READINGS

Alsenas, Linda. 2008. *Gay America: Struggle for Equality.* New York: Amulet Press.
Friedman, Lawrence M. 1993. *Crime and Punishment in American History.* New York: Basic Books.
Pinello, Daniel. 2003.*Gay Rights and American Law.* New York: Cambridge Univ. Press.

CROSS REFERENCES

Child Custody; Ettelbrick, Paula Louise; Marriage.

GENERAL ACCOUNTING OFFICE

The GENERAL ACCOUNTING OFFICE (GAO), created by the Budget and ACCOUNTING Act of 1921 (31 U.S.C.A. 41), was vested with all powers and duties of the six auditors and the COMPTROLLER of the Treasury, as stated in the act of July 31, 1894 (28 Stat. 162), and other statutes extending back to the original Treasury Act of 1789 (1 Stat. 65).

The 1921 act broadened the AUDIT activities of the government and established new responsibilities for reporting to Congress.

The scope of the activities of the General Accounting Office (GAO) was further extended by the Government Corporation Control Act (31 U.S.C.A. 841 [1945]), the Legislative Reorganization Act of 1946 (31 U.S.C.A. 60), the Accounting and Auditing Act of 1950 (31 U.S.C.A. 65), the Legislative Reorganization Act of 1970 (31 U.S.C.A. 1151), the Congressional Budget and IMPOUNDMENT Control Act of 1974 (31 U.S.C.A. 1301), the General Accounting Office Act of 1974 (31 U.S.C.A. 52c), and other legislation.

The GAO is under the control and direction of the comptroller general of the United States and the deputy comptroller general of the United States, who are appointed by the president with the advice and consent of the Senate for terms of 15 years.

The GAO has the following basic purposes: to assist Congress, its committees, and its members in carrying out their legislative and oversight responsibilities, consistent with its role as an independent, nonpolitical agency in the legislative branch; to carry out legal, accounting, auditing, and claims-settlement functions with respect to FEDERAL government programs and operations as assigned by Congress; and to make recommendations that are designed to provide for more efficient and effective government operations. It has more than 3,100 employees working in Washington, D.C. and 11 other cities. Its 2009 budget was $507 million.

Direct Assistance to Congress

The GAO directly assists Congress and its committees, members, and officers upon request. This assistance can come in any of the forms described in the following paragraphs.

Legislation may be enacted to direct the GAO to examine a specific matter; special audits, surveys, and reviews may be performed for the committees, members, or officers of Congress; professional staff members may be assigned to assist committees in conducting studies and investigations; the comptroller general or his or her representatives may testify before committees on matters considered to be within the special competence of the GAO; and committees or members may request comments on, or assistance in, drafting proposed legislation or other advice in legal and legislative matters. Further, the GAO responds to numerous requests from congressional sources for information relating to, or resulting from, its work, and it provides advice on congressional, administrative, and financial operations.

The Congressional Budget and Impoundment Control Act of 1974 specified numerous additional ways in which the GAO is to assist Congress: (1) provide information, services, facilities, and personnel (as mutually agreed) to the CONGRESSIONAL BUDGET OFFICE; (2) assist congressional committees in developing statements of legislative objectives and goals and methods for assessing and reporting actual program performance; (3) assist such committees in analyzing and assessing federal agency program reviews and evaluation studies; (4) develop and recommend methods for review and evaluation of government programs; (5) conduct a continuing program to identify needs of committees and members of Congress for FISCAL, budgetary, and program-related information; (6) assist congressional committees in developing their information needs; (7) monitor recurring reporting requirements of the Congress; (8) develop, in cooperation with the Congressional Budget Office, the Treasury, and the OFFICE OF MANAGEMENT AND BUDGET, an up-to-date INVENTORY and directory of sources and information systems for fiscal, budgetary, and program-related information; (9) help committees and members to obtain information from such sources and to appraise and analyze it; (10) develop, with the Congressional Budget Office, a central file of data and information to meet recurring requirements of Congress for fiscal, budgetary, and program-related information; (11) review and report to Congress on deferrals and rescissions of budget authority proposed by the president; and (12) BRING SUIT, where necessary, to ensure the availability for obligation of budget authority.

Auditing

In general, the audit authority of the GAO extends to all departments and agencies of the federal government. Exceptions to this audit authority principally involve funds that relate to certain intelligence activities.

Where audit authority exists, the GAO has the right of access to, and examination of, any books, documents, papers, or records of the departments and agencies. The law provides

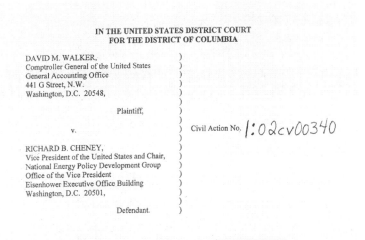

IN THE UNITED STATES DISTRICT COURT
FOR THE DISTRICT OF COLUMBIA

DAVID M. WALKER,   )
Comptroller General of the United States   )
General Accounting Office   )
441 G Street, N.W.   )
Washington, D.C. 20548,   )
)
                          Plaintiff,   )
)
                          v.   )   Civil Action No. 1:02cv00340
)
RICHARD B. CHENEY,   )
Vice President of the United States and Chair,   )
National Energy Policy Development Group   )
Office of the Vice President   )
Eisenhower Executive Office Building   )
Washington, D.C. 20501,   )
)
                          Defendant.   )

COMPLAINT FOR DECLARATORY AND INJUNCTIVE RELIEF

Plaintiff Comptroller General of the United States ("Comptroller General") brings this action for declaratory and injunctive relief and in support of his claims alleges as follows:

NATURE OF THE CASE

1.   This is an action arising under 31 U.S.C. §§ 712, 716, and 717 and the Declaratory Judgment Act, 28 U.S.C. §§ 2201 and 2202, against defendant, Richard B. Cheney, for access to certain records relating to the composition and activities of the National Energy Policy Development Group ("NEPDG"). Defendant is sued in his official capacity as the Vice President of the United States and as the official who served as the Chair of the NEPDG.

that departments and agencies must furnish to the comptroller such general information as he or she may require, including that which is related to their powers, duties, activities, organization, financial transactions, and methods of business.

The GAO has statutory authority to investigate all matters relating to the receipt, disbursement, and application of public funds. Additionally, the audit authority of the GAO covers wholly and partially owned government corporations and certain nonappropriated fund activities. By law, it is authorized and directed to make expenditure analyses of executive agencies in order to enable Congress to determine whether public funds are efficiently and economically administered and expended, and to review and evaluate the results of existing government programs and activities.

The scope of the audit work of the GAO extends not only to the programs and activities that the federal government itself conducts, but also to the activities of state and local

In 2002, former Comptroller General David M. Walker filed suit against then-Vice President Dick Cheney in order to force the release of the Bush administration's energy task force information.

AP IMAGES

GAO's Organizational Chart

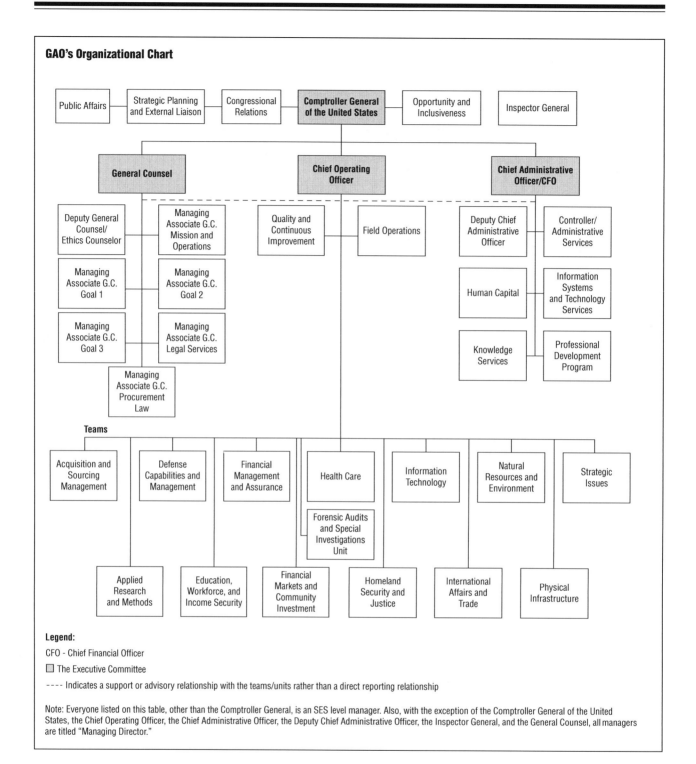

Public Affairs

Strategic Planning and External Liaison

Congressional Relations

Comptroller General of the United States

Opportunity and Inclusiveness

Inspector General

General Counsel

Chief Operating Officer

Chief Administrative Officer/CFO

Deputy General Counsel/ Ethics Counselor

Managing Associate G.C. Mission and Operations

Quality and Continuous Improvement

Field Operations

Deputy Chief Administrative Officer

Controller/ Administrative Services

Managing Associate G.C. Goal 1

Managing Associate G.C. Goal 2

Human Capital

Information Systems and Technology Services

Managing Associate G.C. Goal 3

Managing Associate G.C. Legal Services

Knowledge Services

Professional Development Program

Managing Associate G.C. Procurement Law

Teams

Acquisition and Sourcing Management

Defense Capabilities and Management

Financial Management and Assurance

Health Care

Information Technology

Natural Resources and Environment

Strategic Issues

Forensic Audits and Special Investigations Unit

Applied Research and Methods

Education, Workforce, and Income Security

Financial Markets and Community Investment

Homeland Security and Justice

International Affairs and Trade

Physical Infrastructure

Legend:

CFO - Chief Financial Officer

☐ The Executive Committee

---- Indicates a support or advisory relationship with the teams/units rather than a direct reporting relationship

Note: Everyone listed on this table, other than the Comptroller General, is an SES level manager. Also, with the exception of the Comptroller General of the United States, the Chief Operating Officer, the Chief Administrative Officer, the Deputy Chief Administrative Officer, the Inspector General, and the General Counsel, all managers are titled "Managing Director."

governments, quasi-governmental bodies, and private organizations in their capacity as recipients under, or administrators for, federal aid programs that are financed by loans, advances, grants, and contributions. The interest of the GAO also extends to certain activities of those parties that have negotiated contracts with the government.

The audit activities of the GAO also include examining and settling accounts of the certification, disbursement, and collection officers of the federal government, including determinations involving accountability for improper or illegal expenditures of public funds. Balances that the comptroller general certifies are binding on the EXECUTIVE BRANCH; however, any settled account can be reviewed on motion by the comptroller general or another interested party.

In its audit work, the GAO makes recommendations for greater economy and efficiency in government operations and for improving the effectiveness of government programs. Within this audit authority is a responsibility to report significant matters to Congress for information and use in carrying out its legislative and executive branch surveillance functions.

Accounting

The comptroller general has the following statutory responsibilities with respect to the accounting systems of federal agencies:

- Prescribe the accounting principles, standards, and related requirements to be followed by the agencies
- Cooperate with federal agencies in developing their accounting systems
- Approve agency accounting systems when they are deemed adequate and meet prescribed principles, standards, and related requirements
- Review, from time to time, agency accounting systems in operation
- Conduct—jointly with the Office of Management and Budget, the TREASURY DEPARTMENT, and the Office of Personnel Management—a continuous program to improve accounting and financial reporting in the federal government

By law, the comptroller general cooperates with the secretary of the Treasury and the director of the Office of Management and Budget in developing for use by all federal agencies standardized information and data-processing systems and also standard terminology, definitions, classifications, and codes for federal fiscal, budgetary, and program-related data and information.

Legal Services and Decisions

The legal work of the GAO is centered at the headquarters office in its Office of the General Counsel.

The comptroller general makes final determinations as to the legality of actions taken by federal departments and agencies with regard to accountability for the use of public funds. These determinations are made in connection with actions that are already taken and on an advance basis upon request by certain responsible officers of the government. Decisions of the comptroller general concerning the legality of payments may arise from the audit work of the GAO or may be applied for by the heads of departments or agencies or by certifying and disbursing officers with regard to payments to be made or as a result of congressional inquiries.

The comptroller general also considers questions that arise in connection with the award of government contracts and certain contracts under government grants. Statutory and regulatory procedures precisely define the manner in which these government awards are to be made, and those competing for such awards who believe that requirements have not been met in any particular instance may apply to the comptroller general for a determination.

The legal work of the GAO also covers a wide range of advisory services: to Congress, its committees, and members, with respect to the legal effect of statutory provisions and implications of proposed legislation as well as assistance in drafting legislation; to the JUSTICE DEPARTMENT, primarily in the form of litigation reports on court cases generated by, or related to, the work of the GAO; and to the courts in connection with cases involving the award of government contracts. In addition, there is daily coordination between the staff of the Office of the General Counsel and the audit and operating staffs with regard to the legal consequences of issues raised in the course of reviews of government activities.

Claims Settlement and Debt Collection

The GAO settles claims by and against the United States as required by law. Claims may involve individuals; business entities; or foreign, state, and municipal governments as claimant or debtor. Settlement of these claims by the GAO is binding upon executive branch agencies. However, the comptroller general may review any settled claim on his or her own initiative or at the request of an interested party. Claimants and debtors have further recourse to the Congress or to the courts.

Where an administrative agency has been unable to collect a debt due the government, the debt is certified to the GAO as uncollectible. After determining the amount due the United States, the GAO superintends its recovery, and ultimately makes final settlement and adjustment.

Energy Data Verification

Under the Energy Policy and Conservation Act (42 U.S.C.A. 6201), approved December 22, 1975, the comptroller general is empowered to conduct verification examinations of energy-related information developed by private business concerns under certain circumstances delineated in the act. For the purpose of carrying out this authority, the comptroller general may issue subpoenas, require written answers to INTERROGATORIES, administer oaths, inspect business premises, and inspect and copy specified books and records. Certain enforcement powers are provided, including, for some types of noncompliance, the power to assess civil penalties and to collect such penalties through CIVIL ACTION.

Rules, Regulations, and Decisions

The comptroller general makes such rules and regulations as deemed necessary for carrying on the work of the GAO, including those for the admission of attorneys to practice before it. Under the SEAL of the office, he or she furnishes copies of records from books and proceedings thereof, for use as EVIDENCE in accordance with the act of June 25, 1948 (62 Stat. 946; 28 U.S.C.A. 1733).

The GAO Personnel Act of 1980 (94 Stat. 27; 31 U.S.C.A. 52–1), approved February 15, 1980, requires the comptroller general to establish an independent personnel management system for employees of the GAO. The system would not be subject to regulation or oversight of executive branch agencies. Employee rights, such as appeals from adverse actions, are protected by creation of a GAO Personnel Appeals Board.

The GAO "Policy and Procedures Manual for Guidance of Federal Agencies" is the official medium through which the comptroller general promulgates principles, standards, and related requirements for accounting to be observed by the federal departments and agencies; uniform procedures for use by the federal agencies; and regulations governing the relationships of the GAO with other federal agencies and with individuals and private concerns DOING BUSINESS with the federal government.

All decisions of the comptroller general of general import are published in monthly pamphlets and in annual volumes.

GAO Reports

As required by law, a list of GAO reports issued or released during the previous month is furnished monthly to Congress, its committees, and its members.

Copies of GAO reports are provided without charge to members of Congress and congressional committee staff members; officials of federal, state, local, and foreign governments; members of the press; college libraries, faculty members, and students; and nonprofit organizations.

Since the late 1990s the GAO has worked to place more information on its web site. It has placed a large archive of its reports online and publishes current reports. These include legal decisions, opinions, and a vast array of resources to help both federal agencies and the general public. In addition, it has placed its bid-protest DOCKET online and has established FraudNet, which allows persons to file allegations of government FRAUD online and it has established an email hotline for reporting small business fraud and abuse.

FURTHER READINGS

General Accounting Office Website. Available online at www.gao.gov (accessed May 25, 2009).

CROSS REFERENCES

Congress of the United States; Federal Budget; Office of Management and Budget; Treasury Department.

GENERAL AGREEMENT ON TARIFFS AND TRADE

The GENERAL AGREEMENT ON TARIFFS AND TRADE (GATT) originated with a meeting of 22 nations meeting in 1947 in Geneva, Switzerland. By 2000 there were 142 member nations, with another 30 countries seeking admission. The detailed commitments by each country to limit tariffs on particular items by the amount negotiated and specified in its tariff schedule is the central core of the GATT system of international obligation.

The obligations relating to the tariff schedules are contained in Article II of GATT. For each COMMODITY listed on the schedule of a country, that country agrees to charge a tariff that will not exceed an amount specified in the schedule. It can, if it wishes, charge a lower tariff.

The World Trade Organization (WTO) heavily influences the workings of the GATT treaties through the efforts of various committees. Representatives of member countries of the WTO comprise the Council for the Trade in Goods (Goods Council), which oversees the work of 11 committees responsible for overseeing the various sectors of GATT. The committees focus on such issues as agriculture, sanitary measures, subsidies, customs valuation, and rules of origin.

FURTHER READINGS

Bagwell, Kyle, and Robert W. Staiger. 2002. *The Economics of the World Trading System.* Cambridge, MA: MIT Press.

Irwin, Douglas A., Petros C. Mavroidis, and Alan O. Sykes. 2009. *The Genesis of the GATT.* New York: Cambridge Univ. Press.

World Trade Organization Web site. 2009. Available online at http://www.wto.org/ (accessed September 3, 2009).

CROSS REFERENCES

Commodity; Tariff.

GENERAL APPEARANCE

The act by which a defendant completely consents to the jurisdiction of the court by appearing before it either in person or through an authorized representative thereby waiving any jurisdictional defects that might be raised except for that of the competency of the court.

A GENERAL APPEARANCE differs from a SPECIAL APPEARANCE in which a DEFENDANT agrees to submit to the JURISDICTION of the court for a restricted purpose, such as to test whether the SERVICE OF PROCESS made upon him or her was legally sufficient.

GENERAL AVERAGE LOSS

General average loss refers to the distribution of maritime loss among various interests of vessels and cargo.

The general average rules apply to losses that are incurred for the common benefit of participants in a maritime venture. These rules establish that losses should be shared ratably by those who participate in a venture. The doctrine of GENERAL AVERAGE LOSS is based on the principle that a voluntary sacrifice of a portion of the ship or cargo to save the remaining property and lives should be made good by all interests exposed to the common peril and saved by the sacrifice.

General average loss is the opposite of PARTICULAR AVERAGE LOSS, which applies when a sacrifice was made for a separate interest or for a reason other than the common benefit of vessel and cargo.

CROSS REFERENCES

Admiralty and Maritime Law.

GENERAL CREDITOR

An individual to whom money is due from a debtor, but whose debt is not secured by property of the debtor. One to whom property has not been pledged to satisfy a debt in the event of nonpayment by the individual owing the money.

GENERAL EXECUTION

A court order commanding a public official, such as a sheriff, to take the personal property of a defendant to satisfy the amount of a judgment awarded against such defendant.

When such officer is given the authority to seize only particular property or types of property, the writ or order is sometimes known as a *special execution.*

GENERAL INTENT

In criminal law and tort law, a mental plan to do that which is forbidden by the law.

Unlike offenses that require a SPECIFIC INTENT, it is not necessary that the ACCUSED intend the precise harm or result. It is sufficient if the person meant to do the act that caused the harm or result. For example, BATTERY is a GENERAL INTENT offense. If a DEFENDANT commits a battery that results in harm to the victim, it does not matter if the defendant did not intend the harm.

GENERAL JURISDICTION

The legal authority of a court to entertain whatever type of case comes up within the geographical area over which its power extends.

GENERAL JURISDICTION differs from special or limited JURISDICTION, which is the power of a COURT to hear only certain types of cases, or those in which the AMOUNT IN CONTROVERSY is below a certain sum or that is subject to exceptions.

GENERAL LEGACY

A monetary gift, payable out of the collective assets of the estate of a testator—one who makes a will—and not from a designated source.

Unlike a SPECIFIC LEGACY, a GENERAL LEGACY is not subject to ADEMPTION, extinction that results when a testator revokes his or her intention to leave designated property to another either by altering the property or removing it from the estate.

GENERAL SERVICES ADMINISTRATION

The GENERAL SERVICES ADMINISTRATION (GSA) was established by section 101 of the FEDERAL Property and Administrative Services Act of 1949 (40 U.S.C.A. § 751). The GSA sets policy for and manages government property and records. More specifically, GSA duties include the construction and operation of buildings; procurement and distribution of supplies; utilization and disposal of property; management of transportation, traffic, and communications; and management of the government's automatic data processing resources program. Like a large business CONGLOMERATE, the GSA conducts business in many different areas and operates on different levels of organization: the central Washington, D.C., office, 11 regional offices, and field activities.

The GSA is a large organization, the structure of which consists of several tiers of administrators, offices, bureaus, and support agencies.

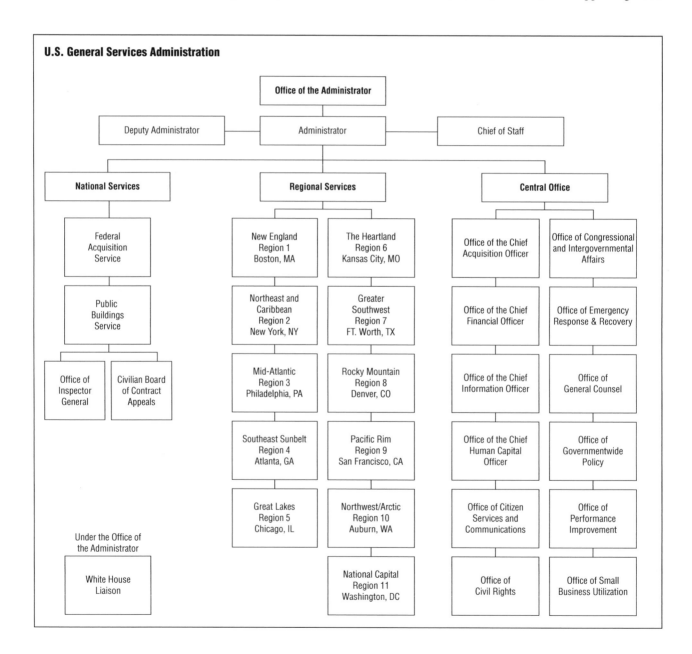

U.S. General Services Administration

- Office of the Administrator
  - Deputy Administrator — Administrator — Chief of Staff

- **National Services**
  - Federal Acquisition Service
  - Public Buildings Service
    - Office of Inspector General
    - Civilian Board of Contract Appeals
  - Under the Office of the Administrator
    - White House Liaison

- **Regional Services**
  - New England Region 1 Boston, MA
  - The Heartland Region 6 Kansas City, MO
  - Northeast and Caribbean Region 2 New York, NY
  - Greater Southwest Region 7 FT. Worth, TX
  - Mid-Atlantic Region 3 Philadelphia, PA
  - Rocky Mountain Region 8 Denver, CO
  - Southeast Sunbelt Region 4 Atlanta, GA
  - Pacific Rim Region 9 San Francisco, CA
  - Great Lakes Region 5 Chicago, IL
  - Northwest/Arctic Region 10 Auburn, WA
  - National Capital Region 11 Washington, DC

- **Central Office**
  - Office of the Chief Acquisition Officer
  - Office of Congressional and Intergovernmental Affairs
  - Office of the Chief Financial Officer
  - Office of Emergency Response & Recovery
  - Office of the Chief Information Officer
  - Office of General Counsel
  - Office of the Chief Human Capital Officer
  - Office of Governmentwide Policy
  - Office of Citizen Services and Communications
  - Office of Performance Improvement
  - Office of Civil Rights
  - Office of Small Business Utilization

The first level in the HIERARCHY of the GSA consists of the administrator, the deputy administrator, and the chief of staff. The administrator is the principal director for the entire organization, assisted by a deputy and chief of staff.

The second tier in the GSA organization consists of four main offices: the Federal Supply Service, Federal Technology Service, Public Buildings Service, and the Office of Governmentwide Policy. These four offices oversee the majority of the agency's work and collectively form the public face of the GSA.

The Federal Supply Service (FSS) provides low-price, quality goods and services to federal departments and agencies. Its services include governmentwide programs for the management of transportation, mail, and travel; audits of transportation; management of a federal fleet; and management of aircraft owned or operated by civilian agencies in support of government missions.

The FSS provides more than $25 billion annually in common-use goods and services to federal agencies. It emphasizes purchasing environmentally safe products, and services and supplies more than 3,000 environmentally oriented products to the federal government, such as retread tires, shipping boxes made with recycled materials, and water-saving devices.

The service also coordinates a worldwide program for the management of government property, through the Office of Property Disposal, which is responsible for allocating excess personal property among the agencies and donating or disposing of property through public sales.

The FSS Interagency Fleet Management Program controls approximately 185,000 vehicles, purchasing more than 58,000 new vehicles annually. The FSS also acts as the government's civilian freight manager by providing rating and routing services to customer agencies and overnight delivery of small packages at reduced rates, and managing the postpayment AUDIT of freight and passenger transportation bills.

Information Technology Service The Federal Technology Service (FTS) directs governmentwide programs for automated data processing and local TELECOMMUNICATIONS equipment and services, coordinates programs for federal records and information management practices, and provides information to the public through the Federal Information Center.

The FTS helps federal agencies manage information resources through the Office of Information Technology INTEGRATION (ITI). The ITI provides assistance through three programs: the Federal Systems Integration and Management System, Federal Computer Acquisition Center, and Federal Information System Support Program. The ITS also procures automatic data processing and telecommunications hardware, software, and services involving information resources of governmentwide agencies.

In addition to technical assistance, the service provides various management assistance programs and policies to governmentwide agencies concerning information-related functions and activities. It is in charge of the GSA's governmentwide telecommunications service and assists with the interagency Information Resources Management infrastructure. It also provides internal information systems management for the GSA.

The FTS's Office of Information Security supports all government activities conducting sensitive and classified national security, diplomatic, and DEFENSE DEPARTMENT missions.

Another program overseen by FTS is the Federal Information Center Program, which is a clearinghouse for information about the federal government. The center answers questions regarding government programs and refers people to the appropriate agency. Depending upon their geographic location, residents may be able to access the center through a toll-free telephone number. Another resource, the Federal Domestic Assistance Catalog Program, provides information on federally operated programs that offer domestic assistance, such as loans, grants, and INSURANCE, to interested persons.

The FTS also offers the Federal Information Relay Service to help hearing-impaired and speech-impaired individuals communicate with the government. The service manages numerous programs that maintain information on equipment, goods, and services bought by the government. The information is available to the public.

The Public Buildings Service (PBS) designs, builds, leases, repairs, and maintains approximately 7,300 federally controlled buildings in the United States. The service is also responsible for property management information systems throughout the government and for the maintenance of public utilities and their costs.

The Office of Governmentwide Policy (OGP) functions to ensure that governmentwide policies allow and encourage agencies to develop and utilize the best, most cost effective management practices for the conduct of their specific programs. The OGP consolidates GSA governmentwide policy-making activities within one central office. These activities include the government's plans for acquiring some $200 billion per year in goods and services, the $8 billion a year the government spends on government travel, and the tens of billions of dollars spent each year on internal administrative management systems. The OGP is focused on re-engineering the traditional policy development model to emphasize collaborative development.

The third tier in the organizational structure of the GSA contains 11 regional offices: New England Region, Northeast and Caribbean Region, Mid-Atlantic Region, Southeast Sunbelt Region, Great Lakes Region, The Heartland Region, Greater Southwest Region, Rocky Mountain Region, Pacific Rim Region, Northwest/Arctic Region, and the National Capitol Region. These offices are distributed to facilitate the work of the GSA in diverse areas of the country.

The fourth level in the structural hierarchy of the GSA consists of ten offices that support all GSA services: the Offices of the Chief Financial Officer, Office of the Chief People Officer, Office of Congressional & Intergovernmental Affairs, Office of Services and Communications, Office of the Chief Information Officer, Office of Small Business Utilization, Office of Performance Improvement, Office of General Counsel, Office of CIVIL RIGHTS, Office of Inspector General, along with the GSA Board of Contract Appeals.

The Office of Portfolio Management manages all aspects of the portfolio management business line at the national level.

FURTHER READINGS

General Services Administration. 2003. *U.S. General Services Administration Guide to Federal Government Sales.* Washington, D.C.:.U.S. Independent Agencies and Commissions.

U.S. General Services Administration. Available online at http://www.gsa.gov (accessed July 25, 2009).

U.S. Government Manual Website. Available online at http://www.gpoaccess.gov/gmanual/index (accessed July 21, 2009).

CROSS REFERENCES

Personal Property; Telecommunications.

GENERAL TERM

A sitting of the court en banc, with the participation of the entire membership of the court rather than the regular quorum. A phrase used in some jurisdictions to signify the ordinary session of a court during which the trial determination of actions occur.

GENERAL TERM is distinguishable from SPECIAL TERM, in that the latter entails the HEARING of motions, which are applications for court orders, arguments, the DISPOSITION of various types of formal business, or the trial of a special list or class of cases.

GENERAL VERDICT

A decision by a jury that determines which side in a particular controversy wins, and in some cases, the amount of money in damages to be awarded.

GENERAL WARRANTY DEED

Another name for a WARRANTY DEED.

GENERAL WELFARE

The concern of the government for the health, peace, morality, and safety of its citizens.

Providing for the WELFARE of the general public is a basic goal of government. The PREAMBLE to the U.S. Constitution cites promotion of the GENERAL WELFARE as a primary reason for the creation of the Constitution. Promotion of the general welfare is also a stated purpose in state constitutions and statutes. The concept has sparked controversy only as a result of its inclusion in the body of the U.S. Constitution.

The first clause of Article I, Section 8, reads, "The Congress shall have Power To lay and collect Taxes, Duties, IMPOSTS and Excises, to pay the Debts and provide for the common Defence and general Welfare of the United States." This clause, called the General Welfare Clause or the SPENDING POWER Clause, does not grant Congress the power to legislate for the general welfare of the country; that is a power reserved to the states through the TENTH AMENDMENT. Rather, it merely allows Congress to spend FEDERAL money for the general welfare. The principle underlying this distinction—the limitation of federal power—eventually inspired the only important disagreement over the meaning of the clause.

According to JAMES MADISON, the clause authorized Congress to spend money, but only to carry out the powers and duties specifically ENUMERATED in the subsequent clauses of Article I, Section 8, and elsewhere in the Constitution, not to meet the seemingly infinite needs of the general welfare. ALEXANDER HAMILTON maintained that the clause granted Congress the power to spend without limitation for the general welfare of the nation. The winner of this debate was not declared for 150 years.

In *United States v. Butler,* 56 S. Ct. 312, 297 U.S. 1, 80 L. Ed. 477 (1936), the U.S. Supreme Court invalidated a federal agricultural spending program because a specific congressional power over agricultural production appeared nowhere in the Constitution. According to the Court in *Butler,* the spending program invaded a right reserved to the states by the Tenth Amendment.

Though the Court decided that *Butler* was consistent with Madison's philosophy of limited federal government, it adopted Hamilton's INTERPRETATION of the General Welfare Clause, which gave Congress broad powers to spend federal money. It also established that determination of the general welfare would be left to the discretion of Congress. In its opinion, the Court warned that to challenge a federal expense on the ground that it did not promote the general welfare would "naturally require a showing that by no reasonable possibility can the challenged legislation fall within the wide range of discretion permitted to the Congress." The Court then obliquely confided, "[H]ow great is the extent of that range … we need hardly remark." "[D]espite the breadth of the legislative discretion," the Court continued, "our duty to hear and to render judgment remains." The Court then rendered the federal agricultural spending program at issue invalid under the Tenth Amendment.

With *Butler* as precedent, the Supreme Court's interest in determining whether congressional spending promotes the general welfare has withered. In *South Dakota v. Dole,* 483 U.S. 203, 107 S. Ct. 2793, 97 L. Ed. 2d 171 (1987), the Court reviewed legislation allowing the secretary of transportation to withhold a percentage of federal highway funds from states that did not raise their legal drinking age to twenty-one. In holding that the statute was a valid use of congressional spending power, the Court in *Dole* questioned "whether 'general welfare' is a judicially enforceable restriction at all."

Congress appropriates money for a seemingly endless number of national interests, ranging from federal courts, policing, IMPRISONMENT, and national security to social programs, environmental protection, and education. No federal court has struck down a spending program on the ground that it failed to promote the general welfare. However, federal spending programs have been struck down on other CONSTITUTIONAL grounds.

FURTHER READINGS

Rosenthal, Albert J. 1987. "Conditional Federal Spending and the Constitution." *Stanford Law Review* 39.

Sky, Theodore. 2004. *To Provide for the General Welfare: A History of the Federal Spending Power.* Newark, DE: Univ. of Delaware Press.

Sorenson, Leonard. 1995. *Madison on the "General Welfare" of America.* New York: Rowman & Littlefield.

CROSS REFERENCES

Congress of the United States; Constitution of the United States; Federal Budget; Federalism.

GENERALLY ACCEPTED ACCOUNTING PRINCIPLES

The standard accounting rules, regulations, and procedures used by companies in maintaining their financial records.

GENERALLY ACCEPTED ACCOUNTING PRINCIPLES (GAAP) provide companies and accountants with a consistent set of guidelines that cover both broad ACCOUNTING principles and specific practices. For example, accountants use GAAP standards to prepare financial statements.

In response to the STOCK MARKET crash of 1929 and the ensuing Great Depression, Congress passed the SECURITIES Act in 1933 and the Securities Exchange Act in 1934. Among other things, these acts established a methodology for standardizing accounting practices among publicly held companies. The task of creating and maintaining accounting standards was handled by the American INSTITUTE of Certified Public Accountants (AICPA) from 1936 until 1973. In 1973, the responsibility was taken over by the Financial Accounting Standards Board (FASB), which was established the same year.

The Financial Accounting Standards Advisory Council (FASAC), which is composed of 33 members from both the public and private sectors, advises the FASB on matters that may affect or influence GAAP rules. These 33 individuals meet quarterly to discuss accounting issues and gather information, which they then present to FASB. Essentially, FASAC serves as FASB's sounding board. FASAC is overseen by the Financial Accounting Foundation, an independent organization whose 16-member board of trustees chooses FASAC's 33 members. The FASB is also monitored by the Corporation Finance division of the SECURITIES AND EXCHANGE COMMISSION (SEC). Among the organizations that influence GAAP rules are the AICPA and the INTERNAL REVENUE SERVICE (IRS).

Other countries have their own GAAP rules, which are set by their versions of the FASB. For example, the Canadian Institute of Chartered Accountants (CICA) sets GAAP standards in Canada.

Publicly held companies are required to conform to GAAP standards. Specifically, the Securities Act and the Securities Exchange Act established a requirement that publicly held companies must undergo an external AUDIT by an independent ACCOUNTANT once per year. In the early 2000s, companies faced increased scrutiny in light of the widely publicized cases involving such major corporations as Enron and WorldCom, along with the firm of Arthur Andersen, one of the world's largest accountancy firms. In the case of Enron, for example, the company manipulated its financial information to give the appearance that revenues were much higher than they actually were. After the company declared BANKRUPTCY in 2001, Arthur Andersen came under attack because its auditors had signed off on Enron's financials despite numerous misgivings. Andersen was found GUILTY of obstruction of justice by a jury in Houston, Texas, in June 2002.

In July 2002, President GEORGE W. BUSH signed the Sarbanes-Oxley Act, which established new regulations for accounting reform and investor protection. Among the provisions of Sarbanes-Oxley was the creation of the five-member Public Company Accounting Oversight Board, overseen by the SEC. Accounting firms that audit publicly held companies are required to register with the board, which has the authority to inspect audits. Sarbanes-Oxley also requires chief executive officers and chief financial officers of publicly held companies to provide a statement attesting to the veracity of their financial statements.

FURTHER READINGS

Financial Accounting Standards Board Web site. Available online at http://www.fasb.org (accessed July 26, 2009).

Schilit, Howard, 2010. *Financial Shenanigans: How to Detect Accounting Gimmicks and Fraud on Financial Reports.* New York: McGraw-Hill.

Squires, Susan E., et al. 2003. *Inside Arthur Andersen: Shifting Values, Unexpected Consequences.* Upper Saddle River, NJ: Prentice-Hall.

United States Securities and Exchange Commission Web site. Available online at http://www.sec.gov (accessed July 26, 2009).

GENETIC ENGINEERING

The human manipulation of the genetic material of a cell.

GENETIC ENGINEERING involves the process of isolating individual DNA fragments, coupling them with other genetic material, and causing the genes to replicate themselves. Introducing this newly created complex to a host cell causes it to multiply and produce clones that can later be harvested and used for a variety of purposes. Current applications of the technology include, but are not limited to, medical investigations of gene structure for the control of genetic disease (particularly through antenatal diagnosis); food crop development to resist plant disease or harsh weather; the creation of new antibiotic and antiviral drugs; genetic cloning to save endangered species; and the development of sustainable energy through bio-fuels. The synthesis of hormones and other proteins (e.g., growth hormone and insulin), which are otherwise obtainable only in their natural state, is also of interest to scientists.

International Codes and Ethical Issues for Society

An international code of ethics for genetic research was first established in the World Medical Association's Declaration of Helsinki in 1964. The guide prohibited outright most forms of genetic engineering and was accepted by numerous U.S. professional medical societies, including the AMERICAN MEDICAL ASSOCIATION (AMA).

In 1969 the AMA promulgated its own ethical guidelines for clinical investigation, key provisions of which conflicted with the Helsinki Declaration. For example, the AMA guidelines proposed that when mentally competent adults were found to be unsuitable subjects for genetic engineering studies, minors or mentally incompetent subjects could be used instead. The Helsinki Declaration did not condone testing on humans.

The growth of genetic engineering in the 1970s aroused international concern, but governments and medical societies took only limited measures to control it. Concern focused on the production of dangerous bacterial mutants that could be used as harmful eugenics tools or WEAPONS. The Genetic Manipulation Advisory Group was established in England based on the recommendations of a prominent medical group, the Williams Committee. Scientists were required to consult this group before carrying out any activity involving genetic manipulation in England. Additional measures required scientific laboratories throughout the world to include physical containment labs to prevent manipulated genes from escaping and surviving in natural conditions. These policies were subsequently adopted in the United States.

In 2000 a group of 138 countries, including the United States, approved the Cartagena Protocol on Biosafety Environment. International concerns over the handling of genetically modified organisms (GMOs) prompted the passage of the protocol. It governs such issues as the safe transfer, handling, use, and disposals of GMOs among member countries.

Another area of developing law, summarized by Sonia Miller in a May 29, 2007, article in *The New York Law Journal*, concerns genetic privacy. With the advancement of genetic engineering technology comes the human benefit of having disease, deformity, and DISABILITY potentially eradicated, enhancing life and health expectancies, and a better world as a whole. However, the same innovation has the potential to be misused for purposes of creating, and perceiving as superior, "designer babies," and genetics-based economic or social communities. Critics of the developing field warn that INSURANCE companies and employers may misuse private genetic information about individuals to discriminate. Both houses in Congress have contemplated LEGISLATION that would prohibit DISCRIMINATION on the basis of genetic information, and would extend privacy and confidentiality requirements. (See, e.g., prior legislative efforts such as the Genetic Information Nondiscrimination Act of 2007 (H.R. 493, S. 358).)

The Breakdown of Regulation: Genetic Inventions and Patents in the United States

In 1980 the U.S. Supreme Court created an economic incentive for companies to develop genetically engineered products by holding that

In 1997, a team of scientists at the Roslin Institute in Edinburgh, Scotland, cloned the first adult mammal, a sheep named Dolly.

AP IMAGES

such products could be patented. In *Diamond v. Chakrabarty*, 447 U.S. 303, 100 S. Ct. 2204, 65 L. Ed. 2d 144, the COURT held that a PATENT could be issued for a novel strain of bacteria that could be used in the cleanup of oil spills. In 1986 the U.S. DEPARTMENT OF AGRICULTURE approved the sale of the first living genetically altered organism. The virus was used as a pseudorabies vaccine, from which a single gene had been cut. Within the next year, the U.S. Patent and Trademark Office announced that non-naturally occurring, non-human, multicellular living organisms, including animals, were patentable under the Patent Act of 1952 (35 U.S.C.A. § 101).

The Department of Agriculture formally became involved in genetic engineering in April 1988, when the Patent and Trademark Office issued the first animal patent, granted on a genetically engineered mouse used in cancer research. U.S. scientists began experiments with the genetic engineering of farm animals, such as creating cows that would give more milk, chickens that would lay more eggs, and pigs that would produce leaner meat. These developments only raised more objections from critics who believed that genetic experimentation on animals violated religious, moral, and ethical principles. In spite of the controversy, the U.S. House of Representatives approved the Transgenic Animal

Patent Reform bill on September 13, 1988. The bill would have allowed exempted farmers to reproduce, use, or sell patented animals, although it prohibited them from selling germ cells, semen, or embryos derived from animals. However, the Senate did not vote on the act, and so it did not become law.

During his campaign for presidency of the United States, then-candidate BARACK OBAMA pledged to require mandatory labeling of all foods containing (GMOs). In 2009 the Obama administration reaffirmed its commitment to this initiative.

Early Developments

In the mid-1990s the international guidelines established by the Declaration of Helsinki were modified to allow certain forms of cell manipulation in order to develop germ cells for therapeutic purposes. Scientists are also exploring genetic engineering as a means of combating the HIV virus.

In 1997 the cloning of an adult sheep by Scottish scientist Ian Wilmut brought new urgency to the cloning issue. Prior to this development, cloning had been successful only with immature cells, not those from an adult animal. The breakthrough raised the prospect of human cloning and prompted an international debate regarding the ethical and legal implications of cloning.

Since the cloning of the sheep, nicknamed "Dolly," scientists have found the process of cloning to be more difficult than expected. After Dolly scientists cloned such animals as cows, pigs, monkeys, cats, and even rare and endangered animals. The process of cloning is complex, involving the replacement of the nucleus of an egg cell with the nucleus of a cell from the subject that will be cloned. This process is meticulous, and the failure rate is high. However, the efforts in such genetic manipulation were not to create or clone animals, but rather to create stronger and healthier animals. Cloning by nuclear transfer and/or transgenic technology involves a process wherein a nucleus from a single cell containing DNA is injected, via nuclear transfer, into an unfertilized egg, with the resulting embryo transferred to the reproductive tract of a healthy specimen.

Evidence suggests that cloned animals have experienced significant health problems, leading to concerns about the vitality of the entire process. Cloned animals tend to be larger at birth, which could cause problems for the female animals giving birth to them. The cloned organisms also tend to become obese at middle age, at least in the case of experimental cloned mice. Moreover, evidence suggests that cloned animals have died because they do not have sufficient IMMUNITY defenses to fight disease.

Dolly lived for six years before dying in February 2003, which is about half of the normal life expectancy of a sheep. Proponents of the cloning experiments suggest that cloning opens a number of possibilities in scientific research, including the nature of certain diseases and the development of genetically enhanced medications. Scientists have also successfully cloned endangered animals. In 2001 an Italian group cloned an endangered form of sheep, called the European mouflon. About a year and a half earlier, an American company, Advanced Cell Technology, tried unsuccessfully to clone a rare Asian ox. The cloning was initially successful, but the animal died of dysentery 48 hours after birth.

In November 2001 scientists first successfully inserted the DNA from one human cell into another human egg. Although the eggs began to replicate, they died shortly after the procedure. Human cloning has caused the most intense debate on the issue, with the debate focusing upon scientific, moral, and religious concerns over this possibility. Scientists do not expect that human cloning will be possible for several years.

In early 2005 the British government granted approval to Professor Ian Wilmut of Edinburgh's Roslin INSTITUTE (the scientist behind the cloning of "Dolly") to clone human embryos for medical research. Despite palpable public outcry, the government was quick to point out that human reproductive cloning remained illegal, but approval could be granted where embryos were created as a source of stem cells to treat or cure disease (therapeutic cloning). Wilmut planned to use these stem cells for investigation into Motor Neurone Disease (MND).

Recent Developments

Perhaps one of the most promising areas of genetic engineering, and one warranting scientific, legal, and ethical caution, is that of stem cell research. The term refers to a process wherein humans (or animals) can regenerate, repair, or replace their own diseased or aged organs, limbs, or tissue through the development and cloning of their own adult stem cells (extracted from their bone marrow). Early genetic experiments involved human embryos (embryonic stem cells), and the scientific community as well as the general public remained divided on the issue. The form of stem cell research that continues to spawn controversy evolves around usage of embryonic stem cells (ESCs) that are removed and harvested for research when an embryo is less than 15 days old.

Research funding had been politically polarized in the past, with celebrities such as Michael J. Fox and former first lady Nancy Reagan urging voters to further the cause. The issue gained extensive media coverage during the 2004 U.S. presidential election campaigns between Senator John Kerry (D–Mass.) and INCUMBENT President GEORGE W. BUSH. The Bush administration firmly reiterated its position that ESC research posed an ethical question, and that taxpayer dollars would not be used to fund the destruction of human embryos, irrespective of their origin. In the end, FEDERAL support for such research was granted, but only using embryos that had been donated from in vitro fertilization clinics and already in federal research custody, that would otherwise have been discarded. In March 2009 President Barack Obama signed into law EXECUTIVE ORDER No. 13505, Removing Barriers to Responsible Scientific Research Involving Human Stem Cells, which expressly revoked the previous administration's restrictive Executive Order 13435 of June 2007.

The 2009 Albert Lasko Basic Medical Research Award for advancements in genetic engineering research went to regenerative technology advances that do not rely human reproductive embryos, but rather use transferred DNA coding capable of instructing special cells to form stem cells, which, in turn, are coded to regenerate as specific organs or tissues. The related Lasko Clinical Medical Research Award went for stem cell research leading to a revolutionary cancer treatment for certain types of leukemia. The global market for such advancements, according to *Genetic Engineering & Biotechnolgy News*, was estimated at $700 million.

A new field of genetic engineering involves the creation of synthetic genes (synthetic genomics). As of 2009, their application was limited to non-human experiments involving alternative energy resources. Likewise, genetic manipulation of existing crops has resulted in the development of experimental crop plants that utilize nitrogen more efficiently, thus requiring less fertilizer in poor soils. Salt-tolerant and drought-tolerant crops are also under development. Of note is the research into turning plant wastes into fuel and boosting oil yields from algae grown in ponds.

Significant State Laws

Certain states have passed laws restricting genetic engineering. By the early 1990s, six states had enacted laws designed to curb or prohibit the spread of genetically engineered products in the marketplace (see Ill. Ann. Stat. ch. 430, § 95/1 [Smith-Hurd 1995]; Me. Rev. Stat. Ann. tit. 7, § 231 et seq. [West 1995]; Minn. Stat. Ann. § 116C.91 et seq. [West 1995]; N.C. Gen. Stat. § 106-765-780 [Supp. 1991]; Okla. Stat. Ann. tit. 2, §§ 2011–2018 [West 1996]; Wis. Stat. Ann. § 146.60 [West 1996]). North Carolina's law sets the most comprehensive restrictions on genetic engineering. Resembling the earlier measures proposed by organizations such as England's Genetic Manipulation Advisory Group, it requires scientists to hold a permit for any release of a genetically engineered product outside a closed-containment enclosure. The North Carolina statute has been cited as a possible model for advocates of comprehensive federal regulations.

In September 2008 California enacted its first law related to genetic engineering, the Farmers Protection Act, AB541. The bill protects farmers from lawsuits relating to the drift (through weather elements) of GE pollen or seed onto their property, often contaminating their crops with patent-protected genetically modified seeds or pollens.

FURTHER READINGS

Beauchamp, Tom L., and James F. Childress. 1983. *Principles of Biomedical Ethics.* Oxford and New York: Oxford University Press.

"Better World: Learning to Love Genetic Engineering." *New Scientist,* September 14, 2009.

"2009 Lasko Awards Recognize Promise of Stem Cells-Global Market Could Top $700 Million." *Genetic Engineering & Biotechnolgy News,* September 14, 2009.

Darvall, Leanna. 1993. *Medicine, Law, and Social Change.* Aldershot, England: Dartmouth.

Harder, Ben. 2002. "Scientific Pitfalls Complicate Cloning Debate." *National Geographic.*

Mason, John Kenyon, and R.A. McCall-Smith. 1994. *Law and Medical Ethics*. London: Butterworths.

Mason, John Kenyon, and R.A. McCall-Smith. 1987. *Butterworths Medico-Legal Encyclopedia*. London: Butterworths.

Paley, Eric R. 1993. "Rethinking Utility: The Expediency of Granting Patent Protection to Partial CDNA Sequences." *Syracuse Law Review*.

Office of the White House. 2009. "Executive Order No. 13505, Removing Barriers to Responsible Scientific Research Involving Human Stem Cells." Text available online at http://www.whitehouse.gov/ ... /Removing-Barriers-to-Responsible-Scientific-Research-Involving-Human-Stem-Cells/; website home page: http://www.whitehouse.gov/ (accessed August 10, 2009)

Ratnoff and Smith. 1968. "Human Laboratory Animals: Martyrs for Medicine." *Fordham Law Review* 36.

Smith, George P., II. 1993. *Bioethics and the Law*. Lanham, Md.; New York; and London: University Press of America.

Smith, George P., II. 1981. *Genetics, Ethics, and the Law*. Gaithersburg, Md.: Associated Faculty Press.

Trivedi, Bijal. 2001. "Human Embryos Cloned by U.S. Company, But Don't Survive." *National Geographic*.

CROSS REFERENCE

Genetic Screening.

GENETIC SCREENING

The scientific procedure of examining genetic makeup to determine whether an individual possesses genetic traits that indicate a tendency toward acquiring or carrying certain diseases or conditions. In 2001, scientists first published the complete human genome map (a human's genetic blueprint), greatly advancing the capability and use of genetic screening, manipulation, and replication.

Genetic testing of humans facilitates the discovery and treatment of genetic defects, both before and after birth. CIVIL RIGHTS proponents, employers, and those who suffer from genetic diseases have debated GENETIC SCREENING because the procedure poses practical and theoretical legal, economic, and ethical problems. Some theorists, for example, have suggested that genetic screening could improve society if it were made mandatory before hiring or MARRIAGE. Others say that to mandate this practice would be unconstitutional. Genetic screening is a dynamic, rather than static, field of medical and scientific experimentation and application that clearly involves scientific, legal, and ethical interests that may differ or compete. Accordingly, each new milestone or discovery warrants commensurate review of these interests for both beneficial and potentially detrimental consequences.

Federal and State Legislation

The earliest national and state legislation concerning genetic screening was enacted in the 1970s. The legislation focused on voluntary genetic testing. The laws generally protect the interests of those who suffer from genetic disease, offer FEDERAL and state subsidies for counseling, and support research in genetic diseases.

In 1976 Congress passed the National Sickle Cell Anemia, Cooley's Anemia, Tay-Sachs, and Genetic Diseases Act (42 U.S.C.A. § 300b-1 et seq.), which permitted the use of public funds for voluntary genetic screening and counseling programs. State legislatures passed measures, with certain exceptions, requiring genetic screening of school-age children for sickle cell anemia. New York enacted a law that provides for premarital testing to identify carriers of the defective sickle cell gene (N.Y. Dom. Rel. Law §13aa [McKinney 1977]). Other states provided for voluntary premarital testing for the sickle cell disease (e.g., Cal. Health & Safety Code § 325-331 [West 1978]); Ga. Code Ann. § 19-3-40 [1974]). Such legislation often included provisions for voluntary, funded counseling (see Va. Code Ann. § 32.1-68 [Michie]).

With the advent of new technology in genetics came increasing concern about its application. In 1996 Congress passed the all-encompassing HEALTH INSURANCE Portability and Accountability Act (HIPAA) (P.L.104-191). One key provision barred group INSURANCE plan administrators from using individual employees' genetic information as a factor when writing group policies (unless such information already resulted in the diagnosis of a illness). However, the bill addressed neither individual policies and premiums nor the use of genetic information in the workplace.

Consequently, in 2000 President BILL CLINTON signed EXECUTIVE ORDER 13145, prohibiting DISCRIMINATION in federal employment based on genetic information. However, according to the National Human Genome Research INSTITUTE (a division of the National Institutes of Health), 39 states had enacted bills addressing genetic discrimination in health insurance (see, e.g., Alabama Code §27–53–2,4; Alaska Statutes Annotated §21.54.100; Louisiana REVISED STATUTES Annotated §22.213.6,7, and so on). Another 27 states had passed bills addressing genetic discrimination in the workplace.

The Constitution, Civil Rights, and Scientific Theory

In 1981 and again in 2002, Congress held hearings to identify potential problems of widespread genetic screening. Subsequent legal and medical discussion has focused on the ethics of certain practices such as eugenics, a form of GENETIC ENGINEERING that involves the systematic programming of genes to create a specific life form or the use of living animals for experimentation. House and Senate committees had pending bills before Congress (S. 318, S. 382) hoping to create national legislation addressing prohibited uses of genetic screening.

One potential problem with genetic screening arises in its use by employers. Although an employer considering hiring an individual with a genetic disease often relies primarily on economic issues, the practice of screening prospective employees and eliminating those with defective genes may be discriminatory because some genetic diseases afflict certain ethnic and racial groups more often than others. G-6-PD DEFICIENCY, for example, occurs most frequently in blacks and persons of Mediterranean descent. If screening excludes persons with G-6-PD deficiency, it will have a stronger effect on those groups. This practice could violate Title VII of the Civil Rights Act of 1964 (42 U.S. C.A. §§ 2000e et seq.).

In early 2001 the first federal court lawsuit of its kind was filed against a private company alleging violations under the Americans with Disabilities Act (ADA), P.L. 101-336 and several state laws. According to the suit, which settled in 2002, employer Burlington Northern Santa Fe Railroad began furtively testing the blood of workers with carpal tunnel syndrome. At least 18 employees claimed to have been subjected to nonconsensual genetic testing. Still, other courts have permitted limited use of genetic screening as an adjudicatory aid in disputes. In a South Carolina CHILD CUSTODY case, a judge ordered a woman to undergo genetic testing for Huntington's disease, because the result could impact her ability to care for the children. While some experts would argue that these factors are important to proper legal and personal decision making, others question where the line will be drawn.

Nevertheless, some legal scholars maintain that compulsory genetic screening programs violate the Constitution. They assert, for example,

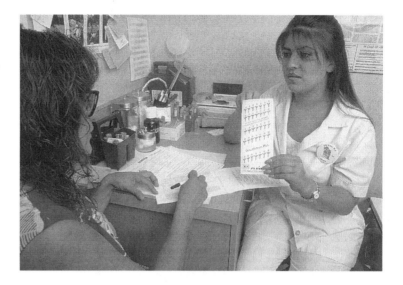

A doctor and patient discuss genetic screening for Down's syndrome. As a result of cases such as Haymon v. Wilkerson, doctors have increased their use of genetic counseling and fetal screening.

PHOTOEDIT

that taking a child's blood sample constitutes a physical invasion of the body in violation of the FOURTH AMENDMENT. Compulsory counseling programs for parents, they say, interfere with the fundamental rights to marry and procreate. The critics of screening propose that less intrusive voluntary programs together with education could accomplish the same objectives.

Even though genetic screening involves at least a minor intrusion into an individual's body and may involve a search within the meaning of the Fourth Amendment, proponents of genetic science maintain that such searches are not unreasonable if executed in a proper manner and justified by a legitimate STATE INTEREST (see *Schmerber v. California*, 384 U.S. 757, 86 S. Ct. 1826, 16 L. Ed. 2d 908 [1966] [holding that a compulsory blood test to determine INTOXICATION of an automobile driver is not an unreasonable search]). Proponents of mandatory screening and counseling agree that these practices could interfere with the right to procreate. However, they suggest that the state's interests in improving the quality of a population's genetic pool in order to minimize physical suffering and reduce the number of economically dependent persons justifies the INFRINGEMENT on the civil liberties of individuals.

Amniocentesis and the Abortion Debate

A specific form of genetic screening known as amniocentesis raised fundamental CONSTITUTIONAL issues when first introduced; in the twenty-first century, however, it is considered standard operating procedure for older women to undergo amniocentesis when they have conceived for the first time. Amniocentesis consists of inserting a needle through the abdominal wall of a pregnant woman into the amniotic sac containing the fetus, withdrawing a sample of the sac fluid, analyzing it for genetic characteristics, and determining whether the fetus has certain genetic defects. If amniocentesis reveals a genetically defective fetus, the parents may choose to abort it or carry it to term. Children born with genetic defects have brought legal claims against their parents for the tort of WRONGFUL LIFE, or WRONGFUL BIRTH.

Before the advent of amniocentesis, wrongful life actions generally failed (*Pinkney v. Pinkney*, 198 So. 2d 52, [Fla. App. 1967] [refusing to recognize tort of wrongful life for extramarital child plaintiff against father] and *Zepeda v. Zepeda*, 41 Ill. App. 2d 240, 190 N. E.2d 849 [1963], *cert. denied*, 379 U.S. 945, 85 S. Ct. 444, 13 L. Ed. 2d 545 [1964]). The development of procedures such as amniocentesis, coupled with a shift in societal attitudes toward ABORTION, has led to successful claims for wrongful life. For example, in *Haymon v. Wilkerson*, 535 A.2d 880 (D.C. App. 1987), a mother brought a wrongful birth action against a physician after her child was born with Down's syndrome. The court of appeals held that the mother was entitled to recover extraordinary medical and health care expenses incurred as a result of the child's mental and physical abnormalities. As a result of cases such as *Haymon*, doctors have increased their use of genetic counseling and prenatal testing.

The Future of Genetic Screening

In 1993 the Nobel Prize for chemistry was awarded to Kary Mullis for his development of a technique known as polymerase chain reaction, a method for rapidly isolating and copying any DNA sequence out of a sample that may contain thousands of other genes. This technology is rapidly developing for application not only in eugenics but also for gene manipulation to correct defective gene sequences in many diseases or conditions (nanotechnology). Researchers at Oxford University's Wellcome Trust Centre for Human Genetics announced in 2003 the development of a methodology for concurrently evaluating the functional significance of millions of noncoding polymorphisms that exist in the human genome. This development is expected to contribute greatly to the determination of genetic susceptibility to disease and assessing future health risk through genetic screening.

On the legal front, Congress passed the Genetic Information Nondiscrimination Act of 2008 (GINA), (Pub.L. 110-343), in 2008. The law addresses concerns about discrimination that might keep some people from getting useful genetic tests that could benefit their health. The law also enables people to take part in research studies without worrying that their DNA information might be used against them when applying for health insurance or for a job. However, the law does not cover life insurance, DISABILITY insurance, and long-term care insurance. It sets a minimum standard of protection that must be met in all states, but it does not weaken the protections provided by any state law concerning these issues. The law also established the Genetic Nondiscrimination Study Commission, which will be appointed in 2014 to review the developing science of genetics and to make recommendations to Congress regarding whether to provide a disparate-impact CAUSE OF ACTION under this statute.

FURTHER READINGS

"A Comparison of Enacted State Genetic Discrimination Legislation." 2001. Council for Responsible Genetics (summer). Available online at www.gene-watch.org (accessed July 26, 2003).

Hawkins, Dana. 2001. "The Dark Side of Genetic Testing." *U.S. News & World Report* 130.

Higgins, Michael. 1998. "Tempest in a Tube." *ABA Journal* 84.

Jones, Nancy. 2008. *Genetic Discrimination*. Hauppauge, New York:Nova Science Publishers.

Reilly, Philip R. 1993. "Public Policy and Legal Issues Raised by Advances in Genetic Screening and Testing." *Suffolk University Law Review* (winter).

Stewart, Alison. 2007. *Genetics, Health Care and Public Policy*.New York: Cambridge University Press.

CROSS REFERENCES

American Medical Association; Disability Discrimination; Employment Law; Fetal Rights; Privacy; Search and Seizure.

GENEVA CONVENTIONS, 1949

The horrors of WORLD WAR II led nations to recognize that existing rules governing the conduct of warfare were inadequate to cover a prolonged and expanded conflict. The resulting efforts to codify new restrictions on belligerent conflict led to the four conventions concluded at Geneva, Switzerland, in 1949. These four treaties related to (1) the treatment of prisoners of war; (2) the alleviation of the suffering of wounded and sick combatants in the field; (3) the alleviation of the suffering of the wounded, sick, and shipwrecked members of the armed forces at sea; and (4) the protection of civilian persons during war.

The International Committee of the Red Cross was active in organizing the conferences and preparing draft treaties that resulted in the final conventions. In addition, the International Red Cross assumed responsibility under portions of the conventions to serve as a neutral party to observe compliance with the conventions and to perform humanitarian tasks.

According to Swedish researchers, 95 percent of all deaths in WORLD WAR I were suffered by soldiers. In World War II, the figure dropped to 50 percent—the remaining deaths were those of civilians when their cities (e.g., London, Coventry, Dresden, Hiroshima, Nagasaki) were bombed. Unfortunately, the statistics worsened. The civilian deaths from the Korean is usually estimated at two to three million, and estimates place the number of civilian deaths from the VIETNAM WAR at approximately 365,000. Between 1974 and 1977 the Diplomatic Conference on the Reaffirmation and Development of International Humanitarian Law, meeting in Geneva, adopted two protocols to be added to the 1949 Geneva Conventions. One applies to international armed conflicts and the other to non-international armed conflicts. Both significantly provide for enhanced protection of the non-combatant, civilian populations.

Yet another concern for the effectiveness of the Geneva Conventions surfaced over the years. It became increasingly evident that, despite "grave breaches" of protocols, the Geneva Conventions lacked enforcement power. Moreover, those nations ratifying the conventions (59 initial signatories in 1949) were usually not the offenders. (With the end of the COLD WAR and the collapse of the Soviet Union, each of the newly independent states that succeeded the former Soviet Union has adhered to the conventions and, excepting Lithuania and Azerbaijan, the additional protocols.) Many of the crimes against humanity were (and are) being committed by warring factions within a country, resulting in genocides, ethnic or religious antagonism, and ultimately the collapse of state structures. In these circumstances, RATIFICATION by the prior state ENTITY means little.

With a world community that in 2010 comprised more than 180 sovereign states, a major overhaul of the Geneva Conventions remained elusive. However, the world community has united to create newer entities such as the International Criminal Tribunal for the Former Yugoslavia in 1993 and the adoption in Rome of the STATUTE of the INTERNATIONAL CRIMINAL COURT in 1998. These entities have ADJUDICATION and sentencing authority, which gives some enforcement power to prosecute and punish those who commit the crimes against humanity outlined in the conventions and protocols. However, the power to identify, pursue, and apprehend suspected violators varies, depending on the circumstances.

FURTHER READINGS

Bugnion, Francis. 2000. "The Geneva Conventions of 12 August 1949: From the 1949 Diplomatic Conference to the Dawn of the New Millennium." *International Affairs* 76.

Goldstein, Richard. 2002. "International Law and Justice in America's War on Terrorism." *Social Research* 69.

Jinks, Derek. 2008. *The Rules of War: The Geneva Conventions in the Age of Terror.* New York: Oxford Univ. Press.

Pictet, Jean S., ed. 1958. *The Geneva Conventions of 12 August 1949: Commentary.* Geneva, Switzerland: International Committee of the Red Cross. Available online at http://www.loc.gov/rr/frd/Military_Law/Geneva_conventions-1949.html; website home page: http://www.loc.gov (accessed September 4, 2002).

CROSS REFERENCES

International Court of Justice; International Law.

GENOCIDE

The crime of destroying or conspiring to destroy a national, ethnic, racial, or religious group.

GENOCIDE can be committed in a number of ways, including killing members of a group or causing them serious mental or bodily harm, deliberately inflicting conditions that will bring about a group's physical destruction, imposing measures on a group to prevent births, and forcefully transferring children from one group to another.

Genocide is a modern term. Coined in 1944 by Polish scholar of INTERNATIONAL LAW Raphael Lemkin, the word is a combination of the Greek *genos* (race) with the Latin *cide* (killing). In his book, *Axis Rule in Occupied Europe*, Lemkin offered the definition of "a coordinated plan of different actions aiming at the destruction of essential foundations of the life of national

The bodies of Rwandan genocide victims before burial in a mass grave. In just 100 days in 1994, an estimated 800,000 Tutsis and moderate Hutus were killed by members of the Hutu majority.

AP IMAGES

groups, with the aim of annihilating the groups themselves" (Lemkin 1944, 79). The book studied in particular detail the methodology of the Nazi German genocide against European Jews, among whom were his parents. Later, he served as an advisor to both the U.S. War Department and the NUREMBERG TRIALS of Nazi leaders for WAR CRIMES. He dedicated his life to the development of international conventions against genocide.

The contemporary archetype of modern genocide is the Holocaust, in which German Nazis starved, tortured, and executed an estimated six million European Jews, as well as millions of other ethnic and social minorities, as part of an effort to develop a master Aryan race. Immediately upon coming to power in Germany in 1933, the Nazis began a systematic effort to eliminate Jews from economic life. The Nazis defined persons with three or four Jewish grandparents as being Jewish, regardless of their religious beliefs or affiliation with the Jewish community. Those with one or two Jewish grandparents were known as Mischlinge, or mixed-breeds. As non-Aryans, Jews and Mischlinge lost their jobs and their Aryan clients, and were forced to liquidate or sell their businesses.

With the onset of WORLD WAR II in 1939, the Germans occupied the western half of Poland, forcing nearly two million Jews to move into crowded, captive ghettos. Many of these Jews died of starvation and disease. In 1941 Germany invaded the Soviet Union. The Nazis dispatched 3,000 troops to kill Soviet Jews on the spot, most often by shooting them in ditches or ravines on the outskirts of cities and towns.

Meanwhile the Nazis began to organize what they termed a final solution to the Jewish question in Europe. German Jews were required to wear a yellow star stitched on their clothing and were deported to ghettos in Poland and the Soviet Union. Death camps equipped with massive gas chambers were constructed at several sites in occupied Poland, and large crematories were built to incinerate the bodies. Ultimately the Nazis transported millions of Jews to concentration camps, in crowded freight trains. Many did not survive the journey. Once at the death camps, many more died from starvation, disease, shooting, or routine gassings, before Allied forces liberated the survivors and forced the Nazis to surrender in 1945.

Following the exterminations of World War II, the UNITED NATIONS passed a resolution in an effort to prevent such atrocities in the future. Known as the Convention on the Prevention and Punishment of the Crime of Genocide (78 U.N.T.S. 278 [Dec. 9, 1948]), the resolution recognized genocide as an international crime and provided for its punishment. Proposed and partially formulated by Lemkin, who had lobbied nations tirelessly for its adoption, the convention also criminalized CONSPIRACY to commit genocide, direct and public incitement to commit genocide, attempted genocide, and complicity in genocide. Its definition of genocide specified that a person must intend to destroy a national, ethnic, racial, or religious group. Thus, casualties of war are not necessarily victims of genocide, even if they are all of the same national, ethnic, racial, or religious group. The convention requires signatory nations to enact laws to punish those found GUILTY of genocide, and allows any signatory state to ask the United Nations to help prevent and suppress acts of genocide.

The convention was, by itself, ineffective. Article XI of the convention requires the United Nations' member countries to ratify the DOCUMENT, which many did not do for nearly 50 years. The United States did not ratify the convention until 1988. Before doing so, it conditioned its obligations on certain understandings: (1) that the phrase INTENT *to destroy* in the convention's definition of genocide means "a SPECIFIC INTENT to destroy"; (2) that the term *mental harm* used in the convention as an example of a genocidal tactic, means "permanent impairment of mental faculties through drugs or torture"; (3) that an agreement to grant EXTRADITION, which is part of the convention, extends only to acts recognized as criminal under both the country requesting extradition and the country to which the request is made; and (4) that acts in the course of armed conflict or war do not constitute genocide unless they are performed with the specific intent to destroy a group of people.

On November 4, 1988, the United States passed the Genocide Implementation Act of 1987 (18 U.S.C.A. § 1091 [1994]). This act created "a new FEDERAL offense that prohibits the commission of acts with the specific intent to destroy, in whole or in substantial part, a national, ethnic, racial or religious group; and to provide adequate penalties for such acts" (S. Rep. No. 333, 100th Cong., 2d Sess. 1 [1988], *reprinted in* 1988 U.S.C. C.A.N. 4156).

In 1990 the U.S. Congress passed the IMMIGRATION and Nationality Act (INA) (8 U.S. C.A. § 1182), a comprehensive reform of immigration laws. As part of this reform, Congress mandated that ALIENS guilty of genocide are excluded from ENTRY into the United States, or deported when discovered. However, the INA lacks a clear definition of genocide, referring only to the U.N. convention drafted more than 40 years earlier.

The unclear definition of genocide makes its prevention and punishment difficult. Whether massive, and often barbaric, loss of life within ethnic, national, religious, or racial groups rises to the crime of genocide—or is simply an unpleasant by-product of war—is open to debate. Until international trials in the late 1990s, the Holocaust of Nazi Germany was the only example recognized throughout the international community as genocide.

Apart from the Holocaust, there have been a number of other events that at least some commentators have described as genocide. These include the devastation of numerous Native American tribes through battles with European settlers and exposure to their diseases; the killing of some 1.5 million Armenians by the Turks during and after WORLD WAR I; the deaths of approximately 1.7 million Cambodians under the Khmer Rouge regime in Cambodia between 1975 and 1979; the killing of hundreds of thousands of civilians during the VIETNAM WAR; the deaths of more than 20,000 Christian Orthodox Serbs, Muslims, and Roman Catholic Croats in "ethnic cleansing" arising out of the civil war in Croatia and Bosnia-Herzegovina during the early 1990s; and the deaths of more than one million Rwandan civilians in ethnic clashes between the Hutu and Tutsi peoples, also during the early 1990s.

During the 1990s, the United Nations Security Council twice convened international tribunals to prosecute genocide and other flagrant humanitarian violations. The International Criminal Tribunals for Former Yugoslavia (ICTY) and Rwanda (ICTR) were convened in 1992 in Arusha, Tanzania, and in 1994 in the Hague, The Netherlands, respectively. As the first courts of their type since World War II, their work, which sought to fix personal responsibility for mass murder, continued into the new millennium.

Given the vast scope and complicated nature of trying crimes of genocide, neither body has moved swiftly. By 2003 the ICTR had indicted 52 people and had completed nine trials stemming from the Rwanda slaughter, while also becoming the first international court in history to hand down a CONVICTION for genocide. By comparison, the ICTY had indicted 87 people and had concluded 23 trials. During 2002 worldwide attention focused upon the opening of the ICTY's long-awaited trial of former Serbian President Slobodan Milosevic, ACCUSED of ordering atrocities in Bosnia, Croatia, and Kosovo at various times between 1991 and 2001. Arrested after flouting the tribunal's INDICTMENT for two years, Milosevic's delivery to the Hague in 2001 made him the highest-ranking European leader since the Nazi era to face trial for war crimes.

Humanitarians, politicians, and international legal scholars are struggling to find an effective way to prevent and punish genocide. Many have called for revising the genocide convention to better meet the needs of the current political, social, and economic environment, by creating a broader definition of genocide and establishing procedural guidelines. Still others have proposed international military INTERVENTION in order to prevent or stop genocide.

FURTHER READINGS

BBC News. 2003. February 20; "The Charges against Milosevic." *BBC News World Edition.* Available online at http://www.news.bbc.co.uk/2/hi/europe/1402790.stm; website home page: http://www.news.bbc.co.uk (accessed July 26, 2009).

Chrisopoulos, Paul. J. 1995. "Giving Meaning to the Term 'Genocide's as it Applies to U.S. Immigration Policy." *Loyola of Los Angeles International & Comparative Law Journal* (October).

Heidenrich, John G. "The Father of 'Genocide'—and Its Biggest Foe." *The Christian Science Monitor* (June 27, 2001).

Kennicott, Philip. "Nearly Nine Decades after the Massacres, a Battle Still Rages to Define 'Genocide'." *The Washington Post.* (November 24, 2002). Available online at http://www.washingtonpost.com/ac2/wp-dyn?pagename=article&node=&contentId=A26543-2002Nov22&notFound=true; website home page: http://www.washingtonpost.com (accessed July 26, 2009).

Lemkin, Raphael. 1944. "Genocide." In *Axis Rule in Occupied Europe: Laws of Occupation—Analysis of Government—Proposals for Redress.* Washington, D.C.: Carnegie Endowment for International Peace. Available online at http://www.preventgenocide.org/lemkin/AxisRule1944-1.htm; website home page: http://www.preventgenocide.org (accessed July 26, 2009).

Yacoubian, George S., Jr. 2003. "Evaluating the Efficacy of the International Criminal Tribunals for Rwanda and the Former Yugoslavia." *World Affairs* 165 (January 1).

CROSS REFERENCES

Hitler, Adolf; International Law; Nuremberg Trials; United Nations.

GENTLEMEN'S AGREEMENT

Although agreements between individuals often create legally binding commitments, instances may arise in which mutual promises yield no legally enforceable agreement. Sometimes called "gentlemen's agreements," parties may honor them because moral obligations compel observance or because future relations will be more difficult if the present arrangement is broken. International organizations likewise may depend on such informal arrangements so as to maintain COMITY among members.

Occasionally the enabling treaties that create an international organization will leave some procedural or VOTING matter unresolved. Rather than amend the formal DOCUMENT, which is usually a difficult task, an informal working agreement will develop to resolve a particular problem. As long as the consensus holds to honor the informal agreement, there is no need to embody it into a legal document.

GERRYMANDER

The process of dividing a particular state or territory into election districts in such a manner as to accomplish an unlawful purpose, such as to give one party a greater advantage.

State constitutions or amendments to those constitutions empower state legislatures, and sometimes state or federal courts, to apportion and reapportion election districts. This generally means that states may draw and redraw the lines around election districts for offices ranging from local to congressional. It can also mean that states may calculate and recalculate the numbers of representatives in election districts. Any form of unfair APPORTIONMENT may be called gerrymandering, but generally, a GERRYMANDER is understood to be invalid redistricting.

Redistricting is usually used to adjust the populations of election districts to achieve equality in representation among those districts. Sometimes, however, it is used for unlawful ulterior motives. Then it crosses the line to become gerrymandering.

The classic example of a gerrymander is a legislative redistricting scheme designed to benefit the party in power. Assume that a state legislature has redrawn its VOTING districts to divide and fold all communities that vote predominantly Democratic into larger communities that vote Republican. This is a political gerrymander. Such redistricting decreases the likelihood of Democratic representation in the state legislature because the Democratic vote in each new district is diluted by the predominant Republican vote.

The term *gerrymander* was inspired by an 1812 Massachusetts redistricting scheme that favored the party of Governor Elbridge Gerry. Portraitist Gilbert C. Stuart noted that one new election district had the shape of a salamander. Stuart drew an outline of the district, put a salamander's head on one end, and called the creature a Gerry-mander.

The gerrymander has been used by state legislatures ever since. It thrived all the way through the 1950s, when many southeastern states were reapportioned in an effort to weaken the voting power of African Americans. This usually involved the drawing of complex, irregularly shaped election districts. A legislature could divide and fold predominantly African American communities into surrounding districts with large blocs of white voters. Such schemes diluted the vote of African Americans, placed their representation in faraway communities, and effectively prevented African Americans from expressing their collective will in ELECTIONS.

In 1960 the U.S. Supreme Court struck down the first gerrymander scheme it reviewed, in *Gomillion v. Lightfoot,* 364 U.S. 339, 81 S. Ct. 125, 5 L. Ed. 2d 110 (1960). In *Gomillion,* the Alabama legislature altered the city limits of Tuskegee to remove all but four of the city's 400 African American voters. It changed the city limits of Tuskegee, for election purposes, from a square to, according to the Court, "an uncouth twenty-eight-sided figure." According to the Court, the redistricting discriminated against African Americans and violated the EQUAL PROTECTION Clause of the FOURTEENTH AMENDMENT.

Gomillion did not establish that the drawing of election districts was always a proper matter for the courts. Before *Gomillion,* the Court had refused to review gerrymandering claims, holding that the issue of reapportionment was political and beyond the reach of the courts. The Court heard *Gomillion* only because the issue of racial DISCRIMINATION lifted the controversy out of the arena traditionally beyond the power of the courts.

In 1962 the U.S. Supreme Court took the first step in establishing its right to review all districting, with its decision in BAKER V. CARR, 369 U.S. 186, 82 S. Ct. 691, 7 L. Ed. 2d 663. At issue in *Baker* was a decades-old Tennessee apportionment. According to urban Tennessee voters, the outdated apportionment was a "silent gerrymander" or a "malapportionment." Although the population in urban election districts had increased, Tennessee had made no changes to reflect this population shift; thus, sparsely populated rural districts had the same representation in the state legislature as did densely populated urban districts. The Court in *Baker* did not reach a decision on the validity of the Tennessee districting; *Baker* established only that the issue of districting was JUSTICIABLE and not merely a political question.

The Court next established the "one person, one vote" requirement for FEDERAL elections, in *Wesberry v. Sanders,* 376 U.S. 1, 84 S. Ct. 526, 11 L. Ed. 2d 481 (1964). This requirement, which held that voting districts should be roughly equal in population, was extended to the states in REYNOLDS V. SIMS, 377 U.S. 533, 84 S. Ct. 1362, 12 L. Ed. 2d 506 (1964). In *Wesberry,* the Court struck down a Georgia redistricting statute (Ga. Code § 34-2301) because its voting districts were unequal in population. Georgia's Fifth Congressional District, largely populated by

The Gerry-mander.

[○ A new species of Monster, which appeared in Essex South District in January last.

Portraitist Gilbert C. Stuart's depiction of an 1812 Massachusetts redistricting scheme favoring the political party of Governor Elbridge Gerry was the inspiration for the term gerrymander.

LIBRARY OF CONGRESS

African Americans, was two to three times the size of other districts in the state. As a result, the African Americans in the Fifth District received less representation in Congress than persons in the other districts. According to the Court, this violated Article I, Section 2 of the U.S. CONSTITUTION, which states that U.S. Representatives were to be "apportioned among the several States ... according to their respective Numbers" (*Wesberry*).

Since these seminal cases, courts have become intimately involved in the review of apportionment, reapportionment, and redistricting. In their review of districting schemes, courts use CENSUS figures to compare election district populations for equality of representation. Courts also examine census figures for racial populations and compare overall percentages with percentages in election districts.

Courts have developed redistricting principles that favor compact, contiguous election districts that respect already existing municipal BOUNDARIES. Gerrymanders may be easy to recognize because they usually produce election districts that are irregularly shaped. However, not all irregularly shaped election districts are the result of gerrymanders. Indeed, Congress has encouraged the creation of "majority-minority" voting districts, which often call for an inventive drawing of election districts. Majority-minority districts are those in which racial minorities constitute the majority of votes.

Under section 4(b) of the Voting Rights Act (79 Stat. 438, *as amended* [42 U.S.C.A. § 1973b (b)]), some states, or specified counties in some states, may need to preclear redistricting plans with the attorney general or the U.S. district court for the DISTRICT OF COLUMBIA. The states subject to preclearance are those that have historically used constraints such as poll taxes and literacy tests in an effort to exclude minority voters.

Section 4(b) of the Voting Rights Act presses the issue of redistricting based on race. The Supreme Court has responded by questioning the constitutionality of the provision. In *Shaw v. Reno,* 509 U.S. 630, 113 S. Ct. 2816, 125 L. Ed. 2d 511 (1993), a group of white North Carolina voters challenged the creation of two North Carolina majority-minority districts, which had the approval of the ATTORNEY general. One of the districts at issue had the shape of a "bug splattered on a windshield" (*Shaw*). The other district was so thin in parts that one legislator remarked, "If you drove down the interstate with both car doors open, you'd kill most of the people in the district" (*Shaw*). According to the Court, the redistricting was a racial gerrymander because it could not be explained by anything other factor than race. The holding of the Court emphasized that redistricting based entirely on race, with no respect for other redistricting principles, was a violation of the Equal Protection Clause and therefore invalid.

The Supreme Court reaffirmed and extended the *Shaw* holding in *Miller v. Johnson,* 515 U.S. 900, 115 S. Ct. 2475, 132 L. Ed. 2d 762 (1995). In *Miller,* the state of Georgia had complied with the redistricting provisions of the Voting Rights Act, but still found its redistricting scheme struck down by the U.S. Supreme Court as a racial gerrymander. As a designated state under the act, Georgia reapportioned three times before the attorney general accepted a plan. In its first two plans, Georgia drew two districts in which the majority of the voting population was African American. The scheme eventually accepted by the attorney general contained three congressional districts in which the majority of the voting population was African American. According to the Court, the redistricting was a racial gerrymander because its guiding principle was racial division, even

though the new election districts were not bizarrely shaped.

The controversy over the North Carolina redistricting plan considered in *Shaw v. Reno* continued throughout the decade, even after the Court's decision in *Miller v. Johnson.* Three years after the Court ruled in *Shaw,* a three-judge panel in federal district court in North Carolina reviewed the state's districting plan, but again found it to be CONSTITUTIONAL. The Supreme Court reversed the decision for a second time in SHAW V. HUNT, 517 U.S. 899, 116 S. Ct. 1894, 135 L. Ed. 2d 207 (1996) and found that the redrawing of the district into bizarre-looking shapes violated the Equal Protection Clause.

The North Carolina legislature constructed a new districting plan with a district 71 miles long, where African Americans comprised a 47 percent majority, compared with 57 percent in the original plan. White voters again contested the plan, and the three-judge panel in the North Carolina district court found that the plan violated the Equal Protection Clause because, according to the court, the legislature used race as a motivating factor in drawing the districts. The Supreme Court, per Justice CLARENCE THOMAS, however, disagreed. In *Hunt v. Cromartie,* 526 U.S. 541, 119 S. Ct. 1545, 143 L. Ed. 2d 731 (1991), the Court held that the motivation of the legislature was in dispute. The white plaintiffs were required to prove that the district was drawn "with an impermissible motive." Moreover, the plaintiffs had to prove that race was the "predominant factor" motivating the legislature. The plaintiffs had the burden of showing, through direct and CIRCUMSTANTIAL EVIDENCE, this racial motivation.

On REMAND, the three-judge panel conducted a full HEARING to determine the intention of the legislature when it drafted the district. After the hearing the panel again ruled that the plan used race as a predominant factor, which is constitutionally impermissible. The Supreme Court reviewed the case for the fourth and final time in *Easley v. Cromartie,* 532 U.S. 234, 121 S. Ct. 1452, 149 L. Ed. 2d 430 (2001), this time concluding that the three-judge panel's findings were clearly erroneous and must be reversed. The Court held that a largely black district is constitutional if it is drawn to satisfy political rather than racial motives.

The issues in North Carolina and Georgia are by no means unique to those states. In 1975

Congress enacted a law (Pub. L. No. 94-171) that requires the Census Bureau to provide redistricting data to each state after each decennial census, the last of which occurred in 2000. Between 1990 and 2000, the percentage of white Americans increased at a lower level than any other race or ethnicity, including African American, Hispanic American, Asian, American Indian, and Native Hawaiian. After the census figures were released, each state underwent a lengthy and costly process of redistricting, and many of these plans were contested in court.

Redistricting raises not only racial and ethnic concerns, but also concerns over the political motivation of these plans. Some claim that the system has become one in which politicians, through redistricting, now choose their voters before the voters choose their politicians. Partisanship is often at the core of these controversies. For example, due in large part to Republican-drafted districts in Texas, the Texas House of Representatives in 2002 came under control of Republicans for the first time in more than a century. Texas courts and those in many other states saw numerous lawsuits filed contesting these districting plans, and these contests were not expected to end for quite some time.

FURTHER READINGS

Clarkowski, Andrew J. 1995. "Shaw v. Reno and Formal Districting Criteria: A Short History of a Jurisprudence That Failed in Wisconsin." *Wisconsin Law Review.*

Fuentes-Rohwer, Luis. 2003. Doing Our Politics in Court: Gerrymandering, "Fair Representation,' and an Exegesis into the Judicial Role." *Notre Dame Law Review* 78 (January).

Hamilton, Jeffrey G. 1994. "Deeper into the Political Thicket: Racial and Political Gerrymandering and the Supreme Court." *Emory Law Journal* 43 (fall).

Harvard Law Review Association. 1995. "Voting Rights and Race-based Districting." *Harvard Law Review* 109.

Lewis, Terrence M. 1996. "Standard of Review under the Fifth Amendment Equal Protection Component: Adarand Expands the Application of Strict Scrutiny." *Duquesne Law Review* 34.

Stockman, Eric J. 1993. "Constitutional Gerrymandering: Fonfara v. Reapportionment Commission." *Connecticut Law Review* 25.

CROSS REFERENCES

Equal Protection; Voting.

GI BILL

The GI BILL created a comprehensive package of benefits, including financial assistance for higher education, for veterans of U.S. military service. The benefits of the GI Bill are intended to help veterans readjust to civilian life following service to their country and to encourage bright, motivated men and women to volunteer for military duty. This legislation came in two parts: the Servicemen's Readjustment Act of 1944 and the Montgomery GI Bill.

Servicemen's Readjustment Act of 1944

The first GI Bill was proposed and drafted by the AMERICAN LEGION, led by former Illinois governor John Stelle, during WORLD WAR II. The public remembered a post-World War I recession, when millions of veterans returned to face unemployment and homelessness. Twice as many veterans would return from World War II, and widespread economic hardship was a real concern. A healthy postwar economy, it seemed, would depend on providing soldiers with a means to support themselves once they were back home.

Newspaper tycoon William Randolph Hearst became the bill's most ardent and vocal supporter. Hearst and his nationwide string of newspapers lobbied the public and members of Congress to support those who served their country, and his effort was a success. The bill unanimously passed both chambers of Congress in the spring of 1944. President FRANKLIN D. ROOSEVELT signed the bill into law on June 22, 1944, just days after the D-Day invasion of Normandy (Servicemen's Readjustment Act of 1944, ch. 268, 58 Stat. 284).

The original GI Bill offered veterans up to $500 per year for college tuition and other educational costs—ample funding at the time. An unmarried veteran also received a $50-per-month allowance for each month spent in uniform; a married veteran received slightly more. Other benefits included mortgage subsidies, enabling veterans to purchase homes with relative ease.

Despite initial misgivings over its success, the GI Bill proved to be enormously effective. Prior to its passage, detractors feared that paying the education expenses of veterans would lead to overcrowding at colleges, which before World War II were accessible predominantly to members of society's upper class. Critics were concerned that veterans would wreak havoc on educational standards and

A group of military veterans line up to purchase books under the GI Bill, which originally provided up to $500 per year for tuition, books, and supplies to veterans attending college after service in WWII.

BETTMANN/CORBIS

overburden campuses with their lack of preparation for the rigors of higher learning.

College campuses did become grossly overcrowded in the postwar years: Approximately 7.8 million World War II veterans received benefits under the original GI Bill, and 2.2 million of those used the program for higher education. By 1947 half of all college students were veterans. Prefabricated buildings and Quonset huts were used as classrooms, and military barracks were often converted into dormitories. However, having spent a large part of their youth engaged in battle, World War II veterans were highly motivated. GIs in their late twenties and early thirties returned to the United States in droves, anxious to catch up with their nonmilitary peers, marry, settle down, and support a family. The benefits provided by the GI Bill facilitated these goals.

Veterans were not the only beneficiaries of the GI Bill. Colleges, with increased enrollments, received years of financial security following its enactment. Veterans demanded more practical college course work, and this need led to a changed concept of higher education, with more emphasis on DEGREE programs such as business and engineering. The lines of race, class, and RELIGION blurred as higher education became attainable for all veterans. No longer was a college degree—and the higher paying jobs that normally follow it—limited to members of the upper class. FEDERAL income increased as the average income of taxpayers in the United States increased, and as the veterans graduated from colleges, women and members of minorities enrolled to fill the gaps they left. The GI Bill's mortgage subsidies led to an escalated demand for housing and the development of suburbs. One-fifth of all single-family homes built in the 20 years following World War II were financed with help from the GI Bill's loan guarantee program, symbolizing the emergence of a new middle class.

Montgomery GI Bill

Following the United States involvement in the VIETNAM WAR and the end of the military DRAFT in 1973, the number of qualified young adults willing to voluntarily serve in the military declined. In 1984 Representative G. V. ("Sonny") Montgomery (D-MS), chairman of the House Veterans Affairs Committee, proposed a new GI Bill to encourage military service, even in times of peace. That year President RONALD REAGAN signed into law the Montgomery GI Bill (38 U.S.C.A. § 1401), which as of the early 2000s continues to provide optional benefits for qualified U.S. veterans.

The Montgomery GI Bill is a voluntary plan that requires a contribution from the soldier who chooses to take part. Upon ENTRY into the ARMED SERVICES, including the NATIONAL GUARD and military reserves, participants may elect to have their military pay reduced by $100 each month of the first 12 months of service. This sacrifice makes them eligible to receive up to $400 a month for 36 months toward tuition and other educational expenses. To receive these benefits, soldiers must receive an honorable DISCHARGE, earn a high school diploma or its equivalent, and serve in active duty for the length of their enlistment. The federal government supplies funding but does not set standards or administer the plan; the Veterans Administration determines whether a veteran is eligible, and the COLLEGES AND UNIVERSITIES (including religious and vocational schools) make admissions policies and keep track of expenditures.

Effects of the GI Bill

The GI Bill, in both its versions, is widely regarded as a success. Military recruiters routinely promote its benefits as a way to attract and enlist the best and brightest young adults: In 1996, 95 percent of new armed services recruits were high school graduates and 94.8 percent of eligible recruits chose to enroll in the education program. (Three-fourths of all women and men who have enlisted since the program began have enrolled.)

In 2000 President BILL CLINTON signed an amendment to the Montgomery GI Bill that allows for a "Top-Up" benefit. This benefit, which equals the difference between the total cost of a particular course and the amount of tuition assistance paid by the military, effectively allows enrollees to receive 100 percent tuition assistance. In 2001 President GEORGE W. BUSH signed two additional bills. The Veterans' Opportunities Act of 2001 (Pub. L. 107-14) became law on June 5, 2001 and the 21st Century GI Enhancement Act (Pub. L. 107-103) became law on December 27, 2001. Both bills amended Title 38 to provide greater benefits to service men and women.

Beneficiaries of the GI Bill include Presidents GEORGE H. W. BUSH and GERALD R. FORD; VICE PRESIDENT ALBERT GORE Jr.; Chief Justice WILLIAM H. REHNQUIST and Justice JOHN PAUL STEVENS, both of the U.S. Supreme Court; SECRETARY OF STATE Warren M. Christopher; journalists David Brinkley and John Chancellor; actors Clint Eastwood, Paul Newman, and Jason Robards Jr.; and former Dallas Cowboys football coach Tom Landry.

FURTHER READINGS

Asch, Beth J., C. Christine Fair, and M. Rebecca Kilburn. 2000. *An Assessment of Recent Proposals to Improve the Montgomery GI Bill.* Santa Monica, CA: Rand. Available online at http://www.rand.org/pubs/documented_briefings/DB301/; website home page: http://www.rand.org (accessed July 26, 2009).

Bennett, Michael J. 1999. *When Dreams Come True: The GI Bill and the Making of Modern America.* Washington, D.C.: Potomac.

Evans, Philip G., II. 1989. "The New GI Bill: The Trojan Horse of the 1980s?" *The Army Lawyer* 17 (October).

Hyman, Harold M. 1986. *American Singularity: The 1787 Ordinance, the 1862 Homestead and Morrill Acts, and the 1944 GI Bill.* Athens: Univ. of Georgia Press.

United States Department of Veterans Affairs. *GI Bill.* Available online at http://www.gibill.va.gov (accessed July 26, 2009).

CROSS REFERENCES

Armed Services; Veterans Affairs Department.

GIBBONS V. OGDEN

Gibbons v. Ogden, 22 U.S. (9 Wheat.) 1, 6 L. Ed. 23, was a LANDMARK decision of the Supreme Court that defined the scope of power given to Congress PURSUANT to the COMMERCE CLAUSE of the Constitution.

Ogden brought an action to enjoin Gibbons from continuing to run his steamships, which were licensed in the coastal trade under a 1793 act of Congress. The state courts granted Ogden the INJUNCTION, and the case was brought on APPEAL to the Supreme Court.

In 1800 the state of New York enacted a statute that gave ROBERT LIVINGSTON and Robert Fulton a monopoly—an exclusive right—to have their steamboats operate on the state waterways. Aaron Ogden owned a steamboat company and had received a license from Livingston and Fulton to conduct a business between ports in New York City and New Jersey. Ogden had formerly been in business with Thomas Gibbons, who started his own steamship company that operated between New York and New Jersey, in direct competition with Ogden.

DANIEL WEBSTER, the ATTORNEY for Gibbons, argued that the issuance of the injunction was wrongful because the laws that authorized the monopoly were enacted in violation of the COMMERCE Clause of the Constitution. This clause gave Congress, not the states, the power to regulate commerce among the states. The term *commerce* included not only buying and selling but also navigation necessary to bring about such transactions.

In the majority opinion drafted by Chief Justice JOHN MARSHALL, the Court agreed with this definition of commerce and then reasoned that because Congress was vested with the power to regulate commerce, there could be no INFRINGEMENT of this power other than that specified in the Constitution. States cannot act in this area without express permission of Congress. The actions of New York State were an unauthorized INTERFERENCE with the power of Congress to regulate commerce, and therefore, the Court reversed the DECREE of the state court and dismissed the injunction against Gibbons.

GIDEON V. WAINWRIGHT

Gideon v. Wainwright, 372 U.S. 335, 83 S. Ct. 792, 9 L. Ed. 2d 799, is a 1963 U.S. Supreme Court decision that established an indigent criminal defendant's right, under the SIXTH AMENDMENT of the U.S. Constitution, to COUNSEL in state criminal trials.

In 1961 Clarence Earl Gideon was charged in a Florida state court with breaking into and entering a poolroom with INTENT to commit a misdemeanor, a combination of offenses that constituted a FELONY under Florida law. He could not afford a lawyer, and he requested to have one appointed by the court. Nearly 20 years earlier, the U.S. Supreme Court had held in *Betts v. Brady*, 316 U.S. 455, 62 S. Ct. 1252, 86 L. Ed. 1595 (1942), that an ordinary person could do an adequate job of defending himself or

herself. A court-appointed lawyer was required only if the DEFENDANT had mental or physical deficiencies, the case was unusually complicated, or the case involved "special circumstances." None of these exceptions applied to Gideon, the Florida trial court ruled, and thus his request for counsel was denied.

Gideon conducted his own DEFENSE and was found GUILTY of the charges. He then filed a handwritten petition with the Supreme Court of Florida, seeking to overturn his CONVICTION on the ground that the trial court's refusal to appoint an ATTORNEY for him denied him the rights "guaranteed by the Constitution and the BILL OF RIGHTS by the United States Government." The state supreme court denied Gideon's petition.

While in prison, Gideon, using law books available to him, drafted a petition for writ of CERTIORARI to the U.S. Supreme Court. (The petition is the legal DOCUMENT in which a person requests the Supreme Court to hear an APPEAL. The Court has the discretion to accept or decline the appeal.) According to Anthony Lewis's acclaimed book on the case, *Gideon's Trumpet* (1964), in the handwritten petition Gideon stated that it "just was not fair" that he had no lawyer at his trial. The petition was granted, and ABE FORTAS, who would later serve as an ASSOCIATE JUSTICE on the Court, was appointed to argue Gideon's case.

In a unanimous decision, the Supreme Court overruled *Betts*, holding the guarantee of counsel to be a FUNDAMENTAL RIGHT under the U.S. Constitution. The Court ruled that the Due Process Clause of the FOURTEENTH AMENDMENT required that the Sixth Amendment, which guarantees indigent defendants the RIGHT TO COUNSEL in FEDERAL criminal proceedings, be interpreted to include indigent defendants in state criminal trials. In his majority opinion, Justice Hugo L. Black wrote, "[R]eason and reflection require us to recognize that in our ... system of criminal justice, any person hailed into court, who is too poor to hire a lawyer, cannot be assured a fair trial unless counsel is provided." Black further pointed out that the government hires attorneys to prosecute defendants, and individuals charged with crimes who are financially unable to hire attorneys to defend themselves, both "strong indications ... that lawyers in criminal courts are necessities, not luxuries."

Gideon was later retried with a court-appointed lawyer representing him and was found not guilty.

Following *Gideon,* it was unclear whether the decision applied only to indigent defendants facing felony convictions and not to individuals charged with lesser crimes. Nine years later, that issue was clarified in *Argersinger v. Hamlin,* 407 U.S. 25, 92 S. Ct. 2006, 32 L. Ed. 2d 530 (1972). In *Argersinger,* the Supreme Court expanded its holding in *Gideon,* RULING that the Sixth Amendment right to appointed counsel extended to misdemeanor cases in which the person charged may face IMPRISONMENT, unless the defendant makes a "knowing and intelligent waiver" of his or her right to counsel. The Court concluded that an ACCUSED in a misdemeanor trial likewise has a strong need for representation and that *Gideon* should apply "to any criminal trial, where an accused is deprived of his liberty."

Argersinger was limited a few years later by *Scott v. Illinois,* 440 U.S. 367, 99 S. Ct. 1158, 59 L. Ed. 2d 383 (1979). In *Scott,* the Supreme Court held that the Sixth Amendment right to counsel extends only to cases where "actual imprisonment" is imposed, and not to cases where the "mere threat of imprisonment" exists (where the crime charged authorizes a possible JAIL sentence).

FURTHER READINGS

Lentine, John A. 2003. "Gideon v. Wainwright at Forty—Fulfilling the Promise?" *American Journal of Trial Advocacy* 26 (spring).

Meares, Tracey L. 2003. "What's Wrong with Gideon?" *Univ. of Chicago Law Review* 70 (winter).

The Oyez Project Web site. *Gideon v. Wainwright,* 372 U.S. 335 (1963). Available online at http://www.oyez.org/cases/1960-1969/1962/1962_155/; website home page: http://www.oyez.org (accessed September 4, 2009).

CROSS REFERENCES

Criminal Procedure; Due Process of Law; Public Defender.

GIFT

A voluntary transfer of property or of a property interest from one individual to another, made gratuitously to the recipient. The individual who makes the gift is known as the donor, and the individual to whom the gift is made is called the donee.

If a GRATUITOUS transfer of property is to be effective at some future date, it constitutes a mere promise to make a gift that is unenforceable due to lack of consideration. A present gift of a FUTURE INTEREST is, however, valid.

DIVISION OF CORRECTIONS

CORRESPONDENCE REGULATIONS

MAIL WILL NOT BE DELIVERED WHICH DOES NOT CONFORM WITH THESE RULES

No. 1 -- Only 2 letters each week, not to exceed 2 sheets letter-size 8 1/2 x 11" and written *on one side only,* and if ruled paper, do not write between lines. *Your complete name* must be signed at the close of your letter. *Clippings, stamps, letters* from other people, *stationery* or *cash must not be enclosed* in your letters.

No. 2 -- All *letters* must be addressed in the *complete prison name* of the inmate. *Cell number,* where applicable, and *prison number* must be placed in lower left corner of envelope, with your complete name and address in the upper left corner.

No. 3 -- *Do not send any packages without a Package Permit.* Unauthorized *packages* will be destroyed.

No. 4 -- *Letters* must be written in English only.

No. 5 -- *Books, magazines, pamphlets,* and *newspapers* of reputable character will be delivered *only if* mailed direct from the publisher.

No. 6 -- *Money* must be sent in the form of *Postal Money Orders* only, in the inmate's complete prison name and prison number.

INSTITUTION ______ CELL NUMBER ______

NAME ______ NUMBER ______

In The Supreme Court of The United States
— — — Washington D.C.
clarence Earl Gideon | Petitioner | Petition for a writ
vs. | of Certiorari Directed
H.G. Cochran, Jr, as | To The Supreme Court
Director, Divisions | State of Florida.
of corrections State |
of Florida |

No. 890 Misc.
OCT. TERM 1961
U.S. Supreme Court

To: The Honorable Earl Warren, Chief Justice of the United States

Comes now the petitioner, Clarence Earl Gideon, a citizen of The United states of America, in proper person, and appearing as his own counsel. Who petitions this Honorable Court for a Writ of Certiorari directed to The Supreme Court of The State of Florida. To review the order and Judgement of the court below denying The petitioner a writ of Habeus Corpus.

Petitioner submits That The Supreme Court of The United States has The authority and jurisdiction to review The final Judgement of The Supreme Court of The State of Florida the highest court of The State Under sec. 344(B) Title 28 U.S.C.A. and Because the "Due process clause" of the

Clarence Earl Gideon's handwritten petition for a writ of certiorari filed with the U.S. Supreme Court in 1961.

COLLECTION OF THE SUPREME COURT OF THE UNITED STATES

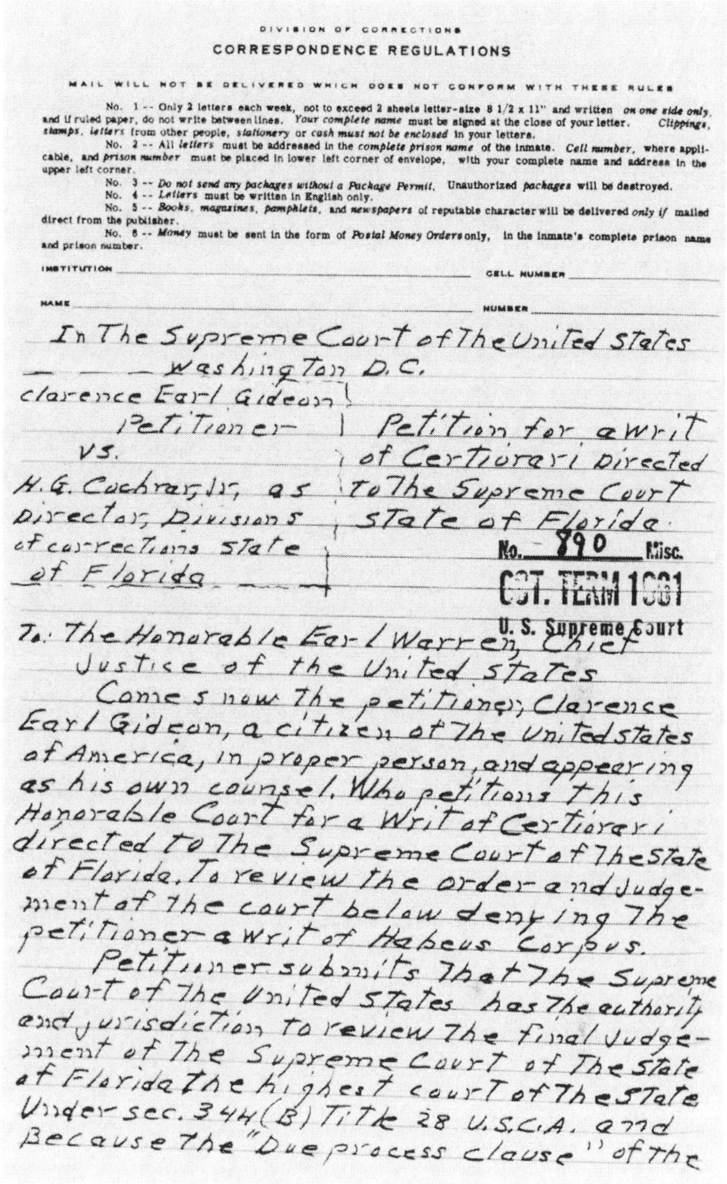

Rules of Gift-Giving

Three elements are essential in determining whether or not a gift has been made: *delivery,* DONATIVE INTENT, and *acceptance* by the DONEE. Even when such elements are present, however, courts will set aside an otherwise valid gift if the circumstances suggest that the DONOR was, in actuality, defrauded by the donee, coerced to make the gift, or strongly influenced in an unfair manner. In general, however, the law favors enforcing gifts because every individual

has the right to dispose of personal property as he or she chooses.

Delivery Delivery of a gift is complete when it is made directly to the donee, or to a THIRD PARTY on the donee's behalf. In the event that the third person is the donor's agent, BAILEE, or trustee, delivery is complete only when such person actually hands the property over to the donee.

A delivery may be actual, IMPLIED, or symbolic, provided some affirmative act takes place. If, for example, a man wishes to give his grandson a horse, an actual delivery might take place when the donor hires someone to bring the horse to the grandson's farm. Similarly, the SYMBOLIC DELIVERY of a car as a gift can take place when the donor hands the keys over to the donee.

Delivery can only occur when the donor surrenders control of the property. For example, an individual who expresses the desire to make a gift of a car to another but continues to drive the car whenever he or she wishes has not surrendered control of the car.

A majority of states are practical about the requirement of a delivery. Where the donor and the donee reside in the same house, it ordinarily is not required that the gift be removed from the house to establish a delivery. If the donee has possession of the property at the time that the donor also gives the person ownership, there is no need to pass the property back and forth in order to make a legal delivery. Proof that the donor relinquished all claim to the gift and recognized the donee's right to exercise control over it is generally adequate to indicate that a gift was made.

In instances where delivery cannot be made to the donee, as when the person is out of the country at the time, delivery can be made to someone else who agrees to accept the property for the donee. If the individual accepting delivery is employed by the donor, however, the court will make the ASSUMPTION that the donor has not rendered control of the property and that delivery has not actually been made. The individual accepting delivery must be holding the property for the donee and not for the donor.

In situations where the donee does not have legal capacity to accept delivery, such delivery can be made to an individual who will hold it for him or her. This might, for example, occur in the case of an infant.

Donative Intent Donative intent to make a gift is essentially determined by the donor's words, but the courts also consider the surrounding circumstances, the relationship of the parties, the size of the gift in relation to the amount of the donor's property as a whole, and the behavior of the donor toward the property subsequent to the purported gift.

The donor must have the legal capacity to make a gift. For example, infants or individuals judged to be unable to attend to their own affairs have a legal DISABILITY to make a gift.

In addition, an intent to make a gift must actually exist. For example, a LANDLORD who rents a house to a tenant does not have the intent to give such premises to the tenant, even though the tenant takes possession for an extended period of time. Similarly, a gift to the wrong person will not take effect. If an individual mistakenly gives gold jewelry to an imposter who is believed to be a niece, the gift is invalid because there was no intention to benefit anyone but the niece.

The intent must be present at the time the gift is made. For example, if one person promises to give a house to an artist "someday," the promise is unenforceable because there is no intent to make an effective gift at the time the promise is made. The mere expectation that something will someday be given is not legally adequate to create a gift.

Acceptance The final requirement for a valid gift is acceptance, which means that the donee unconditionally agrees to take the gift. It is necessary for the donee to agree at the same time the delivery is made. The gift can, however, be revoked at any time prior to acceptance.

A court ordinarily makes the assumption that a gift has been accepted if the gift is beneficial, or unless some event has occurred to indicate that it is not.

Types of Gifts

The two principal categories of gifts are INTER VIVOS gifts and CAUSA MORTIS gifts.

Inter vivos gifts *Inter vivos* is Latin for "between the living" or "from one living person to another." A gift inter vivos is one that is perfected and takes effect during the lifetime of the donor and donee and that is IRREVOCABLE when made. It is a voluntary transfer of property, at no cost to the donee, during the normal course of the donor's life.

A gift inter vivos differs from a sale, a loan, or BARTER since something is given in exchange for the benefit in each of such transfers. Whether the value given is a money price, a percentage interest or an equivalent item of property, or a promise to repay, the element of exchange makes such transfers something other than a gift.

There are a number of special types of inter vivos gifts. Forgiveness of a debt is a gift of the amount of money owed, and delivery can be accomplished by destroying the promissory note signed by the debtor and handing it over to him or her. A share of stock in a corporation may ordinarily be given to someone else by having ownership transferred to the person on the books of the corporation or by having a new stock certificate issued in the person's name. A life INSURANCE policy can generally be given to someone by delivering the policy, but it is more expedient to express in writing that all interest in the policy is assigned, or transferred, to the donee and to notify the insurance company to that effect. Certain states require these formalities because insurance is strictly regulated by state law. Gifts of land can only be made by written transfer.

A donor can limit an inter vivos gift in certain ways. For example, he or she might give someone a LIFE ESTATE in his or her property. When the donee dies, the property reverts to the donor. A donor cannot place other restrictions on a gift if the restrictions would operate to make the gift invalid. If, for example, the donor reserves the power to revoke a gift, there is no gift at all.

Causa Mortis Gifts A gift *causa mortis* (Latin for "in contemplation of approaching death") is one that is made in anticipation of IMMINENT death. This type of gift takes effect upon the death of the donor from the expected disease or illness. In the event that the donor recovers from the peril, the gift is automatically revoked. Gifts causa mortis only apply to personal property.

A donor who is approaching death might make a gift by putting his or her intention in writing. This procedure is likely to be followed, when, for example, the donee is in another state, and personal delivery is thereby impractical. The delivery requirement is frequently relaxed when a causa mortis gift is involved, since a donor is less likely to be able to make an actual delivery as his or her death approaches.

A symbolic delivery is frequently sufficient to show that a gift was made, provided at least some effort to make a delivery is exercised. The OVERT ACT aids a court in its DETERMINATION as to whether a delivery has been made.

The difference between a gift causa mortis and a *testamentary gift* made by will is that a will transfers ownership subsequent to the death of the donor, but a gift causa mortis takes effect immediately. In most states, the donee becomes legal owner of the gift as soon as it is given, subject only to the condition that the gift must be returned if the donor does not actually die.

The requirements of a *causa mortis* gift are essentially the same as a gift *inter vivos*. In addition, such a gift must be made with a view toward the donor's death, the donor must die of the ailment, and there must be a delivery of the gift.

Gifts *causa mortis* are usually made in a very informal manner and are frequently made because dying people want to be certain that their dearest possessions go to someone they choose.

A donor who is approaching death might make a gift by putting his or her intention in writing. This procedure is likely to be followed, when, for example, the donee is in another state, and personal delivery is thereby impractical. The courts only permit the donee to keep the gift if the donor clearly intended the gift to take effect at the time it was made. If the gift is made in writing in a will and is intended to become effective only after the donor dies, the gift is a testamentary one. The law in each JURISDICTION is very strict about the features that make a will valid. One requirement, for example, is that the will must be signed by witnesses. If the donor writes down that he or she is making a gift, but the writing is neither an immediate gift nor a witnessed will, the donee cannot keep the gift.

The delivery requirement is frequently relaxed when a *causa mortis* gift is involved, because a donor is less likely to be able to make an actual delivery as his or her death approaches. A symbolic delivery is frequently sufficient to show that a gift was made, provided at least some effort to make a delivery is exercised. The overt act aids a court in its determination as to whether a delivery has been made.

A gift *causa mortis* is only effective if the donor actually dies. It is not necessary that the donor die immediately, but the person must die of a condition or danger that existed when the gift was made and without an intervening recovery. The donee becomes legal owner of the property in most states from the time the gift is made. The person must, however, later return the gift if the donor does not actually die. If the donor changes his or her mind and revokes the gift, or recovers from the particular illness or physical INJURY, the gift is invalid. A donor also has the right to require that debts or funeral expenses be paid out of the value of the gift.

FURTHER READINGS

Bove, Alexander A. 2005. *The Complete Book of Wills, Estates, and Trusts.* New York: Henry Holt.

Hyland, Richard. 2009. *Gifts A Study in Comparative Law.* New York: Oxford Univ. Press.

Internal Revenue Service. 2008. Publication 950, *Introduction to Estate and Gift Taxes.* Available online at http://www.irs.gov/publications/p950/index.html; website home page: http://www.irs.gov (accessed September 4, 2009).

"Landlord's Estate May Include Tenant's Improvements to Lease Property." 2002. *Tax Return Preparer's Letter* (July).

GIFT TAX

See ESTATE AND GIFT TAXES.

GIFTS TO MINORS ACT

The GIFTS TO MINORS ACT has been enacted in every state (with only minor variations) that facilitates the management of money given to infants.

Initially, in 1955 and 1956, thirteen states enacted a law called an *Act Concerning Gifts of SECURITIES to Minors.* The New York Stock Exchange and the Association of Stock Exchange Firms sponsored the development of the law, to make it possible to donate shares of stock to children without the creation of a formal trust. The scope of the law was subsequently expanded to encompass all gifts to minors.

The law allows the individual giving the property to choose an adult in whom he or she has confidence to serve as custodian of the property for the infant. The custodian has authority to collect, hold, manage, invest, and reinvest the property.

The custodian may pay out some of the money for the child's support, if necessary, and must manage the funds reasonably. The custodian must maintain accurate records of transactions and pay over the property when the child reaches majority. A custodian is not permitted to use any of the money personally or for anyone else except the child, nor can the person commingle the property with his or her own.

A professional custodian, such as a trust company or an ATTORNEY serving as GUARDIAN of the property for the minor, can be remunerated out of the child's property. Such a custodian is, however, held to a higher standard of care in management of the property. Other business people who deal with the custodian in management of the property are not responsible for ascertaining that the custodian has authority to act.

When a custodian resigns, dies, or is removed from the position by court order, another custodian can be appointed as a successor. Before dying, a custodian can designate who his or her successor will be, or a court may appoint one. A petition to appoint a new custodian can be filed in court by the individual who initially made the gift, by an adult member of the child's family, by a guardian, or generally by the child if the child is over fourteen years of age.

The AGE OF MAJORITY varies from one state to another. Within some states, the age of majority is not the same for all purposes, so it is necessary to check the Gifts to Minors Act in the state in which the child resides.

❖ GIGNOUX, EDWARD THAXTER

During his 30-year career in the federal courts, EDWARD THAXTER GIGNOUX developed a reputation as an articulate, compassionate, and competent trial judge. He was also a leader in the fields of judicial ethics, court administration, and trial practice and technique. He showcased his skills in a number of high-profile cases—including the CONTEMPT trial of Abbie Hoffman and other defendants known as the CHICAGO EIGHT (*In re Dellinger*, 370 F. Supp. 1304, N.D. Ill., E.D. [1973]).

Gignoux was born in Portland, Maine, on June 28, 1916. He graduated cum laude from Harvard College in 1937 and went on to Harvard Law School, where he was editor of the *Harvard Law Review.* He graduated magna cum laude from the law school in 1940 and began his legal career with the firm of Slee, O'Brian, Hellings, and Ulsh, in Buffalo. After a year in Buffalo, he joined the Washington, D.C., firm of Covington, Burling, Rublee, Acheson, and Shorb.

WORLD WAR II interrupted Gignoux's Washington, D.C., career after just a few months. In 1942, Gignoux joined the U.S. Army. During his three-year tour of duty with the First Cavalry Division in the Southwest Pacific, he rose to the rank of major and was awarded the Legion of Merit and the Bronze Star.

After the war, Gignoux returned to Covington, Burling, in Washington, D.C., to resume the PRACTICE OF LAW, but a bout with malaria, contracted during his years in service, forced a return to his native Maine for convalescence. As his health returned, Gignoux joined the Portland, Maine, firm of Verrill, Dana, Walker, Philbrick, and Whitehouse, and he married Hildegard Schuyler.

Gignoux and his wife had two children as they settled into life in Portland. In addition to practicing law, Gignoux was named assistant corporation counsel for the city of Portland, and he was twice elected to a three-year term on the Portland City Council, serving from 1949 to 1955.

By 1957 Gignoux was well-known and respected in Maine legal and political circles, and he was a logical choice to fill a vacancy on the FEDERAL bench. He was appointed U.S. district judge for the District of Maine in August 1957 by President DWIGHT D. EISENHOWER, and he served as Maine's only federal court judge for the next 20 years.

One of the first cases he heard as a federal judge was an antitrust action brought by the federal government against the Maine

Edward T. Gignoux.
AP IMAGES

Lobstermen's Association—an important group in a very visible industry (*United States v. Maine Lobstermen's Ass'n,* 160 F. Supp. 115 [D. Me. 1957]). A jury found the lobstermen GUILTY, but Gignoux, showing both wisdom and compassion early on, managed to satisfy both parties when he imposed only a small fine on the defendants. Gignoux was also a central figure in Indian settlement claims in his native state, and he was instrumental in establishing that several tribes in Maine were "federal" rather than "colonial" Indians, thus making them eligible for millions of dollars each year in federal housing, education, and health care benefits

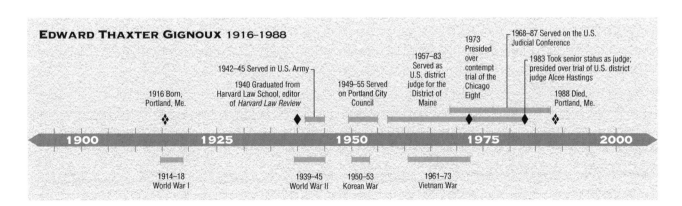

EDWARD THAXTER GIGNOUX 1916–1988

1916 Born, Portland, Me.

1940 Graduated from Harvard Law School, editor of *Harvard Law Review*

1942–45 Served in U.S. Army

1949–55 Served on Portland City Council

1957–83 Served as U.S. district judge for the District of Maine

1973 Presided over contempt trial of the Chicago Eight

1968–87 Served on the U.S. Judicial Conference

1983 Took senior status as judge; presided over trial of U.S. district judge Alcee Hastings

1988 Died, Portland, Me.

1900   1925   1950   1975   2000

1914–18 World War I

1939–45 World War II

1950–53 Korean War

1961–73 Vietnam War

(*Joint Tribal Council v. Morton*, 528 F.2d 370 [1st Cir. 1975]). Prior to the Gignoux decision, Maine Indians were considered "colonial" Indians and not the Indians of the frontier that Congress meant to protect in the Nonintercourse Act. Gignoux ruled in 1975 that the statute did apply, thus making some previous land transactions illegal and making the Maine tribes "federal" Indians.

Gignoux's reputation as a trial judge spread quickly. According to one of his former law clerks, lawyers and other judges packed his courtroom during their spare time to watch Gignoux's performance.

Gignoux was serious about the fair and equitable administration of justice. Throughout the 1960s and 1970s, he served the U.S. Judicial Conference. The Judicial Conference is the principal machinery through which the federal court system operates, establishing the standards policies governing the federal JUDICIARY. In recognition of his efforts with the Conference, Gignoux recieved the Devitt Award in 1987.

Gignoux's work with the Judicial Conference brought him national recognition, and in 1970 he was considered for a nomination to the U.S. Supreme Court. Although he was not appointed, he did make an impression on future Court justice DAVID H. SOUTER. When Souter filled out a questionnaire in preparation for his confirmation HEARING 20 years later, he noted a voting-rights case that he had argued in 1970 before Gignoux. He said, "It was one of the most gratifying events of my life, for the argument included a genuinely dialectical exchange between the great JURIST and me."

As Gignoux's reputation grew, Chief Justice WARREN E. BURGER called on him to preside over some very political, and potentially explosive, cases. In 1973 Warren appointed him to preside over the contempt trial of Abbie Hoffman, Bobby Seale, Jerry Rubin, Tom Hayden, David Dellinger, Rennie Davis, Lee Weiner, and John Froines. These 1960s radicals known as the Chicago Seven (even though there were eight of them) had already been tried and convicted for their participation in violent demonstrations at the 1968 Democratic National Convention, in Chicago. Following their trial, contempt charges were filed against the individuals and their lawyer, WILLIAM M. KUNSTLER, for their behavior in court. Gignoux found only Hoffman, Rubin, Dellinger, and their lawyer to be in contempt,

> TRIALS WHICH PROCEED IN ACCORDANCE WITH THE LAW, THE RULES OF EVIDENCE AND THE STANDARDS OF DEMEANOR NOT ONLY REAFFIRM THE INTEGRITY AND VIABILITY OF THE JUDICIAL PROCESS, BUT ALSO SERVE TO INSURE THE ABILITY OF EACH ONE OF US TO PROTECT THE RIGHTS AND LIBERTIES WE ENJOY AS CITIZENS.
> —EDWARD GIGNOUX

but he did not impose additional sentences on the parties involved, saying that their CONVICTION and their previous time served were punishment enough.

On June 1, 1983, after 25 years on the federal bench, Gignoux took senior (or semiretired) status, but he continued to hear cases around the country and to serve on the TEMPORARY EMERGENCY COURT OF APPEALS, which heard cases from district courts on the Emergency Natural Gas Act of 1977. Gignoux's ability to uphold both the letter and the spirit of the law, against overwhelming political and social pressures, was still very much IN EVIDENCE when, during his first year of "retirement," he was asked to preside over the trial of U.S. district judge Alcee L. Hastings (see IMPEACHMENT [sidebar]). Hastings, who was later acquitted of CONSPIRACY to solicit a bribe and of obstruction of justice, was the first sitting U.S. judge to face criminal charges. Although pressured to drop the charges throughout the trial, Gignoux said that "the court is entirely persuaded that the government has submitted evidence that is sufficient to sustain a finding by the jury of guilty." Also during the *Hastings* trial, Gignoux rejected one of the first serious efforts to open a federal court trial to TELEVISION coverage; Gignoux believed that he was prohibited by federal law from permitting cameras in the courtroom.

Gignoux died on November 4, 1988, in Portland, Maine. Shortly before his death, the city renamed the federal courthouse there in his honor. Gignoux was acknowledged by friend and circuit judge Frank M. Coffin as an "inspiration" and as a jurist who served honorably and well "in the most demanding and delicate of trial situations."

❖ GILBERT, CASS

Cass Gilbert was the U.S. architect responsible for the traditional style and regal proportions seen in many of the nation's finest public buildings—including the Supreme Court Building, in Washington, D.C. His remarkable body of work included FEDERAL, state, municipal, educational, and religious structures as well as facilities designed for commercial, industrial, and private USE. Gilbert believed strongly that architecture should serve the established political and social order; much of his work continues to serve its public purpose decades after its conception and completion.

Gilbert was born November 24, 1859, in Zanesville, Ohio, where his grandfather, Charles Champion Gilbert, was the first mayor. He attended school in Zanesville until the death of his father, Samuel Augustus Gilbert, in 1868. At that time, his mother, Elizabeth Fulton Wheeler, apprenticed him to an architectural firm in St. Paul, Minnesota. There he completed his education and trained as a surveyor. In 1878 Gilbert enrolled at the Massachusetts INSTITUTE of Technology, where he studied architecture for one year.

Income from occasional surveying work allowed Gilbert to embark, in 1879, on the customary grand tour of Europe, undertaken by many young men of his social standing and economic means. He traveled in England, France, and Italy and was exposed to many of the classic architectural styles that would later dominate his work.

Upon his return to the United States, Gilbert was employed as a draftsman by the New York architectural firm of McKim, Mead, and White, where he was influenced by name partner and noted architect Stanford White. His association with this firm gave him an opportunity to hone his skills and to learn the business side of running an architectural enterprise. Seeing his promise, the firm sent him to St. Paul in 1881 to oversee a building project.

By December 1882 Gilbert had severed ties with McKim, Mead and formed a partnership with St. Paul architect James Knox Taylor. Together, Gilbert and Taylor pursued both institutional and residential work, but they were unable to succeed financially. The business partnership dissolved. Well organized and efficient, Gilbert found that he preferred to

Cass Gilbert.
LIBRARY OF CONGRESS.

work alone; he did not form another professional partnership during his career. His architectural work from this period included the Dayton Avenue Church, St. Paul (1888); St. Martin's by the Lake, Minneapolis (1888); and the Lightner House, St. Paul (1893).

Gilbert did establish a personal partnership, on November 29, 1887, when he married Julia T. Finch. Their growing family—which ultimately included Emily, Elizabeth Wheeler, Julia Swift, and Cass, Jr.—added to the financial burdens of the struggling architect. To supplement his income from design work, Gilbert sold watercolors. He had begun painting during his European travels, and he was known locally as a talented artist.

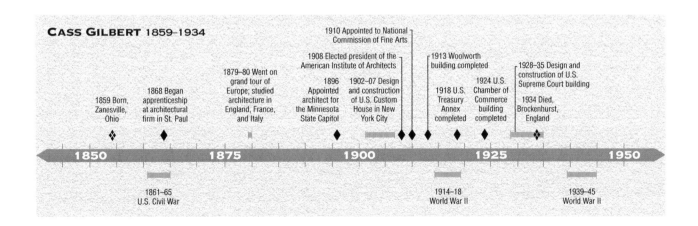

CASS GILBERT 1859–1934

1859 Born, Zanesville, Ohio

1868 Began apprenticeship at architectural firm in St. Paul

1879–80 Went on grand tour of Europe; studied architecture in England, France, and Italy

1896 Appointed architect for the Minnesota State Capitol

1902–07 Design and construction of U.S. Custom House in New York City

1908 Elected president of the American Institute of Architects

1910 Appointed to National Commission of Fine Arts

1913 Woolworth building completed

1918 U.S. Treasury Annex completed

1924 U.S. Chamber of Commerce building completed

1928–35 Design and construction of U.S. Supreme Court building

1934 Died, Brockenhurst, England

1850   1875   1900   1925   1950

1861–65 U.S. Civil War

1914–18 World War II

1939–45 World War II

In 1896 Gilbert landed the job that would launch him to national prominence: He was appointed architect for the Minnesota State Capitol Building, in St. Paul. The majestic domed structure that he created was immensely popular. Both its scale and detail were considered appropriate for its public purpose. His success convinced Gilbert that he was ready to compete in New York.

Shortly after moving to New York, Gilbert was among those invited to submit plans for the U.S. Custom House. He won the competition, but not without controversy. Other firms involved in the competition thought Taylor, then architect of the Treasury Building, in Washington, D.C., had unfairly influenced the choice of his former partner. Despite the controversy, Gilbert was eventually awarded other commissions, including the Union Club and the West Street Building, in New York, and the Essex County Courthouse, in Newark, New Jersey.

He also began to play a role in organizations associated with his profession, being elected president of the American Institute of Architects in 1908. At various points in his career, he was an active member of the Architectural League of New York, Academy of Design, National Institute of Arts and Letters, Academy of Arts and Letters, Royal Institute of British Architects, Royal Institute of Canada, Architectural Society of Liverpool, Royal Academy of Arts, and French Legion of Honor.

Although Gilbert entered, and won, a number of competitions during his career, most of his work came from his professional associations and his power of persuasion. His pursuit of the contract for the Woolworth Building, in New York, is just one example of his tenacious nature. HEARING that Frank W. Woolworth was going abroad before naming an architect for his new building, Gilbert booked passage on the same boat; he had a signed contract in hand before the boat docked.

The Woolworth Building, with its tremendous height and inventive use of terra-cotta, was a huge success. It was the tallest building in the world and it towered over the New York skyline for almost 20 years. The building made Gilbert a celebrity and substantially increased the demand for his professional services. The Scott Memorial Fountain, Detroit (1914); Detroit Public Library (1917); Brooklyn Army Terminal (1918); St. Louis Public Library (1921); and a host of other schools, banks, libraries, museums, and municipal structures were commissioned in the years following his completion of the Woolworth Building in 1913.

In 1910 Gilbert was appointed to the National Commission of Fine Arts by President WILLIAM HOWARD TAFT. He was reappointed for another term by President Woodrow Wilson in 1914. Through this association, Gilbert secured some of his most prestigious work, including the U.S. Treasury Annex (1918), Chamber of COMMERCE (1924), and, finally, the Supreme Court Building.

In 1928 Chief Justice and former president William Howard Taft became chairman of the Supreme Court Building Commission, created by Congress to build a permanent home for the nation's High Court. Taft remembered Gilbert's work on the National Commission of Fine Arts and selected him to design the new Court building.

The structure envisioned by Gilbert was a monumental temple of justice—one that evoked the power, authority, and solemnity of the Court. His design, which filled the square-block site, featured a neo-classical white marble structure with an enormous central hall housing the courtroom. Two symmetrical wings on either side of the central hall contained offices, libraries, and other Court functions. The focus of the Court chamber was an elevated bench, which looked out on seating for more than three hundred spectators.

The interior layout of the building separated the justices' private areas from the public areas, and was designed to facilitate grand entrances into the courtroom. The building's private areas contained three-room office suites, a robing room, underground parking and entrances, temperature- and humidity-controlled library and DOCUMENT storage facilities, and pressrooms.

Gilbert's architectural sketches were approved by the commission in 1929, and construction began in 1931. The building was not completed until after Gilbert's death in 1934; Gilbert's son, Cass, Jr., supervised the final stages of the project.

The Supreme Court Building opened its doors to the public on Monday, October 7,

1935. Initially, the building was criticized for both its size and its exterior embellishment. To a large extent, the size was dictated by the site: Gilbert strove to complement the scale of the ADJACENT LIBRARY OF CONGRESS and of other buildings in the Capitol complex. Charges of wasted space in the halls and corridors, and excessive seating in the courtroom, have diminished with time. The building's exterior embellishment featured prominent legal figures and themes and was executed by some of the finest artists and sculptors of the day. It is said that one of the toga-clad figures depicted on the building bears the likeness of the architect himself.

As a space designed for hearing arguments and holding public discussion, the large courtroom was also criticized for its poor acoustics. Time and improved sound technology have diminished this criticism. In the early 2000s, the Supreme Court Building is considered the pinnacle of Gilbert's work and is one of the nation's finest public buildings.

While developing the Supreme Court Building, Gilbert also continued to work in New York and across the country. During this period he designed the New York Life INSURANCE Building, the U.S. Courthouse in New York City, the GEORGE WASHINGTON Memorial Bridge, and the state capitol buildings in Arkansas and West Virginia.

Biographer Egerton Swartwout described Gilbert as "purposely impressive in manner and rather pompous at times." This description could as easily be applied to the public buildings Gilbert designed. Gilbert's work stayed true to the traditional themes that inspired him as a young man traveling in Europe. Though his Woolworth Building and other commercial structures contributed to the evolution of the modern skyscraper, Gilbert was not a fan of the modern functional architecture that emerged in the 1920s. The turmoil of WORLD WAR I and the economic difficulties of the 1920s were said to have solidified Gilbert's commitment to classic traditional style.

Still much in demand by those who shared his architectural vision, Gilbert died suddenly May 17, 1934, on a golf holiday at Brockenhurst, England, at age seventy-five. He is buried in New York City. His personal and professional papers are housed at the Library of Congress—across the street from his Supreme Court Building.

FURTHER READINGS

Blodgett, Geoffrey. 2005. *Cass Gilbert, Architect, Conservative at Bay.* Journal of American History 72 (December)

———. 2001. *Cass Gilbert: The Early Years.* St. Paul, MN: Minnesota Historical Society.

Bluestone, Daniel M. 1988. "Detroit's City Beautiful and the Problem of Commerce." *Journal of the Society of Architectural Historians* 47, no. 3 (September).

Gaskie, Margaret F. 1981. "The Woolworth Tower." *Architectural Record* (November).

Irish, Sharon Lu. "Cass Gilbert's Career in New York, 1899–1905." Ann Arbor, MI: Univ. Microfilms.

———. 1989. "A Machine That Makes the Land Pay: The West Street Building in New York." *Technology and Culture* 30.

———. 1973. "Mr. Woolworth's Tower: The Skyscraper as Popular Icon." *Journal of Popular Culture.*

Jones, Robert Allan. 1976. *Cass Gilbert, Midwestern Architect in New York.* Ph.D. dissertation, Case Western Reserve Univ.

McGurn, Barrett. 1982. "Slogans to Fit the Occasion." Washington, D.C.: Supreme Court Historical Society.

Murphy, P. 1981. "Minnesota's Architectural Favorite Son." *Architecture: the AIA Journal* 3.

Myers, Rex C. 1976. "The Montana Club: Symbol of Elegance." *The Magazine of Western History* 26, no. 4 (autumn).

Thompson, Neil B. 2005. *Minnesota's State Capitol: The Art and Politics of a Public Building.* Minneapolis: Minnesota Historical Society.

Tunick, Susan, and Jonathan Walters. 1982. *The Wonderful World of Terra Cotta.* Historic Preservation.

❖ GILLETT, EMMA MELINDA

Emma Melinda Gillett was a remarkable ATTORNEY who helped establish one of the first co-educational law schools in the United States. In 1896, Gillett and a colleague, ELLEN SPENCER MUSSEY, sponsored a series of lectures in Washington, D.C., for local women interested in law. Despite social pressures against women in the legal profession, Gillett and Mussey held the lectures for two years. They expanded their curriculum and created Washington College of Law, a co-educational INSTITUTION that later became part of American University.

Gillett was born July 30, 1852, in Princeton, Wisconsin. After her father, Richard J. Gillett, died in 1854, Gillett moved to Girard, Pennsylvania, with her mother, Sarah Ann Gillett, and family. Like Mussey, Gillett attended Lake Erie Seminary in Painesville, Ohio. Upon graduation in 1870, Gillett became a public school teacher.

After ten years of teaching, she decided to move to Washington, D.C., to pursue a LEGAL EDUCATION and career. Her plans were thwarted by the refusal of most district law schools to admit women. Gillett overcame the obstacle by

THE MAJORITY OF THE [WOMEN] PRACTITIONERS WHO ARE STICKING TO THEIR WORK AND PLODDING ON [THEIR] WAY TO SUCCESS ARE UNMARRIED.
—EMMA GILLETT

enrolling at Howard University Law College, a well-known, predominantly African American institution that did accept female students. Gillett earned a law degree from Howard in 1882 and a master of law degree in 1883. She began a successful law practice in Washington, D.C., and became VICE PRESIDENT of the D.C. region of the previously all-male AMERICAN BAR ASSOCIATION. She also was elected president of the Women's BAR ASSOCIATION of the DISTRICT OF COLUMBIA.

Both Gillett and Mussey had been denied admission to the all-male, all-white law schools in Washington, D.C., which likely motivated the women to form the Washington College of Law. Three additional motivating factors have also been identified. First, women's voluntary associations had experienced significant growth during the latter part of the nineteenth century. Second, opportunities for women in higher education had expanded. Third, the women's SUFFRAGE movement had grown considerably.

Gillett and Mussey established a co-educational institution, rather than a women-only law school. They believed that admitting both men and women as students, as well as hiring male faculty and administrators, were necessary to promote gender equality. Perhaps as important, Gillett and Mussey knew that admitting men as students and employing men in faculty and administrative positions were necessary to promote the long-term success of the school. Fifteen years after its establishment, in fact, the number of men enrolled in the school outnumbered the number of women, due largely to the fact that two other law schools in Washington, D.C., began to admit women as students. Nevertheless, only women served as deans of the Washington College of Law until 1947. Washington College

of Law earned accreditation from the American Bar Association in 1940 and became a part of American University in 1949.

Gillett succeeded Mussey as dean of the law school in 1913, heading the institution for ten years. Gillett died on January 23, 1927, in Washington, D.C., at the age of 74.

FURTHER READINGS

Clark, Mary L. 1998. "The Founding of the Washington College of Law: The First Law School Established by Women for Women." *American Univ. Law Review* 47, no. 3.

"Emma Melinda Gillett." 1927. *Women Lawyers' Journal.* Available online at http://www.stanford.edu/group/WLHP/articles/gillettobit.htm; website home page: http://www.stanford.edu (accessed July 26, 2009).

"Emma M. Gillett." History of WCL. *Washington College of Law.* Available online at http://www.wcl.american.edu/history/gillett.cfm; website home page: http://www.wcl.american.edu (accessed September 4, 2009).

❖ GILPIN, HENRY DILWORTH

Henry Dilworth Gilpin served as attorney general of the United States from 1840 to 1841 under President MARTIN VAN BUREN. He was born April 14, 1801, in Lancaster, England. He and his parents, Joshua Gilpin and Mary Dilworth Gilpin, boarded a ship for the United States in 1802. The Gilpins were aristocratic and socially prominent, not a struggling immigrant family. Gilpin's grandfather Thomas Gilpin was a manufacturer and businessman who had been shipping goods to U.S. harbors since colonial days. He was among those who helped to plan and execute the construction of the Chesapeake and Delaware Canal (which connects the head of Chesapeake Bay with the Delaware River estuary and thereby shortens sea routes to Baltimore from the north and from Europe). Gilpin's father, an author and poet with

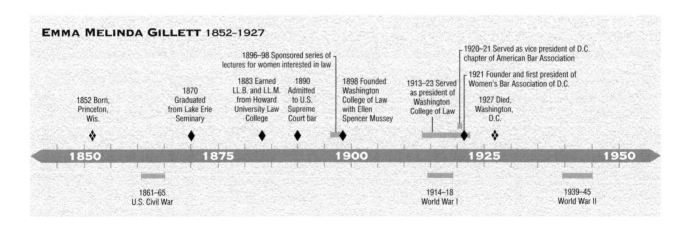

EMMA MELINDA GILLETT 1852–1927

1852 Born, Princeton, Wis.

1870 Graduated from Lake Erie Seminary

1883 Earned LL.B. and LL.M. from Howard University Law College

1890 Admitted to U.S. Supreme Court bar

1896–98 Sponsored series of lectures for women interested in law

1898 Founded Washington College of Law with Ellen Spencer Mussey

1913–23 Served as president of Washington College of Law

1920–21 Served as vice president of D.C. chapter of American Bar Association

1921 Founder and first president of Women's Bar Association of D.C.

1927 Died, Washington, D.C.

1850   1875   1900   1925   1950

1861–65 U.S. Civil War

1914–18 World War I

1939–45 World War II

published works in both England and the United States, dabbled in a number of artistic and business ventures in the United States. He eventually settled in Pennsylvania, where he ran a successful papermaking business.

Gilpin was brought up near Philadelphia and was educated at the University of Pennsylvania. He graduated as valedictorian of his class in 1819 and began to study law with a local ATTORNEY. In 1822 he was admitted to the bar but he did not establish a practice. Instead, he went to work as an agent for the Chesapeake and Delaware Canal Company. The position allowed him to travel and to pursue the literary interests encouraged by his father. From 1826 to 1832 he wrote detailed accounts of his visits to Harper's Ferry, the Shenandoah Valley, Weyer's Cave, Natural Bridge, Lexington, Charlottesville, Fredericksburg, Washington, D.C., and other locations in the Atlantic and southern states. His writings were collected by his father and later published in a seven-volume work called *Atlantic Souvenirs* (1826–1832).

Gilpin's pedigree and business interests permitted him to mix with prominent citizens wherever he traveled. During this early period of travel, he met and married Eliza Johnson, of New Orleans. In 1826 he attended—and wrote a famous account of—President John Quincy Adams's inaugural ball and public reception. On subsequent trips to the nation's capital, he developed an interest in politics by writing profiles of men like HENRY CLAY, DANIEL WEBSTER, and ANDREW JACKSON.

Gilpin was a great admirer of Jackson and was active in Jackson's successful bid for the presidency in 1828. In appreciation for Gilpin's

Henry D. Gilpin.
LIBRARY OF CONGRESS

support, Jackson named him to the board of directors of the Second National BANK OF THE UNITED STATES. The First National Bank, located in Gilpin's hometown of Philadelphia, was established as the nation's central bank in 1816 during the financial crisis after the WAR OF 1812. It had opened in 1791 and closed in 1811 after its renewal CHARTER was successfully challenged by agricultural interests who were not served by the bank's commercial focus.

Like its predecessor, the Second National Bank had strong opposition. Jackson believed that it had become too powerful, and he wanted to diminish its influence by withdrawing FEDERAL funds and depositing the money in selected state

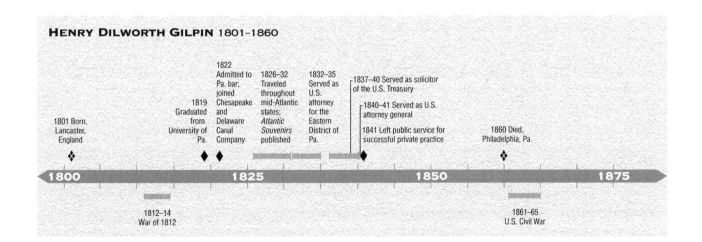

HENRY DILWORTH GILPIN 1801–1860

1801 Born, Lancaster, England

1819 Graduated from University of Pa.

1822 Admitted to Pa. bar; joined Chesapeake and Delaware Canal Company

1826–32 Traveled throughout mid-Atlantic states; *Atlantic Souvenirs* published

1832–35 Served as U.S. attorney for the Eastern District of Pa.

1837–40 Served as solicitor of the U.S. Treasury

1840–41 Served as U.S. attorney general

1841 Left public service for successful private practice

1860 Died, Philadelphia, Pa.

1812–14 War of 1812

1861–65 U.S. Civil War

1800   1825   1850   1875

banks. The Bank War, as the debate over the bank's role in the federal economy came to be called, was a central issue in Jackson's second presidential campaign. Jackson's re-election, along with the presence of his ally Gilpin on the board, ensured the bank's DEMISE. Gilpin successfully pressed Jackson's arguments against the INSTITUTION, and the renewal of the bank's charter was rejected. The bank closed in 1836 when its charter expired.

Gilpin's willingness to act as Jackson's chief spokesman at the height of the Bank War resulted in his removal from the board in the bank's final years. To fill the void left by his removal, Gilpin renewed his interest in the PRACTICE OF LAW, and from 1832 to 1835 he served as U.S. attorney for the Eastern District of Pennsylvania. He also pursued a number of land-investment and business opportunities in the Michigan Territory.

Jackson named Gilpin territorial governor of Michigan in 1835, but the president's opponents in Congress blocked the confirmation. It was not until President Van Buren was elected a year later that Gilpin returned to a role in the federal government.

Van Buren named Gilpin to be SOLICITOR of the U.S. Treasury in 1837 and elevated him to serve as attorney general of the United States from 1840 to 1841. As in his early years, Gilpin continued to chronicle his experiences. The *Gilpin Reports,* published in 1837, and the *Opinions of Attorneys-General of the United States,* published in 1840, record his service to the Van Buren administration.

Gilpin's term as attorney general increased the demand for his legal services, and after leaving the CABINET, he devoted the last 20 years of his life to the practice of law. He also continued to oversee development of the Chesapeake and Delaware Canal Company, where he rose to the positions of secretary and director.

Gilpin retained a lifelong interest in politics and the DEMOCRATIC PARTY and served as a DELEGATE to the party's national convention in 1844. Gilpin tutored his younger brother, William, in the study of the law and was instrumental in launching the latter's political career. His brother went on to become the governor of Colorado.

Gilpin died on January 29, 1860, in Philadelphia, Pennsylvania.

I KNOW FEW THINGS MORE STRIKING IN THE HISTORY OF HUMANKIND THAN THAT KINDLING ENTHUSIASM WHICH, SPRINGING FROM ONE INDIVIDUAL...SWAYS THE CONDUCT OF IMMENSE BODIES OF MEN.
—HENRY GILPIN

FURTHER READINGS

Gerdts, William H. 1983. "The American 'Discourses' A Survey of Lectures and Writings on American Art, 1770–1858." *American Journal of Art* 15, no. 3.

Gray, Ralph D. 1968. "A Tour of Virginia in 1827. Letters of Henry D. Gilpin to his Father." *Virginia Magazine of History and Biography* 76, no.3 (October).

Gray, Ralph D., ed. 1965. *Washington in 1825: Observations by Henry D. Gilpin.* Delaware Historical Society.

Rimini, Robert V. 1967. *Andrew Jackson and the Bank War.* New York: Norton.

Tobias, Clifford I. 1975. "Henry D. Gilpin: Governor in and over the Territory of Michigan." *Michigan History.*

———. 1975. *Henry D. Gilpin and the Bank War, A Study in Reform Politics.* Cleveland, Ohio: Case Western Reserve Univ. Press.

❖ GINGRICH, NEWTON LEROY

With his election as Speaker of the U.S. House of Representatives in January 1995, NEWTON LEROY GINGRICH (R-Ga.) became a powerful politician. Assuming control of the first Republican majority in the House since 1952, Gingrich ruled that body during his first year with an authority not seen since the nineteenth century. The veteran congressman from Georgia used his new position to proclaim the arrival of an era in which his conservative agenda—including lower taxes, decentralized government, and deep cuts in social programs—would fundamentally alter the fabric of U.S. society.

Since his arrival on the Washington, D.C., scene in 1979 as a brash and combative new member of Congress, Gingrich has shaped and guided Republican efforts on Capitol Hill. With an affinity for both intellectual debate and backroom deal making, this white-haired former professor provided the vision, verve, and ideas that built a Republican majority. His opponents, however, ACCUSED him of posessing a lack of concern for poor and disadvantaged persons, as well as an overly optimistic view of technology and the free market. Observers have described his actions in Congress as alternately brilliant and petty, leaving many to wonder whether he will be a passing footnote or a pivotal chapter in U.S. political history.

Gingrich was born June 17, 1943, in Harrisburg, Pennsylvania. His parents, Newton C. McPherson and Kathleen Daugherty McPherson, were separated after only three days of MARRIAGE. Gingrich's mother remarried three years after his birth, and her new husband, Robert Bruce Gingrich, adopted Gingrich. Gingrich's adoptive father was a career army officer, and the family moved frequently, living in Kansas, France, Germany, and Fort Benning, Georgia.

In 1958 the 15-year-old Gingrich accompanied his family on a trip to Verdun, France, site of the bloodiest battle of WORLD WAR I. Deeply moved by the story and scene of the battle, along with a visit to rooms filled with bones of the dead, Gingrich experienced an epiphany that he later described as "the driving force which pushed me into history and politics, and molded my life." The day after this visit, he told his family that he would run for Congress, because politicians could prevent such senseless bloodshed.

At age 19, Gingrich, who was then an undergraduate at Emory University, married his former high school math teacher, Jackie Battley. The couple had two daughters, Linda Kathleen and Jacqueline Sue. Gingrich completed his bachelor of arts degree at Emory in 1965 and obtained a doctor of philosophy degree in modern history at Tulane University in 1971. A liberal, reform-minded Republican in these years, Gingrich worked for Nelson A. Rockefeller's 1968 presidential campaign in Louisiana.

Gingrich took his first college teaching job at West Georgia College, in Carrollton, Georgia, with one eye toward an eventual seat in Congress. He nevertheless became a popular teacher at West Georgia, and founded environmental studies and future studies programs.

In 1974 and 1976, Gingrich ran for a seat in the U.S. House from Georgia's Sixth District, a rural and suburban region on the northern outskirts of Atlanta. Still voicing moderate and even liberal positions, he was endorsed in 1974

Newt Gingrich.
CALLISTA GINGRICH, GINGRICH PRODUCTIONS

by the liberal newspaper the *Atlanta Constitution.* He narrowly lost both ELECTIONS. In a move that some have called a calculated ploy to gain political office, Gingrich cast himself as a conservative for the 1978 election. In his platform he called for lower taxes and opposed the Panama Canal Treaty. He beat the Democratic contender by 7,600 votes, earning a seat in the 96th Congress.

Shortly after his election, Gingrich and his wife separated. He married Marianne Ginther in 1981.

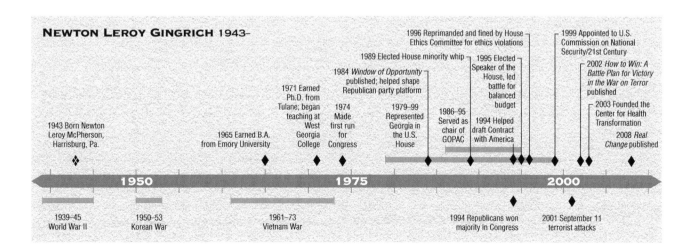

NEWTON LEROY GINGRICH 1943–

1943 Born Newton Leroy McPherson, Harrisburg, Pa.

1965 Earned B.A. from Emory University

1971 Earned Ph.D. from Tulane; began teaching at West Georgia College

1974 Made first run for Congress

1979–99 Represented Georgia in the U.S. House

1984 *Window of Opportunity* published; helped shape Republican party platform

1986–95 Served as chair of GOPAC

1994 Helped draft Contract with America

1995 Elected Speaker of the House, led battle for balanced budget

1989 Elected House minority whip

1996 Reprimanded and fined by House Ethics Committee for ethics violations

1999 Appointed to U.S. Commission on National Security/21st Century

2002 *How to Win: A Battle Plan for Victory in the War on Terror* published

2003 Founded the Center for Health Transformation

2008 *Real Change* published

1950   1975   2000

1939–45 World War II

1950–53 Korean War

1961–73 Vietnam War

1994 Republicans won majority in Congress

2001 September 11 terrorist attacks

In Washington, D.C., Gingrich joined a number of Republican first-year Congress members eager to leave their mark on the political landscape. Unafraid of making enemies, he vigorously attacked Democrats and sometimes his own party, criticizing it for a complacent acceptance of its minority status in Congress. He called instead for an aggressive effort to build a Republican majority, a feat he would orchestrate 16 years later.

In February 1983 Gingrich began meeting regularly with other young conservatives in an organization they called the Conservative Opportunity Society—a name designed to contrast with "liberal WELFARE state," the favorite target for their ideological barbs. Gingrich and other young Republicans also gained notoriety for their creative use of the Cable-Satellite Public Affairs Network (C-SPAN), which broadcast live proceedings of the House. This group used the "special orders" period of the House, during which members of Congress may read items into the record, as a platform to denounce Democrats and advance their own views. Although they were actually reading their material before an empty House chamber, Gingrich and his colleagues attempted to create the impression that they were making unchallenged arguments to specific Democrats. House Speaker Thomas P. ("Tip") O'Neill Jr. (D-Mass.) responded by ordering the C-SPAN cameras to periodically pan the empty chamber.

By 1984 Gingrich had developed the basic outlines of his conservative philosophy. He published his views in a book, *Window of Opportunity,* cowritten with his wife, Marianne, and David Drake. It remains an excellent guide to Gingrich's thought. In it, he exhibited, in addition to a strong belief in the efficacy of the free market, a strong devotion to technology as an answer to social ills. He wrote of a "window of opportunity" represented by "breakthroughs in computers, biology, and space." Among his futuristic proposals was an ambitious space program, including a lunar research base by 2000.

He contrasted this vision of a bright future with a "window of vulnerability" that opened onto an alternative future of Soviet expansionism and U.S. decline. This dystopia was to be prevented by large-scale WEAPONS programs such as Star Wars, also known as the Strategic DEFENSE Initiative, and the dismantling of welfare programs and excessive TAXATION. The seventh

> WE MUST MAKE GOVERNMENT MORE EFFICIENT, MAKING SURE TAXPAYERS GET THEIR MONEY'S WORTH.
> —NEWT GINGRICH

chapter of the book, "Why Balancing the Budget Is Vital," foreshadowed a 1995–96 showdown between Gingrich and President BILL CLINTON over the FEDERAL BUDGET.

At the 1984 Republican National Convention in Dallas, Gingrich gained national attention as he led a move to make the party platform more conservative, successfully inserting planks against tax increases and ABORTION. He won still more influence in 1986 when he became chair of GOPAC, a Republican POLITICAL ACTION COMMITTEE that serves as a principal source of funding for Republican candidates across the United States. The organization, which Gingrich once called "the Bell Labs of politics," also provided the means for him to spread his conservative gospel. GOPAC has distributed printed and audiovisual works by Gingrich to hundreds of Republican candidates. In the early and mid-1990s, it came under investigation by the FEDERAL ELECTION COMMISSION for alleged improprieties, including illegal assistance to Gingrich during his 1990 election campaign. Gingrich stepped down as the head of GOPAC in 1995.

In 1987 Gingrich took on a major Washington, D.C., figure when he accused House Speaker Jim Wright (D-Tex.) of ethics violations. Gingrich claimed that Wright had violated House rules in his dealings with a Texas developer and in the manner by which he had profited from sales of a book. Gingrich's foes immediately attacked him as an irresponsible upstart, but he remained unwavering in his attacks. As he later told a newspaper, "I didn't come here to pleasantly rise on an escalator of self-serving compromises." Gingrich won a major coup in 1989 when the House Ethics Committee formally charged Wright with 69 ethics violations and Wright resigned from the House.

That same year, Gingrich lobbied for and won (by two votes) the position of House minority whip, making him the second highest-ranking Republican in the House of Representatives. This victory represented an important step in his transformation from party pugilist to party leader. However, Gingrich himself soon became the object of a House Ethics Committee probe of alleged violations of House rules on outside gifts and income. The allegations focused on his earnings from two books, including *Window of Opportunity.* Later that year, Gingrich was investigated again by the same committee for improperly transferring congressional staff to work on his reelection campaigns. In both cases, the committee did not find sufficient grounds to reprimand Gingrich.

Gingrich nearly suffered defeat in the elections of 1990 and 1992, winning the former CONTEST by fewer than 1,000 of the 156,000 votes cast. But these narrow victories were followed by a much wider reaching victory for both Gingrich and his party in 1994.

Gingrich had done much to lay the groundwork for his 1994 win, particularly through his organization of the CONTRACT WITH AMERICA, a ten-point plan of action that was intended to give Republicans a unified front against their Democratic opponents. The contract called for such measures as tax breaks, a balanced budget amendment to the Constitution, a presidential line-item VETO, term limits for members of Congress, get-tough proposals on crime, reduction of government regulations, welfare reform, military budget increases, and more. In September 1994 Gingrich gathered more than 300 Republican candidates for Congress to sign the contract on Capitol grounds.

The big GOP win in 1994 gave the party a gain of 54 seats and majority status in the House. In January 1995 Gingrich was voted Speaker of the House. His leadership soon led to a dramatic change in House protocol. Wresting control from committee chairs by placing loyal associates—many of them first-year Republican Congress members—on key committees, Gingrich became one of the most powerful speakers since the nineteenth century, at times virtually dictating the content of legislation.

Riding the crest of publicity attached to his new position, Gingrich published two books, *To Renew America* (1995) and *1945* (1995). *To Renew America* was a best-selling work communicating Gingrich's vision for the country. It presents a thesis that cultural elites have torn down the traditional culture of U.S. society. It also contains his already familiar calls to balance the FEDERAL budget and decentralize the federal BUREAUCRACY by returning power to states and localities. The book *1945* is a "what if" novel that explores what the consequences would have been if Nazi Germany had been triumphant in WORLD WAR II.

Gingrich, eager to make his mark as Speaker, initiated a 100-day plan to enact the Contract

with America into law. He passed nine of the ten items of the contract through the House, but only three—the Congressional Accountability Act (Pub. L. No. 104-1, 109 Stat. 3), the Unfunded Mandates Reform Act (Pub. L. No. 104-4, 109 Stat. 48), and the Paperwork Reduction Act (Pub. L. No. 104-13, 109 Stat. 163)—were signed into law by the president.

Gingrich fought especially hard for one element of the contract: a balanced budget amendment to the Constitution. After its defeat in the Senate, he organized a Republican plan to balance the federal budget in seven years. This plan included tax reductions and deep cuts in federal social programs. Most controversial were provisions requiring large cuts to such programs as MEDICARE and MEDICAID, which provide health care to elderly, disabled, and poor people. Over the course of 1995, President Clinton gradually adopted the goal of a seven-year balanced budget plan—a change of mind that symbolized the pervasive power of the Republican agenda.

When President Clinton vetoed the House budget plan late in 1995, Gingrich and his Republican colleagues refused to compromise their budget priorities. As a result, the federal government was forced to shut down nonessential services for lack of funding. The budget showdown forced national parks, agencies, and other elements of the federal government to close their doors. Gingrich came under fire as people complained of undelivered paychecks and other problems. The impasse ended in January 1996, when Gingrich and Clinton reached a compromise that allowed provisional funding of the federal government and abandoned the seven-year goal of balancing the budget.

In 1995 *Time* magazine named Gingrich its Man of the Year, a fitting recognition of the Speaker's large role in shaping the national political agenda. Such power had not translated into universal public approval for Gingrich, however, particularly given the unpopularity of the federal government shutdown.

President Clinton and Congress, despite their collective ideological differences, managed to achieve a budget surplus in 1998, years ahead of expectations. The surpluses grew from $69 billion in 1998 to $122.7 billion in 1999. Nevertheless, Gingrich's popularity dwindled during the late 1990s, due in large part to his policies and brash personality.

Republicans maintained control over Congress in the 1996 and 1998 elections, but the margin of the majority following the 1998 elections was the narrowest in more than 30 years. Fellow Republican members of Congress largely blamed Gingrich for the difficulties during the elections. Amid increasing dissension, Gingrich resigned both as the Speaker of the House and as a representative in 1999.

After he left politics, Gingrich founded the Gingrich Group, a communications and management consulting firm based in Atlanta. In 2003 he founded the Center for Health Transformation, described as a collection of private and public sector leaders dedicated to a twenty-first-century intelligent health system. In 2007 Gingrich founded American Solutions for Winning the Future, a nonprofit organization dedicated to developing solutions to America's challenges and mobilizing the grassroots energy to implement them. Gingrich serves as chair of the organization and also as a senior fellow for both the American Enterprise INSTITUTE in Washington, D.C., and the Hoover INSTITUTION at Stanford University. In 2001 he was named a distinguished visiting scholar at the National Defense University. He has served as a political analyst in the media and is generally recognized for his expertise in such areas as world history, military issues, and international affairs.

Gingrich has written 13 FICTION and nonfiction books since leaving office, including the New York Times best sellers *Winning the Future* (2005) and *Real Change* (2008), and the best-selling active history novels *Gettysburg* (2003), *Pearl Harbor* (2007), and *Days of Infamy* (2008). He resides in Virginia with his third wife, Callista, who serves as the president of Gingrich Productions.

FURTHER READINGS

Gingrich, Newt. 2008. *Real Change: From the World That Fails to the World That Works.* Washington, D.C.: Regnery Publishing, Inc.

———. 2006. *Rediscovering God in America.* Franklin, TN: Integrity House.

———. 2005. *Winning the Future: A 21st Century Contract with America.* Washington, D.C.: Regnery Publishing, Inc.

———. 1995. *To Renew America.* New York: HarperCollins.

Gingrich, Newt, with David Drake and Marianne Gingrich. 1984. *Window of Opportunity.* Tom Doherty Associates.

Gugliotta, Guy, and Juliet Eilperin. 1998. "Gingrich Steps Down in Face of Rebellion." *Washington Post* (November 7).

"The Long March of Newt Gingrich." *PBS: Frontline.* Available online at http://www.pbs.org/wgbh/pages/frontline/newt; website home page: http://www.pbs.org (accessed July 26, 2009).

1995–1996 Official Congressional Directory, 104th Congress. 1995. Washington, D.C.: U.S. Government Printing Office.

Wilkins, David. 1991. "Newt Gingrich." *Newsmakers 1991.* Edited by Louise Mooney. Detroit: Gale Research.

CROSS REFERENCES

Contract with America; Election Campaign Financing.

GINNIE MAE

See GOVERNMENT NATIONAL MORTGAGE ASSOCIATION.

❖ GINSBURG, DOUGLAS HOWARD

Douglas Howard Ginsburg became the chief judge of the U.S. Court of Appeals for the DISTRICT OF COLUMBIA in 2001 after serving as an associate judge since 1986. In 1987 his nomination to the SUPREME COURT OF THE UNITED STATES was derailed by questions about his inexperience and about his personal life.

Ginsburg was born May 25, 1946, in Chicago. He grew up in Chicago, where he graduated from the prestigious Latin School in 1963. After high school, he entered Cornell University, in Ithaca, New York, but he left college in the mid-1960s to open the nation's first computerized dating service. After achieving success with the company, which was named Operation Match, Ginsburg sold his interest and returned to Cornell, earning his bachelor's degree in 1970. From there, he went to the University of Chicago Law School, where he received his doctor of JURISPRUDENCE degree in 1973.

Ginsburg served as a law clerk to U.S. circuit judge Carl McGowan from 1973 to 1974, and to Justice THURGOOD MARSHALL, of the U.S. Supreme Court, from 1974 to 1975. In 1975 he became an assistant professor of law at Harvard Law School, and in 1981 he was promoted to the rank of professor. He left academia to become a deputy assistant attorney general for regulatory affairs in the U.S. DEPARTMENT OF JUSTICE, Antitrust Division, in 1983. A year later he was appointed administrator for information and regulatory affairs of the OFFICE OF MANAGEMENT AND BUDGET, where he served for one year before returning to the Antitrust Division of the JUSTICE DEPARTMENT in 1985. In 1986 President RONALD REAGAN named him a judge of the U.S.

Court of Appeals for the District of Columbia Circuit.

At this point in his career, Ginsburg seemed to be settling into a predictable future on the FEDERAL bench. But there was to be a short detour along the way. In 1987, to the surprise of almost everyone, Reagan nominated him to replace retiring Justice Lewis F. Powell Jr. on the U.S. Supreme Court.

Ginsburg's nomination followed months of intense, sometimes acrimonious questioning by the SENATE JUDICIARY COMMITTEE of Judge ROBERT H. BORK, Reagan's first nominee. During these hearings, the Senate had departed from its traditional advice-and-consent role and closely questioned Bork on philosophical and doctrinal matters never before addressed in confirmation proceedings. Bork had a long paper trail, with years of scholarly writings that revealed him to be a strict, conservative constructionist on CONSTITUTIONAL matters, just the type of Justice Reagan wanted on the Court to carry his vision of judicial restraint into the next century. However, members of the Senate, openly concerned with his conservative political ideologies, eventually rejected Bork's nomination.

Stung by the Senate's rejection of Bork, Reagan and his aides were determined to find a nominee who would fulfill their requirement of judicial restraint but who had no "history" that would make their choice vulnerable to attack. They thought they had just the person they needed in Ginsburg and, although Ginsburg had less than a year's experience as a judge, Reagan nominated him for the vacancy.

Douglas Ginsburg.
MARK WILSON/
NEWSMAKERS/GETTY
IMAGES

Ginsburg's nomination ran into difficulty almost immediately. Senators raised the obvious issues of his youth and inexperience and voiced concern about how his scanty judicial record made him a tabula rasa on constitutional matters. A conflict-of-interest question was raised when newspapers reported that at the Justice Department he had handled a major case involving the cable TV industry while he held a $140,000 INVESTMENT in a Canadian cable TV company. Then, too, it began to look as if he might be opposed by some conservatives

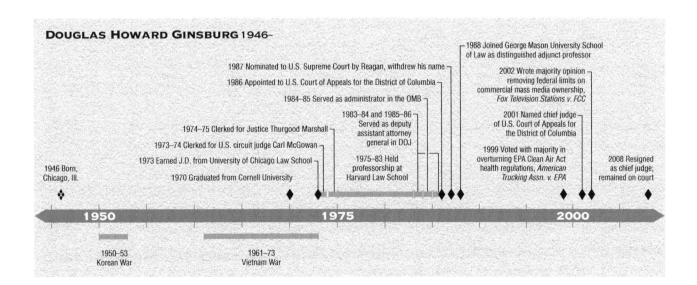

DOUGLAS HOWARD GINSBURG 1946–

1988 Joined George Mason University School of Law as distinguished adjunct professor

1987 Nominated to U.S. Supreme Court by Reagan, withdrew his name

1986 Appointed to U.S. Court of Appeals for the District of Columbia

2002 Wrote majority opinion removing federal limits on commercial mass media ownership, *Fox Television Stations v. FCC*

1984–85 Served as administrator in the OMB

1983–84 and 1985–86 Served as deputy assistant attorney general in DOJ

2001 Named chief judge of U.S. Court of Appeals for the District of Columbia

1974–75 Clerked for Justice Thurgood Marshall

1973–74 Clerked for U.S. circuit judge Carl McGowan

1973 Earned J.D. from University of Chicago Law School

1975–83 Held professorship at Harvard Law School

1999 Voted with majority in overturning EPA Clean Air Act health regulations, *American Trucking Assn. v. EPA*

2008 Resigned as chief judge; remained on court

1946 Born, Chicago, Ill.

1970 Graduated from Cornell University

1950   1975   2000

1950–53 Korean War

1961–73 Vietnam War

because his wife, a physician, had reportedly performed some abortions. The death knell for Ginsburg's nomination sounded when he admitted that he had smoked marijuana "on a few occasions" while he was a student and during his early days on the faculty at Harvard.

Faced with the embarrassment of backing a nominee who had admitted illicit drug use, the White House dispatched Secretary of Education William J. Bennett to urge Ginsburg to withdraw his name from consideration. Ginsburg complied, issuing a statement in which he said that the scrutiny of his personal life would continue to draw attention away from more relevant questions. "My views on the law and on what kind of Supreme Court justice I would make have been drowned out in the clamor," he stated. He commended Reagan and his wife, Nancy Reagan, for "leading the fight against illegal drugs," adding, "I fully support their effort and I hope that the young people of this country, including my own daughters, will learn from my mistake and heed their message."

The swift and unfortunate DEMISE of Ginsburg's nomination was a sobering lesson for the Reagan administration. The president reacted by nominating an experienced and uncontroversial moderate, Judge ANTHONY M. KENNEDY, who was quickly and easily confirmed. Many feel that the Senate's handling of the Bork and Ginsburg nominations set a precedent for later investigations of presidential appointees and established a breadth and depth of scrutiny that some say are outside the scope allowed by the Constitution. The Senate continued its method of scrutiny with CLARENCE THOMAS in 1991.

After his withdrawal, Ginsburg returned to his position on the District of Columbia Circuit. In July 2001, after serving as an associate judge for nearly 15 years, he ascended to the position of chief judge, which he held until February 2008. As of 2009 he is still serving on the court as a judge, but David E. Sentelle has taken over as chief. Ginsburg has also maintained an active interest in LEGAL EDUCATION, serving as a part-time instructor at Harvard University, Columbia University, the University of Chicago, and GEORGE MASON University in Virginia. He teaches courses in antitrust, administrative law, and jurisprudence. In addition, Ginsburg is the author of numerous legal casebooks and other texts, focusing primarily upon antitrust and economic regulation.

> IT IS A CARDINAL PRINCIPLE OF OUR SYSTEM OF CRIMINAL LAW THAT THE FACTS ARE SETTLED BY THE TRIER OF FACT, BE IT A JURY OR A JUDGE, AND ARE NOT ORDINARILY TO BE DETERMINED BY A REVIEWING COURT.
> —DOUGLAS GINSBURG

Ginsburg is married to Hallee Perkins Morgan Ginsburg, and has three children. He is a member of the Illinois State BAR ASSOCIATION, the Massachusetts State Bar Association, the American Economic Association, and the Honor Society of Phi Kappa Phi. Ginsburg is also an honorary member of the District of Columbia Bar Association.

FURTHER READINGS

Groner, Jonathan. 2001. "Edwards Passing the Torch." *Legal Times* (June 11).

Krauthammer, Charles. 1987. "The Ginsburg Test: Bad Logic." *Time* (November 23).

❖ GINSBURG, RUTH BADER

RUTH BADER GINSBURG was appointed ASSOCIATE JUSTICE of the U.S. Supreme Court in 1993. Ginsburg was the first person nominated to the Court by President BILL CLINTON, filling the vacancy created by the retirement of Justice BYRON R. WHITE. As an ATTORNEY prior to her appointment, Ginsburg won distinction for her advocacy of women's rights before the Supreme Court.

Ginsburg was born March 15, 1933, in Brooklyn, daughter of Nathan Bader, a furrier and haberdasher, and Celia (Amster) Bader. Ginsburg attended New York public schools and then Cornell University. She married Martin Ginsburg after graduating from Cornell in 1954, and gave birth to a daughter, Jane Ginsburg, before entering Harvard Law School in 1956. Ginsburg was an outstanding student and was elected president of her class at the prestigious Harvard Law School. After her second year, she transferred to Columbia Law School, following her husband, who had taken a position with a New York City law firm. Ginsburg was elected to the Columbia LAW REVIEW and graduated first in her class. She was admitted to the New York bar in 1959.

Despite her academic brilliance, New York law firms refused to hire Ginsburg because she was a woman. She finally got a position as a law clerk to a federal district court judge. In 1961 Ginsburg entered the academic field as a research associate at Columbia Law School. In 1963, she joined the faculty of Rutgers University School of Law, where she served as a professor until 1972.

In 1972 Ginsburg's career shifted to that of an advocate. As the director of the Women's Rights Project of the AMERICAN CIVIL LIBERTIES UNION, she developed and used a strategy of showing that laws that discriminated between men and women were often based on stereotypes that were unfair to both sexes. In the early to mid-1970s, Ginsburg argued six women's rights cases before the U.S. Supreme Court, winning five of them.

FRONTIERO V. RICHARDSON, 411 U.S. 677, 93 S. Ct. 1764, 36 L. Ed. 2d 583 (1973), illustrates the type of cases Ginsburg argued before the Court. In *Frontiero*, a female Air Force officer successfully challenged statutes (10 U.S.C.A. §§ 1072, 1076; 37 U.S.C.A. §§ 401, 403) that allowed a married serviceman to qualify for higher housing benefits even if his wife was not dependent on his income, while requiring a married servicewoman to prove her husband's dependence before receiving the same benefit. The Supreme Court voted 8–1 to overturn the law.

President JIMMY CARTER appointed Ginsburg to the U.S. Court of Appeals for the DISTRICT OF COLUMBIA Circuit in 1980. In this position Ginsburg proved to be a judicial moderate, despite her reputation as a women's rights advocate. She supported a woman's right to choose to have an ABORTION, but disagreed with the framework of ROE V. WADE, 410 U.S. 113, 93 S. Ct. 705, 35 L. Ed. 2d 147, the 1973 decision that gave women that right. She generally sided with the government in criminal cases, but supported CIVIL RIGHTS issues. She was a model of judicial restraint, preferring legislative solutions to social problems, instead of judge-made solutions.

Ruth Bader Ginsburg.
STEVE PETTEWAY, COLLECTION OF THE SUPREME COURT OF THE UNITED STATES

President Clinton nominated Ginsburg to the Supreme Court in 1993, and she was easily confirmed. Her tenure on the High Court has been consistent with her service on the court of appeals. She has remained a judicial moderate with a strong emphasis on protecting civil rights. In UNITED STATES V. VIRGINIA, 518 U.S. 515, 116 S. Ct. 2264, 135 L. Ed. 2d 735 (1996), Ginsburg wrote the majority opinion, which ordered the all-male Virginia Military INSTITUTE (VMI) to admit women or give up state

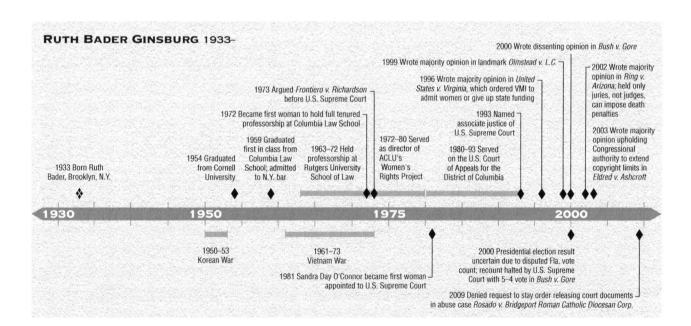

RUTH BADER GINSBURG 1933–

2000 Wrote dissenting opinion in *Bush v. Gore*

1999 Wrote majority opinion in landmark *Olmstead v. L.C.*

2002 Wrote majority opinion in *Ring v. Arizona;* held only juries, not judges, can impose death penalties

1996 Wrote majority opinion in *United States v. Virginia,* which ordered VMI to admit women or give up state funding

1973 Argued *Frontiero v. Richardson* before U.S. Supreme Court

1972 Became first woman to hold full tenured professorship at Columbia Law School

1993 Named associate justice of U.S. Supreme Court

2003 Wrote majority opinion upholding Congressional authority to extend copyright limits in *Eldred v. Ashcroft*

1959 Graduated first in class from Columbia Law School; admitted to N.Y. bar

1963–72 Held professorship at Rutgers University School of Law

1972–80 Served as director of ACLU's Women's Rights Project

1980–93 Served on the U.S. Court of Appeals for the District of Columbia

1954 Graduated from Cornell University

1933 Born Ruth Bader, Brooklyn, N.Y.

1930   1950   1975   2000

1950–53 Korean War

1961–73 Vietnam War

1981 Sandra Day O'Connor became first woman appointed to U.S. Supreme Court

2000 Presidential election result uncertain due to disputed Fla. vote count; recount halted by U.S. Supreme Court with 5–4 vote in *Bush v. Gore*

2009 Denied request to stay order releasing court documents in abuse case *Rosado v. Bridgeport Roman Catholic Diocesan Corp.*

funding. This decision also affected the Citadel, South Carolina's state-run all-male military school, and was a decisive blow to state-sponsored SEX DISCRIMINATION. Ginsburg rejected a proposal by VMI that it establish a separate military program for women. Such a program would be unequal, Ginsburg concluded, because it would rely on stereotypes about women and would not provide an equal education. She stated, "Women seeking and fit for a VMI-quality education cannot be offered anything less under the state's obligation to afford them genuinely equal protection."

Ginsburg has written for the majority in nearly 100 opinions. One of her most far-reaching opinions was the INTELLECTUAL PROPERTY case of *New York Times v. Tasini*, 533 U.S. 483, 121 L. Ed. 2d 2381, 150 L. Ed. 2d 500 (2001). The Tasini opinion upheld a 1999 federal appeals court decision, which found that the New York Times Company and its codefendants had violated the copyrights of Tasini and five other freelance writers by reproducing their work online on their own websites, and through subscription databases such as Lexis-Nexis. Ginsburg's opinion states that publishing the same article in print and on electronic formats are separate publishing events for purposes of COPYRIGHT law. Consequently, the authors should be compensated for each publishing event. The suit was brought forward by freelance writers who complained that their work was posted on the INTERNET without their permission and, in some cases, earned extra revenue for publishers who sold access to the archived material.

Ginsburg also has contributed nearly 40 dissenting opinions, including a strong DISSENT to the majority opinion in BUSH V. GORE, 531 U.S. 98, 121 S. Ct. 525, 148 L. Ed. 2d 388 (2000). The *Bush* opinion played a primary role in determining the outcome of the 2000 election in favor of GEORGE W. BUSH. Ginsburg's dissent in the *Bush* case rested on the notion that "federal courts [should] defer to state high courts' interpretations of their state's own law."

Justice Ginsburg holds honorary degrees from a number of institutions, including American University, Hebrew Union College, Amherst College, and Georgetown University. She has also been an active BAR ASSOCIATION member, serving on the Board of Editors of the AMERICAN BAR ASSOCIATION journal, and as

secretary, board member, and executive committee member of the American Bar Foundation. In addition, Ginsburg is a well-respected author and editor, writing on such topics as conflict of laws, CONSTITUTIONAL LAW, and CIVIL PROCEDURE.

In 2005 Ginsberg wrote the majority decision in a 6–3 Supreme Court RULING that protects LEGAL AID for poor defendants that are convicted but want to APPEAL.

In 1999, at the age of 66, Justice Ginsburg was diagnosed with colorectal cancer. She received radiation and chemotherapy treatments, and underwent surgery in September 1999. Upon recovery, she returned to her duties on the bench. On February 5, 2009, she underwent surgery related to pancreatic cancer. Ginsburg's tumor was discovered at an early stage, and expert medical opinions have been optimistic about her recovery

Since joining the Court, Ginsburg has supported gender equality, separation of church and state and workers rights, opposed property rights expansion, and moved to protect workers against overzealous prosecutors more often than a majority of her colleagues.

FURTHER READINGS

Baugh, Joyce Ann, et al. 1994. "Justice Ruth Bader Ginsburg: A Preliminary Assessment." *University of Toledo Law Review* 26 (fall).

Biskupic, Joan. 1999. "A High Court of Recovery." *Washington Post* (September 20).

Campbell, Amy Leigh. 2004. *Raising the Bar: Ruth Bader Ginsburg and the ACLU Women's Rights Project.* Bloomington, IN: Xlibris Corporation.

Kay, Herma Hill. 1999. "Equal Treatment: In the 1970s, Ruth Bader Ginsburg Sought to Do Something Radical: Level the Legal Playing Field for Men and Women." *American Lawyer* 21 (December).

Kushner, James A. 2003. "Introducing Ruth Bader Ginsburg and Predicting the Performance of a Ginsburg Court." *Southwestern University Law Review* 32 (spring).

O'Connor, Karen, and Barbara Palmer. 2001. "The Clinton Clones: Ginsburg, Breyer, and the Clinton Legacy." *Judicature* 84 (March-April).

GITLOW V. NEW YORK

Gitlow v. New York, 268 U.S. 652, 45 S. Ct. 625, 69 L. Ed. 1138, is a 1925 decision by the Supreme Court that upheld the constitutionality of criminal anarchy statutes.

The DEFENDANT, Benjamin Gitlow, was a member of the Left Wing Section, a splinter group of the SOCIALIST PARTY. The group formed in opposition to the party's DOMINANT policy of

THE GREATEST FIGURES OF THE AMERICAN JUDICIARY HAVE BEEN INDEPENDENT THINKING INDIVIDUALS WITH OPEN BUT NOT EMPTY MINDS — INDIVIDUALS WILLING TO LISTEN AND LEARN.

— RUTH BADER GINSBURG

"moderate socialism," and criticized the party for its insistence on introducing SOCIALISM through the legislative process. The Left Wing Section advocated change through militant and revolutionary means. It viewed mass industrial revolution as the mechanism by which the parliamentary state would be destroyed and replaced by a system of communist socialism.

Gitlow was responsible for publishing and disseminating the group's views. He did so in such pamphlets as the "The Left Wing Manifesto." The manifesto was also published in *The Revolutionary Age,* the official paper of the Left Wing. The opinions expressed in these publications formed the bases for the defendant's convictions under Sections 160 and 161 of the penal law of New York, which were the criminal anarchy statutes.

Section 160 defined criminal anarchy and prescribed that the verbal or written advocacy of the doctrine be treated as a FELONY. Section 161 delineated the conduct that constituted the crime of advocacy of criminal anarchy and stated that its punishment be IMPRISONMENT, a fine, or both. The proscribed conduct consisted of the verbal or written advertisement or teaching of the duty, necessity, or propriety of overthrowing organized government by violence, ASSASSINATION, or other unlawful acts. A person was also prohibited from publishing, editing, knowingly circulating, or publicly displaying any writing embodying this doctrine.

There was a two-count INDICTMENT against Gitlow. The first charged that the defendant had advocated, advised, and taught the duty, necessity, and propriety of unlawfully overthrowing organized government through "The Left Wing Manifesto." The second count charged that he had printed, published, knowingly circulated, and distributed *The Revolutionary Age,* containing the writings set forth in the first count advocating the doctrine of criminal anarchy.

In his APPEAL, Gitlow argued that Left Wing publications had resulted in no real action. Because they were merely utterances, he contended that the New York state laws violated the right of free speech protected by the FIRST AMENDMENT. In sustaining the defendant's CONVICTION, the U.S. Supreme Court assumed that the Due Process Clause of the FOURTEENTH AMENDMENT prevented the states from impairing the freedoms guaranteed by the First Amendment. The Court also noted that the statutes did not penalize the "utterance or publication of ABSTRACT doctrine or academic theory having no propensity to INCITE concrete action." It found that Gitlow's publications used language advocating, advising, or teaching the overthrow of organized government by unlawful means, and that such language IMPLIED an urging to action.

The Court reasoned that revolutionary actions called for in Gitlow's publications, including mass industrial uprisings and political mass strikes, implied the use of force and violence. Such actions are inherently unlawful in a democratic system of government. It ruled that freedom of expression does not grant an individual the ABSOLUTE right to speak or publish, nor does it offer unqualified IMMUNITY from punishment for every possible utterance or publication. The state, in the exercise of its police power, is allowed to punish anyone who abuses the FREEDOM OF SPEECH and press by utterances that are adverse to the public WELFARE, tend to corrupt public morals, incite to crime, or breach the public peace. As part of its primary and essential right of self-preservation, a state can penalize any expression that imperils the foundations of organized government and threatens its overthrow by unlawful means. The Court cautioned, however, that enforcement of state statutes cannot be arbitrary or unreasonable.

In subsequent cases (for example, *Brandenburg v. Ohio,* 395 U.S. 444, 89 S. Ct. 1827, 23 L. Ed. 2d 430 [1969]; *Hess v. Indiana,* 414 U.S. 105, 94 S. Ct. 326, 30 L. Ed. 2d 303 [1973]), the Court rejected the "dangerous tendency" doctrine it formulated in *Gitlow,* that incitement to action is implicit in utterances that advocate unlawful acts. The Court subsequently held that states may only prohibit utterances that directly incite lawless action or advocate individuals to imminently take lawless action.

FURTHER READINGS

Levinson, Nan. 2006. *Outspoken: Free Speech Stories.* Berkeley: Univ. of California Press.

The Oyez Project Web site. *Gitlow v. New York, 268 U.S. 652 (1925).* Available online at http://www.oyez.org/cases/ 1901-1939/1922/1922_19; website home page: http:// www.oyez.org (accessed September 4, 2009).

Tedford, Thomas L., and Dale A. Herbeck. 2009. *Freedom of Speech in the United States.* State College, PA: Strata.

CROSS REFERENCES

Anarchism; Communism; Due Process of Law; Incorporation Doctrine.

❖ GLANVILL, RANULF

English COMMON LAW developed partly in response to the pioneering work of RANULF GLANVILL. As chief justiciar, Glanvill was the legal and financial minister of England under Henry II. He is commonly associated with the first important treatise on practice and procedure in the king's courts: *Tractatus de legibus et consuetudinibus regni Angliae* (Treatise on the laws and customs of the realm of England). Historians agree that Glanvill is probably not the author of the *Tractatus,* which first appeared circa 1188, but he is thought to have been instrumental in its creation. Early U.S. law owes much to ENGLISH LAW, which became greatly simplified and available to common people during Glanvill's tenure.

Glanvill was probably born at Stratford St. Andrew, near Saxmundham, Suffolk, England. Although few details are known about his life, it is recorded that he had bumpy political fortunes. He was sheriff of Yorkshire from 1163 to 1170, but lost his authority following an official inquiry into the corruption of sheriffs. He regained it by helping raise troops against Scottish invaders in 1173–74, and his reward from King Henry II was a series of increasingly important appointments: justice of the king's court, itinerant justice in the northern circuit, and ambassador to the court in Flanders. In 1180, Glanvill's ascent to power seemed complete when he became legal and financial minister, but a new king, Richard I, threw him in prison. He ransomed his way out, and then died of illness on a Crusade at Acre, in what is now Israel, in 1190.

For a few centuries before Glanvill became influential, English law was mired in FEUDALISM. Under this political and military system, justice was administered in crude forms: trial by combat, which operated under the assumption that God would favor the righteous party, and trial by ordeal, which, in one of its forms, posed the question of innocence as a test of whether a person's wounds could heal within three days. By the twelfth century, feudalistic law was dying. The local courts still adhered to its methods, but the king's courts offered a superior form of justice that was at once less bloody and less superstitious. This was a writ-based, or formulary, system. It allowed litigants to frame a complaint in terms of a particular action, which had its own WRIT and established modes of PLEADING and trial. Although primitive by modern standards, the formulary system represented a considerable advance for its time. But such justice was chiefly available to great lords; commoners had to resort to the local courts.

As chief justiciar, Glanvill sought to extend the benefits of the king's courts to ordinary people. He accomplished this through a system of itinerant royal justices, and the results revolutionized English legal procedure. As the feudal forms fell into disuse, they were replaced with a dominant system of central courts that followed uniform procedure throughout the realm and made English law simpler and better.

The *Tractatus* played a crucial role in this improvement. In fourteen books, it covered each of the eighty distinct writs used in the king's courts. One important writ, for example, was the grand ASSIZE, a procedure for settling land disputes that replaced the feudal practice of battle with a form of jury system. The treatise offered this commentary on its value: "It takes account so effectively of both human life and civil condition that all men may preserve the rights which they have in any free tenement, while avoiding the doubtful outcome of battle. In this way, too, they may avoid the greatest of

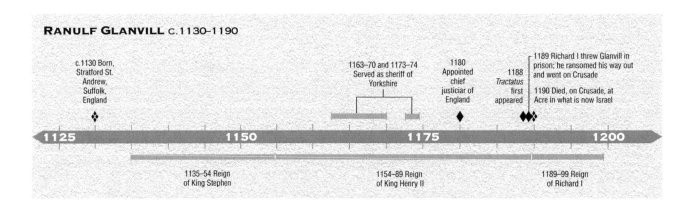

RANULF GLANVILL C.1130–1190

| c.1130 Born, Stratford St. Andrew, Suffolk, England | 1163–70 and 1173–74 Served as sheriff of Yorkshire | 1180 Appointed chief justiciar of England | 1188 *Tractatus* first appeared | 1189 Richard I threw Glanvill in prison; he ransomed his way out and went on Crusade / 1190 Died, on Crusade, at Acre in what is now Israel |

| 1125 | 1150 | 1175 | 1200 |

| 1135–54 Reign of King Stephen | 1154–89 Reign of King Henry II | 1189–99 Reign of Richard I |

all punishments, unexpected and untimely death." As with other writs, the *Tractatus* painstakingly spelled out how the grand assize worked. Directed at practitioners of law, the *Tractatus* sought to encourage them to adopt these new "royal benefit[s] granted to the people by the goodness of the king."

The simplicity and clarity of the *Tractatus* helped lead England to a common law. Although records from the period associate Glanvill with the treatise, scholars believe he is unlikely to have written it. The real author may have been his nephew, Hubert Walter, who was the archbishop of Canterbury, or even a later justiciar, Geoffrey Fitzpeter. However, its authorship is of secondary importance to its effect. Besides encouraging the spread of unified procedure, it provided the foundation for later classics, in particular Henry de Bracton's thirteenth-century treatise on English law and custom, *De legibus et consuetudinibus Angliae*.

FURTHER READINGS

Beames, John. 1900. *A Translation of Glanville*. Washington, D.C.: John Byrne.

de Glanvill, Ranulf. 1996. *Tractatus de legibus et consuetudinibus regni Angliae*. English translation available at http://www.vi.uh.edu/pages/bob/elhone/glanvill.html; web site home page: http://www.vi.uh.edu (accessed on July 26, 2009).

Scrutton, Thomas Edward. 1885. *The Influence of the Roman Law on the Law of England*. Cambridge, U.K.: Cambridge Univ. Press.

GLASS-STEAGALL ACT

The Glass-Steagall Act, also known as the Banking Act of 1933 (48 Stat. 162), was passed by Congress in 1933 and prohibits commercial banks from engaging in the investment business.

It was enacted as an emergency response to the failure of nearly 5,000 banks during the Great Depression. The act was originally part of President Franklin D. Roosevelt's NEW DEAL program and became a permanent measure in 1945. It gave tighter regulation of national banks to the Federal Reserve System; prohibited bank sales of SECURITIES; and created the FEDERAL DEPOSIT INSURANCE CORPORATION (FDIC), which insures bank deposits with a pool of money appropriated from banks.

Beginning in the 1900s, commercial banks established security affiliates that floated bond issues and underwrote corporate stock issues. (In underwriting, a bank guarantees to furnish a definite sum of money by a definite date to a

business or government entity in return for an issue of bonds or stock.) The expansion of commercial banks into securities underwriting was substantial until the 1929 STOCK MARKET crash and the subsequent Depression. In 1930 the BANK OF THE UNITED STATES failed, reportedly because of activities of its security affiliates that created artificial conditions in the market. In 1933 all of the banks throughout the country were closed for a four-day period, and 4,000 banks closed permanently.

As a result of the bank closings and the already devastated economy, public confidence in the U.S. financial structure was low. In order to restore the banking public's confidence that banks would follow reasonable banking practices, Congress created the Glass-Steagall Act. The act forced a separation of commercial and investment banks by preventing commercial banks from underwriting securities, with the exception of U.S. Treasury and federal agency securities, and municipal and state general-obligation securities. More specifically, the act authorizes Federal Reserve banks to use government obligations and COMMERCIAL PAPER as collateral for their note issues, in order to encourage expansion of the currency. Banks also may offer advisory services regarding investments for their customers, as well as buy and sell securities for their customers. However, information gained from providing such services may not be used by a bank when it acts as a lender. Likewise, investment banks may not engage in the business of receiving deposits.

A group of congressmen look on as President Franklin D. Roosevelt signs the Glass-Steagall Act on June 16, 1933. Senators Carter Glass (light suit) and Henry S. Steagall stand on either side of the president.
BETTMANN/CORBIS.

A bank is defined as an institution organized under the laws of the United States, any state of the United States, the District of Columbia, any territory of the United States, Puerto Rico, Guam, American Samoa, or the Virgin Islands, that both accepts demand deposits (deposits that the depositor may withdraw by check or similar means for payment to third parties or others) and is engaged in the business of making commercial loans (12 U.S.C.A. § 1841 (c)(1) [1988]). Investment banking consists mostly of securities underwriting and related activities; making a market in securities; and setting up corporate mergers, acquisitions, and restructuring. Investment banking also includes services provided by brokers or dealers in transactions in the secondary market. A secondary market is one where securities are bought and sold subsequent to their original issuance.

Despite attempts to reform Glass-Steagall, the legislature has not passed any major changes—although it has passed bills that relax restrictions. Banks may now set up brokerage subsidiaries, and UNDERWRITE a limited number of issues such as asset-backed securities, corporate bonds, and commercial paper.

The Glass-Steagall Act restored public confidence in banking practices during the Great Depression. However, many historians believe that the commercial bank securities practices of the time had little actual effect on the already devastated economy and were not a major contributor to the Depression. Some legislators and bank reformers argued that the act was never necessary, or that it had become outdated and should be repealed.

Congress responded to these criticisms in passing the Gramm-Leach-Bilely Act of 1999, which made significant changes to Glass-Steagall. The 1999 law did not make sweeping changes in the types of business that may be conducted by an individual bank, broker-dealer or insurance company. Instead, the act repealed the Glass-Steagall Act's restrictions on bank and securities-firm affiliations. It also amended the Bank HOLDING COMPANY Act to permit affiliations among financial services companies, including banks, securities firms and insurance companies. The new law sought financial modernization by removing the very barriers that Glass-Steagall had erected.

FURTHER READINGS

Cintron, Ivan. 1995. "Bankers Hope Reform Helps Shatter Glass." *Nashville Business Journal* (September 4).

Class, Edgar. 1995. "The Precarious Position of the Federal Deposit Insurance Corporation after O'Melveny and Myers v. FDIC." *Administrative Law Journal of the American Univ.* (summer).

Eaton, David M. 1995. "The Commercial Banking-related Activities of Investment Banks and Other Nonbanks." *Emory Law Journal* 44 (summer).

Feibelman, Adam. 1996. "The Dukes of Moral Hazard." *Memphis Business Journal* (July 1).

Smoot, James R. 1996. "Financial Institutions Reform in the Wake of Valic." *Creighton Law Review* (February).

Sullivan, Edward D. 1995. "Glass-Steagall Update: Proposals to Modernize the Structure of the Financial Services Industry." *Banking Law Journal* 112 (November–December).

"U.S. Bank Law Overhaul Not Provoking Big Changes—Meyer." 2001. *Reuters Business Report* (February 15).

Woelful, Charles J. 1994. *Encyclopedia of Banking and Finance.* 10th ed. New York: McGraw-Hill.

CROSS REFERENCES

Banks and Banking; Federal Reserve Board; Glass, Carter.

❖ GLASS, CARTER

Carter Glass sponsored important banking laws of the twentieth century, among them the Glass-Steagall Acts of 1932 and 1933 (48 Stat. 162). He wrote and sponsored the legislation that established the Federal Reserve System in 1913. He was also a key player in making amendments to the system during the decades following its establishment. A Virginia Democrat, he served as secretary of the treasury under Woodrow Wilson and was a member of the House of Representatives and the Senate.

Glass was born January 4, 1858, in Lynchburg, Virginia, the youngest of twelve children. His mother, Augusta Christian Glass, died when he was two years old, and Glass was raised by a sister ten years older than he. His father, Robert H. Glass, was the editor of the *Daily Republic.*

Following the Civil War, Glass's father turned down an offer of reappointment to his old position as postmaster general, because he did not want to be on the payroll of the nation he had just fought. Having lived through a financially strapped childhood during the Reconstruction period, Glass would as an adult consistently oppose strong centralized control by the federal government except in emergencies.

Glass left school at age 14 to begin a printer's apprenticeship at his father's paper. He completed his apprenticeship in 1876 when the family moved to Petersburg, Virginia. Glass soon moved back to Lynchburg to work as an auditor for the railroad. In 1880 he became the city editor, and then the editor, of the *Lynchburg News.* With savings and the financial backing of friends, he purchased that newspaper in 1888. The same year he married Aurelia McDearmon Caldwell, a teacher. In the early 1890s Glass bought and consolidated other Lynchburg newspapers.

In 1899 Glass was elected to the Virginia state senate, where he was put on the committee of finance and banking. During his career as a state legislator, he was an active debater on suffrage for African Americans, the subject of the Fourteenth and Fifteenth Amendments to the U.S. Constitution. He supported restricting voting rights for illiterate former slaves on the theory that these votes were used by those in power to maintain their power. He also argued in defense of the EIGHTEENTH AMENDMENT, prohibiting the sale of alcohol. In 1933, however, he voted for its appeal on the grounds that it was futile to maintain a law that could not be enforced.

In 1902 Glass was elected to the U.S. House of Representatives, where he served until 1918. In 1904 he was appointed to the Banking and Currency Committee. He devoted the next several years to studying the topic of banking, and introduced few bills during this period.

The U.S. banking system of the late nineteenth and early twentieth centuries was unstable, leading to a series of banking panics over a 34-year span. By the end of the nineteenth century, banks were largely independent from, and often in competition with, one another. The relatively young U.S. banking system was burdened primarily with a lack of flexibility in lending (or rediscounting) policies and currency availability,

Carter Glass.
AP IMAGES

as well as weak supervision and inadequate check collection systems.

In the first decade of the twentieth century, Glass began crafting a bill to address the need for banking reform. In 1912 WOODROW WILSON was elected PRESIDENT OF THE UNITED STATES. Glass, now chair of the House Banking Committee, enlisted and got Wilson's support for his reform bill.

The Federal Reserve Act, 12 U.S.C.A. § 221 et seq., the most radical banking reform bill in U.S. history, was passed into law December 23, 1913. In presenting his bill to the House, Glass said in his closing remarks, "I have tried to reconcile conflicting views, to compose all friction and technical knowledge of the banker, the wisdom of the philosopher, and the rights of the people."

According to its preamble, Glass's bill was created to "provide for the establishment of

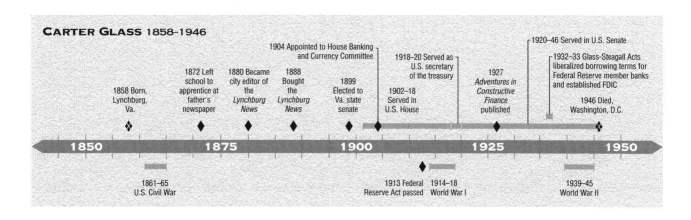

CARTER GLASS 1858–1946

1858 Born, Lynchburg, Va.

1872 Left school to apprentice at father's newspaper

1880 Became city editor of the *Lynchburg News*

1888 Bought the *Lynchburg News*

1899 Elected to Va. state senate

1902–18 Served in U.S. House

1904 Appointed to House Banking and Currency Committee

1918–20 Served as U.S. secretary of the treasury

1927 *Adventures in Constructive Finance* published

1920–46 Served in U.S. Senate

1932–33 Glass-Steagall Acts liberalized borrowing terms for Federal Reserve member banks and established FDIC

1946 Died, Washington, D.C.

1850　1875　1900　1925　1950

1861–65 U.S. Civil War

1913 Federal Reserve Act passed

1914–18 World War I

1939–45 World War II

Federal reserve banks, to furnish an elastic currency, to afford means of rediscounting COMMERCIAL PAPER, to establish a more effective supervision of banking in the United States, and for other purposes." It provided the establishment of up to 12 Federal Reserve banks (district banks) to develop policy with the seven-member FEDERAL RESERVE BOARD in Washington, D.C. (This board's title was later changed to the Federal Reserve Board of Governors.) Glass's plan also required all nationally chartered banks to be members of the Federal Reserve System and weakened the power of private banks. Although the Federal Reserve System would be criticized for failing to stave off the Great Depression in the 1930s, it would be credited with helping control the effects of a 1987 stock plunge.

During the years leading up to WORLD WAR I, Glass headed a committee that investigated the act's effectiveness and made amendments as needed. Three test cases in 1923 and 1926 resulted in various changes in the act, which continues to be altered as circumstances dictate.

Glass was appointed Secretary of the Treasury in late 1918 and worked to develop and promote a new "Victory loan" under Wilson's administration (which was renamed "Fifth Liberty Loan" because the V looked like the Roman numeral for 5) as World War I drew to a close. These loans were bonds that the U.S. government encouraged Americans to buy to help generate revenue for war debts and for rebuilding war-torn Europe. In February 1920, Glass resigned as secretary and accepted a vacant seat in the U.S. Senate.

In early 1920, an election year, sentiments against Wilson grew. A movement took hold to select Glass as the Democratic presidential candidate. But Glass, a strong supporter and close friend of Wilson's throughout his lifetime, did not support the effort. WARREN G. HARDING, a critic of the Federal Reserve Board, was elected president in 1920.

In the late 1920s, conditions began to develop that would lead to a STOCK MARKET crash and the subsequent Great Depression. In fall 1928 Glass wrote an article addressing his concern that the Reserve System was being misused for financial speculation. In early 1929 he gave a speech on the Senate floor warning of financial disaster and urging that action be taken against individuals abusing the system in gambling ventures.

THE MAIN PURPOSE OF THE [GLASS-STEAGALL] BILL . . . WAS TO PREVENT . . . THE USE OF THE FEDERAL RESERVE BANKING FACILITIES FOR STOCK-GAMBLING PURPOSES.
—CARTER GLASS

Glass also began work on amendments to reduce the consequences of the disaster he suspected was coming. This work resulted in the Glass-Steagall Acts of 1932 and 1933, sponsored by Glass and Representative Henry B. Steagall. The Glass-Steagall Acts marked the third time in early U.S. history that a major crisis precipitated banking reform. (The first was the Civil War and the development of the National Banking System; the second was the panic of 1907 and the development of the Federal Reserve Act.)

The act of 1932 liberalized terms under which member banks could borrow from the Federal Reserve System. The act of 1933, also called the Banking Act of 1933, established the FEDERAL DEPOSIT INSURANCE CORPORATION. This institution guaranteed bank depositors' savings, separated commercial banking from investment banking and insurance underwriting, regulated interests on time deposits, and increased the power of the Federal Reserve Board.

Glass served in the Senate until 1946. He died May 28, 1946.

FURTHER READINGS

Brostoff, Steven. 1995. "Bank Bill May Limit Comptroller Power." *National Underwriter Property and Casualty—Risk and Benefits Management* (June 12).

"Insurers Back the Right Man, Still Lost Glass-Steagall Fight." 1996. *Best's Review, Life-Health Insurance Edition* (August).

McConnell, Bill. 1996. "Glass-Steagall Repeal, Wider Powers Depend on Push by Congress' Leaders." *American Banker* (October 22).

———. 1996. "GOP Congressional Victories Seen as Boost for Glass-Steagall Repeal." *American Banker* (November 7).

Palmer, James E., Jr. 2007. *Carter Glass: Unreconstructed Rebel.* Whitefish, MT: Kessinger.

CROSS REFERENCE

Banks and Banking.

GLEANING

Harvesting for free distribution to the needy, or for donation to a nonprofit organization for ultimate distribution to the needy, an agricultural crop that has been donated by the owner.

Gleaning raises legal liability issues, especially with respect to the quality of the food donated and any harmful effects that may come from donated food. A group of statutes known as Good Samaritan laws are meant to encourage the donation of food and groceries to nonprofit charitable agencies by minimizing the number of legal actions against donors and distributors of foods.

Prior to 1990, every state and the District of Columbia had some form of statutory protection from liability for charitable food donation and distribution. These statutes were exceptions to the COMMON LAW or statutory rule of STRICT LIABILITY for distributing food or any other defective product that causes injury. The statutes vary greatly from jurisdiction to jurisdiction. Some provide liability only for gleaners' or donors' GROSS NEGLIGENCE or intentional acts, while others provide liability for mere NEGLIGENCE. Others limit liability if the donor reasonably inspects the donated food at the time the donor makes the donation and has no actual or constructive knowledge of any defective condition.

But the inconsistency of the existing state laws prompted gleaners and donors who volunteer time and resources to help feed hungry people to express concern that their charitable work put themselves at legal risk. In 1996 Congress passed federal legislation providing uniform protection to gleaners, citizens, businesses, and nonprofit organizations that act in GOOD FAITH to donate, recover, and distribute excess food.

The Bill Emerson Good Samaritan Food Donation Act (the Act), P.L. 104-210 (October 1, 1996), was named in honor of the late congressman who supported efforts to expand food donations to the poor and to protect those who make donations. It converted the Model Good Samaritan Food Donation Act to permanent law and incorporated it into section 22 of the Child Nutrition Act of 1966 (P.L. 89-642, October 11, 1966). The Child Nutrition Act of 1966 was an anti-hunger initiative begun during the President LYNDON B. JOHNSON administration as part of its "War on Poverty" and has been amended numerous times.

Congress passed the act in late September 1996 and President BILL CLINTON signed the bill into law on October 1, 1996. The act encourages citizens to donate food and grocery products to nonprofit organizations such as homeless shelters, soup kitchens, and churches for distribution to needy individuals.

The act promotes food recovery by limiting donors' liability to cases of gross negligence or intentional misconduct. In the absence of gross negligence or intentional misconduct, donors, gleaners, and nonprofit organizations are not subject to civil or criminal liability arising from the nature, age, packaging, or condition of food that is apparently wholesome. It also establishes basic nationwide uniform definitions pertaining to donation and distribution of nutritious foods and helps to assure that donated foods meet quality and labeling standards of federal, state, and local laws and regulations.

The 1996 law encourages and protects gleaning by excluding from civil or criminal liability a person or nonprofit food organization that, in good faith, donates or distributes donated foods for food relief. The law does not supersede state or local health regulations and its protections do not apply to an injury or death due to gross neglect or intentional misconduct.

As a federal law, the act takes precedence over individual states' Good Samaritan laws, but it may not entirely replace such statutes. The act creates a uniform minimum level of protection from liability for donors and gleaners. But state Good Samaritan laws may still provide protection for donors and gleaners above and beyond that guaranteed in the federal statute.

FURTHER READINGS

Feeding America Web site. Available online at http://www. feedingamerica.org (accessed July 27, 2009).

USDA Gleaning and Food Recovery. "A Citizen's Guide to Food Recovery." Available online at http://www.usda. gov/news/pubs/gleaning/content.htm; website home page: http://www.usda.gov (accessed July 27, 2009).

U.S. Department of Agriculture. 2009. "The Emerson Good Samaritan Food Donation Act." Available online at http://www.usda.gov/news/pubs/gleaning/ seven.htm; http://www.usda.gov/news (accessed September 4, 2009).

CROSS REFERENCES

Good Samaritan Doctrine; Liability.

GLOSS

An annotation, explanation, or commentary on a particular passage in a book or document, which is ordinarily placed on the same page or in the margin to elucidate or amplify the passage.

GOING CONCERN VALUE

The value inherent in an active, established company as opposed to a firm that is not yet established.

The value of the assets of a business considered as an operating whole.

As a component of business value, going concern value recognizes the many advantages that an existing business has over a new business, such as avoidance of start-up costs and improved operating efficiency. In this sense, the going concern value of a firm represents the difference between the value of an established firm and the value of a start-up firm.

Going concern value also indicates the value of a firm as an operating, active whole, rather than merely as distinct items of property. U.S. BANKRUPTCY law, for example, has recognized the need to preserve going concern value when reorganizing businesses in order to maximize recoveries by creditors and shareholders (11 U.S.C.A. § 1101 et seq.). Bankruptcy laws seek to preserve going concern value whenever possible by promoting the reorganization, as opposed to the liquidation, of businesses.

Going concern value also implies a firm's ability to generate income without interruption, even when ownership has changed (*Butler v. Butler*, 541 Pa. 364, 663 A.2d 148 [Pa. 1995]).

Going concern value is distinguished from the concept of GOOD WILL, which refers to the excess value of a business that arises from the favorable disposition of its customers. Good will may include the value of such business elements as trade names, trade brands, and established location.

FURTHER READINGS

Bernstein, Donald S., and Nancy L. Sanborn. 1993. *The Going Concern in Chapter 11.* New York: Practising Law Institute.

Oswald, Lynda J. 1991. "Goodwill and Going-concern Value: Emerging Factors in the Just Compensation Equation." *Boston College Law Review* 32 (March).

Venuti, Elizabeth K. 2004. "The Going-Concern Assumption Revisited." *The CPA Journal* 40. Available online at http://www.nysscpa.org/cpajournal/2004/504/essentials/p40.htm; website home page: http://www.nysscpa.org (accessed September 4, 2009).

GOING PUBLIC

Altering the organization of a corporation from ownership and control by a small group of people, as in a close corporation, to ownership by the general public, as in a publicly held corporation.

When a corporation goes public, it opens up the sale of shares of its stock to the public at large.

❖ GOLDBERG, ARTHUR JOSEPH

Arthur Joseph Goldberg served as a justice of the U.S. Supreme Court from 1962 to 1965. A distinguished LABOR LAW attorney, Goldberg also served as secretary of labor in the administration of President JOHN F. KENNEDY from 1961 until his judicial appointment and as ambassador to the UNITED NATIONS from 1965 to 1968 during the administration of President LYNDON B. JOHNSON. Johnson persuaded a reluctant Goldberg to resign from the Supreme Court to accept the U.N. assignment.

Goldberg was born August 8, 1908, in Chicago, to Russian immigrants. He graduated from Northwestern University Law School in 1929 and entered the field of labor law in Chicago. Goldberg gained national attention in 1939 as counsel to the Chicago Newspaper Guild during a strike. He served in the Office of Strategic Services during WORLD WAR II and then returned to his labor practice in 1944.

In 1948 he became general counsel for the United Steelworkers of America, a position he held until 1961. The steelworkers union was an important union during a time when U.S. heavy industry was thriving. Strikes or the threat of strikes in the steel industry had national repercussions. Goldberg proved adept in his role as general counsel, skillfully negotiating strike settlements, consolidating gains through COLLECTIVE BARGAINING, and helping with public relations.

From 1948 to 1955 Goldberg also was general counsel for the Congress of Industrial Organizations (CIO), which contained most nontrade unions, such as those controlling manufacturing and mining jobs. The CIO had been created when the TRADE UNION members of the American Federation of Labor (AFL) showed no interest in organizing these industries. There was a great deal of friction between the CIO and the AFL, yet the leadership of both organizations realized that a unified labor movement was a necessity. Goldberg was a principal architect of the 1955 merger of the CIO and AFL into the AFL-CIO. He then served as a special counsel to the AFL-CIO's INDUSTRIAL UNION department from 1955 to 1961.

In 1961 President Kennedy appointed Goldberg secretary of labor. During the less than two years that Goldberg held this office, he saw congressional approval of an increase in the MINIMUM WAGE, and the reorganization of the Office of Manpower Administration (now the Employment and Training Administration). When Justice FELIX FRANKFURTER retired from the Supreme Court in 1962, Kennedy appointed

Goldberg to the "Jewish seat." The so-called Jewish seat began with the 1939 appointment of Felix Frankfurter, who was Jewish, to succeed Justice BENJAMIN CARDOZO, also Jewish. It was assumed that for political reasons, Democratic presidents would appoint a Jewish person to that vacancy. This tradition ended with the appointment of ABE FORTAS.

The appointment of the liberal Goldberg, replacing the conservative Frankfurter, turned a four-justice liberal minority on the Court into a five-justice liberal majority, which was led by Chief Justice EARL WARREN. Goldberg became known as an innovative judicial thinker who moved the Court toward liberal activism. He usually joined the majority of WARREN COURT justices in extending the Court's rulings into areas previously considered the realm of the states and of Congress. He was also an able negotiator within the Court, helping to smooth the way in reaching difficult and controversial decisions.

Goldberg was a firm supporter of CIVIL RIGHTS and civil liberties. His best-known opinion came in the areas of CRIMINAL LAW and CRIMINAL PROCEDURE, when he wrote the majority opinion in ESCOBEDO V. ILLINOIS, 378 U.S. 478, 84 S. Ct. 1758, 12 L. Ed. 2d 977 (1964). In this case the Court struck down a MURDER conviction because the DEFENDANT had been denied the right to confer with his lawyer after his arrest. This decision was a major step toward the landmark decision in MIRANDA V. ARIZONA, 384 U.S. 436, 86 S. Ct. 1602, 16 L. Ed. 2d 694 (1966), which gave suspects the right to be advised of their constitutional rights to remain silent, to have a lawyer appointed, and to have a lawyer present during interrogation.

Arthur Goldberg.
LIBRARY OF CONGRESS

Goldberg believed in the constitutional right of due process. In a dissenting opinion in *United States v. Barnett,* 376 U.S. 681, 84 S. Ct. 984, 12 L. Ed. 2d 23 (1964), he argued that federal judges should not be allowed to use their contempt power to send persons to jail. When punishment for contempt of court could be meted out, the person held in contempt should be entitled to a jury trial. Although he did not prevail in *Barnett,* his dissent drew attention to the abuses of this practice and helped reduce it.

In 1965 Goldberg appeared to have a promising judicial career. Yet he became one

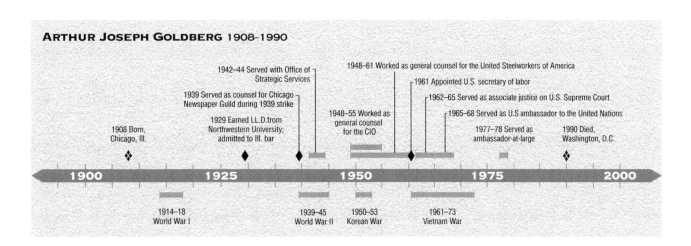

ARTHUR JOSEPH GOLDBERG 1908–1990

1942–44 Served with Office of Strategic Services

1939 Served as counsel for Chicago Newspaper Guild during 1939 strike

1929 Earned LL.D. from Northwestern University; admitted to Ill. bar

1908 Born, Chicago, Ill.

1948–55 Worked as general counsel for the CIO

1948–61 Worked as general counsel for the United Steelworkers of America

1961 Appointed U.S. secretary of labor

1962–65 Served as associate justice on U.S. Supreme Court

1965–68 Served as U.S ambassador to the United Nations

1977–78 Served as ambassador-at-large

1990 Died, Washington, D.C.

1900   1925   1950   1975   2000

1914–18 World War I

1939–45 World War II

1950–53 Korean War

1961–73 Vietnam War

of the few justices to give up his lifetime appointment to the Supreme Court for a reason other than retirement. In the summer of 1965, President Johnson asked Goldberg to resign from the Court and accept the U.S. ambassadorship to the United Nations, promising a larger role in foreign policy than was traditionally given to the U.N. delegate. Goldberg did so reluctantly and regretfully. When Johnson appointed his friend and political confidant Abe Fortas to replace Goldberg, many believed this had been the primary motive in offering Goldberg the U.N. post.

Goldberg's major achievement as U.N. ambassador was his aid in drafting Security Council RESOLUTION No. 242 (22 SCOR 8–9, U.N. Doc. S/INF/Rev. 2), passed in November 1967, concerning peace measures in the Middle East. Goldberg tried continually and unsuccessfully to make the United Nations play a role in a peace process that would end the VIETNAM WAR. His efforts were met with disfavor by Johnson and by Johnson's advisers. Frustrated and disappointed by the failure of these efforts and the escalation of the war, Goldberg resigned his U.N. position in 1968.

After his resignation Goldberg joined a New York City law firm and also served in 1968 and 1969 as president of the American Jewish Committee, a national HUMAN RIGHTS organization. He ran for governor of New York in 1970 as the Liberal-Democrat candidate, but incumbent Nelson A. Rockefeller soundly defeated him. He then returned to Washington, D.C., where he resumed a PRIVATE LAW practice.

In 1977 and 1978, Goldberg was a U.S. ambassador-at-large in the administration of President JIMMY CARTER. Following this assignment, he became deeply involved in the international human rights movement, a cause he pursued until his death.

Goldberg wrote several books, including *AFL-CIO Labor United* (1956), *Defense of Freedom* (1966), and *Equal Justice: The Warren Era of the Supreme Court* (1972). He died January 19, 1990, in Washington, D.C.

FURTHER READINGS

Cushman, Clare. 2001. *The Supreme Court Justices.* Washington, D.C.: Supreme Court Historical Society.

Moynihan, Daniel Patrick, ed. 1966. *The Defenses of Freedom: The Public Papers of Arthur J. Goldberg.* New York: Harper & Row.

Stebenne, David L. 1996. *Arthur J. Goldberg: New Deal Liberal.* New York: Oxford Univ. Press.

GOLDEN PARACHUTE

An agreement that provides key executives with generous severance pay and other benefits in the event that their employment is terminated as a result of a change of ownership at their employer corporation; known more formally as a change-of-control agreement.

Golden parachutes are provided by a firm's BOARD OF DIRECTORS and, depending on the laws of the state in which the company is incorporated, may require shareholder approval. These agreements compensate executives in the event that they lose their job or quit because they have suffered a reduction in power or status following a change of ownership of their employer corporation. Some golden parachutes are triggered even if the control of the corporation does not change completely; such parachutes open after a certain percentage of the corporation's stock is acquired.

Golden parachutes have been justified on three grounds. First, they may enable corporations that are prime takeover targets to hire and retain high-quality executives who otherwise would be reluctant to work for them. Second, because the parachutes add to the cost of acquiring a corporation, they may discourage takeover bids. Finally, if a takeover bid does occur, executives with a golden parachute are more likely to respond in a manner that will benefit the shareholders. Without a golden parachute, executives might resist a takeover that would be in the interests of the shareholders, in order to save their own job.

As golden parachutes have grown increasingly lucrative, they have come under criticism from shareholders who argue that they are a waste of corporate assets. These shareholders point out that managers already have a fiduciary duty to act in the best interests of their shareholders and should not require golden parachutes as an incentive. Especially suspect are large parachutes that are awarded once a takeover bid has been announced. Critics charge that these last-minute parachutes are little more than going-away presents for the executives and may encourage them to work for the takeover at the expense of the shareholders.

As the practice of offering golden parachutes became more and more common in the 1980s, efforts to place restrictions on the agreements increased. Many of these efforts stemmed from the realization that the practice, which had once showed positive stock returns for shareholders, was now producing negative stock returns.

On February 6, 1996, the FEDERAL DEPOSIT INSURANCE CORPORATION (FDIC) issued a final rule that restricted troubled banks, thrifts, and holding companies from making golden parachute payments. Exceptions to the rule are allowed for individuals who have qualified for pension and retirement plans. Other exceptions permit the FDIC to enforce the spirit of the law by allowing legitimate payments but stopping payments that might be considered abusive or improper. The rule also prevents FDIC-insured institutions from paying the legal expenses of employees who are the subject of related enforcement proceedings. The rule went into effect on April 1, 1996.

Congress likewise restricted the use of golden parachutes in the Emergency Economic Stabilization Act of 2008, the rescue plan for the U.S. economy. The Act allows financial institutions to sell their troubled assets to the federal government either through a direct purchase or at an auction. If the federal government purchases troubled assets from an institution by direct purchase and receives a meaningful equity or debt position in the company, no golden parachutes are permitted for senior executives. This ban on golden parachutes expires when the government no longer holds an equity or debt position in the company. The result is different, however, if the federal government buys more than $300 million in troubled assets through an auction or bidding process. In that scenario, the Act prohibits the institution from entering into any new golden parachute agreements, but it allows golden parachute agreements in place prior to the acquisition of assets to remain in effect. A senior executive receiving such golden parachute payments faces profound tax ramifications as a result, including an excise tax and loss of a tax deduction.

The restrictions on golden parachutes were included in the Emergency Economic Stabilization Act to face public outrage at the notion that institutions benefiting from taxpayer funds would terminate executives and allow them to depart with excessive golden parachutes. These concerns arose amidst news coverage suggesting that at least six major financial institutions participating in the bailout program had plans to pay their top executives billions of dollars.

FURTHER READINGS

Emergency Economic Stabilization Act of 2008. Available online at www.gpo.gov (accessed May 19, 2009).

Mogavero, Damian J., and Michael F. Toyne. 1995. "The Impact of Golden Parachutes on Fortune 500 Stock Returns: A Reexamination of the Evidence." *Quarterly Journal of Business and Economics* 34: 4.

"New Powers: FDIC Cuts Down Golden Parachutes." 1995. *The Banking Attorney.* 5: 12.

Reid, Pelosi Call on Paulson to Strengthen Golden Parachute Restrictions on Financial Institutions Receiving Taxpayer Funds. Available online at democrats.senate.gov (accessed May 19, 2009).

Hulbert, Mark. 2007. "Why Backdated Options Might Be Contagious." *New York Times* (Jan. 21).

Rosen, Kenneth M. 2008. "'Who Killed Katie Couric?' and Other Tales from the World of Executive Compensation Reform." *Fordham Law Review* 76 (May).

Scannell, Kara and Joann S. Lublin. 2008. "SEC Unhappy with Answer on Executive Pay." *Wall Street Journal* (Jan. 21) B1.

❖ GOLDMAN, EMMA

EMMA GOLDMAN was a crusader for ANARCHISM, feminism, and the labor movement. She was also an essayist and is best known as the first editor of *Mother Earth,* a magazine providing a forum for feminist and anarchist writers.

Goldman was born June 27, 1869, in Kaunas, Lithuania, a province of the Russian Empire, during the early stages of revolt against czarism and the rise in popularity of COMMUNISM. The seeds of the Bolshevik revolt were already being sown in the towns and villages throughout the country where discontent with czarist rule was strongest. Goldman, who described herself as a born rebel, came into the world as the third daughter of Abraham Goldman and Taube Goldman. Her parents' marriage, like many Jewish Orthodox unions of the time, had been arranged.

Goldman suffered the fate of being a female in a culture that valued males. When she was young, her father made no effort to disguise his disappointment at having still another daughter instead of the much-prized son he hoped for. He has been described as hot tempered and impatient, particularly with Goldman's rebelliousness, which she showed at an early age. He was a traditional Jewish father, and he planned to arrange a marriage for his daughter when she was 15. Goldman, however, had different ideas: She longed for an education and hoped

Emma Goldman.
LIBRARY OF CONGRESS

half hours daily at a salary of $2.50 per week. She lived in a crowded apartment with her two sisters and her brother-in-law. Their working and living conditions, as well as those of others even more destitute, sparked her interest in anarchism and the labor movement, which was in its infancy. She joined radical groups agitating for an eight-hour workday and other improvements in factory conditions.

Goldman was intensely interested in the Haymarket Square incident in Chicago in 1886. A labor rally called by a small group of anarchists was interrupted by a bomb explosion and gunfire. When it was over, seven police officers and four spectators were dead and 100 were injured. Eight anarchists were tried and convicted of inciting a riot. Four of the convicted were hanged, one committed suicide in prison, and the other three served prison sentences. Spurred by her outrage at this alleged injustice, Goldman began attending anarchist meetings and reading the militant anarchist newspaper *Die Freiheit* (Freedom). She felt herself irresistibly drawn to the movement, and in the summer of 1889, at the age of 20, she moved to New York City to be near the center of anarchist activity.

After arriving in New York, Goldman befriended Johann J. Most, a well-known anarchist and publisher of *Die Freiheit*. She also met Alexander Berkman, who became her lover and with whom she remained close throughout her life. By this time, she was known as Red Emma, and she was followed by detectives wherever she went. She wrote, traveled, and lectured to promote anarchism and the labor movement. In 1893 she was briefly jailed for

someday to marry someone she loved. Goldman described her mother as cold and distant, but also strong and assertive, and she may have served as a role model for Goldman's own forthright manner.

After spending her childhood in Kaunas, Königsberg, and St. Petersburg, Goldman emigrated to the United States in 1885 with a sister. They joined another sister who had settled in Rochester, New York, where Goldman found work in a coat factory, sewing ten-and-a-

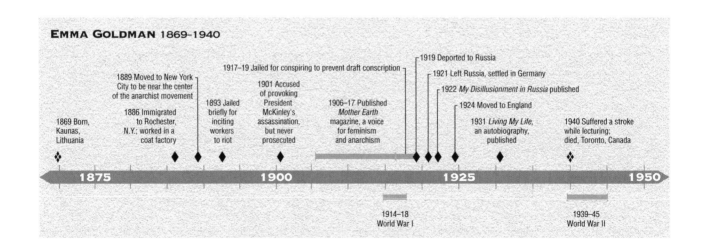

EMMA GOLDMAN 1869–1940

1869 Born, Kaunas, Lithuania

1886 Immigrated to Rochester, N.Y.; worked in a coat factory

1889 Moved to New York City to be near the center of the anarchist movement

1893 Jailed briefly for inciting workers to riot

1901 Accused of provoking President McKinley's assassination, but never prosecuted

1906–17 Published *Mother Earth* magazine, a voice for feminism and anarchism

1917–19 Jailed for conspiring to prevent draft conscription

1919 Deported to Russia

1921 Left Russia, settled in Germany

1922 *My Disillusionment in Russia* published

1924 Moved to England

1931 *Living My Life*, an autobiography, published

1940 Suffered a stroke while lecturing; died, Toronto, Canada

1875   1900   1925   1950

1914–18 World War I

1939–45 World War II

inciting workers to riot. After her release from jail, she traveled to Vienna to train as a nurse and midwife. She then returned to New York and resumed her lecturing. In 1901 she was accused of provoking the ASSASSINATION of President WILLIAM MCKINLEY, because the assassin had attended one of her lectures. No charges were ever brought against her, but newspapers throughout the United States portrayed her as an evil traitor because of her controversial ideas.

In 1906 Goldman published the first issue of a magazine that was to serve as a platform for feminist and anarchist ideas. She called her venture *Mother Earth,* and within six months, it became a leading voice for feminism and anarchism. With Berkman, Goldman published the magazine until 1917, while she continued to travel, write, and lecture. During this time she carried on an eight-year relationship with Ben Reitman, Chicago's King of the Hobos, a well-known anarchist and labor activist who became her manager. Goldman had long since given up her idealistic notions about marriage. She had been married twice to the same man, both times with disastrous results, and had carried on a number of love affairs. Goldman preferred the impermanence and freedom of short-term affairs and wrote in more than one essay that marriage was women's greatest enemy because it robbed them of their independence.

The entry of the United States into WORLD WAR I in 1917 precipitated a wave of hostility toward leftists, pacifists, anarchists, and foreigners. Legislation such as the Selective Service Act, the ESPIONAGE Act, and the SEDITION Act were passed during 1917 and 1918 in order to suppress opposition to the war or the draft and to restrict certain civil liberties. Heedless of the repressive mood of the country, Goldman and Berkman, along with Leonard D. Abbott and Eleanor Fitzgerald, organized the No-Conscription League to oppose "all wars by capitalist governments." In the June 1917 issue of *Mother Earth,* they declared, "We will resist conscription by every means in our power, and we will sustain those who ... refuse to be conscripted." As a result of their antiwar activities, Goldman and Berkman were arrested and charged with conspiring to prevent draft registration. They were tried and convicted and each received the maximum sentence of two years in prison and $10,000 in fines. In December 1919, in the wake of a RED SCARE that led to the arrest and DEPORTATION of hundreds of leftists, anarchists, and labor organizers, Goldman and Berkman were deported to Russia.

Goldman was optimistic about resuming life in Russia now that the czar had been toppled by the Bolsheviks, but her hopes quickly dissipated as the realities of the new government became apparent. In her opinion, "the old cruel regime ... had simply been replaced by a new, equally cruel one." She and Berkman left Russia in 1921 and eventually went to Germany. During their years in Germany, Goldman lectured and wrote a book, *My Disillusionment in Russia* (1923), detailing her disillusionment with Bolshevik rule.

In 1924 Goldman moved to England, but she longed to return to the United States. Accepting an offer of marriage to James Colton, a staunch Scottish anarchist she had known for many years, provided her with an opportunity for British citizenship and the possibility of obtaining a British passport. She hoped to make her way to Canada and somehow gain entry into the United States. During the 1920s and 1930s, she traveled through Europe, writing and lecturing, and in 1931 she published her autobiography, *Living My Life.*

Goldman's wish to return to the United States was granted for a brief 90-day lecture tour in 1934, after which she returned to Europe. In 1940, while on a trip to Canada to enlist support for the anti-Franco forces in Spain, Goldman suffered a stroke. She died several months later, on May 14, 1940, in Toronto. Her body was allowed to be returned to the United States for burial in Chicago near the graves of other anarchists she admired.

FURTHER READINGS

The Emma Goldman Papers. Berkeley Digital Library. Available online at http://www.sunsite3.berkeley.edu/Goldman; website home page: http://www.sunsite3.berkeley.edu (accessed July 27, 2009).

Falk, Candace, et al., ed. 2003. *Emma Goldman: A Documentary History of the American Years.* Berkeley: Univ. of California Press.

Forster, Margaret. 1986. *Significant Sisters: The Grassroots of Active Feminism 1839–1939.* New York: Penguin Putnam.

Goldman, Emma. 2006. *Living My Life.* New York: Penguin.

Wexler, Alice. 1984. *Emma Goldman: An Intimate Life.* New York: Pantheon.

CROSS REFERENCE

Haymarket Riot.

ALL WARS ARE WARS AMONG THIEVES WHO ARE TOO COWARDLY TO FIGHT AND WHO THEREFORE INDUCE THE YOUNG MANHOOD OF THE WHOLE WORLD TO DO THE FIGHTING FOR THEM.
—EMMA GOLDMAN

◊ GOLDWATER, BARRY MORRIS

Barry Morris Goldwater was a former U.S. senator and presidential nominee. During almost 40 years in public life, he became the outspoken and controversial leader of the conservative wing of the REPUBLICAN PARTY.

Goldwater was born January 1, 1909, in Phoenix, Arizona. His paternal ancestors were Orthodox Jewish innkeepers who emigrated from Poland in the mid-1800s to join the California gold rush. Goldwater's father, Baron Goldwater, managed the family's general store in Phoenix. This store was the humble beginning of what would become an enormously profitable chain, Goldwater's Department Stores. Goldwater's mother, Josephine Williams, was a nurse who raised Goldwater and his siblings in her Episcopalian faith. A woman who loved outdoor activities, she took her children hiking and camping throughout Arizona and taught them the colorful history of the region. From her Goldwater acquired an abiding love of the Southwest and a deep appreciation of its people and its beauty.

Goldwater was a mediocre student who preferred sports and socializing to studying. At Phoenix Union High School, he was elected president of his first-year class, but the principal advised his father that Goldwater should probably attend school elsewhere the following year. Against his strenuous objections, his parents sent him to Staunton Military Academy in Virginia. There he excelled at athletics and did better academically than anyone expected, being named best all-around cadet in 1928.

Goldwater loved the military and dreamed of attending West Point. But when he graduated from Staunton, his father was in ill health, and Goldwater instead enrolled at the University of Arizona, at Tucson, to be near his home.

His father died before he had finished his first year in college. Goldwater left school a year later to enter the family business.

With his father gone, Goldwater turned to an uncle for advice and direction. He quickly worked his way up from junior clerk, to general manager in 1936, and to president in 1937. Under his leadership, Goldwater's became Phoenix's premier department store and leading specialty shop. Goldwater pioneered the five-day workweek and instituted many progressive fringe benefits for his employees, including health and life insurance, profit sharing, and use by employees of a vacation ranch. Also, Goldwater's was the first Phoenix store to hire African Americans as salesclerks.

Goldwater entered politics in 1949 when he was elected to the Phoenix City Council as a reform candidate. He was surprised to find that he loved politics. In 1950 he managed Howard Pyle's successful campaign for governor of Arizona. In 1952 he was elected to the U.S. Senate on the strength of voter dissatisfaction with Democratic president HARRY TRUMAN and the KOREAN WAR. Elected as a Republican, Goldwater described himself as "not a me-too Republican" but one "opposed to the superstate and to gigantic, bureaucratic, centralized authority." He quickly developed a reputation for "outspoken unreliability" because even his Republican colleagues could not predict what he might say.

A maverick who spoke his mind regardless of consequences, Goldwater was the personification of the Western ideal of rugged individualism. He opposed any intrusion by the federal government in what he considered to be the state's domain. While in the Senate, he consistently opposed federal spending for social programs, argued that contributions to SOCIAL

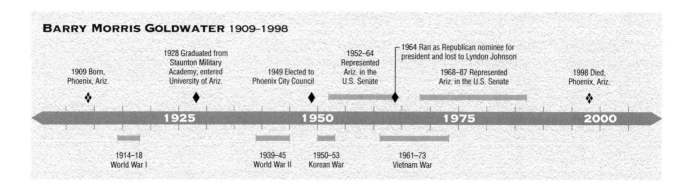

BARRY MORRIS GOLDWATER 1909–1998

1909 Born, Phoenix, Ariz.

1928 Graduated from Staunton Military Academy; entered University of Ariz.

1949 Elected to Phoenix City Council

1952–64 Represented Ariz. in the U.S. Senate

1964 Ran as Republican nominee for president and lost to Lyndon Johnson

1968–87 Represented Ariz. in the U.S. Senate

1998 Died, Phoenix, Ariz.

1925   1950   1975   2000

1914–18 World War I

1939–45 World War II

1950–53 Korean War

1961–73 Vietnam War

SECURITY should be voluntary, and contended that medical programs for poor and elderly people would lead to socialized medicine. "I do not undertake to promote welfare, for I propose to extend freedom," he said. Throughout his career, Goldwater sought to reduce the role of government in citizens' lives by eliminating unnecessary laws and social programs.

One of Goldwater's most controversial actions in the Senate was his staunch defense of Senator JOSEPH R. MCCARTHY, a notorious Communist hunter whose committee, through innuendo and guilt by association, ruined the lives and careers of many U.S. citizens by labeling them Communists or Communist sympathizers. Goldwater was criticized for trying to forestall a Senate vote on censuring McCarthy and then voting against the CENSURE.

In 1958 Goldwater was easily reelected to the Senate despite a concerted campaign to defeat him by organized labor, a group he distrusted and criticized. By that time he had established himself as the outspoken leader of conservative Republicans. His statements were frequently off-the-cuff, sometimes contradictory, and always quotable. He has been credited with saying that Walter P. Reuther, a labor movement leader, was a bigger threat than the Communists; that Supreme Court chief justice EARL WARREN, noted for his liberal opinions, was a socialist; and that Cuban premier Fidel Castro was just another Communist who needed a shave. He was notoriously disdainful of what he called the Eastern establishment, who, according to him, were elitist and out of touch with the rest of the United States. He supported a strong military, and opposed efforts to lower defense spending and increase social spending. His detractors scoffed at him, but his followers were fiercely devoted, perhaps because his nonintellectual, candid style reflected their own values.

While in the Senate, Goldwater befriended JOHN F. KENNEDY, and, though they disagreed vehemently, they remained close friends until Kennedy's death. Goldwater had hoped to run against Kennedy in 1964; the two had discussed the possibility of traveling the country together on an old-fashioned debating tour. When Kennedy was assassinated, Goldwater lost his desire to run. He felt he could not beat LYNDON B. JOHNSON. Nonetheless, supporters persuaded him to run.

Barry Goldwater.
LIBRARY OF CONGRESS

At the 1964 Republican convention in San Francisco, Goldwater was unanimously nominated after an intense floor fight. In his acceptance speech, he uttered the words that would haunt him during the coming campaign and paint him, perhaps unfairly, as a one-dimensional warmonger. "I would remind you," he said, "that extremism in the defense of liberty is no vice. And let me remind you also that moderation in the pursuit of justice is no virtue." Johnson and the Democrats blasted Goldwater as a trigger-happy extremist who was willing to drop bombs whenever and wherever necessary to defend the interests of the United States.

Capitalizing on the country's growing unease with the war in Vietnam, the Johnson campaign developed a television commercial that many feel ushered in a new era of negative campaign advertising. The commercial showed a young girl standing in a field plucking petals from a daisy. A background voice recited an ominous countdown. Finally, the child evaporated in a mushroom cloud, and viewers were urged to vote for Johnson because, "The stakes are too high for you to stay home." Goldwater acknowledged later that the Johnson campaign effectively exploited the public's fear of his militancy. "In fact," he said with sardonic wit, "if I hadn't known Goldwater, I'd have voted against the s.o.b. myself."

Goldwater was defeated by Johnson in a landslide, carrying only Arizona and five southern states. He was unapologetic about his "extremism" speech, saying, "Protecting freedom is what this country has been about. We'll go to any extent to protect it. I know people were thinking 'nuclear' when I said [extremism,] but … I think it had to be said, and I never lost any sleep over it." The final irony, of course, is that Johnson escalated the war in Vietnam, and it dragged on until 1973. According to Goldwater, Johnson's Vietnam policy cost the country far more money and lives than if Goldwater, the supposed warmonger, had been elected.

After his loss to Johnson, Goldwater returned to Arizona and private life. Although his defeat was stunning, and he was treated like a pariah by other Republicans, he was undaunted. "Politics has never been the making or breaking point of my life," he said. "I worked hard to make Arizona a better state and my country a better country. If I failed, I've taken the criticism." He returned to politics in 1968 when he easily won the Senate seat vacated by retiring Democrat Carl Hayden. As an older and somewhat more moderate statesman, he relished his positions as chair of the ARMED SERVICES Committee, the Intelligence Committee, the Communications Subcommittee, and the Indian Affairs Committee. He continued to work against big government and in favor of a free market economy. Summing up his opposition to federal control, he said, "All the great civilizations fell when people lost their initiative because government moved in to do things for them."

Goldwater served in the Senate for almost 20 additional years and left with his reputation and his convictions intact. "I was luckier than hell—politics is mostly luck—and I made a lot of friends," he said. "It would be hard for me to name an enemy in Congress. People disagreed with me violently, but we remained very good friends." In addition to a loyal conservative following, Goldwater's friends included liberal Democrats Morris Udall, Daniel Inouye, EDWARD M. KENNEDY, Walter F. Mondale, and HUBERT H. HUMPHREY. One conservative Goldwater removed from his list of friends was RICHARD M. NIXON. Unable to accept Nixon's failings or forgive his deceptions during the WATERGATE crisis, Goldwater called the scandal "one of the saddest

> A GOVERNMENT THAT IS BIG ENOUGH TO GIVE YOU ALL YOU WANT IS BIG ENOUGH TO TAKE IT ALL AWAY.
> —BARRY GOLDWATER

moments of my life. For 20 years or so, he and I worked hand in glove all over this land—not to help Nixon, not to help Goldwater, but to help the Republican Party and our country. But I was slow to see the real Nixon."

Goldwater retired from the Senate when his term ended in 1987 and returned to his home in Paradise Valley, Arizona, overlooking Phoenix. He remained active, although slowed somewhat by arthritis. In the 1990s he took up an unlikely new cause: gay rights. "The big thing is to make this country … quit discriminating against people just because they're gay," he asserted. "You don't have to agree with it, but they have a constitutional right to be gay. And that's what brings me into it." Always a strict constructionist when it came to the Constitution, Goldwater felt that his defense of gay rights was consistent with his lifelong devotion to individual freedom. Then governor of Oregon Barbara Roberts said that because people do not expect someone like Goldwater to speak up for gay rights, they look at the issue in a new light when he does. "He causes people to focus on the real issue," she said. "Should the country that celebrates life, liberty and the pursuit of happiness allow DISCRIMINATION for a group of Americans based on sexual preference?" Goldwater's position on gay rights put the former conservative standard-bearer squarely in conflict with religious conservatives who opposed any effort to outlaw discrimination against homosexuals.

Goldwater died at the age of 89 on May 29, 1998. He was a member of many organizations, including the Royal Photographic Society, the American Association of Indian Affairs, and the VETERANS OF FOREIGN WARS. He was honorary cochairman of Americans against Discrimination, a lobbying effort aimed at securing gay rights. He and his second wife, Susan Goldwater, lived in Paradise Valley, Arizona, at the time of his death.

FURTHER READINGS

Goldwater, Barry M. 1979. *With No Apologies.* New York: Morrow.

Goldwater, Barry M., with Jack Casserly. 1988. *Goldwater.* New York: Doubleday.

Perlstein, Rick. 2009. *Before the Storm: Barry Goldwater and the Unmaking of the American Consensus.* Washington, D.C.: Nation.

CROSS REFERENCE

Gay and Lesbian Rights.

❖ GOMPERS, SAMUEL

Samuel Gompers, a founding member and longtime president of the American Federation of Labor (AFL), was instrumental in broadening the goals of the labor movement in the United States. He used his gifts as an organizer and speaker to consolidate numerous unions into one umbrella organization that lobbied successfully for improved working conditions for all tradesmen.

The son of Dutch immigrants, Gompers was born in London on January 26, 1850. He attended school briefly but began working at age 10. Initially apprenticed to a shoemaker, he chose instead to become a cigarmaker like his father. The family moved to New York in 1863, and within a year Gompers had joined the Cigar Makers' National Union.

At around this time many trades were beginning to form unions, but their power was limited because as small, individual groups they had little clout. By the 1880s, leaders of the various unions decided that by uniting in common cause they would make for a stronger political force. Late in 1881, several unions joined together to form the Federation of Organized Trades and Labor Unions (FOTLU). Gompers, who had proven himself an able leader in the cigarmakers' union, was elected an officer of FOTLU.

FOTLU was a first step for organizing unions but it was too loosely connected to have any real influence. In 1886 FOTLU was restructured into the American Federation of Labor (AFL), and Gompers was elected president. Except for a one-year hiatus in 1895, Gompers remained AFL president for the rest of his life.

Samuel Gompers.
LIBRARY OF CONGRESS

As AFL president, Gompers steered the organization toward practical goals. He was interested in securing living wages for union members, an eight-hour work day, comprehensive CHILD LABOR LAWS, equal pay for women and men, and compulsory school attendance for children. To that end, he lobbied tirelessly for these and other improvements for working men and women.

Gompers steered clear of political issues (although in 1899 the AFL did endorse women's suffrage). Many left-wing labor leaders thought that Gompers was too timid and ineffective, too tied to the mainstream. Anarchist EMMA

I WONDER WHETHER ANY OF US CAN IMAGINE WHAT WOULD BE THE ACTUAL CONDITION OF THE WORKING PEOPLE OF OUR COUNTRY TODAY WITHOUT THEIR ORGANIZATIONS TO PROTECT THEM.
—SAMUEL GOMPERS

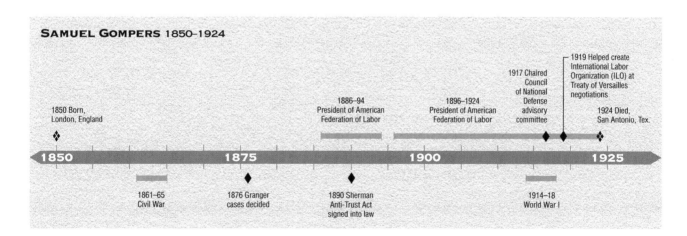

SAMUEL GOMPERS 1850–1924

1850 Born, London, England

1886–94 President of American Federation of Labor

1896–1924 President of American Federation of Labor

1917 Chaired Council of National Defense advisory committee

1919 Helped create International Labor Organization (ILO) at Treaty of Versailles negotiations

1924 Died, San Antonio, Tex.

1850   **1875**   **1900**   **1925**

1861–65 Civil War

1876 Granger cases decided

1890 Sherman Anti-Trust Act signed into law

1914–18 World War I

GOLDMAN wrote that the AFL had not "grasped the social abyss which separates labor from its masters, an abyss which can never be bridged by the struggle for mere material gains." But under Gompers's leadership, labor made significant sustainable gains at the state and federal level. Workers' compensation laws were enacted to assist those injured on the job; wages were raised; and the eight-hour day became law for a growing number of workers (including federal employees in 1912). In 1913, the federal government created the LABOR DEPARTMENT, and, in 1914, it passed the Clayton Antitrust Act, which protected union members from prosecution under the Sherman Antitrust Act. That same year, industrialist Henry Ford initiated the eight-hour workday (at $5 per day) at his automobile plant.

When the United States entered WORLD WAR I in 1917, Gompers chaired an advisory committee of the Council of National Defense, which was created to coordinate industry and resources in wartime, and called on employers and employees to stand united and not take advantage of the war to make unreasonable demands. He traveled to Europe during the war to examine labor conditions, and after the war, in 1919, he attended the negotiations for the TREATY OF VERSAILLES, where he was instrumental in the creation of the International Labor Organization (ILO). He attended the Congress of the Pan-American federation of Labor in Mexico City in December 1924. He collapsed on December 8 and was brought to San Antonio, Texas, where he died on December 13.

FURTHER READINGS

Goldman, Emma. 1925. "Samuel Gompers." In The Road to Freedom. *The Emma Goldman Papers*, Vol. 1, March. Available online at http://www.sunsite.berkeley.edu/ Goldman/Writings/Essays/gompers.html; http://www. sunsite.berkeley.edu (accessed July 27, 2009).

Kaufman, Stuart Bruce. 1973. *Samuel Gompers and the Origins of the American Federation of Labor.* Westport, CT: Greenwood.

Mandel, Bernard. 1980. *Samuel Gompers: A Biography.* Yellow Springs, Ohio: Antioch.

CROSS REFERENCES

Craft Union; Industrial Union; Labor Union; Trade Union.

❖ GONZALES, ALBERTO R.

Alberto R. Gonzales served as U.S. attorney general from 2005 to 2007. GEORGE W. BUSH tapped Gonzales to the position to succeed JOHN ASHCROFT, and upon his confirmation, Gonzales became the first Hispanic American to serve as U.S. attorney general. Several controversies arose during Gonzales's tenure, leading to his resignation on September 17, 2007.

Born August 4, 1955, in San Antonio, Texas, Gonzales grew up in Houston. Neither of his parents finished elementary school, and Gonzales's father died from a work accident in 1982. After graduating from high school, Gonzales joined the U.S. Air Force. While he was stationed in Alaska, two Air Force Academy graduates told him he should seek an appointment to the academy. Gonzales entered the academy, but soon found out that his vision was no longer good enough to become a pilot. As a result, he turned his attention to a career in law and applied to Rice University, from which he graduated in 1979. Gonzales was the first in his family to attend college, but he did not stop there. Upon graduation, he went on to Harvard Law School. He then joined the firm of Vinson and Elkins and practiced general corporate business law with the firm for the next thirteen years.

In 1990 Gonzales gained the attention of Bush's father, president GEORGE H. W. BUSH, but Gonzales declined a job offer at the White House to remain in private practice and focus on making partner at the law firm. However, when the younger Bush offered him the opportunity to be legal counsel for the governor five years later, Gonzales accepted. Over the next five years, Bush showed strong support for Gonzales, eventually appointing him as Texas SECRETARY OF STATE and then as a justice on the Texas Supreme Court. There was little doubt that Gonzales had become part of Bush's innermost circle when Bush called on Gonzales again, in 2000, to serve as the White House counsel. Traditionally, the counsel to the White House garners little media attention unless there is a scandal. As described by Daniel Klaidman and Tamara Lipper in *Newsweek,* "the president's lawyer typically offers discreet advice on legislation and helps the White House staff steer clear of ethical land mines."

Gonzales came to public attention with his efforts to prevent details of Vice President Dick Cheney's energy commission from being revealed. More notoriously, his memo on the torture of prisoners taken in the so-called war on terror, which described the Geneva Conventions as "quaint" and "obsolete," raised strong opposition from the left, whose members felt that such comments were in part responsible for the prisoner abuse cases in Iraq. Gonzales also cleared a JUSTICE DEPARTMENT memo that stated that the president was not bound by laws against torture when incarcerating people described as "enemy combatants."

After the resignation of John Ashcroft following Bush's 2004 election victory, Bush nominated Gonzales in November 2004 to take the position of attorney general. Senate Democrats on the Judiciary Committee challenged his confirmation and unanimously voted against his nomination. However, the full Senate confirmed his nomination by a vote of 60-36. At the time of his appointment, Gonzales was seen as a more moderate appointment than Ashcroft, as Gonzales was not opposed to AFFIRMATIVE ACTION or ABORTION, two subjects of particular Republican objection.

In 2005 and 2006, Gonzales led an eventually successful effort to advocate the reauthorization of the USA PATRIOT Act. However, his position with regard to civil rights in relation to national security continued to cause a stir. The *New York Times* in 2005 reported that Bush had authorized the National Security Agency (NSA) to conduct warrantless searches on individuals within the United States. Gonzales responded to the report by noting that the program was supported by the broad war powers given to Bush following the 2001 terrorist attacks. In July 2006 Gonzales testified before the Senate that Bush had blocked the

Alberto Gonzales.
AP IMAGES

Justice Department from investigating the spying program. Gonzales was one of the government officials who had authority to review the program every 45 days. Facing pressure from Congress, Gonzales in 2007 announced that the NSA warrantless eavesdropping program would be reviewed by a secret national intelligence court.

In addition to the controversy surrounding Gonzales' handling of the eavesdropping program, Gonzales became embroiled in a dispute over the sudden dismissal of several U.S. attorneys. He reportedly met in November 2006 to discuss the dismissal of eight prosecutors in a plan approved by the White House about a week later. On December 7, 2006, the Justice Department dismissed these eight attorneys, providing no reason for the firings.

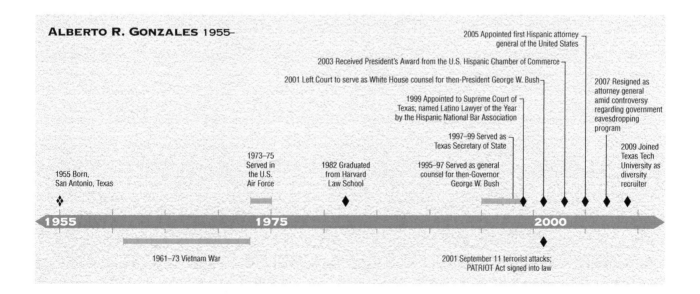

ALBERTO R. GONZALES 1955–

2005 Appointed first Hispanic attorney general of the United States

2003 Received President's Award from the U.S. Hispanic Chamber of Commerce

2001 Left Court to serve as White House counsel for then-President George W. Bush

1999 Appointed to Supreme Court of Texas; named Latino Lawyer of the Year by the Hispanic National Bar Association

2007 Resigned as attorney general amid controversy regarding government eavesdropping program

1997–99 Served as Texas Secretary of State

1973–75 Served in the U.S. Air Force

1982 Graduated from Harvard Law School

1995–97 Served as general counsel for then-Governor George W. Bush

2009 Joined Texas Tech University as diversity recruiter

1955 Born, San Antonio, Texas

1955   1975   2000

1961–73 Vietnam War

2001 September 11 terrorist attacks; PATRIOT Act signed into law

Reports later showed that the majority of those who were dismissed were given favorable evaluations during the periods of time that they held their positions. As the controversy continued to heat up, Deputy Attorney General Paul McNulty testified that the attorneys were dismissed due to poor performance rather than political reasons.

Senator Charles Schumer (D-N.Y.) led an investigation into the attorneys' firings. He criticized the Justice Department for what he concluded were politically motivated decisions. Calls for Gonzales's resignation became more prevalent in March 2007. Arlen Specter (R-Pa.), the top Republican on the SENATE JUDICIARY COMMITTEE, openly questioned whether Gonzales's tenure as attorney general had run its course. Another Republican, Senator John Sununu (R-NH), openly called for Gonzales's resignation.

Gonzales responded to allegations about the dismissal of the attorneys by noting that though he should be held accountable, he was not involved with seeing memos or with other discussions about the proposed firings. About two months later, evidence surfaced that Gonzales indeed saw memos about the firings and had consulted with aides prior to the dismissals. Moreover, former Deputy Attorney General James Comey testified that in 2004 Gonzalez had pressured then attorney general Ashcroft to approve the eavesdropping program. This occurred while Ashcroft was hospitalized in an intensive-care unit.

Congressional Democrats stepped up their efforts to pressure Gonzales to resign. House and Senate members introduced no-confidence votes in both chambers of Congress. Nonetheless, Bush continued to express support for Gonzales. Amid accusations of PERJURY for his earlier testimony, however, Gonzales finally gave in and announced his resignation on August 27, 2007. Bush claimed that Gonzales's name had been "dragged through the mud for political reasons," but even some Republican lawmakers said that the time for the resignation had come.

Gonzales gave numerous speeches during the two years following his resignation, but he reportedly had difficulty finding a position at a law firm. In July 2009 Texas Tech University announced that it had hired Gonzales to serve as diversity recruiter. He was also scheduled to teach a political science course.

YOU DO THE BEST YOU CAN, LOOKING AT PRECEDENT, IN TRYING TO ANTICIPATE WHERE THE SUPREME COURT IS GOING TO DRAW THE BALANCE BETWEEN THE PROTECTION OF CIVIL LIBERTIES AND PROTECTING THE NATIONAL SECURITY, AND IN SOME CASES WE GUESSED WRONG.
—ALBERTO GONZALES

FURTHER READINGS

Johnston, David. 2007. "Dismissed U.S. Attorneys Praised in Evaluations." *New York Times*. February 25.
Myers, Steven Lee, and Philip Shenon. 2007. "Embattled Attorney General Resigns." *New York Times*. August 27.

GOOD BEHAVIOR

Orderly and lawful action; conduct that is deemed proper for a peaceful and law-abiding individual.

The definition of good behavior depends upon how the phrase is used. For example, what constitutes good behavior for an elected public officer may be quite different from that expected of a prisoner who wants to have his or her sentence reduced or to earn privileges.

The CONSTITUTION OF THE UNITED STATES provides that federal judges shall hold their offices during good behavior, which means that they cannot be discharged but can be impeached for misconduct.

GOOD CAUSE

Legally adequate or substantial grounds or reason to take a certain action.

The term *good cause* is a relative one and is dependent upon the circumstances of each individual case. For example, a party in a legal action who wants to do something after a particular STATUTE OF LIMITATIONS has expired must show good cause, or justification for needing additional time. A serious illness or accident might, for example, constitute good cause.

An employee is said to be discharged for good cause if the reasons for the termination are work related. However, if the employer simply did not like the employee's personality, this would not ordinarily constitute good cause, unless the employee held a position, such as a salesperson, for which a likable personality was required.

GOOD FAITH

Honesty; a sincere intention to deal fairly with others.

Good faith is an abstract and comprehensive term that encompasses a sincere belief or MOTIVE without any MALICE or the desire to DEFRAUD others. It derives from the translation of the Latin term BONA FIDE, and courts use the two terms interchangeably.

The term *good faith* is used in many areas of the law but has special significance in COMMERCIAL LAW. A good faith purchaser for value is protected by the UNIFORM COMMERCIAL CODE, which every state has adopted. Under sections 1-201(9) and 2-403 of the code, a merchant may keep possession of goods that were bought from a seller who did not have title to the goods, if the merchant can show he or she was a good faith purchaser for value. To meet this test, the person must be a merchant, must have demonstrated honesty in the conduct of the transaction concerned, and must have observed reasonable commercial standards of fair dealing in the trade. A buyer would likely meet these requirements if the purchase proceeded in the ordinary course of business. If, on the other hand, the purchase took place under unusual or suspicious circumstances, a court might conclude that the buyer lacked good faith.

Where a nonmerchant purchases property that the seller lacks LEGAL TITLE to convey, the issue of good faith is known both as the INNOCENT PURCHASER doctrine and as the bona fide purchaser doctrine. If the purchaser acquires the property by an honest contract or agreement and without knowledge of any defect in the title of the seller, or means of knowledge sufficient to charge the buyer with such knowledge, the purchaser is deemed innocent.

In both commercial and noncommercial law, persons who in good faith pay a FRAUDULENT seller VALUABLE CONSIDERATION for property are protected from another person who claims legal title to the property. If a court establishes the purchaser's good faith defense, the person who claims title has recourse only against the fraudulent seller. Strong PUBLIC POLICY is behind the good faith defense. Good faith doctrines enhance the flow of goods in commerce, as under them, buyers are not required, in the ordinary course of business, to go to extraordinary efforts to determine whether sellers actually have good title. A purchaser can move quickly to close a deal with the knowledge that a fraudulent seller and a legitimate titleholder will have to sort the issue out in court. Of course, the purchaser will be required to demonstrate to the court evidence of good faith.

Good faith is also central to the COMMERCIAL PAPER (checks, drafts, promissory notes, certificates of deposit) concept of a HOLDER IN DUE COURSE. A holder is a person who takes an instrument, such as a check, subject to the reasonable belief that it will be paid and that there are no legal reasons why payment will not occur. If the holder has taken the check for value and in good faith believes the check to be good, she or he is a holder in due course, with sole right to recover payment. If, on the other hand, the holder accepts a check that has been dishonored (stamped with terms such as "insufficient funds," "account closed," and "payment stopped"), she or he has knowledge that something is wrong with the check and therefore cannot ALLEGE the check was accepted in the good faith belief that it was valid.

In LABOR LAW, the National Labor Relations Act of 1935 (29 U.S.C.A. § 151 et seq.) mandates good faith bargaining by every union and employer in order to reach agreement. In corporate law, the BUSINESS JUDGMENT RULE is based on good faith. This principle makes officers, directors, managers, and other agents of a corporation immune from liability to the corporation for losses incurred in corporate transactions that are within their authority and power to make, when sufficient evidence demonstrates that those transactions were made in good faith. As in commercial law, the use of good faith in this case enhances corporate business practices, as agents of a corporation are free to act quickly, decisively, and sometimes wrongly to advance the interests of the corporation. Good faith insulates corporate officers from disgruntled shareholders.

FURTHER READINGS

Bristow, David I., and Reva Seth. 2000–2001. "Good Faith in Negotiations." *Dispute Resolution Journal* 55 (November-January). Available online at http://findarticles.com/p/articles/mi_qa3923/is_200011/ai_n8963898/; website home page: http://findarticles.com (accessed July 27, 2009).

Carter, Roger L. 2002. "Oh, Ye of Little (Good) Faith: Questions, Concerns and Commentary on Efforts to Regulate Participant Conduct in Mediations." *Journal of Dispute Resolution* 2002 (fall).

Compliance News. Available online at http://www.compliancenews.com/ (accessed September 4, 2009).

GOOD SAMARITAN DOCTRINE

A principle of tort law that provides that a person who sees another individual in imminent and serious danger or peril cannot be charged with negligence if that first person attempts to aid or rescue the injured party, provided the attempt is not made recklessly.

The Good Samaritan doctrine is used by rescuers to avoid civil LIABILITY for injuries arising from their NEGLIGENCE. Its purpose is to encourage emergency assistance by removing the threat of liability for damage done by the assistance. However, the assistance must be reasonable; a rescuer cannot benefit from the Good Samaritan doctrine if the assistance is reckless or grossly negligent.

Three key elements support a successful invocation of the Good Samaritan doctrine: (1) the care rendered was performed as the result of the emergency, (2) the initial emergency or injury was not caused by the person invoking the defense, and (3) the emergency care was not given in a grossly negligent or reckless manner.

Assume that a person has slipped on ice and broken a vertebra. The victim is unconscious, the accident has occurred in a desolate area, and the weather is dangerously cold. A passerby finds the injured person and moves the person to warmth and safety, but in the process aggravates the spinal injury. In a civil suit by the victim seeking damages for the additional injury, the passerby may successfully defeat the claims under the Good Samaritan doctrine.

The Good Samaritan doctrine is also used as a defense by persons who act to prevent or contain property damage. Assume that a passerby notices a fire has started just outside a cabin in the wilderness. If the passerby breaks into the cabin to look for a fire extinguisher, the passerby will not be liable for damage resulting from the forced entry. However, if the passerby runs down the cabin with a bulldozer to extinguish the fire, this will probably be considered grossly negligent or reckless, and the Good Samaritan doctrine will not provide protection from a civil suit for damages to the cabin.

The line separating negligence from GROSS NEGLIGENCE or RECKLESSNESS is often thin. *Hardingham v. United Counseling Service of Bennington County*, 672 A. 2d 480 (Vt. 1995), illustrates the negligent acts that the Good Samaritan doctrine protects. In this case, the PLAINTIFF, David Hardingham, sued United Counseling Service (UCS) when he became blind after drinking windshield wiper fluid. Hardingham, a recovering alcoholic, was employed by UCS as an emergency services counselor. When Hardingham began drinking again, employees of UCS went to his apartment and discovered him in an inebriated condition. During their visit, they saw Hardingham drink windshield wiper fluid. They called the police, who took Hardingham to a hospital. At the hospital, none of the UCS

workers informed medical authorities that Hardingham had drunk the dangerous fluid. Doctors did not learn until the next day that Hardingham had overdosed on methanol, a component of windshield wiper fluid, and Hardingham eventually lost his sight.

Hardingham never got a chance to present his case to a jury. The Chittenden Superior Court granted SUMMARY JUDGMENT to UCS, holding that there was insufficient evidence to support an ALLEGATION of gross negligence by the organization. The Supreme Court of Vermont affirmed this decision. According to the court, the actions of the defendants "probably saved plaintiff's life." Although the defendants may have been negligent in failing to disclose that Hardingham had swallowed enough methanol to threaten his life, "no REASONABLE PERSON could conclude that defendants showed indifference to plaintiff or failed to exercise even a slight degree of care."

Justice John Dooley dissented, arguing that the case presented a QUESTION OF FACT for a jury to decide. The defendants "failed to tell the emergency room physician the most significant fact that wasn't obvious from plaintiff's condition—that plaintiff had consumed windshield wiper fluid." Dooley lamented that "the greatest difficulty plaintiff faces in this case is to persuade us to accept that 'good samaritans' should ever be liable."

Section 324 of the Second Restatement of Torts describes the Good Samaritan doctrine in an inverse fashion. According to section 324, a person is subject to liability for physical harm resulting from the failure to exercise reasonable care if the failure increases the risk of harm, if the rescuer has a duty to render care, or if others are relying on the rescuer.

Many states are content to follow the Good Samaritan doctrine through their COMMON LAW or through similar previous cases. Some states have general statutes mandating the doctrine. Utah, for example, has a Good Samaritan act, which provides in part that

> [a] person who renders emergency care at or near the scene of, or during an emergency, gratuitously and in GOOD FAITH, is not liable for any civil damages or penalties as a result of any act or omission by the person rendering the emergency care, unless the person is grossly negligent or caused the emergency. (Utah Code Ann. § 78-11-22).

Some states have enacted statutes that protect specific emergency care or assistance. Indiana, for example, protects the emergency care of veterinarians (Ind. Code § 15-5-1.1-31). Alabama provides IMMUNITY to those who assist or advise in the mitigation of the effects of the discharge of hazardous materials (Ala. Code § 6-5-332.1). Some states also provide protection to those participating in the cleanup of oil spills. In 1990, Congress passed the Oil Pollution Act (Pub. L. No. 101-380, 33 U.S.C.A. §§ 2701–2761 [1994]), which gave immunity from liability to persons who participate in oil cleanup efforts. Like any Good Samaritan law, the statute does not protect a person who is grossly negligent or reckless.

FURTHER READINGS

Crawley, Annette Teichert. 1993. "Environmental Auditing and the 'Good Samaritan' Doctrine: Implications for Parent Corporations." *Georgia Law Review* 28 (fall).

Landes, William M., and Richard A. Posner. 2001. "Harmless Error." *Journal of Legal Studies* 30 (January). Available online at http://www.law.uchicago.edu/files/files/101.WML_.Harmless.pdf; website home page: http://www.law.uchicago.edu (accessed July 27, 2009).

White, Christopher H. 2002. "No Good Deed Goes Unpunished: The Case for Reform of the Rescue Doctrine." *Northwestern Univ. Law Review* 97 (fall).

GOOD TIME

The amount of time deducted from time to be served in prison on a given sentence, at some point after the prisoner's admission to prison, contingent upon good behavior or awarded automatically by the application of a statute or regulation. Good time can be forfeited for misbehavior. In some jurisdictions, prisoners may not earn good time during their first year of their sentence.

GOOD WILL

The favorable reputation and clientele of an established and well-run business.

The value of good will is ordinarily determined as the amount a purchaser will pay for a business beyond the monetary value of its tangible property and money owed to it.

Good will is regarded as a property interest in and of itself, although it exists only in connection with other property, such as the name or location of the operation. Good will exists even in a situation where the business is not operating at a profit. Certain courts refuse to recognize good will that arises out of the personal qualities of the owner. For example, a physician cannot sell good will when selling the office building and other physical assets of his or her practice, because the physician's reputation is based solely upon personal professional abilities.

A transfer of good will from one individual to another can take place as a bequest in a will or through a sale. Ordinarily, when an individual sells the property to which good will is connected, it is automatically transferred to the buyer. However, the buyer and seller can alter this arrangement or specify details in their sale agreement. A former owner of a business has no right to interfere with the subsequent owner's enjoyment of good will following a sale transferring good will, even in the event that the sales contract does not specifically so indicate. In the event that the purchaser wants to prevent the seller from establishing a competing business in the same vicinity, the purchaser must bargain for such a provision in the contract. An agreement not to compete, sometimes called RESTRICTIVE COVENANT, differs from good will. However, an individual who sells the good will of his or her business is not permitted to solicit former clients or customers or lead them to believe that he or she is still running the same business.

GOODS

Items; chattels; things; any personal property.

Goods is a term of flexible context and meaning and extends to all tangible items.

❖ GORE, ALBERT ARNOLD, JR.

He has been a reporter, an environmentalist, a congressman, and served as vice PRESIDENT OF THE UNITED STATES, but Al Gore may go down in history as the unsuccessful candidate in possibly the most contested presidential race the United States has ever seen. Having spent the majority of his life in the political ring, Gore made two unsuccessful bids for the presidency. The first came in 1988, when he was a fledgling senator; the second was in 2000, following two terms as vice president under BILL CLINTON. In the protracted 2000 race, Gore won the popular vote, but lost the electoral vote to GEORGE W. BUSH. He became the third candidate in history to receive the greatest share of the popular vote, but lose the presidency. In 2002 Gore announced that he would not try for the office a

Al Gore.
AP IMAGES

although he opposed the intervention of the United States in the VIETNAM WAR.

While stationed in Vietnam, Gore served as an army reporter. After Gore left the military service in 1971, the *Nashville Tennessean* hired him as an investigative reporter and, later, as an editorial writer. In addition to his journalism career, Gore was a home builder, a land developer, and a livestock and tobacco farmer.

Gore married his college sweetheart, Mary Elizabeth "Tipper" Aitcheson, in 1970. Tipper Gore holds a B.A. degree from Boston University and an M.A. in psychology from George Peabody College at Vanderbilt University. She is actively involved in a number of issues, including AIDS, education, and homelessness. She has also has been a longtime advocate for mental health, and gained national attention in the 1980s through her efforts to influence the record industry to rate and label obscene and violent lyrics. She was cofounder of the Parents' Music Resource Center, which monitors musical and video presentations that glorify casual sex and violence. The Gores have four children: Karenna, Kristin, Sarah, and Albert III.

Interested in RELIGION and philosophy, Gore enrolled in the Graduate School of Religion at Vanderbilt University during the 1971–72 academic year. In 1974, he entered Vanderbilt's law school but left to enter elective office two years later.

third time, claiming, "there are many other exciting ways to serve."

Gore was born in Washington, D.C., on March 31, 1948. His father, Albert Gore Sr., at the time served as a Democratic member of the U.S. House of Representatives from Tennessee. The senior Gore was to serve in the House and the Senate for nearly three decades. His mother was Pauline LaFon Gore. She had the distinction of being one of the first women to graduate from the law school at Vanderbilt University.

Gore attended St. Alban's Episcopal School for Boys in Washington, D.C., where he was an honor student and captain of the football team. In 1969 he received a B.A. with honors in government from Harvard University. He was interested in becoming a writer, rather than following his father's footsteps as a politician. After graduation he enlisted in the army,

In 1976 Gore ran for a seat in the U.S. House of Representatives. He won the primary election against eight other candidates and went on to win in the general election. He ran successfully in the three following elections. Gore claimed some early attention in 1980 when he was assigned to study nuclear arms as a member of the House Intelligence Committee.

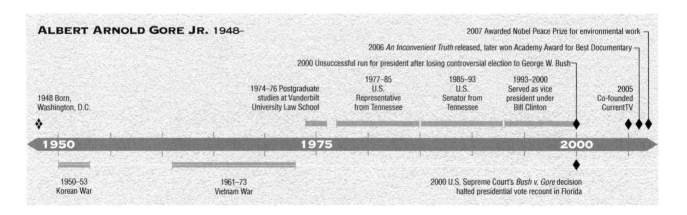

ALBERT ARNOLD GORE JR. 1948–

2007 Awarded Nobel Peace Prize for environmental work

2006 *An Inconvenient Truth* released, later won Academy Award for Best Documentary

2000 Unsuccessful run for president after losing controversial election to George W. Bush

1948 Born, Washington, D.C.

1974–76 Postgraduate studies at Vanderbilt University Law School

1977–85 U.S. Representative from Tennessee

1985–93 U.S. Senator from Tennessee

1993–2000 Served as vice president under Bill Clinton

2005 Co-founded CurrentTV

1950   1975   2000

1950–53 Korean War

1961–73 Vietnam War

2000 U.S. Supreme Court's *Bush v. Gore* decision halted presidential vote recount in Florida

He researched and eventually published a comprehensive manifesto on arms restructuring for future security, which was published in the February 1982 issue of Congressional Quarterly. In 1984, Gore campaigned for a seat in the U.S. Senate that had just become vacant. He won that office with a large margin of votes.

While in Congress, Gore focused on several issues, including health care and environmental reform. He worked for nuclear ARMS CONTROL AND DISARMAMENT, as well as other strategic defense issues. He also stressed the potential of new technologies, such as biotechnology and computer development.

As the decade came to a close, Gore set his sights on the race for the 1988 presidential election. Only 39 years old at the time, he ran on traditional domestic Democratic views and was tough on foreign policy issues. He failed, however, to develop a national theme for his campaign and was criticized for changing positions on issues. Gore was successful in gaining public support in the primaries during the early spring and won more votes than any other candidate in southern states. However, he obtained only small percentages of votes in other states and withdrew from the presidential nomination campaigns in mid-April.

Two years later Gore won election to a second term in the U.S. Senate. He chose not to seek the presidency in 1992, citing family concerns (his son Albert had been hit by an automobile and was seriously injured). It was during this time that Gore wrote the book *Earth in the Balance: Ecology and the Human Spirit*, which expressed his concern, ideas, and recommendations on conservation and the global environment. In the book he wrote about his own personal and political experiences and legislative actions on the environmental issue. One of Gore's statements in the book that sums up his philosophy regarding the environment and human interaction is, "We must make the rescue of the environment the central organizing principle for civilization."

In the summer of 1992, Bill Clinton selected Gore as his vice presidential nominee. The choice startled many people because it ended a long-standing pattern of a candidate choosing a vice presidential nominee to "balance the ticket." Both men were of the same age, region, and reputation and moderate in political outlook. Gore did balance Clinton's strength, however, by bringing to the ticket his experience in foreign and defense policy, expertise in environmental and new technology matters, and an image as an unwavering family man.

Clinton and Gore won the election in 1992, and Gore was inaugurated as the 45th vice president on January 20, 1993. At the age of 44 years, he became one of the youngest people to hold the position. Clinton and Gore were reelected in 1996, running against Republicans Bob Dole and Jack Kemp.

During his time as vice president, Gore continued to stress environmental concerns. In 1997, the White House launched an effort to start producing a report card on the health of the nation's ecosystems. This project was carried out by an environmental think tank and initiated by Gore.

That same year, however, Gore's reputation was somewhat tarnished when he was accused of and admitted to making fund-raising telephone calls from the White House during the 1996 presidential campaign. Gore held a press conference on March 3, 1997, to defend his actions, saying there was nothing illegal about what he had done, although he admitted it may not have been a wise choice. Gore was also criticized for toasting Li Peng, initiator of the Tiananmen Square Massacre, during a trip to China. In September 1997 Buddhist nuns testified before the Senate panel investigating the abuses of campaign fund-raising. The nuns admitted that donors were illegally reimbursed by their temple following a fund-raiser attended by Gore, and that they had destroyed or altered records to avoid embarrassing their temple. Some believe these incidents further damaged Gore's reputation.

Despite questions of impropriety, Gore announced his candidacy for president in 1999. By early 2000 he had secured the majority of Democratic delegates for the 2000 elections. Gore chose Connecticut Senator Joseph Lieberman as his running mate to face Texas governor George W. Bush and Richard Cheney, former secretary of defense. Although Bush took an early lead in the polls, the Gore campaign closed the gap. Gore sought not only to demonstrate his compassion in a variety of speeches, but also to distance himself from Clinton. As the November 7 election approached, most observers predicted a deadlock.

During the afternoon of November 7, 2000, it appeared as if Gore would win the election,

NO MATTER HOW HARD THE LOSS, DEFEAT MIGHT SERVE AS WELL AS VICTORY TO SHAKE THE SOUL AND LET THE GLORY OUT.
—AL GORE

and several media outlets declared him the unofficial winner. However, vote tallies from the late afternoon and early evening revealed that Bush had closed the gap. By the evening of November 7, the totals showed that although Gore had won the popular vote, Bush won the ELECTORAL COLLEGE. Gore immediately requested a recount of the votes in the state of Florida, where voting procedures had caused a great deal of controversy. For the next month, the results of the election hung in the balance as both sides postured in a series of court disputes. However, the U.S. Supreme Court, in BUSH V. GORE, 531 U.S. 98, 121 S. Ct. 525, 148 L. Ed. 2d 388 (2000), overturned an order by the Florida Supreme Court requiring a recount of ballots in several counties. Gore then conceded the election to Bush.

In 2001 Gore accepted a position at the Columbia Graduate School of Journalism as a visiting professor. He has also accepted teaching positions at universities in his home state of Tennessee. Although many observers expected him to run again for president in the 2004 elections—and although a number of grassroots organizations had urged his running—Gore announced in December 2002 that he would not enter the race. "I personally have the energy and drive and ambition to make another campaign, but I don't think it's the right thing for me to do," he said in an interview with the CBS program *60 Minutes*. "I think that a campaign that would be a rematch between myself and President Bush would inevitably involve a focus on the past that would in some measure distract from the focus on the future that I think all campaigns have to be about."

By 2006 Gore had reinvented himself as a leading, vocal environmentalist. That year, his global warming documentary, *An Inconvenient Truth*, was wildly popular. It became the third highest grossing documentary of all time. *An Inconvenient Truth* won Gore and the other filmmakers an Academy Award for best documentary and numerous other awards. The film was not Gore's only media work. He was also the creator of Current TV, an interactive cable network targeted at young people. In addition, Gore was the co-organizer of July 7, 2007, Live Earth: The Concert for a Climate in Crisis. This media event in which live concerts took place on all seven continents and aired world-wide to raise awareness about environmental issues.

With the success of *An Inconvenient Truth*, as well as its companion book of the same name, Gore was repeatedly asked if he would run for president in 2008. He denied any further political ambitions and never sought the presidency in 2008. He found it easier to push for environmental change outside of political office. However, call for Gore to run only increased after he was the co-winner of the 2007 Nobel Peace Prize for his environmental work. Instead, Gore has continued his activist work and he joined the venture capital firm, Kleiner Perkins Caufield & Byers, as a partner in November 2007. For all his success and influence, *Time* magazine named him runner-up to person of the year in 2007. His most recent book, *Our Choice: A Plan to Solve the Climate Crisis*, was pubished in November 2009.

FURTHER READINGS

Gore, Al. 2007. *The Assault on Reason*. New York: Penguin Press.

"Gore Says He Won't Run in 2004." 2002. CNN.com: Inside Politics. Available online at <www.cnn.com/2002/ALLPOLITICS/12/15/gore/index.html> (accessed August 18, 2009).

Turque, Bill. 2000. *Inventing Al Gore: A Biography*. Boston: Houghton Mifflin.

GOVERNMENT INSTRUMENTALITY DOCTRINE

A rule that provides that any organization run by a branch of the government is immune from taxation.

GOVERNMENT NATIONAL MORTGAGE ASSOCIATION

The Government National Mortgage Association (GNMA), also known as Ginnie Mae, is a corporation wholly owned by the federal government. Created by the Housing and Urban Development Act of 1968, 825 Stat. 491, GNMA is designed to support the federal government's housing programs by establishing a secondary market for the sale and purchase of residential mortgages.

During the late 1960s, the federal government expressed concern that available credit for low-income housing was insufficient to meet the growing demand. In response, GNMA began issuing certificates to obtain additional funds for government-backed, low-income mortgages. GNMA certificates entitle their holders to receive a portion of the income derived from a residential mortgage pool approved by the government.

A residential mortgage pool consists of a group of mortgages that are issued by private lenders, including commercial banks and savings and loan institutions. Each mortgage pool includes 1,000 residential mortgages.

The revenue generated by the sale of these pools helps make additional credit available for low-income residential mortgages insured by government agencies such as the Federal Housing Administration (FHA), the Department of Veterans Affairs (VA), and the Farmers Home Administration. The DEPARTMENT OF HOUSING AND URBAN DEVELOPMENT, which is responsible for administering GNMA, oversees the entire program.

GNMA mortgage pools and mortgage-backed SECURITIES (MBSs) are considered stable investments by securities dealers and investors alike. The timely payment of principal and interest on each mortgage is guaranteed by GNMA and the full faith and credit of the federal government. GNMA enjoys unlimited authority to borrow funds from the U.S. Treasury in order to make good on this guarantee.

By developing a stable and viable secondary market for government-backed residential mortgages, GNMA has originated more than $2.8 trillion in securities trading. The revenue generated through this secondary market has enabled millions of low-income families to purchase homes and provided the U.S. Treasury with annual receipts sometimes exceeding $400 million.

In 1994 President BILL CLINTON outlined the National Homeowners Strategy, which spurred GNMA to undertake an intense and sweeping review of its practices and programs. In addition, GNMA has been working to satisfy internal mandates that require it to enhance its customer service, improve its relations with other businesses, and better market its securities. GNMA has incorporated the latest technology and automation to achieve these goals and has hired consultants to market its residential mortgage pools.

GNMA continues to streamline its documentation procedures and make efforts to eliminate paperwork, such as accepting electronic confirmation of insurance rather than relying on paper insurance certificates. It has begun an ambitious program to increase home ownership by minority families. Since its inception in 1968, GNMA has given more than 35 million families access to affordable mortgage costs.

GNMA's mortgage-backed securities (MBSs) fared better than others during the housing FORECLOSURE and mortgage crisis of 2008 and early 2009 because GNMA's are the only ones to carry the full faith and credit GUARANTY of the United States government. In fact, as investors fled the private mortgage securities market (led by private lenders without government backing) following its collapse, GNMA actually grew in 2009. It announced that for the first six months of 2009, it had provided nearly $207 billion of liquidity to the MBS secondary market, compared with $107 billion for the first six months of 2008.

FURTHER READINGS

Benson, John D. 1991. "Ending the Turf Wars: Support for a CFTC/SEC Consolidation." *Villanova Law Review* 36.

Ginnie Mae. 2009. Available online at tp://www.ginniemae. gov/about.asp?section=about; website home page: http://www.ginniemae.gov/ index.asp (accessed September 10, 2009).

Hadaway, Beverly L., and Paula C. Murray. 1986. "Mortgage Backed Securities: An Investigation of Legal and Financial Issues." *Journal of Corporation Law* 11.

Malloy, Robin P. 1986. "The Secondary Mortgage Market: A Catalyst for Change in Real Estate Transactions." *Southwestern Law Journal* 39.

CROSS REFERENCES

Corporations; Credit; Guarantor; Foreclosure; Mortgage

GOVERNMENT PRINTING OFFICE

Since the mid-nineteenth century, one government establishment has existed to fill the printing, binding, and distribution needs of the federal government. Established on June 23, 1860, by Congressional JOINT RESOLUTION No. 25, the Government Printing Office (GPO) has provided publication supplies and services to the U.S. Congress, the executive departments, and all other agencies of the federal government. The definition of the duties set forth in the 1860 resolution has stayed essentially the same over the years, with only one amendment in all that time, 44 U.S.C.A. § 101 et seq.

The GPO is overseen by the Congressional Joint Committee on Printing. The head of the GPO works under the title *public printer* and is appointed by the PRESIDENT OF THE UNITED STATES with the consent of the Senate. The public printer is also legally required to be a "practical

Government Printing Office

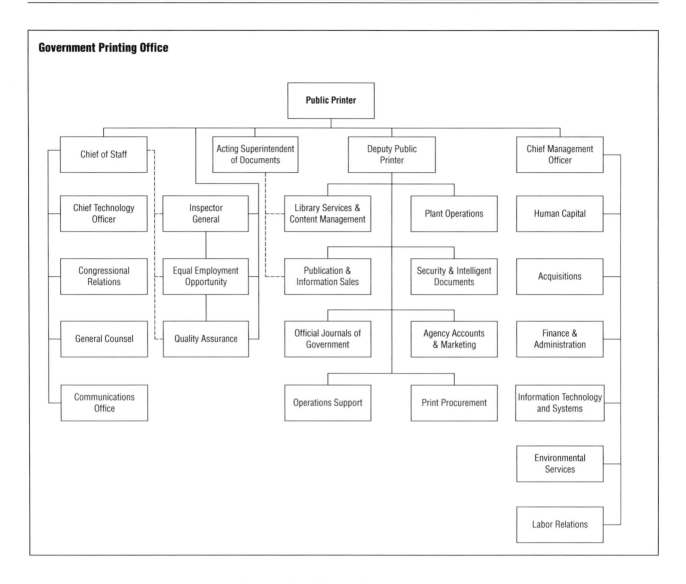

printer versed in the art of bookbinding" (44 U.S.C.A. § 301).

The GPO uses a variety of printing and binding processes, including electronic photo composition; letterpress printing; Linotype and hand composition; photopolymer platemaking; offset photography; stripping, platemaking, and presswork; and manual and machine bookbinding. The GPO also provides supplies such as blank paper and ink to federal agencies, prepares catalogs, and sells and distributes some publications to civilians.

The GPO offers catalogs that detail publications available to the public. All catalogs are available from the superintendent of documents at the GPO. The *GPO Sales Publications Reference File,* which is issued biweekly on magnetic tape, lists the author, the title, and subject information for each new publication. A more

comprehensive listing, the *Monthly Catalog of U.S. Government Publications,* serves as an index to all the publications handled by the GPO.

The GPO also offers two free catalogs for people who are interested in new or popular publications: *U.S. Government Books* and *New Books.* The first lists the titles of best-selling government publications, and the second is a bimonthly listing of government publications for sale.

The approximately 20,000 publications listed in these catalogs can be purchased by mail from the GPO's superintendent of documents. In addition, the books and catalogs published by the GPO can be purchased at the approximately two-dozen GPO bookstores open to the public. Most of the bookstores are located in government hub cities such as Washington, D.C., Atlanta, Chicago, Dallas, Houston, and Los Angeles. Publications are also available for public perusal at select depository libraries around the United States.

Owing to the large volume of documents produced by the various federal agencies, the GPO does not handle all of the printing and binding services for the government. In some instances, the GPO takes bids from commercial suppliers and awards contracts to those with the lowest bids. From there, the GPO serves as a connection between ordering agencies and contractors. The booklet *How to Do Business with the Government Printing Office* provides a background and instructions for contracting with the GPO and submitting bids. The booklet can be requested from any GPO regional printing procurement office. Any printing or binding contract inquiries can be directed to one of 13 offices, located in Atlanta; Boston; Chicago; Columbus, Ohio; Dallas; Denver; Hampton, Virginia; Los Angeles; New York; Philadelphia; St. Louis; San Francisco; and Seattle.

Since the mid-1990s many of the documents published by the GPO have been available in electronic formats. During the mid-1990s, GPO distributed CD-ROM products containing government documents to thousands of American libraries. Many of these documents are now available through GPO's Web site, known as *GPO Access*. The site contains hundreds of thousands of individual documents from the various federal departments and agencies. It has become particularly useful for attorneys who need to locate such information as administrative regulations and LEGISLATIVE HISTORY of federal statutes.

FURTHER READINGS

"Keeping America Informed: The United States Government Printing Office." Available online at http://www.access. gpo.gov/congress/gpopub250-2.pdf; website home page: http://www.access.gpo.gov (accessed July 27, 2009).

U.S. Government Manual Website. Available online at http:// www.gpoaccess.gov/gmanual/index (accessed July 21, 2009).

U.S. Government Printing Office. 2001. *Guide to Federal Publishing.* Washington, D.C.: Government Printing Office.

CROSS REFERENCES

Congress of the United States; Legislative History.

GRAB LAW

State statutory provisions and common-law principles that govern the aggressive use of legal and equitable remedies, such as attachment and garnishment, by creditors to collect payment from debtors.

State laws governing debtor and creditor transactions emphasize the importance of prompt action by creditors to ensure payment of the debtor's outstanding debts. For example, the first creditor to attach the debtor's property is most likely to be paid. The quicker the creditor acts to seize or "grab" the debtor's assets, the greater the chance the creditor's claims will be satisfied. As a result, grab law has come to designate aggressive, but legal, methods used by creditors to enforce their rights to payment against delinquent debtors.

GRACE PERIOD

In insurance law, a period beyond the due date of a premium (usually thirty or thirty-one days) during which the insurance is continued in force and during which the payment may be made to keep the policy in good standing. The grace period for payment of the premium does not provide free insurance or operate to continue the policy in force after it expires by agreement of the parties. Grace period may also refer to a period of time provided for in a loan agreement during which default will not occur even though a payment is overdue.

GRADUATED TAX

Tax structured so that the rate increases as the amount of income of taxpayer increases.

GRAFT

A colloquial term referring to the unlawful acquisition of public money through questionable and improper transactions with public officials.

Graft is the personal gain or advantage earned by an individual at the expense of others as a result of the exploitation of the singular status of, or an influential relationship with, another who has a position of public trust or confidence. The advantage or gain is accrued without any exchange of legitimate compensatory services.

Behavior that leads to graft includes BRIBERY and dishonest dealings in the performance of public or official acts. Graft usually implies the existence of THEFT, corruption, FRAUD, and the lack of integrity that is expected in any transaction involving a public official.

GRAND JURY

A panel of citizens that is convened by a court to decide whether it is appropriate for the government to indict (proceed with a prosecution against) someone suspected of a crime.

An American institution since the colonial days, the grand jury has long played an important role in CRIMINAL LAW. The FIFTH AMENDMENT to the U.S. Constitution says that a person suspected of a federal crime cannot be tried until a grand jury has determined that there is enough reason to charge the person. Review by a grand jury is meant to protect suspects from inappropriate prosecution by the government, since grand jurors are drawn from the general population. It has been criticized at times as failing to serve its purpose.

The grand jury system originated in twelfth-century England, when King Henry II enacted the ASSIZE of Clarendon in order to take control of the courts from the Catholic Church and local nobility. The proclamation said that a person could not be tried as a criminal unless a certain number of local citizens appeared in court to accuse him or her of specific crimes. This group of citizens, known as the grand assize, was very powerful: It had the authority to identify suspects, present evidence personally held by individual jurors, and determine whether to make an ACCUSATION. Trial was by ordeal, so accusation meant that conviction was very likely. (Trial by ordeal involved subjecting the DEFENDANT to some physical test to determine guilt or innocence. For example, in ordeal by water, a suspect was thrown into deep water: if he or she floated, the verdict was guilty; if the suspect sank, the verdict was innocent.)

The grand assize was not designed to protect suspects, and it changed very little over the next five hundred years. Then, in 1681, its reputation began to evolve. An English grand jury denied King Charles II's wish for a public hearing in the cases of two Protestants accused of TREASON for opposing his attempts to reestablish the Catholic Church. The grand jury held a private session and refused to indict the two suspects. This gave the grand jury new respect as a means of protection against government bullying (although ultimately in those particular cases, the king found a different grand jury willing to indict the suspects).

After this small act of rebellion, the grand jury became known as a potential protector of people facing baseless or politically motivated prosecution. The early colonists brought this concept to America, and by 1683, all colonies had some type of grand jury system in place. Over the next century, grand juries became more sympathetic to those who resisted British rule. In 1765, for example, a Boston grand jury refused to indict leaders of protests against the STAMP ACT, a demonstration of resistance to colonialism.

The grand jury was considered important enough to be incorporated into the U.S. Constitution, and has remained largely unchanged. Grand juries are used in the federal and most state courts. Federal grand juries use a standard set of rules. States are free to formulate their own pretrial requirements, and they vary greatly in the number of grand jurors they seat, the limits they place on the deliberations of those jurors, and whether a grand jury is used at all. federal courts use a grand jury that consists of 23 citizens but can operate with a QUORUM of 16. Twelve jurors' votes are required for an INDICTMENT. States use a grand jury consisting of as few as five but no more than 23 members. Grand juries are chosen from lists of qualified state residents of LEGAL AGE, who have not been convicted of a crime, and who are not biased against the subject of the investigation.

The usual role of a grand jury is to review the adequacy of evidence presented by the PROSECUTOR and then decide whether to indict the suspect. In some cases, a grand jury decides which charges are appropriate. Generally, grand jurors do not lead investigations, but can question WITNESSES to satisfy themselves that evidence is adequate and usable. The prosecutor prepares a BILL OF INDICTMENT (a list explaining the case and possible charges) and presents evidence to the grand jury. The jurors can call witnesses, including the target of the investigation, without revealing the nature of the case. They call witnesses by using a document called a SUBPOENA. A person who refuses to answer the grand jury's questions can be punished for contempt of court. However, no witness need answer incriminating questions unless that witness has been granted IMMUNITY. In federal courts, the jurors may accept hearsay and other evidence that is normally not admissible at trial.

If the grand jury agrees that there is sufficient reason to charge the suspect with a crime, it returns an indictment carrying the words *true bill.* If there is insufficient evidence to satisfy the grand jury, it returns an indictment carrying the words *no bill.*

Seldom do grand juries issue documents. However, when given a judge's permission to do so, they may use a report to denounce the conduct of a government figure or organization against whom an indictment is not justified or allowed. This occurred in 1973, when U.S. district court judge John J. Sirica allowed the grand jury investigating the WATERGATE scandals to criticize President Richard Nixon's conduct in covering up the involvement of his administration in the June 17, 1972, BURGLARY of the Democratic National Committee headquarters in the Watergate Apartment and Hotel complex. The judge recommended that the report be forwarded to the House Judiciary Committee to assist in proceedings to IMPEACH the president. Many states allow the issuance of grand jury reports, but limit their use: The target must be a public official or institution who can be denounced only where statutory authority exists, and the resulting document can be released publicly only with a judge's approval.

In February 1996, for the first time in history, a first lady of the United States was required to appear before a grand jury. HILLARY RODHAM CLINTON testified for four hours before a federal grand jury on the disappearance and reappearance of billing records related to her representation of a failed investment institution that was under scrutiny when she was an attorney in Arkansas. Her testimony was part of the WHITEWATER investigation, which examined past financial dealings of Hillary Rodham Clinton, President BILL CLINTON, and others.

Critics have complained that the grand jury offers witnesses and suspected criminals insufficient protection. The cause of the controversy is the set of rules that govern the operation of federal grand juries. For example, a prosecutor manages the work of the grand jury, which some say is contradictory since the job of prosecutor is to prove a defendant's guilt. Another contradiction, according to critics, is that a defense attorney does not represent the suspect. Instead, prosecutors may be required in state grand jury proceedings to present, on behalf of the suspect, information that they feel is exculpatory (so strong that it could create a REASONABLE DOUBT that the suspect committed the crime); however, the U.S. Supreme Court

has held that federal prosecutors are not required to do so in federal grand jury proceedings (*United States v. Williams,* 504 U.S. 36 [1992]). In arguing that a suspect should be charged, prosecutors may make arguments and use information that would normally not be admissible during a trial. Witnesses who are called before a grand jury are not allowed to have an attorney present when they testify. This holds true for a witness who may be a suspect. A final concern is that grand juries meet in secret, and a formal record of federal grand jury proceedings is not usually provided to the suspect even after indictment.

Critics of the current system claim that justice is ill served by these rules. They say that ambitious prosecutors may be tempted to misuse the powers of a nonprofessional grand jury to harass, trap, or wear down witnesses. For example, activists who opposed the VIETNAM WAR during the 1960s and 1970s accused the JUSTICE DEPARTMENT of abusing the grand jury system as it searched for information about political dissidents. The activists believed that the department used the power and secrecy of the grand jury to intimidate witnesses and fish for evidence. Members of the news media, the business community, and organized labor, have also criticized the institution.

Supporters of the current system say that the secrecy of the grand jury's work prevents several things, including a suspect from escaping, attempts to influence jurors, and the coaching or intimidation of witnesses. Supporters also contend that the system encourages candid testimony and protects the privacy of innocent suspects who are later cleared. Regarding witnesses' lack of LEGAL REPRESENTATION, supporters of the STATUS QUO point out that delay, disruption, and rehearsed testimony would lessen the efficiency of the grand jury's work and would result in a MINITRIAL. Similar arguments have been made against limiting evidence that would not be admissible at trial. In addition, federal courts have held that because the rights of a suspect are adequately protected during trial, where the strength or weakness of evidence determines the verdict, no examination of grand jury indictment proceedings is necessary.

Grand juries also face criticism in the area of jury selection, especially with high-profile cases. Criticism focuses on bias and a lack of

SHOULD THE GRAND JURY BE ABOLISHED?

Though the grand jury has existed in the United States since the colonial period, and the FIFTH AMENDMENT to the U.S. Constitution requires its use in federal criminal proceedings, it has come under increasing attack. Critics charge that it no longer serves the functions the Framers intended, and therefore should be abolished. Defenders admit there may be some problems with it, but contend that these can be remedied.

Critics aim their attacks at both federal and state grand juries. They note that a grand jury has two functions. One is to review evidence of criminal wrongdoing and to issue an INDICTMENT if the evidence is sufficient. The other is to be an investigative arm of the government, helping the PROSECUTOR gather evidence. Critics contend that in both areas contemporary grand juries have failed.

In reviewing evidence of criminal wrongdoing, a grand jury is supposed to act as a shield against ill-conceived or MALICIOUS prosecutions. Yet critics charge that grand juries typically rubber-stamp the prosecution's moves, indicting anyone the prosecutor cares to bring before it.

Historically the grand jury was not dominated by a professional prosecutor. Without a strong attorney leading the way, the grand jury was forced to be independent and diligent in reviewing evidence brought before it.

Critics note that many states abolished all or part of the grand jury's jurisdiction at the end of the nineteenth century, in large part because the process had come increasingly under the control of prosecutors. States acknowledged that a professional criminal prosecutor did not need a grand jury's assistance in the charging process. The prosecutor was capable of making an independent, DISINTERESTED review of the need to bring charges. Though 48 states have grand juries as part of their criminal justice system, many of these judicial bodies are now reserved for serious felonies, usually first-degree MURDER.

Those who favor ABOLITION of the grand jury argue that the domination of the prosecutor has led to a passivity that destroys the legitimacy of the grand jury concept. Most grand jurors have little background in law and must rely on the prosecutor to educate them about the applicable law and help them apply the law. In addition, at the federal level, there are very complex criminal laws, like the Racketeer Influenced and Corrupt Organizations statute. Even lawyers find many of these laws difficult to fathom, yet grand jurors are expected to understand them and apply them to intricate fact situations. Not surprisingly, charge the critics, the grand jury tends to follow the prosecution's advice.

Critics point out that though the Fifth Amendment requires a grand jury indictment for all federal crimes, the accused may waive this requirement and accept charges filed by a prosecutor alone on all but capital crimes. Waivers are frequent, and most prosecutions of even serious offenses are initiated by federal prosecutors. Therefore, critics argue that it makes no sense to take additional time and money for a grand jury to convene and participate in a hollow ritual.

For its critics the grand jury has declined from a proactive community voice to a passive instrument of the prosecution. Though the U.S. Supreme Court may talk about the historic importance of the grand jury in Anglo-American justice, few academics defend the institution based on its current performance. Faced with this poor performance, the critics argue that abolition is the best course. It would make the prosecutor directly accountable for the charging decision and remove the illusion that grand jurors are in control.

Defenders of the grand jury acknowledge that there are problems with the modern system, but insist the grand jury is worth saving. Despite its shortcomings the grand jury still allows citizens to help make important community decisions. Though critics may deplore prosecutorial domination of grand juries, they overgeneralize when they call the grand juries rubber stamps for the state. Congress recognized the competency and importance of citizen input when, in the ORGANIZED CRIME Control Act of 1970 (18 U.S.C.A. §§ 3332–3333), it authorized the creation of "special" grand juries to investigate organized crime, return indictments if warranted, and issue reports on the results of their investigations.

Supporters also believe that the critics overemphasize the importance of the grand jury in acting as a shield against government OPPRESSION. The key function of the grand jury is to enhance the legitimacy of the criminal charges that are returned. Prosecutors use the grand jury to gain community support for charges that might otherwise be perceived as based on racial bias, political motivation, or prosecutorial vindictiveness. A grand jury review may also help a prosecutor avoid bringing charges where the formal requisites of a crime are present but the community's moral sense would regard charges as unjust.

Some supporters of the grand jury admit that it could be improved by severing the close tie between prosecutor and jurors. They point out that Hawaii provides grand juries with their own attorney. Such a "grand jury counsel" provides independent legal advice and acts as a buffer between jurors and prosecutors. This, in turn, makes grand juries more independent and gives their indictments more credibility. Some scholars have argued that though using such a system nationwide would cost more, the added expense would be a small price to pay to reinvigorate the grand jury and restore it to its proper role as a voice of the community.

Hearsay Evidence: Admissible before a Grand Jury?

The rules of evidence prohibit the introduction of most hearsay evidence in a criminal trial. (Hearsay is evidence given by a person concerning what someone else said outside of court.) However, when Frank Costello, alias Francisco Castaglia, a notorious organized crime figure of the 1940s and 1950s, argued that his conviction for federal income tax evasion should be overturned because the grand jury that indicted him heard only hearsay evidence, the Supreme Court rejected his claim (*Costello v. United States,* 350 U.S. 359, 76 S. Ct. 406, 100 L. Ed. 397 [1956]).

Prior to his trial, Costello asked to inspect the grand jury record. He claimed there could have been no legal or competent evidence before the grand jury that indicted him. The judge refused the request. At trial, Costello's attorneys established that three investigating officers were the only witnesses to testify before the grand jury. These officers summarized the vast amount of evidence compiled by their investigation and introduced computations showing, if correct, that Costello had received far greater income than he had reported. Their summaries clearly constituted hearsay, because the three officers had no firsthand knowledge of the transactions upon which their computations were based. Therefore, Costello alleged a violation of the Fifth Amendment, and asked that hearsay evidence be barred from grand jury proceedings.

Justice Hugo L. Black, in his majority opinion, rejected these claims, noting that "neither the Fifth Amendment nor any other constitutional provision prescribes the kind of evidence upon which grand juries must act."

balance in the selection process. The requirement that grand juries be unbiased has evolved since 1807, when Vice President AARON BURR was indicted as a traitor. Burr insisted that the evidence against him be heard by an "impartial" jury as guaranteed in the SIXTH AMENDMENT to the Constitution. He successfully challenged many jurors on the all-Republican grand jury that had been selected. Burr was willing to accept jurors who were familiar with some details of his famous case but who claimed they had not drawn any conclusions about it. (Although he was indicted, Burr was eventually acquitted at trial.)

In the early twenty-first century, an unbiased grand jury means one that comprises people who have no prior familiarity with the facts of the case. Critics of this requirement say that it greatly limits the quality of people who are chosen to sit, since many intelligent, engaged, and otherwise ideal candidates for a grand jury also follow the news. On June 24, 1994, a California state judge dismissed a grand jury that was considering whether to indict former athlete and media personality O. J. SIMPSON for the MURDER of his ex-wife and her friend. The judge was responding to concerns, of both the prosecutor and the defendant, that grand jurors had been exposed to PRETRIAL PUBLICITY that might prejudice them—such as transcripts of 911 calls made by Simpson's ex-wife after he broke down the back door to her house.

After numerous struggles to balance grand juries racially and by gender, federal CASE LAW provides that "a defendant may challenge the array of grand jurors ... on the ground that the grand jury was not selected, drawn or summoned in accordance with law, and may challenge an individual juror on the ground that the juror is not legally qualified" (*Estes v. United States,* 335 F.2d 609, *cert. denied,* 379 U.S. 964, 85 S. Ct. 656, 13 L. Ed. 2d 559).

There have been suggestions that the federal grand jury should be abolished, but this action seems unlikely because it would change the BILL OF RIGHTS for the first time. In addition, the investigative and indicting roles of the courts have to be performed by some entity, and an alternative entity may be less desirable than the grand jury. Some states have abolished grand juries or provided alternatives. For example, in some states, prosecutors are allowed to file an information, which is a formal list of charges, usually submitted with notice of some kind of PROBABLE CAUSE hearing.

Other suggestions for change at the federal level may experience more success. Among those promoted by groups such as the AMERICAN BAR ASSOCIATION are:

- Better instructions from judges to jurors about the grand jury's powers and its independence from prosecutors
- Reports by prosecutors on the performance of the grand jury system
- Increased access to grand jury transcripts for suspects who are eventually indicted
- Expanded safeguards against abuse of witnesses, including education about their rights and the presence of their attorneys
- Notification of targets of investigations that they are targets
- Optional rather than mandatory appearances by targets of investigations
- An end to the requirement that prosecutors present defense evidence, and replacement with a requirement that grand jurors be informed that the defense was not represented in the hearing.

FURTHER READINGS

Beale, Sara Sun, et al. 1997. *Grand Jury Law and Practice.* 2d ed. Eagan, MN: West.

Brenner, Susan W. 1995. "The Voice of the Community: A Case for Grand Jury Independence." *Virginia Journal of Social Policy and the Law* 3 (fall). Available online at http://campus.udayton.edu/~grandjur/recent/lawrev.htm; website home page: http://campus.udayton.edu (accessed July 27, 2009).

Farrel, Lyn, ed. 2002. *The Federal Grand Jury.* New York: Nova.

Goldstein, Howard W. 1998. *Grand Jury Practice.* New York: Law Journal Seminars-Press.

Iraola, Roberto. 2003. "Terrorism, Grand Juries, and the Federal Material Witness Statute." *St. Mary's Law Journal* 34 (winter).

Leipold, Andrew D. 1995. "Why Grand Juries Do Not (and Cannot) Protect the Accused." *Cornell Law Review* 80 (January). Available online at http://freedomlaw.com/GRANDJRY.html; website home page: http://freedomlaw.com (accessed July 27, 2009).

Simmons, Ric. 2002. "Re-Examining the Grand Jury: Is There Room for Democracy in the Criminal Justice System?" *Boston Univ. Law Review* 82 (February).

Skolnik, Sam. 1999. "Grand Jury: Power Shift?" *Legal Times* (April 12). Available online at http://www.truthinjustice.org/grandjury.htm; website home page: http://www.truthinjustice.org (accessed July 27, 2009).

U.S. Department of Justice, National Institute of Justice Office of Development, Testing and Dissemination. *Grand Jury Reform: A Review of Key Issues.* Washington, D.C.: U.S. Government Printing Office.

Worden, Amy. 2000. "Lawyers Target 'Lawless' Federal Grand Juries." *ABP News Online.* Available online at http://www.crimelynx.com/gjref.html; website home page: http://www.crimelynx.com (accessed July 27, 2009).

CROSS REFERENCE

Clarendon, Constitutions of.

GRAND LARCENY

A category of larceny—the offense of illegally taking the property of another—in which the value of the property taken is greater than that set for petit larceny.

At COMMON LAW, the punishment for grand larceny was death. In the early 2000s, grand LARCENY is a statutory crime punished by a fine, imprisonment, or both.

GRANDFATHER CLAUSE

A portion of a statute that provides that the law is not applicable in certain circumstances due to preexisting facts.

Grandfather clauses, which were originally intended to prevent black people from voting, were named for provisions adopted by the constitutions of some states. Such amendments sought to interfere with an individual's right to vote by setting forth difficult requirements. For example, common requirements were ownership of a large amount of land or the ability to read and write portions of the state and federal constitutions. The name *grandfather clause* arose from the exceptions that were made for veterans of the Civil War. If the veterans were qualified to vote prior to 1866, their descendants were also qualified. Thus, in effect, if a person's grandfather could vote, he could vote without further restrictions.

These statutes accomplished precisely what was intended, because nearly all slaves and their descendants were disqualified from voting because they could not satisfy the statutory requirements.

In the 1915 case of *Guinn v. United States,* 238 U.S. 347, 35 S. Ct. 926, 59 L. Ed. 1340, the SUPREME COURT OF THE UNITED STATES examined a grandfather clause that was added to the Oklahoma constitution shortly following its admission to the Union. The 1910 CONSTITU-TIONAL AMENDMENT required that prospective voters pass a literacy test in order to qualify to vote. However, anyone who was entitled to vote on January 1, 1866, or any time earlier under any form of government, or who at that time lived in a foreign country, was exempt from satisfying the literacy test requirement. The lineal descendants of such exempted persons also were exempt from such a requirement. In reality, the amendment recreated and perpetu-ated the very conditions that the FIFTEENTH AMENDMENT was intended to destroy, even though race was never mentioned as a voter qualification.

The Court held that the clause was in violation of the Fifteenth Amendment, which states that "the right of citizens of the United States to vote shall not be denied or abridged by the United States or by any State on account of race, color, or previous condition of servitude." Oklahoma argued that states had the power to set forth voter qualifications. Therefore, the statute in controversy did not violate the Fifteenth Amendment because race was not mentioned as a voter qualification. The Supreme Court was in agreement that states have the right to determine who is qualified to vote; however, they are permitted to do so only within constitutional limits. The limit that proscribes consideration of the race of voters extends to sophisticated as well as simple-minded DISCRIMINATION, and equality under the law cannot be based upon whether a person's grandfather was a free man.

Oklahoma undertook to change its law following this decision. The revised statute said that everyone who was able to vote as a result of the grandfather clause automatically contin-ued to be eligible and those who had been denied voting rights were given 12 days in 1916 to register to vote. If they were out of the county where they resided or if they were prevented from registering by sickness or unavoidable circumstances, they were given an additional 50 days in 1916 to register. After that time black persons who tried to register to vote were turned away, because the time to register outside the grandfather clause had ended in 1916.

In the 1939 case of *Lane v. Wilson*, 307 U.S. 268, 59 S. Ct. 872, 83 L. Ed. 1281, the Supreme Court rejected Oklahoma's new scheme, calling

it another example of an attempt by a state to thwart equality in the right to vote regardless of race or color. The Court ruled that the proposed remedy, in the form of such a limited registration period, was inadequate. A group of citizens who lacked the habits and traditions of political independence deserved a greater opportunity to register to vote.

The term *grandfather clause* in its current application refers to a legislative provision that permits an exemption based upon a preexisting condition. For example, through the application of grandfather clauses, certain prerogatives are extended to those regularly engaged in a particular profession, occupation, or business that is regulated by statute or ordinance. Such a clause might allow an individual, who has been in continuous practice in a particular profession for a specific period, to circumvent certain licensing requirements.

GRANGER MOVEMENT

The Granger Movement was begun in the late 1860s by farmers who called for government regulation of railroads and other industries whose prices and practices, they claimed, were monopolistic and unfair. Their efforts contrib-uted to a growing public sentiment against monopolies, which culminated in the passage of the Sherman Act (or SHERMAN ANTI-TRUST ACT) of 1890, 15 U.S.C.A. §§ 1–7.

In 1867 the American farmer was in desperate straits. Needing better educational opportunities and protection from exorbitant prices charged by middlemen, the farmers decided to form an independent group to achieve their goals.

Oliver Hudson Kelley, a former employee of the AGRICULTURE DEPARTMENT, organized a group called the Patrons of Husbandry. Membership was open to both men and women, and each local group was known as a Grange. Each Grange chose officers, and the goal of each meeting was to present news of educational value to the farmer.

Kelley traveled across the country establish-ing Granges; he found his greatest support in Minnesota. The Granges soon evolved into the national Granger Movement. By 1873 all but four states had Granges.

The main problems confronting the Granger Movement concerned corporate ownership of

grain elevators (used for the storage of crops) and railroads. These corporations charged high prices for the distribution and marketing of agricultural goods, and the farmer had no recourse but to pay. By 1873, the movement was becoming political, and the farmers formed an alliance, promising to support only political candidates who shared the interests of farmers; if that failed, they vowed to form their own parties.

Granger-supported candidates won political victories, and, as a result, much legislation protective of their interests was passed. Their biggest gain occurred in 1876, when the U.S. Supreme Court decreed in Munn v. Illinois, 94 U.S. (4 Otto.) 113, 24 L. Ed. 77, that states had the right to intervene in the regulation of public businesses. The law affected the prices of elevator charges, grain storage, and other services vital to the livelihood of the farmers.

In addition to political involvement, the Grangers established stores and cooperative elevators and employed the services of agents who secured special prices for the Grangers. These endeavors were not as successful as their previous undertakings, and the attempt to manufacture farm machinery depleted the finances of the movement. As a result, the Granger Movement began to wane in 1876.

CROSS REFERENCE

Agricultural Law.

THE WAR IS OVER—
THE REBELS ARE OUR
COUNTRYMEN AGAIN.
—ULYSSES S. GRANT

GRANT

To confer, give, or bestow. A gift of legal rights or privileges, or a recognition of asserted rights, as in treaty.

In the law of property, the term *grant* can be used in a deed to convey land, regardless of the number and types of rights conferred or the promises made by the transferor to the transferee. It is a comprehensive term that encompasses more specific words of transfer, such as assign, bargain, and devise.

A *public land grant* is a conveyance of ownership or other rights and privileges in publicly owned property to members of the general public who come under the qualifications of the statute that makes the land available. Such a grant is ordinarily noted in a public record, such as a charter or patent. In order to properly trace the ownership of property, it is sometimes necessary to determine each successive owner following the first grant.

A *private grant* is a grant of public land by a public official to a private individual as a type of reward or prize.

❖ GRANT, ULYSSES SIMPSON

Ulysses Simpson Grant, originally known as Hiram ULYSSES GRANT, was a U.S. general, the commander of the Union army during the last part of the Civil War, and the PRESIDENT OF THE UNITED STATES from 1869 to 1877. During his presidency Grant's reputation was tarnished by political corruption and scandal in his administration. Though he was never personally involved with any scandal, his failure to choose trustworthy advisers hurt his presidency.

Grant was born April 27, 1822, in Point Pleasant, Ohio. Raised in nearby Georgetown, he was educated at local and boarding schools. In 1839 he accepted an appointment to the Army's military academy at West Point, though he did not intend to become a soldier. The appointment allowed him to obtain the education he could not afford otherwise. He graduated in 1843 and began his military career with a tour of duty during the Mexican War of 1846–48, in which he distinguished himself in battle. After the war he was assigned to Fort Humboldt, California. During his time in California, Grant became lonely, and it has been alleged he had a drinking problem. He resigned his commission in 1854 and made several unsuccessful attempts at alternative careers, including farming and real estate. In 1860 he moved to Galena, Illinois, where he worked in his father's leather goods store.

With the outbreak of the Civil War in 1861, Grant returned to the military as a colonel in the Illinois Volunteers. He soon was promoted to brigadier general. Grant's first major victory came in February 1862, when his troops captured Forts Henry and Donelson, Tennessee, forcing General Simon B. Buckner, of the CONFEDERACY, to accept unconditional surrender. As a result Grant was promoted to major general.

Grant fought in the Battles of Shiloh and Corinth before forcing the surrender of Vicksburg, Mississippi, on July 4, 1862. In 1863 his forces triumphed over those of General Braxton Bragg, of the Confederacy, at Chattanooga, Tennessee.

Grant's leadership was welcomed by President ABRAHAM LINCOLN, who had endured a succession of commanders of the Union army who refused to wage an aggressive war. In March 1864 Lincoln promoted Grant to lieutenant general and gave him command over the entire Union army. In that year Grant scored another major military triumph. He commanded the Army of the Potomac against the forces of General Robert E. Lee, of the Confederacy, in the Wilderness Campaign, a series of violent battles that took place in Virginia. Battles at Spotsylvania, Cold Harbor, Petersburg, and Richmond produced heavy Union casualties, but Lee's smaller army was devastated. On April 9, 1865, at Appomattox Courthouse, Lee surrendered his forces, signaling an end to the Civil War.

After the war Grant enforced the Reconstruction laws of Congress in the Southern

Ulysses S. Grant.
LIBRARY OF CONGRESS

military divisions. President ANDREW JOHNSON appointed him secretary of war in 1867, but Grant soon had a falling out with the president. Grant aligned himself with the REPUBLICAN PARTY and became its presidential candidate in 1868. He defeated Democrat Horatio Seymour, former governor of New York, by a small popular vote margin. At age 46, he was the youngest man yet elected president. He was reelected in 1872, easily defeating Horace Greeley.

Though Grant's intentions were good, it soon became clear that his political and administrative skills did not match his military acumen. Despite his interest in CIVIL SERVICE reform, he followed his predecessors in using political patronage to fill positions in his

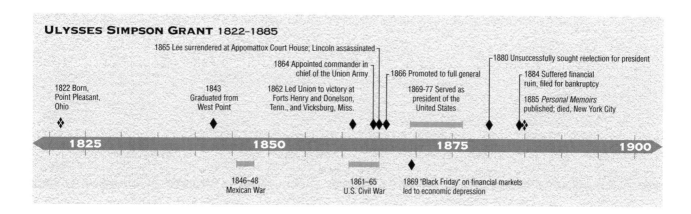

ULYSSES SIMPSON GRANT 1822–1885

1822 Born, Point Pleasant, Ohio

1843 Graduated from West Point

1862 Led Union to victory at Forts Henry and Donelson, Tenn., and Vicksburg, Miss.

1864 Appointed commander in chief of the Union Army

1865 Lee surrendered at Appomattox Court House; Lincoln assassinated

1866 Promoted to full general

1869–77 Served as president of the United States

1880 Unsuccessfully sought reelection for president

1884 Suffered financial ruin, filed for bankruptcy

1885 *Personal Memoirs* published; died, New York City

1825 1850 1875 1900

1846–48 Mexican War

1861–65 U.S. Civil War

1869 "Black Friday" on financial markets led to economic depression

administration. Many of his appointees were willing to use their office for personal profit.

Grant's reputation was first tarnished in 1869 when financiers Jay Gould and James Fisk attempted to corner the gold market and drive up the price. Their plan depended on keeping the federal government's gold supply off the market. They used political influence within the Grant administration to further their scheme. When Grant found out about it, he ordered $4 million of government gold sold on the market. On September 24, 1869, known as Black Friday, the price of gold plummeted, which caused a financial panic.

During Grant's second term, more scandal erupted. Vice President Schuyler Colfax was accused of taking bribes in the Crédit Mobilier scandal, which involved a diversion of profits from the Union Pacific Railroad. And Grant's private secretary, Orville E. Babcock, was one of 238 persons indicted in the Whiskey Ring conspiracy, which sought to defraud the federal government of liquor taxes. Babcock was acquitted after Grant testified on his behalf. Finally, Grant accepted the resignation of Secretary of War William W. Belknap shortly before Belknap was impeached on charges of accepting a bribe.

In domestic policy Grant attempted to resolve the tensions between North and South. He supported AMNESTY for Confederate leaders, and he tried to enforce federal CIVIL RIGHTS legislation that was intended to protect the newly freed slaves. In foreign policy he settled long-standing difficulties with Great Britain, in the 1871 Treaty of Washington.

After leaving office in 1877, Grant spent his time traveling and writing. He made a world tour in 1878 and 1879. In 1880 he unsuccessfully sought the Republican party's nomination for president. In 1881 he bought a home in New York City and became involved in the investment firm of Grant and Ward, in which his son, ULYSSES S. GRANT, Jr., was a partner. He invested his personal fortune with the firm and encouraged others to invest as well. In 1884 the firm collapsed. Partner Ferdinand Ward had swindled all the funds from the investors. Grant was forced to file for BANKRUPTCY.

Needing money, Grant contracted with his friend Mark Twain to write his memoirs. Despite the debilitations of throat cancer, Grant was able to complete his *Personal Memoirs*

THE WAR IS OVER—
THE REBELS ARE OUR
COUNTRYMEN AGAIN.
—ULYSSES S. GRANT

shortly before his death on July 23, 1885, in Mount McGregor, New York. His memoir was well received and is now recognized as a classic military autobiography. Grant and his wife, Julia Dent Grant, are buried in Grant's Tomb, in New York City, which was proclaimed a national memorial in 1959.

FURTHER READINGS

Perret, Geoffrey, 1997. *Ulysses S. Grant: Soldier & President.* New York: Random House.

Scaturro, Frank J. 1999. *President Grant Reconsidered.* Lanham, MD: Madison.

Smith, Jean Edward. 2002. *Grant.* New York: Simon & Schuster.

GRANTEE

An individual to whom a transfer or conveyance of property is made.

In a case involving the sale of land, the buyer is commonly known as the grantee.

GRANTING CLAUSE

The portion of an instrument of conveyance, such as a deed, containing the words that transfer a present interest from the grantor to the grantee.

GRANTOR-GRANTEE INDEX

A master reference book, ordinarily kept in the office of official records of a particular county, which lists all recorded deeds as evidence of ownership of real property.

This index contains the volume and page number where an instrument can be found in the record books. The grantor-grantee index is frequently used to conduct a TITLE SEARCH on property. By consulting the index, an individual can trace the conveyance history of the property and determine whether or not it is encumbered.

GRANTOR

An individual who conveys or transfers ownership of property.

In real PROPERTY LAW, an individual who sells land is known as the grantor.

GRATUITOUS

Bestowed or granted without consideration or exchange for something of value.

The term *gratuitous* is applied to deeds, bailments, and other contractual agreements.

A *gratuity* is something given by someone who has no obligation to give and can be used in reference to a bribe or tip.

GRATUITOUS LICENSEE

An individual who is permitted, although not invited, to enter another individual's property and who provides no consideration in exchange for such permission.

For example, a person who obtains the permission of the owner of a parcel of land to park his or her car on such land for a few hours is a gratuitous licensee. Because the driver of the vehicle was not invited by the owner, he or she is not an invitee, and since the driver has obtained the owner's permission, he or she is not committing a TRESPASS. If the driver does not pay for the permission to park, the license to do so is thereby considered GRATUITOUS.

GRATUITY

Money, also known as a tip, given to one who provides services and added to the cost of the service provided, generally as a reward for the service provided and as a supplement to the service provider's income.

Legend suggests that the term "tip" originated from an innkeeper's sign, "To Insure Promptness." Traditionally, patrons gave gratuity to those providing services in order to ensure faster service. Gratuity has always been defined by local custom and etiquette, never by law. Individuals who work for gratuity include those who provide a wide variety of services, including, for example, waiters and waitresses, bartenders, hotel employees, and cab drivers.

Gratuity is customarily designed to ensure that patrons receive the best service possible. The custom allows service providers to be rewarded for providing good service and lets patrons penalize those who provide poor service. The amount of gratuity depends upon the type of service, though tips are usually determined by the total cost of service provided. Proper etiquette suggests that patrons should tip between ten to twenty percent of the total bill. Without gratuity, service providers may have no incentive to provide a higher level of service than necessary.

The system of tipping has been the subject of extensive commentary and debate. For example, Eleanor Roosevelt suggested to those Americans traveling in foreign lands, "a fair tip, or one a little on the generous side, will leave a pleasant feeling and respect for you in the one who receives it. A lavish one will create a secret disrespect and add to the reputation Americans have for trying to buy their way into everything." Scholars have focused their attention on many aspects of tipping, including the satisfaction of the patron when he or she leaves a tip for the services provided.

Tips and other forms of gratuity constitute TAXABLE INCOME and must be reported by those who receive them. Although the current federal MINIMUM WAGE for most employees is $5.15 per hour, this number is reduced to $2.13 per hour for most tipped employees. Since these tipped employees generally receive more than $3 per hour in compensation from gratuity, they seldom receive less than the minimum wage paid to other types of employees. However, if the combined amount of tips and wages comes to less than $5.15 per hour, the employer is required to make up the difference under regulations established by the U.S. LABOR DEPARTMENT. Employees must claim the amount of tips they receive to the employer and must report these amounts when they file their tax returns.

Patrons have, on occasion, brought suit over the practices of service providers of adding gratuity to bills. For example, in *Searle v. Wyndham International, Inc.*, 126 Cal. Rptr. 2d 231 (Cal. App. 2002), patrons of a hotel ordered room service, which included taxes, a seventeen percent service charge, and a room delivery charge. The bill also provided a line whereby the patrons could add gratuity to the bill, even though the service charge was gratuity paid to the server. The patrons sued the hotel, claiming that the practice was deceptive because it did not indicate that the service charge constituted gratuity and that the service charge constituted obligatory gratuity, which the patrons claimed should be voluntary. The court held that the practice was neither deceptive nor FRAUDULENT, holding in favor of the hotel.

FURTHER READINGS

Hernandez, Arnold. 2006. "Employer Tips on Employee Tip Income." Available online at http://www.arnoldhernandez.com/article_employee_tip_income_lawyer.php; website home page: http://www.arnoldhernandez.com (accessed September 4, 2009).

Lake, Holly R., Cindy J. Morgan, and Regan E. Forester. 2008. "The Difference between Employees and Independent Contractors." *Country Bar Update* 28, no. 1

(December). Available online at http://www.crimelynx.com/gjref.html; website homepage: http://www.crimelynx.com (accessed July 27, 2009).

Morgan, Daniel L., and Yale F. Goldberg. 1990. *Employees and Independent Contractors.* Chicago: CCH.

CROSS REFERENCES

Labor Department; Independent Contractor.

GRATZ V. BOLLINGER

The Supreme Court's decision in Gratz v. Bollinger struck down an affirmative action policy at the University of Michigan because it violated the equal protection clause.

The Supreme Court's decision in *Gratz v. Bollinger* (539 U.S. 244, 123 S. Ct. 2411, 156 L. Ed. 257 [2003]) was one of two major AFFIRMATIVE ACTION cases decided on June 23, 2003. Both *Gratz* and *Grutter v. Bollinger* (539 U.S. 306, 123 S. Ct. 2325, 156 L. Ed. 2d 304 [2003]) involved the use of racial preferences at the University of Michigan. The *Gratz* decision concluded that the University's undergraduate admissions policy violated the EQUAL PROTECTION clause.

In 1995 Jennifer Gratz, a white student, sought admission to the University of Michigan as an undergraduate. The university has approximately 25,000 applicants each year for 5,000 undergraduate slots. Gratz's grades, college entrance scores, and community and school activities were such that the school did not dispute Gratz's ALLEGATION that she would have been admitted had she been a minority.

Michigan's undergraduate admissions policy was based on a points system, with 150 points available. Underrepresented ethnic and racial groups automatically received 20 points. Other points could be given to scholarship athletes and socio-economically disadvantaged applicants. The largest number of points was reserved for academic credentials. Gratz's attorneys called the 20-point bonus for ethnicity or race a "super bonus" equivalent to a full extra point of a student's grade point average. In the 2002 freshman class, about 17 percent of the students were minorities.

Gratz won her case in federal district court in 2001. The court ruled that the school erred in "using race as a factor in admissions to remedy the present effects of past discrimination." The university appealed, but the Sixth CIRCUIT COURT of Appeals did not rule on the appeal before the Supreme Court agreed to hear both *Gratz* and *Grutter*.

The cases represented the first instances where the Court had reviewed the affirmative action issue addressed in REGENTS OF THE UNIVERSITY OF CALIFORNIA V. BAKKE (438 U.S. 265, 98 S. Ct. 2733, 57 L. Ed. 2d 750 [1978]). In *Bakke*, the Court invalidated the admission plan of the medical school at the University of California, Davis, because it set aside 16 places for minority students. The Supreme Court ruled that the quota system violated the CIVIL RIGHTS of a white student who sought admission. However, the Court also ruled that race could be factor that a school considers during the admission process.

Like the issue in *Bakke*, the issue in *Gratz* and *Grutter* focused on whether a compelling STATE INTEREST existed to promote diversity or whether the equal protection clause mandates that one ethnic, minority, gender, or age group cannot receive special advantages over another. In *Gratz* and *Grutter*, the Court determined that diversity is a compelling state interest.

However, the Court reached different conclusions when it came to Michigan's different admissions systems. With regard to the undergraduate policy, the Court in *Gratz* determined that the point system violated the equal protection clause. According to Chief Justice WILLIAM H. REHNQUIST, the university's use of race in its admission policy was not narrowly tailored to achieve the university's interest in promoting diversity. The policy did not provide for individualized consideration of each applicant, which is what the Court had identified as an essential requirement under *Bakke*.

Justices JOHN PAUL STEVENS, DAVID H. SOUTER, and RUTH BADER GINSBURG dissented in *Gratz*. Stevens and Souter argued that the case should be dismissed on jurisdictional grounds because the plaintiffs had already enrolled in other schools by the time they brought suit against the University of Michigan. Justice Ginsburg wrote a separate dissent arguing that Michigan's policy did not violate the equal protection clause.

FURTHER READINGS

Lee, Francis Graham. 2003. *Equal Protection: Rights and Liberties under the Law.* Santa Barbara, Calf.: ABC-CLIO.

Perry, Barbara A. 2007. *The Michigan Affirmative Action Cases.* Lawrence: Univ. Press of Kansas.

Stohr, Greg. 2004. *A Black and White Case: How Affirmative Action Survived Its Greatest Legal Challenge.* Princeton, N.J.: Bloomberg Press.

CROSS REFERENCES

Affirmative Action; Grutter v. Bollinger

GRAVAMEN

The basis or essence of a grievance; the issue upon which a particular controversy turns.

The gravamen of a criminal charge or complaint is the material part of the charge.

In English ecclesiastical law, the term *gravamen* referred to a grievance of which the clergy complained before the bishops in convocation.

❖ GRAY, HORACE

Horace Gray gained prominence as a Massachusetts jurist and a U.S. Supreme Court justice. In his 53-year career as a lawyer and judge, Gray earned a reputation as an expert on LEGAL HISTORY and precedent.

Gray was born in the prosperous Beacon Hill neighborhood of Boston on March 24, 1828. His grandfather, William Gray, was a prominent merchant and shipowner, and his father, Horace Gray, was a successful manufacturer. His uncle, Francis Calley Gray, gained fame for discovering the original Liberties of the Massachusetts Colony in New England, the first constitution of the colony, which was drawn up by NATHANIEL WARD and adopted in 1641.

Gray attended Harvard College, in Cambridge, Massachusetts. In 1848 he entered Harvard Law School; he received his law degree one year later. After two years of working in various law offices, Gray opened his own firm in Boston, where he practiced law until 1864. In addition to practicing law, Gray worked as reporter and editor of the *Massachusetts Reports,* a collection of court opinions and commentary on Massachusetts CASE LAW.

The position of reporter of the *Massachusetts Reports* traditionally led to a seat on the

Horace Gray.

PHOTOGRAPH BY HARRIS AND EWING. COLLECTION OF THE SUPREME COURT OF THE UNITED STATES

state supreme court, and that tradition played out for Gray. In 1864 he was named to the Supreme Judicial Court of Massachusetts by Governor John A. Andrew. At age 36, Gray was the youngest appointee in the history of that court.

As a justice, Gray was formal and stern. He required conservative dress in his court, and he lectured lawyers on their conduct. He demanded that attorneys arrive prepared, and he asked frequent questions from the bench. Gray's opinions were thorough and well documented. In 1873 Gray assumed the position of chief justice of the Supreme Judicial Court of Massachusetts.

In 1881 President JAMES GARFIELD was looking for a nominee for the U.S. Supreme Court, to

[I]T BEHOOVES THE COURT TO BE CAREFUL THAT IT DOES NOT UNDERTAKE TO PASS UPON POLITICAL QUESTIONS, THE FINAL DECISION OF WHICH HAS BEEN COMMITTED BY THE CONSTITUTION TO THE OTHER DEPARTMENTS OF THE GOVERNMENT.
—HORACE GRAY

HORACE GRAY 1828–1902

1873 Became chief justice of Mass. Supreme Judicial Court

1881–1902 Served as associate justice of the U.S. Supreme Court

1851–64 Practiced law in the private sector

1854–61 Served as reporter of Mass. Supreme Judicial Court

1884 Wrote majority opinion

1864–81 Served on Mass. Supreme Judicial Court

1892 Wrote majority opinion in *Nishimura Ekiu v. United States*

1849 Earned law degree from Harvard Law

1828 Born, Boston, Mass.

1845 Graduated from Harvard College

opinion in *Juilliard v. Greenman*

1902 Died, Nahant, Mass.

1825　1850　1875　1900　1925

1861–65 U.S. Civil War

1914–18 World War I

replace the ailing justice NATHAN CLIFFORD. Garfield was considering Gray and asked for copies of his opinions. Considering such self-promotion unseemly, Gray refused to send anything to Garfield. After Garfield's death in September 1881, Senator George F. Hoar recommended Gray to the new president, CHESTER A. ARTHUR, and Arthur nominated Gray as Clifford's replacement.

Gray authored many opinions on important issues of the day, including cases involving industry, IMMIGRATION, and state-federal relations. One lasting opinion written by Gray involved the power of the federal government to issue paper money. In *Juilliard v. Greenman*, 110 U.S. 421, 4 S. Ct. 122, 28 L. Ed. 204 (1884), the High Court established that the United States, through Congress, had the power to issue paper money against its own credit during times of peace as well as times of war.

The *Juilliard* opinion revealed Gray's strong nationalist sentiment, which became a hallmark of Gray's service on the Court. Gray tended to promote the rights of the United States in its own endeavors and in its relations with other countries. He led the Court in upholding a federal law limiting the immigration of Chinese into the United States (*Nishimura Ekiu v. United States*, 142 U.S. 651, 12 S. Ct. 336, 35 L. Ed. 1146 [1892]). In *Fong Yue Ting v. United States*, 149 U.S. 698, 13 S. Ct. 1016, 37 L. Ed. 905 (1893), Gray dismissed the notion that resident ALIENS could claim the protection of the U.S. Constitution. Gray also wrote the opinion in *Hilton v. Guyot*, 159 U.S. 113, 16 S. Ct. 139, 40 L. Ed. 95 (1895), in which the Court held that the United States did not have to recognize judgments obtained in France, because France did not recognize judgments obtained in the United States.

Gray never attained the legendary status enjoyed by some Supreme Court justices, perhaps because of his unwillingness to stray beyond the bounds of precedent and author far reaching opinions that change the course of the law. He died September 15, 1902, in Nahant, Massachusetts.

FURTHER READINGS

Friedman, Leon, and Fred L. Israel, eds. 1995. *The Justices of the United States Supreme Court: Their Lives and Major Opinions*, Volumes I–V. New York: Chelsea House.

"Horace Gray." 1992. *The Supreme Court of the United States: Its Beginnings and Its Justices, 1790–1991*. Washington, D.C.: Commission of the Bicentennial of the U.S. Constitution, Library of Congress.

Jacobs, Roger, comp. 1981. *Memorials of the Justices of the Supreme Court of the United States*. Vol. 2. Littleton, CO: Rothman.

❖ GRAY, JOHN CHIPMAN

JOHN CHIPMAN GRAY served as a member of the Harvard Law School faculty for more than four decades. He was an expert on the law of real property, and his works are still cited as PERSUASIVE AUTHORITY today.

John Chipman Gray was born July 14, 1839, in Brighton, Massachusetts, son of Horace and Sarah Russell (Gardner) Gray. He was the grandson of "Billy" Gray, shipowner and one-time lieutenant governor of the Commonwealth of Boston. Gray's older half-brother, HORACE GRAY, later became a Supreme Court justice.

When he was still a young boy, Gray's father experienced a financial setback. This did not, however, discourage Gray from seeking higher education. After attending Boston Latin School, he went to Harvard University, earning a bachelor of arts degree in 1859 and a bachelor of laws degree in 1861. Gray also received

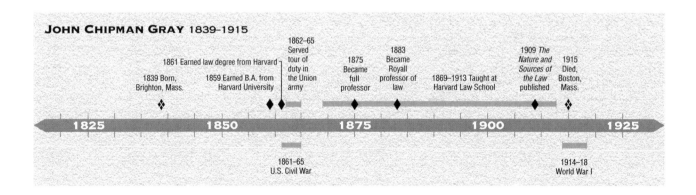

JOHN CHIPMAN GRAY 1839–1915

1839 Born, Brighton, Mass.

1859 Earned B.A. from Harvard University

1861 Earned law degree from Harvard

1862–65 Served tour of duty in the Union army

1875 Became full professor

1883 Became Royall professor of law

1869–1913 Taught at Harvard Law School

1909 *The Nature and Sources of the Law* published

1915 Died, Boston, Mass.

1825   1850   1875   1900   1925

1861–65 U.S. Civil War

1914–18 World War I

honorary doctor of laws degrees from Yale University in 1894 and Harvard in 1895.

After his ADMISSION TO THE BAR in 1862, Gray served a tour of military duty in the Civil War before establishing his legal practice in Boston in 1865. The law firm, Ropes & Gray, still exists and is a major national law firm, with offices in Boston, New York, Washington, D.C., and San Francisco. Four years after establishing the firm, Gray became a member of the faculty of the Harvard Law School. He served as a lecturer from 1869 to 1871 before becoming a law professor in 1875. He was named the Royall professor of law in 1883, a position he held until 1913. This chair is named after Isaac Royall, who funded the first chair in law at Harvard Law School, and it remains one of the most prestigious chairs of any law school in the United States.

Chipman's specialty was real PROPERTY LAW, and his works about future interests are still largely regarded as classic works. Among his more notable publications about future interests are *Restraints on the Alienation of Property* (1883) and *The Rule against Perpetuities* (1886), reprints of which are still available in the early 2000s. His most noteworthy publication, however, is *The Nature and Sources of the Law* (1909), which is widely considered one of the more significant works on the nature of COMMON LAW.

On February 25, 1915, two years after retiring from teaching, Gray died in Boston, Massachusetts.

FURTHER READINGS

Albert, Ropes, and Gray Boyden. 1942. *Ropes-Gray, 1865–1940*. Boston: Lincoln & Smith.

Gray, John Chipman. 1886. *The Rule against Perpetuities*. Reprint, 2009. Ithaca, NY: Cornell Univ. Press.

"John Chipman Gray." 1915. *Harvard Law Review* 6 (April).

Moran, Gerald P. 2009. *John Chipman Gray: The Harvard Brahmin of Property Law*. Durham, NC: Carolina Academic.

GRAY PANTHERS

Founded in 1970, the Gray Panthers is a national organization dedicated to social justice for old and young people alike. However, the Gray Panthers is best known for work on behalf of older persons. It has lobbied and litigated against AGE DISCRIMINATION in the areas of retirement, housing, and health care. The group's broad liberal agenda reflects the politics of its founder, Margaret E. "Maggie" Kuhn (1905–1995), who built the fledgling organization into a powerful

A member of the Gray Panthers takes part in a 1984 Boston rally calling for the elimination of mandatory retirement ages in public and private sector jobs. The Gray Panthers support a variety of issues including affordable housing and creation of a national health system.

AP IMAGES

force in local and national politics. At the time of her death in 1995, Kuhn's success as an organizer, leader, spokeswoman, and author had built the Gray Panthers into an organization with 70,000 members in 85 chapters nationwide. Although the organization is strongest at the grassroots level, its relatively small seven-member national staff has effected significant changes in federal law.

The protest era of the VIETNAM WAR gave rise to the Gray Panthers. In 1970, 65-year-old Margaret E. Kuhn was forced by the federal mandatory retirement law to end her 22-year career in the United Presbyterian Church. However, she did not want to retire. In response Kuhn helped form a loose-knit organization called Consultation of Older and Younger Adults for Social Change. Its primary goals were changing the mandatory retirement age and uniting people of all ages to seek an end to the Vietnam War. As the group gained recognition, the press coined the term "gray panthers," comparing it to the radical black activist group, the Black Panthers. Kuhn adopted the name in 1972.

The Gray Panthers developed a broad political agenda. Among its goals were affordable housing, the creation of a national health system, nursing home reform, and CONSUMER PROTECTION.

Lobbying efforts soon established the group's reputation on Capitol Hill. In 1978 it helped secure passage of an amendment to the

Age DISCRIMINATION in Employment Act of 1967, which raised the mandated retirement age from 65 to 70. In 1981 the Gray Panthers added a representative to the U.N. Economic and Social Council. In 1990 it moved its headquarters to Washington, D.C.

Throughout the 1980s and early 1990s, the Gray Panthers backed efforts ranging from the passage of gay CIVIL RIGHTS legislation to the legalization of the medical use of marijuana by those who are ill. Its members also lobbied strongly during President Bill Clinton's first term for the creation of a NATIONAL HEALTH CARE system.

The organization was also active in the courts. It joined numerous cases by filing friend-of-the-court briefs and brought its own suits. Perhaps its most significant victory came in 1980, in *Gray Panthers v. Schweiker* (652 F.2d 146 [D.C. Cir. 1980]), a CLASS ACTION suit brought to change MEDICARE regulations. At issue was how the government informed older patients when Medicare reimbursements were denied: Under federal law, benefits of less than $100 could be denied for reimbursement with only a form letter, which was thick with jargon (42 U.S.C.A. § 1395 et seq.). In 1979 the Gray Panthers contended that this notification scheme was a violation of their constitutional due process rights. The DEFENDANT, the Department of Health, Education, and Welfare, maintained that it had a congressional mandate to set restraints on the program; any further form of notification would be too expensive, it argued. After losing the initial court case, the Gray Panthers successfully argued on appeal for improved written communication and an oral hearing at which they could explain their side of the dispute.

As of 2009, the Gray Panthers have identified a host of issues for its organizational focus: health care, family security, peace, civil rights, political integrity and economic justice, education, jobs and workers rights, and the environment.

FURTHER READINGS

Gray Panthers. Available online at www.graypanthers.org (accessed September 23, 2009).

Kuhn, Maggie. 1991. *No Stone Unturned: The Life and Times of Maggie Kuhn.* New York: Ballantine.

❖ GRAY, WILLIAM HERBERT, III

From 1979 to 1991 William H. Gray served as U.S. representative from Pennsylvania's Second Congressional District. Gray, a liberal Democrat, chaired the powerful House Budget Committee during his last six years in Congress. In those years, he fought against the administrations of Republican presidents RONALD REAGAN and GEORGE H.W. BUSH to preserve Democratic spending priorities. An African American, Gray also became a leader on U.S. policy toward Africa. He helped create and pass laws that imposed harsh sanctions on South Africa for its policies of apartheid.

William Herbert Gray III was born August 20, 1941, in Baton Rouge, Louisiana. His father was a clergyman and an educator who served as president of Florida Normal and Industrial College in St. Augustine and of Florida A&M College in Tallahassee. His mother, Hazel Yates Gray, worked as a high school teacher. In 1949 the family moved to Philadelphia, where Gray's father became pastor of Bright Hope Baptist Church. Gray's grandfather had served in the same post since 1925, and Gray would follow his grandfather and father to the Bright Hope pulpit in 1972.

Gray attended Franklin and Marshall College, in Lancaster, Pennsylvania, where he served an internship in the office of Representative Robert N. C. Nix Jr. (D-Pa.). Although Gray felt stimulated by his brief experience in politics, he followed his father and grandfather into the ministry after his graduation in 1963. In 1964 he became assistant pastor of the Union Baptist Church, in Montclair, New Jersey. He went on to earn a master of divinity degree from Drew Theological School, in Madison, New Jersey, in 1966, and a master of theology degree from Princeton Theological Seminary in 1970.

While working as a minister, Gray became active in community projects, winning particularly high praise for his efforts to improve housing for low-income African Americans. In 1970 he brought suit against a landlord in Montclair who had refused to rent to him because of his race. The New Jersey Superior Court awarded Gray financial damages in a decision that set a national precedent (*Gray v. Serruto Builders, Inc.*, 110 N.J. Super. 297, 265 A.2d 404 [1970]). Gray also served as a lecturer at several New Jersey colleges and as an assistant professor at Saint Peter's College, in Jersey City, New Jersey.

After his father's death in 1972, Gray became pastor of Bright Hope Baptist Church and continued his involvement in community politics. Convinced that he could accomplish more in a position of greater power, Gray decided to challenge his former employer, Nix, in 1976 for the Democratic nomination to represent Pennsylvania's Second Congressional District. He lost the primary by only 339 votes. In 1978 he challenged Nix in the primary again and won, and then earned a decisive victory over his Republican opponent in the general election.

In the House, Gray became a member of the Foreign Affairs, District of Columbia, and Budget Committees and was an active member of the Congressional Black Caucus. On the Budget Committee, he brokered crucial budget compromises between the House and Senate and developed a keen understanding of the intricacies of the federal government's money matters. An unapologetic liberal, he fought doggedly against the conservative policies of President Reagan.

On January 4, 1985, Gray was elected chair of the powerful Budget Committee. During budget negotiations that year, he salvaged many programs that the Reagan administration and the Republican-controlled Congress sought to cancel, including Urban Development Action grants and the Appalachian Development Program. He also froze the defense budget at the previous year's level in order to reduce the budget deficit. Gray opposed the Gramm-Rudman-Hollings Act, also known as the Balanced Budget and Emergency Deficit Control Act, 2 U.S.C.A. §§ 901 et seq., however, calling it a "flawed doomsday machine" that would destroy worthwhile programs. The law mandated automatic budget cuts unless specific deficit-reduction targets were met. Gray argued that the act led to budget padding and discouraged efficient management.

William H. Gray III.
AP IMAGES

In 1987 Gray whittled the budget deficit down to $137 billion, $7 billion under the Gramm-Rudman-Hollings ceiling. He accomplished this through military spending reductions and tax increases. In negotiations for the budget of fiscal year 1989—the year in which the FEDERAL BUDGET first exceeded $1 trillion—Gray successfully lobbied for more tax increases to meet the Gramm-Rudman-Hollings targets.

Gray worked throughout his congressional career to increase aid to black Africa. In 1980 he became the first rookie member of Congress to create a new government program, when

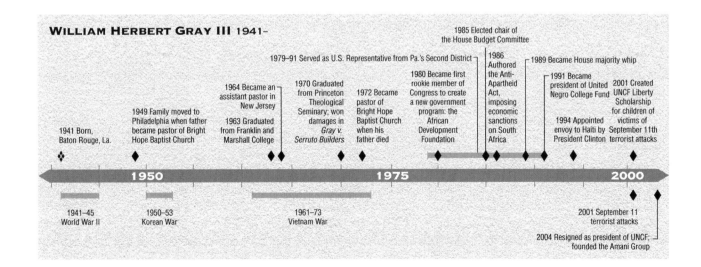

WILLIAM HERBERT GRAY III 1941–

1985 Elected chair of the House Budget Committee

1979–91 Served as U.S. Representative from Pa.'s Second District

1986 Authored the Anti-Apartheid Act, imposing economic sanctions on South Africa

1989 Became House majority whip

1980 Became first rookie member of Congress to create a new government program: the African Development Foundation

1970 Graduated from Princeton Theological Seminary; won damages in *Gray v. Serruto Builders*

1972 Became pastor of Bright Hope Baptist Church when his father died

1964 Became an assistant pastor in New Jersey

1963 Graduated from Franklin and Marshall College

1991 Became president of United Negro College Fund

2001 Created UNCF Liberty Scholarship for children of victims of September 11th terrorist attacks

1949 Family moved to Philadelphia when father became pastor of Bright Hope Baptist Church

1994 Appointed envoy to Haiti by President Clinton

1941 Born, Baton Rouge, La.

1950

1975

2000

1941–45 World War II

1950–53 Korean War

1961–73 Vietnam War

2001 September 11 terrorist attacks

2004 Resigned as president of UNCF; founded the Amani Group

he sponsored the bill that established the African Development Foundation (22 U.S.C.A. §§ 290h-1). The foundation sent aid directly to African villages. In 1984 he sponsored legislation that sent emergency food aid to Ethiopia. Gray also exerted a great deal of influence over African affairs, authoring and promoting passage of the Anti-Apartheid Act (22 U.S.C.A. §§ 5001 et seq.), which imposed economic sanctions on South Africa for its policies of racial SEGREGATION. The act passed in 1986 over President Reagan's veto. In addition, Gray worked to foster better relations between African and Jewish Americans.

As he rose in the House, Gray became increasingly influential in the DEMOCRATIC PARTY. In 1988 he chaired the panel that drafted the party platform at the Democratic National Convention. The following year he was named to the powerful position of House majority whip.

Gray encountered difficulties when unconfirmed rumors of financial wrongdoing surfaced in 1988. He left Congress in 1991, surprising many who had predicted that he would continue to rise in the House. The same year, Gray became president and chief executive officer of the United Negro College Fund (UNCF), the nation's oldest higher education assistance organization for African Americans, a position he held until June 2004. More than half of the $1.8 billion raised throughout the organization's history (which spans more than 50 years) took place during Gray's tenure. He was instrumental in establishing a number of new research and funding programs, and he ensured that administrative costs remained below 15 percent of the fund's total revenues.

In 1994 President BILL CLINTON appointed him envoy to Haiti. Gray advocated using economic sanctions against that country's military dictatorship in order to restore President Jean-Bertrand Aristide to power.

Gray has continued to be active in public affairs, and he sits on several corporate boards, such as Dell Inc., J.P. Morgan Chase & Co., Prudential Financial Inc., Visteon Corporation and Pfizer Inc. He is Chairman of the Amani Group (a consulting and advisory firm), a position he has held since August 2004.

Throughout his career, Gray has received numerous awards, including the MARTIN LUTHER KING Jr. Award for Public Service in 1985. And, in its December 1999 issue, *Ebony* magazine

named him one of the 100 Most Important Blacks in the World in the 20th Century. Gray also has received honorary degrees from more than 60 colleges. Despite his heavy work schedule over the years, he has continued to preach sermons at Bright Hope Baptist Church in Philadelphia at least two Sundays per month.

Gray married Andrea Dash in 1971. The couple has three sons.

GREAT COMPROMISE OF 1787

See SHERMAN COMPROMISE.

GREAT SOCIETY

In May 1964 President LYNDON B. JOHNSON gave a speech at the University of Michigan in Ann Arbor in which he outlined his domestic agenda for the United States. He applauded the nation's wealth and abundance but admonished the audience that "the challenge of the next half century is whether we have the wisdom to use that wealth to enrich and elevate our national life, and to advance the quality of American civilization." Johnson's agenda was based on his vision of what he called "the Great Society," the name by which the agenda became popularly known.

Part of the Great Society agenda was based on initiatives proposed by Johnson's predecessor, JOHN F. KENNEDY, but Johnson's vision was comprehensive and far-reaching. Johnson wanted to use the resources of the federal government to combat poverty, strengthen CIVIL RIGHTS, improve public education, revamp urban communities, and protect the country's natural resources. In short, Johnson wanted to ensure a better life for all Americans. He had already begun his push toward this goal with his "War on Poverty," a set of initiatives announced in 1964 and marked by the passage of the Economic Opportunity Act of 1964. This act authorized a number of programs including Head Start; work-study programs for college students; Volunteers in Service to America (VISTA), a domestic version of the Peace Corps; and various adult job-training programs. Johnson's Great Society proposal was ambitious, even by his standards—as a seasoned politician, he had a well-earned reputation for getting things done. Not only that, he had to win the 1964 presidential election before he could enact his ideas.

Johnson sought affordable health care for all, stronger civil rights legislation, more

THE DIFFERENCE
BETWEEN MYSELF
AND OLD-LINE FOLKS
IS THAT I
UNDERSTAND THAT
THE POLITICAL
PROCESS IS PUTTING
TOGETHER
COALITIONS.
—WILLIAM H. GRAY

benefits for the poor and the elderly, increased aid to education, economic development, urban renewal, crime prevention, and stronger conservation efforts. To many, Johnson's initiative seemed to be the most sweeping change in federal policy since Franklin D. Roosevelt's NEW DEAL in the 1930s.

The Great Society theme was the foundation of his campaign in the 1964 presidential election. Johnson's Republican opponent, BARRY GOLDWATER, campaigned on a promise of reducing the size and scope of the federal government. In the end, Johnson's campaign for the Great Society was convincing enough that he carried 46 states and won 61 percent of the popular vote in November.

Johnson outlined his Great Society programs during his State of the Union address in January 1965, and over the next several months progress followed quickly. MEDICARE was introduced to provide healthcare funding to SENIOR CITIZENS. The Elementary and Secondary Education Act was signed into law, guaranteeing increased funding to disadvantaged students. The Housing and Urban Development (HUD) program was created to bring affordable housing to the inner cities. The Highway Beautification Act was signed, providing funding to clear the nation's highways of blight. Along with that went legislation to regulate air and water quality. The Civil Rights Act of 1965 prohibited DISCRIMINATION on the basis of race, color, and gender.

Johnson chose John Gardner to head the Department of Health, Education, and Welfare (HEW). Gardner, who was sworn in on July 27, 1965, was a psychologist, an authority on education, and had previously been head of the Carnegie Corporation. Widely respected by members of both parties (he was a Republican) Gardner helped carry out Johnson's goals and agenda; in some circles he was known as the "engineer of the Great Society."

Johnson's Great Society made a genuine difference in the lives of millions of Americans, and many of its initiatives are still integral to U.S. society in the twenty-first century. But the programs were expensive, costing billions of dollars, and many of Johnson's opponents said that the programs only added new layers of BUREAUCRACY to an already oversized government. A more pressing issue, however, was the VIETNAM WAR. What was supposed to have been a

short-term exercise had now gone on for several years with financial and human cost. The war was highly unpopular with a large portion of American society, and the energy needed to keep the war effort going drained resources from the programs of the Great Society. The departure of Gardner from HEW was a blow to Johnson, especially since after Gardner left HEW he spoke out publicly against the war.

The 1960s also saw an upsurge in racial unrest. Despite the sweeping civil rights initiatives Johnson had launched, many poor blacks felt it was not enough. Racial unrest in major cities led to several riots, and it was clear that there was a great deal of pent-up anger and FRUSTRATION that could not simply be legislated away.

Faced with mounting criticism because of Vietnam, Johnson chose not to run for re-election in 1968. The shadow of Vietnam hung over him until his death five years after, and it was only later that the American people were able to appreciate fully the scope and importance of Johnson's role in shaping the Great Society.

FURTHER READINGS

Andrew, John A. 1998. *Lyndon Johnson and the Great Society.* Chicago: Dee.

Califano, Joseph A. 2000. *The Triumph and Tragedy of Lyndon Johnson: The White House Years.* College Station: Texas A&M Univ. Press.

Unger, Irwin. 1996. *The Best of Intentions: The Triumphs and Failures of the Great Society under Kennedy, Johnson, and Nixon.* New York: Doubleday.

CROSS REFERENCES

Civil Rights; Civil Rights Movement.

GREEN CARD

The popular name for the Alien Registration Receipt Card issued to all immigrants entering the United States on a non-temporary visa who have registered with and been fingerprinted by the Immigration and Naturalization Service. The name green card *comes from the distinctive coloration of the card.*

CROSS REFERENCE

Aliens.

GREEN PARTY

The Green Party blossomed as an outgrowth of the environmental and conservation movement of the 1970s and 1980s. In 1970 Charles Reich published *The Greening of America,* a popular extended essay that effectively inserted

Former congresswoman Cynthia McKinney ran for president in 2008 as the Green Party candidate. Her running mate was Rosa Clemente.

AP IMAGES

environmentalism into politics. Reich, along with anarchist Murray Bookchin, helped inspire a worldwide environmental movement. Throughout the 1970s and 1980s, environmental activists, calling themselves Greens, began to work within the political system to advance environmental causes around the globe.

The Green Party first achieved electoral success in Germany in the early 1980s. German Green Party candidates were elected to public office on platforms that stressed four basic values: ecology, social justice, grassroots democracy, and nonviolence. In the mid-1990s the Green Party was established in more than 50 countries, and Green Party politicians held seats in approximately nine European parliaments.

In the United States, Greens originally were reluctant to move into electoral politics. Throughout the 1970s and most of the 1980s, they teamed with military and NUCLEAR POWER protesters to promote their agendas from outside the formal political system. In 1984 the Greens began to discuss the organization of a political party, and in 1985 the organization fielded its first candidates for elective office in North Carolina and Connecticut. The U.S. Greens became known as the Association of State Green Parties.

In 1996, in response to the need for a national Green presence, the organization's name changed to the Green Party of the United States. The U.S. Green Party expanded the European platform to forge its own identity. According to its Website, the party offers a proactive approach to government based on ten key values: ecological wisdom; grassroots democracy; social justice and equal opportunity; nonviolence; decentralization; small-scale, community-based economics and economic justice; feminism and gender equity; respect for diversity; personal and global responsibility; and future focus and sustainability. Each state and local chapter of the party adapts these goals to fit its needs.

The Green Party of the United States also extended its reach in the 1990s and into the 2000s. In 1996 the party fielded candidates in 17 states and in the District of Columbia. It increased its national profile the same year by nominating RALPH NADER as its candidate for president. Nader accepted the nomination, but stipulated that he would not become a member of the Green Party and that he did not feel obliged to follow faithfully its political platform. Nader ran a no-frills campaign, eschewing advertising and usually traveling alone to speak at various locales. He accepted no taxpayer money and spent approximately $5,000 on the campaign. With political activist Winona LaDuke as his running mate, Nader appeared on the ballot in 21 states and in the District of Columbia. The ticket also received write-in votes in all but five states. Nader and LaDuke lost to the Democratic incumbents, President BILL CLINTON and Vice President AL GORE.

Nader and LaDuke ran again in the 2000 presidential election, again on the Green Party platform. Nader raised more than $8 million for the campaign, about $30 million less than REFORM PARTY candidate Pat Buchanan. Nader received the third highest number of votes with 2,882,955, representing 2.74 percent of the total vote. By comparison, Buchanan received a total of 448,895.

David Cobb, legal counsel for the party, was its 2004 presidential candidate, receiving the nomination after a divisive battle with Nader. His name appeared on only 28 state ballots, down from 44 in 2000. The party suffered a dramatic loss of support, with Cobb receiving only 119,859 votes. The decline continued in the 2009 presidential election, when Cynthia McKinney, a former congresswoman, received only 161,603 votes.

On the local level, the Green Party has realized some electoral success. As of 2009, there are 193 Greens serving in state and local government.

FURTHER READINGS

Burchell, John. 2002. *The Evolution of Green Politics.* London: Earthscan Publications.

Green Party of the United States. Available online at www. greenpartyus.org (accessed September 23, 2009).

Herrnson, Paul S., and John C. Green, eds. 1998. *Multiparty Politics in America.* Lanham, Md.: Rowman & Littlefield.

CROSS REFERENCES

Environmental Law; Independent Parties

Jack Greenberg.
COURTESY OF JACK GREENBERG

❖ GREENBERG, JACK

Jack Greenberg is a CIVIL RIGHTS attorney and professor of law who was on the front lines of the struggle to eliminate racial DISCRIMINATION in U.S. society. He served for 35 years as an assistant counsel and as director-counsel of the NAACP LEGAL DEFENSE AND EDUCATIONAL FUND (LDF).

Greenberg was born December 22, 1924, in New York City. His parents, Bertha Rosenberg and Max Greenberg, were immigrants from Eastern Europe who stressed to their children the importance of education. Although they were not involved in civil rights or politics, they inculcated in their children a deep concern for disadvantaged people. This early awareness of the plight of society's less fortunate ignited Greenberg's desire to take up the civil rights cause.

Greenberg grew up in Brooklyn and the Bronx, and he was educated at public elementary and high schools before receiving his bachelor of arts from Columbia University in 1945. He then entered the U.S. Navy and served in the Pacific as a deck officer, participating in the invasion of Iwo Jima. After the war ended, he enrolled at Columbia Law School and earned his bachelor of laws in 1948. While in law school, Greenberg enrolled in a seminar called

Legal Survey, which established the course of his future career. The course offered students the opportunity to work for civil liberties and civil rights organizations, doing legal research and writing memorandums, complaints, and briefs. While taking the course, Greenberg became acquainted with THURGOOD MARSHALL, who at the time was the LDF's director. When a staff attorney resigned her position, Greenberg was recommended as a replacement. His career in civil rights, as well as his lasting friendship with Marshall, was launched.

Greenberg began his work at the LDF with only a vague idea about the types of cases he would handle. He was quickly plunged into the ugly reality of racial discrimination. His first cases required him to travel regularly to the

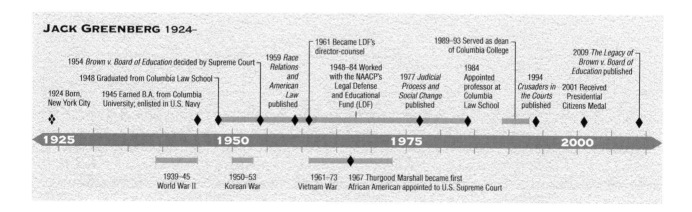

JACK GREENBERG 1924–

1924 Born, New York City

1945 Earned B.A. from Columbia University; enlisted in U.S. Navy

1948 Graduated from Columbia Law School

1954 *Brown v. Board of Education* decided by Supreme Court

1959 *Race Relations and American Law* published

1948–84 Worked with the NAACP's Legal Defense and Educational Fund (LDF)

1961 Became LDF's director-counsel

1977 *Judicial Process and Social Change* published

1984 Appointed professor at Columbia Law School

1989–93 Served as dean of Columbia College

1994 *Crusaders in the Courts* published

2001 Received Presidential Citizens Medal

2009 *The Legacy of Brown v. Board of Education* published

1939–45 World War II

1950–53 Korean War

1961–73 Vietnam War

1967 Thurgood Marshall became first African American appointed to U.S. Supreme Court

South to defend African Americans against various racially motivated charges. While on those trips, he experienced racial discrimination firsthand, as the African American lawyers with whom he traveled were not allowed to stay at hotels for whites or eat at restaurants for whites.

Upon seeing the deplorable accommodations African Americans were forced to accept because of legal SEGREGATION, Greenberg, who is white, soon realized that the LDF had a definite plan underlying its apparently random selection of disparate cases. The fund's ambitious goal was nothing less than the complete repudiation of PLESSY V. FERGUSON, 163 U.S. 537, 16 S. Ct. 1138, 41 L. Ed. 256, the infamous 1896 Supreme Court case that established the separate-but-equal doctrine, which legitimized segregation at all levels of society.

During the 1930s and 1940s, NAACP and LDF lawyers concentrated on desegregating higher education. Greenberg was involved in important cases that allowed the integration of professional schools in Maryland, Missouri, Oklahoma, Texas, Louisiana, North and South Carolina, and many other states. The LDF then set its sights on state-supported undergraduate schools. The first big case that Greenberg handled on his own involved the integration of the University of Delaware. The LDF's ASSAULT on segregated education culminated with the landmark 1954 Supreme Court decision in BROWN V. BOARD OF EDUCATION, 349 U.S. 294, 75 S. Ct. 753, 99 L. Ed. 1083, in which Greenberg was a major participant.

Greenberg and the LDF argued on behalf of African Americans in countless cases, with Greenberg appearing before the U.S. Supreme Court more than 40 times. During the 1960s and 1970s, Greenberg won important cases abolishing discrimination in housing, health care, employment, and public accommodations. Also during this time, the fund launched a full-scale effort to abolish the death penalty because of its disproportionate effect on blacks. The LDF was ultimately successful, but the victory was short-lived. By the 1980s most of the states that had used CAPITAL PUNISHMENT before it was outlawed had reinstated it under new terms considered constitutionally acceptable by the Supreme Court.

In 1961, when Marshall was appointed to the federal judiciary, Greenberg was named director-counsel of the LDF, a position he held

until 1984, when he resigned to become a professor at Columbia Law School. During his last ten years at the LDF, he concentrated the group's energies on preventing the reversal of laws and court rulings that had finally outlawed discrimination in all forms. In 1989 Greenberg was named dean of Columbia College, a post he held until 1993, when he returned to the faculty of the law school.

Greenberg's position as one of a small number of white lawyers involved in the LDF's struggles against racial discrimination was not a point of contention until 1982, when he was asked to co-teach a course in race and legal issues at Harvard Law School. The Black Law Students Association picketed the opening of the course, protesting the use of a white lawyer to present it. Greenberg led the course as planned, although some students boycotted. He encountered similar hostility when he was slated to teach a similar course at Stanford the following year, and so he declined the Stanford position. The protests were apparently a reflection of the feelings of younger black students and lawyers that whites had no credibility to speak about the African American struggle for equality. Greenberg was unfazed by the objections.

A man of many and varied interests, Greenberg has written several books, including *Race Relations and American Law* (1959), *Judicial Process and Social Change* (1977), and *Crusaders in the Courts: How a Dedicated Band of Lawyers Fought for the Civil Rights Revolution* (1994). He also coauthored a cookbook, *Dean Cuisine, or the Liberated Man's Guide to Fine Cooking* (1990), and studies Mandarin Chinese. He was married from 1950 to 1969 to Sema Ann Tanzer, with whom he had four children. He now lives in Manhattan with Deborah M. Cole, whom he married in 1970. They have two children.

Greenberg has received numerous awards throughout his career, including the Thurgood Marshall Award from the AMERICAN BAR ASSOCIATION in 1996. In recognition of his 50 years of defending civil and HUMAN RIGHTS, President BILL CLINTON awarded Greenberg the Presidential Citizens Medal in January 2001. This award honors individuals who have performed "exemplary deeds of service" to the United States in the areas of medicine and health, education, RELIGION, disability advocacy, government service, the environment, civil rights, and human rights.

I THINK THAT THE LAW HAS BEEN AN IMMENSE FORCE FOR SOCIAL CHANGE WITH REGARD TO RACE.
—JACK GREENBERG

Greenberg continues to teach at Columbia University Law School and has served as a visiting professor at more than ten American and foreign universities. He has earned a number of honorary law degrees and, as of 2009, continues to serve as a senior director of the LDF.

FURTHER READINGS

Greenberg, Jack. 2004. *Brown v. Board of Education: Witness to a Landmark Decision.* New York: Twelve Tables Press.

———. 1994. *Crusaders in the Courts: How a Dedicated Band of Lawyers Fought for the Civil Rights Revolution.* New York: Basic Books.

Greenberg, Jack, and Kendall Thomas, eds. 2009. *The Legacy of Brown v. Board of Education: Reflections and Colloquy.* New York: Twelve Tables Press.

Greenberg, Jack, with Stanley Corngold and Benno Wagner, eds. 2008. *Franz Kafka: The Office Writings.* New Jersey: Princeton Univ. Press.

CROSS REFERENCES

NAACP; School Desegregation.

GREENMAIL

A corporation's attempt to stop a takeover bid by paying a price above market value for stock held by the aggressor.

Greenmail is a practice in corporate MERGERS AND ACQUISITIONS. Like BLACKMAIL, the concept after which it is named, greenmail is money paid to an aggressor to stop an act of aggression. In the case of greenmail, the aggressor is an investor attempting to take over a corporation by buying up a majority of its stock, and the money is paid to stop the takeover. The corporation under attack pays an inflated price to buy stock from the aggressor, known popularly as a corporate raider. After the greenmail payment, the takeover attempt is halted. The raider is richer; the corporation is poorer but retains control. During a great wave of corporate mergers in the 1980s, the practice of paying greenmail became controversial. Critics viewed it as harmful to U.S. business interests. Portraying the transaction as little more than a bribe, they argued that some corporate raiders began takeover bids simply to earn profits through greenmail. Corporate shareholders also protested the practice. By the mid-1990s, state legislatures had taken the lead in opposing greenmail through legislation.

The increase in corporate mergers in the 1980s made the hostile corporate takeover a familiar event. Before the decade's multi-billion-dollar takeovers, corporate mergers usually involved a mutual agreement. In contrast, hostile takeovers ignore the target corporation's management. One form of hostile takeover involves stock. Whoever owns the most stock controls the corporation. Instead of entering negotiations with management, corporate raiders go to the corporation's stockholders with offers to buy their stock. Not only the means but also the goals of these acquisitions differ from those of earlier acquisitions. Prior to the 1980s, mergers generally occurred when larger interests bought up smaller competitors in similar industries, with an eye toward dominating a particular market. In hostile takeovers, corporate raiders often intend to break up and sell a corporation after the takeover is complete. Their interest commonly lies in earning enormous short-term profits from selling a company's assets, motivating corporations to try to protect themselves against takeovers.

Greenmail is one of an array of strategies, ranging from changing corporate bylaws to acquiring debt that makes the corporation a less attractive target, used to deter raiders. It is an expensive alternative, as was illustrated when investor Saul P. Steinberg attempted to take over the Disney Corporation in 1984. Steinberg was known for his concerted efforts in the takeover field, having previously targeted Chemical Bank and Quaker State. In March 1984 his purchase of 6.3 percent of Disney's stock triggered concern at the corporation that a takeover was in progress. Disney management quickly announced an approximately $390 million acquisition of its own that would make the company less attractive. After this maneuver failed, Disney's directors ultimately bought Steinberg's stock to stop the takeover. Steinberg earned a profit of about $60 million.

The Disney case illustrates a major criticism of greenmail: Other stockholders blame corporate directors for showing undue favoritism to corporate raiders, who are paid exorbitant sums for stock whereas the stockholders are not. This criticism formed the basis of a lawsuit that produced one of the few court decisions condemning greenmail outright. In 1984 Disney stockholders sued the corporation's directors as well as Steinberg and his fellow investors, seeking to recover the amount paid as greenmail. They won an injunction from the Superior Court of Los Angeles County, which placed Steinberg's profits from the sale in a trust. The verdict was upheld on appeal (*Heckmann v. Ahmanson,* 168 Cal. App. 3d 119, 214 Cal. Rptr. 177 [Cal. Ct.

App. 1985]). In ordering the profits put in a trust, the court sought "to prevent unjust enrichment" that would otherwise "reward [Steinberg] for his wrongdoing." In 1989 Steinberg settled with the plaintiffs for approximately $21.1 million.

Although greenmail's heyday was in the 1980s, it continued to be controversial in the 1990s. Criticism of greenmail grew out of a larger condemnation of the way in which corporate raiders had rewritten the rules of mergers and acquisitions in an avaricious, shortsighted manner. Some critics viewed this trend harshly. In his 1995 work on the subject, Professor David C. Bayne portrayed greenmail as a pact involving embezzlement by corporate directors and blackmail by corporate raiders. Bayne said greenmail is "nothing other than a recondite species of the broader genus Corporate BRIBERY, and as such is intrinsically illegitimate." States increasingly viewed greenmail in the same light. Most states had enacted antitakeover laws, and several had anti-greenmail provisions. The Ohio and Pennsylvania laws were among the toughest, requiring raiders to return greenmail profits to the target corporation (Ohio Rev. Code Ann. § 1707.043 [Anderson Supp. 1990]; 15 Pa. Cons. Stat. Ann. §§ 2571–2576 [Purdon Supp. 1991]). Some people doubt the constitutionality of these laws, and the issue of greenmail remains far from settled.

FURTHER READINGS

Bayne, David Cowan. 2001. "Traffic in Corporate Control—Greenmail: Damages and the Disposition of the Bribe." *Univ. of Detroit Mercy Law Review* 78 (summer).

———. 1995. "Traffic in Corporate Control—Greenmail: The Definition of the Reverse Premium-Bribe." *Univ. of Dayton Law Review* 20 (spring).

Crain, Mark E. 1991. "Disgorgement of Greenmail Profits: Examining a New Weapon in State Anti-Takeover Arsenals." *Houston Law Review* 28 (July).

"Securities and Exchanges: Greenmail." 1991. *United States Law Week* 60 (November 5).

GREGG V. GEORGIA

Modern U.S. death penalty jurisprudence begins with the U.S. Supreme Court's decision in *Gregg v. Georgia*, 428 U.S. 153, 96 S. Ct. 2909, 49 L. Ed.2d 859 (1976). In that landmark case, the Court rejected the idea that CAPITAL PUNISHMENT is inherently CRUEL AND UNUSUAL PUNISHMENT under the EIGHTH AMENDMENT. In addition, it endorsed new state death penalty statutes that sought to address the criticisms that the Court had raised in FURMAN V. GEORGIA, 408 U.S. 238, 92 S. Ct. 2726, 33

L. Ed.2d 346 (1972). These statutes split the criminal trial into a guilt phase and a penalty phase, gave jurors specific aggravating and mitigating factors to consider in deliberating the death penalty, and mandated appellate review with designated factors for the court to consider. Finally, the states removed capital punishment as a sentencing option for crimes other than MURDER. Since *Gregg*, the issues surrounding the death penalty have turned on procedural fairness rather than questions of societal values.

By the early 1970s, the death penalty had been removed from the statute books in many countries, including Austria, Denmark, Great Britain, Portugal, Switzerland, Brazil, and Venezuela. In the United States, criticism of the arbitrary administration of capital punishment and its application to crimes other than murder led to judicial challenges based on the Eighth Amendment's Cruel and Unusual Punishment proscription. The number of executions had dwindled, and public opinion polls suggested that the death penalty was no longer as popular. Therefore, opponents were optimistic when the U.S. Supreme Court struck down three death sentences in *Furman*.

However, the Court's manner of deciding the case revealed a split in the way that the justices looked at the death penalty. *Furman*, which came on a 5–4 vote, was issued as a *per curiam* decision, which takes the form of a brief, unsigned opinion. Such a decision does not have as great a precedential value as a signed opinion, as it indicates that the court was deeply divided over the reasons that went into its ultimate decision either to affirm or reverse a decision. Each justice filed a separate opinion, with only Justices William Brennan and THURGOOD MARSHALL declaring that the death penalty is intrinsically cruel and unusual punishment. Others on the Court who reversed the sentences indicated that capital punishment might be constitutional if the states administered it fairly and rationally so as to serve legitimate societal needs.

Georgia set out to address these concerns, and its legislature passed a comprehensive death-penalty-reform law. It established a BIFURCATED TRIAL process, in which guilt or innocence is to be decided first. If the DEFENDANT were found guilty of a capital crime, the jury then entered a penalty phase. The state developed a list of 14 "aggravating circumstances," any one of which could justify the death penalty. The jury had to find BEYOND A REASONABLE DOUBT that an aggravating circumstance applied. The defendant was also given the opportunity to present "mitigating circumstances" to the jury in hopes of overcoming the aggravating circumstances. These included the youth of the defendant, the defendant's cooperation with police, and the defendant's emotional state at the time of the crime. If the jury imposed the death penalty, the Georgia Supreme Court was mandated to review the decision. It was told to consider whether passion or prejudice influenced the sentence, whether the evidence of aggravating circumstances was sufficient, and whether the penalty was disproportional or excessive in comparison to similar cases and defendants.

The new law was applied at the trial of Troy Gregg for two counts each of armed ROBBERY and murder. Gregg was convicted, and during the penalty phase the PROSECUTOR offered evidence of aggravating circumstances. The jury found beyond a REASONABLE DOUBT that Gregg had committed the murders during the commission of another capital crime and for the purpose of taking a victim's property. These two circumstances sustained the death-penalty verdict. On appeal, the Georgia Supreme Court upheld the sentence, finding that the verdict was fair, based on the three factors it was instructed to review. However, it sustained the death penalty on only the second aggravating circumstance. It threw out the armed-robbery circumstance because the death penalty had rarely been imposed for that crime. Gregg then appealed to the U.S. Supreme Court.

The U.S. Supreme Court upheld the decision on a 7–2 vote. Justice POTTER STEWART announced the judgment of the Court in an opinion joined by two other justices. Four justices agreed with the AFFIRMANCE, but for different reasons. Stewart retraced the *Furman* decision and noted that only two justices had taken an absolutist position against the death penalty. The Court then declared that the death penalty was not inherently cruel and unusual punishment. The Eighth Amendment incorporated a "basic concept of dignity," which was consistent with the purposes of deterrence and of retribution. As long as it was proportional to the severity of the crime, the death penalty was not unconstitutional. Stewart also stated that legislatures do not have to prove that capital punishment deters crime; nor must they enact the least severe penalty possible.

Finally, Stewart noted a telling change in U.S. public opinion, demonstrating that the public supported capital punishment. The rush of legislatures to modify their death penalty statutes did not take place in a vacuum.

Having disposed of the threshold issue, Stewart examined the Georgia statutory framework. He found the framework constitutional, as each element worked to prevent the arbitrary and disproportionate death sentences criticized in *Furman*. Gregg had argued that other elements undercut the statutory framework. These included prosecutorial discretion, plea-bargaining and executive CLEMENCY. Stewart rejected these arguments, noting that the Georgia law required the jury to consider aggravating and mitigating factors as applied to the individual defendant.

Justices Brennan and Marshall again dissented on absolutist grounds, arguing that the time had passed for the state to execute criminals.

FURTHER READINGS

Hall, Kermit L. 2008. *The Magic Mirror: Law in American History.* 2d ed. New York: Oxford Univ. Press.

Janda, Kenneth, Jeffrey M. Berry, and Jerry Goldman. 2006. *The Challenge of Democracy: Government in America.* Belmont, CA: Wadsworth.

Stephens, Otis H., Jr., and John M. Scheb II. 2002. *American Constitutional Law.* Belmont, CA: Wadsworth.

❖ GREGORY, THOMAS WATT

THOMAS WATT GREGORY served as attorney general of the United States under President Woodrow Wilson from 1914 to 1919. Because his term of office coincided with the entry of the United States into WORLD WAR I, Gregory's JUSTICE DEPARTMENT experienced tremendous growth. He presided over the creation of a war emergency division within the DEPARTMENT OF JUSTICE, and he watched the FEDERAL BUREAU OF INVESTIGATION (FBI) grow to five times its prewar size as he worked to enforce U.S. laws pertaining to ESPIONAGE, SEDITION, SABOTAGE, trading with the enemy, and selective service compliance—in addition to pursuing the general interests of the U.S. government.

It is fitting that Gregory's service to the United States came in a time of war. Born November 6, 1861, in Crawfordsville, Mississippi, he was, in many ways, a child of war. His father, Francis Robert Gregory, a physician and Confederate army captain, was killed during the early days of the Civil War. His mother, Mary Cornelia

CRITICISM OF THE COURTS FOR THEIR ADMINISTRATION OF THE WAR LAWS CAN HARDLY BE CALLED AN ATTACK ON THE FORM OF GOVERNMENT OF THE UNITED STATES.
—THOMAS GREGORY

Thomas W. Gregory.
LIBRARY OF CONGRESS.

law at the University of Virginia. In 1885 he received a bachelor of laws degree from the University of Texas. Later that year, he opened a law office in Austin, Texas.

In the early 1890s Gregory began forming some important partnerships. On February 22, 1893, he married Julia Nalle, the daughter of Captain Joseph Nalle, an Austin native. They had two sons, Thomas Watt Gregory, Jr., and Joseph Nalle Gregory, and two daughters, Jane Gregory and Cornelia Gregory. He also formed a law partnership with Robert L. Batts. Together, they successfully represented the state of Texas against Waters-Pierce Oil Company, a SUBSIDIARY of Standard Oil of New York, charged with violating Texas antitrust laws. The company was found guilty and enjoined from doing further business in Texas. The case was appealed, and was ultimately affirmed by the U.S. Supreme Court (*Waters-Pierce Oil Co. v. Texas,* 212 U.S. 86, 29 S. Ct. 220, 53 L. Ed. 417 [1909]). The company paid a heavy fine and ceased to operate in Texas.

While partnered with Batts, Gregory also served as assistant city attorney of Austin, from 1891 to 1894. As his reputation grew, he was offered a number of political appointments, including the assistant attorney generalship of Texas in 1892 and a state judgeship in 1894. Wanting to serve on a national level, he declined them all.

To further his personal and professional goals, Gregory served as a Texas delegate to the Democratic national conventions of 1904 and 1912. In 1910 he began working in DEMOCRATIC PARTY circles to secure a presidential nomination for Wilson. He actively promoted a Wilson candidacy throughout his state—and because of Gregory's considerable influence, Texas went on

Watt Gregory, a delicate woman mourning the loss of her first child, was unable to cope with news of her husband's death. As she drifted in and out of melancholy, the upbringing of her remaining child, Gregory, fell to her father, Major Thomas Watt, a Mississippi planter.

By all accounts, Gregory's grandfather was a stern taskmaster with a strong commitment to education. Gregory graduated from Southwestern Presbyterian University, in Clarksville, Tennessee, in 1883. Driven to please his grandfather, he had completed his course work in just two years. From 1883 to 1884 he studied

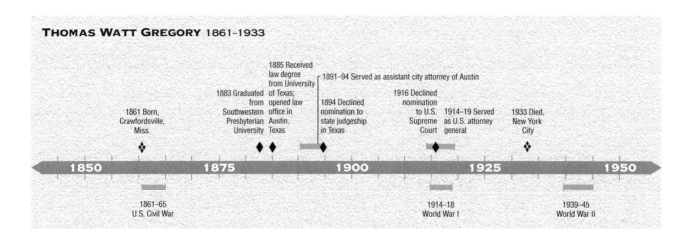

THOMAS WATT GREGORY 1861–1933

1885 Received law degree from University of Texas; opened law office in Austin, Texas

1883 Graduated from Southwestern Presbyterian University

1891–94 Served as assistant city attorney of Austin

1894 Declined nomination to state judgeship in Texas

1916 Declined nomination to U.S. Supreme Court

1914–19 Served as U.S. attorney general

1861 Born, Crawfordsville, Miss.

1933 Died, New York City

1850   1875   1900   1925   1950

1861–65 U.S. Civil War

1914–18 World War I

1939–45 World War II

to elect a delegation that would hold fast for Wilson at the Baltimore convention. In 1913 Gregory was rewarded for his efforts. President Wilson's attorney general, JAMES C. MCREYNOLDS, made Gregory a special assistant and asked him to spearhead an action against the New York, New Haven, and Hartford Railroad for monopolizing transportation in New England. Using his experience from the *Waters-Pierce* case in Texas, Gregory negotiated a settlement. As a result of his work, the railroad gave up control of several rail lines, trolley lines, and coastal shipping interests.

Gregory was named attorney general of the United States by President Wilson in 1914. McReynolds, his predecessor (and former University of Virginia classmate), created the vacancy by accepting Wilson's appointment to the U.S. Supreme Court.

When WORLD WAR I broke out in Europe, the first act of the Department of Justice was to create a war emergency division responsible for circumventing the work of agents of foreign governments, and preventing or suppressing violations of U.S. neutrality. When the United States entered the war, the roles and responsibilities of the Department of Justice and the FBI were expanded to deal with the enforcement of espionage, sedition, sabotage, and trading-with-the-enemy laws. The passage of selective service legislation further increased the department's reach. Reports from Gregory's tenure reveal that his officers arrested sixty-three hundred spies and conspirators; detained 2,300 ALIENS in Army detention camps; filed 220,747 actions against men who failed to comply with draft laws; and uncovered the activities of a group securing government and supply contracts through illegal means.

Under Gregory, the Department of Justice also organized and oversaw the operations of a volunteer SECRET SERVICE called the American Protective League. In addition to his wartime responsibilities, Gregory continued to watch domestic issues. He initiated several antitrust suits, including actions against the International Harvester Company and anthracite coal operators. Gregory also secured reforms in the administration of federal prisons while in office.

Like his predecessor, Gregory was eventually offered a Supreme Court appointment by President Wilson; unlike his predecessor, he declined. In refusing the vacancy created by the resignation of Justice Charles E. Hughes in 1916, Gregory cited his failing hearing and his inability to tolerate the confining life dictated by the position. Gregory liked to speak his mind and thought he would be unable to temper the expression of his opinions.

On March 4, 1919, Gregory resigned from the cabinet at the request of President Wilson. During the war, Gregory had treated pacifists and other opponents of the war ruthlessly; his tough, no-compromise demeanor had been suited to the times. But, as the war drew to a close, Wilson and others wanted to replace him with an attorney general more suited to postwar needs abroad and peacetime needs at home.

In a gesture of respect and esteem, President Wilson invited Gregory to attend the postwar Paris Peace Conference as an adviser. In the spirit of reconciliation, Gregory urged Wilson to enlist the support of Republican business leaders in the peace efforts and to include them on the advisory team.

Upon his return from the peace conference, Gregory remained in Washington, D.C., and returned to the PRACTICE OF LAW. But ill health and age forced a retirement after just a few years. He spent his last years in Houston, Texas, where he continued to advise local attorneys on antitrust matters and to lecture at the University of Texas.

Gregory died of pneumonia on February 26, 1933, in New York City, while on a trip to meet with president-elect FRANKLIN D. ROOSEVELT.

FURTHER READINGS

Anders, Ivan. 1989. "Thomas Watt Gregory and the Survival of His Progressive Faith." *Southwestern Historical Quarterly* 93. Available online at http://www.tshaonline.org/shqonline/apager.php?vol=093&pag=023; website home page: http://www.tshaonline.org/ (accessed July 27, 2009).

Gould, Lewis L. 1992. *Progressives and Prohibitionists: Texas Democrats in the Wilson Era.* Austin: Univ. of Texas Press.

Gregory, Thomas Watt. *Thomas Watt Gregory Papers.* Austin: Southwest Collection, Texas Tech Univ.

❖ GRIER, ROBERT COOPER

Robert Cooper Grier served as an associate justice of the U.S. Supreme Court from 1846 to 1870. Grier is best remembered for his unusual actions during the deliberation of DRED SCOTT V. SANDFORD, 60 U.S. (19 How.) 393, 15 L. Ed. 691 (1857).

THE EVIDENCE OF [FRAUD] IS ALMOST ALWAYS CIRCUMSTANTIAL. NEVERTHELESS . . . IT PRODUCES CONVICTION IN THE MIND OFTEN OF MORE FORCE THAN DIRECT TESTIMONY.
—ROBERT GRIER

Robert C. Grier.
THE LIBRARY OF
CONGRESS

Grier was born March 5, 1794, in Cumberland County, Pennsylvania. He graduated from Dickinson College in 1812 and was admitted to the bar in Bloomsburg, Pennsylvania, in 1817. A year later, he relocated to Danville, Pennsylvania, and established a successful law practice. In 1833, he was appointed judge of the Allegheny County, Pennsylvania, district court, where he remained until 1846.

With the death in 1844 of Supreme Court justice HENRY BALDWIN, who was a Pennsylvania native, President JAMES POLK sought to appoint a Democrat from that state. After failing to find a candidate who could pass Senate confirmation, Polk turned in 1846 to the noncontroversial and relatively unknown Grier.

During his term on the Supreme Court, Grier held a centrist position. A strong believer

in states' rights, he generally was opposed to federal legislation that intruded on state police powers. This philosophy led him to side with the Southern states in upholding their right to keep slaves and to recapture runaway slaves who had escaped to Northern states.

Grier has been criticized for his actions during the deliberation of *Dred Scott,* generally recognized as the most important pre–Civil War case concerning the legitimacy of SLAVERY and the rights of African Americans. The circumstances of the ruling as well as the ruling itself increased the division between the Northern and Southern states.

Dred Scott was a slave owned by an army surgeon, John Emerson, who resided in Missouri. In 1836 Emerson took Scott to Fort Snelling, in what is now Minnesota but was then a territory in which slavery had been expressly forbidden by the Missouri Compromise legislation of 1820. In 1846 Scott sued for his freedom in Missouri state court, arguing that his residence in a free territory released him from slavery. The Missouri Supreme Court rejected his argument, and Scott appealed to the U.S. Supreme Court.

Grier and the other members of the Court heard arguments on *Dred Scott* in 1855 and 1856. A key issue was whether African Americans could be citizens of the United States, even if they were not slaves. Grier did not want to address the citizenship issue, but other justices who were Southerners wanted the Court's vote to transcend sectional lines. Justice JOHN CATRON took the unusual and unethical step of asking President JAMES BUCHANAN to lobby Grier on this issue. Buchanan wrote to Grier, who in turn breached the separation between the executive and judicial branches by replying

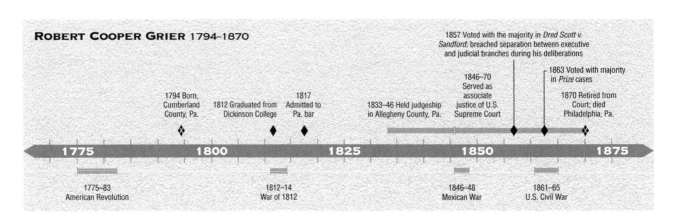

ROBERT COOPER GRIER 1794–1870

1857 Voted with the majority in *Dred Scott v. Sandford*; breached separation between executive and judicial branches during his deliberations

1846–70
Served as
associate
justice of U.S.
Supreme Court

1863 Voted with majority
in *Prize* cases

1794 Born,
Cumberland
County, Pa.

1812 Graduated from
Dickinson College

1817
Admitted to
Pa. bar

1833–46 Held judgeship
in Allegheny County, Pa.

1870 Retired from
Court; died
Philadelphia, Pa.

◆ 1775   1800   1825   1850   1875 ◆

1775–83
American Revolution

1812–14
War of 1812

1846–48
Mexican War

1861–65
U.S. Civil War

to the president. Grier agreed to side with the majority, which held that there was no power under the Constitution to grant African Americans citizenship. Grier set out in detail how the Court would rule on the case. Buchanan, in his inaugural address on March 4, 1857, mentioned the case. When the decision was released two days later, opponents of the decision attributed the president's remarks to inside information provided by Chief Justice ROGER B. TANEY. In fact, Grier was the informer.

Although Grier was sympathetic to Southern concerns, he remained a Unionist. During the Civil War, Grier voted to support the power of the president to enforce a blockade of the Confederate shoreline. The *Prize* cases, 67 U.S. 635, 17 L. Ed. 459; 70 U.S. 451, 18 L. Ed. 197; 70 U.S. 514, 18 L. Ed. 200; 70 U.S. 559, 18 L. Ed. 220 (1863), involved the disposition of vessels captured by the Union navy during the blockade of Southern ports ordered by President ABRAHAM LINCOLN in the absence of a congressional declaration of war. Under existing laws of war, the Union could claim the vessels as property only if the conflict was a declared war. The Supreme Court rejected prior law and ruled that the president has the authority to resist force without the need for special legislative action. Grier noted that the "[p]resident was bound to meet [the Civil War] in the shape it presented itself, without waiting for the Congress to baptize it with a name; and no name given to it by him or them could change the fact."

Grier's health began to fail in 1867. He retired in 1870, after members of the Court requested that he resign because he could no longer carry out his duties. He died on September 25, 1870, in Philadelphia.

GRIEVANCE PROCEDURE

A term used in labor law to describe an orderly, established way of dealing with problems between employers and employees.

Through the grievance procedure system, workers' complaints are usually communicated through their union to management for consideration by the employer.

❖ GRIGGS, JOHN WILLIAM

John William Griggs was a prominent New Jersey lawyer and politician who served as attorney general of the United States under President WILLIAM MCKINLEY.

Griggs was born July 10, 1849, near Newton, Sussex County, New Jersey. His father, Daniel Griggs, descended from the colonial founders of Griggstown, New Jersey. His mother, Emeline Johnson Griggs, also had early roots in New Jersey; she descended from militiaman and Revolutionary War soldier Henry Johnson.

As a young man, Griggs attended the Collegiate Institute, in Newton. He later entered Lafayette College, and graduated in 1868. After college, he studied law in Newton with Representative Robert Hamilton, of New Jersey, and Socrates Tuttle. Griggs completed his legal studies in 1871 and entered into practice with Tuttle.

In 1874 Griggs was established well enough to marry Carolyn Webster Brandt, the daughter of a successful Newton businessman. They had three children.

Griggs's early association with Congressman Hamilton sparked a lifelong interest in politics. While working for Hamilton, Griggs established himself as an able campaigner and gifted speech maker. By 1874 Griggs had decided to stop

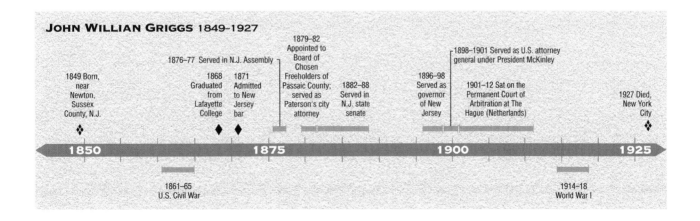

JOHN WILLIAN GRIGGS 1849–1927

1849 Born, near Newton, Sussex County, N.J.

1876–77 Served in N.J. Assembly

1868 Graduated from Lafayette College

1871 Admitted to New Jersey bar

1879–82 Appointed to Board of Chosen Freeholders of Passaic County; served as Paterson's city attorney

1882–88 Served in N.J. state senate

1896–98 Served as governor of New Jersey

1898–1901 Served as U.S. attorney general under President McKinley

1901–12 Sat on the Permanent Court of Arbitration at The Hague (Netherlands)

1927 Died, New York City

1850   1875   1900   1925

1861–65 U.S. Civil War

1914–18 World War I

John W. Griggs.
LIBRARY OF CONGRESS

campaigning for others and to throw his own hat into the ring. In 1875, he was elected to the New Jersey Assembly, the lower house of the New Jersey Legislature, where he became chairman of the Committee on the Revision of the Laws. Griggs's special area of expertise was the laws governing elections. He returned to the assembly for a final term in 1877.

At the end of his final term, Griggs opened a law office in Paterson, New Jersey, and resolved to take a break from politics. His resolve was short-lived. In 1879, he was appointed to the Board of Chosen Freeholders of Passaic County, and he served as legal counsel to the city of Paterson from 1879 to 1882.

In 1882 Griggs was elected to the first of two terms in the New Jersey state senate. He served as president of the senate in 1886, and in that capacity presided over several high-profile IMPEACHMENT trials resulting from allegations of corruption in state government.

As a state senator, Griggs worked to pass legislation forcing railroads and other large corporations to bear a larger share of the state's tax burden. He was known as a centrist who moderated many of the radical measures proposed by New Jersey's liberal Democratic governor Leon Abbett.

Griggs was a delegate to the Republican National Convention of 1888, and he worked actively to further the political agenda of presidential candidate BENJAMIN HARRISON. After the election, he was among those considered for a Supreme Court nomination by President Harrison. When the nomination did not materialize, Democratic governor George Theodore Werts offered him a seat on New Jersey's highest court. Historians have speculated that Griggs discouraged the Supreme Court nomination, and declined appointment to the New Jersey high court, because of his wife's ill health. She died in 1891.

In 1893 Griggs married Laura Elizabeth Price, with whom he eventually had two children. With the support of his new wife and of campaign manager Garret A. Hobart, Griggs made a run for the governor's office in 1894. In 1895 he became the first Republican to be elected governor of New Jersey since the Civil War.

The victory brought Griggs to national prominence. In 1898 he resigned his office to accept President McKinley's appointment as attorney general of the United States.

As attorney general, Griggs rendered early opinions on the controversial practice of presidential impoundment, which is an action or failure to act by the president that effectively prevents the use of congressionally appropriated funds and thereby thwarts the effectiveness of legislation that should have been funded. Griggs advised the president to look beyond a bill's specific language and consider the intent of Congress in determining whether an expenditure of funds was mandatory or discretionary. Upon examination of intent, Griggs often counseled against impoundment (see 22 Op. Att'y Gen. 295, 297 [1899]).

Griggs's work with a body of litigation known as the *Insular* cases established some of the guiding principles of INTERNATIONAL LAW by defining geographic limits to the protections afforded by the U.S. Constitution. (The *Insular* cases concerned disputes involving the island possessions of the U.S. government.)

Because of his expertise in the field of international law, Griggs was among the first members appointed to the Permanent Court of Arbitration at The Hague. He served, when called on, from 1901 to 1912. While on the court, he also maintained a law practice in New York City and was involved in many lucrative business ventures. Griggs served as president of the Marconi Wireless Telegraph Company prior to its dissolution, and he was general counsel and director of the Radio Corporation of America at the time of his death in New York City on November 28, 1927.

FURTHER READINGS

Griggs, John William. 1901. *In the Supreme Court of the United States: The Relations Which the United States Sustains under the Constitution to Acquired Territory.* Washington.

Kramer, Irwin R. 1990. "The Impoundment Control Act of 1974: An Unconstitutional Solution to a Constitutional Problem." *Univ. of Missouri–Kansas City Law Review* 58 (winter).

Raymond, John M., and Barbara J. Frischholtz. 1982. "Lawyers Who Established International Law in the United States, 1776–1914." *American Journal of International Law* 76 (October). Available online at http://www.questia.com/PM.qst?a=o&d=79254210; website home page: http://www.questia.com (accessed July 29, 2009).

GRISWOLD V. CONNECTICUT

Griswold v. Connecticut, 381 U.S. 479, 85 S. Ct. 1678, 14 L. Ed. 2d 510 (1965), was a landmark Supreme Court decision that recognized that a married couple has a right of privacy that cannot be infringed upon by a state law making it a crime to use contraceptives.

Two Connecticut statutes provided that any person who used, or gave information or assistance concerning the use of, contraceptives was subject to a fine, imprisonment, or both. Estelle T. Griswold, an executive with the state Planned Parenthood League, and a physician who worked at a league center were arrested for violating these laws, even though they gave such information to married couples.

They were convicted and fined $100 each. The state appellate courts upheld their convictions and they appealed to the Supreme Court on the ground that the statutes violated the FOURTEENTH AMENDMENT. The Supreme Court recognized that the appellants had standing to raise the issue of the constitutional rights of married couples because they had a professional relationship with such people.

Addressing the propriety of its review of such legislation, the Court reasoned that although it is loath to determine the need for state laws affecting social and economic conditions, these statutes directly affected sexual relations between a married couple and the role of a physician in the medical aspects of such a relationship. Such a relationship is protected from intrusion by the government under the theory of a right to privacy. This right, while not specifically guaranteed by the Constitution, exists because it may be reasonably construed from certain amendments contained in the BILL OF RIGHTS.

The FIRST AMENDMENT guarantees of FREEDOM OF SPEECH and press implicitly create the right of freedom of association since one must be allowed to freely associate with others in order to fully enjoy these specific guarantees. The THIRD AMENDMENT prohibition against the quartering of soldiers in a private home without the owner's consent is an implicit acknowledgment of the owner's right to privacy. Both the FOURTH AMENDMENT protection against unreasonable searches and seizures and the FIFTH AMENDMENT SELF-INCRIMINATION Clause safeguard a person's privacy in his or her home and life against government demands. The NINTH AMENDMENT states that the enumerated constitutional rights should not be interpreted as denying any other rights retained by the people.

The Court created the right of privacy from the penumbras of these specific rights, which it deemed created zones of privacy. The statutory regulation of a marital relationship by the state was an invasion of the constitutional right of a married couple to privacy in such a relationship, a relationship that historically American law has held sacred. The means by which the state chose to regulate contraceptives—by outlawing their use, rather than their sale and manufacture—was clearly unrelated to its goal and would detrimentally affect the marital relationship. The question of enforcement of such statutes also was roundly criticized since it would mandate government inquiry into "marital bedrooms."

Because of the invalidity of such laws, the Supreme Court reversed the judgments of the state trial and appellate courts and the convictions of the appellants.

FURTHER READINGS

Kalman, Laura. 1994. "Review: The Promise and Peril of Privacy." *Reviews in American History* 22.

Loewy, Arnold H. 2003. "Morals Legislation and the Establishment Cluase." *Alabama Law Review* 55.

Tushnet, Mark. 2008. *I Dissent: Great Opposing Opinions in Landmark Supreme Court Cases.* Boston: Beacon.

Yeh, Jessica I., and Sindy S. Chen. 2002. "Contraception." *Georgetown Journal of Gender and the Law* 3 (spring).

CROSS REFERENCES

"Griswold v. Connecticut" (Appendix, Primary Document); Husband and Wife; Penumbra.

❖ GROESBECK, WILLIAM SLOCOMB

Thrust into the national spotlight by the IMPEACH-MENT trial of President ANDREW JOHNSON in 1868, defense attorney WILLIAM SLOCOMB GROESBECK won wide renown for his stirring defense of the president. Prior to the trial, Groesbeck was known chiefly for his law practice in Ohio and for a single term in Congress. His friendship with Johnson led to his last-minute substitution on the president's defense team. Delivered while he was ill, Groesbeck's CLOSING ARGUMENT is remembered for its brilliance and passion.

Groesbeck was born July 24, 1815, in Schenectady, New York, and studied law at Miami University, in Ohio. After graduating in 1834, he began practicing at the age of 19 in Cincinnati. As a liberal Republican, he served in Congress from 1857 to 1859, but then lost his bid for reelection. He remained active in party politics as a leader of the Union Democrats, served as a delegate at the fruitless peace convention in 1861 that sought to prevent the Civil War, and won election as a senator in the Ohio state legislature in 1862.

Groesbeck befriended Johnson during the war and became a natural choice for defending Johnson during his 1868 impeachment trial. Johnson trusted and respected the younger man. He had even briefly considered ousting treasury secretary Hugh McCulloch and giving McCulloch's job to Groesbeck. When the distinguished lawyer JEREMIAH SULLIVAN BLACK resigned from Johnson's impeachment defense team amid scandal, Johnson turned to Groesbeck.

Like the rest of Johnson's defense team, Groesbeck served without a fee. The task facing the attorneys was immense. After assuming the presidency in 1865 following Abraham Lincoln's ASSASSINATION, Johnson had embarked on a moderate, slow-paced policy of reform. The bitter politics of the Reconstruction era, however, had sapped both his popularity and his power. Radical Republicans in Congress overruled his policies and, in 1867, with the stage set for a dramatic confrontation, they established the TENURE OF OFFICE ACT (14 Stat. 430) over his veto. This law severely limited executive power. It required the president to ask the Senate for permission before removing any federal official whose appointment the Senate had approved, and it also provided that presidential cabinet members would serve one month past the expiration of the president's term.

In August 1867, Johnson rejected the authority of the act when he requested the removal of Secretary of War EDWIN M. STANTON, on the ground that Stanton had secretly conspired with Johnson's political enemies. Stanton refused to step down, so Johnson removed him from office and replaced him with ULYSSES S. GRANT. The Radical Republicans swiftly sought revenge. Three days later, the House of Representatives voted to IMPEACH Johnson, making him the first president in U.S. history to stand trial on impeachment charges. The U.S. Senate then adopted 11 ARTICLES OF IMPEACHMENT, the most serious of which was violation of the Tenure of Office Act.

Groesbeck played a key role in trial preparation. Like his colleagues, he advised Johnson not to appear at trial—a recommendation the president followed. Groesbeck remained silent in the Senate until all the evidence had been presented, and on April 25 he delivered the second closing argument. (Because there was no precedent for an impeachment trial of a president, the Senate allowed several defense attorneys to present closing arguments.)

Groesbeck's speech was a masterpiece of simplicity and eloquence. He noted that there had only been five impeachment trials since

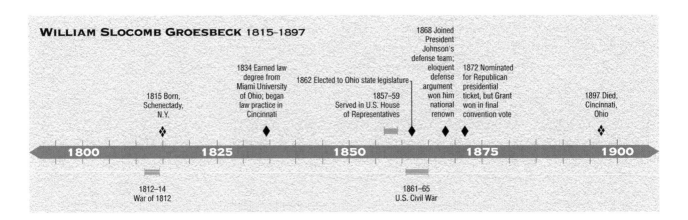

WILLIAM SLOCOMB GROESBECK 1815–1897

1815 Born, Schenectady, N.Y.

1834 Earned law degree from Miami University of Ohio; began law practice in Cincinnati

1862 Elected to Ohio state legislature

1857–59 Served in U.S. House of Representatives

1868 Joined President Johnson's defense team; eloquent defense argument won him national renown

1872 Nominated for Republican presidential ticket, but Grant won in final convention vote

1897 Died, Cincinnati, Ohio

1800   1825   1850   1875   1900

1812–14 War of 1812

1861–65 U.S. Civil War

the organization of the government, and urged the Senate to leave political judgments to the citizenry. Despite suffering from an illness, he deftly countered each of the 11 charges.

When Groesbeck addressed the Tenure of Office Act, he turned the tables on the Senate. He argued that the Senate had always had the power to deal with Stanton's dismissal and replacement without resorting to impeachment. What Johnson had done, argued Groesbeck, was simply to remove a member of the cabinet who had been unfriendly to him, both personally and politically. Johnson had made an AD INTERIM (temporary) appointment to last for a single day, an appointment the Senate could have terminated whenever it saw fit. The Senate, argued Groesbeck, possessed the power to control the situation all along. Surely, in light of this, Johnson's act was no crime.

Groesbeck continued with a peroration comparing Johnson to Lincoln and even invoking Christ's crucifixion. Then he praised Johnson's contribution to the nation in time of war: "How his voice rang out in this hall for the GOOD CAUSE, and in denunciation of rebellion. But he ... was wanted for greater peril, and went into the very furnace of the war ... Who of you have done more? Not one."

The speech stunned the Senate. Supporters surrounded Groesbeck. His argument was praised in the national press, with the *New York Herald* calling it "the most eloquent ... heard in the Senate since the palmy days of oratory" (as quoted in Bowers 1929, 189). Likewise, the *Nation* regarded it as the defense's most effective moment. Johnson, too, was deeply pleased, and Groesbeck assured him that he would be acquitted. When the Senate voted on May 16 and May 26, Johnson escaped impeachment by a margin of one vote.

Following the trial, Groesbeck's political fortunes briefly soared. In 1872 he was nominated for the presidency by liberal Republicans but failed to garner enough support. He died on July 7, 1897, in Cincinnati.

FURTHER READINGS

Bowers, Claude G. 2001. *The Tragic Era.* New York: Simon.

Castel, Albert. 1979. *The Presidency of Andrew Johnson.* Lawrence: Univ. Press of Kansas.

Dewitt, David M. 2007. *The Impeachment and Trial of Andrew Johnson.* Whitefish, MT: Kessinger.

Milton, George F. 1930. *The Age of Hate: Andrew Johnson and the Radicals.* New York: Coward-McCann.

Stryker, Lloyd P. 2007. *Andrew Johnson: A Study in Courage.* Whitefish, MT: Kessinger.

GROSS

Great; culpable; general; absolute. A thing in gross exists in its own right, and not as an appendage to another thing. Before or without diminution or deduction. Whole; entire; total; as in the gross sum, amount, weight—as opposed to net. Not adjusted or reduced by deductions or subtractions.

Out of all measure; beyond allowance; flagrant; shameful; as a gross dereliction of duty, a gross injustice, gross carelessness or negligence. Such conduct as is not to be excused.

GROSS ESTATE

All the real and personal property owned by a decedent at the time of his or her death.

The calculation of the value of the gross estate is the first step in the computation that determines whether any estate tax is owed to federal or state governments. Federal and state laws define gross estate for purposes of TAXATION. Under federal law, the gross estate includes proceeds of life insurance policies that are payable to the decedent's estate, as well as policies to which the decedent retained "incidents of ownership" until his or her death, such as the right to change beneficiaries or to borrow against the CASH SURRENDER VALUE of the policy.

CROSS REFERENCE

Estate and Gift Taxes.

GROSS INCOME

The financial gains received by an individual or a business during a fiscal year.

For INCOME TAX purposes, gross income includes any type of monetary benefit paid to an individual or business, whether it be earned as a result of personal services or business activities or produced by investments and capital assets. The valuation of gross income is the first step in computing whether any federal or state income tax is owed by the recipient.

GROSS NEGLIGENCE

An indifference to, and a blatant violation of, a legal duty with respect to the rights of others.

Gross negligence is a conscious and voluntary disregard of the need to use reasonable care, which is likely to cause foreseeable grave injury or harm to persons, property, or both. It is conduct that is extreme when compared with ordinary NEGLIGENCE, which is a mere failure to

Hugo Grotius.
LIBRARY OF CONGRESS

exercise reasonable care. Ordinary negligence and gross negligence differ in degree of inattention, while both differ from willful and wanton conduct, which is conduct that is reasonably considered to cause injury. This distinction is important, since contributory negligence—a lack of care by the PLAINTIFF that combines with the defendant's conduct to cause the plaintiff's injury and completely bar his or her action—is not a defense to willful and wanton conduct but is a defense to gross negligence. In addition, a finding of willful and wanton misconduct usually supports a recovery of PUNITIVE DAMAGES, whereas gross negligence does not.

❖ GROTIUS, HUGO

Hugo Grotius, also known as Huigh de Groot, achieved prominence as a Dutch jurist and statesman and is regarded as the originator of INTERNATIONAL LAW.

Grotius was born April 10, 1583, in Delft, Netherlands. A brilliant student, Grotius attended the University of Leiden, received a law degree at the age of fifteen, and was admitted to the bar and began his legal practice at Delft in 1599. It was at this time that he became interested in international law, and, in 1609, wrote a preliminary piece titled *Mare liberum,* which advocated freedom of the seas to all countries.

In 1615 Grotius became involved in a religious controversy between two opposing groups, the Remonstrants, Dutch Protestants who abandoned Calvinism to follow the precepts of their leader, Jacobus Arminius, and the Anti-Remonstrants, who adhered to the beliefs of Calvinism. The dispute extended to politics, and when Maurice of Nassau gained control of the government, the Remonstrants lost popular support. Grotius, a supporter of the Remonstrants, was imprisoned in 1619. Two years later he escaped, seeking safety in Paris.

In Paris, Grotius began his legal writing, and in 1625 produced *De jure belli ac pacis,* translated as "Concerning the Law of War and Peace." This work is regarded as the first official text of the principles of international law, wherein Grotius maintained that NATURAL LAW is the basis for legislation for countries as well as individuals. He opposed war in all but extreme cases and advocated respect for life and the ownership of property. The main sources for his theories were the Bible and history.

Grotius spent the remainder of his years in diplomatic and theological endeavors. From 1635 to 1645 he represented Queen Christina of Sweden as her ambassador to France. He pursued his religious interests and wrote several theological works. Grotius died August 28, 1645, in Rostock, Germany.

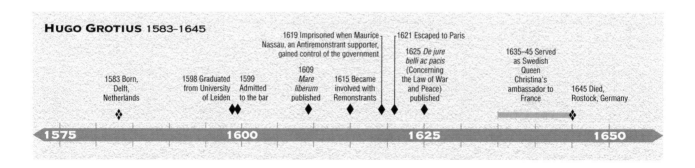

HUGO GROTIUS 1583–1645

1583 Born, Delft, Netherlands

1598 Graduated from University of Leiden

1599 Admitted to the bar

1609 *Mare liberum* published

1615 Became involved with Remonstrants

1619 Imprisoned when Maurice Nassau, an Antiremonstrant supporter, gained control of the government

1621 Escaped to Paris

1625 *De jure belli ac pacis* (Concerning the Law of War and Peace) published

1635–45 Served as Swedish Queen Christina's ambassador to France

1645 Died, Rostock, Germany

1575   1600   1625   1650

GROUND RENT

Perpetual consideration paid for the use and occupation of real property to the individual who has transferred such property, and subsequently to his or her descendants or someone to whom the interest is conveyed.

Ground rent agreements have sometimes required the payment of rent for a term of 99 years, with renewal at the option of the party who pays it. In this type of agreement, the LESSOR retains title to the property. Large structures, such as hotels and office buildings, are ordinarily built on land under ground rent leases.

The concept of a ground rent arrangement is English in origin. Its original purpose was an attempt by feudal tenants to put themselves in the role of lords over lower tenants. This was proscribed by a law passed in 1290 that made every tenant a subject only to the overlord.

In the United States, the only states where the ground rent system has been used to any great extent are Maryland and Pennsylvania. These agreements were initially popular as a method of encouraging renters to improve the property, because they could own the buildings while paying rent on the land. The courts enforced the ground rent agreements, and they gained popularity with investors who purchased and sold shares in ground rent agreements.

Although the ground rent system was not used in New York, the state courts did recognize comparable *manorial* or *perpetual* leases. A deed setting up a ground rent arrangement might indicate that it is to last for 99 years, but because most agreements are automatically renewable, ground rents can last forever.

An obligation to pay the rent can terminate if (1) the individual entitled to receive rent forfeits such a right in a deed or other instrument; (2) the land is taken by EMINENT DOMAIN and the individual entitled to receive rent is compensated for the loss; (3) the agreement setting up the rent is breached and is thereafter unenforceable; or (4) the landowner also becomes the individual entitled to receive the rent or buys back the right to receive rents.

Under the COMMON LAW, rents that were not demanded for a number of years could not be collected, since the law assumed that they had been paid.

The term *ground rent* is currently applied to a lease for land upon which the tenant constructs a building. While the landlord continues to own the land, the tenant owns all of the structures and pays rent for the ground only.

GROUNDS

The basis or foundation; reasons sufficient in law to justify relief.

Grounds are more than simply reasons for wanting a court to order relief. They are the reasons specified by the law that will serve as a basis for demanding relief. For example, a woman may sue her neighbor for TRESPASS on the ground that his fence was erected beyond his boundary line. Her real reason for suing may be that she does not like the loud music that he plays on his stereo, and she wants to cause him trouble. If his fence actually encroaches on her property, however, she has grounds for a CAUSE OF ACTION based on the trespass.

GROUP LEGAL SERVICES

Legal services provided under a plan to members, who may be employees of the same company, members of the same organization, or individual consumers.

Group legal services resembles group HEALTH INSURANCE. It is an all-purpose, general coverage: for an annual fee, members are entitled to low-cost or free consultation with an attorney. Several forms of group legal services exist, ranging from employee-provided benefits to commercially marketed plans. These vary in scope, price, and availability. The first plans appeared in the early 1970s, for unions, which negotiated for them as employee benefits and have remained their primary users. Over the following two decades, the concept expanded as lawyers saw an opportunity for a nontraditional way to market their services. By the mid-1980s, the rise of commercial plans aimed at other groups sparked considerable interest in the legal profession, the media, and the public. Approximately 10 percent of U.S. citizens belonged to some form of plan in the 1990s, and observers expected that percentage to increase as more vendors entered the market to cater to consumers.

For several decades, the legal profession resisted the plans and sought to restrict them. State bars opposed them because the organization of the plans requires the imposition of an intermediary between the attorney and the client, which they saw as violative of the traditional attorney-client relationship. As the first groups to realize the advantages of using the plans, unions encountered stiff opposition in several states. Beginning in the early 1960s, however, the CIVIL RIGHTS MOVEMENT and a series of U.S. Supreme Court decisions removed these barriers.

The Court's decision in *NAACP v. Button*, 371 U.S. 415, 83 S. Ct. 328, 9 L. Ed. 2d 405 (1963), struck down a Virginia law that had prevented the National Association for the Advancement of Colored People (NAACP) from providing staff lawyer services to members. *Brotherhood of Railroad Trainmen v. Virginia ex rel. Virginia State Bar*, 377 U.S. 1, 84 S. Ct. 1113, 12 L. Ed. 2d 89 (1964), struck down an injunction that prohibited legal services activities of the union on First and FOURTEENTH AMENDMENT grounds. In *United Mine Workers District 12 v. Illinois State Bar Ass'n*, 389 U.S. 217, 88 S. Ct. 353, 19 L. Ed. 2d 426 (1967), the Court permitted the union to collectively sponsor legal services for members' workers' compensation claims, holding that restrictions imposed by the Illinois State Bar Association were unconstitutional under the FIRST AMENDMENT. In response, the legal profession slowly loosened restrictions in its Model Code of PROFESSIONAL RESPONSIBILITY and Model Rules of Professional Conduct. By the mid-1970s, most of the special restrictions were gone.

These trends cleared the way for a broad expansion of group legal services. The chief benefit of such plans is discounted legal fees. Legal advice is often expensive. As in group health insurance, volume produces savings: the buying power of a large membership can lower the costs to individuals. This feature figured prominently in an expansion of the plans into commercial markets in the 1980s. Moreover, although individuals with low incomes are sometimes entitled to LEGAL AID, and affluent individuals can usually afford a lawyer, members of the middle class are often hit hard by legal bills. Thus, marketers of group legal services have tried to appeal to middle-class consumers through such outlets as banks and credit card companies.

Federal and state regulations govern plans for group legal services. Employer-provided plans fall under the EMPLOYEE RETIREMENT INCOME SECURITY ACT (ERISA) (29 U.S.C.A. § 1001 et seq.). Enacted in 1974, ERISA protects employees' pension rights and imposes strict fiduciary requirements on their group legal services. Other types of plans are subject to state laws, which generally impose light regulation and follow the legal profession's Model Rules of Professional Conduct in such areas as ethics and ATTORNEY-CLIENT PRIVILEGE.

FURTHER READINGS

American Bar Association Governmental Affairs Office. 2009. "Access to Legal Services: Group and Prepaid Services." Washington, D.C.: American Bar Association.

Costich, Julia Field. 1993–94. "Joint State-Federal Regulation of Lawyers: The Case of Group Legal Services under ERISA." *Kentucky Law Journal* 82 (winter).

Schwartz, Alec M. 1989. "Lawyer's Guide to Prepaid Legal Services." *Legal Economics* (July/August).

❖ GRUNDY, FELIX

Felix Grundy served as U.S. attorney general from 1838 to 1839. A prominent criminal attorney, Grundy also served as a judge, state legislator, and U.S. senator. His brief service as attorney general took place during the administration of President MARTIN VAN BUREN.

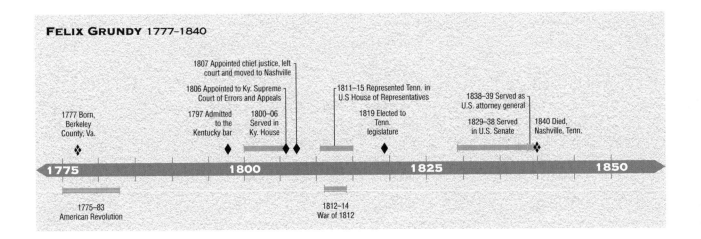

FELIX GRUNDY 1777–1840

1807 Appointed chief justice, left court and moved to Nashville

1806 Appointed to Ky. Supreme Court of Errors and Appeals

1811–15 Represented Tenn. in U.S House of Representatives

1838–39 Served as U.S. attorney general

1777 Born, Berkeley County, Va.

1797 Admitted to the Kentucky bar

1800–06 Served in Ky. House

1819 Elected to Tenn. legislature

1829–38 Served in U.S. Senate

1840 Died, Nashville, Tenn.

1775 1800 1825 1850

1775–83 American Revolution

1812–14 War of 1812

Grundy was born September 11, 1777, in Berkeley County, Virginia (now West Virginia). His family moved to Kentucky in 1780. Although he had little early formal education, he studied law and was admitted to the Kentucky bar in 1797. An able advocate, he soon developed a reputation as an outstanding criminal lawyer.

In 1799 he was elected a delegate to the Kentucky state constitutional convention, where he played a prominent role. In 1800 he was elected to the Kentucky House of Representatives. He served in the house until 1806, when he was appointed associate justice of the state supreme court of errors and appeals. He was made chief justice in 1807, but left the court that same year and moved to Nashville.

Grundy established a law practice in Nashville before politics again became paramount. He was elected to the U.S. House of Representatives in 1811 and was reelected in 1813. During these years in Congress, Grundy was a strong advocate of territorial expansion, seeking to add Florida and Canada to the United States. He was also a supporter of the WAR OF 1812, against Great Britain.

After resigning from Congress in 1815, Grundy returned to Nashville and his law practice. JAMES POLK, future PRESIDENT OF THE UNITED STATES, apprenticed under Grundy during this period. In 1819 Grundy was elected to the Tennessee legislature, and in 1820 he acted as a commissioner to settle the boundary line between Kentucky and Tennessee.

During the 1820s Grundy concentrated on his law practice, while working to strengthen the DEMOCRATIC PARTY and to promote the candidacy of Tennessean ANDREW JACKSON for president. Though Jackson lost his first bid in 1824, he easily won in 1828 and 1832. In 1829 Grundy was appointed to a vacancy in the U.S. Senate, and in 1833 he was reelected.

Grundy remained in the Senate until 1838, when President Van Buren appointed him to serve as attorney general. Van Buren, who had been Jackson's vice president, had little success as president. An economic depression, called the Panic of 1837, crippled the U.S. economy for most of his four-year term. Grundy, sensing the fading political fortunes of Van Buren, resigned his position in December 1839 and returned to his seat in the Senate.

Grundy died in Nashville, December 19, 1840.

Felix Grundy.
LIBRARY OF CONGRESS.

THE PROSECUTOR'S STATEMENT WAS BUT ANOTHER ILLUSTRATION OF COLD-BLOODED YANKEE CHARACTER.
—FELIX GRUNDY

GRUTTER V. BOLLINGER

The Supreme Court's decision in Grutter v. Bollinger upheld the use of race as a factor in admitting students at the University of Michigan's law school.

The case of *Grutter v. Bollinger* (539 U.S. 306, 123 S. Ct. 2325, 156 L. Ed. 2d 304 [2003]) was a significant AFFIRMATIVE ACTION decision that upheld the University of Michigan law school's use of race as a factor in admitting students. The decision in *Grutter* occurred on the same day that the Court in *Gratz v. Bollinger* (539 U.S. 244, 123 S. Ct. 2411, 156 L. Ed. 257 [2003]) struck down the affirmative action policy used for undergraduate students at the University of Michigan.

The cases of *Gratz* and *Grutter* established guidance the Court has given regarding use of affirmative action in admissions programs. For many years, this issue was governed by the Court's decision in REGENTS OF THE UNIVERSITY OF CALIFORNIA V. BAKKE (438 U.S. 265, 98 S. Ct. 2733, 57 L. Ed. 2d 750 [1978]). In *Bakke*, the Court ruled that the admission plan of the medical school at the University of California, Davis, violated the EQUAL PROTECTION clause because it established a quota regarding the number of positions that the school had to set aside for minority applicants. The Court's PLURALITY opinion established that schools must make individualized considerations rather than rely on quotas.

Barbara Grutter, a Michigan resident, applied for admission to the University of Michigan's law school for admission for the 1997–1998 school year. Grutter is white. She was first placed on a wait list, then later learned that her application had been denied. Grutter brought suit on her own behalf as well as others from "disfavored racial groups" who were denied admission due to the law school's stated policy of using different admissions standards in part based on race. Grutter alleged that Michigan's policies amounted to reverse racial DISCRIMINATION because she was white and that the school violated her rights under the equal protection clause of the FOURTEENTH AMENDMENT.

The stated goal of the law school's admission policy was as follows: "to admit a group of students who individually and collectively are among the most capable students applying to American law schools in a given year." Moreover, the policy sought the admission of "a mix of students with varying backgrounds and experiences who will respect and learn from each other." The law school policy committed the school to ethnic and racial diversity and made "special reference to the inclusion of students from groups which have been historically discriminated against, like African Americans, Hispanics and Native Americans."

A Michigan federal district court judge ruled in Grutter's favor. Judge Bernard Friedman ruled that the "use of race as a factor in its admissions decision is unconstitutional and a violation of Title VI of the 1964 CIVIL RIGHTS Act." He discounted the university's rationale for its admissions process—to produce a racially diverse student population. He said that the school's rationale did not establish a compelling STATE INTEREST. In the alternative, if the rationale did constitute a compelling state interest, the law school had failed to narrowly tailor its use of race to achieve that interest.

The Sixth CIRCUIT COURT of Appeals reversed the district court's opinion in May 2002 in a 5–4 decision. The Supreme Court agreed to review both Gratz and Grutter, and the Court handed down decisions on the cases on the same day.

The Court determined that the undergraduate student policy challenged in Gratz violated the equal protection clause, but the Court ruled that the Michigan law school's policy was constitutional. According to the majority opinion in Grutter, written by Justice Sandra Day O'Connor, the law school policy "bears the hallmarks of a narrowly tailored plan." The admissions policy did not insulate certain categories of applicants from competition with other applicants. Rather, the Court found that the law school engaged in a "highly individualized, holistic review of each applicant's file, giving serious consideration to all the ways an applicant might contribute to a diverse education environment ... [and] affords this individualized consideration to applicants of all races." Michigan's law school policy succeeded where the undergraduate policy failed because, O'Connor wrote, the law school "awards no mechanical predetermined diversity 'bonus'" based on race or ethnicity.

Chief Justice WILLIAM H. REHNQUIST argued that the law school's admission policy was unconstitutional because "[i]n practice, the ... program bears little or no relation to its asserted goal of achieving 'critical mass' ... of each underrepresented minority group."

FURTHER READINGS

Lee, Francis Graham. 2003. *Equal Protection: Rights and Liberties under the Law*. Santa Barbara, Calf.: ABC-CLIO.

Perry, Barbara A. 2007. *The Michigan Affirmative Action Cases*. Lawrence: Univ. Press of Kansas.

Stohr, Greg. 2004. *A Black and White Case: How Affirmative Action Survived Its Greatest Legal Challenge*. Princeton, N.J.: Bloomberg Press.

CROSS REFERENCES

Affirmative Action; Gratz v. Bollinger.

GUARANTEE

One to whom a guaranty is made. This word is also used, as a noun, to denote the contract of guaranty or the obligation of a guarantor, and, as a verb, to denote the action of assuming the responsibilities of a guarantor.

GUARANTY

As a verb, to agree to be responsible for the payment of another's debt or the performance of another's duty, liability, or obligation if that person does not perform as he or she is legally obligated to do; to assume the responsibility of a guarantor; to warrant.

As a noun, an undertaking or promise that is collateral to the primary or principal obligation and that binds the guarantor to performance in the event of nonperformance by the principal obligor.

A guaranty is a contract that some particular thing shall be done exactly as it is agreed to be done, whether it is to be done by one person or another, and whether there be a prior or principal contractor or not.

GUARANTY CLAUSE

A provision contained in a written document, such as a contract, deed, or mortgage, whereby one individual undertakes to pay the obligation of another individual

The stipulation contained in Article IV, Section 4, of the U.S. Constitution, in which the federal government promises a republican form of government to every state and the defense and protection of the federal government if domestic violence occurs.

GUARDIAN

A person lawfully invested with the power, and charged with the obligation, of taking care of and managing the property and rights of a person who,

because of age, understanding, or self-control, is considered incapable of administering his or her own affairs.

GUARDIAN AD LITEM

A guardian appointed by the court to represent the interests of infants, the unborn, or incompetent persons in legal actions.

Guardians are adults who are legally responsible for protecting the well-being and interests of their ward, who is usually a minor. A guardian ad litem is a unique type of guardian in a relationship that has been created by a court order only for the duration of a legal action. Courts appoint these special representatives for infants, minors, and mentally incompetent persons, all of whom generally need help protecting their rights in court. Such court-appointed guardians figure in

---

Guaranty

FOR GOOD CONSIDERATION, and as an inducement for _____ (Creditor),

to extend credit to _____ (Customer), it is hereby agreed that the undersigned does hereby guaranty to Creditor the prompt, punctual and full payment of all monies now or hereinafter due Creditor from Customer.

Until termination, this guaranty is unlimited as to amount or duration and shall remain in full force and effect notwithstanding any extension, compromise, adjustment, forbearance, waiver, release or discharge of any party obligor or guarantor, or release in whole or in part of any security granted for said indebtedness or compromise or adjustment thereto, and the undersigned waives all notices thereto.

The obligations of the undersigned shall be at the election of Creditor, shall be primary and not necessarily secondary and Creditor shall not be required to exhaust its remedies as against Customer prior to enforcing its rights under this guaranty against the undersigned.

The guaranty hereunder shall be unconditional and absolute and the undersigned waive all rights of subrogation and set-off until all sums under this guaranty are fully paid. The undersigned further waives all suretyship defenses or defenses in the nature thereof, generally.

In the event payments due under this guaranty are not punctually paid upon demand, then the undersigned shall pay all reasonable costs and attorney's fees necessary for collection, and enforcement of ths guaranty.

If there are two or more guarantors to this guaranty, the obligations shall be joint and several and binding upon and inure to the benefit of the parties, their successors, assigns and personal representatives.

The guaranty may be terminated by any guarantor upon fifteen (15) days written notice of terminination, mailed certified mail, return receipt requested to the Creditor. Such termination shall extend only to credit extended beyond said fifteen (15) day period and not to prior extended credit, or goods in transit received by Customer beyond said date, or for special orders placed prior to said date notwithstanding date of delivery. Termination of this guaranty by any guarantor shall not impair the continuing guaranty of any remaining guarantors of said termination.

Each of the undersigned warrants and represents it has full authority to enter into this guaranty.

This guaranty shall be binding upon and inure to the benefit of the parties, their successors, assigns and personal representatives.

This guaranty shall be construed and enforced under the laws of the State of _____.

Signed this _____ day of _____, 20_____.

In the presence of:

_____   _____
Witness   Guarantor

_____   _____
Witness   Guarantor

A sample guaranty.

ILLUSTRATION BY GGS CREATIVE RESOURCES. REPRODUCED BY PERMISSION OF GALE, A PART OF CENGAGE LEARNING.

divorces, child neglect and abuse cases, PATERNITY suits, contested inheritances, and so forth, and are usually attorneys.

The concept of guardian AD LITEM grew out of developments in U.S. law in the late nineteenth century. Until then, the COMMON LAW had severely restricted who could bring lawsuits in federal courts; it was easiest to sue in states through equity courts. Changes in the 1870s relaxed these standards by bringing federal codes in line with state codes, and in 1938, the Federal Rules of CIVIL PROCEDURE removed the old barriers by establishing one system for civil actions. Rule 17(c) addresses the rights of children and incompetent persons in three ways. First, it permits legal guardians to sue or defend on the behalf of minors or incompetent individuals. Second, it allows persons who do not have such a representative to name a "next friend," or guardian ad litem, to sue for them. And third, it states that federal courts "shall appoint a guardian ad litem for an infant or incompetent person not otherwise represented in an action or shall make such other order as it deems proper for [his or her] protection." In practice, the courts have interpreted this last provision broadly: The term *infants* is taken to mean unborn children and all minors. In addition, courts can exercise discretion; they are not required to appoint a guardian ad litem.

In the 1970s and 1980s the importance of the guardian ad litem grew in response to increased concern about children's welfare. Two social developments brought about this growth: a rise in DIVORCE cases, and greater recognition of the gravity of CHILD ABUSE and neglect. Because states had generally modeled their civil court processes on the Federal Rules of Civil Procedure, the role of guardian ad litem was well established. But now, states began moving toward stronger legislation of their own. By the 1990s many states had enacted laws specifying the guardians' qualifications, duties, and authority. Equally important, these laws spelled out requirements for the appointment of guardians ad litem in abuse cases. As a leader in the area, Florida enacted legislation in 1990 providing funding for the training of guardians ad litem (State of Florida Guardian Ad Litem Program Guidelines for FAMILY LAW Case Appointment, Fla. Stat. § 61.104). In 1993, after hearing an appeal in a particularly horrifying abuse case, the Supreme Court of West Virginia set forth guidelines for guardians

ad litem in its decision (*In Re Jeffrey R. L.*, 190 W. Va. 24, 435 S.E.2d 162 [1993]).

Guardians ad litem have extensive power and responsibility. Their duties are greatest in cases involving children, where they investigate, attend to the child's emotional and legal needs, monitor the child's family, and seek to shield the child from the often bruising experience of a lawsuit. Their function as OFFICERS OF THE COURT is also extensive: in addition to compiling relevant facts, interviewing WITNESSES, giving testimony, and making recommendations to the court on issues of custody and visitation, they ensure that all parties comply with court orders. Given the rigors of the task, which is often voluntary or low paid, it is not surprising that courts have traditionally had difficulty finding adequate numbers of qualified individuals to serve as guardians ad litem.

In the mid-1990s the role of guardian ad litem provoked new concerns. Whereas many attorneys perceived a need for guardians ad litem to be appointed in all CHILD CUSTODY proceedings, others expressed caution about the risk of lawsuits. Particularly for attorneys serving as guardians ad litem in divorce cases, this risk was high: parents upset with the result of a custody ruling might sue the guardian, just as a number of parties had in the 1980s brought action against government agencies involved in child welfare cases. Lawyers worried that the guardian ad litem system had become potentially dangerous for those whose rights it had been designed to protect, some of society's weakest members.

FURTHER READINGS

Callahan, Cindy, and Vince Wills. 2003. "Searching for Answers about the Role of the Guardian ad Litem." *The Maryland Bar Journal* 36 (May-June).

Goldenberg, Renee, and Nancy Palmer. 1995. "Guardian ad Litem Programs: Where They Have Gone and Where They Are Going." *Florida Bar Journal* 69 (December).

Kearns, Bridget. 2002. "A Warm Heart But a Cool Head: Why a Dual Guardian ad Litem System Best Protects Families Involved in Abused and Neglected Proceedings." *Wisconsin Law Review* 2002 (May-June).

Lorenson, Rick. 1994. "Court Defines Role of Guardian ad Litem in Abuse and Neglect Cases." *West Virginia Lawyer* (November).

Prescott, Dana. 1995. "Family Law Guardian ad Litem: Defenses to Tort Claims." *Fairshare* (January).

Wright, Charles Alan, and Arthur R. Miller. 2004. *Federal Practice and Procedure: Federal Rules of Civil Procedure.* Eagan, MN: West.

CROSS REFERENCE

Civil Procedure.

GUARDIAN AND WARD

The legal relationship that exists between a person (the guardian) appointed by a court to take care of and manage the property of a person (the ward) who does not possess the legal capacity to do so, by reason of age, comprehension, or self-control.

The term *guardian* refers to a person appointed by a court to manage the affairs of another person who is unable to conduct those affairs on his or her own behalf. The term is most often applied to a person who is responsible for the care and management of an infant, which in legal terms is a person below the AGE OF MAJORITY. Thus, children who have not reached adulthood (usually age 18 or 21) must, with some exceptions, have a legal guardian.

Courts also appoint guardians to supervise the property and personal well-being of adults who cannot manage their affairs. Persons incapacitated because of mental or physical illness, drug or alcohol abuse, or other disability may require the appointment of a guardian to ensure the conservation of their PERSONAL PROPERTY and to oversee their day-to-day personal care. The term *conservator* is often used for a person designated to manage the property of an adult who is unable to do so.

The law of guardianship is based on the COMMON LAW and has been the province of state government. This law has been modified by state statutes. For example, Section V of the UNIFORM PROBATE CODE, a model set of procedures governing the administration of trusts and estates, contains rules that guide courts in managing guardianships. The Uniform Probate Code (1969), adopted by virtually every state, has done much to streamline probate law. In 1982, provisions of the code were updated via the Uniform Guardianship and Protective Proceedings Act (UGPPA). As legislation changed, and issues arose concerning the protection of wards, the UGPPA underwent scrutiny. The act was revised over the course of several years and, in 1997, it was officially approved by the National Conference of Commissioners on Uniform State Laws. The act updated procedures for appointing guardians and conservators and provided due process protection for adults who are incapacitated.

There are two basic types of guardians: of the person and of the property. A guardian of the person has custody of the ward and responsibility for the ward's daily care. A guardian of the property has the right and the duty to hold and manage all property belonging to the ward. A ward usually has a general guardian, who supervises both the person and the property, but in some circumstances it is necessary and convenient to divide responsibilities.

Persons for Whom a Guardian Is Appointed

A guardian cannot be appointed for a person unless that person is in need of supervision by a representative of the court. The natural guardian of a child is the child's parent. A parent can lose this status by neglect or ABANDONMENT. In addition, when both parents die, leaving a minor child, the court will often appoint a guardian.

Guardians can also be appointed in medical emergencies. If a parent refuses to permit necessary treatment for a child, such as a blood transfusion or vaccination, the court can name a temporary guardian to consent to such treatment. An adult has the right to refuse medical treatment, even if his or her life is in immediate danger. However, if there is evidence that the adult is not thinking clearly or is not making the decision voluntarily, a guardian can be appointed to make the decision.

Selection of a Guardian

Courts of GENERAL JURISDICTION in most states have the authority to appoint guardians. Typically, probate courts and juvenile courts hear cases involving guardianship. Probate courts, which oversee the administration of the estates of decedents, are the most common forum for the appointment of guardians. Juvenile courts decide on the appointment of guardians when a child has been removed from the home because of abuse or neglect, or has been declared a ward of the court. Generally, a court can appoint a guardian for a minor wherever the child lives. If a child lives in one state and has title to real estate in another state, a guardian can be appointed where the property is, in order to manage it.

A parent can appoint a guardian, usually by naming the guardian in a will. Some state laws allow a child to choose his or her own guardian if the child is over a certain age, usually 14. A court must approve the choice if the proposed guardian is suitable, even if the court believes someone else would be a better choice. Before approving the child's choice, however, the court must satisfy itself that the child understands the effect of the nomination and that the choice is not detrimental to the child's interests or contrary to law.

Guardianship statutes specify which persons have the right to ask a court to appoint a guardian for a certain child. Most of these laws list people who would be expected to have an interest in the child's welfare, usually relatives. Some statutes are more general, permitting applications to be filed by "any person." A court must examine a PETITION to determine whether the person applying for appointment as guardian really has the child's interest at heart.

Factors in Choosing a Guardian

The choice of a guardian for a child is guided by the needs of the ward. The ward's age, affections for certain people, education, and morals are all important considerations. Courts prefer to allow a child to remain with a competent person who has been caring for the child rather than disrupt a stable home. Courts also examine the financial condition, health, judgment, morals, and character of the person who seeks guardianship of the ward. Although age alone is not a determining factor, it may be material to the individual's ability to fulfill the duties of guardian for the entire period of guardianship. Affluence is not a prerequisite for a guardian, although a guardian must be reasonably secure financially. As a rule, courts attempt to entrust the care of a child to someone with the same religious background as the child's.

A divorced parent is not disqualified from appointment as guardian of a child's property simply because the DIVORCE decree has awarded the other parent custody. The court almost always favors a parent over other relatives or someone not related to the child unless there is reason to believe the parent is not a fit guardian. A close family member is not disqualified from caring for a child whose property he or she is eligible to inherit, unless it appears that he or she is unkind to the child or concerned only with the wealth to be gained from the child's property.

Sometimes the responsibilities of guardianship are divided between two people. In one case, a mother continued to have custody of her children after her husband's death, but the court refused her request to be appointed guardian of the children's estates because she dissipated the family allowance. A parent can also be disqualified under different statutes for "notoriously bad conduct," by "willfully and knowingly abandoning the child," or for "failing to maintain the child" when he or she has the financial ability to contribute to the child's support.

Manner and Length of Appointment

Once a guardian is selected, he or she can be required to take an oath of office before performing the duties of guardian. Statutes generally require a guardian to post a bond, that is, pay the court a sum of money out of which a ward can be reimbursed if the guardian fails to perform the duties faithfully. These laws also permit the court to waive this requirement if the ward's property is of relatively little value or if the guardian managing the property is a financial corporation, such as a bank or a TRUST COMPANY.

The formal appointment of a guardian is completed when the court issues the guardian a certificate called letters of guardianship. The naming of a guardian in a parent's will is only a nomination. The court must issue the letters of guardianship before a guardian has the legal authority to act.

Generally, a guardian's authority continues as long as the ward is below the LEGAL AGE of majority. If the ward marries before reaching the age of majority, guardianship of the person ends. Under the law of some states, guardianship of the property continues until he or she reaches the age of majority. For an adult ward, guardianship ends when a court determines the ward no longer needs supervision.

A guardian can be divested of authority whenever a court is convinced that he or she has neglected the duties of guardian or mismanaged property. In some cases, courts have ordered partial removal. For example, a father who has squandered money that should have remained in his children's bank accounts can continue to have personal guardianship of them, while someone else acts as guardian of their property.

Duties and Responsibilities of a Guardian

Generally, a guardian acts as guardian of both the person and the property of the ward, but in some circumstances these duties are split. When acting as guardian of the person, a guardian is entitled to custody and control of the ward. Some statutes make a specific exception when a child has a living parent who is suitable to provide daily care. The guardian then manages the child's property, and the parent retains custody. The rights and responsibilities associated with the child's daily care belong to the parent, but the guardian makes major decisions affecting long-term planning for the minor.

A guardian of the person of a child can prevent certain people from seeing the ward, but a court will not allow unreasonable restrictions. A guardian also has the right to move to a different state with the child, but can be required to appear in court prior to relocation and give assurances regarding the child's care. A guardian has the duty to provide for the child's support, education, and religious training. Courts permit a guardian to use income and interest earned by the child's assets to pay for the child's needs, but they are reluctant to permit the guardian to spend the principal. A parent is primarily responsible for the support of a child, so when a parent is living, his or her money must be used before the child's resources are spent. The child has a right to receive all of his or her property upon reaching the age of majority, unless restrictions are imposed by a will or a trust instrument.

A general guardian or a guardian of the property is considered a fiduciary—a person who occupies a position of trust and is legally obligated to protect the interests of the ward in the same manner as his or her own interests. A guardian cannot invest the ward's money in speculative ventures, agree not to sue someone who owes the ward money, or neglect LEGAL PROCEEDINGS, tax bills, or the maintenance of land, crops, or buildings that are part of the ward's estate. In addition, a guardian cannot allow someone else to maintain a business that the ward inherited or permit someone else to hold on to property belonging to the ward, without supervising such transactions. A guardian must earn income from the ward's property by making secure investments.

A guardian must take inventory and collect all the assets of the ward. Where permitted by law, title is taken in the ward's name. Otherwise, the guardian owns the property "as guardian" for the ward, which indicates that the guardian has the LEGAL RIGHT to hold or sell the property but must not use it for his or her personal benefit. The guardian must determine the value of the property and file a list of assets and their estimated value with the court. The guardian must collect the assets promptly, and is liable to

the ward's estate for any loss incurred owing to a failure to act promptly.

In general, a guardian does not have the authority to make contracts for the ward without specific permission from the court. If the child is party to a lawsuit, a guardian cannot assent to a settlement without first submitting the terms to the court for approval. A guardian must deposit any money held for the ward into an interest-bearing bank account separate from the guardian's own money. A guardian is also prohibited from making gifts from the ward's estate.

Generally, a guardian cannot tie up the ward's money by purchasing real estate, but can lend the money to someone else buying real estate if the property is sufficient security for the loan. A guardian cannot borrow money for personal use from the ward's estate. A guardian can lease property owned by the ward, but ordinarily the lease cannot extend beyond the time the ward reaches the age of majority. A guardian cannot mortgage real property or permit a LIEN on personal property of the ward. A guardian can sell items of the ward's personal property, but must receive the permission of the court to sell the ward's real estate.

At the end of the guardianship period, a guardian must account for all transactions involving the ward's estate. The guardian is usually required to file interim reports periodically with the court, but a final report must be filed and all property turned over to the ward when the ward has reached the age of majority. If the guardian has not managed the property in an ethical manner, the ward, upon reaching adulthood, may sue for waste, conversion, or embezzlement. If the management of the ward's assets was not illegal but resulted in losses, the guardian must reimburse the ward. If the guardian has managed the assets correctly, the guardian is entitled to be paid out of the ward's estate for his or her services.

Finally, whenever a guardian participates in a lawsuit for the ward, he or she sues or is sued only "as guardian," and not personally. For example, if the ward sues a physician for MALPRACTICE and recovers damages, the money does not belong to the guardian even though he or she initiated the lawsuit for the ward. In the same way, if someone obtains a judgment for damages against the ward, the money must come from the ward's property, not from the guardian. If both the guardian and the ward are parties in one lawsuit, the guardian participates in the action as both a guardian and an individual.

FURTHER READINGS

Barnes, Alison McChrystal. 2003. "The Liberty and Property of Elders: Guardianship and Will Contests as the Same Claim." *The Elder Law Journal* 11 (spring).

———. 2003. "Ward and Guardian." *Elder's Advisor* (winter).

Frolik, Lawrence A. 2001. "Promoting Judicial Acceptance and Use of Limited Guardianship." *Stetson Law Review* 31 (spring).

McConnell, Joyce E. 1998. "Securing the Care of Children in Diverse Families: Building on Trends in Guardianship Reform." *Yale Journal of Law and Feminism* 10 no. 1 (summer).

Morgan, Rebecca C. 2007. "The Uniform Guardianship and Protective Proceedings Act of 1997—Ten Years of Developments." *Stetson Law Review* 37, no. 1.

Zimmy, George H., and George T. Grossberg, eds. 1998. *Guardianship of the Elderly: Psychiatric and Judicial Aspects.* New York: Springer.

GUEST STATUTES

Widely adopted in the 1920s and 1930s, guest statutes were state laws that strictly limited LIABILITY in car accidents. These laws curtailed the legal rights of "guests"—nonpaying passengers such as friends or neighbors—who brought lawsuits against drivers after being hurt. Generally speaking, they prevented guests from suing car drivers or owners except in cases of a very high degree of NEGLIGENCE. Mere ordinary carelessness was an insufficient ground for a suit: If a guest was injured when a driver momentarily failed to pay attention and crashed the car, most states would reject a lawsuit. The net effect of guest statutes was to protect drivers and insurance companies while leaving injured passengers, for the most part, out of luck. Constitutional challenges to the laws frequently appeared in state and federal courts throughout the middle of the twentieth century, but courts waited until the 1970s and 1980s to begin narrowing and ultimately striking down the statutes in wholesale numbers.

The first guest statutes appeared in 1927, in Connecticut and Iowa (1927 Conn. Pub. Acts 4404, ch. 308, § 1 [repealed 1937]; Iowa Code Ann. § 321.494 [Supp. 1983]). Coinciding with a burst in manufacturing that increased the number of automobiles produced, the laws arose to meet the growing number of suits resulting from car accidents. By 1939, the last year in which a guest statute was enacted, 33 states had such laws or court precedents of

comparable effect. The rationale behind the statutes was that a driver's liability should be limited: Mere carelessness was seen as so commonplace that drivers in all accidents would be held liable for hurting their passengers were that the standard. For an injured passenger to surmount the barriers of a guest statute, greater evidence would have to be shown. A lawsuit would have to prove that the driver's actions were much more than careless—that they were grossly or willfully negligent. Other states went further, setting the standard as willful or wanton misconduct. In essence, little short of an utter disregard for safety or a desire to run someone off the road would hold up in court in a civil suit.

Thus, in one typical 1943 case, the Iowa guest statute prevented a passenger from recovering for injury. On May 30, 1942, a four-door Plymouth carrying five teenagers along a narrow, twisty gravel road went out of control, hit a bridge, and turned over. Driving was 17-year-old Fabian Gehl. Seconds before the accident, Gehl had leaned over to pick up a cigarette from the floor of the car. John Neyens, an 18-year-old passenger who was injured in the accident, sued Gehl. Under the guest statute, Neyens had to convince a jury that Gehl's behavior was reckless. At trial, the jury ruled in favor of the DEFENDANT, finding that reaching down for a cigarette, smashing the car into a bridge, and rolling it over was something short of reckless. On appeal, Neyens lost again (*Neyens v. Gehl et al.,* 235 Iowa 115, 15 N.W.2d 888 [1944]).

Over the years, guest statutes caused considerable controversy. When they were defended at all, it was to argue that they were needed to prevent drivers and passengers from colluding to bring FRAUDULENT claims against insurers. Critics took a different tack: they argued that guest statutes unfairly protected drivers and insurance companies, while leaving injured passengers and the survivors of dead passengers with no compensation for their losses. The distinction between paying and nonpaying passengers seemed arbitrary: Why should friends given a ride in a car be unable to recover damages when, for example, commuters riding in a bus were able to do so? In many states, even cattle being transported to market enjoyed greater legal protection than a guest in a car. But such arguments fell on deaf ears for many years. As early as 1929, the U.S. Supreme Court rejected a constitutional challenge to a guest statute on due process grounds (*Silver v. Silver,* 280 U.S. 117, 50 S. Ct. 57, 74 L. Ed. 221), and as late as 1977, it refused to hear another challenge because it did not pose a substantial FEDERAL QUESTION (*Hill v. Garner,* 434 U.S. 989, 98 S. Ct. 623, 54 L. Ed. 2d 486 [mem.]).

Nonetheless, the death knell for guest statutes began in the 1970s. As the concept of liability evolved, state legislatures began providing other means for passengers to seek compensation, and a few repealed their guest laws. Reacting to these changes, courts began to carve out exceptions in existing guest statutes, and ultimately to overturn the laws on constitutional grounds. Thus, the Supreme Court of Utah said, when striking down Utah's guest statute in 1984, "The original scope of the guest statute has been substantially narrowed, and its application to any particular guest is both problematic and irrational" (*Malan v. Lewis,* 693 P.2d 661). By 1996 only Alabama still had a guest statute (Ala. Code § 32-1-2).

FURTHER READINGS

Edwards, Linda L., J. Stanley Edwards, and Patricia Kirtley Wells. 2008. *Tort Law for Legal Assistants.* Farmington Hills, MI: Cengage Learning.

Emanuel, Steven. 2008. *Emanuel Law Outlines: Torts.* Frederick, MD: Aspen.

"Letter from Friedrich K. Juenger, Professor of Law, Univ. of California at Davis, to Harry C. Sigman, Esq., September 16, 1994." Reprinted in *Vanderbilt Journal of Transnational Law* 28 (May 1995).

GUILTY

Blameworthy; culpable; having committed a tort or crime; devoid of innocence.

An individual is guilty if he or she is responsible for a delinquency or a criminal or civil offense. When an accused is willing to accept legal responsibility for a criminal act, he or she pleads guilty. Similarly, a jury returns a verdict of guilty upon finding that a DEFENDANT has committed a crime. In the event that a jury is not convinced that a defendant has committed a crime, jurors can return a verdict of *not guilty,* which does not mean that the individual is innocent or that the jurors are so convinced, but rather that they do not believe sufficient evidence has been presented to prove that the defendant is guilty.

In civil lawsuits, the term *guilty* does not imply criminal responsibility but refers to misconduct.

GUN CONTROL

Government regulation of the manufacture, sale, and possession of firearms.

The SECOND AMENDMENT to the U.S. Constitution is at the heart of the issue of gun control. The Second Amendment declares that "A well regulated MILITIA, being necessary to the security of a free State, the right of the people to keep and bear Arms, shall not be infringed."

For decades, a debate raged over the meaning of these words. To many, the language of the amendment appeared to grant to the people the absolute right to bear arms. Others, however, believed it only protected the right of states to form a state militia. The U.S. Supreme Court had never fully addressed the issue head-on. It did issue a ruling in 1939 (*United States v. Miller,* 307 U.S. 174, 59 S. Ct. 816, 83 L. Ed. 1206 [1939]) that endorsed the state militia viewpoint, but it never explicitly addressed the limits of gun control until 2008. In *District of Columbia v. Heller,* No. 07-290, __U.S.__, 128 S.Ct. 2783, 171 L.Ed.2d 637 (2008), the Court struck down a Washington, D.C. ordinance that banned the possession of handguns in the district and declared that people have an individual right to possess firearms that the state cannot take away. The decision put in doubt thousands of gun control laws in the United States, though reasonable regulation of firearms remains viable. Outright bans on firearms, however, appear to be in question.

Congress, state legislatures, and local governing bodies have passed laws restricting the right to bear arms since the early days of the republic. Kentucky passed the first state legislation prohibiting the carrying of concealed WEAPONS, in 1813. By the end of the 1990s, firearms were regulated by approximately 23,000 federal, state, and local laws.

State and local firearms laws have varied widely. Thirteen states prohibit only the carrying of concealed handguns. At the other end of the spectrum, three Chicago suburbs—Morton Grove, Oak Park, and Evanston—ban handgun ownership outright. Generally, firearms regulations are more restrictive in large metropolitan areas.

State and local firearms laws and ordinances include outright bans of certain firearms, prohibitions on the alteration of certain firearms, and restrictions on the advertising of guns. State gun-control laws also address the

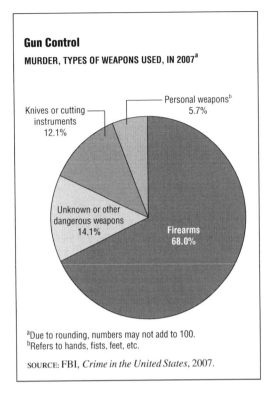

Gun Control

MURDER, TYPES OF WEAPONS USED, IN 2007[a]

Personal weapons[b]
5.7%

Knives or cutting
instruments
12.1%

Unknown or other
dangerous weapons
14.1%

Firearms
68.0%

[a]Due to rounding, numbers may not add to 100.
[b]Refers to hands, fists, feet, etc.

SOURCE: FBI, *Crime in the United States*, 2007.

THEFT of handguns, the inheritance of firearms, the use of firearms as collateral for loans, the possession of firearms by ALIENS, the discharge of firearms in public areas, and the alteration of serial numbers or other identifying marks on firearms. States generally base their power to control firearms on the police-power provisions of their constitutions, which grant to the states the right to enact laws for public safety.

Congress derives its power to regulate firearms in the COMMERCE CLAUSE, in Article I, Section 8, Clause 3, of the U.S. Constitution. Under the Commerce Clause, Congress may regulate commercial activity between the states and commerce with foreign countries. In reviewing federal legislation enacted pursuant to the Commerce Clause, the U.S. Supreme Court has given Congress tremendous leeway. Congress may enact criminal statutes regarding firearms if the activity at issue relates to interstate transactions, affects interstate commerce, or is such that control is necessary and proper to carry out the intent of the Commerce Clause.

In 1927 Congress passed the Mailing of Firearms Act, 18 U.S.C.A. § 1715, which banned the shipping of concealable handguns through the mail. Congress followed this with the NATIONAL FIREARMS ACT OF 1934 (ch. 757, 48 Stat.

1236–1240 [26 U.S.C.A. § 1132 et seq.]), which placed heavy taxes on the manufacture and distribution of firearms. One year later, Congress prohibited unlicensed manufacturers and dealers from shipping firearms across state borders, with the Federal Firearms Act of 1938 (ch. 850, § 2(f), 52 Stat. 1250, 1251).

In 1968, after the assassinations of President JOHN F. KENNEDY, CIVIL RIGHTS activists Malcolm X and MARTIN LUTHER KING Jr., and Senator ROBERT F. KENNEDY, Congress responded to the public outcry by passing the Gun Control Act of 1968 (GCA) (Pub. L. No. 90-615, § 102, 82 Stat. 1214 [codified at 18 U.S.C.A. §§ 921–928]). This act repealed the Federal Firearms Act and replaced it with increased federal control over firearms. Title I of the Act requires the federal licensing of anyone manufacturing or selling guns or ammunition. Title I also prohibits the interstate mail-order sale of guns and ammunition, the sale of guns to minors or persons with criminal records, and the importation of certain firearms. Title II of the Act imposes the same restrictions on other destructive devices, such as bombs, grenades, and other explosive materials.

Between 1979 and 1987, a total of 693,000 people in the United States were assaulted by criminals armed with handguns. Statistics such as this, as well as high-profile shootings, such as that of President RONALD REAGAN and his aide, James Brady, in 1981, led to pressure for further gun-control measures.

The congressional enactment in 1993 of the Brady Handgun Violence Prevention Act, Pub. L. No. 103-159, 107 Stat. 1536, marked the first significant federal gun-control legislation since the GCA in 1968. The Act was named for James Brady, the White House press secretary who was critically and permanently injured in 1981 during an ASSASSINATION attempt on President Ronald Reagan. The Brady Act amended the GCA, requiring the U.S. attorney general to establish a national instant background-check system and immediately put into place certain interim provisions until the federal system became operational. Under these interim provisions, a firearms dealer who sought to transfer a handgun was required to obtain from the proposed purchaser a statement, known as a Brady Form, that contained the name, address, and date of birth of the purchaser along with a sworn statement that the purchaser was not among those classes of persons prohibited from purchasing a handgun. The dealer was then required to verify the purchaser's identity and to provide the "chief law enforcement officer" (CLEO) within the jurisdiction with a copy of the Brady Form. With some exceptions, the dealer was required to wait five business days before completing the sale, unless the CLEO notified the dealer that there was no apparent reason to believe that the transfer would be illegal.

A number of CLEOs objected to these interim provisions. Jay Printz of Montana and Richard Mack of Arizona, both CLEOs, filed actions in federal court challenging the constitutionality of the parts of the Brady Act requiring CLEOs to accept Brady Forms. In both cases, the district courts held that the provision requiring CLEOs to conduct background checks were unconstitutional. However, the U.S. Court of Appeals for the Ninth Circuit consolidated the two cases and reversed these decisions, finding none of the Brady Act's interim provisions unconstitutional.

The U.S. Supreme Court, in *Printz v. United States*, 521 U.S. 898, 117 S. Ct. 2365, 138 L. Ed. 2d 914 (1997), reversed the Ninth Circuit, ruling that the interim provisions were unconstitutional. The Court, per Justice ANTONIN SCALIA, believed that the interim provisions disturbed the separation and equilibrium of powers among the three branches of the federal government. Under the Constitution, the president is to administer the laws enacted by Congress. The Brady Act "effectively transfers this responsibility to thousands of CLEOs in the 50 states," leaving the president with no meaningful way of controlling the administration of the law. Accordingly, CLEOs could not be required to accept Brady Forms from firearms dealers.

Other provisions of the Brady Act have also come under attack in the courts on constitutional grounds. For example, in *Gillespie v. City of Indianapolis*, 185 F.3d 693 (7th Cir. 1999), a former police officer challenged the act's prohibition of persons convicted of DOMESTIC VIOLENCE offenses from possessing a firearm in or affecting interstate commerce. Gerald Gillespie, the PLAINTIFF in the suit, was convicted of domestic violence and, as a result, lost his job as a police officer. Although the U.S. Court of Appeals for the Seventh Circuit found

In its first substantial pronouncement on gun control, the Supreme Court ruled in 2008 that in-home gun possession for the purpose of self-defense is an American constitutional right.
AP IMAGES

that Gillespie had standing to bring the suit challenging the Brady Act, it noted that the Second Amendment was intended to ensure protection by a militia for the people as a whole. Because it could not find a reasonable relationship between ownership of a particular gun and the preservation and efficiency of a state militia, Gillespie's claim failed. Other lower federal courts have similarly held that the Second Amendment does not prohibit the federal government from imposing some restrictions on private gun ownership.

In August 1994, Congress passed legislation banning so-called ASSAULT weapons under Title XI of the Public Safety and Recreational Firearms Use Protection Act (Pub. L. No. 103-322, 108 Stat. 1796 [codified as amended in scattered sections of 42 U.S.C.A.]). This act bans the manufacture, sale, and use of 19 types of semiautomatic weapons and facsimiles, as well as certain high-capacity ammunition magazines.

In 1995, the U.S. Supreme Court set additional limits on gun control with its landmark decision in *United States v. Lopez*, 514 U.S. 549, 115 S. Ct. 1624, 131 L. Ed. 2d 626. In *Lopez*, the Court ruled that Congress had exceeded its authority under the Commerce Clause in passing a law that criminalized the possession of a firearm within 1,000 feet of a school (Gun-Free School Zones Act of 1990 [18 U.S.C.A. § 922(1)(1)(A)]). The Court held that because such gun possession was not an economic activity that significantly affected interstate commerce, it was beyond Congress's power to regulate.

The debate over gun control entered a new phase when, beginning in 1998, major U.S. cities brought lawsuits against the gun industry. Frustrated by decades of meager progress in gun control, as well as mounting costs in law enforcement and health care, mayors from such cities as New Orleans, Miami, Chicago, San Francisco, Cleveland, and Cincinnati looked beyond traditional regulation and tried litigation as a means to recoup the millions of dollars that the cities spend each year in coping with gun violence. The cities hoped to emulate the success of state governments in winning record settlements from the tobacco industry. In February 1999 they were encouraged when a federal jury returned the first-ever verdict holding gun makers liable for damages caused by the use of their products in a crime. But as many more cities considered filing suits, the gun industry fought back with LOBBYING and launched pre-emptive strikes in state legislatures against future lawsuits.

Many of the lawsuits were dismissed. The gun industry enjoyed two victories in 2000 as judges dismissed suits brought by the cities of Philadelphia and Chicago. Charging the industry with a public NUISANCE, both cities sought to recover the public costs of gun violence, including medical care, police protection, emergency services, and prison costs. The cities argued that gun manufacturers and distributors were responsible for these costs because they knowingly or negligently sold guns to dealers who then supplied them to criminals. A judge in the Cook County CIRCUIT COURT dismissed Chicago's claim because Chicago had failed to prove that gun manufacturers were responsible for public costs resulting from criminal gun violence. Likewise, a Pennsylvania judge dismissed Philadelphia's lawsuit because under the Pennsylvania Uniform Firearms Act—for which the gun industry lobbied—the state of Pennsylvania has the sole authority to regulate the industry.

State and federal appellate courts have generally held in favor of gun manufacturers as well. The California Supreme Court, in *Merrill v. Navegar, Inc.*, 28 P.3d 116 (Cal. 2001), held that gun manufacturers cannot be held legally responsible when their products are used for criminal activity. The closely watched case stemmed from a 1993 shooting rampage in a San Francisco office tower that left eight people dead and six wounded. Similarly, the U.S. Court of Appeals for the Third Circuit, in *Camden County Board of Chosen Freeholders v. Beretta U.S. A. Corp.*, 273 F.3d 536 (3d Cir. 2001), upheld the dismissal of a suit brought by Camden County, New Jersey, which had accused several gun manufacturers of creating a public nuisance

and acting negligently in its distribution of handguns. The Third Circuit also upheld the dismissal of the suit brought by the city of Philadelphia in *City of Philadelphia v. Beretta U.S.A. Corp.*, 277 F.3d 415 (3d Cir. 2002).

Some lawsuits involving gun manufacturers were settled out of court. In March 2000, under pressure from many lawsuits nationwide, Smith & Wesson, the nation's oldest and largest manufacturer of handguns, entered into a settlement to end many of the cases. Under the agreement, Smith & Wesson agreed to place tamper-proof serial numbers on handguns to prevent criminals from scratching them off. It also promised to manufacture its handguns with trigger locks to prevent them from being fired by unauthorized users.

The landmark *Heller* case was a legal challenge to the District of Columbia's gun control laws. In 1976 the district enacted firearms control regulations that banned residents from owning handguns, automatic firearms, and high-capacity semi-automatic firearms. The law also prohibited possession of unregistered firearms. For those with lawfully registered handguns, the law required owners to keep the firearm unloaded and disassembled or otherwise bound by a trigger lock.

Six residents of the District of Columbia challenged the law. Four plaintiffs wanted to have guns in their homes to provide SELF-DEFENSE, whereas another plaintiff wanted to keep a gun assembled in his home without a trigger lock. A final plaintiff, Dick Heller (the named plaintiff in the Supreme Court action), wanted to possess a gun both at home and in his capacity as a special police officer. The U.S. district court for the District of Columbia ruled against the plaintiffs in 2004, but in 2007 the U.S. Court of Appeals for the District of Columbia ruled that the D.C. restrictions on handguns violated the Second Amendment. In a lengthy opinion by Judge Laurence H. Silberman, the court ruled that the Second Amendment provided an individual right and that the D.C. statute violated this individual right. Silberman based his reasoning primarily on the text of the amendment itself. *Parker v. Dist. of Columbia*, 478 F.3d 370 (D.C. Cir. 2007).

The Supreme Court, in a 5–4 decision, upheld the appeals court and agreed that the Second Amendment gives individuals the right to possess firearms. Justice Antonin Scalia,

TAKE THAT! AND THAT! THE GUN CONTROL DEBATE CONTINUES

Gun control motivates one of U.S. law's fiercest duels.

Arguments favoring control range from calls for regulation to support for total disarmament. At the most moderate point of the spectrum is the idea that government should regulate who owns guns and for what purpose, a position held by the lobby Handgun Control Incorporated (HGI), which helped write the Brady law. This kind of monitoring is far too little for one antigun group, the Coalition to Stop Gun Violence, which demands a complete ban on manufacturing and selling guns to the general public. The opposition leaves room for only very slight compromise. The NATIONAL RIFLE ASSOCIATION (NRA)—the most powerful opponent of gun control—generally fights any restrictive measure. The NRA has opposed efforts to ban so-called cop-killer bullets, which can pierce police safety vests. It has supported background checks at the time of purchase, yet only if these are done instantly so as not to inconvenience the vast majority of gun buyers. Even more adamant is the group Gun Owners of America, which opposes any legal constraints.

With so many laws on the books, the question of gun control's constitutionality would seem already settled. Yet this is where the gun control debate begins. The SECOND AMENDMENT reads, "A well regulated MILITIA, being necessary to the security of a free State, the right of the people to keep and bear Arms, shall not be infringed." Does this mean citizens have a constitutional right to own guns? The gun lobby says yes.

A minority of legal scholars believe that the framers of the BILL OF RIGHTS meant to include citizens along with "a well regulated Militia" in the right to bear arms. One supporter of this view is Professor Sanford Levinson, of the University of Texas, who argues that the Second Amendment is intended to tie the hands of government in restricting private ownership of guns. He charges that liberal academics who support gun control read only the Constitution's Second Amendment so narrowly.

The majority view is more restrictive in its reading. It pictures the Second Amendment as tailored to a specific right, namely, that of states to equip and maintain a state NATIONAL GUARD. Harvard law professor Laurence Tribe argues that "[t]he Second Amendment's preamble makes it clear that it is not designed to create an individual right to bear arms outside of the context of a state-run militia."

This argument has a leading advantage over the minority position: It is what the U.S. Supreme Court has consistently held for over fifty years.

In the 1939 case of *United States v. Miller*, 307 U.S. 174; 59 S. Ct. 816, 83 L. Ed. 1206 (1939)—the only modern Supreme Court case to address the issue—a majority of the Court refused to find an individual constitutional right to bear arms.

Because the meaning of the Second Amendment seems well settled, the dispute has turned to pragmatics. How well does gun control work, if it works at all? Measuring lives saved by gun control is practically impossible; it is only possible to count how many lives are lost to gun violence. Advocates generally claim that the fact that lives are lost to guns and the possibility that even one life may be saved through gun control are justification enough for legislation. They can quantify gains of another sort under the Brady law. In early 1995 the JUSTICE DEPARTMENT estimated that background checks had kept 40,000 felons from buying handguns, a figure derived from information provided by the state and local authorities who ran the checks.

Opponents say gun control is a gross failure. They argue that it never has kept criminals from buying guns illegally. Instead, they say, prohibition efforts have only been nuisances for law-abiding gun owners: city ordinances such as Chicago's that ban handgun sales send buyers to the suburbs, and the Brady law's five-day waiting period amounts to another unfair penalty. Moreover, opponents rebut arguments about gun violence by insisting that guns are actually used to protect their owners from harm. The NRA's chief lobbyist has argued that the SELF-DEFENSE effectiveness of guns is proved by "the number of crimes thwarted, lives protected, injuries prevented, medical costs saved and property preserved."

Settling the gun control debate is no more likely than solving the problem of crime itself. In fact, only the latter could ever bring about the former. After all, it is violent crime, more than accidental gun deaths involving children, that animates the gun control movement. On this point, the two sides agree briefly and then diverge once again. Both want tougher action on crime. The key difference is that gun control opponents want such measures to include almost every traditional means available—more police officers, more prisons, and longer prison sentences—except the control of guns. Advocates believe there can be no effective anticrime measures without gun control.

writing for the majority, focused on the text of the amendment. Scalia stated:

The Second Amendment is naturally divided into two parts: its prefatory clause and its operative clause. The former does not limit the latter grammatically, but rather announces a purpose. The Amendment could be rephrased, 'Because a well regulated Militia is necessary to the security of a free State, the right of the people to keep and bear Arms shall not be infringed.' Although this structure of the Second Amendment is unique in our Constitution, other legal documents of the founding era, particularly individual-rights provisions of state constitutions, commonly included a prefatory statement of purpose.

Scalia pointed out that the Second Amendment is one of three places in the BILL OF RIGHTS where the phrase "the right of the people" is used. The two other instances include the Assembly-and-Petition Clause of the FIRST AMENDMENT and the Search-and-Seizure Clause of the FOURTH AMENDMENT. In each instance, the phrase referred to an individual right, rather than a collective right. In addition, prior draft versions of the Second Amendment clearly referred to the right to bear arms as an individual right. Therefore, the Second Amendment provided individual, rather than collective, rights.

Based on this conclusion, the Court ruled that the D.C. handgun ban and the trigger-lock requirement both violated the Second Amendment. The total handgun ban effectively prohibited an entire class of "arms" that citizens use for lawful self-defense. The trigger-lock requirement made it impossible for citizens to use guns for self-defense, thus rendering this restriction unconstitutional as well.

FURTHER READINGS

Doherty, Brian. 2008. *Gun Control on Trial: Inside the Supreme Court Battle over the Second Amendment.* Washington, D.C.: Cato Institute.

Dolan, Edward F., and Margaret M. Scariano. 1994. *Guns in the United States.* New York: Watts.

Halbrook, Stephen P. 2008. *The Founders' Second Amendment: Origins of the Right to Bear Arms.* New York: Ivan R. Dee.

Kopel, David B., et al. 2003. *Supreme Court Gun Cases.* Phoenix, Ariz: Bloomfield Press.

Lott, John R., Jr. 2000. *More Guns, Less Crime: Understanding Crime and Gun-Control Laws.* 2d ed. Chicago: Univ. of Chicago Press.

Spitzer, Robert. 2007. *The Politics of Gun Control.* 4th ed. Washington, D.C.: CQ Press.

CROSS REFERENCE

Weapons.

HABEAS CORPUS

[Latin, You have the body.] *A writ (court order) that commands an individual or a government official who has restrained another to produce the prisoner at a designated time and place so that the court can determine the legality of custody and decide whether to order the prisoner's release.*

A WRIT of habeas corpus directs a person, usually a prison warden, to produce the prisoner and justify the prisoner's detention. If the prisoner argues successfully that the incarceration is in violation of a constitutional right, the court may order the prisoner's release. Habeas corpus relief also may be used to obtain custody of a child or to gain the release of a detained person who is insane, is a drug addict, or has an infectious disease. Usually, however, it is a response to imprisonment by the criminal justice system.

A writ of habeas corpus is authorized by statute in federal courts and in all state courts. An inmate in state or federal prison asks for the writ by filing a PETITION with the court that sentenced him or her. In most states, and in federal courts, the inmate is given the opportunity to present a short oral argument in a hearing before the court. He or she also may receive an evidentiary hearing to establish evidence for the petition.

The habeas corpus concept was first expressed in the MAGNA CARTA, a constitutional document forced on King John by English landowners at Runnymede on June 15, 1215. Among the liberties declared in the Magna Carta was that "No free man shall be seized, or imprisoned, or disseised, or outlawed, or exiled, or injured in any way, nor will we enter on him or send against him except by the lawful judgment of his peers, or by the law of the land." This principle evolved to mean that no person should be deprived of freedom without DUE PROCESS OF LAW.

The writ of habeas corpus was first used by the COMMON-LAW COURTS in thirteenth- and fourteenth-century England. These courts, composed of legal professionals, were in competition with feudal courts, which were controlled by local landowners, or "lords." The feudal courts lacked procedural consistency, and on that basis, the COMMON LAW courts began to issue writs demanding the release of persons imprisoned by them. From the late fifteenth to the seventeenth centuries, the common law courts used the writ to order the release of persons held by royal courts, such as the Chancery, Admiralty courts, and the STAR CHAMBER.

The only reference to the writ of habeas corpus in the U.S. Constitution is contained in Article I, Section 9, Clause 2. This clause provides, "The Privilege of the Writ of Habeas Corpus shall not be suspended, unless when in Cases of Rebellion or Invasion the public Safety may require it." President ABRAHAM LINCOLN

A sample application for habeas corpus.
ILLUSTRATION BY GGS CREATIVE RESOURCES. REPRODUCED BY PERMISSION OF GALE, A PART OF CENGAGE LEARNING.

Application for Habeas Corpus

STATE OF NORTH CAROLINA

File No. ______

______ County

In The General Court Of Justice
☐ District ☐ Superior Court Division

STATE VERSUS				**APPLICATION AND WRIT OF HABEAS CORPUS AD PROSEQUENDUM**
Name of Defendant				
Race	*Sex*	*Date of Birth*	*Social Security No.*	
Name of Agency in Whose Custody Defendant Confined ☐ *N.C. DOC* ☐ *Sheriff of* *County*				

File No.	Offense(s) CHARGES PENDING FOR TRIAL

APPLICATION

To Any Judge Of The Trial Division Named Above:

The defendant named above is confined in the custody of the agency named above. The prosecutor requests that a Writ of Habeas Corpus Ad Prosequendum be issued to the agency, requiring that the defendant be delivered, on the court date and at the time and place shown below, to the court in which the charge(s) referred to above are pending.

Court Date	*Court Time* ☐ AM ☐ PM	*Date of Application*
Location of Court		*Signature of Prosecutor*

WRIT

To the Agency Named Above:
The defendant named above is confined in your custody. Upon application of the prosecutor named above, you are ORDERED to deliver the defendant to the custody of the sheriff of this county so that the defendant may be brought before this Court on the court date and at the time and place referred to above.

To: ☐ **The Sheriff of this County** ☐ **Other** ______
You are **ORDERED** to serve this writ upon the agency named above; to take the defendant into custody and bring him before this Court on the date and at the time and place shown above and, when the court proceeding has been completed and the defendant is released by the court, to return the defendant to the custody of that agency unless the court directs otherwise.

Date	*Court*	*Name (Type or Print)*
☐ *District Court Judge*	☐ Superior Court Judge	*Signature*

RETURN OF SERVICE

I certify that this Writ was received and served as follows.

Date Writ Received	*Date Writ Served on Custodian*	*Date of Return of Service*
Name of Person Served		*Signature of Person Making Return of Service*
Date Def. Received from Custodian	*Date Def. Returned to Custodian*	☐ Deputy Sheriff ☐ Other

AOC-CR-223, Rev. 10/96
©1997 Administrative Office of the

Original-Custodian Copy-District Attorney Copy-File

suspended the writ in 1861, when he authorized his Civil War generals to arrest anyone they thought to be dangerous. In addition, Congress suspended it in 1863 to allow the Union army to hold accused persons temporarily until trial in the civilian courts. The Union army reportedly ignored the statute suspending the writ and conducted trials under MARTIAL LAW.

In 1789 Congress passed the JUDICIARY ACT OF 1789 (ch. 20, § 14, 1 Stat. 73 [codified in title 28 of the U.S.C.A.]), which granted to federal courts the power to hear the habeas corpus petitions of federal prisoners. In 1867 Congress passed the Habeas Corpus Act of February 5 (ch. 28, 14 Stat. 385 [28 U.S.C.A. §§ 2241 et seq.]). This statute gave federal courts the power to issue habeas corpus writs for "any person . . . restrained in violation of the Constitution, or of any treaty or law of the United States." The U.S. Supreme Court has interpreted it to mean that federal courts may hear the habeas corpus petitions of state prisoners as well as federal prisoners.

The writ of habeas corpus is an EXTRAORDI-NARY REMEDY because it gives a court the power to release a prisoner after the prisoner has been processed through the criminal justice system, with all its procedural safeguards and appeals. For this reason, the burden is initially on the petitioning prisoner to prove that he or she is being held in violation of a constitutional right. If the PETITIONER can meet this burden with sufficient evidence, the burden then shifts to the warden to justify the imprisonment.

A prisoner may file a petition for a writ of habeas corpus with the sentencing court only after exhausting all appeals and motions. Federal courts may receive a petition from a state prisoner, but not until the petitioner has attempted all available appeals and motions and habeas corpus petitions in the state courts. Federal prisoners must exhaust all available appeals and motions in the federal sentencing court and federal appeals courts before filing a habeas corpus petition with the sentencing court. If the first petition is denied, the inmate may petition the appeals courts.

A petition for a writ of habeas corpus is a CIVIL ACTION against the jailer. It is neither an appeal nor a continuation of the criminal case against the prisoner. It is not used to determine guilt or innocence. Rather, the purpose is solely to determine whether the confinement is in violation of a constitutional right. This is significant because it limits the scope of complaints that a petitioner may use as a basis for the writ.

Violation of the Due Process Clauses of the Fifth and Fourteenth Amendments is the most common basis for a writ of habeas corpus. Prosecutorial misconduct, juror MALFEASANCE, and ineffective assistance of counsel are common due process grounds for the writ. FIFTH AMEND-MENT grounds include failure of the police to give *Miranda* warnings before in-custody questioning (in violation of the right against SELF-INCRIMINA-TION), and multiple trials (in violation of the DOUBLE JEOPARDY prohibition). The EIGHTH AMEND-MENT right against CRUEL AND UNUSUAL PUNISHMENT is another common ground for habeas corpus relief, especially in cases involving the death penalty or a lengthy prison term.

There are several notable restrictions on the writ's application. FOURTH AMENDMENT violations of the right against unreasonable SEARCH AND SEIZURE cannot be raised in a habeas corpus petition. Prisoners are not entitled to a court-appointed attorney for habeas corpus petitions. Newly developed constitutional principles will not be applied retroactively in habeas corpus cases except where doubt is cast on the guilt of the prisoner. Delay in filing a habeas petition may result in its dismissal if the government is prejudiced (i.e., made less able to respond) by the delay. In addition, the petitioner must be in custody to request a writ of habeas corpus. This rule prevents a prisoner from challenging a conviction through habeas corpus after serving out a sentence for the conviction.

The law of habeas corpus is ever changing. In the 1990s the U.S. Supreme Court took steps to further limit the writ's application. In *Keeney v. Tamayo-Reyes,* 504 U.S. 1, 112 S. Ct. 1715, 118 L. Ed. 2d 318 (1992), the Court held that a habeas corpus petitioner is not entitled to an evidentiary hearing in federal court unless he or she can show two things: a reason for failing to develop evidence at trial, and actual prejudice to the prisoner's defense as a result of the failure. In *Herrera v. Collins,* 506 U.S. 390, 113 S. Ct. 853, 122 L. Ed. 2d 203 (1993), the Court held that a claim of actual innocence is not a basis for federal habeas corpus relief. This means that newly discovered evidence alone does not entitle a petitioner to federal habeas corpus relief.

The availability and import of habeas corpus in state courts is also subject to change through

Rubin "Hurricane" Carter

Federal courts grant writs of habeas corpus only when grave constitutional violations have occurred. The granting of Rubin "Hurricane" Carter's habeas petition in 1985 freed him from almost 20 years of imprisonment for a crime he maintains he did not commit.

Carter was a top-ranked middleweight boxer when he and John Artis were arrested in 1966 and charged with murdering three people in Paterson, New Jersey. Carter and Artis were African American; the victims were white. Carter and Artis claimed they were the victims of racism and a police frame-up, but they were convicted of murder and sentenced to life imprisonment.

Carter fought his conviction in state court, but the verdict was upheld. In 1974 he published *The Sixteenth Round: From Number 1 Contender to Number 45472*. The book became a national best-seller and drew attention to his case. In 1975 Bob Dylan wrote and recorded the song "Hurricane," which recounted Carter's arrest and trial and characterized Carter as an innocent man. This publicity, along with an investigation by the New Jersey public defenders' office, led to a motion for a new trial. The motion was granted, but Carter and Artis were convicted again in 1976. Carter remained imprisoned; Artis was paroled in 1981.

After all state appeals were exhausted, the only remaining avenue for relief was to file for a writ of habeas corpus in federal court. In November 1985 Judge H. Lee Sarokin ruled that the second murder trial convictions were unconstitutional because the prosecution had been allowed to imply that guilt could be inferred by the defendants' race and because the prosecution withheld polygraph evidence that could have been used to impeach the credibility of their "star witness" (*Carter v. Rafferty,* 621 F. Supp. 533 [D. N.J. 1985]). Judge Sarokin therefore granted habeas corpus, overturned the convictions, and ordered "Immediate release from custody with prejudice."

The State of New Jersey appealed to the Third Circuit Court of Appeals, asking to reverse Sarokin's ruling and requesting that Carter remain incarcerated until a final ruling. The Third Circuit rejected both appeals. New Jersey appealed to the U.S. Supreme Court, which also refused to overturn. The state chose not to attempt a third prosecution of Carter and Artis. Carter moved to Canada where he headed the Association for the Defense of the Wrongly Convicted.

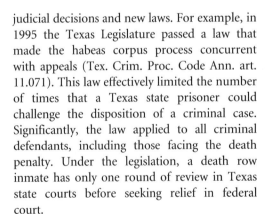

judicial decisions and new laws. For example, in 1995 the Texas Legislature passed a law that made the habeas corpus process concurrent with appeals (Tex. Crim. Proc. Code Ann. art. 11.071). This law effectively limited the number of times that a Texas state prisoner could challenge the disposition of a criminal case. Significantly, the law applied to all criminal defendants, including those facing the death penalty. Under the legislation, a death row inmate has only one round of review in Texas state courts before seeking relief in federal court.

In 1996 Congress passed the Anti-Terrorism and Effective Death Penalty Act (AEDPA) (Pub. L. No. 104-132, 110 Stat. 1214). Congress sought to streamline post-conviction appeals proceedings and to curtail the time that prisoners could use to seek habeas corpus relief. Since the enactment of the law, the U.S. Supreme Court has been called upon to interpret a number of the AEDPA provisions; these rulings primarily have addressed technical details of the workings of the new law, but the Court has endorsed the AEDPA and removed jurisdiction from the lower federal courts to hear many habeas petitions. The Court upheld the constitutionality of the AEDPA in *Felker v. Turpin,* 518 U.S. 651, 116 S. Ct. 2333, 135 L. Ed. 2d 827 (1996).

The habeas corpus provisions represent a major shift in federal-state judicial relations, for Congress directed that federal courts generally defer to state court judgments on questions of federal CONSTITUTIONAL LAW in criminal cases. The AEDPA established a "deference" standard, which mandates that the federal courts, in reviewing state court convictions, defer to a state court ruling on the merits of any habeas corpus claim. This deferral includes questions of fact and of law, as well as mixed questions of FACT AND LAW. A federal court must defer unless the state court ADJUDICATION of the claim resulted in a decision that was contrary to, or involved an unreasonable application of, clearly established federal law, as determined by the U.S. Supreme Court; or if the state conviction resulted in a decision that was based on an unreasonable determination of the facts in light of the evidence presented in the state court proceeding.

The AEDPA also contains a number of specific rules for habeas corpus review. The act provides for a one-year filing deadline for non-capital habeas corpus petitions. The time starts running at the conclusion of direct review or the expiration of time for seeking such review. The law requires a certificate of appealability from a circuit judge or justice before a petitioner may appeal from denial of relief. The petitioner must make a substantial showing of denial of a constitutional right, and the certificate must be issue-specific. The AEDPA also allows federal courts to deny relief with respect to unexhausted claims but may not grant relief if the claim is unexhausted. The habeas petitioner can avoid exhaustion only if there is no available state remedy, or if the remedy is ineffective to protect the petitioner's rights. If there is no state remedy because of a procedural default, federal review is still prohibited.

The AEDPA also places restrictions on the ability of a petitioner to obtain an evidentiary hearing on a claim where the prisoner failed to develop the factual basis. Because state court fact-findings are presumed to be correct, the petitioner must rebut the PRESUMPTION by clear and convincing evidence. To obtain an evidentiary hearing, the petitioner must show that the claim relies on a new rule made retroactive by the U.S. Supreme Court or that the factual predicate could not have been discovered earlier through due diligence. Moreover, in all cases, the petitioner must show by clear and convincing evidence that, but for the alleged error for which a hearing is sought, no reasonable factfinder would have found the petitioner guilty of the underlying offense. This is a steep hurdle for a habeas petitioner to overcome.

The AEDPA also seeks to prevent the abuse of habeas corpus by limiting the number of times a prisoner may ask for a writ. A successive habeas petition may not be filed in district court unless the petitioner is authorized to do so by a three-judge panel of the Court of Appeals. The U.S. Supreme Court, in *Felker*, characterized this provision as an acceptable "gatekeeping" mechanism. If petitioners make a PRIMA FACIE showing that they satisfy the exceptions against successive petitions, then they may proceed; otherwise, the court must dismiss the petition. If a successive claim was presented in a prior petition, it must be dismissed; no exceptions are authorized by the AEDPA. Though the AEDPA provides some narrow exceptions to this rule, any claim must establish by clear and convincing evidence that, but for the error, no reasonable factfinder would have found the petitioner guilty of the underlying offense.

In habeas petitions from death row inmates, the AEDPA imposes additional rules beyond those already described. The rules apply to states that establish certain standards for competence of counsel. For states to benefit from these additional limitations, they must provide a mechanism for appointment and compensation of competent counsel in state post-conviction proceedings or for appointment of counsel to handle the appeal and post-conviction remedies in a unitary proceeding. Once the state court has made an appointment of counsel, a federal court that would have jurisdiction over the case may enter a stay of execution. The stay expires if a timely petition is not filed, if the prisoner properly waives the right to pursue federal habeas relief, or if relief is denied at any stage of federal review. Once a stay vacates under any of those circumstances, a new one may not be imposed unless the petitioner can overcome the presumption against successive petitions.

The AEDPA sets a time limit for habeas petition in capital cases: The petition must be filed within 180 days after final state court AFFIRMANCE on direct review. In addition, the AEDPA requires that capital habeas cases be given priority over all non-capital matters, and it imposes time limits on resolution. These include a decision by the district court within 180 days after the petition is filed, although the court may extend its time by no more than 30 days. Failure by the district court to act within the time limits may be enforced by a petition for writ of mandate. More importantly, a court of appeals must decide the case within 120 days after the reply BRIEF is filed; any petition for rehearing must be decided within 30 days after the petition is filed, or 30 days after any requested RESPONSIVE PLEADING is filed. If rehearing or rehearing EN BANC is granted, the case must be decided within 120 days after the order granting such rehearing. In addition, the time limits are applicable to all first petitions, successive petitions, and habeas cases considered on remand from a court of appeals or the U.S. Supreme Court.

The AEDPA has changed the legal landscape for prisoners seeking writs of habeas corpus. Petitioners must act within set deadlines, and they must attempt to place all issues in dispute before the first habeas-reviewing federal court or risk the chance of being rejected in a successive petition.

A protracted habeas corpus case invoking AEDPA was that of *Miller-El v. Cockrell,* 537 U. S. 322 (2003). In that case, Thomas Miller-El, a Texas death-row inmate, was able to successfully invoke the standard of review under AEDPA to get his case remanded for a new hearing on his claim of racial bias in the jury selection (systematic exclusion of African-Americans). On remand, the Fifth CIRCUIT COURT of Appeals in 2004 held that Miller-El had failed to show, by clear and convincing evidence, that the state court's finding of no DISCRIMINATION was erroneous. Two years later, in *Miller-El v. Dretke,* 545 U.S. 231 (2005), the Supreme Court reversed the Fifth Circuit, finding that the state trial court's interpretation of the facts (in finding no discrimination) was both unreasonable and erroneous under AEDPA.

In *Munaf v. Geren,* No. 06-1666; 553 U.S. ___, 128 S.Ct 2207 (2008) the U.S. Supreme Court was again faced with another case testing the scope of habeas corpus within the context of the international war on terror. In this case, the Supreme Court held that a U.S. citizen may file a petition for habeas corpus to challenge his detention by American military forces taking part in a multinational force (MNF) overseas.

FURTHER READINGS

Freedman, Eric M. 2001. *Habeas Corpus: Rethinking the Great Writ of Liberty.* New York: New York University Press.

Harrington, James C., and Anne More Burnham. 1995. "Texas's New Habeas Corpus Procedure for Death-Row Inmates: Kafkaesque—and Probably Unconstitutional." *St. Mary's Law Journal* 27 (fall).

Jones, Andrew A. 1994. "Federal Habeas Corpus Evidentiary Hearings: Has the Court Deliberately Bypassed Section 2254(D)?" *Wisconsin Law Review* (January-February).

Morse, Charles R. 1993. "Habeas Corpus and 'Actual Innocence': *Herrera v. Collins,* 113 S. Ct. 853 (1993)." *Harvard Journal of Law and Public Policy* 16 (autumn).

Statsinger, Steven M. 2007. *Habeas Corpus.* 2d ed. Louisville, CO: National Institute for Trial Advocacy.

HABEAS CORPUS ACT

The Habeas Corpus Act was an English statute enacted in 1679 during the reign of King Charles II. It was subsequently amended and supplemented by enactments of Parliament that permitted, in certain cases, a person to challenge the legality of his or her imprisonment before a court that ordered the person to appear before it at a designated time so that it could render its decision. The Habeas Corpus Act served as the precursor of habeas corpus provisions found in U.S. federal and state constitutions and statutes that safeguard the guarantee of personal liberty.

HABENDUM CLAUSE

The portion of a deed to real property that begins with the phrase To have and to hold *and that provides a description of the ownership rights of the transferee of such property.*

Whereas a GRANTING CLAUSE contains the words of transfer of an interest, a habendum clause defines the estate granted and declares the extent of the interest conveyed. For example, such a clause might say: "To have and to hold the premises herein granted unto the party of the second part, and to the female heirs of the party of the second part forever." This particular habendum clause qualifies the estate granted by limiting its inheritability to the female heirs of the grantee.

HABITABILITY

Fitness for occupancy. The requirement that rented premises, such as a house or apartment, be reasonably fit to occupy.

A warranty of habitability is an implied promise by a landlord of residential premises that such premises are fit for human habitation. It exists in a majority of states, either by statute or CASE LAW, and implies that the premises are free from any condition that is unsafe or unsanitary. A breach of this warranty would, for example, occur if none of the toilets were in working order or if the roof of a house was in total disrepair.

A warranty of habitability begins at the commencement of the tenancy and continues for its duration.

HABITUAL

Regular or customary; usual.

A *habitual* drunkard, for example, is an individual who regularly becomes intoxicated as opposed to a person who drinks infrequently. A *habitual criminal* is a legal category that has been created by a number of state statutes by which serious penalties can be imposed on individuals who have been repeatedly convicted of a designated crime.

HAGUE TRIBUNAL

The Hague Tribunal was an ARBITRATION court established for the purpose of facilitating immediate recourse for the settlement of international disputes. As of 2009 the term is often used to refer to the International Criminal Tribunal for the Former Yugoslavia (ICTY), which has prosecutorial and adjudicatory powers. Both entities are commonly referred to transitionally as the Hague Tribunal, although technically speaking, they are not the same.

The Hague Tribunal was established by the Hague Peace Conference in 1899 to provide a permanent court accessible at all times for the resolution of international differences. The court was granted jurisdiction over all arbitration cases, provided the parties thereto did not decide to institute a special tribunal. In addition, an international bureau was established to act as a registry for the tribunal and to serve as the channel of communications with respect to the meetings of the court.

The Hague Tribunal is considered permanent due to the fact that there is a permanent list of members from among whom the arbitrators are chosen. In 1907, at the Second Hague Conference, it was provided that of the two arbitrators selected by each of the parties, only one could be a national of the state appointing him or her.

In 1993 the UNITED NATIONS (UN) Security Council passed a resolution to establish within The Hague, Netherlands, an ad hoc international 14-judge court expressly mandated to prosecute and adjudicate WAR CRIMES, GENOCIDE, and crimes against humanity committed on the territory of the former Yugoslavia. This International Criminal Tribunal for the Former Yugoslavia (ICTY) is often referred to as the Hague Tribunal. (Subsequent resolutions have increased the court to 16 members as well as a special force of AD LITEM judges.) The tribunal is composed of three chambers and an appeal chamber. Judges are elected by the UN Assembly but are nominated for four-year terms by their respective countries.

The UN Security Council also chooses a PROSECUTOR who, in the name of the tribunal, brings indictments. The tribunal has power to impose prison sentences up to life but has no power to impose the death penalty. Sentences meted by the tribunal are served in various prison systems of several nations with whom the tribunal has made formal arrangements. The tribunal has no policing power or police force and relies for these on the mandated cooperation of various states for arrests, documents, and compulsory producing of WITNESSES. It operates on an annual budget of approximately $100 million.

As of 2009 the tribunal had indicted more than 160 defendants (several in custody awaiting trial) and has obtained 60 convictions. It had completed 34 trials, for which 29 persons were found guilty. (Of the 29 convictions, 18 were Serbs; nine were Croats; and two were Bosnian Muslims.) One of the most notorious defendants, former Yugoslav president Slobodan Milosevic, went on trial in 2002 on 66 separate charges of grave crimes, including genocide and other atrocities allegedly involving Slovenia, Bosnia, Croatia, Serbia, and Kosovo. His trial dragged on, in part because Milosevic defended himself without legal counsel. A verdict was never reached, as Milosevic died on March 11, 2006. Other completed trials included that of General Radislav Krystic, found guilty of genocide in the Srebrenica massacres of as many as 8,000 persons; Croatian General Tihomir Blaskic, found guilty of the massacre of villagers in Ahmici; and General Stanislav Galic, allegedly involved in the killing of civilians in Sarajevo. Former President Radovan Karadzic of the Bosnian Serb Republic eluded capture until 2008. He was captured in Belgrade, Serbia, and transported to The Hague. The other most wanted DEFENDANT, Ratko Mladic, former commander of the Bosnian Serb army, remains at large as of 2009, despite a $5 million reward for his capture by the U.S. government and $1 million by the Serbian government.

The tribunal expects to try Karadzic in early 2012 and believes it will complete its final trials and appellate work sometime in 2013.

FURTHER READINGS

International Criminal Tribunal for the former Yugoslavia (ICTY), www.icty.org (accessed September 23, 2009).
"The Lesson of Slobodan Milosevic's Trial and Tribulation." 2003. *Economist* 366.
Wald, Patricia M. 2002. "Punishment of War Crimes by International Tribunals." *Social Research* 69.

CROSS REFERENCES

Arbitration; International Court of Justice; International Law; Jurisdiction.

❖ HAMER, FANNIE LOU TOWNSEND

FANNIE LOU HAMER worked for voter registration for African Americans in the U.S. South and helped establish the Mississippi Freedom DEMOCRATIC PARTY (MFDP), which successfully challenged the all-white Democratic party in Mississippi.

Hamer was born October 6, 1917, in Montgomery County, Mississippi. She was the twentieth and youngest child of Jim Townsend and Lou Ella Townsend, who were sharecroppers in rural Mississippi. Hamer grew up in a tar paper shack and slept on a cotton sack stuffed with dry grass. She first went into the cotton fields to work when she was six years old, picking thirty pounds of cotton a week. By the time she was 13 years old, Hamer was picking 200 to 300 pounds of cotton each week.

Because of her family's poverty, she was forced to end her formal education after the sixth grade.

In 1944, when she was 27, Hamer married Perry ("Pap") Hamer, a sharecropper on a nearby plantation owned by the Marlowe family, near Ruleville, Mississippi. Hamer spent the next 18 years working in the fields chopping cotton. Her husband also ran a small saloon, and they made liquor to sell.

In August 1962 Hamer attended a meeting sponsored by the SOUTHERN CHRISTIAN LEADERSHIP CONFERENCE (SCLC) and the STUDENT NONVIOLENT COORDINATING COMMITTEE (SNCC, pronounced Snick). The SCLC was founded in 1957 by a group of black ministers led by MARTIN LUTHER KING, JR., and coordinated the CIVIL RIGHTS activ-ities of ministers. SNCC was organized in 1960 by students and other young people, and SNCC workers had recently come to Ruleville to organize voter registration drives. At that time only five percent of African Americans in Mississippi who were old enough to vote had been allowed to register. Ten days later a group of white men rode through the town and fired 16 shots into the homes of those involved in the black voting drive. That night Hamer fled to her niece's house 40 miles away. A few weeks later, SNCC workers brought her to the SNCC annual conference in Nashville. She later returned to the Marlowe plantation, where she found that her husband had been fired from his job and her family had lost its car, furniture, and house.

Hamer then became a field secretary for SNCC in Ruleville, earning $10 per week, and

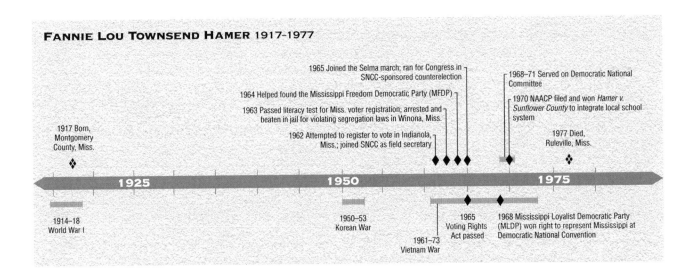

FANNIE LOU TOWNSEND HAMER 1917–1977

1917 Born, Montgomery County, Miss.

1962 Attempted to register to vote in Indianola, Miss.; joined SNCC as field secretary

1963 Passed literacy test for Miss. voter registration; arrested and beaten in jail for violating segregation laws in Winona, Miss.

1964 Helped found the Mississippi Freedom Democratic Party (MFDP)

1965 Joined the Selma march; ran for Congress in SNCC-sponsored counterelection

1968–71 Served on Democratic National Committee

1970 NAACP filed and won *Hamer v. Sunflower County* to integrate local school system

1977 Died, Ruleville, Miss.

1925   1950   1975

1914–18 World War I

1950–53 Korean War

1961–73 Vietnam War

1965 Voting Rights Act passed

1968 Mississippi Loyalist Democratic Party (MLDP) won right to represent Mississippi at Democratic National Convention

began organizing a poverty program. She worked with the local people, educating them about their right to vote, and she became an effective fund-raiser for SNCC, traveling to northern towns to speak about life as an African American in Mississippi, and participating in civil rights demonstrations across the country. Hamer and her associates were often harassed, intimidated, and even beaten.

Hamer helped found the Council of Federated Organizations, which brought large numbers of white northerners into Mississippi in the summer of 1964, known as Freedom Summer. These volunteers helped with voter registration and other civil rights activities, and their work focused national attention on the SEGREGATION still rampant in the South.

In April 1964, Hamer helped found the Mississippi Freedom Democratic party. The MFDP was organized as an alternative to the all-white Mississippi Democratic party, which barred African Americans from its activities. The MFDP planned to challenge the regular Democratic party's right to represent Mississippi at the Democratic National Convention in Atlantic City, New Jersey, in August 1964 and hoped to win the right to be seated as the state's legal delegation. Before leaving for Atlantic City, the MFDP held its own convention and elected 64 African Americans and four whites as delegates to the national convention. Hamer was elected vice chairwoman.

Democratic president LYNDON B. JOHNSON, who was running for reelection in 1964, became worried that the MFDP would disrupt party unity and cause him to lose the election to Republican senator BARRY M. GOLDWATER. Johnson went to work to stop the MFDP by having his supporters threaten and harass MFDP supporters on the Credentials Committee, which was scheduled to hear the MFDP's case at the convention. In nationally televised proceedings before the committee, Hamer testified about the difficult life of African Americans in Mississippi and how they were prevented from participating in the political process. She also described a brutal beating she received while in jail for violating segregation laws. The beating left Hamer nearly blind in one eye.

Following Hamer's testimony, viewers from across the United States telegrammed their delegates, urging them to support the MFDP. Realizing he would now have to deal with the

Fannie Lou Hamer.
LIBRARY OF CONGRESS

NEW PARTY, Johnson worked out a settlement that called for the seating of two at-large delegates from the MFDP and a pledge that segregated delegations would not be seated at the 1968 convention. Hamer spoke out strongly against the compromise, and the delegation voted to reject it.

Following the 1964 convention, Hamer continued her work in the CIVIL RIGHTS MOVEMENT. In March 1965 she joined King and hundreds of others in a 54-mile march from Selma, Alabama, to Montgomery, Alabama. She also traveled with a SNCC delegation to Africa.

Back in Ruleville, Hamer and two other women ran for Congress against white congressmen in a special counterelection organized by SNCC. In the Democratic primary, their names were not on the ballot because the Mississippi election commission said they did not have enough signatures of registered voters on their petitions, and the white candidates won. In the SNCC election, however, the women's names were listed on the ballot, and they won. The women pressed their claim to be seated in Congress in Washington, D.C. They argued that Mississippi county registrars had refused to certify the signatures of black voters on their petitions. In September 1965, after nine months of investigation into their claim that the state had illegally obstructed their attempts to place their names on the ballot, the U.S. House of Representatives rejected their challenge by a margin of eighty-five votes.

In August 1968, Hamer again traveled to the Democratic National Convention in Chicago as a member of the alternative Mississippi delegation, renamed the Mississippi Loyalist Democratic party (MLDP). Again, the party went before the Credentials Committee seeking recognition, and again, a compromise was offered, this time to seat 21 members of each delegation. The MLDP refused to compromise, and this time, the regular delegation was unseated. When Hamer finally took her seat at the convention, she received a standing ovation.

Hamer went on to serve on the Democratic National Committee from 1968 until 1971. She also continued her civil rights work in Mississippi. In May 1970 Hamer and officials of the National Association for the Advancement of Colored People (NAACP) in Indianola filed a CLASS ACTION lawsuit in federal district court, claiming that the Sunflower County, Mississippi, school districts maintained a dual school system for black and white students and that black teachers and principals were not adequately protected against losing their jobs. The suit asked the court to order that one integrated school system be established and maintained. In *Hamer v. Sunflower County* (N.D. Miss., June 15, 1970), the district court, relying heavily on data in a report from a biracial committee headed by Hamer, ordered the county to merge its schools into one public school system. The U.S. Court of Appeals for the Fifth Circuit affirmed the district court in *United States v. Sunflower County School District*, 430 F.2d 839 (5th Cir. 1970).

Hamer continued to work for the poor in Ruleville, organizing poverty programs, raising money for low-income housing, and starting a day care center. Her favorite project was the Freedom Farm Cooperative. She started the farm with 40 acres, which eventually increased to 650 acres on which 5,000 people grew their own food.

In 1976 Hamer was honored in Ruleville on Fannie Lou Hamer Day. She died March 14, 1977, in Mound Bayou, Mississippi, from heart disease, cancer, and diabetes. Engraved on the headstone of her grave in Ruleville are the words "I am Sick and Tired of Being Sick and Tired."

FURTHER READINGS

Lee, Chana Kai. 1999. *For Freedom's Sake: The Life of Fannie Lou Hamer.* Urbana: Univ. of Illinois Press.

Mills, Kay. 2007. *This Little Light of Mine.* Lexington, KY: Univ. Press of Kentucky.

Rubel, David. 1990. *Fannie Lou Hamer: From Sharecropping to Politics.* Englewood Cliffs, NJ: Silver Burdett.

CROSS REFERENCES

Civil Rights Movement; Voting.

❖ HAMILTON, ALEXANDER

Alexander Hamilton, as a lawyer, politician, and statesman, left an enduring impression on U.S. government. His birth was humble, his death tragic. His professional life was spent forming basic political and economic institutions for a stronger nation. As a New York delegate at the Constitutional Convention, Hamilton advocated certain powers for the central government. His principles led to his rise as chief spokesperson for the FEDERALIST PARTY. The party had a short life span, but Hamilton's beliefs carried on through his famous FEDERALIST PAPERS. In these documents he advocated broad constitutional powers for the federal government, including national defense and finance. According to Hamilton, a lesser degree of individual human liberties and CIVIL RIGHTS would follow federal powers. His deemphasis of freedom put him at odds with other Founders, especially Thomas Jefferson's Democrats. However, he backed his beliefs with a strong record of public service from the Revolution onward. Through his contributions in the U.S. Army, in the TREASURY DEPARTMENT, and as a lawyer, many still recognize him as a commanding architect of the United States government.

Hamilton was born January 11, 1757, on Nevis Island, in the West Indies. His parents never married. His father, the son of a minor Scottish noble, drifted to the West Indies early in his life and worked odd jobs throughout the Caribbean. His mother died in the Indies when he was 11. Hamilton spent his early years in poverty, traveling to different islands with his father. At the age of 14, while visiting the island of St. Croix, he met a New York trader who recognized his natural intelligence and feisty spirit. The trader made it possible for

Hamilton to go to New York in pursuit of an education.

Hamilton attended a preparatory school in New Jersey and developed contacts with men who had created a movement seeking colonial independence. When he later entered King's College (now Columbia University), he became active in the local patriot movement. The American Revolution had been brewing in the background, and Hamilton took a keen interest in the battles that flared between the colonists and the British around Boston in 1775. Instead of graduating from college, he opted to join a volunteer MILITIA company.

He reported for orders to General George Washington's chief of artillery, Colonel Henry Knox. In his duties, Hamilton assisted in the famous crossing of the ice-jammed Delaware River on Christmas Night, 1776. Knox called Hamilton to Washington's attention. In March 1777, Hamilton was appointed aide to the commander in chief. With Washington, Hamilton learned his first lessons on the need for central administration in dealing with crises.

He also took advantage of his contacts with General Philip Schuyler, a wealthy and influential man within the military. In March 1780, Schuyler's young daughter, Elizabeth Schuyler, agreed to marry Hamilton. The relationship provided Hamilton with both additional contacts inside U.S. politics and generous financial gifts from his father-in-law.

Hamilton came to resent the limits of his position as aide to Washington and aspired to greater challenges. A minor reprimand afforded him the opportunity to resign from his services in April 1781. Hamilton had already received an education beyond anything that King's or any

Alexander Hamilton.
LIBRARY OF CONGRESS

other college could have offered. However, he went to New York with his wife and took up the study of law in early 1782. In July of that year, he was admitted to the bar.

As a lawyer and as an intellectual who commanded growing respect, Hamilton represented New York in the CONTINENTAL CONGRESS of 1782, in Philadelphia. Here, he spoke with an ally, a young Virginian, JAMES MADISON. The two expounded on the merits of strong central administration. Most of the other delegates represented the common fears of citizens in the United States—apprehensions about the abusive tendencies of strong central powers and, more important, the possibility of oppression in

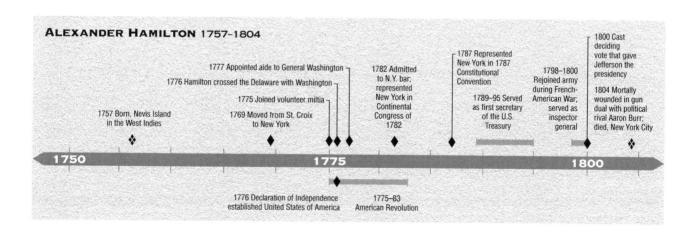

ALEXANDER HAMILTON 1757–1804

1777 Appointed aide to General Washington

1776 Hamilton crossed the Delaware with Washington

1775 Joined volunteer militia

1757 Born, Nevis Island in the West Indies

1769 Moved from St. Croix to New York

1782 Admitted to N.Y. bar; represented New York in Continental Congress of 1782

1787 Represented New York in 1787 Constitutional Convention

1789–95 Served as first secretary of the U.S. Treasury

1798–1800 Rejoined army during French-American War; served as inspector general

1800 Cast deciding vote that gave Jefferson the presidency

1804 Mortally wounded in gun dual with political rival Aaron Burr; died, New York City

1750

1775

1800

1776 Declaration of Independence established United States of America

1775–83 American Revolution

the future. Hamilton and Madison failed to sway a majority of the delegates to vote for their ideas. In the end, the Congress adopted the ARTICLES OF CONFEDERATION, a body of principles intended to knit the new states into a union that was only loosely defined.

Hamilton left Philadelphia frustrated. He returned to New York, built a thriving law practice, and gained fame as a legal theorist. In 1787 he spent a term in the New York Legislature and joined the movement designed to create a new Constitution. During this time, Madison and John Jay—a future chief justice on the U.S. Supreme Court—helped Hamilton draft a series of essays called *The Federalist Papers*. The essays stand as fundamental statements of U.S. political philosophy.

The Articles of CONFEDERATION had already begun to show inadequacies, as the federal government had no real power to collect the money necessary for its own defense. The authors of *The Federalist Papers* argued that a strong federal government would constitute not a tyranny but an improvement over the current system of relatively weak rule. Their arguments helped allay the commonly held fears about central power.

At the 1787 Constitutional Convention in Philadelphia, Hamilton again served as a delegate from New York. This time, his ideas were received with more favor. In the drafting of the new Constitution, and the creation of a more effective government, many of Hamilton's Federalist beliefs came into play. In the area of defense, for example, Article I, Section 8, of the Constitution read, "The Congress shall have Power . . . To raise and support Armies . . . To provide and maintain a Navy . . . To provide for organizing, arming, and disciplining, the Militia." The role of the government in raising finances to do these things would put Hamilton's ideas to the test.

Hamilton took on the test personally. In 1789, when President Washington began to assemble the new federal government, he asked Hamilton to become the nation's first secretary of the treasury. For the following six years, Hamilton developed a fiscal and economic system based on a national coinage, a national banking system, a revenue program to provide for the repayment of the national debt, and measures to encourage industrial and commercial development. He

sought a vigorous, diversified economy that would also provide the nation with the means to defend itself. He stirred a considerable amount of controversy with certain proposals, such as the need for tariffs on imports, several kinds of excise taxes, the development of natural resources, a friendship with England, and opposition to France during the French Revolution. However, without such a concrete agenda, many historians have argued, the United States could not have survived its years of initial development.

Because of Hamilton's decisive stance on some issues, a split occurred between, and even within, political parties. Hamilton and JOHN ADAMS spoke the ideas of the Federalists. Madison joined Jefferson in the DEMOCRATIC-REPUBLICAN PARTY. Even though Hamilton had previously worked alongside SECRETARY OF STATE Jefferson, the two were now, as Washington noted, "daily pitted in the cabinet like two cocks." Hamilton stressed the need for a strong central government, while Jefferson emphasized individuals' rights. Their rivalry, among the most famous political clashes in U.S. history, led to a significant and ongoing level of frustration for both sides. Because of the deadlock, Hamilton retired from his secretarial position in 1795 and returned to the PRACTICE OF LAW.

Through his service in government and his connections with the Schuyler family, Hamilton became a prominent and prosperous lawyer. His practice extended to wealthy clients in New York and in other states, both individuals and partnerships. It resembled the practices of modern corporate lawyers, because he also represented banks and companies.

The bulk of his civil practice took place in maritime litigation, which boomed with European interests in the U.S. market. His most important admiralty case involved the sale and export to Europe of large quantities of cotton and indigo. Defendants Gouveneur and Kemble had incurred damages to the head merchant in their trade, Le Guen. Hamilton took on the case as attorney for Le Guen. He was assisted by AARON BURR, with whom he had worked in New York.

In *Le Guen v. Gouveneur*, Hamilton helped the merchant successfully sue his agents for $120,000—at the time, one of the largest awards in a personal damage suit. JAMES KENT, chancellor

REAL LIBERTY IS NEITHER FOUND IN DESPOTISM OR THE EXTREMES OF DEMOCRACY, BUT IN MODERATE GOVERNMENTS.
—ALEXANDER HAMILTON

of the New York bar, remembered Hamilton's performance in the trial as displaying "his reasoning powers...his piercing criticism, his masterly analysis, and...his appeals to the judgment and conscience of the tribunal." A grateful Le Guen wanted to pay Hamilton a fee commensurate with the size of the judgment. Hamilton refused anything more than $1,500. Burr took a much larger fee at his own discretion. This was the beginning of strained developments between Hamilton and Burr that would result in a future, climactic confrontation.

As a private citizen, Hamilton had amassed considerable power. In letters to politicians and newspapers, he continued to make a number of government-related proposals. At least four of them figured into future developments in the U. S. political structure. First, he suggested dividing each state into judicial districts as subdivisions of the federal government's judicial branch. Second, he proposed consolidating the federal government's revenues, ships, troops, officers, and supplies as assets under its control. Third, he pushed for the enlargement of the legal powers of the government by making certain already existing laws permanent, particularly the law authorizing the government to summon militias to counteract subversive activities and insurrections. Finally, he proposed the addition of laws that would give the courts power to punish SEDITION. Through letters to leaders and citizens, as through his *Federalist Papers,* Hamilton's ideas were received, although not always easily, into the political mainstream.

In 1798 the United States prepared for war with France. Hamilton decided to rejoin the Army as a major general. He was assigned the additional duties of inspector general until 1800. In 1800 Jefferson campaigned for president with Hamilton's former partner in the Le Guen settlement, Burr, as his running mate. The two received identical numbers of electoral votes for the 1800 presidential election. At that time all candidates ran for the presidency. The winner became president and the individual in second place became vice president. Hamilton, an elector for New York, refused to go along with the Federalists' plans to deny Jefferson the presidency. Hamilton voted for Jefferson instead of Burr, partly because he could stand Burr even less than his ideological rival. Jefferson won the election.

In 1804 Burr ran for governor of New York and became embittered by more of Hamilton's insults during the campaign. When Burr lost again, he challenged Hamilton to a duel. On July 11, 1804, the two men met at Weehawken Heights, New Jersey. Hamilton received a mortal wound from Burr's pistol shot, and died in New York City the next day.

As the United States evolved in political, legal, and economic dimensions, Hamilton's contributions remained part of its basic structure. His legacy went on to affect the way the rest of the world interpreted the proper role of government. Numerous political experiments took place in the following centuries, but still, Hamilton's notions of a strong central government made other systems appear weak in comparison. In a letter to the *Washington Post* on January 28, 1991, biographer Robert A. Hendrickson asserted that Hamilton's doctrine lives up to its model status as "a beacon of freedom and financial success in the modern world. It has peacefully discredited agrarianism, COMMUNISM, and totalitarianism."

FURTHER READINGS

Brookhiser, Richard. 2000. *Alexander Hamilton, American.* New York: Free Press.

Chernow, Ron. 2004. *Alexander Hamilton.* New York: Penguin.

Cooke, Jacob Ernest. 1982. *Alexander Hamilton: A Profile.* New York: Scribner.

Emery, Noemie. 1982. *Alexander Hamilton: An Intimate Portrait.* New York: Putnam.

Epstein, David F. 2007. *The Political Theory of the Federalist.* Chicago: Univ. of Chicago Press.

Flaumenhaft, Harvey. 1992. *The Effective Republic, Administration and Constitution in the Thought of Alexander Hamilton.* Durham, NC: Duke Univ. Press.

Randall, Willard Sterne. 2003. *Alexander Hamilton: A Life.* New York: HarperCollins.

CROSS REFERENCES

Constitution of the United States; "Federalist, Number 10" and "Federalist, Number 78" (Appendix, Primary Documents).

HAMMER V. DAGENHART

At the beginning of the twentieth century, U.S. reformers sought to end the practice of child labor. Young children were sent into factories and mines to work long hours for low wages. Aside from the physical demands placed upon children, labor robbed them of a chance to obtain an education. Some states enacted laws to regulate child labor, but others ignored these efforts and found competitive advantages in having a cheap supply of labor. Congress finally responded in 1916, when it passed the Keating-Owen Child Labor Act, of September 1, 1916, c. 432, 39 Stat. 675. The statute prohibited the use of interstate commerce for goods and materials made with child labor. Congress believed that the Constitution's COMMERCE CLAUSE permitted it to act to regulate child labor, but the U.S. Supreme Court thought differently. In *Hammer v. Dagenhart*, 247 U.S. 251, 38 S. Ct. 529, 62 L. Ed. 1101 (1918), the Court ruled the act unconstitutional, basing its decision on a constricted interpretation of the Commerce Clause and an expansive view of state governments' powers. The decision provoked Justice OLIVER WENDELL HOLMES to write one of the most significant dissenting opinions in the history of the U.S. Supreme Court.

Roland H. Dagenhart filed a lawsuit in North Carolina on behalf of his sons Reuben and John, challenging the Keating-Owen Act. Under the provisions of the law, his two sons would have been barred from working in a cotton mill, as one son was under 14 years old and the older son was under 16 years of age. Dagenhart asked the U.S. district court to strike down the law as unconstitutional as a violation of the Commerce Clause and the TENTH AMENDMENT. The relevant part of the law prohibited the shipment of goods in interstate or foreign commerce if "within thirty days prior to the time of removal of such product" children had been employed or permitted to help make them. The law applied to children under the age of 16 who worked in mines; to children under the age of 14 who worked in mills, canneries, workshops, factories or manufacturing establishments; and to children between 14 and 16 years of age who worked more than eight hours per day, more than six days in any week, or after 7 p.m. or before 6 a.m. These provisions effectively barred the Dagenhart sons from working and thereby deprived the family of needed income. The district court agreed with Dagenhart and held the act unconstitutional.

The Supreme Court, in a 5–4 decision, upheld the district court's ruling. Justice WILLIAM DAY, in his majority opinion, agreed that the Commerce Clause gives Congress the power to regulate commerce among the states and with foreign countries. However, the power to regulate did not mean that Congress had the power to prohibit certain commerce. Day acknowledged that prior Court rulings had upheld federal laws that banned the movement of certain goods in interstate commerce but these decisions rested "upon the character of the particular subjects" at issue. In *Champion v. Ames*, 188 U. S. 321, 23 Sup. Ct. 321, 47 L. Ed. 492 (1903), the Court had upheld a law that banned the movement of lottery tickets in interstate commerce. In *Hipolite Egg Co. v. United States*, 220 U. S. 45, 31 Sup. Ct. 364, 55 L. Ed. 364 (1911) the Court sustained the constitutionality of the Pure Food and Drug Act, which prohibited the shipping of impure foods and drugs in interstate commerce. The Court had also upheld the MANN ACT in *Hoke v. United States*, 227 U. S. 308, 33 Sup. Ct. 281, 57 L. Ed. 523 (1913). This law prohibited the movement of women in interstate commerce for the purposes of PROSTITUTION. Finally, the Court had sustained a federal law that regulated the shipment of intoxicating liquors in interstate commerce. Justice Day noted that in this decision, *Clark Distilling Co. v. Western Maryland Railway Co.*, 242 U. S. 311, 37 Sup. Ct. 180, 61 L. Ed. 326 (1917), the Court had agreed that Congress could prohibit the shipment of liquor but only because of the "exceptional nature of the subject here regulated."

Advocates of the child LABOR LAW believed that all of these decisions supported the right of Congress to ban the products of child labor in interstate commerce, but Justice Day concluded otherwise. The key to the prior rulings was that interstate commerce was needed to accomplish the "harmful results." With the child labor, law the goods in question were harmless. The effect of the act was to regulate child labor rather than to regulate transportation in interstate commerce. In the Court's view, this was an impermissible effect because of its definition of "commerce." The manufacture of goods and the mining of coal were not commerce, only the transportation of such things were.

Justice Day was troubled by the expansive reading of the Commerce Clause by Congress. If the Court had upheld this law, "all manufacture intended for interstate shipment would be brought under federal control." He concluded that the framers of the Constitution would never have envisioned such a broad grant of authority, for it undercut the power of the states to regulate commerce within their borders. In addition, the Tenth Amendment reserved powers to the states' governments, which included regulations "relating to the internal trade and affairs of the States." Thus, the Court's reading of the Commerce Clause and the Tenth Amendment combined to defeat the constitutionality of the child labor law. It was up to the states to regulate child labor; Day noted that North Carolina had acted on the issue by prohibiting children younger than 12 years of age from working. A contrary interpretation would have had catastrophic consequences to the federal system of powers. Day concluded that "our system of government [would] be practically destroyed" if Congress could use the Commerce Clause to effect changes in work conditions within the states.

Justice Oliver Wendell Holmes, in a dissenting opinion joined by three other justices, could barely contain his contempt for the majority's interpretation. He faulted the Court for imposing personal values "upon questions of policy and morals." In a famous statement, Holmes declared: "I should have thought that if we were to introduce our own moral conceptions where, in my opinion, they do not belong, this was preeminently a case for upholding the exercise of all its powers by the United States." Holmes rejected the idea that Congress could not prohibit the movement of goods in interstate commerce, whether the products were judged harmful in themselves or the result of a harmful practice. He stated that "Regulation means the prohibition of something," and then referred to prior rulings where the Court had upheld federal laws that had prohibited actions contrary to the wishes of Congress. In his view, Congress had sufficient authority to regulate child labor. The states were free to regulate their internal affairs, but once goods crossed state lines, the Commerce Clause gave Congress the authority to regulate these shipments.

The U.S. Supreme Court reversed *Dagenhart* in *United States v. Darby*, 312 U.S. 100, 312 U.S. 657, 61 S. Ct. 451 (1941). In its ruling, the Court acknowledged the "powerful and now classic dissent of Mr. Justice Holmes."

❖ HAND, BILLINGS LEARNED

Learned Hand served as a U.S. district court judge from 1909 to 1924 and on the U.S. CIRCUIT COURT of Appeals from 1924 to 1951. Although he was a great and respected legal figure, he was never appointed to the U.S. Supreme Court.

Hand cannot be classified as a liberal or conservative because he did not allow his personal biases to affect his judicial positions. He was careful to base his decisions on PUBLIC POLICY and laws as he understood them, and he did not believe it was the court's job to create public policy. To Hand's way of thinking, human values are relative. Although one value—such as protecting young people from obscenity—may prevail in a certain case, it might not prevail in another. And he felt that the role of court decisions should be to provide realistic guidelines on which to base future decisions.

Hand was born January 27, 1872, in Albany, New York. His was a distinguished family, with both his grandfather and his father being lawyers and Democrats. He was an only child, and his father died when he was fourteen. Hand attended private schools and graduated with honors and a degree in philosophy from Harvard in 1893. He graduated from Harvard Law School with honors in 1896. A year later he began practicing law in the state of New York.

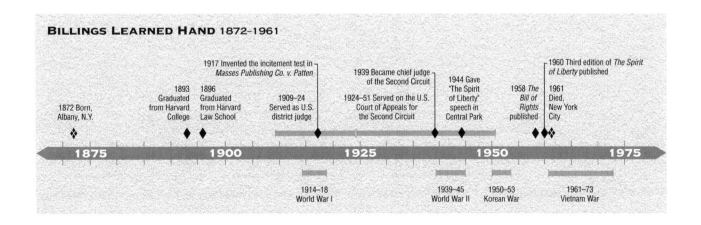

BILLINGS LEARNED HAND 1872–1961

1872 Born, Albany, N.Y.

1893 Graduated from Harvard College

1896 Graduated from Harvard Law School

1917 Invented the incitement test in *Masses Publishing Co. v. Patten*

1909–24 Served as U.S. district judge

1924–51 Served on the U.S. Court of Appeals for the Second Circuit

1939 Became chief judge of the Second Circuit

1944 Gave "The Spirit of Liberty" speech in Central Park

1958 *The Bill of Rights* published

1960 Third edition of *The Spirit of Liberty* published

1961 Died, New York City

1875 1900 1925 1950 1975

1914–18 World War I

1939–45 World War II

1950–53 Korean War

1961–73 Vietnam War

Billings Learned Hand.
LIBRARY OF CONGRESS

In 1902 Hand married Frances A. Fincke and moved to New York City. Although successful, he found law practice to be boring. In 1909 newly elected president WILLIAM HOWARD TAFT appointed Hand to a federal judgeship. At age 37, Hand was one of the youngest appointees ever. He served the court for 15 years.

A few years after his appointment, Hand supported Theodore Roosevelt's Bull Moose party presidential candidacy against Taft and became the Progressive party's candidate for chief judge of the New York Court of Appeals. He undertook this first and last political venture of his career because of a concern that big business would control the nation. Whatever Hand's reasons, Taft never forgot Hand's "disloyalty," and many believe that this act cost Hand his first chance to serve on the Supreme Court in 1922. Taft, who was then the chief justice of the U.S. Supreme Court, urged President WARREN G. HARDING not to nominate Hand.

Throughout his career, Hand chose to follow his conscience while knowing he would forfeit promotions as a result. For example, in 1917 Hand decided *Masses Publishing Co. v. Patten,* 244 F. 535 (S.D.N.Y. 1917), *rev'd* 246 F. 24 (2d Cir. 1917). *Masses* was the first test of a new law, the ESPIONAGE ACT OF 1917 (Act of June 15, 1917, ch. 30, 40 Stat.

217). This act outlawed making "false statements with intent to interfere with the operation or success of the military or naval forces . . . when the United States is at war." It also allowed the U.S. mail to ban materials containing such statements. Editors of an antiwar magazine, *The Masses,* took the New York City postmaster, Thomas G. Patten, to court for refusing to distribute the magazine. Patten argued that the ESPIONAGE Act allowed him to ban the publication.

The *Masses* case came before the Second District at the beginning of WORLD WAR I, when the government viewed criticism of the war as a threat to national security. It came also when Hand was being considered for appointment to the Second Circuit Court of Appeals.

At that time, the legality of written or spoken words was usually judged by the probable result of the words—that is, if the words had the tendency to produce unlawful conduct, then they could be banned. Hand took a different approach: his solution focused on the words themselves, rather than on a guess at the public's reaction to them. He invented what became known as the incitement test: If the words told someone to break the law, if they instructed the person that it was a duty or interest to do so, then they could be banned. *The Masses* magazine praised conscientious objectors and antiwar demonstrators, but it never actually told readers they should behave similarly. For this reason, Hand ruled that the postmaster could not ban the magazine.

Masses was just one of the many opinions Hand wrote that decided issues for which no precedent existed at the Supreme Court level. It is an early example of Hand's strong opinions about free speech—that it should be protected and defined as a critical ingredient to democracy. He struggled for the rest of his career to convince his colleagues of the importance and complexity of issues relating to the FIRST AMENDMENT to the U.S. Constitution.

Hand correctly predicted the consequences of his decision in *Masses* before he announced it. The decision was immediately appealed and reversed by the Second Circuit Court of Appeals, and he did not receive the appointment to that court. But over time the climate of the country and the courts would change, and in the late 1960s the Supreme Court would adopt Hand's incitement test as the standard for evaluating whether speech threatened security.

In 1924 Hand was appointed to the U.S. Circuit Court of Appeals for the Second Circuit. On the court, Hand served with many famous judges, including conservative judge Thomas Walter Swan, Hand's first cousin Augustus Noble Hand, Harrie Brigham Chase, Charles Edward Clark, and JEROME N. FRANK.

With his cousin and Swan, Hand made many widely respected decisions. Some observers credit the craftsmanship of these decisions to the use of preconference memos, which were unique to the Second Circuit at that time. Under this method, each judge reviewed each case and drafted a tentative opinion without consulting the others. Only after each judge had reached an independent conclusion did all the conferring judges exchange memos and meet to discuss the case. This process encouraged more diverse and thorough thinking than with the usual method of approaching cases, in which one judge took the lead early on and drafted a single opinion.

As a circuit court judge, Hand was limited to applying precedents of the Supreme Court and federal statutes in appeals before his court. He felt responsible to the precedents, and once he was sure he understood the basic reason for a law, he stood his ground despite any negative effects the decision might cause.

Hand was again considered for the Supreme Court in 1931, this time by President HERBERT HOOVER. But Hoover felt obliged to offer the position to CHARLES EVANS HUGHES first, with the intention of appointing Hand when Hughes refused. To Hoover's surprise, Hughes accepted.

Hand became senior circuit judge of the circuit court in 1939 when his predecessor, Martin T. Manton, was indicted and eventually imprisoned for accepting bribes. Nine years later, the office of "senior circuit judge" was renamed the office of "chief judge," pursuant to a revision in the federal judicial code. See Act of June 25, 1948, ch. 646, S 46(c), 62 Stat. 869, 871 (1948), codified as amended at 28 U.S.C. S 46(c) (1988). This was the highest position that Hand was to hold in the courts.

Hand's final close call with the Supreme Court came in 1942, when FRANKLIN D. ROOSEVELT was seeking a replacement for Justice JAMES F. BYRNES, whom he had appointed to a cabinet position. Hand was in the running, and his colleagues organized a strong campaign to persuade the president to choose him. However,

in January 1943—the month that Hand turned 71—Roosevelt appointed WILEY B. RUTLEDGE, of Iowa: Rutledge was only 48 years old, and Roosevelt had insisted in 1937 that justices should not serve past age seventy. Ironically, Rutledge died in 1949, whereas Hand was still active and productive for another twelve years.

Hand influenced the Supreme Court profoundly, though he did not serve on it. He was quoted in Supreme Court opinions and widely cited in legal journals. Even during his lifetime, he was widely regarded as one of the greatest judges in the English-speaking world.

In 1944 Hand delivered a public speech that brought his thinking to the attention of people in nonlegal circles. His address, "The Spirit of Liberty," was delivered in New York's Central Park to more than 1 million people. The *New Yorker,* the *New York Times, Life,* and *Reader's Digest* all reprinted portions of his address. Hand also publicly denounced McCarthyism during an address in Albany in 1952.

Hand served on the council of the American Law Institute, a group of law professors, judges, and lawyers who organize and summarize the law in publications called the "Restatements of the Law" and "Model Codes," two bodies of legal authority designed to provide a clear, practice-oriented exposition of legal rules, precedents, and principles.

When Hand retired from the Second Circuit in 1951, he had served as a federal judge longer than anyone else in U.S. history. During his career he had written almost 3,000 legal opinions. They are famous for their careful construction and sharp understanding of all forces at work. He showed an ability to clarify legal concepts, even those in specialized areas such as admiralty (shipping) law, patent law, and IMMIGRATION law.

After he retired, Hand still sat on the federal bench, wrote opinions, and handled a nearly full workload. Toward the end of his life, he complained to a friend that he was only writing 20 to 25 opinions per month, instead of his customary 50 to 60. *The Spirit of Liberty,* a collection of his papers and speeches originally published in 1952 had a third edition in 1960, while his 1958 Oliver Wendell Holmes Lectures at Harvard were published as *The Bill of Rights* (1958).

IF WE ARE TO KEEP OUR DEMOCRACY, THERE MUST BE ONE COMMANDMENT: THOU SHALT NOT RATION JUSTICE.
—BILLINGS LEARNED HAND

Hand died of a heart attack in New York City on August 18, 1961, after more than 50 years of service on the federal bench.

FURTHER READINGS

Griffith, Kathryn P. 1974. *Judge Learned Hand and the Role of the Federal Judiciary*. Norman, OK: Univ. of Oklahoma Press.

Gunther, Gerald. 1998. *Learned Hand: The Man and the Judge*. Cambridge, MA: Harvard Univ. Press.

Hagemann, John F. 1995. "The Judge's Judge." *South Dakota Law Review* 40.

Schick, Marvin. 1978. *Learned Hand's Court*. Westport, CT: Greenwood.

Thomson, James A. 1995. "Learned Hand: Evaluating a Federal Judge." *Northern Kentucky Law Review* 22.

CROSS REFERENCE

Criminal Law.

HARBOR

As a noun, a haven, or a space of deep water so sheltered by the adjacent land and surroundings as to afford a safe anchorage for ships.

As a verb, to afford lodging to, to shelter, or to give a refuge to. To clandestinely shelter, succor, and protect improperly admitted aliens. It may be aptly used to describe the furnishing of shelter, lodging, or food clandestinely or with concealment, and under certain circumstances may be equally applicable to those acts divested of any accompanying secrecy. Harboring a criminal is a crime under both federal and state statutes and a person who harbors a criminal is an accessory after the fact.

❖ HARDING, GEORGE

George Harding is known as the greatest U.S. patent attorney of the late nineteenth century.

Harding was born in Philadelphia on October 26, 1827. He was the son of Jesper Harding, publisher of the *Pennsylvania Inquirer*. Harding attended public schools and graduated from the University of Pennsylvania in 1846. After graduating, he worked as an intern for John Cadwalader, who later became a U.S. district judge, before starting his own law practice.

Harding was admitted to the bar in 1849, and elected secretary of the Law Academy of Philadelphia the same year. Two years later he assisted EDWIN M. STANTON in *Pennsylvania v. Wheeling & Belmont Bridge Co.*, 54 U.S. (13 How.) 518, 14 L. Ed. 249 (1852), before the Supreme Court. With this case he began to gain fame as a patent attorney.

Harding successfully represented Samuel F. Morse in lengthy litigation over Morse's telegraph patent (*O'Reilly v. Morse*, 56 U.S. [15 How.] 62, 14 L. Ed. 601 [1854]). In this case Morse was found to be the "true and original inventor of the Electro-Magnetic Telegraph, worked by the motive power of electromagnetism, and of the several improvements thereon."

In the Cyrus H. McCormick reaper litigation, *McCormick v. Talcott*, 61 U.S. (20 How.) 402, 15 L. Ed. 930 (1858), the attorney on retainer for DEFENDANT John Manny was ABRAHAM LINCOLN. Harding and his associates, lead attorneys for the defense, considered Lincoln too inexperienced to handle the litigation but kept him on because they needed to have a local attorney of record. They promptly removed him to the status of little more than an observer. Historians report that Lincoln was devastated by the treatment he received from the famous lawyers from Philadelphia.

Relying on his expertise in mechanics and chemistry, Harding became known for his

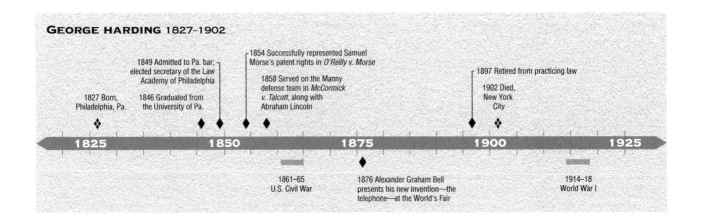

GEORGE HARDING 1827–1902

1827 Born, Philadelphia, Pa.

1846 Graduated from the University of Pa.

1849 Admitted to Pa. bar; elected secretary of the Law Academy of Philadelphia

1854 Successfully represented Samuel Morse's patent rights in *O'Reilly v. Morse*

1858 Served on the Manny defense team in *McCormick v. Talcott*, along with Abraham Lincoln

1897 Retired from practicing law

1902 Died, New York City

1825   1850   1875   1900   1925

1861–65 U.S. Civil War

1876 Alexander Graham Bell presents his new invention—the telephone—at the World's Fair

1914–18 World War I

courtroom demonstrations. To explain some of the patent issues being litigated, he would perform chemical experiments or demonstrate working models of the machines in question. Some of the models he brought into the courtroom were a miniature telephone system, a miniature grain field and reaper, and a furnace. In *Burr v. Duryee*, 68 U.S. (1 Wall.) 531, 17 L. Ed. 650 (1864), Justice ROBERT C. GRIER noted that the "large museum of exhibits in the shape of machines and models" brought in by Harding were critical to giving the Court "a proper understanding of the merits of the controversy."

Harding was as much a showman as an orator and was able to use humor to create interest in patent litigation. He was listed as counsel in more than 100 cases heard before the federal circuit courts of appeal and the Supreme Court.

Harding retired from practice in 1897 at age 70. He died five years later on November 17, 1902, in New York City.

George Harding.
LIBRARY OF CONGRESS

✧ HARDING, WARREN GAMALIEL

Warren Gamaliel Harding served as the twenty-ninth PRESIDENT OF THE UNITED STATES, from 1921 to 1923. Harding, who also served one term in the U.S. Senate, presided over an administration that achieved little and that was tainted by political corruption.

Harding was born November 2, 1865, on a farm at Caledonia (now Blooming Grove), Morrow County, Ohio, the eldest of eight children. He attended Ohio Central College. Harding then tried teaching, reading the law, selling insurance, and working as a journalist. He became the editor and publisher of the *Marion Star,* in Ohio, in 1884.

In 1891 Harding married Florence Kling DeWolfe, the daughter of a prominent Marion banker. DeWolfe was a divorcée, five years Harding's senior, with great ambitions for Harding. She helped build the *Marion Star* into a prosperous newspaper and encouraged Harding to enter REPUBLICAN PARTY politics.

Harding was elected to the Ohio Senate in 1898, and was elected lieutenant governor of the state in 1903. He ran unsuccessfully for governor in 1910. His national political standing rose over the next decade. At the Republican National Convention in 1912, he was selected to nominate President WILLIAM HOWARD TAFT for a second term. (In 1921, he would nominate Taft

AMERICANS OUGHT EVER BE ASKING THEMSELVES ABOUT THEIR CONCEPT OF THE IDEAL REPUBLIC.
—WARREN G. HARDING

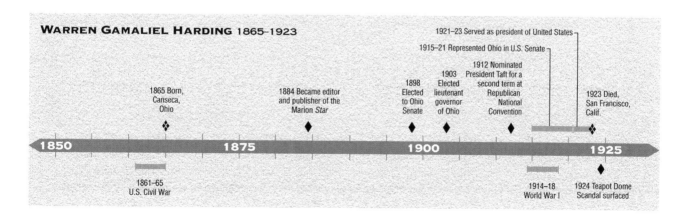

WARREN GAMALIEL HARDING 1865–1923

1921–23 Served as president of United States
1915–21 Represented Ohio in U.S. Senate

1865 Born, Caniseca, Ohio

1884 Became editor and publisher of the Marion Star

1898 Elected to Ohio Senate

1903 Elected lieutenant governor of Ohio

1912 Nominated President Taft for a second term at Republican National Convention

1923 Died, San Francisco, Calif.

1850   1875   1900   1925

1861–65 U.S. Civil War

1914–18 World War I

1924 Teapot Dome Scandal surfaced

Warren G. Harding.
LIBRARY OF CONGRESS

to serve as chief justice of the U.S. Supreme Court.) In 1914 he was elected to the U.S. Senate. Regarded as a fine public speaker, he gave the keynote address at the 1916 Republican National Convention.

As a U.S. senator, Harding was well liked by his colleagues but demonstrated little interest in the legislative process. He introduced no major bills during his six-year term, and was frequently absent. His politics followed the Republican mainstream: favoring high tariffs on imports and opposing the LEAGUE OF NATIONS and the federal regulation of commerce.

At the 1920 Republican National Convention, in Chicago, most of the delegates favored Governor Frank O. Lowden, of Illinois; Major General Leonard Wood, formerly army chief of staff; or Senator Hiram W. Johnson, of California, for president. After four ballots, the convention was deadlocked. Early in the morning, in what Harding campaign manager HARRY M. DAUGHERTY called a smoke-filled room, the party leaders agreed on Harding as a compromise candidate. The convention agreed to the selection and nominated Governor CALVIN COOLIDGE, of Massachusetts, as Harding's vice presidential running mate.

Harding defeated the DEMOCRATIC PARTY nominee, Governor James M. Cox, of Ohio, in the November 1920 election. Harding campaigned from the front porch of his home in Marion, avoiding any specifics on his domestic political agenda. Instead, he promised the United States a return to "normalcy."

Harding's presidency was marked by the delegation of responsibilities to his cabinet chiefs. Rejecting the strong executive leadership style of Presidents THEODORE ROOSEVELT and Woodrow Wilson, Harding relied on a distinguished group of men, including Secretary of Commerce HERBERT HOOVER, SECRETARY OF STATE CHARLES EVANS HUGHES, and Secretary of Agriculture Henry C. Wallace. These and other cabinet heads helped lead the government away from wartime emergency conditions. In 1921 Secretary Hughes convened the Washington Conference on Naval Disarmament. The members of the conference—England, France, Italy, Japan, and the United States—agreed to limit their naval warships in fixed ratios.

In June 1923 Harding began a cross-country speaking tour, in hopes of reviving Republican party fortunes, which had taken a beating in the 1922 congressional election. On the trip, he received a secret telegram that disclosed an impending scandal for his administration concerning a Senate investigation of oil leases. In Seattle, Harding fell ill, presumably of food poisoning. His train stopped in San Francisco, where doctors reported Harding had pneumonia. On August 2, Harding died. No autopsy was made, leaving the exact cause of death unknown. Vice President Coolidge succeeded Harding as president.

The scandals that stained the Harding administration largely became public after Harding's death. One involved Attorney General Daugherty, who in 1926 was tried twice on charges he had committed improprieties in administering the Office of the Alien Property Custodian. Both trials ended in a HUNG JURY.

The TEAPOT DOME SCANDAL was the most troubling. Secretary of the Interior Albert B. Fall, a wealthy New Mexico attorney, had left the U.S. Senate in 1921 to join Harding's cabinet. In 1924 he was indicted for criminal conspiracy and BRIBERY. It was alleged that he accepted a $100,000 bribe from oil producers Harry F. Sinclair and Edward Doheny in exchange for leasing government-owned oil reserves at Teapot Dome, Wyoming, and Elk Hills, California, to the pair's oil companies at unusually favorable terms. Fall was acquitted of the conspiracy charge in 1926, but was convicted of accepting bribes in 1929. He served two years in prison and paid a fine.

President Harding's short term of office and the scandals that befell his political appointees have left his administration remembered more for its corruption than for its achievements.

FURTHER READINGS

Dean, John W. 2004. *Warren G. Harding*. Waterville, ME: Thorndike.

"Harding a Farm Boy Who Rose by Work." 1923. *The New York Times* (August 3, 1923). Available online at http://www.nytimes.com/learning/general/onthisday/bday/1102.html; website home page: http://www.nytimes.com (accessed September 4, 2009).

Watkins, T.H. 1992. *Righteous Pilgrim: The Life and Times of Harold Ickes, 1874–1952*. New York: Holt.

❖ HARLAN, JOHN MARSHALL

JOHN MARSHALL HARLAN served as justice of the U.S. Supreme Court from 1877 to 1911. Harlan, a native of Kentucky, is best remembered for his dissenting opinions in cases that upheld restrictions on the civil rights of African Americans, most notably in PLESSY V. FERGUSON, 163 U.S. 537, 16 S. Ct. 1138, 41 L. Ed. 256 (1896). Harlan's dissents served to enlarge his judicial reputation as attitudes and laws changed concerning state-mandated SEGREGATION.

Harlan was born in Boyle County, Kentucky, on June 1, 1833. The son of a prominent lawyer and politician, Harlan graduated from Centre College and then studied law at Transylvania University, both located in Kentucky. He was admitted to the Kentucky bar in 1853. As a young man, Harlan sought his own political career. He was elected a county judge

John Marshall Harlan.
LIBRARY OF CONGRESS

in 1858, but relocated to Louisville in 1861 to establish a successful law practice.

With the beginning of the Civil War in 1861, Harlan joined the Union army as a lieutenant colonel and commanded a company of infantry volunteers. Upon the death of his father, he resigned his commission and returned to his law practice in Louisville. There, he became an active member of the REPUBLICAN PARTY. He made two unsuccessful efforts at getting himself elected governor of Kentucky, but proved more successful at helping others, securing the presidential nomination of RUTHERFORD B. HAYES at the 1876 Republican National Convention.

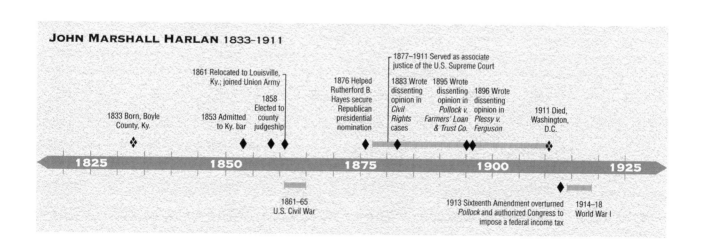

JOHN MARSHALL HARLAN 1833–1911

1833 Born, Boyle County, Ky.

1853 Admitted to Ky. bar

1858 Elected to county judgeship

1861 Relocated to Louisville, Ky.; joined Union Army

1861–65 U.S. Civil War

1876 Helped Rutherford B. Hayes secure Republican presidential nomination

1877–1911 Served as associate justice of the U.S. Supreme Court

1883 Wrote dissenting opinion in *Civil Rights* cases

1895 Wrote dissenting opinion in *Pollock v. Farmers' Loan & Trust Co.*

1896 Wrote dissenting opinion in *Plessy v. Ferguson*

1911 Died, Washington, D.C.

1913 Sixteenth Amendment overturned *Pollock* and authorized Congress to impose a federal income tax

1914–18 World War I

1825   1850   1875   1900   1925

Hayes took office in 1877, after a difficult election. One of his first acts was to appoint Harlan to the U.S. Supreme Court. Harlan, at age forty-four, joined a Court that, for the length of his tenure, was economically conservative and philosophically opposed to the enlargement of federal power. In addition, the Court deferred to the policies of southern states on racial segregation.

During his long tenure on the bench, Harlan gained prominence as a frequent dissenter. With a temperament that was better suited to leading than following, Harlan did not have the ability to negotiate compromise. Instead, he relied on his dissenting opinions to voice his often prophetic judgments.

In POLLOCK V. FARMERS' LOAN & TRUST CO., 157 U.S. 429, 15 S. Ct. 673, 39 L. Ed. 759 (1895), the Court held that the federal INCOME TAX was unconstitutional. Harlan dissented, arguing that the Court was ignoring precedent and acting as a legislator rather than a court. He noted that "the practical effect of the decision today is to give to certain kinds of property a position of favoritism and advantage." Harlan was vindicated in 1913 when the SIXTEENTH AMENDMENT overturned *Pollock* and authorized Congress to impose a federal income tax.

In 1883 the Supreme Court struck down Congress's attempt to outlaw racial DISCRIMINATION in places of public accommodation, including hotels, taverns, restaurants, theaters, streetcars, and railroad passenger cars. The majority decided in the CIVIL RIGHTS CASES, 109 U.S. 3, 3 S. Ct. 18, 27 L. Ed. 835 (1883), that the Civil Rights Act of 1875 violated the FOURTEENTH AMENDMENT. It determined that the amendment prohibited only official, state-sponsored discrimination and could not reach discrimination practiced by privately owned places of public accommodation.

Justice Harlan, in his dissent, argued that segregation in public accommodations was a "badge of slavery" for the recently freed African Americans, and that the act could be constitutionally justified by looking to the THIRTEENTH AMENDMENT. This amendment gave Congress the authority to outlaw all "badges and incidents" of SLAVERY. Harlan pointed out that before the Civil War, the Supreme Court protected the rights of slaveholders. Less than twenty years after the ABOLITION of slavery, the Court refused to extend its power and authority to protect the former slaves. Not until the passage of title II of the Civil Rights Act of 1964 (42 U.S.C.A. § 2000a et seq.) would the federal government ultimately achieve the desegregation of public accommodations.

Harlan's most famous dissent came in *Plessy*. At issue in this case was an 1890 Louisiana law that required passenger trains operating within the state to provide "equal but separate" accommodations for "white and colored races." The Supreme Court upheld the law on a 7–1 vote, thus putting a stamp of approval on all laws that mandated racial segregation. In his majority opinion, Justice HENRY B. BROWN concluded that the Fourteenth Amendment "could not have intended to abolish distinctions based upon color, or to enforce social, as distinguished from political, equality."

Justice Harlan, the lone dissenter, responded that the "arbitrary separation of citizens on the basis of race" was equivalent to the imposition of a "badge of servitude" on African Americans. He cut through the legal arguments to proclaim that the real intent of the law was not to give equal accommodations but to compel African Americans "to keep to themselves." He concluded that this was unacceptable because "our Constitution is color-blind, and neither knows nor tolerates classes among citizens."

Sixty years later, Harlan's vision was embraced by the Supreme Court in BROWN V. BOARD OF EDUCATION, 347 U.S. 483, 74 S. Ct. 686, 98 L. Ed. 873 (1954), when it overturned *Plessy* and rejected the "separate-but-equal" doctrine. With *Brown*, the modern CIVIL RIGHTS MOVEMENT gained its first major victory, setting the stage for the dismantling of the JIM CROW LAWS, which had required racial discrimination in the South.

Justice Harlan also taught CONSTITUTIONAL LAW at Columbian University (now George Washington University) and served on the Bering Sea Arbitration Tribunal of 1893, which resolved a dispute between the United States and Great Britain over the hunting of seals inhabiting the Bering Sea area of Alaska.

Harlan died October 14, 1911. His grandson, JOHN MARSHALL HARLAN II, also served on the Supreme Court.

FURTHER READINGS

Chin, Gabriel J. 1999. "The First Justice Harlan by the Numbers: Just How Great Was 'the Great Dissenter?'" *Akron Law Review* 32 (summer): 629–55.

OUR CONSTITUTION IS COLOR-BLIND, AND NEITHER KNOWS NOR TOLERATES CLASSES AMONG CITIZENS. IN RESPECT OF CIVIL RIGHTS, ALL CITIZENS ARE EQUAL BEFORE THE LAW.
—JOHN MARSHALL HARLAN

Harlan, Malvina Shanklin. 2002. *Some Memories of a Long Life, 1854–1911.* New York: Modern Library.

Harlan, Malvina Shankin, and Linda Przybyszewski. 2001. "Memoir: Some Memories of a Long Life, 1854–1911." *Journal of Supreme Court History* 26 (July): 97–212.

Przybyszewski, Linda. 1999. *The Republic According to John Marshall Harlan.* Chapel Hill: Univ. of North Carolina Press.

John Marshall Harlan II.
AP IMAGES

❖ HARLAN, JOHN MARSHALL, II

John Marshall Harlan II served as an associate justice of the U.S. Supreme Court from 1955 to 1971. Harlan was the grandson of U.S. Supreme Court Justice JOHN MARSHALL HARLAN. He was a conservative voice during the WARREN COURT era, arguing for judicial restraint in the face of court decisions that changed the landscape of U.S. civil and CRIMINAL LAW.

Harlan was born May 20, 1899, in Chicago. His father, John Maynard Harlan, was a successful lawyer and reform Republican politician who served as a Chicago alderman. Harlan was educated at boarding schools in Canada and Princeton University. After graduating from Princeton in 1920, he attended Oxford University on a Rhodes Scholarship and studied JURISPRUDENCE.

On his return to the United States, Harlan was hired by Root, Clark, Buckner, and Howard, a prominent New York City law firm. Emory Buckner, a partner in the firm and its chief litigator, encouraged Harlan to attend law school. Harlan graduated from New York Law School in 1924 and was admitted to the bar in 1925.

At Root, Clark, Harlan worked assiduously to master the fine points of litigation. His attention to detail and careful preparation won

him Buckner's admiration. In 1925, when Buckner became U.S. attorney for New York's Southern District, Harlan joined his legal staff. One of Harlan's primary duties was enforcing the National Prohibition Act (aka the VOLSTEAD ACT, 41 Stat. 305, which outlawed the possession, sale, transportation of, and importation of intoxicating liquors.

Harlan returned to Root, Clark in 1927. During the 1930s he emerged as the law firm's top trial attorney. He became the attorney of choice for many major U.S. corporations.

During WORLD WAR II, Harlan headed the Army Air Corps's operations analysis section, which developed ways of improving the accuracy of military bombings of Germany. Following the war, he returned to his law practice.

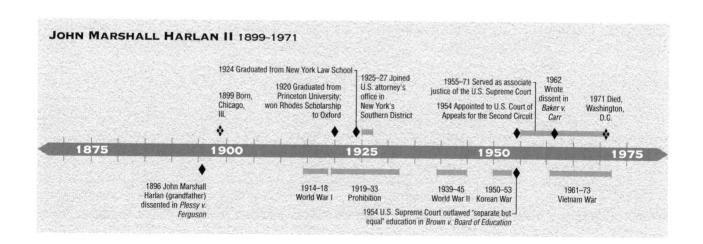

JOHN MARSHALL HARLAN II 1899–1971

1924 Graduated from New York Law School

1920 Graduated from Princeton University; won Rhodes Scholarship to Oxford

1899 Born, Chicago, Ill.

1925–27 Joined U.S. attorney's office in New York's Southern District

1955–71 Served as associate justice of the U.S. Supreme Court

1954 Appointed to U.S. Court of Appeals for the Second Circuit

1962 Wrote dissent in *Baker v. Carr*

1971 Died, Washington, D.C.

1875   1900   1925   1950   1975

1896 John Marshall Harlan (grandfather) dissented in *Plessy v. Ferguson*

1914–18 World War I

1919–33 Prohibition

1939–45 World War II

1950–53 Korean War

1961–73 Vietnam War

1954 U.S. Supreme Court outlawed "separate but equal" education in *Brown v. Board of Education*

Harlan's connections with REPUBLICAN PARTY politicians, including President DWIGHT D. EISENHOWER's attorney general, HERBERT BROWNELL, JR., led to a judicial career. In 1954 Eisenhower accepted Brownell's recommendation and appointed Harlan to the U.S. Court of Appeals for the Second Circuit.

Harlan's tenure on the circuit court of appeals was unremarkable and brief. When Justice ROBERT H. JACKSON died in October 1954, Eisenhower appointed Harlan to the U.S. Supreme Court. Harlan was confirmed by the U.S. Senate in 1955.

Harlan took his seat at a time when the Supreme Court, under Chief Justice EARL WARREN, had aroused the anger of advocates of racial segregation. The previous year, in BROWN V. BOARD OF EDUCATION, 347 U.S. 483, 74 S. Ct. 686, 98 L. Ed. 873 (1954), a unanimous Court had rejected the concept of "separate but equal," signaling the end of the JIM CROW LAWS that had required RACIAL DISCRIMINATION throughout the South. The decision vindicated Harlan's grandfather, who had written the lone dissent to the Supreme Court's decision in PLESSY V. FERGUSON, 163 U.S. 537, 16 S. Ct. 1138, 41 L. Ed. 256 (1896), upholding an 1890 Louisiana law requiring passenger trains to provide "equal but separate" accommodations for "white and colored races."

In his first years on the Court, Harlan and Justice FELIX FRANKFURTER often voted together, counseling judicial restraint. They believed in the concepts of FEDERALISM (the division of power between the state and federal governments) and SEPARATION OF POWERS (the division of power between the legislative, executive, and judicial branches of the federal government). After Frankfurter left the Court in 1962, Harlan became the lone advocate of these concepts. As the Warren Court reshaped U.S. law, Harlan often dissented, arguing that the Court was granting too much power to the federal government and to the judicial branch.

As a conservative jurist, Harlan respected precedent. He sought to limit the reach of decisions by linking constitutional interpretation with the facts of a case. In this way, lower courts would be restrained from applying an interpretation to other contexts. This refusal to overgeneralize an interpretation led him to dissent in the ONE-PERSON, ONE-VOTE case of BAKER V. CARR, 369 U.S. 186, 82 S. Ct. 691, 7 L.

Ed. 2d 663 (1962). The majority in *Baker* held that the federal district court had jurisdiction to consider a claim that a state statute apportioning state legislative districts violated the plaintiffs' right to EQUAL PROTECTION guaranteed by the FOURTEENTH AMENDMENT. Noting that the majority has disregarded considerable precedent, the dissent asserted that the claim was a nonjusticiable POLITICAL QUESTION.

Harlan died December 29, 1971, in Washington, D.C.

CROSS REFERENCES

Apportionment; Judicial Review.

HARMLESS ERROR

The legal doctrine of harmless error is found in the Federal Rules of CRIMINAL PROCEDURE, extensive CASE LAW, and state statutes. It comes into use when a litigant appeals the decision of a judge or jury, arguing that an error of law was made at trial that resulted in an incorrect decision or verdict. The appellate court then must decide whether the error was serious enough to strike down the decision made at trial. Review for harmless error involves a complicated test that applies to state and federal laws as well as rules of procedure. If an error is held to be serious, the appellate court is likely to set aside the decision of the trial court and may order a new trial. If it deems the error harmless, the appellate court affirms the lower court's decision. The doctrine of harmless error thus prevents an unnecessary new trial when the error alleged would not have affected the outcome at trial.

Harmless error jurisprudence grew out of a late-nineteenth-century development in ENGLISH LAW. Before 1873, English courts automatically reversed decisions in cases where an error was committed at trial. In 1873, Parliament put an end to this practice in civil cases by permitting reversals only in cases of substantial error. As the author Raymond A. Kimble has noted, U.S. law slowly adopted the idea in order to limit the number of retrials in U.S. courts.

In 1919 Congress first applied the harmless error doctrine to federal appellate courts, ordering them "to give judgment after an examination of the record without regard to errors or defects which do not affect the substantial rights of the parties" (28 U.S.C.A. § 2811 [1988]). By the midtwentieth century, harmless error jurisprudence was growing. The U.S. Supreme Court first moved toward establishing harmless error analysis in the 1946 case of *Kotteakos v. United States,* 328 U.S. 750, 66 S. Ct. 1239, 90 L. Ed. 1557, but left doubt about its applicability to constitutional errors. It began to remove this doubt in 1967 in the landmark case of *Chapman v. California,* 386 U.S. 18, 87 S. Ct. 824, 17 L. Ed. 2d 705. The Court in *Chapman* ruled that defendants were not necessarily entitled to a new trial simply because constitutional violations had occurred at trial. It directed appellate courts to dismiss arguments about certain constitutional errors when these "are so unimportant and insignificant that they may, consistent with the Federal Constitution, be deemed harmless, not requiring automatic reversal of a conviction." However, the Supreme Court put an important condition on this analysis: the appellate court had to be certain BEYOND A REASONABLE DOUBT that the error did not affect the outcome of the case.

Even decades after *Chapman,* determining whether a constitutional error is harmless remains a complicated task. This is because harmless error has no single, uniform definition. Courts must resort to one of two distinct tests— and sometimes a third that combines both of them. The first test asks whether the error influenced the verdict. If the error did not have even a minimal effect on the verdict, it is harmless. The second test considers the evidence of guilt found in the trial record. If the evidence is overwhelming and untainted, the defendant's guilt is considered to be the most important factor, and the error is harmless. The third test is a balancing test in which the court weighs the error's effect on the verdict against the untainted evidence. The court may emphasize either element in this test, and the outcome of the test will reflect which is considered stronger.

The harmless error doctrine has continued to evolve since the late 1960s. For many years, there was still uncertainty about which constitutional errors at trial could be subject to harmless error analysis, but the Supreme Court has clarified this by allowing most constitutional errors to be reviewed under the doctrine. Some of its decisions have proved controversial. In the 1991 case of *Arizona v. Fulminante,* 499 U.S. 279, 111 S. Ct. 1246, 113 L. Ed. 2d 302, for example, it included coerced confessions under the scope of harmless error review. This decision curtailed the ability of criminal defendants to overturn their conviction by arguing that the police used physical or emotional force to win a CONFESSION. As a result, appellate courts are free to determine if the jury had enough evidence besides the challenged confession to convict a DEFENDANT. As part of a general trend, this expansion of the scope of harmless error analysis has raised complaints about the proper role of appellate review.

FURTHER READINGS

Cooper, Jeffrey O. 2002. "Searching for Harmlessness: Method and Madness in the Supreme Court's Harmless Constitutional Error Doctrine." *Univ. of Kansas Law Review* 50 (January).

Kimble, Raymond A. 1995. "Casenote: Harmless Error." *Seton Hall Constitutional Law Journal* (spring).

Landes, William M., and Richard A. Posner. 2001. "Harmless Error." *Journal of Legal Studies* 30 (January). Available online at http://www.law.uchicago.edu/files/files/101.WML_.Harmless.pdf; website home page: http://www.law.uchicago.edu (accessed July 27, 2009).

Mitchell, Gregory. 1994. "Against 'Overwhelming' Appellate Activism: Constraining Harmless Error Review." *California Law Review* (October).

CROSS REFERENCE

Criminal Procedure.

❖ HARMON, JUDSON

Judson Harmon was an attorney, judge, and two-time Ohio governor with presidential aspirations. He served as attorney general of the United States under President Grover Cleveland from 1895 to 1897.

Harmon was born February 3, 1846, in Newton, Hamilton County, Ohio, the oldest of eight children of BENJAMIN FRANKLIN Harmon and Julia Bronson Harmon. Because his father was a teacher, the young Harmon was schooled at home. Later, when his father entered the ministry, Harmon attended public schools. An apt student, he was enrolled at Denison University by the age of 16, and he graduated in 1866.

The Civil War was an ever present intrusion on Harmon's college years. Funds for education were scarce, and young men were needed on the battlefield, not in the classroom. Harmon often earned money between terms by serving with local MILITIA units responsible for defending his home district against Southern raids. He was profoundly affected by the ASSASSINATION of President ABRAHAM LINCOLN in 1865. When Lincoln's body lay in state in Springfield, Ohio, Harmon went through the line of mourners

THE FUNDAMENTAL PRINCIPLE OF INTERNATIONAL LAW IS THE ABSOLUTE SOVEREIGNTY OF EVERY NATION, AS AGAINST ALL OTHERS, WITHIN ITS OWN TERRITORY.
—JUDSON HARMON

Judson Harmon.
LIBRARY OF CONGRESS

three times. Years later, he said that he had been in awe—and that he had never seen such a crowd of sad and disheartened people.

After graduating from college, Harmon moved to Columbus, Ohio, and followed his father into the teaching profession. He lasted a year. Upon deciding to pursue a legal career, he moved to Cincinnati and read law in the office of George Hoadly. He received his law degree at Cincinnati Law School in 1869, and he was admitted to the Ohio bar the following year. In June 1870, Harmon married Olivia Scobey, of Hamilton, Ohio, and settled into the life of a successful young attorney.

After seven years of practice, Harmon was elected judge of the COMMON PLEAS court in

Cincinnati; two years later, he was elected to the local superior court. He left the bench in 1887 when his teacher and mentor, Hoadly, was elected governor of Ohio. To help his old friend with the transition to public office, Harmon assumed Hoadly's caseload at the firm of Hoadly, Johnson, and Colston. At Hoadly's urging, Harmon also took a greater interest in national politics. Though Harmon had originally supported the REPUBLICAN PARTY on war issues, he found himself unable to support its program of Reconstruction after the Civil War. By 1887 Harmon was closely associated with Hoadly's supporters, the conservative faction of the DEMOCRATIC PARTY in Ohio.

Harmon's ties to the governor and the state Democratic party reaped rewards. In June 1895 President Cleveland appointed Harmon to succeed RICHARD OLNEY as attorney general of the United States. In this office, Harmon established a national reputation as a lawyer. As attorney general, he directed several major antitrust prosecutions, including one against the Trans-Missouri Freight Association (*United States v. Trans-Missouri Freight Ass'n,* 166 U.S. 290, 17 S. Ct. 540, 41 L. Ed. 1007 [1897]) and one against the Addyston Pipe and Steel Company (*United States v. Addyston Pipe & Steel Co.,* 78 Fed. 712 [E.D. Tenn. 1897]).

In *United States v. Texas,* 162 U.S. 1, 16 S. Ct. 725, 40 L. Ed. 867 (1896), a WATER RIGHTS case, he espoused a theory of absolute territorial sovereignty that has come to be known as the Harmon doctrine. Harmon said, "[T]he rules, principles and precedents of international law imposed no liability or obligation on the United States" to let parts of the waters that were diverted upstream by the United States flow to Mexico. According to Harmon, nations had

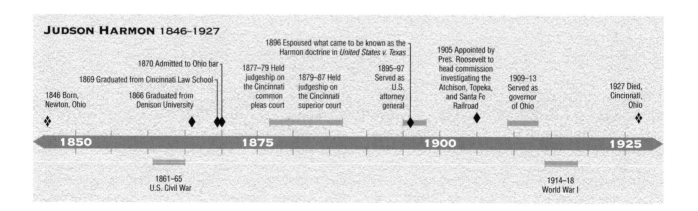

JUDSON HARMON 1846–1927

1846 Born, Newton, Ohio

1866 Graduated from Denison University

1869 Graduated from Cincinnati Law School

1870 Admitted to Ohio bar

1877–79 Held judgeship on the Cincinnati common pleas court

1879–87 Held judgeship on the Cincinnati superior court

1896 Espoused what came to be known as the Harmon doctrine in *United States v. Texas*

1895–97 Served as U.S. attorney general

1905 Appointed by Pres. Roosevelt to head commission investigating the Atchison, Topeka, and Santa Fe Railroad

1909–13 Served as governor of Ohio

1927 Died, Cincinnati, Ohio

1850   1875   1900   1925

1861–65 U.S. Civil War

1914–18 World War I

exclusive jurisdiction and control over the uses of all waters within their boundaries. (Since Harmon's time, the Harmon doctrine has been largely superseded by the concepts of state responsibility and global citizenship.)

Following his term as attorney general, Harmon resumed practice in Cincinnati, but he was never far from the national spotlight. In 1905 he was appointed by President THEODORE ROOSEVELT to head a commission investigating the business practices of the Atchison, Topeka, and Santa Fe Railroad. Harmon helped to trace a million dollars in kickbacks—or rebates, as they were then called—to a railroad traffic manager named Paul Morton. The commission's findings embarrassed the president because Morton had left the railroad to become Roosevelt's secretary of the Navy. Harmon urged prosecution of the responsible railroad officials, but Roosevelt interceded, and charges were never brought. Harmon was disappointed in the president's actions. He believed that individuals were accountable for their activities, even when those activities were carried out on behalf of a corporate entity. Harmon's observation that "guilt is always personal" became a theme in his subsequent political campaigns.

By 1908 Harmon had reasserted himself in the politics of his home state. His reputation as a conservative Democrat made him the logical person to help the Democrats challenge the long-standing Republican control of Ohio state politics.

At the Ohio state Democratic convention of May 1908, Harmon became the nominee of his party. He went on to win the gubernatorial election over a Republican incumbent—even though a Republican presidential candidate, WILLIAM HOWARD TAFT, carried the state. In his first term as governor, Harmon waged war on corporate GRAFT and corruption and created a state office of business administration.

Harmon won a second term easily—even though former president Roosevelt, still bearing a grudge from the Morton incident, came to Ohio to assist the opposition. In his second term, Harmon remained conservative but began to feel the pressures of the Progressive wave sweeping the nation. This Progressive movement was made up of those who supported more government involvement and oversight in programs aimed at helping ordinary citizens.

Bowing to that pressure, his administration supported a number of popular measures, including a federal INCOME TAX amendment; a law consolidating boards overseeing the state's penal, benevolent, and reformatory institutions; and a corrupt practices act to safeguard against voting violations. Harmon's signature was also attached to a model workers' compensation act, a measure for the direct popular election of U.S. senators, and a statute creating a public utility commission.

In 1912 Harmon decided to seek his party's nomination for PRESIDENT OF THE UNITED STATES at the Democratic National Convention in Baltimore. After he declared his opposition to the statewide application of initiative and referendum in Ohio, many Progressive leaders in his home state doubted his viability as a national candidate. (Initiative is the power of the people to propose bills and laws and to enact or reject them at the polls independent of legislative assembly; referendum is the process of referring constitutional or legislative proposals to the electorate for decision.) WILLIAM JENNINGS BRYAN, leader of the national Progressive movement, denounced Harmon as a reactionary. Harmon nevertheless went to the national convention assured of support from both Ohio and New York delegates, but he failed to win the nomination.

By throwing his hat into the national ring, Harmon had given up the opportunity to run for a third term as governor of Ohio. The election of James M. Cox as governor later in 1912 marked the end of Harmon's political career.

Harmon returned to Cincinnati, resumed practice, and began teaching at Cincinnati Law School. He was often asked to reconsider his withdrawal from public life, but he firmly declined all opportunities to do so. Harmon died in Cincinnati on February 22, 1927.

FURTHER READINGS

Burke, James L. 1973. "Judson Harmon: The Dilemma of a Constructive Conservative." *Cincinnati Historical Society Bulletin* 31. Available online at http://library.cincy-museum.org/starweb/journals/servlet.starweb; website home page: http://library.cincymuseum.org (accessed July 28, 2009).

Cohen, Jonathan E. 1991. "International Law and the Water Politics of the Euphrates." *New York Univ. of International Law and Politics* (fall).

Jusdon Harmon Papers, 1908–1912. Cincinnati Historical Society.

Benjamin Harrison.
LIBRARY OF CONGRESS

McCaffrey, Stephen C. 1996. "The Harmon Doctrine One Hundred Years Later: Buried, Not Praised." *Natural Resources Journal* 36, no. 3 (fall).

❖ HARRISON, BENJAMIN

On March 4, 1889, Benjamin Harrison was sworn in as the twenty-third PRESIDENT OF THE UNITED STATES. Forty-eight years to the day earlier, his grandfather, WILLIAM H. HARRISON, had become the ninth U.S. president. His grandfather's presidency ended after only one month when he died from complications due to a pneumonia he developed after delivering his inaugural address in the rain. Harrison's presidency lasted a full four-year term, ushering in sweeping legislative changes, signaling a return of the REPUBLICAN PARTY to the White

House, and laying the groundwork for the foreign policy of the late 1800s.

Harrison was born August 20, 1833, in Ohio. After graduating from Miami University, in Oxford, Ohio, he moved to Indianapolis to practice law. There he became involved in Republican politics, serving as city attorney, secretary of the Republican state committee, and supreme court reporter for Indiana. During the Civil War, he joined the Union Army. Within a month he was promoted to colonel and commanding officer of the Seventieth Indiana Regiment. He fought under General William T. Sherman and was promoted to brevet brigadier general in February 1865. After the war he returned to Indianapolis to pursue his legal career.

Harrison lost the race for governor of Indiana in 1876, but made a successful bid for a Senate seat in 1881. He held his Senate position for only one term, failing to win reelection in 1887. This loss did not deter ardent Republican supporters who wanted to see Harrison in the White House.

In 1888 Harrison ran against the incumbent Democratic president, Grover Cleveland. Harrison was the surprise nominee of the Republican party, a second choice after James G. Blaine, who declined to run again after having lost to Cleveland in 1884. Following a very close race, Harrison won 233 electoral votes; although Cleveland took the popular vote, he won only 168 electoral votes.

In the 1888 election, the Republican party gained control of Congress. During the first two years of Harrison's presidency, Congress enacted into law almost everything contained in the 1888 Republican platform. This was one of the most active Congresses in history. The

THE BOTTOM PRINCIPLE...OF OUR STRUCTURE OF GOVERNMENT IS THE PRINCIPLE OF CONTROL BY THE MAJORITY. EVERYTHING ELSE ABOUT OUR GOVERNMENT IS APPENDAGE, IT IS ORNAMENTATION.
—BENJAMIN HARRISON

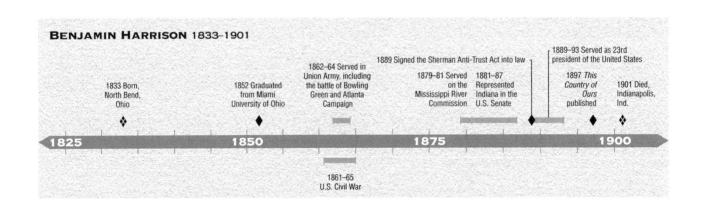

BENJAMIN HARRISON 1833–1901

1833 Born, North Bend, Ohio

1852 Graduated from Miami University of Ohio

1862–64 Served in Union Army, including the battle of Bowling Green and Atlanta Campaign

1889 Signed the Sherman Anti-Trust Act into law

1879–81 Served on the Mississippi River Commission

1881–87 Represented Indiana in the U.S. Senate

1889–93 Served as 23rd president of the United States

1897 *This Country of Ours* published

1901 Died, Indianapolis, Ind.

1825   1850   1875   1900

1861–65 U.S. Civil War

central themes of Harrison's campaign had been nationalism and tariff protection. The Democrats favored tariff reduction, whereas the Republicans steadfastly favored a system of protection. The tariff existing at the time Harrison took office produced more income than was needed to run the government and was the cause of much bipartisan debate. In 1889 Harrison signed the McKinley Tariff Act, which raised CUSTOMS DUTIES to an average of 49.5 percent, higher than any previous tariff. The act contained more than 400 amendments, including provisions for reciprocal trade agreements. It found favor with few Republicans, causing a rift within the party.

One issue in Harrison's term that enjoyed bipartisan support was antitrust legislation. During the late 1800s, business combinations known as trusts were created and began taking over large shares of the market. Both Republicans and Democrats perceived trusts as destructive of competition, and each party's platform was antimonopoly in 1888. In 1889 Senator JOHN SHERMAN introduced antitrust legislation to restrain interstate trusts. On July 2, 1889, Harrison signed the SHERMAN ANTI-TRUST ACT into law. This was the first major piece of legislation enacted during his term, and it remains in effect more than 120 years after its adoption. Historians view the Sherman Anti-Trust Act as the most important piece of legislation of the Fifty-first Congress.

During Harrison's term legislation providing for federal supervision of all congressional elections was defeated several times. The legislation had been drafted to ensure the voting rights of blacks as mandated by the FIFTEENTH AMENDMENT. Harrison was a strong supporter of the bill and also of legislation to ensure education for southern blacks, which was also defeated. These were the last significant attempts to provide these CIVIL RIGHTS until the 1930s.

With regard to foreign policy, Harrison had an aggressive attitude and little patience for drawn-out diplomatic negotiations. He helped convince several European countries to lift their restrictions on the importation of U.S. pork products, thus increasing U.S. exports of pork from approximately 47 million pounds in 1891 to 82 million pounds in 1892. Harrison also played a part in solving disputes between the United States, England, and Canada regarding seal hunting in the Bering Sea. And his tenacity proved successful in avoiding a war with Chile in 1892. Harrison's attitude toward foreign relations was emulated by THEODORE ROOSEVELT and other politicians.

When Harrison sought reelection in 1892, Cleveland once again opposed him. This time Cleveland emerged the victor.

Harrison has been described as an aloof loner, lacking in personal magnetism, but a man of great intellect. After he failed to secure a second term as president, he was revered as an elder statesman, giving lectures and acting as chief counsel for Venezuela in a boundary dispute with British Guiana. After a bout with pneumonia, Harrison died March 13, 1901, in Indianapolis, Indiana.

FURTHER READINGS

Lyle, Jack. 1996. "Benjamin Harrison First ISBA President." *Res Gestae* 39 (January).

Moore, Chieko, and Hester Anne Hale. 2006. *Benjamin Harrison: Centennial President.* New York: Nova.

Socolofsky, Homer E., and Allan B. Spetter. 1987. *The Presidency of Benjamin Harrison.* Lawrence: Univ. Press of Kansas.

❖ HARRISON, ROBERT HANSON

Robert Hanson Harrison was a lawyer and judge who was one of George Washington's original six appointments to the U.S. Supreme Court.

Harrison was born in 1745, in Charles County, Maryland. Though little has been written about his upbringing and education, it is known that he established a successful law practice in Alexandria, Virginia, where Washington became a client and close friend. Harrison later served as Washington's personal secretary throughout much of the Revolutionary War. He resigned from this post in March 1781 to become chief justice of the General Court of Maryland.

On September 24, 1789, President Washington signed the JUDICIARY ACT OF 1789 into law. This act established the Supreme Court, consisting of a chief justice and five associate justices. The act also established lower federal circuit and district courts and gave the Supreme Court the power to review, as well as affirm or reverse, the rulings of those courts. On the day the law was enacted, Washington nominated his longtime friend Harrison to the Court.

Robert H. Harrison.
LIBRARY OF CONGRESS.

ROBERT H. HARRISON WAS COMMISSIONED AN ASSOCIATE JUSTICE OF THE U.S. SUPREME COURT ON SEPTEMBER 28, 1789. BUT HE NEVER SERVED IN THAT CAPACITY.

The Senate confirmed Harrison's nomination two days later with little debate. Harrison initially declined the appointment because of poor health, but Washington persuaded him to accept the seat. A week after Harrison departed for New York City to begin work on the Court, he was stricken with a sudden illness and was forced to again decline the appointment. Washington eventually appointed JAMES IREDELL to the seat intended for Harrison.

Despite illness, Harrison remained chief justice of the General Court of Maryland until his death on April 2, 1790. During his tenure on the Maryland court, Harrison dealt mainly with real estate law and other legal matters; he had little opportunity to write about more sweeping issues of CONSTITUTIONAL LAW. As a result, his legal record indicates little about the effect he would have had if he had been able to serve his appointed term on the U.S. Supreme Court.

FURTHER READINGS

Congressional Quarterly. 2004. *Guide to the U.S. Supreme Court.* 4th ed. Washington, D.C.: Congressional Quarterly.

Degregorio, William A. 2009. *The Complete Book of U.S. Presidents.* New York: Barricade.

Elliott, Stephen P., ed. 1986. *A Reference Guide to the United States Supreme Court.* New York: Facts on File.

❖ HARRISON, WILLIAM HENRY

William Henry Harrison was the ninth president of the United States. He served the shortest term of any U.S. president, dying just a month after assuming office.

Harrison was born February 9, 1773, in Charles City County, Virginia, the youngest of seven children in a distinguished plantation family. His father, BENJAMIN HARRISON V, served in the House of Burgesses before the American Revolution, was later a member of the CONTINENTAL CONGRESS, and was a signer of the DECLARATION OF INDEPENDENCE. Harrison was tutored at home in his early years. In 1787, at age 14, he entered Hampden-Sydney College for premedical studies, intending to become a doctor. In 1791 he enrolled at the University of Pennsylvania Medical School to study under Dr. BENJAMIN RUSH, a noted physician. Later that year, following his father's death and without funds to continue school, Harrison decided to enlist in the Army and was commissioned an ensign in the First Infantry, serving in the Northwest Territory.

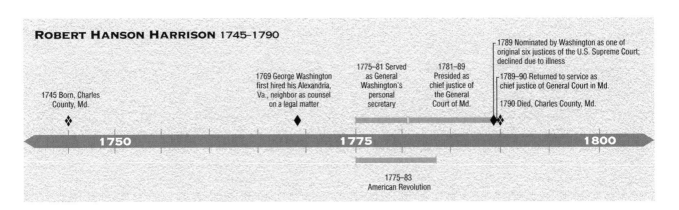

ROBERT HANSON HARRISON 1745-1790

1745 Born, Charles County, Md.

1769 George Washington first hired his Alexandria, Va., neighbor as counsel on a legal matter

1775–81 Served as General Washington's personal secretary

1781–89 Presided as chief justice of the General Court of Md.

1789 Nominated by Washington as one of original six justices of the U.S. Supreme Court; declined due to illness

1789–90 Returned to service as chief justice of General Court in Md.

1790 Died, Charles County, Md.

1750   1775   1800

1775–83 American Revolution

Harrison rose quickly through the ranks of the military, becoming a lieutenant in 1792 and acting as aide-de-camp to Major General Anthony ("Mad Anthony") Wayne, who was responsible for pacifying the Ottawa, Chippewa, Shawnee, and Pottawatomie tribes. At the Battle of Fallen Timbers, in August 1794, Harrison was responsible for holding the line against the tribes and received an official commendation from General Wayne for his efforts. He was later promoted to captain, but in 1798 resigned from the Army.

Following his distinguished military service, Harrison was appointed territorial secretary of the Northwest Territory by President JOHN ADAMS. The position paid well ($1,200 per year), but Harrison did not find it particularly challenging. In 1799, he was appointed the territory's first delegate to Congress, a nonvoting position that authorized him only to introduce legislation and participate in debate. Harrison made the most of his office, introducing and lobbying for passage of the Harrison Land Act of 1800, which opened the Northwest Territory to settlers and offered land for sale in small, affordable tracts and on reasonable credit terms.

In 1800 Harrison was appointed governor of the Indiana Territory. In his twelve years in the post, Harrison successfully negotiated a number of Indian treaties that opened to white settlers millions of acres in southern Indiana and Illinois. Despite the treaties, the threat of uprisings continued, and in November 1811 Harrison led a force of a thousand men, largely militiamen and volunteers from Kentucky and Indiana, against the Indian CONFEDERACY. Harrison's troops, taken by surprise, were

William Henry Harrison.
THE LIBRARY OF CONGRESS

attacked by the confederacy forces in an early morning raid. In more than two hours of intense fighting, Harrison's men beat back their opponents, suffering more than two hundred casualties. The conflict, known as the Battle of Tippecanoe, put an end to Native American resistance to white settlement in the region—and earned Harrison the nickname Old Tippecanoe.

Soon after the WAR OF 1812 broke out, Harrison was again on the front lines of a major military operation. He was commissioned a major general of the Kentucky MILITIA, then made a brigadier general in command of the

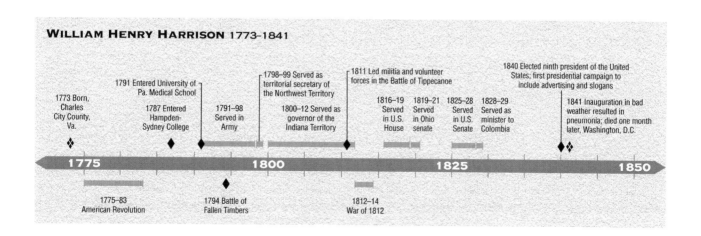

WILLIAM HENRY HARRISON 1773–1841

1773 Born, Charles City County, Va.

1787 Entered Hampden-Sydney College

1791 Entered University of Pa. Medical School

1791–98 Served in Army

1798–99 Served as territorial secretary of the Northwest Territory

1800–12 Served as governor of the Indiana Territory

1811 Led militia and volunteer forces in the Battle of Tippecanoe

1816–19 Served in U.S. House

1819–21 Served in Ohio senate

1825–28 Served in U.S. Senate

1828–29 Served as minister to Colombia

1840 Elected ninth president of the United States; first presidential campaign to include advertising and slogans

1841 Inauguration in bad weather resulted in pneumonia; died one month later, Washington, D.C.

1775   1800   1825   1850

1775–83 American Revolution

1794 Battle of Fallen Timbers

1812–14 War of 1812

Northwest frontier. In 1813 he was promoted to major general. Harrison's biggest battle of the war was at the Thames River, in Ontario, where he defeated a force of seventeen hundred British troops and secured the Northwest for the United States. Harrison was proclaimed a national hero and left the military to resume a career in politics.

In 1816 Harrison won a seat in the U.S. House of Representatives, where he served as chairman of the Militia Committee, advocating universal military training and sponsoring a relief bill for veterans and war widows. He also opposed laws that would restrict SLAVERY. In 1819 Harrison left the House to serve as an Ohio state senator. After a year in office, he ran for the U.S. Senate but was defeated. He also lost a close election for the U.S. House in 1822. In 1825 he was elected to the U.S. Senate. As a senator, Harrison once again focused on military issues, using his influence as chairman of the Committee on Military Affairs to lobby for increases in Army pay and an expansion of the Navy.

After three years in the Senate, Harrison turned to foreign service, accepting an appointment as minister to Colombia. Harrison's tenure in South America was brief, because of political instability within Colombia and concerns within the U.S. government that he was sympathetic to revolutionaries plotting to overthrow the Colombian president. He was recalled to Washington, D.C., in 1829.

After returning to the United States, Harrison retired to his farm in Ohio and suffered a series of financial setbacks and family tragedies, including the death of his oldest son. But he remained interested in politics. In 1836 he ran unsuccessfully for president, losing to MARTIN VAN BUREN. In 1840 he again ran against Van Buren, with JOHN TYLER as his running mate. The race has been viewed by historians as the first modern presidential campaign, one with advertising and slogans, including the famous Tippecanoe and Tyler, Too, a reference to Harrison's strong military record on the frontier. Harrison and Tyler won the election with 53 percent of the popular vote.

Harrison was inaugurated amid great enthusiasm and gave one of the longest inaugural speeches in history (nearly an hour and a half) outdoors in early March without a hat, gloves, or an overcoat. He soon came down with a cold,

which grew progressively worse and eventually developed into pneumonia. He died less than a month later, on April 4, 1841, in Washington, D.C., at age 68.

FURTHER READINGS

Calhoun, Charles William. 2005. *Benjamin Harrison: The 23rd President 1889–1893.* New York: Macmillan.

Degregorio, William A. 2009. *The Complete Book of U.S. Presidents.* New York: Barricade.

Green, Meg. 2007. *William H. Harrison.* Breckenridge, CO: Twenty-First Century.

❖ HASTIE, WILLIAM HENRY

William Henry Hastie was one of the twentieth century's leading African American lawyers and jurists. He served on the U.S. Court of Appeals for the Third Circuit from 1949 to 1971, becoming the first African American to sit on a federal appellate court. Hastie also distinguished himself as an educator, a CIVIL RIGHTS attorney, and a public servant. He successfully argued major CIVIL RIGHTS CASES before the U.S. Supreme Court and was a leader in the effort to desegregate the U.S. military during WORLD WAR II. With CHARLES HAMILTON HOUSTON, his second cousin, Hastie dramatically improved the standing and reputation of Howard University Law School during the 1930s and 1940s.

Hastie was born in Knoxville, Tennessee, on November 17, 1904. In 1916 his family moved to Washington, D.C., so that he could attend Dunbar High School. Thus began an education at the same schools Houston had attended before him. Hastie graduated from Dunbar as class valedictorian in 1921 and went on to distinguish himself at Amherst College, where he graduated in 1925, again as valedictorian.

After college Hastie spent two years teaching mathematics and science at a New Jersey school, then enrolled at Harvard Law School. There he served on the editorial board of the *Harvard LAW REVIEW*, becoming only the second African American to do so. He received a bachelor of laws degree from Harvard in 1930 and a doctor of jurisprudence degree in 1933.

Hastie then joined Houston's Washington, D.C., law firm. He also worked as an instructor at Howard University Law School, where Houston served as vice dean. Together, Hastie and Houston mentored scores of young black lawyers, including THURGOOD MARSHALL, who

SEE THAT THE GOVERNMENT DOES NOT ACQUIRE TOO MUCH POWER. KEEP A CHECK UPON YOUR RULERS. DO THIS, AND LIBERTY IS SAFE.
—WILLIAM HENRY HARRISON

would become a leading civil rights lawyer and a U.S. Supreme Court justice.

Throughout the 1930s and 1940s, Hastie worked as an activist for African American civil rights. In 1933 he founded the New Negro Alliance, a group that organized pickets and boycotts of white businesses to force increased hiring of African Americans. He worked with Houston, Marshall, and other members of the National Association for the Advancement of Colored People (NAACP) to devise legal strategies to fight racism in employment, housing, and education. With regard to segregation in schools, Hastie and his NAACP colleagues focused first on graduate education. Hastie unsuccessfully argued one of the first SCHOOL DESEGREGATION cases, *Hocutt v. Wilson* (N.C. Super. Ct. 1933), *unreported,* which involved the attempt of a student, Thomas R. Hocutt, to enter the University of North Carolina.

In 1933 Secretary of the Interior Harold L. Ickes recruited Hastie to work for the INTERIOR DEPARTMENT as assistant solicitor. While in that position, Hastie fought against segregated dining facilities in the department and helped draft the Organic Act of 1936 (48 U.S.C.A. § 1405 et seq.), which restructured the government of the Virgin Islands and gave that territory greater autonomy. In 1937, as a result of this work, he was appointed to the federal district court of the Virgin Islands, becoming the first African American to be named a federal judge.

Hastie left this position in 1939 when he was named dean of Howard University Law School. A year later he returned to government service as civilian aide to the secretary of war. Charged

William H. Hastie.
AP/WORLD WIDE PHOTOS

with rooting out racial discrimination in the military, Hastie identified and attacked discrimination against African Americans such as unequal promotion, segregation in unequal training facilities, and violent assaults by police officers and civilians. Unsatisfied with the government response to his proposals to eliminate discrimination, Hastie resigned from his position in protest in 1943. However, his reports on racism in the military attracted national notice, and in 1944 the Army high command ordered that African American officers be trained alongside white officers.

Following his work in the military, Hastie continued to practice law and plead civil rights cases for the NAACP. Hastie and Marshall won several key cases before the U.S. Supreme Court. In *Smith v. Allwright,* 321 U.S. 649, 64 S. Ct. 757, 88 L. Ed. 2d 987 (1944), Hastie and Marshall persuaded the Court that the practice of holding all-white party primaries, which effectively denied African Americans the right

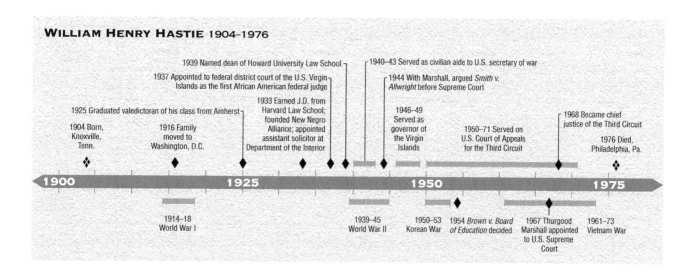

WILLIAM HENRY HASTIE 1904–1976

1939 Named dean of Howard University Law School

1937 Appointed to federal district court of the U.S. Virgin Islands as the first African American federal judge

1940–43 Served as civilian aide to U.S. secretary of war

1944 With Marshall, argued *Smith v. Allwright* before Supreme Court

1925 Graduated valedictoran of his class from Amherst

1933 Earned J.D. from Harvard Law School; founded New Negro Alliance; appointed assistant solicitor at Department of the Interior

1904 Born, Knoxville, Tenn.

1916 Family moved to Washington, D.C.

1946–49 Served as governor of the Virgin Islands

1950–71 Served on U.S. Court of Appeals for the Third Circuit

1968 Became chief justice of the Third Circuit

1976 Died, Philadelphia, Pa.

1900   1925   1950   1975

1914–18 World War I

1939–45 World War II

1950–53 Korean War

1954 *Brown v. Board of Education* decided

1967 Thurgood Marshall appointed to U.S. Supreme Court

1961–73 Vietnam War

to vote, was unconstitutional. The case set a vital precedent for later Supreme Court civil rights decisions.

Hastie and Marshall won another major victory in *Morgan v. Virginia,* 328 U.S. 373, 66 S. Ct. 1050, 90 L. Ed. 1317 (1946), in which the Court struck down a Virginia law (Virginia Code of 1942, §§ 4097z–4097dd) requiring racial segregation on buses. Hastie and Marshall argued that the law imposed an improper burden on interstate commerce. Despite this ruling DE FACTO (actual) segregation continued on buses in the South.

From 1946 to 1949 Hastie served as governor of the Virgin Islands. In 1949 President HARRY S. TRUMAN appointed Hastie to the U.S. Court of Appeals for the Third Circuit. He was sworn in as an interim appointee that year and was confirmed by the Senate in 1950. In 1968 Hastie was named chief justice of the court of appeals. After retiring from the court in 1971, Hastie devoted himself to public interest law, including programs to provide legal aid for consumers, environmentalists, and minorities. He died April 14, 1976 in Philadelphia, Pennsylvania.

Hastie was awarded more than 20 honorary degrees, including ones from Amherst and Harvard. He received the NAACP's Spingarn Medal in 1943 and was elected a fellow of the American Academy of Arts and Sciences in 1952.

ALWAYS BE PREPARED. YOUR OPPONENT WILL HAVE THE ADVANTAGE OF COLORLESSNESS. —WILLIAM HENRY HASTIE

FURTHER READINGS

Cohen, Mark S. 1986. *Review of William Hastie: Grace under Pressure by Gilbert Ware.* Michigan Law Review 84 (February–April).

Tushnet, Mark V. 1985. "Being First." Review of William Hastie: Grace Under Pressure by Gilbert Ware. *Stanford Law Review* 37 (April).

Ware, Gilbert. 1984. *William Hastie: Grace under Pressure.* New York: Oxford Univ. Press.

HATCH ACT

Enacted in 1939, the HATCH ACT (5 U.S.C.A. 7324) curbs the political activities of employees in federal, state, and local governments. The law's goal is to enforce political NEUTRALITY among civil servants: the act prohibits them from holding public office, influencing elections, participating in or managing political campaigns, and exerting UNDUE INFLUENCE on government hiring. Penalties for violations range from warnings to dismissal. The law's restrictions have always been controversial. Critics have long argued that the act violates the FIRST AMENDMENT freedoms of government employees. The U.S. Supreme Court has disagreed, twice upholding the law's constitutionality. Congress has amended the Hatch Act several times since 1939. In 1993, a number of amendments to the act sought to limit the effects of political patronage in federal hiring.

The Hatch Act grew out of nineteenth-century concerns about the political activities of federal employees. As early as 1801, President THOMAS JEFFERSON issued an executive order that said federal workers should neither "influence the votes of others, nor take part in the business of electioneering." He saw such activities as "inconsistent with the spirit of the Constitution." Jefferson was primarily concerned with what government employees did while in office; subsequently, concerns developed in another area. Throughout the nineteenth century, appointments to the federal bureaucracy were viewed as the natural spoils of political success. The prevalent awarding of jobs for political loyalty created a so-called spoils system and, ultimately, a reaction against it.

The long process of neutralizing politics in federal employment continued into the twentieth century. Attempts began with the Pendleton Act of 1883 (22 Stat. 403), a comprehensive anti-patronage law named after its sponsor, Senator GEORGE H. PENDLETON, who argued that "the spoils system needs to be killed or it will kill the republic" (14 Cong. Rec. 206 [1882]). The law sought to eliminate patronage by insulating federal employees from coercion. It provided that they could not be fired for refusing to work on behalf of a candidate or for choosing not to make campaign contributions. In 1907, President THEODORE ROOSEVELT instituted even broader controls through Executive Order 642. Its two major prohibitions addressed employees in the executive CIVIL SERVICE and the larger class of federal civil servants. The former were forbidden to use their authority to interfere in elections, and the latter were barred from taking part in political management or campaigning. This order marked the first time that federal employees had limits placed on their First Amendment right to engage in political speech.

The passage of the Hatch Act in 1939 combined the prohibitions of earlier executive orders and the Pendleton Act. The act includes restrictions on political activity for the whole federal bureaucracy. The act stated, "[N]o officer or employee in the EXECUTIVE BRANCH of the Federal government, or in any agency or department thereof, shall take any active part in political management or in political campaigns" (ch. 410, § 9(a)). The measure received bipartisan support in a response to concern about the New Deal—President Franklin D. Roosevelt's economic program for relieving the effects of the Great Depression—which significantly increased the ranks of federal employees. Congress wanted to rein in Roosevelt's power, especially following allegations that he had used Works Progress Administration employees to influence the 1938 congressional elections. Opponents of patronage in general and enemies of Roosevelt in particular thought the NEW DEAL represented an opportunity for the president to meddle with elections while perpetuating his hold on the White House.

Congress increased the scope of the Hatch Act in 1940 by extending its restrictions to employees of state and local governments that receive federal funds (Act of July 19, 1940, ch. 640, 54 Stat. 767), although it cut back certain applications of this measure in 1974. At various times it has also increased or decreased the penalties for Hatch Act violations—notably, by including suspension without pay as a lesser penalty. In 1993 Congress made yet more changes aimed at curtailing patronage in jobs: Amendments to 5 U.S.C.A. § 3303 restricted elected officials from making unsolicited recommendations for job applicants seeking federal employment. States, meanwhile, have broadly incorporated the principles of the Hatch Act in their own statutes, which have also undergone revision over time.

Debate over the Hatch Act has been vigorous since its inception. Critics have portrayed it as an unfair restriction on the First Amendment rights of government employees, especially violative of their FUNDAMENTAL RIGHT to engage in political speech. This argument formed the basis of an early suit that the U.S. Supreme Court heard in 1947, *United Public Workers of America v. Mitchell*, 330 U.S. 75, 67 S. Ct. 556, 91 L. Ed. 754. In sustaining the legality of the Hatch Act, the Court balanced individual speech rights against the "elemental need for order," and found the latter more important. The Court rejected another challenge to the law in 1973 in *United States Civil Service Commission*

v. National Ass'n of Letter Carriers, 413 U.S. 548, 93 S. Ct. 2880, 37 L. Ed. 2d 796. Opponents continued to attack these rulings throughout the 1990s. "Unfortunately for those individuals who have chosen a career in the federal public service," argued author Michael Bridges in a 1993 LAW REVIEW article, "the Court has found that Congress may place an asterisk beside their First Amendment rights."

In 2002, Green Party candidate Roger Merle, a U.S. Postal Service employee, challenged the Hatch Act in an unsuccessful attempt to win a seat in the U.S. House of Representatives.

AP IMAGES

FURTHER READINGS

Bridges, Michael. 1993. "Release the Gags: The Hatch Act and Current Legislative Reform." *Capital Univ. Law Review* (winter).

Feinstein, Andrew A., and Douglas K. Nelson. 1988. "Hatch Act Reform." *Federal Bar News and Journal* (July/August).

Gely, Rafael, and Timothy D. Chandler. 2000. "Restricting Public Employees' Political Activities: Good Government or Partisan Politics?" *Houston Law Review* 37 (fall). Available online at http://www.houstonlawreview.org/archive/downloads/37-3_pdf/HLR37P775.pdf; website home page: http://www.houstonlawreview.org (accessed

Polley, James D. 1994. "Hatch Act Reform Amendments of 1993." *Prosecutor* (September/October).

Segal, Lydia. 1997. "Can We Fight the New Tammany Hall?: Difficulties of Prosecuting Political Patronage and Suggestions for Reform. *Rutgers Law Review* 50 (winter).

HATE CRIME

A crime motivated by racial, religious, gender, sexual orientation, or other prejudice.

Hate crimes are based, at least in part, on the defendant's belief regarding a particular status of the victim. Hate-crime statutes were first passed by legislatures in the late 1980s and

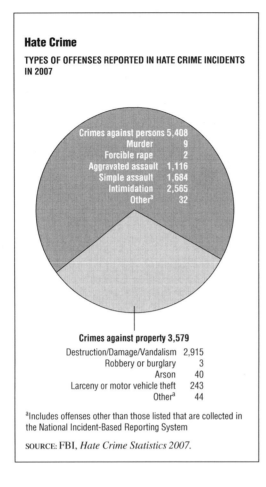

Hate Crime

TYPES OF OFFENSES REPORTED IN HATE CRIME INCIDENTS IN 2007

Crimes against persons 5,408
Murder   9
Forcible rape   2
Aggravated assault 1,116
Simple assault   1,684
Intimidation   2,565
Other[a]   32

Crimes against property 3,579

Destruction/Damage/Vandalism	2,915
Robbery or burglary	3
Arson	40
Larceny or motor vehicle theft	243
Other[a]	44

[a]Includes offenses other than those listed that are collected in the National Incident-Based Reporting System

SOURCE: FBI, *Hate Crime Statistics 2007.*

early 1990s in response to studies that indicated an increase in crimes motivated by prejudice. By 2009, 45 states, the District of Columbia, and the federal government have some form of hate-crime statute. (Only Arkansas, Georgia, Indiana, South Carolina, and Wyoming do not have hate-crime laws.) Many localities have also enacted their own hate-crime ordinances.

The precise definition of HATE CRIME varies from state to state. Some states define a hate crime as any crime based on a belief regarding the victim's race, RELIGION, color, disability, sexual orientation, national origin, or ancestry. Some states exclude crimes based on a belief regarding the victim's sexual orientation. Others limit their definition to certain crimes such as harassment, ASSAULT, and damage to property. In all states, the victim's actual status is irrelevant. For example, if a victim is attacked by someone who believes that the victim is gay, the attack is a hate crime whether or not the victim is actually gay. The federal government's hate-crime statute limits federal jurisdiction over hate crimes to assaults based on race, color,

religion, or national origin. In April 2009 the House of Representatives, at the urging of President BARACK OBAMA, passed an amendment that would broaden the law to include attacks based on a victim's sexual orientation, gender identity, or mental or physical ability. As of May 2009, the Senate had not voted on the measure.

Generally, there are four types of hate-crime statutes. One type criminalizes hate crime, one type enhances criminal sanctions, another provides a civil CAUSE OF ACTION for victims, and the last mandates only the collection of hate crime data. One version defines a hate crime as a discrete offense and provides stiff punishment for the offense. Under Ohio's statute, for example, any person who commits menacing, aggravated menacing, criminal damage or criminal endangerment, criminal mischief, or telephone harassment "by reason of the race, color, religion, or national origin of another person or group of persons" is guilty of the hate crime termed ethnic intimidation (Ohio Rev. Code Ann. § 2927.12 [Baldwin 1996]). The gravity of ethnic intimidation is always one degree higher than a base offense. For example, menacing is a MISDEMEANOR of the fourth degree, but menacing based on ethnicity is a more serious offense, classified in Ohio as a misdemeanor of the third degree.

Another type of hate-crime law enhances punishment for certain offenses that are motivated by hate. In Wisconsin, for example, defendants who intentionally select their victims based at least in part on the victims' race, religion, color, disability, sexual orientation, national origin, or ancestry are subject to more severe penalties than they would receive in the absence of such hate-based intent (Wis. Stat. § 939.645 [1995]). Thus in Wisconsin, for a class A misdemeanor based on hate, the maximum fine is $10,000, and the maximum period of imprisonment is two years in jail or prison (Wis. Stat. Ann. § 939.645(2)(a)), whereas an ordinary class A misdemeanor is punishable by a maximum fine of $10,000 or up to nine months in jail, or both (§ 939.51(3)(a)). For a class B misdemeanor, a less serious crime, the maximum fine is $1,000, and the maximum imprisonment is 90 days in jail. If the class B misdemeanor is a hate crime, the maximum fine is $10,000, and the maximum sentence is one year in jail.

There are laws in 31 states that allow a victim to file a civil lawsuit for injuries caused by a hate crime. It is possible that the perpetrator of a hate crime will serve time behind bars and be legally required to pay the victims thousands of dollars in damages.

A third type of hate-crime statute simply requires the collection of statistics. At the federal level, the Hate Crime Statistics Act of 1990 (Pub. L. No. 101-275, 104 Stat. 140 [28 U.S.C.A. § 534 (1990)]) requires the JUSTICE DEPARTMENT to collect statistics on crimes that manifest evidence of prejudice. Data must be acquired for crimes based on race, religion, disability, sexual orientation, or ethnicity. The purpose of the act is to provide the data necessary for Congress to develop effective policies against hate-motivated violence, to raise public awareness, and to track hate-crime trends.

Laws against hate crimes might conflict with rights under the FIRST AMENDMENT to the U.S. Constitution. Generally, the First Amendment protects a citizen's right to the free expression of thoughts. However, the courts have ruled that First Amendment rights may give way to the greater public good. For example, there is no First Amendment protection for someone who falsely yells "Fire!" in a crowded theater, because such speech endangers the safety of others. Such expression might give rise to a DISORDERLY CONDUCT charge or similar charge. In determining the constitutionality of hate-crime legislation, one primary question is whether the prohibited speech deserves First Amendment protection.

In 1997 the federal government documented 9,861 hate crimes based on the victims' religion, ethnicity, gender, sexual orientation, and disability. More than half of these crimes were motivated by racial bias, and over 1,000 were based on sexual orientation. These statistics were illustrated in a pair of hate crimes that drew national attention. The deaths of James Byrd Jr. and Matthew Shepard appeared to be quintessential hate crimes.

Byrd was walking along a street in his Jasper, Texas, community late at night in June 1998 when he was given a ride by three white men in a pick-up truck: The men beat him and chained him by his ankles (with a towing chain) to the back of their truck and dragged him for nearly three miles. Byrd was decapitated and dismembered as he was dragged behind the truck. He had been alive and conscious when it all began. All three of the

Rev. Larry Hill looks over the remains of his Greenville, N.C., church in 1996. During the 1990s, arsonists targeted African-American churches in a rash of church burnings classified as racial hate crimes.

AP IMAGES

perpetrators were on parole at the time and had extensive criminal records. It was alleged that at least two of the men had affiliations with racist groups, such as the Aryan Nation and the KU KLUX KLAN, and displayed white-supremacist tattoos. All three were convicted of MURDER, and two were sentenced to death.

Matthew Shepard was a 21-year-old college student at the University of Wyoming in Laramie. On October 12, 1998, he died, in part, because he was a homosexual. On October 6, 1998, two men in their early twenties entered a local bar, where Shepard was already drinking. The men, pretending to be gay, approached Shepard who eventually left with them. The men then drove him to a deserted area, where they tied him to a fence and pistol-whipped him until his skull collapsed. They took his wallet and shoes and obtained his address so that they could rob his apartment. Shepard was discovered 18 hours later, still tied to the fence. He never regained consciousness. The pair were charged with first-degree murder, kidnapping, and aggravated ROBBERY. Both men pleaded guilty to the charges and were sentenced to serve two consecutive life sentences, escaping a possible death sentence.

The U.S. Supreme Court has been called upon to examine the constitutionality of hate-crime laws. In 1992 the Court struck down a St. Paul, Minnesota, ordinance on the ground that it violated the First Amendment (*R.A.V. v. City of St. Paul*, 505 U.S. 377, 112 S. Ct. 2538, 120 L. Ed. 2d 305 [1992]). In *R.A.V.* several juvenile defendants were tried and convicted after they allegedly assembled a crude, wooden cross and

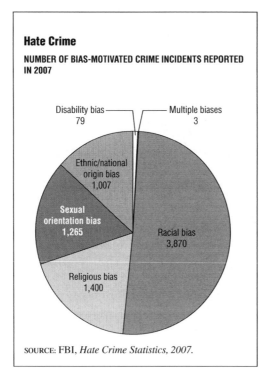

Hate Crime

NUMBER OF BIAS-MOTIVATED CRIME INCIDENTS REPORTED
IN 2007

Disability bias
79

Multiple biases
3

Ethnic/national
origin bias
1,007

Sexual
orientation bias
1,265

Racial bias
3,870

Religious bias
1,400

SOURCE: FBI, *Hate Crime Statistics, 2007.*

set it on fire in the yard of an African American family in St. Paul. The teenagers were arrested and charged under St. Paul's Bias-Motivated Crime Ordinance (Minn. Legis. Code § 292.02). Under the ordinance, a person who placed "on public or private property a symbol, object, appellation, characterization or graffiti, including, but not limited to, a burning cross or Nazi swastika" and who had reason to know that the display would arouse anger or alarm in others based on "race, color, creed, religion or gender" was guilty of a misdemeanor.

The trial court dismissed the charge on the grounds that it was overbroad and unconstitutionally content-based. Specifically, the court ruled that the statute criminalized too much behavior and infringed on First Amendment rights of free speech. The city of St. Paul appealed to the Minnesota Supreme Court, which reversed the trial court's ruling. The teenagers then appealed to the U.S. Supreme Court.

The high court was unanimous in striking down the St. Paul ordinance. However, it was divided in its legal reasoning. According to the majority opinion, the ordinance violated the First Amendment. Justice ANTONIN SCALIA, writing for the majority, declared the statute unconstitutional because it prohibited "otherwise permitted

speech solely on the basis of the subjects the speech addresses." Scalia illustrated this point by noting that a government may proscribe libelous speech, but that it may not proscribe only libelous speech that is critical of the government. The St. Paul ordinance violated this constitutional rule by proscribing only hate speech delivered through symbols.

In a separate opinion, the concurring justices argued that the majority opinion weakened previous First Amendment jurisprudence. Specifically, the majority opinion protected fighting words, a form of speech that provokes hostile encounters and is not protected by the First Amendment. By holding that "lawmakers may not regulate some fighting words more strictly than others because of their content," the majority had forced legislatures to criminalize all fighting words in order to legally prohibit the most dangerous ones.

According to the concurring justices, the statute was merely overbroad—that is, it legitimately regulated unprotected speech, but it also impermissibly prohibited speech that can cause only hurt feelings or resentment. With more careful wording, the concurring justices argued, hate-crime laws could pass constitutional muster. However, under the Court's majority opinion, this did not seem possible.

In 1993 the Supreme Court revisited hate-crime legislation and unanimously adopted a coherent approach. In *State v. Mitchell,* 508 U.S. 476, 113 S. Ct. 2194, 124 L. Ed. 2d 436 (1993), Todd Mitchell, a young black man from Kenosha, Wisconsin, was convicted of aggravated BATTERY and received an increased sentence under the Wisconsin hate-crime statute. The incident at issue began with Mitchell asking some friends, "Do you all feel hyped up to move on some white people?" Shortly thereafter, Mitchell spotted Gregory Reddick, a 14-year-old white male, walking on the other side of the street. Mitchell then said to the group, "You all want to fuck somebody up? There goes a white boy; go get him." The group attacked Reddick. Reddick suffered extensive injuries, including brain damage, and was comatose for four days.

Mitchell appealed his conviction to the Wisconsin Supreme Court, which held that the hate-crime statute violated the First Amendment. The state of Wisconsin appealed to the U.S. Supreme Court, which reversed the Wisconsin Supreme Court's ruling. The high court ruled that the Wisconsin statute was constitutional because it was directed at conduct, not expression. The court distinguished the *R.A.V.* case by explaining that the St. Paul ordinance was impermissibly aimed at expression. The primary purpose of the St. Paul ordinance was to punish specifically the placement of certain symbols on property. This violated the rule against content-based speech legislation. The Wisconsin law, by contrast, merely allowed increased sentences based on motivation, which is always a legitimate consideration in determining a criminal sentence.

Some states have mandated that a jury decide whether a DEFENDANT was motivated by bias, while others have authorized the trial judge to decide bias motivation. In *Apprendi v. New Jersey*, 530 U.S. 466, 120 S. Ct. 2348, 147 L. Ed. 2d 435 (2000), the U.S. Supreme Court examined a New Jersey statute that gave judges the power to decide bias. The Court ruled this practice unconstitutional, requiring that a jury decide the issue based on the reasonable-doubt standard of proof.

Vineland, New Jersey, police arrested Charles C. Apprendi Jr. in December 1994 after he fired eight shots into the home of an African American family in his otherwise all-white neighborhood. No one was injured in the shooting, and Apprendi admitted that he had fired the shots. In his confession, he told police that he had wanted to send a message to the black family that they did not belong in his neighborhood. Later, however, Apprendi claimed that police had pressured him into making that statement. He contended that he had had no racial motivation for the shooting but rather fired into the house when its purple front door attracted his attention.

Apprendi pleaded guilty to a firearms charge and to having processed a bomb in his house. Although the offenses carried a maximum sentence of ten years in prison, the prosecutor invoked the New Jersey hate-crime law and asked that the judge increase the sentence. The judge agreed and imposed a 12-year prison term, stating that prosecutors had shown, by a preponderance of the evidence, that Apprendi's act had been racially motivated. Apprendi appealed the sentence, arguing that he could be given such an enhanced sentence only if prosecutors presented evidence to a jury that proved, BEYOND A REASONABLE DOUBT, that he had fired the weapon out of racial bias. The

prosecutor contended that the hate-crime law punished motive, which has been regarded as a sentencing issue for the judge to resolve.

The U.S. Supreme Court, on a 5–4 vote, reversed the New Jersey Supreme Court and found the hate-crime provision to be unconstitutional. Justice JOHN PAUL STEVENS, writing for the majority, stated that any factor, except for a prior conviction, "that increases the maximum penalty for a crime must be charged in an indictment, submitted to a jury, and proven beyond a reasonable doubt." Justice Stevens based the court's decision on the Fourteenth Amendment's Due Process Clause and the Sixth Amendment's right to trial by a jury. Taken together, these two provisions entitle a criminal defendant to a jury determination that "he is guilty of every element of the crime, with which he is charged, beyond a REASONABLE DOUBT. Although judges do have the right to exercise discretion in sentencing, they must comply with sentencing provisions contained in state criminal statutes. Justice Stevens noted the "novelty of the scheme that removes the jury from the determination of a fact that exposes the defendant to a penalty exceeding the maximum he could receive if punished according to the facts reflected in the jury VERDICT alone."

The subject of cross burning returned to the U.S. Supreme Court again in *Virginia v. Black,*538 U.S. 343, 123 S. Ct. 1536, 155 L. Ed. 2d 535 (2003). The court, in a ruling aimed primarily at the Ku Klux Klan, upheld a Virginia statute that made it a felony to burn a cross "on the property of another, a highway or other public place . . . with the intent of intimidating any person or group." The 6–3 decision meant that the state could prosecute and convict two white men who had burned a four-foot-high cross in the backyard of an African American family. The family moved away after the incident. Justice Sandra Day O'Connor, in her majority opinion, held that the context of the cross burning determined whether it could be protected as constitutionally protected political speech. The First Amendment would protect a cross burning at a political rally, but it would not protect what had occurred in this case, which was criminal intimidation.

Hate-crime laws complicate the work of police officers by requiring them not only to capture criminals and to investigate their criminal acts, but also to conduct a broad

IN FOCUS

DO HATE-CRIME LAWS RESTRICT FIRST AMENDMENT RIGHTS?

The U.S. Supreme Court's upholding of the state "hate-crime" law in *Wisconsin v. Mitchell,* 508 U.S. 476, 113 S. Ct. 2194, 124 L. Ed. 2d 436 (1993), has not stopped some legal commentators from arguing that such laws violate the FIRST AMENDMENT of the U.S. Constitution. Though these critics generally admit that hate crimes are on the rise, they believe that laws that increase the severity of punishment on the basis of the motives of the perpetrator create a dangerous precedent for government interference with freedom of expression and thought. Defenders of hate-crime laws reject these fears, claiming that the laws deal with criminal conduct and are meant to send a message that discrimination will not be tolerated.

Critics of the laws have articulated a number of reasons for their opposition, some constitutional, some practical. The foremost concern is that hate-crime laws violate a person's right to freedom of thought. These statutes enhance the penalties for conduct already punished under state law when the perpetrator is motivated by a type of bigotry the legislature finds offensive. Therefore, if a rich man assaults a homeless person because he hates the poor, the rich man can be charged only with ASSAULT, because the legislature has not specifically found bigotry against the poor to be offensive. However, if a man assaults an African American because he hates persons of that race, he can be charged with assault and intimidation, which carries a more severe penalty, or his sentence for assault can be increased, because the legislature has penalized a racially discriminatory motive. For the critics of hate-crime laws, this result reveals that the legislature is regulating the defendant's thoughts, in violation of the First Amendment.

Critics also charge that the focus on motive distorts the traditional rules of CRIMINAL LAW. In the past, criminal law was interested in a defendant's mental state only to the extent that it would reveal whether the DEFENDANT had engaged in deliberate conduct. As a general rule, the motive of a crime has never been considered an element that must be proved at trial. Whether a person robbed a bank to buy food for a family or to pay back a gambling debt is considered irrelevant. The key state-of-mind question is whether the person intended to rob the bank.

Some critics also ask what good the additional penalty will do for persons convicted of hate crimes. If a person is filled with prejudices, extra time spent in prison is not likely to help eradicate those beliefs; it may, in fact, reinforce them. These critics do not believe that hate-crime laws seek to deter criminal activity. They feel that instead such laws appear to seek retribution for acts of violence motivated by racism, sexism, anti-Semitism, and homophobia. The critics contend the retribution model is not compatible with the modern goals of the criminal and penal systems.

Another criticism is that hate-crime laws do not address deeper forces within society that create prejudice. Some social psychologists believe that prejudice and the behavior that may accompany it are caused by a combination of social, economic, and psychological conflicts. Adding more punishment for those who act on their prejudice may give the community the illusion it is dealing with the problem, but, in fact, hate-crime laws do little to help change thought and behavior.

Defenders of hate-crime laws reject the idea that they are taking away anyone's First Amendment rights. They note that in *Mitchell* the Supreme Court rejected as "too speculative a hypothesis" the "chilling effect" argument, which maintains that these laws chill, or inhibit, free thought and speech. The Court also cited precedent that permitted the "evidentiary use of speech to establish the elements of a crime or to prove motive or intent." This means that persons are free to express their ideas, no matter how repugnant, but when they engage in unlawful conduct based on these beliefs, they surrender their First Amendment rights.

Defenders also believe that hate-crime laws, like other criminal laws, are aimed at preventing harmful acts. The focus is not on stifling disagreeable and prejudicial beliefs or biases, but on preventing the particularly harmful effects of hate crimes. Even critics of the laws admit that hate-crime violence is often brutal and severe. Defenders argue that increasing the penalties for this type of behavior is therefore justified.

Supporters of hate-crime laws point out, as did the Supreme Court in *Mitchell,* that most of the statutes use the same language as title VII of the CIVIL RIGHTS Act of 1964 (42 U.S.C.A. § 2000e et seq.). Why, they ask, is it acceptable to penalize employment discrimination that is based on racism and bigotry, but not criminal acts based on similar biases? The courts have long upheld federal and state discrimination laws as acceptable methods of penalizing conduct and promoting nondiscriminatory practices. Intentional employment discrimination requires a person to communicate his or her bias. Supporters conclude that once a person verbalizes a prejudice and acts on it, the state is free to regulate that conduct.

investigation of their personal life to determine whether a crime was motivated by prejudice. This determination can be difficult to make, and most laws offer little assistance in defining motivation.

The extra investigative work required by hate-crime laws also touches on privacy issues and the boundaries of police investigations. Defendants who have been accused of a hate crime may have their home and workplace searched for information on group memberships, personal and public writings, and reading lists, and for other personal information that may have been inadmissible at trial before the advent of the hate-crime statute.

Advocates of hate-crime laws concede that those laws do not root out all hate crimes, but they note that no CRIMINAL LAW is completely effective. They also contend that the difficulty in determining prejudiced motivation is no different from the difficulty that judges and juries face every day in determining whether the evidence presented in a case supports the charge. Supporters dismiss free speech and privacy concerns by reminding detractors that protections for such categories of rights regularly give way when public safety requires their restriction. According to advocates of hate-crime laws, fighting hatred and prejudice is an important government function, especially when hatred and prejudice motivate victimization.

FURTHER READINGS

Bell, Jeannine. 2002. *Policing Hatred: Law Enforcement, Civil Rights, and Hate Crime.* New York: New York Univ. Press.

Grattet, Ryken, and Valerie Jenness. 2001. "Examining the Boundaries of Hate Crime Law: Disabilities and the 'Dilemma of Difference.'"*Journal of Criminal Law and Criminology* 91 (spring): 653.

Lawrence, Frederick M. 2002. *Punishing Hate: Bias Crimes under American Law.* New York: Harvard Univ. Press.

Levin, Jack. 2006.*The Violence of Hate.* 2d ed. New York: Allyn and Bacon.

Shepard, Judy. 2009. *The Meaning of Matthew: My Son's Murder in Laramie, and a World Transformed.* New York: Hudson Street Press.

CROSS REFERENCES

Criminal Law; Freedom of Speech; Motive; Prejudice.

HAVE AND HOLD

The opening words, or habendum clause, found in a deed to real property, which describes the ownership rights of the individual to whom such property is being conveyed.

HAWKERS AND PEDDLERS

A hawker *is an individual who sells wares by carrying them through the streets. The person's ordinary methods of attracting attention include addressing the public, using placards, labels, and signs, or displaying merchandise in a public place. A* peddler *is defined as a retail dealer who brings goods from place to place, exhibiting them for sale. The terms are frequently defined in state statutes or city ordinances and are often used interchangeably.*

An individual is ordinarily considered to be a peddler in the legal sense if he or she does not have a fixed place of conducting business, but regularly carries the goods for sale with himself or herself. The wares must be offered for immediate sale and delivery and must be sold to customers as opposed to dealers who sell such wares. The goods may be bartered rather than sold for cash.

A single act of selling is generally insufficient to make the salesperson a peddler. Such individual must be engaged in this type of selling as a regular occupation or business, although it need not be the person's sole or main business. In addition, the individual, in order to be considered a hawker or peddler, need not earn sufficient funds for support from the business, nor does the business need to gain a profit in order for the individual to be considered a hawker or peddler.

The business of peddling has traditionally been distinguished from the service delivery of perishable goods, such as eggs, milk, or bakery products. An individual who delivers this type of perishable goods to regular customers is not considered a peddler. When, however, an individual travels from house to house, and sells goods to different persons in small quantities, the person is a peddler, even though he or she might make daily sales to somewhat regular customers. For example, a person who sharpens knives or an ice cream truck driver might fall into this category.

The individual who actually engages in the solicitation, makes the sale, and delivers the goods is the peddler, irrespective of whether the person owns the goods or is an agent or employee of the owner. An agent who sells his or her principal's merchandise can be considered a peddler; however, a principal who does not make sales calls or deliver merchandise is not. Ordinarily, an individual

George E. C. Hayes.
AP IMAGES

must be issued to the individual who is actually engaged in the peddling. It is not transferrable. In order for an applicant to obtain a license, the person must establish certain facts, such as acceptable moral character. Some statutes and ordinances require a person seeking a license to take a prescribed oath, give a bond, or deposit a particular amount of money.

Licensing statutes and ordinances often exempt certain individuals from their requirements; persons within the exempt classes need not obtain licenses. Such exemptions include persons selling goods or articles they have made themselves, honorably discharged or disabled veterans, poor or generally disabled persons, and clergy. The exemption is personal and cannot be extended to agents or employees of the licensed person.

❖ HAYES, GEORGE E. C.

George E. C. Hayes was an attorney and CIVIL RIGHTS activist, and a member of the team of lawyers who argued the landmark SCHOOL DESEGREGATION cases before the U.S. Supreme Court in 1954.

Hayes was born July 1, 1894, in Richmond, and lived most of his life in Washington, D.C., where he attended public schools. He graduated from Brown University, in Providence, in 1915 and received his law degree from Howard University in 1918. While at Howard, he attained one of the highest academic averages on record there.

Hayes's involvement in the burgeoning CIVIL RIGHTS MOVEMENT began in the 1940s. As a member of the District of Columbia Board of Education from 1945 to 1949, he worked to

[THE COUNTENANCING OF SCHOOL SEGREGATION] BY FEDERAL LAWMAKERS…WAS A MATTER OF POLITICS…IT WAS DONE AS AN EXPEDIENT.
—GEORGE E. C. HAYES

who merely solicits orders or sells by sample but does not deliver the goods sold is not considered a peddler.

Municipalities are permitted to set forth reasonable regulations concerning hawking and peddling within their borders. It may be required for such salespeople to obtain licenses; however, municipalities cannot prohibit the business through the requirement of an excessive fee.

In situations where a license is required, a peddler or hawker must obtain it prior to the time when he or she begins to sell wares and it

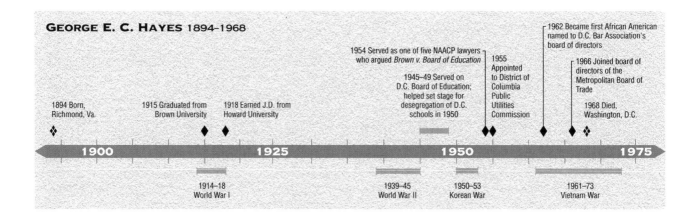

GEORGE E. C. HAYES 1894–1968

1962 Became first African American named to D.C. Bar Association's board of directors

1954 Served as one of five NAACP lawyers who argued *Brown v. Board of Education*

1955 Appointed to District of Columbia Public Utilities Commission

1966 Joined board of directors of the Metropolitan Board of Trade

1945–49 Served on D.C. Board of Education; helped set stage for desegregation of D.C. schools in 1950

1894 Born, Richmond, Va.

1915 Graduated from Brown University

1918 Earned J.D. from Howard University

1968 Died, Washington, D.C.

1900   1925   1950   1975

1914–18 World War I

1939–45 World War II

1950–53 Korean War

1961–73 Vietnam War

desegregate the schools in the nation's capital. Through his efforts, he met the National Association for the Advancement of Colored People (NAACP) lawyers who were mounting desegregation battles in other states. Their work culminated in the U.S. Supreme Court's landmark decision in BROWN V. BOARD OF EDUCATION, 347 U.S. 483, 74 S. Ct. 686, 98 L. Ed. 873 (1954). Hayes was one of five NAACP lawyers, including THURGOOD MARSHALL and James Nabrit, Jr., who convinced the High Court that segregation in public schools was unconstitutional. The *Brown* decision, repudiating the long-established "separate-but-equal" doctrine, marked the beginning of the end of segregation in all public accommodations. After the decision was handed down, Hayes and the other NAACP lawyers continued to press for immediate desegregation and urged the Court not to grant the states' appeals for a delay in implementation of the changes.

In 1954 Hayes clashed with Senator JOSEPH R. MCCARTHY, a Wisconsin Republican who headed the Senate Subcommittee on Investigations. McCarthy, looking into possible Communist infiltration of the armed services, accused Annie Lee Moss, a civilian employee of the Army Signal Corps, of Communist affiliation. Hayes defended Moss, who repeatedly denied the allegations against her. He sharply criticized McCarthy's investigative methods and presumption that Moss was guilty. Ultimately, Moss was cleared of the charges, and the secretary of defense restored her to a position with the Army.

Hayes has been described as independent and a "quiet pioneer." He was a lifelong Republican, choosing an unusual affiliation for an African American civil rights activist. In 1955 President DWIGHT D. EISENHOWER appointed him to a post on the District of Columbia Public Utilities Commission, and Hayes thus became the first African American in nearly one hundred years to serve in a municipal agency in the District of Columbia. In 1962 the District of Columbia Bar Association named him to its board of directors, making him the first African American to hold office in that group.

Hayes had open and sometimes bitter differences with the younger, more militant activists who assumed leadership of the civil rights movement in the early 1960s. In 1966 they criticized him for accepting membership on the previously segregated board of directors of the Metropolitan Washington Board of Trade, one of the District of Columbia's most conservative groups. As Howard University counsel, he advised and assisted his friend Nabrit, then president of Howard, in his handling of the black power student uprising on the campus in 1967.

Hayes was highly respected among his colleagues, who knew him to be calm, diligent, modest, and unassuming. He was noted for his elegance in language, manner, and dress, and he projected an image of intelligence and confidence. In addition to holding a long tenure as counsel to Howard University, Hayes acted as counsel to the NAACP for many years. He died December 20, 1968, in Washington, D.C.

❖ HAYES, RUTHERFORD BIRCHARD

Rutherford Birchard Hayes was a respected and successful lawyer in his home state of Ohio. He achieved further success while serving in the Union Army during the U.S. CIVIL WAR, and he went on to gain prominence as a politician from Ohio. His service as governor of Ohio and as a member of the U.S. House of Representatives led to his election as the nineteenth PRESIDENT OF THE UNITED STATES.

Hayes was born October 4, 1822, in Delaware, Ohio. His father, Rutherford Hayes, died before Hayes was born and Hayes was raised by his mother, Sophia Birchard Hayes, with the help of his uncle, Sardis Birchard, a bachelor. Hayes was enrolled at Norwalk Academy, a Methodist school in Ohio, in the spring of 1836. The next year he joined Isaac Webb's Preparatory School, in Middletown, Connecticut, where Sardis aided with his tuition. In 1838 Hayes enrolled at Kenyon College, in Gambier, Ohio. He graduated first in his class in August 1842 and delivered the valedictory address. After graduating he studied French and German on his own.

He went on to Harvard Law School in 1843 and was later admitted to the Ohio bar. He began practicing law in Lower Sandusky (now Fremont), Ohio, as a partner of Ralph P. Buckland, a leading legal figure in the town. He assumed an active role in politics in 1848 when he worked to elect ZACHARY TAYLOR, the Whig candidate for president. In 1849 he established a law office in Cincinnati, and eventually he became a prominent attorney in

POLITICS AND LAW ARE MERELY RESULTS, MERELY THE EXPRESSION OF WHAT THE PEOPLE WISH.
—RUTHERFORD B. HAYES

Rutherford B. Hayes.
LIBRARY OF CONGRESS

the city. In 1852 he was chosen to examine candidates for admission to the Ohio bar. Later that year he married Lucy Webb, whom he had known for nearly eight years.

Hayes developed into a leading and somewhat radical figure in Ohio politics. Like many Republicans he opposed SLAVERY but saw no need to punish the South. He chose other avenues in the fight to end slavery, offering his services to the Underground Railroad, which helped Southern slaves escape to freedom in the North. In 1853 he defended a number of escaped slaves in court. He went on to form a well-known Cincinnati law firm, Corwine, Hayes, and Rogers.

In the 1860 presidential campaign, he worked for the election of ABRAHAM LINCOLN, but with no great enthusiasm. After Lincoln's election at the beginning of the Civil War, Hayes wrote in his diary, "Six states have 'seceded.' Let them go." Nevertheless, when the war broke out, Hayes became active in the Union's military effort to unify the nation. In 1862 he was promoted to full colonel and given command of the Twenty-third Ohio Regiment. Hayes was wounded four times, once seriously, during the war. His composure in battle gained him the respect of those who served under him.

Hayes's popularity helped his political career. On October 19, 1864, he was elected to the U.S. House of Representatives for the Second Congressional District of Ohio. He was reelected in 1866. In 1867 the Ohio REPUBLICAN PARTY nominated Hayes as its candidate for governor. He gained considerable support from Radical Republicans who, like Hayes, opposed President Andrew Johnson's vetoes of legislation calling for MILITARY GOVERNMENT in the South. On January 13, 1868, Hayes was inaugurated as governor of Ohio. He was reelected governor in 1870 and again in 1875.

Hayes favored a sound fiscal policy with regard to the use of public money, and he opposed public funds for Catholic schools. These issues struck a chord with Republicans throughout the United States, who sought to extend his fiscal policies to the federal level. He received the Republican nomination for president in 1876, to run against SAMUEL J. TILDEN of New York.

Even before election results were in, Hayes wrote in his diary that he feared a contested

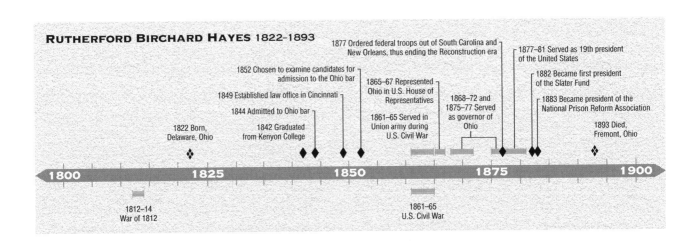

RUTHERFORD BIRCHARD HAYES 1822–1893

1877 Ordered federal troops out of South Carolina and New Orleans, thus ending the Reconstruction era

1877–81 Served as 19th president of the United States

1852 Chosen to examine candidates for admission to the Ohio bar

1865–67 Represented Ohio in U.S. House of Representatives

1882 Became first president of the Slater Fund

1849 Established law office in Cincinnati

1868–72 and 1875–77 Served as governor of Ohio

1883 Became president of the National Prison Reform Association

1844 Admitted to Ohio bar

1861–65 Served in Union army during U.S. Civil War

1893 Died, Fremont, Ohio

1822 Born, Delaware, Ohio

1842 Graduated from Kenyon College

1800   1825   1850   1875   1900

1812–14 War of 1812

1861–65 U.S. Civil War

election and perhaps even an armed conflict because of it. He apparently anticipated the most complicated election in the nation's history. On November 7, 1880, election results showed that Tilden had won 4.300 million popular votes to Hayes's 4.036 million, giving Tilden 184 electoral votes (one short of the needed majority) and Hayes 166.

A congressional election committee was designated to determine the winner of the election. After months of deliberation, Republicans managed to sway the committee by filling it with Republican loyalists. On March 2, 1877, Congress declared Hayes and his vice presidential candidate, William Almon Wheeler, of New York, the winners of the 1876 election.

In his inaugural address, Hayes stressed the importance of settling the problems left by Union occupation of Southern states. In April 1877 he ordered federal troops out of South Carolina and New Orleans. The era of the Reconstruction of the South initiated by former president ULYSSES S. GRANT was over.

During Hayes's administration he renewed the economic policy of satisfying the public debt with government currency, and he opposed measures passed by Congress to freely coin silver. Hayes reformed the process for appointing civil servants. He also signed legislation permitting women to practice law before the Supreme Court.

Hayes refused to run for reelection in 1880, and retired from politics. However, he continued to contribute to the landscape of American life. In 1882 he became the first president of the Slater Fund, founded to aid African American education programs in the South. He later gave a scholarship to a promising young man, W. E. B. Du Bois, who went on to attend Fisk and Harvard Universities and ultimately became a leading figure in the National Association for the Advancement of Colored People (NAACP). In 1883 Hayes became the first president of the National Prison Reform Association, a post he held for nearly ten years. Hayes was also a trustee of Ohio Wesleyan and Ohio State Universities.

On January 14, 1893, Hayes suffered severe chest pain while in Cleveland on business for Western Reserve and Ohio State Universities. His son Webb C. Hayes accompanied him to Speigel Grove, in Fremont, Ohio, where his wife had been buried three years earlier. On January 17 Hayes died, at the age of 70.

FURTHER READINGS

Barnard, Harry. 1994. *Rutherford B. Hayes and His America.* Newton, CT: American Political Biography.

Bishop, Arthur. 1969. *Rutherford B. Hayes, 1822–1893.* Dobbs Ferry, NY: Oceana.

Clancy, Herbert J. 1958. *The Presidential Election of 1880.* Chicago: Loyola Univ. Press.

Davison, Kenneth E. 1972. *The Presidency of Rutherford B. Hayes.* Westport, CT: Greenwood.

Hoogenboom, Ari Arthur. 1988. *The Presidency of Rutherford B. Hayes.* Lawrence: Univ. Press of Kansas.

———. 1995. *Rutherford B. Hayes, Warrior and President.* Lawrence: Univ. Press of Kansas.

Morris, Roy. 2003. *Fraud of the Century: Rutherford B. Hayes, Samuel Tilden, and the Stolen Election of 1876.* New York: Thorndike.

HAYMARKET RIOT

In the HAYMARKET RIOT of May 4, 1886, the police clashed violently with militant anarchists and labor movement protesters in Chicago. Seven policemen and several protesters were killed, leading to MURDER convictions for seven radicals, four of whom were executed. The strong public and state reaction against the Haymarket protesters has been called the first RED SCARE in U.S. history, and their trial has been widely critized for improper procedure and prosecutorial excess.

The Haymarket Riot grew out of labor unrest that had been brewing since the 1870s. Unhappy with difficult working conditions and feeling the pressure of economic depression, workers had engaged in periodic strikes. Strong, sometimes violent police opposition to these strikes led to greater labor militancy. Radicals became increasingly convinced that the struggle between labor and capital had come to a head and that the time for revolution was near. Many anarchists publicly advocated the use of explosives to bring down the capitalist system.

In 1886, a broad coalition of labor organizations joined to campaign for an eight-hour workday. On May 1, 1886, this coalition initiated a general strike throughout the United States, the effects of which were particularly strong in Chicago. On May 3, fighting broke out at the McCormick Reaper Works in Chicago, and at least two workers were killed by the police.

Outraged at these killings, anarchists, members of the labor movement, and other radicals met for a rally in Chicago's Haymarket Square on May 4. The rally was peaceable until the police attempted to disperse the crowd. Then a

The Haymarket Riot took place in Chicago on May 4, 1886. Seven policemen and several protesters were killed, and the event led to the execution of four radicals.

LIBRARY OF CONGRESS

bomb was thrown into the police ranks, killing seven officers and wounding 60 more. The police fired in response, killing and wounding like numbers of participants.

In an ensuing crackdown against the labor movement, the police arrested hundreds of anarchists and other radicals. Two leading anarchist newspapers were put out of business, and their staffs were imprisoned. Finally, eight noted Chicago radicals and anarchists, including nationally known radical leaders August Spies and Albert Parsons, were indicted for the murder of one of the policemen at Haymarket Square. Public opinion turned swiftly against the protesters, in part because seven of the eight defendants in the case were foreign-born.

The trial in the criminal court of Cook County began on June 21, 1886. Despite a lack of evidence linking them directly to the bombing, seven of the eight were convicted of murder and sentenced to death, and the eighth was sentenced to 15 years in prison. The defendants were held liable for the murder on the ground that they had incited the bombing through inflammatory public speech.

The defendants appealed their case to the Illinois Supreme Court which upheld the lower court's decision on September 14, 1887 (*Spies v. People*, 122 Ill. 1, 12 N.E. 865). Supporters of the defendants undertook a CLEMENCY campaign that gathered 40,000 petition signatures. Under pressure from all sides, Governor Richard Oglesby, of Illinois, pardoned two of the seven sentenced to death but sustained the sentences of the other five. One of the seven committed

suicide shortly before the date of execution by detonating a small dynamite bomb smuggled to him by a friend. The other four, including Spies and Parsons, were hanged on November 11, 1887.

The three remaining Haymarket defendants were pardoned in 1893 by Governor John Peter Altgeld, of Illinois, who also issued a report condemning the trial as unfair. He noted that the presiding judge was clearly biased against the defendants, that the defendants were not proved to be guilty of the crime with which they were charged, and that the jury was "packed" by state prosecutors with members who were prejudiced against the defendants. Later legal scholars have supported Altgeld's conclusions.

The questionable jury selection practices in the Haymarket trial, which allowed the seating of jurors who were clearly prejudiced against the defendants, were struck down by a later decision of the Illinois Supreme Court (*Coughlin v. People*, 144 Ill. 140, 33 N.E. 1 [1893]).

FURTHER READINGS

Green, James R. 2006. *Death in the Haymarket: A Story of Chicago, the First Labor Movement and the Bombing that Divided Gilded Age America.* New York: Pantheon

Landsman, Stephan. 1986. "When Justice Fails." *Michigan Law Review* 84 (February–April).

Wish, Harvey. 1976. "Haymarket Riot." In *Dictionary of American History.* Edited by Louise B. Ketz. New York: Scribner.

CROSS REFERENCES

Anarchism; Darrow, Clarence Seward; Goldman, Emma; Labor Law; Labor Union.

❖ HAYNSWORTH, CLEMENT FURMAN, JR.

Clement Furman Haynsworth Jr. was a controversial judge on a federal appellate court who was nominated for a seat on the U.S. Supreme Court but failed to win confirmation.

Born October 30, 1912, in Greenville, South Carolina, and raised in South Carolina, Haynsworth graduated from Furman University in 1933 and from Harvard Law School in 1936. He then returned to his home state and practiced law there for nearly 20 years. In 1957 President DWIGHT D. EISENHOWER appointed Haynsworth to the U.S. Court of Appeals for the Fourth Circuit. Haynsworth became chief judge of the court in 1964.

In May 1969 Associate Justice ABE FORTAS, whose earlier nomination to become chief justice was withdrawn amid charges of financial impropriety and CONFLICT OF INTEREST, resigned his seat on the U.S. Supreme Court after new charges of UNETHICAL CONDUCT were raised. Later that summer, President RICHARD M. NIXON nominated Haynsworth to succeed Fortas.

Reaction to Haynsworth's nomination was mixed. Some commentators thought him to be a competent nominee, if not particularly distinguished, whereas others expressed disappointment at his conservative judicial views. No U.S. Supreme Court nominee had been denied confirmation since 1930, and it initially appeared that Haynsworth would be confirmed with little debate.

In the confirmation hearings that followed, however, Haynsworth faced serious conflict-of-interest allegations. It was disclosed that he had participated in two cases involving subsidiaries of companies in which he held stock. Senators opposing his nomination also revealed that Haynsworth had purchased stock in a corporation after he had voted in its favor in a decision but before the decision was announced by the court. In addition, labor and CIVIL RIGHTS groups voiced opposition to Haynsworth's nomination, contending that he did not support their causes. Nevertheless, the SENATE JUDICIARY COMMITTEE narrowly approved Haynsworth's appointment in a 10–7 vote.

In November 1969 the full Senate, mindful of the controversy that had surrounded Fortas's ethical improprieties, rejected Haynsworth's nomination by a vote of 55–45. This was the widest margin of defeat ever for a Supreme Court nominee.

Haynsworth's failure to win confirmation was widely viewed as a major political setback for President Nixon. A second Nixon nominee for the Fortas seat, Judge G. Harrold Carswell,

Clement F. Haynsworth Jr.
AP IMAGES

another southern conservative, was widely viewed as unqualified for the Court and his nomination was also defeated. The vacancy was finally filled in May 1970 by Judge HARRY A. BLACKMUN, of the Eighth CIRCUIT COURT of Appeals, who was confirmed unanimously.

Following his defeat, Haynsworth returned to the court of appeals. He became a senior judge in 1981, and he remained with the court until his death November 22, 1989, at the age of 77.

FURTHER READINGS

Fourth Circuit History. "Remembering the Fourth Circuit Judges: A History from 1941 to 1998." 1998. *Washington and Lee Law Review* 55 (spring).

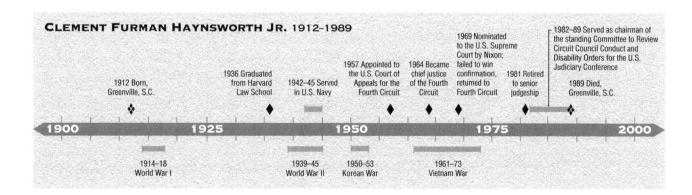

CLEMENT FURMAN HAYNSWORTH JR. 1912–1989

1912 Born, Greenville, S.C.

1936 Graduated from Harvard Law School

1942–45 Served in U.S. Navy

1957 Appointed to the U.S. Court of Appeals for the Fourth Circuit

1964 Became chief justice of the Fourth Circuit

1969 Nominated to the U.S. Supreme Court by Nixon; failed to win confirmation, returned to Fourth Circuit

1981 Retired to senior judgeship

1982–89 Served as chairman of the standing Committee to Review Circuit Council Conduct and Disability Orders for the U.S. Judiciary Conference

1989 Died, Greenville, S.C.

1900   1925   1950   1975   2000

1914–18 World War I

1939–45 World War II

1950–53 Korean War

1961–73 Vietnam War

William H. Hays.
CORBIS.

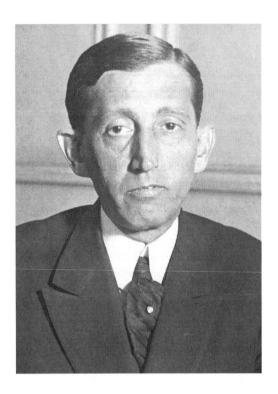

Frank, John Paul. 1991. *Clement Haynsworth, the Senate, and the Supreme Court.* Charlottesville, VA: Univ. of Virginia Press.

Kotlowski, Dean J. 1996. "Trial by Error: Nixon, the Senate, and the Haynsworth Nomination." *Presidential Studies Quarterly* 26, no. 1.

❖ HAYS, WILLIAM HARRISON

William Harrison Hays is mainly known for his establishment of the code through which motion picture producers regulated themselves, thereby avoiding outside CENSORSHIP.

Hays was born in Sullivan, Indiana, on November 5, 1879, to John T. Hays and Mary Cain Hays. He first gained attention through a series of increasingly important positions within the Indiana REPUBLICAN PARTY. In February 1918 his party career culminated in his appointment as chairman of the Republican National Committee. From that position he aided in the 1920 election of WARREN G. HARDING as president of the United States. As reward for his service, Harding appointed Hays U.S. postmaster general in March 1921, after which Hays relinquished his position as Republican chairman.

At this time a widely reported series of sex scandals contributed to a growing perception that the movie industry was out of control and out of step with U.S. society. With more than 30 state legislatures considering bills to censor movies, producers intervened to repair their image. In March 1922 they hired Hays, known as a teetotaler and an elder in the Presbyterian Church, to head the Motion Picture Producers and Distributors of America (MPPDA) at $100,000 per year. With his high political profile, his personal moral characteristics, and his connections with businesspeople, including Hollywood executives, Hays was seen as an outsider who could restore public confidence in the morality of the movie industry.

The effort to head off federal or local censorship through hiring Hays was successful. In 1930 the Hays Office, as it became commonly known, coordinated the Production Code among the producers of movies to provide rules for the film industry's self-regulation. The 1930 code had no enforcement mechanism. Still, the hiring of Hays, the goodwill implied in the code, and a lack of cooperation and

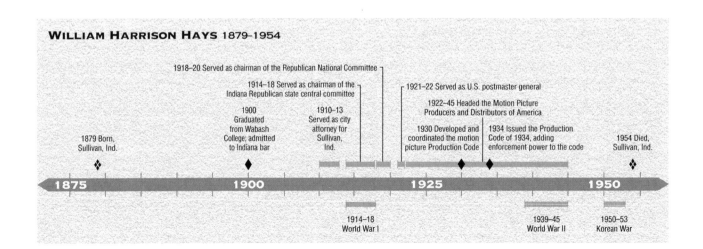

WILLIAM HARRISON HAYS 1879–1954

1918–20 Served as chairman of the Republican National Committee

1914–18 Served as chairman of the Indiana Republican state central committee

1921–22 Served as U.S. postmaster general

1922–45 Headed the Motion Picture Producers and Distributors of America

1900 Graduated from Wabash College; admitted to Indiana bar

1910–13 Served as city attorney for Sullivan, Ind.

1930 Developed and coordinated the motion picture Production Code

1934 Issued the Production Code of 1934, adding enforcement power to the code

1879 Born, Sullivan, Ind.

1954 Died, Sullivan, Ind.

1875　　　1900　　　1925　　　1950

1914–18 World War I

1939–45 World War II

1950–53 Korean War

agreement among reformers, mainly Protestant, dissipated any danger of censorship in the early 1930s.

In 1934, with box office receipts down as the Great Depression widened, Hays responded to a renewed call for morality in the movies spearheaded by the Catholic Church's Legion of Decency. Operating with support from parish priests, from the church hierarchy, and from Protestant and Jewish reform groups, the Legion avoided efforts at government legislated censorship. Rather, it threatened to call for boycotts of films that failed to satisfy its requirements for moral behavior. Hays issued the Production Code of 1934, which added enforcement power to his earlier code. Though the 1934 code provided for fines and suggested that scripts should be preapproved by the Hays Office, its real strength lay in requiring that a film receive the Hays Code Purity Seal of Approval in order to be shown in any movie theater owned by the studios. With the movie industry vertically integrated, so that studios controlled both a large segment of film production and the most successful and profitable movie theaters nationwide, even foreign and nonstudio films were submitted for code approval.

The Hays code went through refinements and shifts in emphasis, both before and after the addition of enforcement in 1934. In general, it was designed to protect impressionable moviegoers by clamping down on sex, language, and violence on screen, with rules relating to sex being particularly stringent. One overarching rule was that sympathetic portrayals of sinners or criminals were prohibited; transgressors had to be punished appropriately for their sins by the end of each film.

Hays maintained his partnership in Hays and Hays, a law firm begun by his father, throughout his tenure with the MPPDA. In 1945 he left his position as head of the MPPDA. He died in Indiana on March 7, 1954.

FURTHER READINGS

Bergman, Andrew. 2007. *We're in the Money: Depression America and Its Films.* Chicago: Dee.

Christensen, Terry, and Peter J. Haas. 1987. *Projecting Politics: Political Messages in American Films.* Armonk, New York: Sharpe.

Crisler, B.R. 1984. "Portrait of an Indiana Lawyer." In *The New York Times Encyclopedia of Film: 1937–1940.* Edited by Gene Brown. New York: Times.

Maltby, Richard. 1993. "'Grief in the Limelight'. Al Capone, Howard Hughes, the Hays Code, and the Politics of the Unstable Text." In *Movies and Politics: The Dynamic Relationship,* edited by James Combs. New York: Garland.

Sklar, Robert. 1994. *Movie-Made America: A Cultural History of American Movies.* Rev. New York: Vintage.

❖ HAYWOOD, MARGARET AUSTIN

Margaret Haywood was a senior judge for the Superior Court of the District of Columbia. She also was the first African American woman to attain a top leadership position in a biracial U.S. church, the United Church of Christ.

MARGARET AUSTIN HAYWOOD was born October 8, 1912, in Knoxville, Tennessee. When she was eight, she and her parents moved to Washington, D.C. Although she was aware of segregation, her loving home life helped her to grow up feeling secure and self-confident. Haywood's parents, Mayme F. Austin and J. W. M. Austin, were able to provide her with a relatively

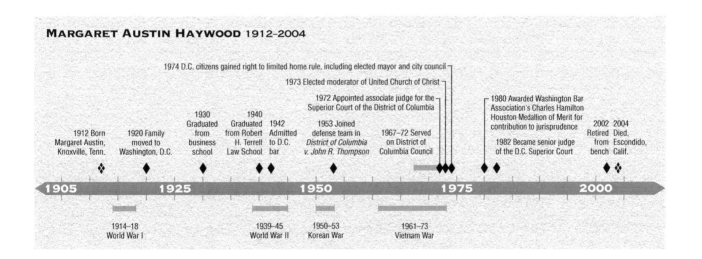

MARGARET AUSTIN HAYWOOD 1912–2004

1974 D.C. citizens gained right to limited home rule, including elected mayor and city council
1973 Elected moderator of United Church of Christ
1972 Appointed associate judge for the Superior Court of the District of Columbia
1980 Awarded Washington Bar Association's Charles Hamilton Houston Medallion of Merit for contribution to jurisprudence

1912 Born Margaret Austin, Knoxville, Tenn.
1920 Family moved to Washington, D.C.
1930 Graduated from business school
1940 Graduated from Robert H. Terrell Law School
1942 Admitted to D.C. bar
1953 Joined defense team in *District of Columbia v. John R. Thompson*
1967–72 Served on District of Columbia Council
1982 Became senior judge of the D.C. Superior Court
2002 Retired from bench
2004 Died, Escondido, Calif.

1905   1925   1950   1975   2000

1914–18 World War I
1939–45 World War II
1950–53 Korean War
1961–73 Vietnam War

Margaret A. Haywood.

comfortable childhood, although her father lost his job in 1929. After two years, he found another job with the Works Progress Administration, helping people obtain public assistance. Reading the letters people wrote to her father detailing their plights, Haywood learned that it was necessary to listen to people in order to help them.

Haywood was always an independent decision maker. While she was in high school, her teachers encouraged her to become a teacher, the best career option for black women in the 1930s. However, Haywood's interests lay elsewhere, for reasons that were both practical and compelling. At the height of the Great Depression, in 1930, she came out of business school with no job and no money for college. She married and had a daughter, but the marriage, as she described it, "was disastrous." Before long, she found herself divorced and raising a child alone. "I wanted my daughter to have a good education, but I was earning only $15 a week as a secretary," she said. "That's when I began to think about going into law."

Determined to provide economic security for her daughter and herself, Haywood enrolled in Robert H. Terrell Law School, an institution for African American students where she could attend classes at night and work during the day.

During her first two years at Terrell, she was the only female student; during the last two years, she was one of two female students. This did not deter her, and she graduated from Terrell with her Bachelor of Laws degree in 1940.

After her admission to the District of Columbia bar in 1942, Haywood joined a well-known African American law firm. She quickly realized that the firm expected her to specialize in domestic relations cases, whereas she was interested in practicing in other fields. Unwilling to compromise, she left the security of the firm and opened her own general practice, where she handled the full range of legal cases. In the early 1950s, she participated in the landmark CIVIL RIGHTS case *District of Columbia v. John R. Thompson Co.*, 345 U.S. 921, 73 S. Ct. 784, 97 L. Ed. 2d 1353 (1953), which confirmed the validity of post–Civil War laws that prohibited segregation. For her efforts, Haywood received threats from the KU KLUX KLAN and was labeled a communist.

Haywood had practiced law for more than 25 years before President LYNDON B. JOHNSON appointed her to a part-time post on the District of Columbia Council. She served in that capacity from 1967 to 1972, during a time when the governance of the district was being reevaluated and reorganized. The revamped system of government, including an elected mayor and the council on which Haywood served, was approved in 1974.

In 1972 President RICHARD M. NIXON appointed Haywood as associate judge for the Superior Court of the District of Columbia, the district's highest trial court. The following year, the United Church of Christ elected her its moderator, making her the first African American woman to hold such a high position in a biracial U.S. church. As moderator, she presided over 728 delegates to the church's ninth biennial general synod, or governing council. Her position with the church was a two-year unsalaried post, which she combined with her duties on the court.

In 1982 Haywood achieved the rank of senior judge of the District of Columbia Superior Court. As a senior judge in the 2000s, Haywood continued to participate in judicial proceedings.

Haywood received honorary degrees from several institutions, including Elmhurst College (1974), Carleton College (1975), Catawba

College (1976), and Doane College (1979). In addition, she was the recipient of many honors and awards. These include a National Association for the Advancement of Colored People (NAACP) trophy in 1950, the Women's Bar Association's Woman Lawyer of the Year award in 1972, induction into the District of Columbia Women's Commission Hall of Fame, and the Washington Bar Association's Charles Hamilton Medallion of Merit for contribution to jurisprudence in 1980. In October 2002 the Standing Committee on Fairness and Access to D.C. Courts presented Haywood with its Trailblazer Award for her contributions to her profession and her community and, in particular, her continued commitment to ensuring equal access to the court system.

Haywood died of renal failure on January 9, 2004, in Escondido, California, at the age of 91.

FURTHER READINGS

Berry, Dawn Bradley. 1996. *The 50 Most Influential Women in American Law.* Los Angeles: Contemporary Books.

Drachman, Virginia G. 1998. *Sisters in Law: Women Lawyers in Modern American History.* Cambridge, Mass.: Harvard Univ. Press.

Smith, Jessie Carney. 2002. *Black Firsts: 4,000 Ground-Breaking and Pioneering Historical Events.* Canton, MI: Visible Ink.

✧ HAYWOOD, WILLIAM DUDLEY

Labor leader Bill Haywood was regarded as a radical in the growing labor movement in the United States. A public figure throughout most of his life, Haywood was the central figure in two famous court cases.

Haywood was born in 1869 in Salt Lake City, Utah. In 1896, Haywood, a coal miner, became an active participant in the Western

William D. Haywood.
LIBRARY OF CONGRESS

Federation of Miners. He rapidly rose to prominence in the federation, securing offices of leadership by 1904. His tactics were militant in nature, as was evidenced by the violence of the Cripple Creek strike that occurred in Colorado in 1904.

In 1905 former Idaho Governor Frank Steunenberg was killed by an explosion caused by a bomb hidden in his home by Harry Orchard. Orchard admitted his guilt and implicated three leaders of the Western Federation of Miners: President Charles H. Moyer,

IT IS THE HISTORIC MISSION OF THE WORKING CLASS TO DO AWAY WITH CAPITALISM.
—WILLIAM HAYWOOD

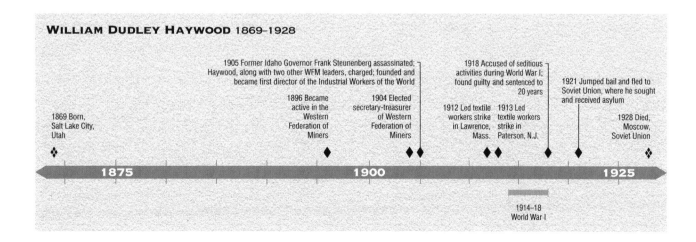

WILLIAM DUDLEY HAYWOOD 1869–1928

1905 Former Idaho Governor Frank Steunenberg assassinated; Haywood, along with two other WFM leaders, charged; founded and became first director of the Industrial Workers of the World

1896 Became active in the Western Federation of Miners

1904 Elected secretary-treasurer of Western Federation of Miners

1918 Accused of seditious activities during World War I; found guilty and sentenced to 20 years

1921 Jumped bail and fled to Soviet Union, where he sought and received asylum

1869 Born, Salt Lake City, Utah

1912 Led textile workers strike in Lawrence, Mass.

1913 Led textile workers strike in Paterson, N.J.

1928 Died, Moscow, Soviet Union

1875   1900   1925

1914–18 World War I

Secretary-Treasurer Haywood, and retired leader George A. Pettibone. These men were abducted from Denver and taken to Boise, Idaho, to stand trial. The Haywood-Moyer-Pettibone case took on national significance for two reasons: (1) it involved a radical labor organization, and (2) eminent attorney CLARENCE DARROW acted as defense attorney. The three men were subsequently acquitted (*Pettibone v. Nichols*, 203 U.S. 192, 27 S. Ct. 111, 51 L. Ed. 148 [1906]).

The INDUSTRIAL WORKERS OF THE WORLD (IWW) was established in 1905, and Haywood was the founder and director of this labor organization. He was a proponent of group action and class struggle, and he abhorred compromise. He continued to use violence in his fight for labor, and led two infamous textile workers' strikes in Lawrence, Massachusetts (1912), and in Paterson, New Jersey (1913).

Haywood and other members of his IWW organization attempted to become members of the SOCIALIST PARTY but were rejected for their theories of violent action.

In 1918 Haywood was again on trial. One hundred sixty-five IWW leaders, including Haywood, were accused of seditious activities during WORLD WAR I. Haywood was found guilty and sentenced to spend the next 20 years in prison.

Haywood was free on bail in 1921, pending the date of a new trial, when he escaped and sought asylum in the Soviet Union. He died in Moscow seven years later.

H.B.

See HOUSE BILL.

HEAD OF HOUSEHOLD

An individual in one family setting who provides actual support and maintenance to one or more individuals who are related to him or her through adoption, blood, or marriage.

The designation *head of household*, also termed *head of family*, is applied to one whose authority to exercise family control and to support the dependent members is founded upon a moral or legal obligation or duty.

Head of household is also a filing status for federal income taxpayers. There are five basic categories of tax statuses: (1) single persons; (2) heads of households; (3) married taxpayers

filing joint returns; (4) married taxpayers filing separate returns; and (5) surviving spouses. Each of these persons pays at different rates. The tax rates for single persons are ordinarily higher than rates for heads of household, while rates for a husband and wife filing a joint return are lower.

In order for an individual to qualify as head of household for income tax purposes, the person need not be unmarried all year as long as the person is unmarried on the final day of the tax year. In addition, the person must support and maintain a household to the extent that his or her monetary contribution exceeds one-half of the total cost of maintenance. The person's home must be the main place of residence of one relative, with the exception of a mother and father, for the whole year. Relatives include children, grandchildren, stepchildren, brothers and sisters, half brothers or half sisters, and stepbrothers and stepsisters. The individual's parents need not reside in the same home as the taxpayer for him or her to claim this status, provided the person meets the support requirements specified.

Homestead exemption statutes, which have been passed in a majority of jurisdictions, permit a head of household to designate a house and land as a homestead and exempt it from execution for general debts in the event of BANKRUPTCY. In addition, some states make available property tax exemptions for homestead property. Such statutes often require the formal recording of a declaration of homestead.

HEADNOTE

A brief summary of a legal rule or a significant fact in a case that, among other headnotes that apply to the case, precedes the full text opinion printed in the reports or reporters. A syllabus to a reported case that summarizes the points decided in the case and is placed before the text of the opinion.

Each jurisdiction usually determines whether headnotes are part of the law or only an editorial device to facilitate research. Most headnotes are included by private publishers and do not constitute a part of an opinion. The most notable publisher that employs headnotes is the West Group in the National Reporter System, which publishes cases from practically every jurisdiction. Use of headnotes in the National Reporter System is generally consistent, regardless of the jurisdiction. The Reporter of Decisions for the United States Supreme Court also prepares a syllabus for Supreme Court decisions, when feasible, at the time an opinion is issued. The syllabus summarizes the points of law addressed in each case, but does not constitute a part of the opinion and does not constitute BINDING AUTHORITY.

HEALTH AND HUMAN SERVICES DEPARTMENT

The Department of Health and Human Services (HHS) is the cabinet-level department of the EXECUTIVE BRANCH of the federal government most involved with the health, safety, and welfare of the U.S. population. A wide variety of HHS agencies administer more than 300 programs, which focus on such initiatives as providing financial assistance, health care, and advocacy to those in need; conducting medical and social science research; assuring food and drug safety; and enforcing laws and regulations related to human services.

The HHS originated in the Department of Health, Education, and Welfare (HEW), which was created in 1953. In 1980, the DEPARTMENT OF EDUCATION Organization Act (20 U.S.C.A. § 3508) redesignated HEW as the Department of Health and Human Services.

The secretary of HHS advises the president of the United States on the federal government's health, welfare, and income security plans, policies, and programs. He or she directs HHS staff in carrying out department programs and activities and promotes public understanding of HHS goals, programs, and objectives. The secretary administers these functions through the Office of the Secretary and the individual agencies of the HHS: the Administration on Aging; Administration for Children and Families; the CENTERS FOR MEDICARE & MEDICAID SERVICES; the Agency for Healthcare Research and Quality; the Centers for Disease Control and Prevention; the Agency for Toxic Substances and Disease Registry; the FOOD AND DRUG ADMINISTRATION; the Health Resources and Services Administration; the Indian Health Service; the National Institutes of Health; the SUBSTANCE ABUSE AND MENTAL HEALTH SERVICES ADMINISTRATION; and the Program Support Center. The Social Security Administration, once located within HHS, became an independent agency in 1995.

Office of the Secretary

The Office of the Secretary of the HHS includes the offices of the assistant secretaries, the inspector general, and the general counsel. Individuals in these offices, along with other senior officials at HHS, assist the secretary with the overall management responsibilities of the HHS and aid in the day-to-day operations of the department. For example, the Program Support Center (PSC), which is part of the Office of the Assistant Secretary for Administration and Management, offers support services in such areas as human resources and financial management.

In addition, the Office for Civil Rights administers and enforces laws that prohibit discrimination in federally assisted health and human services programs. These laws include Title VI of the Civil Rights Act of 1964 (42 U.S.C.A. § 2000d et seq.), which prohibits discrimination with regard to race, color, or national origin in programs and activities receiving federal financial assistance; the Age Discrimination Act of 1975 (42 U.S.C.A. § 6101 et seq.); and the Americans with Disabilities Act of 1990 (42 U.S.C.A. § 12101 et seq.).

The secretary is accountable to Congress and to the public for departmental expenditures of taxpayers' money. Thus, the secretary and other members of the HHS staff often testify before congressional committees, make speeches before national organizations interested in and affected by HHS policy, and meet with the press and the public to explain HHS actions. The secretary and the HHS staff also prepare special reports, sometimes at the request of the president, on national problems related to health and human services. In addition, the secretary is required by law to submit to the president and to Congress periodic reports that explain how tax money was spent to address and solve a particular problem and whether progress on the problem was achieved.

The headquarters of the HHS department is located in Washington, D.C., and ten regional HHS offices are located throughout the United States. The regional directors of these offices represent the secretary in any official HHS dealings with state and local government organizations. They promote a general understanding of HHS programs, policies, and objectives; advise the secretary on the potential local effects of HHS policies and decisions; and provide administrative services and support to HHS programs and activities in the regions.

Health and Human Services Department

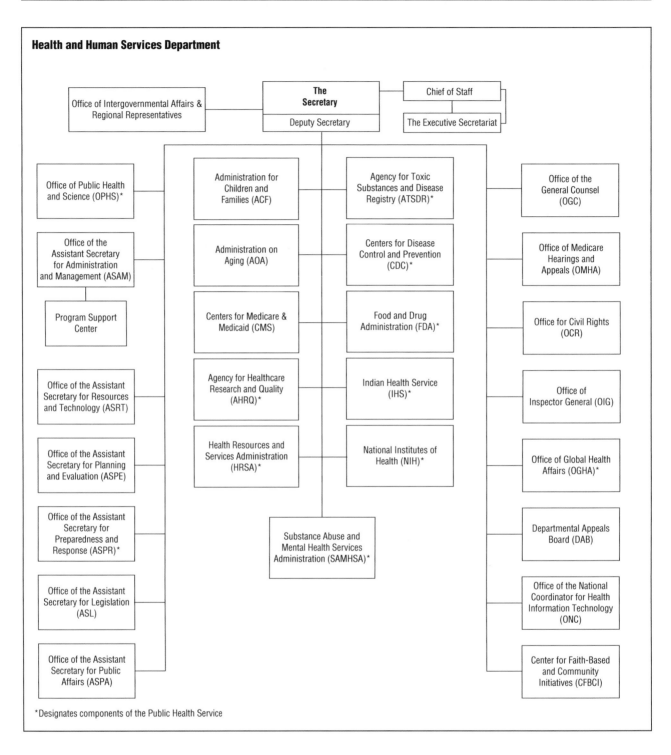

Administration on Aging

The Administration on Aging (AOA) is the principal agency of the HHS designated to carry out the provisions of the Older Americans Act of 1965, as amended (42 U.S.C.A. § 3001 et seq.). The Older Americans Act was enacted to promote the well-being of older U.S. citizens by providing services and programs designed to help them live independently in their homes and communities. The act also empowers the federal government to distribute funds to the states for supportive services for older people. The AOA advises the secretary and other federal departments and agencies on the characteristics, circumstances, and needs of older citizens; develops policies and programs to promote the welfare of older citizens and advocates for their needs in HHS policy development and planning; and administers to the states grants that establish at the state and local levels programs providing services to older citizens, such as group meals and nutrition education. The AOA also administers programs providing legal and protective services for older people.

Administration for Children and Families

The Administration for Children and Families (ACF) was created in 1991 and is headed by the assistant secretary for children and families, who reports to the secretary of the HHS. The ACF consists of several component administrations, including the Administration on Children, Youth, and Families (ACYF), which advises the secretary, through the assistant secretary, on matters relating to the welfare of children and families, and administers grant programs to help the states provide child welfare services as well as foster care and adoption assistance. The ACYF also administers state grant programs for the prevention of CHILD ABUSE; the Head Start Program, which appropriates funds for health, education, nutrition, social, and other services to economically disadvantaged children and their families; and programs providing services to prevent drug abuse among youth. In addition, the ACYF supports and encourages in the private and voluntary sectors programs for children, youth, and families.

Other components of the ACF include the Administration on Developmental Disabilities (ADD) and the Administration for Native Americans (ANA). ADD advises the secretary of the HHS on matters relating to persons with developmental disabilities and their families and helps provide services to such individuals. ADD also helps the states provide services at the local level through grants and other programs. ANA represents the concerns of Native Americans and serves as the focal point within the HHS for providing developmental, social, and economic strategies to support Native American self-determination and self-sufficiency. ANA administers grant programs to Indian tribes and other Native American organizations in both urban and rural areas and acts as a liaison with other federal agencies on Native American affairs.

Another component of the ACF is the Office of Child Support Enforcement (OCSE), which advises the secretary on matters relating to child support enforcement and provides direction and guidance to state offices for child enforcement programs. The OCSE helps states develop programs establishing and enforcing support obligations by locating absent parents, establishing paternity, and collecting child support payments.

Medicare and Medicaid

The Centers for Medicare & Medicaid Services (CMS) replaced the former Health Care Financing Administration in 2001. It was created to oversee the Medicare Program and the federal portion of the Medicaid Program. Medicare provides HEALTH INSURANCE for U.S. citizens age 65 or older, for younger people receiving Social Security benefits, and for persons needing dialysis or kidney transplants. Medicaid covers healthcare expenses for recipients of Temporary Assistance for Needy Families (formerly Aid to Families with Dependent Children), as well as for low-income pregnant women and other individuals whose medical bills qualify them as medically needy. Through these programs, the HCFA serves 68 million older, disabled, and poor U.S. citizens. In addition, a quality assurance program administered by the CMS develops health and safety standards for providers of healthcare services authorized by Medicare and Medicaid legislation.

Public Health Service Agencies

The Office of Public Health and Science (OPHS) oversees 12 civilian offices and the Commissioned Corps of the U.S. PUBLIC HEALTH SERVICE. The Public Health Service was first established in 1798 to create hospitals to care for U.S. merchant seamen. OPHS provides assistance in implementing and coordinating decisions for the Public Health Service and coordination of population-based health, clinical divisions; It also provides oversight of research conducted or supported by the department. In addition, it implements several programs to provide population-based public health services; OPHS provides direction and policy oversight, through the SURGEON GENERAL, for the Commissioned Corps.

Over time legislation has substantially broadened the number and scope of agencies that deal with public health. These include the Agency for Healthcare Research and Quality, which produces and disseminates information

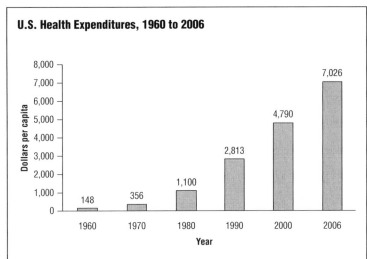

U.S. Health Expenditures, 1960 to 2006

SOURCE: U.S. Department of Health and Human Services, Centers for Disease Control and Prevention, National Center for Health Statistics, *Health, United States*, 2008.

ILLUSTRATION BY GGS CREATIVE RESOURCES. REPRODUCED BY PERMISSION OF GALE, A PART OF CENGAGE LEARNING.

about the quality, medical effectiveness, and cost of health care, and the Centers for Disease Control and Prevention (CDC), which provides leadership in the prevention and control of disease outbreak and responds to public health emergencies.

Other agencies dealing with public health include the Agency for Toxic Substances and Disease Registry, which carries out the health-related responsibilities of the Comprehensive Environmental Response, Compensation, and Liability Act of 1980 (CERCLA) (42 U.S.C.A. § 9601 et seq.), as well as the Food and Drug Administration (FDA), which is charged with protecting the health of the nation against unsafe foods, drugs, cosmetics, and other hazards.

The Health Resources and Services Administration (HRSA) focuses on ensuring that people without resources or living in underserved areas (e.g., rural areas) receive quality health care. There are more than three thousand HRSA-funded centers throughout the United States. The health status of Native Americans and Alaska Natives is the concern of the Indian Health Service. The Indian Health Service administers a comprehensive healthcare delivery system for these groups, developing and managing programs to meet their health needs.

The National Institutes of Health (NIH) is the principal biomedical research agency of the federal government. Included within the NIH are the National Cancer Institute; National Heart, Lung, and Blood Institute; National Institute of Child Health and Human Development; and other institutes conducting research in the areas of alcohol and drug abuse, mental health, communication and neurological disorders, and aging.

The Substance Abuse and Mental Health Services Administration (SAMHSA) provides national leadership in the prevention and treatment of addictive and mental disorders, through programs and services for individuals who suffer from these disorders. Within SAMHSA are several component centers designated to carry out its purposes, including the Center for Substance Abuse Prevention, Center for Substance Abuse Treatment, and Center for Mental Health Services. SAMHSA is also served by the Office of Management, Planning, and Communications, which is responsible for the financial and administrative management of SAMHSA components, monitors and analyzes legislation affecting these components, and oversees SAMHSA public affairs activities.

FURTHER READINGS

"Health and Human Services Department." *The New York Times* (September 4, 2009). Available online at http://topics.nytimes.com/topics/reference/timestopics/organizations/h/health_and_human_services_department/index.html; website home page: http://topics.nytimes.com (accessed September 4, 2009).

U.S. Department of Health and Human Services. Available online at www.hhs.gov (accessed December 21, 2009).

U.S. Government Manual. Available online at www.gpoaccess.gov/gmanual (accessed December 21, 2009).

HEALTH CARE FINANCING ADMINISTRATION

See CENTERS FOR MEDICARE & MEDICAID SERVICES.

HEALTH CARE LAW

Health care law involves many facets of U.S. law, including torts, contracts, antitrust, and insurance. According to statistics from the California Health Care Foundation (CHCF), health care expenditures reached $2.2 trillion dollars in 2007, or $7,421 per person in the U.S. Per-person costs jumped 81 percent between 1997 and 2007. If costs are not controlled, the CHCF estimates that health spending will reach 20 percent of the country's gross domestic product by 2018.

Medical Malpractice

One major area within health care law is MEDICAL MALPRACTICE, which is professional misconduct or lack of skill in providing medical treatment or services. The victims of medical MALPRACTICE seek compensation for their physical or emotional injuries, or both, through a NEGLIGENCE action.

A DEFENDANT physician may be found liable for medical malpractice if the PLAINTIFF patient can establish that there was in fact a patient-physician relationship; that the physician breached (i.e., violated or departed from) the accepted standard of medical care in the treatment of the patient; that the patient suffered an injury for which he or she should be compensated; and that the physician's violation of the standard of care was the cause of the injury.

To protect themselves against the massive costs of such claims, physicians purchase malpractice insurance. Physicians' malpractice premiums total billions of dollars each year and add substantially to the cost of health care in the United States. In some specialties, such as obstetrics, 50 percent of the cost for medical services goes for the provider's malpractice premiums. Many physicians, faced with the rising tide of malpractice premiums, practice "defensive medicine" by ordering tests and procedures that might not be necessary, so that the records will show that they did all they could. Several studies have estimated the cost of defensive tests and procedures at tens of billions of dollars per year.

Medical malpractice liability can extend to hospitals and even to health maintenance organizations (HMOs). In the case of severe injuries, this can provide a plaintiff patient with an additional source of compensation. One complicating element is a historical doctrine that disallows the corporate practice of medicine—which in effect, and sometimes in actuality through statutes, prohibits the employment of physicians. In states that disallow the corporate practice of medicine, plaintiffs may not bring medical malpractice claims against HMOs or hospitals based on a physician's treatment, because the doctors are not considered employees.

Because every state prohibits the practice of medicine without a license, and because a corporate or business entity may not obtain a license to practice medicine, the historical model provided that all physicians were independent contractors (i.e., separate economic entities), even in their role on the medical staff of a hospital. Without an explicit employer-employee relationship, the liability of a physician for malpractice most likely could not be imputed (i.e., passed along to) a hospital.

The legal theory of *respondeat superior* holds an employer liable for the negligent acts of an employee who acts within the SCOPE OF EMPLOYMENT. Historically, as most physicians were not employees, this theory of liability was often defeated in medical malpractice suits. Today, however, most courts look beyond the title given to the relationship, and to the control that the hospital or health care organization exerts over the physician in question, to determine whether the relationship is more like that of an employer and employee (e.g., where the processes and treatment decisions are tightly prescribed by the organization, and liability may be imputed) or whether it is truly that of an independent contractor and a client (e.g., where the physician acts alone to accomplish a particular end result, and liability may not be imputed).

The legal theory of ostensible agency can also attach liability to a hospital or health care organization for an individual physician's malpractice. No employer-employee relationship needs to be shown here. Ostensible agency liability is created where the principal (the hospital or health care organization) represents or creates the appearance to third persons that the physician is an agent of the principal, subject to the principal's control. This theory focuses on the reasonable expectations and beliefs of the patient, based on the conduct of the hospital or health care organization. The actual relationship of the physician and the hospital or organization is immaterial.

Most states have enacted legislation that modifies the common law action of medical malpractice, in an attempt to stem the rising tide of lawsuits. Restrictions on plaintiff patients include shorter statutes of limitations (i.e., times within which a lawsuit must be filed after injury) than those provided for in common law actions, and a required affidavit from a physician expert witness, certifying that the applicable standard of care in the particular case was violated by the defendant physician and that the violation caused the plaintiff patient's injuries.

Even with legislation in these states, the costs of medical malpractice liability have increased, and, in some parts of the country, skyrocketed. Doctors in some areas claim that liability insurance is so high that they refuse to accept patients, move their practice to another state, or even retire early. Insurance companies that provide malpractice insurance claim that multi-million-dollar judgments in medical malpractice cases, coupled with lawsuits deemed frivolous by the companies, have been the root cause of the increase in rates.

Several states have considered and passed legislation under the pretext of major tort reform. California law provides a model that several states have followed. In 1975, the California legislature enacted the Medical Injury Compensation Reform Act (MICRA), which capped non-economic damages—which include damages for pain and suffering, and even death—at $250,000. Many states that have followed California's lead have limited such damages to between $250,000 and $350,000. In 2001, President GEORGE W. BUSH called for major reform on a national level, requesting that Congress enact legislation that could create a national cap of $250,000 on non-economic damages in all medical malpractice cases. These efforts failed. Other proposals include limiting the recovery of attorney's fees in medical malpractice cases, restricting the liability of a doctor who provides emergency care, and limiting the recovery of attorneys in medical malpractice cases.

These efforts are not without their critics. Skeptics point out that in some states, the cap on non-economic damages has not resulted in lower premiums on malpractice insurance, and that bad business practices of insurance companies have been as or more responsible for the rise in liability insurance premiums as the multi-million-dollar judgments. Without major insurance reform, say these critics, the local and national tort reform efforts will not provide what they promise.

Physician Malpractice Records

In the past, it was very difficult for patients to discover malpractice information about their physicians. The federal government maintains the National Practitioners Data Bank, which lists doctors and malpractice claims in excess of $20,000, along with state disciplinary records. Its list is not made available to the public, but it is provided to state medical boards, hospitals, and other organizations that grant credentials. Because of the great demand by patients for this information, many states are enacting legislation that makes it readily available. For example, the state of Washington provides access to physician information through several sources: insurance company claims records, which are required by law to be reported to the state; the National Practitioners Data Bank; and the state board of medicine, which administers physician licensing and discipline. Massachusetts created a similar system, called the Physician's Profiles Project, and other states, including Florida, California, and New York, are considering the same kind of initiative.

A Physician's Duty to Provide Medical Treatment

Medical malpractice dominates the headlines, but a more basic legal question involving medical care is the affirmative duty, if any, to provide medical treatment. The historical rule is that a physician has no duty to accept a patient, regardless of the severity of the illness. A physician's relationship with a patient was understood to be a voluntary, contracted one. Once the relationship was established, the physician was under a legal obligation to provide medical treatment and was a fiduciary in this respect. (A fiduciary is a person with a duty to act primarily for the benefit of another.)

Once the physician-patient relationship exists, the physician can be held liable for an intentional refusal of care or treatment, under the theory of abandonment. (Abandonment is an intentional act; negligent lack of care or treatment is medical malpractice.) When a treatment relationship exists, the physician must provide all necessary treatment to a patient unless the relationship is ended by the patient or by the physician, provided that the physician gives the patient sufficient notice to seek another source of medical care. Most doctors and hospitals routinely ensure that alternative sources of treatment—other doctors or hospitals—are made available for patients whose care is being discontinued.

The discontinuation of care involves significant economic issues. Reimbursement procedures often limit or cut off the funding for a particular patient's care. Under the diagnosis-related group (DRG) system of MEDICARE, part A, 42 U.S.C. § 1395c, a hospital is paid a pre-set amount for the treatment of a particular diagnosis, regardless of the actual cost of treatment. Patients who are covered by private insurance or HMOs may lose their coverage if they fail to pay premiums. Physicians and hospitals must act carefully when this happens, because the fiduciary nature of the relationship between provider and patient is not changed by a patient's unexpected inability to pay. Health care providers must notify a patient and even must help to secure alternative care when funds are not reimbursed as expected.

A Hospital's Duty to Provide Medical Treatment

The historical rule for hospitals is that they must act reasonably in their decisions to treat patients. Hospitals must acknowledge that a common practice of providing treatment to all emergency patients creates among members of a community an expectation that care will be provided whenever a person seeks care in an "unmistakable emergency." Seeking alternative care in a time-sensitive emergency situation could result in avoidable permanent injury or death, so it is not surprising that hospitals are held to a more flexible "reasonable duty" standard in their admission of patients for treatment.

Owing to the high cost of emergency room care, many private hospitals in the early 1980s began refusing to admit indigent patients and instead had them transferred to emergency rooms at municipal or county hospitals. This practice, known as "patient dumping," has since been prohibited by various state statutes, and also by Congress as part of the Consolidated Omnibus Budget Reconciliation Act of 1985 (COBRA) (Public Law No. 99-272), in a section titled Emergency Medical Treatment and Active Labor Act (EMTALA) (§ 9121(b), codified at 42 U.S.C.A. § 1395dd). Under EMTALA, hospitals that receive federal assistance, maintain charitable nonprofit tax status, or participate in Medicare are prevented from denying emergency treatment based solely on an individual's inability to pay. EMTALA allowed private enforcement actions (i.e., lawsuits by individuals) and civil penalties (i.e., fines) for hospitals that violate its provisions. Patients who must receive medical treatment include people whose health is in "serious jeopardy" and pregnant women in active labor. The EMTALA duty to provide treatment may be relieved only if a patient is stabilized to the point where a transfer to another hospital will result in "no material deterioration of [his or her] condition."

The U.S. Supreme Court ruled in *Roberts v. Galen of Virginia, Inc.*, 525 U.S. 249, 119 S. Ct. 685, 142 L. Ed. 2d 648 (1999), that patients who have an emergency medical condition who are transferred from a hospital before being stabilized may sue the hospital under the EMTALA. The Court interpreted EMTALA to allow any patient to sue under the stabilization requirement, even those who are not emergency room victims of patient dumping. Under the decision, a patient may recover if a hospital transfers the patient without stabilizing his or her condition, regardless of whether the doctor who signed the transfer order did so because the patient lacked HEALTH INSURANCE, or for any other improper purpose. Lower federal courts have conflicted over other aspects of the EMTALA, including whether the plaintiff must prove an improper motive when a hospital fails to screen an emergency patient. The High Court has not resolved all of these conflicts.

Similar federal statutes require that hospitals treat all patients who have the ability to pay. Federal law prohibits discrimination on the basis of race, color, or national origin, by any program that receives federal financial assistance (42 U.S.C.A. § 2000d). Almost all hospitals receive this kind of funding, and many derive half or more of their revenue from Medicare or MEDICAID. Section 504 of the Rehabilitation Act of 1973 (29 U.S.C.A. § 794) prohibits federally funded programs and activities (including hospitals that receive federal funds) from excluding any "otherwise handicapped individual... solely by reason of his handicap."

The broad definition of "handicap" is "physical or mental impairment that substantially limits one or more of a person's major life activities." This has been construed to include ACQUIRED IMMUNE DEFICIENCY SYNDROME (AIDS) and asymptomatic HIV. Thus, hospitals that receive federal aid may not deny treatment to patients who are HIV-positive or who have AIDS. At the state level, similar legislation protects access to all state-licensed health care facilities and to the services of treating physicians.

Antitrust and Monopoly

The same antitrust and monopoly laws that govern businesses and corporations apply to physicians, hospitals, and health care organizations.

Sherman Act The SHERMAN ANTI-TRUST ACT of 1890 (15 U.S.C.A. § 1) prohibits conspiracies in RESTRAINT OF TRADE that affect interstate commerce. Often, physicians who are denied admittance to, or who are expelled from, the medical staff of a hospital file a lawsuit in federal court, against the medical staff and the hospital, claiming violation of the Sherman Act.

To understand why this kind of federal action applies in this situation, one must first understand the unique relation of doctors to hospitals. Doctors generally do not work for a particular hospital, but instead enjoy staff, or "admitting," privileges at several hospitals. They are accepted for membership on a medical staff by the staff itself, pursuant to its bylaws. The process of selecting and periodically re-evaluating medical staff members (called "credentialing" or "peer review") can result in a denial of admittance to, or expulsion from, the medical staff.

Physicians who are denied admittance to, or expelled from, a hospital's medical staff and file a claim of Sherman Act violation in federal court are essentially claiming that they are being illegally restrained from their trade (i.e., practicing medicine). It is the unique relation between doctors and hospitals, described earlier, that satisfies the first element of a Sherman Act violation, which is that a conspiracy must exist. Normally, a single business cannot conspire with itself to restrain trade—a conspiracy requires a concerted, or joint, effort between or among two or more entities. Because physicians, as independent contractors, constitute individual economic entities, when they vote as a medical staff to admit or expel a physician, they are acting in the concerted, or joint, fashion described by the statute.

The second element of a Sherman Act violation is that a restraint of trade must occur. One rule states that any restraint of trade, especially in the commercial arena, may be viewed as per se (i.e., inherently) illegal. However, courts often have resorted to comparative analysis to balance the pro-competitive versus anticompetitive effects of a medical staff's decision. For example, if a physician has a history of incompetent or unethical behavior, then a denial of medical staff privileges can be independently justified. However, if there is only one hospital in a small town, and the physician in question meets all qualifications for ethics and competence, a denial of medical staff privileges may well constitute illegal restraint of trade.

The final element of a Sherman Act violation, that the action must substantially affect interstate commerce, is a jurisdictional requirement, which means that if it is not satisfied, the federal court has no jurisdiction to hear the dispute, and the Sherman Act does not apply. Courts are split as to whether a medical staff's decision to grant or deny medical staff privileges satisfies this element. Some courts view the practice of a single physician to have a minimal, rather than the required substantial, effect on interstate commerce, and hold that the jurisdictional element is not met. Other courts focus on the activity of the entire hospital (e.g., receipt of federal funds, purchase of equipment from other states, and reimbursement from national insurance companies) and find that the jurisdictional element is met.

Challenged medical staffs and hospitals often raise the "state-action" exemption, which exempts from federal antitrust law activities required by state law or regulations. Many states mandate the peer-review process, even at private hospitals, but in order for an exemption based on this mandate to negate a finding of a Sherman Act violation, the state must supervise the process closely.

Clayton Act Section 7 of the Clayton Anti-Trust Act of 1914 (15 U.S.C.A. § 18) prohibits mergers if they "lessen competition or tend to create a monopoly." To be valid, a merger must not give a few large firms total control of a particular market, because of the risks of PRICE-FIXING and other forms of illegal COLLUSION. Market-share statistics control merger analysis, and they are based on a "relevant market." The CLAYTON ACT can prohibit a national hospital-management company from purchasing several hospitals in one town, and it can even prohibit joint ventures between hospitals and physicians or between formerly competing groups of practicing physicians.

Several exceptions apply to these prohibitions. If a hospital is on the verge of BANKRUPTCY and certain closure, but for the merger, then the merger will be allowed. Nonprofit hospitals long enjoyed complete exemption from Section 7 of the Clayton Act, but now federal district courts are split as to whether the act applies to nonprofit hospitals. In any case, a careful market analysis that shows that particular relevant markets do not overlap—and hence do not lessen competition or create a monopoly—can be used as evidence to uphold a merger decision between two or more health care entities.

Health Care Insurance

A trend toward "managed care" and away from "fee-for-service" medicine has been sparked by significant changes in the health insurance industry. Health care insurance originated in the 1930s with Blue Cross (hospitalization coverage) and Blue Shield (physician services coverage). It traditionally has stayed out of the provision of health care services and has served as a third-party indemnitor for health care expenses; that is, in exchange for the payment of a monthly premium, a health care insurance company agrees to indemnify, or be responsible for, its insured's health care costs pursuant to the specific provisions in the health insurance policy purchased.

Skyrocketing costs in health care spurred public and private reform. The federal Medicare Program introduced diagnosis-related-groups (DRGs) in 1983, which for the first time set predetermined limits on the amounts that Medicare would pay to hospitals for patients with a particular diagnosis. Employers seeking lower health care costs for employees have increasingly chosen managed care options like HMOs and preferred provider organizations (PPOs), both of which use cooperation and joint efforts among patients, health care providers, and payers to manage health care delivery so as to reduce costs by eliminating administrative inefficiency as well as unnecessary medical treatment.

Health care law will continue to be affected by the country's move toward managed care as the predominant health care delivery model. For example, HMOs' potential liability for medical malpractice could increase because many HMOs operate on a "staff model" whereby physicians are explicitly hired as "employees," thus making it easier to demonstrate *respondeat superior* liability for the negligent acts of their physicians. In addition, many HMOs exercise greater control over the discretion of individual physicians with regard not only to primary care but also to specialist referrals and the prescribing of certain drugs. The historical bright line forbidding the corporate practice of medicine is thus blurred even further by managed care.

HMOs operate on a prepaid basis, making monthly capitation (i.e., per patient) payments to participating physicians and physician groups. PPOs operate on a reduced-fee schedule, offering lower fees for patients who seek care from a "preferred provider," who functions both as a primary care doctor and as a gatekeeper for such tasks as specialist referrals. Both use "networks" of physicians and health care providers. The standard duty to provide medical care applies to physicians in these networks, but new issues arise regarding the payment or reimbursement of expenses. Some managed-care plans offer limited "out-of-network" benefits, and some offer none at all. Should an employer change health plans, an employee with an established physician-patient relationship might find that the treating physician is not part of the new provider's network. If the patient cannot or will not cover subsequent medical costs independently, who has the responsibility to secure alternative treatment for the patient? Who should pay for that treatment? These questions have not yet been resolved. Many patients in this situation start over again with a new physician, out of economic necessity, and many are not happy about that involuntary termination of the physician-patient relationship.

Another potential issue for physician networks and "integrated delivery systems" (which include primary care physicians, specialists, and hospitals) is price-fixing, which has traditionally been held to be per se illegal under the Sherman Act. PPOs are under particular scrutiny in this regard, as a PPO is a group of health care providers who agree to discounted fees in exchange for bulk business (e.g., medical care for all of a particular company's employees). These providers are individual economic entities, and as such they must exercise great care in the concerted, joint effort of setting prices and fees, in order to avoid accusations of conspiracy to restrain trade through illegal price-fixing. Likewise, integrated delivery systems must be ever mindful of Clayton Act prohibitions against monopolies, and they must carefully tailor their joint ventures and other agreements to minimize their anticompetitive effects on relevant markets.

Forty-five states have passed so-called Patients' Bill of Rights—legislation to improve patients' rights under private health insurance plans. However, efforts to enact a federal BILL OF RIGHTS have proven unsuccessful. In 2003 the

U.S. Supreme Court, in *Kentucky Association of Health Plans v. Miller*, 538 U.S. 329, 123 S. Ct. 1471, 155 L. Ed. 2d 468 (2003), reviewed a provision of Kentucky's Health Care Reform Act that sought to regulate HMOs. The HMO in the case claimed that Kentucky's law was preempted by the EMPLOYEE RETIREMENT INCOME SECURITY ACT of 1974 (ERISA). The Court disagreed, holding that the Kentucky law regulated insurance, rather than an employee retirement plan, and thus that the ERISA preemption does not apply.

FURTHER READINGS

Jonas, Stephen. Ed. 2007. *An Introduction to the U.S. Health Care System.* 6th ed. New York: Springer.

Pozgar, George. 2006. *Legal Aspects of Health Care Administration.* 10th ed. New York: Jones and Bartlett.

Sultz, Harry & Young, Kristina. 2008. & *Health Care USA: Understanding Its Organization and Delivery.* 6th ed. New York: Jones and Bartlett.

CROSS REFERENCES

Abortion; Animal Rights; Death and Dying; Drugs and Narcotics; Fetal Rights; Fetal Tissue Research; Food and Drug Administration; Physicians and Surgeons.

HEALTH INSURANCE

Health insurance originated in the Blue Cross system that was developed between hospitals and schoolteachers in Dallas in 1929. Blue Cross covered a pre-set amount of hospitalization costs for a flat monthly premium and set its rates according to a "community rating" system: Single people paid one flat rate, families another flat rate, and the economic risk of high hospitalization bills was spread throughout the whole employee group. The only requirement for participation by an employer was that all employees, whether sick or healthy, had to join, again spreading the risk over the whole group. Blue Shield was developed following the same plan to cover ambulatory (i.e., non-hospital) medical care.

The Blue Cross/Blue Shield plans were developed to complement the traditional method of paying for health care, often called "fee-for-service." Under this method, a physician charges a patient directly for services rendered, and the patient is legally responsible for payment. The Blue Cross/Blue Shield plans are called "indemnity plans," meaning they reimburse the patient for medical expenses incurred. Indemnity insurers are not responsible directly to physicians for payment, although physicians typically submit claims information to the insurers as a convenience for their patients. For insured patients in the fee-for-service system, two contracts are created: one between the doctor and the patient, and one between the patient and the insurance company.

Traditional property and casualty insurance companies did not offer health insurance because with traditional rate structures, the risks were great, and the returns uncertain. After the Blue Cross/Blue Shield plans were developed, however, the traditional insurers noted the community rating practices and realized that they could enter the market and attract the healthier community members with lower rates than the community rates. By introducing health screening to identify the healthier individuals, and offering lower rates to younger individuals, these companies were able to lure lower-risk populations to their health plans. This left the Blue Cross/Blue Shield plans with the highest-risk and costliest population to insure. Eventually, the Blue Cross/Blue Shield plans also began using risk-segregation policies and charged higher-risk groups higher premiums.

During the 1960s Congress enacted the MEDICARE program to cover health care costs of older patients, and MEDICAID to cover health care costs of indigent patients (Pub. L. No. 81-97). The federal government administers the Medicare Program and its components: Part A, which covers hospitalization, and Part B, which covers physician and outpatient services. The federal government helps the states fund the Medicaid Program, and the states administer it. Medicare Part A initially covered 100 percent of hospitalization costs, and Medicare Part B covered 80 percent of the usual, customary, and reasonable costs of physician and outpatient care.

Under both the fee-for-service system of health care delivery, where private indemnity insurers charge premiums and pay the bills, and the Medicare-Medicaid system, where taxes fund the programs, and the government pays the bills, the relationship between the patient and the doctor remains distinct. Neither the doctor nor the patient is concerned about the cost of various medical procedures involved, and fees for services are paid without significant oversight by the payers. In fact, if more services are performed by a physician under a fee-for-service system, the result is greater total fees.

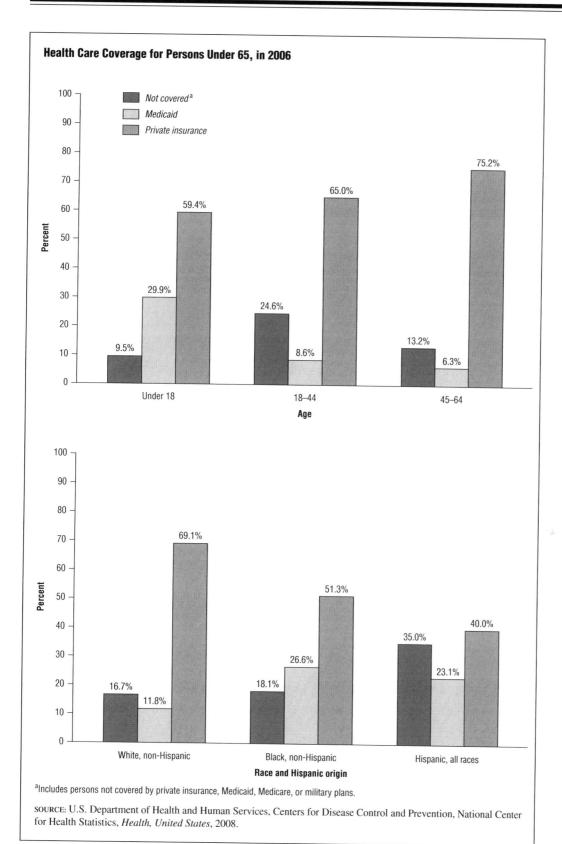

Health Care Coverage for Persons Under 65, in 2006

Legend:
- Not covered[a]
- Medicaid
- Private insurance

Chart 1 — by Age (Percent):

Under 18: Not covered 9.5%, Medicaid 29.9%, Private insurance 59.4%
18–44: Not covered 24.6%, Medicaid 8.6%, Private insurance 65.0%
45–64: Not covered 13.2%, Medicaid 6.3%, Private insurance 75.2%

Chart 2 — by Race and Hispanic origin (Percent):

White, non-Hispanic: Not covered 16.7%, Medicaid 11.8%, Private insurance 69.1%
Black, non-Hispanic: Not covered 18.1%, Medicaid 26.6%, Private insurance 51.3%
Hispanic, all races: Not covered 35.0%, Medicaid 23.1%, Private insurance 40.0%

[a]Includes persons not covered by private insurance, Medicaid, Medicare, or military plans.

SOURCE: U.S. Department of Health and Human Services, Centers for Disease Control and Prevention, National Center for Health Statistics, *Health, United States*, 2008.

ILLUSTRATION BY GGS CREATIVE RESOURCES. REPRODUCED BY PERMISSION OF GALE, A PART OF CENGAGE LEARNING.

From 1960 to 1990, per capita medical costs in the United States rose 1,000 percent, which was four times the rate of inflation. As a consequence, a different way of paying for health care rose to prominence. "Managed care," which had been in existence as long as indemnity health insurance plans, became the health plan of choice among U.S. employers who sought to reduce the premiums paid for their employees' health insurance.

Managed care essentially creates a triangular relationship among the physician, patient (or member), and payer. Managed care refers primarily to a prepaid health-services plan where physicians (or physician groups or other entities) are paid a flat per-member, per-month (PMPM) fee for basic health care services, regardless of whether the patient seeks those services. The risk that a patient is going to require significant treatment shifts from the insurance company to the physicians under this model.

Managed care is a highly regulated industry. It is regulated at the federal level by the Health Maintenance Organization Act of 1973 (Pub. L. No. 93-222) and by the states in which it operates. The health maintenance organization (HMO) is the primary provider of managed care, and it functions according to four basic models:

1. The staff-model HMO employs physicians and providers directly, and they provide services in facilities owned or controlled by the HMO. Physicians under this model are paid a salary (not fees for service) and share equipment and facilities with other physician-employees.

2. The group-model HMO contracts with an organized group of physicians who are not direct employees of the HMO, but who agree to provide basic health care services to the HMO's members in exchange for capitation (i.e., PMPM) payments. The capitation payments must be spread among the physicians under a pre-determined arrangement, and medical records and equipment must be shared.

3. The individual-practice-association (IPA) model HMO is based around an association of individual practitioners who organize to contract with an HMO, and as a result treat the HMO's patients on a discounted fee-for-service basis. Although there is no periodic limit on the amount of payments from the HMO, the physicians in an IPA must have an explicit agreement that determines the distribution of HMO receipts and sets forth the services to be performed.

4. The direct-service contract/network HMO model is the most basic model. Under this variation, an HMO contracts directly with individual providers to provide service to the HMO's patients, on either a capitated or discounted fee-for-service basis.

All four of these models share one very important feature of HMOs: The health care providers may not bill patients directly for services rendered, and they must seek any and all reimbursement from the HMO.

Another form of managed care is the preferred provider organization (PPO). A PPO does not take the place of the traditional fee-for-service provider (as does a staff model HMO) and does not rely on capitated payments to providers. Instead, a PPO contracts with individual providers and groups to create a network of providers. Members of a PPO may choose any physician they wish for medical care, but if they choose a provider in the PPO network, their co-payments—predetermined, fixed amounts paid per visit, regardless of treatment received—are significantly reduced, thus providing the incentive to stay in the network. No federal statutes govern PPOs, but many states regulate their operations. There are three basic PPO models:

1. In a gatekeeper plan, a patient must choose a primary-care provider from the PPO network. This provider tends to most of the patient's health care needs and must authorize any referrals to specialists or other providers. If the patient "self-refers" without authorization, the cost savings of the PPO will not apply.

2. The open-panel plan, on the other hand, allows a patient to see different primary-care physicians and to self-refer within the PPO network. The financial penalties for seeking medical care out of the PPO network are much greater in this less-structured model than in the gatekeeper model.

3. The exclusive-provider plan shifts onto the patient all of the costs of seeking medical care from a non-network provider, and in this respect it is very similar to an HMO plan.

Other forms of health care delivery that encompass features of managed care include point-of-service (POS) plans and physician-hospital organizations (PHOs). A POS plan is a combination of an HMO and an indemnity insurance plan, allowing full coverage within the network of providers and partial coverage outside of it. A patient must choose one primary-care physician and might pay a higher monthly rate to the POS if the physician is not in the HMO network. Another version of the POS plan creates "tiers" of providers, which are rated by cost-effectiveness and quality of patient outcomes. A patient may choose a provider from any tier and then will owe a monthly premium payment set to the level of that tier.

A PHO is very similar to an IPA in that it is an organization among various physicians (or physician groups) and a hospital, set up to contract as a unit with an HMO. Physician-hospital networks, within HMOs or through PHO contracts, further the managed-care mission of "vertical integration," which is the coordination of health care (and payment for that care) from primary care through specialists to acute care and hospitalization.

Managed care has affected Medicare as well as private health care. In 1983 Congress changed the payment system for Medicare, Part A, from a fee-for-service-paid-retroactively system to a prospective payment system, which fixes the amount that the federal government will pay based on a patient's initial diagnosis, not on the costs actually expended (Pub. L. No. 98-369). Medical diagnoses are grouped according to the medical resources that are usually consumed to treat them, and from that grouping is determined a fixed amount that Medicare will pay for each diagnosis. Although this system is applicable only to the acute-care hospital setting, it is clearly an example of shifting the risk of the cost of health care from the payer (in this case, Medicare) to the provider, which is an important element of managed care. In addition, many HMOs now offer Medicare managed-care plans, and many older citizens opt for these plans because of their paperless claims and pre-set co-payments for physician visits and pharmaceuticals.

The most recent development in the area of health insurance is the medical savings account (MSA), a pilot program that was created by the Health Insurance Portability and Accountability Act of 1996 (Pub. L. No. 104-191). The premise behind the MSA is to take the bulk of the financial risk, and premium payments, away from the managed-care and indemnity insurers; and to allow individuals to save money, tax free, in a savings account for use for medical expenses. Individuals or their employers purchase major-medical policies, medical insurance policies with no coverage for medical expenses until the amount paid by the patient exceeds a pre-determined maximum amount, such as $2,500 per year. These policies have extremely high deductibles and correspondingly low monthly premiums. The participants take the money that they would have spent on higher premiums and deposit it in an MSA. This money accrues through monthly deposits and also earns interest, and it can be spent only to pay for medical care. The major-medical policy applies if a certain amount equal to the high deductible is expended or if the account is depleted. MSAs do not incorporate any of the cost-controlling aspects of managed-care organizations, and instead depend on competition among providers for patients (who are generally more cost-conscious about spending their own money) to encourage efficient health-care delivery and to discourage unnecessary expense.

Litigation has resulted from insurance companies seeking to place limits for certain conditions. The decision by the U.S. Court of Appeals for the Seventh Circuit in *Doe and Smith v. Mutual of Omaha Insurance Co.,* 179 F.3d 557 (7th Cir. 1999), cert. denied, 120 S. Ct. 845 (2000), concerns AIDS caps insurance policies. At issue in the case was whether the Americans with Disabilities Act (ADA) covers the content of insurance policies. The plaintiffs, who sued under the pseudonyms John Doe and Richard Smith, argued that Mutual of Omaha Company had discriminated against them by selling them insurance policies with lifetime caps on AIDS-related expenditures. John Doe's policy had a lifetime AIDS cap of $100,000, and Richard Smith's policy had a cap of $25,000. Other health insurance policies sold by the company had lifetime caps for other diseases of $1 million. The Seventh Circuit found that AIDS caps do not violate the ADA. The court found that Doe and Smith had not been discriminated against, because the company had offered them an insurance policy. The ADA, the court determined, would only prohibit Mutual of Omaha from singling out

HEALTHCARE REFORM

Healthcare reform has been a contentious political issue since the 1940s. Whereas most industrialized countries have single-payer systems, where the government administers and finances healthcare, the U.S. system has been built on employer-paid healthcare insurance sold by private companies. Under single-payer plans, such as used in Canada, everyone is provided benefits and no one has to pay deductibles or co-payments. Single-payer plans reduce overhead expenses because the government pays the medical costs directly to the provider, eliminating the middle-person, which in the United States are HEALTH INSURANCE companies. Efforts to establish a single-payer system in the United States have been unsuccessful, as opponents warn of socialized medicine and the loss of free choice. Meanwhile, healthcare costs rise every year, putting financial strains on employers and their employees. More than 47 million people in the United States did not have health insurance in 2009. By the 2008 presidential election, healthcare reform was a hot political topic. The election of BARACK OBAMA as president meant that healthcare legislation would be on the congressional agenda in 2009. As the year unfolded, five committees in the House and Senate worked on reform plans. By the end of 2009, it appeared likely that a major reform will would be passed in early 2010.

In the late 1940s, President HARRY TRUMAN proposed that the United States adopt a single-payer plan. His proposal went nowhere, and healthcare remained an issue left to state regulation and the marketplace. The passage of the MEDICARE Act in 1965 inserted the federal government into healthcare, paying for the healthcare of all citizens 65 and older. Medicare was opposed by Republicans, who believed it was a major step toward single-payer, socialized medicine. Medicare proved, however, to be a popular program; though the program is government-run, senior citizens have the ability to choose healthcare providers.

The healthcare debate rekindled with the election of BILL CLINTON as president in 1992. His wife, HILLARY RODHAM CLINTON, led a White House committee that drafted a reform initiative. The result was a complex proposal that sought to guarantee universal coverage by requiring employers to insure all full-time workers. The plan would have established a national health board and a government agency that would have set the maximum amount health insurers could increase premiums each year. Employers and insurance companies mounted an effective lobbying campaign that killed off the proposal.

From the mid-1990s to the 2008 presidential campaign, there was much talk about healthcare reform, but neither major party displayed interest in proposing comprehensive reform. They noted that Clinton's failure to pass his proposal weakened him politically and contributed to the Republicans taking over the House of Representatives for the first time since the late 1940s. Congress did pass in 1997 the State Children's Health Insurance Program (SCHIP), which provides matching funds to states to pay for health insurance for families with children. In 2009 the program was given a large infusion of money, so as to insure millions more. Nevertheless, more persons complained that they could not afford health insurance premiums or that they were denied coverage for a pre-existing medical condition. A significant number of individuals filed for BANKRUPTCY due to medical bills for catastrophic illnesses. Reforms at the state level proved difficult to combat these problems.

Republicans argued that the best way to reform healthcare was to open the market. As of late 2009, each state regulates insurers. Some states have stronger regulations than others, but the overall effect has been a lack of competition; insurers select the states that they find most beneficial and ignore the rest. Republicans, such as 2008 presidential nominee Senator JOHN MCCAIN, proposed that state regulation be relaxed so a person in Minnesota could have the choice of buying a healthcare policy from any insurer in the country. In addition, he proposed moving from the employer-based model to an expanded federal healthcare savings account system that would be combined with federal subsidies and tax breaks.

However, there was movement toward some type of government solution that mandated universal coverage. The state of Massachusetts enacted healthcare reform in 2006. Under the plan, almost all residents are required to purchase healthcare coverage. If they fail to comply, residents must pay a penalty. By 2008, 439,000 previously uninsured residents had insurance. Employers with more than ten employees are required to make a "fair and reasonable contribution" to the payment of health premiums. The costs of the program were higher than anticipated, but by 2009

disabled people and refusing to sell them insurance. The court ruled that the ADA did not prohibit the company from offering disabled parties insurance policies with different terms and conditions from other people. The court held the plaintiffs were not denied a policy because they had AIDS but rather were denied coverage for certain AIDS treatments.

only 4.1 percent of Massachusetts residents lacked health insurance, the lowest rate in the United States.

President Obama put healthcare at the top of his agenda when he entered the White House. Though he sought a plan with universal coverage, cost controls, and tougher regulations of health insurance practices, he did not propose a specific plan but left it to Congress to determine the details. Seeking to avoid the Clinton debacle, Obama gambled that Congress could write a comprehensive plan with bipartisan support. As the year progressed and competing ideas surfaced, it became clear that virtually all Republicans would oppose legislation written by the Democratic majorities in the House and Senate. However, moderate and conservative Democrats also raised concerns about the scope and cost of the proposals that were in five committees.

By March 2009 the committee chairs had reached consensus on what the legislation should contain. Like Massachusetts, the plan would require universal coverage and carry penalties for those who do not comply. The health insurance industry insisted on this element, as millions of healthy young adults who will not use healthcare much would pay for the increased costs that would come with insurance reforms. Such reforms included preventing insurers from dropping sick policy holders, denying claims and coverage for pre-existing conditions, and removing yearly and life-time caps on benefits.

Another major component of the emerging proposal was the creation of health insurance exchanges. The exchanges would introduce competition into the private health insurance market. An individual with no coverage, the self-employed, and small business owners would purchase coverage from one of the companies in an exchange. The exchange would have competing providers offering different plans with varying benefit levels

and prices. Insurers would not be able to discriminate based on a person's health history or future risk. Plans would have to be certified as meeting a minimum level of comprehensiveness. The hope was that competition would drive down healthcare costs because the exchanges, with thousands or millions of participants, would leverage the same bargaining power as large employers.

However, one contentious issue began to dominate the debate: the public option. House Democrats proposed that the government compete with private insurers for the same pool of people in the health insurance exchange. Advocates believed the only way to generate meaningful competition and lower costs was for the government to enter the market. Economies of scale and bargaining power, coupled with the fact that the government would not have to earn a profit for shareholders, meant that a public option would be a serious competitor. Opposition to the public option from the health-care industry, Republicans, and some Democrats, especially in the Senate, put reform in doubt as the summer of 2009 progressed. Some influential Democratic senators announced that the public option would not be in the final bill, whereas some House Democrats insisted they would not vote for any reform bill that did not contain it.

On November 7, 2009, the House passed its healthcare bill on a vote of 220-215, which indicated a number of conservative Democrats opposed it. To achieve passage, Speaker of the House Nancy Pelosi agreed to several compromises to gain some conservative Democrat votes. One restricted ABORTION coverage in subsidized plans. Another change barred the public option plan from offering rates just above what Medicare pays; instead, it would have to negotiate rates as insurers do. The CONGRESSIONAL BUDGET OFFICE (CBO) projected the plan would reduce the federal deficit over the next ten years by $109 billion.

The Senate debate began in late November and concluded with an early morning vote on December 24, 2009. Though the Democratic majority is 60 seats, several conservative Democrats objected to the public option and refused to vote for the bill if it contained such a provision. As an alternative, a group of senators floated the idea of people ages 55 to 64 "buying in" to Medicare. The opposition of Senator Joseph Lieberman killed that idea. Senator Ben Nelson became the last holdout, the sixtieth vote. The conservative from Nebraska forced the removal of a provision that would have stripped the insurance industry of its antitrust exemption. He also forced the addition of language that gives states the right to block plans covering abortion coverage from their health exchanges.

The final vote, 60 to 39, was a major victory for President Obama yet potential roadblocks lay ahead. Because the two bills differed, a conference committee was to meet in early January 2010 to reconcile differences. Commentators expected House Democrats to drop the public option and work towards a final bill that would satisfy conservative Senate Democrats. If the legislation were to be enacted, many of its key provisions would not begin until 2014. Even if enacted, 24 million people would remain uninsured in 2019, with about one-third of them illegal immigrants.

In March 2010, President Obama signed health insurance reform legislation (P.L. 111-148, the Patient Protection and Affordability Act of 2010).

FURTHER READINGS

Jonas, Stephen, ed. 2007. *An Introduction to the U.S. Health Care System.* 6th ed. New York: Springer.

Pozgar, George. 2006. *Legal Aspects of Health Care Administration.* 10th ed. New York: Jones and Bartlett.

Sultz, Harry, and Kristina Young. 2008. *Health Care USA: Understanding Its Organization and Delivery.* 6th ed. New York: Jones and Bartlett.

Federal health care reform has been a contentious issue since the early 1990s. The Clinton administration's reform efforts failed, and the issue was not a major focus of either major political party until the 2008 presidential election. President BARACK OBAMA signed into law in February 2009 the Children's Health Insurance Program Reauthorization Act of 2009, better known as the State Children's Health Insurance Program or SCHIP. The law continues health insurance coverage for six to seven million children and increases that coverage to four million more children. President Obama also asked Congress to work with him to pass comprehensive health care reform in 2009, with the goal of providing affordable health insurance to every American. Such an effort would involve massive government funding and oversight. Republican leaders in Congress have advocated a different approach, which would move away from employer-paid health insurance. Instead, individuals and families would be given tax-credits, which would be used to purchase health insurance. Proponents argue that this is a less expensive approach and that it would not involve the government.

In March 2010, President Obama signed health insurance reform legislation (P.L. 111-148, the Patient Protection and Affordability Act of 2010).

FURTHER READINGS

Jonas, Stephen, ed. 2007. *An Introduction to the U.S. Health Care System.* 6th ed. New York: Springer.

Pozgar, George. 2006. *Legal Aspects of Health Care Administration.* 10th ed. New York: Jones and Bartlett.

Sultz, Harry & Young, Kristina. 2008. & *Health Care USA: Understanding Its Organization and Delivery.* 6th ed. New York: Jones and Bartlett.

CROSS REFERENCES

Health Care Law; Physicians and Surgeons.

HEALTH MAINTENANCE ORGANIZATION

See HEALTH CARE LAW; HEALTH INSURANCE; MANAGED CARE.

HEARING

A legal proceeding where an issue of law or fact is tried and evidence is presented to help determine the issue.

Hearings resemble trials in that they ordinarily are held publicly and involve opposing parties. They differ from trials in that they feature more relaxed standards of evidence and procedure, and take place in a variety of settings before a broader range of authorities (judges, examiners, and lawmakers). Hearings fall into three broad categories: judicial, administrative, and legislative. Judicial hearings are tailored to suit the issue at hand and the appropriate stage at which a legal proceeding stands.

Administrative hearings cover matters of rule making and the adjudication of individual cases. Legislative hearings occur at both the federal and state levels and are generally conducted to find facts and survey public opinion. They encompass a wide range of issues relevant to law, government, society, and public policy.

Judicial hearings take place prior to a trial in both civil and criminal cases. Ex parte hearings provide a forum for only one side of a dispute, as in the case of a TEMPORARY RESTRAINING ORDER, whereas adversary hearings involve both parties. Preliminary hearings, also called preliminary examinations, are conducted when a person has been charged with a crime. Held before a magistrate or judge, a PRELIMINARY HEARING is used to determine whether the evidence is sufficient to justify detaining the accused or discharging the accused on bail. Closely related are detention hearings, which can also determine whether to detain a juvenile. Suppression hearings take place before trial at the request of an attorney seeking to have illegally obtained or irrelevant evidence kept out of trial.

Administrative hearings are conducted by state and federal agencies. Rule-making hearings evaluate and determine appropriate regulations, and adjudicatory hearings try matters of fact in individual cases. The former are commonly used to garner opinion on matters that affect the public—as, for example, when the ENVIRONMENTAL PROTECTION AGENCY (EPA) considers changing its rules. The latter commonly take place when an individual is charged with violating rules that come under the agency's jurisdiction—for example, violating a pollution regulation of the EPA, or, if incarcerated, violating behavior standards set for prisoners by the Department of Corrections.

Some blurring of this distinction occurs, which is important given the generally more relaxed standards that apply to some administrative hearings. The degree of formality required of an administrative hearing is determined by the liberty interest at stake: The greater that interest, the more formal the hearing. Notably, rules limiting the admissibility of evidence are looser in administrative hearings than in trials. Adjudicatory hearings can admit, for example, hearsay that generally would not be permitted at trial. (Hearsay is a statement by a witness who does not appear in person, offered by a third party who does appear.) The Administrative Procedure

Act (APA) (5 U.S.C.A. § 551 et seq.) governs administrative hearings by federal agencies, and state laws largely modeled upon the APA govern state agencies. These hearings are conducted by a civil servant called a HEARING EXAMINER at the state level and known as an administrative law judge at the federal level.

Legislative hearings occur in state legislatures and in the U.S. Congress, and are a function of legislative committees. They are commonly public events, held whenever a lawmaking body is contemplating a change in law, during which advocates and opponents air their views. Because of their controversial nature, they often are covered extensively by the media.

Not all legislative hearings consider changes in legislation; some examine allegations of wrongdoing. Although lawmaking bodies do not have a judicial function, they retain the power to discipline their members, a key function of state and federal ethics committees. Fact finding is ostensibly the reason for congressional hearings into public scandals. Often, however, critics will argue that these hearings are staged for attacking political opponents. Throughout the twentieth century, legislative hearings have been used to investigate such things as allegations of Communist infiltration of government and industry (the House Un-American Activities Committee hearings) and abuses of power by the EXECUTIVE BRANCH (the WATERGATE and WHITEWATER hearings).

CROSS REFERENCE

Administrative Law and Procedure.

HEARING EXAMINER

An employee of an administrative agency who is charged with conducting adjudicative proceedings on matters within the scope of the jurisdiction of the agency.

Hearing examiners are employees of federal, state, and local administrative agencies who act as judges to resolve conflicts that are within the jurisdiction of their particular agency. Hearing examiners have also been called hearing officers, and since the 1980s, they are commonly referred to as administrative law judges (ALJs).

The growth of administrative law started with the creation of the federal INTERSTATE COMMERCE COMMISSION and the FEDERAL TRADE COMMISSION in the late nineteenth century.

Administrative law burgeoned in the 1930s, as President Franklin D. Roosevelt's NEW DEAL policies led to the establishment of EXECUTIVE BRANCH agencies that were charged with regulating the economy and overseeing social welfare policies. Since the 1930s, all levels of government have established administrative agencies.

ALJs are governed by the Administrative Procedure Act (5 U.S.C.A. § 551 et seq. [1966]). They are appointed through a professional merit selection system that requires high test scores and, in many instances, experience in the particular regulatory program in which they wish to serve. Once appointed, ALJs may not be removed or disciplined, except for GOOD CAUSE. These parameters are meant to shield administrative law from political appointments and political pressure.

Hearing examiners serve in different adjudicative areas and are involved in all types of government activity, from the administration of environmental regulations to the review of UNEMPLOYMENT COMPENSATION claims. For example, when an agency is charged with issuing permits, appropriate procedures are set out in administrative regulations. If there are objections to the granting of a permit, a hearing may be held to determine the merits of the application. A HEARING EXAMINER conducts the hearing, enforces appropriate rules of evidence and procedure, and issues a decision. This decision may be appealed to a higher level of authority in the agency, and if that does not resolve the issue, to a court proceeding in the judicial branch.

Even though they are not as insulated from political pressures as judicial branch judges, hearing examiners seek to maintain their independence. During the Reagan administration, in the 1980s, this independence was challenged in the SOCIAL SECURITY Administration's (SSA's) disability review section. SSA officials, concerned with perceived inconsistencies and inaccuracies in disability rulings, singled out for review federal ALJs who rendered the highest percentage of decisions favorable to claimants. The review program received much criticism for allegedly putting subtle pressure on the ALJs to rule against claimants more often. Though the most intrusive features of the program were abandoned, the program itself served as a reminder that ALJs were part of an administrative agency and not independent, judicial branch decision makers.

HEARSAY

A statement made out of court that is offered in court as evidence to prove the truth of the matter asserted.

It is the job of the judge or jury in a court proceeding to determine whether evidence offered as proof is credible. Three evidentiary rules help the judge or jury make this determination: (1) Before being allowed to testify, a witness generally must swear or affirm that his or her testimony will be truthful. (2) The witness must be personally present at the trial or proceeding in order to allow the judge or jury to observe the testimony firsthand. (3) The witness is subject to CROSS-EXAMINATION at the option of any party who did not call the witness to testify.

In keeping with the three evidentiary requirements, the Hearsay Rule, as outlined in the FEDERAL RULES OF EVIDENCE, prohibits most statements made outside a courtroom from being used as evidence in court. This is because statements made out of court normally are not made under oath, a judge or jury cannot personally observe the demeanor of someone who makes a statement outside the courtroom, and an opposing party cannot cross-examine such a declarant (the person making the statement). Out-of-court statements hinder the ability of the judge or jury to probe testimony for inaccuracies caused by ambiguity, insincerity, faulty perception, or erroneous memory. Thus, statements made out of court are perceived as untrustworthy.

Hearsay comes in many forms. It may be a written or oral statement; it also includes gestures. Essentially anything intended to assert a fact is considered a statement for the purposes of the Hearsay Rule. A nodding of the head may be a silent assertion of the word *yes*. A witness pointing to a gun may be asserting, "That is the MURDER weapon." Even silence has been accepted as a statement, as when a passengers' failure to complain was offered to prove that a train car was not too cold (*Silver v. New York Central Railroad*, 329 Mass. 14, 105 N.E.2d 923 [1952]).

Not all out-of-court statements or assertions are impermissible hearsay. If an attorney wishes the judge or jury to consider the fact that a certain statement was made, but not the truthfulness of that statement, the statement is not hearsay and may be admitted as evidence. Suppose a hearing is held to determine a woman's mental competence. Out of court, when asked to identify herself, the woman said, "I am the pope." There is little question that the purpose of introducing that statement as evidence is not to convince the judge or jury that the woman actually is the pope; the truthfulness of the statement is irrelevant. Rather, the statement is introduced to show the woman's mental state; her belief that she is the pope may prove that she is not mentally competent. In contrast, a defendant's out-of-court statement "I am the murderer," offered in a murder trial to prove that the DEFENDANT is the murderer, is hearsay.

The Federal Rules of Evidence outline the various types of statements that are excluded by the Hearsay Rule, and are thus admissible in court. These exceptions apply to circumstances believed to produce trustworthy assertions. Some hearsay exceptions are based on whether the declarant of the statement is available to testify. For example, a witness who has died is unavailable. A witness who claims some sort of testimonial privilege, such as the ATTORNEY-CLIENT PRIVILEGE, is also unavailable to testify, as is the witness who testifies to lack of memory regarding the subject matter, or is too physically or mentally ill to testify. These definitions fall under Rule 804 of the Federal Rules of Evidence. There are also situations where hearsay is allowed even though the declarant is available as a witness. These situations are outlined under Rule 803 of the Federal Rules of Evidence.

Hearsay Exceptions: Declarant Unavailable

1. ***Former Testimony***. Testimony given as a witness at another hearing in the same or a different proceeding, or in a deposition, is admissible when the declarant is unavailable, provided the party against whom the testimony is now being offered had the opportunity to question or cross-examine the witness (Fed. R. Evid. 804(b1)).

2. ***Statement Under Belief of Impending Death***. A statement made by a declarant who, when making the statement, believed death to be imminent, is admissible to show the cause or circumstances of the death. For example, the statement "Horace shot me," made moments before the declarant died, is admissible for the purpose of proving

that Horace committed murder (Fed. R. Evid. 804(b2)).

3. **Statement against Interest**. A statement that, at the time of its making, was contrary to the declarant's pecuniary or proprietary interest, or that subjected the declarant to civil or criminal liability, is admissible if the declarant is unavailable to testify. For example, the statement "I never declare all my income on my tax returns" could subject the declarant to criminal tax FRAUD liability, and is thus an admissible statement against interest (Fed. R. Evid. 804(b3)).

4. **Statement of Personal or Family History**. A statement concerning the declarant's own birth, adoption, MARRIAGE, divorce, legitimacy, or similar fact of personal family history is admissible hearsay when the declarant is unavailable to testify (Fed. R. Evid. 804(b4)).

Hearsay Exceptions: Availability of Declarant Immaterial

1. **Present Sense Impression**. "A statement describing or explaining an event or condition made while the declarant was perceiving the event or condition, or immediately thereafter," is admissible hearsay (Fed. R. Evid. 803(1)). An example is the statement "That green pickup truck is going to run that red light."

2. **Excited Utterance**. "A statement relating to a startling event or condition made while the declarant was under the stress of excitement caused by the event or condition" is admissible hearsay (Fed. R. Evid. 803(2)). For example, "The robber is pointing a gun at the cop!" is admissible.

3. **Then Existing Mental, Emotional, or Physical Condition**. A statement of the declarant's then existing intent, plan, motive, design, mental feeling, pain, or bodily health is admissible (Fed. R. Evid. 803(3)). Generally, however, a statement of memory or belief to prove the fact remembered or believed is not. For example, "After eating at that restaurant, I'm feeling rather ill" could be admitted under this exception. But the out-of-court statement "I believe Julie to be the murderer" would not be admitted under this exception.

4. **Statements for Purposes of Medical Diagnosis or Treatment**. A statement describing medical history, or past or present symptoms, pain, or sensations, or the general character of the cause or external source of those symptoms, is admissible (Fed. R. Evid. 803(4)). For example, this statement made to a physician following an accident is admissible: "I slipped and fell on the ice, and then my left leg became numb."

5. **Recorded Recollection**. "A memorandum or record concerning a matter about which a witness once had knowledge but now has insufficient recollection to enable the witness to testify fully and accurately" is admissible (Fed. R. Evid. 803(5)). The record must have been made when the matter was fresh in the witness's memory and must reflect that knowledge correctly. One example is a detailed phone message.

6. **Business Records**. A record, report, or memo of a business activity made by an individual who regularly conducts the business activity is exempt from the hearsay prohibition under this rule (Fed. R. Evid. 803(6). Written minutes of a business meeting are a common example. The normal absence of information contained in these types of business records may also be excluded from the hearsay prohibition (Fed. R. Evid. 803(7)).

7. **Public Records and Reports**. A record, report, statement, or data compilation, in any form, of a public office or agency, setting forth the activities of the office or agency or matters for which there is a legal duty to report, is admissible. Voting records of a city council are an example. Matters observed by law enforcement personnel in criminal cases are excluded under this rule (Fed. R. Evid. 803(8)).

8. **Records of Vital Statistic**. A data compilation, in any form, of births, fetal deaths, other deaths, or marriages, if the report is made to a public office pursuant to requirements of the law, is a hearsay exception (Fed. R. Evid. 803(9)).

9. **Records of Religious Organizations**. A statement contained in a regularly kept record of a religious organization may be exempt from the prohibition against

hearsay. Some examples are statements of birth, marriage, divorce, death, legitimacy, ancestry, relationship by blood or marriage, or similar facts of personal or family history (Fed. R. Evid. 803(11)).

10. ***Marriage, Baptismal, and Similar Certificates***. "Statements of fact contained in a certificate that the maker performed a marriage or other ceremony or administered a sacrament, made by a clergyman, public official, or other person authorized by the rules or practices of a religious organization or by law to perform the act certified, and purporting to have been issued at the time of the act or within a REASONABLE TIME thereafter," are admissible (Fed. R. Evid. 803(12)).

11. ***Family Records***. "Statements of fact concerning personal or family history contained in family Bibles, genealogies, charts, engravings on rings, inscriptions on family portraits, engravings on urns, crypts, or tombstones" are hearsay exceptions (Fed. R. Evid. 803(13)).

12. ***Records of Documents Affecting an Interest in Property***. A record purporting to establish or affect an interest in property, such as a notice of a tax lien placed on a house, is admissible hearsay if the record is a record of a public office and an applicable statute authorizes the recording of documents of that kind in that office.

13. ***Statements in Ancient Documents***. A statement in a document in existence 20 years or more, the authenticity of which is established, is admissible hearsay. One example is a statement in a letter written 30 years ago, provided the letter's authenticity can be proved.

14. ***Market Reports, Commercial Publications***. "Market quotations, tabulations, lists, directories, or other published compilations, generally used and relied upon by the public or by persons in particular occupations," are exceptions to the rule against hearsay (Fed. R. Evid. 803 (17)).

15. ***Learned Treatises***. Statements contained in a published treatise, periodical, or pamphlet on a subject of history, medicine, or other science or art, established as a reliable authority by the testimony or admission of an expert witness, are admissible (Fed. R. Evid. 803(18)).

16. ***Reputation Concerning Personal or Family History***. A reputation among members of a person's family by blood, adoption, or marriage, or among a person's associates, or in the community, concerning the person's birth, adoption, marriage, divorce, death, ancestry, or legitimacy is an exception to the rule against hearsay. For example, the out-of-court statement "My sister was adopted," although hearsay, is admissible (Fed. R. Evid. 803 (19)).

17. ***Reputation Concerning Boundaries or General History***. "Reputation in a community, arising before the controversy, as to boundaries of or customs affecting lands in the community, and reputation as to events of general history important to the community or state or nation in which located," are admissible (Fed. R. Evid. 803(20)). For example, "Stein's land extends south to the river" involves the reputation of a land's boundary and falls within this exception.

18. ***Reputation as to Character***. The "reputation of a person's character among associates or in the community" is admissible hearsay (Fed. R. Evid. 803(21)). One example is the statement "Sergei has never said a dishonest word."

19. ***Judgment of Previous Conviction***. A PLEA or judgment of guilt for a crime punishable by death or imprisonment of more than one year is admissible hearsay (Fed. R. Evid. 803(22)).

Hearsay Exceptions When the Declarant Is Unavailable to Testify

1. ***Former Testimony***. Testimony given as a witness at another hearing in the same or a different proceeding, or in a deposition, is admissible when the declarant is unavailable, provided the party against whom the testimony is now being offered had the opportunity to question or cross-examine the witness (Fed. R. Evid. 804(1)).

2. ***A Statement Made under the Belief of Impending Death***. A statement made by a declarant who, when making the statement, believed death to be imminent, is admissible

Nicole Brown Simpson's Journals: Inadmissible as Hearsay

During the 1995 criminal trial of O. J. Simpson, the prosecution argued that Simpson killed his former wife Nicole Brown Simpson, and that the murder was the culmination of a long pattern of domestic violence. The prosecution discovered in a safe-deposit box journals that Brown Simpson had written concerning her problems with Simpson. The journals contained graphic language and described episodes of physical violence and threats committed by Simpson. They appeared to be a powerful demonstration of the couple's relationship, yet they were never entered into evidence at the criminal trial, and Simpson was acquitted in the killings of his former wife and her friend Ronald Lyle Goldman.

The journals were inadmissible because they constituted hearsay evidence. The rules of evidence are generally the same in every state and federal jurisdiction. In California, where Simpson's criminal trial was held, hearsay evidence cannot be admitted unless it meets the requirements of a well-defined exception.

Oral hearsay (what one person tells another about a third person) is the same as written hearsay. In her journal Brown Simpson told readers what Simpson did to her. With her death, there was no way for the defense to challenge her memory, perception, and sincerity about what she had written. The rules of evidence view such nonchallengeable out-of-court statements as unreliable when they are intended to prove the truth of the matter they assert—here, that Simpson had beaten Brown Simpson, stalked her, and made her fear for her life.

For the same reasons, the journals were not admitted at Simpson's civil trial in 1997, in which he was found liable for the wrongful deaths of Brown Simpson and Goldman.

CROSS REFERENCE

Simpson, O. J.

to show the cause or circumstances of the death. For example, the statement "Horace shot me," made moments before the declarant died, is admissible for the purpose of proving that Horace committed murder (Fed. R. Evid. 804(2)).

3. *A Statement against the Declarant's Interest.* A statement that, at the time of its making, was contrary to the declarant's pecuniary or proprietary interest, or that subjected the declarant to civil or criminal liability, is admissible if the declarant is unavailable to testify. For example, the statement "I never declare all my income on my tax returns" could subject the declarant to criminal tax fraud liability, and is thus an admissible statement against interest (Fed. R. Evid. 804(3)).

4. *A Statement of Personal or Family History.* A statement concerning the declarant's own birth, adoption, marriage, divorce, legitimacy, or similar fact of personal family history is admissible hearsay when the declarant is unavailable to testify (Fed. R. Evid. 804(4)).

FURTHER READINGS

Binder, David F. 2002–2008. *Hearsay Handbook.* Eagan, MN: West.

Cleary, Edward W., ed. 1987. *McCormick on Evidence.* 5th ed. Eagan, MN: West.

Darden, Christopher, with Jess Walter. 1996. *In Contempt.* New York: HarperCollins.

Fenner, G. Michael. 2009. *The Hearsay Rule.* Durham, NC: Carolina Academic.

Friedman, Richard D. 1998. "Truth and Its Rivals in the Law of Hearsay and Confrontation." *Hastings Law Journal* 49 (March).

Kessel, Gordon Van. 1998. "Hearsay Hazards in the American Criminal Trial: An Adversary-Oriented Approach." *Hastings Law Journal* 49 (March).

Waltz, Jon R., and Roger C. Park. 2009. *Evidence: Cases and Materials.* 11th ed. New York: Foundation.

Ziemer, David. 2002. "Hearsay Statements Must Be Considered Individually." *Wisconsin Law Journal* (October 2).

HEARST, PATTY

In the 1990s she could be seen in John Waters's motion picture *Crybaby,* and heard as an off-screen caller to a radio talk show on the TV series *Frasier.* She had appeared on the runways of Paris as a fashion model, wearing a sequined evening gown designed by friend Thierry Mugler. Her story had been told as a movie, *Patty Hearst,* in which she was played by Natasha Richardson, and even as an opera, Anthony Davis's *Tania.* Ever since the 1970s, Patricia Campbell Hearst has been very much in the public eye.

On February 4, 1974, Hearst, the 19-year-old daughter of Randolph A. Hearst and Catherine C. Hearst, of the Hearst newspaper chain, was kidnapped by a tiny group of political extremists who called themselves the Symbionese Liberation Army (SLA). They locked Hearst in a closet for many weeks, where she was taunted, sexually assaulted, and raped repeatedly. The SLA held her for an unusual form of ransom: They demanded that the Hearst family distribute millions of dollars of food to poor and needy people of the San Francisco Bay area. Although the Hearsts complied with this and other SLA demands, the young woman did not return to her parents. Instead, she sent them a tape recording in which she announced that she had decided to become a revolutionary, join the SLA, and go underground.

On April 15, 1974, the members of the SLA, accompanied by Hearst, robbed the Hibernia Bank in San Francisco. A month later, a botched shoplifting attempt at a sporting goods store by SLA members Bill Harris and Emily Harris led the police to the SLA hideout. A gunfight ensued, and all six SLA members inside at the time were killed. Only Hearst, the Harrises, and Wendy Yoshimura survived.

Sixteen months later, and 18 months after her abduction, Hearst was arrested by the FEDERAL BUREAU OF INVESTIGATION after an investigation that had covered the entire United States. She was tried by jury for armed bank ROBBERY, convicted, and sentenced to seven years in prison. On February 1, 1979, after Hearst had served approximately two years of the original sentence, President JIMMY CARTER, stopping short of a full pardon, commuted her sentence.

Hearst claimed at her 1976 federal trial for armed bank robbery that she had, in fact, undergone no political conversion. She claimed that even as she stood in the Hibernia Bank cradling a rifle in her arms, she remained the same person who, only a few months earlier, had chosen the china and crystal patterns for her upcoming marriage. Her defense, orchestrated by her attorneys, F. Lee Bailey and Albert Johnson, was that she had been brainwashed. This defense did not exist in law and had only been attempted in "collaboration-with-the-enemy" charges against U.S. prisoners of war during the KOREAN WAR. As in the Korean War cases, the Hearst attorneys were forced to add a defense that was allowed by law: duress. The crux of the defense's case was that Hearst, owing to brainwashing or coercion, had not had criminal intent when she participated in the bank robbery.

Three defense psychiatrists testified that the DEFENDANT had not been responsible for her actions; two prosecution psychiatrists testified that she had been responsible. The young woman testified that she had been in fear of her life as she stood inside the Hibernia Bank. The judge instructed the jurors,

> You are free to accept or reject the defendant's own account of her experience with her captors.... Duress or coercion may provide a legal excuse for the crime charged against her. But a compulsion must be present and immediate...a well-founded fear of death or bodily injury with no possible escape from the compulsion.

The jury found her guilty BEYOND A REASON-ABLE DOUBT, thereby implicitly stating its belief that she had acted intentionally and voluntarily in robbing the Hibernia Bank; she had been neither brainwashed nor forced to participate.

In August 1987 Hearst filed a petition for a pardon before President RONALD REAGAN. Her attorney, George Martinez, stated that "she wants to put it all behind her. And she wants to get some indication that there is now complete understanding by the government of the extraordinary circumstances under which she participated" in the Hibernia Bank robbery. In 1977, as governor of California, Reagan had called for executive CLEMENCY for Hearst; he was thus considered Hearst's best chance for a pardon. But Reagan left office in 1988 without granting the pardon. Hearst's petition then fell to George H. W. Bush, who also failed to grant the pardon. Hearst finally received her pardon when she was among a list of controversial people, including Marc Rich, that President BILL CLINTON pardoned on his last day in office.

In 1996 Hearst was a member of the Screen Actors Guild and lived just 50 miles outside of Manhattan with her husband and former bodyguard, Bernard Shaw, and her two children. In 2004 the documentary *Guerrilla: The Taking of Patty Hearst* was released, which told the story of Hearst and the SLA within the context of the 1970s.

FURTHER READINGS

Bancroft, David P. 1985. *Post Traumatic Stress Disorders, and Brainwashing as State of Mind Defenses in Criminal, and Civil Fraud Cases,* by David P. Bancroft. In Litigation and Administrative Practice Course Handbook series: Criminal Law and Urban Problems, PLI order no. C4-4174.

"Clinton Defends Pardons, Saying Individuals 'Paid in Full' for Crimes." 2001. *CNN* Web site (January 21). Available online at http://www.cnn.com/2001/ALLPO-LITICS/stories/01/21/clinton.pardons; website home page: http://www.cnn.com (accessed July 29, 2009).

Freedman, Suzanne. 2002. *The Bank Robbery Trial of Heiress Patty Hearst: A Headline Court Case.* Berkeley Heights, NJ: Enslow.

HEART BALM ACTS

Statutes that abrogate or restrict lawsuits brought by individuals who seek pecuniary damages to salve their broken hearts.

Heart balm actions are founded on the precept that the law disfavors any intrusion with the marital relationship or family ties. Such suits include actions for BREACH OF MARRIAGE PROMISE, ALIENATION OF AFFECTION, CRIMINAL CONVERSATION, and seduction.

Breach of Marriage Promise

Breach of promise actions are based on the theory that a promise made should be kept. A subscription to this principle, however, defeats the purpose of the engagement period prior to MARRIAGE that is designed to determine whether or not the couple is sufficiently compatible to get married. In certain situations, however, one party might take advantage of the other, as where a woman becomes engaged to a man merely for the purpose of gaining access to substantial wealth. In such cases, breach of promise actions can be utilized to compensate the individual who has been injured from such a relationship. A number of states, however, have eliminated breach of marriage promise suits.

Alienation of Affection and Criminal Conversation

A legal action may be brought against an individual who intrudes upon a marital relationship. Alienation of affection means interfering in such manner as to win away the love of a husband or wife from his or her spouse.

Criminal conversation is ADULTERY. Conversation is used to mean sexual relations in this context. These actions were designed to protect the sanctity of marriage and the family relationship. In the early 2000s, suits for alienation of affection and criminal conversation have been abolished in most states.

Seduction

The right to sue for seduction belonged to a father who could bring an action against a man who had sexual relations with his daughter.

At common law, the daughter did not ordinarily have the right to sue on her own behalf. A woman who was seduced by a marriage promise could sue for breach of promise if the marriage did not take place. If she became sexually involved with a man due to force or duress, she might be able to bring action for RAPE or ASSAULT. The general rule was, however, that regardless of whether the woman was an adult or a minor, her seduction was regarded as an injury to her father.

In early cases, a father was permitted to be awarded pecuniary damages only as compensation for services that he lost as a result of the seduction. Subsequently, fathers were also allowed to recover COMPENSATORY DAMAGES for medical expenses, as well as damages for distress or sorrow.

Seduction suits are very seldom brought in modern times and have been abolished by some states. One of the primary reasons for this is that they publicize the individual's humiliation.

Limitations on Heart Balm Actions

A majority of judges and legal scholars are in agreement that all heart balm suits should be eliminated. Most states have enacted heart balm statutes that place limitations upon the amount of recovery. The ABOLITION of heart balm suits does not, however, prevent either individual from recovering gifts made in contemplation of marriage. Many states have ruled that gifts, such as engagement rings, must be recovered if the promise to marry is revoked.

HEAT OF PASSION

A phrase used in criminal law to describe an intensely emotional state of mind induced by a type of provocation that would cause a reasonable person to act on impulse or without reflection.

A finding that a person who killed another acted in the heat of passion will reduce MURDER to MANSLAUGHTER under certain circumstances. The essential prerequisites for such a reduction are that the accused must be provoked to a point of great anger or rage, such that the person loses his or her normal capacity for self-control; the circumstances must be such that a REASONABLE PERSON, faced with the same degree of PROVOCATION, would react in a similar manner; and finally, there must not have been an opportunity for the accused to have "cooled off" or regained self-control during the period between the provocation and the killing.

The RULE OF LAW that adequate provocation may reduce murder to manslaughter was developed by the English courts. It was a means of avoiding the severity of the death penalty, a fixed punishment for murder under the common law, when the act of killing was caused by natural human weakness.

The type of provocation considered serious enough to induce a heat of passion offense varies slightly from one jurisdiction to another, although the usual test is reasonableness. Depending upon the circumstances, ASSAULT, BATTERY, ADULTERY, and illegal arrest are illustrative of what may be held to be sufficient provocation. In almost all cases, the reasonableness of a provocation is a decision made by a jury.

HEDGE FUND

Hedge funds are private, loosely regulated investment pools that solicit funds from wealthy individuals and other investors and invests these funds on their behalf.

Hedge funds are investment monies managed by an individual or a business for the benefit of wealthy clients who place large amounts of money to the pool. Though hedge funds look much like mutual funds, they have not been subject to government regulation. Only wealthy individuals or investment companies participate in hedge funds because of the high minimum investment, which is usually at least $1 million and sometimes as much as $5 million. Hedge funds seek high returns on their investments, but they also employ investment strategies that seek to minimize losses when there is a large market downswing. The fact that hedge funds are loosely regulated makes them prone to manipulation by unethical fund managers. The downfall of Bernard Madoff and his hedge fund in 2008 revealed that Madoff was really running a PONZI SCHEME. With the collapse of the U.S. financial markets in the fall of 2008, Madoff and a string of other hedge fund managers were exposed as con artists, leaving their clients with little or no equity.

The differences between highly regulated mutual funds, which draw much of their money from retirement account deposits and institutional investors, and hedge funds are significant. Mutual funds must register with the SECURITIES AND EXCHANGE COMMISSION (SEC) and are subject to rigorous oversight. All prospective mutual fund investors must receive a prospectus containing specific information about the fund's management, holdings, fees and expenses, and performance. Hedge funds are not required to register with the SEC, nor do they have to file periodic reports with the commission. Hedge funds issue SECURITIES in private offerings and under federal securities law are treated much differently than mutual funds. However, even hedge funds are governed by federal laws that prohibit FRAUD, and fund managers have the same fiduciary duties as mutual fund investment managers.

A major difference between hedge funds and mutual funds is what funds can charge for their services. Fees for mutual funds are subject to regulation, and investors must be provided with a fee table that can be compared with fees of other mutual funds. Hedge funds can charge whatever they like. Besides an asset-based fee, hedge fund managers usually charge an annual performance fee of between 15 percent and 25 percent of profits. This means that if the value of the fund goes up, managers can earn millions and, in some cases, hundreds of millions of dollars.

The fact that hedge fund managers can become extremely wealthy makes them take higher risks than mutual fund managers. The SEC restricts the ability of mutual funds to leverage or borrow against the value of the securities in their portfolios. In contrast, hedge funds are not constrained and have relied on leveraging and high-risk strategies. The economic collapse of 2008 left many hedge funds in dire financial straits, as the value of their securities, which were pledged as COLLATERAL on loans, plummeted. A number of hedge funds went out of business as a result of these financial practices. Hedge fund investors, including pension funds, university endowments, and other institutional investors, were big losers. The attraction of extraordinary returns led them to ignore the potential risks.

In response to these hedge fund abuses, Congress began to draft reform legislation in 2009. Though both the House and Senate moved forward with competing plans, passage of a bill was not expected until 2010. The TREASURY DEPARTMENT proposed legislation that identified key elements of reform: hedge funds, private equity funds, venture capital funds, and other private pools of capital must register with the SEC if they have more than $30 million of assets under management. Investment advisers will be also be required to follow new reporting, record-keeping, compliance, and disclosure requirements as well as CONFLICT OF INTEREST and anti-fraud prohibitions.

FURTHER READINGS

Larimore, James N., ed. 2008. *Securities and Exchange Commission: Programs and Operations.* New York: Nova Science.

Securities and Exchange Commission. Available online at www.sec.gov (accessed December 26, 2009).

Seligman, Joel. 2003. *The Transformation of Wall Street: A History of the Securities and Exchange Commission and Modern Corporate Finance.* 3d ed. New York: Aspen.

Western, David. 2004. *Booms, Bubbles, and Busts in the U.S. Stock Market.* New York: Routledge.

Winer, Kenneth B., and Samuel J. Winer. 2004. *Securities Enforcement: Counseling & Defense.* Newark, N.J.: LexisNexis.

CROSS REFERENCES

Ponzi Scheme; Securities and Exchange Commission

❖ HEGEL, GEORG WILHELM FRIEDRICH

Philosopher GEORG WILHELM FRIEDRICH HEGEL had a profound effect on modern thought. Hegel wrote his earliest work in 1807 and his groundbreaking *Philosophy of Right* in 1827. An idealist, he explored the nature of rationality in an attempt to create a single system of thought that would comprehend all knowledge. Among his chief contributions was developing the hegelian dialectic, a three-part process for revealing reason that ultimately influenced nineteenth- and twentieth-century theories of law, political science, economics, and literature. Especially in the late twentieth century, scholars debated the ideas of Hegel for their relevance to contemporary legal issues.

Born August 27, 1770, in Stuttgart, Germany, Hegel achieved fame in his lifetime as a teacher and writer. The son of a German government official, he was originally a divinity student who later turned to philosophy. He worked as a tutor in his twenties, and later as a school principal and a professor at German universities in Heidelberg and Berlin. At the same time, he wrote far-ranging and lengthy books, including *Science of Logic* (1812–16) and *Encyclopedia of the Philosophical Sciences* (1817), which contains every element of his system of philosophy. He died November 14, 1831, in Berlin.

Hegel's theories arose partly in response to those of his predecessor, the Prussian philosopher IMMANUEL KANT. Believing that perception alone could determine what is real, Kant had provided a concept of reason that Hegel was able to use in building a complete theoretical system. In doing so Hegel created his own form of the dialectic (a method of critical reasoning), which he divided into three parts. Essentially, it held: (1) A thesis (idea) encourages the development of its reverse, or antithesis. (2) If

THE HISTORY OF THE WORLD IS NONE OTHER THAN THE PROGRESS OF THE CONSCIOUSNESS OF FREEDOM.
—GEORG HEGEL

Georg Hegel.
LIBRARY OF CONGRESS.

these two combine, they form an entirely new thesis, or synthesis. (3) This synthesis is the beginning of a new series of developments. Hegel believed that life eternally forms itself by setting up oppositions.

Hegel's system has special implications for the progress of history, particularly the evolution of people and government. He believed that the ideal universal soul can be created through logic that is based on his dialectic. This, he argued, was the foundation of all development. Using his three-part dialectic, he laid out the development of society. Hegel's thesis was that the primary goal of persons is to acquire property, and the pursuit of property by all persons necessitates the antithesis of this goal, laws. The association of persons and laws

produces a synthesis, called ethos, that combines the freedom and interdependence of the people and creates a state. According to Hegel, the state is above the individual. Allowed to reach its highest form of development, Hegel believed, the state evolves into a monarchy (a government ruled by a single person, often called a king or queen).

Hegel's view of government is at odds with the historical course pursued by the United States. In fact, he was a critic of the individualism at the heart of the American Revolution. But his ideas have nonetheless had an immeasurable effect on modern thought in the United States as well as Europe. He saw human history as the progression from bondage to freedom, attainable only if the will of the individual is made secondary to the will of the majority. This view shaped the development of the philosophy of idealism in the United States and Europe. Hegel's dialectic was also adapted by KARL MARX as the basis for Marx's economic theory of the struggle of the working class to achieve revolution over the owners of the means of production. In the twentieth century, Hegel inspired the academic methodology called deconstructionism, used in fields ranging from literature to law as a means to interpret texts.

Although Hegel was largely ignored or attacked by U.S. legal scholars for two centuries, the 1950s brought a new interest in his ideas that has grown in the ensuing decades. Generally speaking, scholars have examined his work for its views on liberalism and the concepts of freedom and responsibility. Hegelian thought has been used to address everything from historical problems such as SLAVERY to

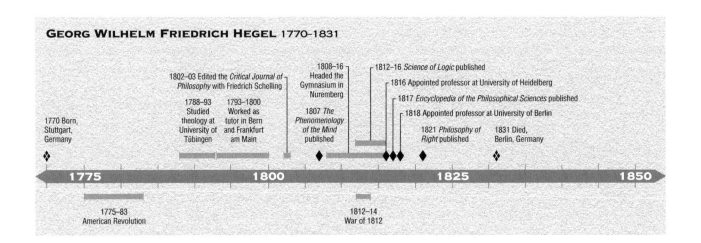

GEORG WILHELM FRIEDRICH HEGEL 1770–1831

1770 Born, Stuttgart, Germany

1788–93 Studied theology at University of Tübingen

1793–1800 Worked as tutor in Bern and Frankfurt am Main

1802–03 Edited the *Critical Journal of Philosophy* with Friedrich Schelling

1807 *The Phenomenology of the Mind* published

1808–16 Headed the Gymnasium in Nuremberg

1812–16 *Science of Logic* published

1816 Appointed professor at University of Heidelberg

1817 *Encyclopedia of the Philosophical Sciences* published

1818 Appointed professor at University of Berlin

1821 *Philosophy of Right* published

1831 Died, Berlin, Germany

1775 ◆ 1800 ◆◆◆ ◆ ◆ 1825 ◆◆ 1850

1775–83 American Revolution

1812–14 War of 1812

contemporary issues in contracts, property, torts, and CRIMINAL LAW. It has also influenced the CRITICAL LEGAL STUDIES movement.

FURTHER READINGS

Althaus, Horst. 2000. *Hegel: An Intellectual Biography.* Michael Tarsh, trans. Cambridge, UK: Polity.

Carlson, David Gray. 1999–2000. "How to Do Things with Hegel." *Texas Law Review* 78 (May).

———. 1992. "The Hegelian Revival in American Legal Discourse." *Univ. of Miami Law Review* 46 (March).

Hegel, Georg. 1977. *The Difference between Fichte's and Schelling's System of Philosophy.* Translated by H.S. Harris and Walter Cerf. Albany, NY: State Univ. of New York Press.

Hoffheimer, Michael H. 1995. "Hegel's First Philosophy of Law." *Tennessee Law Review* 62 (summer).

McCracken, Chad. 1999. "Hegel and the Autonomy of Contract Law." *Texas Law Review* 77 (February).

Pinkard, Terry. 2001. *Hegel: A Biography.* Cambridge; New York: Cambridge Univ. Press.

CROSS REFERENCE

Jurisprudence.

HEIGHTENED SCRUTINY

Heightened scrutiny is a standard of judicial review for a challenged law or policy in which the court presumes the law to be invalid unless the law furthers an important government interest in a way that is substantially related to that interest.

Heightened scrutiny is also known as intermediate scrutiny because it is the middle level of three tests developed by the Supreme Court to decided constitutional questions. The lowest level of constitutional review is the RATIONAL BASIS TEST, whereas the highest level is the STRICT SCRUTINY test. The outcome of a case where constitutional arguments are made often depends on which level of review is applied. The Supreme Court has identified issues that qualify for one of these three tests.

The least rigorous of the three, the rational basis test, is employed in cases where a PLAINTIFF alleges that the legislature has made an arbitrary or irrational decision. Plaintiffs rarely succeed because this test gives great deference to the legislative branch. The legislature's reasons for enacting a law may be misguided or clearly wrong, but as long as the body did not act arbitrarily, the Court will not overturn statutes on constitutional grounds.

The most rigorous test is called strict scrutiny. The Supreme Court has mandated that courts apply strict scrutiny when fundamental rights are at issue. The Court has identified the right to vote, the right to travel, and the right to privacy as fundamental rights. In addition, when a law or policy makes distinctions based on a SUSPECT CLASSIFICATION, strict scrutiny must be applied. Race, national origin, alienage, and religious affiliation are suspect classifications. However, gender, age, and disability are not. Unlike rational basis, the government has the burden of proving that the suspect law is narrowly tailored and the least restrictive means to further a compelling government interest.

Heightened scrutiny was developed by the Supreme Court to deal with classifications that did not, in the Court's view, reach the level of race and other suspect classifications. The test was announced in *Craig v. Boren* (429 U.S., 97 S. Ct. 451, 50 L.Ed.2d 397 [1976]). *Boren* dealt with an Oklahoma law that treated women differently than men. Because the Court was unwilling to make gender a suspect classification but did not believe rational basis was the proper standard of review, it came up with heightened scrutiny.

The law prohibited the sale of "nonintoxicating" 3.2 beer to males under the age of 21 but permitted females over the age of 18 to buy it. The law was challenged as discriminatory under the EQUAL PROTECTION clause of the FOURTEENTH AMENDMENT by three plaintiffs: two men, who were over 18 but under 21, and a female beer vendor. In a 7–2 vote with four concurring opinions, the Court ruled that the law was unconstitutional. Oklahoma attempted to show the legislature had a rational basis for enacting a law it believed would reduce drunk driving. It provided statistics showing that arrests of males 18 to 20 years of age outnumbered those of females of similar age by a factor of nine for "drunk" driving (2 percent versus 18 percent), by a factor of eighteen for "driving under the influence," and by a factor of ten for public drunkenness.

Justice William Brennan, in his majority opinion, announced that gender-based classifications were subject to a higher level of scrutiny than provided by the rational basis test. For the law to survive, the state would have to show that classifying by gender "must serve important governmental objectives and must be substantially related to those objectives." This test was somewhat less rigorous than strict scrutiny.

Justice Brennan applied the test to the facts of the case and concluded the law was unconstitutional. He agreed that the state had an important government interest in keeping people from driving while intoxicated. The statistical evidence demonstrated that there was a problem with underage drinking and driving, but it failed to show that the law was "substantially related to those objectives."

The heightened or intermediate scrutiny test has been applied to a number of gender-based classifications. In *Mississippi University for Women v. Hogan* (458 U.S. 718, 102 S. Ct. 3331; 73 L. Ed. 2d 1090), the Supreme Court held that the single-sex admission policy of a Mississippi University violated the equal protection clause. In this case, an otherwise qualified male nursing school candidate was denied admission because of his gender. Mississippi did have two coeducational schools of nursing, but he would have had to relocate because of they were in other parts of the state. The federal district court used the rational basis test, ruling that maintaining the nursing school as a single-sex school had a rational relationship to the state's legitimate interest "in providing the greatest practical range of educational opportunities for its female student population." In addition, the single-sex policy was not arbitrary. The Supreme Court applied the heightened scrutiny test and concluded that the state had an important government interest in providing educational options for all its residents. However, the single-sex admission policy was not substantially related to that interest. The Court noted that there must be an "exceedingly persuasive justification" for gender-based classification to be judged constitutional.

Heightened scrutiny has also been applied to legal restrictions based on illegitimacy. In *Caban v. Mohammed* (441 U.S. 380, 99 S. Ct. 1760, 60 L. Ed. 2d 297 [1979]), the state of New York had a law that only allowed mothers to block adoptions of children born out of wedlock, regardless of the relationship between the children and the natural father. In this case, the unwed mother and father lived together for five years and had two children. The father acknowledged paternity on the birth certificate. When the couple later separated, the mother retained custody of the children, but the father visited the children regularly. When the mother married another man, the husband sought to adopt the children. The father opposed the adoption, but the trial court granted the adoption based on the best interests of the children.

The Supreme Court ruled that the law violated the equal protection clause because the father had a relationship with the children fully comparable to that of the mother. The law was unequal because the mother had an absolute veto over an out-of-wedlock child, whereas the father was required to prove that it was in the best interest of the child for the child not to be adopted. The state could not give the mother an absolute veto, while forcing the father to show child's best interest before he could retain parental rights.

FURTHER READINGS

Flack, Horace Edgar. 2003. *The Adoption of the Fourteenth Amendment.* Birmingham, Ala.: Palladium Press.
Langran, Robert. 2003. *The Supreme Court: A Concise History.* New York: Peter Lang.
Tribe, Lawrence. 2008. *The Invisible Constitution.* New York: Oxford Univ. Press.

CROSS REFERENCES

Rational Basis Test; Strict Scrutiny; Suspect Classification.

HEIR

An individual who receives an interest in, or ownership of, land, tenements, or hereditaments from an ancestor who has died intestate, through the laws of descent and distribution. At common law, an heir was the individual appointed by law to succeed to the estate of an ancestor who died without a will. It is commonly used in the early 2000s in reference to any individual who succeeds to property, either by will or law.

An *heir of the body* is an heir who was either conceived or born of the individual who has died, or a child of such heir. This type of heir is anyone who descends lineally from the decedent, excluding a surviving spouse, adopted children, and collateral relatives. Ordinarily, property can be given by will to anyone named or can be shared by all heirs, but historically, the owner of an entail could only pass his or her property on to heirs of the body. This type of inheritance is largely abolished by statute in the early twenty-first century.

HELD

In relation to the opinion of a court, decided.

The holding in a particular case is the ultimate decision of a court of a justiciable controversy.

✧ HELMS, JESSE ALEXANDER, JR.

The career of Jesse Alexander Helms Jr. is unique in post-World War II U.S. politics. Few legislators have fought as relentlessly, caused as much uproar, or arguably, had as much influence as the ultraconservative Republican from North Carolina. As a fiery radio editorialist in the 1960s, Helms waged a one-man war on liberalism. His notoriety helped him win a historic 1972 Senate race, a breakthrough in a state that had not elected a Republican in the twentieth century, and three reelections followed. He emerged not only as a party leader but as an independent legislator with his own tough agenda on social issues and foreign policy.

Born October 18, 1921, in the small segregated town of Monroe, North Carolina, Helms was named for his formidable father. JESSE HELMS Sr. was the town's police and fire chief, and he exacted obedience from Monroe and his two sons alike. "My father was a six-foot, two-hundred pound gorilla," Helms affectionately said. "When he said, 'Smile,' I smiled." His mother, Ethel Mae Helms, marshaled her family off to the First Baptist Church twice a week. In Helms's childhood, Monroe still romantically celebrated Confederate Memorial Day, and patriotism, regional pride, RELIGION, and racial separation were formative influences on the boy. He showed early promise in writing, by high school already reporting for the local newspaper.

Journalism held such interest for Helms that he quit Wake Forest College in 1939 to work on the *Raleigh News and Observer.* The 20-year-old moved up rapidly. By 1941 he was assistant city

Jesse Helms.
U.S. SENATE HISTORICAL OFFICE

editor of the *Raleigh Times,* the city's smaller, more conservative paper. Then Pearl Harbor intervened. Accepted by the U.S. Navy for limited duty in recruitment and public speaking, Helms made a crucial discovery: he was good at broadcasting. Starting in 1948, he began a new career as a radio news director at station WRAL in Raleigh.

Helms soon moved from the role of political observer to that of political insider. His reporting in the vicious, racially divided 1950 Democratic primary race for the Senate led to accusations that he had doctored a photo of the wife of the loser, Frank Graham, so that she appeared to be dancing with a black man—a fatal blow to the candidate's chances in the segregated state. Helms denied it. The winner,

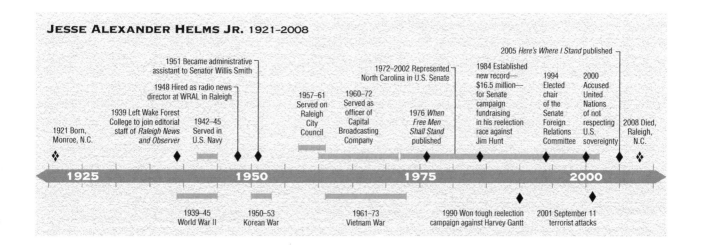

JESSE ALEXANDER HELMS JR. 1921–2008

2005 *Here's Where I Stand* published

1951 Became administrative assistant to Senator Willis Smith

1972–2002 Represented North Carolina in U.S. Senate

1984 Established new record— $16.5 million— for Senate campaign fundraising in his reelection race against Jim Hunt

1948 Hired as radio news director at WRAL in Raleigh

1994 Elected chair of the Senate Foreign Relations Committee

2000 Accused United Nations of not respecting U.S. sovereignty

1939 Left Wake Forest College to join editorial staff of *Raleigh News and Observer*

1957–61 Served on Raleigh City Council

1960–72 Served as officer of Capital Broadcasting Company

1976 *When Free Men Shall Stand* published

1921 Born, Monroe, N.C.

1942–45 Served in U.S. Navy

2008 Died, Raleigh, N.C.

1925   1950   1975   2000

1939–45 World War II

1950–53 Korean War

1961–73 Vietnam War

1990 Won tough reelection campaign against Harvey Gantt

2001 September 11 terrorist attacks

Senator Willis Smith, took him to Washington as his administrative assistant in 1951. Working in the Senate propelled Helms closer to a political career.

From 1953 to 1960 Helms was a lobbyist and editorialist for the North Carolina Bankers Association. He had an opportunity to exercise his politics in a weekly column and at the same time held his first elective office, on the Raleigh City Council, where, although nominally a Democrat, he opposed virtually all taxes.

The great turning point in Helms's life came in 1960. As the executive vice president of the Capital Broadcasting Company, he began broadcasting fierce radio editorials on radio station WRAL. Here, for the next 12 years, he developed views that would last the rest of his life. These broadcasts were fire and brimstone. In much the same way that radio host Rush Limbaugh criticized liberals in the 1990s, Helms attacked liberal trends in the 1960s. He referred to the 1960s as "this time of the fast buck and the 'New Morality'—the age of apathy and indifference, the season of disdain for simple virtues and common honesty."

What riled Helms most was the CIVIL RIGHTS MOVEMENT. Carried across the state of North Carolina, Helms's attacks on desegregation were reprinted in newspapers under such titles as "Nation Needs to Know of Red Involvement in Race Agitation!" The liberal media were to blame, Helms reasoned, and if they would stop distorting the truth, then "there would be millions around the world who would change their minds about race relations in the South." Despite his own biases, Helms and WRAL survived repeated complaints to the FEDERAL COMMUNICATIONS COMMISSION.

It was only a matter of time before the conservative Helms gave up on the DEMOCRATIC PARTY. In 1972, he switched parties and ran for the U.S. Senate as a Republican. Helms liked to tell his radio listeners that he had never voted for a Democrat for president, and now, with the decidedly liberal George S. McGovern as the Democratic nominee, he had even more reason to sever his symbolic ties to the party. McGovern stood for everything that Helms detested: support for welfare and ABORTION, and opposition to the war in Vietnam. To Helms, such views were typical of the way liberalism betrayed traditional values, and why he could not remain a Democrat.

When Helms jumped ship, he took an extreme gamble. North Carolina—indeed, the South as a whole—had been the Democratic Party's stronghold for generations. In fact, not since the late nineteenth century had the state elected a Republican senator. Helms changed everything. One key to his beating the favorite, Democrat Nick Galifianakis (by only 120,000 votes), was Helms's use of national politics. The presidential election offered excellent coattails upon which to ride. Helms allied himself with Republican candidate RICHARD M. NIXON, linking Galifianakis with the highly unpopular McGovern. Galifianakis saw a much different, and worse, kind of tarring at work. He accused the Helms campaign of using his Greek American ethnicity to imply that he was not a loyal U.S. citizen.

Not surprisingly, Helms's first term in Washington, D.C., established the same hard-line politics of his broadcasting career. He was soon nicknamed Senator No for voting against federal spending—with the exception of support for the military and farmers. He opposed federal aid to education, food stamps for striking workers, government-subsidized abortion, and the creation of the CONSUMER PROTECTION Agency.

Returning politics to traditional values would be the hallmark of his career, a philosophy outlined in his 1976 book, *When Free Men Shall Stand*. During his first term in the U.S. Senate, he introduced an amendment designed to circumvent the Supreme Court's decisions banning prayer in public schools. Although the effort failed, it paid personal dividends: Helms came to the attention of conservative organizations and contributors who would be increasingly supportive of him over the next two decades. He saw no conflict with his faith in opposing government aid to the needy. He believed it was the role of the private individual to help others, as he and his wife, Dorothy Helms, had done by adopting a nine-year-old orphan with cerebral palsy. In Congress he voted against federal aid to disabled people and against school lunch programs.

Unlike some social conservatives, Helms had an equal passion for foreign policy. He was staunchly anti-communist, a belief that formed the basis for his opposition to any cooperation between the United States and left-wing governments. He opposed President Nixon's historic opening of ties to China. Supporting right-wing

WE ARE LIVING IN AN AGE WHERE ANYTHING GOES.
—JESSE HELMS

governments—even those associated with abuses of HUMAN RIGHTS, such as Turkey, or with all-white rule, such as Rhodesia and South Africa—made more sense to him.

Helms gained influence as his career progressed. By the late 1970s he was already shaping the Republican presidential platform behind the scenes. In Senate votes, he could openly defy the party on nominations and policy decisions. Helms had little fear of the party leadership because he was building a national base of support. He did this with the help of a powerful insider in national politics, Richard A. Viguerie, publisher of the *Conservative Digest.* Viguerie was an early advocate of using direct-mail techniques, a marketing tool borrowed from business. As campaign manager for Helms in 1978, he blanketed the United States with letters asking for support. It worked, fantastically. Helms raised $6.2 million for his successful 1978 reelection, two-thirds of it from outside of North Carolina. Politicians of all kinds soon followed his lead in using this powerful technology.

In the 1980s the importance of direct mail to Helms grew in proportion to the rise of conservative Christian politics. Analysts called this emerging constituency the New Right. It favored mandating school prayer, outlawing abortion, and preventing gays and lesbians from acquiring equal rights. Helms tapped its members with dramatic fund-raising letters. By 1982, Helms could count on great support for brash, independent actions in the Senate: filibustering against the renewal of the Voting Rights Act, for example, or attaching a school prayer amendment to the annual extension of the national debt.

The 1980s was a period of great activity for Helms in domestic policy. He railed against the National Endowment for the Arts (NEA) for funding art that he found offensive, chiefly that of the gay photographer Robert Mapplethorpe and of the artist Andres Serrano, whose work *Piss Christ* depicted a crucifix submerged in urine. The national controversy he engendered continued to divide liberals and conservatives well into the 1990s. He also led a highly publicized attempt to take over CBS, exhorting conservatives to buy up stock in order to end liberal bias in news reporting. He introduced antiabortion legislation that made him the leading enemy of pro-abortion forces, which began demonizing Helms in their own direct-mail

campaigns. He was most successful in agriculture policy. Helms won continued backing for tobacco price supports, an issue key to one of his most active advocates, the tobacco industry.

In a combative 1990 reelection campaign, Helms nearly lost to African American Harvey Gantt. The former Democratic mayor of Charlotte was ahead of Helms until the last weeks of the campaign, when Helms's forces mailed 125,000 postcards to voters warning them that they could be prosecuted for FRAUD if they voted improperly. At least 44,000 cards were sent to black voters, according to the U.S. DEPARTMENT OF JUSTICE, which sent observers to the state to ensure fair elections. Helms edged out Gantt by just over 100,000 votes. In 1992 the JUSTICE DEPARTMENT ruled that the Helms campaign had violated federal CIVIL RIGHTS and voting laws by intimidating, threatening, and discouraging African Americans from voting. Helms's office denied that he was involved in the mailings.

Helms was an outspoken critic of President BILL CLINTON. The Republican takeover of Congress in November 1994 gave him chairmanship of the Foreign Relations Committee, a powerful post from which he could authorize money for foreign aid, make recommendations on ambassadors and foreign treaties, and control the budget of the STATE DEPARTMENT. Almost immediately, he blasted the president as unfit to conduct foreign policy and warned that Clinton "better have a bodyguard" if he planned to visit North Carolina military bases. Politicians from both parties denounced the remark, which came on the anniversary of the ASSASSINATION of President JOHN F. KENNEDY. Helms called his statement a "mistake," but refused to apologize.

Despite surgery for serious health problems, Helms seemed eager to enter more battles. He was reelected to another term in 1996, again defeating Harvey Gantt. He served on the Foreign Relations Committee until 2001. During his tenure as chair, the committee approved 143 treatises (although some were later rejected or returned to the president), confirmed 477 presidential nominations for ambassadorships and other administrative posts, and conducted 597 hearings.

In 2001, after serving on the Senate for 30 years, Helms announced that he would not seek reelection in the 2002 elections. He continued,

Henry II of England.

Dole won a heated race in the nation's most expensive congressional campaign.

Helms married the former Dorothy Jane Coble in 1942, with whom he had three children and seven grandchildren. They were longtime cerebral palsy advocates, and were actively involved with the Jesse Helms Center in Wingate, North Carolina. The nonprofit center promotes free enterprise, representative democracy, and traditional values.

Here's Where I Stand, which came out in 2005, is Helms's memoir of his life, his ideological positions, and his political career. He died on July 4, 2008.

FURTHER READINGS

Furgurson, Ernest B. 1996. *Hard Right: The Rise of Jesse Helms.* New York: Norton.

The Jesse Helms Center. Available online at www.jessehelmscenter.org (accessed August 18, 2009).

Snider, William D. 1985. "Helms & Hunt: The North Carolina Senate Race, 1984." Chapel Hill, N.C.: Univ. of North Carolina Press.

Wagner, John. 2003. "Helms Looks Back." *The News & Observer* (January 3).

CROSS REFERENCES

Election Campaign Financing; Republican Party.

HENCEFORTH

From this time forward.

The term *henceforth*, when used in a legal document, statute, or other legal instrument, indicates that something will commence from the present time to the future, to the exclusion of the past.

❖ HENRY II OF ENGLAND

King Henry II was born March 5, 1133, in Le Mans, France. He reigned from 1154 to 1189 and founded the Plantagenet dynasty of English

however, to spark controversy even in the final year of his term as senator. He allegedly made some racially charged comments to the press, not dissimilar to those made by Senator TRENT LOTT at the birthday celebration of Senator Strom Thurmond. (These comments eventually cost Lott his position as Senate majority leader). Helms also openly criticized the lifestyles of homosexuals. Nevertheless, many conservatives celebrated his numerous accomplishments prior to his retirement in 2003. And no one could deny the indelible imprint he left on U.S. politics.

Helms supported Elizabeth Dole, wife of former Senator Bob Dole, as his successor in the 2002 senatorial election in North Carolina.

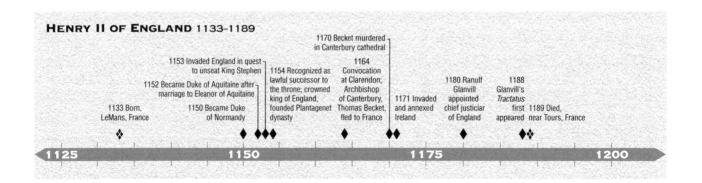

HENRY II OF ENGLAND 1133–1189

1133 Born, LeMans, France

1150 Became Duke of Normandy

1152 Became Duke of Aquitaine after marriage to Eleanor of Aquitaine

1153 Invaded England in quest to unseat King Stephen

1154 Recognized as lawful successor to the throne; crowned king of England, founded Plantagenet dynasty

1164 Convocation at Clarendon; Archbishop of Canterbury, Thomas Becket, fled to France

1170 Becket murdered in Canterbury cathedral

1171 Invaded and annexed Ireland

1180 Ranulf Glanvill appointed chief justiciar of England

1188 Glanvill's *Tractatus* first appeared

1189 Died, near Tours, France

1125   1150   1175   1200

rulers. Henry's many innovations in civil and CRIMINAL PROCEDURE had a lasting effect upon ENGLISH LAW and his expansion of the royal court system made royal justice available throughout England.

Building upon the earlier tradition of the inquest, Henry issued several assizes, or ordinances, that introduced the procedures that eventually developed into the GRAND JURY. He also developed a number of writs to bring cases from the feudal courts of the barons into the royal courts. In addition, Henry sent itinerant justices on regular circuits through the kingdom to make royal justice more easily obtainable.

Henry's expansion of royal justice did, however, bring him into conflict with THOMAS BECKET, the archbishop of Canterbury, who opposed the king's efforts to punish members of the clergy who had been convicted of crimes in ECCLESIASTICAL COURTS and removed from their clerical status. Becket was murdered in 1170 by some of the king's men, though apparently not at his command, and Henry thereafter gave up his efforts to punish members of the clergy. Henry died July 6, 1189, near Tours, France.

Patrick Henry.
AP/WORLD WIDE PHOTOS

❖ HENRY, PATRICK

Patrick Henry was a leading statesman and orator at the time of the American Revolutionary War. Several of Henry's speeches have remained vivid documents of the revolutionary period, with "Give me liberty or give me death" his most remembered statement.

Henry was born May 29, 1736, in Hanover County, Virginia. Though Henry attended public school for a short time, he was largely

taught by his father, who had a good education. From 1751 to 1760 Henry was a storekeeper and farmer. When his business and farming ventures failed, he turned to the study of law, and received his license to practice in 1760.

Within three years Henry had become a prominent attorney, owing in great measure to his oratorical skills. He was drawn to politics, and was elected to the Virginia House of Burgesses in 1765. In this colonial legislature, Henry became an outspoken critic of British policies toward the 13 colonies. He introduced

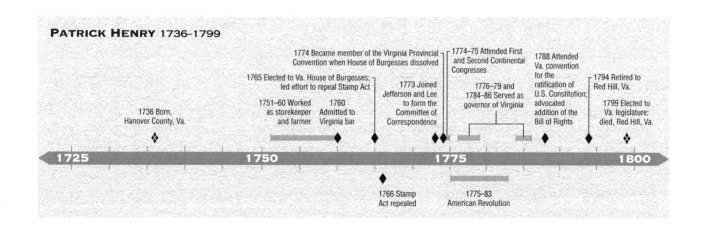

PATRICK HENRY 1736–1799

1774 Became member of the Virginia Provincial Convention when House of Burgesses dissolved

1774–75 Attended First and Second Continental Congresses

1788 Attended Va. convention for the ratification of U.S. Constitution; advocated addition of the Bill of Rights

1765 Elected to Va. House of Burgesses; led effort to repeal Stamp Act

1773 Joined Jefferson and Lee to form the Committee of Correspondence

1776–79 and 1784–86 Served as governor of Virginia

1794 Retired to Red Hill, Va.

1751–60 Worked as storekeeper and farmer

1760 Admitted to Virginia bar

1799 Elected to Va. legislature; died, Red Hill, Va.

1736 Born, Hanover County, Va.

1725   1750   1775   1800

1766 Stamp Act repealed

1775–83 American Revolution

seven resolutions against the STAMP ACT, which levied a tax by requiring that stamps be affixed to documents and other papers. In one speech opposing the act, he stated, "If this be TREASON, make the most of it."

Henry's efforts led the Virginia House of Burgesses to pass five of the seven resolutions he introduced. All seven resolutions were reprinted in newspapers as the Virginia Resolves. Colonial businesspeople, in support of the resolves, agreed not to import British goods until the Stamp Act was repealed. Trade diminished, and business owners refused to use the stamps on business documents. Faced with organized resistance in the colonies, and the displeasure of British businesses that had lost trade, the British Parliament repealed the Stamp Act on March 4, 1766.

Henry grew more radical after the repeal of the act, arguing that the colonies should break away from Great Britain. In 1773 he joined with THOMAS JEFFERSON and Richard Henry Lee to form the Committee of Correspondence to transmit messages throughout the colonies. When the House of Burgesses was dissolved in 1774 he became a member of the Virginia Provincial Convention, which advocated revolution. Before this convention, he made his most famous remarks, words that became the clarion call that led the colonies into revolution: "I know not what course others may take, but as for me, give me liberty or give me death."

During 1774 and 1775 Henry attended the First CONTINENTAL CONGRESS as a member of the Virginia delegation, advocating military mobilization. When the Second Continental Congress convened in 1775, he helped draft the legislation that organized the Continental Army. In 1776 he also helped draft the Virginia Constitution.

In 1776 Henry was elected governor of the newly independent commonwealth of Virginia. A tireless administrator, Henry worked vigorously to meet the demands of the Revolutionary War. As commander in chief, he recruited the state's quota of 6,000 men for the Continental Army, plus the state militia's allotment of five thousand soldiers.

After the war, Henry continued as governor, eventually serving five terms. During his second term, Henry provided supplies to George Rogers Clark for his expedition to the Northwest Territory. Clark rid the territory of British control.

In 1788 Henry attended the Virginia convention for the ratification of the U.S. Constitution. Henry opposed ratification, fearing that it imperiled the rights of states and individuals, but Virginia ratified it. Henry successfully advocated the addition of the BILL OF RIGHTS to the document. This first ten amendments to the Constitution protect the rights of states and individuals, allowing Henry to support the Constitution.

Following ratification, Henry was offered many government posts, but was forced to resume his Virginia law practice to rescue himself from personal debt. He quickly became a wealthy man, because his fame attracted many clients. In 1794 he retired to his estate at Red Hill, near Appomattox, Virginia. Despite his new wealth, Henry refused pleas to resume public service, turning down President George Washington's request to serve as chief justice of the U.S. Supreme Court.

Washington finally persuaded Henry to seek election to the Virginia legislature. Henry won election in 1799. He died June 6, 1799, before he could take office.

FURTHER READINGS

Mayer, Henry. 2001. *A Son of Thunder: Patrick Henry and the American Republic.* New York: Grove.

Rivkin, Victoria. 1998. "Patrick Henry." *New York Law Journal* 220 (August 24): 4.

Wirt, William. 2009. *Sketches of the Life and Character of Patrick Henry.* Carlisle, MA: Applewood.

HEREAFTER

In the future.

The term *hereafter* is always used to indicate a future time—to the exclusion of both the past and present—in legal documents, statutes, and other similar papers.

HEREDITAMENT

Anything that can be passed by an individual to heirs.

There are two types of hereditaments: corporeal and incorporeal.

A *corporeal hereditament* is a permanent tangible object that can be seen and handled and is confined to the land. Materials, such as coal, timber, stone, or a house are common examples of this type of hereditament.

THE BATTLE, SIR, IS NOT TO THE STRONG ALONE; IT IS TO THE VIGILANT, THE ACTIVE, THE BRAVE.
—PATRICK HENRY

An *incorporeal hereditament* is an intangible right, which is not visible but is derived from real or PERSONAL PROPERTY. An easement is a classic example of this type of hereditament, since it is the right of one individual to use another's property and can be inherited.

HERITAGE FOUNDATION

The HERITAGE FOUNDATION is a research and educational institute, popularly known as a "think tank," whose mission is to formulate and promote conservative public policies based on the principles of free enterprise, limited government, individual freedom, traditional values, and a strong national defense. Founded in 1973, the Heritage Foundation has proven to be effective, gaining national influence during the administrations of Presidents RONALD REAGAN and GEORGE H.W. BUSH. This influence grew in the 1990s, as conservative Republicans gained control of Congress in 1994. Speaker of the House NEWT GINGRICH of Georgia declared just after the 1994 election, "Heritage is, without question, the most far-reaching conservative organization in the country in the war of ideas, and one which has had a tremendous impact not just in Washington, but literally across the planet."

The Heritage Foundation is a nonpartisan, tax-exempt institution and is governed by an independent board of trustees. It relies on the private financial support of individuals, foundations, and corporations for its income and accepts no government funds and performs no contract work. Currently it receives support from more than 200,000 contributors. Its headquarters are in Washington, D.C.

The staff of the Heritage Foundation includes policy and research analysts who examine issues in a wide variety of fields, including the legislative and executive branches of government, domestic policy, education, corporations, foreign policy, the UNITED NATIONS, Asian studies, and other areas of public concern. Once the researchers have made their findings, the foundation markets the results to its primary audiences: members of Congress, key congressional staff members, policy makers in the EXECUTIVE BRANCH, the news media, and the academic and policy communities.

The Heritage Foundation publicizes its work through weekly, monthly, and quarterly periodicals, including *Policy Review*. It also provides public speakers to promote its positions and convenes conferences and meetings on policy issues.

The Heritage Foundation has played an important role in advancing conservative ideas, especially after the election of Republican majorities in the U.S. House of Representatives and Senate in 1994. The Republican "Contract with America" agenda sought major changes in the size and power of the federal government. Heritage Foundation staff played a key role behind the scenes in helping to craft and refine legislative proposals. The overhaul of the system of agricultural subsidies and the first comprehensive rewriting of the telecommunications law embraced free-market approaches advocated by the foundation. Its research and proposals also shaped the 1996 welfare reform bill. This was followed by a period of intensive fund-raising and recruitment of members in such initiatives as the Leadership for America campaign. This activity led to the Heritage Foundation exceeding its two-year goal of $85 million in donations. In 2001 the Heritage Foundation actively supported a program of sweeping federal tax reforms that were eventually signed into law by President GEORGE W. BUSH.

FURTHER READINGS

Berkowitz, Bill. 2008. "The Heritage Foundation at 35." (March 3).

The Heritage Foundation. Available online at http://www.heritage.org (accessed July 29, 2009).

"The Think Tank Index." 2009. *Foreign Policy*.

CROSS REFERENCE

Lobbying.

HIERARCHY

A group of people who form an ascending chain of power or authority.

Officers in a government, for example, form an escalating series of ranks or degrees of power, with each rank subject to the authority of the one on the next level above. In a majority of hierarchical arrangements, there are a larger number of people at the bottom than at the top.

Originally, the term was used to mean government by a body of priests. Currently, a hierarchy is used to denote any body of individuals arranged or classified according to capacity, authority, position, or rank.

A. Leon Higginbotham.

❖ HIGGINBOTHAM, ALOYISUS LEON, JR.

A. Leon Higginbotham Jr. was an attorney, a scholar, and a federal judge. His distinguished judicial career culminated in his attaining the rank of chief judge of the U.S. Court of Appeals for the Third Circuit.

Higginbotham was born February 25, 1928, in Trenton, New Jersey. Although he attended segregated public schools, his mother was determined that he would receive the same opportunities available to white students. "She knew that education was the sole passport to a better life," he said. No African American student had been admitted to the academic high school program in Trenton because Latin, a requirement for the program, was not offered at the black elementary schools. But Higginbotham's mother fought for her son's right to enroll and finally convinced the principal to allow him into the program. Higginbotham had no doubt that his mother's advocacy made a difference in the outcome of his life. "When I see students who went to [elementary school] with me now working as elevator operators or on street maintenance," he said, "I often wonder what their future would have been if the school had offered Latin."

After finishing high school, Higginbotham decided to become an engineer and enrolled at Purdue University, in West Lafayette, Indiana. A winter spent sleeping in an unheated attic with 11 other African American students caused him to rethink his career goals. "One night, as the temperature was close to zero, I felt that I could suffer the personal indignities and denigration no longer," he wrote in the preface to his book, *In the Matter of Color: The Colonial Period* (1978). He spoke to the university president, who told him the law did not require the university to "let colored students in the dorm." Higginbotham was advised to accept the situation or leave. "How could it be that the law would not permit twelve good kids to sleep in a warm dormitory?" he wondered. He decided then and there to abandon engineering and pursue a career in law.

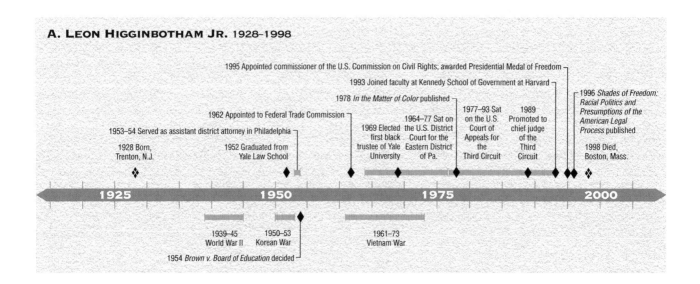

A. LEON HIGGINBOTHAM JR. 1928–1998

1995 Appointed commissioner of the U.S. Commission on Civil Rights; awarded Presidential Medal of Freedom

1993 Joined faculty at Kennedy School of Government at Harvard

1978 *In the Matter of Color* published

1977–93 Sat on the U.S. Court of Appeals for the Third Circuit

1989 Promoted to chief judge of the Third Circuit

1996 *Shades of Freedom: Racial Politics and Presumptions of the American Legal Process* published

1962 Appointed to Federal Trade Commission

1964–77 Sat on the U.S. District Court for the Eastern District of Pa.

1969 Elected first black trustee of Yale University

1953–54 Served as assistant district attorney in Philadelphia

1928 Born, Trenton, N.J.

1952 Graduated from Yale Law School

1998 Died, Boston, Mass.

1925   1950   1975   2000

1939–45 World War II

1950–53 Korean War

1961–73 Vietnam War

1954 *Brown v. Board of Education* decided

Higginbotham left Purdue to attend Antioch College, in Ohio, where he studied sociology, earning his bachelor of arts degree in 1949. He went on to Yale Law School, and received his bachelor of laws degree in 1952. Another incident that helped galvanize his commitment to racial equality occurred shortly after his graduation from Yale. He was a job candidate for a prominent Philadelphia law firm that did not know he was black until he arrived for the interview. Although the partner who spoke with him praised his qualifications, he told Higginbotham he could not do anything for him except direct him to local African American law firms who might hire him.

Discouraged but not daunted, Higginbotham began his legal career as an assistant district attorney in Philadelphia and then became a partner in a law firm that handled business, church, and CIVIL RIGHTS CASES. President JOHN F. KENNEDY made him a commissioner with the FEDERAL TRADE COMMISSION in 1962; he was the youngest person ever appointed to the post and the first African American. The same year, the U.S. Junior Chamber of Commerce named him one of its ten outstanding young men. In 1964 President LYNDON B. JOHNSON named him a U.S. district judge for the Eastern District of Pennsylvania; at age 36, he was the youngest federal judge to be appointed in three decades. In 1977 President JIMMY CARTER elevated him to the U.S. Court of Appeals for the Third Circuit, which encompasses Pennsylvania, New Jersey, Delaware, and the Virgin Islands.

Higginbotham's distinguished judicial career was capped in 1989 when he was promoted to chief judge for the Third CIRCUIT COURT of Appeals. At the time, he was the only African American judge directing one of the federal judiciary's 12 circuits. His ascendancy was hailed by many who saw it as proof that the U.S. judicial system was becoming more inclusive. Guido Calabresi, dean of Yale Law School, praised him as "a first-rate judge, a sensitive judge, who is powerful in style and analytically strong." But some African American lawyers felt that too much emphasis was placed on Higginbotham's skin color and on the racial import of his promotion. "There is no more significance to it than anybody else becoming Chief Judge," said THURGOOD MARSHALL, associate justice of the U.S. Supreme Court. "I think he is a great lawyer and a very great judge. Period."

Higginbotham was an outspoken proponent of CIVIL RIGHTS and racial equality. In 1990 he declined to officiate at a MOOT COURT competition at the University of Chicago Law School because, he said, Chicago was the only one of the top ten schools in the United States that "for two decades has not had even one black professor in either a tenured position or a tenure-track position."

Higginbotham's devotion to civil rights was evident in his criticism of Justice CLARENCE THOMAS, a conservative African American whose nomination to the U.S. Supreme Court in 1991 provoked criticism and controversy. In an article titled "An Open Letter to Justice Clarence Thomas from a Federal Judicial Colleague" (*U. Pa. L. Rev.*, Jan. 1992), Higginbotham called upon Thomas to remain cognizant of his responsibilities as an African American on the Supreme Court. He reminded Thomas of the discrimination both men's grandfathers had faced and of Thomas's debt to the CIVIL RIGHTS MOVEMENT, commenting that without the movement, "probably neither you nor I would be Federal judges today." He was also sharply critical of Thomas's record. He noted that after studying nearly all of Thomas's speeches and writings, "I could not find one shred of evidence suggesting an insightful understanding on your part of how the evolutionary movement of the Constitution and the work of the civil rights organizations have benefited you."

During his career, Higginbotham was awarded more than 60 honorary degrees; in 1969, he became the first African American elected to the board of trustees of Yale University. He was also a tireless lecturer, teaching at various times over the course of 20 years at the University of Pennsylvania, University of Michigan, Stanford, New York University, and Yale. In addition, Higginbotham was well known for his prolific writings, including more than one hundred articles. His book *In the Matter of Color* received several national and international awards. In 1996, he published *Shades of Freedom: Racial Politics and Presumptions of the American Legal Process.*

In 1993 Higginbotham retired from the circuit court and formed an association with the law firm of Paul, Weiss, Rifkind, Wharton, & Garrison in New York City. In 1995 President BILL CLINTON awarded Higginbotham the Presidential Medal of Freedom, the nation's highest

BROWN CHANGED THE MORAL TONE OF AMERICA; BY ELIMINATING THE LEGITIMIZATION OF STATE-IMPOSED RACISM IT IMPLICITLY QUESTIONED RACISM WHEREVER IT WAS USED.
—A. LEON HIGGINBOTHAM

civilian award. In the same year, President Clinton appointed him to serve a six-year term as a commissioner of the U.S. COMMISSION ON CIVIL RIGHTS. Higginbotham died of a stroke on December 14, 1998, in Boston, Massachusetts.

FURTHER READINGS

"A. Leon Higginbotham Jr., Federal Judge, is Dead at 70." *The New York Times* (December 15, 1998).

Diver, Colin S. 1999 "A. Leon Higginbotham (1928–1998): A Tribute." *The Pennsylvania Gazette.* Available online at http://www.upenn.edu/gazette/0399/higginbotham. html; website home page: http://www.upenn.edu (accessed July 29, 2009).

Higginbotham, A. Leon. 1996. *Shades of Freedom: Racial Politics and Presumptions of the American Legal Process.* New York: Oxford Univ. Press.

HIGH CRIMES AND MISDEMEANORS

The offenses for which presidents, vice presidents, and all civil officers, including federal judges, can be removed from office through a process called impeachment.

A depiction of the 1868 impeachment proceedings against President Andrew Johnson. The Senate's vote on the 11th Article of Impeachment fell short of the two-thirds majority needed to impeach Johnson. Two other articles were later defeated.

LIBRARY OF CONGRESS

The phrase *high crimes and misdemeanors* is found in the U.S. CONSTITUTION. It also appears in state laws and constitutions as a basis for disqualification from holding office. Originating in English common law, these words have acquired a broad meaning in U.S. law. They refer to criminal actions as well as any serious misuse or abuse of office, ranging from TAX EVASION to OBSTRUCTION OF JUSTICE. The ultimate authority for determining whether an offense constitutes a ground for IMPEACHMENT rests with Congress.

The exact meaning of the phrase cannot be found in the Constitution itself. Article II, Section 4, establishes, "The President, Vice President and all civil Officers of the United States, shall be removed from Office on Impeachment for, and Conviction of, TREASON, BRIBERY, or other High Crimes and Misdemeanors." *Treason* and *bribery* are specific, but *high crimes and misdemeanors* is not. In fact, considerable debate occupied the Framers of

the Constitution over the issue of impeachment, and the wording of the grounds for impeachment was itself controversial. A proposed offense of maladministration was rejected as being too vague and susceptible to political abuse. Finally, they chose to use a phrase from English common law that had no precisely settled meaning at the time yet at least connoted serious offenses.

The reason for the choice lies in the Framers' approach to the larger question of impeachment. Although borrowing language from the law they knew best, they explicitly chose not to imitate the English model of impeachment. Traditionally, this approach had allowed the British Parliament to conduct a simple review of charges and then remove officials by a majority vote. Instead, the Framers intended for removal from office to be the final step in a two-part process that began in the House of Representatives and, if charges should result, ended in a trial-like hearing before the U.S. Senate. Thus, two goals would be achieved: a full public inquiry into allegations, and, if necessary, the adjudication of those charges requiring a two-thirds majority for removal.

Generally, debate over the phrase *high crimes and misdemeanors* has split into two camps. The minority view is held by critics who undertake a literal reading of the Constitution. They maintain that *high crimes* means what it says—criminal activity—and argue that the Framers wanted only criminal activities to be the basis for impeachment. The generally accepted viewpoint is much broader. It defines high crimes and misdemeanors as any serious abuse of power— including both legal and illegal activities. Supporters of this reading believe that because impeachment is a public inquiry, first and foremost, it is appropriate to read the phrase broadly in order to provide the most thorough inquiry possible. Thus, a civil officer may face impeachment for misconduct, violations of oath of office, serious incompetence, or, in the case of judges, activities that undermine public confidence or damage the integrity of the judiciary.

The vagueness of the standard has left much interpretive power to Congress. In 1868 President ANDREW JOHNSON underwent impeachment proceedings when he ordered the firing of his secretary of war. His opponents charged that this order violated the TENURE OF OFFICE ACT, which set the tenure of certain officials. Johnson escaped conviction in the Senate by only one

vote, but the attempt to IMPEACH him quickly came to be seen as a politically motivated mistake. In 1974 the House Judiciary Committee recommended that the full House of Representatives approve ARTICLES OF IMPEACHMENT against President RICHARD M. NIXON. It did not cite any single impeachable offense, but instead found a broad pattern of wrongdoing: Nixon had conspired with his advisers to obstruct federal and congressional investigations of the WATERGATE break-in, the burglarizing of the Democratic National Committee headquarters in Washington, D.C., which was eventually linked to the Nixon administration. Nixon resigned from office before the process could continue.

The dispute over what constitutes a high crime or MISDEMEANOR reemerged in 1998 when the House Judiciary Committee voted to recommend that the House begin impeachment proceedings against President BILL CLINTON. The House concurred with the recommendation, which included charges of perjury and obstruction of justice. Legal commentators debated for weeks about whether these charges were the type of high crimes and misdemeanors contemplated by the language of the Constitution, but the House nevertheless approved two of the four articles of impeachment. The trial then moved to the Senate, which failed to garner the necessary two-thirds majority to remove Clinton from office.

FURTHER READINGS

Coulter, Ann H. 2002. *High Crimes and Misdemeanors: The Case against Bill Clinton.* New York: Perseus.

Isenbergh, Joseph. 1999. "Impeachment and Presidential Immunity from Judicial Process." *Yale Law and Policy Review* 18.

Smith, Alexa J. 1995. "Federal Judicial Impeachment: Defining Process Due." *Hastings Law Journal* 46 (January).

Tushnet, Mark V. 1995. "Clarence Thomas: The Constitutional Problems." *George Washington Law Review* (March).

Williams, Victor. "Third Branch Independence and Integrity Threatened by Political Branch Irresponsibility." 1995. *Seton Hall Constitutional Law Journal* (summer).

HIGHWAY

A main road or thoroughfare, such as a street, boulevard, or parkway, available to the public for use for travel or transportation.

The nature of a public way is determinable from its origin, as well as the intention and

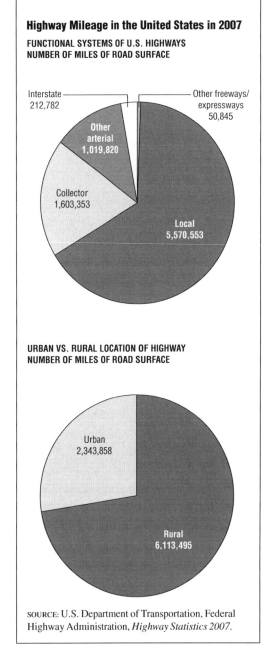

Highway Mileage in the United States in 2007

FUNCTIONAL SYSTEMS OF U.S. HIGHWAYS
NUMBER OF MILES OF ROAD SURFACE

Interstate 212,782

Other freeways/ expressways 50,845

Other arterial 1,019,820

Collector 1,603,353

Local 5,570,553

URBAN VS. RURAL LOCATION OF HIGHWAY
NUMBER OF MILES OF ROAD SURFACE

Urban 2,343,858

Rural 6,113,495

SOURCE: U.S. Department of Transportation, Federal Highway Administration, *Highway Statistics 2007.*

the owner of the property subject to the consent of public authorities. Prior to the time that any statutory procedure for the establishment of highways was devised, prescription and dedication were the methods used in common law. Currently, most highways are created by statute.

Extended Use or Prescription

One method of establishing a highway or public road is through prescription—the extended use of a piece of land for a certain length of time by the public, absent the owner's consent.

The actual number of persons using the road or the frequency or extent of such use is immaterial provided the property is openly and continuously used as a road with no restrictions. In addition, such public use must not be interrupted by acts of the owner that are designed to stop the use of his or her property as a public highway. For example, the posting of several "no trespassing" signs around the land and the erection of a fence would most likely prevent a highway from being recognized. Verbal objections alone, or unsuccessful attempts to curtail use as a highway, are ordinarily insufficient.

Any property subject to the right of the state to lay out a public way over it can become a highway by extended use if the conditions prescribed by statute are met. The public is given an easement in the land as a highway, and the width and extent of a highway are determined by the extent of its actual use for such purposes.

Statute

The creation of highways is a function of the government that stems from its power of eminent domain—the authority to take private property for public use. The legislature makes the determination needed for public use and convenience and provides for establishment of highways by local boards or courts. In deciding whether the need for a highway exists, factors for consideration include topography, soil character, population, location, condition, convenience of highways already established or proposed, and the probable extent of use.

In the absence of statutory authorization, a highway cannot be constructed through lands of the state, or property that has already been designated for public use, such as a park. Additionally, some state laws proscribe the

plans of the appropriate authorities and the use to which it has been put. If a particular road or highway is designated as private, its character will not be altered if it is actually a public road or highway. Private roads are intended for use by a few private individuals, as distinguished from highways that are for public use.

It is essential that a highway be established in a manner recognized by the particular jurisdiction, whether it be by extended use—prescription—or by dedication to the public by creation of highways through residences, buildings used for trade, gardens, or orchards.

Public Authorities

Public officials, such as state highway commissioners, act on behalf of the particular county or municipal corporation upon which the state has conferred power to establish highways.

A highway and road district is a subdivision of the state, which the legislature creates to facilitate the administration of highways. The legislature defines and sets the territorial extent, limits, and boundaries of the road or highway district, and, generally, only lands that will be benefited are included. Highway boards and commissions are ordinarily responsible for the construction, improvement, and maintenance of highways.

Abandonment, Alteration, and Vacation

The right of the public to use a highway may be forfeited by *abandonment*. Nonuse might be considered abandonment under statutory provisions. The evidence that a highway is in such a dangerous state of disrepair for a number of years that the public stops using it and a county fails to repair it constitutes abandonment in some jurisdictions. Where provided by statute, delay in opening a highway might be regarded as abandonment if it extends over an unreasonable length of time.

An *alteration* of a highway ordinarily refers to a change in its course that the state may effect in exercise of its POLICE POWER. A proceeding for a change or alteration in a public road generally will not be brought unless the change will further safety, convenience, or other public interests.

Vacation of a highway occurs when its existence is terminated by the direct action of public officials. The authority to vacate is generally delegated to the appropriate authorities or local agencies. Certain statutes make the provision that highways may be vacated by a vote of the town in a town meeting. Ordinarily, highways cannot be vacated unless they are useless, inconvenient, or burdensome, and the grounds are usually regulated by statutes. A highway that has been laid out but not constructed may be discontinued due to a change of circumstances, such as where a variation in traffic patterns makes the proposed highway unnecessary.

Title

The public only acquires the right to use a highway, whereas title to the land remains with the owner, subject to the public's rights. When a highway is constructed, the public has the RIGHT OF WAY as well as privileges incident thereto, including the right to construct, improve, and repair the highway. When a highway is abandoned or discontinued, however, total and unlimited ownership reverts to the true owner.

An individual whose land abuts a public highway might have special rights, including the right to a reasonable passageway to the highway from his or her land.

Construction and Maintenance

The construction and maintenance of highways are assumed by either the state, local communities, or a specifically designated agency. The actual plan of work in constructing, maintaining, or repairing highways is in the discretion of the highway authorities, whereas the state legislature determines their routes. The designation and location of a federally-aided state highway must be in accordance with federal and state law. A state, in its construction of a highway under the federal-aid primary system might be required to obtain the approval of federal agencies if the highway has a marked effect on the environment. The authorities may make provisions for the drainage of surface waters and for the building of ditches and culverts.

The construction and repair of public roads may be funded by general TAXATION, because the public roads are for a public purpose. The power to impose highway taxes vests in the legislature, and funds may be raised from vehicle taxes, gasoline taxes, property taxes, the sale of bonds, or by special assessments on the property for the amount necessary to cover the costs of construction or improvement.

In 1998 Congress enacted a law (Transportation Equity Act for the 21st Century, Public Law (105-178) that required states to enact .08 as the blood alcohol count (BAC) needed to constitute the crime of driving while intoxicated. States that did not lower their BAC to meet this standard would lose federal highway funds. By 2005 all of the states had met this new federal standard.

The U.S. TRANSPORTATION DEPARTMENT, established by Congress, works with the states to establish and maintain a national highway system (23 U.S.C.A. § 101 et seq.). Federal revenues pay for most of the national highway system. Congress may withhold portions of these funds if states do not enact certain laws related to highways or highway use and affecting interstate commerce. For example, Congress may withhold funding if a state does not set the minimum age for alcohol consumption at 21 years; suspend, for at least six months, the driver's license of persons convicted of drug offenses; or prohibit driving under the influence of alcohol.

Obstruction

Any unauthorized obstruction that hinders the use of a public highway, such as a fence, gate, or ditch, is illegal and constitutes a NUISANCE. Officials may, however, lawfully obstruct highways temporarily under their jurisdictions for a reasonable period to make necessary repairs or improvements. Anyone who causes or allows an obstruction to be placed on a public highway is liable and may be enjoined to compel its removal.

In addition, the authorities or private individuals who have sustained special damages—financial or other losses that differ from those incurred by the public—may sue for damages against one who obstructs a highway. What constitutes SPECIAL DAMAGES is dependent upon the facts of each case. Special injury might exist where the obstruction blocks access to the plaintiff's property. In a number of jurisdictions the obstruction of highways is a criminal offense.

Use

The state has the power to control and regulate the use of public highways, provided its regulations do not constitute an unreasonable interference with the right of travel or impede interstate commerce. The state may determine the character of motor vehicles that use its highways and may properly exclude vehicles weighing in excess of a maximum set by statute. A reasonable tax may be imposed on vehicles based on their excess weight in order to compensate the state for the additional costs of maintaining the highway as a result of the severe wear and tear placed on the road by such vehicles. To protect the public health, the state may prohibit trucks that transport chemicals or explosives from driving through populated or residential areas. The secretary of transportation regulates the safety performance of all commercial motor carriers transporting explosives or dangerous articles, such as flammable or radioactive materials, in interstate or foreign commerce. The state may restrict the speed of vehicles, or proscribe parking alongside the highway except in emergencies. Bicycles used on highways may be subject to reasonable restrictions, such as the requirement that they be equipped with lights at night.

The *law of the road* is composed of a system of rules and regulations based upon the traditional practices and customs that govern safe travel on highways. The law is often embodied in statutes or government regulations and is regarded as being so well-known that there is a legal presumption that everyone knows it. Highway travelers, therefore, may properly make the assumption that other travelers will observe the law and comply with rules and regulations. When an individual fails to observe the law of the road without justification, he or she will be held liable for injuries precipitated by the NEGLIGENCE. A violation of a particular rule of the road may be justified by special circumstance.

FURTHER READINGS

King, Ledyard. "Delay of Road Bill Will Cost States." *USA Today* (September 23, 2003). Available online at http://www.usatoday.com/news/washington/2003-09-23-road money_x.htm; website home page: http://www.usatoday.com (accessed July 29, 2009).

Lynch, James. 1986. "The Federal Highway Beautification Act after Metromedia." *Emory Law Journal* 35.

Queary, Paul. "Seat Belt Law Comes under Fire." *Seattle Post-Intelligencer* (August 4, 2003). Available online at http://www.usatoday.com/news/washington/2003-09-23-roadmoney_x.htm; website home page: http://www.usatoday.com (accessed July 29, 2009).

CROSS REFERENCES

Automobiles; National Transportation Safety Board.

HIJACKING

The seizure of a commercial vehicle—airplane, ship, or truck—by force or threat of force.

Hijacking is the modern term for "piracy." It is derived from the phrase "High, Jack!" which is a command to raise one's hands before being robbed. The word gained popular currency during Prohibition (1920–33), when bootleggers commandeered truckloads of liquor from each other, and reappeared when political activists began to seize commercial airplanes in the 1960s.

Airplane Hijacking

The first U.S. airplane hijacking occurred in 1961. The number of such incidents, also known as skyjackings or air piracies, grew during the 1960s, with 40 attempts made in 1969. Many of the early hijacking incidents involved persons seeking to divert airplanes to Cuba, where they could gain asylum. These hijackings became so numerous that the phrase "Take me to Havana" entered popular culture.

In 1973 the United States and Cuba were able to reach an agreement that allows either country to request the EXTRADITION of a hijacker. The agreement came about through an exchange of diplomatic notes. It was in Cuba's interest to make the agreement because many Cubans had hijacked planes from Cuba and forced them to fly to the United States. The agreement allows either country to take into account EXTENUATING CIRCUMSTANCES when the hijackers acted "for strictly political reasons and were in real and imminent danger of death without a viable alternative, provided there was no financial EXTORTION or physical injury" to crew, passengers, or other persons (12 *I.L.M.* 370–76, No. 2 [March 1973]).

In addition to this agreement, the United States, in 1961, made the hijacking of an airplane a federal crime. Under the Aircraft Piracy Act (18 U.S.C.A. § 32), the attempted or successful execution of the following actions is considered hijacking: damaging an aircraft; placing or bringing a destructive device or substance on an aircraft; damaging or interfering with an air navigation facility, or equipment and property used in connection with the operation of an aircraft; committing an act of violence against or otherwise injuring an individual on an aircraft; or making threats or statements that they know are false against or about the safety of an aircraft that is already in flight.

Hijacking has not been confined to the United States and Cuba. In 1970 hijackers seized more than 90 planes around the world. The growth of international TERRORISM, specifically in the Middle East, led to widely publicized hijackings. In these situations hijackers sought the satisfaction of political demands and a platform to air their views. In 1970 members of the Popular Front for the Liberation of Palestine hijacked three airliners and flew two of them to an airstrip in the desert near Amman, Jordan, while blowing up the third in Cairo, Egypt after releasing the passengers and crew. Several days later another plane was hijacked. The hijackers demanded the release of Palestinian prisoners in European prisons and in Israeli jails. When their demands were not met, they removed the passengers from the airliners and destroyed the planes one by one.

Faced with increased numbers of air hijackings, the international community sought to negotiate agreements that would prevent hijackers from finding safe haven. The 1970 Hague Convention for the Suppression of Unlawful Seizure of Aircraft (22 U.S.T. 1641, T.I.A.S. 7192 [effective in the United States in 1971]) deals specifically with the hijacking of aircraft in flight. The 1971 Montreal Convention for the Suppression of Unlawful Acts against the Safety of Civil Aviation (24 U.S.T. 564, T.I.A.S. 7570 [effective in the United States in 1973]) addresses attacks on or SABOTAGE of civil aircraft either in flight or on the ground, or destruction of or damage to air navigation facilities when this is likely to endanger the safety of aircraft in flight. Either the state of registration or the state in which the aircraft lands can exercise jurisdiction. The state having the hijackers in custody must prosecute or extradite them. A state may decline to extradite if it considers the offense political, or may prefer not to extradite to a state that imposes the death penalty, but in either of these cases, it is obligated to prosecute the offenders.

The United States passed the Antihijacking Act of 1974 (49 U.S.C.A. § 1301 et seq.) to implement these international conventions. This act seeks to prevent nations from adopting a permissive posture toward illegal activities such as the commandeering of aircraft, by providing penalties for hijackers and for nations that shield or fail to take adequate precautions against hijackers. The act gives the president the power to terminate air service between an offending nation and the United States if the president determines that the offending nation has acted inconsistently with its obligations under the antihijacking conventions. Since the signing of these international conventions in the 1970s, airplane hijacking fell sharply, especially in the United States.

Hijacking, however, reached a new level on SEPTEMBER 11, 2001, when terrorists commandeered four commercial airplanes and crashed them into the World Trade Center in New York, the Pentagon in Washington, D.C., and a field in Pennsylvania. The United States was stunned and the definition of hijacking came into serious question. Prior to the attacks, experts generally found that if pilots adhered to the hijackers' demands, violence was less likely to occur. In this case, however, there was no negotiation. In effect, the hijackers proved that planes can be used as missiles, causing mass violence not only to those aboard a plane, but to thousands of others located in or near a target of terrorism. As a result, national security became an immediate priority, and regulations and security measures were quickly implemented in the hopes of preventing similar attacks.

Prior to September 11, airline security fell under the purview of the FEDERAL AVIATION ADMINISTRATION (FAA). After the attacks, Congress passed the Aviation and Transportation Act (Pub. L. No. 107-71; codifed at 49 U.S.C.A. §§ 40101 et. seq.), which among other things transferred this authority from the FAA to the Transportation Security Administration (TSA). One year later, Congress enacted the Homeland Security Act of 2002, Pub. L. No. 107-296 (codified in scattered sections of 6 U.S.C.A.), which included additional provisions for the prevention of hijacking. For example, Title XIV of the act, known as the Arming Pilots Against Terrorism Act, qualified certain volunteer pilots as federal law enforcement officers in order to protect cockpits in the case of an attempted hijacking.

New approaches to the prevention of airline hijacking led to a tightening of security in U.S. airports. Persons using an airport must now generally show identification several times before boarding a plane. And, because the terrorists in the September 11 attacks used a common household item (box cutters), many articles that could potentially be used as a weapon are now prohibited or restricted.

Ship Hijacking

Ship hijacking is rare, but the seizure of the *Achille Lauro* proved that it can happen. The Italian cruise ship was commandeered on October 7, 1985, by four members of a faction of the Palestine Liberation Organization. The hijackers boarded the ship posing as tourists, and waited until the ship was off the Egyptian coast before taking its crew and passengers hostage. They threatened to kill the hostages if Israel did not meet their demand to release 50 Palestinian prisoners. They also threatened to blow up the ship if anyone attempted a rescue mission. When the hijackers' demands were not met the next day, they shot and killed Leon Klinghoffer, a U.S. citizen who was partially paralyzed and used a wheelchair. They dumped Klinghoffer's body in the sea.

Denied access to a Syrian port, the hijackers sailed to Alexandria, where they surrendered to Egyptian authorities. The hijackers were allowed to leave Egypt for Italy to stand trial, where they were convicted for violating an Italian statute that made terrorist kidnapping illegal. The hijacker who confessed to killing Klinghoffer was sentenced to 30 years in prison.

FURTHER READINGS

Karber, Phillip A. 2002. "Reconstructing Global Aviation in an Era of the Civil Aircraft as a Weapon of Destruction." *Harvard Journal of Law and Public Policy* 25, no. 2.

Niles, Mark C. 2002. "On the Hijacking of Agencies (and Airplanes): The Federal Aviation Administration, 'Agency Capture,' and Airline Security." *American Univ. Journal of Gender, Social Policy, and the Law* 10.

Taillon, J. Paul D. 2002. *Hijacking and Hostages: Government Responses to Terrorism.* Santa Barbara, CA: Praeger.

❖ HILL, ANITA FAYE

A little-known law professor testifying before a U.S. Senate committee in 1991 became a cause célèbre when she accused a respected U.S. Supreme Court nominee of SEXUAL HARASSMENT. Anita Faye Hill became a household name during the televised confirmation hearings of U. S. Supreme Court candidate CLARENCE THOMAS, the second African American in U.S. history to be tapped for the High Court. Hill, who is also African American, was calm and articulate as she withstood an intense grilling by the all-male, all-white SENATE JUDICIARY COMMITTEE. Despite skepticism and open hostility from some of the senators, Hill stood firm on her account of sexually explicit remarks and behavior by Thomas, her former boss. Conservatives reviled Hill, feminists revered her—and by the end of the hearings, U.S. citizens of all political persuasions had a keener awareness of the problem of sexual harassment in the workplace.

Nothing in Hill's background prepared her for the unremitting media attention she received during and after the Thomas confirmation hearings. The youngest of Albert Hill and Erma Hill's 13 children, she was an extremely private person. Hill was born July 30, 1956, and raised on a struggling family farm near Morris, Oklahoma. Her religious parents emphasized the importance of hard work, strong moral values, and education. Intelligent and disciplined, Hill was valedictorian of her high school class and an honor student at Oklahoma State University, in Stillwater, where she graduated in 1977 with a degree in psychology. After college, Hill attended Yale University Law School on a scholarship from the National Association for the Advancement of Colored People (NAACP).

Hill graduated from law school with honors in 1980, and worked briefly for the Washington, D.C., law firm of Wald, Harkrader, & Ross. In 1981 she left private practice to become special counsel to the assistant secretary in the U.S. Department of Education's Office of CIVIL RIGHTS. The assistant secretary was Thomas. It was during this time that Thomas asked her out and, according to Hill, sexually harassed her. In 1982 Thomas was appointed chair of the EQUAL EMPLOYMENT OPPORTUNITY COMMISSION (EEOC), and Hill moved to the EEOC with her boss in what she felt was a necessary career step.

In 1983 Hill decided to leave Washington, D.C., to become a law professor at Oral Roberts University. In 1986 she accepted a teaching position at the University of Oklahoma. Although full professorship and tenure are normally granted at Oklahoma after six years, Hill achieved both in just four years.

Anita Faye Hill.
SCOTT WINTROW/GETTY IMAGES

Hill's transformation from legal scholar to feminist icon came about after Thomas was offered the career opportunity of a lifetime. President GEORGE H. W. BUSH nominated Thomas, then a federal appeals court judge, to fill an opening on the U.S. Supreme Court. During the mandatory Senate investigation of Thomas, Hill disclosed in private sessions the alleged incidents of sexual harassment by Thomas. Reports of Hill's private testimony were leaked to a National Public Radio reporter.

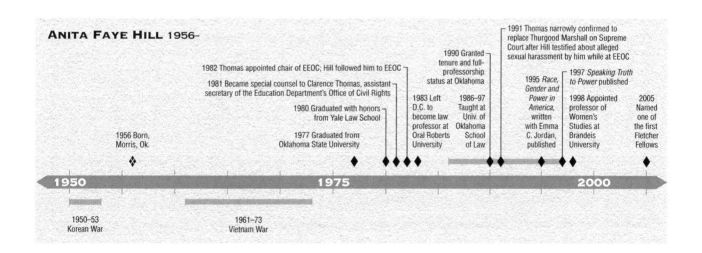

ANITA FAYE HILL 1956–

1956 Born, Morris, Ok.

1977 Graduated from Oklahoma State University

1980 Graduated with honors from Yale Law School

1981 Became special counsel to Clarence Thomas, assistant secretary of the Education Department's Office of Civil Rights

1982 Thomas appointed chair of EEOC; Hill followed him to EEOC

1983 Left D.C. to become law professor at Oral Roberts University

1986–97 Taught at Univ. of Oklahoma School of Law

1990 Granted tenure and full-professorship status at Oklahoma

1991 Thomas narrowly confirmed to replace Thurgood Marshall on Supreme Court after Hill testified about alleged sexual harassment by him while at EEOC

1995 *Race, Gender and Power in America*, written with Emma C. Jordan, published

1997 *Speaking Truth to Power* published

1998 Appointed professor of Women's Studies at Brandeis University

2005 Named one of the first Fletcher Fellows

1950

1975

2000

1950–53 Korean War

1961–73 Vietnam War

When Hill's allegations became public, they stood as a potential roadblock to Thomas's confirmation.

During a live broadcast of the Senate hearings, Hill's personal motives, character, and politics were scrutinized relentlessly. Both Hill and Thomas brought in witnesses to support their separate versions of events. Thomas angrily denied Hill's charges and accused the senators of conducting a media circus and a "high tech lynching." Hill stood by her story, despite the accusations of some senators who suggested that she was delusional. Her testimony was detailed and graphic. In a clear, dispassionate manner, she described Thomas's alleged interest in pornographic films and bragging comments about his sexual performance. She steadfastly denied that she was lying or prone to fantasies.

Despite Hill's damaging testimony, Thomas weathered the hearings and received Senate confirmation by a narrow margin on October 15, 1991. Hill returned to the University of Oklahoma Law School and tried to resume her quiet private life.

Immediately after the Hill-Thomas hearings, only 24 percent of the registered voters who responded to a *Wall Street Journal*–NBC News poll indicated that they believed Hill; 40 percent thought Thomas was telling the truth. Just one year after Thomas's confirmation, public opinion had changed. In a 1992 *Wall Street Journal*–NBC News poll, 44 percent of the people interviewed sided with Hill and 34 percent believed Thomas. One possible explanation for this shift in loyalties was the nation's year-long posthearing examination of the nature and effects of sexual harassment. Perhaps as more people became aware of the problem and more women revealed their own encounters with sexual harassment, Hill's credibility increased.

To some, the Hill-Thomas hearings illustrated the almost insurmountable difficulty in bringing a sexual harassment claim; to others, they showed how vulnerable men are to false accusations by women with ulterior motives. Although some women were discouraged after witnessing Hill's treatment by the Senate panel, others found the courage to file their own sexual harassment complaints after watching Hill's example.

Hill left the University of Oklahoma in 1996. She served as a visiting professor at the University of California's Institute for the Study of Social Change before accepting a position as a professor at Brandeis University's Heller School for Social Policy and Management. She has published extensively in the areas of international COMMERCIAL LAW, BANKRUPTCY, and civil rights, and has engaged in a number of speaking engagements and other presentations. Hill also has offered commentary in such publications as *Newsweek*, *The New York Times*, and *The Boston Globe*. In 1997 she authored *Speaking Truth to Power*, in which she recounts her experiences as a witness in the confirmation hearing for Clarence Thomas.

For a decade after the release of her book, Hill disappeared from the public eye and focused on her work at Brandeis University, where she teaches social policy, women's studies, and law. In 2007 Thomas released an autobiography, *My Grandfather's Son: A Memoir*, which contained passages in which he criticized Hill and her legal team for engaging in a liberal character ASSAULT against him. During Thomas's promotional tour, he repeated his accusations against Hill and the members of the media who supported her. Hill responded to Thomas's statements in a series of media interviews and also decided to publish an op-ed article in the *New York Times*, in which she reaffirmed her accusations and expressed surprise that Thomas was still defending his actions by defaming his accusers. "In the portion of his book that addresses my role in the Senate hearings into his nomination," Hill wrote in her article, "Justice Thomas offers a litany of unsubstantiated representations and outright smears that Republican senators made about me when I testified before the Judiciary Committee."

In the wake of Thomas's biography, Hill expressed hope that her experience and actions have contributed to positive developments for working women in the United States. As she stated in the conclusion to her article, "My belief is that in the past 16 years we have come closer to making the resolution of these issues an honest search for the truth, which, after all, is at the core of all legal inquiry." Speaking in her biography about the importance of the Thomas trials for women's rights, Hill said, "More than anything else, the Hill-Thomas hearing of October 1991 was about finding our voices and breaking the silence forever."

WE NEED TO TURN THE QUESTION AROUND TO LOOK AT THE HARASSER, NOT THE TARGET. WE NEED TO BE SURE THAT WE CAN GO OUT AND LOOK AT ANYONE WHO IS A VICTIM OF HARASSMENT... AND SAY, 'YOU DO NOT HAVE TO REMAIN SILENT ANYMORE.'
—ANITA HILL

FURTHER READINGS

Hill, Anita. 1997. *Speaking Truth to Power*. New York: Doubleday.

Smitherman, Geneva, ed. 1995. *African American Women Speak Out on Anita Hill-Clarence Thomas*. Detroit: Wayne State Univ. Press.

⬦ HILL, OLIVER WHITE, SR.

Oliver W. Hill is an African American attorney who was instrumental in the CIVIL RIGHTS struggles of the 1950s and 1960s.

Oliver White Hill Sr. was born May 1, 1907, in Richmond, Virginia. He received his bachelor of art degree from Howard University in 1931, then continued at Howard and received his doctor of jurisprudence degree in 1933. The following year, he opened a law practice in Roanoke, Virginia, which he later moved to Richmond. He became active in such organizations as the National Association for the Advancement of Colored People (NAACP) and the Urban League as well as the local faction of the DEMOCRATIC PARTY. Hill served a two-year stint in the military from 1943 to 1945, then returned to private practice.

In August 1947 Hill ran for the Virginia House of Delegates. He lost that election by a mere 190 votes, missing an opportunity to become the first African American to occupy a seat in Virginia's general assembly since 1890. He returned to politics the following year, and on June 10, 1948, he was elected to a seat on Richmond's city council. With that victory, he became the first African American elected to office in Richmond since Reconstruction.

Hill's election was significant because at least 2,000 of the 9,000 voters who backed him were white. Such racial crossover voting was unprecedented at the time, but Hill had made an effort to appeal to voters from all races.

Oliver White Hill.
AP IMAGES

He shrewdly realized that many whites, some motivated by moral conviction and others by simple pragmatism, understood that change was imminent in the South. The treatment of African American soldiers during WORLD WAR II had forced harsh scrutiny on a system that was coming to an end. "There is rising in the South a large body of white citizens who recognize the importance of extending constitutional guarantees to Negroes in order to strengthen their own economic and political security," he said.

During his stint on the Richmond council, Hill was voted the second-most-effective member of the nine-member body. But his triumph was short-lived: In 1950 he lost his bid for reelection. Later, he was a popular contender for appointment to a vacancy on the council, but because of his uncompromising position on civil rights, he was denied the appointment. African American leaders in Richmond were

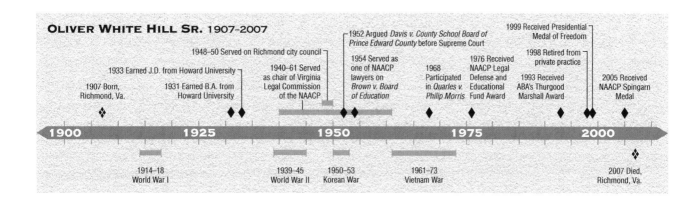

OLIVER WHITE HILL SR. 1907–2007

1907 Born, Richmond, Va.

1931 Earned B.A. from Howard University

1933 Earned J.D. from Howard University

1940–61 Served as chair of Virginia Legal Commission of the NAACP

1948–50 Served on Richmond city council

1952 Argued *Davis v. County School Board of Prince Edward County* before Supreme Court

1954 Served as one of NAACP lawyers on *Brown v. Board of Education*

1968 Participated in *Quarles v. Philip Morris*

1976 Received NAACP Legal Defense and Educational Fund Award

1993 Received ABA's Thurgood Marshall Award

1998 Retired from private practice

1999 Received Presidential Medal of Freedom

2005 Received NAACP Spingarn Medal

2007 Died, Richmond, Va.

1914–18 World War I

1939–45 World War II

1950–53 Korean War

1961–73 Vietnam War

1900 | 1925 | 1950 | 1975 | 2000

angered by the rejection, and much of the racial tension that had characterized Richmond before Hill's 1948 victory was rekindled.

Hill returned to his law practice and joined the ranks of the pioneers in the fight for civil rights. During a career that has spanned six decades, he has been involved in many of the landmark cases that secured constitutional rights for minorities in housing, education, and employment. As a member of the Richmond Democratic Committee, he worked diligently to secure minority voting rights and to encourage involvement in political activity. From 1940 to 1961 Hill served as chair of the Virginia Legal Commission of the NAACP and participated in such celebrated legal battles as BROWN V. BOARD OF EDUCATION, 347 U.S. 483, 74 S. Ct. 686, 98 L. Ed. 873 (1954), abolishing segregated public schools, and *Quarles v. Philip Morris,* 279 F. Supp. 505 (ED. Va.), a 1968 case establishing the right of minorities to equal employment opportunities. In August 1955, because of his participation in *Brown,* a fiery cross, the symbol of the KU KLUX KLAN, was burned on the front lawn of his home.

In 1952 President HARRY S. TRUMAN named Hill to the Committee on Government Contract Compliance. This organization was charged with policing the enforcement of federal contract clauses barring racial or religious discrimination in employment. Hill also served, under President JOHN F. KENNEDY, as assistant to the commissioner of the Federal Housing Administration. He returned to his law practice after Kennedy's death.

Hill received numerous awards and recognitions during his long and distinguished career, including the Howard University Alumni Award (1950), National Bar Association Lawyer of the Year Award (1959), Washington Bar Association CHARLES H. HOUSTON Medallion of Merit (1976), NAACP LEGAL DEFENSE AND EDUCATIONAL FUND Award (1976), NAACP William Ming Advocacy Award (1980), National Council of Christians and Jews Brotherhood Citation (1982), American Bar Association's THURGOOD MARSHALL Award (1993), Urban League of Richmond Lifetime Achievement Award (1994), NAACP Spingarn Medal (2005), and the University of Richmond Law School Oliver W. Hill Social Justice Award (2007).

In 1999 Hill received the highest civilian award awarded in the United States, the Presidential Medal of Freedom. President BILL CLINTON said of Hill, "Throughout his long and rich life, he has challenged the laws of our land and the conscience of our country. He has stood up for equal pay, better schools, fair housing— for everything that is necessary to make America truly, one, indivisible and equal."

Hill retired from the full-time PRACTICE OF LAW in 1998, at the age of 91. In an interview with *Virginia Lawyer* in 1998, he said, "Most of the time you get your satisfaction when you find that people need your help and you voluntarily help them. We never turned down any cases. Even when we were supposed to get paid, and sometimes we didn't."

Hill and his late wife, Beresenia A. Walker Hill, had one son, Oliver W. Hill Jr., and three grandchildren. He died August 5, 2007.

FURTHER READINGS

Dalpino, Laura E. 1999. "Virginia Leader and Legend Honored by the President." *Virginia Lawyer* (October).

HIROHITO

Hirohito was the emperor of Japan from 1926 to 1989. His reign encompassed a period of Japanese militarism that resulted in Japan's participation in WORLD WAR II, the United States' dropping of atomic bombs on Hiroshima and Nagasaki, and the United States' MILITARY OCCUPATION of Japan following Japan's defeat. After World War II, Hirohito's authority changed, and he was reduced to a ceremonial figure.

Hirohito was born in Tokyo on April 29, 1901, and was educated in Japan. He became emperor on December 25, 1926, at a time when Japanese parliamentary government suggested that democracy and international cooperation would continue to grow. However, forces within the military sought to dominate the government and embark on a course of expansionism within Asia. Though he had private misgivings about the rise of militarism, Hirohito took no action to stop the generals. His advisers were concerned that imperial opposition would lead to the military overthrow of the monarchy.

As the 124th direct descendant of Japan's first emperor, Jimmu, Hirohito was considered sacred and was referred to as Tenno Heika, meaning "son of heaven." Because Hirohito was unwilling to exercise his divine authority against

I DECIDED TO GO TO LAW SCHOOL TO SEE WHAT I COULD DO ABOUT TRYING TO GET THE SUPREME COURT TO CHANGE ITS MIND.
—OLIVER W. HILL

the military, the Japanese army invaded China in 1937 and in 1940 joined in a military alliance with the Axis powers. The alliance led to Japan's participation in World War II and its attack on Pearl Harbor and the United States on December 7, 1941.

The attack on the United States led to severe consequences for Japanese Americans. On February 19, 1942, President FRANKLIN D. ROOSEVELT issued Executive Order No. 9066, forcing the relocation of all 112,000 Japanese Americans living on the West Coast (including 70,000 U.S. citizens) to detention camps in places such as Jerome, Arkansas, and Heart Mountain, Wyoming. Roosevelt issued the order after U.S. military leaders, worried about a Japanese invasion, argued that national security required such drastic action.

The U.S. Supreme Court upheld the forced relocation in KOREMATSU V. UNITED STATES, 323 U.S. 214, 65 S. Ct. 193, 89 L. Ed. 194 (1944). Justice Hugo L. Black noted that curtailing the rights of a single racial group is constitutionally suspect, but in this case military necessity justified the exclusion of Japanese Americans from the West Coast. In retrospect historians have characterized the removal and detention as the most drastic invasion of individual CIVIL RIGHTS by the government in U.S. history.

Hirohito gradually became more open, within the inner circles of government, about his desire to end the war, especially after the United States inflicted numerous military defeats on Japan. But many members of the military wished to fight until the very end. With the United States' dropping of atomic bombs on Hiroshima and Nagasaki in August 1945, Hirohito pushed for the surrender of Japan. On August 15 he broadcast Japan's surrender to the Allied forces. He broadcast to the Japanese people additional messages that were credited for the smooth transfer of power from Japan to the U.S. military occupation force, under the leadership of General Douglas MacArthur.

Although Hirohito was implicated in Japanese war plans, he was exonerated in the WAR CRIMES trials of 1946–48. He had changed the importance of the monarchy in 1946, when he publicly renounced his divine authority. The 1947 constitution that was written for Japan by MacArthur and his advisers had transformed Hirohito from a sovereign with supreme authority into a "symbol of the state," and

Hirohito, emperor of Japan from 1926 to 1989, in his coronation robes.

placed control of the government in the hands of elected officials. Hirohito had endorsed the change, which reduced the emperor to a ceremonial figure.

Hirohito embraced the ceremonial role. He traveled widely and became more accessible. He also pursued his interest in marine biology. He died on January 7, 1989.

FURTHER READINGS

Bix, Herbert P. 2001. *Hirohito and the Making of Modern Japan.* New York, NY: HarperCollins.

Dower, John W. 2000. *Embracing Defeat: Japan in the Wake of World War II.* New York: Norton.

Executive Order No. 9066. 1942. *Federal Register 7:1407.* Available online at http://www.english.illinois.edu/maps/poets/g_l/haiku/9066.htm; website home page: http://www.english.illinois.edu (accessed July 29, 2009).

CROSS REFERENCE

Japanese American Evacuation Cases.

HISS, ALGER

For the United States, the prosecution of ALGER HISS was a pivotal domestic event of the COLD WAR. A former high-ranking federal official with a seemingly impeccable reputation, Hiss was accused in 1948 of having spied for the Soviet Union. The charges shocked the nation. Not only had Hiss held government positions of extreme importance, but he was also one of the architects of postwar international relations,

having helped establish the UNITED NATIONS. He steadfastly maintained his innocence in hearings before the House Un-American Activities Committee (HUAC). But a relentless probe by the committee's lead investigator, Representative RICHARD M. NIXON, of California, led to a GRAND JURY investigation. In 1950, Hiss was convicted of two counts of perjury, for which he served 44 months in prison. His case became a cause célàbre for liberals, who regarded him as a victim of the era's anti-Communist hysteria. It also fueled a passion for anti-Communist investigations and legislation that preoccupied Congress for the next several years.

Before coming under suspicion, Hiss had a meteoric rise in public service. A Harvard graduate in 1929, the INTERNATIONAL LAW specialist served in the Departments of Agriculture and Justice from 1933 to 1936. He then moved to the STATE DEPARTMENT, where he assumed the post of counselor at global conferences during WORLD WAR II. In 1945 Hiss advised President FRANKLIN D. ROOSEVELT at the Yalta Conference, at which the Allied powers planned the end of the war. He was 41 years old. Next came a leading role in the establishment of the United Nations, appointment to the administration of the U.S. Office of Special Political Affairs, and, in 1946, election to the presidency of the Carnegie Endowment for International Peace. As a statesman, Hiss had proved himself in

no small way; his career had earned him the highest confidence of his government in times of crisis.

But soon Hiss was swept up in a round of damaging public accusations. By the late 1940s the U.S. House of Representatives had spent several years investigating Communist influence in business and government. This was the work of HUAC, first established in 1938 and increasingly busy in the years of suspicion that followed World War II. In August 1948 HUAC heard testimony from Whittaker Chambers, an editor at *Time* magazine, who had previously admitted to spying for the Soviet Union. Now Chambers fingered Hiss. He charged that Hiss had secretly been a Communist party member in the 1930s, and most dramatically, he accused Hiss of giving him confidential State Department documents to deliver to the Soviets in 1938.

Accusations of Communist affiliation were common at HUAC hearings—in a sense, they were its chief business. The process of naming names was triggered by the committee's threat of legal action against witnesses who did not cooperate. But even by HUAC's standards, the accusations against Hiss were spectacular. Furthermore, Chambers had evidence. He offered the committee microfilm of the confidential documents, which he claimed had been prepared on Hiss's own typewriter. The charges particularly excited committee member Nixon, a California freshman, who used them to establish his credentials as a tough anti-Communist. In a highly publicized event, Chambers took Nixon to his Maryland farm, where the microfilm was hidden in a hollow pumpkin. Hiss was soon called before HUAC to be grilled by Nixon. He denied Chambers's accusations and dramatically questioned Chambers himself in a vain attempt to clear his name.

A grand jury was impaneled and held hearings in December 1948. Because of the STATUTE OF LIMITATIONS, Hiss could not be tried on charges of ESPIONAGE in 1948 for allegedly passing documents to the Soviets in 1938. But the grand jury returned a two-count indictment of perjury: It charged that he had lied about giving Chambers the official documents in 1938, and when claiming that he had not even seen Chambers after January 1, 1937.

After his first trial in 1948 ended in a hung jury, Hiss was retried in 1950 (*United States v.*

Hiss, 88 F. Supp. 559 [S.D.N.Y. 1950]). Hiss's defense hinged on portraying Chambers, the government's primary witness, as unreliable. He claimed that Chambers was a psychopathic personality prone to chronic lying. In what became the seminal ruling of its kind, the court admitted psychiatric evidence for the reason of discrediting the witness. But despite challenging Chambers's credibility, the validity of Chambers's testimony, and the accuracy of other evidence, Hiss was convicted. Sentenced to five years in prison, he served nearly four years. His career in law and public service was ruined. He spent the next two decades working as a salesman while writing books and giving lectures.

The question of Hiss's guilt has divided intellectuals for decades. Hiss always maintained his innocence—in 1957, when he published a memoir, *In the Court of Public Opinion,* and even more in 1975, when, with prominent help, he successfully sued for reinstatement to the bar of Massachusetts (*In re Hiss,* 368 Mass. 447, 333 N.E.2d 429). Since 1975, some wordsmiths have used FEDERAL BUREAU OF INVESTIGATION files to argue in favor of or against Hiss's guilt: notably, author Allan Weinstein in *Perjury* (1978) and editor Edith Tiger in *In Re Alger Hiss* (1979).

The *Hiss* case profoundly affected the politics of its era. It gave impetus to anti-Communist sentiment in Washington, D.C., which led to more hearings before HUAC as well as legislation such as the McCarran Act (50 U.S.C.A. § 781 et seq.), intended as a crackdown on the American Communist party. The case also helped launch the careers of Nixon and of Senator JOSEPH R. MCCARTHY, of Wisconsin, providing the latter with ammunition for an infamous crusade against alleged Communist infiltration of the federal government.

Hiss died November 15, 1996, in New York City.

FURTHER READINGS

Alden, Bill. 1999. "'Historical Interest' Held to Justify Access to Notes of Hiss Grand Jury." *New York Law Journal* 221 (May 14).

Biography of President Richard Nixon. 2005. The Richard Nixon Library & Birthplace Foundation web site. Available online at http://www.nixonlibraryfoundation.org/index.php?src=gendocs&link=Rnbio; website home page: http://www.nixonlibraryfoundation.org (accessed July 29, 2009).

Dresser, Rebecca. 1990. "Personal Identity and Punishment." *Boston Univ. Law Review* 70 (May).

Hiss, Tony. 1999. *The View from Alger's Window: A Son's Memoir.* New York: Knopf.

Schrecker, Ellen. 1994. *The Age of McCarthyism: A Brief History with Documents.* Boston: St. Martin's. Available online at http://www.writing.upenn.edu/~afilreis/50s/schrecker-age.html; website home page: http://www.writing.upenn.edu (accessed July 29, 2009).

Weinstein, Allen. 1997. *Perjury: The Hiss-Chambers Case.* New York: Random House.

CROSS REFERENCES

Cold War; Communism; Rosenbergs Trial.

HITLER, ADOLF

Adolf Hitler ruled Germany as a dictator from 1933 to 1945. Hitler's National Socialist (Nazi) German Workers' party was based on the idea of German racial supremacy and a virulent anti-Semitism. Hitler's regime murdered more than 6 million Jews and others in concentration camps and started WORLD WAR II.

Hitler was born in Braunauam Inn, Austria, on April 20, 1889, the son of a minor government official and a peasant woman. A poor student, Hitler never completed high school. In 1907 he moved to Vienna and tried to make a living as an artist. He was unsuccessful and had to work as a day laborer to support himself. During this period Hitler immersed himself in anti-Jewish and antidemocratic literature. He was also a passionate German nationalist who believed that Austria should be merged with Germany so as to unite the German people.

In 1913 he moved to Munich. He gave up his Austrian citizenship and enlisted in the German army when WORLD WAR I began in 1914. He rose to lance corporal in his infantry regiment, won the Iron Cross, and was wounded in 1917. When Germany admitted defeat and signed the armistice terminating World War I in November 1918, Hitler was in a hospital, temporarily blinded by a mustard gas attack and suffering from shock. Outraged at the defeat, Hitler blamed Jews and Communists for stabbing the German army in the back.

Other members of the German army felt the same way. After his discharge from the hospital, Hitler was assigned to spy on politically subversive activities in Munich. In 1919 he joined a small nationalist party. The German Workers' party was transformed in 1920 by Hitler into the National Socialist German

Adolf Hitler salutes Nazi soldiers in Nuremberg, Germany, in 1938. Hitler ruled Germany as the nation's chancellor from 1933 to 1945.

U.S. HOLOCAUST
MEMORIAL MUSEUM

Workers' party. The Nazis advocated the uniting of all German people into one nation and the repudiation of the Versailles treaty, which the Allies had forced Germany to sign. This treaty imposed large reparations on Germany and restricted the size of its armed forces.

In 1923 the Nazis tried to capitalize on political and economic turmoil in Germany. On November 8 Hitler called for a Nazi revolution. The beer hall *putsch* (revolution), named for its place of origin, failed because Hitler had no military support. When he led 2,000 storm troopers in revolt, the police opened fire and killed 16 people. Hitler was arrested and sentenced to five years in prison for TREASON.

While in prison Hitler wrote *Mein Kampf* (My Struggle), a rambling book that was both an autobiography and a declaration of his political beliefs. He made his intentions plain: If he was to assume control of Germany, he would seek to conquer much of Europe and he would destroy the Jewish race. He rejected democracy and called for a dictatorship that would be able to withstand an ASSAULT by COMMUNISM.

Hitler served only nine months in prison, as political pressure forced the Bavarian government to commute his sentence. He was set free in December 1924.

From 1924 to 1928 Hitler and the Nazis had little political success. The Great Depression, which started in late 1929, was the catalyst for Hitler's rise to power. As the economy declined, Hitler railed against the Versailles treaty and a conspiracy of Jews and Communists who were destroying Germany. By 1932 the Nazis had become the strongest party in Germany. On January 30, 1933, Hitler was named chancellor, or prime minister, of Germany.

Many German leaders believed that Hitler could be controlled by industrialists and the German army. Instead, Hitler quickly moved to make Germany a one-party state and himself the führer (leader). He abolished labor unions, imposed government CENSORSHIP, and directed that Nazi propaganda dominate the press and the radio. The gestapo, Hitler's secret police, waged a war of terror on Nazi opponents. Jews were fired from jobs, placed in concentration camps, and driven from Germany. By 1934 Hitler was securely in charge.

The majority of Germans supported Hitler enthusiastically. He restored full employment, rebuilt the German economy, and allowed Germans to escape the feelings of inferiority instilled after World War I.

Hitler broke the Versailles treaty and proceeded with a massive buildup of the German armed forces. In 1936 he reclaimed the Rhineland from French control, and in 1938 he annexed Austria to Germany. Also in 1938 he took over the German areas of Czechoslovakia, and in 1939 he annexed all of that country. When he invaded Poland on September 1, 1939, Great Britain and France declared war on Germany. World War II had begun.

During the early years of Hitler's regime, some prominent U.S. citizens had believed he was a positive force for Germany. As Hitler became more aggressive and war clouds appeared, U.S. isolationists argued against involvement. People such as aviator Charles A. Lindbergh argued for an America First policy.

Concerns about Nazism led in part to the SMITH ACT (54 Stat. 670) in 1940. Nazi sympathizers organized groups such as the Silvershirts and the German-American Bund, raising the specter of subversion. The Smith Act required aliens to register with and be fingerprinted by the federal government. More important, it made it illegal not only to conspire to overthrow the government, but to advocate or conspire to advocate to do so. The U.S. Supreme Court upheld the constitutionality of the act in *Dennis v. United States,* 341 U.S. 494, 71 S. Ct. 857, 95 L. Ed. 1137 (1951).

Hitler's quick and easy conquest of western Europe in 1940 left Great Britain alone. With the Japanese attack on Pearl Harbor on December 7, 1941, the United States and Great Britain became allies in World War II. They were joined by the Soviet Union, which Hitler had invaded in June 1941. In 1942 the war turned against Hitler. North Africa and then Italy were lost to the Allies. In June 1944 the Allies invaded France and were soon nearing Germany. On the eastern front, the Soviet army moved toward Berlin. During these last years of the war, Hitler directed the extermination of Jews and other "undesirables" in concentration camps.

On July 20, 1944, Hitler escaped an ASSASSINATION attempt. As the military situation crumbled, Hitler realized that defeat was inevitable. While Soviet troops entered Berlin in April 1945, Hitler married his longtime mistress, Eva Braun. On April 30 the two committed suicide. Their bodies were burned by Hitler's aides.

FURTHER READINGS

Anthes, Louis. 1998. "Publicly Deliberative Drama: The 1934 Mock Trial of Adolf Hitler for 'Crimes against Civilization'." *American Journal of Legal History* 42 (October).

Giblin, James Cross. 2002. *The Life and Death of Adolf Hitler.* New York: Clarion Books.

Kershaw, Ian. 1999. *Hitler.* New York: Norton.

Welch, David. 2001. *Hitler: Profile of a Dictator.* London; New York: Taylor & Francis.

CROSS REFERENCES

Hirohito; Mussolini, Benito; Nuremberg Trials.

❖ HOAR, EBENEZER ROCKWOOD

Ebenezer Rockwood Hoar served as attorney general of the United States from 1869 to 1870 under President ULYSSES S. GRANT.

Hoar was born February 21, 1816, in Concord, Massachusetts. His grandfather, Captain Samuel Hoar, was a Revolutionary War hero. His father, Samuel Hoar, Jr., was a Harvard graduate, a Massachusetts state senator, a U.S. representative—and a lifelong activist in partisan politics. Hoar's father was affiliated with the FEDERALIST PARTY until it disappeared after the WAR OF 1812, was associated with the WHIG PARTY in the 1830s, was an organizer of the Massachusetts Free-Soil party in the 1840s, and joined the REPUBLICAN PARTY toward the end of his life.

Hoar's educational path, professional career, and political interests closely mirrored those of his father. Hoar graduated from Harvard College in 1835 and from Harvard Law School in 1839. He was admitted to the bar in 1840 and he practiced law in Concord and Boston. His father's legal and political connections allowed him to try cases with leading attorneys of his day, including RUFUS CHOATE and DANIEL WEBSTER.

Like his father, Hoar began his political career at the state level. In the early 1840s, he was elected to the Massachusetts state senate. His chance remark that he would rather be a Conscience Whig than a Cotton Whig gave the former name to the antislavery arm of the Whig party. By 1848 he was working with his father

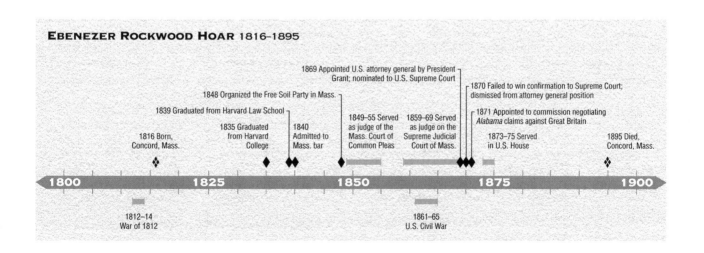

EBENEZER ROCKWOOD HOAR 1816-1895

1869 Appointed U.S. attorney general by President Grant; nominated to U.S. Supreme Court

1848 Organized the Free Soil Party in Mass.

1870 Failed to win confirmation to Supreme Court; dismissed from attorney general position

1839 Graduated from Harvard Law School

1871 Appointed to commission negotiating *Alabama* claims against Great Britain

1835 Graduated from Harvard College

1849–55 Served as judge of the Mass. Court of Common Pleas

1859–69 Served as judge on the Supreme Judicial Court of Mass.

1816 Born, Concord, Mass.

1840 Admitted to Mass. bar

1873–75 Served in U.S. House

1895 Died, Concord, Mass.

1800   1825   1850   1875   1900

1812–14 War of 1812

1861–65 U.S. Civil War

to organize the Free-Soil party in Massachusetts. This party emerged in the late 1840s to oppose the extension of SLAVERY in newly acquired western territories and to curb the resulting legislative and electoral power that expansion would bring to southern cotton and tobacco interests.

From 1849 to 1855 Hoar served as a judge of the Massachusetts Court of COMMON PLEAS. In 1859 he was named to the Supreme Judicial Court of Massachusetts. During his early years on the bench, Hoar took a special interest in the skills of the young lawyers who appeared before him. He was known to write to them—or their mentors—critiquing their courtroom appearances. After hearing OLIVER WENDELL HOLMES, JR., for the first time, Hoar wrote to Holmes's father, telling him that Holmes "made a very creditable appearance." Hoar also noted that the young Holmes's argument in the case at hand had been "a little savoring of experimental philosophy."

In March 1869 Hoar was named attorney general of the United States by President Grant. Hoar was popular with the public and thoroughly qualified to serve but he was also independent and outspoken. As attorney general, he severely alienated patronage-seeking senators when he insisted on filling nine new circuit judgeships with competent judges rather than using the positions as opportunities for political paybacks.

When a vacancy on the U.S. Supreme Court occurred shortly after Hoar became attorney general, President Grant offered him the seat. Hoar's formal nomination in December 1869 drew expected opposition from the Senate. Citing Hoar's effort to eliminate government patronage, as well as his opposition to the IMPEACHMENT of President ANDREW JOHNSON, conservative Republican senators were especially vocal in their disapproval.

When a second vacancy on the High Court opened while Hoar's nomination was pending, the Senate moved quickly to see that President Grant named a candidate for that vacancy who was more to their liking. Their choice was the late president Abraham Lincoln's secretary of war, EDWIN M. STANTON. In exchange for Grant's nomination and support of Stanton, the Senate agreed to confirm Hoar.

The Senate pushed ahead on Stanton's nomination, confirming him in less than four hours, but Stanton never took his seat on the Court. Just four days after his confirmation, he suffered a fatal heart attack. Meanwhile, the Senate continued to debate Hoar's suitability for the position. "[R]egarding a dead Justice of its choosing to be an insufficient half of a bargain," it rejected Hoar by a vote of 33–24 on February 3, 1870.

The battle between President Grant and the Senate over Hoar's Supreme Court nomination remained a source of antagonism even after the vote. To end the fight and to cultivate Senate support for his other programs, Grant dismissed Hoar as attorney general in July 1870.

Hoar understood the political reasons for Grant's decision and he maintained a cordial relationship with the president. For his part, Grant remembered both Hoar's legal skills and his allegiance. Grant called on Hoar again in 1871 to serve on a joint commission to negotiate the treaty of arbitration that eventually settled the United States' *Alabama* claims against Great Britain.

Following the Civil War, relations between the United States and Great Britain were jeopardized by U.S. claims that England should pay for damages done during the war by the *Alabama* and other Confederate ships—which had been accorded belligerency status by Great Britain. (In INTERNATIONAL LAW, belligerency refers to the status of DE FACTO statehood attributed to a body of insurgents, by which their hostilities are legalized). Hoar served as the Grant administration's liaison with senators who urged a hard-line approach to settling the claims. He was influential in convincing Grant to deny belligerency status to insurgents in Cuba (as Britain had done to the CONFEDERACY), because the action would weaken the U.S. bargaining position with England during the treaty negotiations.

Following his work on the treaty, Hoar returned to his home in Massachusetts. As a Republican candidate, he sought and won a seat in the U.S. House, which he subsequently held from December 1, 1873, to March 3, 1875. His brother, George Frisbie Hoar, was serving as a representative from Massachusetts at the same time, having been elected in 1868.

After leaving office, Hoar continued to be active in local and national Republican politics until his death, on January 31, 1895, in Concord.

✧ HOBBES, THOMAS

Sixteenth-century political theorist, philosopher, and scientist THOMAS HOBBES left a stark warning to succeeding generations: strong central authority is the necessary basis for government. In several influential works of legal, political, psychological, and philosophical theory, Hobbes's view of society and its leaders was founded on pessimism. He saw people as weak and selfish, and thus in constant need of the governance that could save them from destruction. These ideas profoundly affected the Federalists during the early formation of U.S. law. The Federalists turned to Hobbes's work for justification for passage of the U.S. Constitution as well as for intellectual support for their own movement in the years following that passage. Today, Hobbes is read not only for his lasting contributions to political-legal theory in general but for the ideas that helped shape U.S. history.

Born on April 5, 1588, in Westport, Wiltshire, England, the son of an Anglican clergyman, Hobbes was a prodigy. By the age of 15, he had entered Oxford University; by 20, he was appointed tutor to a prominent family, a post he would later hold with the Prince of Wales. His considerable output of work began with English translations of FRANCIS BACON and Thucydides while he was in his late thirties. Soon, mathematics interested him, and his travels brought him into contact with some of the greatest minds of his age: Galileo and René Descartes. His writing canvassed many subjects, such as language and science, to arrive at a general theory of people and their leaders. The most influential works of this polymath came in the 1650s: *Leviathan, or the Matter, Form, and Power of a Commonwealth, Ecclesiastical and Civil* (1651), *De Corpore* (1655), and

Questions Concerning Liberty, Necessity, and Chance (1656). Hobbes died December 4, 1679, at age 91.

Hobbes was a supreme pessimist. To him, people were inherently selfish; they struggled constantly against one another for survival. "[T]he life of a man," he wrote in his masterwork, *Leviathan,* "is solitary, poor, nasty, brutish and short." Thus, people could not survive on their own in the state of nature. This foundation led him to a theory of the law: only by submitting to the protection of a sovereign power could individuals avoid constant anarchy and war. The sovereign's authority would have to be absolute. Law derived from this authority rather than from objective truth, which he argued did not exist. All citizens of the state were morally bound to follow the sovereign's authority; otherwise, law could not function. Hobbes chose the leviathan (a large sea animal) to represent the state, and he maintained that like a whale, the state could only be guided by one intelligence: its sovereign's.

The influence of Hobbes's ideas varied dramatically over the seventeenth and eighteenth centuries. English politicians and clerics derided him as a heretic. But his theories eventually lent support to loyalists who wanted to preserve the Crown's control over the American colonies: Thomas Hutchinson, the last royal governor of Massachusetts, viewed the upstart challengers to royal authority in a Hobbesian light. Later, Hobbes proved useful to the other side: After the American Revolution, his ideas influenced the Federalists in their arguments for adoption of the federal Constitution in 1787. Embracing Hobbes's pessimism, the Federalists saw the American people as

THE CONDITION OF MAN ... IS A CONDITION OF WAR OF EVERYONE AGAINST EVERYONE.
—THOMAS HOBBES

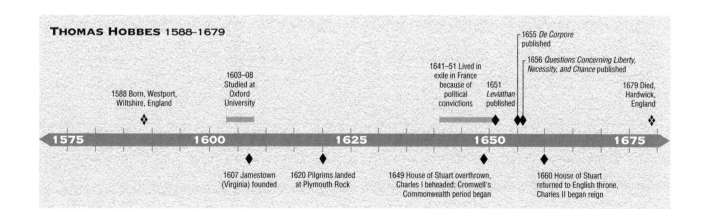

THOMAS HOBBES 1588–1679

1655 *De Corpore* published

1656 *Questions Concerning Liberty, Necessity, and Chance* published

1641–51 Lived in exile in France because of political convictions

1651 *Leviathan* published

1679 Died, Hardwick, England

1603–08 Studied at Oxford University

1588 Born, Westport, Wiltshire, England

1575   1600   1625   1650   1675

1607 Jamestown (Virginia) founded

1620 Pilgrims landed at Plymouth Rock

1649 House of Stuart overthrown, Charles I beheaded; Cromwell's Commonwealth period began

1660 House of Stuart returned to English throne, Charles II began reign

unable to survive as a nation without a strong central government that would protect them from foreign powers.

Hobbes is still taught, and scholars continue to discuss contemporary legal issues in the light of his critique. Particularly relevant are his insights into the form of law and the interrelationship of law and politics, and his subtle explorations of language and meaning.

FURTHER READINGS

Dyzenhaus, David. 2001. "Hobbes and the Legitimacy of Law." *Law and Philosophy* 20 (September).

———. 1998. "Now the Machine Runs Itself: Carl Schmitt on Hobbes and Kelsen." *Cardozo Law Review* 16 (August). Available online at http://papers.ssrn.com/sol3/papers.cfm?abstract_id=1244505; website home page: http://papers.ssrn.com (accessed July 29, 2009).

Hobbes, Thomas. 1651. *Leviathan, or the Matter, Form, and Power of a Commonwealth, Ecclesiastical and Civil.* Reprint, 1982. New York: Viking.

Malcolm, Noel. 2002. *Aspects of Hobbes.* New York: Oxford Univ. Press.

Martinich, A.P. 2008. *Hobbes: A Biography.* New York: Cambridge Univ. Press

Robinson, Reginald Leamon. 1993. "The Impact of Hobbes's Empirical Natural Law on Title VII's Effectiveness: A Hegellian Critique." *Connecticut Law Review* 25 (spring).

Rutten, Andrew. 1997. "Anarchy, Order, and the Law: A Post-Hobbesian View." *Cornell Law Review* 82 (July).

❖ HOFFA, JAMES RIDDLE

One of the most powerful labor leaders in U.S. history, JAMES RIDDLE HOFFA ruled with brawn and charisma for 14 years as president of the International Brotherhood of Teamsters, Chauffeurs, Warehousemen, and Helpers of America. From 1957 to 1971, Hoffa bound the loose-knit Teamsters into a cohesive organization that won higher wages and tremendous bargaining power for its members. Loved by his union rank and file, he was thought ruthless, cunning, and corrupt by his enemies, among them law enforcement leaders such as ROBERT F. KENNEDY. Federal investigators pursued Hoffa for several years because of his reputed ties to ORGANIZED CRIME. He dodged conviction until being found guilty in 1964 on unrelated charges of jury tampering and MALFEASANCE in a real estate deal. He began serving a 13-year prison sentence in 1967, which President RICHARD M. NIXON commuted in late 1971. In 1975 Hoffa disappeared mysteriously.

Hoffa rose from obscure origins to stand in the national spotlight. He was born February 14, 1913, in Brazil, Indiana, where his family lived by modest means. His father, a coal driller, died of an occupational respiratory disease when Hoffa was seven. The second of four children, Hoffa, an athletic, shy, B-student, quit school after the ninth grade to work full-time as a stock boy in a department store.

In 1930, while still a teenager, Hoffa became a freight handler in a warehouse of the Kroger Grocery and Baking Company in Clinton, Indiana. Here came a turning point in his life, brought on by what he called a need for self-preservation in the face of meager pay and poor working conditions. The young man soon led the other warehousemen in a successful strike that would become a part of the Hoffa legend: By refusing to unload a shipment of perishable strawberries, they forced the company to accede to their demands. With his prowess as an organizer quickly recognized, Hoffa left the warehouse in 1932 to become a full-time Teamster organizer in Detroit, Michigan. The four coworkers who had helped him carry off

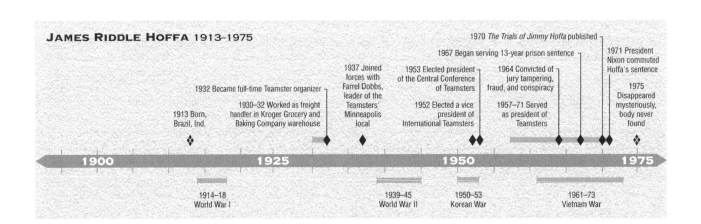

JAMES RIDDLE HOFFA 1913–1975

1913 Born, Brazil, Ind.

1930–32 Worked as freight handler in Kroger Grocery and Baking Company warehouse

1932 Became full-time Teamster organizer

1937 Joined forces with Farrel Dobbs, leader of the Teamsters' Minneapolis local

1952 Elected a vice president of International Teamsters

1953 Elected president of the Central Conference of Teamsters

1957–71 Served as president of Teamsters

1964 Convicted of jury tampering, fraud, and conspiracy

1967 Began serving 13-year prison sentence

1970 *The Trials of Jimmy Hoffa* published

1971 President Nixon commuted Hoffa's sentence

1975 Disappeared mysteriously, body never found

1900   1925   1950   1975

1914–18 World War I

1939–45 World War II

1950–53 Korean War

1961–73 Vietnam War

the strike at Kroger left with him and remained on his staff throughout his career.

Hoffa found his new work difficult in the beginning. During the 1930s opposition to labor organizers was fierce and often violent. Clashes with management strikebreakers and police officers would turn bloody—Hoffa himself was beaten up 24 times, by his count, during his first year alone. Describing this "war" in his 1970 autobiography, *The Trials of Jimmy Hoffa*, he recalled, "Managements didn't want us around . . . and the police, recognizing who the big taxpayers were and responding to orders of politicians who knew quite well where the big contributions came from, seemed not only willing but anxious to shove us around." Tenacity, bullish strength, and a persuasive personal style were traits that helped him not only survive opposition but win new recruits to his side.

In the Depression era, the Teamsters were loosely organized in isolated areas. In 1937 Hoffa joined forces with the Trotskyite leader of the Minneapolis local Teamsters, Farrel Dobbs, a socialist who was successfully unionizing drivers in the Midwest. Hoffa helped Dobbs organize long-haul highway truck drivers under the Central States Drivers Council. However, Hoffa was never above using strong-arm tactics, and later, when it served him, he would help the federal government suppress the Trotskyites.

Whether with management or with rival unions, Hoffa's policy was toughness. By 1941 he was making his first contacts with organized crime figures, as his biographer, Arthur A. Sloane, documented: That year, he enlisted the help of Detroit mobsters—the so-called East Side Crowd—to drive a rival union out of town. Thereafter, dealings with mobsters became regular. Never admitting any illegality, Hoffa nonetheless did not hide these connections. In later years, he claimed, "I'm no different than the banks, no different than the insurance companies, no different than the politicians."

Hoffa ascended to power during the 1940s. He became vice president of the Central States Drivers Council, then president of the Michigan Conference of Teamsters, later an examiner of the Teamster's books, and eventually president of the Teamsters Joint Council 43 in Detroit. In 1952 he was elected an International Teamsters vice president. By 1953, as president of the

Jimmy Hoffa.
AP IMAGES

Central Conference of Teamsters, he was the chief negotiator for truck drivers in 20 states. Over the next decade, Hoffa set about centralizing the Teamsters. As his power grew, local union leaders were encouraged to call Hoffa for authorization to hold strikes. The national bargaining unit that he created amassed such clout that it forged the trucking industry's first national contract in January 1964.

Although his gains were resisted by industry leaders, Hoffa won a reputation for being faithful to contracts. Within the Teamsters, the rank and file respected the gains he won for them and regarded him with open affection. At rallies and in interviews, he employed a speaking style more polished than his ninth-grade education might have suggested, gravelly yet authoritative. Frequently referring to himself in the third person, he would often boast, "Hoffa can take care of Hoffa."

But Hoffa was also running into trouble. Prompted by allegations of labor RACKETEERING, the U.S. Senate began investigating several unions in January 1957. Nationally televised hearings were conducted by the Senate Select Committee on Improper Activities in the Labor or Management Field—popularly known as the McClellan Committee, after its presiding officer, Senator JOHN LITTLE MCCLELLAN. Over two years, the committee uncovered widespread corruption in the Teamsters. Teamster president Dave Beck resigned; he was later convicted of larceny, embezzlement, and income TAX EVASION. Hoffa, succeeding Beck as president, faced months of intense questioning by Senator JOHN F. KENNEDY and the committee's chief counsel, ROBERT KENNEDY.

The committee alleged that Hoffa had used union funds for his own profit, accepted payoffs from trucking companies, and associated with convicted labor racketeer John Dioguardi. Pressed by the Kennedys during hearings that had an air of open animosity, Hoffa admitted nothing. Just before one of his scheduled appearances, FEDERAL BUREAU OF INVESTIGATION (FBI) agents arrested him on charges of trying to bribe a lawyer to leak confidential committee memos to him. Robert Kennedy announced he would jump off the dome of the Capitol building if the union leader was not convicted. When Hoffa was acquitted after a four-month trial, his attorney offered to send Kennedy a parachute.

The McClellan Committee report condemned Hoffa and the Teamsters. One result was the passage of more stringent legislation concerning unions; another was the expulsion of the Teamsters from the American Federation of Labor and Congress of Industrial Organizations (AFL-CIO). For Hoffa, the hearings marked the beginning of a feud between himself and Robert Kennedy that would deepen upon the latter's appointment in 1960 as attorney general. Kennedy devoted considerable resources within the U.S. JUSTICE DEPARTMENT to prosecuting Hoffa, whom he described as heading a conspiracy of evil. Despite several indictments, Hoffa escaped conviction until 1964. First, he was convicted of jury tampering and sentenced to eight years in prison. The manner in which the conviction was obtained later brought a rebuke from U.S. Supreme Court chief justice EARL WARREN: the U.S. Justice Department used a jailed Teamster member to trap Hoffa. At a second 1964 trial, Hoffa received an additional five years for FRAUD and conspiracy in the handling of a Teamster benefit fund.

In March 1967, with his appeals exhausted, Hoffa began serving his 13-year sentence in Lewisburg Federal Penitentiary, in Pennsylvania. Hoffa refused to relinquish control of the Teamsters. He was denied parole three times. Then, in December 1971, President Nixon

IN THE OLD DAYS ALL YOU NEEDED WAS A HANDSHAKE. NOWADAYS YOU NEED FORTY LAWYERS.
—JIMMY HOFFA

commuted his sentence on the condition that he refrain from union activities until the year 1980. His attorneys worked to reverse the limitation, while he campaigned on behalf of prison reform. But he never regained power.

In 1975 Hoffa drove to a suburban Detroit restaurant to meet reputed crime figure Anthony ("Tony Pro") Provenzano. Hoffa's car was found later, but he was never seen again. For several years, the FBI maintained an open file on Hoffa, yet it never solved the mystery. Theories about his disappearance abound, including the belief that Hoffa was buried underneath the goalposts at the Meadowlands football stadium, in New Jersey. In the 1980s, Hoffa's daughter Barbara Ann Crancer, an associate CIRCUIT COURT judge in Missouri, filed a lawsuit to force the FBI to release the records of its investigation of Hoffa's death. She was unsuccessful in her efforts. In 1989, the retiring FBI chief in Detroit, Kenneth P. Walton, told the press that he knew the identity of Hoffa's killer. But Walton said the case would never be prosecuted because doing so would compromise the security of FBI sources and informants.

Hoffa's legacy is still controversial. Critics charged that the script for the 1993 film dramatization of his life, by screenwriter David Mamet, celebrated Hoffa while purposely ignoring the extent of his involvement with crime figures. Also in 1993, the longtime suspicion that Hoffa had been involved in a plot to assassinate President Kennedy generated renewed interest. Frank Ragano, a former mob lawyer, claimed that he personally delivered a message from Hoffa to two mobsters, which read "kill the president." Such speculation has never been substantiated, but another aspect of Hoffa's legacy is beyond doubt. Although he was enormously successful in building the Teamsters, his association with mobsters left a stain on the union that would linger for decades to come. Not until the late 1980s, when the federal government took control of the union's national elections, did the Teamsters begin to emerge from the shadow of organized crime.

In September 2001 *The Detroit News* reported that DNA EVIDENCE placed Hoffa in a car driven by a longtime friend on the day of his disappearance. The investigation was reopened but no further progress was made. In March

2002 the FBI announced that it would no longer continue its efforts to find and prosecute those who had caused Hoffa's disappearance and that the case would be referred to state officials for possible charges.

In 1998 Jimmy Hoffa's son, James Phillip Hoffa, carried on the family tradition when he was elected president of the Teamsters Union. He was sworn in by his sister, Barbara Ann, in May 1999. In 2001 Hoffa was reelected with almost two-thirds majority vote.

FURTHER READINGS

A&E Home Video. *Hoffa: The True Story.* 2004. DVD.

Hoffa, James R. 1970. *The Trials of Jimmy Hoffa.*

"Members Celebrate New Era for Teamsters." 1999. *Teamster Magazine* (July).

PBS Frontline. "JFK, Hoffa, and the Mob." 1993. Video cassette and DVD.

Sinclair, Norman, and David Shepardson. "New Clue Might Mean Charges in Hoffa Death." *The Detroit News* (September 7, 2001).

CROSS REFERENCES

Labor Law; Labor Union.

❖ HOFFMAN, WALTER EDWARD

Federal district judge WALTER EDWARD HOFFMAN "single-handedly cleared a legendary backlog" of cases in the late 1950s by "working around the clock and seven days a week." A firm believer that justice delayed is often justice denied, Hoffman created the "rocket docket" system to move cases through his courtroom more efficiently. Hoffman's workaholic spirit came to characterize his court—and years after his retirement, the Eastern District of Virginia was still one of the fastest and most efficient courts in the United States. (Studies conducted in the 1980s by the Administrative Office of the U.S. Courts showed that the Eastern District of Virginia consistently beat all other federal jurisdictions in elapsed time between the filing of litigants' papers and the start of a civil trial.) Owing in large part to the timesaving tactics developed by Hoffman, the Eastern District of Virginia, which stretches from Northern Virginia to the North Carolina line and includes Alexandria, Norfolk, and Richmond courts, in 1987 averaged only five months (compared with a national average of 14 months) from the filing of a case to the start of its trial. The court also maintained one of the lowest reversal rates in the country.

Speed, efficiency, and the ability to juggle a wide variety of tasks simultaneously were lifelong character traits of the man who developed the rocket docket. He was born July 18, 1907, in Jersey City, New Jersey. After completing a bachelor of science degree in economics at the University of Pennsylvania in 1928, Hoffman attended the Marshall-Wythe School of Law, at the College of William and Mary. He later transferred to Washington and Lee University School of Law, where he received a bachelor of laws degree in 1931.

In 1931 he joined the Norfolk law firm of Rumble and Rumble and also began teaching law on a part-time basis at the College of William and Mary. In 1935 he and a colleague established the law firm of Breeden and Hoffman; their partnership thrived until Hoffman was appointed to the federal bench in 1954. While practicing law, Hoffman continued to teach—and he took an active role in the Norfolk and Portsmouth Bar Association, serving as president in 1948. He also maintained memberships in the Virginia Bar Association and the AMERICAN BAR ASSOCIATION, serving on numerous committees and taking leadership

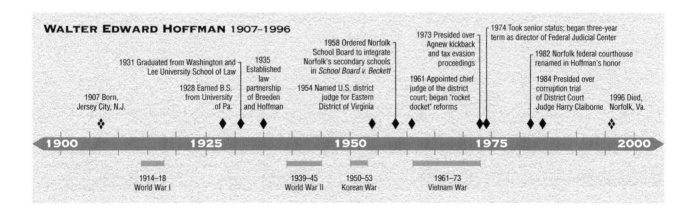

WALTER EDWARD HOFFMAN 1907–1996

1907 Born, Jersey City, N.J.

1928 Earned B.S. from University of Pa.

1931 Graduated from Washington and Lee University School of Law

1935 Established law partnership of Breeden and Hoffman

1954 Named U.S. district judge for Eastern District of Virginia

1958 Ordered Norfolk School Board to integrate Norfolk's secondary schools in *School Board v. Beckett*

1961 Appointed chief judge of the district court; began "rocket docket" reforms

1973 Presided over Agnew kickback and tax evasion proceedings

1974 Took senior status; began three-year term as director of Federal Judicial Center

1982 Norfolk federal courthouse renamed in Hoffman's honor

1984 Presided over corruption trial of District Court Judge Harry Claiborne

1996 Died, Norfolk, Va.

1900   1925   1950   1975   2000

1914–18 World War I

1939–45 World War II

1950–53 Korean War

1961–73 Vietnam War

roles when called upon to do so. His committee work brought Hoffman to the attention of the national legal community, and before long, he was considered for a federal judgeship.

Hoffman was named U.S. district judge for the Eastern District of Virginia on September 3, 1954. Soon after his appointment, the issue of SCHOOL DESEGREGATION came to his court. In 1958 he ordered the Norfolk School Board to admit 17 black students to white secondary schools (*School Board v. Beckett,* 260 F.2d 18 [1958]). The schools were immediately closed under state laws intended to thwart integration, and Hoffman became the target of segregationist attacks from around the country. Despite public and private pressure to do otherwise, Hoffman held firm in his order and in his denial of a request by the school to delay admitting the 17 students until the following year.

In the late 1950s both the volume of cases on his docket and their volatile nature prompted Hoffman to explore ways of delivering more timely justice in his jurisdiction. He made a personal commitment to clear his own backlog of cases and to put future trials on a tighter schedule. His marathon court sessions to achieve this goal are now judicial legend. As he worked to clear his backlog, Hoffman began to develop courtroom procedures and a philosophy for speeding justice. He also began to seek out professional colleagues with similar concerns. To that end, he volunteered to serve on the U.S. Judicial Conference Advisory Committee on Criminal Rules in 1960.

When Hoffman became chief judge in 1961, he put his theories into practice. On July 31 of that year, he wrote an open letter to attorneys in his jurisdiction: "[W]ith an excess of 750 civil and admiralty cases pending on the dockets … it is apparent that there must be a drastic change in procedure relating to the preparation of cases for trial." The next day, he issued a lengthy order that became the basis for the rocket docket system—an order that has sped up justice in Virginia ever since.

The foundation of Hoffman's system was setting firm trial dates and keeping them. Hearings and trials were scheduled early; and pretrial investigation was limited, as were the number of character and expert witnesses at trial. Stipulations were encouraged so that time would not be wasted proving facts that

all parties agreed to accept. And Hoffman made it clear to all parties that delaying tactics would not be tolerated in his court. "We decided we didn't want to miss a single trial date," he recalled in 1987, "and we still don't."

Hoffman felt that delays are costly because "lawyers are less keen, witnesses are harder to locate, and every type of confusion and slip-up is more likely." Critics of Hoffman's approach said that the pace of litigation in his court favored large law firms and businesses with access to vast legal resources, and that too often his system allowed little time to negotiate a settlement before trial. But the vast majority of litigators in Hoffman's jurisdiction praised his methods. In 1968 the Virginia Trial Lawyers Association presented him with its annual award, for his contributions to the advancement of justice in Virginia.

Although speedy justice was important to Hoffman, he also recognized that the quality of justice ultimately rested on the quality of judges and of judicial education. Perhaps for this reason, he joined the Board of Directors of the FEDERAL JUDICIAL CENTER in 1972, and served as director of the center from 1974 to 1977. As director he was responsible for the development and delivery of seminars instructing new judges on both law and administrative issues. Hoffman took a central role in many of the seminars, drawing on his experience to lead discussions and alert attendees to the difficulties encountered, and errors made, by inexperienced judges.

Hoffman took senior (or semiretired) status in 1974. As a senior judge he accepted assignments to district and circuit courts throughout the federal system. In his capacity as senior judge, he was involved in a number of high-profile cases, including the criminal prosecutions of former vice president Spiro T. Agnew for TAX EVASION, former U.S. district judge Harry E. Claiborne for tax evasion, former Charleston mayor Mike Roark for cocaine possession and OBSTRUCTION OF JUSTICE, and former West Virginia governor Arch A. Moore, Jr., for EXTORTION, MAIL FRAUD, tax FRAUD, and obstruction of justice.

Even at senior status, Hoffman often heard more cases than many of his younger colleagues. "He's regarded as one of the premier federal trial judges in the United States," said

FOR MANY, DEFENDANTS AS WELL AS PLAINTIFFS, JUSTICE DELAYED MAY BE JUSTICE DENIED OR JUSTICE MITIGATED IN QUALITY.
—WALTER HOFFMAN

U.S. district judge John T. Copenhaver, Jr., at one of the many award ceremonies acknowledging Hoffman's lifelong contributions to the bench. In 1976 the American Judicature Society presented Hoffman with the Herbert Harley Award for aiding the effective administration of justice throughout the United States.

In 1977 the U.S. Judicial Conference passed a resolution commending Hoffman's past services to the judiciary, with special emphasis on his services as director of the Federal Judicial Center. Also in 1977 Hoffman began a 15-year tenure on the TEMPORARY EMERGENCY COURT OF APPEALS, and he returned to the College of William and Mary as a visiting professor. In 1982 the U.S. Senate voted to rename the federal courthouse in Norfolk in his honor. Hoffman responded by saying he doubted "that a single United States senator knew what he was voting for" that day.

In 1984 Hoffman became the second recipient of the Devitt Distinguished Service to Justice Award, which is administered by the American Judicature Society. This award—named for Edward J. Devitt, former chief U.S. district judge for Minnesota—acknowledges the dedication and contributions to justice made by all federal judges, by recognizing the specific achievements of one judge who has contributed significantly to the profession. Hoffman was acknowledged for improving the quality of justice through efficient judicial administration.

In his late eighties, Hoffman had slowed his pace, but he continued to hear some cases in the nation's federal courts. Hoffman died November 21, 1996, in Norfolk, Virginia. He was married to Helen Caulfield Hoffman and was the father of two children.

FURTHER READINGS

Almanac of the Federal Judiciary. 2001. Frederick, MD: Aspen.

Federal Judicial Center. "Walter Edward Hoffman." *Biographical Directory of Federal Judges.* Available online at http://www.fjc.gov/servlet/tGetInfo?jid=1066; website home page: http://www.fjc.gov (accessed September 4, 2009).

Saxon, Wolfgang. "Walter E. Hoffman, 89, Dies; Judge in Agnew Proceeding." *The New York Times* (November 24, 1996).

HOLD HARMLESS AGREEMENT

An agreement or contract in which one party agrees to hold the other free from the responsibility for any liability or damage that might arise out of the transaction involved.

For example, a company might agree in an employee's contract to pay the judgment if the person is successfully sued for injuries sustained by a PLAINTIFF if the employee is acting within the scope of his or her authority on company time.

In certain cases, particular parties may not, however, be exempted from liability. For example, a provision exempting a common carrier from all liability for loss would ordinarily be void, as against public policy.

Hold harmless agreements are ordinarily contained in leases and easements.

HOLD OVER

To continue in possession of an office and exercise the functions associated therewith following the expiration of the term thereof. To retain possession as a tenant of real property following the termination of the lease or tenancy at will.

A *hold over tenant* is also known as a *tenant at sufferance,* since the tenant has no estate or title to the property but only possession thereof.

HOLDER

An individual who has lawfully received possession of a commercial paper, such as a check, and who is entitled to payment on such instrument.

A holder is distinguishable from a HOLDER IN DUE COURSE since, in addition to possession of the instrument, the latter takes it for value, in GOOD FAITH, and in the absence of any notice that there is any claim against it or that it is overdue or has been dishonored, which means that payment of it has been refused.

❖ HOLDER, ERIC H., JR.

Following the 2008 presidential election of BARACK OBAMA, Eric Holder was nominated for the post of U.S. attorney general, succeeding MICHAEL MUKASEY. Holder became the first African American to head the DEPARTMENT OF JUSTICE.

Holder was born January 21, 1951, and raised in a working-class section of Queens, New York. His parents had both emigrated from Barbados. By virtue of excellent academic work, he was accepted into the academically elite Stuyvesant High School in Manhattan, and

Eric Holder.
CHIP SOMODEVILLA/
GETTY IMAGES

after graduation he enrolled at Columbia University. There he majored in American history and earned top grades. He spent his spare time absorbing black culture at such notable Harlem landmarks as the Apollo Theater and the Abyssinian Baptist Church. Feeling a responsibility toward less fortunate black Americans, Holder began spending his Saturday mornings at a Harlem youth center and taking young people on trips around the city. He joined the Concerned Black Men, a national organization dedicated to helping minority youngsters.

Holder received his bachelor's degree in 1973 and immediately was accepted into Columbia's law school. When he graduated from that institution in 1976, he decided to join the Department of Justice. At the time, he figured he would work there two or three years and then take a position in a private firm. Holder joined the relatively new division, the Public Integrity Unit. "It was formed … with WATERGATE still ringing in everyone's ears," he told the *Chicago Tribune.* The Public Integrity attorneys were charged with prosecuting high-level corruption cases, often involving respected public figures. Among those Holder helped to prosecute were former South Carolina congressman John W. Jenrette, in the notorious "Abscam" case in the late 1970s, and a Philadelphia judge who accepted monetary gifts to "fix" cases. The people Holder prosecuted while with Public Integrity included FEDERAL BUREAU OF INVESTIGATION (FBI) agents, politicians, ORGANIZED CRIME figures, and even a fellow JUSTICE DEPARTMENT lawyer. Holder thought he would stay in this job for two years, but instead he remained for twelve.

In 1988 President RONALD REAGAN appointed Holder to the Superior Court of the District of Columbia. The rotating judgeship involved a wide range of cases, from murders and armed robberies to nonpayment of CHILD SUPPORT and school truancy. The job proved particularly difficult for a man committed to helping African Americans in the city. Holder's sentiments as a judge—both sympathetic and pragmatic—helped endear him to the District of Columbia's political leaders. Many of these politicians felt that the district should have a black U.S. attorney, preferably a local citizen who had demonstrated loyalty to the area. Holder was just that person, and he had even

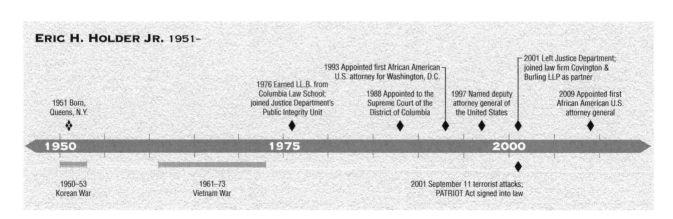

ERIC H. HOLDER JR. 1951–

1951 Born,
Queens, N.Y.

1976 Earned LL.B. from
Columbia Law School;
joined Justice Department's
Public Integrity Unit

1993 Appointed first African American
U.S. attorney for Washington, D.C.

1988 Appointed to the
Supreme Court of the
District of Columbia

1997 Named deputy
attorney general of
the United States

2001 Left Justice Department;
joined law firm Covington &
Burling LLP as partner

2009 Appointed first
African American U.S.
attorney general

1950   1975   2000

1950–53
Korean War

1961–73
Vietnam War

2001 September 11 terrorist attacks;
PATRIOT Act signed into law

worked at the Department of Justice. After the presidential swearing-in of BILL CLINTON in 1993, congressional delegate ELEANOR HOLMES NORTON commissioned a panel of Washington, D.C., lawyers and civic activists to make recommendations for the district's U.S. attorney slot. The panel chose Holder, and Norton passed his name along to the president. Holder was one of three candidates interviewed for the position, and the only qualm expressed about him was his lack of leadership experience.

Late in 1993 Clinton announced that he had chosen Holder to be the first black U.S. attorney for Washington, D.C. Holder provided direction for the prosecution of numerous local criminal suspects, ranging from local drug dealers to those who might wish to harm the president.

Holder became involved in a number of public incidents from the moment he took office. Soon after taking office, he presided over a complicated Justice Department investigation of FRAUD involving the post office in the House of Representatives. The investigation focused on an influential congressman, Illinois Democrat Dan Rostenkowski, who was indicted on charges that he misused official House accounts. As chairman of the congressional Ways and Means Committee, Rostenkowski was in a position to help the Clinton administration to implement its agenda for health care reform. Nonetheless, Holder persisted with the investigation and even widened its scope. He told the *Washington Post* that matters of criminal prosecution must be handled without regard to partisan politics. "The idea that a Democratic U.S. attorney is going to do something different than a Republican U.S. attorney is pretty close to ridiculous," he observed.

In 1997 Clinton nominated Holder to fill the position of deputy attorney general of the United States, immediately under Attorney General JANET RENO. At the time, a stumbling block to Holder's appointment was his position against the death penalty. However, he stated his willingness to put aside his personal beliefs to uphold the Constitution and the laws determined by Congress. Holder received unanimous confirmation by the Senate.

Holder was involved with some controversial pardons under the Clinton administration. As a result, Holder left the Justice Department

for some years during the Bush administration. As a citizen and litigation partner at the private firm of Covington and Burling in Washington, D.C., he represented such clients as Merck and the National Football League. He also served as a special investigator in a case involving a casino development in Rosemont, Illinois.

While in private practice, Holder grew increasingly critical of the Justice Department under President GEORGE W. BUSH. Like many citizens, for example, Holder disagreed with the U.S. use of waterboarding on prisoners at Guantanamo.

In 2009 he was nominated to the position of U.S. attorney general by President Barack Obama. Holder stated that if confirmed, he would seek to prosecute terrorists being held at Guantanamo Bay in U.S. courts, offering them full trials. He also pledged that fighting TERRORISM would be his top priority.

The controversial pardons issued by Clinton, apparently at Holder's recommendation, were a stumbling block in the hearings before his appointment. In 1999 Holder had supported CLEMENCY for 16 Puerto Rican militants; an FBI agent who had worked on that investigation stated in the *New York Times* that he was "outraged" by the clemency decision. Holder, however, held to his decision, defending it as "reasonable." Those who were granted clemency had been sentenced from 16 to 20 years, and none had been accused of crimes that resulted in the death penalty.

The other pardon, however, was a source of greater contention. Marc Rich was a financier who fled to Switzerland to avoid being prosecuted for tax related charges. Rich's wife had made a large donation to Clinton's library. Holder stated that his advice on the case, given before he knew all the facts, was "neutral, leaning toward favorable," a statement used as support by the Clinton administration and now regretted by Holder. Louis J. Freeh, who had been head of the FBI from 1993 to 2001, spoke in support of Holder, recognizing that the pardon of Rich was corrupt but that the guilt lay with former president Clinton rather than Holder. Freeh believed that Holder had learned from the mistake and would never allow himself to be put in that situation again.

Despite these controversies, Holder was confirmed to the position of attorney general

THOUGH THIS NATION HAS PROUDLY THOUGHT OF ITSELF AS AN ETHNIC MELTING POT IN THINGS RACIAL, WE HAVE ALWAYS BEEN, AND WE, I BELIEVE, CONTINUE TO BE, IN TOO MANY WAYS, ESSENTIALLY A NATION OF COWARDS. THOUGH RACE-RELATED ISSUES CONTINUE TO OCCUPY A SIGNIFICANT PORTION OF OUR POLITICAL DISCUSSION, AND THOUGH THERE REMAIN MANY UNRESOLVED RACIAL ISSUES IN THIS NATION, WE, AVERAGE AMERICANS, SIMPLY DO NOT TALK ENOUGH WITH EACH OTHER ABOUT THINGS RACIAL.
—ERIC HOLDER

in a Senate vote of 75 to 21. Upon his appointment, Holder immediately began working to separate the Justice Department under his leadership from the work of the department under the Bush administration. He was made one of the leaders in the initiative to close the Guantanamo Bay detention center. He sought to investigate corruption inside the Justice Department, particularly surrounding a scandal in which eight U.S. attorneys were abruptly dismissed. Holder dismissed charges of corruption against former Alaska senator Ted Stevens due to a failure by the prosecution to provide critical information to the defense lawyers. The dismissal of the case of Stevens, a Republican, served not only as a symbolic statement against political alliances in the Justice Department, but also as a precedent for fixing bad cases that did not follow proper procedures.

Holder promised to revitalize the Department of Justice's CIVIL RIGHTS Division. There were internal reports that 63 attorneys were hired into that division based on their political affiliations. Holder pledged to look into the case against former senior civil rights lawyer Bradley Scholzman over accusations of making false statements to Congress, which the department refused to investigate. Patrick Leahy (D-VT) praised Holder's appointment as attorney general in the *New York Times*, stating that the appointment was "a statement that we all want to restore the integrity and competence of the Justice Department and to restore another critical component—the American people's confidence in federal law enforcement."

FURTHER READINGS

"Eric H. Holder." *Contemporary Black Biography*. Volume 9. Gale Research, 1995.

Lichtblau, Eric, and David Johnston. 2008. "Pardon Is Back in Focus for the Justice Nominee." *New York Times*. December 2.

HOLDER IN DUE COURSE

An individual who takes a commercial paper for value, in good faith, with the belief that it is valid, with no knowledge of any defects.

The UNIFORM COMMERCIAL CODE (UCC) defines a holder in due course as one who takes an instrument for value in GOOD FAITH absent any notice that it is overdue, has been dishonored, or is subject to any defense against it or claim to it by any other person.

HOLDING

A comprehensive term applied to the property, whether real, personal, or both, owned by an individual or a business. The legal principle derived from a judicial decision. That part of the written opinion of a court in which the law is specifically applied to the facts of the instant controversy. It is relied upon when courts use the case as an established precedent in a subsequent case.

A holding is distinguishable from dicta, which is language in the opinion relating some observation or example that may be illustrative, but which is not part of the court's judgment in the case.

HOLDING COMPANY

A corporation that limits its business to the ownership of stock in and the supervision of management of other corporations.

A holding company is organized specifically to hold the stock of other companies and ordinarily owns such a dominant interest in the other company or companies that it can dictate policy. Holding companies must comply with the federal antitrust laws that proscribe the secret and total acquisition of the stock of one corporation by another, since this would lessen competition and create a monopoly.

HOLIDAY

A day of recreation; a consecrated day; a day set apart for the suspension of business.

A *legal holiday* is a day set aside by statute for recreation, the cessation of work, or religious observance. It is a day that is legally designated as exempt from the conduct of all judicial proceedings, service of process, and the demand and protest of COMMERCIAL PAPER. A prohibition against conducting public business transactions on holidays does not, however, have an effect upon private business. Private transactions will not, therefore, be invalidated solely because they are conducted on a holiday.

❖ HOLMES, OLIVER WENDELL, JR.

Oliver Wendell Holmes Jr. was a justice of the U.S. Supreme Court and legal philosopher who has become a celebrated legal figure. His writings on jurisprudence have shaped discussions on the nature of law, and his court opinions have been studied as much for their style as for their intellectual content. Though Holmes has been widely praised, he does have critics who contend that he paid too much deference to the power of the state to control individual freedom.

Holmes was born March 8, 1841, in Boston. His father, Oliver Wendell Holmes Sr., was a well-known physician, a lecturer at Harvard Medical School, an author who was widely read in England and the United States, and a founder of the *Atlantic Monthly.* Holmes attended private school and then Harvard College, graduating in 1861. With the outbreak of the Civil War in 1861, Holmes enlisted as an officer in the Twentieth Massachusetts Volunteer Infantry.

His military service was difficult. Holmes was wounded three times, twice almost fatally, and suffered from dysentery. In 1863 he accepted a position as an aide to a Union general, and he served in that capacity until 1864. He resigned his commission before the end of the war and returned, exhausted, to Boston, where he began preparations for a legal career.

He attended Harvard Law School and graduated in 1866. He was admitted to the Massachusetts bar in 1867. Because of inherited wealth Holmes had the financial luxury of pursuing his intellectual interests. He edited the twelfth edition of jurist James Kent's *Commentaries on American Law* (1873) and wrote many articles for the *American Law Review.* Following his marriage to Fanny Dixwell in 1873, Holmes joined a prominent Boston law firm, where he practiced COMMERCIAL LAW.

Holmes did not abandon his inquiries into the nature of law. He was invited to Boston to

Oliver Wendell Holmes.
LIBRARY OF CONGRESS

present a series of lectures on the law, which were published in 1881 as *The Common Law.* This volume is the most renowned work of legal philosophy in U.S. history. It allowed Holmes systematically to analyze, classify, and explain various aspects of U.S. common law, ranging from torts to contracts to crime and punishment.

In *The Common Law,* Holmes traced the origins of the common law to ancient societies where liability was based on feelings of revenge and the subjective intentions of a morally blameworthy wrongdoer. For example, Holmes observed that in such societies creditors were permitted to cut up and divide the body of a debtor who had breached the terms of a

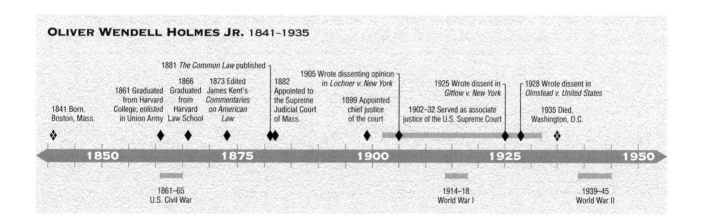

OLIVER WENDELL HOLMES JR. 1841–1935

1841 Born, Boston, Mass.

1861 Graduated from Harvard College; enlisted in Union Army

1866 Graduated from Harvard Law School

1873 Edited James Kent's *Commentaries on American Law*

1881 *The Common Law* published

1882 Appointed to the Supreme Judicial Court of Mass.

1899 Appointed chief justice of the court

1905 Wrote dissenting opinion in *Lochner v. New York*

1902–32 Served as associate justice of the U.S. Supreme Court

1925 Wrote dissent in *Gitlow v. New York*

1928 Wrote dissent in *Olmstead v. United States*

1935 Died, Washington, D.C.

1850   1875   1900   1925   1950

1861–65 U.S. Civil War

1914–18 World War I

1939–45 World War II

contract. Advanced societies, Holmes noticed, no longer settle contractual disputes in such a barbaric fashion. These societies have evolved to the point where liability is now premised on objective and external standards that separate moral responsibility from legal obligation, and wholly eliminate concerns regarding the actual guilt of the wrongdoer. Holmes noted that common-law principles require judges and juries to interpret contractual relations from the perspective of an average person with ordinary intelligence, regardless of how a particular agreement may have actually been understood or performed by the parties themselves.

The importance of *The Common Law* rests in its rejection of the idea that law is a logical system and that legal systems obey the rules of logic. In his most famous quotation, Holmes concluded,

> The life of the law has not been logic: it has been experience. The felt necessities of the time, the prevalent moral and political theories, intuitions of public policy, avowed or unconscious, even the prejudices which judges share with their fellow-men, have had a good deal more to do than the syllogism in determining the rules by which men should be governed.

Holmes's jurisprudence led to the conclusion that judges first make decisions and then come up with reasons to explain them. His approach, which has been characterized as cynical, touched a nerve with succeeding generations of legal scholars. He had a profound effect on the development of sociological jurisprudence and LEGAL REALISM. Sociological jurisprudence and legal realism were twentieth-century schools of thought that emphasized the need to examine social, economic, and political forces rather than confine the study of law to logic and abstract thought.

Holmes joined the faculty of the Harvard Law School in 1882, then left after one semester to accept an appointment as justice on the Supreme Judicial Court of Massachusetts, the highest tribunal in the state. In 1899 he was appointed chief justice of that court, and he served in that position until 1902, when President THEODORE ROOSEVELT named him to the U.S. Supreme Court.

His service on the Supreme Court gave Holmes the opportunity to apply his philosophy. He believed that judges should not impose their private beliefs on law, especially law created by a legislature. When reviewing the constitutionality of legislation, Holmes said a legislature can do whatever it sees fit unless a law it enacts is not justified by any rational interpretation of, or violates an express prohibition of, the Constitution (*Tyson & Brothers United Theatre Ticket Offices v. Banton*, 273 U.S. 418, 47 S. Ct. 426, 71 L. Ed. 718 [1927]). Holmes was skeptical about his ability to determine the "goodness or badness of laws" passed by the legislature, and felt that in most situations he had no choice but to practice judicial restraint and defer to the desires of the popular will.

Holmes's dissenting opinion in LOCHNER V. NEW YORK, 198 U.S. 45, 25 S. Ct. 539, 49 L. Ed. 937 (1905), is recognized as his most famous opinion. It is based on the idea of judicial restraint. In *Lochner* Holmes disagreed with the majority, which struck down a New York law that limited the number of hours a baker could work during a week. The majority held that the law violated the "liberty of contract" guaranteed by the FOURTEENTH AMENDMENT, which provides that no state is to "deprive any person of life, liberty, or property, without due process of law" (§ 1). In his dissent Holmes suggested that the majority had based its decision on its members' personal ideological preference for freedom of contract, and not on the Constitution. He said it was improper to overturn a legislative act simply because the Court embraced an economic theory antagonistic to government work regulations.

But Holmes rarely deferred to the popular will in cases raising free speech questions under the FIRST AMENDMENT. If the law must correspond to powerful interests in society, Holmes reasoned, then all facets of society must be given a fair opportunity to compete for influence through the medium of public speech. In GITLOW V. NEW YORK, 268 U.S. 652, 45 S. Ct. 625, 69 L. Ed. 1138 (1925), Holmes dissented from a decision upholding the conviction of a man who had been arrested for violating the New York Criminal Anarchy Law (N.Y. Penal Law §§ 160, 161 [ch. 88, McKinney 1909; ch. 40, Consol. 1909]) by advocating the establishment of a socialist government. In his dissent he argued for "the free trade in ideas" as the best way of testing the truth of particular beliefs. He stated that FREEDOM OF SPEECH must be permitted unless it is intended "to produce a clear and imminent danger." This "clear-and-imminent-danger" test for subversive advocacy was first

IF THERE IS ANY PRINCIPLE OF OUR CONSTITUTION THAT MORE IMPERATIVELY CALLS FOR ATTACHMENT THAN ANY OTHER IT IS THE PRINCIPLE OF FREE THOUGHT—NOT FREE THOUGHT FOR THOSE WHO AGREE WITH US BUT FOR THE THOUGHT THAT WE HATE.
—OLIVER WENDELL HOLMES JR.

labeled by Holmes as the "clear-and-present-danger" test in SCHENCK V. UNITED STATES, 249 U.S. 47, 39 S. Ct. 247, 63 L. Ed. 470 (1919). It remains influential as a way of protecting what Holmes termed the marketplace of ideas.

Holmes also contributed to modern FOURTH AMENDMENT jurisprudence. In OLMSTEAD V. UNITED STATES, 277 U.S. 438, 48 S. Ct. 564, 72 L. Ed. 944 (1928), the Supreme Court ruled that incriminating evidence illegally obtained by the police was admissible against a DEFENDANT during prosecution. Foreshadowing the Court's later recognition of an EXCLUSIONARY RULE that prohibits prosecutors from using illegally obtained evidence during trial, Holmes wrote that the "government ought not to use evidence" that is "only obtainable by a criminal act" of the police. While acknowledging the legitimate objectives of law enforcement, Holmes concluded that it was "a less[er] evil that some criminals should escape than that the government should play an ignoble part."

Despite Holmes's substantial reputation, he is not without critics. BUCK V. BELL, 274 U.S. 200, 47 S. Ct. 584, 71 L. Ed. 1000 (1927), is the case most frequently cited to point out faults in his jurisprudence. In his majority opinion in *Buck*, Holmes upheld the constitutionality of a state statute (Va. Law of March 20, 1924, ch. 394) authorizing the sterilization of "feeble-minded" (mentally retarded) persons. Reviewing the family history of Carrie Buck, her mother, and her daughter, Holmes stated, "Three generations of imbeciles are enough." He believed that sterilization was the best way to end the procreation of mentally retarded persons, and in looking at these three generations of women he believed they were all mentally retarded. Later evidence suggested that none of the three were in fact mentally retarded. The case also suggested that deference to legislative acts, such as forced sterilization, was not an unfettered good and that questions of morality and justice have a place in the law, despite Holmes's protests to the contrary.

Holmes's jurisprudence also suggested that the law is what the government says it is. This approach, called LEGAL POSITIVISM, was called into question in the 1930s and 1940s with the rise of totalitarian regimes in Germany and Italy and the rule of Stalin in the Soviet Union. Many legal scholars criticized positivism as lacking a basis in morality and fundamental societal values.

Holmes retired from the Supreme Court in 1932. He died in Washington, D.C., on March 6, 1935, two days before his 94th birthday.

FURTHER READINGS

Alschuler, Albert W. 2000. *Law without Values: The Life, Work, and Legacy of Justice Holmes.* Chicago: Univ. of Chicago Press.

Burton, David H. 1998. *Taft, Holmes, and the 1920s Court: An Appraisal.* Madison, NJ: Fairleigh Dickinson Univ. Press.

Coper, Michael. 2003. "The Path of the Law: A Tribute to Holmes." *Alabama Law Review* 54 (spring).

George, Robert P. 2003. "Holmes on Natural Law." *Villanova Law Review* 48 (February). Available online at http://www.law.harvard.edu/students/orgs/jlpp/Vol31_No1_Georgeonline.pdf; website home page: http://www.law.harvard.edu (accessed July 30, 2009)

Kellogg, Frederic R. 2002. "Holmes, Common Law Theory, and Judicial Restraint." *John Marshall Law Review* 36 (winter).

CROSS REFERENCES

Clear and Present Danger; Judicial Review; Labor Law; "The Path of the Law" (Appendix, Primary Document).

HOLOGRAPH

A will or deed written entirely by the testator or grantor with his or her own hand and not witnessed.

State laws vary widely in regard to the status of a holographic will. Some states absolutely refuse to recognize any will not in compliance with the formal statutory requirements pertaining to the execution of the will. Many states that do not recognize holographic wills executed by their own citizens within their borders will nevertheless admit a holographic will to probate if it was validly executed in accordance with the statutory requirements of another jurisdiction that recognizes such wills.

HOME RULE

The right to local self-government including the powers to regulate for the protection of the public health, safety, morals, and welfare; to license; to tax; and to incur debt.

Home rule involves the authority of a local government to prevent state government intervention with its operations. The extent of its power, however, is subject to limitations prescribed by state constitutions and statutes.

When a municipality or other political subdivision has the power to decide for itself

Tom Ridge, former secretary of the Department of Homeland Security, unveils the agency's five-level, color-coded warning system on March 12, 2002.

AP IMAGES

whether to follow a particular course of action without receiving specific approval from state officials, it acts pursuant to such powers. For example, a town exercises its home rule powers when it puts the issue of allowing the sale of alcoholic beverages within its borders on the ballot.

HOMELAND SECURITY DEPARTMENT

There were gaps in the U.S. system for detecting and deterring terrorist acts in the homeland, which became clear on SEPTEMBER 11, 2001. The DEPARTMENT OF HOMELAND SECURITY was the GEORGE W. BUSH administration's plug for those gaps.

The department's main goal is to protect U.S. citizens against terrorists. It brings together personnel from 22 agencies to protect the nation's borders, help state and local safety officials better respond to catastrophes, research treatments against biological threats, and coordinate intelligence on terrorists. The administration's rationale: better communication is the key to achieving those goals; the Department of Homeland Security is the key to better communication.

In January 2002 Republicans drafted legislation to create the department. In November of that year, the U.S. House and Senate passed the Homeland Security Act, and President Bush signed it. The cabinet department melded 22 agencies as varied as the Coast Guard, the Customs Service, the IMMIGRATION and NATURALIZATION Service, and the Transportation Security

Administration. It was the biggest change in U.S. government since the DEPARTMENT OF DEFENSE was created in 1947.

Former Pennsylvania governor and Vietnam veteran Tom Ridge became the first secretary of the department. In March 2002 Ridge revealed the Homeland Security Advisory System, which formally merged into the department in 2003. The system is based upon five alerts, which are each given a color reflecting the applicable threat level. Under the system, green is considered to be a low threat, blue is a guarded threat, yellow is an elevated threat, orange is a high threat, and red is a severe threat. Since the system's inception, the threat level has never been green or blue, and it has predominantly stayed at yellow.

James Loy and Michael Chertoff followed Tom Ridge as subsequent secretaries of the department. Loy and Chertoff likewise served under President Bush. After BARACK OBAMA was elected President in 2008, Janet Napolitano became the secretary of the department.

By 2008 the department had grown to include many compartments. These compartments are focused generally on information sharing and analysis, prevention and protection, preparedness and response, research, commerce and trade, travel security, and immigration. The department employs 216,000 individuals and is one of the nation's largest cabinet departments.

The department has faced criticism primarily on the grounds of its alleged inefficiency. In 2008, media reports indicated that the department was responsible for $15 million worth of failed contracts from projects such as baggage screening and trailers for Hurricane Katrina evacuees.

In 2009 the department released warnings to law enforcement agencies that right-wing extremism poses an increasing threat to the United States. Information released by the department reflected that right-wing terrorists were growing in number, as the result of recruitment campaigns based upon fears related to a down economy. The recruitment is also said to be based on racism related to the election of Obama, the nation's first African American President. In the final week of the year, Napolitano came under severe criticism for commenting, "The system worked," after security checks in Amsterdam had failed to stop a Nigerian passenger from boarding a transatlantic flight, bound for Detroit, with a syringe and explosive chemicals, which he ignited while the plane was in the air. The passenger's father had alerted the American authorities about the dangers that he feared his son posed, weeks before the incident.

FURTHER READINGS

Cmar, Thomas. 2002. "Office of Homeland Security." *Harvard Journal on Legislation* 39 (summer): 455–74.

Department of Homeland Security Annual Performance Report. for Fiscal Years 2008-2010. Available online at www.dhs.gov (accessed May 21, 2009).

Jarrett, Peggy Roebuck, comp. 2003. *The Department of Homeland Security: A Compilation of Government Documents Relating to Executive Reorganization.* Buffalo, N.Y.: W.S. Hein.

May, Randolph J. 2002. "Will We Be Safe at Home?" *Legal Times* 25 (Sept. 2): 38.

Moore, John Norton. 2010. *Legal Issues in the Struggle Against Terror.* Durham: University of North Carolina Press.

Nemeth, Charles P. 2010. *Homeland Security: An Introduction to Principles and Practice.* Boca Raton, Fla.: Auerback Publications.

CROSS REFERENCES

Ridge, Thomas Joseph; Terrorism.

HOMELESS PERSON

An individual who lacks housing, including one whose primary residence during the night is a supervised public or private facility that provides temporary living accommodations; an individual who is a resident in transitional housing; or an individual who has as a primary residence a public or private place not designed for, or ordinarily used as, a regular sleeping accommodation for human beings.

The National Coalition for the Homeless (NCH), which publishes reports and studies of the homeless, has noted that several national estimates of homelessness exist at any given time, and depending on the source, there are inconsistencies in the numbers. The best estimates translate to a figure approximating one percent of the U.S. population annually; the Coalition, estimating "on the high end" in its September 2009 report, put that number at 3.5 million persons.

According to the U.S. Conference of Mayors Report for 2008, 19 of the 25 cities reporting experienced an increase in homelessness between 2007 and 2008. Twelve of the 25 cities reported an increase due to housing foreclosures, and had to turn people away due to lack

of capacity. (Another six reporting cities lacked sufficient data to make a determination as to reasons for increased numbers.) On average, over 90 percent of persons living on the streets were single adults; two percent were unaccompanied minors. The average length of stay for single men in emergency shelters was 69 days; for women, 51 days, and for families, 70 days.

Unemployment, cutbacks in social service programs, a lack of affordable housing, and the deinstitutionalization of mentally ill patients are some of the circumstances that have led to people living in shelters or on the streets. There is no fair stereotype of homeless persons: They include the young and old, individuals and entire families, and all races and ethnicities. According to the U.S. Conference of Mayors Report for 2008 (as reported in the September 2009 updated statistics kept by the NCH), the homeless population was estimated to be 42 percent African American; just under 40 percent white; 13 percent Hispanic; four percent Native American; and two percent Asian, these figures varying widely according to the area of the country. Additionally, the report indicated that 13 percent of homeless individuals in the reporting cities were physically disabled, while one in four (26 percent) was considered mentally ill. Nineteen percent were victims of DOMESTIC VIOLENCE, 13 percent were veterans, and two percent were HIV-positive. The same report indicated that approximately 19 percent of homeless people were employed. By sheer number alone, the rights of these persons have become important societal and legal issues.

A homeless man sleeps on a park bench. Several states have enacted local laws recognizing the right to shelter, but state agencies, due to expense and overcrowding, often cannot keep up with the demand.

AP IMAGES

Shelter

Although federal law provides for emergency shelter for homeless families in most states, there is no federal or constitutional right to shelter. In 1987 the Stewart B. McKinney Homeless Assistance Act (42 U.S.C.A. § 11301) was passed to provide public resources and programs to assist the homeless population. Under the act, the federal government is required to provide underutilized public buildings for use by people who are homeless. In *National Law Center v. United States Department of Veterans Affairs*, 964 F.2d 1210 (D.C. Cir. 1992), a homeless rights group sought to enforce compliance with the MCKINNEY ACT. The court agreed with the plaintiffs and held that the government must comply with the McKinney Act by allowing homeless people access to underused federal property.

Because the federal courts have refused to recognize a federal constitutional right to shelter, several states have enacted their own laws to recognize such a right. Many of these statutes require that cities provide shelter for people who are homeless, but they do not outline enforcement procedures. Although statutes require state agencies to provide shelter, the agencies often cannot keep up with the demand, citing expense and overcrowding. In *Atchison v. District of Columbia*, 585 A.2d 150 (D.C. App. 1991), a court imposed daily fines on a shelter for failure to provide services. The level of fines combined with the cost of litigation stimulated the adoption of an emergency act that allowed the agency to provide a shelter program based on the availability of funds.

Economic Assistance

Public assistance for the homeless remains a prominent political issue. As the government began cutting welfare programs, people who were homeless found it increasingly difficult to rise above the poverty level. In addition, substantial cuts to welfare programs created the possibility that more people would be forced into homelessness.

Existing public assistance programs often fail to help those who are homeless. Some programs require that recipients have temporary or permanent addresses, effectively eliminating otherwise eligible recipients. Some people who are homeless are provided temporary housing in "welfare hotels." A welfare hotel is inexpensive housing that is used for temporary instances. In 1995 federal legislation was introduced to control welfare spending and to reduce welfare dependence. (H.R. 1157, 104th Cong., 1st Sess.). The features of this legislation included discontinuing welfare benefits to certain groups and creating state demonstration projects to reduce the number of homeless families in welfare hotels.

The mortgage and FORECLOSURE crises of 2008 and 2009 prompted specific response. The American Recovery and Reinvestment Act of 2009 (P.L. 111-5) created a $1.5 billion Homelessness Prevention and Rapid Re-Housing Program (HPRP) intended to assist families either homeless or facing homelessness with emergency funds for rent payments, security deposits, utility bills, and other housing expenses. The program was to be administrated through the DEPARTMENT OF HOUSING AND URBAN DEVELOPMENT (HUD). Additionally, the Protecting Tenants at Foreclosure Act (H.R. 1247) was enacted in May 2009 to protect tenants living in foreclosed properties.

Education

One alarming aspect of the growth of the homeless population is the increasing numbers of families and children who have nowhere to live. Children are more strongly affected by homelessness than are adults because they are less able to overcome a lack of food, shelter, health care, and education. Many children in homeless families lack the transportation, documentation, and even clothing needed to attend public schools.

State residency guidelines typically require children to attend school within the district in which their parent or guardian lives. Homeless children cannot meet these residency requirements. Because education is often critical to overcoming poverty and homelessness, the McKinney Act specifically addresses the issue of education for children who are homeless. The act ensures that these children have every opportunity for a public school education. It requires states to revise their residency requirements in order to give such children a free education.

Another barrier to the education rights of children without a home is the inability to track education and medical records. Students can be refused enrollment if they have no documentation of previous schooling. The McKinney Act requires local education agencies to maintain records that can be readily available when a student moves to a new school district. Under the act, children must also have equal access to special-education programs in the public school system.

Voting

The right to vote is expressly stated in the U.S. Constitution. Because most states require that a citizen have a permanent residence in order to vote, the right to vote is often denied to people who are homeless. The right to vote provides a way for a person who is homeless to be heard—by electing public officials who are sympathetic to the concerns of people who are without a home.

New Jersey was one of the first states to allow people who are homeless the right to vote. The only requirement is that they meet the age and residency requirement of the state's constitution. They can satisfy the residency requirement by specifying a place they regard as home and providing the name of at least one contact who can verify their residence in that place.

By 1994, 13 states had legislation protecting the voting rights of people who are homeless. In *Collier v. Menzel,* 176 Cal. App. 3d 24, 221 Cal. Rptr. 110 (1985), three persons who were homeless listed a local park as their address on a voter-registration card. The court held that they had satisfied the residency requirement because they had indicated a fixed habitation in which they intended to remain for an extended period. In addition, even though a city ordinance prohibited camping and sleeping overnight in the park, the court held that denying the voter registration would violate EQUAL PROTECTION.

The 2004 and 2008 national elections were fraught with allegations that certain nonprofit "voter registration" groups had exceeded their authority in their efforts to recruit new voting registrants. For example, in the weeks leading up to the 2006 national elections, the media televised several instances of third-party groups bestowing money and gifts on inner-city and/or homeless persons in return for their efforts to register and vote, many times with a commitment to vote for a certain party or issue.

Antihomeless Legislation

With an increased homeless population comes increased concern on the part of members of the general public when they find members of that population loitering on the streets. Vagrancy ordinances were passed to keep people who are homeless from staying too long in any one location. Many of these statutes have been labeled antihomeless legislation because they particularly target behavior over which some homeless people have no control.

In *Papachristou v. Jacksonville,* 405 U.S. 156, 92 S. Ct. 839, 31 L. Ed. 2d 110 (1972), eight homeless people challenged their conviction for violating a vagrancy ordinance. The U.S. Supreme Court held that the ordinance was vague and that it criminalized otherwise innocent conduct. In this and similar cases, the Court has stated that these "crimes" do not cause any harm to others that outweighs the violation of the rights of the individuals arrested.

Protections against an illegal SEARCH AND SEIZURE also apply to people who are homeless and to their belongings, even though their belongings might not be located in a traditional home setting. In *State v. Mooney,* 218 Conn. 85, 588 A.2d 145 (1991), police officers searched belongings of a homeless man that were found under a bridge embankment. As a result of the search, the man was arrested and charged with ROBBERY and felony MURDER. The man appealed his conviction, claiming that it had been an illegal search because the police had lacked a warrant to search his home, a cardboard box. The court agreed with the man that he had a reasonable expectation of privacy in the contents of his belongings. It disagreed, however, with his contention that he had an expectation of privacy in the bridge abutment area.

When people without a home are arrested and jailed, their property is often destroyed or stolen while they are incarcerated. Laws that target people who are homeless are thus viewed as unreasonable searches and seizures of property. In *Pottinger v. City of Miami,* 810 F. Supp. 1551 (S.D. Fla. 1992), a CLASS ACTION suit was brought on behalf of thousands of homeless people. The court agreed that certain city ordinances unfairly targeted those people and that resulting arrests and seizures of property were in violation of their constitutional rights.

Another rising statistic is that of hate crimes against the homeless. The NCH reported that in 2006 alone, the number of attacks had risen 65 percent. For the first six months of 2008, there were 26 reported assaults on homeless persons, 13 of which resulted in deaths. As of late-2009, no federal legislation had yet been passed, but a few states had acted individually. For example, Alaska was the most recent state to classify a homeless person as a "vulnerable person," which serves to enhance punishment for crimes against them.

Finally, there appeared to be an increasing trend for many urban areas to enact legislation prohibiting the homeless from begging or panhandling among the general public. As of 2008, of the 224 cities surveyed in a NCH study, 43 percent prohibited begging and/or aggressive panhandling in particular public places; 39 percent had loitering laws; 27 percent prohibited sitting or lying down in certain public places; and 28 percent prohibited camping out in particular public places.

FURTHER READINGS

Baker, Donald E. 1990–91. "Anti-Homeless Legislation: Unconstitutional Efforts to Punish the Homeless." *University of Miami Law Review* 45 (November 1990–January 1991).

Hanrahan, Patricia M. 1994. "No Home? No Vote. Homeless Are Often Denied That Most Basic Element of Democracy." *Human Rights* 21 (winter).

Jarrett, Beth D., and Wes R. Daniels. 1993. "Law and the Homeless: An Annotated Bibliography." *Law Library Journal* 85 (summer).

Mathews, K. Scott. 1991. "Rights of the Homeless in the 1990s: What Role Will the Courts Play?" *University of Missouri–Kansas City Law Review* 60 (winter).

National Coalition for the Homeless. 2009. "Fact Sheets." Available online at http://www.nationalhomeless.org/factsheets/; website home page: http://www.nationalhomeless.org/ (accessed September 25, 2009,).

Siebert, Patricia. 1986. "Homeless People: Establishing Rights to Shelter." *Law and Inequality Journal* 4.

Tolme, Paula. 2003. "Banning Begging." *Newsweek* 141.

Wright, James. 2009. *Address Unknown: The Homeless in America.* New Brunswick, NJ: Transaction Publishers.

HOMEOWNER'S WARRANTY

An insurance protection program offered by a number of builders of residential dwellings in the United States.

Homeowner's warranty, commonly known as HOW, was developed by the Home Owner's Warranty Corporation and protects the original homeowner of a new home for a period of ten years against major structural defects. If such defects occur, the builder, and not the original buyer, is financially responsible for their repair. In a number of states, similar warranty protection is afforded by statute.

HOMESTEAD

The dwelling house and its adjoining land where a family resides. Technically, and pursuant to the modern homestead exemption laws, an artificial estate in land, created to protect the possession and enjoyment of the owner against the claims of creditors by preventing the sale of the property for payment of the owner's debts so long as the land is occupied as a home.

Laws exempting the homestead from liability for debts of the owner are strictly of U.S. origin. Under the English common law, a homestead right, a personal right to the peaceful, beneficial, and uninterrupted use of the home property free from the claims of creditors, did not exist. Homestead rights exist only through the constitutional and statutory provisions that create them. Nearly every state has enacted such provisions. The earliest ones were enacted in 1839 in the Republic of Texas.

Homestead exemption statutes have been passed to achieve the public policy objective of providing lodgings where the family can peacefully reside irrespective of financial adversities. These laws are predicated on the theory that preservation of the homestead is of greater significance than the payment of debts.

Property tax exemptions, for all or part of the tax, are also available in some states for homesteaded property. Statutory requirements prescribe what must be done to establish a homestead.

A probate *homestead* is one that the court sets apart out of the estate property for the use of a surviving spouse and the minor children or out of the real estate belonging to the deceased.

A *homestead corporation* is an enterprise organized for the purpose of acquiring lands in large tracts; paying off encumbrances, charges attached to and binding real property; improving and subdividing tracts into homestead lots or parcels; and distributing them among the shareholders and for the accumulation of a fund for such purposes.

HOMESTEAD ACT OF 1862

The HOMESTEAD ACT OF 1862 was a landmark in the evolution of federal agriculture law. Passed by Congress during the Civil War, it had an idealistic goal: it sought to shape the U.S. West by populating it with farmers. The law's Northern supporters had pursued a vision of taming the rough frontier for several decades, as a means both to create an agrarian base there and to break the institution of SLAVERY that was entrenched in the South. To achieve this end, they engineered a vast giveaway of public lands. The HOMESTEAD Act provided 160 acres of land for a small filing fee and a modest investment of time and effort. The overly optimistic law failed in several ways. Most important, it was exploited by railroads and other powerful interests for profit. After making basic changes to it Congress finally repealed the law in 1977.

The Homestead Act arose from the struggle between the North and the South that culminated in the Civil War (1861–65). During this struggle, the nation followed two competing paths of agricultural development: the industrialized North favored giving public lands to individual settlers, while the South clung to its tradition of slave labor. From the early 1830s, Northern proponents of the free distribution of public land, organized around the Free-Soil party and later in the REPUBLICAN PARTY, had their ideas blocked by Southern opponents. The secession of Southern states in 1861 cleared the way for passage of the Homestead Act in 1862, against a backdrop of other important legislation that would define national agriculture policy for the next century: the Morrill Land-Grant College Act, the PACIFIC RAILROAD ACT, and the creation of the AGRICULTURE DEPARTMENT. The Homestead Act went into effect on January 1, 1863, just as President ABRAHAM LINCOLN signed the EMANCIPATION PROCLAMATION freeing slaves.

In this context of controversy and war, the Homestead Act offered a simple plan to achieve the goals of the North. As yet not fully settled, western states would be populated with a flood of homesteaders—individual farmers whose hard work would create a new agricultural industry. On its face, the law was generous. Anyone who was at least 21 years of age, the head of a family, or a military veteran was qualified to claim land; moreover, citizens and immigrants alike were entitled to participate. They paid a small filing fee in return for the temporary right to occupy and farm 160 acres. The land did not become theirs immediately; the law stipulated that it had to be improved,

Between the passage of the Homestead Act of 1862 and the year 1934, more than 1.6 million homestead applications were filed by settlers such as this family in Custer County, Nebraska (c. 1870–89).

BETTMANN/CORBIS.

and only after living on and maintaining it for five years would the homesteader gain ownership. Proponents viewed the law with an almost utopian fondness: Through the federal government's largesse, a new West would be created.

In actual application, the act did not achieve this happy outcome. Although the East offered sufficient rainfall, the West was unforgiving. There, harsh land and arid conditions made farming 160 acres a dismal prospect for the settlers, who lived in houses usually made of sod. Often, they simply needed more acreage in order to succeed. In addition, homesteaders seldom had the best land. By bribing residents who bought the land for them, or simply by filing fraudulent claims, speculators managed to reap the lion's share of land at public expense. It is estimated that only a quarter of the trillion acres made available through the Homestead Act ever served their intended purpose. The bulk of this land went to corporate interests, particularly in the railroad and timber industries, rather than individual settlers.

The Homestead Act left a complicated legacy to U.S. law. Its passage was a triumph for Northern states in their decades-long battle to control the destiny of national agricultural policy. But its limitations and its exploitation meant that the vision of those states could scarcely be realized. Congress made changes to the law during its 105-year history—chiefly, modifying the limits on acreage that it made available—but these amendments did little to alter the act's net effect on the course of national agricultural policy. The law was finally repealed in 1977. Popularly romanticized during the nineteenth century and even into the twentieth, the Homestead Act is now widely viewed by scholars as a failed experiment and a lesson in the contrasts between the intentions and outcomes of law.

FURTHER READINGS

Buckley, F.H. 1995. "The American Fresh Start." *Southern California Interdisciplinary Law Journal* 4 (fall).

Chen, Jim. 1995. "Of Agriculture's First Disobedience and Its Fruit." *Vanderbilt Law Review* 48 (October).

Nore, Michael J. "'Burn This without Fail': The Downfall of Oregon's Sen. John H. Mitchell." 1995. *Oregon State Bar Bulletin* (October).

CROSS REFERENCES

Agricultural Law; Railroad.

HOMICIDE

The killing of one human being by another human being.

Although the term *homicide* is sometimes used synonymously with MURDER, homicide is broader in scope than murder. Murder is a form of criminal homicide; other forms of homicide might not constitute criminal acts. These homicides are regarded as justified or excusable. For example, individuals may, in a necessary act of SELF-DEFENSE, kill a person who threatens them with death or serious injury, or they may be commanded or authorized by law to kill a person who is a member of an enemy force or who has committed a serious crime. Typically, the circumstances surrounding a killing determine whether it is criminal. The intent of the killer usually determines whether a criminal homicide is classified as murder or MANSLAUGHTER and at what degree.

English courts developed the body of common law on which U.S. jurisdictions initially relied in developing their homicide statutes. Early English common law divided homicide into two broad categories: FELONIOUS and non-felonious. Historically, the deliberate and premeditated killing of a person by another person was a felonious homicide and was classified as murder. Non-felonious homicide included justifiable homicide and excusable homicide. Although justifiable homicide was considered a crime, the offender often received a pardon. Excusable homicide was not considered a crime.

Under the early common law, murder was a felony that was punishable by death. It was defined as the unlawful killing of a person with "malice aforethought," which was generally defined as a premeditated intent to kill. As U.S. courts and jurisdictions adopted the English common law and modified the various circumstances that constituted criminal homicide, various degrees of criminal homicide developed. Modern statutes divide criminal homicide into two broad categories: murder and manslaughter. Murder is further divided into the first degree, which typically involves a premeditated intent to kill, and the second degree, which typically does not involve a premeditated intent to kill. Manslaughter normally involves an unintentional killing that resulted from a person's CRIMINAL NEGLIGENCE or reckless disregard for human life.

All homicides require the killing of a living person. In most states, the killing of a viable fetus is generally not considered a homicide unless the fetus is first born alive. In some states, however, this distinction is disregarded and the killing of an unborn viable fetus is classified as homicide. In other states, statutes separately classify the killing of a fetus as the crime of feticide.

The law generally requires that the death of the person occur within a year and a day of the fatal injury. This requirement initially reflected a difficulty in determining whether an initial injury led to a person's death, or whether other events or circumstances intervened to cause the person's death. As FORENSIC SCIENCE has developed and the difficulty in determining cause of death has diminished, many states have modified or abrogated the year-and-a-day rule.

Justifiable or Excusable Homicide

A homicide may be justifiable or excusable by the surrounding circumstances. In such cases, the homicide will not be considered a criminal act. A justifiable homicide is a homicide that is commanded or authorized by law. For instance, soldiers in a time of war may be commanded to kill enemy soldiers. Such killings are considered justifiable homicide unless other circumstances suggest that they were not necessary or that they were not within the scope of the soldiers' duty. In addition, a public official is justified in carrying out a death sentence because the execution is commanded by state or federal law.

A person is authorized to kill another person in self-defense or in the defense of others, but only if the person reasonably believes that the killing is absolutely necessary in order to prevent serious harm or death to himself or herself or to others. If the threatened harm can be avoided with reasonable safety, some states require the person to retreat before using DEADLY FORCE. Most states do not require retreat if the individual is attacked or threatened in his or her home, place of employment, or place of business. In addition, some states do not require a person to retreat unless that person in some way provoked the threat of harm.

Police officers may use deadly force to stop or apprehend a fleeing felon, but only if the suspect is armed or has committed a crime that involved the infliction or threatened infliction of serious injury or death. A police officer may not use deadly force to apprehend or stop an individual who has committed, or is committing, a MISDEMEANOR offense. Only certain felonies are considered in determining whether deadly force may be used to apprehend or stop a suspect. For instance, a police officer may not use deadly force to prevent the commission of larceny unless other circumstances threaten him or other persons with imminent serious injury or death.

Excusable homicide is sometimes distinguished from justifiable homicide on the basis that it involves some fault on the part of the person who ultimately uses deadly force. For instance, if a person provokes a fight and subsequently withdraws from it but, out of necessity and in self-defense, ultimately kills the other person, the homicide is sometimes classified as excusable rather than justifiable. The distinction between justifiable homicide and excusable homicide has largely disappeared, and only the term *justifiable homicide* is widely used.

Other Defenses

Other legal defenses to a charge of criminal homicide include insanity, necessity, accident, and intoxication. Some of these defenses may provide an absolute defense to a charge of criminal homicide; some will not. For instance, a successful defense of voluntary intoxication generally allows an individual to avoid prosecution for a premeditated murder, but typically it will not allow an individual to escape liability for any lesser charges, such as second-degree murder or manslaughter. As with any defense to

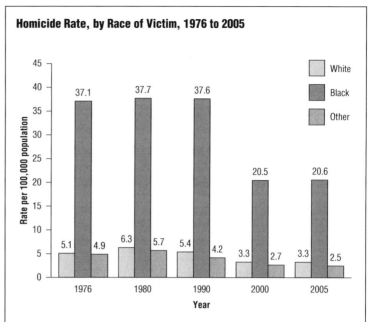

Homicide Rate, by Race of Victim, 1976 to 2005

SOURCE: U.S. Department of Justice, Bureau of Justice Statistics, *Homicide Trends in the United States*, available online at http://www.ojp.usdoj.gov/bjs/homicide/homtrnd.htm#contents (accessed on August 14, 2009).

a criminal charge, the accused's mental state is a critical determinant of whether he or she had the requisite intent or mental capacity to commit a criminal homicide.

ILLUSTRATION BY GGS CREATIVE RESOURCES. REPRODUCED BY PERMISSION OF GALE, A PART OF CENGAGE LEARNING.

Euthanasia and Physician-Assisted Suicide

The killing of oneself is a suicide, not a homicide. If a person kills another person in order to end the other person's pain or suffering, the killing is considered a homicide. It does not matter if the other person is about to die or is terminally ill just prior to being killed; the law generally views such a killing as criminal. Thus, a "mercy killing," or act of EUTHANASIA, is generally considered a criminal homicide.

As medical technology advances and the medical profession is able to prolong life for many terminally ill patients, a person's right to die by committing suicide with the help of a physician or others has become a hotly contested issue. In the 1990s, the issue of physician-assisted suicide came to the forefront of U.S. law. Dr. JACK KEVORKIAN, a Michigan physician, helped approximately 130 patients to commit suicide. Michigan authorities prosecuted Kevorkian for murder on a number of occasions, but because aiding, assisting, or causing a suicide is generally considered to be separate from homicide, Kevorkian initially avoided conviction. In 1999 he was convicted of second-degree murder following the nationally televised broadcast of a videotape showing Kevorkian injecting a lethal drug into a patient. In 2000 the *New England Journal of Medicine* revealed a study showing that 75 percent of the 69 Kevorkian-assisted deaths that were investigated were of victims who were not suffering from a potentially fatal disease; five had no discernible disease at all. Instead, it appeared that many of the suicides were the result of depression or psychiatric disorder.

In 1997 Oregon was the first state to adopt a statute permitting physician-assisted suicide. Although the statute was a source of considerable controversy, the U.S. Supreme Court upheld the law in a 2006 decision. The Supreme Court, in the case of *Gonzales v. Oregon*, did not make any broad determinations with respect to the right to die. Instead, the decision focused on the government's attempt to use the federal Controlled Substances Act (CSA) to undermine the Oregon law allowing for physician-assisted suicide. The Supreme Court held that the government could not use the CSA to prosecute physicians that provide deadly doses of medicine to terminally ill patients. In 2008 Washington became the second state to establish a law allowing for physician-assisted suicide.

FURTHER READINGS

Chan, Samantha. 2000. "Rates of Assisted Suicides Rise Sharply in Oregon." *Student BMJ* 11.

FAQs about the Death With Dignity Act. State of Oregon. Available online at http://www.oregon.gov (accessed June 10, 2009).

Garland, Norman M. 2009. *Criminal Law for the Criminal Justice Professional*. 2nd Ed. New York: McGraw-Hill.

Kadish, Sanford H., ed. 1983. *Encyclopedia of Crime and Justice*. Vol. 2. New York: Free Press.

Lafave, Wayne R., and Austin W. Scott, Jr. 1986. *Substantive Criminal Law*. Vol. 2. St. Paul, MN: West.

Loewy, Arnold H. 2003. *Criminal Law in a Nutshell*. 4th Ed. St. Paul, MN: West.

"New Revelations about Dr. Death." 2000. *Macleans* 113.

Torcia, Charles E. 1994. *Wharton's Criminal Law*. 15th ed. New York: Clark, Boardman, Callaghan.

CROSS REFERENCES

Death and Dying; Insanity Defense.

HONOR

As a verb, to accept a bill of exchange, or to pay a note, check, or accepted bill, at maturity. To pay or to accept and pay, or, where a credit so engages,

to purchase or discount a draft complying with the terms of the draft.

As a noun, in old ENGLISH LAW, *a seigniory of several manors held under one baron or lord paramount. Also those dignities or privileges, degrees of nobility, knighthood, and other titles that flow from the crown.*

In the United States, the customary title of courtesy given to judges, and occasionally to some other officers, as, "his honor," "your honor," "honorable."

HONORARY TRUST

An arrangement whereby property is placed in the hands of another to be used for specific non-charitable purposes where there is no definite ascertainable beneficiary—one who profits by the act of another—and that is unenforceable in the absence of statute.

Trusts for the erection of monuments, the care of graves, the saying of Masses, or the care of specific animals, such as a cat, dog, or horse, are examples of honorary trusts. Honorary trusts for the benefit of specific animals differ from charitable trusts that have as a trust purpose the benefit of animals in general. In many jurisdictions, legislation validates special provisions for the upkeep of graves and monuments. Similarly, trusts for the saying of Masses are upheld as charitable trusts.

As a general rule, the designated trustee, one appointed or required by law to execute a trust, can effectuate the intent of the settlor—one who creates a trust—if he or she chooses to do so. Since there is no beneficiary who can enforce the trust, the implementation of the purposes of the trust depends upon the honor of the trustee. If the person does not execute the trust duties, he or she holds the property for the settlor or the settlor's heirs on the theory of a RESULTING TRUST.

Jurisdictions differ as to the extent to which honorary trusts will be recognized, if at all. Honorary trusts are usually limited by considerations of public policy. For instance, they cannot exist beyond the period of the RULE AGAINST PERPETUITIES, and their amounts cannot be unreasonably large for the purpose to be accomplished. The purpose must also be that of a reasonably normal testator and cannot be capricious.

A settlor bequeaths $1,000 to a trustee to care for the settlor's cat and dog, and $1,000 for the purpose of maintaining the settlor's home in the same condition as of the instant of his death for 20 years thereafter, with all windows and doors blocked shut. Upon the settlor's death, the residuary legatee inherits any money that remains in the estate after all other claims are paid and makes claims to both sums of money under these testamentary provisions. A court will find that the residuary legatee has no right to the $1,000 left for the cat and dog unless the trustee refuses to fulfill the obligations of caring for the dog and cat. The residuary legatee is, however, entitled to the other $1,000. Neither of these provisions of the settlor's will created a private trust.

As a general rule, the beneficiary of a private trust must be competent to come into court either in person or by guardian and enforce the trust duties against the trustee. Neither the cat nor the dog can appear in court. Some states permit provisions for reasonable sums to specific animals to be valid honorary trusts as long as public policy is not violated. If the trustee fails to properly execute his or her duties, he or she holds the property in resulting trust for the heirs or NEXT OF KIN of the decedent. In this example, if the trustee spends the $1,000 in caring for the dog and cat, he or she is not liable, but if he or she does not, a court will order the trustee to turn the money over to the residuary legatee as the beneficiary of a resulting trust. If the purpose of an intended honorary trust is capricious, the trust will fail. In this case, there is no legitimate end to be served by keeping the settlor's home boarded up for 20 years. The purpose is capricious and the trust fails. Therefore, the $1,000 set aside for this purpose is held by the trustee in resulting trust for the residuary legatee who must receive it.

Benjamin Hooks.
CHIP SOMODEVILLA/
GETTY IMAGES

❖ HOOKS, BENJAMIN LAWSON

CIVIL RIGHTS advocate Benjamin Lawson Hooks is best known as the forceful executive director of the National Association for the Advancement of Colored People (NAACP) from 1977 to 1993. Before he led the NAACP, Hooks made a virtual career out of shattering U.S. racial barriers. He was the first African American ever appointed to a Tennessee criminal court and the first African American named to the FEDERAL COMMUNICATIONS COMMISSION (FCC). Hooks was also an ordained minister, a television host and producer, a savings and loan administrator, a public speaker, and a fast-food executive.

Hooks was born January 31, 1925, in Memphis. As an African American living under JIM CROW LAWS, he experienced the daily

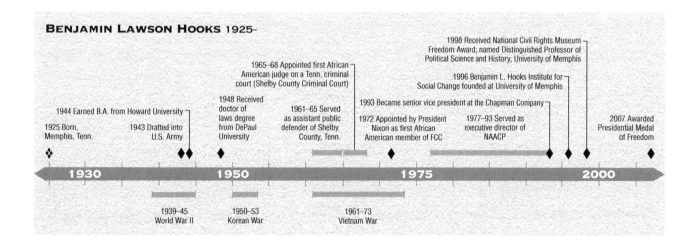

BENJAMIN LAWSON HOOKS 1925–

1925 Born, Memphis, Tenn.

1943 Drafted into U.S. Army

1944 Earned B.A. from Howard University

1948 Received doctor of laws degree from DePaul University

1961–65 Served as assistant public defender of Shelby County, Tenn.

1965–68 Appointed first African American judge on a Tenn. criminal court (Shelby County Criminal Court)

1972 Appointed by President Nixon as first African American member of FCC

1993 Became senior vice president at the Chapman Company

1977–93 Served as executive director of NAACP

1996 Benjamin L. Hooks Institute for Social Change founded at University of Memphis

1998 Received National Civil Rights Museum Freedom Award; named Distinguished Professor of Political Science and History, University of Memphis

2007 Awarded Presidential Medal of Freedom

1930   1950   1975   2000

1939–45 World War II

1950–53 Korean War

1961–73 Vietnam War

indignities of southern segregation. His parents, Bessie Hooks and Robert B. Hooks, raised their seven children with high moral and academic standards. After high school, Hooks enrolled at LeMoyne College, in Memphis, but his college career was interrupted by WORLD WAR II. Hooks was drafted into the U.S. Army in 1943 and rose to the rank of staff sergeant.

After his military service, Hooks attended Howard University, in Washington, D.C., and graduated with a bachelor of arts degree in 1944. Hooks then traveled to Chicago to study law at DePaul University. Although Hooks wanted to enroll in a Tennessee law school, he could not do so because law schools in Tennessee refused to admit African Americans. Hooks graduated with a doctor of laws degree from DePaul in 1948. In 1949, he moved back to Memphis and started his own law practice. In 1952, he married Frances Dancy, and later, they had one child, Patricia.

During the 1950s Hooks became active in the growing national CIVIL RIGHTS MOVEMENT. Along with MARTIN LUTHER KING Jr., Hooks served on the Board of Directors for the SOUTHERN CHRISTIAN LEADERSHIP CONFERENCE. During this time, Hooks also became an ordained Baptist minister and accepted a call as pastor of the Middle Baptist Church in Memphis. Adding to an already busy life, Hooks became vice president of a savings and loan association he helped found in Memphis in 1955.

In 1961 Hooks took over as assistant public defender of Shelby County. His role led to an appointment in 1965 by Governor Frank G. Clement of Tennessee to the Shelby County Criminal Court. With this appointment, Hooks became the first African American to serve as judge on the Tennessee criminal bench. In 1966 he was elected on his own to a full eight-year term. In the meantime, Hooks became minister of the Greater New Mount Moriah Baptist Church in Detroit. He flew to Detroit twice a month to lead his congregation.

In 1968 Hooks resigned his criminal court judgeship to become president of Mahalia Jackson Chicken Systems, a fast-food franchise. In 1972, he was appointed by President RICHARD M. NIXON to become a member of the previously all-white FCC, the federal agency that licenses and regulates radio, television, satellite communications, telephones, and telegraph transmissions. This position allowed him to focus public attention on the image of African Americans in radio and television and to increase minority jobs in broadcasting.

In 1977 Hooks assumed the position with which he is most commonly identified: executive director of the NAACP. Following in the footsteps of the retiring ROY WILKINS, Hooks accepted the job because he deeply respected the NAACP and because he wanted to complete some of the unfinished business of the equal rights movement. A tireless worker, Hooks spent long days in the NAACP Baltimore headquarters performing what he called the "killing job."

During Hooks's tenure the NAACP expressed concern over homelessness, drug abuse, inadequate education, and neighborhood safety. Hooks lamented the rise of an intractable urban underclass and warned that the promise of jobs and economic independence for African Americans must be met soon.

Hooks's important accomplishments with the NAACP include his work in convincing Congress to impose sanctions against South Africa's system of apartheid, for legislation creating fair housing rights, and for a federally recognized holiday to celebrate the life and work of Martin Luther King Jr.

Hooks's achievements with the NAACP took on a special significance in view of the political conservatism that prevailed during his fifteen-year tenure as its head—a period when RONALD REAGAN and GEORGE H. W. BUSH were in the White House. Hooks vowed to keep the NAACP true to its progressive mission. In fact, under his leadership, the NAACP refused to endorse the nomination of African American CLARENCE THOMAS to the U.S. Supreme Court because Thomas's views were too conservative.

By the time Hooks retired from the NAACP in 1993, its membership had grown to more than 500,000 people in over 2,200 chapters across the United States. Hooks was gratified by the results of a 1992 survey in which the NAACP earned an 86 percent approval rating among those polled. The organization worked hard to counter criticism that it was mired in the past and out of touch with African American youths.

When Hooks retired from the NAACP post in April 1993, the 64 members of the NAACP Board of Directors elected Benjamin F. Chavis Jr., as his successor. Hooks left the NAACP to embark on yet another career challenge—as a senior vice president at the Chapman Company, a minority controlled brokerage and investment banking firm with offices in seven cities.

THERE WILL ALWAYS BE A NEED FOR THE NAACP. ONCE WE THOUGHT THERE WOULD COME A TIME WHEN OUR WORK WOULD BE FINISHED. BUT RACISM STILL EXISTS AND INEQUALITY IS STILL BUILT INTO THIS SOCIETY.
—BENJAMIN L. HOOKS

The NAACP experienced turmoil in 1994 when a SEXUAL HARASSMENT lawsuit was filed against Chavis. Chavis resigned and was replaced in 1996 by Kweisi Mfume who functioned as president and CEO. Throughout the controversy Hooks remained supportive of the NAACP.

After retiring from the NAACP, Hooks remained active. In addition to the Spingarn Medal which he was awarded in 1986, Hooks received numerous awards and more than 25 honorary degrees, and he has served as president of the National Civil Rights Museum. In 1996 the Benjamin L. Hooks Institute for Social Change was established at the University of Memphis. The purpose of the institute is to promote understanding of the civil rights movement and the quest for HUMAN RIGHTS. Hooks also served as the chairman of the Board of Directors of the National Civil Rights Museum.

In 2007 Hooks was awarded the Presidential Medal of Freedom, the nation's highest civilian honor, by President GEORGE W. BUSH. "Dr. Hooks was a calm yet forceful voice for fairness, opportunity, and personal responsibility. He never tired or faltered in demanding our nation live up to its founding ideals of liberty and equality," said Bush when he presented Hooks with the award.

Hooks died April 15, 2010, in his home in Memphis, Tennessee.

FURTHER READINGS

"Benjamin Hooks, Leading Jurist and Civil Rights Leader." *Voice of America.* February 26, 2008.

Bigelow, Barbara Carlisle, ed. 1992. *Contemporary Black Biography.* Vol. 2. Detroit: Gale Research.

Biography of Dr. Benjamin L. Hooks. *Benjamin Hooks Institute for Social Change.* Available online at http://benhooks.memphis.edu/drhooks.html (accessed November 25, 2009).

Kluger, Richard. 1976. *Simple Justice.* New York: Random House.

Orfield, Gary, Susan E. Eaton, and Elaine R. Jones. 1997. *Dismantling Desegregation: The Quiet Reversal of Brown v. Board of Education.* New York: New Press.

Schwartz, Bernard. 1986. *Swann's Way: The School Busing Case and the Supreme Court.* New York: Oxford University Press.

❖ HOOVER, HERBERT CLARK

Herbert Clark Hoover was the thirty-first PRESIDENT OF THE UNITED STATES, serving from 1929 to 1932. A wealthy mining engineer, Hoover directed humanitarian relief efforts during and after World Wars I and II. His presidency was devastated by the stock market crash of 1929 and the ensuing Great Depression.

Hoover was born August 10, 1874, in West Branch, Iowa. His father and mother died when he was young, and he was raised by an uncle in Oregon. He entered the first first-year class at Stanford University and graduated in 1895 with a degree in mining engineering. He became an expert on managing and reorganizing mines throughout the world. He spent time in Australia and China before setting up his own engineering firm in London in 1908. By 1914 Hoover had become a millionaire.

Hoover became involved in relief work during WORLD WAR I. In 1914 he served as director of the American Relief Commission in England, which helped one hundred twenty thousand U.S. citizens return home after being stranded at the outbreak of the war. The British government then asked him to lead the Commission for Relief in Belgium. His main achievement during this period was the distribution of supplies to civilian victims of the war in Belgium and France.

After the United States entered the war in 1917, President WOODROW WILSON named Hoover U.S. food administrator. In this capacity Hoover coordinated the production and conservation of food supplies that could be used for the war effort. Hoover also chaired the European Relief and Reconstruction Commission, directing activities of numerous relief departments and organizing the distribution of provisions. After the war Hoover coordinated the American Relief Administration. This agency provided food to millions during the famine of 1921 in the Soviet Union.

Hoover's humanitarian efforts made him an international figure. Democrats and Republicans sought to make him a presidential candidate in 1920, but Hoover rejected their offers. Instead, in 1921 he accepted the position of secretary of commerce in the administration of President WARREN G. HARDING, a Republican. Hoover was an energetic administrator, reorganizing the department and expanding its oversight into commercial aviation, highway safety, and radio broadcasting. He chaired commissions that established the Hoover Dam and the St. Lawrence Seaway.

In 1928 Hoover won the Republican presidential nomination. He easily defeated Democrat Alfred E. Smith, on a platform of continued economic prosperity and support for Prohibition.

FREE SPEECH DOES NOT LIVE MANY HOURS AFTER FREE INDUSTRY AND FREE COMMERCE DIE.
—HERBERT HOOVER

Herbert Hoover.

Hoover devoted the early days of his presidency to improving the economic conditions of farmers. He advocated foreign tariffs on imported farm products as a way to protect domestic farm prices. Congress went beyond Hoover's recommendation and in 1930 enacted the Hawley-Smoot Tariff Act (19 U.S.C.A. § 1303 et seq.), which placed tariffs on nonfarm products as well. The act severely damaged U.S. foreign trade.

The control of Prohibition pursuant to the EIGHTEENTH AMENDMENT and the VOLSTEAD ACT (41 Stat. 305 [1919]) had become a serious problem by 1929. ORGANIZED CRIME had seized the opportunity to sell illegal alcohol. The only way large-scale liquor and speakeasy traffic could flourish was with the cooperation of law enforcement, so state and local law enforcement agencies were tainted with corruption. In 1929 Hoover established the National Commission on Law Observance and Law Enforcement, appointing GEORGE W. WICKERSHAM to direct an investigation of the effectiveness of law enforcement practices in the United States. The WICKERSHAM COMMISSION report was an important inquiry into the practices of the U.S. criminal justice system. The report examined all facets of police work and, for the first time, discussed police brutality and the "third degree" method of interrogating suspects. The report called for the professionalization of police.

The U.S. economy appeared to be robust in 1929, but a rising stock market had been built on stock purchases financed by widespread borrowing. When the stock market crashed on October 29, individuals, banks, and other economic institutions were devastated. Hoover sought to inspire public confidence by meeting with business leaders and by proclaiming that the economic downturn would be brief.

Hoover's prediction was wrong. The United States slid into the worst economic depression in its history. Hoover resisted massive federal intervention because he believed that the economy would correct itself. He did approve some federal public works projects that provided jobs, but he opposed federal aid to the

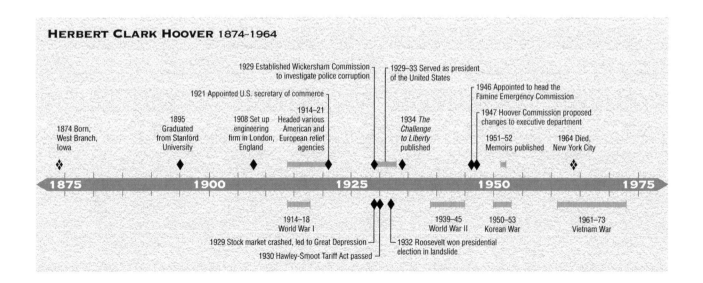

HERBERT CLARK HOOVER 1874–1964

1874 Born, West Branch, Iowa

1895 Graduated from Stanford University

1908 Set up engineering firm in London, England

1914–21 Headed various American and European relief agencies

1921 Appointed U.S. secretary of commerce

1929 Established Wickersham Commission to investigate police corruption

1929–33 Served as president of the United States

1934 *The Challenge to Liberty* published

1946 Appointed to head the Famine Emergency Commission

1947 Hoover Commission proposed changes to executive department

1951–52 Memoirs published

1964 Died, New York City

1875 · 1900 · 1925 · 1950 · 1975

1914–18 World War I

1929 Stock market crashed, led to Great Depression

1930 Hawley-Smoot Tariff Act passed

1932 Roosevelt won presidential election in landslide

1939–45 World War II

1950–53 Korean War

1961–73 Vietnam War

unemployed. In his view private charity should help those who had fallen on hard times.

In 1932, with 12 million people out of work and hundreds of banks failing, Hoover created the Reconstruction Finance Corporation (RFC) to extend loans to revitalize industry and to keep banks from going into BANKRUPTCY. Congress authorized the RFC to loan up to $300 million to states for relief. Many persons viewed these actions as too little and too late.

The troubles of the Hoover administration culminated in the Bonus Army March on Washington, D.C. In 1932 World War I veterans demanded monetary bonuses that had been promised them in 1924, even though the bonuses were not scheduled to be paid until 1945. The House of Representatives had passed a bill authorizing early payment, and the veterans sought to pressure the Senate to follow suit. More than 15,000 veterans, in desperate need of funds, organized a march on Washington, D.C., to secure immediate payment from the government. The "bonus army" constructed a makeshift city and declared that its members were ready to stay until their goal was achieved. Hoover dispatched federal troops to destroy the encampment and drive the veterans out of the nation's capital. For doing so he received nationwide criticism.

The REPUBLICAN PARTY nominated Hoover for a second term in 1932, but his candidacy attracted little enthusiasm. The DEMOCRATIC PARTY nominee, New York Governor FRANKLIN D. ROOSEVELT, mounted a vigorous campaign against Hoover's economic policies, calling for a "new deal" for U.S. citizens. Roosevelt promised to balance the budget, provide relief to the unemployed, help the farmer, and repeal Prohibition. He carried 42 of the 48 states.

Hoover was angered by Roosevelt's NEW DEAL, which made the federal government the dominant player in the national economy. In 1934 he published *The Challenge to Liberty*, which attacked Roosevelt and his policies. He then withdrew from public life until 1946, when President HARRY S. TRUMAN asked him to return to relief work. Hoover subsequently directed the Famine Emergency Commission, which distributed food supplies to war-torn nations. In 1947 Truman authorized him to investigate the executive department of the U.S. government. The resulting Hoover Commission proposed changes in the EXECUTIVE BRANCH that saved money and streamlined government.

Hoover had a continuing interest in the Hoover Institution on War, Revolution, and Peace, which he founded at Stanford in 1919 and which remains an important research center. He published his memoirs in three volumes (1951–52) and *The Ordeal of Woodrow Wilson* (1958).

Hoover lived longer after leaving the presidency than did any other president. He died at age 90 on October 20, 1964, in New York City.

FURTHER READINGS

Hawley, Ellis, ed. 1974–1977. *Herbert Hoover: Containing the Public Messages, Speeches, and Statements of the President*, 4 vols. Washington, D.C.: U.S. Government Printing Office.

Leuchtenberg, William E. 2009. *Herbert Hoover*. New York: Times.

Walch, Timothy, ed. 2003. *Uncommon Americans: The Lives and Legacies of Herbert and Lou Henry Hoover*. Santa Barbara, CA: Praeger.

❖ HOOVER, JOHN EDGAR

John Edgar Hoover served from 1924 to 1972 as the director of the FEDERAL BUREAU OF INVESTIGATION (FBI). During his long tenure, Hoover built the FBI into a formidable law enforcement organization, establishing standards for the collection and evaluation of information that made the FBI an effective crime fighting agency. However, Hoover's reputation was tarnished by his collection of damaging information on prominent politicians and public figures for his personal use, and by his aggressive investigation of CIVIL RIGHTS leaders and left-wing radicals.

Hoover was born January 1, 1895, in Washington, D.C. Following graduation from high school, he turned down a scholarship from the University of Virginia, electing to stay home and study law at night at GEORGE WASHINGTON University. In 1916 he received a bachelor of laws degree. In 1917 he added a master of laws degree. Upon graduation from college, Hoover joined the U.S. JUSTICE DEPARTMENT.

Hoover started in a minor position, but his intelligence, energy, and mastery of detail were quickly noticed by his superiors. By 1919 he had risen to the rank of special assistant attorney general. During these early years, Hoover first became involved with the suppression of

WE ARE A FACT-GATHERING ORGANIZATION ONLY. WE DON'T CLEAR ANYBODY. WE DON'T CONDEMN ANYBODY.
—J. EDGAR HOOVER

J. Edgar Hoover.
LIBRARY OF CONGRESS

political radicals, assisting Attorney General A. Mitchell Palmer in the arrest and deportation of left-wing aliens. In 1919 he was appointed chief of the department's General Intelligence Division (GID), a unit designated by Palmer to hunt down radicals. Within three months Hoover collected the names of 150,000 alleged subversives. Armed with this information, federal agents conducted nationwide dragnets, arresting over ten thousand people. Critics argued that these Palmer Raids violated civil liberties. Nevertheless, thousands of persons were deported. By 1921 the GID had nearly half a million names of persons suspected of subversive activities.

In 1924 Hoover was appointed acting director of the Bureau of Investigation (BI), the forerunner of the FBI. The BI was a weak agency, hampered by limited investigatory powers, the inability of its agents to carry weapons, and the swelling of its rank with

political appointments. After several scandals revealed the extent of the BI's problems, Attorney General HARLAN F. STONE appointed Hoover to clean up the agency.

Though only 29, Hoover met the challenge head-on. He began a thorough reorganization of the bureau, imposing strict discipline on his employees. Hoover's goal was to establish a professional law enforcement agency of unquestioned integrity. Between 1924 and 1935, he introduced a series of innovations that changed national law enforcement. Hoover established a national fingerprint collection, the first systematic database that federal, state, and local agencies could use to match FINGERPRINTS at crime scenes with those on file at the bureau. He also created a crime laboratory, which developed scientific procedures for obtaining forensic evidence. Finally, Hoover made a point of changing the character of his agents. He established a training academy for new agents, who were selected on the basis of their qualifications, not on their political connections. Agents were required to be college educated and to maintain the highest standard of personal and professional ethics.

As the agency became more professional, its jurisdiction increased. In 1935 President FRANKLIN D. ROOSEVELT signed crime bills giving agents the authority to carry guns and make arrests, and in the same year, the bureau officially became the FBI. During the 1930s Hoover moved from internal reorganization to external promotion of himself and his agency. The gangster era, from 1920 to 1935, ended in the arrest or killing of well-publicized hoodlums such as John Dillinger, Pretty Boy Floyd, and Bonnie and Clyde. Hoover and his G-men were celebrated for these exploits in newspapers, radio, newsreels, and Hollywood

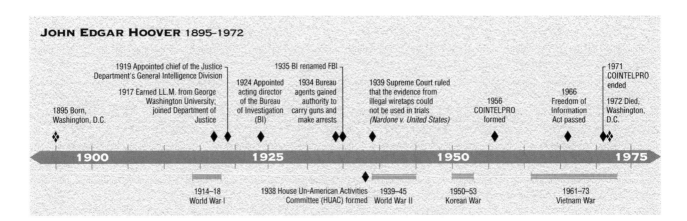

JOHN EDGAR HOOVER 1895–1972

1895 Born, Washington, D.C.

1917 Earned LL.M. from George Washington University; joined Department of Justice

1919 Appointed chief of the Justice Department's General Intelligence Division

1924 Appointed acting director of the Bureau of Investigation (BI)

1934 Bureau agents gained authority to carry guns and make arrests

1935 BI renamed FBI

1939 Supreme Court ruled that the evidence from illegal wiretaps could not be used in trials (*Nardone v. United States*)

1956 COINTELPRO formed

1966 Freedom of Information Act passed

1971 COINTELPRO ended

1972 Died, Washington, D.C.

1900   1925   1950   1975

1914–18 World War I

1938 House Un-American Activities Committee (HUAC) formed

1939–45 World War II

1950–53 Korean War

1961–73 Vietnam War

movies, establishing Hoover as the nation's leading crime fighter.

Hoover's focus shifted to political subversion and foreign ESPIONAGE during WORLD WAR II. Again, the FBI was celebrated in the news media and popular culture, this time for tracking down Nazi saboteurs and spies. With the end of World War II and the beginning of the COLD WAR with the Soviet Union, Hoover directed his efforts at rooting out Communist subversives. Harkening back to his early work with Palmer, Hoover's zealousness for this task led him to make alliances with the House Un-American Activities Committee; anti-Communist politicians such as Representative RICHARD M. NIXON, of California, and Senator JOSEPH R. MCCARTHY, of Wisconsin; and members of the news media who were eager to print Hoover's inside information.

During the 1950s Hoover concentrated on anti-Communist initiatives, ignoring calls to investigate the growth of ORGANIZED CRIME. He published *Masters of Deceit* (1958), a book that articulated his views on what he perceived to be the Communist conspiracy to overthrow the U.S. government. He established the FBI's Counterintelligence Program (COINTELPRO) to disrupt the U.S. Communist party and to discredit its members through informants, disinformation, and anonymous letters and telephone calls. He also enlisted the cooperation of the INTERNAL REVENUE SERVICE to conduct selective tax audits of people he suspected of being Communists. Critics of Hoover argued—and continue to argue—that he went beyond law enforcement in these efforts, using so-called dirty tricks to undermine the reputation of persons he believed to be subversive.

Despite these charges Hoover remained a powerful federal official. His use of wiretaps on phones, and of other forms of ELECTRONIC SURVEILLANCE, provided him with a wealth of information on the private affairs of many prominent political figures. Hoover shared some of this information with his political allies, but much of it remained in his private files. Over time many politicians came to fear Hoover, who they believed might have incriminating information about them that could destroy their political careers. Armed with these files, Hoover enjoyed immense power in the 1950s and 1960s.

With the birth of the modern CIVIL RIGHTS MOVEMENT, Hoover discovered what he considered another subversive group. He became convinced that MARTIN LUTHER KING, JR., was a pawn of the Communist conspiracy. He had agents follow King and record sexual encounters in various hotel rooms. King's SOUTHERN CHRISTIAN LEADERSHIP CONFERENCE offices were wiretapped and burglarized by the FBI many times, all in the hope of finding information that would discredit King. Though Hoover's efforts proved futile, they demonstrated his ability to use the FBI as his personal tool.

During the 1960s Hoover also had the FBI investigate the KU KLUX KLAN and other white supremacist groups. The same techniques used against King and other alleged subversives were also employed against right-wing radicals who threatened physical violence. And with the growth of opposition to the VIETNAM WAR in the 1960s, Hoover targeted war protesters.

Presidents LYNDON B. JOHNSON and Richard M. Nixon allowed Hoover to serve past the mandatory retirement age. During his last years, Hoover was criticized for his authoritarian administration of the FBI. Agents who displeased him could be banished to an obscure FBI field office or discharged. Perhaps most troubling was his refusal to investigate organized crime with the same resources expended on politically subversive organizations.

Hoover died May 2, 1972, in Washington, D.C.

FURTHER READINGS

Gentry, Curt. 2001. *J. Edgar Hoover: The Man and the Secrets.* New York: Norton.

Powers, Richard G. 1987. *Secrecy and Power: The Life of J. Edgar Hoover.* New York: Free Press.

Wannall, Ray. 2000. *The Real J. Edgar Hoover: For the Record.* Paducah, KY: Turner.

CROSS REFERENCES

Communism; Forensic Science.

❖ HORNBLOWER, WILLIAM BUTLER

William Butler Hornblower was a noted corporate and trial lawyer who was nominated to the U.S. Supreme Court but failed to win confirmation.

Hornblower was born May 13, 1851, in Paterson, New Jersey, with an unusually distinguished family background. His great-grandfather was a member of the Congress of the CONFEDERATION and a judge, his grandfather was a chief justice of the Supreme Court of New Jersey, his father was a noted theologian and pastor, and his mother was a descendant of Revolutionary leaders and colonial judges. In addition, one of his uncles was JOSEPH P. BRADLEY, an associate justice of the U.S. Supreme Court, and another was Lewis B. Woodruff, a highly respected federal CIRCUIT COURT judge.

Hornblower was first educated at prestigious preparatory schools and in 1871 graduated with honors from the College of New Jersey (later known as Princeton University). At the encouragement of Bradley and Woodruff, he then entered Columbia University to study law. In 1875 he graduated with distinction, was admitted to the bar, and became a trial lawyer with the New York City firm of Caton and Eaton, where he had been a clerk while a law student. In 1888 he founded the firm of Hornblower and Byrne. Throughout his legal career, Hornblower represented a number of major corporate clients, including the New York Life Insurance Company; the Chicago, Milwaukee, and St. Paul Railway Company; the New York Security and Trust Company; and several tobacco companies. He also served on many public commissions, held office in state and national bar associations, and was active in the DEMOCRATIC PARTY.

In 1893 President Grover Cleveland nominated Hornblower to succeed SAMUEL BLATCHFORD, who had died, as an associate justice of the U.S. Supreme Court. Given his long and distinguished career, Hornblower appeared headed for easy confirmation, but a bitter political battle intervened to prevent Hornblower from taking the seat.

A year before his nomination to the Court, Hornblower had been appointed to a New York City Bar Association committee convened to investigate Judge Isaac H. Maynard. Maynard was accused of improper conduct in a contested election while he was deputy attorney general. The investigation ultimately led to Maynard's defeat for a seat on the New York Court of Appeals. David B. Hill, a powerful New York senator and a close friend of Maynard's, retaliated against Hornblower for his role in the investigation by vigorously campaigning against Hornblower's nomination. Hill's efforts were successful: the Senate rejected Hornblower's nomination by a vote of 30–24.

In 1895 President Cleveland nominated Hornblower for another vacancy on the Court. This time, Hornblower declined the nomination, citing the financial sacrifice he would incur if he left his very lucrative law practice.

In 1914 Hornblower was nominated to the New York Court of Appeals and was confirmed unanimously by the New York state senate. He took his seat on the court in March, but left after only one week owing to illness. He died two months later, on June 16, 1914, in Litchfield, Connecticut.

HORNBOOK

A primer; a book explaining the basics, fundamentals, or rudiments of any science or branch of knowledge. The phrase hornbook law is a colloquial designation of the rudiments or general principles of law.

A colloquial reference to a series of textbooks that review various fields of law in summary, narrative form, as opposed to casebooks, which are designed as primary teaching tools and include many reprints of court opinions.

[T]HE INDEPENDENCE OF THE JUDICIARY IS THE KEYSTONE OF OUR FORM OF GOVERNMENT, THAT IF THE KEYSTONE IS REMOVED THE WHOLE STRUCTURE IS IN DANGER OF DISINTEGRATION AND DESTRUCTION.
—WILLIAM HORNBLOWER

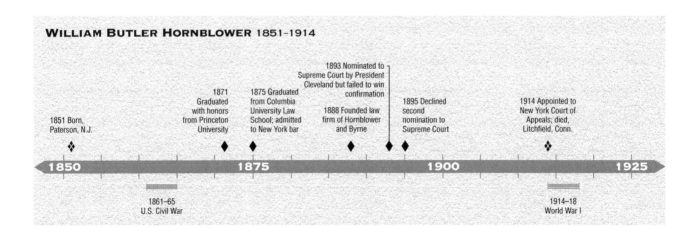

WILLIAM BUTLER HORNBLOWER 1851–1914

1851 Born, Paterson, N.J.

1871 Graduated with honors from Princeton University

1875 Graduated from Columbia University Law School; admitted to New York bar

1888 Founded law firm of Hornblower and Byrne

1893 Nominated to Supreme Court by President Cleveland but failed to win confirmation

1895 Declined second nomination to Supreme Court

1914 Appointed to New York Court of Appeals; died, Litchfield, Conn.

1850   1875   1900   1925

1861–65 U.S. Civil War

1914–18 World War I

HOSTAGES

Persons taken by an individual or organized group in order to force a state, government unit, or community to meet certain conditions: payment of ransom, release of prisoners, or some other act.

The taking of hostages, whether during wartime or periods of peace, is generally condemned under INTERNATIONAL LAW.

HOSTILE FIRE

In insurance law, a combustion that cannot be controlled, that escapes from where it was initially set and confined, or one that was not intended to exist.

A hostile fire differs from a FRIENDLY FIRE, which burns in a place where it was intended to burn, such as one confined to a fireplace or furnace.

HOSTILE WITNESS

A witness at a trial who is so adverse to the party that called him or her that he or she can be cross-examined as though called to testify by the opposing party.

The FEDERAL RULES OF EVIDENCE provide that witnesses who are hostile, or adverse, can be interrogated through the use of leading questions.

HOT LINE AGREEMENT, 1971

The original "hot line" agreement was a memorandum of understanding between the United States and the Soviet Union reached in 1963 to establish a direct communications link between the governments of the two nations.

The need for such a communications channel was evident in the CUBAN MISSILE CRISIS of 1962 and its establishment was viewed as a means of forestalling an unnecessary resort to force. The 1971 hot line agreement updated the 1963 accord by increasing the communications capability between the two governments. It called for the addition of two separate circuits of communications employing a U.S. and a Russian satellite system.

CROSS REFERENCE

Cold War.

HOT PURSUIT

A doctrine that provides that the police may enter the premises where they suspect a crime has been

The doctrine of hot pursuit provides that in certain cases police may enter, without a warrant, premises where they suspect a crime has been committed.

CORBIS.

committed without a warrant when delay would endanger their lives or the lives of others and lead to the escape of the alleged perpetrator; also sometimes called fresh pursuit.

Countless crime dramas have portrayed police officers in a high-speed chase barking into their radio that they are "in hot pursuit" of a suspect. This popular image says little about the legal rule of hot pursuit. As established by the U.S. Supreme Court, the rule is an important exception to the freedoms guaranteed by the FOURTH AMENDMENT. That constitutional provision safeguards citizens against excessive police intrusion into their life and property. Its foremost protection is the SEARCH WARRANT, which must be obtained from a judge or magistrate before the police can conduct most searches. Under special circumstances, the rule of hot pursuit gives the police extra powers to enter private property and conduct a search without a warrant. The rule recognizes practical limitations on Fourth Amendment rights in light of the realities of police work, especially in emergencies, but it stops far short of giving the police complete freedom to conduct warrantless searches.

As a powerful deterrent to the ABUSE OF POWER, the Fourth Amendment is designed to prevent the rise of a police state. The requirement that police officers obtain search warrants prevents arbitrary violations of freedom, applying equally to federal and state authority. Yet this freedom is not absolute. In the twentieth century, the Supreme Court has carved out a few exceptions to its protections. These exceptions exist under "exigent circumstances": the emergencylike demands of specifically defined situations that call for immediate response by the police, who must have PROBABLE CAUSE to conduct a search. Generally, these are circumstances under which obtaining a search warrant would be impractical—ranging from those requiring officers to frisk suspects for weapons to those requiring officers to stop and search automobiles—as well as when suspects explicitly consent or imply consent to a search.

Hot pursuit is one such exigent circumstance. It usually applies when the police are pursuing a suspected felon into private premises or have probable cause to believe that a crime has been committed on private premises. The Supreme Court stated that "'hot pursuit' means some sort of a chase, but it need not be an extended hue and cry 'in and about the public streets'" (*United States v. Santana*, 427 U.S. 38, 96 S. Ct. 2406, 49 L. Ed. 2d 300 [1976]). Hot pursuit also applies when the lives of police officers or others are in danger. Thus, the Court has recognized two specific conditions that justify warrantless searches under the rule of hot pursuit: the need to circumvent the destruction of evidence, and the need to prevent the loss of life or serious injury.

The Supreme Court enunciated the rule of hot pursuit in 1967, in *Warden v. Hayden*, 387 U.S. 294, 87 S. Ct. 1642, 18 L. Ed. 2d 782. It had used the term before, but in *Warden*, it explicitly condoned a certain form of this warrantless search. In this case, police officers pursuing a suspected armed robber were told that he had entered a dwelling moments before their arrival. They entered the dwelling, searched it and seized evidence, and then apprehended the suspect in bed. The man alleged in court that the warrantless search of the premises had violated his Fourth Amendment rights. When the case reached the Supreme Court, it disagreed, justifying the search under exigent circumstances.

Since *Warden*, lower courts have applied the rule to determine whether police officers acted reasonably or unreasonably when conducting a search without obtaining a search warrant. Other cases have permitted warrantless entry and arrest in hot pursuit under different circumstances: when the police saw a suspect standing in her doorway who retreated inside carrying a package that contained marked money from a drug sting (*United States v. Santana*, 427 U.S. 38, 96 S. Ct. 2406, 49 L. Ed. 2d 300 [1976]); when the police had probable cause to arrest a suspect because he fit the description of an assailant who had threatened others and fled arrest (*United States v. Lopez*, 989 F.2d 24 (1st Cir. 1993), *cert. denied*, 510 U.S. 872, 114 S. Ct. 201, 126 L. Ed. 2d 158 [1993]); and when a police officer at the threshold of an apartment viewed a narcotics deal taking place inside (*United States v. Sewell*, 942 F.2d 1209 [7th Cir. 1991]).

Although hot pursuit expands the powers of the police to conduct warrantless searches, it does so under strict circumstances. Its purpose is grounded in practical necessity; it does not give law officers license to ignore constitutional safeguards. Courts make the final determination of whether a warrantless search is permissible, and they will reject misuses of the rule. One improper use of hot pursuit occurred in *O'Brien v. City of Grand Rapids*, 23 F.3d 990 (6th Cir. 1994). In this case, police officers pursued a suspect to his house, called for backup, surrounded the residence, and ultimately spent six hours in a standoff without seeking a search warrant. The court held that the suspect could not have fled the scene and that the officers had no fear of destruction of evidence or of a threat to safety. Thus, no exigent circumstances authorized their warrantless search.

FURTHER READINGS

Apol, John, and Magistrate Judge Paul J. Komives. 2002. "Criminal Procedure." *Michigan State–D.C.L College of Law Review* (summer).

Department of the Army. 1987. "Warrantless Searches and Seizures." Pamphlet 27-22.

Jenson, Travis N. 1998. "Cooling the Hot Pursuit: Toward a Categorical Approach." *Indiana Law Journal* 73 (fall).

Poulantzas, Nicholas M. 2002. *The Right of Hot Pursuit in International Law*. 2d ed. New York: Springer.

Search and Seizure Update. 2009. *New York: Practising Law Institute*. Available online at http://www.pli.edu (accessed July 30, 2009).

CROSS REFERENCE

Search and Seizure.

HOTCHPOT

The process of combining and assimilating property belonging to different individuals so that the property can be equally divided; the taking into consideration of funds or property that have already been given to children when dividing up the property of a decedent so that the respective shares of the children can be equalized.

HOUSE ARREST

Confinement to one's home or another specified location instead of incarceration in a jail or prison.

House arrest has been used since ancient times as an alternative to criminal imprisonment, often imposed upon people who either were too powerful or too influential to be placed in an actual prison. Hereditary rulers, religious leaders, and political figures, whose imprisonment might spur a revolt by loyalists, would be confined to their homes where they could live comfortably and safely but without any influence. House arrest does not always lessen influence, however. For example, Aung San Suu Kyi, a political leader from Myanmar, was placed under house arrest from 1989 to 1995, and again from 2000 to 2002, by the nation's military junta. On both occasions, the international community successfully exerted pressure on the government to release Suu Kyi, a peace activist and Nobel laureate.

The term *house arrest* can also refer to electronic monitoring programs in which a convicted criminal is sentenced to home confinement instead of prison, for a specified period. The criminal wears an electronic ankle bracelet (for which he usually bears maintenance costs) that monitors movement and sends a signal to a central computer if the house arrest is violated. Examples of crimes that could warrant house arrest include white-collar crimes such as FRAUD or embezzlement. This type of sentence can be a cost-effective way of punishing criminals who pose no threat to others and thus do not need to be imprisoned at the state's expense.

The justice system is more closely scrutinized when high-profile public figures are sentenced to house arrest. Boxer Riddick Bowe (ASSAULT AND BATTERY), television personality Martha Stewart (lying to investigators about a stock sale), and investment swindler Bernard Madoff (fraud) were all sentenced to house arrest for varying lengths of time for their offenses. Paris Hilton (driving under the influence) initially convinced a sheriff that she was entitled to house arrest due to a medical condition she suffered. A court later called the release a mistake and ordered her back to jail, after many members of the media and the public criticized the release as preferential treatment for a celebrity.

HOUSE OF REPRESENTATIVES

The lower chamber, or larger branch, of the U.S. Congress, or a similar body in the legislature of many of the states.

The U.S. House of Representatives forms one of the two branches of the U.S. Congress. The House comprises 435 members who are elected to two-year terms. The U.S. Constitution vests the House with the sole power of introducing bills for raising revenue, making it one of the most influential components of the U.S. government.

Members

According to Article I, Section 2, of the U.S. Constitution, a member of the House must be at least twenty-five years of age and a U.S. citizen for seven years before his or her election. In addition, representatives must reside in the state that they represent. Members of the House are generally called congressmen, congresswomen, or representatives.

During the First Congress (1789–91), the House had sixty-five members, each representing approximately 30,000 people. Until 1929 the law required the number of members in the House to increase in proportion to the national population. That year Congress passed the Permanent APPORTIONMENT Act (46 Stat. 21, 26, 27), which limited the size of the House to 435 representatives. During the 1990s each House member represented an average of 572,000 people.

Reapportionment or redistribution of House seats—a process whereby some states lose House representatives while others gain them—occurs after census figures have been collected. The Constitution requires that a census be conducted every ten years (art. 1, § 2). Each state must have at least one representative.

Puerto Rico elects a nonvoting resident commissioner to the House for a four-year term. Nonvoting delegates from American Samoa,

The First U.S. House of Representatives, 1789–1791: Setting Precedent for Future Lawmakers

In the early twenty-first century, the U.S. House of Representatives is known as an institution with established traditions and procedures. It has 435 members, standing committees, rules for evaluating legislation, and well-defined relations with the Senate, the president, and the executive agencies of the federal government. However, the structure and operations of the House have not always been well established. In 1789, as it began the task of creating laws for a new nation, the House had no precedent to guide it.

The House of Representatives first convened April 1, 1789, in New York City. Representatives slowly made the long journey to New York, and the First House eventually reached a total of 65 members. Fifty-five representatives belonged to the Federalist party, and ten allied themselves with the Anti-Federalist party.

The new House members were not without experience in legislative matters. Fifty-two had served in a state legislature, the Continental Congress, or the Constitutional Convention. Their legislative experience proved invaluable during this First Congress, because the Constitution gave them only limited guidance on how to establish the House. It was up to the representatives to work out the details of an effective lawmaking body.

On its first day in session, the House elected its officers, choosing Frederick A. C. Muhlenberg, of Pennsylvania, as its first Speaker. On succeeding days it established rules relating to debate, legislation, committees, and cooperation with the Senate. It also defined the duties of the Speaker, modeling that position after the Speaker of the English House of Commons. The Speaker was to preside over House sessions, preserve order, resolve disputed points, and appoint certain committees.

The lack of precedent made operations difficult for the First House. James Madison, of Virginia, a principal Framer of the Constitution and a leading member of the First House, complained, "In every step the difficulties arising from novelty are severely experienced.... Scarcely a day passes without some striking evidence of the delays and perplexities springing merely from the want of precedents."

Madison was confident that the House would resolve its problems, however, concluding, "Time will be a full remedy for this evil."

The House gradually found ways to improve the problems cited by Madison and others. One important solution was the development of committees. The first legislation passed by the House was created by the Committee of the Whole—that is, the entire House acting as one large committee. Representatives soon found that this was a cumbersome way to pass legislation. When meeting as the Committee of the Whole, they could consider only one piece of legislation at a time. Moreover, the chamber often became bogged down by seemingly endless debate as each member sought to join the argument.

The House responded to this predicament by creating temporary committees to research and draft legislation, forming a separate committee for each bill. This relieved the entire chamber of the necessity of debating every detail of each piece of legislation. The contemporary House, by contrast, has permanent, or standing, committees, each of which handles many bills. The sole standing committee to come out of the first House was the Committee on Elections.

With these and other changes, the First House of Representatives was able to accomplish many tasks of vital importance to the young nation. Together with the Senate, it passed 60 statutes, including laws that founded the Departments of War, Treasury, and Foreign Affairs. The House also established its power to give limited orders to executive agencies, such as when it requested Secretary of the Treasury Alexander Hamilton to report on issues such as the federal debt, plans to promote manufacturing, and the establishment of a national mint. No less important, under the leadership of James Madison, it drafted the first ten amendments to the Constitution, known as the Bill of Rights.

The House has changed greatly in more than two centuries, but the foundation built by the first representatives remains. Their innovations have become flexible traditions that allow the House to maintain order even as it evolves and adapts to new situations.

the District of Columbia, Guam, and the Virgin Islands are elected to a two-year term. These special representatives are allowed to participate in debates and vote in committees.

Committees

House committees are responsible for most of the work involved in the creation of new laws. After a bill is introduced in the House, it is referred to a committee. The committee studies the bill and may hold public hearings on it or suggest amendments. If the bill has the support of a majority of committee members, it is reported to the House, which then debates it and votes on it. The Committee on Rules determines how long a bill may be debated and the procedure by which it is amended.

The number of standing, or permanent, House committees has varied over time. In 1800 five standing committees existed. By 1910 the number of standing committees had increased to sixty-one. Between 1950 and the 1990s, the total stabilized at nineteen to twenty-two. During the 104th Congress (1995–97), there were nineteen standing committees in the House: Agriculture; Appropriations; Banking and Financial Services; Budget; Commerce; Economic and Educational Opportunities; Government Reform and Oversight; House Oversight; International Relations; Judiciary; National Security; Resources; Rules; Science; Small Business; Standards of Official Conduct; Transportation and Infrastructure; Veterans' Affairs; and Ways and Means.

Each committee has an average of eight to ten subcommittees. Committee membership is determined by a vote of the entire House, and committee chairs are elected by the majority party. The House may also create special committees, including investigative committees.

Officers

The Speaker of the House has the most powerful position in the House and is traditionally the leader of the majority party. The Speaker interprets and applies House rules and refers bills to committees. Party leadership positions in the House include the majority and minority leaders, or floor leaders, and the majority and minority whips.

The elected officers of the House include the clerk, the sergeant at arms, and the doorkeeper. The clerk oversees the major legislative duties of the House. He or she takes all votes and certifies the passage of bills, calls the House to order at the commencement of each Congress, administers legislative information and reference services, and supervises television coverage of House floor proceedings. The sergeant at arms, a member of the U.S. Capitol Police Board, is the chief law enforcement officer for the House. The sergeant maintains order in the House and arranges formal ceremonies such as presidential inaugurations and joint sessions of Congress. The doorkeeper monitors admission to the House and its galleries and organizes the distribution of House documents.

FURTHER READINGS

Office of the Clerk, U.S. House of Representatives Website. "House History." Available online at http://clerk.house. gov/art_history/house_history/index.html; website home page: http://clerk.house.gov (accessed July 30, 2009).

U.S. House of Representatives. 1994. Committee on House Administration. *History of the United States House of Representatives, 1789–1994.* 103d Cong. 2d sess. H.Doc. 103–324.

Zelizer, Julian E. 1006. *On Capitol Hill: The Struggle to Reform Congress and its Consequences.* New York: Cambridge Univ. Press.

CROSS REFERENCES

Apportionment; Congress of the United States; Constitution of the United States.

HOUSE UN-AMERICAN ACTIVITIES COMMITTEE (HUAC)

See COMMUNISM "House Un-American Activities Committee" (In Focus).

HOUSEBREAKING

The act of using physical force to gain access to, and entering, a house with an intent to commit a felony inside.

In most states, housebreaking that occurs at night constitutes the crime of BURGLARY. Some statutes expand the definition of housebreaking to include breaking out of a house after entry has been achieved without the use of physical force, such as when access was gained under FALSE PRETENSES.

HOUSEHOLD

Individuals who comprise a family unit and who live together under the same roof; individuals who dwell in the same place and comprise a family, sometimes encompassing domestic help; all those who are under the control of one domestic head.

For the purposes of insurance, the terms *family* and *household* are frequently used interchangeably.

CROSS REFERENCE

Head of Household.

HOUSING AND URBAN DEVELOPMENT DEPARTMENT

The DEPARTMENT OF HOUSING AND URBAN DEVELOPMENT (HUD) is the principal federal agency responsible for programs concerned with housing needs, fair housing opportunities, and improving and developing U.S. communities.

HUD was established in 1965 by the Department of Housing and Urban Development Act (42 U.S.C.A. § 3532–3537). Its major functions include insuring mortgages for single-family and multifamily dwellings and extending loans for home improvements and for the purchase of mobile homes; channeling funds from investors into the mortgage industry through the GOVERNMENT NATIONAL MORTGAGE ASSOCIATION; and making loans for the

construction or rehabilitation of housing projects for older and handicapped persons. HUD also provides federal housing subsidies for low- and moderate-income families, makes grants to states and local communities for development activities related to housing, and promotes and enforces laws, policies, and regulations supporting fair housing and equal housing opportunities.

HUD is administered under the supervision and direction of a cabinet-level secretary appointed by the president. The secretary of HUD formulates recommendations for housing and community development policy and works with the Executive Office of the President and other federal agencies to ensure that housing policies are consistent with other economic and fiscal policies of the government. In addition, the secretary encourages private enterprise to serve the housing and community development needs of the nation whenever possible and promotes the use of initiatives within the state, local, and private sectors to spur the growth of housing and community development resources. Equally important, the secretary ensures equal access to housing and promotes nondiscrimination. The secretary also oversees the FEDERAL NATIONAL MORTGAGE ASSOCIATION

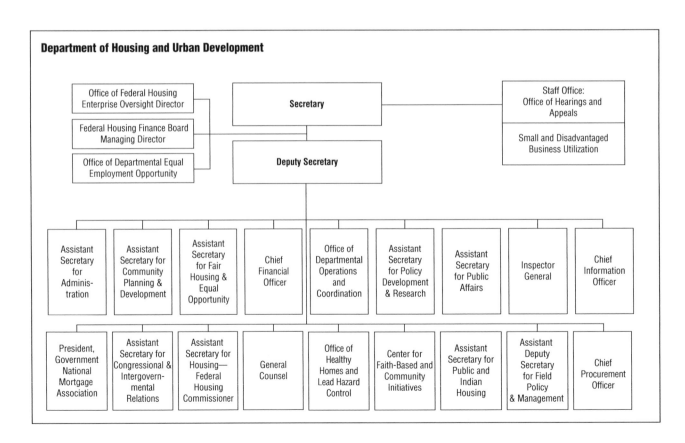

Department of Housing and Urban Development

(FNMA). FNMA, also known as Fannie Mae, was chartered by Congress in the late 1960s as a stockholder-owned, privately managed corporation to provide a secondary market for home mortgages. Fannie Mae purchases home mortgages and then issues SECURITIES funded by the monthly principal and interest payments of homeowners.

Several program areas within HUD carry out the department's goals and functions. The assistant secretary for housing, who also acts as the federal housing commissioner, underwrites property improvement loans and loans for manufactured homes and administers programs that help provide housing for special groups, including the elderly, the disabled, and the chronically mentally ill. The assistant secretary also administers housing programs to assist low-income families who are having difficulties affording housing and to protect consumers against fraudulent practices of land developers and promoters.

The assistant secretary for community planning and development implements a number of programs, including the Community Development Block Grant (CDBG) Program for local communities. The CDBG Program was established in 1974 to meet a wide variety of community development needs, including the need to expand economic opportunities for persons of low and moderate income by helping to provide them with decent and affordable housing. Block grants can be used to revitalize neighborhoods in blighted areas as well as to meet other community development needs.

The assistant secretary for community planning and development also implements Hope for Ownership of Single Family Homes, which helps low-income persons become homeowners by providing federal assistance to help finance the purchase and rehabilitation of single-family homes at affordable prices. A similar program administered by the Community Planning and Development area of HUD is Home Investment in Affordable Housing, which also provides federal assistance to localities and Indian tribes for housing rehabilitation, assistance to first-time home buyers and funding for the new construction of rental housing in areas where such housing is needed. Other programs provide assistance for procuring both transitional and permanent housing for homeless people and for relocating property owners displaced by federal projects under the Uniform Relocation Assistance and Real Property Acquisition Policies Act of 1970 (42 U.S.C.A. § 4601 et seq.).

The assistant secretary for community planning and development is also responsible for implementing the Neighborhood Development Demonstration Program, which was designed to determine the ability of neighborhood organizations to fund and implement neighborhood development activities. The program uses cooperative efforts and monetary support from individuals, businesses, and nonprofit organizations in conjunction with federal matching funds to encourage neighborhood organizations to become more self-sufficient in their development activities.

The assistant secretary for policy development and research evaluates and analyzes existing and proposed HUD programs and policies. The office of this secretary conducts field studies to determine the effectiveness of HUD programs through cost-benefit research and provides the secretary of HUD with economic, legal, and policy analyses of issues related to the department's oversight responsibilities.

The Office of Lead-Based Paint Abatement develops policy, conducts research, and drafts regulations to increase awareness of the dangers associated with lead-based paint poisoning and to develop safe and effective methods for the detection and abatement of lead-based paint poisoning. It also encourages state and local governments to develop programs for public education and hazard reduction surrounding such poisoning.

The assistant secretary for fair housing and equal opportunity administers fair housing laws and regulations prohibiting discrimination in public and private housing on the basis of race, color, RELIGION, sex, national origin, handicap, or familial status. This assistant secretary thus acts as the principal adviser to the secretary of HUD on all matters relating to CIVIL RIGHTS and equal opportunity in housing. The assistant secretary also administers equal employment opportunity laws and regulations that prohibit discrimination on the basis of race, color, religion, sex, national origin, handicap, or age.

The assistant secretary for public and Indian housing administers a number of programs to help meet the housing needs of Native Americans. These programs include the Comprehensive Improvement Assistance Grant

Program, which helps modernize and upgrade low-income housing projects; the Resident Initiatives Program, which supports resident participation in the management of properties, economic development, and other services, including programs to help ensure drug-free neighborhoods; and other programs that determine eligibility for public housing.

The Government National Mortgage Association (GNMA), another component of HUD, is a government corporation that guarantees mortgages issued by private lenders. In addition, through its mortgage-backed securities programs, Ginnie Mae, as it is known, works to promote and expand the housing market by increasing the supply of credit available for housing by channeling funds from the securities market into the mortgage market.

HUD headquarters are located in Washington, D.C., and ten HUD field offices are located throughout the United States. Each field office is headed by a secretary's representative, who is responsible for the management of the office and reports directly to the secretary. The representatives carry out the objectives of HUD as they relate to state and local governments and monitor the potential local effects of HUD policies and decisions.

In 1998 HUD opened the HUD Enforcement Center to take action against HUD-assisted multifamily property owners and other HUD fund recipients who violate laws and regulations. In the same year, Congress also approved Public Housing reforms to reduce segregation by race and income, encourage and reward work, bring more working families into public housing, and increase the availability of subsidized housing for very poor families. Subsequently, HUD increased its funding for low income family housing, as well as tax credits to developers of affordable single family homes.

FURTHER READINGS

"Articles about the Housing and Urban Development." *The New York Times* (September 4, 2009). Available online at http://topics.nytimes.com/topics/reference/timesto pics/organizations/h/housing_and_urban_development_ department/index.html; website home page: http:// topics.nytimes.com (accessed September 4, 2009).

Housing and Urban Development Department. "Homes & Communities." Available online at http://www.hud.gov (accessed July 30, 2009).

Office of the Federal Register (U.S.). 2009. *Code of Federal Regulations, Title 24, Housing and Urban Development,* Pt. 500–699, Revised as of April 1, 2009.

CROSS REFERENCES

Civil Rights; Federal National Mortgage Association; Government National Mortgage Association.

❖ HOUSTON, CHARLES HAMILTON

Charles Hamilton Houston was a law professor and CIVIL RIGHTS lawyer who argued many landmark cases on behalf of the National Association for the Advancement of Colored People (NAACP).

Houston was born September 3, 1895, in Washington, D.C. His father, William Houston, was trained as a lawyer and worked for a while as a records clerk to supplement the family's income; his mother, Mary Ethel Houston, worked as a hairdresser. Houston's father eventually began practicing law full-time and later became a law professor at Howard University, a predominantly black institution located in Washington, D.C. An only child, Houston received his primary and secondary education in segregated Washington, D.C., schools. After graduating from high school, he received a full scholarship to the University of Pittsburgh. At the urging of his parents, he instead entered Amherst College, where he was the only black student enrolled. An outstanding student, he was elected Phi Beta Kappa, and graduated magna cum laude in 1915.

After Amherst, Houston taught English composition and literature at Howard for two years. In 1917, shortly after the United States entered WORLD WAR I, Houston left teaching for military service. He enrolled in an officer candidate school for blacks, established at Des Moines. After four months of training, Houston became a first lieutenant in the infantry and was assigned to duty at Camp Meade, Maryland. He later entered field artillery school, despite the widely held belief that blacks could not serve effectively as field artillery officers.

Houston served in France until 1919, then returned to the United States to enroll at Harvard Law School. He was one of the few black students admitted at that time. His outstanding academic record earned him a place on the editorial board of the *Harvard Law Review,* making him the first black student to be so honored. In 1922 he received a bachelor of laws degree cum laude. He remained at Harvard for an additional year of graduate study, and earned a doctor of juridical science degree in 1923. He then won a fellowship to study for a year at the

University of Madrid, where he earned a doctor of CIVIL LAW degree.

In 1924, his studies completed, Houston was admitted to the bar of the District of Columbia and became his father's partner in the law firm of Houston and Houston. He quickly developed a successful practice, specializing in trusts and estates, probate, and landlord-tenant matters. He also taught law part-time at Howard University. In 1929 he left law practice to become an associate professor and vice dean of the School of Law at Howard. In 1932 he became dean, a post he held until 1935.

While at Howard, Houston worked to upgrade the law school's facilities, reputation, and academic standards and was instrumental in securing full accreditation for the school. He also found time to participate in important CIVIL RIGHTS CASES. He helped write the brief for *Nixon v. Condon*, 286 U. S. 73, 52 S. Ct. 484, 76 L. Ed. 984 (1932), in which the U.S. Supreme Court held that a "whites-only" primary election was unconstitutional. He also helped argue *Norris v. Alabama*, 294 U.S. 587, 55 S. Ct. 579, 79 L. Ed. 1074 (1935), where the Court overturned the convictions of nine black men charged with RAPE, because Alabama's systematic exclusion of blacks from juries violated the FOURTEENTH AMENDMENT of the Constitution.

In 1935 Houston left Washington, D.C., to become the first special counsel for the NAACP, headquartered in New York City. As special counsel, Houston initiated legal challenges in support of civil rights and argued landmark cases before the U.S. Supreme Court, including *Missouri ex rel. Gaines v. Canada*, 305 U.S. 337, 59 S. Ct. 232, 83 L. Ed. 208 (1938). In *Gaines*,

Charles Hamilton Houston.
FISK UNIVERSITY LIBRARY

the Supreme Court ruled that a state could not exclude a black applicant from a state-supported all-white law school. Houston also argued *Shelley v. Kraemer*, 334 U.S. 1, 68 S. Ct. 836, 92 L. Ed. 1161 (1948). In the *Shelley* decision, the Court held that a clause in a real estate contract prohibiting the sale of property to nonwhites could not be enforced by state courts. Houston was widely praised for the thorough and sometimes painstaking preparation of his legal briefs and his impassioned oral arguments before the Court.

WHETHER ELECTED OR APPOINTED, PUBLIC OFFICIALS SERVE THOSE WHO PUT AND KEEP THEM IN OFFICE. WE CANNOT DEPEND UPON THEM TO FIGHT OUR BATTLES.
—CHARLES HAMILTON HOUSTON

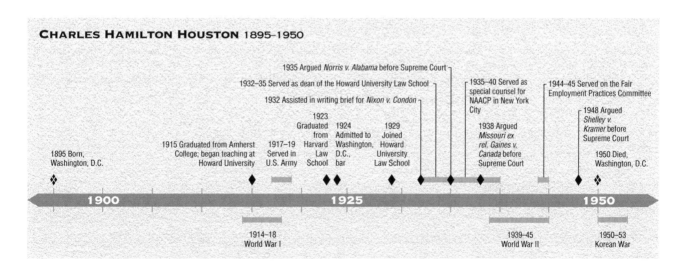

CHARLES HAMILTON HOUSTON 1895–1950

1935 Argued *Norris v. Alabama* before Supreme Court

1932–35 Served as dean of the Howard University Law School

1932 Assisted in writing brief for *Nixon v. Condon*

1935–40 Served as special counsel for NAACP in New York City

1944–45 Served on the Fair Employment Practices Committee

1923 Graduated from Harvard Law School

1924 Admitted to Washington, D.C., bar

1929 Joined Howard University Law School

1938 Argued *Missouri ex rel. Gaines v. Canada* before Supreme Court

1948 Argued *Shelley v. Kramer* before Supreme Court

1895 Born, Washington, D.C.

1915 Graduated from Amherst College; began teaching at Howard University

1917–19 Served in U.S. Army

1950 Died, Washington, D.C.

1900

1925

1950

1914–18 World War I

1939–45 World War II

1950–53 Korean War

In 1940 Houston left the NAACP to return to private practice in Washington, D.C., though he remained a member of the NAACP's national legal committee. He was succeeded as special counsel by THURGOOD MARSHALL, a colleague at the NAACP whom he had taught at Howard and who later became the first African American justice on the U.S. Supreme Court. Houston remained active in civil rights work, winning before the U.S. Supreme Court two cases that struck down racially discriminatory practices by the railroads: *Steele v. Louisville and Nashville Railroad Company*, 323 U.S. 192, 65 S. Ct. 226, 89 L. Ed. 173 (1944), and *Tunstall v. Brotherhood of Locomotive Firemen*, 323 U.S. 210, 65 S. Ct. 235, 89 L. Ed. 187 (1944).

In 1944 Houston was appointed by President FRANKLIN D. ROOSEVELT to the Fair Employment Practices Committee (FEPC). He resigned the following year after a dispute with President HARRY S. TRUMAN over alleged discriminatory hiring practices on the part of the Capital Transit Company, of Washington, D.C. Capital Transit Company was the transportation system in Washington, D.C. Houston alleged that it engaged in discriminatory policies by not hiring black workers or promoting current black workers to positions as bus operators or streetcar conductors. The FEPC wanted to issue a directive ending discrimination. Truman did not respond to Houston's efforts to have the directive issued, so Houston resigned from the FEPC. Truman finally did respond, maintaining that, because Capital Transit had earlier been seized under the War Labor Dispute Act because of a labor dispute, enforcement of the order ending discrimination should be postponed.

After battling heart disease for several years, Houston died in Washington, D.C., on April 22, 1950, at the age of 54.

FURTHER READINGS

Congressional Quarterly. 2004. *Guide to the U.S. Supreme Court*. 4th ed. Washington, D.C.: Congressional Quarterly.

Elliott, Stephen P., ed. 1986. *A Reference Guide to the United States Supreme Court*. New York: Facts on File.

Fairfax, Roger A., Jr. 1998. "Wielding the Double-Edged Sword: Charles Hamilton Houston and Judicial Activism in the Age of Legal Realism." *Harvard Blackletter Law Journal* 14 (spring).

Jones, Nathaniel R. 2001. "The Sisyphean Impact on Houstonian Jurisprudence." *Univ. of Cincinnati Law Review* 69 (winter).

McNeil, Genna Rae. 1983. *Groundwork: Charles Hamilton Houston and the Struggle for Civil Rights*. Philadelphia: Univ. of Pennsylvania Press.

Smith, J. Clay, Jr., and E. Desmond Hogan. 1998. "Remembered Hero, Forgotten Contribution: Charles Hamilton Houston, Legal Realism, and Labor Law." *Harvard Blackletter Law Journal* 14 (spring).

CROSS REFERENCE

Powell v. Alabama.

❖ HOWARD, BENJAMIN CHEW

Benjamin Chew Howard was a lawyer who served as the Supreme Court reporter of decisions from 1843 to 1861.

Howard, born November 5, 1791, in Baltimore, was the son of a distinguished Revolutionary War officer and the grandson of the president of the Pennsylvania Court of Errors and Appeals before the Revolution. Howard earned bachelor's and master's degrees from the College of New Jersey (later known as Princeton University). In 1812 he began the study of law, which was interrupted by military

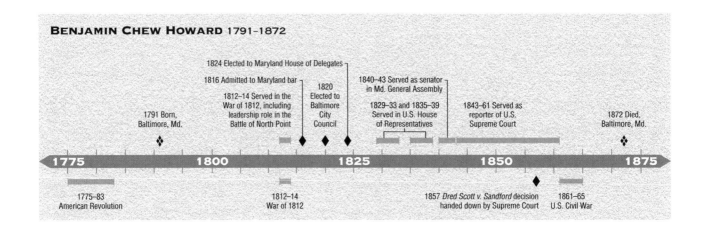

BENJAMIN CHEW HOWARD 1791–1872

1824 Elected to Maryland House of Delegates

1816 Admitted to Maryland bar

1812–14 Served in the War of 1812, including leadership role in the Battle of North Point

1820 Elected to Baltimore City Council

1840–43 Served as senator in Md. General Assembly

1829–33 and 1835–39 Served in U.S. House of Representatives

1843–61 Served as reporter of U.S. Supreme Court

1791 Born, Baltimore, Md.

1872 Died, Baltimore, Md.

◀ 1775   1800   1825   1850   1875 ▶

1775–83 American Revolution

1812–14 War of 1812

1857 *Dred Scott v. Sandford* decision handed down by Supreme Court

1861–65 U.S. Civil War

service during the WAR OF 1812. Howard was a captain in the war and played a prominent role in the defense of Baltimore during the Battle of North Point, fought in September 1814.

Following the war, Howard resumed his legal studies. He was admitted to the Maryland bar in 1816. Active in the Maryland DEMOCRATIC PARTY, in 1820, he was elected to the Baltimore City Council, and in 1824 he won a seat in the Maryland House of Delegates. In 1829 he was elected to the U.S. Congress, where he served four terms. During his time in Congress, he was chairman of the House Foreign Relations Committee for several years. In 1840 he left Congress to return to Maryland state politics, serving as a senator in the Maryland General Assembly. In January 1843 he resigned before the expiration of his term, to become reporter of the U.S. Supreme Court, a position created by Congress in 1816.

As reporter Howard was primarily responsible for editing, publishing, and distributing the Court's opinions. He replaced Richard Peters, who was fired after he disagreed with several of the justices about whether their opinions should be published in the reports. Howard, though highly praised for publishing thorough and well-edited reports, did create a controversy of his own when he refused to include the complete arguments raised by both sides in a fugitive slave case decided by the Court, thus calling his impartiality into question.

In Howard's day the reporter was paid a modest yearly salary and usually earned additional income selling copies of the bound volume in which an important case appeared or printing the opinion separately in a pamphlet for sale to the public. When the *Dred Scott* decision outlawing SLAVERY was issued by the U. S. Supreme Court in 1857, the U.S. Senate sought to publicize it as broadly as possible and printed 20,000 copies for free distribution to the public (DRED SCOTT V. SANDFORD, 60 U.S. [19 How.] 393, 15 L. Ed. 691 [1856]). Howard protested strongly that his income from the sale of the opinion would suffer from the competition. As a result the Senate voted to pay him $1,500 in compensation and agreed not to distribute its version until Howard's bound volume and pamphlet version were made available.

Howard, who edited 24 volumes of reports, remained active in politics while Supreme COURT

Benjamin C. Howard.
COLLECTION OF THE SUPREME COURT OF THE UNITED STATES

REPORTER. He resigned from the Court in 1861 to run as the Democratic candidate for governor of Maryland. Following his defeat, Howard retired from public life. He died March 6, 1872, in Baltimore.

H.R.

See HOUSE OF REPRESENTATIVES.

HUD

See HOUSING AND URBAN DEVELOPMENT, DEPARTMENT OF.

❖ HUGHES, CHARLES EVANS

The long public career of CHARLES EVANS HUGHES prepared him to be a powerful chief justice of the U.S. Supreme Court. Hughes was a legal and political dynamo. Beginning as a lawyer and law professor in New York in the 1880s, he became known nationally for his role in investigating power utilities and the insurance industry. He went on to a career in national and international affairs—first as a two-term governor of New York, second as a Republican nominee for president, and third as SECRETARY OF STATE. He was twice appointed to the U.S. Supreme Court, serving as an associate justice from 1910 to 1916 and as chief justice from 1930 to 1941. His intellectual vigor and strong hand guided the Court through the critical period of the NEW DEAL

Charles Evans Hughes.
PHOTOGRAPH BY HARRIS & EWING. COLLECTION OF THE SUPREME COURT OF THE UNITED STATES

era when it made significant changes in its views on the constitutional limits on government power.

Hughes was born April 11, 1862, in Glen Falls, New York. Educated at Columbia University Law School, he spent his twenties and thirties in private practice and teaching law at Columbia and Cornell Universities. His expertise was in COMMERCIAL LAW and by the time he was in his forties he had built a considerable reputation in that area. The New York state legislature chose him in 1905 to lead public investigations of the gas and electrical utilities

in New York City and to probe the state's insurance industry. His work not only resulted in groundbreaking regulatory plans, later highly influential across the United States, but also catapulted Hughes into a political career. He immediately ran for governor of New York and twice won election to that office as a politician known for independence of mind and commitment to administrative reform. In 1910 his second term as governor had not yet expired when he stepped down and accepted President William Howard Taft's appointment to the Supreme Court.

This move characterized the lifelong tension between Hughes's attractions to the legal and political spheres. He left public office to join the Court; later he would leave the Court to run for office again, then return to the Court as chief justice. In his nearly seven years on the Court as an associate justice, he displayed a flexibility of thought that led him to side at times with liberals and at times with the conservative majority. His most significant opinions turned on the issue of federal power. In particular, these opinions weighed the extent to which the COMMERCE CLAUSE of the Constitution gave the federal government authority to regulate the national economy. The opinions were delivered in the *Minnesota* and *Shreveport Rate* cases, in which the Court's decisions laid the groundwork for the expansion of federal regulation in the years to come (*Simpson v. Shepard,* 230 U.S. 352, 33 S. Ct. 729, 57 L. Ed. 1511 [1913]; *Houston, East & West Texas Railway Co. v. United States,* 234 U.S. 342, 34 S. Ct. 833, 58 L. Ed. 1341 [1914]).

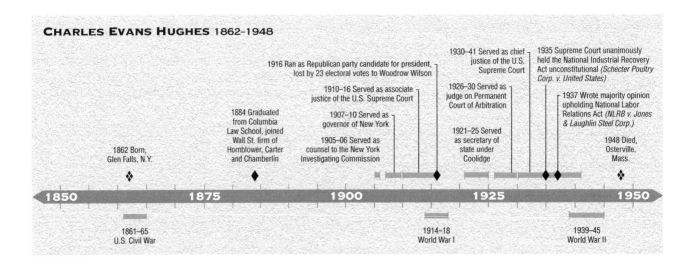

CHARLES EVANS HUGHES 1862–1948

1930–41 Served as chief justice of the U.S. Supreme Court

1935 Supreme Court unanimously held the National Industrial Recovery Act unconstitutional *(Schecter Poultry Corp. v. United States)*

1916 Ran as Republican party candidate for president, lost by 23 electoral votes to Woodrow Wilson

1926–30 Served as judge on Permanent Court of Arbitration

1937 Wrote majority opinion upholding National Labor Relations Act *(NLRB v. Jones & Laughlin Steel Corp.)*

1910–16 Served as associate justice of the U.S. Supreme Court

1884 Graduated from Columbia Law School, joined Wall St. firm of Hornblower, Carter and Chamberlin

1907–10 Served as governor of New York

1921–25 Served as secretary of state under Coolidge

1948 Died, Osterville, Mass.

1862 Born, Glen Falls, N.Y.

1905–06 Served as counsel to the New York Investigating Commission

1850　　**1875**　　**1900**　　**1925**　　**1950**

1861–65 U.S. Civil War

1914–18 World War I

1939–45 World War II

The middle years of Hughes's career saw tumultuous change. In 1916 he stepped down from the Court to return to politics. Although he had not actively sought the Republican Party's nomination for president, the party drafted him, and he reluctantly agreed to run against WOODROW WILSON. Despite a hard-fought campaign, Hughes lost the close election and returned to private practice. His respite from public service was brief. In 1921 President WARREN G. HARDING appointed Hughes secretary of state, a difficult position because of the challenges facing the United States in the aftermath of WORLD WAR I: the war debt, reparations, the newly established Soviet Union, and especially relations with East Asia. Naval disarmament ranked high among Hughes's concerns. In 1921 and 1922 he organized the Washington Conference, which for nearly a decade curbed naval growth and brought stability to the western Pacific.

The final chapter in Hughes's career returned him to the Supreme Court. Hughes served as secretary of state to Harding's successor, CALVIN COOLIDGE, then resigned in 1925 to work in private practice. Between that and his next stint on the Court, he published a book-length work entitled The SUPREME COURT OF THE UNITED STATES: Its Foundation, Methods, and Achievements: An Interpretation (1928, reprinted 2000). In 1930 President HERBERT HOOVER nominated him for chief justice. Bitter opponents voiced criticism of Hughes's political career and his resignation but failed to block his appointment in a confirmation vote of 52–26. At age 68, Hughes became the oldest man ever to be chosen chief justice.

The Hughes Court sat during a controversial period in U.S. LEGAL HISTORY. The Depression years had brought misery and a radical federal response. President Franklin D. Roosevelt's economic recovery plans, known collectively as the New Deal, met opposition in Congress and from the justices of the Court. Several pieces of New Deal legislation faced constitutional tests and failed. After unanimously holding unconstitutional the National Industrial Recovery Act (48 Stat. 195 [1933]) in Schechter Poultry Corp. v. United States, 295 U.S. 495, 55 S. Ct. 837, 79 L. Ed. 1570 (1935), the Court provoked a battle with the frustrated president. Roosevelt proposed an increase to the number of seats on the Court, hoping to then pack the Court with justices favorable to his views.

Hughes wrote to the SENATE JUDICIARY COMMITTEE in a move to help thwart Roosevelt's plan.

By taking a largely dim view of both federal and state regulatory power, the Hughes Court differed little from its conservative predecessors. In 1937 this changed dramatically. In upholding the National Labor Relations Act, 29 U.S.C.A. § 151 et seq., Hughes wrote a landmark opinion that greatly strengthened the labor movement (NLRB V. JONES & LAUGHLIN STEEL CORP., 301 U.S. 1, 57 S. Ct. 615, 81 L. Ed. 893 [1937]). Also that year the Court upheld a state MINIMUM WAGE law, in West Coast Hotel v. Parrish, 300 U.S. 379, 57 S. Ct. 578, 81 L. Ed. 703. The Parrish decision was a striking departure from rulings of previous decades. Only 15 years earlier, for example, the Court had refused to force employers of adult women to pay a minimum wage, viewing such a requirement as an unconstitutional infringement of the liberty of contract. The 1937 decisions together have been called a constitutional revolution because they marked a great change in jurisprudence that liberalized the Court's view of government power.

When Hughes retired at last in 1941, at age 80, he had made a powerful impression on the law and on the Court. During his tenure as chief justice, he had shown the same flexibility of mind that marked his period as an associate justice: Siding alternately with liberal and conservative colleagues, he often cast the swing vote. He had clearly run the Court with a strong hand, not only in leading the discussion but frequently in persuading justices to vote with him. Justice FELIX FRANKFURTER, who served under Hughes, likened him to the conductor of an orchestra: "He took his seat at the center of the Court with a mastery, I suspect, unparalleled in the history of the Court."

Hughes died August 27, 1948, in Osterville, Massachusetts. Succeeding generations have compared his bold leadership to that of Chief Justice EARL WARREN, who headed the Court two decades later.

FURTHER READINGS

Hall, Timothy L. 2001. Supreme Court Justices: A Biographical Dictionary. New York: Facts on File.

Perkins, Dexter. 1978. Charles Evans Hughes and American Democratic Statesmanship. Westport, CT: Greenwood.

Schwartz, Bernard. 1995. "Supreme Court Superstars: The Ten Greatest Justices." Tulsa Law Journal 31 (fall).

CROSS REFERENCES

Labor Law; Labor Union; Supreme Court of the United States.

> WHEN WE LOSE THE RIGHT TO BE DIFFERENT, WE LOSE THE PRIVILEGE TO BE FREE.
> —CHARLES EVANS HUGHES

HUMAN RIGHTS

Basic rights that fundamentally and inherently belong to each individual.

HUMAN RIGHTS are freedoms established by custom or international agreement that impose standards of conduct on all nations. Human rights are distinct from civil liberties, which are freedoms established by the law of a particular state and applied by that state in its own jurisdiction.

Specific human rights include the right to personal liberty and DUE PROCESS OF LAW; to freedom of thought, expression, RELIGION, organization, and movement; to freedom from discrimination on the basis of race, religion, age, language, and sex; to basic education; to employment; and to property. Human rights laws have been defined by international conventions, by treaties, and by organizations, particularly the UNITED NATIONS. These laws prohibit practices such as torture, SLAVERY, summary execution without trial, and arbitrary detention or exile.

History

Modern human rights law developed out of customs and theories that established the rights of the individual in relation to the state. These rights were expressed in legal terms in documents such as the English BILL OF RIGHTS of 1688, the U.S. DECLARATION OF INDEPENDENCE of 1776, the U.S. Bill of Rights added to the U.S. Constitution in 1789, and the French Declaration of the Rights of Man and the Citizen added to the French Constitution in 1791.

Human rights law also grew out of earlier systems of INTERNATIONAL LAW. These systems, developed largely during the eighteenth and nineteenth centuries, were predicated on the doctrine of national sovereignty, according to which each nation retains sole power over its internal affairs without interference from other nations. As a result, early international law involved only relations between nation-states and was not concerned with the ways in which states treated their own citizens.

During the late nineteenth and early twentieth centuries, the notion of national sovereignty came under increasing challenge, and reformers began to press for international humanitarian standards. In special conferences such as the Hague Conference of 1899 and 1907, nations created laws governing the conduct of wars and handling of prisoners.

Not until after WORLD WAR II (1939–45) did the international community create international treaties establishing human rights standards. The United Nations, created in 1945, took the lead in this effort. In its charter, or founding document, the United Nations developed objectives for worldwide human rights standards. It called for equal rights and self-determination for all peoples, as well as "universal respect for, and observance of, human rights and fundamental freedoms for all without distinction as to race, sex, language, or religion" (art. 55). The Universal Declaration of Human Rights, adopted by the U.N. General Assembly in 1948, also became an important human rights document.

To develop the U.N. Charter into an international code of human rights law, the international community created a number of multilateral human rights treaties. The two most significant of these are the International Covenant on Civil and Political Rights and the International Covenant on Economic, Social, and Cultural Rights, both put into effect in 1976. These treaties forbid discrimination on the basis of race, color, sex, language, religion, political or other opinion, national or social origin, property, birth, or other status. The two covenants, along with the U.N. Charter, the Universal Declaration of Human Rights, and an accord called the Optional Protocol to the Covenant on Civil and Political Rights (1976), constitute a body of law that has been called the International Bill of Human Rights.

The Covenant on Civil and Political Rights includes protections for the right to life, except after conviction for serious crime (art. 6); freedom from torture and other cruel and inhumane punishment (art. 7); freedom from slavery and prohibition from slave trade (art. 8); freedom from arbitrary arrest or detention (art. 9); humane treatment of prisoners (art. 10); freedom of movement and choice of residence (art. 12); legal standards, including equality before the law, fair hearings before an impartial tribunal, PRESUMPTION OF INNOCENCE, a prompt and fair trial, the RIGHT TO COUNSEL, and the right to review by a higher court; freedom of thought, conscience, and religion (art. 18); and freedom of association, including association in trade unions (art. 22).

The Covenant on Economic, Social, and Cultural Rights protects additional rights, many of which have yet to be realized in poorer countries. These include the right to work (art. 6); to just wages and safe working conditions (art. 7); to SOCIAL SECURITY and social insurance (art. 9); to a decent standard of living and freedom from hunger (art. 11); to universal basic education (art. 13); and to an enjoyment of the cultural life and scientific progress of the country.

The international community has also adopted many other human rights treaties. These include the Convention on the Prevention and Punishment of the Crime of GENOCIDE (1948); the Convention on the Political Rights of Women (1953); the Convention to Suppress the Slave Trade and Slavery (revised 1953); the Convention against Torture and Other Cruel, Inhuman, or Degrading Treatment (1987); the Convention on the Rights of the Child (1990); and the Convention on Protection of the Rights of Migrant Workers (2003).

In addition to worldwide human rights agreements, countries have also established regional conventions. These include the European Convention for the Protection of Human Rights and Fundamental Freedoms, the American Convention on Human Rights, and the African Charter on Human and Peoples' Rights.

The United States and Human Rights

Although the United States was an active participant in the formation and implementation of international human rights organizations and treaties following World War II, and although it ratified selected treaties such as the Convention to Suppress the Slave Trade and Slavery in 1967 and the Convention on the Political Rights of Women in 1976, it did not ratify any of the major rights treaties until 1988, when it approved the Convention on the Prevention and Punishment of the Crime of Genocide. Four years later it ratified the International Covenant on Civil and Political Rights.

The U.S. Senate, which has authority to ratify all treaties, has been slow to review and approve human rights provisions, for a number of reasons. Senators have expressed concern about the effect of international treaties on U.S. domestic law. Article VI of the U.S. Constitution provides, "This Constitution, and the Laws of the United States which shall be made in Pursuance thereof; and all Treaties made, or which shall be made, under the Authority of the United States, shall be the supreme Law of the Land." Treaties therefore stand as federal law, though they are not considered to be law if they conflict with the Constitution (*Reid v. Covert,* 354 U.S. 1, 77 S. Ct. 1222, 1 L. Ed. 2d 1148 [1957]).

Conservative senators blocked early ratification of human rights treaties largely out of concern that the treaties would invalidate racial SEGREGATION laws that existed in the United States until the 1960s. Many human rights advocates claimed that these laws violated existing international treaties. Some senators argued that human rights should fall under domestic authority only and should not be subject to international negotiations. Others contended that ratification of human rights treaties would federalize areas of law better left to the states.

Since the late 1960s such objections in the Senate have been overcome by attaching to treaties modifying terms called reservations, understandings, and declarations (RUDs). RUDs modify the treaties so that their effect on U.S. law will be acceptable to the two-thirds majority required for treaty ratification in the Senate. A reservation, for example, may state that the United States will not accept any element of a treaty found to be in conflict with the U.S. Constitution or existing laws, or that ratification will not federalize areas of law currently controlled by the states.

The U.S. Congress has also enacted its own human rights legislation. Under the leadership of Representative Donald M. Fraser (D-Minn.) during the 1970s, the House Committee on Foreign Affairs added language to the Foreign Assistance Act of 1973 (22 U.S.C.A. § 2151 et seq.) that required the president to cancel military and economic assistance to any government that "engages in a consistent pattern of gross violations of internationally recognized human rights," including torture and arbitrary detention without charges (§§ 2151n, 2304). This new legislation authorized the STATE DEPARTMENT to collect and analyze data on human rights violations. Congress has also passed laws that require cutting off or limiting aid to countries with significant human rights violations.

In 1977 Congress gave human rights greater priority within the executive branch by creating a new State Department office, the Bureau on

TORTURE

No government wants to admit that it has committed torture. Apart from international agreements that ban torture, such as the United Nation's Convention Against Torture, the cruelty inherent in the act of torture can delegitimize the officials who authorize it. Therefore, officials will do what they can to distinguish their interrogations from acts of torture. The Convention Against Torture defines it as "any act by which severe pain or suffering, whether physical or mental, is intentionally inflicted on a person for such purposes as [obtaining information or a confession, intimidation or coercion, or discrimination]." Defining what constitutes "severe pain or suffering" is what drove the torture debate over the U.S. interrogations of suspected terrorists during the administration of President GEORGE W. BUSH.

A 50-page, 2002 memo from the Justice Department's Office of Legal Counsel (OLC) about permissible interrogation tactics brought the Bush administration strong criticism after its release in 2004. The memo, written after the CIA requested legal advice following the SEPTEMBER 11, 2001, TERRORIST ATTACKS, addressed legally defensible methods of interrogation for al Qaeda terrorist suspects. Surprisingly, the memo said that the torture of suspected al Qaeda terrorist "may be justified" and that international laws against torture "may be unconstitutional if applied to interrogation" when used against suspected terrorists. The memo concluded that "certain acts may be cruel, inhuman, or degrading, but still not produce pain and suffering of the requisite intensity" to be classified as torture.

The memo examined various aspects of the Convention Against Torture, as found in title 18, Sections 2340 P 2340A of the United States Code. The memo came in response to questions that arose during the interrogation in early 2002 of al Qaeda operations chief Abu Zubaida. The CIA was frustrated over its lack of progress with the interrogation and wanted to know how far it could legally go without violating the law. Neither the military nor the STATE DEPARTMENT was consulted for assistance in preparation or review of the memo.

The memo stated that physical torture "must be equivalent in intensity to the pain accompanying serious physical injury, such as organ failure, impairment of bodily function, or even death." In other words, torture means "pain that is difficult to endure." According to the memo, in order for psychological methods of interrogation to rise to the level of torture, they must result in "significant psychological harm of a significant duration," meaning the harm must last "months or even years." According to the memo, "a DEFENDANT must specifically intend to cause prolonged mental harm" for the act(s) to be considered torture; "specific intent only to commit the predicate acts that give rise to prolonged mental harm" would not constitute torture. Moreover, if an interrogator "has a GOOD FAITH belief that his actions will not result in prolonged mental harm," he will have valid defense against conviction for unlawful torture. Certain mind-altering drugs, which do not profoundly disrupt the senses or personality, would also be permitted in interrogation.

Another section of the memo examined whether the Convention Against Torture "may be unconstitutional if applied to interrogations of enemy combatants pursuant to the President's Commander-in-Chief powers." The memo concluded that interrogators who engaged in torture could be protected from criminal prosecution.

After the memo was made public, administration officials maintained that the president consistently insisted that all methods of interrogation conform to U.S. and international laws and treaties. HUMAN RIGHTS observers blamed the document for leading to abuses against prisoners at the Abu Ghraib prison in Iraq, in Afghanistan, and at Guantanamo Bay, Cuba, where suspected terrorists were detained.

A December 2004 memo from the OLC superseded, in its entirety, the August 2002 memo. According to the new memo, "torture is abhorrent both to American laws and values and to international norms." The new 17-page memo backed away from any claims in the August 2002 memo that the president might be legally justified in departing from U.S. law on torture in times of war and that there might exist some legally defensible ways around criminal charges for those who employ torture. According to the new memo, the August 2002 memo was wrong when it stated that only "excruciating and agonizing pain" constituted torture. Moreover, the earlier memo was wrong when it said that criminal prosecution would be limited to cases where severe pain was imposed for its own sake, rather than to obtain information.

Human Rights and Humanitarian Affairs, headed by an assistant SECRETARY OF STATE (Pub. L. No. 95-105, 91 Stat. 846). In 1994, the administration of President BILL CLINTON renamed the office the Bureau for Democracy, Human Rights, and Labor. The bureau is charged with administering programs and policies to promote democratic institutions

The new memo stated that U.S. interrogators did not have a defense to allegations of torture by claiming that they were guided by national security reasons. Moreover, the memo prohibited telling a detainee that he could avoid torture only by cooperating. The memo also rejected the prior claim that torture is limited to physical suffering that involves severe physical pain or even death, but says it must be more than "mild and transitory" suffering. Mental suffering need not last months or years, as the original document claimed, and need not be permanent, but "must continue for a prolonged period of time."

The use of torture or what the Bush administration labeled "enhanced interrogation," led to the dropping of charges against one detainee. In May 2008 the top official responsible for overseeing military trials of suspected terrorists held at the U. S. detention prison at Guantanamo Bay, Cuba, dismissed the pending case against Mohammed al-Qahtani because he had been subjected to torture. According to Susan J. Crawford, convening authority of military commissions, interrogation techniques used against Qahtani were authorized at the time (2002), but "his treatment met the legal definition of torture," causing her to order war-crime charges against him dropped.

A military report indicated that Qahtani was threatened with a military working dog, forced to wear a woman's bra, had a thong placed on his head during interrogation, and was told that his mother and sister were "whores." At one point, a leash had been tied to his chains as he was led around a room, forced to perform dog tricks. Additionally, interrogation techniques included sustained isolation, sleep deprivation, and prolonged exposure to cold temperatures. However, it was the fact that Qahtani was hospitalized twice following interrogations that led Crawford to her

conclusion. His diagnosis was bradycardia, a condition in which the heart rates slows to dangerously low levels, leading to heart failure and death. Bradycardia can be directly linked to cold body temperature and fatigue. In October 2006 Qahtani recanted a confession he said he had made after enduring such interrogation methods.

Revelations that some terrorist suspects were water boarded many times also drew criticism. Water boarding is a technique involving the simulation of drowning. It involves binding a person to an inclined board, covering his or her head with cloth or cellophane, and pouring water repeatedly over the face and head. In some cases water actually enters the nose and mouth, but mostly, the sensation of water hitting the face (cloth or cellophane) causes a psychological reaction during which the brain processes information of drowning, which causes a gag reflex similar to choking.

John Yoo, a lawyer with OLC, prepared a memo in 2003 for military interrogators that was similar to its 2002 memo for civilian interrogators. The memo approved of the use of water boarding, as well as head-slapping, sleep deprivation, and exposure to extreme temperatures. However, the OLC officially rejected the "flawed reasoning" in the memo. Nevertheless, the Bush administration contended that the CIA's water boarding against three top al Qaida detainees, Khalid Sheikh Mohammed, Abu Zubaydah, and Abd al-Rahim al-Nashiri was legal. The practice was ended in 2006.

Congress passed the Detainee Treatment Act in 2005, requiring the DEPARTMENT OF DEFENSE to restrict interrogation methods to those set out in the Army Field Manual, which banned coercive interrogations. In 2007 President Bush issued an executive order narrowing the

list of approved techniques for the CIA. Although that list of authorized techniques remained classified, intelligence officials stated that water boarding was not on the list of approved techniques but that President Bush could authorize it during an emergency.

In December 2007 the CIA admitted that it had destroyed video tapes of the interrogations of some key Iraqi detainees. In 2008 the House Judiciary Committee conducted hearings into the meaning and parameters of torture, particularly as applied to detainees held outside the United States. When John Yoo was called to testify, he declared EXECUTIVE PRIVILEGE. David Addington, former chief of staff to Vice President Dick Cheney, could not "recollect" matters of substance or interest. Former CIA director George Tenet testified that the value of water boarding and other "enhanced" methods of interrogation "far exceeded" any other method(s). Former attorney general JOHN ASHCROFT also testified that water boarding was not torture and that it had been approved by JUSTICE DEPARTMENT officials before being employed. All administration officials denied that any illegal "torture" was involved in military interrogations.

When the administration of Barack Obama took office in 2009, it released internal papers showing the extent of interrogative techniques used during the Bush years. President Obama called this a "dark period" in U.S. history and vowed to end it and "move on." To accomplish this objective, Attorney General Eric Holder announced that interrogators would not be prosecuted for their actions. It also became clear the administration had no interest in further investigations.

FURTHER READINGS

Levinson, Sanford, ed. 2006. *Torture: A Collection.* New York: Oxford Univ. Press.

and respect for human rights and workers' rights around the world. It also presents to Congress an annual report on the status of human rights all over the globe.

Nongovernment Organizations

AMNESTY INTERNATIONAL, the CENTER FOR CONSTITUTIONAL RIGHTS, HUMAN RIGHTS WATCH, the International Commission of Jurists, and other international human rights organizations closely monitor states' compliance with human rights standards. These groups also publicize rights violations and coordinate world public opinion against offending states. In many cases they induce governments to modify their policies to meet rights standards.

Domestic human rights organizations such as the Vicaria de Solidaridad, in Chile, and the Free Legal Assistance Group of the Philippines also play a significant role as human rights watchdogs, often at great personal risk to their members.

FURTHER READINGS

Amnesty International Website. Available online at http://www.amnesty.org (accessed July 31, 2009).

Curry, Lynne. 2004. *The Human Body on Trial: A Sourcebook with Cases, Laws, and Documents (on Trial)*. Indianapolis: Hackett.

Golove, David. 2002. "Human Rights Treaties and the U.S. Constitution." *DePaul Law Review* 52 (winter).

Kennedy, David. 2002. "The International Human Rights Movement: Part of the Problem?" *Harvard Human Rights Journal* 15 (spring). Available online at http://www.law.harvard.edu/students/orgs/hrj/iss15/kennedy.shtml; website home page: http://www.law.harvard.edu (accessed July 31, 2009).

State Department. "Bureau of Democracy, Human Rights, and Labor." Available online at http://www.state.gov/g/dr; website home page: http://www.state.gov/ (accessed July 31, 2009).

CROSS REFERENCES

Civil Rights; Genocide; Nuremberg Trials; Tokyo Trial.

HUMAN RIGHTS WATCH

HUMAN RIGHTS WATCH (HRW) investigates HUMAN RIGHTS abuses throughout the world, publishing its findings in books and reports every year. These activities often generate significant coverage in local and international media. This publicity in turn prompts governments to change their policies and practices. In cases of extreme human rights abuses, HRW advocates for the withdrawal of military and economic support from governments that violate the rights of their people.

In international conflicts and other crises, HRW provides current information about conflicts—focusing on the human rights situation on the ground—while the conflicts or crises are underway. The purpose of HRW is to increase the price of human rights abuse, thereby helping to decrease the incidents of such abuses.

HRW is the largest human rights organization based in the United States. HRW employs lawyers, journalists, academics, and country experts of many nationalities and diverse backgrounds, and often leverages the force of allied human rights organizations by joining forces with them to achieve shared human rights goals. As of February 2002, Human Rights Watch employed 189 permanent staff plus short-term fellows and consultants.

Human Rights Watch is an independent, nongovernmental organization. It gains most of its support from contributions from private individuals and foundations worldwide. It accepts no government funds, directly or indirectly, from the United States or any other government. HRW is not an agency of the U.S. government, nor was it founded by the U.S. government. Although HRW frequently calls on the United States to support human rights in U.S. foreign policy, the organization also reports on human rights abuses inside the United States. HRW has made negative reports against the United States in areas such as prison conditions, police abuse, the detention of immigrants, and the imposition of the death penalty.

HRW maintains its headquarters in New York. It also maintains offices in Brussels, Bujumbura, Freetown (Sierra Leone), Kigali, Geneva, London, Los Angeles, Moscow, San Francisco, Santiago de Chile, Tashkent, Tbilisi, and Washington.

Most HRW research is carried out by sending fact-finding teams into countries where there have been allegations of serious human rights abuses. HRW examines the human rights practices of governments of all political stripes, of all geopolitical alignments, and of all ethnic and religious persuasions. HRW documents and denounces murders, disappearances, torture, arbitrary imprisonment, discrimination, and other abuses of internationally recognized human rights.

Not only does HRW encompass the entire globe for its activities, but HRW is interested in enormously complex and diverse issues. For example, HRW follows developments worldwide in women's rights, children's rights, and the flow of arms to abusive forces. Other HRW projects include ACADEMIC FREEDOM, the human rights responsibilities of corporations, international justice, prisons, drugs, and refugees. The unique and independent nature of this international organization enables it to target any and all parties to conflict.

HRW pursues active investigations of human rights abuses in more than 70 countries. Its methods for obtaining human rights information has made it a credible source of information for individuals and governments concerned with human rights. To conduct research, Human Rights Watch sends members of its staff to interview people who have firsthand experience with alleged abuse. Researchers work with local activists and other specialists. Their findings are written up in reports.

HRW reports categorize and describe human rights violations, detail probable causes for the abuses, and make recommendations for ways to end the abuses. HRW has published more than a thousand reports dealing with human rights issues in more than one hundred countries worldwide. HRW has used its investigations to examine human rights violations associated in the following cases: Taliban massacres in Afghanistan; trafficking of Thai women in Asia; RAPE in U.S. prisons; refugees in Sierra Leone; and conflicts in Indonesia, Macedonia, Colombia, Russia, and the Congo.

Since its formation, HRW has focused mainly on upholding civil and political rights. HRW began in 1978 with the founding of its European division, Helsinki Watch (now Human Rights Watch/Helsinki). This was in response to a call for support from groups in Moscow, Warsaw, and Prague, which had been established to monitor compliance in Soviet Bloc countries with the human rights provisions of the landmark Helsinki accords. A few years later, the Reagan administration contended that human rights abuses by certain right-wing governments were more tolerable than those of left-wing governments. Thus, to counter charges of maintaining a double standard between the East and West, HRW formed Americas Watch (now Human Rights Watch/Americas).

By 1987 HRW had developed a powerful set of techniques for pursuing its agenda: painstaking documentation of abuses and aggressive advocacy in the press and with governments, and it employed these techniques all over the world. Over time, the organization grew to cover other regions of the world. Eventually, all the "Watch" committees were united in 1988 to form Human Rights Watch.

Between 1993 and 2003 HRW increasingly addressed economic, social, and cultural rights as well. It is particularly attuned to situations in which its methods of investigation and reporting are most effective. These include cases in which arbitrary or discriminatory governmental conduct lies behind an economic, social and cultural rights violation. In addition to governments, its work also addresses significant economic players and such international financial institutions as the WORLD BANK and multinational corporations such as General Electric.

In the early 2000s, HRW comprises seven major divisions: Africa, the Americas, Arms, Asia, Children, Women, the Middle East and North Africa, and Europe and Central Asia.

FURTHER READINGS

Human Rights Watch. Available online at http://www.hrw.org/ (accessed July 31, 2009).

Human Rights Watch World Report. *2001: Events of 2000 (November 1999–October 2000).* New York: Human Rights Watch. Available online at http://www.hrw.org/legacy/wr2k1/; website home page: http://www.hrw.org (accessed July 31, 2009).

Iriye, Akira. 2004. *Global Community: The Role of International Organizations in the Making of the Contemporary World.* Berkeley: Univ. of California Press.

Pease, Kelly-Kate S. 2009. *International Organizations: Perspectives on Governance in the Twenty-First Century.* Upper Saddle River, NJ: Prentice Hall.

Welch, Claude E., Jr., ed. 2000. *NGOs and Human Rights: Promise and Performance.* Philadelphia: Univ. of Pennsylvania.

CROSS REFERENCE

Human Rights.

❖ HUME, DAVID

David Hume was an eighteenth-century Scottish philosopher, historian, and social theorist who influenced the development of skepticism and empiricism, two schools of philosophical thought. Hume's economic and political ideas influenced Adam Smith, the Scottish economist and theorist of modern capitalism, and JAMES MADISON, the American statesman who helped shape the republican form of government through his work on the U.S. Constitution.

Hume was born August 25, 1711, in Chirnside, near Edinburgh, Scotland. He entered Edinburgh University when he was twelve. He left the university after several years of study and attempted to study law. He did not like the subject, and instead read widely in philosophy. In 1729 he suffered a nervous breakdown. After

THE HEART OF MAN IS MADE TO RECONCILE CONTRADICTIONS.
—DAVID HUME

a prolonged recovery, he moved to France in 1734, where he wrote his first work, *A Treatise on Human Nature*. The book was not published until 1739 and was largely ignored. His next work, *Essays, Moral and Political* (1741), attracted favorable notice. Throughout the 1740s Hume's religious skepticism doomed his chances for a professorship at Edinburgh University. He spent the decade as a tutor and then as secretary to a Scottish general. During this period he wrote several more works of philosophy, including *An Enquiry Concerning the Principles of Morals* (1751).

In 1752 he was made librarian of the Faculty of Advocates Library at Edinburgh. From 1754 to 1762, he published his monumental *History of England,* which for many years was considered the basic text of English history. This work brought him international fame. He later served as secretary to the British counsel in Paris. He died August 25, 1776, in Edinburgh.

As a philosopher, Hume espoused a skeptical viewpoint, distrusting speculation. He believed that all knowledge comes from experience and that the mind contains nothing but a collection of perceptions, that all events are viewed and interpreted through the sensations of the mind. He attacked the principle of causality, which states that nothing can happen or exist without a cause. Hume was willing to admit that one event, or set of sense impressions, always precedes another, but he argued that this did not prove that the first event causes the second. A person can conclude that causality exists, but that conclusion is based on belief, not proof. Therefore, a person cannot expect the future to be similar to the past, because there is no rational basis for that expectation.

Like his philosophical beliefs, Hume's essays on politics and economics were influential in his time. Historians have concluded that James Madison read Hume's *Essays, Moral and Political* and applied some of the ideas from this work while helping write the Constitution and *The Federalist Papers.* Hume was concerned about the formation of factions based on RELIGION, politics, and other common interests. He concluded that a democratic society needs to prevent factions, which ultimately undermine the government and lead to violence. Madison agreed that factions can divide government but came to the opposite conclusion: the more factions the better. In Madison's view more factions made it less likely that any one party or coalition of parties would be able to gain control of government and invade the rights of other citizens. The system of checks and balances contained in the Constitution was part of Madison's plan for placing some limits on factions.

FURTHER READINGS

Allan, James. 1999. "To Exclude or Not to Exclude Improperly Obtained Evidence: Is a Humean Approach More Helpful?" *Univ. of Tasmania Law Review* 18 (October).

Arkin, Marc M. 1995. "'The Intractable Principle': David Hume, James Madison, Religion, and the Tenth Federalist." *American Journal of Legal History* 39.

Mossner, Ernest Campbell. 2001. *The Life of David Hume.* New York: Oxford Univ. Press.

Schmidt, Claudia M. 2004. *David Hume: Reason in History.* State College, PA: Pennsylvania State Univ. Press.

Vermeule, Adrian. 2003. "Hume's Second-Best Constitutionalism." *Univ. of Chicago Law Review* 70, no. 4 (winter).

CROSS REFERENCES

Hobbes, Thomas; Jurisprudence; Locke, John.

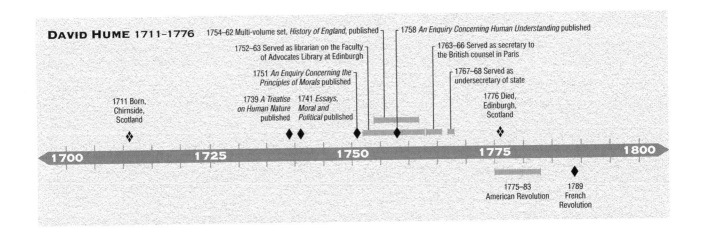

DAVID HUME 1711–1776

1754–62 Multi-volume set, *History of England,* published

1758 *An Enquiry Concerning Human Understanding* published

1752–63 Served as librarian on the Faculty of Advocates Library at Edinburgh

1763–66 Served as secretary to the British counsel in Paris

1751 *An Enquiry Concerning the Principles of Morals* published

1767–68 Served as undersecretary of state

1711 Born, Chirnside, Scotland

1739 *A Treatise on Human Nature* published

1741 *Essays, Moral and Political* published

1776 Died, Edinburgh, Scotland

1700   1725   1750   1775   1800

1775–83 American Revolution

1789 French Revolution

❖ HUMPHREY, HUBERT HORATIO

Hubert Horatio Humphrey served as a U.S. senator from Minnesota and as the thirty-eighth vice president of the United States. From his election to the U.S. Senate in 1948 to his death in 1978, Humphrey was the quintessential COLD WAR liberal. His unsuccessful presidential campaign in 1968 was weakened by his support of President Lyndon B. Johnson's VIETNAM WAR policies.

Humphrey was born in Wallace, South Dakota, on May 27, 1911. He grew up in Doland, South Dakota, where his father ran the local drugstore. He received a degree from the Denver College of Pharmacy in 1933 and helped run the family drugstore before entering the University of Minnesota. After graduating from the University of Minnesota in 1939, he earned a master's degree from Louisiana State University. He taught at the University of Minnesota, Louisiana State University, and Macalester College, in St. Paul, Minnesota, before joining the federal Works Progress Administration in Minnesota in 1941.

Humphrey became a leader in Minnesota DEMOCRATIC PARTY politics during WORLD WAR II. After narrowly losing the Minneapolis mayoral election in 1943, he cemented his position in 1944 when he united the Minnesota Democratic and Farmer-Labor parties into the Democratic Farmer-Labor (DFL) party. The Farmer-Labor party had advocated more radical political policies in the 1930s and 1940s, and had gained national attention through Governor Floyd B. Olson, of Minnesota. In the 1930s Olson and the Farmer-Labor party had advocated more aggressive governmental intervention to deal with the Great Depression. Olson criticized

Hubert H. Humphrey.
LIBRARY OF CONGRESS

President FRANKLIN D. ROOSEVELT for not doing enough to help the nation's unemployed. By the mid-1940s the party had attracted many Communist-influenced members. In 1947 Humphrey and his allies forced the more radical Farmer-Labor members out of leadership positions and ultimately out of the DFL. On a national level, Humphrey helped form Americans for Democratic Action, a liberal organization that trumpeted its anti-Communist credentials.

His political leadership paid quick dividends. In 1945 he was elected mayor of Minneapolis by more than 30,000 votes. He increased his margin of victory to 50,000 in his 1947 reelection campaign. As mayor he rooted out political graft and corruption and began to

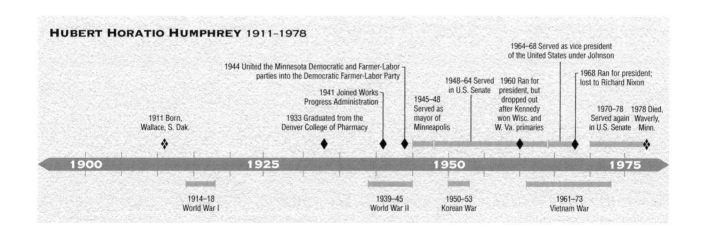

HUBERT HORATIO HUMPHREY 1911–1978

1964–68 Served as vice president of the United States under Johnson

1944 United the Minnesota Democratic and Farmer-Labor parties into the Democratic Farmer-Labor Party

1948–64 Served in U.S. Senate

1960 Ran for president, but dropped out after Kennedy won Wisc. and W. Va. primaries

1968 Ran for president; lost to Richard Nixon

1941 Joined Works Progress Administration

1945–48 Served as mayor of Minneapolis

1911 Born, Wallace, S. Dak.

1933 Graduated from the Denver College of Pharmacy

1970–78 Served again in U.S. Senate

1978 Died, Waverly, Minn.

1900　1925　1950　1975

1914–18 World War I

1939–45 World War II

1950–53 Korean War

1961–73 Vietnam War

implement pieces of his liberal agenda. He secured the passage of the first municipal fair employment act in the United States and gained additional funds for public housing and welfare.

Humphrey galvanized liberal Democrats in 1948 at the Democratic National Convention. Southern Democrats on the platform committee had rejected President Harry S. Truman's CIVIL RIGHTS proposals. Humphrey, a delegate to the convention and a candidate for the U.S. Senate, led a fight from the convention floor to restore the civil rights plank. His passionate oratory helped bring back the proposals and fixed in the public mind the image of Humphrey as a fiery liberal, an image he would evoke the rest of his public career.

He was elected to the Senate in 1948, and found that his aggressive style clashed with the gentleman's-club atmosphere of that institution. A quick learner, he sought the mentorship of LYNDON JOHNSON, soon to be Senate majority leader. Humphrey was reelected to the Senate in 1954 and 1960. In 1960, along with Senator JOHN F. KENNEDY and Johnson, he sought the Democratic presidential nomination. Following victories by Kennedy in the Wisconsin and West Virginia primaries, Humphrey dropped out of the race and stood for reelection to the Senate.

During the Kennedy administration, Humphrey displayed his command of parliamentary procedure and political persuasion. He became assistant majority leader and helped pass the LIMITED TEST BAN TREATY of 1963. Following Kennedy's ASSASSINATION in November 1963, Humphrey worked closely with President Johnson to pass the many pieces of social welfare legislation that Johnson dubbed his GREAT SOCIETY program. Humphrey's plan for providing federal medical insurance to older people, called Medicare, was enacted. Most important, Humphrey played a critical role in securing the passage of the Civil Rights Act of 1964 (42 U.S.C.A. § 2000a et seq.).

In 1964 Johnson selected Humphrey as his vice presidential running mate. Johnson's landslide victory over conservative Republican BARRY M. GOLDWATER promised more liberal legislation. Humphrey worked to enhance civil rights for minorities and increase economic opportunities. But the political climate turned sour with rising protests over Johnson's escalation of U.S. involvement in Vietnam.

Humphrey, who initially doubted the wisdom of U.S. military intervention, became an energetic and unrepentant advocate of Johnson's policies.

Humphrey had always dreamed of becoming president. When President Johnson announced in March 1968 that he would not seek reelection, Humphrey entered the race against Senator EUGENE MCCARTHY, of Minnesota, and Senator ROBERT F. KENNEDY, of New York. McCarthy, a longtime friend and ally of Humphrey's, opposed the Vietnam War, as did Kennedy. Humphrey continued to support it. By May Humphrey had secured enough delegates to win the nomination. In June Kennedy was assassinated.

The Democratic National Convention, in Chicago, was a debacle. Confrontations between antiwar demonstrators and Chicago police officers led to a series of violent outbursts by the police. Though Humphrey won the nomination, he remained staunchly loyal to Johnson and refused to make a clean break on Vietnam policy, which would have won votes from disaffected Democrats. In November Republican RICHARD M. NIXON won the election with 301 electoral votes to Humphrey's 191. Humphrey lost the popular vote by less than one percent.

Following his defeat Humphrey returned to Minnesota and taught again at Macalester College. In 1970 he was reelected to the Senate. In 1972 he campaigned unsuccessfully for the Democratic presidential nomination. Reelected to the Senate again in 1976, Humphrey soon was engaged in a personal battle with cancer. He died at his home in Waverly, Minnesota, on January 13, 1978.

FURTHER READINGS

Halberstam, David. 1993. *The Best and the Brightest.* New York: Ballantine.

Humphrey, Hubert H. 1991. *The Education of a Public Man: My Life and Politics.* Minneapolis: Univ. of Minnesota Press.

Mann, Robert. 1997. *The Walls of Jericho: Lyndon Johnson, Hubert Humphrey, Richard Russell, and the Struggle for Civil Rights.* Boston: Mariner.

O'Neill, William L. 2005. *Coming Apart: An Informal History of America in the 1960s.* Chicago: Dee.

HUNDRED

A political subdivision in old England.

Under the Saxons, each shire or county in England was divided into a number of

THERE ARE NOT ENOUGH JAILS, NOT ENOUGH POLICEMEN, NOT ENOUGH COURTS TO ENFORCE A LAW NOT SUPPORTED BY THE PEOPLE.
—HUBERT H. HUMPHREY

hundreds, which were made up of ten tithings each. The tithings were groups of ten families of freeholders. The hundred was governed by a high constable and had its own local court called the Hundred Court. The most remarkable feature of the hundred was the collective responsibility of all the inhabitants for the crimes or defaults of any individual member.

HUNG JURY

A trial jury duly selected to make a decision in a criminal case regarding a defendant's guilt or innocence, but who are unable to reach a verdict due to a complete division in opinion.

When a jury has been given an adequate opportunity to deliberate and is unable to reach a VERDICT, a retrial takes place at the discretion of the prosecution. The subsequent trial does not constitute a violation of the constitutional prohibition of DOUBLE JEOPARDY.

❖ HUNT, WARD

The legal career of WARD HUNT peaked when he was appointed to the U.S. Supreme Court by President ULYSSES S. GRANT in 1873. Hunt held a seat on the High Court for nine years, until January 1882. Although he was well liked and respected as a diligent lawyer and jurist, Ward's tenure on the Court was unspectacular and marked by a forced retirement.

Hunt was born June 14, 1810, in Utica, New York, to Montgomery Hunt and Elizabeth Stringham Hunt. He studied at the Oxford Academy, in England and the Geneva Academy, in Switzerland. In 1828 he graduated with honors from Union College, in Schenectady,

Ward Hunt.
PHOTOGRAPH BY MATHEW BRADY. COLLECTION OF THE SUPREME COURT OF THE UNITED STATES.

New York. He attended law school in Litchfield, Connecticut. He returned to Utica to work in a local law office, and was admitted to the bar in 1831.

Hunt married Mary Ann Savage in 1837, and they raised three children until her death in 1845. Eight years later he married Maria Taylor. With his partner, Hiram Denio, Hunt ran a successful law practice in Utica for 31 years. While practicing law Hunt became active in politics. He supported the policies of ANDREW JACKSON, who defended the interests of the middle class and served two terms as

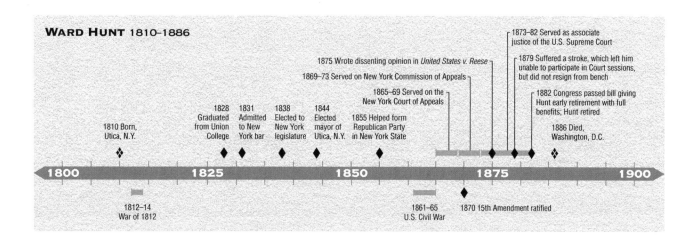

WARD HUNT 1810–1886

1873–82 Served as associate justice of the U.S. Supreme Court

1875 Wrote dissenting opinion in *United States v. Reese*

1879 Suffered a stroke, which left him unable to participate in Court sessions, but did not resign from bench

1869–73 Served on New York Commission of Appeals

1865–69 Served on the New York Court of Appeals

1882 Congress passed bill giving Hunt early retirement with full benefits; Hunt retired

1810 Born, Utica, N.Y.

1828 Graduated from Union College

1831 Admitted to New York bar

1838 Elected to New York legislature

1844 Elected mayor of Utica, N.Y.

1855 Helped form Republican Party in New York State

1886 Died, Washington, D.C.

1800   1825   1850   1875   1900

1812–14 War of 1812

1861–65 U.S. Civil War

1870 15th Amendment ratified

president. In 1838 Hunt was elected to the New York legislature, where he served one term, and in 1844 he was elected mayor of Utica.

In the 1840s Hunt came to differ with the DEMOCRATIC PARTY when he opposed the expansion of SLAVERY and the annexation of Texas. In 1848 Hunt supported the Free-Soil presidential candidacy of ex-Democrat and ex-president MARTIN VAN BUREN, who was defeated. Hunt ran for a spot on the New York Supreme Court in 1853, but he lost the election, a result that observers attributed to his defection from the Democratic party. In 1855 Hunt helped to form the REPUBLICAN PARTY in the state of New York. As a Republican he was elected to the New York Court of Appeals in 1865.

After three years on the New York Court of Appeals, Hunt was promoted to chief justice. A year later, in 1869, the New York court system was reorganized by an amendment to the state constitution, and Hunt was named commissioner of appeals. He held that position for three years, until January 1873, when he replaced fellow New Yorker SAMUEL NELSON as an associate justice on the U.S. Supreme Court.

Hunt had strong ties to the Republican party, and he had risen in the judicial ranks along with the party. At that time the Republican party promoted expansive federal powers. These powers were critical to the abolition of slavery and the defeat of the Confederate forces in the Civil War. However, by the mid-1870s, the nation's appreciation of federal power had waned, and the judiciary began to emphasize the rights of the states. Perhaps as a result of this shift, Hunt, with his Republican views, authored few major opinions.

Hunt delivered his most memorable opinion in *United States v. Reese*, 92 U.S. (2 Otto) 214, 23 L. Ed. 563 (1875). In *Reese* the High Court struck down parts of the Enforcement Act of 1870, a federal act passed to ensure that African Americans would be allowed to vote. The act had been passed by Congress pursuant to the FIFTEENTH AMENDMENT, which provides, "The right of citizens of the United States to vote shall not be denied or abridged by the United States or by any State on account of race, color, or previous condition of servitude." *Reese* was brought by the U.S. government against two inspectors at a municipal election in Kentucky, alleging that they had refused to

receive and count the vote of William Garner, an African American.

According to the majority in *Reese*, the Fifteenth Amendment did not confer on all adult citizens the right to vote. Rather, it merely prevented the state and federal governments from denying the right to vote based on race, color, or previous condition of servitude. Therefore, it was not within the power of the federal government to require that states give the vote to all adult citizens. Because parts of the Enforcement Act did not limit the application of criminal penalties to wrongful refusals based on race, the Court ruled that those parts unconstitutionally infringed on the powers of the states.

Hunt was the only dissenting justice. He argued that the Fifteenth Amendment was intended to confer on all persons the same political rights given to white persons. The guarantee of the right to vote, according to Hunt, was one of those rights. He declared that the persons affected in the case "were citizens of the United States" and that the subject of the case "was the right of these persons to vote, not at specified elections or for specified officers, not for federal officers or for state officers, but the right to vote in its broadest terms." Hunt mournfully concluded that the majority's holding brought "to an impotent conclusion the vigorous amendments on the subject of slavery."

Hunt's defense of African American rights appeared to be short-lived. In another case dealing with the Enforcement Act and decided the same month as *Reese*, he sided with the majority in refusing to enforce the rights of African Americans. In *United States v. Cruikshank*, 92 U.S. (2 Otto) 542, 23 L. Ed. 588 (1875), approximately 100 defendants were alleged to have assaulted two African American men in an attempt to keep the men from voting in a Louisiana state election. This ASSAULT violated provisions of the Enforcement Act that made it a federal offense for persons to band together to prevent a person from exercising any right guaranteed by the Constitution or federal law.

The defendants were charged with violations of the Enforcement Act and convicted at trial, but their convictions were overturned by a U.S. circuit court. On appeal by the United States, the Supreme Court held that legislation

THE CITIZEN OF THIS COUNTRY WHERE NEARLY EVERYTHING IS SUBMITTED TO THE POPULAR TEST AND WHERE OFFICE IS EAGERLY SOUGHT, WHO POSSESSES THE RIGHT TO VOTE, HOLDS A POWERFUL INSTRUMENT FOR HIS OWN ADVANTAGE.
—WARD HUNT

concerning the right to free assembly under the FIRST AMENDMENT was a matter reserved to the states, not to the federal government, and that Congress did not have the right to pass legislation on the matter. In response to the federal government's argument that in this case the mob had intended to prevent the two men from voting on account of their race, the Court declared, "[W]e may suspect that race was the cause of the hostility; but it is not so averred." Hunt could have dissented based on the same reasoning he used in his dissent in *Reese,* but he did not.

Hunt's failure to dissent in the *Cruikshank* case can be explained, in part, by his devotion to precedent. Hunt firmly believed that cases should be decided in accordance with the reasoning employed in previous cases. Because the Court in *Reese* had already struck down portions of the Enforcement Act, further attempts to prosecute under the act would meet a similar fate.

Hunt fell ill with gout in 1877 and missed many Court sessions. In January 1879 he suffered a paralytic stroke that left him temporarily speechless and permanently disabled on one side of his body. Hunt became too sick to function as a justice, but he refused to resign because he had not served long enough to qualify for a pension. In addition, Hunt's sponsor, Senator ROSCOE CONKLING, of New York, was quarreling with President RUTHERFORD B. HAYES, and Hunt did not want to let Hayes appoint Hunt's successor to the Court. Finally, three years after his stroke, Congress passed a special retirement bill that gave Hunt a pension if he agreed to resign within 30 days. Hunt resigned in January 1882, on the day the bill became law. He died March 24, 1886, in Washington, D.C.

FURTHER READINGS

Friedman, Leon, and Fred L. Israel, eds. 1995. *The Justices of the United States Supreme Court: Their Lives and Major Opinions,* Volumes I–V. New York: Chelsea House.

"Horace Gray." 1992. *The Supreme Court of the United States: Its Beginnings and Its Justices, 1790–1991.* Washington, D.C.: Commission of the Bicentennial of the U.S. Constitution, Library of Congress.

Lurie, Jonathan. 2004. *The Chase Court: Justices, Rulings, and Legacy.* Denver, CO: ABC-CLIO.

❖ HUNTER, ELMO BOLTON

Elmo Bolton Hunter, a federal judge, was a leader in national efforts to take party politics out of the state courts through the adoption of judicial merit selection programs. (Under most merit selection systems, a nonpartisan commission of lawyers and nonlawyers evaluates candidates for judicial vacancies and sends recommendations to, usually, a governor, who makes appointments.) In 1990 the American Judicature Society (AJS) funded the first national clearinghouse for information on merit selection; located at AJS headquarters in Chicago, it is known as the ELMO B. HUNTER Center for Judicial Selection. The AJS also gives the Elmo B. Hunter Award annually to a person who has made significant improvement in the judicial selection process.

Hunter was born in St. Louis on October 23, 1915. He attended the University of Missouri, at Columbia, receiving a bachelor of arts degree in 1936 and a bachelor of laws degree in 1938. Elected to Phi Beta Kappa as an undergraduate,

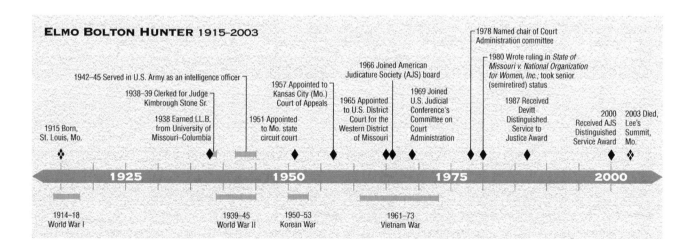

ELMO BOLTON HUNTER 1915–2003

1942–45 Served in U.S. Army as an intelligence officer
1938–39 Clerked for Judge Kimbrough Stone Sr.
1938 Earned LL.B. from University of Missouri–Columbia
1915 Born, St. Louis, Mo.
1957 Appointed to Kansas City (Mo.) Court of Appeals
1951 Appointed to Mo. state circuit court
1965 Appointed to U.S. District Court for the Western District of Missouri
1966 Joined American Judicature Society (AJS) board
1969 Joined U.S. Judicial Conference's Committee on Court Administration
1978 Named chair of Court Administration committee
1980 Wrote ruling in *State of Missouri v. National Organization for Women, Inc.;* took senior (semiretired) status
1987 Received Devitt Distinguished Service to Justice Award
2000 Received AJS Distinguished Service Award
2003 Died, Lee's Summit, Mo.

1925   1950   1975   2000

1914–18 World War I
1939–45 World War II
1950–53 Korean War
1961–73 Vietnam War

he continued his academic excellence in law school. Hunter graduated first in his class and was elected to the ORDER OF THE COIF. He was also a member of the LAW REVIEW and author of numerous articles.

In his final year of law school, Hunter was chosen by the Board of Curators of the University of Missouri to receive the Judge Shepard Barclay Award for "the greatest contribution in moral leadership to the school." Also in 1938, Hunter was selected by the board to represent the University of Missouri—and the state of Missouri—in the Rhodes Scholarship selection competition.

Hunter was admitted to the Missouri bar in 1938 and to the federal bar in 1939. He served as a law clerk to Judge Kimbrough Stone Sr. from 1938 to 1939. Following his ADMISSION TO THE BAR and clerkship, he accepted a position as senior assistant city counselor for Kansas City, Missouri. He left the position in 1940 to pursue graduate work in law, under a Cook Fellowship, at the University of Michigan.

In 1941 Hunter took a job as special assistant to the U.S. district attorney for the Western District of Missouri and Kansas, where he prosecuted war FRAUD cases. After a year he joined the U.S. Army, and he served in military intelligence at the rank of first lieutenant from 1942 to 1945.

After WORLD WAR II he joined the firm of Sebree, Shook, Hardy, and Hunter, and began the PRACTICE OF LAW. He also married Shirley Arnold during these years and fathered his only child, Nancy A. Hunter.

Hunter gave up the practice of law when he was appointed to the state circuit court by Governor Forrest Smith on December 12, 1951. Along with his new judicial duties, Hunter began a ten-year stint as a law instructor at the University of Missouri in 1952. For his work he received the university's Outstanding Alumni Service Award in 1955.

In 1957 he was appointed to the Kansas City Court of Appeals. Following his appointment, Hunter served, by special order, as special judge to the Missouri Supreme Court, and he often sat with the Springfield Court of Appeals and the St. Louis Court of Appeals—and therefore served on every appellate court in the state of Missouri. He also saw every type and variation of political influence brought to bear

on the judges and courts in Missouri. During his years of service in the Missouri courts, he developed an interest in both the judicial selection process and the improved administration of justice.

In August 1965 President LYNDON B. JOHNSON appointed Hunter U.S. district judge for the Western District of Missouri. It was as a federal judge that Hunter began his distinguished commitment to the AJS. He served on the board of the AJS in 1966 and was elected vice president in 1967. He went on to serve as president, and he is the only person in the history of the AJS to have served as both president and chairman of the board, which he did simultaneously in 1969 and 1970. As an AJS leader, Hunter spearheaded the organization's national efforts to promote merit selection systems for judges. He traveled across the United States to promote the concept and practice of merit selection, and he participated in hundreds of citizen conferences to discuss the issue. In conjunction with his efforts to promote merit selection, he was largely responsible for *Who Shall Judge* (1974), the film narrated by E. G. Marshall. In recognition of the role he played in citizen education on this important issue, Hunter received the AJS Herbert Harley Award in 1975.

As a federal judge, Hunter made his presence felt within the U.S. Judicial Conference, which establishes the standards and shapes the policies governing the federal judiciary. Hunter became a member of the Judicial Conference's Committee on Court Administration in 1969 and was named committee chairman in 1978. His appointment as chairman followed his term as chairman of the Subcommittee on Judicial Improvements from 1976 to 1978. Former chief justice WARREN E. BURGER said Hunter was "a credit to all judges who recognize that the delivery of our product is at least as important as the quality of it."

Hunter took senior (or semi-retired) status in 1980, shortly after handing down his noteworthy ruling that the NATIONAL ORGANIZATION FOR WOMEN was within its rights in promoting an economic boycott of Missouri because the state had not approved the proposed EQUAL RIGHTS AMENDMENT (*State of Missouri v. National Organization for Women, Inc.*, 620 F.2d 1301 [8th Cir. 1980]). As a senior judge, Hunter heard the case of a Los Angeles drug dealer

IT IS APPARENT THAT THERE MUST BE A DRAMATIC CHANGE IN PROCEDURE RELATING TO THE PREPARATION OF CASES FOR TRIAL IN ORDER TO EFFECT A SAVING IN COURT TIME, JURY EXPENSE, LAST-MINUTE SETTLEMENT, EXPENSES OF EXPERT WITNESSES, AND MANY OTHER FACTORS.
—ELMO BOLTON HUNTER

caught with PCP at the Kansas City Airport. He sentenced the DEFENDANT to life in prison without parole, marking the first time a federal judge applied the mandatory penalty under the U.S. three-strikes drug law (21 U.S.C.A. § 841 [2000]). Though many said the law violated constitutional protection against CRUEL AND UNUSUAL PUNISHMENT, Hunter disagreed. "I thought about the constitutional aspects," said Hunter. "I am satisfied that the statute is lawful."

In 1987 Hunter received the Devitt Distinguished Service to Justice Award. This award—named for Edward J. Devitt, former chief U.S. district judge for Minnesota—acknowledges the dedication and contributions to justice made by all federal judges, by recognizing the specific achievements of one judge who has contributed significantly to the profession. Hunter was acknowledged for his devotion to public education and to the administration of justice. Devitt said, "[Hunter] has been the mainstay in the judiciary's self-improvement efforts for more than 20 years."

In 1991 the AJS established the Elmo B. Hunter Citizens Center for Judicial Selection. The center conducts and distributes empirical research on a wide range of issues related to judicial selection. In 2000 the AJS honored Hunter with its Distinguished Service Award, given for significant contributions to the AJS and the nation in promoting the effective administration of justice.

Hunter died on December 27, 2003, in Lee's Summit, Missouri. He continued to serve as a judge until the time of his death.

FURTHER READINGS

"AJS Honors Two Who Serve the Judiciary." *The Third Branch.* Available online at http://www.uscourts.gov/ttb/april00ttb/ajshonor.html; website home page: http://www.uscourts.gov (accessed July 31, 2009).

American Judicature Society. "About the Elmo B. Hunter Citizens Center for Judicial Selection." Available online at http://www.ajs.org/selection/sel_about.asp; website home page: http://www.ajs.org (accessed December 29, 2009).

Morris, Mark. 2003. "Judge Elmo Hunter Dies at the Age of 88." *Kansas City Star.* December 29.

CROSS REFERENCE

Judicial Conference of the United States.

HUNTING

The regulation of hunting is a matter reserved to the states as part of their POLICE POWER under

A young hunter with a brace of pheasants. Many states have minimum age requirements for hunting licenses and require completion of a firearm safety course for young applicants.

CORBIS.

the TENTH AMENDMENT to the U.S. Constitution (*Totemoff v. Alaska,* 905 P.2d 954 [Alaska 1995]). Congress maintains statutes that regulate hunting on federal land. States may further regulate the federal lands located within their boundaries so long as their laws do not conflict with federal laws.

South Dakota and Georgia illustrate the sort of hunting laws typically maintained by a state. In South Dakota hunting is regulated by Title 41 of the South Dakota Codified Laws Annotated, Section 41-1-1 et seq. Under Title 41 hunters must obtain from the game, fish, and parks commission a license for the privilege of hunting in South Dakota. Other states maintain similar commissions or boards to implement licensing procedures and policies.

Licensing parameters vary from state to state. Most states have minimum age requirements. In South Dakota, for example, no person under the age of 12 may obtain a license, but an 11-year-old may obtain a license to hunt between September 1 and December 31 if he or she will turn 12 in that period. A child under the age of 16 may obtain a basic game and fish license without cost, but only if he or she has completed a firearms safety course. A parent of the child must apply for the license, and the child may hunt only with a parent, guardian, or responsible adult (§ 41-6-13).

In Georgia any person over the age of 12 may hunt on his or her own land. If a person between the ages of 12 and 15 seeks to hunt, he or she must complete a hunter education course, and then may hunt only with a parent or guardian. This is true even for children between the ages of 12 and 15 who are hunting on the land of their parents or guardians. A person between the ages of 16 and 25 must also complete a hunter education course before obtaining a hunting license.

States may make licensing exceptions for certain persons. In Georgia, for example, persons over the age of 65 may receive a hunting license without paying a fee. Furthermore, persons who are permanently and totally disabled may obtain a hunting or fishing license for free (Ga. Code Ann. § 27-2-4 [1996]).

In some states an additional license must be obtained to hunt certain animals whose populations are of concern to the state. In South Dakota these animals are small game, big game, fur-bearing animals, and migratory waterfowl. An additional license is required for these animals so that the commission can keep track of the number of persons hunting them and conserve their populations.

To control animal populations, state licensing commissions also allow the hunting of certain animals only at certain times of the year. These time periods are called open seasons, and they are set each year by the state regulatory commission. Open seasons limitations sometimes come with special exceptions. In South Dakota, for example, residents do not need a license to hunt game birds on their own land during an open season.

Most states place separate restrictions on resident versus nonresident licensing and hunting for certain animals. In South Dakota, for example, nonresidents may hunt only if they have obtained a special nonresident license. A nonresident may hunt small and big game, waterfowl, and wild turkey. A nonresident must obtain a nonresident predator license to hunt predators, but if the nonresident has a nonresident small-game, big-game, waterfowl, or wild turkey license, the nonresident may hunt predators in the animal group authorized by that license without a separate nonresident predator license (S.D. Codified Laws Ann.

§ 41-6-30). Predators include jackrabbits, prairie dogs, gophers, ground squirrels, coyotes, red foxes, gray foxes, skunks, crows, and porcupines.

States may place additional restrictions on the hunting of certain animals. In Georgia, for example, feral hogs may be hunted only in certain situations. For instance, a hunter may not shoot a feral hog during deer season unless the hunter and all persons accompanying the hunter are each wearing a total of at least 500 square inches of daylight florescent orange material as an outer garment above the waistline. In South Dakota fur-bearing animals are completely off-limits to nonresidents. No person may apply for a license to take protected fur-bearing animals unless he or she has lived in the state for 90 days prior to the application date (§ 41-6-24).

State hunting statutes also specify standards for firearm power. In South Dakota, for example, no one may hunt big game with a muzzle loading rifle that discharges a projectile less than forty-four hundredths of an inch in diameter. No one may hunt big game with buckshot, or with a single ball or rifled slug weighing less than one-half ounce. No self-loading or autoloading firearm that holds more than six cartridges may be used to hunt big game, and no fully automatic weapons may be used to hunt big or small game (§ 41-8-10, -13).

States may enact a variety of other restrictions on hunting. In Georgia, at night, no person may hunt any game bird or game animal except for raccoon, opossums, foxes, and bobcats. Those animals may be hunted at night, but only with a lantern or a light that does not exceed six volts (Ga. Code Ann. § 27-3-24). In South Dakota no dogs may be used in the hunting of big game, no person may use salt to entice big game, and no person may use artificial light in hunting (S.D. Codified Laws Ann. § 41-8-15, -16). However, an animal damage control officer may use an artificial light to take a nuisance animal from land, with the landowner's written permission (§ 41-8-17(3)).

Most states consider hunting a right of residents and a valuable promotional tool for tourism. Many states even have hunter harassment statutes, which punish persons for intentionally distracting hunters. Under such statutes a person may be arrested and prosecuted for attempting to discourage hunters or drive away game.

FURTHER READINGS

Cottriel, Darren K. 1996. "The Right to Hunt in the Twenty-First Century: Can the Public Trust Doctrine Save an American Tradition?" *Pacific Law Journal* 27 (spring).

"Ruling Sought on Indian Hunting, Fishing Rules." September 17, 2003. *CNN.com: U.S. News.*

Ugalde, Aileen M. 1996. "The Right to Arm Bears: Activists' Protests against Hunting." *Univ. of Miami Law Review* 45.

CROSS REFERENCE

Fish and Fishing.

HUNTLEY HEARING

In New York state, a separate proceeding in a criminal action conducted solely for the purpose of determining the admissibility of the extrajudicial statements made by the defendant.

The name *Huntley hearing* is derived from the case of *People v. Huntley,* 15 N.Y. 2d 72, 255 N.Y.S. 2d 838, 204 N.E. 2d 179 (1965), which set forth the hearing requirement.

HURTADO V. CALIFORNIA

An 1884 decision of the Supreme Court, *Hurtado v. California,* 110 U.S. 516, 4 S. Ct. 111, 28 L. Ed. 232, held that states are not required to comply with the FIFTH AMENDMENT provision that a criminal prosecution be initiated by an indictment by a GRAND JURY.

The constitution of California and various penal statutes provided for the prosecution of a person charged with an offense by information after a PRELIMINARY HEARING before a magistrate with rights to counsel and to cross-examine witnesses, or by indictment with or without a preliminary hearing. In February 1882, the district attorney of Sacramento County filed an information against Joseph Hurtado, charging him with the MURDER of Jose Stuardo. Hurtado was arraigned, tried, convicted of the crime, and sentenced to death. He unsuccessfully appealed his conviction throughout state appellate courts and brought a writ of error before the SUPREME COURT OF THE UNITED STATES.

Hurtado alleged that his conviction and sentence were void because they were obtained in violation of his rights to DUE PROCESS OF LAW as guaranteed by the FOURTEENTH AMENDMENT. He was convicted and sentenced on the basis of an information, not an indictment or presentment by a grand jury as required by the Fifth Amendment and, therefore, was deprived by the state of his liberty without due process.

After reviewing English treatises and numerous cases construing the term *due process of law,* the Court affirmed Hurtado's conviction. Only persons accused of federal crimes are entitled to a presentment or indictment of a grand jury. The Court refused to declare the proceedings that led to Hurtado's conviction under state law as violative of due process of law. Like an indictment, the information was "merely a preliminary proceeding," which would bring about a final judgment only as a consequence of a regular trial. Since it served the substantial interest of the prisoner and protected the principles of liberty and justice in a manner comparable to an indictment or presentment by a grand jury, an information satisfied the requirements of due process as guaranteed by the Constitution.

The effect of this decision—that the Fourteenth Amendment guarantee of due process of law does not mandate that an indictment or presentment to a grand jury is necessary for a conviction under state criminal laws to be upheld as legally valid—is still the law after more than 100 years.

HUSBAND AND WIFE

A man and woman who are legally married to one another and are thereby given by law specific rights and duties resulting from that relationship.

The U.S. legal concept of MARRIAGE is founded in English common law. Under common law, when a man and woman married, they became a single person in the eyes of the law—that person being the husband. The duties and benefits afforded a married woman, as well as the restrictions on her freedom, reflected this view. Even in the early twenty-first century, although the EQUAL PROTECTION Clause provides that no state shall "deny to any person within its jurisdiction the equal protection of the laws" (U.S. Const. amend. 14, § 1), the U.S. Supreme Court has never interpreted this to mean that states must treat husbands and wives the same.

There is a strong public policy in favor of marriage. Because of this, a husband and wife are not always able to determine their duties and privileges toward one another; instead, these rights and responsibilities are set forth by special legal principles that define the parameters within which husbands and wives must act.

However, the very concept of the terms *husband* and *wife* became nebulous as four states passed laws granting marriages to same-sex couples (Massachusetts in 2004, Connecticut in 2008, Iowa in 2009, and Vermont in 2009). California voters reversed a court ruling in favor of same-sex marriages in November 2008 (see below).

Support

Under common law, because it was unusual for a wife to have a job and earn her own money, a husband was obliged to provide his wife with "necessaries"—which included food, clothing, and shelter—but only those he deemed appropriate. In the early 2000s, judges have taken the support obligation further and construed the term "necessary" to include any item in furtherance of an established standard of living.

Most jurisdictions make it a criminal offense for a spouse to fail to meet a support obligation. Criminal nonsupport statutes are created to prevent men and women from becoming public charges and are most frequently applied upon the dissolution of a marriage when a spouse does not meet alimony and child-support obligations. Actions for support are rarely initiated by men, although an equal obligation of support applies.

Property

Historically wives were at a disadvantage as property owners. At common law, when a woman married, her personal possessions were considered to be the property of her husband. In addition, the husband was entitled to use the land she owned or subsequently inherited, and to retain rents and profits obtained from it. A married woman's right to own property was not incorporated into U.S. law until the mid-nineteenth century, with the Married Women's Property Acts. These laws allowed husbands to permit their spouses to own separate property. Women were also granted the right to enter contracts, sell land, write wills, sue and be sued, work without their husband's permission and keep their earnings, and, in certain jurisdictions, sue for injuries caused by their husbands.

Ordinarily, questions of who owns what property are brought to court only when a couple is obtaining a divorce. Courts are otherwise reluctant to become involved in property disputes between a husband and wife. Various systems exist in the United States to determine who owns

property in a marriage: a majority of states recognize separate property, whereas some adhere to COMMUNITY PROPERTY or equitable distribution doctrines.

The rule in separate-property states is that each person owns whatever items are in his or her name. In these states, various types of joint spousal ownership are recognized. A TENANCY BY THE ENTIRETY is a form of joint ownership whereby the husband and wife own all the property together. This type of arrangement ordinarily applies to real estate. In a tenancy by the entirety, neither spouse can sell the property or his or her interest in it independently. If the husband or wife dies, the remaining spouse has full survivorship rights.

In states that adhere to community property laws (as of 2009, Arizona, California, Idaho, Nevada, New Mexico, Texas, Washington, and Wisconsin), the husband and wife are each given an equal interest in everything they own with the exception of the separate property of either individual. A majority of the property obtained by a husband and wife during a marriage is considered community property. State law defines precisely what is considered separate property. In general, separate property includes whatever each party brought to the marriage and anything either spouse individually inherits during the marriage.

Equitable distribution is a method of property distribution that considers both the economic and noneconomic contributions of each spouse to the marital relationship, as well as each spouse's needs. It is based on the theory that a marriage should be regarded as a partnership of equal individuals.

Disputes over property ownership may arise when one spouse dies. A majority of jurisdictions have eliminated the common-law rights of dower and curtesy, which require that a spouse receive a specific portion of an estate. As an alternative, when one party leaves a will that disinherits her or his spouse, the survivor ordinarily has the right to acquire an ELECTIVE SHARE of the estate, which typically amounts to approximately one-third of its value. In some jurisdictions, this right is given only to a surviving wife. Elective shares do not prevent the dissipation of an estate prior to death.

In separate-property states, if a husband or wife dies intestate (without leaving a will), statutes provide for the surviving spouse to acquire a specified portion of the decedent's property. A statute might, for example, prescribe that the surviving spouse can acquire a one-half interest in the estate. The size of the portion depends on whether there are surviving children.

The distribution of property between a husband and wife might also be affected by a PREMARITAL AGREEMENT, also called an "antenuptial" or "prenuptial agreement." Premarital agreements are typically entered into by a man and woman before they are married, to arrange for the distribution or preservation of property owned by each spouse in the event of divorce or death.

Sexual Relationship

The most unique aspects of the relationship between a husband and wife are the legal sanctions attached to their sexual relationship. A number of states will grant a divorce based on the ground that a husband or wife was denied sex by his or her spouse. Similarly, an individual is ordinarily able to obtain an annulment if his or her spouse is unable to engage in sexual relations. The right of the state to interfere with the marital sexual relationship is limited by the U.S. Constitution as interpreted by the Supreme Court.

In the landmark case of *Griswold v. Connecticut*, 381 U.S. 479, 85 S. Ct. 1678, 14 L. Ed. 2d 510 (1965), the Court held that state statutes cannot unreasonably intrude into the marital sexual relationship. In this case, Connecticut was not allowed to enforce a statute that made it a crime for a physician to counsel married people on birth control. This was viewed as an unreasonable intrusion into the marital sexual relationship, since the sanctity of the marital relationship would be invaded if the statute were enforced. The Court emphasized the significance and constitutional considerations of privacy in marriage.

It was once thought that the degree of privacy to which a married couple is entitled could be restricted. Although some state statutes have used this reasoning to attempt to prohibit certain sex acts between a husband and wife, such as anal and oral sex, most courts have maintained that married couples have a constitutional privacy right over their marital sexual activities (*Lovisi v. Zahradnick*, 429 U.S. 977, 97 S. Ct. 485, 50 L. Ed. 2d 585) (1976).

A husband and wife have the right to purchase and use birth control devices—although when an individual uses contraceptives or becomes sterilized contrary to his or her spouse's wishes, this might provide grounds for annulment or divorce.

ABORTION has been viewed as an additional restriction on the sexual rights of a husband and wife. A wife's right to choose abortion takes precedence over the husband-and-wife relationship. A husband may not preclude his wife from having a legal abortion, nor may he compel her to have one. The Supreme Court struck down statutory requirements that a husband must be notified of his wife's abortion, in *Planned Parenthood v. Casey*, 505 U.S. 833, 112 S. Ct. 2791, 120 L. Ed. 2d 674 (1992).

At one time, a husband was allowed to have sexual relations with his wife with or without her consent, and for many years courts supported a marital exception to laws against RAPE. Under current law, the fact that the accused party and the victim were husband and wife can no longer be used as a defense to criminal charges. A rape by a husband of his wife might be subject to prosecution as an ASSAULT or, in some cases, as an attempted MURDER. Although all 50 states now criminalize spousal rape, many states still categorize spousal rape as lesser offenses than those ostensibly committed by strangers.

Crimes

Common law put many restrictions on a husband and wife when crimes occurred between them or against the marriage relationship itself. At one time, the courts recognized lawsuits based on "heart balm" acts. In such an action, a husband asserted that a monetary recovery would salve the "broken heart" caused by a third party's intrusion into his marriage. The basis for many of these causes of action was that a husband was being denied his rights to the affections and services of his wife; these lawsuits did not extend to a wife.

A husband once had an actionable injury if anyone induced his wife to leave him, under the theory that he was entitled to sue for damages any person who divested him of a servant. Similarly, a husband was able to bring an action for CRIMINAL CONVERSATION if his wife voluntarily engaged in adultery. The theory was that criminal conversation interferes with a husband's exclusive privilege to obtain sexual services from his wife. The basis of recovery is the public policy in favor of preserving marriage and the family. ALIENATION OF AFFECTION is another seldom-prosecuted action. In this type of action, a husband must prove that another man won his wife away from him, thereby depriving him of love, comfort, and companionship.

Because of the theories that gave rise to such causes of action, very few jurisdictions recognize lawsuits based on HEART BALM ACTS. Yet, even today, TORT LAW retains some special rules for husbands and wives when an outsider causes injury to the marital or family relationship. Consortium is the marital relationship between two people that encompasses their mutual right to support, cooperation, and companionship. An action for loss of consortium is based on the inconvenience of having a debilitated spouse. Husbands and wives have won suits for damages for injuries to their spouse precipitated by such things as MEDICAL MALPRACTICE, automobile accidents, FALSE IMPRISONMENT, and WRONGFUL DEATH.

Under common law, a husband was held responsible for any crimes committed by his wife against a third party. Although a wife had responsibility for crimes she committed, there was a legal presumption that her husband compelled her to perform any act she undertook when he was present. Today, husbands and wives are equally liable for their own criminal actions.

Privileged Communication

The law of evidence includes a privilege extended to a married couple so that neither a husband nor a wife can be compelled to testify against a spouse. This rule was designed to protect intrafamily relations and privacy. In addition, it was meant to promote communication between husbands and wives by making revelations between them strictly confidential.

In 1980 the U.S. Supreme Court, in *Trammel v. United States*, 445 U.S. 40, 100 S. Ct. 906, 63 L. Ed. 2d 186, held that husbands and wives were permitted to testify against one another voluntarily in a federal criminal prosecution. Many states now allow a spouse to testify against a husband or wife, but with the caveat that the testimony is subject to the accused spouse's consent. Other states view the spouse of an accused person as an ordinary witness who can be forced to testify against the accused person.

Domestic Abuse

It was once presumed that a husband should have the right to exert physical control over his wife, if only to protect himself from liability for his wife's actions. Therefore, common law permitted a husband to discipline his wife physically. Interspousal tort immunity made it impossible for a wife to succeed in an action against her husband. It was rare for a wife to accuse her husband of a crime, and a wife was forbidden to testify against her husband. In the early twenty-first century, a wife is almost always permitted to testify against a husband who has been accused of causing intentional injury to her or their child. With interspousal tort immunity all but abrogated in most jurisdictions, husbands and wives can now recover in suits against one another under the theories of FRAUDULENT MISREPRESENTATION, BATTERY, intentional infliction of emotional distress, and NEGLIGENCE.

The common law right of a husband to discipline his wife, combined with interspousal tort immunity, prevented incidents of domestic abuse from becoming public. In addition, victims of domestic abuse often did not reveal the extent of their injuries for fear of reprisals. Little legal relief was available, as courts were hesitant to interfere in the marital relationship. With the ABROGATION of interspousal tort immunity, the U.S. public has become aware of domestic abuse as a nationwide issue.

In some cases, victims of domestic abuse who have injured or killed their spouse as a means of SELF-DEFENSE against violence and abuse have been acquitted of criminal charges. The battered-spouse syndrome is a defense these men and women have asserted. The syndrome is a subcategory of post-traumatic stress disorder. Experts seek to explain why some spouses remain in abusive relationships and others finally use violence to break out of such relationships. Because battered women are typically economically dependent on their husband, they hesitate to seek help until the violence escalates to the point where they believe the only way to free themselves is to kill their abuser.

In 2009 the Supreme Court affirmed the application of the 1996 Lautenberg Amendment to the GUN CONTROL Act of 1968 (which prohibits gun ownership by anyone convicted of a MISDEMEANOR crime of DOMESTIC VIOLENCE, 18 U. S.C. 922(g)(9)), to cover anyone convicted of *any* violent misdemeanor committed against a family member or domestic partner. *United States v. Hayes* No. 07-608, 129 S.Ct. 1079, 172 L.Ed.2d 816 (2009). DEFENDANT Hayes had argued that the amendment only applied to convictions under specific laws proscribing domestic violence, not general laws proscribing violence that just happened to be committed against family members. Also in 2009, the White House announced the appointment of a White House Advisor on Violence Against Women, Lynn Rosenthal, a former executive director of the New Mexico Coalition Against Domestic Violence.

Same-Sex Marriage

In the 1980s and early 1990s, lawsuits were initiated to expand the traditional husband-and-wife relationship, and the rights and privileges that relationship conveys, to partners of the same sex. In a landmark case, *Baehr v. Lewin,* 74 Haw. 645, 852 P.2d 44 (1993), the Hawaii Supreme Court, although rejecting the idea that the Hawaii Constitution gives same-sex couples a FUNDAMENTAL RIGHT to marriage, held that Hawaii's marriage statute (Haw. Rev. Stat. § 572-1) discriminates on the basis of sex by barring people of the same sex from marrying. As a result, such statutes are subject to STRICT SCRUTINY. However, in 1998 Hawaiian voters overwhelmingly approved a CONSTITUTIONAL AMENDMENT that, while not banning same-sex marriage, gave the legislature the power to restrict marriages to opposite-sex couples.

In 1996, largely in response to *Baehr,* Congress passed the Defense of Marriage Act (110 Stat. § 2419), which defines *marriage* as "a legal union between one man and one woman as husband and wife." The term *spouse* is defined as a "person of the opposite sex who is a husband or a wife." In effect, the Defense of Marriage Act states that the federal government does not acknowledge same-sex marriages.

In 2001, however, Vermont became the first state to enact a law recognizing "civil unions" between same-sex couples (23 V.S.A. § 1201 et seq. [2000]). The 2000 law came in response to a 1999 Vermont Supreme Court ruling (*Baker v. Vermont,* 170 Vt. 194, 744 A.2d 864 [1999]),

which found that the benefits and protections guaranteed by the Vermont Constitution for opposite-sex couples extend to same-sex couples. Benefits and protections include access to a spouse's medical, life, and disability insurance; hospital visitation, and other medical decision-making privileges; spousal support; and the ability to inherit property from a deceased spouse without a will.

In October 2008 the Supreme Court of Connecticut ruled that denying same-sex couples the same rights, responsibilities, and designation of being "married" violated the equal protection clause of the state's constitution. *Kerrigan v. Commissioner of Public Health,* SC 17716. Weeks later, in November 2008, the state began to issue marriage licenses to same-sex couples. Connecticut thus became the third state ever to issue marriage licenses to same-sex couples, following Massachusetts (2004) and California (2008). The California Supreme Court had ruled just five months earlier, in May 2008. *In re Marriage Cases,* No. S147999, 183 P.3d 384. However, subsequent to California's court decision, California voters reversed the ruling through Proposition 8, a ballot initiative in the November 2008 elections that would amend California's constitution. California's reversal left only two states permitting same-sex marriages until the Iowa Supreme Court, on April 3, 2009, legalized gay marriages by also ruling that Iowa restrictions violated the state's constitution. This ruling again brought the total to three states upholding such marriages. These three states were followed by Vermont, which also upholds same-sex marriages.

FURTHER READINGS

Chriss, Margaret J. 1993. "Troubling Degrees of Authority: The Continuing Pursuit of Unequal Marital Roles." *Law & Inequality Journal* 12 (December).

Hartog, Hendrik. 2000. *Man and Wife in America: A History.* Cambridge, Mass.: Harvard University Press.

Keane, Thomas M. 1995. "Aloha, Marriage? Constitutional and Choice of Law Arguments for Recognition of Same-Sex Marriages." *Stanford Law Review* 47 (February).

Krause, Harry D. and David D. Meyer. 2007. *Family Law in a Nutshell.* 5th ed. St. Paul, Minn.: West Group.

Nickles, Don. 1996. "Defense of Marriage Act." *Congressional Record* 142.

"Same-Sex Marriages and Civil Unions: On Meaning, Free Exercise, and Constitutional Guarantees." 2002. *Loyola Law Journal* 33.

"Vermont Legislature Legalizes Same-Sex Marriage." 2009. *The Washington Post,* April 7.

Waggoner, Lawrence W. 1994. "Marital Property Rights in Transition." *Missouri Law Review* 59 (winter).

Wanamaker, Laura H. 1994. "*Waite v. Waite:* The Florida Supreme Court Abrogates the Doctrine of Interspousal Immunity." *Mercer Law Review* 45 (winter).

CROSS REFERENCES

Cohabitation; Domestic Violence; Family Law; Gay and Lesbian Rights

HYPOTHECATE

To pledge property as security or collateral for a debt. Generally, there is no physical transfer of the pledged property to the lender, nor is the lender given title to the property, though he or she has the right to sell the pledged property in the case of default.

HYPOTHESIS

An assumption or theory.

During a criminal trial, a hypothesis is a theory set forth by either the prosecution or the defense for the purpose of explaining the facts in evidence. It also serves to set up a ground for an inference of guilt or innocence, or a showing of the most probable motive for a criminal offense.

HYPOTHETICAL QUESTION

A mixture of assumed or established facts and circumstances, developed in the form of a coherent and specific situation, which is presented to an expert witness at a trial to elicit his or her opinion.

When a hypothetical question is posed, it includes all the facts in evidence needed to form an opinion and, based on the assumption that the facts are true, the witness is asked whether he or she can arrive at an opinion, and if so, to state it.

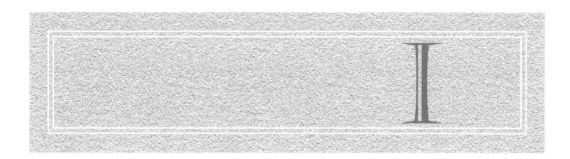

IBID.

An abbreviation of the Latin ibidem, *meaning "in the same place; in the same book; on the same page."*

ICC

See INTERSTATE COMMERCE COMMISSION.

IDEM

Latin, "the same." Typically abbreviated "id.," it is used in legal and scholarly bibliographic citations to indicate a previously cited reference.

IDENTITY THEFT

Identity theft is the assumption of a person's identity in order, for instance, to obtain credit; to obtain credit cards from banks and retailers; to steal money from existing accounts; to rent apartments or storage units; to apply for loans; or to establish accounts using another's name.

An identity thief can steal thousands of dollars in a victim's name without the victim even knowing about it for months or years. Identity thieves are able to accomplish their crimes by doing things such as opening a new credit card account with a false address, or using the victim's name, date of birth, and SOCIAL SECURITY number. When the thief uses the credit card and does not pay the resulting bills, the delinquent account is reported on the victim's credit report.

As increasing numbers of businesses and consumers rely on the INTERNET and other forms of electronic communication to conduct transactions, so too is illegal activity using the very same media on the rise. FRAUDULENT schemes conducted via the Internet are generally difficult to trace and to prosecute, and they cost individuals and businesses millions of dollars each year.

The Internet has facilitated identify theft, but stolen wallets, mail, and physical documents account for a large percentage of stolen information. However, the use of "phishing" by online criminals has proved to be an effective way of stealing personal information. The criminal seeks credit card numbers, passwords, and other information by posing as a trusted entity, such as a financial institution, in e-mails and text messages sent to potential victims. The person is directed through a hyperlink to a Web site that appears to be authentic. If the person provides sensitive information through this Web site, the criminal can gain access to bank and credit accounts. In response, banks and credit card companies have provided more security to customers that try to ensure that the customer will not be tricked.

Identify theft is also facilitated by the illegal acquisition of databases held by financial institutions, credit reporting services, and

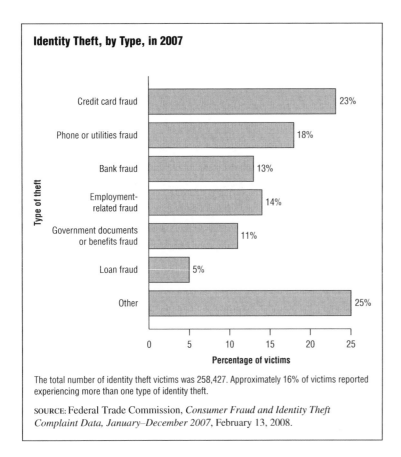

Identity Theft, by Type, in 2007

Type of theft / Percentage of victims:
- Credit card fraud: 23%
- Phone or utilities fraud: 18%
- Bank fraud: 13%
- Employment-related fraud: 14%
- Government documents or benefits fraud: 11%
- Loan fraud: 5%
- Other: 25%

The total number of identity theft victims was 258,427. Approximately 16% of victims reported experiencing more than one type of identity theft.

SOURCE: Federal Trade Commission, *Consumer Fraud and Identity Theft Complaint Data, January–December 2007*, February 13, 2008.

ILLUSTRATION BY GGS CREATIVE RESOURCES. REPRODUCED BY PERMISSION OF GALE, A PART OF CENGAGE LEARNING.

government units. By exploiting security breaches, computer hackers have been able to gain access to credit information, social security numbers, and other details that allow them to drain bank accounts and run up large credit card and phone bills. For example, more than 100 U.S. military officers were involved in a case of identity theft. Defendants in the case illegally acquired the names and social security numbers of the military personnel from a web site, then used the Internet to apply for credit cards issued by a Delaware bank. In another case of identity theft and FRAUD, a DEFENDANT stole personal information from the web site of a federal agency, and then used the information to make applications for an online auto loan through a Florida bank. In 2006 the theft of a laptop computer from a Department of Veterans Affairs (VA) employee set off a national panic as 19 million veterans and current military personnel discovered that their birthdates and social security numbers were at peril. Fortunately, the laptop was recovered, and the FBI concluded that no data had been accessed. However, the VA paid millions for credit insurance to protect the credit of veterans.

In October 1998 Congress passed the Identity Theft and Assumption Deterrence Act of 1998 (Identity Theft Act) 18 U.S.C. § 1028 to address the problem of identity theft. Specifically, the Act amended 18 U.S.C. § 1028 to make it a federal crime when anyone: knowingly transfers or uses, without lawful authority, a means of identification of another person with the intent to commit, or to aid or abet, any unlawful activity that constitutes a violation of federal law, or that constitutes a felony under any applicable state or local law. Violations of the act are investigated by federal investigative agencies such as the U.S. SECRET SERVICE, the FBI, and the U.S. Postal Inspection Service and are prosecuted by the DEPARTMENT OF JUSTICE.

The FEDERAL TRADE COMMISSION (FTC) is the federal clearinghouse for complaints by victims of identity theft. Although the FTC does not have the authority to bring criminal cases, it assists victims of identity theft by providing them with information to help them to resolve the financial and other problems that can result from identity theft. The FTC also may refer victim complaints to other appropriate government agencies and private organizations for further action. It has an identity theft section on its Web site: www.ftc.gov. In 2008, the FTC disclosed that 26 percent of complaints it received involved identity theft.

Consumers can protect themselves from this type of crime by protecting information such as credit card and social security numbers and by shredding mailed offers to obtain credit. They also can check their credit reports for unknown accounts. In the event of identity theft, an alert can be placed on a CREDIT BUREAU that notifies consumers of potential fraudulent activity. Consumers who are victims can also write a statement that will appear on their credit reports explaining the criminal activity. Most banks and major credit card companies have fraud departments with staff who are trained to address these situations, but often the consumer feels that the onus is on him or her to prove lack of wrongdoing, and many victims report frustration at having their credit and lives destroyed by identity theft. A number of states have taken action to make identity theft a state crime. Consumers can also purchase insurance to protect them from financial responsibility for identity theft, but most credit card companies do not charge customers for fraudulent charges.

FURTHER READINGS

Collins, Judith M. 2006 *Investigating Identity Theft: A Guide for Businesses, Law Enforcement, and Victims.* New York: Wiley.

Cullen, Terri. 2007 *The Wall Street Journal Complete Identity Theft Guidebook.* New York: Three Rivers Press.

Stickley, Jim. 2008 *The Truth about Identity Theft.* Upper Saddle River, New Jersey: FT Press.

I.E.

An abbreviation for the Latin id est, *"that is to say, meaning."*

ILLEGAL ALIENS AND IMMIGRATION

See ALIENS.

ILLEGITIMACY

The condition before the law, or the social status, of a child whose parents were not married to each other at the time of his or her birth.

The term *nonmarital child* is also used interchangeably with *illegitimate child.*

English common law placed harsh penalties on an illegitimate child, denying the child inheritance and property rights. Modern law has given the nonmarital child more rights but still differentiates between the marital and nonmarital status. In addition, a rising level of out-of-wedlock births in the United States has drawn the attention of politicians and policy makers.

Common Law and Illegitimacy

A child was considered to be illegitimate at common law if the parents were not married to each other at the time of the child's birth even though the parents were married later.

There was a common-law presumption that a child born of a married woman was legitimate. This presumption was rebuttable, however, upon proof that her husband either was physically incapable of impregnating her or was absent at the time of conception. In addition, a child born of a MARRIAGE for which an annulment was granted was considered illegitimate, because an annulled marriage is void retroactively from its beginning. Furthermore, if a man married a second time while still legally married to his first wife, a child born of the bigamous marriage was illegitimate.

At common law an illegitimate child was a fillius nullius (child of no one) and had no parental inheritance rights. This deprivation was

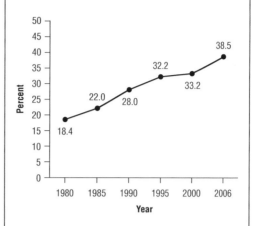

Births to Unmarried Women as Percentage of All Births, 1980 to 2006

Year	Percent
1980	18.4
1985	22.0
1990	28.0
1995	32.2
2000	33.2
2006	38.5

SOURCE: U.S. Department of Health and Human Services, Centers for Disease Control and Prevention, National Center for Health Statistics, *National Vital Statistics Reports*, vol. 57, no. 7, January 2009.

ILLUSTRATION BY GGS CREATIVE RESOURCES. REPRODUCED BY PERMISSION OF GALE, A PART OF CENGAGE LEARNING.

based in part on societal and religious beliefs concerning the sanctity of the marital relationship, as well as the legal principles that property rights were determined by blood relationships. The legal rights and duties of a person born of married parents could be ascertained more accurately than those of a child with an unknown or disputed father. Public policy in favor of maintaining solid family relationships contributed significantly to the preference for a legitimate child.

Modern Law

The harsher aspects of the common law dealing with an illegitimate child have been eliminated, primarily through the application of the EQUAL PROTECTION Clause of the FOURTEENTH AMENDMENT to the U.S. Constitution. In *Levy v. Louisiana,* 391 U.S. 68, 88 S. Ct. 1509, 20 L. Ed. 436 (1968), the Supreme Court ruled that a state statute (La. Civ. Code Ann. Art. 2315) that barred illegitimate children from recovering damages for the WRONGFUL DEATH of their mother, but allowed legitimate children to recover in similar circumstances, was invalid because it denied illegitimate children equal protection of the law.

The Supreme Court also enhanced the right of an illegitimate child to inherit property. Whereas most states had given legitimate and illegitimate children the same right to inherit property from the mother and her family, a number of states did not allow an illegitimate child to inherit property from the father in the absence of a specific provision in the father's will. In *Trimble v. Gordon*, 430 U.S. 762, 97 S. Ct. 1459, 52 L. Ed. 2d 31 (1977), the Supreme Court ruled such provisions in an Illinois statute invalid.

A majority of states now subscribe to the theory that a child born of any union that has the characteristics of a formal marriage relationship is entitled to legitimate status. This theory includes children born of marriages that fail owing to legal technicalities as well as children of void or voidable marriages.

Some states still recognize the validity of COMMON-LAW MARRIAGE, which takes place when a man and woman cohabit for an extensive period, and hold themselves out to the public as being husband and wife even though they were never formally married. In such states children born of such arrangements are considered legitimate. Common-law marriages were a convenient mechanism in the nineteenth century for establishing property rights and legitimating children. Frontier society accepted the economic necessity for permitting such marriages because it was difficult for people on the frontier to obtain a formal marriage license; without common-law marriages, many children would have been declared illegitimate.

Legal Presumption of Legitimacy

The presumption of legitimacy is a strong legal presumption because public policy favors legitimacy to preserve stable family groupings. This presumption can be rebutted only if it can be clearly established that the child in question is illegitimate. A child born to a married couple is presumed to be their legitimate offspring in the absence of a clear demonstration that the husband could not possibly be the father.

Legitimation is the process whereby the status of a child is changed from illegitimate to legitimate. Some statutes provide that a child becomes legitimated upon an open acknowledgment of paternity by the alleged father. In some states an oral admission is sufficient, but in other states a written statement is required. A majority of states prescribe that an acknowledgment must be coupled with an act in order for the child to be declared legitimate. An adequate

act in some states is the marriage of the child's natural parents. Once a child has been determined to be legitimate, he or she is entitled to the same rights and protections as any individual whose legitimacy has never been questioned.

Paternity Actions

A PATERNITY SUIT, or AFFILIATION PROCEEDING, may be brought against a father by an unmarried mother. This CIVIL ACTION is intended not to legitimate the child but to obtain support for the child and often to obtain the payment of bills incident to the pregnancy. Ordinarily, the mother starts the civil lawsuit, but some states allow public authorities to bring a paternity action for the mother if she refuses to do so. If the mother is on welfare, a paternity action is a vehicle for the local government agency to obtain financial assistance from the father.

A paternity action must start within the time prescribed by the STATUTE OF LIMITATIONS, or the mother's right to establish the putative father's paternity and corresponding support obligation will be lost. The evidence needed to establish paternity includes the testimony of the mother, blood and DNA tests, and in some states photographs from which to determine similar facial characteristics of the alleged father and the child.

Legal Rights of Fathers

Whether a father acknowledges paternity or is adjudged to be the father in a paternity action, he has more custody rights today than at common law. At common law fathers were assumed to have little concern for the well-being of their illegitimate offspring. Historically, in most jurisdictions, if a child was illegitimate, the child could be adopted with only the consent of his or her natural mother.

This assumption, as embodied in a New York statute (N.Y. Domestic Relations Law § 111), was challenged in *Caban v. Mohammed*, 441 U.S. 380, 99 S. Ct. 1760, 60 L. Ed. 2d 297 (1979). The key issue was whether the consent of an unwed biological father had to be obtained before an adoption could be finalized. The Supreme Court ruled that a law depriving all unwed fathers of the right to decide against adoption, whether or not they actually took care of the children in question, was unconstitutional and a form of SEX DISCRIMINATION.

Robert L. Johnson's Son? The Rights of Illegitimate Heirs

Robert L. Johnson is an important figure in blues music. Though he recorded only 29 songs before his death in 1938, at age 27, Johnson's songs, voice, and guitar playing have influenced many great musicians, including Muddy Waters, Keith Richards, and Eric Clapton. The Mississippi bluesman's recordings became a commercial success in the late 1960s, and by 1990 his collected works were released on compact discs.

Johnson married twice. Both wives died before he did and left no children. In 1974 Johnson's half-sister, Carrie Thompson, sold the copyrights of his songs and photographs, asserting that she was entitled to his estate. Upon her death in 1983, her half-sister Annye Anderson inherited her purported rights to Johnson's work.

When Anderson finally probated Johnson's estate in 1991, Claud L. Johnson filed a claim stating that he was the illegitimate son of Johnson

and the sole heir of the bluesman. Claud Johnson produced a Mississippi birth certificate from 1931 that lists R. L. Johnson as his father.

But for the U.S. Supreme Court's ruling in *Trimble v. Gordon*, 430 U.S. 762, 97 S. Ct. 1459, 52 L. Ed. 2d 31 (1977), Claud Johnson could not have made his claim. Until *Trimble* Mississippi prohibited illegitimate children from inheriting from their father.

Anderson argued that Claud Johnson's claim should be dismissed because he had waited too long to file it. A county court agreed with Anderson, but the Mississippi Supreme Court reversed the lower court's decision, ruling that the intent of state law was to give the same rights to illegitimate as to legitimate children (*In re Estate of Johnson*, 1996 WL 138615 [Miss.]). The supreme court sent the case back to the county court, which is to determine whether Claud Johnson is the son of Robert Johnson. If so, he is entitled to Robert Johnson's estate.

Artificial Insemination

Legitimacy issues have arisen when a child is conceived by ARTIFICIAL INSEMINATION. This process involves impregnating a woman, without sexual intercourse, with the semen of a donor who might be her husband or another party. Some states adhere to traditional views and consider any child conceived in this manner to be illegitimate, regardless of whether the husband gave his consent to the procedure. Other courts declare that a child is legitimate if the husband consented. A child is most likely considered illegitimate when the mother was unmarried and was artificially inseminated by an unknown donor, and remains unmarried. In most cases of artificial insemination, the father has donated semen anonymously, and his identity is not known.

Current Trends

The rate of illegitimate births in the United States has risen sharply since the early 1970s. In the 1940s fewer than five percent of the total

births were out of wedlock. By the early 2000s, according to statistics compiled by the Center for Health Statistics at the U.S. HEALTH AND HUMAN SERVICES DEPARTMENT, births to unmarried mothers accounted for nearly one-third of all U.S. births.

FURTHER READINGS

Roberts, Patricia G. 1998. "Adopted and Nonmarital Children—Exploring the 1990 Uniform Probate Code's Intestacy and Class Gift Provisions." *Real Property, Probate and Trust Journal* 32 (winter).

Sigle-Rushton, Wendy, and Sara McLanahan. 2002. "The Living Arrangements of New Unmarried Mothers." *Demography* (August). Available online at http://www.northwestern.edu/ipr/jcpr/workingpapers/wpfiles/siglerushton_mclanahan.pdf; website home page: http://www.northwestern.edu (accessed July 31, 2009).

Terry-Humen, Elizabeth, Jennifer Manlove, and Kristen A. Moore. 2001. "Births outside of Marriage: Perceptions vs. Reality." *Child Trends Research Brief* (April). Available online at http://www.childtrends.org/Files/Child_Trends-2001_04_01_RB_BirthsMarriage.pdf; website home page: http://www.childtrends.org (accessed July 31, 2009).

CROSS REFERENCES

Child Custody; Child Support; DNA Evidence; Family Law; Parent and Child.

ILLICIT

Not permitted or allowed; prohibited; unlawful; as an illicit trade; illicit intercourse.

ILLUSORY PROMISE

A statement that appears to assure a performance and form a contract but, when scrutinized, leaves to the speaker the choice of performance or nonperformance, which means that the speaker does not legally bind himself or herself to act.

When the provisions of the purported promise render the performance of the person who makes the promise optional or completely within his or her discretion, pleasure, and control, nothing absolute is promised; and the promise is said to be illusory. For example, a court decided that a promise contained in an agreement between a railroad and an iron producer whereby the railroad promised to purchase as much iron as its board of directors might order was illusory and did not form a contract.

IMMATERIAL

Not essential or necessary; not important or pertinent; not decisive; of no substantial consequence; without weight; of no material significance.

IMMEDIATE CAUSE

The final act in a series of provocations leading to a particular result or event, directly producing such result without the intervention of any further provocation.

For example, if an individual who was driving while intoxicated crashed his or her car and was killed, the immediate cause of death was the crash. The PROXIMATE CAUSE, however, was the individual's state of intoxication.

IMMIGRATION

The entrance into a country of foreigners for purposes of permanent residence. The correlative term EMIGRATION denotes the act of such persons in leaving their former country.

CROSS REFERENCE

Aliens.

IMMIGRATION AND NATURALIZATION

See ALIENS.

IMMINENT

Impending; menacingly close at hand; threatening.

Imminent peril, for example, is danger that is certain, immediate, and impending, such as the type an individual might be in as a result of a serious illness or accident. The chance of the individual dying would be highly probable in such situation, as opposed to remote or contingent. For a gift *causa mortis* (Latin for "in anticipation of death") to be effective, the donor must be in imminent peril and must die as a result of it.

IMMUNITY

Exemption from performing duties that the law generally requires other citizens to perform, or from a penalty or burden that the law generally places upon other citizens.

Sovereign Immunity

SOVEREIGN IMMUNITY prevents a sovereign state or person from being subjected to suit without its consent.

The doctrine of sovereign immunity stands for the principle that a nation is immune from suit in the courts of another country. It was first recognized by U.S. courts in the case of *The Schooner Exchange v. M'Faddon,* 11 U.S. (7 Cranch) 116, 3 L. Ed. 287 (1812). At first, courts espoused a theory that provided absolute immunity from the jurisdiction of a U.S. court for any act by a foreign state. But beginning in the early 1900s, courts relied on the political branches of government to define the breadth and limits of sovereign immunity.

In 1952 the U.S. STATE DEPARTMENT reacted to an increasing number of commercial transactions between the United States and foreign nations by recognizing foreign immunity only in noncommercial or public acts, and not in commercial or private acts. However, it was easily influenced by foreign diplomats who requested absolute sovereign immunity, and the application of sovereign immunity became inconsistent, uncertain, and often unfair.

Complaints about inconsistencies led to the passage of the Foreign Sovereign Immunities Act of 1976 (28 U.S.C.A. §§ 1 note, 1330, 1332, 1391, 1441, 1602–1611). By that act, Congress codified the theory of sovereign immunity, listing exceptions for certain types of acts such as commercial acts, and granted the exclusive power to decide sovereign immunity issues to the courts, rather than to the State Department.

Indian tribes have been granted sovereign immunity status by the United States, and therefore they generally cannot be sued without the consent of either Congress or the tribe. This immunity is justified by two considerations: First, historically, with more limited resources and tax bases than other governments, Indian tribes generally are more vulnerable in lawsuits than are other governments. Second, granting sovereign nation status to tribes is in keeping with the federal policy of self-determination for Indians.

Indian tribes are immune from suit whether they are acting in a governmental or a proprietary capacity, and immunity is not limited to acts conducted within a reservation. However, individual members of a tribe do not receive immunity for their acts; only the tribe itself is immune as a sovereign nation.

Governmental Tort Immunity

Sovereign immunity may also apply to federal, state, and local governments within the United States, protecting these governments from being sued without their consent. The idea behind domestic sovereign immunity—also called governmental tort immunity—is to prevent money judgments against the government, as such judgments would have to be paid with taxpayers' dollars. As an example, a private citizen who is injured by another private citizen who runs a red light generally may sue the other driver for NEGLIGENCE. But under a strict sovereign immunity doctrine, a private citizen who is injured by a city employee driving a city bus has no CAUSE OF ACTION against the city unless the city, by ordinance, specifically allows such a suit.

Governmental tort immunity is codified at the federal level by the FEDERAL TORT CLAIMS ACT (28 U.S.C.A. § 1291 [1946]), and most states and local governments have similar statutes. Courts and legislatures in many states have greatly restricted, and in some cases have abolished, the doctrine of governmental tort immunity.

Official Immunity

The doctrine of sovereign immunity has its roots in the law of feudal England and is based on the tenet that the ruler can do no wrong. Public policy grounds for granting immunity from civil lawsuits to judges and officials in the Executive Branch of government survive even today. Sometimes known as official immunity, the doctrine was first supported by the U.S. Supreme Court in the 1871 case of *Bradley v. Fisher,* 80 U.S. 335, 20 L. Ed. 646. In *Bradley,* an attorney attempted to sue a judge because the judge had disbarred him. The Court held that the judge was absolutely immune from the civil suit because the suit had arisen from his judicial acts. The Court recognized the need to protect judicial independence and noted that malicious or improper actions by a judge could be remedied by impeachment rather than by litigation.

Twenty-five years later, in *Spalding v. Vilas,* 161 U.S. 483, 16 S. Ct. 631, 40 L. Ed. 780 (1896), the Court expanded the doctrine to include officers of the federal Executive Branch. In *Spalding,* an attorney brought a defamation suit against the U.S. postmaster general, who had circulated a letter that criticized the attorney's motives in representing local post-masters in a salary dispute. At that time, the postmaster general was a member of the president's cabinet. The Court determined that the proper administration of public affairs by the Executive Branch would be seriously

Air Force analyst A. Ernest Fitzgerald sued President Nixon for firing him after Fitzgerald disclosed to Congress huge cost overruns in the Defense Department. The Supreme Court held that the president is immune from civil lawsuits arising from official acts performed while in office.

AP IMAGES

crippled by a threat of civil liability and granted the postmaster general absolute immunity from civil suit for discretionary acts within the scope of the postmaster's authority. Federal courts since *Spalding* have continued to grant absolute immunity—a complete bar to lawsuits, regardless of the official's motive in acting—to federal executive officials, so long as their actions are discretionary and within the scope of their official duties.

Members of Congress and state legislators are absolutely immune from civil lawsuits for their votes and official actions. The U.S. Supreme Court, in *Bogan v. Scott-Harris*, 523 U.S. 44, 118 S. Ct. 966, 140 L. Ed. 2d 79 (1998), extended absolute immunity to local legislators (e.g., city council members, and county commissioners) when they act in their legislative, rather than administrative, capacities.

Prosecutors are absolutely immune for their actions during a trial or before a GRAND JURY. However, during the investigatory phase, they are only granted qualified immunity. In *Kalina v. Fletcher*, 522 U.S. 118, 118 S. Ct. 502, 139 L. Ed. 2d 471 (1997), the U.S. Supreme Court ruled that a prosecutor was not entitled to absolute immunity with respect to her actions in making an allegedly false statement of fact in an affidavit supporting an application for an ARREST WARRANT. Policy considerations that merited absolute immunity included both the interest in protecting a prosecutor from harassing litigation that would divert his or her time and attention from official duties and the interest in enabling him or her to exercise independent judgment when deciding which suits to bring and in conducting them in court. These considerations did not apply when a prosecutor became an official witness in swearing to a statement.

However, in *Conn v. Gabbert*, 526 U.S. 286, 119 S. Ct. 1292, 143 L. Ed. 2d 399 (1999), the U.S. Supreme Court held that prosecutors cannot be sued for having lawyers searched or for interfering with the ability to advise a client who is appearing before a grand jury. Prosecutors have a qualified immunity in this situation, based on the two-step analysis that the courts apply to qualified-immunity issues. Under this two-part test, an Executive Branch official will be granted immunity if (1) the constitutional right that allegedly has been violated was not clearly established; and (2) the officer's conduct

was "objectively reasonable" in light of the information that the officer possessed at the time of the alleged violation. The qualified-immunity test is usually employed during the early stages of a lawsuit. If the standard is met, a court will dismiss the case.

Police and prison officials may be granted qualified immunity. In *Hope v. Pelzer*, 536 U.S. 730, 122 S. Ct. 2508, 153 L. Ed. 2d 666 (2002), the U.S. Supreme Court held that Alabama prison officials were not eligible for qualified immunity because they were on notice that their conduct violated established law even in novel factual circumstances. The officials were on notice that tying a prisoner to a hitching post in the prison yard constituted CRUEL AND UNUSUAL PUNISHMENT under the EIGHTH AMENDMENT. Prior court rulings and federal prison policies also made clear that law banning the practice had been clearly established. Therefore, the officials were not qualified for immunity.

In *Saucier v. Katz*, 533 U.S. 194, 121 S. Ct. 2151, 150 L. Ed.2d 272 (2001), the U.S. Supreme Court applied the qualified-immunity test to a claim that a U.S. SECRET SERVICE agent had used excessive force in removing a protester. The Court reasserted its general belief that law officers must be given the benefit of the doubt that they acted lawfully in carrying out their day-to-day activities. Moreover, one of the main goals of qualified immunity is to remove the DEFENDANT from the lawsuit as quickly as possible, thereby reducing legal costs. Justice ANTHONY KENNEDY restated the principle that immunity is not a "mere defense" to liability but an "immunity from suit." Therefore, immunity issues must be resolved as early as possible. As to the first step, Kennedy agreed that the case revealed a "general proposition" that excessive force is contrary to the FOURTH AMENDMENT. However, a more specific inquiry must take place to see whether a reasonable officer "would understand that what he is doing violates that right." As to this second step, Justice Kennedy rejected the idea that because the PLAINTIFF and the officer disputed certain facts, there could be no short-circuiting of this step. He stated that the "concern of the immunity inquiry is to acknowledge that reasonable mistakes can be made as to the legal constraints on particular police conduct." Officers have difficulty in assessing the amount of force that is required in a particular circumstance. If their mistake as to "what the law requires is reasonable, however, the officer is entitled to the immunity defense."

In *Nixon v. Fitzgerald*, 457 U.S. 731, 102 S. Ct. 2690, 73 L. Ed. 2d 349 (1982), the U.S. Supreme Court held that former U.S. president RICHARD M. NIXON was entitled to absolute immunity from liability predicated on his official acts as president. In *Nixon*, a weapons analyst, A. Ernest Fitzgerald, had been fired by the U.S. Air Force after he had disclosed to Congress certain cost overruns within the DEFENSE DEPARTMENT. Fitzgerald sued Nixon and two former presidential aides for wrongful retaliatory termination.

The Court emphasized the singular importance of the duties of the president, and noted that the diversion of the president's energies over concern for private lawsuits "would raise unique risks to the effective functioning of government." It also observed that the president, in view of the visibility of the office, would be an easy target for civil lawsuits. The ensuing personal vulnerability and distraction would prove harmful to the nation.

Despite the Court's grant of absolute immunity to the president for official actions, a president does not have immunity from civil lawsuits for actions that allegedly occurred before becoming president. The Court, in *Clinton v. Jones*, 520 U.S. 681, 117 S. Ct. 1636, 137 L. Ed. 2d 945 (1997), ruled that President BILL CLINTON had to defend himself in a sexual-harassment lawsuit that was based on his alleged actions while governor of Arkansas. Clinton had contended that the lawsuit could not proceed until he left office, but the Court disagreed. The Court pointed out that grants of official immunity are based on a functional analysis, and it would not extend immunity to actions outside of an officeholder's official capacities. Moreover, it concluded that defending the lawsuit would not divert Clinton's energies.

Immunity from Prosecution

State and federal statutes may grant witnesses immunity from prosecution for the use of their testimony in court or before a grand jury. Sometimes, the testimony of one witness is so valuable to the goals of crime prevention and justice that the promise of allowing that witness to go unpunished is a fair trade. For example, a drug dealer's testimony that could help law enforcement to destroy an entire illegal drug-manufacturing network is more beneficial to society than is the prosecution of that lone drug dealer. Although the FIFTH AMENDMENT to the U.S. Constitution grants witnesses a PRIVILEGE AGAINST SELF-INCRIMINATION, the U.S. Supreme Court has permitted prosecutors to overcome this privilege by granting witnesses immunity. Prosecutors have the sole discretion to grant immunity to witnesses who appear before a grand jury or at trial.

States employ one of two approaches to prosecutorial immunity: Use immunity prohibits only the witness's compelled testimony, and evidence stemming from that testimony, from being used to prosecute the witness. The witness still may be prosecuted so long as the prosecutor can obtain other physical, testimonial, or CIRCUMSTANTIAL EVIDENCE apart from the witness's testimony. Transactional immunity completely immunizes the witness from prosecution for any offense to which the testimony relates.

Congressional committees have the power to grant testimonial immunity to witnesses who testify before members of Congress. Congressional investigations into allegations of misconduct—such as the WATERGATE investigations in the 1970s and the Iran-Contra investigations in the 1980s—rely heavily on witness testimony. Whereas prosecutors simply decide whether to grant immunity to a witness, congressional committees must follow more formal procedures. Immunity may be granted only after a two-thirds majority vote by members of the committee. Ten days before the immunized testimony is given, the committee must advise the JUSTICE DEPARTMENT or the INDEPENDENT COUNSEL of its intention to grant immunity.

Family Immunity

At common law, a child could sue a parent for breach of contract and for torts related to property. An adult could sue his or her parent for any tort, whether personal or related to property. In 1891 the Mississippi Supreme Court, in *Hewllette v. George*, 9 So. 885 (1891), held that a child could not seek compensation for PERSONAL INJURY that was caused by a parent's wrongdoing, so long as the parent and child were obligated by their family duties to one another. The decision was based not on precedent but rather on public policy: The court found that such a lawsuit would undermine the "peace of society and of the families composing society." Criminal laws, the court found, were adequate to protect children.

Other states fell in step with Mississippi, adopting parental immunity of varying degrees. Some parental-immunity laws prohibited only claims of negligence, whereas others prohibited lawsuits for intentional torts such as rapes and beatings. The rationale supporting parental-immunity laws includes the need to preserve family harmony and, with the availability of liability insurance, the need to prevent parents and the children from colluding to defraud insurance companies.

Unjust results have led courts in many states that espouse parental immunity to carve out exceptions to the rule. For example, a child usually can sue a parent for negligence when the parent has failed to provide food or medical care, but not when the parent has merely exercised parental authority. Most courts have abolished the parental-immunity defense for car accident claims, and many allow children to sue their parents for negligent business or employment actions. Courts normally permit WRONGFUL DEATH suits to be brought by a child against a parent or by a parent against a child, because death terminates the parent-child relationship. Moreover, most states allow a child to sue a parent for injuries suffered in utero owing to the negligence of the mother.

FURTHER READINGS

Fox, Hazel. 2008. *The Law of State Immunity*. Oxford; New York: Oxford.

Giuttari, Theodore R. 1970. *The American Law of Sovereign Immunity; An Analysis of Legal Interpretation*. Santa Barbara, CA: Praeger.

Sels, John van Loben. 1994. "From Watergate to Whitewater: Congressional Use Immunity and Its Impact on the Independent Counsel." *Georgetown Law Journal* 83.

Stein, Theodore P. 1983. "Nixon v. Fitzgerald: Presidential Immunity as a Constitutional Imperative." *Catholic Univ. Law Review* 32 (spring).

CROSS REFERENCES

Ambassadors and Consuls; Diplomatic Immunity; Feres Doctrine; Husband and Wife; Judicial Immunity.

IMMUNIZATION PROGRAMS

Government immunization programs seek to protect residents from certain diseases by requiring individuals to undergo vaccinations against those diseases. Immunization is the process by which an individual's immune system becomes fortified against agents known as immunogens. Immuniza-
tion can be accomplished through a variety of means, most commonly vaccination. Vaccines against microorganisms that cause diseases help prepare the body's immune system to fight or prevent an infection.

The twentieth century saw great successes in the battle against childhood diseases. For example, pioneering researchers Jonas E. Salk and Albert B. Sabin developed vaccines that brought the dreaded virus poliomyelitis under control. This revolutionary work meant that a once rampant disease now could be stopped with a simple inoculation. In 1952 alone, more than 57,000 cases of polio in the United States left approximately 21,000 people crippled; in 1985, only four cases of polio were reported in the nation. Measles was also effectively halted: It killed more than 2,000 people in 1941 but only two in 1985. And by the end of the 1970s, smallpox was virtually eliminated around the world.

In the 1950s medical breakthroughs resulted in new vaccines to combat such diseases as polio and measles. States responded by requiring immunization for schoolchildren. One result was the near eradication of diseases that had previously been crippling or fatal. A second, unforeseen result was adverse side effects of the vaccines, which led to lawsuits against drug companies. Between the 1960s and late 1980s, millions of dollars in litigation forced drug manufacturers to retreat from the market and prompted government action to help protect companies and ensure their presence in the vaccine market.

Not only the vaccines accomplished this success. Government action helped, by enabling the widespread inoculation of children. By the 1960s, states had begun administering vaccines to school-age children, and their programs ultimately became mandatory. Each state now requires parents to submit a proof of immunization before enrolling their child in school; thus, the majority of young children in the United States are inoculated against such diseases as measles, polio, mumps, meningitis, and diphtheria, pertussis, tetanus, and whooping cough.

Vaccines are never entirely safe. Side effects range from mild to serious: from swelling and fever to brain damage and death. These dangers were recognized early on. Between 1961 and 1963, federal agencies noted occasional serious side effects from polio vaccines. By 1964, the

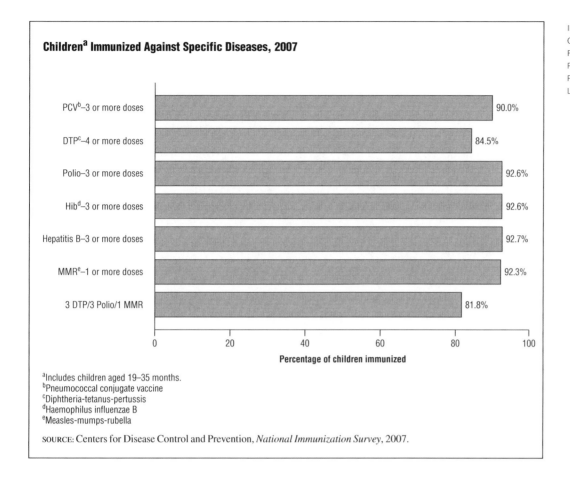

Children[a] Immunized Against Specific Diseases, 2007

PCV[b]–3 or more doses	90.0%
DTP[c]–4 or more doses	84.5%
Polio–3 or more doses	92.6%
Hib[d]–3 or more doses	92.6%
Hepatitis B–3 or more doses	92.7%
MMR[e]–1 or more doses	92.3%
3 DTP/3 Polio/1 MMR	81.8%

Percentage of children immunized

[a]Includes children aged 19–35 months.
[b]Pneumococcal conjugate vaccine
[c]Diphtheria-tetanus-pertussis
[d]Haemophilus influenzae B
[e]Measles-mumps-rubella

SOURCE: Centers for Disease Control and Prevention, *National Immunization Survey*, 2007.

surgeon general's Special Advisory Committee on Oral Poliomyelitis Vaccine found that 53 cases of polio could apparently be linked to the three types of the vaccine.

Public health authorities have nevertheless consistently urged the continuation of vaccine programs, arguing that the extremely minor incidence of adverse side effects is far outweighed by the health and lives they preserve. The Centers for Disease Control estimates, for example, that 1 in 310,000 children is adversely affected by the diphtheria, pertussis, and tetanus (DPT) vaccine. According to the AMERICAN MEDICAL ASSOCIATION, one in 3.2 million doses of polio vaccine will cause paralysis, and one in 1 million doses of measles vaccine will cause brain damage.

Beginning in the 1960s, vaccine-related injuries produced expensive litigation. Aggrieved families brought suit against drug manufacturers, sometimes winning large damages awards. These suits proceeded on a number of theories: NEGLIGENCE, failure to warn, design defect, production defect, breach of warranty, and STRICT LIABILITY. In 1970, for instance, Epifanio Reyes, the father of eight-month-old Anita Reyes, filed suit against Wyeth Laboratories, charging that the company's vaccine had transmitted paralytic polio to his daughter. He claimed strict product liability, breach of warranty, and negligence. The jury returned an award of $200,000, and the VERDICT was upheld on appeal in *Reyes v. Wyeth Laboratories*, 498 F.2d 1264 (5th Cir. 1974).

The lawsuits increased costs for drug companies, which, even when successful in court, faced increased expenses in liability insurance. Fearing greater losses in court, manufacturers fled the vaccine market. Between the mid-1960s and early 1990s, the number of vaccine makers shrank by half. The remaining companies drastically raised the price of vaccines: the DPT vaccine, for instance, sold for $1 a dose in the early 1980s, but had increased to $11 a dose by the end of the decade. The exodus of companies from the market left measles, mumps, and rubella vaccines each with only one manufacturer. This situation raised worries about the possibility of a critical shortage if one of these manufacturers left the market.

Companies were not the only target of lawsuits. In the mid-1970s, the federal government established a vaccine program called the National Swine Flu Immunization Program of 1976 (42 U.S.C.A. § 247 b[j]-[1], *amended by* Pub. L. No. 95-626, 92 Stat. 3574 [1978]), in anticipation of an onslaught of swine flu. To induce manufacturers to produce the drug, the act absolved them of all liability, and the federal government assumed all risk. The epidemic never materialized, but legal problems did. Plaintiffs alleging harmful side effects from the vaccine sued, and the government ended up paying out millions of dollars in settlements. In *Petty v. United States*, 740 F.2d 1428 (1984), for example, the Eighth Circuit upheld a damages award of some $200,000. The Court held that the warnings on the vaccine were inadequate.

Since the time of the swine flu immunization suits, courts and lawmakers have taken actions that have lessened the risks of liability facing drug manufacturers. Courts have restricted the grounds under which litigants can succeed in civil tort actions. Where products are found to be unavoidably unsafe—having obvious benefits yet carrying certain risks—the courts have erected barriers to strict liability claims. The courts have presumed that certain vaccines are unavoidably unsafe and, in some jurisdictions, that warnings provided by drug companies are adequate as long as they meet FOOD AND DRUG ADMINISTRATION (FDA) standards. The Restatement (Second) of Torts mentions the rabies vaccine as one of the products that, "in the present state of human knowledge, are quite incapable of being made safe for their intended and ordinary use," noting,

> Since the disease itself invariably leads to a dreadful death, both the marketing and the use of the vaccine are fully justified, notwithstanding the unavoidable high degree of risk which they involve. Such a product, properly prepared, and accompanied by proper directions and warning, is not defective, nor is it unreasonably dangerous (§ 402A comment k [1965]).

Courts in most jurisdictions follow this standard in determining liability in vaccine cases.

The finding that a vaccine is unavoidably unsafe does not mean that manufacturers are completely absolved of liability. Plaintiffs may still overcome the two barriers of unavoidable danger and compliance with FDA standards. To prevail, they must show that vaccine-related injuries or deaths could have been prevented. Two chief means exist: They must show that the drugmaker engaged in illegal activity or that the drugmaker failed to exercise due care in preparing or marketing the vaccine. Although both are difficult matters to prove, they can be established, as in *Petty*, in which inadequate warnings on the swine flu vaccine were found to be more significant than the fact that the vaccine was unavoidably unsafe.

Congress used a similar liability standard in groundbreaking federal legislation passed in 1986, the National Childhood Vaccine Injury Act (42 U.S.C.A. §§ 300aa-1 et seq.). The act established a federal no-fault compensation program for victims. It sought to stem civil litigation by providing an alternative: Rather than sue drug companies, families alleging injury or death due to a child's compulsory inoculation could file suit in the federal claims court. This alternative reflected not only legal but commercial realities: Congress hoped to maintain an adequate national supply of vaccines by relieving drug companies of risk. The law set the maximum damages award at $250,000 and required plaintiffs to first file suit in the claims court. If successful, plaintiffs could accept the award or reject it in favor of filing a separate CIVIL ACTION. Like the evolving standard in courts, this law protected DEFENDANT drug companies: Their compliance with federal production and labeling standards is an acceptable defense against civil lawsuits, and no strict liability claims are allowed.

Judicial and legislative solutions have thus partially ameliorated the liability risks of drug manufacturers. But by the mid-1990s, concerns remained about the potential for marketing an AIDS vaccine if one was discovered. Some observers called for federal legislation to protect potential manufacturers of an AIDS vaccine, and two states—California (Cal. Health & Safety Code § 199.50) and Connecticut (Conn. Gen. Stat. Ann. § 19a-591b)—extended liability protection to them.

Despite the use of anthrax in October 2001 as a terror weapon, medical and national security experts have always considered the intentional spreading of smallpox to be a far greater danger. In the weeks after the terrorist attacks, the HEALTH AND HUMAN SERVICES DEPARTMENT sought emergency funding for bio-terrorist preparedness, which included urgent production of smallpox vaccine.

Smallpox as a naturally occurring disease was declared eradicated in 1980 after worldwide inoculation programs had successfully defeated it. The United States halted smallpox inoculations in 1972, and those Americans who had them are probably no longer protected, according to medical experts. The active life of the vaccination was considered to be ten years, though recent studies indicate protection may last longer. The GEORGE W. BUSH administration labored for months over the question of reinstituting vaccines. The vaccine itself can be deadly and is not advised for people with weak immune systems, people being treated for cancer, nursing mothers, pregnant women, very young children, or people who have or have ever had eczema or atopic dermatitis. People who live with someone at risk under any of these conditions also should not be vaccinated.

Based on medical studies, experts estimate that 15 out of every 1 million persons vaccinated for the first time could face serious side effects. Several countries are suspected to have varying amounts of smallpox virus, including North Korea, Russia, China, Pakistan, and Iran. The United States had several vials of the virus, according to testimony before Congress, kept under tight security at the Centers for Disease Control and Prevention in Atlanta. A single infected person can spread smallpox. The last major outbreak in an industrialized nation was in Yugoslavia in 1972.

In December 2002 President Bush ordered a national smallpox vaccination program in the United States. Military personnel destined for deployment to the Persian Gulf, Central Asia, and Middle East regions were given the vaccine as states across the country prepared to vaccinate emergency medical and disaster personnel who might have to contend with an outbreak of the disease. Under the plan, there would be voluntary vaccinations of first responders, the fire fighters, police and emergency personnel who are first on the scene at a disaster. Government officials estimated that there were about 10 million first responders nationwide. Secretary of Health and Human Services Tommy Thompson said that there is a stockpile of nearly 15 million doses of an established and licensed vaccine that has been used in the United States for decades. These doses were expected to be administered to military and service personnel. There are some 85 million doses of a new vaccine that would not

be licensed until 2004 and that could be used in case of emergency. The Association of American PHYSICIANS AND SURGEONS issued a statement of support for the president's program. The American Nurses Association, whose members would be some of the personnel offered inoculations in the first phased, said there was insufficient information about the risks for their members to make a clear decision. Some private citizens have been vaccinated under experimental programs, but the vaccine has not been made available to the general public.

Whereas concerns about bioterrorist attacks lessened in the United States since 2001, questions about the ongoing need for any kind of mandatory immunizations have been increasing. In a sense, vaccines have become their own worst enemy. Americans rarely see the debilitating effects from polio and meningitis, causing many parents to become complacent about immunization requirements. Anti-vaccination sentiment is also fueled by controversial and disputed links between immunizations and autism. As a result, increasing numbers of parents are refusing immunizations for their children and seeking legally sanctioned exemptions instead, citing religious and philosophical grounds for their refusal.

State legislatures and government health officials thus face a difficult challenge: respecting individual rights and freedoms while also safeguarding the public welfare. Nearly all 50 states allow vaccination exemptions for religious reasons, and a growing number provide "philosophical" opt-outs as well. However, in all but a handful of jurisdictions, neither objection is seriously documented or verified. Often, the law requires a parent to do no more than simply check a box indicating that he or she does not wish her child to receive immunizations. The rise in parents opting out has caused the American Medical Association (AMA) great concern, with many experts decrying the rise of so-called "exemptions of convenience." In some areas in the United States, nearly one out of five children have not received their recommended vaccines.

Evaluating the impact of growing complacency over immunization programs is complicated by the rise of diseases that mutate as they circle the world. In April 2009 a highly infectious Novel Influenza A (H1N1) virus was discovered to have infected humans in

Mexico. First thought to be a simple variation of swine flu, subsequent cases showed that the virus had mutated, combining with strains of human and bird viruses. By June the mutated virus had spread to the United States, Canada, Europe, Asia, the Middle East, Australia, and South America, leading the World Health Organization (WHO) to declare a global pandemic, the first since 1968. Whereas infections had been confirmed in nearly 45,000 people in more than 90 countries, with 180 deaths being attributed to the virus, a majority of the cases were mild, especially when considering that every year ordinary seasonal influenza kills 36,000 people in the United States alone. The real concern for health officials is the reemergence of a more deadly, mutated version of the virus when flu season hits the northern hemisphere in late 2009 and early 2010. In preparation, government officials and pharmaceutical companies worked together on a vaccine that would target not only the H1N1 swine/bird/human virus that had been discovered, but also a mutated version that may evolve in the future.

FURTHER READINGS

Chaitow, Leon. 1990. *Vaccination and Immunization.* Saffron Walden, UK: C. W. Daniel.

Hauptly, Denis J., and Mary Mason. 1990. "The National Childhood Vaccine Injury Act." *Federal Bar News and Journal* 37 (October).

King, George H. 1989. "A Prescription for Applying Strict Liability: Not All Drugs Deserve Comment K Immunization." *Arizona State Law Journal* 21 (fall).

Krishnan, Shobha S. 2008. *the HPV Vaccine Controversy.* Westport, Conn.: Praeger.

Miller, Neil Z. 2001. *Vaccines: Are They Really Safe and Effective?* Santa Fe, NM: New Atlantean.

Polizzi, Catherine M. 1994–95. "A Proposal for a Federal Aids Immunization Policy." *Journal of Law and Health* 9.

CROSS REFERENCES

Acquired Immune Deficiency Syndrome; Drugs and Narcotics.

IMPANEL

The act of the clerk of the court in making up a list of the jurors who have been selected for the trial of a particular cause. All the steps of ascertaining who shall be the proper jurors to sit in the trial of a particular case up to the final formation.

IMPARTIAL

Favoring neither; disinterested; treating all alike; unbiased; equitable, fair, and just.

IMPEACH

To accuse; to charge a liability upon; to sue. To dispute, disparage, deny, or contradict; as in to impeach a judgment or decree, or impeach a witness; or as used in the rule that a jury cannot impeach its verdict. To proceed against a public officer for crime or misfeasance, before a proper court, by the presentation of a written accusation called articles of impeachment.

In the law of evidence, the testimony of a witness is impeached by earlier statements that the witness has made if they are inconsistent with the statements to which the witness testifies.

IMPEACHMENT

A process that is used to charge, try, and remove public officials for misconduct while in office.

Impeachment is a fundamental constitutional power belonging to Congress. This safeguard against corruption can be initiated against federal officeholders from the lowest cabinet member, all the way up to the president and the chief justice of the U.S. Supreme Court. Besides providing the authority for impeachment, the U.S. Constitution details the methods to be used. The two-stage process begins in the House of Representatives with a public inquiry into allegations. It culminates, if necessary, with a trial in the Senate. State constitutions model impeachment processes for state officials on this approach. At both the federal and state levels, impeachment is rare: From the passage of the Constitution to the mid-1990s, only 50 impeachment proceedings were initiated, and only a third of these went as far as a trial in the Senate. The reluctance of lawmakers to use this power is a measure of its gravity; it is generally only invoked by evidence of criminality or substantial ABUSE OF POWER.

The roots of impeachment date to ancient Athens. Its place in the U.S. Constitution was secured by the influence of English common law on the Framers of the Constitution. Originally, any English subject, politician, or ruler could institute impeachment charges in Parliament. By the fourteenth century, this power became the exclusive domain of the House of Commons and the House of Lords. In 1776, the American colonies included much of the English tradition in state constitutions, but the delegates of the Constitutional Convention hotly debated how best to embody it in the federal Constitution. Their most contentious question was over the offenses that should be considered impeachable.

The result of the Framers' debate was a compromise: They borrowed language from English common law but adapted the grounds of impeachment. These grounds are specified in Article II, Section 4: "The President, Vice President and all civil Officers of the United States, shall be removed from Office on Impeachment for, and Conviction of, Treason, Bribery, or other High Crimes and Misdemeanors." The choice of the phrase "High Crimes and Misdemeanors" left the exact definition of impeachable offenses open to interpretation by Congress. It has invited considerable debate, but it is generally read to mean both indictable offenses and other serious noncriminal misconduct. The latter has included corruption, dereliction of constitutional duty, and violation of limitations on the power of an office. Under the Constitution, federal judges are held to the most exacting standard: They may remain on the bench only "during good Behavior" (art. III, SEC. 1).

Impeachment is conducted in two stages. Impeachment proceedings begin in the House of Representatives (art. I, sec. 2). This stage satisfies the Framers' belief that impeachment should be a public inquiry into charges against an official, and it involves fact-finding at hearings. After accumulating all the evidence, the House votes on whether or not to impeach. A vote against impeachment ends the process. A vote to impeach formally advances the process to its second stage through what is called adoption of the ARTICLES OF IMPEACHMENT. Each article is a formal charge with conviction on any one article being sufficient for removal. The case is then sent to the Senate, which organizes the matter for trial (art. I, sec. 3).

During the trial, the Senate follows unique rules. There is no jury (art. III, sec. 2). Instead, the Senate is transformed into a quasi-judicial body that hears the case, and the impeached official can attend or be represented by counsel. The vice president presides over the trial of any official except the president, and the chief justice of the U.S. Supreme Court presides over the trial of the president. To convict, a two-thirds majority is needed. The punishments for conviction are removal from office and disqualification from holding office again. No presidential pardon is possible (art. II, sec. 2).

Additional criminal charges can be brought against convicted officials, but these are pursued in court and are separate from the impeachment process.

Impeachment is not often pursued. President ANDREW JOHNSON was nearly impeached as a result of a bitter struggle in 1868 between his exercise of executive power and congressional will. He escaped an impeachment conviction in the Senate by a single vote. In 1974 President RICHARD M. NIXON, embroiled in the WATERGATE scandal, resigned rather than face almost certain impeachment. The House Judiciary Committee had recommended that the full House take up three articles of impeachment against Nixon: OBSTRUCTION OF JUSTICE; abuse of constitutional authority; and refusal to answer the committee's subpoenas.

Congress has adopted the articles of impeachment against one senator, William Blount; one cabinet member, William W. Belknap; and one Supreme Court justice, SAMUEL CHASE. It also has voted to impeach a small number of federal appeals and district court judges. In 1989 U.S. district court judge Alcee Hastings, of Miami, became only the twelfth federal judge in U.S. history to be impeached. His case was unique: He was the first African-American to be appointed to the Florida federal bench, and also the only judge to be impeached after an acquittal in a criminal trial. The House voted to adopt 17 articles of impeachment against him in 1988. After Hastings unsuccessfully challenged his impeachment in court in 1989, the Senate convicted him on eight of the articles and removed him from office.

Chief Justice Rehnquist is sworn in by Senator Strom Thurmond on January 7, 1999, to preside over the Senate impeachment trial of President Clinton.

AP IMAGES

HOW WILL THE TRIAL OF BILL CLINTON AFFECT FUTURE IMPEACHMENTS?

Impeachment, the constitutional method for removing presidents, judges, and other federal officers who commit "Treason, Bribery, or other high Crimes and Misdemeanors," requires a majority vote by the House of Representatives, and then conviction by a two-thirds vote in the Senate. President William Jefferson Clinton's impeachment trial was the fifteenth in U.S. history, and the second of a president. ANDREW JOHNSON, the other president to be impeached by the House of Representatives, was acquitted by the Senate in 1868 in a vote that mostly followed party lines. Especially in light of prior impeachments, seven of which ended with the removal of federal judges, Clinton's case will affect the future use of impeachment, the process of impeachment, and the definition of "high Crimes and Misdemeanors."

Clinton's experience, like Johnson's, shows that impeachment can be a tool of political warfare. Although the U.S. Constitution only requires a House majority for impeachment, many scholars and other commentators say it should be a bipartisan effort to remove a president who is dangerous to the nation. However, the world of academia differs from that of politics. In contrast, House Republicans pursued Clinton by disregarding polls that said two-thirds of the nation opposed impeachment. The vote in the House then fell mostly along party lines. Future House majorities could use this precedent and to impeach a political opponent without substantial public support.

The price of the impeachment, however, was high for House Republicans. Speaker Newt Gingrich (R-Ga.) resigned after mid-term elections in November 1998, trimming the Republican House majority to six votes. Then, upon exposure of his own extramarital affair, Speaker-elect Robert L. Livingston (R-La.) resigned on the day of impeachment, urging Clinton to follow his example. Republicans and Democrats alike might hesitate to pursue another unpopular impeachment with so much at risk. However, when Democrats someday control the House of Representatives with a Republican in the White House, the human temptation for revenge will be great. As historian Benjamin Ginsberg observed, "The history of American politics over the last few decades is that the victims of a political attack denounce it as an illegitimate endeavor—but within a few years adopt it themselves. It's like an arms race."

As for the process of impeachment, Clinton's experience may affect the future use of witnesses and the viability of censure. The House Judiciary Committee declined to call a single witness to any of Clinton's misconduct, relying instead in the investigation by INDEPENDENT COUNSEL KENNETH W. STARR. Democrats criticized this procedure, asking how the House could vote on impeachment without an independent investigation. (In fact, the only other time the House failed to conduct an investigation was when it impeached President Johnson, suggesting that such

an approach is political.) During Clinton's trial in the Senate, however, Democrats themselves opposed calling witnesses, a political move motivated by fear that witnesses would reveal something leading to conviction. House managers running the prosecution, who now wanted 15 witnesses after calling none in the House, had to settle for just three. Everyone will remember that lesson next time.

As an alternative to impeachment, Democrats tried to introduce censure resolutions in both the House and Senate. Republicans defeated these efforts. Some said censure was not a legal option, as the U.S. Constitution provides for censure of members of Congress but not presidents. Democrats, however, pointed to past censures of Presidents ANDREW JACKSON, JOHN TYLER, and JAMES BUCHANAN, and suggested that Republican opposition stemmed from a desire to brand Democrats as supporting Clinton's misconduct during upcoming elections.

Any future impeachment, whether of a president, judge, or other civil officer, will revisit the question of what constitutes "high Crimes and Misdemeanors," which is undefined in the U.S. Constitution. Those in favor of impeaching Clinton argued that PERJURY and OBSTRUCTION OF JUSTICE of any kind are impeachable because they subvert the RULE OF LAW, making it impossible to expect lawful behavior from ordinary citizens and even future presidents, who are charged by the Constitution with taking "Care that the

The impeachment and trial of President BILL CLINTON in 1998 and 1999 demonstrated the difficulty of removing an official when the debate becomes politicized. The desire of the House of Representatives to impeach Clinton grew out of actions that had taken place in litigation involving Clinton and Paula Jones. Jones had filed a lawsuit against

Clinton, alleging that he had sexually harassed her when he was governor of Arkansas and she was a state employee. Clinton sought to postpone the suit until he left office but the U.S. Supreme Court, in *Clinton v. Jones*, 520 U.S. 681, 117 S. Ct. 1636, 137 L. Ed. 2d 945 (1997), ruled that a sitting president does not have presidential *immunity* from suit over

Laws be faithfully executed." Those who opposed impeachment said that whereas perjury and obstruction of justice are wrong, they are not impeachable offenses unless they concern the president's official duties and present a danger to the nation.

Clinton's impeachment by the House and acquittal by the Senate thus will affect future interpretation of "high Crimes and Misdemeanors" in many ways. The House Judiciary Committee recommended impeachment for perjury in Clinton's deposition in a civil lawsuit, and for perjury in his criminal GRAND JURY testimony. The House voted to impeach only for the latter, suggesting that perjury in a criminal matter is impeachable, whereas perjury in a civil matter is not.

The Senate, however, voted to acquit Clinton of perjury and obstruction of justice even though most Republicans and Democrats believed Clinton lied under oath and tried to influence the testimony of other witnesses. As explained by Senator Richard H. Bryan (D-Nev.), "The president's conduct is boorish, indefensible, even reprehensible. It does not threaten the republic." This suggests that misconduct, even perjury, that is unrelated to the president's official duties and does not present a danger to the nation is not impeachable.

As such, Clinton's acquittal creates a double standard for impeachment of presidents and judges. In 1986 the House impeached and the Senate convicted Judge Harry E. Claiborne for filing false income tax returns. In 1989 the House impeached and the Senate convicted Judge Walter L. Nixon Jr., for lying under oath about conduct unrelated to his official duties. In neither case did anyone suggest that lying about personal conduct is not an impeachable offense. In fact, the House managers' report concerning Judge Nixon said, "It is difficult to imagine an act more subversive to the legal process than lying from the WITNESS STAND. A judge who violates his testimonial oath and misleads a grand jury is clearly unfit to remain on the bench. If a judge's truthfulness cannot be guaranteed, if he sets less than the highest standard for candor, how can ordinary citizens who appear in court be expected to abide by their testimonial oath." The Senate's acquittal of Clinton suggested that lying about private matters is an impeachable offense for judges, but not for presidents.

Finally, the most significant effect of Clinton's impeachment and acquittal may be to define "high Crimes and Misdemeanors" to mean whatever the public wants. Scholars and politicians argued that the term purposefully is vague and undefined to allow Congress to handle each instance in the best interests of the nation. According to constitutional scholar Laurence H. Tribe, "[u]nless the rights of individuals or minority groups are threatened, our governing institutions are structured to make the sustained will of a significant majority all but impossible to topple—as the failure of the effort to remove President Clinton will dramatically illustrate." Even Senator Orrin G. Hatch (R-Utah), who voted to convict Clinton, said, "It's not just law. It's politics.... And you have to combine those two and say—and this ought to be the prevailing question—what is in the best interest of our country, of our nation, of our people."

FURTHER READINGS

Amar, Akhil Reed. 1999. "On Impeaching Presidents." *Hofstra Law Review* 28 (winter).

Austin, Jan, ed. 1999. *Congressional Quarterly 1998 Almanac.* Washington, D.C.: Congressional Quarterly.

Baker, Peter, and Juliet Eilperin. 1998. "Clinton Impeached." *Washington Post* (December 20).

Carney, James, John F. Dickerson, and Karen Tumulty. 1999. "Nightmare's End." *Time* (February 22).

Cooper, Charles J. 1999. "A Perjurer in the White House?: The Constitutional Case for Perjury and Obstruction of Justice as High Crimes and Misdemeanors." *Harvard Journal of Law and Public Policy* (spring).

Coyle, Marcia. 1999. "Impeachment Lessons for the House Are Stark." *National Law Journal* (February 22).

Gettinger, Stephen. 1999. "Impeachment's Future: Just Another Political Weapon?" *CQ Weekly,* (February 13).

"Impeachment of the President: Interpreting 'High Crimes and Misdemeanors'." 1999. *Congressional Digest* (February).

Marcus, Ruth. 1999. "House Managers Warn of Trial's Future Impact on Presidency." *Washington Post* (January 12).

———. 1999. "Scholars Weigh Likelihood of Future Impeachments." *Washington Post* (February 15).

———. 1999. "With Precedents as a Guide; Senators' Decisions, As Well As Rules, Will Affect Process." *The Washington Post* (January 14).

Samuelson, Robert J. 1998. "Nixon's Revenge." *Washington Post* (December 23).

"Special Report: Impeachment of the President." 1999. *CQ Weekly* (February 13).

Tribe, Laurence H. 1999. "And the Winner Is . . ." *New York Times* (February 12).

"The Verdict; Constitutional Justice." 1999. *New York Times* (February 13).

Weisberger, Bernard A. 1999. "Impeachment Aftermath." *American Heritage* (February).

CROSS REFERENCES

Articles of Impeachment; Sexual Harassment.

conduct unrelated to his official duties. Jones's attorneys then sought to obtain evidence for the trial. Clinton agreed to be deposed in Washington, D.C. on January 17, 1998, the first sitting president to do so. At the deposition, Jones's attorney asked Clinton whether he been involved in a sexual relationship with former White House intern Monica Lewinsky. He denied that there had been such a relationship and made other denials to questions about his conduct with Lewinsky. In written responses to interrogatories, Clinton made similar denials. Within days, the news media reported about allegations of a sexual affair between the president and the intern.

A Challenge to Impeachment

In 1989, federal judge Alcee Hastings was removed from the bench by a Senate vote, becoming the first judge in U.S. history to be impeached after being acquitted in a criminal trial. Hastings vigorously proclaimed his innocence, challenged the proceedings in court, and alleged that racism drove the proceedings.

An appointee of President Jimmy Carter, Hastings joined the U.S. District Court for the Southern District of Florida as its first African American judge in 1979. In 1981, federal prosecutors indicted him on conspiracy to accept a bribe from a Federal Bureau of Investigation agent posing as a defendant in a case before him. They charged Attorney William A. Borders, president of the National Bar Association, with offering the agent a lenient sentence from Hastings in exchange for $150,000. Borders was convicted in 1982. Hastings was acquitted in February 1983.

Hastings's troubles soon deepened. In April 1983, the U.S. Court of Appeals for the Eleventh Circuit set in motion a three-year investigation into charges that Hastings had manufactured evidence for his defense. The probe concluded that he was guilty, and in March 1987, the Judicial Conference of the United States recommended impeachment. The House of Representatives agreed. On August 3, 1988, the full House voted 413–3 to send the case to the Senate with seventeen articles of impeachment, including false testimony, fabrication of false records, and improper disclosure of confidential law enforcement information.

Hastings brought suit, seeking a preliminary injunction from the U.S. District Court for the District of Columbia (*Hastings v. United States Senate,* 716 F. Supp. 38 [1989]). In his three-part complaint, Hastings claimed that (1) the impeachment hearing was procedurally flawed because his trial would be conducted by committee and not by the full body of the Senate; (2) the impeachment hearings violated his Fifth Amendment double jeopardy rights against a second prosecution for the same crime; and (3) he was being denied effective counsel and was entitled to attorneys' fees.

The suit failed. U.S. district judge Gerhard Gesell held that (1) rule XI of the governing Rules of Procedure and Practice in the Senate When Sitting on Impeachment authorizes a committee format but does not prevent the full participation of the Senate; (2) double jeopardy principles did not apply in this case because impeachment is not a criminal proceeding and because Hastings faced separate impeachment charges; and (3) no statute provides for attorneys' fees.

In August 1989, the Senate panel heard twenty-four days of testimony. On October 20, it convicted Hastings on eight of the impeachment articles and removed him from office. Hastings left the bench continuing to profess his innocence, attacking the Senate's handling of evidence, and maintaining that he was the victim of racism.

CROSS REFERENCE

Double Jeopardy.

KENNETH STARR, the INDEPENDENT COUNSEL who was charged with investigating possible criminal activity by President Clinton and First Lady HILLARY RODHAM CLINTON in an Arkansas real estate deal ("Whitewater"), worked with Jones's attorneys to develop evidence that Clinton had lied about the affair with Lewinsky. Starr threatened to SUBPOENA Clinton to testify before a GRAND JURY about possible PERJURY and obstruction of justice, but Clinton voluntarily agreed to appear before the grand jury. On August 17, 1998, Clinton changed his story when Starr questioned him before the grand jury. Clinton admitted that he had been alone with Lewinsky and that they had engaged in "inappropriate intimate contact." Much of Clinton's grand jury testimony contradicted the sworn testimony that he had given at the Jones deposition.

Starr prepared a 453-page report and submitted it to the House of Representatives on September 11, 1998. He accused Clinton of betraying his constitutional duty by engaging in a pattern of "abundant and calculating" lies regarding his relationship with Lewinsky. The report, which contained explicit language, was released on the INTERNET a few days later. The Republican-controlled House Judiciary Committee began deliberating the possibility of impeaching Clinton. On Dec. 11, 1998, after seven days of hearings, the Judiciary Committee voted to recommend the impeachment of President Clinton. On a 21-to-16, straight, party-line vote, the committee approved an article of impeachment claiming that Clinton had committed perjury before the grand jury. The committee passed two more articles, alleging perjury in the Paula Jones suit and obstruction of justice. On December 12, it passed a fourth article, alleging that Clinton had abused his power. On December 19, the full House of Representatives impeached Clinton, charging him with "high crimes and misdemeanors" for lying under oath and obstructing justice by trying to cover up his affair with Lewinsky. The House voted largely along party lines to approve two of the four proposed articles of impeachment.

The Senate began the impeachment trial on January 14, 1999. Thirteen House members, acting as prosecutors, spent three days making opening statements, laying out the case for the Senate to convict President Clinton and to remove him from office. The team of lawyers representing President Clinton spent the following three days presenting their lines of defense. After the Senate questioned both sides for several days, it adjourned the trial until House prosecutors could be take depositions from Lewinsky and others who had been involved in the alleged perjury and obstruction of justice. The Senate, on a 70-30 vote, decided not to call Lewinsky as a witness but permitted videotape excerpts of her testimony to be played at the trial. Both sides played excerpts that it believed to be favorable to its position, which were shown to the U.S. public through the televised deliberations. Closing arguments then were presented, and the Senate moved into closed-door deliberations on February 9, 1999.

On February 19, 1999, the Senate acquitted President Clinton of the two articles of impeachment. Rejecting the perjury charge, ten Republicans and all 45 Democrats voted not guilty. On the obstruction-of-justice charge, the Senate split 50-50. After the VERDICT was announced, Clinton stated that he was "profoundly sorry" for the burden he had imposed on the Congress and the citizens of the United States.

Impeachment remains the ultimate check on the abuse of power. By providing this power to Congress, the Framers drew on a long tradition of democratic skepticism about leaders. These provisions ensure that leaders will serve the people only so long as they respect the law and their offices. In this sense, the power of impeachment also stands ready to thwart tyranny. Calls are occasionally made for reform that would streamline the impeachment process, but its rare invocation and tradition of service make such reform unlikely.

FURTHER READINGS

Aguilar, Narciso M. 2001. *Fundamentals on Impeachment.* Quezon City, Philippines: Central Lawbook.

Baron, Alan I. 1995. "The Curious Case of Alcee Hastings." *Nova Law Review* (spring).

Shea, Pegi Deitz. 2000. *The Impeachment Process.* Philadelphia: Chelsea House.

Smith, Alexa J. 1995. "Federal Judicial Impeachment: Defining Process Due." *Hastings Law Journal* 46 (January).

Strasser, Fred. 1989. "Proud, Unrepentant, Judge Hastings Exits." *The National Law Journal* (November 6).

Villadolid, Oscar S., and Alice Colet Villadolid. 2001. *The Impeachment of a President.* Manila.

CROSS REFERENCES

High Crimes and Misdemeanors; Chase, Samuel, "The Samuel Chase Impeachment Trial" (Sidebar).

IMPEDIMENT

A disability or obstruction that prevents an individual from entering into a contract.

Infancy, for example, is an impediment in making certain contracts. Impediments to MARRIAGE include such factors as CONSANGUINITY between the parties or an earlier marriage that is still valid.

IMPERSONATION

The crime of pretending to be another individual in order to deceive others and gain some advantage.

The crime of false impersonation is defined by federal statutes and by state statutes that differ from jurisdiction to jurisdiction. In some states, pretending to be someone who does not actually exist can constitute false impersonation. For example, suppose Bill attempts to evade prosecution for a crime by giving the arresting officer a fictitious name and address. In Colorado, where "[a] person who knowingly assumes a false or fictitious identity and, under that identity, does any other act intending unlawfully to gain a benefit for himself is guilty of criminal impersonation," Bill could be charged with a crime (Colo. Rev. Stat. Ann. § 18-5-113(1) [West 1996]). In this situation, the benefit Bill hopes to realize is avoiding prosecution, so that element of the offense has been satisfied. To be charged, the DEFENDANT does not need to seek a monetary benefit from the impersonation.

In New York, giving only a fictitious name does not constitute false impersonation. Under New York law, criminal impersonation is committed when an individual "[i]mpersonates another and does an act in such assumed character with intent to obtain a benefit or to injure or defraud another" (N.Y. Penal Law § 190.25 [McKinney 1996]). In other words, it is illegal to impersonate a real person, but not a fictitious one. Thus, if Carol forges Ann's name on checks made out to Ann so that Carol can cash the checks, Carol could be guilty of false impersonation—but only if Ann is a real person. Such laws are designed to protect innocent people from the losses they may incur owing to the wrongful acts of others and to restore any loss of dignity and reputation they may have suffered as a result of impersonation.

Most state laws also provide that the impersonation of a public official is a criminal act. In Texas, impersonating "a public servant with intent to induce another to submit to his pretended official authority or to rely on his pretended official acts" is a crime (Tex. Penal Code Ann. § 37.11 [West 1996]). Depending on the jurisdiction, the public servant being impersonated does not always have to actually exist. For example, suppose Carl pulls over a driver, shows her a fake police badge, and reprimands her for speeding but tells her that he will not arrest her if she pays him $50. Carl's actions constitute the crime of false impersonation, in addition to any other crimes, including extortion, that may apply to the situation. Thousands of criminal reports are filed every year by individuals victimized in various ways by persons impersonating police officers.

Under federal law, pretending to be "an officer or employee acting under the authority of the United States" in order to demand or obtain "any money, paper, document, or thing of value" can result in a fine as well as imprisonment for up to three years (18 U.S.C.A. § 912). Like state false impersonation statutes, the federal law also seeks to protect interests such as the dignity and prestige of individuals, especially those who hold federal office. Federal statutes also prohibit other types of impersonation, including pretending to be a U.S. citizen; pretending to be a U.S. officer or employee attempting to arrest or search a person or search a building; pretending to be a creditor of the United States or a foreign official; and pretending to be an agent or member of 4-H or of the Red Cross.

IMPERTINENCE

Irrelevancy; the flaw of bearing no reasonable relationship to the issues or proceeding at hand.

An *impertinent question* is one that is immaterial or has no logical relation to the issue or controversy before the court.

IMPLEADER

A procedural device used in a civil action whereby a defendant brings into the lawsuit a third party who is not already a party to the action but may ultimately be liable for the plaintiff's claim against the defendant.

Impleader is most commonly used where the third party, often an insurance company, has a duty to indemnify, or contribute to the payment of, the plaintiff's damages. An insurance policy usually provides that if the insured is sued, the insurance company will defend him or her in court and pay any damages owed if he or she is found liable in the action. For example, suppose a person slips and falls on a homeowner's property, suffers an injury, and sues the homeowner. If the homeowner has a homeowner's policy, he may implead his insurance company by filing a third-party complaint for approval by the court. If the court permits the complaint, the insurer is brought into the action. The homeowner is now both the DEFENDANT in the action and a third-party PLAINTIFF. If he is found liable and ordered to pay damages, the insurance company will be expected to pay all or part of those damages.

Impleader, which was known as VOUCHING-IN at common law, is governed by procedural rules on both the state and federal levels. "Vouching in" has its origins in the English common-law practice of "vouching to warranty." A defendant, sued by a plaintiff for the recovery of a certain piece of property, could "vouch in" another party who may have given a warranty of title when the property was sold to the defendant. Similar types of third-party actions began to appear in this country and eventually, in the interests of uniformity, a federal rule of CIVIL PROCEDURE providing for impleader was adopted. Rule 14 of the Federal Rules of Civil Procedure provides that "a defending party, as a third-party plaintiff, may cause a summons and complaint to be served upon a person not a party to the action who is or may be liable to the third-party plaintiff for all or part of the plaintiff's claim against the third-party plaintiff."

State rules of civil procedure regulate the use of impleader in actions commenced in state courts. In Connecticut, for instance, "a defendant in any CIVIL ACTION may move the court for permission to serve a writ, summons and complaint upon a person not a party to the action who is or may be liable to him for all or part of the plaintiff's claim against him" (Conn. R. Super. Ct. 117). Both federal and state court impleader rules are designed to promote judicial economy by disposing of two or more trials in one action, thus eliminating the need for the defendant to sue the third party at a later time.

A third party who is brought into an action through impleader is entitled to defend herself or himself against the claims of both the plaintiff and the defendant, raising whatever defenses may be applicable. An insurance company may allege that the policy issued to the defendant does not cover the acts that gave rise to the lawsuit and thus led the defendant to implead the company. For example, suppose Ann has been sued for allegedly assaulting Susan and has filed an impleader to have her insurance company defend her and pay any damages against her. The insurance company may refuse to defend her on the ground that the policy does not cover intentional acts, such as assaulting another person. If the court agrees, the insurance company will not have to defend Susan or pay any damages that Ann is awarded by the court or a jury.

The court has a great deal of discretion in deciding whether a defendant may implead a third party. The court considers a number of factors, including whether joining the third party will unduly complicate the action, cause delay in deciding the main action (the original suit brought by the plaintiff against the defendant), adversely affect the plaintiff, or confuse the jury. If any of these factors is present, the court may refuse to permit the impleader. The court's decision to grant or deny the impleader will be overturned by an appellate court only if it appears that the lower court abused its discretion.

FURTHER READINGS

"Pleadings and Motions, Rule 14." *Federal Rules of Civil Procedure*. Ithaca, NY: Cornell Univ. Law School.

Wicks, James M., and Marie Zweig. 1999. "Impleader Practice in New York: Does It Really Discourage Piecemeal Litigation?" *New York State Bar Journal* 71 (February): 44.

Yeazell, Stephen C. 1998. *Federal Rules of Civil Procedure 2009 Statutory Supplement*. Frederick, MD: Aspen.

IMPLIED

Inferred from circumstances; known indirectly.

In its legal application, the term *implied* is used in contrast with express, where the intention regarding the subject matter is explicitly and directly indicated. When something is implied, its meaning is derived from the words or actions of the individuals involved. For example, when one individual gives another a gift, the recipient's acceptance is implied if he or she performs acts indicating ownership, such as using the gifts.

IMPLIED CONSENT

Consent that is inferred from signs, actions, or facts, or by inaction or silence.

Implied consent differs from express consent, which is communicated by the spoken or written word.

Implied consent is a broadly based legal concept. Whether it is as valid as express consent depends on the situation and the applicable law. For example, the owner of a car generally is liable for an accident caused by someone who drove that car with his or her consent. In many states, that consent can be express or implied, and implied consent may arise from seemingly innocuous actions. For instance, a habit of leaving the keys in the car's ignition may under law imply that the owner

The most common application of implied consent is to laws prohibiting drunk driving. By using a public road, motorists imply consent to submit to tests measuring the existence of alcohol in their blood.

JUSTIN SULLIVAN/GETTY IMAGES

consents to anyone else's—even a car thief's—driving the car.

Corporations that conduct business in a foreign state—that is, any state other than the state of incorporation—impliedly consent to be bound by the laws of the foreign state and to be subject to the foreign state's jurisdiction. The rationale supporting this application of the implied consent rule is basic: a corporation that reaps the benefits of conducting business in a state also should be subject to the laws and the courts of that state. The fact that the corporation has business in the foreign state is all that is needed for a finding of implied consent.

Implied consent as the result of inaction is most commonly found in litigation procedures. For instance, a party to a lawsuit may have the legal right to object to a court hearing that is scheduled to occur before the party has obtained certain crucial documents. But if the party appears at the hearing and allows it to proceed without objecting, the party has waived the right to later object or appeal. By failing to take action to cancel or reschedule the hearing, the party is said to have implied its consent to the hearing.

Perhaps the best known—and most often litigated—application of implied consent involves laws prohibiting driving while intoxicated. Most states have legislation that subjects motorists suspected of driving while under the influence of alcohol or illicit drugs to blood, breath, or urine tests. These chemical tests can confirm the existence and the level of drugs or alcohol in a driver's body, and can be used as evidence against the driver. Pursuant to these

state statutes, known as implied consent laws, anyone who drives on public roads or highways has, by that action, impliedly consented to such tests. Once stopped or arrested for suspicion of driving while impaired, a person must submit to a test or face revocation or suspension of his or her driver's license.

Implied consent statutes have been attacked for a variety of constitutional reasons, usually unsuccessfully. Courts have held that the statutes do not violate a driver's FOURTH AMENDMENT protection from unreasonable SEARCH AND SEIZURE, or FIFTH AMENDMENT right against SELF-INCRIMINATION. The statutes usually are upheld on due process grounds, although courts have struck down statutes that permit the revocation of a license without a hearing. Arguments that implied consent laws are an invasion of privacy or an undue burden on interstate commerce have also been rejected by the courts.

Courts generally look to one of two theories supporting the validity of implied consent laws. According to the first theory, driving on public roads and highways is a privilege, not a right. Only those who adhere to state laws, including laws prohibiting driving while intoxicated, are entitled to the driving privilege. Under the second theory, courts consider implied consent laws to be a reasonable regulation of driving pursuant to the state's POLICE POWER, so long as the laws do not violate due process. Courts have weighed the interests of society against the interests of individuals, and have determined that drunk or drug-impaired drivers are enough of a danger to society that a slight infringement on the liberty of individuals is justifiable.

The liberty of individuals is protected somewhat by the requirement that before a law officer can request a blood, urine, or breath test, the officer must have reasonable grounds to believe that the driver is intoxicated. What constitutes reasonable grounds is determined on a case-by-case basis. If a driver loses her or his license after refusing to comply with a chemical test and a court later finds that reasonable grounds for the test did not exist, the court can invalidate the revocation or suspension of the license.

Courts generally hold that a revocation or suspension of a license caused by a driver's refusal to test for drugs or alcohol is separate and distinct from a prosecution for driving while intoxicated. Therefore, in most states, it makes no difference whether a driver pleads guilty to, is convicted of, or is acquitted of the crime: refusing to take a test for chemical impairment may result in a revoked or suspended license, and this punishment must be paid despite a subsequent acquittal of driving while intoxicated or in addition to any punishment that comes as a result of a conviction.

Many states require that a law officer warn a driver of the consequences of refusing to take a chemical test, and if that warning is not given, the license cannot be revoked or suspended. Some states offer drivers a limited right to consult an attorney before deciding whether to take a sobriety test. This right is not absolute, since a significant delay would render ineffective a blood, urine, or alcohol test. Several states offer drivers the opportunity for a second opinion—the right to have an additional test performed by the driver's choice of physicians.

States differ in their approach to implied consent laws, but their goal is the same: keeping dangerously impaired drivers off the roads. Courts and legislatures are reluctant to frustrate this goal.

FURTHER READINGS

Faden, Ruth R., and Tom L. Beauchamp. 1986. *A History and Theory of Informed Consent.* New York: Oxford Univ. Press.

Fuller, M. Elizabeth. 1985. "Implied Consent Statutes: What Is Refusal?" *American Journal of Trial Advocacy* 9 (spring).

Implied Consent.org Web site. 2009. Available online at http://www.impliedconsent.org/ (accessed September 4, 2009).

CROSS REFERENCE

Automobiles.

IMPLIED WARRANTY

A promise, arising by operation of law, that something that is sold will be merchantable and fit for the purpose for which it is sold.

Every time goods are bought and sold, a sales contract is created: the buyer agrees to pay, and the seller agrees to accept, a certain price in exchange for a certain item or number of items. Sales contracts are frequently oral, unwritten agreements. The purchase of items such as a candy bar hardly seems worth the trouble of drafting an agreement spelling out the buyer's expectation that the candy bar will be fresh and edible. Implied warranties protect the buyer whether or not a written sales contract exists.

Implied Warranty of Merchantability

Implied warranties come in two general types: merchantability and fitness. An implied warranty of merchantability is an unwritten and unspoken guarantee to the buyer that goods purchased conform to ordinary standards of care and that they are of the same average grade, quality, and value as similar goods sold under similar circumstances. In other words, merchantable goods are goods fit for the ordinary purposes for which they are to be used. The UNIFORM COMMERCIAL CODE (UCC), adopted by most states, provides that courts may imply a warranty of merchantability when (1) the seller is the merchant of such goods, and (2) the buyer uses the goods for the ordinary purposes for which such goods are sold (§ 2-314). Thus, a buyer can sue a seller for breaching the implied warranty by selling goods unfit for their ordinary purpose.

There is rarely any question as to whether the seller is the merchant of the goods sold. Nevertheless, in *Huprich v. Bitto*, 667 So.2d 685 (Ala. 1995), a farmer who sold defective horse feed was found not to be a merchant of horse feed. The court stated that the farmer did not hold himself out as having knowledge or skill peculiar to the sale of corn as horse feed, and therefore was not a merchant of horse feed for purposes of determining a breach of implied warranty of merchantability.

The question of whether goods are fit for their ordinary purpose is much more frequently litigated. Thomas Coffer sued the manufacturer of a jar of mixed nuts after he bit down on an unshelled filbert, believing it to have been shelled, and damaged a tooth. Coffer argued in part that the presence of the unshelled nut among shelled nuts was a breach of the implied warranty of merchantability. Unquestionably, Coffer was using the nuts for their ordinary purpose when he ate them, and unquestionably, he suffered a dental injury when he bit the filbert's hard shell. But the North Carolina appellate court held that the jar of mixed nuts was nonetheless fit for the ordinary purpose for which jars of mixed nuts are used (*Coffer v. Standard Brands*, 30 N.C. App. 134, 226 S.E.2d 534 [1976]). The court consulted the state agriculture board's regulations and noted that the peanut industry allows a small amount of unshelled nuts to be included with shelled nuts without rendering the shelled nuts inedible or adulterated. The court also noted that shells are a natural incident to nuts.

The policy behind the implied warranty of merchantability is basic: sellers are generally better suited than buyers to determine whether a product will perform properly. Holding the seller liable for a product that is not fit for its ordinary purpose shifts the costs of nonperformance from the buyer to the seller. This motivates the seller to ensure the product's proper performance before placing it on the market. The seller is better able to absorb the costs of a product's nonperformance, usually by spreading the risk to consumers in the form of increased prices.

The policy behind limiting the implied warranty of merchantability to the goods' ordinary use is also straightforward: a seller may not have sufficient expertise or control over a product to ensure that it will perform properly when used for nonstandard purposes.

Implied Warranty of Fitness

When a buyer wishes to use goods for a particular, nonordinary purpose, the UCC provides a distinct implied warranty of fitness (§ 2-315). Unlike the implied warranty of merchantability, the implied warranty of fitness does not contain a requirement that the seller be a merchant with respect to the goods sold. It merely requires that the seller possess knowledge and expertise on which the buyer may rely.

For example, one court found that horse buyers who indicated to the sellers their intention to use the horse for breeding were using the horse for a particular, nonordinary purpose (*Whitehouse v. Lange*, 128 Idaho 129, 910 P.2d 801 [1996]). The buyers soon discovered that the horse they purchased was incapable of reproducing. Because the court found this use of the horse to be nonordinary, the buyers were entitled to an implied warranty of fitness.

Before a court will imply a warranty of fitness, three requirements must be met: (1) the seller must have reason to know of the buyer's particular purpose for the goods; (2) the seller must have reason to know of the buyer's reliance on the seller's skill and knowledge in furnishing the appropriate goods; and (3) the buyer must, in fact, rely on the seller's skill and knowledge. Even when these requirements are met, courts will not imply a warranty of fitness under certain circumstances. A buyer

who specifies a particular brand of goods is not entitled to an implied warranty of fitness. Also, a buyer who has greater expertise than the seller regarding the goods generally is precluded from asserting an implied warranty of fitness, as is a buyer who provides the seller with specifications, such as a blueprint or design plan, detailing the types of material to be used in the goods.

FURTHER READINGS

Biddle, Arthur. 2009. *A Treatise on the Law of Warranties in the Sale of Chattels.* Charleston, SC: BiblioBazaar.

Davidson, Charles Darwin. 2006. "Often Overlooked Implied Warranties Apply to a Host of Sales." *Arkansas Business* (June 27).

Gonzales, Vincent M. 1987. "The Buyer's Specifications Exception to the Implied Warranty of Fitness for a Particular Purpose: Design or Performance?" *California Law Review* 61 (November).

IMPORT QUOTAS

Import quotas are a form of protectionism. An import quota fixes the quantity of a particular good that foreign producers may bring into a country over a specific period, usually a year. The U.S. government imposes quotas to protect domestic industries from foreign competition. Import quotas are usually justified as a means of protecting workers who otherwise might be laid off. They also can raise prices for the consumer by reducing the amount of cheaper, foreign-made goods imported and thus reducing competition for domestic industries of the same goods.

The GENERAL AGREEMENT ON TARIFFS AND TRADE (GATT) (61 Stat. A3, T.I.A.S. No. 1700, 55 U.N. T.S. 187), which was opened for signatures on October 30, 1947, is the principal international multilateral agreement regulating world trade. GATT members were required to sign the Protocol of Provisions Application of the General Agreement on Tariffs and Trades (61 Stat. A2051, T.I.A.S. No. 1700, 55 U.N.T.S. 308). The Protocol of Provisions set forth the rules governing GATT and it also governs import quotas. This agreement became effective January 1, 1948, and the United States is still bound by it. GATT has been renegotiated seven times since its inception; the most recent version became effective July 1, 1995, with 123 signatories.

Import quotas once played a much greater role in global trade, but the 1995 renegotiation of GATT has made it increasingly difficult for a country to introduce them. Nations can no longer impose temporary quotas to offset surges in imports from foreign markets. Furthermore, an import quota that is introduced to protect a domestic industry from foreign imports is limited to at least the average import of the same goods over the last three years. In addition, the 1995 GATT agreement identifies the country of an import's origin in order to prevent countries from exporting goods to another nation through a third nation that does not have the same import quotas. GATT also requires that all import quota trade barriers be converted into tariff equivalents. Therefore, although a nation cannot seek to deter trade by imposing arbitrary import quotas, it may increase the tariffs associated with a particular import.

In the United States, the decade from the mid-1980s to the mid-1990s saw import quotas placed on textiles, agricultural products, automobiles, sugar, beef, bananas, and even underwear—among other things. In a single session of Congress in 1985, more than 300 protectionist bills were introduced as U.S. industries began voicing concern over foreign competition.

Many U.S. companies headquartered in the United States rely on manufacturing facilities outside of the country to produce their goods. Because of import quotas, some of these companies cannot get their own products back into the United States. While such companies lobby Congress to change what they consider to be an unfair practice, their opposition argues that this is the price to be paid for giving away U.S. jobs to foreign countries.

Nearly every country restricts imports of foreign goods. For example, in 1996—even after the new version of GATT went into effect—Vietnam restricted the amount of cement, fertilizer, and fuel and the number of automobiles and motorcycles it would import. The import quotas of foreign countries can adversely affect U.S. industries that try to sell their goods abroad. The U.S. economy has suffered because of foreign import quotas on canned fruit, cigarettes, leather, insurance, and computers. In a market that has become overcrowded with U.S. entertainment, the European Communities have chosen to enforce import quotas on U.S.-made films and television in an effort to encourage Europe's own industries to become more competitive.

FURTHER READINGS

Benenson, Bob. 1994. "Free Trade Carries the Day As GATT Easily Passes." *Congressional Quarterly Weekly Report* 52 (November 26).

Prepared testimony of Allan I. Mendelowitz. 1995. Federal News Service, congressional hearings testimony (June 14).

"Provisions: GATT Implementing Bill." 1994. *Congressional Quarterly Weekly Report* 52 (November 26).

Reinke, John J. 1985. "An Analysis of the Conflicts between Congressional Import Quotas and the General Agreement on Tariffs and Trade." *Fordham International Law Journal* 9.

IMPOSSIBILITY

A legal excuse or defense to an action for the breach of a contract; less frequently, a defense to a criminal charge of an attempted crime, such as attempted robbery or murder.

Historically, a person who entered a contract was bound to perform according to his or her promised duties, regardless of whether it became impossible to do so. Thus, early U.S. courts did not recognize the defense of impossibility of performance. Courts noted that if the parties to a contract had desired to take into account any events that may develop after they reached an agreement, then they should have accounted for such contingencies in the contract.

As contract law developed over the twentieth century—and in response to increasing commercial activities—courts began to recognize impossibility as a valid defense to an action for breach of a contract. This defense did not normally apply if one party found it unexpectedly difficult or expensive to perform according to the contract; rather, it applied only when the basis or subject matter of the contract was destroyed or no longer existed. In addition, the defense of impossibility became available only if objective impossibility existed. Objective impossibility occurred when the contractual obligation could not actually be performed. Objective impossibility is often referred to by the statement "The thing cannot be done." For example, if a musician promised to play a concert at a specific concert hall but the concert hall subsequently burned down, it would be impossible to perform according to the contractual agreement and the musician would be excused from performing at that particular venue. Subjective impossibility exists when only one of the parties to a contract subjectively believes that she or he cannot complete the required performance. For example, if a musician believed that he had not practiced sufficiently to perform a successful concert, this belief would not excuse the musician from performing the concert. The statement "I cannot do it" frequently refers to the state of mind present in a case involving subjective impossibility.

Modern U.S. law uses the term *impracticability* synonymously with the term *impossibility*, primarily because some things may not be absolutely impossible to perform but are nevertheless impracticable to complete. Thus, the general rule is that a thing may be impossible to perform when it would not be practicable to perform. A contractual obligation is impracticable "when it can only be done at an excessive and unreasonable cost" (*Transatlantic Financing Corp. v. United States,* 363 F.2d 312 [D.C. Cir. 1966]).

When a party raises the defense of impracticability, courts generally determine three things: first, whether something unexpected occurred after the parties entered the contract; second, whether the parties had assumed that this thing would not occur; and third, that the unexpected occurrence made performance of the contract impracticable. Some widely recognized occurrences that would normally provide a defense of impracticability are the death or illness of one of the necessary parties, the unforeseeable destruction of the subject matter of the contract (perhaps by an "act of God"), or a supervening illegality.

Impossibility has been used as a defense to charges of attempted crimes. Historically, courts recognized that a party could not be convicted of criminal attempt if the actual crime was legally impossible to accomplish. For example, if a person was accused of attempting to receive stolen property but the property was not actually stolen, the defense of legal impossibility could arise. Legal impossibility is distinguished from factual impossibility, where facts unknown to the person attempting to commit a crime render the crime factually impossible to complete. For example, if a pickpocket attempts to steal a wallet but no wallet is present, factual impossibility may exist. Courts generally have recognized legal impossibility as a defense to a criminal attempt, but not factual impossibility. They reasoned that because a person attempting to commit a crime had formed the required intent to commit the crime, it was irrelevant that the crime was factually impossible to complete.

Impossibility as a defense to a criminal attempt has largely been rejected by modern U.S. statutes and courts. The Model Penal Code—which many states have adopted since its introduction in 1962—expressly rejects impossibility as a defense to the charge of criminal attempt (§ 5.01 [1995]).

FURTHER READINGS

Bello, Christopher. 1985. "Construction and Application of State Statute Governing Impossibility of Consummation as Defense to Prosecution for Attempt to Commit Crime." *American Law Review* 41.

Berliant, Marcus, and Paul Rothstein. 2003. "Possibility, Impossibility, and History In the Origins of the Marriage Tax." *National Tax Journal* 56 (June). Available online at http://www.entrepreneur.com/tradejournals/article/106701001.html; website home page: http://www.entrepreneur.com (accessed August 1, 2009).

"Modern Status of the Rules Regarding Impossibility of Performance as Defense in Action for Breach of Contract." 1962. *American Law Reports* 84.

IMPOSTOR RULE

Under Uniform Commercial Code, Article 3, Sect. 404(a), a rule stating that if an impostor endorses a negotiable instrument and receives payment in good faith, the drawer of the instrument is responsible for the loss. An example would be if an individual impersonates a person for whom a check has been cut or misrepresents himself as that person's agent. If the impostor receives the check, endorses it, and cashes it at the drawer's bank, the drawer is responsible for the loss, because the bank accepted the endorsement in good faith. The bank may be responsible for a percentage of the loss if it failed to exercise "ordinary care"; for example, if the bank did not check the impostor's identification. The imposter rule is based on the assumption that between the bank and the drawer, the drawer is in a better position to prevent the loss. Also spelled imposter rule.

IMPOSTS

Taxes or duties; taxes levied by the government on imported goods.

Although *impost* is a generic term, which can be used in reference to all taxes, it is most frequently used interchangeably with CUSTOMS DUTIES.

IMPOUNDMENT

An action taken by the president in which he or she proposes not to spend all or part of a sum of money appropriated by Congress.

The current rules and procedures for impoundment were created by the Congressional Budget and Impoundment Control Act of 1974 (2 U.S.C.A. § 601 et seq.), which was passed to reform the congressional budget process and to resolve conflicts between Congress and President RICHARD M. NIXON concerning the power of the executive branch to impound funds appropriated by Congress. Past presidents, beginning with THOMAS JEFFERSON, had impounded funds at various times for various reasons, without instigating any significant conflict between the executive and the legislative branches. At times, such as when the original purpose for the money no longer existed or when money could be saved through more efficient operations, Congress simply acquiesced to the president's wishes. At other times, Congress or the designated recipient of the impounded funds challenged the president's action, and the parties negotiated until a political settlement was reached.

Changes during the Nixon Administration

The history of accepting or resolving impoundments broke down during the Nixon administration for several reasons. First, President Nixon impounded much greater sums than had previous presidents, proposing to hold back between 17 and 20 percent of controllable expenditures between 1969 and 1972. Second, Nixon used impoundments to try to fight policy initiatives that he disagreed with, attempting to terminate entire programs by impounding their appropriations. Third, Nixon claimed that as president, he had the constitutional right to impound funds appropriated by Congress, thus threatening Congress's greatest political strength: its power over the purse. Nixon claimed, "The Constitutional right of the President of the United States to impound funds, and that is not to spend money, when the spending of money would mean either increasing prices or increasing taxes for all the people—that right is absolutely clear."

In the face of Nixon's claim to impoundment authority and his refusal to release appropriated funds, Congress in 1974 passed the Congressional Budget and Impoundment Control Act, which reformed the congressional budget process and established rules and procedures for presidential impoundment. In general, the provisions of the act were designed to curtail the power of the president in the budget process, which had been steadily growing throughout the twentieth century.

The Impoundment Control Act divides impoundments into two categories: deferrals and rescissions. In a deferral, the president asks Congress to delay the release of appropriated funds; in a rescission, the president asks Congress to cancel the appropriation of funds altogether. Congress and the president must follow specific rules and procedures for each type of impoundment.

Deferrals

To propose a deferral, the president must send Congress a request identifying the amount of money to be deferred, the program that will be affected, the reasons for the deferral, the estimated fiscal and program effects of the deferral, and the length of time for which the funds are to be deferred. Funds cannot be deferred beyond the end of the fiscal year, or for so long that the affected agency could no longer spend the funds prudently.

In the original Impoundment Control Act, the president was allowed to defer funds for any reason, including opposition to a specific program or for general policy goals, such as curtailing federal spending. Congress retained the right to review deferrals, and a deferral could be rejected if either the House or the Senate voted to disapprove it. In 1986 several members of Congress and a number of cities successfully challenged the constitutionality of these deferral procedures in *City of New Haven v. United States,* 809 F.2d 900 (D.C. Cir. 1987). *New Haven* was based on a 1981 case, *INS v. Chadha,* 454 U.S. 812, 102 S. Ct. 87, 70 L. Ed. 2d 80, in which the Supreme Court ruled that one-house vetoes of proposed presidential actions are unconstitutional. The *Chadha* ruling invalidated Congress's right to review and disapprove deferrals. In response, Congress took away most of the president's deferral power through provisions in the Balanced Budget and Emergency Deficit Control Reaffirmation Act of 1987 (2 U.S.C.A. § 901 et seq.) (otherwise known as Gramm-Rudman-Hollings II). These provisions allow presidential impoundment for only three reasons: to provide for special contingencies, to achieve savings through more efficient operations, and when such deferrals are specifically provided for by law. The president can no longer defer funds for policy reasons.

Once the president sends a message to Congress requesting a deferral, the comptroller general must submit a report on the proposed deferral to Congress. A proposed deferral is automatically considered to be approved unless the House or the Senate passes legislation specifically disapproving it. If the president still refuses to spend appropriated funds after Congress has formally disapproved of a deferral, the comptroller general has the power to sue the president in federal court.

Rescissions

The rules and procedures for rescissions are very similar to those for deferrals. As with a deferral, the president must send Congress a message proposing a rescission. In this message, the president must detail how much money is to be rescinded, the department or agency that was targeted to receive the money, the specific project or projects that will be affected by the rescission, and the reasons for the rescission. The comptroller general handles a rescission as she or he would a deferral, preparing a report on the rescission for Congress. Unlike a deferral, a rescission must be specifically approved by both houses of Congress within forty-five legislative days after the message requesting the rescission is received. Congress can approve all, part, or none of the proposed rescission. If either house disapproves the rescission or takes no action on it, the president must spend the appropriated funds as originally intended. If the president refuses to do so, the comptroller general can sue the president in federal court.

Legislative Line Item Veto Act of 1995

The Legislative Line Item Veto Act of 1995 (Pub. L. No. 104-130, 110 Stat. 1200), signed by President BILL CLINTON on April 9, 1996, and made effective January 1, 1997, affects the way impoundments are handled. The Line Item Veto Act does not actually give the president the authority to veto individual line items, which would require a CONSTITUTIONAL AMENDMENT. It does, however, give the president the functional equivalent, allowing the president to veto, or rescind, specific items in appropriations bills, as well as targeted tax breaks affecting one hundred or fewer people and new entitlement programs. The president proposes these rescissions to Congress and they become effective in 30 days unless Congress passes a bill rejecting them. The president can in turn veto any congressional bill of disapproval, and Congress can override that veto with a two-thirds vote in both houses. Under the Line Item Veto Act, therefore, Congress still retains the ultimate power to override the president's rescission requests, but the president enjoys significantly enhanced rescission authority.

FURTHER READINGS

Collender, Stanley E. 1994. *The Guide to the Federal Budget, Fiscal 1995.* Washington, D.C.: Urban Institute Press.

Pfiffner, James P. 1979. *The President, the Budget, and Congress: Impoundment and the 1974 Budget Act.* Boulder, CO: Westview.

Schick, Allen. 2007. *The Federal Budget: Politics, Policy, Process.* Baltimore, MD: Hopkins Fulfillment Services.

Shuman, Howard E. 1984. *Politics and the Budget.* Englewood Cliffs, NJ: Prentice-Hall.

CROSS REFERENCES

Congress of the United States; Federal Budget; Separation of Powers.

IMPRACTICABILITY

Substantial difficulty or inconvenience in following a particular course of action, but not such insurmountability or hopelessness as to make performance impossible.

Rule 23 of the Federal Rules of CIVIL PROCEDURE establishes impracticability as one of the grounds for permitting a CLASS ACTION in federal courts. "[T]he class is so numerous that joinder of all members is impracticable." In such a situation, the court will permit a few individuals who have made a motion to it to represent in one lawsuit a large number of persons who will be similarly affected by the legal outcome of the particular action. The group to be represented must be so large that there would be significant problems or impracticability in bringing each member before the court to appear as a party to the action. For purposes of certification as a class, the prospective representatives must show that joinder can be accomplished only with substantial difficulty, expense, and hardship, but not that such joinder cannot be done at all. State procedural rules also require that joinder of all prospective class members be impracticable before permitting the commencement of a class action in state courts.

In the law governing sales, the UNIFORM COMMERCIAL CODE allows either party to a contract to be excused from the legal obligations created by it where performance becomes impracticable because an unexpected event has occurred, such as a severe shortage of supplies due to unexpected and continual flooding.

CROSS REFERENCE

Impossibility.

IMPRIMATUR

[Latin, Let it be printed.] A license or allowance, granted by the constituted authorities, giving permission to print and publish a book. This allowance was formerly necessary in England before any book could lawfully be printed, and in some other countries is still required.

IMPRISONMENT

Incarceration; the act of restraining the personal liberty of an individual; confinement in a prison.

Imprisonment can be effected without the application of physical restraint by verbal compulsion coupled with the display of available force. The tort of FALSE IMPRISONMENT involves the illegal arrest or detention of an individual without a warrant, by an illegal warrant, or by an illegally executed warrant, either in a prison or any place used temporarily for such purpose, or by force and constraint without actual confinement.

IMPROVEMENTS

Additions or alterations to real property that increase the value thereof.

Improvements to land, for example, might include the planting of crops, the construction of fences, and the digging of wells.

IMPUTED

Attributed vicariously.

In the legal sense, the term *imputed* is used to describe an action, fact, or quality, the knowledge of which is charged to an individual based upon the actions of another for whom the individual is responsible rather than on the individual's own acts or omissions. For example, in the law of agency, the actions of an agent performed during the COURSE OF EMPLOYMENT will be attributed to the agent's principal. The doctrine of imputed NEGLIGENCE makes one person legally responsible for the negligent conduct of another.

IMPUTED KNOWLEDGE

The comprehension attributed or charged to a person because the facts in issue were open to discovery and it was that person's duty to apprise himself or herself of them; more accurately described as knowledge.

For example, if the stairway leading to a retail store is defective and a patron is injured on the stairway, the store owner cannot evade liability for the patron's injury by denying knowledge of the defect. Because the store owner is subject to a duty to discover and rectify the defect in an area known to be used by the public, knowledge of the defect is imputed to the store owner.

In the law of agency, notice of facts brought to the attention of an agent (a person authorized by another, known as a principal, to act for him or her), within the scope of the agent's authority or employment, is usually imputed to his or her principal.

IMPUTED NOTICE

Information regarding particular facts or circumstances that the law permits to affect the legal rights of a person who has no firsthand knowledge of them but who should have learned of them because his or her agent or representative had direct knowledge of that information and a duty to report it to him or her.

IN BLANK

Absent limitation or restriction.

The term *in blank* is used in reference to negotiable instruments, such as checks or promissory notes. When such COMMERCIAL PAPER is endorsed in blank, the designated payee signs his or her name only. The paper is not made payable to any one individual in particular, but anyone who presents it for payment is entitled to be paid.

IN CAMERA

In chambers; in private. A judicial proceeding is said to be heard in camera *either when the hearing is had before the judge in his or her private chambers or when all spectators are excluded from the courtroom.*

IN COMMON

Shared in respect to title, use, or enjoyment; without apportionment or division into individual parts. Held by several for the equal advantage, use, or enjoyment of all.

A TENANCY IN COMMON is ownership of real property by two or more persons, each of whom holds an undivided interest in such property.

IN EVIDENCE

Facts, documents, or exhibits that have been introduced before and accepted by the court for consideration as probative matter.

IN EXTREMIS

[Latin, In extremity.] A term used in reference to the last illness prior to death.

A CAUSA MORTIS gift is made by an individual who is in extremis.

IN FORMA PAUPERIS

[Latin, In the character or manner of a pauper.] A phrase that indicates the permission given by a court to an indigent to initiate a legal action without having to pay for court fees or costs due to his or her lack of financial resources.

IN KIND

Of the same class, category, or species.

A loan is repaid *in kind* when a substantially similar article is returned by the borrower to the lender.

IN LIEU OF

Instead of; in place of; in substitution of. It does not mean in addition to.

IN LOCO PARENTIS

In loco parentis *is a Latin phrase that can be translated in English as "in the place of a parent." The phrase refers to the legal doctrine under which an individual assumes parental rights, duties, and obligations regarding a child without going through the formalities of legal adoption.*

In loco parentis is a legal doctrine describing a relationship similar to that of a parent to a child. It refers to an individual who assumes parental status and responsibilities for another individual, usually a young person, without formally adopting that person. For example, legal guardians are said to stand in LOCO PARENTIS with respect to their wards, creating a

relationship that has special implications for insurance and workers' compensation law.

By far the most common usage of in loco parentis pertains to teachers and students. For hundreds of years, the English common-law concept shaped the rights and responsibilities of public school teachers: Until the late nineteenth century, their legal authority over students was as broad as that of parents. Changes in U.S. education, concurrent with a broader reading by courts of the rights of students, had brought the concept into disrepute by the 1960s. Cultural changes, however, brought a resurgence of the doctrine in the twenty-first century.

Taking root in colonial American schools, in loco parentis was an idea derived from English common law. The colonists borrowed it from the English ideal of schools having not only educational but also moral responsibility for students. The idea especially suited the puritanical values of the colonists, and after the American Revolution, it persisted in elementary and high schools, colleges, and universities. The judiciary respected it: Like their English counterparts, U.S. courts in the nineteenth century were unwilling to interfere when students brought grievances, particularly regarding rules, discipline, and expulsion.

In 1866, for instance, one court stated, "A discretionary power has been given, ... [and] we have no more authority to interfere than we have to control the domestic discipline of a father in his family" (*People ex rel. Pratt v. Wheaton College*, 40 Ill. 186). Well into the twentieth century, courts permitted broad authority to schools and showed hostility to the claims of student plaintiffs. In dismissing a claim by a restaurant owner against a college, the Kentucky Supreme Court found that a college's duties under in loco parentis gave it the power to forbid students to patronize the restaurant (*Gott v. Berea College*, 156 Ky. 376, 161 S.W. 204 [1913]).

Two important shifts in society and law diminished the effect of the doctrine. One was the evolution of educational standards. Beginning in the late 1800s and advancing rapidly during the mid-1900s, the increasing secularization of schools brought an emphasis on practical education over moral instruction. At a slower rate, courts adapted to this change, according greater rights to students than were previously recognized.

The first to benefit were students in higher education, through rulings such as the landmark *Dixon v. Alabama State Board of Education* (294 F.2d 150 [5th Cir. 1961]). In *Dixon,* the U.S. Court of Appeals for the Fifth Circuit extended due process rights to students at tax-supported colleges, ruling that the Constitution "requires notice and some opportunity for hearing" before students can be expelled for misconduct. After *Dixon,* courts largely turned to contract law for adjudicating disputes between students and their institutions.

Other changes came as well. Partly in reaction to free speech movements, courts began to recognize that students at public colleges and universities, as well as public secondary schools, were entitled to full enjoyment of their First and FOURTH AMENDMENT rights. For example, in ruling that high school students could not be expelled for wearing black armbands to protest the VIETNAM WAR, the U.S. Supreme Court held, in 1969, that students do not "shed their constitutional rights … at the schoolhouse gate" (*Tinker v. Des Moines Independent Community School District*, 393 U.S. 503, 89 S. Ct. 733, 21 L. Ed. 2d 731). In 1975, the Court held in *Goss v. Lopez* (419 U.S. 565, 95 S. Ct. 729, 42 L. Ed. 2d 725) that the suspension of high school students for alleged disruptive or disobedient conduct required some sort of notice of charges and a prior hearing.

But the underlying premise of in loco parentis did not disappear completely from public schools. For example, in 1977 the Supreme Court held that the disciplinary paddling of public school students was not a CRUEL AND UNUSUAL PUNISHMENT prohibited by the EIGHTH AMENDMENT (*Ingraham v. Wright*, 430 U.S. 651, 97 S. Ct. 1401, 51 L. Ed. 2d 711) and that students who were disciplined in a school setting were not denied due process under the FOURTEENTH AMENDMENT. Since then, several cases have challenged this ruling, and U.S. district courts have attempted to clarify the rights of students regarding CORPORAL PUNISHMENT (*Hall v. Tawney*, 621 F. 2d 607, 613 [4th Cir. 1980]; *Garcia v. Miera*, 817 F. 2d 650, 653 [10th Cir. 1987]; and *Neal ex real. Neal v. Fulton County Board of Education* 229 F. 3d 1069 [11th Cir. 2000]).

In the 1980s, new issues involving the in loco parentis doctrine arose at public schools, colleges, and universities. The Reagan administration's war on drugs led to the passage of the Drug-Free Schools and Campuses Act of 1989 (Pub. L. 101-226, December 12, 1989, 103 Stat. 1928). The act bans the unlawful use, possession, or distribution of drugs and alcohol by students and employees on school grounds and college campuses. As a result, most campuses began to enforce ZERO TOLERANCE drug polices. In 1995 the Supreme Court ruled that high schools were permitted to conduct random drug testing of student athletes (*Vernonia School District v. Acton*, 515 U.S. 646, 115 S. Ct. 2386, 132 L. Ed. 2d 564). According to the Court, such testing does not violate the reasonable SEARCH AND SEIZURE clause of the Fourth Amendment because students in school are under state supervision, and as such, the state (and the school) is responsible for their well-being. The Court extended permissable drug testing to any student who wishes to participate in extracurricular activities in *Board of Education, Pottawatomie County v. Earls* (536 U. S. 822, 122 S. Ct. 2559, 153 L. Ed. 2d 735 [2002]).

By the 1990s and into the 2000s, the loco parentis doctrine seemed to be in full force as schools attempted to safeguard students. Many institutions enacted controversial rules governing dress codes and so-called hate speech, all in the name of protecting students. Violence on campuses, however, became a very real threat. In 1994 Congress enacted a federal policy toward weapons on school grounds when it passed the Gun-Free Schools Act of 1994 (Pub. L. 103-382, Title I, § 101, October 20, 1994, 198 Stat. 3907). According to the act, schools are required to expel students who are found in possession of a gun. After the 1999 Columbine, Colorado, shootings, reinforcement of this act escalated, and schools enforced zero tolerance policies toward the possession of any article that may pose a potential threat. As a result, students have been expelled from school for having such items as nail files, plastic knives, and model rockets. Although many students and parents filed lawsuits in protest, most cases were denied since, according to the courts, school authorities have the right to maintain school safety.

FURTHER READINGS

Bickel, Robert D., and Peter F. Lake. 1999. *The Rights and Responsibilities of Modern Universities: Who Assumes the Risk of College Life?* Durham, N.C.: Carolina Academic Press.

Fellmeth, Robert. 2006. *Child Rights & Remedies: How the U.S. Legal System Affects Children.* 2d. ed. Atlanta: Clarity Press.

Lake, Peter F. 2001. "The Special Relationship(s): Between a College and a Student: Law and Policy Ramifications for the Post In Loco Parentis College." *Idaho Law Review* 37 (summer): 531–55.

Pardeck, John. 2006 *Children's Rights: Policy and Practice.* 2d. ed. New York: Routledge.

Ramsey, Sarah, and Douglas Abrams. 2008. *Children and the Law in a Nutshell.* 3d. ed. St. Paul, Minn.: West.

CROSS REFERENCES

Children's Rights; Colleges and Universities; Guardian and Ward; Infants; Juvenile Law; Schools and School Districts.

IN MEDIAS RES

[Latin, Into the heart of the subject, without preface or introduction.]

IN PARI DELICTO

[Latin, In equal fault.] A descriptive phrase that indicates that parties involved in an action are equally culpable for a wrong.

When the parties to a legal controversy are *in pari delicto,* neither can obtain affirmative relief from the court, because both are at equal fault or of equal guilt. They will remain in the same situation they were in prior to the commencement of the action.

IN PARI MATERIA

[Latin, Upon the same subject.] A designation applied to statutes or general laws that were enacted at different times but pertain to the same subject or object.

Statutes *in pari materia* must be interpreted in light of each other because they have a common purpose for comparable events or items.

IN PERPETUITY

Of endless duration; not subject to termination.

The phrase *in perpetuity* is often used in the grant of an easement to a utility company.

IN PERSONAM

[Latin, Against the person.] A lawsuit seeking a judgment to be enforceable specifically against an individual person.

An *in personam* action can affect the defendant's personal rights and interests and substantially all of his or her property. It is based on the authority of the court, or jurisdiction, over the person as an individual rather than jurisdiction over specific property

owned by the person. This contrasts with in rem jurisdiction, or actions that are limited to property of the DEFENDANT that is within the control of the court. A court with *in personam* jurisdiction in a particular case has enough power over the defendant and his or her property to grant a judgment affecting the defendant in almost any way.

IN RE

[Latin, In the matter of.] Concerning or regarding. The usual style for the name of a judicial proceeding having some item of property at the center of the dispute rather than adverse parties.

For example, proceedings to determine various claims to the assets of a bankrupt company could be called *In re Klein Company,* or *In the matter of Klein Company.*

Sometimes *in re* is used for a proceeding where one party makes an application to the court without necessarily charging an adversary. This may be done, for example, where a couple seeks to adopt a child or an adult wants to change his or her name.

Such actions may instead use the English translation "in the matter of" or the Latin words ex parte. The final decision on the style to be used for a particular lawsuit is usually made by the clerk of the court.

IN REM

[Latin, In the thing itself.] A lawsuit against an item of property, not against a person (in personam).

An action *in rem* is a proceeding that takes no notice of the owner of the property but determines rights in the property that are conclusive against all the world. For example, an action to determine whether certain property illegally imported into the United States ought to be forfeited can be captioned *United States v. Thirty-nine Thousand One Hundred and Fifty Cigars.* The object of the lawsuit is to determine the disposition of the property, regardless of who the owner is or who else might have an interest in it. Interested parties might appear and make out a case one way or another, but the action is *in rem,* against the things.

In rem lawsuits can be brought against the property of debtors in order to collect what is owed, and they are begun for the partition of real property, foreclosure of mortgages, and the enforcement of liens. They may be directed against real or PERSONAL PROPERTY. *In rem* actions are permitted only when the court has control of the property or where its authority extends to cover it. For example, the courts in Kansas may determine rights to a farm in Kansas, but not the ownership of a cannery in Texas. The *in rem* jurisdiction of a court may be exercised only after parties who are known to have an interest in the property are notified of the proceedings and have been given a chance to present their claim to the court.

IN SPECIE

Specific; specifically. Thus, to decree performance in specie is to decree specific performance. In kind; in the same or like form. A thing is said to exist in specie when it retains its existence as a distinct individual of a particular class.

IN TERROREM

[Latin, In fright or terror; by way of a threat.] A description of a legacy or gift given by will with the condition that the donee must not challenge the validity of the will or other testament.

Conditions of such nature, labeled in terrorem clauses, are ordinarily regarded as threats, since the potential loss of the gift is thought to provoke fear or dread of litigation over the will in the recipient.

INADMISSIBLE

That which, according to established legal principles, cannot be received into evidence at a trial for consideration by the jury or judge in reaching a determination of the action.

Evidence, for example, that is obtained as a result of an unlawful SEARCH AND SEIZURE is inadmissible, as is hearsay.

INADVERTENCE

The absence of attention or care; the failure of an individual to carefully and prudently observe the progress of a court proceeding that might have an effect upon his or her rights.

The term *inadvertence* is generally used in reference to a ground upon which a judgment may be set aside or vacated under the Rules of Federal CIVIL PROCEDURE or state rules of civil procedure.

INALIENABLE

Not subject to sale or transfer; inseparable.

That which is inalienable cannot be bought, sold, or transferred from one individual to another. The personal rights to life and liberty guaranteed by the CONSTITUTION OF THE UNITED STATES are inalienable. Similarly, various types of property are inalienable, such as rivers, streams, and highways.

INC.

An abbreviation for incorporated; having been formed as a legal or political entity with the advantages of perpetual existence and succession.

CROSS REFERENCE

Corporations.

INCAPACITY

The absence of legal ability, competence, or qualifications.

An individual incapacitated by infancy, for example, does not have the legal ability to enter into certain types of agreements, such as MARRIAGE or contracts.

Under provisions of workers' compensation laws, the term *incapacity* refers to the inability to find and retain employment due to a disease or injury that prevents the performance of the customary duties of a worker.

INCARCERATION

Confinement in a jail or prison; imprisonment.

Police officers and other law enforcement officers are authorized by federal, state, and local lawmakers to arrest and confine persons suspected of crimes. The judicial system is authorized to confine persons convicted of crimes. This confinement, whether before or after a criminal conviction, is called "incarceration." Juveniles and adults alike are subject to incarceration.

A jail is a facility designed to confine persons after arrest and before trial, or for a short period upon conviction for a lesser offense. A prison is built to house persons for longer periods of time following conviction for a more serious offense. Jails also may be called "detention centers," and prisons may be called "correctional facilities" or "penitentiaries." Regardless of their name, their function is generally the same: to lock up accused and convicted criminals.

An African-American man incarcerated in one of New York's Rikers Island jails. Critics of wholesale incarceration point out that correctional facility inmates are disproportionately African American.

MICHAEL S. YAMASHITA/ CORBIS.

The pretrial detention of accused criminals is an ancient practice. From the fifth century to the tenth century, persons accused of crimes in England were confined in jail through the end of trial unless they had property to pledge. If they pledged property, the court held it in order to ensure their appearance at trial, and they were released from jail. After the conquest of England by William the Conqueror in 1066, local sheriffs determined who deserved pretrial release. This practice continued until the thirteenth century, when widespread favoritism and abuse by the sheriffs led to the enactment of uniform procedures concerning pretrial release.

The custom of jailing criminal defendants was continued in the American colonies. The payment of bail as a condition of pretrial release was also adopted. In 1791, the EIGHTH AMENDMENT to the U.S. Constitution was ratified, stating in part that "[e]xcessive bail shall not be required … nor cruel and unusual punishments inflicted." This language constituted the only provision in the Constitution directly addressing jails and incarceration.

There were no prisons in the United States before the Constitution was written in 1789. Convicted criminals were sentenced to forms of punishment more colorful than incarceration. Punishment for serious crimes included banishment from the community; public pillory, which was detention in a wooden device that held the head and hands by closing around the neck and wrists; and CORPORAL PUNISHMENT, which was designed to disfigure the offender using measures such as whipping, branding, or slicing off the body part thought to be responsible for the crime. The most serious crimes were punishable by death.

The first prison in the United States was built in Philadelphia in 1790, when the Walnut Street Jail added a new cell house to its existing jail and devoted the new cells to the confinement of convicted criminals. Established by the nonviolent Quakers as an alternative to capital punishment, prison was originally intended to be a progressive setting for hard work, reflection, self-examination, and spiritual guidance. However, by the 1820s prison had become the punishment most feared by criminal defendants. Federal, state, and local governments were free to confine convicts and accused criminals in the most inhumane of conditions. A convict was considered a slave of the state, with no rights other than to be kept alive.

Until the 1960s, courts were reluctant to review the procedures, conditions, and treatment of persons held in jails and prisons. At that time, perhaps inspired by progressive social discourse and a growing emphasis on rehabilitation over punishment, courts began to scrutinize the actions of jailers and prison officials. They found numerous constitutional violations, including violations of due process, of the FIRST AMENDMENT guarantee of FREEDOM OF SPEECH, and of the Eighth Amendment.

Violence against prisoners was commonplace. Prisoners were beaten with leather straps; forced to consume milk of magnesia; handcuffed to fences or cells for long periods in uncomfortable positions; made to stand, sit, or lie on crates or stumps for long periods; and shot at, to force them to keep moving or to remain standing. In one prison, officials made inmates strip naked, hosed them down with water, and then turned a fan on them while they were naked and wet (*Gates v. Collier*, 501 F.2d 1291 [5th Cir. 1974]).

Jail and prison inmates also had to endure brutal living conditions. The Charles Street Jail, in Boston, represented incarceration at its

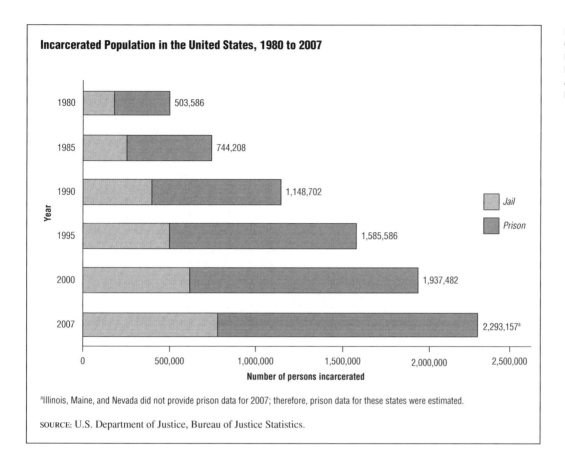

Incarcerated Population in the United States, 1980 to 2007

- 1980: 503,586
- 1985: 744,208
- 1990: 1,148,702
- 1995: 1,585,586
- 2000: 1,937,482
- 2007: 2,293,157[a]

Legend: Jail / Prison

Y-axis: Year
X-axis: Number of persons incarcerated (0, 500,000, 1,000,000, 1,500,000, 2,000,000, 2,500,000)

[a]Illinois, Maine, and Nevada did not provide prison data for 2007; therefore, prison data for these states were estimated.

SOURCE: U.S. Department of Justice, Bureau of Justice Statistics.

worst. Originally erected in 1848, Charles Street contained both pretrial detainees and convicts serving sentences of less than one year. The building was constructed of several tiers comprising long rows of cells. The cells were made of four walls of stone: three of them solid, and one with two small openings. Both wall openings were barred, and in some cases also had screens covering them. There were no heat vents in the cells; the only heat came from a blower at either end of the tier. One inmate commented that in winter, rain puddles that formed on the floor turned to ice.

The cells were eight feet wide, 11 feet long, and ten feet high. Each contained two beds, a sliver of open floor space between the beds, approximately one foot of open floor space at the end of one bed, and a sink and a toilet at the end of the other bed. The beds consisted of two iron slats covered by an old, soiled mattress with no protective cover. The sinks had no hot water. Many of the toilets had no seats, and many either leaked or did not flush. These conditions attracted cockroaches, water bugs, and rats. The electrical system was antiquated and lacked a

backup generator, so power outages were common.

In 1971 inmates of the jail, then known as the Suffolk County Jail, sued the Suffolk County sheriff, the Massachusetts commissioner of correction, the mayor of Boston, and nine city councilors. The inmates claimed that the conditions in the jail amounted to punishment, and, because the detainees were presumed innocent, the punishment violated the Due Process Clause of the FOURTEENTH AMENDMENT. The inmates further argued that the conditions constituted CRUEL AND UNUSUAL PUNISHMENT in violation of the Eighth Amendment. The federal district court in Massachusetts agreed, ruling that the conditions unnecessarily and unreasonably infringed on the most basic liberties of presumptively innocent citizens (*Inmates of Suffolk County Jail v. Eisenstadt*, 360 F. Supp. 676 [1973]).

The *Suffolk County* decision was followed by several rounds of litigation. More than 25 years after the original complaint was filed, the matter of the Charles Street Jail was still not finished. The major obstacle to improving the conditions was double-bunking, or the practice of placing two prisoners in a cell originally intended for one. Ultimately, the court allowed double-bunking in some cells, in an order that became final on June 14, 1999.

The procedures leading to incarceration in jail or prison vary, but certain procedural features are common to all jurisdictions. Many criminal defendants are released mere hours after being jailed if they agree to return for future proceedings. Other defendants are released after the first hearing before a judge, who orders them to return for future court dates. Still other defendants may be ordered by a judge to be held in jail until they pay a sum of money to secure their appearance at future proceedings. This sum of money is called "bail." A DEFENDANT held on bail may obtain a release from jail by paying the full bail amount, or by paying a percentage of the bail amount to a licensed bail agent, who then pays the full amount to the court. If the defendant is unable to post bail, he or she is held in jail until the case is resolved.

The U.S. Supreme Court ruled in *Atwater v. City of Lago Vista*, 532 U.S. 318, 121 1536, 149 L. Ed. 2d 549 (2001) that police can arrest and temporarily incarcerate a person charged with a minor offense that is punishable by a fine and no incarceration. Gail Atwater, a 16-year resident of Lago Vista, Texas, was driving her pickup truck through a residential area of town. In the front seat with her were her 3-year-old son and 5-year-old daughter. Neither the children nor Atwater was wearing a seatbelt, for which Lago Vista police officer Bart Turek stopped Atwater. Turek, who had pulled Atwater over several months before, on a mistaken belief that her child was not seat-belted, approached the truck in a loud and abusive manner, stating that Atwater was going to jail for her offense. When she asked to take her frightened children to a friend's house nearby, Turek denied the request. After a neighbor saw what was happening and took the children to her house, Turek handcuffed Atwater, placed her in the squad car, and took her to the police station. At the station, she removed her shoes, jewelry, and eyeglasses and emptied her pockets. Officers then took her "mug shot" and placed her in a jail cell. After an hour, she was taken before a magistrate and released on $310 bail. She later pleaded guilty to the seatbelt offenses and was fined $50.

Atwater sued under a federal CIVIL RIGHTS law, arguing that her arrest and incarceration had been unconstitutional. Her lawsuit was dismissed by the lower federal courts, and the U.S. Supreme Court upheld these rulings in a 5–4 vote. Justice DAVID SOUTER, writing for the majority, concluded that neither common law nor prior precedent provided any grounds for placing limits on police authority to arrest individuals for minor criminal offenses.

A person confined to jail while awaiting trial is called a "pretrial detainee." Where the crime alleged is particularly heinous, the judge may deny bail and order the defendant held until the case is resolved. Depending on the size and complexity of the case, a pretrial detainee may be confined in jail for several months, or sometimes even years.

Juveniles are usually held in separate facilities, called "juvenile detention centers." However, not all states provide special facilities to keep minors separate from adults. Furthermore, if a juvenile is certified to stand trial as an adult, he or she may be transferred from the juvenile detention center to an adult detention facility. If found guilty, a certified juvenile may be sentenced to adult prison.

If a criminal defendant is convicted, he or she may be sentenced to additional incarceration. Persons convicted of serious crimes are usually sentenced to at least one year in prison. For serious offenses, an inmate may receive a prison sentence of several years to life, or a life term without the possibility of parole. For less-serious offenses, the sentence may consist of continued confinement in jail or in a similar secure facility for up to one year. In most states, a jail sentence does not exceed one year; other states allow jail sentences to last more than two years.

There are different levels of security within the jail and prison systems. Inmates in jail and prison are screened and then classified according to security concerns. For example, persons who present a danger to themselves or others may be placed in isolation under 24-hour surveillance, and persons with infectious diseases may be quarantined in a separate cell block.

Most jurisdictions operate minimum-, medium-, and maximum-security prisons: Security in these facilities ranges from relaxed to strict. The placement of a convict will depend on many factors, including the nature of the offense; perceived gang activity; and the defendant's personal and criminal history, sexual orientation, and physical and mental health. In some cases, a judge may order a defendant to serve time at a specific prison.

The security measures in jail and prison vary. They include inspection of mail, searches of body cavities, searches of the inmate's cell, short-term placement in restraints, administration of psychotropic drugs if no alternative methods for security are available, limitations on the possession of personal effects, and placement in solitary confinement.

Daily life in jail and prison is strictly regulated. Physical contact visits are usually reserved for well-behaved inmates in minimum- and medium-security facilities. In most facilities, inmates are not allowed to have physical contact with visitors. Visits are conducted through wire mesh, or through heavy glass by means of a telephone. Inmates are usually shackled at the hands and feet when they are moved from one part of the facility to another.

Federal and state laws address a minimum of issues concerning the operation of jails and prisons. Most legislatures and courts prefer to leave the matter of confinement to jail and prison administrators. Some prison administrators, or wardens, try to share political power with inmates, in order to avoid prison violence and uprisings. The general trend, however, is to limit prisoners' rights and freedoms. Sometimes lawmakers regulate the warden-inmate relationship with a law or ordinance. For example, some municipalities have overruled prison officials by passing laws that grant gay pretrial detainees the right to visit with their same-sex partners.

In most jurisdictions, judges have a wide range of incarceration options. As an alternative to jail or prison, many states have created boot camps. These facilities, sometimes known as "shock camps", emphasize hard work and physical conditioning. They are generally reserved for first-time offenders. The theory advanced for boot camps is rehabilitation: They attempt to instill in inmates a sense of pride and capability. They also attempt to avoid turning youthful transgressors into experienced, hardened criminals by keeping them out of jail and prison, and therefore away from the influence of more serious offenders or career criminals.

Many states use home confinement as an alternative to institutional confinement. Home confinement allows a defendant to live at home and go to work while being monitored through an electronic bracelet. The bracelet is usually worn around the ankle and detects the defendant's whereabouts at all times. If the defendant fails to comply with the conditions of the home confinement, the court may resentence the defendant to jail or prison.

Some states have halfway houses to help inmates re-enter society after incarceration. These facilities are situated in communities. Their doors are not locked, but if an inmate fails to comply with the rules, he or she may be returned to jail or prison for the remainder of his or her sentence.

If a defendant needs drug or alcohol treatment, a judge may sentence the defendant to stay at a treatment center specializing in drug and alcohol dependency. This is another alternative to incarceration in a correctional facility. If the defendant fails to comply with the rules of the treatment center or fails to remain sober, the judge may resentence the defendant to jail or prison.

Jail and prison can be more difficult for some inmates than others. Persons who are accused or convicted of sexual ASSAULT on a minor are often targets of violence. Youthful inmates are commonly raped. Short of requiring solitary confinement for all detainees and convicts, officials have found few solutions to the violence that occurs when accused and convicted criminals are grouped together in small spaces.

Incarceration may severely disrupt the equilibrium of mentally or physically ill persons. Jail and prison officials are not liable for the death or injury of an inmate because of lack of health care unless the staff exhibited deliberate indifference to the needs of the inmate. An inmate may be forced to take psychotropic drugs if that would be the least intrusive means available to control violent behavior.

Hunger strikes are common in jail and prison. Some inmates who participate in these strikes want to die, whereas others wish to call attention to a particular issue. The chief legal issue in these situations is whether officials may force-feed an inmate. In most cases, courts uphold the right of the government to keep prisoners alive as being necessary to the effective administration of the criminal justice system. In other cases, courts have not upheld that right. In Georgia, for example, a prisoner's right to privacy includes the right to starve to death (*Zant v. Prevatte*, 248 Ga. 832, 286 S.E.2d 715 [1982]).

The United States imprisons more people per capita than any other country. By 2009, 2.3 million people were behind bars. The record prison population figures were driven by tough policies that mandate long terms for drug offenders and other criminals. Many critics of the increase in incarceration argue that confinement serves only to "dehabilitate" convicts and breed more crime. According to these critics, incarceration too often turns individuals capable of rehabilitation into angry, vindictive persons. By the time many inmates are released from incarceration, they have been deprived of a means of self-support. Stripped of self-respect and resources, many ex-convicts find it nearly impossible to lead anything other than a life of crime and despair.

Other critics of wholesale incarceration point out that jail and prison inmates are disproportionately African American. In 2009, one in nine African American men between the ages of 20 and 34 were incarcerated, compared to one in 30 other men of the same age.

Still other critics emphasize the unfairness reflected in the disparity between the tremendous number of drug offenders in jail and prison, compared with the small number of white-collar criminals incarcerated. For example, in 1991 the federal courts sentenced more than 14,000 defendants to prison terms for drug offenses, compared with fewer than 5,500 persons for FRAUD, embezzlement, and RACKETEERING crimes.

Following the SEPTEMBER 11TH ATTACKS in 2001, the federal government mobilized to fight a WAR ON TERRORISM. President GEORGE W. BUSH authorized the indefinite detention of enemy combatants in a 2002 military order. One person captured by U.S. forces in Afghanistan was Yaser Esam Hamdi, who claimed he was a U.S. citizen. Hamdi sought his release from indefinite incarceration in a military prison. The U.S. Court of Appeals for the Fourth Circuit ruled that Hamdi could be held as an ENEMY COMBATANT and that his citizenship did not change his status. The Supreme Court overturned this decision in *Hamdi v. Rumsfeld*, 542

U.S. 507, 124 S.Ct. 2633, 159 L.Ed.2d 578 (2004), ruling that U.S. citizens held as enemy combatants may challenge their detention in U.S. courts.

In a series of cases, the Supreme Court considered the rights of enemy combatants incarcerated at Guantanamo Bay, Cuba, who were not U.S. citizens. The Bush Administration claimed that they had no legal rights. The Court disagreed. In *Rasul v. Bush* 542 U.S. 466, 124 S. Ct. 2686, 159 L. Ed. 2d 548 (2004), the Court ruled that the federal habeas statute applied to non-citizen detainees. Congress responded with the Detainee Treatment Act of 2005, stripping the federal courts of jurisdiction over HABEAS CORPUS petitions filed by the Guantanamo detainees. The Supreme Court, in *Boumediene v. Bush*, 553 U.S.___, 128 S.Ct. 2229, 171 L.Ed.2d 41(2008), ruled that the act and a similar 2006 statute were unconstitutional.

FURTHER READINGS

Palmer, John. 2006.*Constitutional Rights of Prisoners.*8th ed. New York: Anderson Pub. Co.

Pew Center on the States.2008. *One in 100: Behind Bars in America 2008.*Washington, D.C.

Potts, Jeff. 1993. "American Penal Institutions and Two Alternative Proposals for Punishment." *South Texas Law Review* 34.

Richardson, Louise. Ed. 2006.*The Roots of Terrorism.*New York: Routledge.

Sturm, Susan P. 1993. "The Legacy and Future of Corrections Litigation." *University of Pennsylvania Law Review* 142.

CROSS REFERENCES

Juvenile Law; Sentencing.

INCEST

The crime of sexual relations or marriage taking place between a male and female who are so closely linked by blood or affinity that such activity is prohibited by law.

Incest is a statutory crime, often classified as a felony. The purpose of incest statutes is to prevent sexual intercourse between individuals related within the degrees set forth, for the furtherance of the public policy in favor of domestic peace. The PROHIBITION of intermarriage is also based upon genetic considerations, since when excessive inbreeding takes place, undesirable recessive genes become expressed and genetic defects and disease are more readily perpetuated. In addition, the incest taboo is universal in human culture.

RAPE and incest are separate offenses and are distinguished by the fact that mutual consent is required for incest but not for rape. When the female is below the AGE OF CONSENT recognized by law, however, the same act can be both rape and incest.

The proscribed degrees of incest vary among the different statutes. Some include parent and child, brother and sister, uncle and niece, or aunt and nephew, and first cousins. In addition, intermarriage and sexual relations are also frequently prohibited among individuals who are related by half-blood, including brothers and sisters and uncles and nieces of the half-blood.

In a number of jurisdictions, incest statutes extend to relationships among individuals related by affinity. Such statutes proscribe sexual relations between stepfathers and stepdaughters, stepmothers and stepsons, or brothers- and sisters-in-law, and such relations are punishable as incest. It is necessary for the relationship of affinity to exist at the time the intermarriage or sexual intercourse occurs in order for the act to constitute incest. In the event that the relationship has terminated prior to the time that the act takes place, the intermarriage or sexual intercourse is not regarded as incest.

Affinity ordinarily terminates upon the divorce or death of the blood relation through whom the relationship was formed. Following the divorce or death of his spouse, it is not a violation of incest statutes for a man to marry or have sexual relations with his stepdaughter or his spouse's sister.

Certain statutes require that the individual accused of incest have knowledge of the relationship. In such cases, both parties need not be aware that their actions are incestuous in order for the party who does know to be convicted.

When intermarriage is prohibited by law, it need not be proved that sexual intercourse took place in order for a conviction to be sustained, since the offense is complete on intermarriage. In statutes that define incest as the intermarriage or CARNAL KNOWLEDGE of individuals within the prohibited degrees, incest can be committed either by intermarriage or sexual relations.

Some state laws provide that the crime of incest is not committed unless both parties consent to it. When the sexual relations at issue were accomplished by force, the act constitutes rape, and the individual accused cannot be convicted of incest.

It is no defense to incest that the woman had prior sexual relations or has a reputation for unchastity. Similarly, voluntary drunkenness, moral insanity, or an uncontrollable impulse are insufficient defenses.

Punishment for a conviction pursuant to an incest statute is determined by statute.

INCHOATE

Imperfect; partial; unfinished; begun, but not completed; as in a contract not executed by all the parties.

INCIDENT OF OWNERSHIP

Some aspect of the exclusive possession or control over the disposition or use of property that demonstrates that the person with such exclusive rights has not relinquished them.

A person who has kept the right to change the beneficiaries on his or her life insurance policy has retained an incident of ownership and is, therefore, considered the owner of the policy.

INCIDENTAL

Contingent upon or pertaining to something that is more important; that which is necessary, appertaining to, or depending upon another known as the principal.

Under workers' compensation statutes, a risk is deemed incidental to employment when it is related to whatever a worker must do in order to fulfill the employment contract, but is not the primary function that the worker was hired to do.

INCITE

To arouse; urge; provoke; encourage; spur on; goad; stir up; instigate; set in motion; as in to incite a riot. Also, generally, in criminal law to instigate, persuade, or move another to commit a crime; in this sense nearly synonymous with abet.

INCOME

The return in money from one's business, labor, or capital invested; gains, profits, salary, wages, etc.

The gain derived from capital, from labor or effort, or both combined, including profit or gain through sale or conversion of capital. Income is not a gain accruing to capital or a growth in the value of the investment, but is a profit, something of exchangeable value, proceeding from the property and being received or drawn by the recipient for separate use, benefit, and disposal. That which comes in or is received from any business, or investment of capital, without reference to outgoing expenditures.

INCOME SPLITTING

The right, created by provisions of federal tax laws, given to married couples who file joint returns to have their combined incomes subject to an income tax at a rate equal to that which would be imposed if each had filed a separate return for one-half the amount of their combined income.

Income splitting was devised as a result of legislation enacted by Congress in 1948 to equalize the federal TAXATION of married couples who lived in common-law states and who paid higher taxes than couples who lived in COMMUNITY PROPERTY states and, as a result, have the tax benefits of income splitting.

INCOME TAX

A charge imposed by government on the annual gains of a person, corporation, or other taxable unit derived through work, business pursuits, investments, property dealings, and other sources determined in accordance with the Internal Revenue Code or state law.

Taxes have been called the building block of civilization. In fact, taxes existed in Sumer, the first organized society of record, where their payment carried great religious meaning. Taxes were also a fundamental part of ancient Greece and the Roman Empire. The religious aspect of TAXATION in Renaissance Italy is depicted in the Brancacci Chapel, in Florence. The fresco *Rendering of the Tribute Money* depicts the gods approving the Florentine INCOME TAX. In the United States, the federal tax laws are set forth in the INTERNAL REVENUE CODE and enforced by the INTERNAL REVENUE SERVICE (IRS).

History

The origin of taxation in the United States can be traced to the time when the colonists were heavily taxed by Great Britain on everything from tea to legal and business documents that were required by the STAMP TAX. The colonists' disdain for this taxation without representation (so-called because the colonies had no voice in the establishment of the taxes) gave rise to revolts such as the Boston Tea Party. However, even after the Revolutionary War and the adoption of the U.S. Constitution, the main source of revenue for the newly created states was money received from customs and excise taxes on items such as carriages, sugar, whiskey, and snuff. Income tax first appeared in the United States in 1862, during the Civil War. At that time, only about one percent of the population was required to pay the tax. A flat-rate income tax was imposed in 1867. The income tax was repealed in its entirety in 1872.

Income tax was a rallying point for the Populist party in 1892 and had enough support two years later that Congress passed the Income Tax Act of 1894. The tax at that time was two percent on individual incomes in excess of $4,000, which meant that it reached only the wealthiest members of the population. The Supreme Court struck down the tax, holding that it violated the constitutional requirement that direct taxes be apportioned among the states by population (Pollock v. Farmers' Loan & Trust, 158 U.S. 601, 15 S. Ct. 912, 39 L. Ed. 1108 [1895]). After many years of debate and compromise, the SIXTEENTH AMENDMENT to the Constitution was ratified in 1913, providing Congress with the power to lay and collect taxes on income without apportionment among the states. The objectives of the income tax were the equitable distribution of the tax burden and the raising of revenue.

Since 1913 the U.S. income tax system has become very complex. In 1913 the income tax laws were contained in 18 pages of legislation; the explanation of the TAX REFORM ACT OF 1986 was more than 1,300 pages long (Pub. L. 99-514, Oct. 22, 1986, 100 Stat. 2085). Commerce Clearing House, a publisher of tax information, released a version of the Internal Revenue Code in the early 1990s that was four times thicker than its version in 1953.

Changes to the tax laws often reflect the times. The flat tax of 1913 was later replaced with a GRADUATED TAX. After the United States entered WORLD WAR I, the War Revenue Act of 1917 imposed a maximum tax rate for individuals of 67 percent, compared with a rate of 13 percent in 1916. In 1924 Secretary of the Treasury Andrew W. Mellon, speaking to Congress about the high level of taxation, stated,

The present system is a failure. It was an emergency measure, adopted under the pressure of war necessity and not to be counted upon as a permanent part of our revenue structure.... The high rates put pressure on taxpayers to reduce their TAXABLE INCOME, tend to destroy individual initiative and enterprise, and seriously impede the development of productive business.... Ways will always be found to avoid taxes so destructive in their nature, and the only way to save the situation is to put the taxes on a reasonable basis that will permit business to go on and industry to develop.

Consequently, the Revenue Act of 1924 reduced the maximum individual tax rate to 43 percent (Revenue Acts, June 2, 1924, ch. 234, 43 Stat. 253). In 1926 the rate was further reduced to 25 percent.

The Revenue Act of 1932 was the first tax law passed during the Great Depression (Revenue Acts, June 6, 1932, ch. 209, 47 Stat. 169). It increased the individual maximum rate from 25 to 63 percent and reduced personal exemptions from $1,500 to $1,000 for single persons, and from $3,500 to $2,500 for married couples. The NATIONAL INDUSTRIAL RECOVERY ACT OF 1933 (NIRA), part of President Franklin D. Roosevelt's NEW DEAL, imposed a five percent excise tax on dividend receipts, imposed a capital stock tax and an excess profits tax, and suspended all deductions for losses (June 16, 1933, ch. 90, 48 Stat. 195). The repeal in 1933 of the EIGHTEENTH AMENDMENT, which had prohibited the manufacture and sale of alcohol, brought in an estimated $90 million in new liquor taxes in 1934. The SOCIAL SECURITY ACT OF 1935 provided for a wage tax, half to be paid by the employee and half by the employer, to establish a federal retirement fund (Old Age Pension Act, Aug. 14, 1935, ch. 531, 49 Stat. 620).

The Wealth Tax Act, also known as the Revenue Act of 1935, increased the maximum tax rate to 79 percent, the Revenue Acts of 1940 and 1941 increased it to 81 percent, the Revenue Act of 1942 raised it to 88 percent, and the Individual Income Tax Act of 1944 raised the individual maximum rate to 94 percent.

The post-World War II Revenue Act of 1945 reduced the individual maximum tax from 94 percent to 91 percent. The Revenue Act of 1950, during the KOREAN WAR, reduced it to 84.4 percent, but it was raised the next year to 92 percent (Revenue Act of 1950, Sept. 23, 1950,

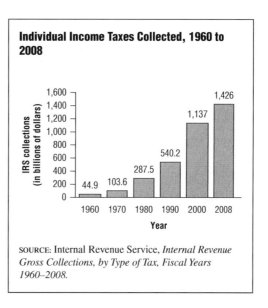

Individual Income Taxes Collected, 1960 to 2008

SOURCE: Internal Revenue Service, *Internal Revenue Gross Collections, by Type of Tax, Fiscal Years 1960–2008.*

ILLUSTRATION BY GGS CREATIVE RESOURCES. REPRODUCED BY PERMISSION OF GALE, A PART OF CENGAGE LEARNING.

ch. 994, Stat. 906). It remained at this level until 1964, when it was reduced to 70 percent.

The Revenue Act of 1954 revised the Internal Revenue Code of 1939, making major changes that were beneficial to the taxpayer, including providing for CHILD CARE deductions (later changed to credits), an increase in the charitable contribution limit, a tax credit against taxable retirement income, employee deductions for business expenses, and liberalized depreciation deductions. From 1954 to 1962, the Internal Revenue Code was amended by 183 separate acts.

In 1974 the EMPLOYEE RETIREMENT INCOME SECURITY ACT (ERISA) created protections for employees whose employers promised specified pensions or other retirement contributions (Pub. L. No. 93-406, Sept. 2, 1974, 88 Stat. 829). ERISA required that, in order to be tax deductible, the employer's plan contribution must meet certain minimum standards as to employee participation and vesting and employer funding. ERISA also approved the use of individual retirement accounts (IRAs) to encourage tax-deferred retirement savings by individuals.

The Economic Recovery Tax Act of 1981 (ERTA) provided the largest tax cut up to that time, reducing the maximum individual rate from 70 percent to 50 percent (Pub. L. No. 97-34, Aug. 13, 1981, 95 Stat. 172). The most sweeping tax changes since WORLD WAR II were enacted in the Tax Reform Act of 1986. This bill was signed into law by President RONALD REAGAN and was designed to equalize the tax treatment of various assets, eliminate tax shelters, and lower marginal rates. Conservatives wanted the act to provide a single, low tax rate that could be applied to everyone. Although this single, flat rate was not included in the final bill, tax rates were reduced to 15 percent on the first $17,850 of income for singles and $29,750 for married couples, and set at 28 to 33 percent on remaining income. Many deductions were repealed, such as a deduction available to two-income married couples that had been used to avoid the "marriage penalty" (a greater tax liability incurred when two persons filed their income tax return as a married couple rather than as individuals). Although the personal exemption exclusion was increased, an exemption for elderly and blind persons who itemize deductions was repealed. In addition, a special capital gains rate was repealed, as was an investment tax credit that had been introduced in 1962 by President JOHN F. KENNEDY.

The Omnibus Budget Reconciliation Act of 1993, the first budget and tax act enacted during the Clinton administration, was vigorously debated, and passed with only the minimum number of necessary votes (Pub. L. No. 103-66, Aug. 10, 1993, 107 Stat. 312). This law provided for income tax rates of 15, 28, 31, 36, and 39.6 percent on varying levels of income and for the taxation of SOCIAL SECURITY income if the taxpayer receives other income over a certain level. In 2001 Congress enacted a major income tax cut at the urging of President GEORGE W. BUSH. Over the course of 11 years, the law reduces marginal income tax rates across all levels of income. The 36 percent rate will be lowered to 33 percent, the 31 percent rate to 28 percent, the 28 percent rate to 25 percent. In addition, a new bottom 10 percent rate was created. (Economic Growth and Tax Relief Reconciliation Act of 2001, Pub. L. No. 107-16, 115 Stat. 38.)

Since the early 1980s, a flat-rate tax system, rather than the graduated bracketed method, has been proposed. (The graduated bracketed method is the one that has been used since graduated taxes were introduced: the percentage of tax differs based on the amount of taxable income.) The flat-rate system would impose one rate, such as 20 percent, on all income and would eliminate special deductions, credits, and exclusions. Despite firm support by some, the flat-rate tax has not been adopted in the United States.

Computation of Income Tax

Regardless of the changes made by legislators since 1913, the formula for computing the amount of tax owed has remained basically the same. To determine the amount of income tax owed, certain deductions are taken from an individual's gross income to arrive at an adjusted gross income, from which additional deductions are taken to arrive at the taxable income. Once the amount of taxable income has been determined, tax rate charts determine the exact amount of tax owed. If the amount of tax owed is less than the amount already paid through tax prepayment or the withholding of taxes from paychecks, the taxpayer is entitled to a refund from the IRS. If the amount of tax owed is more than what has already been paid, the taxpayer must pay the difference to the IRS.

Calculating the gross income of restaurant employees whose income is partially derived from gratuities left by customers has led to disputes with the IRS and employers over how much they should contribute in Federal Insurance Contribution Act (FICA) taxes. Although customers pay these tips directly to employees, federal law deems the tips to have been wages paid by the employer for FICA tax purposes. Employers are imputed to have paid large sums of money they never handled and for which they have no way of ascertaining the exact amount. The Supreme Court, in *United States v. Fior D'Italia*, 536 U.S. 238, 122 S. Ct. 2117, 153 L. Ed. 2d 280 (2002), upheld the IRS "aggregate method" of reporting tip income. Instead of requiring the IRS to make individual determinations of unreported tips for each employee when calculating FICA tax, the Court held that the IRS could make employers report their gross sales on a monthly statement to help determine tip income. Employees also must report their tip income monthly on a form. The IRS then uses these two pieces of information to calculate what the employer needs to contribute in FICA tax.

Gross Income The first step in computing the amount of tax liability is the determination of gross income. Gross income is defined as "all income from whatever source derived," whether from personal services, business activities, or capital assets (property owned for personal or business purposes). Compensation for services in the form of money, wages, tips, salaries, bonuses, fees, and commissions constitutes income. Problems in defining income often arise when a taxpayer realizes a benefit or compensation that is not in the form of money.

An example of such compensation is the fringe benefits an employee receives from an employer. The Internal Revenue Code defines these benefits as income and places the burden on the employee to demonstrate why they should be excluded from gross income. Discounts on the employer's products and other items of minimal value to the employer are usually not considered income to the employee. These benefits (which include airline tickets at nominal cost for airline employees and merchandise discounts for department store employees) are usually of great value to the employee but do not cost much for the employer to provide, and build good relationships between the employee and the employer. As long as the value to the employer is small, and the benefit generates goodwill, it usually is not deemed to be taxable to the employee.

The value of meals and lodging provided to an employee and paid for by an employer is not considered income to the employee if the meals and lodging are furnished on the business premises of the employer for the employer's convenience (as when an apartment building owner provides a rent-free apartment for a caretaker who is required to live on the premises). However, a cash allowance for meals or lodging that is given to an employee as part of a compensation package is considered compensation and is counted as gross income. An employer's payment for a health club membership is also included in gross income, as are payments to an employee in the form of stock. An amount contributed by an employer to a pension, qualified stock bonus, profit-sharing, annuity, or bond purchase plan in which the employee participates is not considered income to the employee at the time the contribution is made, but will be taxed when the employee receives payment from the plan. Medical insurance premiums paid by an employer are generally not considered income to the employee. Although military pay is taxable income, veterans' benefits for education, disability and pension payments, and veterans' insurance proceeds and dividends are not included in gross income.

Other sources of income directly increase the wealth of the taxpayer and are taxable. These sources commonly include interest earned on bank accounts; dividends; rents; royalties from copyrights, trademarks, and patents; proceeds from life insurance if paid for a reason other than the death of the insured; annuities; discharge from the obligation to pay a debt owed (the amount discharged is considered income to the debtor); recovery of a previously deductible item, which gives rise to income only to the extent the previous deduction produced a tax benefit (this is commonly referred to as the "tax benefit rule" and is most often used when a taxpayer has recovered a previously deducted bad debt or previously deducted taxes); gambling winnings; lottery winnings; found property; and income from illegal sources. Income from prizes and awards is taxable unless the prize or award is made primarily in recognition of religious, charitable, scientific, educational, artistic, literary, or civic achievement; the recipient was chosen, without any action on his or her part, to enter the selection process; and the recipient is not required to render substantial future services as a condition to receiving the prize or award. For example, recipients of Nobel Prizes meet these criteria and are not taxed on the prize money they receive.

In some situations a taxpayer's wealth directly increases through income that is not included in the determination of income tax. For example, gifts and inheritances are excluded from income in order to encourage the TRANSFER OF ASSETS within families. However, any income realized from a gift or inheritance is considered income to the beneficiary—most notably rents, interest, and dividends. In addition, most scholarships, fellowships, student loans, and other forms of financial aid for education are not included in gross income, perhaps to equalize the status of students whose education is funded by a gift or inheritance, and of students who do not have the benefit of such assistance. Cash rebates to consumers from product manufacturers and most state UNEMPLOYMENT COMPENSATION benefits are also not included in gross income.

Capital gains and losses pose special considerations in the determination of income tax liability. Capital gains are the profits realized as a result of the sale or exchange of a capital asset. Capital losses are the deficits realized in such transactions. Capital gains and losses are determined by establishing a taxpayer's basis in the property. Basis is generally defined as the taxpayer's cost of acquiring the property. In the case of property received as a gift, the donee basically steps into the shoes of the donor and is deemed to have the same basis in the property as did the donor. The basis is subtracted from the amount realized by the sale or other disposition of the property, and the difference is either a gain or a loss to the taxpayer.

Capital gains are usually included in gross income, with certain narrow exclusions, and capital losses are generally excluded from gross income. An important exception to this favorable treatment of capital losses occurs when the loss arises from the sale or other disposition of property held by the taxpayer for personal use, such as a personal residence or jewelry. When a capital gain is realized from the disposition of property held for personal use, it is included as income even though a capital loss involving the same property cannot be excluded from income. This apparent discrepancy is further magnified by the fact that capital losses on business or investment property can be excluded from income. Consequently, there have been many lawsuits over the issue of whether a personal residence, used at some point as rental property or for some other income producing use, is deemed personal or business property for income tax purposes.

Taxpayers age 55 or older who sell a personal residence in which they have resided for a specific amount of time can exclude their capital gains. This is a one-time exclusion, with specific dollar limits. Consequently, if future, greater gains are anticipated, a taxpayer age 55 or older may choose to pay the capital gains tax on a transaction that qualifies for the exclusion but produces smaller capital gains.

Even though a capital gain on a personal residence is realized, it may be temporarily deferred from inclusion in gross income if the taxpayer buys and occupies another home two years before or after the sale, and the new home costs the same as or more than the old home. The gain is merely postponed. This type of transaction is called a "rollover." The gain that is not taxed in the year of sale will be deducted from the cost of the new home, thereby establishing a basis in the property that is less than the price paid for the home. When the new home is later sold, the amount of gain recognized at that time will include the gain

that was not recognized when the home was purchased by the taxpayer.

Deductions and Adjusted Gross Income Once the amount of gross income is determined, the taxpayer may take deductions from the income in order to determine adjusted gross income. Two categories of deductions are allowed. Above-the-line deductions are taken in full from gross income to arrive at adjusted gross income. Below-the-line, or itemized, deductions are taken from adjusted gross income and are allowed only to the extent that their combined amount exceeds a certain threshold amount. If the total amount of itemized deductions does not meet the threshold amount, those deductions are not allowed. Generally, above-the-line deductions are business expenditures, and below-the-line deductions are personal, or nonbusiness, expenditures.

The favorable tax treatment afforded business and investment property is also evident in the treatment of business and investment expenses. Ordinary and necessary expenses are those incurred in connection with a trade or business. Ordinary and necessary business expenses are those that others engaged in the same type of business incur in similar circumstances. With regard to deductions for expenses incurred for investment property, courts follow the same type of "ordinary-and-necessary" analysis used for business expense deductions, and disallow the deductions if they are personal in nature or are capital expenses. Allowable business expenses include insurance, rent, supplies, travel, transportation, salary payments to employees, certain losses, and most state and local taxes.

Personal, or nonbusiness, expenses are generally not deductible. Exceptions to this rule include casualty and theft losses that are not covered by insurance. Certain expenses are allowed as itemized deductions. These below-the-line deductions include expenses for medical treatment, interest on home mortgages, state income taxes, and charitable contributions. Expenses incurred for tax advice are deductible from federal income tax, as are a wide array of state and local taxes. In addition, an employee who incurs business expenses may deduct those expenses to the extent they are not reimbursed by the employer. Typical unreimbursed expenses that are deductible by employees include union dues and payments for mandatory uniforms. Alimony payments may be taken as a deduction by the payer and are deemed to be income to the recipient; however, CHILD SUPPORT payments are not deemed income to the parent who has custody of the child and are not deductible by the paying parent.

Contributions made by employees to an INDIVIDUAL RETIREMENT ACCOUNT (IRA) or by self-employed persons to Keogh plans are deductible from gross income. Allowable annual deductions for contributions to an IRA are lower than allowable contributions to a Keogh account. Contributions beyond the allowable deduction are permitted; however, amounts in excess are included in gross income. Both IRAs and Keogh plans create tax-sheltered retirement funds that are not taxed as gross income during the taxpayer's working years. The contributions and the interest earned on them become taxable when they are distributed to the taxpayer. Distribution may take place when the taxpayer is 59 and one-half years old, or earlier if the taxpayer becomes disabled, at which time the taxpayer will most likely be in a lower tax bracket. Distribution may take place before either of these occurrences, but if so, the funds are taxable immediately, and the taxpayer may also incur a substantial penalty for early withdrawal of the money.

Additional Deductions and Taxable Income
Once adjusted gross income is determined, a taxpayer must determine whether to use the standard deduction or to itemize deductions. In most cases, the standard deduction is used, because it is the most convenient option. However, if the amount of itemized deductions is substantially more than the standard deduction and exceeds the threshold amount, a taxpayer will receive a greater tax benefit by itemizing.

After the standard deduction or itemized deductions are subtracted from adjusted gross income, the income amount is further reduced by personal and dependency exemptions. Each taxpayer is allowed one personal exemption. A taxpayer may also claim a dependency exemption for each person who meets five specific criteria: the dependent must have a familial relationship with the taxpayer; have a gross income that is less than the amount of the deduction, unless he or she is under nineteen years old or a full-time student; receive more than one-half of his or her support from the taxpayer; be a citizen or resident of the United States, Mexico, or Canada; and, if married, be unable to file a joint return with his or her spouse. Each exemption is valued at a certain dollar amount, by which the taxpayer's taxable income is reduced.

Tax Tables and Tax Owed Once the final deductions and exemptions are taken, the resulting figure is the taxpayer's taxable income. The tax owed on this income is determined by looking at applicable tax tables. This figure may be reduced by tax prepayments or by an applicable tax credit. Credits are available for contributions made to candidates for public office; child and dependent care; earned income; taxes paid in another country; and residential energy. For each dollar of available credit, a taxpayer's liability is reduced by one dollar.

Refund or Tax Owed Finally, after tax prepayments and credits are subtracted, the amount of tax owed the IRS or the amount of refund owed the taxpayer is determined. The taxpayer's tax return and payment of tax owed must be mailed to the IRS by April 15 unless an extension is sought. Taxpayers who make late payments without seeking an extension will be charged interest on the amount due and may be charged a penalty. A tax refund may be requested for up to several years after the tax return is filed. A refund is owed usually because the taxpayer had more tax than necessary withheld from his or her paychecks.

Tax Audits The IRS may audit a taxpayer to verify that the taxpayer correctly reported income, exemptions, or deductions on the return. The majority of returns that are audited are chosen by computer, which selects those that have the highest probability of error. Returns may also be randomly selected for audit or may be chosen because of previous investigations of a taxpayer for TAX EVASION or for involvement in an activity that is under investigation by the IRS. Taxpayers may represent themselves at an audit, or may have an attorney, certified public accountant, or the person who prepared the return accompany them. The taxpayer will be told what items to bring to the audit in order to answer the questions raised. If additional tax is found to be owed and the taxpayer disagrees, he or she may request an immediate meeting with a supervisor. If the supervisor supports the audit findings, the taxpayer may appeal the decision to a higher level within the IRS or may take the case directly to court.

Tax Rebates The Economic Stimulus Act of 2008, P.L. 110-185, 122 Stat. 613 was intended to provide several forms of economic stimulus to individuals and businesses following a national recessive state in 2007 and 2008. Among other things, the act provided for tax rebates to low- and middle-income taxpayers and tax incentives to stimulate business investments. Specifically, most taxpayers with qualifying income received a rebate, in the form of a government-issued check, of $300 per person ($600 per married couple) as well as $300 per dependent under the age of 17.

Moreover, with respect to businesses, the Act provided for a 50 percent special depreciation allowance for property placed in service after December 31, 2007, but generally before January 1, 2009. It also created new depreciation limits on business vehicles and special Section 179 expensing.

FURTHER READINGS

Adams, Charles. 1998. *Those Dirty Rotten Taxes: The Tax Revolts that Built America.* New York: Free Press.

Cataldo, Anthony J., and Arline A. Savage. 2001. *U.S. Individual Federal Income Taxation: Historical, Contemporary, and Prospective Policy Issues.* New York: JAI.

Chirelstein, Marvin A. 2002. *Federal Income Taxation: A Law Student's Guide to the Leading Cases and Concepts.* 9th ed. New York: Foundation Press.

Internal Revenue Service. 2008. "2008 Economic Tax Benefits to Businesses." Press release, February 21, 2008. Available online at http://www.irs.gov/newsroom/article/0,,id=179227,00.html; website home page: http://www.irs.gov/newsroom/ (accessed September 20, 2009)

Ivers, James F., ed. 2008. *Income Tax Fundamentals 2009.* 27th ed. Mason, OH: South-Western.

Whittenburg, Gerald E., and Martha Altus-Buller. 1994. *Income Taxes: Concise History and Primer.* Baton Rouge, La.: Claitor's.

Willan, Robert M. 1994. *Income Taxes: Concise History and Primer.* Baton Rouge, La.: Claitor's.

CROSS REFERENCES

Tax Avoidance; Tax Court; Taxpayer Bill of Rights.

INCOMPATIBILITY

The inability of a husband and wife to cohabit in a marital relationship.

INCOMPETENCY

The lack of ability, knowledge, legal qualification, or fitness to discharge a required duty or professional obligation.

The term *incompetency* has several meanings in the law. When it is used to describe the mental condition of a person subject to LEGAL PROCEEDINGS, it means the person is neither able to comprehend the nature and consequences of the proceedings nor adequately able to help an attorney with his defense. When it is used to describe the legal qualification of a person, it means the person does not have the legal capacity to enter a contract. When it is employed to describe a professional duty or obligation, it means that the person has demonstrated a lack of ability to perform professional functions.

Mental Incompetency

A person who is diagnosed as being mentally ill, senile, or suffering from some other debility that prevents them from managing his own affairs may be declared mentally incompetent by a court of law. When a person is judged to be incompetent, a guardian is appointed to handle the person's property and personal affairs.

The legal procedure for declaring a person incompetent consists of three steps: (1) a motion for a competency hearing, (2) a psychiatric or psychological evaluation, and (3) a competency hearing. Probate courts usually handle competency proceedings, which guarantee the allegedly incompetent person DUE PROCESS OF LAW.

In CRIMINAL LAW a defendant's mental competency may be questioned out of concern for the defendant's welfare or for strategic legal reasons. The defense may request a competency hearing so that it can gather information to use in PLEA BARGAINING, to mitigate a sentence, or to prepare for a potential INSANITY DEFENSE. The prosecution may raise the issue as a preventive measure or to detain the DEFENDANT so that a weak case can be built into a stronger one.

A motion for a competency hearing must be made before sentencing takes place. In federal court a motion for a hearing will be granted "if there is a reasonable cause to believe that the defendant may be suffering from a mental disease or defect rendering him mentally incompetent" (18 U.S.C.A. § 4241 (a)). A psychiatric or psychological evaluation is then conducted, and a hearing is held on the matter. If the court finds that the defendant is incompetent, the defendant will be hospitalized for a reasonable period of time, usually no more than four months. The goal is to determine whether the defendant's competence can be restored.

This type of mental commitment is authorized by the U.S. Supreme Court only for defendants who "probably soon will be able to stand trial" (*Jackson v. Indiana,* 406 U.S. 715, 92 S. Ct. 1845, 32 L. Ed. 2d 435 [1972]). The possibility that a defendant committed a serious crime does not warrant an extended commitment period, because that would violate the defendant's due process rights.

At the end of a four-month commitment, if it appears that the defendant's competence can be restored but more time is needed to do so, the defendant may be hospitalized for an additional 30 days to 18 months. The length of stay varies by state. If a hospital director certifies that the defendant's competence has been restored, the court holds another hearing. If the court agrees the defendant is competent, they are released and a criminal trial date is set. Such a competency ruling cannot be used as evidence against the defendant if they later pleads insanity as a defense in the criminal trial. (An insanity defense refers to the defendant's inability to know or appreciate right from wrong at the time of the alleged crime.)

The *Jackson* ruling also specified that "treatment must stop if there is no substantial probability that the defendant will regain trial competence in the near future." If that decision is reached, the defendant can continue to be detained only if they are declared permanently incompetent in a civil commitment proceeding.

The development of powerful drugs has given the government the opportunity to medicate mentally incompetent defendants to the point whre they are competent to stand trial. By 2003, the federal government was medicating hundreds of defendants each year but a small number objected to medication. The Supreme Court, in *Sell v. United States* 539 U.S. ___, 123 S. Ct., 2174, 156 L. Ed. 2d 197 (2003), issued a major setback to prosecutors, when it placed strict guidelines on medicating defendants accused of less serious, nonviolent crimes.

Legal Incapacity

CIVIL LAW requires a person to be legally competent in order to enter a contract, sign a will, or make some other type of binding legal commitment. A person may be judged incompetent by virtue of age or mental condition.

In contract law a person who agrees to a transaction becomes liable for duties under the contract unless they are legally incompetent. A person under the age of 18 or 21 (depending on the jurisdiction) is not bound by the legal duty to perform the terms of a contract he signed and is not liable for breach of contract. Public policy deems it desirable to protect an immature person from liability for contracts that he or she is too inexperienced to negotiate.

If a party does not comprehend the nature and consequences of the contract when it is formed, they are regarded as having mental incapacity. A distinction must be made between persons who have been adjudicated incompetent by a court and had a guardian appointed, and persons who are mentally incompetent but have not been so adjudicated. A person who has been declared incompetent in a court proceeding lacks the legal capacity to enter into a contract with another. Such a person is unable to consent to a contract, because the court has determined that he does not understand the obligations and effects of a contract. A contract made by such a person is void and without any legal effect. If there has been no adjudication of mental incompetency, a contract made by a mentally incapacitated individual is voidable by them. This means that the person can legally declare the contract void, making it unenforceable. However, a voidable contract can be ratified by the incompetent person if the person recovers the capacity to contract.

Contract law also holds that a contract made by an intoxicated person is voidable, as the person was incompetent at the time the contract was formed.

A MARRIAGE contract may be annulled if one of the parties was legally incompetent. Grounds for incompetency include age (under the AGE OF MAJORITY), mental incompetence such as insanity, and a preexisting marriage.

A person who executes a will must be legally competent. The traditional recital in a will states that the testator (the maker of the will) is of "sound mind." This language attempts to establish the competency of the testator, but the issue may be challenged when the will is probated.

Professional Obligation

Lawyers, doctors, teachers, and other persons who belong to a profession are bound either by professional codes of conduct or by contracts that contain standards of conduct. A professional person who fails to meet the duties required of that profession may be judged incompetent. Such a ruling by a court, a professional disciplinary board, or an employer may result in professional discipline, including loss of a license to practice, demotion, or termination of employment.

FURTHER READINGS

Grisso, Thomas. 2003. *Evaluating Competencies: Forensic Assessments and Instruments.* 2d ed. New York: Plenum.

Hubbard, Karen L., Patricia A. Zapf, and Kathleen A. Ronan. 2003. "Competency Restoration: An Examination of the Differences between Defendants Predicted Restorable and Not Restorable to Competency." *Law and Human Behavior* 27 (April).

Moriarty, Jane Campbell, ed. 2001. *The Role of Mental Illness in Criminal Trials: Insanity & Mental Incompetence.* New York: Routledge.

Scott, Charles L. 2003. "Commentary: A Road Map for Research in Restoration of Competency to Stand Trial." *Journal of the American Academy of Psychiatry and the Law* 31 (March). Available online at http://www.jaapl.org/cgi/reprint/31/1/36; website home page: http://www.jaapl.org (accessed August 1, 2009).

Tewksbury, Jane E., et al. 2001. *Going to Trial: Criminal Defendants & Mental Illness: Competency and Criminal Responsibility.* Boston, MA: Massachusetts Continuing Legal Education.

INCOMPETENT EVIDENCE

Probative matter that is not admissible in a legal proceeding; evidence that is not admissible under the Federal Rules of Evidence. That which the law does not allow to be presented at all, or in connection with a particular matter, due to lack of originality, a defect in the witness or the document, or due to the nature of the evidence in and of itself.

INCONSISTENT

Reciprocally contradictory or repugnant.

Things are said to be inconsistent when they are contrary to each other to the extent that one implies the negation of the other. For example, a city ordinance might be inconsistent with a state statute; or two defenses to a crime, such as the defenses of alibi and SELF-DEFENSE, are inconsistent.

INCONTESTABILITY CLAUSE

A provision in a life or health insurance policy that precludes the insurer from alleging that the policy, after it has been in effect for a stated period (typically two or three years), is void because of misrepresentations made by the insured in the application for it.

An incontestability clause prevents an insurer from denying benefits on the ground of MISREPRESENTATION in the application. The clause applies only when the policy has been in effect for a specified period of time. This time period, the contestability period, is usually two or three years.

Most states maintain statutes that require an incontestability clause in life and health insurance contracts. The incontestability clause strikes a balance between providing predictable coverage and protecting the right of insurers to select the precise risks they seek to insure.

Most incontestability clauses are limited by a provision stating that the contestability period must be completed within the lifetime of the insured. With this nuance the insurer is able to contest a claim for benefits after the contestability period has lapsed if the insured dies before the end of that period. This protects insurers from providing benefits to someone who was already so ill at the inception of the policy that he or she died less than two years later. It means that the insurer may contest the flow of insurance benefits to the insured's heirs.

Another common caveat to incontestability clauses limits the period of disability. Under this provision any disability that begins prior to the expiration of the contestability period will toll the period. In other words, if an insured becomes physically disabled before the end of the contestability period, the clock stops ticking and the insurer may challenge claims during the illness and beyond. Without such language, an insured could always avoid contestability by waiting until the contestability period has expired before filing a claim.

Finally, some incontestability clauses contain a FRAUD exception. Such a clause might read, "After two years from the date of issue of this policy, only FRAUDULENT misstatements made by the applicant may be used to void the policy or deny a claim that commences after the expiration of the two-year period." Generally, fraud is a false representation calculated to deceive another into acting against her or his legal interest. Statements that are inaccurate but made without the intent to deceive are not fraudulent.

The difference between fraud and simple misstatement can only be found in the facts of a particular case. In *Paul Revere Life Insurance Co. v. Haas,* 137 N.J. 190, 644 A.2d 1098 (1994), the Paul Revere Company brought an action against Gilbert K. Haas, when it discovered that Haas had made false statements in his insurance application. Haas had received a policy on March 5, 1987, and on December 1, 1990, started a claim for disability payments related to a progressive eye disease. The company sought to rescind the policy or to secure a DECLARATORY JUDGMENT from the court that the policy did not cover Haas's disease.

The New Jersey law on incontestability clauses gave insurers two options: one reserving contestability in case of fraud, the other reserving contestability if the insured became disabled within the contestability period (N.J. Stat. Ann. § 17B:26-5 [West]). The Paul Revere Company chose to bring action under the disability provision.

The facts indicated that Haas had made false statements on his policy application. He had declared that he had not had "any surgical operation, treatment, special diet, or any illness, ailment, abnormality, or injury … within the past five years." Investigations by the insurance company revealed that Haas had been diagnosed and treated for retinitis pigmentosa as much as four years prior to applying for the policy. According to the New Jersey Supreme Court, neither incontestability option mandated in section 17:B-26-5 of the New Jersey Statutes Annotated could be construed to allow coverage for disabilities that an insured knew existed but concealed on the policy application. The court held that Haas's policy continued in effect because the insurer had not proved its case under the disability provision, but that the incontestability clause did not prevent the insurer from contesting Haas's claims under the fraud provision.

FURTHER READINGS

Postel, Theodore. 2001. "Insurance Incontestability Clause." *Chicago Daily Law Bulletin* 147 (August 28).

Schuman, Gary. 1995. "Health and Life Insurance Applications: Their Role in the Claims Review Process." *Defense Counsel Journal* 62.

Yu, Kay Kyungsun. 1999. "The Incontestability Clause and the Battle against Insurance Fraud." *For the Defense* 41 (September).

INCORPORATE

To formally create a corporation pursuant to the requirements prescribed by state statute; to confer a corporate franchise upon certain individuals.

INCORPORATION BY REFERENCE

The method of making one document of any kind become a part of another separate document by alluding to the former in the latter and declaring that the former shall be taken and considered as a part of the latter the same as if it were completely set out therein.

It is common drafting practice to incorporate by reference an existing writing into a pleading, contract, or other legal document in order to save space. The incorporating document, rather than copying the exact words of the existing document, describes it, and a photocopy is often attached to the incorporating document. This standard practice, however, encounters difficulty with the requirements prescribed by law for a will. If the will is a holograph—a document disposing of property that is written with one's own hand and not witnessed—the attachment might not be in the handwriting of the deceased and, therefore, invalid. If the will is formal, an attachment might violate the requirement that the testator (one who makes a will) or the witnesses subscribe (sign at the end of the will) the attachment. If subscription is not required, the incorporated document raises the question whether the testator has declared it to be a part of the will if it was not present at the time the will was signed.

The document that is incorporated is usually not treated as a part of the will itself but as an external source from which the meaning of the will can be determined. This maintains the distinction between actual incorporation, an integration achieved by extensive copying of a document into the pages that constitute the will, and INCORPORATION BY REFERENCE, which is a figurative rather than literal integration. Incorporation by reference is treated as if it were actually integrated.

Fear of FRAUDULENT substitutions is probably the basis for the legal insistence upon compliance with certain conditions in order to incorporate a document into a will by reference. Certain requirements exist for incorporation by reference into a will. The document to be incorporated must exist at the time the will is executed. The will must manifest the intention of the testator to incorporate the provisions of the incorporated document. The incorporated document must be sufficiently described to permit its identification. Some courts emphasize that the incorporated document comply with the description. Some, but not all, statutes require that the incorporating document refer to the incorporated document as being in existence in addition to the requirement mentioned earlier that it actually be in existence.

Most states currently allow incorporation by reference into wills upon compliance with the foregoing conditions. In the states that permit holographic wills, most allow the incorporation by reference of nonholographic material, even if actual incorporation would otherwise invalidate the will because it is not entirely in the handwriting of the deceased.

INCORPORATION DOCTRINE

A constitutional doctrine whereby selected provisions of the Bill of Rights are made applicable to the states through the Due Process Clause of the Fourteenth Amendment.

The doctrine of selective incorporation, or simply the INCORPORATION DOCTRINE, makes the first ten amendments to the Constitution—known as the Bill of Rights—binding on the states. Through incorporation, state governments largely are held to the same standards as the federal government with regard to many constitutional rights, including the FIRST AMENDMENT freedoms of speech, RELIGION, and assembly, and the separation of church and state; the FOURTH AMENDMENT freedoms from unwarranted arrest and unreasonable searches and seizures; the FIFTH AMENDMENT PRIVILEGE AGAINST SELF-INCRIMINATION; and the SIXTH AMENDMENT right to a speedy, fair, and public trial. Some provisions of the Bill of Rights—including the requirement of indictment by a GRAND JURY (Sixth Amendment) and the right to a jury trial in civil cases (Seventh Amendment)—have not been applied to the states through the incorporation doctrine.

Until the early twentieth century, the BILL OF RIGHTS was interpreted as applying only to the federal government. In the 1833 case *Barron ex rel. Tiernon v. Mayor of Baltimore,* 32 U.S. (7 Pet.) 243, 8 L. Ed. 672, the Supreme Court expressly limited application of the Bill of Rights to the federal government. By the mid-nineteenth century, this view was being challenged. For example, Republicans who were opposed to southern state laws that made it a crime to speak and publish against SLAVERY alleged that such laws violated First Amendment rights regarding FREEDOM OF SPEECH and FREEDOM OF THE PRESS.

For a brief time following the ratification of the FOURTEENTH AMENDMENT in 1868, it appeared that the Supreme Court might use the PRIVILEGES AND IMMUNITIES Clause of the Fourteenth Amendment to apply the Bill of Rights to the states. However, in the SLAUGHTER-HOUSE CASES, 83 U.S. (16 Wall.) 36, 21 L. Ed. 394 (1873), the first significant Supreme Court ruling on the Fourteenth Amendment, the Court handed down an extremely limiting interpretation of that clause. The Court held that the clause created a distinction between rights associated with state citizenship and rights associated with U.S., or federal, citizenship. It concluded that the Fourteenth Amendment prohibited states from passing laws abridging the rights of U.S. citizenship (which, it implied, were few in number) but had no authority over laws abridging the rights of state citizenship. The effect of this ruling was to put much state legislation beyond the review of the Supreme Court.

Instead of applying the Bill of Rights as a whole to the states, as it might have done through the Privileges and Immunities Clause, the Supreme Court has gradually applied selected elements of the first ten amendments to the states through the Due Process Clause of the Fourteenth Amendment. This process, known as selective incorporation, began in earnest in the 1920s. In GITLOW V. NEW YORK, 268 U.S. 652, 45 S. Ct. 625, 69 L. Ed. 1138 (1925), one of the earliest examples of the use of the incorporation doctrine, the Court held that the First Amendment protection of freedom of speech applied to the states through the Due Process Clause. By the late 1940s, many civil freedoms, including freedom of the press (NEAR V. MINNESOTA, 283 U.S. 697, 51 S. Ct. 625, 75 L. Ed. 1357 [1931]), had been incorporated into the Fourteenth Amendment, as had many of the rights that applied to defendants in criminal cases, including the right to representation by counsel in capital cases (POWELL V. ALABAMA, 287 U.S. 45, 53 S. Ct. 55, 77 L. Ed. 158 [1931]). In 1937, the Court decided that some of the privileges and immunities of the Bill of Rights were so fundamental that states were required to abide by them through the Due Process Clause (*Palko v. Connecticut,* 302 U.S. 319, 58 S. Ct. 149, 82 L. Ed. 288).

In 1947 the Court rejected an argument that the Fifth Amendment's right against SELF-INCRIMINATION applied to the states through the

Fourteenth Amendment (*Adamson v. People of the State of California*, 332 U.S. 46, 67 S. Ct. 1672, 91 L. Ed. 2d 1903 [1947]). However, in one of the most famous dissents in history, Justice HUGO L. BLACK argued that the Fourteenth Amendment incorporated all aspects of the Bill of Rights and applied them to the states. Justice FELIX FRANKFURTER, who wrote a concurrence in *Adamson,* disagreed forcefully with Black, arguing that some rights guaranteed by the Fourteenth Amendment may overlap with the guarantees of the Bill of Rights, but are not based directly upon such rights. The Court was hesitant to apply the incorporation doctrine until 1962, when FRANKFURTER retired from the Court. Following his retirement, most provisions of the Bill of Rights were eventually incorporated to apply to the states.

FURTHER READINGS

Amar, Akhil Reed. 2002. "2000 Daniel J. Meador Lecture: Hugo Black and the Hall of Fame." *Alabama Law Review* 1221. Available online at http://www.law.yale.edu/documents/pdf/2002Hugo.pdf; website home page: http://www.law.yale.edu (accessed August 1, 2009).

Epstein, L., and T. Walker. 2006. *Constitutional Law for a Changing America.* Washington, D.C.: CQ Press.

Lindern, Doug. 2009. "The Incorporation Debate." *Exploring Constitutional Conflicts.* Available online at http://www.law.umkc.edu/faculty/projects/ftrials/conlaw/incorp.htm; website home page: http://www.law.umkc.edu (accessed September 5, 2009).

CROSS REFERENCE

Due Process of Law.

INCORPOREAL

Lacking a physical or material nature but relating to or affecting a body.

Under common law, incorporeal property were rights that affected a tangible item, such as a CHOSE IN ACTION (a right to enforce a debt).

Incorporeal is the opposite of corporeal, a description of the existence of a tangible item.

INCREMENTAL

Additional or increased growth, bulk, quantity, number, or value; enlarged.

Incremental cost is additional or increased cost of an item or service apart from its actual cost. When applied to the price of gas, the incremental cost includes the actual cost of gas to the distributors plus the expenses incurred in

its transportation as well as any taxes imposed upon it.

INCRIMINATE

To charge with a crime; to expose to an accusation or a charge of crime; to involve oneself or another in a criminal prosecution or the danger thereof; as in the rule that a witness is not bound to give testimony that would tend to incriminate him or her.

INCULPATE

To accuse; to involve in blame or guilt.

When an individual who has committed a crime imputes guilt upon another individual, he or she is thereby inculpating such individual.

INCUMBENT

An individual who is in current possession of a particular office and who is legally authorized to discharge the duties of that office.

INCUR

To become subject to and liable for; to have liabilities imposed by act or operation of law.

Expenses are incurred, for example, when the legal obligation to pay them arises. An individual incurs a liability when a money judgment is rendered against him or her by a court.

INDEFEASIBLE

That which cannot be defeated, revoked, or made void. This term is usually applied to an estate or right that cannot be defeated.

INDEFINITE TERM

A prison sentence for a specifically designated length of time up to a certain prescribed maximum, such as one to ten years or 25 years to life.

INDEMNIFY

To compensate for loss or damage; to provide security for financial reimbursement to an individual in case of a specified loss incurred by the person.

Insurance companies indemnify their policyholders against damage caused by such things as fire, theft, and flooding, which are specified

by the terms of the contract between the company and the insured.

INDEMNITY

Recompense for loss, damage, or injuries; restitution or reimbursement.

An *indemnity* contract arises when one individual takes on the obligation to pay for any loss or damage that has been or might be incurred by another individual. The *right to indemnity* and the *duty to indemnify* ordinarily stem from a contractual agreement, which generally protects against liability, loss, or damage.

CROSS REFERENCE

Damages.

INDENTURE

An agreement declaring the benefits and obligations of two or more parties, often applicable in the context of bankruptcy and bond trading.

The term *indenture* primarily describes secured contracts and has several applications in U.S. law. At its simplest, an indenture is an agreement that declares benefits and obligations between two or more parties. In BANKRUPTCY law, for example, it is a MORTGAGE or DEED OF TRUST that constitutes a claim against a debtor. The most common usage of indenture appears in the bond market. Before a bond is issued, the issuer executes a legally binding indenture governing all of the bond's terms. Finally, the concept of indenture has an ignominious place in the history of U.S. labor. Indentured servants of the seventeenth and eighteenth centuries were commonly European workers who contracted to provide labor for a number of years and in return received passage to the American colonies as well as room and board.

As an investment product that is used to raise capital, a bond is simply a written document by which a government, corporation, or individual promises to pay a definite sum of money on a certain date. The issuer of a bond, in cooperation with an underwriter (i.e., a financial organization that sells the bond to the public), prepares in advance an indenture outlining the terms of the bond. The issuer and the underwriter negotiate provisions such as the interest rate, the maturity date, and any restrictions on the issuer's actions. The last detail is especially important to corporate bonds because corporations accrue liability upon becoming bond issuers and therefore seek to have the fewest possible restrictions placed on their business behavior by the terms of the indenture. As a consequence, potential buyers of corporate bonds should know what the indenture specifies before buying them.

Federal law governs these indentures. For 50 years, the Trust Indenture Act of 1939 (TIA) (15 U.S.C.A. § 77aaa) was the relevant law. Significant changes in financial markets prompted Congress to amend the TIA through the SECURITIES Act Amendments of 1990 (Pub. L. No. 101-550, 1990; 104 Stat. 2713), which included the Trust Indenture Reform Act (Pub. L. No. 101-550, 104 Stat. 2713). The reforms simplified the writing of indentures, recognized the increasing internationalization of corporations by creating opportunities for foreign institutions to serve as trustees, and revised standards for conflicts of interest. The reforms also broadened the authority of the SECURITIES AND EXCHANGE COMMISSION.

In early American history, indenture was a form of labor contract. Beginning during the colonial period, employers in the largely agricultural economy faced a labor shortage.

They addressed it in two ways: by buying slaves and by hiring indentured servants. The former were Africans who were brought to the colonies against their will to serve for life; the latter were generally Europeans from England and Germany who had entered multiyear employment contracts. From the late sixteenth century to the late eighteenth century, approximately half of the 350,000 European immigrants to the colonies were indentured servants. During the seventeenth century, these servants outnumbered slaves.

An indentured servant agreed to a four- to seven-year contract, and in return received passage from Europe and guarantees of work, food, and lodging. Colonial courts enforced the contracts of indentured servants, which were often harsh. Employers were seen as masters, and the servants had not only to work for them but also to obey their orders in all matters. For some, indentured servitude was not a VOLUNTARY ACT. Impoverished women and children were pressed into servitude, as were convicts. Nevertheless, this servitude was not equivalent to SLAVERY. Slaves remained slaves for life, whereas indentured servants were released at the end of their contracts. Moreover, as parties to a contract, indentured servants had rights that slaves never enjoyed. The practice of indentured servitude persisted into the early nineteenth century.

FURTHER READINGS

Ballam, Deborah A. 1996. "Exploding the Original Myth Regarding Employment-at-Will: The True Origins of the Doctrine." *Berkeley Journal of Employment and Labor Law* 17, no. 1.

———. 1995. "The Traditional View on the Origins of the Employment-at-Will Doctrine: Myth or Reality?" *American Business Law Journal* 33 (fall).

Riger, Martin. 1990. "The Trust Indenture as Bargained Contract: The Persistence of Myth." *Journal of Corporation Law* 16 (winter).

INDEPENDENCE

One of the essential attributes of a state under INTERNATIONAL LAW is external sovereignty—that is, the right to exercise freely the full range of power a state possesses under international law. Recognition of a state as independent necessarily implies that the recognizing states have no legal authority over the independent state. The status of a fully independent state should be contrasted with that of dependent or vassal states, where a superior state has the legal authority to impose its will over the subject, or inferior, state.

INDEPENDENT AUDIT

A systematic review of the accuracy and truthfulness of the accounting records of a particular individual, business, or organization by a person or firm skilled in the necessary accounting methods and not related in any way to the person or firm undergoing the audit.

INDEPENDENT CONTRACTOR

A person who contracts to do work for another person according to his or her own processes and methods; the contractor is not subject to another's control except for what is specified in a mutually binding agreement for a specific job.

An independent contractor contracts with an employer to do a particular piece of work. This working relationship is a flexible one that provides benefits to both the worker and the employer. However, there are drawbacks to the relationship as well. The decision to hire or work as an independent contractor should be weighed carefully. Properly distinguishing between employees and independent contractors has important consequences, and the failure to maintain the distinction can be costly.

Taxes

The status of independent contractor carries with it many tax ramifications. For example, an employee shares the costs of SOCIAL SECURITY and MEDICARE taxes with his or her employer; whereas an independent contractor is responsible for the entire amounts. Yet independent contractors generally qualify for more business deductions on their federal income taxes than do employees. Also, independent contractors must pay estimated taxes each quarter, whereas employees generally have taxes withheld from their paychecks by their employer.

One important disadvantage of working as an independent contractor is that standard employment benefits—such as health, life, dental, and disability insurance; funded retirement plans; paid vacation time; and paid maternity or paternity leave—are not available. Independent contractors may fund their own benefits, but not on a tax-free basis—whereas many benefits provided by employers to employees are, by law, tax free.

Labor Relations

Congress and the states have enacted numerous laws geared toward protecting employees. The National Labor Relations Act (29 U.S.C.A. § 152(3)) protects employees and union members from unfair bargaining practices; Title VII of the CIVIL RIGHTS Act of 1964 (42 U.S.C.A. § 2000 et seq.) protects employees from discrimination on the basis of race, sex, RELIGION, and national origin; the AGE DISCRIMINATION in Employment Act (20 U.S.C.A. § 623) protects employees from age discrimination; the FAIR LABOR STANDARDS ACT (29 U.S.C.A. § 203) establishes MINIMUM WAGE and overtime standards; the EMPLOYEE RETIREMENT INCOME SECURITY ACT of 1974 (29 U.S.C.A. § 1002) ensures the security of employee retirement funds; and the Occupational Safety and Health Act (29 U.S.C.A. § 652) protects employees from environmental work hazards. Most states also have unemployment and workers' compensation laws, which obligate employers to pay, directly or indirectly, for medical treatment or lost wages, or both, for employees who are injured while at work or who lose their job. None of these laws protect independent contractors. And because compliance often comes at great expense, employers can significantly reduce their liability and increase their profit margin by hiring independent contractors rather than employees.

Economics and Social Policy

Although not protected by law to the extent of an employee, an independent contractor has far greater control over elements such as work hours and work methods. Unlike most employees, an independent contractor may opt to work at night or on weekends, leaving weekdays free. An independent contractor may choose to wear blue jeans or a business suit, take one week of vacation or 30 weeks, or interrupt work to attend a child's school play or to go to the beach. Moreover, although the other contracting party retains control over the finished work product, an independent contractor has exclusive control over the actual work process. Decisions such as whether to work for one person or several, whether to work a little or a lot, whether to accept or reject an undesirable work project, and how much money to charge are made by the independent contractor.

The other party, in turn, enjoys mainly profit-related advantages by hiring an independent contractor instead of an employee. For one

thing, an employer need not provide an independent contractor with vacation time, pension, insurance, or other costly benefits. Management costs that ordinarily go toward training and overseeing large numbers of employees decrease when independent contractors do the work. Some say that because independent contractors benefit directly from their hard work, the quality of their work may be higher than it is for full-time employees who might be less motivated. And by hiring independent contractors, an employer enjoys the greater ease and flexibility to expand and contract the workforce as demand rises and falls.

Tort Liability

The common-law doctrine of RESPONDEAT SUPERIOR holds an employer liable for the negligent acts of its employee. Generally, under COMMON LAW, the hiring party is not responsible for the NEGLIGENCE of an independent contractor. The Restatement (Second) of Torts identifies a few exceptions to this rule. The hiring party may be liable when, owing to its failure to exercise reasonable care to retain a competent and careful contractor, a THIRD PARTY is physically harmed. Also, when an independent contractor acts pursuant to orders or directions negligently given by the hiring party, the latter may be held liable. Notwithstanding the exceptions, the hiring party's risk of liability is greatly reduced by hiring independent contractors rather than employees.

Defining the Independent Contractor

No consistent, uniform definition distinguishes an employee from an independent contractor. Some statutes contain their own definitions. The U.S. Supreme Court has held that when a statute contains the term *employee* but fails to define it adequately, there is a presumption that traditional agency-law criteria for identifying master-servant relationships apply (*National Mutual Insurance Co. v. Darden*, 503 U.S. 318, 112 S. Ct. 1344, 111 L. Ed. 2d 581 [1992]).

One comprehensive test that takes into account agency-law criteria and numerous other factors courts have created to define independent contractor status was developed by the INTERNAL REVENUE SERVICE (IRS). Known collectively as the 20-factor test, the enumerated criteria generally fall within three categories: control (whether the employer or the worker has control over the work performed), organization (whether the worker is integrated into the business), and economic realities (whether the worker directly benefits from his or her labor). The 20 factors serve only as a guideline. Each factor's degree of importance varies depending on the occupation and the facts involved in a particular case.

Twenty-factor Test

1. A worker who is required to comply with *instructions* about when, where, and how he or she must work is usually an employee.

2. If an employer *trains* a worker—requires an experienced employee to work with the worker, educates the worker through correspondence, requires the worker to attend meetings, or uses other methods—this normally indicates that the worker is an employee.

3. If a worker's services are *integrated* into business operations, this tends to show that the worker is subject to direction and control and is thus an employee. This is the case particularly when a business's success or continuation depends to a large extent on the performance of certain services.

4. If a worker's services must be *rendered personally*, there is a presumption that the employer is interested in the methods by which the services are accomplished as well as in the result, making the worker an employee.

5. If an employer *hires, supervises, and pays assistants* for a worker, this indicates control over the worker on the job, making the worker an employee.

6. A *continuing relationship* between a worker and an employer, even at irregular intervals, tends to show an employer-employee relationship.

7. An employer who sets *specific hours of work* for a worker exhibits control over the worker, indicating that the worker is an employee.

8. If a worker is working *substantially full-time* for an employer, the worker is presumably not free to do work for other employers and is therefore an employee.

9. Work performed on an *employer's premises* suggests the employer's control over a worker, making the worker an employee. This is especially true when work could be done elsewhere. However, the mere fact that work is done off the employer's premises does not necessarily make the worker an independent contractor.

10. If a worker is required to perform services in an *order or sequence* set by an employer, the employer has control over the worker that demonstrates an employer-employee relationship.

11. A worker who is required to submit regular *oral or written reports* to an employer is likely an employee.

12. *Payment by the hour, week, or month* tends to indicate that a worker is an employee; payment made by the job or on a straight commission points to an independent contractor.

13. A worker is ordinarily an employee if an employer pays for the worker's *business or travel expenses*.

14. An employer who furnishes a worker with significant *tools, materials, or other equipment* tends to show that the worker is an employee.

15. A worker who *significantly invests* in facilities used to perform services and not typically maintained by employees (such as office space) is generally an independent contractor.

16. A worker who can *realize a profit or loss* resulting from his or her services is generally an independent contractor.

17. A worker who performs *for more than one firm at a time* is generally an independent contractor.

18. If a worker makes his or her *services available to the general public* on a regular and consistent basis, that worker is generally an independent contractor.

19. An employer's *right to discharge* a worker tends to show that the worker is an employee. An employee must obey an employer's instructions in order to stay employed; an independent contractor can be fired only if the work result fails to meet the agreed-upon specifications.

20. If a worker has the *right to terminate* his or her relationship with an employer at any time without incurring liability, such as breach of contract, that worker is likely an employee.

FURTHER READINGS

Fishman, Stephen. 2008. *Working for Yourself: Law and Taxes for Independent Contractors, Freelancers, and Consultants.* 4th ed. Berkeley, CA: Nolo.

Fishman, Stephen, and Amy Delpo. 2003. *Hiring Independent Contractors: The Employers' Legal Guide.* 3d ed. Berkeley, CA: Nolo.

Nunnallee, Walter H. 1992. "Why Congress Needs to Fix the Employee/Independent Contractor Tax Rules." *North Carolina Central Law Journal* 20.

Pacynski, Rick A. 1993. "Legal Challenges in Using Independent Contractors." *Michigan Bar Journal* 72 (July).

Payton, Janet G. 2001. "Checklist for Determining Independent Contractor Status." *Corporate Counsel's Quarterly* 17 (October).

Ringquist, Neil A. 1997. *Independent Contractor or Employee?: A Practitioner's Guide.* Chicago: CCH.

Sheppard, Lee A. 1999. "Resolving the Independent Contractor Dispute for the Future." *Tax Notes* 83 (May).

Treasury Department. Internal Revenue Service. 1987. *Revenue Ruling 87–41: Employment Status Under Section 530(D) of the Revenue Act of 1978.* Washington, D.C.: U.S. Government Printing Office. Available online at http://www.medlawplus.com/legalforms/instruct/revrul87-41.htm; website home page: http://www.medlawplus.com (accessed August 1, 2009).

Wood, Robert W. 2005. *Legal Guide to Independent Contractor Status.* Frederick, MD: Aspen Press.

CROSS REFERENCES

Employment Law; Labor Law; Master and Servant.

INDEPENDENT COUNSEL

An attorney appointed by the federal government to investigate and prosecute federal government officials.

Before 1988, independent counsel were referred to as special prosecutors. In 1988 Congress amended the ETHICS IN GOVERNMENT ACT OF 1978 (Ethics Act) (92 Stat. 1824 [2 U.S.C.A. §§ 701 et seq.]) to change the title to *independent counsel.* This change was made because lawmakers considered the term *special prosecutor* to be too inflammatory.

Independent counsel are attorneys who investigate and prosecute criminal activity in government. They hold people who make and implement laws accountable for their own criminal activity.

The need for independent counsel arises from the CONFLICT OF INTEREST posed by having the established criminal justice system investigate government misconduct. Prosecutors and law enforcement agencies work under the authority of government leaders. When government leaders are accused of wrongdoing, these entities face conflicting duties: the duty to uphold the laws on the one hand, versus the duty of loyalty to superiors on the other. Independent counsels do not answer to the government officials they are assigned to investigate, and therefore they avoid much of this conflict of interest. One potential element for bias remains: the political affiliations of the accused government official and the independent counsel. The people rely on independent counsel's duty as members of the bar to uphold the laws and the U.S. CONSTITUTION, to overcome any similarities or differences in political beliefs. Independent counsel who appear to be motivated by political or other bias may be dismissed.

President ULYSSES S. GRANT was the first to appoint independent counsel to investigate high-level federal government officials. In 1875, Grant's personal secretary, Orville E. Babcock, was indicted in federal district court on charges of accepting bribes. Babcock had allegedly arranged favorable tax treatment for a group of moonshiners who were known as the Whiskey Ring. Grant removed the federal district attorney and replaced him with an independent counsel, who finished the investigation and the trial.

In the early 1920s, another bribery scandal, known as Teapot Dome, led to the appointment of an independent counsel. President WARREN G. HARDING appointed independent counsel to investigate the sale of oil-rich federal lands. The independent counsel's investigation led to the prosecution of Harding's secretary of the interior, Albert B. Fall.

In its later days, President Harry S. Truman's administration labored under allegations of corruption. Specifically, officials in the INTERNAL REVENUE SERVICE and the Tax Division of the JUSTICE DEPARTMENT were accused of giving favorable treatment to tax evaders. Attorney General J. Howard McGrath appointed a special assistant attorney to investigate. When the special prosecutor sought to investigate McGrath, McGrath fired him. Truman then fired McGrath and refused to pursue the matter.

The WATERGATE scandals of the 1970s gave Congress the incentive to create the first statutory framework for investigating government officials. In 1973, newspaper reports concerning a burglary at the Democratic National Committee headquarters in the Watergate Hotel in Washington,

D.C., implicated officials in the administration of President RICHARD M. NIXON. Attorney General ELLIOT L. RICHARDSON appointed ARCHIBALD COX, a Harvard law professor, as independent counsel to investigate the situation.

Cox endeavored to uncover the facts surrounding Watergate. As it became apparent that White House officials were involved in the episode, Cox was forced to investigate the president himself. When Cox asked Nixon for White House tape recordings, Nixon sought to have Cox fired. One weekend in October 1973, in a turn of events later known as the Saturday Night Massacre, Richardson and Deputy Attorney General William D. Ruckelshaus resigned rather than carry out Nixon's order to fire Cox. That same night, SOLICITOR GENERAL ROBERT H. BORK, who had just become acting head of the DEPARTMENT OF JUSTICE, carried out Nixon's request and fired Cox.

Nixon then appointed LEON JAWORSKI to be the second independent counsel to investigate Watergate. Like Cox, Jaworski sought Nixon's White House tapes. After a court battle that reached the U.S. Supreme Court in *United States v. Nixon,* 418 U.S. 683, 94 S. Ct. 3090, 41 L. Ed. 2d 1039 (1974), Jaworski successfully subpoenaed the tapes. Nixon resigned the office of president shortly thereafter.

After the Saturday Night Massacre and the Watergate matter, it became obvious that independent counsel were necessary to check government misconduct. In 1978 Congress passed the Ethics Act to establish, on the federal level, a statutory scheme for policing the EXECUTIVE BRANCH.

Ethics in Government Act

Under the Ethics Act, the process of appointing independent counsel began when the attorney general received information on criminal activity. The attorney general could investigate all violations of CRIMINAL LAW other than minor misdemeanors and minor violations. This permission included special ethics laws that applied to executive branch officials, such as laws that make it illegal for an executive branch official to receive money from a person if the official has arranged for that person to be employed by the federal government.

There had to be sufficient credible information of criminal activity to constitute grounds for an investigation, and the information had to

Patrick Fitzgerald has held the position of special counsel since 2003. The U.S. Department of Justice Office of Special Counsel replaced the Office of the Independent Counsel in 1999.
AP IMAGES

pertain to the president, the vice president, a member of the president's CABINET, a high-level executive officer, a high-level Justice Department official, the director or deputy director of the CENTRAL INTELLIGENCE AGENCY, the commissioner of the Internal Revenue Service, any person with a personal or financial relationship with the attorney general or any other officer in the Department of Justice, or the president's campaign chair or treasurer.

Once the attorney general received credible inculpatory information, the attorney general had to decide within 30 days whether to investigate the matter. If the attorney general determined that the matter warranted an investigation, he had to begin an investigation. The attorney general could not conduct this initial investigation for more than 150 days. At the close of the investigation, the attorney general submitted a report to the Independent Counsel Division of the U.S. Court of Appeals for the District of Columbia Circuit. The members of this three-judge panel were appointed by the chief justice of the U.S. Supreme Court.

In the report, the attorney general requested or declined the appointment of independent counsel on the matter. A court could not review this decision. If the attorney general requested independent counsel, the panel appointed one and defined the scope of the investigation. Generally, the panel limited the counsel's investigation to certain persons or certain issues.

The appointment of independent counsel was unusual because the Department of Justice already is required to police the executive branch. In theory, the attorney general is an independent official. In practice, however, he usually is a political ally of the president. Like other executive branch officials, the attorney general is appointed by the president and reports to the president. Because the attorney general decided whether independent counsel should be appointed by the panel, an investigation could be influenced by the executive branch. An attorney general might have been reluctant to recommend the prosecution of a political ally. However, if enough sources exerted sufficient pressure, the attorney general could be forced to avoid the appearance of favoritism by requesting the appointment of independent counsel.

The appointment of independent counsel was often politically charged, in large part because independent counsel investigated executive branch officials and their political operatives. When politicians are investigated, an invariable response is that the investigation is politically motivated. Nevertheless, most politicians considered independent counsel to be crucial to conveying at least the appearance of propriety in the executive branch. The danger of independent counsel is that they may be called for on a regular basis by politicians who are opposed to the president, for the sole purpose of demoralizing the executive branch and gaining an electoral advantage.

Once appointed, independent counsel could proceed as any other prosecutor. Counsel filed criminal charges in the U.S. District Court for the District of Columbia and had the power to SUBPOENA witnesses, and to grant immunity to witnesses.

Under the Ethics Act, only the attorney general could fire independent counsel. Independent counsel could be dismissed only for GOOD CAUSE or because a physical or mental condition prevented counsel from performing the position's duties. Dismissed independent counsel had the right to appeal to the U.S. District Court for the District of Columbia.

The first government officials investigated under the new Ethics Act were two officials in the administration of President JIMMY CARTER. After investigating allegations of drug use and conflict of interest, the independent counsel declined to file criminal charges.

In May 1986 an official in the administration of President RONALD REAGAN mounted a challenge to the Ethics Act. Theodore B. Olson, a former assistant attorney general in the administration, argued that the executive branch had the power to conduct all criminal investigations, and that it was unconstitutional for Congress to give the JUDICIARY the power to appoint independent prosecutors. The U.S. Supreme Court disagreed, RULING that the Ethics Act was constitutional because the attorney general, an officer within the executive branch, had the power to remove independent counsel and therefore retained ultimate control (*Morrison v. Olson*, 487 U.S. 654, 108 S. Ct. 2597, 101 L. Ed. 2d 569 [1988]).

The list of federal government officials investigated or prosecuted by independent counsel under the Ethics Act is long and ever growing. In December 1987 Michael Deaver, former aide to President Reagan, was convicted of perjury after prosecution by independent counsel. In February 1988 Lyn Nofziger, another presidential aide, was convicted of ethical violations. Nofziger's conviction was later overturned on appeal. President Reagan's attorney general EDWIN MEESE III resigned in July 1988 after an investigation by independent counsel James McKay. Although Meese was not prosecuted, McKay stated in his report to the panel that he believed that Meese had broken the law by helping a company in which Meese owned stock, Wedtech Corporation, to solicit contracts with the U.S. military.

In December 1986, before he resigned, Meese appointed Lawrence E. Walsh as independent counsel to investigate and prosecute wrongdoing in the burgeoning Iran-Contra scandal, which involved trading arms to Iranians and diverting the proceeds to fund a covert war in Nicaragua. Walsh was able to obtain several convictions of high-level Reagan administration officials, but some of those were overturned on appeal.

The administration of President BILL CLINTON was heavily investigated by independent counsel. In 1994, Donald C. Smaltz was appointed as independent counsel to investigate Clinton's secretary of agriculture, Mike Espy. The independent counsel was directed to investigate whether Espy had accepted gifts from organizations and individuals with business pending before the DEPARTMENT OF AGRICULTURE and whether Espy had committed any crimes connected to, or arising out of, the investigation, such as OBSTRUCTION OF JUSTICE and false testimony or statements.

In October 1994, just a few months after Smaltz began work, Espy resigned his office. Nevertheless, the investigation of Espy and several associates continued. Over the next four years, Smaltz spent more than $17 million to bring 30 counts of corruption against Espy. At Espy's 1998 trial, Smaltz produced 70 prosecution witnesses, yet a jury took just nine hours to acquit Espy on all 30 counts.

In January 1994 Robert Fiske Jr. was appointed as independent counsel to investigate the death of White House counsel Vincent Foster and alleged financial misconduct by Clinton and the first lady, HILLARY RODHAM CLINTON. Because the Ethics Act had lapsed, Attorney General JANET RENO herself chose Fiske. When Congress reauthorized the Ethics Act, Reno submitted the matter to the panel, which appointed a new independent counsel, KENNETH W. STARR.

Starr, a former U.S. solicitor general and U.S. district court judge, worked on the Clinton investigation until 1999. He obtained convictions against a number of Clinton associates, but it was not until 1998 that he ensnared President Clinton. Allegations of a sexual affair with a White House intern shifted Starr's work. In January 1998 Clinton was deposed for the SEXUAL HARASSMENT lawsuit filed by Paula Jones. At the deposition, Clinton denied that there had been a sexual relationship with intern Monica Lewinsky. In August 1998 he changed his story when called before Starr's GRAND JURY, but he still would not give details. In the fall, Starr sent his report to the House of Representatives and testified before a House panel. Starr accused the president of having had a sexual affair with the intern. The report, which contained graphic sexual descriptions from Lewinsky, claimed that Clinton had committed perjury and obstruction of justice, and that he had abused his presidential power in an effort to keep the affair from coming to light. This report led to the House passing ARTICLES OF IMPEACHMENT in December 1998. Clinton was acquitted of the charges by the Senate in February 1999.

By the end of Starr's investigation, very few people in Congress or the White House had positive feelings about the Ethics in Government Act. The 1980s and 1990s had seen independent counsel spend years and millions of dollars on seemingly open-ended investigations of official misconduct, usually with little to show for it. Even Starr agreed that the law should expire, testifying to that effect before Congress in April 1999. With no congressional support for its continuation, the act was allowed

to expire on June 30, 1999. Although bills have been introduced seeking to curtail the powers of future independent counsel while requiring greater accountability, Congress has not acted.

With the lapsing of the Ethics in Government Act, the Department of Justice resumed appointing special counsel to investigate alleged criminal acts by executive branch members. The department's Office of Special Counsel has conducted several high-profile investigations into matters including the leaking of the identity of undercover CIA agent Valerie Plame Wilson by members of the Bush Administration. Patrick Fitzgerald, U.S. Attorney for Northern Illinois, was appointed special counsel in December 2003 to investigate the so-called Plame Affair. His investigation ultimately led to the prosecution and conviction of Lewis "Scooter" Libby, Vice President Dick Cheney's chief of staff in 2007.

Congress and Independent Counsel

When Congress is in session, independent counsel do not investigate or prosecute the criminal activities of members of Congress. Instead, Congress polices its members through ethics committees and can expel a member with a two-thirds vote of the member's chamber (U.S. Const. art. I, § 5, cl. 2). Members of Congress cannot be arrested while Congress is in session, except for treason, felony, or BREACH OF THE PEACE (§ 6, cl. 1). When Congress is not in session, members of Congress are not exempt, and they may be prosecuted in the jurisdiction where an alleged offense occurred.

Congress may also investigate official wrongdoing in the executive branch. When Congress and independent counsel are investigating the same persons or events, the matter can become a political tug-of-war, and one investigation can run afoul of the other. For example, if Congress grants immunity to a witness who is under investigation by independent counsel, it becomes difficult for independent counsel to prosecute the witness.

State or Local Independent Counsel

Independent counsel also may be appointed at the state or local level. In Alaska, for example, executive branch officials may be investigated by independent counsel who is appointed by a special personnel board. Governor Sarah Palin was investigated in 2008 by an independent counsel while she was running for Vice President for allegedly seeking to have her former brother-in-law fired from the state police department. The independent counsel exonerated her of ethics violations just days before the presidential election.

In its broadest sense, the term *independent counsel* can describe any attorney who is appointed by one party to represent, prosecute, or bring suit against someone who is connected with that party. For example, in Alaska, a municipal school board is represented by a municipal attorney. If the municipal attorney has a conflict of interest in a particular matter, the school board may appoint independent counsel for that particular matter (§ 29.20.370). Thus, if the municipal attorney owns stock in a construction company that is hired by the school board, the school board might seek a different attorney to handle legal issues associated with that company, in order to avoid the appearance of collusion between government and private business. The new attorney would be called an independent counsel, to describe his or her independence in the matter.

FURTHER READINGS

Danner, Allison Marston. 2003. "Navigating Law and Politics: The Prosecutor of the International Criminal Court and the Independent Counsel." *Stanford Law Review* 55.

Kutler, Stanley I. 1994. "In the Shadow of Watergate: Legal, Political, and Cultural Implications." *Nova Law Review* 18.

Greenberg, Gerald S., ed. 2000. *Historical Encyclopedia of U.S. Independent Counsel Investigations* New York: Greenwood Press.

Sels, John van Loben. 1995. "From Watergate to White-water: Congressional Use Immunity and Its Impact on the Independent Counsel." *Georgetown Law Journal* 83.

Solloway, Robert G. 1988. "The Institutionalized Wolf: An Analysis of the Unconstitutionality of the Independent Counsel Provisions of the Ethics In Government Act of 1978." *Indiana Law Review* 21.

Plame Wilson, Valerie. 2008. *Fair Game: How a Top CIA Agent Was Betrayed by Her Own Government.* New York: Simon & Schuster.

CROSS REFERENCE

Congress of the United States.

INDEPENDENT PARTIES

The current two-party system of Democrats and Republicans evolved during the mid–nineteenth century. Before that, the Democrats squared off against the Whigs, led by HENRY CLAY and DANIEL WEBSTER. The WHIG PARTY was founded around 1834 to oppose the populist policies of Democratic president ANDREW JACKSON. Its members objected to Jackson's views on banking and the designation of federal funds, among other things.

Although the United States has a firmly established two-party system, independent parties play an important role in U.S. politics. Democrats and Republicans win the vast majority of federal, state, and local elections, but independent candidates often reflect popular attitudes and concerns. Most independent parties—also known as third parties—begin in response to a specific issue, candidate, or political philosophy.

Although Whig presidential candidates were successful in 1840 (WILLIAM HENRY HARRISON) and 1848 (ZACHARY TAYLOR), the party survived for less than 40 years. In the 1850s, the Republicans entered the political scene as independents. After Republican Abraham Lincoln's victory in the 1860 U.S. presidential race, the REPUBLICAN PARTY replaced the Whig party as the main party opposing the Democrats. Many northern Whigs joined the Republicans, whereas southern Whigs became aligned with the Democrats.

The platforms and purposes of independent parties, both past and present, vary tremendously. Some independent parties, such as the SOCIALIST PARTY, the Communist Party, and the LIBERTARIAN PARTY, were formed to promote their political world views rather than a single issue or a charismatic leader. The Socialist Party, founded in 1901, has been relatively long-lasting. Its heyday was around 1912, when its candidate, EUGENE V. DEBS, received about six percent of the popular vote in the presidential election. That same year, more than 1,000 Socialists held elected positions throughout the United States.

Other independent parties were founded by dissident progressives from one or both of the major parties. In 1912 progressives in the Republican Party broke off and formed the PROGRESSIVE PARTY, also known as the Bull Moose Party, naming former U.S. president THEODORE ROOSEVELT as its presidential candidate. Roosevelt lost to Democratic nominee Woodrow Wilson in the general election.

In 1924 another progressive party, called the League for Progressive Political Action, was launched. This party backed Senator ROBERT M. LA FOLLETTE of Wisconsin, who received 16 percent of the popular vote while losing to Republican incumbent CALVIN COOLIDGE.

In 1948 progressives in the DEMOCRATIC PARTY formed another Progressive Party. It supported Henry A. Wallace in an unsuccessful bid to unseat incumbent Democratic president HARRY S. TRUMAN.

Other offshoots of the two major parties include the Locofocos, or Equal Rights Party, and the Mugwumps. The Locofocos emerged from the Democratic Party in the early nineteenth century. They supported stricter bank regulation and antitrust laws. The Mugwumps broke from the Republican Party in the 1884 presidential campaign and supported the Democratic nominee Grover Cleveland. Their name was derived from the Algonquian word for *big chief.* The Mugwumps' defection contributed to the Democrats' victory.

Some independent candidates transcend their party affiliation. Billionaire H. Ross Perot captured the public's attention during the 1992 presidential election, which was won by Democrat BILL CLINTON. Of the 19 million U.S. citizens who voted for Perot, few cast their ballot in support of his independent party. People voted for Perot, the person, as an alternative to Clinton and the Republican incumbent GEORGE H.W. BUSH. Perot ran again as an independent in 1996.

An independent candidate and a specific issue are often inextricably linked. This was the case in 1968, with Alabama governor GEORGE WALLACE and his American Independent Party. Wallace was a vocal opponent of CIVIL RIGHTS. His position on segregation and states' rights and his bold personality were the sum total of the party.

Other important social issues have spawned independent parties. Before the CIVIL WAR, the Liberty Party was created by abolitionists to outlaw SLAVERY. Similarly, the Free-Soil Party—which later became part of the Republican Party—was started in 1848 to prevent the extension of slavery into new U.S. territories and states. Bigotry was the driving force behind the Know-Nothing Party—also called the American Party—formed in 1849 to pursue discrimination against immigrants and Roman Catholics. The name referred to the secrecy surrounding the group: Members were instructed to say, "I don't know," if asked about the party. The PROHIBITION PARTY was formed in 1869 by temperance activists who wanted to ban the sale and consumption of alcohol.

On the other end of the ideological spectrum were the Dixiecrats. Led by Strom Thurmond, these were a group of southern Democrats who were opposed to President Truman's civil rights policies. The Dixiecrats splintered from the main party in 1948.

The effect of an independent party on a presidential race varies. In 1912 independent candidate Theodore Roosevelt of the Bull Moose Party, won more votes than Republican nominee WILLIAM HOWARD TAFT, and in effect delivered the election to Democratic challenger Woodrow Wilson. In other presidential elections, independents made barely a ripple. For example, in 1872 the Prohibition party candidate received a mere 5,600 votes.

In the remarkable presidential election of 2000, independent candidates played prominent and controversial roles. On the political right, author and media commentator PATRICK BUCHANAN ran on the REFORM PARTY ticket, espousing a mixture of social conservatism, labor support, and international isolationism. On the left, progressive activist and consumer advocate RALPH NADER received the GREEN PARTY nomination. Declaring the two main parties to be almost identical, Nader appealed to liberals and youth with his idealistic speeches on corporate influence and the erosion of democracy.

Although neither third-party candidate was invited to the official presidential debates between Democrat AL GORE and Republican GEORGE W. BUSH, no one foresaw their ultimate impact upon the election. After the bitter deadlock in Florida between Gore and Bush produced ballot disputes, recounts, and lawsuits, the totals in that critical state revealed that Nader had taken enough votes there and elsewhere to tip the decision to Bush. Furthermore, Buchanan also scored heavily in a Gore stronghold, leading the conservative candidate to explain that the votes were probably due to poorly designed ballots.

In terms of sheer votes, both Nader and Buchanan fared poorly. Nader captured only three percent of the vote, and Buchanan less than one percent. As a result, neither of their parties qualified for federal matching funds for the 2004 elections, a fate surely likely to hamper their effectiveness at a time when money is of major significance in running political campaigns.

Nader in particular earned the enmity of many Democrats who viewed him as a spoiler. Even his former allies took to the pages of *The Nation* and other liberal publications to denounce him for undermining Gore's chances. Nader was unrepentant. In his 2002 book, *Crashing the Party: How to Tell the Truth and Still Run for President*, Nader defended his candidacy as an intellectually and morally superior choice to what he deemed the corruption of the Democrats and Republicans.

In the 2004 election, Nader ran as an independent, rather than the Green Party candidate. Nader was accompanied on the ballot by several other third-party candidates, including Michael Peroutka of the CONSTITUTION PARTY, Michael Badnarik of the Libertarian Party, and David Cobb of the Green Party. Although Nader fared the best of the third-party candidates, earning third place in the election, he garnered a mere 0.38 percent of the vote.

To the extent that the 2004 election reflected a declining interest in independent parties, that trend continued into the following presidential election. In 2008 Nader again ran as an independent candidate, accompanied on the ballot by Bob Barr for the Libertarian Party, Chuck Baldwin for the CONSTITUTION Party, and Cynthia McKinney for the Green Party. Again, Nader came in third, earning 0.56 percent of the vote. With the exception of Nader, the 2008 third-party candidates were given little media attention. Some critics fault the media for ignoring those candidates altogether, thereby eliminating them from any discussion related to the race.

If the contemporary appeal of independent parties has proven underwhelming, their ability to influence close races is one argument for their significance. This impact is felt even more sharply in an age of vast voter apathy. For all the hubbub generated by the 2000 election controversy, only 51 percent of registered voters bothered to vote that year. Independent parties may find that their ability to control slight percentage points in elections translates into broader political power to shape debate and even to nudge the mainstream parties toward their positions.

Some citizens are reluctant to vote for an independent candidate, believing that such a gesture is futile. Indeed, the odds of winning either the popular or electoral vote are slim. Still, the political dialogue generated by independent candidates is a meaningful contribution to the democratic process. Even when independent candidates lose the election, the public is treated to ideas and perspectives that are seldom broached by the mainstream parties.

FURTHER READINGS

Bass, Harold F. 2000. *Historical Dictionary of United States Political Parties.* Lanham, MD: Scarecrow Press, Inc.

Cohen, Ted. 2002. "Nader: It's Too Early to Decide on '04 Run." *Portland Press Herald* (June 20): 10B.

Douglas, William. 2000. "Unapologetic Nader Faces Anger over His Fla. Role." *Newsday* (November 9): A48.

Engelhardt, Joel, and Scott McCabe. 2001. "Over-Votes Cost Gore the Election in Florida: A Palm Beach Post Analysis of 19,125 Ballots That Were Punched More Than Once." *The Palm Beach Post* (March 11): 1A.

"Reform Party Eyes Survival Challenge: Conference Hopes to Revive Fortunes." 2001. *The Washington Times* (July 26).

Thornburgh, Nathan. 2008. "Could Third-Party Candidates Be Spoilers?" *Time* (November 3): 10B.

Thornburgh, Nathan. 2008. "Can the Libertarians Go Mainstream?" *Time* (May 21)

Wilson, James Q. 1992. *American Government: Institutions and Policies.* Lexington, MA: Heath.

CROSS REFERENCE

Election Campaign Financing

INDETERMINATE

That which is uncertain or not particularly designated.

INDEX

A book containing references, alphabetically arranged, to the contents of a series or collection of documents or volumes; or a section (normally at the end) of a single volume or set of volumes containing such references to its contents.

Statistical indexes are also used to track or measure changes in the economy (for example, the Consumer Price Index) and movement in stock markets (for example, Standard & Poor's Index). Such indexes are usually keyed to a base year, month, or other period of comparison.

In mortgage financing, the term is used to determine adjustable-rate mortgage (ARM) interest rates after the discount period ends. Common indexes for ARMs are one-year Treasury securities and the national average cost of funds to savings and loan associations.

INDEX TO LEGAL PERIODICALS

The set of volumes that lists what has appeared in print from 1926 to the present in the major law reviews and law-oriented magazines in various countries—usually organized according to author, title, and subject, and containing a table of cases.

The *Index to Legal Periodicals*, published by the H. W. Wilson Company of New York, aids individuals who are conducting legal research by enabling them to search the contents of past and currently published periodicals, thereby providing access to secondary source materials. The index is bound every three years, with annual supplements and ADVANCE SHEETS for every month except September.

The *Index to Legal Periodicals* is also available in an on-line form through the Online Computer Library Center, Inc., based in Dublin, Ohio. The database contains records of articles from more than 900 journals and more than 1,400 monographs; the total number of records exceeds 500,000. The earliest articles date back to 1981.

FURTHER READINGS

"Index to Legal Periodicals Full Text." 2009. *H.W. Wilson* Web site. Available online at http://www.hwwilson.com/Databases/legal.htm; http://www.hwwilson.com (accessed September 5, 2009).

Kunz, Christina L., et al. 2008. *The Process of Legal Research.* 7th ed. New York: Wolters Kluwer Law & Business.

INDIAN CHILD WELFARE ACT

The Indian Child Welfare Act (ICWA), passed by Congress in 1978, intended to limit the historical practice of removing Native American children from their tribe and family and placing them in a non-Indian family or institution (25 U.S.C.A. §§ 1901–1963). The stated purpose of the act is to "[p]rotect the best interests of Indian children and to promote the stability and security of Indian tribes." The act seeks to achieve these goals through three principal methods: by establishing minimum federal standards for when Indian children can be removed from their family; by placing children who are removed in a foster or adoptive home that reflects the unique values of Indian culture; and by providing assistance to family services programs operated by Indian tribes.

The impetus behind the passage of the ICWA was a widespread recognition of the failure of the federal government's historical policy of removing Indian children from their family and tribe and attempting to assimilate them into white culture by placing them in a white family or institution. Since the late 1800s, a large percentage of Indian children had been taken from their home and placed in a boarding school off their tribal reservation in order to teach them white culture and practices. In many cases government authorities removed Indian children from their family because of vague allegations of neglect, when in fact the children's treatment reflected cultural differences in child rearing practices, and not neglect or abuse. In addition, the practice of removing Indian children from their tribe placed the very existence of the tribes in JEOPARDY.

The ICWA was written with the belief that it was in the best interests of Indian children for them to remain with their tribe and maintain their Indian heritage. To foster this goal, the ICWA enacts minimal federal standards for when Indian children can be removed from their family and seeks to ensure that children who are removed are placed in a foster or adoptive home that reflects the unique values of Indian culture. Examples of these standards include giving custodial preference to a child's extended family or tribal members, requiring remedial programs to prevent the breakup of Indian families, and requiring proof "beyond a reasonable doubt" that continued custody of a child will result in serious emotional or physical harm to the child.

To prevent a resumption of the practice of removing Indian children from their home, Congress, in the ICWA, gave tribal courts exclusive jurisdiction over the adoption and custody of Indian children who reside or are domiciled within their tribe's reservation, unless some federal law provides to the contrary (*domiciled* refers to a permanent residence while *residing* may be in a temporary residence). One such contrary law is Public Law 280 (28 U.S.C.A. § 1360). This law made certain tribes in Alaska, California, Minnesota, Nebraska, Oregon, and Wisconsin subject to state jurisdiction. ICWA allows these tribes to reassume jurisdiction over CHILD CUSTODY proceedings by petitioning the secretary of the interior.

Tribes also have exclusive jurisdiction over such proceedings when they involve an Indian child who is a ward of the tribal court, regardless of where the child resides. Custody proceedings covered by the act include foster care placement, the termination of parental rights, and pre-adoptive and adoptive placement; the act does not govern custody proceedings in DIVORCE settlements. The ICWA applies both to children who are tribal members and to children who are eligible for tribal membership; eligibility for tribal membership is determined by individual tribes.

In cases involving Indian children who neither reside nor are domiciled within a tribal reservation, tribal courts and state courts possess CONCURRENT JURISDICTION. This question of jurisdiction has resulted in several important JUDICIAL interpretations of the ICWA. One significant interpretation was the 1989 U.S. Supreme Court decision *Mississippi Band of Choctaw Indians v. Holyfield,* 490 U.S. 30, 109 S. Ct. 1597, 104 L. Ed. 2d 29, which declared that because Congress had clearly enacted the law to protect Native American families and tribes, tribal jurisdiction preempted both state authority and the wishes of the parents of the children at issue. The case involved twins born off the reservation to unmarried parents, who voluntarily consented to having the children adopted by a non-Indian family. The Supreme Court ruled that children born to unmarried parents are considered to share the domicile of the mother, and since the mother in this case was domiciled on the reservation, the tribal court had jurisdiction over the placement of the children, even if it opposed the parents' wishes.

In a significant state case, the Minnesota Supreme Court in August 1994 followed the reasoning in *Holyfield,* rejecting a white couple's petition to adopt three Ojibwa (also called Chippewa or Anishinabe) sisters (*In re S. E. G.,* 521 N.W.2d 357). The court ruled in favor of the Leech Lake band of Chippewa, which had contested the adoption, holding that the ICWA dictated that adopted Indian children should be raised within their own culture. Although non-Indian families may adopt Indian children in very limited circumstances if they prove there is "good cause," the court held that such GOOD CAUSE cannot be based on the European value of family permanence.

In some cases, however, courts have given less weight to the provisions of the ICWA, instead RULING in favor of state jurisdiction over Indian children. In 1995, for example, the Illinois Supreme Court ruled that the ICWA does not mandate exclusive jurisdiction for tribal courts in custody hearings when the location of the children's domicile is in question. *In re Adoption of S. S. & R. S.,* 167 Ill. 2d 250, 212 Ill. Dec. 590, 657 N.E.2d 935, involved two children of an unmarried Indian mother and non-Indian father, who had been living with their father. When the father died, his sister and brother-in-law sought to adopt the children. The mother's tribe, the Fort Peck tribe in Montana, objected and claimed jurisdiction over the proceeding. The Illinois Supreme Court ruled against the tribe, holding that because the children had never been domiciled on the mother's reservation and because the mother had "abandoned" the children, state law preceded tribal court jurisdiction. The court thus limited the scope of the ICWA in Illinois.

FURTHER READINGS

Bennett, Michele K. 1993. "Native American Children: Caught in the Web of the Indian Child Welfare Act." *Hamline Law Review* 16 (spring).

Gallagher, Brian D. 1994. "Indian Child Welfare Act of 1978: The Congressional Foray into the Adoption Process." *Northern Illinois Univ. Law Review* 15 (fall).

Goldsmith, Donna J. 2002. "In the Best Interests of an Indian Child: The Indian Child Welfare Act." *Juvenile & Family Court Journal* 53 (fall).

Graham, Lorie. 2008. "Reparations and the Indian Child Welfare Act." *Harvard Human Rights Journal* 21; Suffolk Univ. Law School Research Paper No. 07-22. Available online at http://papers.ssrn.com/sol3/papers.cfm?abstract_id=1126774; website home page: http://papers.ssrn.com (accessed August 1, 2009).

Hemp, Susan J. 1996. "State Court versus Tribal Court Jurisdiction in an Indian Child Custody Case." *Illinois Bar Journal* 84 (April).

Jones, B.J., and John G. Richardson. 1997. *The Indian Child Welfare Act: A Cultural and Legal Education Program.* Williamsburg, VA: National Center for State Courts.

Ujke, David M. 1993. "Tribal Court Jurisdiction in Domestic Relations Matters Involving Indian Children: Not Just a Matter of Comity." *Wisconsin Lawyer* 66 (August).

CROSS REFERENCES

Child Custody; Native American Rights.

INDICIA

Signs; indications. Circumstances that point to the existence of a given fact as probable, but not certain. For example, indicia of partnership *are any circumstances which would induce the belief that a given person was in reality, though not technically, a member of a given firm.*

The term is much used in CIVIL LAW in a sense nearly or entirely synonymous with CIRCUMSTANTIAL EVIDENCE. It denotes facts that give rise to inferences, rather than the inferences themselves.

INDICTMENT

A written accusation charging that an individual named therein has committed an act or omitted to do something that is punishable by law.

An indictment is found and presented by a GRAND JURY legally convened and sworn. It originates with a prosecutor and is issued by the grand jury against an individual who is charged with a crime. Before such individual

Indictment

STATE OF NORTH CAROLINA

_____ County

STATE VERSUS

Name And Address Of Defendant

File No.

In The General Court Of Justice
Superior Court Division

**NOTICE OF RETURN OF
BILL OF INDICTMENT**

G.S. 15A-630, 15A-941(d)

To The Defendant Named Above:

Take notice that the grand jury of the county named above has returned the attached True Bill(s) of Indictment charging you with the offense(s) specified.

You are informed that there are important time limitations on your right to discovery of the evidence against you. *(See G.S. 15A-902, which is printed on the reverse.)*

This Notice is issued upon the order of the presiding judge.

You will be arraigned on the charges contained in this Indictment only if you file a written request for arraignment with the Clerk of Superior Court not later than twenty-one (21) days after the Indictment is served on you. If you do not file a written request for arraignment within that time, the court will enter a not guilty plea on your behalf.

You must appear in Superior Court at the date, time and place shown below to answer the charges in this Indictment.

NOTE: *If an earlier court date is set in a release order, you must appear at that time also.*

Date Of Hearing	*Time Of Hearing*	*Place Of Hearing*
	☐ AM ☐ PM	

NOTE: *Attach True Bill(s) of Indictment and a copy of the Order of Arrest, if appropriate.*

Date Issued

Signature

☐ *Deputy CSC*   ☐ *Assistant CSC*   ☐ *Clerk Of Superior Court*

CERTIFICATE OF NOTICE

I certify that I issued a copy of this Notice to the defendant named above at the address shown by:

☐ 1. Mailing it through the U.S. Postal Service.

☐ 2. Attaching it to an Order for Arrest to be served on the defendant.

☐ 3. Other: *(specify)*

Date	*Signature*	
		☐ *Deputy CSC* ☐ *Assistant CSC* ☐ *Clerk Of Superior Court*

AOC-CR-215, Rev. 10/04
©2004 Administrative Office of the Courts

Original-File   Copy-Defendant
(Over)

[continued]

A sample indictment.

Indictment

G.S. 15A-902 Discovery Procedure

"(a) A party seeking discovery under this Article must, before filing any motion before a judge, request in writing that the other party comply voluntarily with the discovery request. A written request is not required if the parties agree in writing to voluntarily comply with the provisions of Article 48 of Chapter 15A of the General Statutes. Upon receiving a negative or unsatisfactory response, or upon the passage of seven days following the receipt of the request without response, the party requesting discovery may file a motion for discovery under the provisions of this Article concerning any matter as to which voluntary discovery was not made pursuant to request.

(b) To the extent that discovery authorized in this Article is voluntarily made in response to a request or written agreement, the discovery is deemed to have been made under an order of the court for the purposes of this Article.

(c) A motion for discovery under this article must be heard before a superior court judge.

(d) If a defendant is represented by counsel, the defendant may as a matter of right request voluntary discovery from the State under subsection (a) of this section not later than the tenth working day after either the probable-cause hearing or the date the defendant waives the hearing. If a defendant is not represented by counsel, or is indicted or consents to the filing of a bill of information before the defendant has been afforded or waived a probable-cause hearing, the defendant may as a matter of right request voluntary discovery from the State under subsection (a) of this section not later than the tenth working day after the later of:

    (1) The defendant's consent to be tried upon a bill of information, or the service of notice upon the defendant that a true bill of indictment has been found by the grand jury, or

    (2) The appointment of counsel.

For the purposes of this subsection a defendant is represented by counsel only if counsel was retained by or appointed for the defendant prior to or during a probable-cause hearing or prior to or execution by the defendant of a waiver of a probable-cause hearing.

(e) The State may as a matter of right request voluntary discovery from the defendant, when authorized under this Article, at any time not later than the tenth working day after disclosure by the State with respect to the category of discovery in question.

(f) A motion for discovery made at any time prior to trial may be entertained if the parties so stipulate or if the judge for good cause shown determines that the motion should be allowed in whole or in part."

G.S. 15A-941(d) Arraignment Before Judge Only Upon Written Request

"(d) A defendant will be arraigned in accordance with this section only if the defendant files a written request with the clerk of superior court for an arraignment not later than 21 days after service of the bill of indictment. If a bill of indictment is not required to be served pursuant to G.S. 15A-630, then the written request for arraignment must be filed not later than 21 days from the date of the return of the indictment as a true bill. Upon the return of the indictment as a true bill, the court must immediately cause notice of the 21-day time limit within which the defendant may request an arraignment to be mailed or otherwise given to the defendant and to the defendant's counsel of record, if any. If the defendant does not file a written request for arraignment, then the court shall enter a not guilty plea on behalf of the defendant."

AOC-CR-215, Side Two, Rev. 10/04
©2004 Administrative Office of the Courts

may be convicted, the charge must be proved at trial BEYOND A REASONABLE DOUBT.

The purpose of an indictment is to inform an accused individual of the charge against him or her so that the person will be able to prepare a defense.

INDIRECT EVIDENCE

Probative matter that does not proximately relate to an issue but that establishes a hypothesis by showing various consistent facts.

CROSS REFERENCE

Evidence.

INDISPENSABLE PARTY

An individual who has an interest in the substantive issue of a legal action of such a nature that a final decree cannot be handed down without that interest being affected or without leaving the controversy in a condition whereby its final determination would be totally unconscionable.

For example, a HUSBAND AND WIFE seeking to dissolve a MARRIAGE are indispensable parties to their own DIVORCE action.

INDIVIDUAL RETIREMENT ACCOUNT

The individual retirement account (IRA) is a means by which an individual can receive certain federal tax advantages while investing for retirement.

The federal government has several reasons for encouraging individuals to save money for their retirement. For one, the average life span of a U.S. citizen continues to increase. Assuming that the average age of retirement does not change, workers who retire face more years of retirement and more years to live without a wage or salary.

Uncertainty over the future of the federal SOCIAL SECURITY system is another reason. U.S. workers generally contribute deductions from their paychecks to the Social Security fund. In theory, this money will come back to them, usually upon their retirement. But a substantial number of politicians, economists, and scholars contend that the Social Security fund is being drained faster than it is being filled and that it will go broke in a number of years, leaving retirees to survive without government assistance.

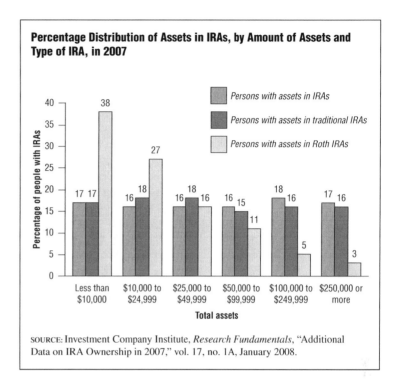

Percentage Distribution of Assets in IRAs, by Amount of Assets and Type of IRA, in 2007

SOURCE: Investment Company Institute, *Research Fundamentals*, "Additional Data on IRA Ownership in 2007," vol. 17, no. 1A, January 2008.

ILLUSTRATION BY GGS CREATIVE RESOURCES. REPRODUCED BY PERMISSION OF GALE, A PART OF CENGAGE LEARNING.

Regardless of its future, many people consider the retirement benefits of Social Security to be inadequate, and they look for other methods of funding their retirement years. Many employers offer retirement plans. These plans vary in form but generally offer retirement funds that grow with continued employment. Yet this benefit is not always available to workers. A changing economy has caused some employers to cut back on retirement plans or to cut them out completely. Often, part-time, new, or temporary workers do not qualify for an employer's retirement plan, and individuals who are self-employed may not choose this job benefit or be able to afford it.

To help people prepare for their retirement, Congress in 1974 established individual retirement accounts (IRAs) (EMPLOYEE RETIREMENT INCOME SECURITY ACT [ERISA] [codified in scattered sections of 5, 18, 26, and 29 U.S.C.A.]). These accounts may take a variety of forms, such as savings accounts at a bank, certificates of deposit, or mutual funds of stocks. Initially, IRAs were available only to people who were not participating in an employer-provided retirement plan. That changed in 1981, when Congress expanded the IRA provisions to include anyone, regardless of participation in an employer's retirement plan (Economic Recovery Tax Act [ERTA] [codified in scattered sections of 26, 42, and 45 U.S.C.A.]). The goal of ERTA was to promote an increased level of personal retirement savings through uniform discretionary savings arrangements.

A movement to bolster the FEDERAL BUDGET by eliminating many existing tax shelters prompted portions of the TAX REFORM ACT OF 1986 (codified in scattered sections of 19, 25, 26, 28, 29, 42, 46, and 49 U.S.C.A.) and another change in IRA laws. This time, Congress limited some of the IRA's tax advantages, making them unavailable to workers who participate in an employer's retirement plan or whose earnings meet or exceed a certain threshold. Yet other tax advantages remain, and the laws still allow anyone to contribute to an IRA, making it a popular investment tool.

It is difficult to understand the advantages that an IRA offers without understanding a few basics about federal INCOME TAX law. Generally, a person calculating the amount of tax that he or she owes to the government first determines the amount of income received in the year. This is normally employment income. Tax laws allow the individual to deduct from this figure amounts paid for certain items, such as charitable contributions or interest on a MORT-GAGE. Some taxpayers choose to take a single STANDARD DEDUCTION rather than numerous itemized deductions. In either case, the taxpayer subtracts any allowable deductions from yearly income and then calculates the tax owed on the remainder.

Taking deductions is only one of the ways in which a taxpayer may reduce taxes by investing in an IRA. But IRAs have proven to be popular with taxpayers. This popularity has prompted expansion of the federal tax rules to encourage additional savings and investment through IRAs. In 2003, there were 11 types of IRAs:

1. Individual Retirement Account
2. Individual Retirement Annuity
3. Employer and Employee Association Trust Account
4. Simplified Employee Pension (SEP-IRA)
5. Savings Incentive Match Plan for Employees IRA (SIMPLE IRA)
6. Spousal IRA
7. Rollover IRA (Conduit IRA)
8. Inherited IRA
9. Education IRA
10. Traditional IRA
11. Roth IRA

Despite the many variations, the two most important remain the traditional IRA and the Roth IRA.

As of 2009, single filers may deduct Traditional IRA contributions as long as their income is less than $101,000 (to qualify for a full contribution) or $110,000 to $121,000 to qualify for a partial contribution. Joint filers may deduct IRA contributions as long as their ADJUSTED GROSS INCOME is less than $159,000 (to qualify for a full contribution). If their adjusted GROSS INCOME is between $159,000 and $176,000, they may qualify for a partial contribution. IRA contribution limits were capped at $5,000 from 2008 through 2010.

Various plans may constitute employer-maintained retirement plans, such as standard pension plans, profit-sharing or stock-bonus plans, annuities, and government retirement plans. Someone who does not participate in such a plan—whether by choice or not—is entitled to contribute to an IRA up to $5,000 per year or 100 percent of her or his annual income, whichever is less. The amount contributed during the taxable year may then be taken as a deduction.

A married taxpayer who files a joint TAX RETURN with a spouse who does not work may deduct contributions toward what is called a spousal IRA, or an IRA established for the spouse's benefit. If neither spouse is a participant in an employer-provided retirement plan, up to $10,000 may be deductible.

Taxpayers who contribute to Traditional IRAs usually realize tax benefits even when the law does not permit them to take deductions. That is because income earned on Traditional IRA contributions is not taxed until the funds are distributed, which usually occurs at retirement. Income that is allowed to grow, untaxed, for several years, grows faster than income that is taxed each year.

To avoid abuses and excessive tax shelters, Congress has placed limits on the extent to which IRAs can be used as a financial tool. Individuals with IRAs may currently make contributions limited to $5,000 per year; contributions exceeding that amount are subject to strict financial penalties by the INTERNAL REVENUE SERVICE each year until the excess is corrected. The owner of an IRA generally may not withdraw funds from that account until age 59 1/2. Premature distributions are subject to a 10-percent penalty in addition to regular income tax. Taxpayers may be able to avoid this premature distribution penalty by "rolling over," or transferring, the distribution amount to another IRA within 60 days.

An individual may elect not to withdraw IRA funds at age 59 1/2. However, the law requires IRA owners to withdraw IRA money at age 70 1/2, either in a lump sum or in periodic (at least annual) payments based on a life-expectancy calculation. Failure to comply with this rule can result in a 50 percent penalty on the amount of the required minimum distribution. Contributions to an IRA must stop at age 70 1/2.

In 1997 Congress provided for a new type of IRA—the Roth IRA, named for former Senator William V. Roth Jr. The Roth IRA was part of the Taxpayer Relief Act of 1997 (Pub. L. No. 105-34, 111 Stat. 788 [codified as amended in scattered sections of 26 U.S.C.]). Contributions to a Roth IRA are not deductible from gross income, and the Roth IRA allows no deductions for contributions. Instead, Roth IRAs provide a benefit that is unique among retirement savings schemes: If a taxpayer meets certain requirements, all earnings from the IRA are tax-free when the taxpayer or his or her beneficiary withdraws them. There are other benefits as well, such as no early distribution penalty on certain withdrawals, and no need to take minimum distributions after age 70 1/2.

The chief advantage of the Roth IRA is the ability to have investment earnings escape TAXATION. However, taxpayers may not claim a deduction when they contribute to Roth IRAs. Whether it is more advantageous to use Roth IRAs or traditional IRAs depends on each taxpayer's personal situation. It also depends on what assumptions the taxpayer makes about the future, such as future tax rates and the taxpayer's earnings in the interim.

Individuals may open a Roth IRA if they are eligible for a regular contribution to a Roth IRA or a rollover or conversion to a Roth IRA. Taxpayers are eligible to make regular contributions to a Roth IRA even if they participate in a retirement plan maintained by their employer. In 2009, these contributions may be as much as $5,000 ($6,000 if 50 or older by the end of the year). There are just two requirements: the taxpayer or taxpayer's spouse must have compensation or alimony income equal to the amount contributed; and the taxpayer's modified adjusted gross income may not exceed certain limits. These limits are the same as in traditional IRAs: $101,000 for single individuals and $159,000 for married individuals filing joint returns. In 2009, the amount that a taxpayer may contribute is reduced gradually and then completely eliminated when the taxpayer's modified adjusted gross income exceeds $120,000 (single) or $176,000 (married filing jointly).

In 2009, a traditional IRA may be converted to a Roth IRA if modified adjusted gross income is $100,000 or less and if the taxpayer is either single or files jointly with his or her spouse. However, beginning in 2010, the $100,000 cap is eliminated. Although taxpayers converting traditional IRAs to Roth IRAs must pay tax in the year of the conversion, the long-term savings may greatly outweigh the conversion tax.

FURTHER READINGS

Internal Revenue Service Website, www.irs.gov (accessed September 19, 2009).

Levy, Donald R., and Avery E. Neumark. 2000. *Quick Reference to IRAs, 1999.* New York: Panel.

Pope, Thomas. 2008. *Prentice Hall's Federal Taxation 2009: Comprehensive.* 22d ed. New York: Prentice Hall.

INDIVIDUALS WITH DISABILITIES EDUCATION ACT OF 1975

See DISABILITY DISCRIMINATION.

INDORSE

To sign a paper or document, thereby making it possible for the rights represented therein to pass to another individual. Also spelled endorse.

INDORSEMENT

A signature on a commercial paper or document.

An indorsement on a NEGOTIABLE INSTRUMENT, such as a check or a PROMISSORY NOTE, has the effect of transferring all the rights represented by the instrument to another individual. The ordinary manner in which an individual endorses a check is by placing his or her signature on the back of it, but it is valid even if the signature is placed somewhere else, such as on a separate paper, known as an allonge, which provides a space for a signature.

The term *indorsement* is also spelled *endorsement.*

Indorsement

In Blank

John Doe
or
Pay to bearer
                John Doe

Special

Pay to Richard Roe or order
                John Doe
or
Pay to the order of Richard Roe
                John Doe
or
Pay to Richard Roe
                John Doe

Restrictive

Pay Richard Roe only
                John Doe
or
For deposit only
                John Doe

Qualified

Pay to Richard Roe without recourse
                John Doe

Conditional

Pay to Acme Company on completion of bulding contract
                John Doe

Indorsement Without Recourse

Without recourse in any event and without representation or warranty whatsoever.
                or
                John Doe
                Without Recourse
                Date

INDUCEMENT

An advantage or benefit that precipitates a particular action on the part of an individual.

In the law of contracts, the inducement is a PLEDGE or promise that causes an individual to enter into a particular agreement. An *inducement to purchase* is something that encourages an individual to buy a particular item, such as the promise of a price reduction. Consideration is the inducement to a contract.

In CRIMINAL LAW, the term *inducement* is the motive, or that which leads an individual to engage in criminal conduct.

INDUSTRIAL UNION

A labor organization composed of members employed in a particular field, such as textiles, but who perform different individual jobs within their general type of work.

CROSS REFERENCE
Labor Union.

INDUSTRIAL WORKERS OF THE WORLD

The Industrial Workers of the World—also known as the IWW, or the Wobblies—is a radical LABOR UNION that had its beginnings in Chicago in 1905.

An outgrowth of the Western Federation of Mines, the IWW was created by WILLIAM D. HAYWOOD, EUGENE V. DEBS, and Daniel DeLeon. Its membership was open to all workers, skilled or unskilled, with no restrictions as to race, occupation, ethnic background, or sex. The Wobblies opposed the principles of capitalism and advocated SOCIALISM. They followed the tenets of syndicalism, a labor movement that evolved in Europe before WORLD WAR I. The syndicalists sought to control industry through labor organizations. In their view the state represented oppression, which had to be replaced by the union as the essential element of society. To achieve their goals, the syndicalists advocated practices such as strikes and slowdowns.

The Wobblies adopted many of the ideologies of syndicalism and employed direct-action methods, such as propaganda, strikes, and boycotts. They rejected more peaceful means of achieving labor's goals, such as arbitration and COLLECTIVE BARGAINING.

From 1906 to 1928, the IWW was responsible for 150 strikes, including a miners' strike in Goldfield, Nevada, from 1906 to 1907; a textile workers' strike in Lawrence, Massachusetts, in 1912; a 1913 silk workers' strike in Paterson, New Jersey; and a miners' strike in Colorado from 1927 to 1928.

During World War I, the IWW began to lose much of its strength. Its members were against the military, and many were convicted of draft evasion, seditious activities, and espionage. In addition, many members left the organization to join the Communist party. By 1930, the IWW was no longer regarded as an influential labor force. Nevertheless, it still exists today.

Despite its radicalism, the IWW was responsible for several gains for organized labor. It brought together skilled and unskilled workers into one union; it achieved better working conditions and a shorter work week in many areas of labor, particularly in the lumber field; and it set a structural example that would be followed by future labor unions.

INFAMY

Notoriety; condition of being known as possessing a shameful or disgraceful reputation; loss of character or good reputation.

At COMMON LAW, infamy was an individual's legal status that resulted from having been convicted of a particularly reprehensible crime, rendering him or her incompetent as a witness at a trial. Infamy, by statute in certain jurisdictions, produces other legal disabilities and is sometimes described as CIVIL DEATH.

INFANCY

Minority; the status of an individual who is below the legal age of majority.

At COMMON LAW, the age of legal majority was 21, but it has been lowered to 18 in most states of the United States. Infancy indicates the condition of an individual who is legally unable to do certain acts. For example, an infant might not have the legal capacity to enter into certain contracts. Similarly, infancy is a ground for annulment of a MARRIAGE in certain jurisdictions.

Although many states have lowered the AGE OF MAJORITY for most purposes to 18, they frequently retain the right to mandate support of a child by a parent beyond that age in the aftermath of DIVORCE.

INFANTS

Infants are persons who are under the age of legal majority—at common law 21 years, now generally 18 years. According to the sense in which this term is used, it may denote the age of the person, the contractual disabilities that non-age entails, or the person's status with regard to other powers or relations.

Modern laws respecting the rights, obligations, and incapacities of children are rooted in ancient customs and practices. In 1765, SIR WILLIAM BLACKSTONE, in his *Commentaries on the Laws of England,* wrote that parents owe their children three duties: maintenance, protection, and education. In the early twenty-first century, these three duties continue and have been expanded by JUDICIAL and legislative

---

What it Costs to Raise a Child to Age 18

A Two-Parent Family	
Earning[a]	Will Spend
Less than $45,800 a year	$148,320
$45,800 to $77,100 a year	$204,060
More than $77,100 a year	$298,680

[a]Earning refers to before-tax income.

SOURCE: U.S. Department of Agriculture, Center for Nutrition Policy and Promotion, *Expenditures on Children by Families,* 2007.

ILLUSTRATION BY GGS CREATIVE RESOURCES. REPRODUCED BY PERMISSION OF GALE, A PART OF CENGAGE LEARNING.

---

advancements. The notion of children's rights has evolved into a highly controversial and dynamic area of law.

COMMON LAW held an infant, also called a minor or child, to be a person less than 21 years of age. Currently, most state statutes define the AGE OF MAJORITY to be 18. Although a person must attain the age of majority to vote, make a will, or hold public office, children are increasingly being recognized by society, legislatures, and the courts as requiring greater protections and deserving greater rights than they were afforded under common law. The law is caught in a tug-of-war between two equally compelling and worthy societal interests: the desire to protect children from harmful situations and from their own immaturity and lack of experience, on the one hand, and the desire to give children as much autonomy as they can bear as soon as they can bear it, on the other.

Legal Rights of Children

Children do have the right to own and acquire property by sale, gift, or inheritance. Often property is given to a child as a beneficiary of a trust. In the case of trusts, a trustee manages the trust assets for the child until the child reaches majority or otherwise meets the requirements specified in the trust for managing the property for herself or himself.

Children also have the right to enter into contracts. Because the law seeks to protect children from adverse consequences due to their lack of knowledge, experience, and maturity, an adult who enters into a contract with a child may be unable to enforce the contract against the child, whereas the child can enforce the contract against the adult if the adult breaches it. However, when a child enters into a contract for necessities (i.e., food, shelter, clothing, and medical attention) or with a bank, the child is legally bound and cannot later disaffirm or negate the contract. In addition, some state statutes provide that all contracts relating to a child's business are enforceable. This arrangement allows a child the opportunity to begin a business. Aside from these limited exceptions, a child may negate a contract before, and even sometimes soon after, reaching the age of majority.

Children have the right to bring lawsuits seeking legal redress for injuries they have suffered or for rights that have been violated. Most jurisdictions require a child to have a representative during the litigation process. This representative, called a *guardian ad litem* or NEXT FRIEND, advises and guides the child.

The right of a child to sue for personal injuries has been extended to cover prenatal injuries. Moreover, if an injured fetus is born alive and then dies as a result of her or his prenatal injuries, the child's parents may sue for the WRONGFUL DEATH of the child. Criminal sanctions may also apply. As of 2009, more than 36 states had enacted *fetal homicide* legislation creating a separate criminal offense for actions taken against a woman that result in the death of, or harm to, her fetus.

However, in civil suits for MEDICAL MALPRACTICE, such a legal premise is not as simple as it may appear. First, depending upon the stage of development, the fetus may or may not be a viable person—with independent legal rights—in the eyes of the law. This controversial issue was addressed in August 2002, when President GEORGE W. BUSH signed into law the Born-Alive Infants Protection Act (P.L. 107-207), ensuring that every infant born alive, including an infant who survives an ABORTION procedure, is considered a person under federal law. The significance of this trend (treating the fetus as a separate person) is in recognizing that the unborn infant has distinct and independent rights. In prior cases and in other jurisdictions, compensation for harm to a fetus has been granted to the mother (or parents) under the legal theory of a *derivative* right stemming from the legal duty owed to the mother.

A second essential element of a malpractice action is the need to show that a professional doctor-patient relationship existed between an allegedly injured patient and the treating physician. This relationship establishes that a duty was owed by the physician to his patient. In matters of obstetrics, a doctor-patient relationship naturally exists between a pregnant woman and her treating physician. If she suffers harm or injury as a result of alleged malpractice and that harm or injury carries over to her unborn child, states permit recovery for both. But the question remained what if the mother suffers no harm or injury as a result of alleged malpractice, yet injury or harm is independently sustained by the developing fetus or newborn.

This question has been addressed by several state courts. In the 2001 case of *Nold v. Binyon* (31 P.3d 274), the Kansas Supreme Court held that a physician has a doctor-patient relationship with both mother and any developing fetus she intends to carry to a healthy full term. In *Nold,* the infant in question was born with hepatitis B, which was transmitted from her infected mother. Tests given to the mother prior to the baby's birth indicated that the virus was present. Normal treatment is to administer gamma globulin and a vaccine at birth; the infant received neither and so contracted the virus.

Although states may recognize a child's right to sue for prenatal injuries, the vast majority of states do not allow WRONGFUL LIFE actions. In a wrongful life lawsuit, the child sues a doctor for NEGLIGENCE or malpractice for failing to diagnose the child's mother with a disease that injured the child before birth or for failing to diagnose a severe, disabling condition of the child before birth. The argument continues that if the doctor had informed the child's parents of the child's condition, the mother would have had an abortion rather than deliver a child with such a debilitating condition. The child's theory in a wrongful life lawsuit is that life with the injury or debilitating condition is worse than no life at all and that he or she would have been better off having not been born.

As examples, the New Jersey Supreme Court has denied wrongful life claims, stating that "there is no precedent in appellate judicial pronouncements that holds a child has a FUNDAMENTAL RIGHT to be born as a whole, functional human being," and it is almost impossible to calculate the damages in such a case (*Gleitman v. Cosgrove* 49 N.J. 22, 227 A.2d 689 [1967]). In contrast, in *Curlender v. Bio-Science Laboratory* (106 Cal. App. 3d 811, 165 Cal. Rptr. 477 [1980]), a California court allowed a child with Tay-Sachs disease to recover for wrongful life, stating that to deny such a claim "permits a wrong with serious consequential injury to go wholly unaddressed." This court would not accept the "impossibility of measuring damages" as the sole reason to deny the child's claim.

A child may bring a lawsuit seeking EMANCIPATION from his or her parents. Emancipation is a doctrine based on ancient ROMAN LAW. An emancipated minor is a child who is entirely self-supporting and who has the LEGAL RIGHT and duty to oversee his or her own behavior. An emancipated minor's parents surrender the right to the care, custody, and earnings of the child. Once emancipated, the child is precluded from demanding that his or her parents continue to support him or her. Historically, an express agreement between the PARENT AND CHILD, the MARRIAGE of the child, the entry of the child into the armed forces, or responsible conduct on the part of the child were all sufficient factors in seeking emancipation. In the early 2000s, the doctrine is seen as a mechanism for ending troubled parent-child relationships and a way to alleviate the difficult task of finding foster families for older teenagers who have been taking care of themselves.

Child Protection

Although children do not have a constitutional right to a safe home, a permanent, stable family, or quality care, significant strides have been made to improve the lives of children. The right of a state to ensure the WELFARE of the children within its boundaries stems from the ancient concept of *parens patriae*, which means "the father of his country," and was used to describe the relationship between a king and his subjects. As of 2009, this right is limited by the parents' legal right to be free from government intrusion in the raising and rearing of their children. The state's intervention is justified, however, if a parent is not living up to his or her responsibilities or when a child is endangered, neglected, or abused. The courts may then place the child in temporary foster care and require the parent to get assistance to remedy the problem or may terminate the parent's rights to the child if that is found to be in the best interests of the child.

In 1960 the federal government spent only a few million dollars on child protective services. By 1980 this expenditure had risen to more than $325 million. This dramatic increase probably did not reflect an actual increase in the incidence of child abuse but rather the effects of laws requiring health care and social workers to report all suspicions of child abuse, an increase in public awareness of the problem and a broadening of the definition of child abuse.

Nevertheless, some abused or neglected children were remaining unidentified and not receiving timely or effective protection from the state, and in some instances, the state was found to be not responsible for these mistakes. For example, in 1989 the U.S. Supreme Court held that the due process clause did not impose an affirmative duty on the state to protect a four-year-old boy from his father's violence (*DeShaney v. Winnebago County Department of Social Services*, 489 U.S. 189, 103 L. Ed. 2d 249, 109 S. Ct. 998). In that case, a child named Joshua was beaten so severely that half of his brain was destroyed and he became permanently brain-damaged and profoundly retarded. A social worker assigned to the family had noted signs of past abuse and several trips to the emergency room but had taken no action to remove Joshua from his family home. Chief Justice WILLIAM H. REHNQUIST stated that the due process clause "is phrased as a limitation on the State's power to act, not as a guarantee of certain minimal levels of safety and security."

While figures are difficult to tally, the estimated 2007 cost of child abuse was $104 billion. In 2007 approximately 5.8 million children were involved in an estimated 3.2 million child abuse reports and allegations. In 2009, billions of state and federal dollars were spent on child protective services; federal expenditures alone were more than $21 billion in 2009; and other funds were directed to prevention programs. While more agencies have been created to handle the increased caseload, many reports are still screened out, and caseworkers must prioritize among the cases they do eventually receive. State and federal funds are also allotted for children whose parents are financially unable to provide for their basic needs, such as food, shelter, and medical attention. The Temporary Assistance for Needy Families (TANF) program grants federal money to needy parents to provide these basic needs for their children.

While the U.S. CONSTITUTION does not mention the right of children to an education, every state has adopted compulsory education laws. The strides in securing education for children occurred at the same time that CHILD LABOR LAWS were beginning to eradicate the exploitation of children in sweatshops. By the mid-1800s, several states had passed laws restricting the number of hours children could work and requiring children who worked to also attend school for a minimum number of months each year. However, because each state had different laws and competition was fierce among states eager to attract industry, many of the laws regarding child labor were not enforced. After several unsuccessful attempts at passing effective child labor laws, Congress passed the FAIR LABOR STANDARDS ACT (FLSA), 29 U.S.C.A. § 201 et seq., which places restrictions on the hours children may work and age limitations for children performing particular jobs and employed in certain hazardous occupations. As of 2009, every state has child labor laws—most of which are patterned after the FLSA, although some differences do exist.

The same concern for children that brought about these protections was responsible for the creation of the juvenile justice system. From the founding of the United States until the end of the nineteenth century, children who were charged with a crime were treated the same as adults. The juvenile justice system arose from an emerging conviction that rehabilitation, not punishment, would better serve the child and the state. In the early 2000s, juvenile court systems had been adopted by every state. These courts hear cases involving status offenses, abuse, dependency, neglect, and termination of parental rights. Status offenses are legal infractions based solely on the age of the person, such as truancy and curfew violations. Children in the juvenile justice system have the constitutional rights of notice, counsel, PRIVILEGE AGAINST SELF-INCRIMINATION, determination of guilt BEYOND A REASONABLE DOUBT, and protection against DOUBLE JEOPARDY. However, juveniles continued not to have a federal constitutional right to a jury trial and were not generally afforded bail.

All state juvenile codes provide for a juvenile to be removed from the juvenile justice system and transferred to the adult criminal courts, depending on the offense the juvenile allegedly committed or the juvenile's prior history of delinquent behavior. Once this move is made, the juvenile is entitled to all the constitutional protections afforded adults accused of crimes, such as bail and the right to a trial by jury, which may be more sympathetic and less likely to convict than would a juvenile court judge.

Constitutional Rights of Children in the Educational Setting

Traditionally, it was assumed that students would behave and express themselves in acceptable ways, and thus their constitutional rights did not need to be recognized or protected in any official manner. Since the 1960s, this notion has tended to be ignored. The Supreme Court has recognized that students do not shed their constitutional rights upon crossing the school-house threshold. The Court has recognized that schools function as a "market-place of ideas" and that FIRST AMENDMENT rights must receive "scrupulous protection if we are not to strangle the free mind at its source and teach youth to discount important principles of our government as mere platitudes" (Tinker v. Des Moines Independent Community School District 393 U.S. 503, 21 L. Ed. 2d 731, 89 S. Ct. 733 [1969]).

The rights of students to wear black armbands in protest of the VIETNAM WAR, to dance, and to use obscene and vulgar language on campus are but a few of the many First Amendment issues that have been litigated. In addition, debates over school prayer, RELIGION in a public school curriculum, and government aid to parochial schools all affect the education children receive. Many court decisions limit the FOURTH AMENDMENT rights of students with regard to searches for drugs, to drug testing, and to searches of their lockers.

Age of Legal Medical Consent

Traditionally, children have been deemed legally incapable of consenting to their own medical care or treatment. In general, parents have the authority to decide whether their minor children will receive medical treatment. Common law recognized an exception to the need for parental consent in cases of emergency. Statutory law has created more exceptions to this requirement, namely in cases where a child is emancipated, married, pregnant, or a parent. In addition, several states have enacted "minor treatment statutes," which typically provide that from 14 to 17 years of age, a minor may consent to ordinary medical treatment. When a parent refuses to consent to medical attention for a seriously ill or dying child, even if on religious grounds, the states may act according to their *parens patriae* power and obtain a court order to secure the necessary medical treatment.

Owing to a high incidence of venereal diseases among teenagers, all states have adopted statutes authorizing minors to consent to the treatment of sexually transmitted diseases. Similarly, most states have laws allowing a child to seek treatment for alcohol or drug abuse without parental consent.

Constitutional guarantees of the right to abortion extend to minors, as does the right to privacy. The Supreme Court has upheld state statutes that require the consent of only one parent if the statutes also offer an expeditious judicial bypass procedure (a hearing before a judge in which the minor requests that parental consent be waived). States can no longer absolutely require two-parent notification or consent before a minor may undergo an abortion.

The Right to Testify

A child is permitted to testify in court if the judge believes that the child comprehends the meaning and importance of telling the truth, is sufficiently mature, and is able to recall and communicate her or his thoughts effectively. Most states do not have a specific age at which children are allowed to testify; consequently, even very young children are allowed to be placed under OATH and testify in court if the judge determines that these requirements have been met.

FURTHER READINGS

Fellmeth, Robert. 2006. *Child Rights & Remedies: How the U.S. Legal System Affects Children.* 2d. ed. Atlanta: Clarity Press.

Jackson, Anthony. 1995. "Action for Wrongful Life, Wrongful Pregnancy, and Wrongful Birth in the United States and England." *Loyola of Los Angeles International and Comparative Law Journal* 17 (April).

Pardeck, John. 2006 *Children's Rights: Policy and Practice.* 2d. ed. New York: Routledge.

Smock, Erica, Priscilla Smith, and Bebe J. Anderson. 2003. "The Legal Status of the Fetus: Implications for Medical Personnel." Center for Reproductive Rights. Available online at http://apha.confex.com/apha/131am/techprogram/paper_69510.htm (accessed October 1, 2009).

CROSS REFERENCES

Adoption; Child Custody; Children's Rights; Child Support; Family Law; Fetal Rights; in Loco Parentis; Juvenile Law; Parent and Child; Schools and School Districts; Welfare; Wrongful Birth; Wrongful Pregnancy.

INFERENCE

In the law of evidence, a truth or proposition drawn from another that is supposed or admitted to be true. A process of reasoning by which a fact or proposition sought to be established is deduced as a logical consequence from other facts, or a state of facts, already proved or admitted. A logical and reasonable conclusion of a fact not presented by direct evidence but which, by process of logic and reason, a trier of fact may conclude exists from the established facts. Inferences are deductions or conclusions that with reason and common sense lead the jury to draw from facts which have been established by the evidence in the case.

INFERIOR COURT

This term may denote any court subordinate to the chief appellate tribunal in the particular judicial system (e.g., trial court); but it is also commonly used as the designation of a court of special, limited, or statutory jurisdiction, whose record must show the existence and attaching of jurisdiction in any given case.

INFIRMITY

Flaw, defect, or weakness.

In a legal sense, the term *infirmity* is used to mean any imperfection that renders a particular transaction void or incomplete. For example, if a deed drawn up to transfer ownership of land contains an erroneous description of it, an infirmity exists in the transaction.

INFORMATION

The formal accusation of a criminal offense made by a public official; the sworn, written accusation of a crime.

An information is tantamount to an indictment in that it is a sworn written statement which charges that a particular individual has done some criminal act or is guilty of some criminal omission. The distinguishing characteristic between an information and an indictment is that an indictment is presented by a GRAND JURY, whereas an information is presented by a duly authorized public official.

The purpose of an information is to inform the accused of the charge against him, so that the accused will have an opportunity to prepare a defense.

INFORMATION AGENCY

See U.S. INFORMATION AGENCY.

INFORMATION AND BELIEF

A standard phrase added to qualify a statement made under oath; a phrase indicating that a statement is made, not from firsthand knowledge but, nevertheless, in the firm belief that it is true.

For example, an affidavit may be needed at some point in a lawsuit even though the individual (whether a party to or a witness in the lawsuit) who has firsthand information is out of the country on business. In many such circumstances that individual's attorney may make an affidavit for him or her. The attorney must indicate that the individual is swearing only to facts that he or she has been told and believes to be true; in other words, on INFORMATION AND BELIEF.

INFORMED CONSENT

Assent to permit an occurrence, such as surgery, that is based on a complete disclosure of facts needed to make the decision intelligently, such as knowledge of the risks entailed or alternatives.

The name for a fundamental principle of law that a physician has a duty to reveal what a reasonably prudent physician in the medical community employing reasonable care would reveal to a patient as to whatever reasonably foreseeable risks of harm might result from a proposed course of treatment. This disclosure must be afforded so that a patient—exercising ordinary care for his or her own welfare and confronted with a choice of undergoing the proposed treatment, alternative treatment, or none at all—can intelligently exercise judgment by reasonably balancing the probable risks against the probable benefits.

INFRA

[Latin, Below, under, beneath, underneath.] A term employed in legal writing to indicate that the matter designated will appear beneath or in the pages following the reference.

INFRACTION

Violation or infringement; breach of a statute, contract, or obligation.

The term *infraction* is frequently used in reference to the violation of a particular statute

for which the penalty is minor, such as a parking infraction.

INFRINGEMENT

The encroachment, breach, or violation of a right, law, regulation, or contract.

The term is most frequently used in reference to the invasion of rights secured by copyright, patent, or trademark. The unauthorized manufacture, sale, or distribution of an item protected by a copyright, patent, or trademark constitutes an infringement.

INGROSSING

The act of making a perfect copy of a particular instrument, such as a deed, lease, or will, from a rough draft so that it may be properly executed to achieve its purpose.

INHERENT

Derived from the essential nature of, and inseparable from, the object itself.

An object that is *inherently dangerous* is one that possesses potential hazard by its mere existence, such as explosives. By contrast, other objects are dangerous only when used in a negligent manner, such as a pipe wrench or baseball bat. The rule of STRICT LIABILITY is applied when accidents arise from objects that are inherently dangerous.

INHERIT

To receive property according to the state laws of intestate succession from a decedent who has failed to execute a valid will, or, where the term is applied in a more general sense, to receive the property of a decedent by will.

INHERITANCE

Property received from a decedent, either by will or through state laws of intestate succession, where the decedent has failed to execute a valid will.

INITIATIVE

A process of a participatory democracy that empowers the people to propose legislation and to enact or reject the laws at the polls independent of the lawmaking power of the governing body.

The purpose of an initiative, which is a type of election commenced and carried out by the people, is to permit the electorate to resolve

A sample informed consent form.

Informed Consent/Consent to Release Information for Research

**U.S. Department of Justice
Federal Bureau of Prisons**

INFORMED CONSENT/CONSENT TO RELEASE INFORMATION FOR RESEARCH

A. Information about the study (to be filled out by the researcher).

Using everyday language, provide a clear and concise description of the study covering each of the following areas in a separate section or paragraph. You should modify the format and specific details in order to best represent your research project. The language used should be clearly written and easy to read with a ninth grade or lower vocabulary level.

1. Introduction:

Researcher's name and organizational affiliation. Title, purpose, and anticipated uses of the results of the study. If a BOP project, indicate the general authority permitting the Bureau to conduct the research [18 U.S.C. 4001(b) and 18 U.S.C.4042(a)]. See the **"What is this study about and why are you doing it?"** section of the example.

2. Procedures:

Description of the procedures involved and the duration of the participation. Clearly describe what will happen during the study from the perspective of the participant. When needed or unclear, identify which procedures are experimental. See the **"What are you asking me to do if I agree to be in this study?"** section of the example.

3. Benefits:

Description of possible benefits, to participants and others, to be gained from the study. Participation incentives are not considered benefits and are not allowed when the participants are inmates. See the **"How will this study help me?"** and the **"Why should I participate in this study?"** sections of the example.

4. Risks or discomforts:

Description of possible risks or discomforts from participating in the study. Potential risks or discomforts may include—but are not limited to—physical risk, psychological risk, emotional risks, breach of confidentiality, etc. See the **"Are there any risks or can I get hurt by being in the study?"** section of the example.

5. Steps taken to alleviate risks or discomforts:

Description of the steps taken to reduce the risks to the participants. For the majority of research conducted in the Bureau of Prisons, the primary risk to participants is from a breach of confidentiality. This issue should be addressed when appropriate. See the **"What steps are you taking to reduce these risks or discomforts?"** section of the example.

6. Required Information:

If not already included, ensure the following important information is included in the consent document when appropriate.

- Your participation is voluntary, and you may refuse to participate at any time without penalty.

- (If inmate participants) Your decision whether or not to participate will not affect your release date or parole eligibility.

- (If inmate participants) If you decide not to participate or to stop participating, you will be returned to your regular assignment as soon as possible.

- (If identifiable data is obtained) All information (if exceptions, describe in the descriptive section above and note here) will be handled in the strictest confidence, and only the researchers working on the project will have access to information that is traceable to you.

- (If identifiable data is obtained) The only exception to this policy of confidentiality is information about intent to commit a future crime or to hurt yourself or someone else (If other exceptions, include them as well).

- Your data will be used for research purposes only, and you will not be individually identifiable in any reports or publications (if exceptions, describe in the descriptive section above and note here).

- (If anonymous data) Please help us make sure you cannot be identified as a participant in this study; PLEASE DO NOT write your name or register number (if inmate) on any of the following pages.

See the **"What else do I need to know?"** section of the example.

7. Contact Information:

Provide an opportunity for participants to ask questions. For questions about the study, list an address for someone knowledgeable about the study (e.g., the researcher, the major advisor, etc.). For concerns about the study, you must note that the participants can contact the Chief Psychologist of the institution. If the Chief Psychologist is a study investigator, then the Bureau's Research Review Board must be listed as a contact. You should note that the participant will receive a copy of the consent form if s/he chooses, or if an anonymous study, note that the participant may detach and keep the consent information if s/he chooses. See the **"Whom can I contact with questions or concerns?"** section of the example.

[continued]

Informed Consent/Consent to Release Information for Research

B. Signatures.

    1. Written consent:

        Add the following to the consent form when the IRB determines that written consent is required:

Participant's Agreement: I have read the above information (or it has been read aloud to me). The study has been explained to me. My questions have been answered. I voluntarily agree to be in this study.

Name (Printed)	
Signature	Date

    2. Written consent with witness signature:

        In addition to the participant's agreement, add the following when the consent form is read aloud to a participant because s/he is a poor reader:

Witness's Statement: The information in this consent form was accurately conveyed to the participant.

Witness's Name Printed	Witness's Signature

    3. Written consent including access to files or other special procedures:

        In addition to the participant's agreement, add the following when the consent procedure includes access to files:

        I give the researcher permission to review my central file for the reason described in this consent form.

Name (printed)	Register #
Signature	Date

In addition to the participant's agreement, use the following format to include permission for special procedures (note—these are examples):

I consent to the following (initial the items you agree to, and cross-out the items you do not agree to)

_____ My test results can be added to my Psychology Services file for future treatment purposes.

_____ I would like feedback from the researcher regarding my literacy needs.

---

questions where their elected representatives fail to do so or refuse to proceed with a change that the public desires.

INJUNCTION

A court order by which an individual is required to perform, or is restrained from performing, a particular act. A writ framed according to the circumstances of the individual case.

An injunction commands an act that the court regards as essential to justice, or it prohibits an act that is deemed to be contrary to good conscience. It is an EXTRAORDINARY REMEDY, reserved for special circumstances in which the temporary preservation of the STATUS QUO is necessary.

An injunction is ordinarily and properly elicited from other proceedings. For example, a landlord might bring an action against a tenant for waste, in which the right to protect the landlord's interest in the ownership of the premises is at issue. The landlord might apply to the court for an injunction against the tenant's continuing harmful use of the property. The injunction is an ancillary remedy in the action against the tenant.

Injunctive relief is not a matter of right, but its denial is within the discretion of the court. Whether or not an injunction will be granted varies with the facts of each case.

The courts exercise their power to issue injunctions judiciously, and only when necessity exists. An injunction is usually issued only in cases where IRREPARABLE INJURY to the rights of an individual would result otherwise. It must be readily apparent to the court that some act has been performed, or is threatened, that will produce irreparable injury to the party seeking the injunction. An injury is considered irreparable when it cannot be adequately compensated by an award of damages. The pecuniary damage that would be incurred from the threatened action need not be great, however. If a loss can be calculated in terms of money, there is no irreparable injury. The consequent refusal by a court to grant an injunction is, therefore, proper. Loss of profits alone is insufficient to establish irreparable injury. The potential destruction of property is sufficient.

Injunctive relief is not a remedy that is liberally granted, and, therefore, a court will always consider any hardship that the parties will sustain by the granting or refusal of an injunction. The court that issues an injunction may, in exercise of its discretion, modify or dissolve it at a later date if the circumstances so warrant.

Types of Injunction

Preliminary A *preliminary* or *temporary injunction* is a provisional remedy that is invoked to preserve the subject matter in its existing condition. Its purpose is to prevent dissolution of the plaintiff's rights. The main reason for use of a preliminary injunction is the need for immediate relief.

Preliminary or temporary injunctions are not conclusive as to the rights of the parties, and they do not determine the merits of a case or decide issues in controversy. They seek to prevent threatened wrong, further injury, and irreparable harm or injustice until such time as the rights of the parties can be ultimately settled. Preliminary injunctive relief ensures the ability of the court to render a meaningful decision and serves to prevent a change of circumstances that would hamper or block the granting of proper relief following a trial on the merits of the case.

A motion for a preliminary injunction is never granted automatically. The discretion of the court should be exercised in favor of a temporary injunction, which maintains the status quo until the final trial. Such discretion should be exercised against a temporary injunction when its issuance would alter the status quo. For example, during the Florida presidential-election controversy in 2000, the campaign of GEORGE W. BUSH asked a federal appeals court for a preliminary injunction to halt the manual counting of ballots. It sought a preliminary injunction until the U.S. Supreme Court could decide on granting a permanent injunction. In that case, *Siegel v. Lepore*, 234 F.3d 1163 (11th Cir. 2000). the U.S. Court of Appeals for the Eleventh Circuit refused to grant the injunction, stating that the Bush campaign had not "shown the kind of serious and immediate injury that demands the extraordinary relief of a preliminary injunction."

Preventive Injunctions An injunction directing an individual to refrain from doing an act is *preventive, prohibitive, prohibitory,* or *negative.* This type of injunction prevents a threatened injury, preserves the status quo, or restrains the continued commission of an ongoing wrong, but it cannot be used to redress a consummated wrong or to undo that which has already been done.

The Florida vote count in the presidential election of 2000 again serves as a good example. There, the Bush campaign sought preventive injunctions to restrain various counties from performing recounts after the Florida results had been certified. The Bush campaign did not attempt to overturn results already arrived at, but rather attempted to stop new results from coming in. In turn, the Gore campaign attempted to obtain a preventive injunction to prevent Florida's SECRETARY OF STATE from certifying the election results.

Mandatory Injunctions Although the court is vested with wide discretion to fashion injunctive relief, it is also restricted to restraint of a contemplated or threatened action. It also might compel SPECIFIC PERFORMANCE of an act. In such a case, it issues a mandatory injunction, commanding the performance of a positive act. Because mandatory injunctions are harsh, courts do not favor them, and they rarely grant them. Such injunctions have been issued to compel the removal of buildings or other structures wrongfully placed upon the land of another.

Permanent Injunctions A *permanent* or *perpetual* injunction is one that is granted by the judgment that ultimately disposes of the injunction suit, ordered at the time of final judgment. This type of injunction must be final relief. Permanent injunctions are perpetual, provided that the conditions that produced them remain permanent. They have been granted to prevent blasting upon neighboring premises, to enjoin the dumping of earth or other material upon land, and to prevent pollution of a water supply.

An individual who has been licensed by the state to practice a profession may properly demand that others in the same profession subscribe to the ethical standards and laws that govern it. An injunction is a proper remedy to prevent the illegal practice of a profession, and the relief may be sought by either licensed practitioners or a professional association. The illegal PRACTICE OF LAW, medicine, dentistry, and architecture has been stopped by the issuance of injunctions.

Acts that are injurious to the public health or safety may be enjoined as well. For example, injunctions have been issued to enforce laws providing for the eradication of diseases in animals raised for food.

The government has the authority to protect citizens from damage by violence and from fear through threats and intimidation. In some states, an injunction is the proper remedy to bar the use of violence against those asserting their rights under the law.

Acts committed without JUST CAUSE that interfere with the carrying on of a business may be enjoined if no other adequate remedy exists. A TRADE SECRET, for example, may be protected by injunction. An individual's right of personal privacy may be protected by an injunction if there is no other adequate remedy, or where a specific statutory provision for injunctive relief exists. An individual whose name or picture is used for advertising purposes without the individual's consent may enjoin its use. The theory is that injunctive relief is proper because of a celebrity's unique property interest in the commercial use of his or her name and likeness (i.e., their right of publicity).

Restraining Orders A RESTRAINING ORDER is granted to preserve the status quo of the subject of the controversy until the hearing on an application for a temporary injunction. A TEMPORARY RESTRAINING ORDER is an extraordinary remedy of short duration that is issued to prevent unnecessary and irreparable injury. Essentially, such an order suspends proceedings until an opportunity arises to inquire whether an injunction should be granted. Unless extended by the court, a temporary restraining order ceases to operate upon the expiration of the time set by its terms.

Contempt

An individual who violates an injunction may be punished for contempt of court. A person is not guilty of contempt, however, unless he or she can be charged with knowledge of the injunction. Generally, an individual who is charged with contempt is entitled to a trial or a hearing. The penalty imposed is within the discretion of the court. Ordinarily, punishment is by fine, imprisonment, or both.

FURTHER READINGS

Stoll-DeBell, Kirstin. 2010. *Injunctive Relif: Temporary Restraining Orders and Preliminary Injunctions.* Washington, D.C.: American Bar Association.

Suro, Robert, and Jo Becker. "Florida Legislature Ready to Intervene; Special Session on Electors to Convene on Friday." *Washington Post* (December 7, 2000).

Waterman, Thomas Whitney, and Robert Henley Eden. 2008. *A Compendium of the Law and Practice of Injunctions.* Charleston, SC: BiblioBazaar.

CROSS REFERENCE

Equity.

INJURE

To interfere with the legally protected interest of another or to inflict harm on someone, for which an action may be brought. To damage or impair.

The term *injure* is comprehensive and can apply to an injury to a person or property.

CROSS REFERENCE

Tort Law.

INJURIOUS FALSEHOOD

A fallacious statement that causes intentional damage to an individual's commercial or economic relations.

Any type of defamatory remark, either written or spoken, that causes pecuniary loss to an individual through disparagement of a particular business dealing.

For example, the early cases on INJURIOUS FALSEHOOD involved oral aspersions cast upon an individual's ownership of land, which prevented the individual from leasing or selling it. This tort has also been called *disparagement of property, slander of goods,* and *trade libel.*

Injurious falsehood is distinguishable from the more general harm to reputation in LIBEL AND SLANDER.

INJURY

A comprehensive term for any wrong or harm done by one individual to another individual's body, rights, reputation, or property. Any interference with an individual's legally protected interest.

A civil injury is any damage done to person or property that is precipitated by a breach of contract, NEGLIGENCE, or breach of duty. The law of torts provides remedies for injury caused by negligent or intentional acts.

An *accidental injury* is an injury to the body caused unintentionally. Within the meaning of workers' compensation acts, it is an injury occurring in the COURSE OF EMPLOYMENT.

One who is injured might be able to recover damages against the individual who caused him or her harm, because the law seeks to provide a remedy for every injury.

INLAND WATERS

Canals, lakes, rivers, water courses, inlets, and bays that are nearest to the shores of a nation and subject to its complete sovereignty.

Inland waters, also known as internal waters, are subject to the total sovereignty of the country as much as if they were an actual part of its land territory. A coastal nation has the right to exclude foreign vessels, subject to the right of entry in times of distress.

Whether or not particular waters are to be regarded as inland waters has traditionally been dependent upon historical and geographical factors. Certain types of shoreline configurations have been regarded as confining bodies of water, such as bays. In addition, there has been a recognition that other areas of water that are closely connected to the shore may be regarded as inland waters based upon the manner in which they have been treated by the coastal nation, although they do not meet any exact geographical test. Historic title to inland waters can be claimed only in situations when the coastal nation has asserted and maintained dominion and control over those waters.

CROSS REFERENCES

Navigable Rivers; Water Rights.

INNKEEPER

An individual who, as a regular business, provides accommodations for guests in exchange for reasonable compensation.

An inn is defined as a place where lodgings are made available to the public for a charge, such as a hotel, motel, hostel, or guest house. A *guest* is a transient who receives accommodations at an inn, transiency being the major characteristic distinguishing him or her from a boarder. In order for the relationship of innkeeper and guest to be established, the parties must intend to have such a relationship. The individual accommodated must be received as a guest and must obtain accommodations in such capacity. The individual need not, however, register.

An innkeeper must accept all unobjectionable individuals offering themselves as guests, provided the innkeeper has available accommodations and the guests are willing to pay the reasonable charges. Proper grounds for a refusal to receive a proposed guest are ordinarily restricted to either lack of accommodations or the unsuitability of the guest.

It is improper and a violation of an individual's CIVIL RIGHTS for an innkeeper to refuse accommodations on the basis of race, creed, or color. Upon assignment to a room, a guest is entitled to its exclusive occupancy for all lawful purposes, subject to the right of the innkeeper to enter the room for proper purposes, such as to assist the police in their investigation of a crime.

Compensation

An innkeeper is permitted to charge a reasonable compensation only, and must ordinarily fulfill his or her entire obligation prior to being entitled to the compensation. In the event that a guest does not pay, the innkeeper has a lien on the guest's property. Such a lien ordinarily extends to all property brought by the guest to the inn and generally continues until the debt is satisfied unless the innkeeper voluntarily surrenders the goods. The innkeeper may remove a guest upon refusal to pay his or her bill but cannot, however, use excessive force.

Liability

An innkeeper has an obligation to reasonably protect guests from injury while at the inn. This duty of reasonable care mandates vigilance in protection of the guests from foreseeable risks. The innkeeper must protect guests from injury at the hands of other guests and from assaults and negligent acts of his or her own employees. The obligation to protect guests is not met merely by warning them, but must be coupled with a policing of the premises.

An innkeeper must take reasonable care regarding the safety of the guests' property and must warn guests of any hidden dangers that can be reasonably foreseen. This duty includes making inspections to ascertain that the premises are safe. The innkeeper is liable for any injuries arising from his or her failure to comply with fire regulations. Reasonably safe means of ingress and egress must be provided.

An innkeeper is required to use reasonable care to keep the hallways, passageways, and stairways well lighted and free from obstructions or hazards. An innkeeper who furnishes appliances or furniture for the convenience of guests must maintain them in a reasonably safe condition. Similar duties are required in connection with plumbing apparatus and swimming pools.

Reasonable care must be exercised by an innkeeper in the operation and maintenance of an elevator, which means that the elevator must be inspected and repaired to keep it in safe condition. The obligation to maintain the premises in a reasonably safe condition applies to windows and screens that are defective or insecurely fastened. Failure to have protective window grills or to guard air shafts located on a roof does not, however, necessarily constitute NEGLIGENCE.

The prevalent COMMON LAW view makes an innkeeper liable as an insurer for all PERSONAL PROPERTY brought by the guest to the inn that is lost through the innkeeper's fault. There is no liability, however, if the guest assumes the entire and exclusive care, control, and possession of his or her property. State laws have been enacted with respect to the liability of innkeepers for the property of their guests. Generally the statutes modify the common law by limiting the innkeeper's liability to a specified amount and by requiring deposit of valuables. Guests must have notice of any limitations of the innkeeper's liability.

INNOCENT

Absent guilt; acting in good faith with no knowledge of defects, objections, or inculpative circumstances.

A person accused of and prosecuted for the commission of a crime is presumed innocent until proved guilty BEYOND A REASONABLE DOUBT.

INNOCENT PURCHASER

An individual who, in good faith and by an honest agreement, buys property in the absence of sufficient knowledge to charge him or her with notice of any defect in the transaction.

An individual is an innocent or good-faith purchaser when he or she buys something, paying VALUABLE CONSIDERATION, without actual or constructive notice of any legal infirmity in the sale. The purchaser of a gold bracelet for $500 from a jewelry store cannot be charged with notice that the bracelet was stolen.

INNS OF CHANCERY

Ancient preparatory colleges where qualified clerks studied the drafting of writs, which was a function of the officers of the Court of Chancery.

Students attended Inns of Chancery to learn the basics of law and to qualify for admission after two years of instruction to the INNS OF COURT to which the Inn of Chancery was attached. The role of the Inns of Chancery in the English LEGAL EDUCATION process significantly declined in the eighteenth and nineteenth centuries.

INNS OF COURT

Organizations that provide preparatory education for English law students in order to teach them to practice in court.

Inns of Court were founded in the beginning of the fourteenth century. Membership in an inn is tantamount to membership in an integrated bar association in the United States. Inns of Court have a COMMON COUNCIL of LEGAL EDUCATION, which gives lectures and holds examinations. Currently, inns have the exclusive authority to confer the degree of *barrister-at-law*, a prerequisite to practice as an advocate or counsel in the superior courts in England.

INOPERATIVE

Void; not active; ineffectual.

The term *inoperative* is commonly used to indicate that some force, such as a statute or contract, is no longer in effect and legally binding upon the persons who were to be, or had been, affected by it.

INQUEST

An inquiry by a CORONER *or medical examiner, sometimes with the aid of a jury, into the cause of a violent death or a death occurring under suspicious circumstances. Generally an inquest may result in a finding of natural death, accidental death, suicide, or murder. Criminal prosecution may follow when culpable conduct has contributed to the death.*

The body of jurors called to inquire into the circumstances of a death that occurred suddenly, by violence, or while imprisoned. Any body of jurors called to inquire into certain matters. (A GRAND JURY *is sometimes called a grand inquest, for example.)*

The determination or findings of a body of persons called to make a legal inquiry or the report issued after their investigation.

The foundation of the modern jury system can be traced back to the Carolingian empire of medieval Europe during the eighth to the tenth centuries. The monarchs used a procedure called inquest, or inquisition, to help them consolidate their authority in the realm. They called together the people of the countryside and required them to recite what they considered to be the immemorial rights of the king. Once these rights were ascertained, they were adopted by the government and considered established. There was no accusation, VERDICT, or judgment in these proceedings, but the inquest fixed the right of the government to obtain information from its citizens.

The Norman invaders were not long on English soil when they used the inquest to compile the DOMESDAY BOOK, a census compiled between 1085 and 1086 to record the ownership of land throughout the kingdom.

For this inquiry, citizens were called and required to give testimony under OATH about their land and PERSONAL PROPERTY.

The inquest was also used in local courts in England during the Middle Ages. Because a person could not be tried for a crime until accused, a panel of four men from each village and twelve from each hundred appeared before the court and charged certain individuals with crimes. The panel members appeared voluntarily, however, and were not summoned by a public officer as is done for an inquest today. Then in 1166 a law called the Assize of Clarendon made the inquest procedure mandatory. The panel of men was required to appear before local sheriffs and make regular accusations on their oaths. These cases then were tried in the royal courts because of the king's special interest in keeping the peace. This procedure was the origin of the modern GRAND JURY.

A further step in consolidating the king's powers came with creation of the office of the coroner, so named for its service to the crown. In the Middle Ages the coroner was a powerful local official who kept records of appeals from lower courts, accusations, hangings, and public financial matters. He held inquests to investigate royal rights concerning fish, shipwrecks, treasure trove, and unexplained deaths. The purpose of such inquests was always to determine the extent of the king's financial interests. Anytime there was a death, the crown took whatever object had caused the death and all of the personal property of anyone who committed suicide or was convicted of a felony. From this early function of fiscal administration, the coroner today has become primarily responsible for managing dead bodies, but the inquest is still the procedure the coroner uses for investigation.

CROSS REFERENCE

Clarendon, Constitutions of.

INQUIRY, COMMISSIONS OF

Individuals employed, during conciliation, to investigate the facts of a particular dispute and to submit a report stating the facts and proposing terms for the resolution of the differences.

INQUISITORIAL SYSTEM

A method of legal practice in which the judge endeavors to discover facts while simultaneously representing the interests of the state in a trial.

The inquisitorial system can be defined by comparison with the adversarial, or accusatorial, system used in the United States and Great Britain. In the ADVERSARY SYSTEM, two or more opposing parties gather evidence and present the evidence, and their arguments, to a judge or jury. The judge or jury knows nothing of the litigation until the parties present their cases to the decision maker. The DEFENDANT in a criminal trial is not required to testify.

In the inquisitorial system, the presiding judge is not a passive recipient of information. Rather, the presiding judge is primarily responsible for supervising the gathering of the evidence necessary to resolve the case. He or she actively steers the search for evidence and questions the witnesses, including the respondent or defendant. Attorneys play a more passive role, suggesting routes of inquiry for the presiding judge and following the judge's questioning with questioning of their own. Attorney questioning is often brief because the judge tries to ask all relevant questions.

The goal of both the adversarial system and the inquisitorial system is to find the truth. But the adversarial system seeks the truth by pitting the parties against each other in the hope that competition will reveal it, whereas the inquisitorial system seeks the truth by questioning those most familiar with the events in dispute. The adversarial system places a premium on the individual rights of the accused, whereas the inquisitorial system places the rights of the accused secondary to the search for truth.

The inquisitorial system was first developed by the Catholic Church during the medieval period. The ECCLESIASTICAL COURTS in thirteenth-century England adopted the method of adjudication by requiring witnesses and defendants to take an inquisitorial OATH administered by the judge, who then questioned the witnesses. In an inquisitorial oath, the witness swore to truthfully answer all questions asked of him or her. The system flourished in England into the sixteenth century, when it became infamous for its use in the Court of the STAR CHAMBER, a court reserved for complex, contested cases. Under the reign of King Henry VIII, the power of the Star Chamber was expanded, and the court used torture to compel the taking of the inquisitorial oath. The Star Chamber was eventually eliminated as repugnant to basic liberty, and England gradually moved toward an adversarial system.

After the French Revolution, a more refined version of the inquisitorial system developed in France and Germany. From there it spread to the rest of continental Europe and to many African, South American, and Asian countries. The inquisitorial system is now more widely used than the adversarial system. Some countries, such as Italy, use a blend of adversarial and inquisitorial elements in their court system.

The court procedures in an inquisitorial system vary from country to country. Most inquisitorial systems provide a full review of a case by an appeals court. In civil trials under either system of justice, the defendant, or respondent, may be required to testify. The most striking differences between the two systems can be found in criminal trials.

In most inquisitorial systems, a criminal defendant does not have to answer questions about the crime itself but may be required to answer all other questions at trial. Many of these other questions concern the defendant's history and would be considered irrelevant and inadmissible in an adversarial system.

A criminal defendant in an inquisitorial system is the first to testify. The defendant is allowed to see the government's case before testifying, and is usually eager to give her or his side of the story. In an adversarial system, the defendant is not required to testify and is not entitled to a complete examination of the government's case.

A criminal defendant is not presumed guilty in an inquisitorial system. Nevertheless, since a case would not be brought against a defendant unless there is evidence indicating guilt, the system does not require the PRESUMPTION OF INNOCENCE that is fundamental to the adversarial system.

A trial in an inquisitorial system may last for months as the presiding judge gathers evidence in a series of hearings.

The decision in an inquisitorial criminal trial is made by the collective vote of a certain number of professional judges and a small group of lay assessors (persons selected at random from the population). Neither the prosecution nor the defendant has an opportunity to question the lay assessors for bias. Generally, the judges vote after the lay assessors vote, so that they do not influence the conclusions of the lay assessors. A two-thirds majority is usually required to convict a criminal defendant, whereas a unanimous VERDICT is the norm in an adversarial system.

The inquisitorial system does not protect criminal defendants as much as the adversarial system. This is true even though, prosecutors in the inquisitorial system do not have a personal incentive to win convictions for political gain, which can motivate prosecutors in an adversarial system. Most scholars agree that the two systems generally reach the same results by different means.

FURTHER READINGS

Moskovitz, Myron. 1995. "The O.J. Inquisition: A United States Encounter with Continental Criminal Justice." *Vanderbilt Journal of Transnational Law* 28.

Sward, Ellen E. 1989. "Values, Ideology, and the Evolution of the Adversary System." *Indiana Law Journal* 64.

Van Koppen, Peter J., and Steven Penrod. 2003. *Adversarial Versus Inquisitorial Justice.* New York: Springer.

CROSS REFERENCES

Criminal Procedure; Due Process of Law.

INSANITY DEFENSE

A defense asserted by an accused in a criminal prosecution to avoid liability for the commission of a crime because, at the time of the crime, the person did not appreciate the nature or quality or wrongfulness of the acts.

The insanity defense is used by criminal defendants. The most common variation is cognitive insanity. Under the test for cognitive insanity, a DEFENDANT must have been so impaired by a mental disease or defect at the time of the act that he or she did not know the nature or quality of the act, or, if the defendant did know the nature or quality of the act, he or she did not know that the act was wrong. The vast majority of states allow criminal defendants to invoke the cognitive insanity defense.

Another form of the insanity defense is volitional insanity, or IRRESISTIBLE IMPULSE. A defense of irresistible impulse asserts that the defendant, although able to distinguish right from wrong at the time of the act, suffered from a mental disease or defect that made him or her incapable of controlling her or his actions. This defense is common in crimes of vengeance. For example, suppose that a child has been brutally assaulted. If an otherwise conscientious and law-abiding mother shoots the perpetrator, the mother may argue that she was so enraged that she became mentally ill and incapable of exerting self-control. Very few states allow the volitional insanity defense.

The insanity defense should not be confused with incompetency. Persons who are incompetent to stand trial are held in a mental institution until they are considered capable of participating in the proceedings.

The insanity defense also should be kept separate from issues concerning mental retardation. The U.S. Supreme Court ruled in 2002 in *Atkins v. Virginia*, 536 U.S. 304, 122 S. Ct. 2242,

153 L. Ed. 2d 335 (2002) that the execution of mentally retarded criminals constituted "cruel and unusual punishment" and that it was prohibited by EIGHTH AMENDMENT. But if a person is acquitted by reason of insanity, execution is not an option.

The insanity defense reflects the generally accepted notion that persons who cannot appreciate the consequences of their actions should not be punished for criminal acts. Most states regulate the defense with statutes, but a few states allow the courts to craft the rules for its proper use. Generally, the defense is available to a criminal defendant if the judge instructs the jury that it may consider whether the defendant was insane when the crime was committed. The judge may issue this instruction if the defendant has produced sufficient evidence at trial to justify the theory. Sufficient evidence invariably includes EXPERT TESTIMONY by psychologists and psychiatrists.

John Hinckley Jr. was prosecuted for the attempted assassination of President Ronald Reagan in 1981. His acquittal by reason of insanity sparked public outcry, ultimately leading Congress to pass the Insanity Defense Reform Act.

AP IMAGES

When invoking insanity as a defense, a defendant is required to notify the prosecution. In some states, sanity is determined by the judge or jury in a separate proceeding following the determination of guilt or innocence at trial. In other states, the defense is either accepted or rejected in the VERDICT of the judge or jury. Even if evidence of insanity does not win a verdict of not guilty, the sentencing court may consider it as a mitigating factor.

History

"Complete madness" was first established as a defense to criminal charges by the COMMON LAW courts in late-thirteenth-century England. By the eighteenth century, the complete madness definition had evolved into the "wild beast" test. Under that test, the insanity defense was available to a person who was "totally deprived of his understanding and memory so as not to know what he [was] doing, no more than an infant, a brute, or a wild beast" (Feigl 1995, 161).

By 1840 most jurisdictions had refined the wild beast test to cognitive insanity and supplemented that with irresistible-impulse insanity. However, in 1843 a well-publicized ASSASSINATION attempt in England caused Parliament to eliminate the irresistible-impulse defense. Daniel M'Naghten, operating under the delusion that Prime Minister Robert Peel wanted to kill him, tried to shoot Peel but shot and killed Peel's secretary instead. Medical testimony indicated that M'Naghten was psychotic, and the court acquitted him by reason of insanity (*M'Naghten's Case*, 8 Eng. Rep. 718 [1843]). In response to a public furor that followed the decision, the House of Lords ordered the Lords of Justice of the Queen's Bench to craft a new rule for insanity in the CRIMINAL LAW.

What emerged became known as the M'Naghten rule. This rule migrated to the United States within a decade of its conception, and it stood for the better part of the next century. The intent of the *M'Naghten* rule was to abolish the irresistible-impulse defense and to limit the insanity defense to cognitive insanity. Under the *M'Naghten* rule, insanity was a defense if

> at the time of the committing of the act, the party accused was labouring under such a defect of reason, from a disease of the mind, as not to know the nature and quality of the act he was doing; or, if he did know it, that he did not know he was doing what was wrong.

Through the first half of the twentieth century, the insanity defense was expanded again. Courts began to accept the theories of psychoanalysts, many of whom encouraged recognition of the irresistible-impulse defense. Many states enacted a combination of the *M'Naghten* rule supplemented with an irresistible-impulse defense, thereby covering both cognitive and volitional insanity.

The insanity defense reached its most permissive standard in *Durham v. United States*, 214 F.2d 862 (D.C. Cir. 1954). The *Durham* rule excused a defendant "if his unlawful act was the product of mental disease or mental defect." The *Durham* rule was lauded by the mental health community as progressive because it allowed psychologists and psychiatrists to contribute to the JUDICIAL understanding of insanity. But it was also criticized for placing too much trust in the opinions of mental health professionals. Within seven years of its creation, the rule had been explicitly rejected in 22 states. It is now used only in New Hampshire.

In 1964 the American Law Institute (ALI) began to reassess the insanity defense in the course of promoting a new MODEL PENAL CODE. What emerged from the Model Penal Code Commission was a compromise between the narrow *M'Naghten* test and the generous *Durham* rule. The ALI test provided that a person was not responsible for criminal conduct if, at the time of the act, the person lacked "substantial capacity" to appreciate the conduct or to conform the conduct to the RULE OF LAW. The ALI test provided for both cognitive and volitional insanity. It also required only a lack of substantial capacity, less than complete impairment. The ALI version of the insanity defense was adopted by more than half the states and all but one federal circuit.

Several years later, another dramatic event led to another round of restrictions on the insanity defense. In 1981 John W. Hinckley Jr. attempted to assassinate President RONALD REAGAN. Hinckley was prosecuted and acquitted of all charges by reason of insanity, and a resulting public outcry prompted Congress to enact legislation on the issue. In 1984 Congress passed the Insanity Defense Reform Act (Insanity Act), 18 U.S.C.A. § 17 to abolish the irresistible-impulse test from federal courts. Initially, Reagan had called for a total abolition of mental illness as a defense to criminal charges, but his administration backed down from this position after intense lobbying by various professional organizations and trade associations.

The Insanity Act also placed the burden on the defendant to prove insanity. Before the Insanity Act, federal prosecutors bore the burden of proving the defendant's sanity BEYOND A REASONABLE DOUBT.

Most states joined Congress in reevaluating the insanity defense after Hinckley's acquittal. The legislatures of these states modified and limited the insanity defense in many and varied ways. Some states shifted the BURDEN OF PROOF, and some limited the applicability of the defense in the same manner as Congress did. A few states abolished the defense entirely. Chief Justice WILLIAM H. REHNQUIST, of the U.S. Supreme Court, opined in a dissent that it is "highly doubtful that due process requires a State to make available an insanity defense to a criminal defendant" (*Ake v. Oklahoma*, 470 U.S. 68, 105 S. Ct. 1087, 84 L. Ed. 2d 53 [1985]).

The Supreme Court was presented with an opportunity to clarify this area of the law in *Clark v. Arizona*, 548 U.S. 735, 126 S.Ct. 2709, 165 L. Ed. 2d 842 (2006). The case centered on an Arizona law that, while affording criminal defendants the right to raise insanity as a defense, articulated a legal standard for insanity that encapsulated only half of the M'Naghten defense. A.R.S. § 13-502(A). Arizona's insanity defense was stated solely in terms of the defendant's capacity to tell whether a criminal act was right or wrong. The act did not allow defendants to argue that they were insane because they failed to comprehend what they were doing while committing the act. Eric Clark, who was convicted of first-degree MURDER in an Arizona court, challenged the Arizona law, arguing that due process affords defendants the right to assert either prong of the M'Naghten defense against criminal charges brought by the state or federal government.

In a 6–3 decision authored by Justice DAVID SOUTER, the Court upheld the law. "[D]ue process imposes no single canonical formulation of legal insanity," the Court observed. In fact, the court said that because a survey of state and federal defenses relating to cognitive incapacity shows such a wide and varied landscape, "it is clear that no particular formulation has evolved into a baseline for due process, and that the insanity rule, like the conceptualization of criminal offenses, is substantially open to state choice." The defendant could point to no evidence that was excluded, the court emphasized, including his expert and lay testimony regarding his delusions, which tended to support a description of him as lacking the capacity to understand that the police officer was a human being. And, the court added, there was no doubt that the trial court considered the evidence as going to an issue of cognitive capacity. The Court concluded that the defendant had his DAY IN COURT and was able to fully present an insanity defense under existing Arizona law.

Similarly, the court ruled that the Due Process Clause does not dictate to state courts how they must receive evidence bearing on a crime charged against a defendant raising insanity as a defense. In *Clark*, the trial court applied a state common law rule of evidence called the *Mott* rule to prevent the defendant from introducing medical testimony showing that his alleged cognitive incapacity negated the specific-intent element of his first-degree murder charge, also known as the MENS REA element. The purpose of the *Mott* rule, the Court said, is to enable jurors to distinguish between a defense of insanity, which requires proof of cognitive incapacity, and a defense of not guilty, which can be established simply by showing that the prosecution failed to prove every element of the offense charged. Allowing the defense to offer proof of the defendant's cognitive incapacity to negate the *mens rea* element would only serve to confuse the jurors, and the state acted within its power by establishing a rule of evidence to prevent this outcome.

Consequences

When a party successfully defends criminal charges on a ground of insanity, the consequences vary from jurisdiction to jurisdiction. Usually, the defendant is committed to a mental institution. On the average, a defendant found not guilty by reason of insanity and committed to a mental institution is confined for twice as long as is a defendant who is found guilty and sent to prison. Very few acquitted insanity defendants are given supervised release, and even fewer are released directly following their verdict.

IS THERE A NEED FOR THE INSANITY DEFENSE?

Though the insanity defense is rarely invoked in criminal trials, it remains a controversial issue. Legislators and the public generally question the need for the defense after a DEFENDANT in a highly publicized MURDER case is found not guilty by reason of insanity. For example, when John Hinckley successfully used the defense after shooting President RONALD REAGAN to impress the actress Jodie Foster, there was a public outcry. Legal and medical commentators have divided opinions about the need for the insanity defense.

Those who wish to retain it note that 48 of the 50 states have some type of insanity defense. This, they claim, is evidence of the need for such a defense. The public is given a distorted view of who uses the defense and how it is employed. In fact about one percent of criminal defendants invoke the defense. More important, criminals rarely "beat the rap" by PLEADING insanity. When an insanity defense is employed, it means the defendant admits committing the criminal behavior and is now seeking a not guilty VERDICT on the basis of his state of mind. If the jury does not agree, the defendant will be convicted, and generally will serve a longer sentence than will someone convicted of the same crime who has not pleaded insanity.

Juries find for only about 20 percent of the defendants who plead insanity. Even this figure does not reflect the reality that many insanity pleas are the result of PLEA bargains, which indicates that prosecutors agree that such pleas are sometimes appropriate.

Finally, the fact that most highly publicized cases involve murder disguises the true demographics: 60 to 70 percent of insanity pleas are for crimes other than murder. They range from ASSAULT to shoplifting.

All these myths have led to the belief that criminals can avoid punishment by claiming insanity. The truth is that the insanity defense is a risky one at best.

Apart from combating these myths, advocates of the insanity defense contend that a fundamental principle of CRIMINAL LAW is at stake. The insanity defense is rooted in the belief that conviction and punishment are justified only if the defendant deserves them. The basic precondition for punishment is that the person who committed the criminal behavior must have responsibility as a moral agent. When a person is so mentally disturbed that her irrationality or compulsion is impossible to control, that person lacks responsibility as a moral agent. It would be unfair to punish a person in such an extreme condition.

Based on this argument, proponents of the insanity defense do not support its application to a person who willingly consumes a powerful hallucinogen and then commits a criminal act. Nor would they allow its application to a person who is able to control a mental disorder through medication but fails to do so. But they do support the defense for a person who unwittingly consumes hallucinogens and then commits a crime.

Some opponents attack the insanity defense for confusing psychiatric and legal concepts, in the process undermining the moral integrity of the law. Both sides agree that the word *insane* is a legal, not medical, term. It is too simplistic to describe a severely mentally ill person merely as insane, and the vast majority of people with a mental illness would be judged sane if current legal tests for insanity were applied. The legal tests for insanity, moreover, require that a defendant's mental condition become so impaired that the fact finder

may conclude the person has lost his or her free will. Because free will is not a concept that can be explained in medical terms, it may be impossible for a psychiatrist to determine if the mental impairment affected the defendant's capacity for voluntary choice. Without a way to measure insanity, it makes no sense to let prosecution and defense psychiatrists spar over the issue. A jury's decision based on psychiatrists' opinions may be grounded on unreliable evidence.

Another major argument against the insanity defense challenges its supposed moral basis. Critics contend that modern criminal law is concerned more with the consequences of crime and less with moral imperatives. If a person commits a criminal act, that person should be convicted. Mental illness can be taken into consideration at the time of sentencing. This line of reasoning supports laws that several states have adopted, which abolish the insanity defense and replace it with a new verdict of guilty but insane. This verdict carries a criminal penalty. It allows the judge to determine the length of imprisonment, which occurs in a hospital prison, and shifts the burden to the defendant to prove he is no longer dangerous or mentally ill in order to be released.

Finally, critics argue that the insanity plea is a rich person's defense. Only wealthy defendants can retain high-priced psychiatric experts. Persons represented by public defenders are usually afforded a psychiatric examination for the defense, but they may not get the same quality of exam, nor are they typically able to hire more than one examiner. Because a two-tiered criminal justice system is morally repugnant, critics contend that the insanity defense must be abolished.

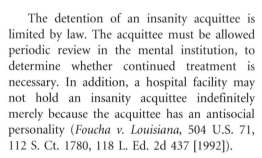

Colin Ferguson

Colin Ferguson was convicted in March 1995 for crimes associated with a massacre in Long Island, New York, on December 7, 1993. Ferguson killed six persons and injured nineteen after opening fire with an automatic pistol on a crowded commuter train.

Ferguson's trial was marked with controversy. He discharged his court-appointed attorneys, who believed him mentally incompetent to stand trial, and was allowed by the judge to act as his own attorney. He dropped the insanity defense prepared by his attorneys and argued that a mysterious gunman had committed the shootings.

His bizarre courtroom behavior appeared to contradict the judge's conclusion that Ferguson was competent to stand trial. Though many witnesses identified Ferguson as the gunman, he insisted a white man had taken the gun from his bag while he slept, shot the passengers, and then escaped, leaving Ferguson, who is black, to take the blame. During the trial he asserted that he had been charged with ninety-three counts only because the crime occurred in 1993.

Attorneys Ronald L. Kuby and William M. Kunstler, whom Ferguson had discharged, had asked the judge before trial to find that Ferguson's paranoia and delusional state made him mentally incompetent to stand trial. Yet Ferguson refused to be examined by either prosecution or defense psychiatrists, believing he was not insane. The judge allowed Ferguson to stand trial, believing he could understand the nature of the charges against him and could assist in his own defense.

The detention of an insanity acquittee is limited by law. The acquittee must be allowed periodic review in the mental institution, to determine whether continued treatment is necessary. In addition, a hospital facility may not hold an insanity acquittee indefinitely merely because the acquittee has an antisocial personality (*Foucha v. Louisiana,* 504 U.S. 71, 112 S. Ct. 1780, 118 L. Ed. 2d 437 [1992]).

The procedural framework in Massachusetts illustrates the consequences that come with the insanity defense. Under chapter 123, section 16, of the Massachusetts General Laws Annotated, the court may order a person found not guilty by reason of insanity (an insanity acquittee) to be hospitalized for 40 days for observation and examination. During this period, the district attorney or the superintendent of the mental hospital may petition the court to have the insanity acquittee committed to the hospital. If the judge orders the commitment, the acquittee is placed in the hospital for six months.

After the first six months have expired, the commitment is reviewed again, and then once a year thereafter. If the superintendent of the mental health facility moves to discharge the acquittee, the district attorney must respond with any objections within 30 days of notice from the superintendent. The mental health facility is authorized to restrict the movement of criminal defendants and insanity acquittees, so a commitment is tantamount to incarceration.

Defendants' Rights

When PLEADING insanity, a defendant might not want to present the best possible image at trial. In *Riggins v. Nevada,* 504 U.S. 127, 112 S. Ct. 1810, 118 L. Ed. 2d 479 (1992), defendant David Riggins was charged with robbing and murdering Las Vegas resident Paul Wade. After being taken into custody, Riggins complained that he was hearing voices in his head and that he was having trouble sleeping. A psychiatrist at the jail prescribed 100 milligrams per day of Mellaril, an antipsychotic drug. By the time of trial, the psychiatrist was prescribing 800 milligrams per day of Mellaril.

Just before trial, Riggins's attorney moved the court to suspend administration of the Mellaril. Riggins was pleading not guilty by reason of insanity, and his attorney wanted the jury to see Riggins in his natural state. According to one psychiatrist, Dr. Jack Jurasky, Riggins "would most likely regress to a manifest psychosis and become extremely difficult to manage" if he were taken off Mellaril.

The court denied the motion, and Riggins was convicted and sentenced to death. The Nevada Supreme Court affirmed Riggins's convictions and death sentence. On appeal to the U.S. Supreme Court, the convictions were reversed. According to the high court, Nevada had violated Riggins's due process rights under the Sixth and Fourteenth Amendments. In the absence of evidence that the treatment was medically appropriate and essential for Riggins's own safety or the safety of others, and without an exploration of less intrusive alternatives, the trial court had erred by denying Riggins's liberty interest in freedom from antipsychotic drugs.

According to the court, the administration of the Mellaril jeopardized a number of Riggins's trial rights. Not only was it possible that the Mellaril had affected Riggins's outward appearance, and thus his defense, but the high daily dosage of Mellaril also might have affected Riggins's testimony, his ability to communicate with his attorney, and his ability to follow the proceedings. Although the defense had been allowed to present expert testimony on the nature of Riggins's mental condition, the Court concluded that the compromise of Riggins's trial rights was reversible error.

Uses and Abuses

Victims of abuse often allege temporary insanity in defending their own violent behavior. For example, in 1994, Virginia resident Lorena Bobbitt, charged with severing her husband's penis with a knife, was acquitted of ASSAULT charges on the ground of temporary insanity. At trial, Bobbitt testified that her husband had abused her physically and emotionally.

Critics complain that the insanity defense is abused by defense attorneys, who use it to free the perpetrators of deliberate criminal acts. However, 95 percent of all persons found not guilty by reason of insanity are detained in hospitals, and in practice, the insanity defense is rarely invoked and rarely successful. The insanity defense is used by defendants in only one percent of all felony cases, and it results in acquittal in only one-quarter of those cases.

Psychopaths and Sociopaths

When most people hear about the insanity defense, they automatically assume that it can be used applied to people commonly referred to as psychopaths and sociopaths. While traditionally there has been a small degree of difference between these two classifications, the American Psychiatric Association's most recent Diagnostic and Statistical Manual—Fourth Edition ("DSM-IV") groups sociopathy and psychopathy under the heading "antisocial personality disorder." The DSM-IV lays out a limited and concise set of diagnostic criteria on which to base the diagnosis of antisocial personality disorder.

According to the DSM-IV, antisocial personality disorder is characterized by pervasive pattern of disregard for, and violation of, the rights of others occurring since age 18, as indicated by three (or more) of the following: (1) failure to conform to social norms with respect to lawful behaviors as indicated by repeatedly performing acts that are grounds for arrest; (2) deceitfulness, as indicated by repeated lying, use of aliases, or conning others for personal profit or pleasure; (3) impulsivity or failure to plan ahead; (4) irritability and aggressiveness, as indicated by repeated physical fights or assaults; (5) reckless disregard for safety of self or others; (6) consistent irresponsibility, as indicated by repeated failure to sustain consistent work behavior or to honor financial obligations; or (7) lack of remorse, as indicated by being indifferent to, or rationalizing, having hurt, mistreated, or stolen from another.

However it is defined, many in the legal community doubt whether the insanity defense covers this kind of behavior at all. The ALI's Model Penal Code test of insanity states that "the terms mental disease or defect do not include an abnormality that is manifested only by repeated criminal or otherwise antisocial conduct." In other words, the criteria laid down by the DSM-IV for antisocial personality disorder would not allow for a claim of insanity under the Model Penal Code, the most widely used insanity test, or in other insanity tests used by states. Thus, sociopaths and psychopaths, while perceived as insane by most people, could likely not use the insanity defense as a defense in a court of law.

For this reason, most celebrated serial killers such as John Wayne Gacy and Ted Bundy, as well as persons whose mental stability seems to be of a questionable nature, such as Ted Kaczynski, have seen their insanity pleas fail or have never used the defense. In fact, in recent years, Hinckley and Bobbitt are among the few celebrated cases who have used the defense successfully. For criminals with antisocial personality disorder, the insanity PLEA simply does not apply.

FURTHER READINGS

American Psychiatric Association. 1994. *Diagnostic and Statistical Manual of Mental Disorders—Fourth Edition.* Washington D.C.: American Psychiatric Press

Bing, Jonathan L. 1996. "Protecting the Mentally Retarded from Capital Punishment: State Efforts since *Penry* and Recommendations for the Future." *New York University Review of Law and Social Change* 22.

Campbell, Emily. 1990. "The Psychopath and the Definition of 'Mental Disease or Defect' Under the Model Penal Code Test of Insanity: A Question of Psychology or a Question of Law?" *Nebraska Law Review* 69

Ellickson, Robert C. 1996. "Controlling Chronic Misconduct in City Spaces: Of Panhandlers, Skid Rows, and Public-Space Zoning." *Yale Law Journal* 105.

Giorgi-Guarnieri, Deborah, et. al. 2002. "Practice Guideline; Forensic Psychiatric Evaluation of Defendants Raising the Insanity Defense." *Journal of the American Academy of Psychiatry and the Law* 30 (June).

Kuby, Ronald L., and William M. Kunstler. 1995. "So Crazy He Thinks He Is Sane: The Colin Ferguson Trial and the Competency Standard." *Cornell Journal of Law and Public Policy* 5.

LaFond, John Q., and Mary L. Durham. 1992. *Back to the Asylum: The Future of Mental Health Law and Policy in the United States.* New York: Oxford Univ. Press.

Melville, John D., and David Naimark. 2002. "Punishing the Insane: The Verdict of Guilty but Mentally Ill." *Journal of the American Academy of Psychiatry and the Law* 30 (December): 553–5.

Morse, Stephen J. 1985. "Excusing the Crazy." *Southern California Law Review* 58.

Phillips, Jean K. Gilles. 2008. "The Insanity of the Mens Rea Model: Due Process and the Abolition of the Insanity Defense." *Pace Law Review* Spring.

Rogers, Richard, and and Daniel Shuman. 2000. *Conducting Insanity Evaluations.* 2d ed. New York: Guilford Press.

Semrau, Stanley, and Judy Gale. 2002. *Murderous Minds on Trial: Terrible Tales from a Forensic Psychiatrist's Case Book.* Toronto, Tonawanda, N.Y.: Dundurn Press.

CROSS REFERENCES

M'naghten Rule.

INSECURITY CLAUSE

Provision in a contract that allows a creditor to make an entire debt come due if there is good reason to believe that the debtor cannot or will not pay.

INSIDER

In the context of federal regulation of the purchase and sale of securities, an insider is anyone who has knowledge of facts not available to the general public.

Insider information refers to knowledge about the financial status of a company that is obtained before the public obtains it, and which is usually known only by corporate officials or other insiders. The use of insider information in the purchase and sale of stock violates federal SECURITIES law.

INSIDER TRADING entails the purchase and sale of corporate shares by officers, directors, and stockholders who own more than 10 percent of the stock of a corporation listed on a national exchange (any association that provides facilities for the purchase and sale of securities, such as the New York Stock Exchange). Insider reports detailing such transactions must be submitted monthly to the SECURITIES AND EXCHANGE COMMISSION.

INSIDER TRADING

Insider trading refers to the illegal practice of a shareholder in a public company who buys or sells stocks in that company as a result of having information unavailable to the general public.

Information is key to making money in the STOCK MARKET. The U.S. stock market is premised on all investors having the same access to information on the performance and activities of corporations. Armed with that information, investors can analyze the data and make their choices. When corporate insiders and their friends trade stocks based on information not available to the general public, they gain an immense advantage in the market. If the stock in a company is likely to fall when the information does become public, insiders who sell before it becomes public minimize their losses; if the information portends a sharp rise in the stock price, purchasing stock at the current price maximize their profits. Because of the unfair advantage built into insider trading, the federal government has imposed civil and criminal sanctions on the practice.

The U.S. laws against inside training are the toughest in the world. State governments took the lead in the nineteenth century against insider training. The federal government did not get involved for many years. When it did, however, the first law against the practice was established not by Congress, but by the Supreme Court, in the 1909 decision of *Strong v. Repide* (213 U.S. 419, 29 S. Ct. 521, 53 L. Ed. 853). In this case, the Court dealt with the sale of stock in the Philippines Sugar Estates Development Company to one of its directors. The director was negotiating at the same time the purchase of stock from the PLAINTIFF and the sale of corporate assets to the Philippines government. The director took elaborate steps to conceal his efforts from both the plaintiff and the government. In the end, he purchased the stock for about one-tenth of its actual value.

The Supreme Court held that based on the facts of this case, "the law would indeed be impotent if the sale could not be SET ASIDE or the DEFENDANT cast in damages for his fraud." This became known as the *special facts* or *special circumstances* rule. The rule made clear that while directors generally had no duty to reveal material facts when trading with shareholders, a duty might rise based on the special circumstances and conduct of the director.

Congress did become involved after the Wall Street Crash of 1929 and the Great Depression of the 1930s. The SECURITIES Exchange Act of 1934 recognized that modern capitalism required more disclosure of information about the stock purchases of corporate executives and directors in their companies. The act established the SECURITIES AND EXCHANGE COMMISSION (SEC) to oversee publicly traded securities and mandated full disclosure of corporate information to promote a stock market that was fair for all investors. The law barred corporate insiders from selling or buying their company's stock while possessing information about the stock that was not available to the public.

Section 10(b) of the Securities Act makes it unlawful for "any person, directly or indirectly, by the use of any means or instrumentality of interstate commerce or the mails" to use or employ in the purchase or sale of securities "any manipulative or deceptive device or contrivance" in violation of SEC rules and regulations. Despite the enactment of this provision, the SEC brought few insider trading cases until the late 1950s. In the late 1950s, the SEC enacted Rule 10b-5, which forbade insiders from trading on material nonpublic information unless they either "disclose or abstain" from trading. The rule has been used ever since to prosecute inside traders.

Despite Rule 10b-5, it is difficult to gather the information necessary to convict someone of insider trading. The SEC monitors all stock trades, looking for suspicious behavior. Moreover, insider trading can involve more people than just corporate officers. The government has prosecuted family members and friends of insiders, as well as journalists who have bought or sold stock based on their reporting of companies. In the current environment, the SEC reviews phone and e-mail records and uses the testimony of informants. The maximum penalties for insider trading are ten years in prison and a $1 million fine. A corporation that is found guilty of insider trading may be fined up to $25 million.

Between 2001 and 2006, the SEC brought 300 charges of insider trading against more than 600 individuals. The prosecution of executives of the energy company Enron led to multiple convictions or PLEA bargains between 2002 and 2006. Author and television personality Martha Stewart was accused of trading stocks based on the advice of the corporation's executive but was ultimately convicted of obstructing justice and lying to investigators. She served five months in prison and six months of HOUSE ARREST.

FURTHER READINGS

Larimore, James N., ed. 2008. *Securities and Exchange Commission: Programs and Operations.* New York: Nova Science.

Securities and Exchange Commission. Available online at www.sec.gov (accessed July 28, 2009).

Seligman, Joel. 2003. *The Transformation of Wall Street: A History of the Securities and Exchange Commission and Modern Corporate Finance.* 3d ed. New York: Aspen.

Western, David. 2004. *Booms, Bubbles, and Busts in the U.S. Stock Market.* New York: Routledge.

Winer, Kenneth B., and Samuel J. Winer. 2004. *Securities Enforcement: Counseling & Defense.* Newark, N.J.: LexisNexis.

CROSS REFERENCES

Securities and Exchange Commission; Stock; Stock Market.

INSOLVENCY

An incapacity to pay debts upon the date when they become due in the ordinary course of business; the condition of an individual whose property and assets are inadequate to discharge the person's debts.

INSPECTION

An examination or investigation; the right to see and duplicate documents, enter land, or make other such examinations for the purpose of gathering evidence.

The inspection of documents relevant to issues in a lawsuit is an important element of discovery.

INSTALLMENT

Regular, partial portion of the same debt, paid at successive periods as agreed by a debtor and creditor.

An *installment loan* is designed to be repaid in certain specified, ordinarily equal amounts over a designated period, such as a year or a number of months.

INSTANT

Current or present.

When composing a legal brief, an attorney might use the phrase *the instant case* in reference to the case currently before the

---

Installment Loan Agreement

PROMISSORY NOTE - INSTALLMENT

_____(city,state,date) FOR VALUE RECEIVED, we the undersigned, jointly and severally, promise to pay to the order of (name of lender), (city, state) , the sum of _____ ($) Dollars with interest on any unpaid balance from (date) at the rate of percent per annum, and payable in equal successive monthly installments of Dollars in lawful money of the United States of America, commencing on the day of each and every month thereafter until paid except the final installment which shall be the balance due on this note.

If any installment be not paid when due, the undersigned promise to pay collection charges of per dollar of each overdue installment, or the actual cost of collection, whichever is greater and the entire amount owing and unpaid hereunder shall at the election of the holder hereof forthwith become due and payable, and notice of such election is hereby waived.

The undersigned promises to pay all reasonable attorney's fees incurred by the holder hereof in enforcing any right or remedy hereunder.

All sums remaining unpaid on the agreed or accelerated date of the maturity of the last installment shall thereafter bear interest at the rate of percent per month. The undersigned authorizes the holder to date and complete this note in accordance with the terms of the loan evidenced hereby, to accept additional co-makers, to release co-makers, to change or extend dates of payment and to grant indulgences all without notice or affecting the obligations of the undersigned, and hereby waives;

    a. Presentment, demand, protest, notice of dishonor and the notice of nonpayment;
    b. The right, if any, to the benefit, or to direct the application of, any security hypothecated to the holder, until all indebtedness of the maker to the holder, howsoever arising shall have been paid;
    c. The right to require the holder to proceed against the maker, or to pursue any other remedy in the holder's power;

And agrees that the holder may proceed against any of the undersigned, directly and independently of the maker and that the cessation of the liability of the maker for any reason other than full payment, or any extension, forbearance, change of rate of interest, acceptance, release, substitution of security, or any impairment or suspension of the holder's remedies or rights against the maker, shall not in anywise affect the liability of any of the undersigned hereunder.

All obligations of the makers if more than one, shall be joint and several.

_____

_____

A sample installment loan agreement.

court to distinguish it from other cases discussed.

INSTIGATE

To incite, stimulate, or induce into action; goad into an unlawful or bad action, such as a crime.

The term *instigate* is used synonymously with abet, which is the intentional encouragement or aid of another individual in committing a crime.

INSTITUTE

To inaugurate, originate, or establish. In civil law, to direct an individual who was named as heir in a will to pass over the estate to another designated person, known as the substitute.

For example, to institute an action is to commence it by the filing of a complaint.

INSTITUTION

The commencement or initiation of anything, such as an action. An establishment, particularly one that is eleemosynary or public by nature.

An institution can be any type of organized corporation or society. It may be private and designed for the profit of the individuals composing it, or PUBLIC and NONPROFIT.

INSTRUCTIONS

Directives given by a judge to a jury during a trial prescribing the manner in which the jurors should proceed in deciding the case at bar. Jury instructions ordinarily include a statement of the questions of fact for determination by the jury, as well as a statement of the laws applicable to the facts of the case.

INSTRUMENT

A formal or legal written document; a document in writing, such as a deed, lease, bond, contract, or will. A writing that serves as evidence of an individual's right to collect money, such as a check.

INSTRUMENTALITY RULE

A principle of corporate law that permits a court to disregard the corporate existence of a subsidiary corporation when it is operated solely for the benefit of the parent corporation, which controls and directs the activities of the subsidiary while asserting the shield of limited liability.

The instrumentality rule, also called the ALTER EGO doctrine, destroys the corporate immunity from liability when the corporate nature of an organization is a sham that brings about injustice. When the rule is applied, the court is considered to pierce the corporate veil.

INSURABLE INTEREST

A right, benefit, or advantage arising out of property that is of such nature that it may properly be indemnified.

In the law of insurance, the insured must have an interest in the subject matter of his or her policy, or such policy will be void and unenforceable since it will be regarded as a form of gambling. An individual ordinarily has an insurable interest when he or she will obtain some type of financial benefit from the preservation of the subject matter, or will sustain pecuniary loss from its destruction or impairment when the risk insured against occurs.

In certain jurisdictions, the INNOCENT PURCHASER of a stolen car, who has a right of possession superior to all with the exception of the true owner, has an insurable interest in the automobile. This is not the case, however, where an individual knowingly purchases a stolen automobile.

Insurable interest is not dependent upon who pays the premiums of the policy. In addition, different people can have separate insurable interests in the same subject matter or property.

INSURANCE

A contract whereby, for specified consideration, one party undertakes to compensate the other for a loss relating to a particular subject as a result of the occurrence of designated hazards.

The normal activities of daily life carry the risk of enormous financial loss. Many persons are willing to pay a small amount for protection against certain risks because that protection provides valuable peace of mind. The term *insurance* describes any measure taken for protection against risks. When insurance takes the form of a contract in an insurance policy, it is subject to requirements in statutes,

Insurance Policy (Motorcycle)

A sample insurance
policy.

COLONIAL MOTOR CYCLE COVER

The Colonial Insurance Company Ltd. (hereinafter referred to as "Colonial") agrees to provide insurance in the Terms and Conditions set out in this Policy during the period of insurance stated in the Schedule or any subsequent period for which the Company may accept a premium.

- The proposal form and declaration signed by you the Insured are the basis of and form part of this contract.
- The policy will operate only in Bermuda.
- This Policy is a Contract of Indemnity between Colonial and you the Insured.
- We welcome you as a policyholder of Colonial.

Stamp Duty chargeable on this Policy under the Stamp Duties Act, 1976 will be paid.

NO CLAIMS DISCOUNT

Provided no claim has arisen under this policy during the previous period of insurance your renewal premium will be discounted as follows: After

1 Claim Free Year	10%
2 Claim Free Years	20%

If only one claim arises in any period of insurance, your No Claim Discount will be reduced to nil.

Your entitlement to No Claims Discount cannot be transferred to anyone else.

The Policy

Definition 'Your Motor Cycle' – The Motor Vehicle described in the Schedule of this Policy.

SECTION 1 – LOSS OR DAMAGE TO YOUR MOTOR CYCLE

Colonial will pay for loss or damage to your motor cycle and its attached accessories and spare parts by:

(a) fire, explosion, malicious damage.
(b) theft,
(c) accidental collision,
(d) any other cause

But Colonial will not pay for:

(a) wear and tear or depreciation,
(b) mechanical or electrical fault or breakdown,
(c) loss of use, cost of alternative transportation
(d) damage to tires by punctures, cuts, bursts or braking,
(e) loss or damage where the driver has been convicted (or a prosecution is pending against the driver) of an offense contrary to section 35, 35A or 35B of the Road Traffic Act, 1947.

Also see "Compulsory Claims Excess" below.

Towing Costs

Colonial will pay for the reasonable cost of removing your motor cycle to the nearest repairer.

Claim Settlement

Colonial has the option to either:

(a) repair your motor cycle,
(b) replace your motor cycle,
(c) pay in cash the amount of the loss or damage.

N.B. Any claim payment will not be for more than the market value of your motor cycle immediately prior to the loss or damage or the Insured's estimated value whichever is the less. The market value is the cost of replacing your motor cycle with another of similar type, age and condition.

The Insured's estimated value at the inception of the Policy is stated in the Schedule. At each renewal of this Policy the Insured's estimated value is as stated on the Certificate of Insurance Form A issued as evidence of the existence of this Policy as required by law.

Compulsory Claims Excess

If loss or damage (excluding fire, explosion, malicious damage or theft) covered by this policy occurs you will be responsible, in respect of each claim, for the amounts specified below:

(a) where the driver is age 26 or over	$50.00
(b) where the driver is under age 26	$100.00

If loss or damage caused by theft occurs you will be responsible in respect of each claim for the amount of $200.00.

Except where the Insured's estimated value exceeds $1500 in which case you will be responsible for the amount of $300.00.

[continued]

A sample insurance policy (continued).

Insurance Policy (Motorcycle)

SECTION 2 – LIABILITY TO THIRD PARTIES

Your Liability
Colonial will indemnify you against your legal liability arising out of an accident in connection with your motor cycle for

an amount of up to BD$5,000,000 (Five Million Dollars) in respect of the total claims arising out of any one accident and/or series of accidents arising out of one event (inclusive of Legal Fees; Costs and Expenses as covered by this Policy)

but subject to

a limit of BD$250,000 (Two Hundred and Fifty Thousand Dollars) in respect of liability for damage to property.

However, in the event of Colonial being required to indemnify you for such liability solely because of the requirements of the Motor Car Insurance (Third Party Risks) Act 1943, then the minimum limits as required of an insurance policy by that Act shall apply.

Other Persons Liability
In the same way, we will indemnify any person permitted by you to drive or use your motor cycle as if they were you provided that the person is not driving or using your vehicle in contravention of any law.

Legal Fees; Costs and Expenses
Colonial will pay all reasonable costs for legal services or any other costs or expenses incurred with our written consent in connection with any incident which might involve legal liability under this policy.

Indemnity to Legal Personal Representatives
In the event of death of any person entitled to indemnity under this section, Colonial will indemnify his/her legal personal representatives.

Liability Not Covered
Colonial will **NOT** indemnify you for:
  (a) liability for damage to your motor cycle or any other property owned by or in the possession of any person claiming indemnity under this section,
  (b) liability covered by any other policy,
  (c) liability for the death of or injury to any person traveling upon or getting on to or off of your motor cycle,
  (d) (i) compensation for damages in respect of judgements delivered or obtained in the first instance otherwise than by a Court of competent jurisdiction within Bermuda,
      (ii) cost and expenses of litigation recovered by any claimant from the insured which are not incurred in and recoverable in Bermuda.

Right of Recovery
You will repay to Colonial all sums it must pay because of any law if Colonial would not have been liable for those payments under the Terms of the Policy

SECTION 3 – GENERAL EXCEPTIONS

Colonial will NOT be liable
  (1) whilst your motor cycle is being driven by
      (a) you unless you hold a license to drive your motor cycle
      (b) any other person driving with your permission who does not hold a license to drive your motor cycle
          unless the driver has held and is not disqualified from holding or obtaining a license.
  (2) whilst your motor cycle is being used otherwise than in accordance with the Limitations as to Use.

Limitations As To Use
Your Motor cycle may be used for social, domestic, and pleasure purposes, and for the Insured's business or profession. The Policy does not cover use for hire or reward, racing, pacemaking, reliability trial and speed testing, or use for any purpose in connection with the Motor Trade.
  (3) for liability which attaches by virtue of an agreement but would not have attached in the absence of such an agreement.
  (4) in respect of loss or destruction of or damage to your motor cycle or any consequential loss or any legal liability directly or indirectly caused or contributed to by or arising from
      (a) ionising radiations or contaminations by radioactivity from any nuclear fuel, or from any nuclear waste from the combustion of nuclear fuel.
      (b) the radioactive toxic explosive or other hazardous properties of any explosive nuclear assembly or nuclear component thereof
      (c) war, invasion, act of foreign enemy, hostilities (whether war be declared or not), civil war, civil commotion, rebellion, revolution, insurrection or military or usurped power except where it is necessary to meet the requirements of The Motor Car Insurance (Third Party Risks) Act 1943.
      (d) earthquake, flood,
      (e) riot or civil commotion.

SECTION 4 – GENERAL CONDITIONS

  (1) Colonial will only provide the insurance described in this Policy if:
      (a) any person claiming indemnity has complied with all its terms, conditions and endorsements.
      (b) the declaration and information given in the proposal form, which forms the basis of the contract, is complete and correct.

[continued]

A sample insurance policy (continued). ILLUSTRATION BY GGS CREATIVE RESOURCES. REPRODUCED BY PERMISSION OF GALE, A PART OF CENGAGE LEARNING.

Insurance Policy (Motorcycle)

(2) You and any other person claiming indemnity must take all reasonable steps to:
   (a) prevent loss or damage
   (b) maintain your motor cycle in an efficient and roadworthy condition.

(3) Colonial must be given free access to examine your motor cycle on request.

(4) Colonial may cancel the policy by sending seven days notice by registered letter to your last known address, in which case you will be entitled to a pro rata refund of premium. You may cancel the policy by notifying Colonial and returning the Certificate of Motor Insurance. Provided no claim has arisen during the period of insurance, you shall be entitled to a return of premium less premium charged at the Company's Short Period rates for the time the policy has been in force.

(5) When an accident, injury, loss, or damage occurs, you must advise Colonial in writing as soon as possible.
   In addition Colonial must be advised immediately of:
   (a) any letter, claim, writ or summons whether civil or criminal received by you or any other person covered by this policy.
   (b) any impending prosecution, coroners inquest, or fatal accident inquiry involving any person covered by this policy.

(6) Any person claiming indemnity must:
   (a) not admit liability or fault nor promise or offer any compensation without our written consent
   (b) give all necessary assistance and information that Colonial may require.

(7) Colonial will be entitled to:
   (a) take over and with full discretion conduct the defence settlement or prosecution of any claim in the name of any person claiming indemnity.
   (b) instruct legal representatives of its own choice in any civil or criminal proceedings arising from any event the subject of a claim under this policy.

(8) If any difference shall arise as to the amount to be paid to you under this policy (liability being otherwise accepted) such difference shall be referred to an arbitrator to be appointed by the parties in accordance with current statutory provisions. Where any difference is by this Condition to be referred to arbitration, the making of an Award shall be a condition precedent to any right of action against Colonial.

SECTION 5 – ENDORSEMENTS

These endorsements apply only if referred to by number in the Schedule.

(1) **Third Party Only**
   Section 1 is cancelled

(2) **Third Party Fire and Theft**
   No claim will be paid under Section 1 except for loss or damage caused by:
   (a) fire, lightning or explosion
   (b) or theft, attempted theft, or as the result of your motor cycle being taken without the consent of the Insured.

(3) **Excluding Named Persons from Driving**
   The policy will not operate whilst your motor cycle is being driven by or is in the charge of any person named in the schedule against this endorsement number.

(4) **Reduction to Third Party Only for Named Drivers**
   Section 1 of the policy will not operate whilst your motor cycle is being driven by or is in the charge of any person named in the schedule against this endorsement number.

(5) **Named Drivers Only**
   The policy will not operate whilst your motor cycle is being driven by or is in the charge of any person other than a person named in the schedule against this endorsement number.

Schedule Attached.

ADMINISTRATIVE AGENCY regulations, and court decisions.

In an insurance contract, one party, the insured, pays a specified amount of money, called a premium, to another party, the insurer. The insurer, in turn, agrees to compensate the insured for specific future losses. The losses covered are listed in the contract, and the contract is called a policy.

When an insured suffers a loss or damage that is covered in the policy, the insured can collect on the proceeds of the policy by filing a claim, or request for coverage, with the insurance company. The company then decides whether or not to pay the claim. The recipient of any proceeds from the policy is called the beneficiary. The beneficiary can be the insured person or other persons designated by the insured.

A contract is considered to be insurance if it distributes risk among a large number of persons through an enterprise that is engaged primarily in the business of insurance. Warranties or service contracts for merchandise, for example, do not constitute insurance. They are not issued by insurance companies, and the risk distribution in the transaction is incidental to the purchase of the merchandise. Warranties and service contracts are thus exempt from strict insurance laws and regulations.

The business of insurance is sustained by a complex system of risk analysis. Generally, this analysis involves anticipating the likelihood of a particular loss and charging enough in premiums to guarantee that insured losses can be paid. Insurance companies collect the premiums for a certain type of insurance policy and use them to pay the few individuals who suffer losses that are insured by that type of policy.

Most insurance is provided by private corporations, but some is provided by the government. For example, the FEDERAL DEPOSIT INSURANCE CORPORATION (FDIC) was established by Congress to insure bank deposits. The federal government provides life insurance to military service personnel. Congress and the states jointly fund MEDICAID and MEDICARE, which are HEALTH INSURANCE programs for persons who are disabled or elderly. Most states offer health insurance to qualified persons who are indigent. The 2008 presidential candidacy of BARACK OBAMA focused largely on a platform of promised health care reform, centered on the insurance industry. In 2009, the Obama administration and Congress struggled with internal power plays along party lines to include a "public option" (government-provided insurance to qualifying persons) in any health care reform package that would ostensibly enhance competition among private insurance companies.

Government-issued insurance is regulated like private insurance, but the two are very different. Most recipients of government insurance do not have to pay premiums, but they also do not receive the same level of coverage available under private insurance policies. Government-issued insurance is granted by the legislature, not bargained for with a private insurance company, and it can be taken away by an act of the legislature. However, if a legislature issues insurance, it cannot refuse it to a person who qualifies for it.

History

The first examples of insurance related to marine activities. In many ancient societies, merchants and traders pledged their ships or cargo as security for loans. In Babylon creditors charged higher interest rates to merchants and traders in exchange for a promise to forgive the loan if the ship was robbed by pirates or was captured and held for ransom.

In postmedieval England, local groups of working people banded together to create "friendly societies," forerunners of the modern insurance companies. Members of the friendly societies made regular contributions to a common fund, which was used to pay for losses suffered by members. The contributions were determined without reference to a member's age, and without precise identification of what claims would be covered. Without a system to anticipate risks and potential liability, many of the first friendly societies were unable to pay claims, and many eventually disbanded. Insurance gradually came to be seen as a matter best handled by a company in the business of providing insurance.

Insurance companies began to operate for profit in England during the seventeenth century. They devised tables to mathematically predict losses based on various data, including the characteristics of the insured and the probability of loss related to particular risks. These calculations made it possible for insurance companies to anticipate the likelihood of claims, and this made the business of insurance reliable and profitable.

The British Parliament granted a monopoly over the business of insurance in colonial America to two English corporations, London Assurance and Royal Exchange. During the 1760s colonial legislatures granted a few American insurance companies permission to operate. Since the Revolutionary War, U.S. insurance companies have grown in number and size, with most offering to insure against a wide range of risks.

Regulation and Control

Until the middle of the twentieth century, insurance companies in the United States were relatively free from federal regulation. According to the U.S. Supreme Court in *Paul v. Virginia*, 75 U.S. (8 Wall.) 168, 19 L. Ed. 357 (1868), the issuing of an insurance policy did not constitute a commercial transaction. This meant that states had the power to regulate the business of insurance. In 1944, the high court held in *United States v. South-Eastern Underwriters Association*, 322 U.S. 533, 64 S. Ct. 1162, 88 L. Ed. 1440, that insurance did, in some cases, constitute a commercial transaction. This meant that Congress had the power to regulate it. The *South-Eastern* holding made the business of insurance subject to federal laws on rate fixing and monopolies.

As of 2010, insurance is governed by a blend of statutes, administrative agency regulations, and court decisions. State statutes often control premium rates, prevent unfair practices by insurers, and guard against the financial insolvency of insurers to protect insureds. At the federal level, the McCarran-Ferguson Act (Pub. L. No. 79-15, 59 Stat. 33 [1945] [codified at 15 U.S.C.A. §§ 1011–1015 (1988)]) permits states to retain regulatory control over insurance, as long as their laws and regulations do not conflict with federal antitrust laws on rate fixing, rate discrimination, and monopolies.

In most states, an administrative agency created by the state legislature devises rules to cover procedural details that are missing from the statutory framework. To do business in a state, an insurer must obtain a license through a registration process. This process is usually managed by the state administrative agency. The same state agency may also be charged with the enforcement of insurance regulations and statutes.

Administrative agency regulations are many and varied. Insurance companies must submit to the governing agency yearly financial reports regarding their economic stability. This requirement allows the agency to anticipate potential insolvency and to protect the interests of insureds. Agency regulations may specify the types of insurance policies that are acceptable in the state, although many states make these declarations in statutes. The administrative agency is also responsible for reviewing the competence and ethics of insurance company employees.

The JUDICIAL branches of governments also shape insurance law. Courts are often asked to resolve disputes between the parties to an insurance contract, and disputes with third parties. Court decisions interpret the statutes and regulations based on the facts of cases, creating many rules that must be followed by insurers and insureds.

Insurance companies may be penalized for violating statutes or regulations. Penalties for misconduct include fines and the loss or suspension of the company's business license. In some states, if a court finds that an insurer's denial of coverage or refusal to defend an insured in a lawsuit was unreasonable, the insurance company may be required to pay court costs, attorneys' fees, and a percentage beyond the insured's recovery.

Types of Insurance

Insurance companies create insurance policies by grouping risks according to their focus. This provides a measure of uniformity in the risks that are covered by a type of policy, which, in turn, allows insurers to anticipate their potential losses and to set premiums accordingly. The most common forms of insurance policies include life, health, automobile, homeowners' and renters', PERSONAL PROPERTY, fire and casualty, marine, and inland marine policies.

Life insurance provides financial benefits to a designated person upon the death of the insured. Many different forms of life insurance are issued. Some provide for payment only upon the death of the insured; others allow an insured to collect proceeds before death.

A person may purchase life insurance on his or her own life for the benefit of a third person or persons. Individuals may even purchase life insurance on the life of another person. For example, a wife may purchase life insurance that will provide benefits to her upon the death of her husband. This kind of policy is commonly obtained by spouses and by parents insuring themselves against the death of a child. However, individuals may only purchase life insurance on the life of another person and name themselves beneficiary when there are reasonable grounds to believe that they can expect some benefit from the continued life of the insured. This means that some familial or financial relationship must unite the beneficiary and the insured. For example, a person may not purchase life insurance on the life of a stranger in the hope that the stranger will suffer a fatal accident.

Health insurance policies cover only specified risks. Generally, they pay for the expenses incurred from bodily injury, disability, sickness, and accidental death. Health insurance may be purchased for oneself and for others.

All automobile insurance policies contain liability insurance, which is insurance against injury to another person or against damage to another person's vehicle caused by the insured's vehicle. Auto insurance may also pay for the loss of, or damage to, the insured's motor vehicle. Most states require that all drivers carry, at a minimum, liability insurance under a no-fault scheme. In states that recognize no-fault insurance, damages resulting from an accident are paid for by the insurers, and the drivers do not have to go to court to settle the issue of damages. Drivers in these states may bring suit over an accident only in cases of egregious conduct, or where medical or repair costs exceed an amount defined by statute.

Homeowners' insurance protects homeowners from losses relating to their dwelling, including damage to the dwelling; personal liability for injury to visitors; and loss of, or damage to, property in and around the dwelling. Renters' insurance covers many of the same risks for persons who live in rented dwellings.

As its name would suggest, personal property insurance protects against the loss of, or damage to, certain items of personal property. It is useful when the liability limit on a homeowner's policy does not cover the value of a particular item or items. For example, the owner of an original painting by Pablo Picasso might wish to obtain, in addition to a homeowner's policy, a separate personal property policy to insure against loss of, or damage to, the painting.

Businesses can insure against damage and liability to others with fire and casualty insurance policies. Fire insurance policies cover damage caused by fire, explosions, earthquakes, lightning, water, wind, rain, collisions, and riots. Casualty insurance protects the insured against a variety of losses, including those related to legal liability, burglary and theft, accidents, property damage, injury to workers, and insurance on credit extended to others. Fidelity and surety bonds are temporary, specialized forms of casualty insurance. A FIDELITY BOND insures against losses relating to the dishonesty of employees, and a surety bond provides protection to a business if it fails to fulfill its contractual obligations.

Marine insurance policies insure transporters and owners of cargo shipped on an ocean, a sea, or a navigable waterway. Marine risks include damage to cargo, damage to the vessel, and injuries to passengers. Inland marine insurance is used for the transportation of goods on land and on landlocked lakes.

Many other types of insurance are also issued. Group health insurance plans are usually offered by employers to their employees. A person may purchase additional insurance to cover losses in excess of a stated amount or in excess of coverage provided by a particular insurance policy. Air-travel insurance provides life insurance benefits to a named beneficiary if the insured dies as a result of the specified airplane flight. Flood insurance is not included in most homeowners' policies, but it can be purchased separately. MORTGAGE insurance requires the insurer to make mortgage payments when the insured is unable to do so because of death or disability.

Contract and Policy

An insurance contract cannot cover all conceivable risks. An insurance contract that violates a statute is deemed contrary to public policy; if it plays a part in some prohibited activity, it will be held unenforceable in court. A contract that protects against the loss of burglary tools or illegal narcotics, for example, is contrary to public policy and thus unenforceable.

Insurable Interest

To qualify for an insurance policy, the insured must have an INSURABLE INTEREST, meaning that the insured must derive some benefit from the continued preservation of the article insured, or stand to suffer some loss as a result of that article's loss or destruction. Life insurance requires some familial and pecuniary relationship between the insured and the beneficiary. Property insurance requires that the insured must simply have a lawful interest in the safety or preservation of the property.

Premiums

Different types of policies require different premiums based on the degree of risk that the situation presents. For example, a policy insuring a homeowner for all risks associated with a home valued at $200,000 requires a higher premium than one insuring a boat valued at $20,000. Although liability for injuries to others might be similar under both policies, the cost of replacing or repairing the boat would be less than the cost of repairing or replacing the home, and this difference is reflected in the premium paid by the insured.

Premium rates also depend on characteristics of the insured. For example, a person with a poor driving record generally has to pay more for auto insurance than does a person with a good driving record. Furthermore, insurers are free to deny policies to persons who present an unacceptable risk. For example, most insurance companies do not offer life or health insurance to persons who have been diagnosed with a terminal illness.

Claims

The most common issue in insurance disputes is whether the insurer is obligated to pay a claim. The determination of the insurer's obligation depends on many factors, such as the circumstances surrounding the loss and the precise coverage of the insurance policy. If a dispute arises over the language of the policy, the general rule is that a court should choose the interpretation that is most favorable to the insured. Many insurance contracts contain an incontestability clause to protect the insured. This clause provides that the insurer loses the right to contest the validity of the contract after a specified period of time.

An insurance company may deny or cancel coverage if the insured party concealed or misrepresented a material fact in the policy application. If an applicant presents an unacceptably high risk of loss for an insurance company, the company may deny the application or charge prohibitively high premiums. A company may cancel a policy if the insured fails to make payments. It also may refuse to pay a claim if the insured intentionally caused the loss or damage. However, if the insurer knows that it has the right to rescind a policy or to deny a claim, but conveys to the insured that it has voluntarily surrendered such right, the insured may claim that the insurer waived its right to contest a claim.

Denial of Claims or Benefits In 2004 the U.S. Supreme Court issued its RULING in an important and closely watched matter involving the liability of Health Maintenance Organizations (HMOs) for NEGLIGENCE in denial of insurance benefits decisions. In *Aetna Health v. Davila*, 542 U.S. 200, the high court unanimously ruled in favor of the HMOs. Technically, the issue decided was a procedural one: whether the federal Employees Retirement Income Security Act (ERISA) preempted a Texas state law that permitted such suits. (The insureds were both provided healthcare insurance benefits through ERISA-regulated employee benefit plans.) The Court ruled that the federal law prevailed, effectively prohibiting suits under state laws. The significance of the Court's procedural decision amounted to a denial of the right of patients to sue for tort damages (e.g., pain and suffering or scarring) caused by such HMO

decisions. Instead, they would be limited to damages allowable under ERISA (e.g., the right to receive the denied treatment). Another case on this subject was the earlier *Pegram v. Herdrich*, 530 U.S. 211 (2000).

In January 2007 a Mississippi jury awarded a married couple $2.5 million in PUNITIVE DAMAGES against State Farm Insurance Company stemming from its denial of a Hurricane Katrina-related homeowners's claim. Although a judge later reduced the punitive damages to $1 million as more reasonably related to the $223,000 in actual damages, this was but a drop in the bucket for State Farm. It still faced more than 600 other Katrina-related lawsuits and 35,000 pending claims still unresolved.

The court ruled that State Farm had failed to meet its burden, under Mississippi law, of proving that the damage to the insured's home was caused by storm-surged water rather than wind, and therefore excluded from coverage. State Farm had argued that the homeowners' policy covered damage from wind but not from water. Further, the policy ostensibly excluded damages that could have been caused by a combination of both, even if the hurricane winds preceded the storm's water damage.

State Farm also argued that the policy at issue categorically excluded any damage caused by negligence. (The storm surge and flooding in the aftermath of Hurricane Katrina are widely believed to have resulted from negligent engineering of levees.) But in the first Katrina-related lawsuit to go to trial (August 2006), a federal judge had ruled that Nationwide Insurance Company was not liable for payment on a policyholder's claims for water damage caused by the hurricane. Later, in November 2006, another federal judge held that water and flood damage caused by Katrina may be covered under those policies that did not specifically exclude damage caused by negligence. State Farm finally announced that it would pay at least $50 million to settle the pending CLASS ACTION involving 35,000 policyholders, and offered another $80 million to settle 640 existing lawsuits.

While the settlements were pending, State Attorney General Jim Hood had repeatedly called for a statewide settlement between all Mississippi policyholders and all insurance companies. Its office had agreed in January 2007 to drop State Farm from the lawsuit it had filed against several insurance companies for their refusal to cover such Katrina damages, in return for State Farm's agreement to settle those claims.

In March 2007, more than a year and a half after the storm, State Farm announced that it would bypass the court and work directly with the state insurance commissioner, George Dale, to reopen pending claims and attempt settlement. Meanwhile, the court denied class-action status to the approximately 640 related lawsuits still pending against State Farm.

Following denial of class-action status, State Farm continued to settle the pending lawsuits individually, either during or shortly before trials that were scheduled to start, in order to avoid the possibility of punitive damages being awarded. In some cases, State Farm agreed to settle the lawsuits after the jury had awarded actual damages to the homeowners, but prior to any determination of punitive damages. The dollar amount of these settlements remained undisclosed.

In November 2007 Louisiana's attorney general filed a massive suit against several insurance companies for alleged and ongoing schemes to avoid fair compensation to victims of Hurricanes Katrina and Rita, in violation of the Louisiana Monopolies Act (an ANTITRUST LAW). Named as defendants in the suit were Allstate Insurance Company; Lafayette Insurance Company; Xactware, Inc.; Marshall & Swift/Boeckh, LLC; Insurance Services Office, Inc.; State Farm Fire and Casualty Company; USAA Casualty Insurance Company; Farmers Insurance Exchange; Standard Fire Insurance Company; and McKinsey & Company. DEFENDANT McKinsey & Company was not an insurer, but rather a New York-based consulting group that allegedly taught insurance companies how to reduce payouts and increase profits. The lawsuit alleged that McKinsey, called the "architect" of sweeping changes in the insurance industry starting in the 1980s, advised its insurer-clients to stop premium leakage by undervaluing claims using the tactics of deny, delay, and defend. The suit claimed that all of the defendant insurance companies had used the services of McKinsey and, therefore, had conspired in a price-fixing scheme. Some of the alleged illegal tactics included coercing policyholders into settling their damage claims for less than actual value, editing engineering assessment reports, delaying and forestalling payments, and forcing policyholders

into costly litigation to challenge their estimates. The case was still pending in 2009.

The lawsuit's filing coincided with local media's investigation into insurance company policies and practices that resulted in record profits despite Katrina and Rita claims. Local WWL news correspondent Dennis Woltering reported that, according to the Consumer Federation of America, Allstate, for example, netted more after-tax income than it had before dealing with the losses from the 2005 hurricanes. In fact, in 2006, when it was still paying claims for Katrina and Rita, its profits jumped to $5 billion. The consumer group also found that between 1996 and 2006, the amount of each premium dollar that Allstate paid back to its policyholders fell from 73 cents per dollar to 59 cents. Such business practices were allegedly uncovered in internal Allstate presentation slides in which McKinsey demonstrated how the insurer could boost profits.

In defense, insurance companies asserted that profits were the result of millions of new policyholders, including auto insurance customers. Allstate responded that when Louisiana insurance officials conducted a market review of its response to Katrina and Rita, they concluded that it was compliant with state statutes, rules, and regulations. However, the state insurance commissioner ordered the company to change its "flawed" property inspection process and to reinstate policyholders after Allstate cancelled the policies of more than 4,700 homeowners.

Other Contractual Provisions

An insurer may have a duty to defend an insured in a lawsuit filed against the insured by a THIRD PARTY. This duty usually arises if the claims in the suit against the insured fall within the coverage of a liability policy.

If a third party caused a loss covered by a policy, the insurance company may have the right to sue the third party in place of the insured. This right is called SUBROGATION, and it is designed to make the party that is responsible for a loss bear the burden of the loss. It also prevents an insured from recovering twice: once from the insurance company, and once from the responsible party.

An insurance company can subrogate claims only on certain types of policies. Property and liability insurance policies allow subrogation because the basis for the payment of claims is

Gene Testing

When a person applies for medical, life, or disability insurance, the insurance company typically requires the disclosure of preexisting medical conditions and a family medical history. In some cases the applicant must undergo a physical examination. Based on this information, the insurance company decides whether to offer coverage and, if so, at what price.

Breakthroughs in genetics now allow persons to be tested for rare medical conditions such as cystic fibrosis and Huntington's disease. In addition, genetic testing can reveal an increased risk of more common conditions, including breast, colon, and prostate cancer; lymphoma; and leukemia. Concerns have been raised that once these tests become affordable, insurance companies will use the results to deny coverage.

Research studies published in the 1990s indicated that persons already had been denied insurance coverage because of the risk of genetic disease. The prospect of widespread genetic discrimination has troubled many professionals in the medical and legal communities. It is unfair, they charge, to deny a person coverage or to charge higher premiums, based on a potential risk of genetic disease that the person is powerless to modify.

The insurance industry, which as of the early 2000s collects medical information on genetic disease through the inspection of medical records and family histories, responds that a fundamental principle in writing insurance is charging people rates that reflect their risks. Doing so means that each applicant pays the fairest possible price, based on individual' characteristics. The industry also notes that the concerns about genetic testing do not come into play with large-group health plans, where rates are based on methods other than individual assessments.

In 2008 Congress resolved the controversy by enacting the Genetic Information Nondiscrimination Acts (GINA). GINA prohibits employers and health insurance companies from discriminating against or refusing coverage to individuals based on the results of genetic testing.

CROSS REFERENCE

Genetic Screening

---

indemnification, or reimbursement, of the insured for losses. Conversely, life insurance policies do not allow subrogation. Life insurance does not indemnify an insured for a loss that can be measured in dollars. Rather, it is a form of investment for the insured and the insured's beneficiaries. A life insurance policy pays only a fixed sum of money to the beneficiary and does not cover any liability to a third party. Under such a policy, the insured stands no chance of double recovery, and the insurance company has no need to sue a third party if it must pay a claim.

Terrorism Insurance

Following the attacks on the World Trade Center and the Pentagon, insurance premiums skyrocketed, especially for tenants of highly visible landmarks like sports arenas and sky-scrapers. The TERRORISM Risk Insurance Act of 2002 (TRIA), Pub. L. No. 107–297, 116 Stat. 2322 (reauthorized in December 2007), established a temporary federal program providing for a shared public and private compensation for insured losses resulting from acts of terrorism. The act provides that insurers must make terrorism coverage available and must provide policyholders with a clear and conspicuous disclosure of the premium charged for losses covered by the program. TRIA caps the exposure of insurance carriers to future acts of foreign terrorism, leaving the federal government to reimburse the insurance company for excess losses up to a maximum of $100 billion per year. Under TRIA as originally written, the TREASURY DEPARTMENT covers 90 percent of terrorism claims when an insurer's exposure exceeds 7 percent of its commercial premiums in 2003, 10 percent of premiums in 2004, and 15 percent in 2005. TRIA has since been extended beyond its original terms, with a new expiration date of December 31, 2014.

TRIA defines an act of terrorism as any act that is certified by the U.S. secretary of the treasury, in concurrence with the U.S. SECRETARY OF STATE and U.S. attorney general. The act of terror must result in damage within the United States, or outside the United States in the case of an airplane or a U.S. mission. A terrorist act must be committed by an individual or individuals acting on behalf of any foreign person or foreign interest. An event must be a violent act or an act that is dangerous to human life, property, or infrastructure. Nuclear, biological, and chemical attacks are not covered, and an event cannot be certified as an act of terrorism unless the total damages exceed $5 million.

FURTHER READINGS

Cady, Thomas C., and Christy H. Smith. 1995. "West Virginia's Automobile Insurance Policy Laws: A Practitioner's Guide." *West Virginia Law Review* 97.

Dixon, Lloyd. 2007. *The Federal Role in Terrorism Insurance: Evaluating Alternatives in an Uncertain World.* Arlington, VA: RAND.

Robinson, Eric L. 1992. "The Oregon Basic Health Services Act: A Model for State Reform?" *Vanderbilt Law Review* 45.

INSURED

The person who obtains or is otherwise covered by insurance on his or her health, life, or property. The insured *in a policy is not limited to the insured named in the policy but applies to anyone who is insured under the policy.*

INSURER

An individual or company who, through a contractual agreement, undertakes to compensate specified losses, liability, or damages incurred by another individual.

An insurer is frequently an insurance company and is also known as an underwriter.

INSURRECTION

A rising or rebellion of citizens against their government, usually manifested by acts of violence.

Under federal law, it is a crime to incite, assist, or engage in such conduct against the United States.

INTANGIBLES

Property that is a "right" such as a patent, copyright, or trademark, or one that is lacking physical existence, such as good will. A nonphysical, non-current asset that exists only in connection with something else, such as the good will of a business.

INTEGRATED

Completed; made whole or entire. Desegregated; converted into a nonracial, nondiscriminatory system.

A contract that has been adopted as a final and complete expression of an agreement between two parties is an INTEGRATED AGREEMENT.

A school that has been integrated has been made into one in which students, faculty, staff, facilities, programs, and activities combine individuals of different races.

CROSS REFERENCE

School Desegregation.

INTEGRATED AGREEMENT

A contract that contains within its four corners the entire understanding of the parties and is subject to the parol evidence rule, which seeks to preserve the integrity of written agreements by refusing to allow the parties to modify their contract through the introduction of prior or contemporaneous oral declarations.

An agreement is integrated when the parties adopt the writing or writings as the final and complete expression of the agreement.

INTEGRATED BAR

The process of organizing the attorneys of a state into an association, membership in which is a condition precedent to the right to practice law.

Integration is usually attained by enactment of a statute that grants authority to the highest court of the state to integrate the bar, or by rule of court in the exercise of its inherent power. When the bar is integrated, all attorneys within an area, which can include a state, a county, or a city, are members.

INTEGRATION

The bringing together of separate elements to create a whole unit. The bringing together of people from the different demographic and racial groups that make up U.S. society.

In most cases, the term *integration* is used to describe the process of bringing together people of different races, especially blacks and whites, in schools and other settings. But it is also used

to describe the process of bringing together people of different backgrounds. A primary purpose of the Americans with Disabilities Act of 1990 (ADA) (42 U.S.C.A. § 12101 et seq.), for example, was to more fully integrate disabled individuals into U.S. society. The House Judiciary Committee's report on the ADA described it as "a comprehensive piece of CIVIL RIGHTS legislation which promises a new future: a future of inclusion and integration, and the end of exclusion and segregation" (H.R. Rep. No. 485, 101st Cong., 2d Sess., pt. 3, at 26 [1990], reprinted in 1990 U.S.C.C.A.N. 445, 449.7).

The term integration is most commonly used in association with the efforts of African-Americans in the United States to eliminate racial SEGREGATION and achieve equal opportunity and inclusion in U.S. society. Often, it has been used synonymously with desegregation to mean the elimination of discriminatory practices based on race. However, although similar, the terms have been used in significantly different ways by the courts, by legal theorists,

and in the context of the CIVIL RIGHTS MOVEMENT. In general, desegregation refers to the elimination of policies and practices that segregate people of different races into separate institutions and facilities. Integration refers not only to the elimination of such policies but also to the active incorporation of different races into institutions for the purpose of achieving racial balance, which many believe will lead to equal rights, protections, and opportunities.

Throughout the civil rights movement in the United States, black leaders have held different opinions about the meaning and value of integration, with some advocating integration as the ultimate goal for black citizens, and others resisting integration out of concern that it would lead to the assimilation of black citizens into white culture and society. In 1934 a disagreement over the value of integration versus segregation led W. E. B. Du Bois—a cofounder of the National Association for the Advancement of Colored People (NAACP) and a leading scholar, writer, and civil rights

Months after the Brown v. Bd. of Ed. Decision, two schools at military bases in Virginia were first opened to black children. Although not yet required of public schools, the Defense Department ordered the racial integration of all schools on military posts.
BETTMANN/CORBIS.

States with the Highest Percentages of Minority Populations, by Race, in 2005

State	Total minority	Black	Hispanic	Asian	Other[a]
Hawaii	76.5%	2.1%	8.0%	40.5%	26.0%
Washington, D.C.	68.9%	55.7%	8.6%	3.0%	1.6%
New Mexico	56.9%	1.8%	43.4%	1.1%	10.5%
California	56.2%	6.2%	35.2%	11.9%	2.8%
Texas	50.8%	11.2%	35.1%	3.2%	1.3%
Maryland	40.8%	28.8%	5.7%	4.7%	1.6%
Georgia	40.4%	29.4%	7.1%	2.6%	1.1%
Mississippi	40.3%	36.8%	1.7%	0.7%	1.0%
Nevada	40.0%	7.2%	23.5%	5.5%	3.8%
Arizona	39.6%	3.2%	28.5%	2.1%	5.8%

[a]Other includes Native Hawaiians/Pacific Islanders, American Indians/Alaskan natives, and persons of more than one race.

SOURCE: National Center for Education Statistics, *Status and Trends in the Education of Racial and Ethnic Minorities*, 2007.

activist—to resign from the NAACP. Du Bois rejected the NAACP's heavy emphasis on integration, calling instead for black citizens to maintain their own churches, schools, and social organizations, and especially to develop their own economic base separate from the mainstream white economy.

After Du Bois's resignation, the NAACP adopted a full-fledged campaign to eliminate segregation and to promote integration. In 1940, NAACP leaders sent to President FRANKLIN D. ROOSEVELT, the secretary of the Navy, and the assistant secretary of war a memorandum outlining provisions for the "integration of the Negro into military aspects of the national defense program." This was the first instance in which the NAACP had specifically used the term *integration* in a civil rights policy pronouncement. After WORLD WAR II, the term *racial integration* became commonly used to describe civil rights issues pertaining to race.

On the legal front, the NAACP focused its efforts on eliminating segregation in the public schools. This campaign was led by THURGOOD MARSHALL, the first director-counsel of the NAACP LEGAL DEFENSE AND EDUCATIONAL FUND and later a U.S. Supreme Court justice. In 1954, Marshall successfully argued the landmark case BROWN V. BOARD OF EDUCATION, 347 U.S. 483, 74 S. Ct. 686, 98 L. Ed. 873, before the U.S. Supreme Court. The RULING in that case declared that racially segregated schools are inherently unequal and thus unconstitutional. Like other NAACP leaders, Marshall was strongly committed to the principle of racial integration. His arguments in *Brown* were heavily based on the work of Kenneth B. Clark, a black social psychologist whose research suggested that black children were stigmatized by being educated in racially segregated schools, causing them to suffer psychological and intellectual harm. Marshall used this theory of "stigmatic injury" to persuade the Court that racially segregated schools were inherently unequal. Although the *Brown* decision called for an end to formal segregation, it did not explicitly call for positive steps to ensure the integration of public schools.

The desegregation momentum begun by *Brown* was enacted into law by the 1964 CIVIL RIGHTS ACT (Pub. L. No. 88-352, 78 Stat. 246), which denied federal funds to any program that discriminated illegally on the basis of race, sex, color, RELIGION, or national origin, outlawing such discrimination not only in public schools but also in areas of public accommodation and employment. To ensure the support necessary for passage of the act, its writers worded the act specifically to emphasize that its purpose was to desegregate, not to integrate. "Desegregation," the act said, was "the assignment of students to public schools . . . without regard to their race," but "not . . . the assignment of students to public schools in order to overcome racial imbalance."

Nevertheless, after the Civil Rights Act was passed, judges and other federal officials enforcing it required schools to go beyond racially neutral desegregation policies to try to remedy past segregation by enforcing a greater degree of racial integration. This policy was established by the U.S. Supreme Court in 1968 in *Green v. County School Board*, 391 U.S. 430, 88 S. Ct. 1689, 20 L. Ed. 2d 716, in which the Court ruled that a school district's desegregation plan was unacceptable under the *Brown* ruling. The *Green* case involved a school district that had two high schools that had previously been segregated by race. When the district changed its rules to allow students to attend the school of their choice, few black students chose to attend the traditionally white school, and no whites chose the black school, thus leaving the schools segregated. In its ruling in *Green,* the Court called the "freedom-of-choice" plan a "deliberate perpetuation of the unconstitutional dual system" and said that school boards had an "affirmative duty to take whatever steps might be necessary to convert to a unitary system in which RACIAL DISCRIMINATION would be eliminated root and branch." Although a freedom-of-choice plan could theoretically be a viable method for converting to a "unitary, nonracial school system," the Court said, it would have to "prove itself in operation," adding that such methods as rezoning might prove speedier, and thus more acceptable. Although the Court did not explicitly require active integration, it suggested that the validity of desegregation plans would be measured by the amount of integration that they actually produced.

This emphasis on achieving specific levels of integration as proof of desegregation was reinforced by the 1971 U.S. Supreme Court ruling in SWANN V. CHARLOTTE-MECKLENBURG BOARD OF EDUCATION, 402 U.S. 1, 91 S. Ct. 1267, 28 L. Ed. 2d 554. In *Swann,* the Court ruled that schools could use methods such as involuntary busing and the altering of attendance zones to achieve specific ratios of racial mixing, as long as those ratios were established as a "starting point[s] in the process of shaping a remedy" for past discrimination.

In a 1974 case, *Milliken v. Bradley,* 418 U.S. 717, 94 S. Ct. 3112, 41 L. Ed. 2d 1069, the Supreme Court made it more difficult for city school districts to achieve racial integration. In *Milliken,* the Court ruled that a federally ordered desegregation remedy could not include suburban schools when a city's school district was officially segregated for reasons other than past illegal discrimination, such as the simple demographics of its residents. In other words, if the surrounding suburban districts had not contributed to past illegal segregation, they could not be held responsible for remedying it. A cross-district remedy, the Court ruled, would be permissible only to correct a cross-district wrong. The effect of *Milliken* has been to allow an increasing amount of resegregation in public schools as housing patterns divide black and white residents between cities and their surrounding suburbs. More recent cases, such as *Missouri v. Jenkins,* 515 U.S. 70, 115 S. Ct. 2038, 132 L. Ed. 2d 63 (1995), have continued to impose strict JUDICIAL limits on the power of the courts to impose and enforce desegregation plans in the public schools.

Despite significant legal victories mandating greater integration, therefore, the actual amount of racial integration in the United States—in the schools and elsewhere—remains limited. In fact, in 2003 the Harvard University Civil Rights Project warned that early school integration gains were actually being reversed. In an 82-page report

titled "A Multiracial Society with Segregated Schools: Are We Losing the Dream?" the multidisciplinary research-and-policy think tank examined trends in federal public school enrollment data from the start of integration efforts through the year 2000. According to its analysis of these figures, the desegregation of black students progressed continuously until the late 1980s. Quantifiable gains from this policy included sharp increases in minority high-school graduations and the narrowing of differences in test scores between white and minority students. Then a process of "resegregation" began.

As argued in the report, resegregation has been marked by several disturbing statistical trends. Whites have clustered in schools with an average of 80 percent white populations, blacks have found themselves more segregated than at any time since the 1970s, and a substantial number of schools have emerged with virtually all non-white student populations. These the authors scathingly designated "apartheid schools" for their institutional resemblance—in terms of economic impoverishment, lack of resources, and social and health problems—to those found under the system of racial segregation enforced in twentieth-century South Africa. The findings also highlighted the isolation of Latino students, who have become the most highly segregated racial group in the public school system.

Most damningly, the Civil Rights Project report diagnosed an intellectual and moral failure in U.S. society to uphold the principles of integration. Not for want of public support was integration being abandoned, the authors argued. Instead, governments had essentially given up: Policy makers had erroneously concluded that enough progress had been made and that more was unattainable. Noting the absence of Congressional action since the early 1970s and the dearth of EXECUTIVE BRANCH enforcement since the Johnson era (with the sole exception of the Carter administration), the authors blamed lawmakers, the Executive Branch, and the courts for allowing integration efforts to wither while resegregation took root. The report called for a renewed focus on desegregation from both state and federal authorities to offer minority students attendance choices among better, more integrated schools.

Such failures have led many black leaders to question whether integration is indeed possible in the United States and whether it would actually benefit African Americans. Those in favor of integration follow in the tradition of Marshall and MARTIN LUTHER KING, JR., who insisted that integration would lead to increased freedom, power, and opportunities for African Americans. "In our society," King insisted, "liberation cannot come without integration and integration cannot come without liberation." More recently, Andrew Young, civil rights activist, former U.N. ambassador, and former mayor of Atlanta, has emphasized that integration does not lead to assimilation. "Those who reject integration," he said, "do so because they see the black community as one-way assimilation." In contrast, he said, "integration is a two-way street, each side contributing their own values, virtues, and traditions."

Other black scholars and political leaders have followed the lead of Du Bois, questioning the value of integration for African-Americans and recommending instead separate black schools, churches, and economic networks. In the 1960s, members of the black power and black nationalist movements, including MALCOLM X, argued that integration was an inappropriate strategy for blacks, who they believed could free themselves from racism and repression only by separating themselves from the mainstream white culture. Integration, they asserted, would result in African Americans being assimilated into the white community. In 1967 for example, STOKELY CARMICHAEL, a leader of the black-power movement, said, "The fact is that integration, as traditionally articulated, would abolish the black community." More recently, some legal theorists of race relations have criticized the theory of stigmatic injury that Marshall presented in *Brown*, contending that it rests on a notion of African American inferiority by asserting that black children can receive an adequate education only in the presence of white children. DERRICK A. BELL, JR., a leading legal theorist on race relations, has been a particularly vocal critic of integrated schools, insisting that they do not meet the needs of African American children, whom, he says, would be better served by increased funding for schools in black neighborhoods, more black teachers and administrators, increased parental involvement, and higher expectations for academic achievement. Many educational experts concur, suggesting that many young black males would receive a higher-quality education by attending black male academies where the approach and curriculum were specifically designed to counter the social and cultural challenges faced by those young men in today's world.

Many of the black leaders who today advocate integration have refined the notion, insisting that it means more than simply mixing black and white students in the same school. Legal scholar john a. powell (who spells his name with only lowercase letters) said that true integration "transforms racial hierarchy" by "[creating] a more inclusive society where individuals and groups have opportunities to participate equally in their communities." Similarly, Ellis Cashmore, a leading scholar of race relations, said integration "describes a condition in which different ethnic groups are able to maintain group boundaries and uniqueness, while participating equally in the essential processes of production, distribution and government." Cashmore conceded, however, that in the United States, this type of integration "remains more of an ideal than a reality."

Cashmore and other current race-relations scholars suggest that integration no longer means simply desegregation but rather that it now includes pluralism. Pluralism, in this context, refers to a condition in which no ethnic hierarchies exist, so there are no ethnic minorities per se; instead, the various groups in society participate equally in the social system, therefore experiencing balance and cohesion rather than contention and resentment. In this sense, said scholar Harold Cruse, "the SEPARATE-BUT-EQUAL doctrine that *Brown* ruled unconstitutional *should* have been supplanted by the truly democratic doctrine of *plural but equal*.

FURTHER READINGS

Brown-Scott, Wendy. 1994. "Justice Thurgood Marshall and the Integrative Ideal." *Arizona State Law Journal* 26.

Carmichael, Stokely, and Charles Hamilton. 1967. *Black Power: The Politics of Liberation in America.* New York: Random House.

Cashmore, Ellis. 1994. *Dictionary of Race and Ethnic Relations.* 3d ed. London: Routledge.

Christian, William. 1994. "Normalization as a Goal: The Americans with Disabilities Act and Individuals with Mental Retardation." *Texas Law Review* 73.

Cruse, Harold. 1987. *Plural but Equal.* New York: Morrow.

Davis, Maia. 2003. "Harvard Study Finds New Segregation." *The Record.* (January 19): A1.

Frankenberg, Erica; Lee, Chungmei; and Orfield, Gary. 20003. "A Multiracial Society with Segregated Schools: Are We Losing the Dream?" *The Civil Rights Project at Harvard University.* (January)

Kimerling, Joshua E. 1994. "Black Male Academies: Re-examining the Strategy of Integration." *Buffalo Law Review* 42.

King, Martin Luther, Jr. 1968. *Where Do We Go from Here—Chaos or Community* Boston: Beacon Press.

Middleton, Michael A. 1995. "*Brown v. Board:* Revisited." *Southern Illinois University Law Journal* 20.

Powell, John A. 1996. "Living and Learning: Linking House and Education." *Minnesota Law Review* 80.

Stewart, Carter M., and S. Felicita Torres. 1996. "Limiting Federal Court Power to Impose School Desegregation Remedies—*Missouri v. Jenkins.*" *Harvard Civil Rights– Civil Liberties Law Review* 31.

Wolters, Raymond. 1996. "Stephen C. Halpern, on the Limits of the Law: The Ironic Legacy of Title VI of the 1964 Civil Rights Act." *American Journal of Legal History* 40.

Young, Andrew. 1995. "Reaffirming Our Faith in Integration." *St. Louis University Law Journal* 39.

CROSS REFERENCES

Disability Discrimination; School Desegregation; Separate But Equal.

INTELLECTUAL PROPERTY

Intangible rights protecting the products of human intelligence and creation, such as copyrightable works, patented inventions, trademarks, and trade secrets. Although largely governed by federal law, state law also governs some aspects of intellectual property.

Intellectual property describes a wide variety of property created by musicians, authors, artists, and inventors. The law of intellectual property typically encompasses the areas of copyright, patents, and trademark law. It is intended largely to encourage the development of art, science, and information by granting certain property rights to all artists, which include inventors in the arts and the sciences. These rights allow artists to protect themselves from infringement, or the unauthorized use and misuse of their creations. Trademarks and service marks protect distinguishing features (such as names or package designs) that are associated with particular products or services and that indicate commercial source.

Copyright laws have roots in eighteenth-century ENGLISH LAW. Comprehensive patent laws can be traced to seventeenth-century England, and they have been a part of U.S. law since the colonial period. The copyright and patent concepts were both included in the U.S. CONSTITUTION. Under Article I, Section 8, Clause 8, of the Constitution, "The Congress shall have Power ... To promote the Progress of Science and useful Arts, by securing for limited Times to Authors and Inventors the exclusive Right to their respective Writings and Discoveries." The first trademark laws were passed by Congress in the late nineteenth century, and they derive their constitutional authority from the COMMERCE CLAUSE.

The bulk of intellectual PROPERTY LAW is contained in federal statutes. Copyrights are protected by the Copyright Act (17 U.S.C.A. §§ 101 et seq. [1994]); patents are covered in the Patent Act (35 U.S.C.A. §§ 101 et seq. [1994]), and trademark protection is provided by the LANHAM ACT (also known as the Trademark Act; 15 U.S.C.A. §§ 1501 et seq. [1994]).

Intellectual property laws give owners the exclusive right to profit from a work for a particular limited period. For copyrighted material, the exclusive right lasts for 70 years beyond the death of the author. The length of the right can vary for patents, but in most cases it lasts for 20 years. Trademark rights are exclusive for ten years and can be continually renewed for subsequent ten-year periods.

Intellectual property laws do not fall in the category of CRIMINAL LAW, *per se.* Some copyright laws authorize criminal penalties, but by and large, the body of intellectual property law is concerned with prevention and compensation, both of which are civil matters. This means that the owner, not the government, is responsible for enforcement.

Intellectual property laws provide owners with the power to enforce their property rights in civil court. They provide for damages when unauthorized use or misuse has occurred. They also provide for injunctions, or court orders, to prevent unauthorized use or misuse.

The property protected by copyright laws must be fixed in a tangible form. For example, a musician may not claim copyright protection for a melody unless it has been written down or somehow actualized and affixed with a recognizable notation or recorded. A formula or device may not receive patent protection unless it has been presented in whole to the U.S. PATENT AND TRADEMARK OFFICE; even then, it must satisfy several tests in order to qualify. A symbol may not receive trademark protection unless it has been placed on GOODS or used in connection with services.

Copyrights

Copyright laws grant authors, artists, composers, and publishers the exclusive right to produce and distribute expressive and original work. Only expressive pieces, or writings, may receive copyright protection. A writing need not

Functionality can be a factor in copyright law. The copyrights to architectural design, for example, are generally reserved for architectural works that are not functional. If the only purpose or function of a particular design is utilitarian, the work cannot be copyrighted. For instance, a person may not copyright a simple design for a water spigot. However, if a person creates a fancy water spigot, the design is more likely to be copyrightable.

Copyrighted material can receive varying degrees of protection. The scope of protection is generally limited to the original work that is in the writing. For example, assume that an artist has created a sculpture of the moon. The sculptor may not prevent others from making sculptures of the moon. However, the sculptor may prevent others from making sculptures of the moon that are exact replicas of his own sculpture.

Copyright protection gives the copyright holder the exclusive right to (1) reproduce the copyrighted work; (2) create derivative works from the work; (3) distribute copies of the work; (4) perform the work publicly; and (5) display the work. The first two rights are infringed whether they are violated in public or in private. The last three rights are infringed only if they are violated in public. *Public* showing is defined under the Copyright Act of 1976 as a performance or display to a "substantial number of persons" outside of friends and family (17 U.S.C.A. § 101).

Infringement of copyright occurs whenever someone exercises the exclusive rights of the copyright owner without the owner's permission. The infringement need not be intentional. Copyright owners usually prove infringement in court by showing that copying occurred and that the copying amounted to impermissible appropriation. These showings require an analysis and comparison of the copyrighted work and the disputed work. Many general rules also relate to infringement of certain works. For example, a character created in a particular copyrighted work may not receive copyright protection unless he or she is developed in great detail and a character in the disputed work closely resembles that character.

The most important exception to the exclusive rights of the copyright holder is the "fair use" doctrine. This doctrine allows the general

Napster, an online company that provided users the ability to share music files freely, was sued by the Recording Industry of America and was eventually forced to changed its business model. Shawn Fanning, founder of Napster, speaks at a February 2001 news conference following a court ruling against the company.
AP IMAGES

be words on paper: In copyright law, it could be a painting, sculpture, or other work of art. The writing element merely requires that a work of art, before receiving copyright protection, must be reduced to some tangible form. This may be on paper, on film, on audiotape, or on any other tangible medium that can be reproduced.

The writing requirement ensures that copyrighted material is capable of being reproduced. Without this requirement, artists could not be expected to know whether they were infringing on the original work of another. The writing requirement also enforces the copyright RULE that ideas cannot be copyrighted: Only the individualized expression of ideas can be protected.

Copyrighted material must be original. This means that there must be something sufficiently new about the work that sets it apart from previous similar works. If the variation is more than trivial, the work will merit copyright protection.

public to use copyrighted material without permission in certain situations. To varying extents, these situations include some educational activities, some literary and social criticism, some parody, and news reporting. Whether a particular use is fair depends on a number of factors, including whether the use is for profit; what proportion of the copyrighted material is used; whether the work is fictional in nature; and what economic effect the use has on the copyright owner.

The rise in electronic publication in the late twentieth century, particularly the widespread use of the INTERNET since the mid 1990s, caused new concerns in the area of copyright. A web site called Napster, which provided a file-sharing system whereby users could trade electronic music files, became one of the most popular sites on the Internet. The company had an estimated 16.9 million worldwide users, and the system accommodated about 65 million downloads. The Recording Industry Association of America sued Napster, eventually causing Napster to close down.

During the late 1990s Congress enacted a series of laws that had significant impacts on the law of copyright. In 1998 Congress enacted the Sonny Bono Copyright Term Extension Act, Pub. L. No. 105-298, 112 Stat. 2827 (17 U.S.C. A. §§ 101 et seq.), which extended the terms of existing and new copyrights by 20 years, against the protests of several lobbying groups. Also in 1998, Congress approved the Digital Millennium Copyright Act (DMCA), Pub. L. No. 105-304, 112 Stat. 2860 (17 U.S.C.A. §§ 101 et seq.), a broad-based piece of legislation designed to bring copyright law into the digital age.

Several years after the lawsuit involving Napster, the issue of file sharing again took center stage in the area of copyright law. In 2005 the U.S. Supreme Court issued a decision in *Metro-Goldwyn-Mayer Studios, Inc. v. Grokster, Ltd.*, wherein it had examined a challenge to a file-sharing system known as Grokster. The software at issue allowed computer users to share files through peer-to-peer networks, meaning that the computers could communicate directly with one another, rather than through a central server. Users of Grokster primarily used the software to share copyrighted video and music files without authorization. Because the Supreme Court found that Grokster had the objective that its software be used to download copyrighted

works without authorization, and took active steps to encourage infringement, it was liable for the infringing acts of its users. In the wake of the Supreme Court decision, Grokster ceased operations. The impact of the Grokster decision is ongoing, but commentators have emphasized the decision's focus on Grokster's behavior, rather than on the technology itself.

Patents

Patent laws encourage private investment in new technologies by granting to artists the right to forbid all others to produce and distribute technological information that is new, useful, and non-obvious. The statutory requirements for patent protection are more stringent than those for copyright protection. Furthermore, because patent protection for commercial products or processes can give a tremendous market advantage to businesses, those seeking patents often find opposition to their applications. Patent protection can be obtained only through the U.S. Patent and Trademark Office (PTO).

The novelty requirement focuses on events that occur prior to the invention. Under Section 102 of the Patent Act, an invention is not novel if it is publicly used, sold, or patented by another inventor within 12 months of the patent application. This definition implements the public policy that favors quick disclosure of technological progress.

Often, two inventors apply for a patent for the same product or process within the same 12-month period. Three factors determine who wins the patent: the date and time that the product or process was conceived; the date and time that the product or process was reduced to practice; and the diligence that was used to pursue patent protection and to perfect the discovery. Generally, the first inventor to conceive the product or process has priority in the application process. However, if the second inventor is the first to reduce the product or process to practice, and the first inventor does not use diligence to obtain patent protection, the second inventor is given priority in the application process.

The utility requirement ensures that the product or process receiving patent protection will have some beneficial use. The inventor must specify in the application a specific utility for the invention. If the application is for a patent on a process, the process must be useful with respect to a product. A process that is new and non-obvious, yet useless, does not increase knowledge or confer any benefit on society.

Non-obviousness is not the same as novelty. Not everything that is novel is non-obvious. Anything that is non-obvious is novel unless it already has been patented. The non-obviousness requirement focuses on existing technology, or "prior art." In determining whether an invention is non-obvious, the PTO analyzes the prior art, examines the differences between the invention and the prior art, and determines the level of ordinary skill in the art. Generally, if an invention is obvious to a person of ordinary skill in the relevant art, it is not patentable.

When an inventor claims that his or her patent has been infringed, the court engages in a two-step process. First, it analyzes all of the relevant patent documents. It then reads the patent documents and compares them with the device or process that is accused of infringement. If each element of the accused device or process substantially duplicates an element in the patented device or process, the court may declare that the patent has been infringed. Infringement can occur only if another person uses, makes, or sells the patented device or process without the permission of the person who has received the patent.

When a patented device or process is infringed, the patent holder, or patentee, may recover in damages an amount equal to a reasonable royalty. If the infringement was willful, the infringing party may be forced to pay three times the reasonable royalty. If successful in court, the patent holder may recover court costs and attorneys' fees. If the patent holder anticipates infringement, he or she may apply for an injunction, which would prohibit a certain party from infringing the patent. An injunction may also be issued after a finding of infringement to prevent repeat infringement.

Trademarks

Trademark laws allow businesses to protect the symbolic information that relates to their goods and services, by preventing the use of such features by competitors. To receive trademark protection, a mark usually must be distinctive. *Distinctiveness* applies to any coined or fanciful word or term that does not closely resemble an existing mark. A mark generally will not receive trademark protection if it is a common or descriptive term used in the marketplace.

To receive trademark protection, a mark must be used in commerce. If two or more marketers claim ownership of a certain mark, the first user of the mark will usually receive the protection. When the mark is known to consumers only in a limited geographic area, it may not receive protection in areas where it is unknown.

Infringement occurs if a mark is likely to cause confusion among consumers. In determining whether confusion is likely, the court examines a number of factors, including the similarity between the two marks in appearance, sound, connotation, and impression; the similarity of the goods or services that the respective marks represent; the similarity of the markets; whether the sale of the goods or services is inspired by impulse or only after careful consideration by the buyer; the level of public awareness of the mark; whether shoppers are actually confused; the number and nature of similar marks on similar goods or services; the length of time of concurrent use without actual confusion on the part of shoppers; and the variety of goods or services that the mark represents (*In re E. I. duPont de Nemours & Co.*, 476 F.2d 1357, 177 U.S.P.Q. 563 [1973]).

Defenses to infringement include fair use and COLLATERAL use. Fair use occurs when the second user, or repossessor, uses a protected mark in a non-conspicuous way to identify a component of a good or service. For example, a restaurant may use a protected mark to advertise that it serves a particular brand of soft drink, without infringing the mark. However, the restaurant may not identify itself by the mark without infringing the mark.

Collateral use is use of the same mark in a different market. For example, assume that a tree surgeon has received trademark protection for the mark Tree Huggers. This protection might or might not prevent a business that sells logging boots from using the same mark. However, if the mark for the boots is written or otherwise appears with the same defining characteristics as the mark for the tree surgeon, it risks being denied trademark protection, depending on whether it can be confused by consumers.

Remedies for infringement of a protected trademark consist of damages for the profits lost owing to the infringement; recovery of the profits realized by the infringer owing to the infringement; and attorneys' fees. A trademark

Napster and Intellectual Property

In early 1999 Shawn Fanning, who was only 18 at the time, began to develop an idea as he talked with friends about the difficulties of finding the kind of MP3 files they were interested in. He thought that there should be a way to create a program that combined three key functions into one. These functions included a search engine, file sharing (the ability to trade MP3 files directly, without having to use a centralized server for storage), and an Internet Relay Chat (IRC), which was a means of finding and chatting with other MP3 users while online. Fanning spent several months writing the code that would become the utility later known world-wide as Napster. Napster became a non-profit on-line music-trading program that became especially popular among college students who typically have access to high-speed Internet connections.

In April 2000 the heavy metal rock group Metallica sued the on-line music-trading Website Napster for copyright infringement. Several universities were also named in this suit. Metallica claimed that these universities violated Metallica's music copyrights by permitting their students to access Napster and illegally trade songs using university servers. A number of universities had banned Napster prior to April 2000 because of concerns about potential copyright infringement and/or because traffic on the Internet was slowing down university servers. Yale University, which was named in the suit, immediately blocked student access to Napster.

Metallica argued that Napster facilitated illegal use of digital audio devices, which the group alleged was a violation of the Racketeering Influenced and Corrupt Organizations (RICO) act, 18 U.S.C. § 1961. Napster responded that the Fair Use Act allows owners of compact discs to use them as they wish. Therefore if an owner of the disc decides to copy it into a computer file, he or she should be allowed to do so. If this file happens to be accessible on the Internet, then others can also access or download it without being guilty of a crime. Napster further claimed that since it made no profit off the trades, it owed no money in royalties. The Ninth Circuit held that Napster's operation constituted copyright infringement.

FURTHER READINGS

Alderman, John. 2001. *Sonic Boom: Napster, P2P, and the Battle for the Future of Music.* New York: Perseus.

Merriden, Trevor. 2001. *Irresistible Forces: The Business Legacy of Napster and the Growth of the Underground Internet.* New York: John Wiley and Sons.

CROSS REFERENCE

Art Law

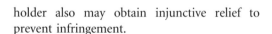

holder also may obtain injunctive relief to prevent infringement.

Other Forms of Intellectual Property

The body of intellectual property law also includes laws relating to trade secrets, UNFAIR COMPETITION, and the right of publicity. TRADE SECRET laws, which function at the state level, protect any formula, pattern, device, or compilation of information that provides a business advantage over competitors who do not use or know of it. A strategy to increase worker productivity, for example, is a trade secret. Trade secrets do not receive patent protection because they are not inventive. Trade secret laws are included in intellectual property laws because, like other intellectual property laws, they prevent the unauthorized use of certain intangible subject matter.

The right of publicity is the right of a person to control the commercial value and exploitation of his or her name, voice, or likeness. Because right-of-publicity laws promote artistic and commercial pursuits, they are included among intellectual property law. These laws are usually reserved for celebrities and other public figures whose name and image are important to their career. By allowing celebrities the right to control the commercial use of their name, voice, and image, right-of-publicity laws protect the commercial potential of entertainers.

Developments

Artists face problems protecting their property in other countries because not all countries subscribe to international agreements regarding intellectual property. This has led to widespread unauthorized copying. In the 1990s China and Mexico were identified as especially serious offenders. In both countries music and films are copied and sold openly without compensation to the creators. The United States threatened to impose trade sanctions against China if it did not observe INTERNATIONAL COPYRIGHT treaties. Such threats illustrate that the United States places a high priority on protecting the right of artists to profit from their work.

FURTHER READINGS

Burgunder, Lee B. 2002. "Reflections on *Napster*: The Ninth Circuit Takes a Walk on the Wild Side." *American Business Law Journal* 39 (summer): 683–707.

Byrne, John G. 1995. "Changes on the Frontier of Intellectual Property Law: An Overview of the Changes Required by GATT." *Duquesne Law Review* 34 (fall): 121–37.

Goldstein, Paul. 2008. *Copyright, Patent, Trademark, and Related State Doctrines: Cases and Materials on the Law of Intellectual Property.* 6th ed. New York: Foundation Press.

Gray, Megan E., and Will Thomas DeVries. 2003. "The Legal Fallout from Digital Rights Management Technology." *Computer and Internet Lawyer* 20 (April): 20–35.

Helprin, Mark. 2009. *Digital Barbarism.* New York: HarperCollins.

Kuney, George W., and Donna C. Looper. 2009. *Mastering Intellectual Property.* Durham, N.C.: Carolina Academic Press.

LaFrance, Mary. 2009. *Understanding Trademark Law.* New Providence, N.J.: LexisNexis.

Lamoureux, Edward Lee, and Steven L. Barron. 2009. *Intellectual Property Law and Interactive Media.* New York: Peter Lang Publishing.

Letterman, G. Gregory. 2001. *Basics of International Intellectual Property Law.* Ardsley, NY: Transnational Publishers.

McJohn, Stephen M., and Roger S. Haydock. 2003. *Intellectual Property: Examples and Explanations.* New York: Aspen.

CROSS REFERENCES

Art Law; Copyright, International; Entertainment Law; Literary Property; Music Publishing; Trade Dress; Trade Name.

INTEMPERANCE

A lack of moderation. Habitual intemperance is that degree of intemperance in the use of intoxicating liquor which disqualifies the person a great portion of the time from properly attending to business. Habitual or excessive use of liquor.

CROSS REFERENCE

Alcohol.

INTENT

A determination to perform a particular act or to act in a particular manner for a specific reason; an aim or design; a resolution to use a certain means to reach an end.

Intent is a mental attitude with which an individual acts, and therefore it cannot ordinarily be directly proved but must be inferred from surrounding facts and circumstances. Intent refers only to the state of mind with which the act is done or omitted. It differs from motive, which is what prompts a person to act or to fail to act. For example, suppose Billy calls Amy names and Amy throws a snowball at him. Amy's intent is to hit Billy with a snowball. Her motive may be to stop Billy's taunts.

The legal importance of what an individual intended depends on the particular area of law. In contract law, for example, the intention of the parties to a written contract is fixed by the language of the contract document.

In TORT LAW, intent plays a key role in determining the civil liability of persons who commit harm. An intentional tort is any deliberate invasion of, or interference with, the property, property rights, personal rights, or personal liberties of another that causes injuries without JUST CAUSE or excuse. In tort an individual is considered to intend the consequences of an act—whether or not she or he actually intends those consequences—if the individual is substantially certain that those consequences will result.

Basic intentional torts include ASSAULT AND BATTERY, conversion of property, FALSE ARREST, FALSE IMPRISONMENT, fraud, intentional infliction of emotional distress, invasion of privacy, and TRESPASS. It is ordinarily not necessary that any wrongful or illegal means be used to accomplish the negative result, provided the wrongful conduct was intentional and was not accompanied by excuse or justification.

In CRIMINAL LAW the concept of criminal intent has been called MENS REA, which refers to a criminal or wrongful purpose. If a person innocently causes harm, then she or he lacks mens rea and, under this concept, should not be criminally prosecuted.

Although the concept of mens rea is generally accepted, problems arise in applying it to particular cases. Some crimes require a very high degree of intent, whereas others require substantially less. LARCENY, for example, requires that the DEFENDANT intentionally take property to which the person knows he or she is not entitled, intending to deprive the rightful owner of possession permanently. On the other hand, negligent HOMICIDE requires only that the defendant negligently cause another's death.

Criminal law has attempted to clarify the intent requirement by creating the concepts of "specific intent" and "general intent." SPECIFIC INTENT refers to a particular state of mind that seeks to accomplish the precise act that the law prohibits—for example, a specific intent to commit RAPE. Sometimes it means an intent to do something beyond that which is done, such as ASSAULT with intent to commit rape. The prosecution must show that the defendant purposely or knowingly committed the crime at issue.

GENERAL INTENT refers to the intent to do that which the law prohibits. It is not necessary for the prosecution to prove that the defendant intended the precise harm or the precise result that occurred. Thus, in most states, a defendant who kills a person with a gun while intoxicated, to the extent that the defendant is not aware of having a gun, will be guilty of second-degree MURDER. The law will infer that the defendant had a general intent to kill.

Criminal law dispenses with the intent requirement in many property-related crimes. Under COMMON LAW the prosecution had to establish that the defendant intended to steal or destroy property. By 1900 many statutes eliminated the "intent-to-defraud" requirement for property crimes. Passing a bad check, obtaining property under FALSE PRETENSES, selling mortgaged property, and embezzling while holding public office no longer required criminal intent.

Criminal law and tort law share the concept of transferred intent. For example, if A shoots a gun at B, intending to strike B, but the bullet hits C, the intent to strike is transferred to the act of shooting C and supplies the necessary intent for either a criminal conviction or a civil tort action. Under the criminal doctrine of transferred intent, the intent is considered to follow the criminal act regardless of who turns out to be the victim. Under the tort doctrine of transferred intent, the defendant is liable for monetary damages to the unintended victim.

INTER ALIA

[Latin, Among other things.] A phrase used in pleading to designate that a particular statute set out therein is only a part of the statute that is relevant to the facts of the lawsuit and not the entire statute.

Inter alia is also used when reporting court decisions to indicate that there were other rulings made by the court but only a particular holding of the case is cited.

INTER VIVOS

[Latin, Between the living.] A phrase used to describe a gift that is made during the donor's lifetime.

In order for an *inter vivos* gift to be complete, there must be a clear manifestation of the giver's intent to release to the donee the object of the gift, and actual delivery and acceptance by the donee.

An *inter vivos* gift is distinguishable from a gift CAUSA MORTIS, which is made in expectation of impending death.

INTEREST

A comprehensive term to describe any right, claim, or privilege that an individual has toward real or personal property. Compensation for the use of borrowed money.

There are two basic types of interest: legal and conventional. *Legal interest* is prescribed by the applicable state statute as the highest that may be legally contracted for, or charged. *Conventional interest* is interest at a rate that has been set and agreed upon by the parties themselves without outside intervention. It must be within the legally prescribed interest rate to avoid the criminal prosecution of the lender for violation of usury laws.

INTEREST ON LAWYERS TRUST ACCOUNT

A system in which lawyers place certain client deposits in interest-bearing accounts, with the interest then used to fund programs, such as legal service organizations who provide services to clients in need.

Originating in Canada and Australia in the 1960s, interest on lawyers trust account (IOLTA) programs made their first appearance in the United States in Florida in 1981. Since then, all 50 states and the District of Columbia have established IOLTA programs. The concept is straightforward. Lawyers routinely place large client deposits—such as escrow accounts—in interest-bearing accounts, with the interest to be paid to the client. Deposits that would individually be too small or too short-term to generate interest are pooled into IOLTA accounts. The interest generated by these funds is then used to fund a variety of public legal services, usually geared toward those who cannot afford lawyers. Nationwide, IOLTA programs earned more than $200 million in interest in 2002.

Over the years IOLTA programs faced challenges from individuals and lawyers who felt that the interest, however small the amount, belonged to the clients. They cited the Fifth Amendment's prohibition against the taking of private property without JUST COMPENSATION. IOLTA proponents countered that, since the deposits individually would yield no interest, the clients were not actually losing money. The U.S. Supreme Court weighed in on March 26, 2003, when it narrowly decided in favor of IOLTAs (*Brown v. Legal Foundation of Washington*, U.S. Supreme Court, 01-1325, 2003). The Court found that the Fifth Amendment's Just Compensation Clause did not apply because without the existence of the IOLTA accounts no other depository accounts would exist, and consequently the clients whose money was being held would not have received any interest.

FURTHER READINGS

Anderson, Tony. 2003. "U.S. Supreme Court Upholds Use of Interest on Lawyer Trust Account." *Wisconsin Law Journal* (April 23).

Greenhouse, Linda. "Method of Legal Services Financing is Challenged before Supreme Court." *The New York Times* (December 10, 2002). Available online at http://www.commondreams.org/headlines02/1210-07.htm; website home page: http://www.commondreams.org (accessed August 1, 2009).

IOLTA.org Web site. Available online at http://www.iolta.org/ (accessed September 5, 2009).

CROSS REFERENCES

Fifth Amendment; Group Legal Services.

INTERFERENCE

In the law of patents, the presence of two pending applications, or an existing patent and a pending application that encompass an identical invention or discovery.

When interference exists, the PATENT AND TRADEMARK OFFICE conducts an investigation to ascertain the priority of invention between the conflicting applications, or the application and the patent. A patent is customarily granted to the earlier invention.

INTERGOVERNMENTAL IMMUNITY DOCTRINE

A principle established under constitutional law that prevents the federal government and individual state governments from intruding on one another's sovereignty. Intergovernmental immunity is intended to keep government agencies from restricting the rights of other government agencies.

The principle of intergovernmental immunity was established by the U.S. Supreme Court in McCulloch v. Maryland, 17 U.S. at 426 (1819), in which Chief Justice JOHN MARSHALL and his fellow justices ruled unanimously that states may not regulate property or operations of the federal government. (Under Maryland state law, banks not chartered by the state were subject to restrictions and taxes; the state government had attempted to impose these restrictions on the Second Bank of the United States.)

The doctrine of intergovernmental immunity is frequently invoked in TAXATION cases. In *Davis v. Michigan Department of Treasury*, 489 U.S. 803 (1989), the U.S. Supreme Court ruled that the state of Michigan was in violation of federal law when it exempted state and local government pensions from taxation but levied taxes on federal government pensions. At the time, more than two dozen other states handled federal pensions in a similar manner.

The doctrine also keeps certain federal entities immune from state laws. The Smithsonian Institution is an example. While not a government agency in the strict sense of what that implies, it is considered an "instrumentality of the United States," and thus under federal jurisdiction. Therefore, the Smithsonian can establish charitable gift annuities and similar funding tools without being required to register under the charitable solicitation laws of individual states.

Intergovernmental immunity also governs the taxation of Native Americans living on federal lands, as well as tribal WATER RIGHTS.

FURTHER READINGS

Anzovin, Steven, and Janet Podell, eds. 1988. *The U.S. Constitution and the Supreme Court.* New York: Wilson.

Engdahl, David E. 1987. *Constitutional Federalism in a Nutshell.* Eagan, MN: West.

"Immunity of Smithsonian Institution from State Insurance Laws." April 25, 1997. *Department of Justice Memorandum.* Available online at http://www.justice.gov/olc/smithsonop2.htm; website home page: http://www.justice.gov (accessed August 1, 2009).

CROSS REFERENCE

States' Rights.

INTERIM

[Latin, In the meantime: temporary; between.]

An *interim dean* of a law school, for example, is an individual who is appointed to fill the office of dean during a temporary vacancy or a period during which the regular dean is absent due to an illness or disability.

INTERIOR DEPARTMENT

The Interior Department is a federal agency responsible for U.S. natural resources and for land owned by the federal government. The department fulfills this responsibility by promulgating and enforcing numerous regulations concerning natural resources and public lands. The head of the department is the secretary of the interior, who sits on the president's CABINET and reports directly to the president.

The Department of the Interior was created by Congress in 1849 (9 Stat. 395 [43 U.S.C.A. § 1451]). Its original duties included supervision

ILLUSTRATION BY GGS CREATIVE RESOURCES. REPRODUCED BY PERMISSION OF GALE, A PART OF CENGAGE LEARNING.

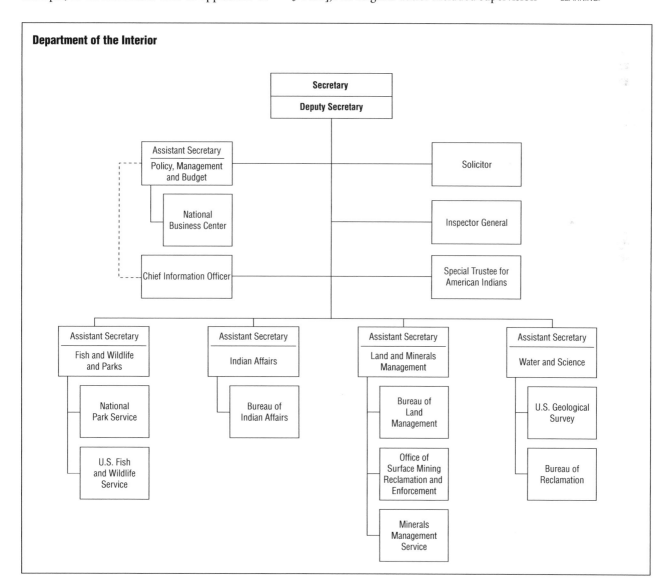

Department of the Interior

A member of the U.S. Fish and Wildlife Service, a division of the Interior Department, prepares to release a salmon into the Connecticut River. The service is concerned with the conservation of species threatened by loss of habitat.

AP IMAGES

of all mining in the United States, the General Land Office, the Office of Indian Affairs, the Pension Office, the Patent Office, the District of Columbia PENITENTIARY, the U.S. census, and accounts for federal court officers. These agencies and duties had little in common except that their focus was within U.S. borders, and they were out of place in other departments.

As a result of the continuing search for streamlined organization in government, the Department of the Interior eventually dropped a number of its original duties and developed an emphasis on natural resources. The department has retained responsibility for mining, federal lands, and American Indian issues. Over the years, it has added several offices and bureaus to help fulfill its responsibilities.

The chief functions of the Department of the Interior include efforts to conserve and develop mineral and water resources; to conserve, develop, and utilize fish and wildlife resources; to coordinate federal and state recreation programs; to preserve and administer scenic and historic areas; to operate the Job Corps Conservation Centers and Youth and Young Adult Conservation Corps Camps, and other youth training programs; to irrigate arid lands; to manage hydroelectric systems; to provide social and economic services to U.S. territories; and to provide programs and services to Native Americans.

The Department of the Interior contains several different offices, departments, and bureaus. The Office of the Secretary includes the Offices of the Deputy Secretary, Assistant

Secretaries, and Inspector General. The inspector general is charged with coordinating and supervising interior audits and with performing inspections to detect fraud and ABUSE. In addition, the inspector general is responsible for supervising the financial activities of U.S. territories such as Guam, American Samoa, and the Virgin Islands. The Office of Hearings and Appeals is also contained within the Office of the Secretary. Persons involved in disputes with the Department of the Interior may have their cases heard at this office.

The hands-on work of the department is performed by several bureaus and services. The Bureau of Reclamation is devoted to the management of water resources. The Bureau of Land Management is in charge of public lands and resources. The U.S. Geological Survey exists to draw a wide variety of maps and to examine and classify public land structures and mineral resources. The Minerals Management Service assesses the value of minerals and supervises mineral recovery. The Office of Surface Mining Reclamation and Enforcement is charged mainly with the operation of a nationwide program on coal mining. The U.S. Bureau of Mines researches mining issues in order to find the best technology for extracting, processing, using, and recycling non-fuel mineral resources. The National Biological Survey conducts research to promote the sound management of plant and animal life. The National Park Service is dedicated to the preservation of national parks, monuments, scenic parkways, preserves, trails, riverways, seashores, lakeshores, and recreation areas. The U.S. Fish and Wildlife Service is devoted primarily to the conservation and enhancement of the nation's fish and wildlife resources.

One controversial function of the department is the oversight of Indian affairs. The Bureau of Indian Affairs (BIA) performs a number of functions that have to do with Native American issues. The Department of the Interior played a dominant role in the drafting of tribal constitutions during the nineteenth century. During the twentieth century, the Bureau of Indian Affairs continued its control over Indian tribes by insisting on review and approval powers over amendments to tribal constitutions.

The BIA's management of an Indian land trust led to a high-profile lawsuit in 1996 over the failure of the BIA to provide Indians with accurate financial accountings of lands held in trust for them by the Department of the Interior. U.S. district court Judge Royce Lamberth has overseen the CLASS ACTION, and by the September 2002 he had had lost patience with the department and Secretary Gale Norton over the lack of effort and honesty in dealing with the issues before the court. In a scathing 267-page RULING, Lamberth concluded that the department and Norton were "either unwilling or unable to administer competently the [Indian] trust." The plaintiffs allege that the BIA cannot account for $137 billions of income due the 500 members of the class, and the district court held the secretary of the interior in contempt, *Cobell v. Norton*, 226 F.Supp.2d 163 (D.D.C.2002). The DC CIRCUIT COURT of Appeals later held that: (1) the secretary was not in criminal contempt of order requiring her to initiate historical accounting project; (2) the secretary did not commit fraud on court, so as to be in criminal contempt, with respect to quarterly status reports; and (3) the secretary did not commit fraud on court, so as to be in criminal contempt, with respect to her representations regarding computer security of trust data (334 F.3d 1128 [D.C.Cir., Jul 18, 2003]).

Like most other federal administrative agencies, the Department of the Interior is controlled by both Congress and the president. Congress created the Department of the Interior, and it could decide to reduce or eliminate it. However, also like most other administrative agencies, the Department of the Interior is a political necessity. Lawmakers are generally well versed in a broad range of topics, but few have the knowledge required to craft the best rules and regulations on, for example, mining or land management. The Department of the Interior possesses such expertise.

At the executive level, the Department of the Interior reports directly to the president, who also exerts control over it. The president has the power to remove and replace department personnel, to propose increases or reductions in responsibilities, and to redirect the department's goals. All of these changes must be approved by Congress.

This dual control over the Department of the Interior makes it subject to political influence. For example, when a new president takes office, he or she will likely make personnel changes in the Department of the Interior to initiate new programs and directions promised in the campaign. Any high-level appointments to administrative agencies will be reviewed by Congress. If a nominee holds views that are contrary to those of the majority in Congress, Congress may reject the nominee, and the president may have to choose one more acceptable to Congress. However, senators and representatives may be reluctant to resist the actions of a newly elected president for fear of alienating the voting public.

Historically, the Department of the Interior has been less concerned with conservation than with development. Interior Secretary Roy O. West commented in 1928 that the Department of the Interior should have been named the Department of Western Development. In the early twentieth century, U.S. citizens became aware that the resources that were needed for modern life were not inexhaustible, and the Department of the Interior gradually recognized the need for conservation. However, the Department of the Interior's original mission of managing development was at odds with conservation, and the department was incapable of concentrating exclusively on conservation. To fill the void created by this situation, Congress created the ENVIRONMENTAL PROTECTION AGENCY (EPA) in 1970.

Although the EPA has taken over the goals of conservation and pollution control, the Department of the Interior is still concerned with environmental matters. In 1987, the department reorganized the Bureau of Reclamation to reflect the bureau's new emphasis on management and conservation instead of construction. In the 1990s, Bruce Babbitt, the secretary of the interior under President BILL CLINTON, made several changes in the Department of the Interior to strengthen its environmental-protection efforts.

Web site: www.doi.gov.

FURTHER READINGS

Friedman, Howard M. 1992. "The Oversupply of Regulatory Reform: From Law to Politics in Administrative Rulemaking." *Nebraska Law Review* 71.

Hines, N. William. 1994. "The Land Ethic and American Agriculture." *Loyola of Los Angeles Law Review* 27.

Interior Department Web site. Available online at http://www.doi.gov (accessed August 1, 2009).

Pommersheim, Frank, and Shermann Marshall. 1992. "Liberation, Dreams, and Hard Work: An Essay on Tribal Court Jurisprudence." *Wisconsin Law Review* 411.

U.S. Government Manual Website. Available online at http://www.gpoaccess.gov/gmanual/ (accessed July 21, 2009).

Volkman, John M. 1987. "Testing New Forms of River Basin Governance: Implication of the Seattle Master Builders Case." *Environmental Law* 17.

CROSS REFERENCES

Environmental Law; Fish and Fishing; Game; Mine and Mineral Law; Native American Rights.

INTERLINEATION

The process of writing between the lines of an instrument; that which is written between the lines of a document.

An interlineation frequently appears in a contract that has been typed and signed. If the parties agree that a sentence is to be inserted between the lines to clarify a particular provision, the new sentence is known as an interlineation. The new line should be initialed and dated to indicate that both parties are aware of and agree to its insertion. An interlineation results in the alteration of an instrument.

CROSS REFERENCE

Alteration of Instruments.

INTERLOCKING DIRECTORATE

The relationship that exists between the board of directors of one corporation with that of another due to the fact that a number of members sit on both boards and, therefore, there is a substantial likelihood that neither corporation acts independently of the other.

Because the same persons occupy seats on the boards of companies that are supposed to compete in the marketplace, there is a potential for violations of federal antitrust acts, particularly the CLAYTON ACT (15 U.S.C.A. §§ 12-27 [1914]) which prohibits the existence of interlocking directorates that substantially reduce commercial competition.

INTERLOCUTORY

Provisional; interim; temporary; not final; that which intervenes between the beginning and the end of a lawsuit or proceeding to either decide a particular point or matter that is not the final issue of the entire controversy or prevent irreparable harm during the pendency of the lawsuit.

Interlocutory actions are taken by courts when a QUESTION OF LAW must be answered by an appellate court before a trial may proceed or to prevent irreparable harm from occurring to a person or property during the pendency of a lawsuit or proceeding. Generally, courts are reluctant to make interlocutory orders unless the circumstances surrounding the case are serious and require timely action.

Interlocutory appeals are restricted by state and federal appellate courts because courts do not want piecemeal litigation. Appeals courts generally review only cases that have reached final judgment in the trial courts. When a COURT ADMINISTRATOR enters final judgment, this certifies that the trial court has ended its review of the case and jurisdiction shifts to the appellate court.

Interlocutory appeals are typically permitted when the trial judge certifies to the appellate court in an interlocutory order that an important question of law is in doubt and that it will substantially affect the final result of the case. Judicial economy then dictates that the court resolve the issue rather than subject the parties to a trial that may be reversed on an appeal from a final judgment.

Appellate courts have the discretion to review interlocutory orders. The federal courts of appeal are governed by the Interlocutory Appeals Act (28 U.S.C.A. § 1292). This act grants discretion to the courts of appeal to review interlocutory orders in civil cases where the district judge states in the order that a controlling question of law is in doubt and that the immediate resolution of the issue will materially advance the ultimate termination of litigation. State appellate courts are governed by statutes and court rules of appellate procedure regarding the review of interlocutory orders.

When an appellate court reviews an interlocutory order, its decision on the matters contained in the order is final. The court enters an interlocutory judgment, which makes that part of the case final. Therefore, if a case proceeds to trial after an interlocutory judgment is entered, and an appeal from the trial court judgment follows, the matters decided by the interlocutory judgment cannot be reviewed by the court again.

Interlocutory orders may be issued in a DIVORCE proceeding to prevent injury or irreparable harm during the pendency of the lawsuit. For example, an interlocutory order may require one spouse to pay the other spouse a designated weekly sum for support, pending a decision on ALIMONY and CHILD SUPPORT. This prevents the spouse and children from being without income during the action.

Courts may also issue interlocutory orders where property is about to be sold or forfeited and a lawsuit has been filed seeking to stop the action. In this type of case, a court will enter an interlocutory injunction, preventing the transfer of property until it has made a final decision. To do otherwise would cause irreparable harm and would complicate LEGAL TITLE to the property if the person contesting the transfer ultimately prevailed.

Thus, though the courts value finality in most proceedings, interlocutory orders and appeals are available to protect important rights and to enhance judicial economy.

INTERMEDIATE-RANGE NUCLEAR FORCES TREATY

The INTERMEDIATE-RANGE NUCLEAR FORCES TREATY of 1987 (INF) was the first NUCLEAR WEAPONS agreement requiring the United States and the Union of Soviet Socialist Republics (U.S.S.R.) to reduce, rather than merely limit, their arsenals of nuclear weapons. Signed by President RONALD REAGAN, of the United States, and General Secretary Mikhail Gorbachev, of the U.S.S.R., on December 8, 1987, the INF Treaty eliminated all land-based nuclear missiles with ranges of between 300 and 3,400 miles. The U.S. Senate quickly ratified the treaty in 1988 by a vote of 93–5.

The INF Treaty marked an historic shift in superpower relations and was the first superpower arms control treaty since 1979. It required the removal of 1,752 Soviet and 859 U.S. short- and intermediate-range missiles, most of which were located in Europe. It was the second superpower agreement to ban an entire class of weapons, the first being the 1972 Biological Weapons Convention. The INF Treaty also contained unprecedented verification procedures, including mandatory exchanges of relevant missile data, on-site inspections, and satellite surveillance.

Soviet concessions in the INF negotiations grew out of Gorbachev's efforts to limit military competition between the United States and the U.S.S.R. The new Soviet willingness to make arms-control concessions was first evident in the 1986 Stockholm Accord, which established various confidence- and security-building measures between the superpowers and their allied

countries, including on-site inspections and advance warning of military movements. In 1988, a year after signing the INF, Gorbachev continued his ambitious program of military cuts by announcing a unilateral reduction of 500,000 troops, including the removal of 50,000 troops and 5,000 tanks from eastern Europe. These developments met with a positive response from the United States and its NORTH ATLANTIC TREATY ORGANIZATION allies, and created an atmosphere that would be conducive to future arms accords, including the CONVENTIONAL FORCES IN EUROPE TREATY of 1990 and the Strategic Arms Reduction Treaties of 1991 and 1993.

Several successor states to the Soviet Union, including Belarus, Kazakhstan, and Ukraine, continue to implement the treaty. Other European nations, including Germany, Hungary, Poland, Czech Republic, and Slovakia, voluntarily destroyed their medium-range missiles in the 1990s. The United States also persuaded Bulgaria to destroy its missiles in 2002. The right of parties to the treaty to conduct on-site inspections expired on May 31, 2001. However, parties still may conduct satellite surveillance to ensure that member states comply with the treaty. The treaty established the Special Verification Commission to implement the treaty, and the commission continues to meet regularly.

FURTHER READINGS

Falkenrath, Richard A. 1995. *Shaping Europe's Military Order: The Origins and Consequences of the CFE Treaty.* Cambridge, MA: Massachusetts Institute of Technology Press.

U.S. President Ronald Reagan and Soviet President Mikhail Gorbachev sign the INF Treaty on December 8, 1987. The treaty called for an elimination of an entire class of short- and intermediate-range nuclear missiles.

AP IMAGES

Sheehan, Michael. 1988. *Arms Control: Theory and Practice.* Cambridge, MA: Blackwell.

Wirth, Timothy E. 1988. *Intermediate-Range Nuclear Forces Treaty and the Conventional Balance in Europe.* Washington, D.C.: U.S. Government Printing Office.

CROSS REFERENCES

Arms Control and Disarmament; Cold War; Conventional Forces in Europe Treaty.

INTERNAL AUDIT

An inspection and verification of the financial records of a company or firm by a member of its own staff to determine the accuracy and acceptability of its accounting practices.

INTERNAL REVENUE CODE

The Internal Revenue Code is the body of law that codifies all federal tax laws, including income, estate, gift, excise, alcohol, tobacco, and employment taxes. These laws constitute title 26 of the U.S. Code (26 U.S.C.A. § 1 et seq. [1986]) and are implemented by the INTERNAL REVENUE SERVICE *through its Treasury Regulations and Revenue Rulings.*

Congress made major statutory changes to title 26 in 1939, 1954, and 1986. Because of the extensive revisions made in the TAX REFORM ACT OF 1986, title 26 is now known as the Internal Revenue Code of 1986 (Pub. L. No. 99-514, § 2, 100 Stat. 2095 [Oct. 22, 1986]).

Subtitle A of the Code contains five chapters on income taxes. The chapters cover normal income taxes and surtaxes, taxes on self-employment income, withholding of taxes on nonresident aliens and foreign corporations, taxes on transfers to avoid income tax, and consolidated returns.

Subtitle B deals with ESTATE AND GIFT TAXES. The rules and regulations concerning the TAXATION of probate estates and gifts are very complicated. This subtitle contains chapters on taxing generation-skipping transfers and rules on special valuation of property.

Subtitle C contains the law of employment taxes. It consists of chapters on general provisions relating to employment taxes and other sections dealing with federal insurance contributions, railroad retirement taxes, and federal unemployment taxes.

Subtitle D covers miscellaneous excise taxes. Its fifteen chapters cover a variety of issues, including retail excise taxes, manufacturers' excise taxes, taxes on wagering, environmental taxes, public charities, private foundations, pension plans, and certain group health plans.

Subtitle E covers alcohol, tobacco, and other excise taxes. Chapter 53 deals with machine guns, destructive devices, and certain other firearms.

Subtitle F contains provisions on procedure and administration. Under this subtitle are twenty chapters that deal with every step of the taxation process, from the setting of filing dates and the collection of penalties for late filing, to criminal offenses and judicial proceedings. The rules for administrative proceedings under the Code are addressed in the appendix to title 26.

Subtitle G addresses the organization of the Congressional Joint Committee on Taxation. Subtitle H contains the rules for the financing of presidential election campaigns. Subtitle I contains the Trust Fund Code.

The Internal Revenue Code has grown steadily since the 1930s. The complexity of its provisions, most of which are written in technical language, has required law and accounting firms to develop specialists in the various areas of taxation.

CROSS REFERENCE

Election Campaign Financing.

INTERNAL REVENUE SERVICE

The Internal Revenue Service (IRS) is the federal agency responsible for administering and enforcing all internal revenue laws in the United States, except those relating to alcohol, tobacco, firearms, and explosives, which are the responsibility of the Alcohol, Tobacco, Firearms, and Explosives Bureau's Tax and Trade division.

The IRS is the largest agency in the TREASURY DEPARTMENT. By the mid-1990s it had approximately 110,000 employees, 650 office locations in the United States, and 12 offices abroad. The agency processes approximately 205 million tax returns and collects more than $1.2 trillion each year.

The U.S. tax system, which the IRS oversees and administers, is based on the principle of voluntary compliance. According to the IRS, this means "that taxpayers are expected to comply with the law without being compelled to do so by action of a federal agent; it does not mean that the taxpayer is free to decide whether or not to comply with the law."

Duties and Powers

The IRS is responsible for enforcing the INTERNAL REVENUE CODE (U.S.C.A. tit. 26), which codifies all U.S. tax laws. Basic IRS activities include serving and educating taxpayers; determining, assessing, and collecting taxes; investigating individuals and organizations that violate tax laws; determining pension plan qualifications and exempt organization status; and issuing rulings and regulations to supplement the Internal Revenue Code.

Historically, Congress has given the IRS unique and wide-ranging powers for administering the U.S. tax system and enforcing its laws. For example, while in a criminal proceeding the government has the burden to prove that the DEFENDANT is guilty BEYOND A REASONABLE DOUBT, in a tax proceeding the burden is on the taxpayer to prove that he or she does not owe the amount claimed by the IRS. The IRS also has the power to impose civil penalties for any of a number of violations of tax law. These penalties are seldom employed, however, and with respect to penalties, the IRS bears the burden of proving that the penalty is justified.

The IRS has the power to collect large amounts of information on U.S. citizens, companies, and other institutions. The most obvious example of this power is that each year all taxpayers must file tax returns containing detailed financial and personal information. Many organizations are also required to notify the IRS of any payments they make to individuals; the IRS receives approximately one billion of these third-party reports annually. The IRS also has the legal authority to order banks, employers, and other institutions to provide information about a taxpayer without having to obtain a warrant from a judge; other law enforcement agencies, such as the FEDERAL BUREAU OF INVESTIGATION and local police forces, must obtain a warrant in such situations.

Another crucial power of the IRS is the ability to withhold taxes automatically from employee paychecks. The IRS was given this authority in 1943, when Congress passed legislation requiring employers to withhold from employees' paychecks the income taxes owed to the government. This withholding requirement was one of several actions taken

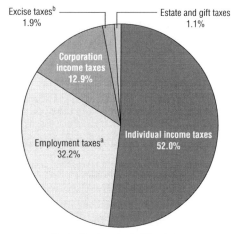

Internal Revenue Gross Collection, by Source, in 2008

Excise taxes[b]
1.9%

Estate and gift taxes
1.1%

Corporation income taxes
12.9%

Individual income taxes
52.0%

Employment taxes[a]
32.2%

Total collections: 2.74 trillion dollars

[a]Includes OASDHI, railroad retirement, and unemployment insurance.

[b]Excludes taxes on alcohol, tobacco, and firearms, now collected by the Bureau of Alcohol, Tobacco, and Firearms and by the Customs Service.

SOURCE: Internal Revenue Service, *Internal Revenue Gross Collections, By Type of Tax, Fiscal Years 2007 and 2008.*

by the government to increase revenue so that it could meet the huge financial requirements for fighting WORLD WAR II. In the early 2000s automatic withholding accounts for the majority of tax dollars paid to the government, with only a small portion sent in with tax returns by April 15, the IRS annual tax deadline. Automatic withholding is important to the government because it enables it to receive a steady stream of tax revenue. It is also useful for enforcing voluntary compliance from taxpayers because the individual's tax burden seems less onerous when taxes owed are subtracted from a paycheck before the check is received.

Organization

The IRS is led by a commissioner, who works in the IRS National Office located in Washington, D.C. The commissioner and his or her chief counsel are appointed by the president and must be approved by the Senate. The chief counsel serves as the chief legal adviser to the IRS. At the next level are regional commissioners, who oversee IRS operations in the four regions into which the country is divided: the

Northeast, Southeast, Midstates, and Western Regions. Within the four regions are 33 district offices, which are responsible for collecting revenue, examining returns, and pursuing criminal investigations within their geographic area. Also located across the country are ten service centers, five submission processing centers, two computing centers, and 23 customer service centers.

In addition to its geographic divisions, the IRS is organized into programs focusing on specific administrative tasks. Several of these, including the Taxpayer Services and Problem Resolution programs, focus on taxpayer assistance and education. Others, including the Examination, Collection, and Criminal Investigation divisions, focus on ensuring taxpayer compliance. Additional IRS programs include Appeals, which attempts to resolve tax controversies without litigation; Statistics of Income, which compiles and publishes data relating to the operation of the Internal Revenue Code; and Tax Practitioner Conduct, which enforces tax laws applying to attorneys, accountants, and taxpayer agents.

History

The IRS was created in 1952, though it was preceded by various other U.S. tax-collecting offices. The earliest incarnation of the IRS was the Office of the Commissioner of Revenue, which was established by Congress in 1792 in response to the request by Secretary of the Treasury ALEXANDER HAMILTON that various tariffs and taxes be created to raise money to pay off the U.S. Revolutionary War debt. Trench Coxe of Pennsylvania was the first person to hold the office. By creating the Office of the Commissioner of Revenue, Congress delegated its constitutional power to "lay and collect taxes, duties, imposts, and excises" to the Treasury Department, which has retained the power ever since (art. 1, § 8, U.S. Constitution).

By the time THOMAS JEFFERSON became president in 1801, the internal revenue program had grown to employ 400 revenue officials, who enforced a wide variety of tax regulations, including taxes on distilled spirits, land, houses, and slaves. Jefferson, a Democrat who fiercely opposed Hamilton and his FEDERALIST PARTY programs, abolished the entire system and relied instead on taxes assessed on imported items for government revenue. When the WAR OF 1812 increased the government's needs for funds, taxes were reimposed on items such as sugar, carriages, liquor, furniture, and other luxury items. At the war's end, all internal taxes and collection offices were abolished, and CUSTOMS DUTIES again became the primary source for government revenue.

When the Civil War broke out in 1861, President ABRAHAM LINCOLN faced a financial crisis because the government needed much more money to finance the war effort than could be raised through customs duties. To address this problem, Congress passed sweeping new tax measures, including the Civil War Revenue Act of August 5, 1861, which authorized the country's first income tax and imposed a DIRECT TAX of $20 million apportioned among the states. The Revenue Act of July 1, 1862, created a wide variety of new taxes. To oversee their collection, Congress created the Bureau of Internal Revenue under the secretary of the treasury. This office, which represents the first form of the modern internal revenue collection system, administered the tax system by dividing the country into 185 collection districts. The commissioner was given the power to enforce tax laws through both seizure and prosecution. George S. Boutwell of Massachusetts was the first commissioner of internal revenue. Boutwell was initially assisted by three clerks. By January 1863 the office had grown to employ nearly 4,000 people, most of whom worked in the field as revenue collectors or property assessors.

When the Civil War ended in 1865, the government's need for revenue was greatly reduced. Taxes were scaled back, the income tax was eliminated, and customs duties again became a sufficient source for federal funds. With the subsequent rise of industrialism and growth of populist political ideas, however, many citizens wanted the government to take a more active role and therefore lobbied for a reestablishment of the income tax to provide greater revenue. Most of the support for an income tax came from southern and western states. Most of the opposition came from the wealthier states whose citizens would be most affected by an income tax—Massachusetts, New Jersey, New York, and Pennsylvania.

After many attempts Congress finally passed a modest income tax in 1894. The Supreme Court quickly ruled it unconstitutional on the ground that it violated the constitutional provision requiring that federal taxes be apportioned equally among the various states. Supporters of the income tax overcame this hurdle in 1913, when Wyoming became the 36th state to ratify the SIXTEENTH AMENDMENT to the Constitution, giving Congress the power to collect taxes without regard to state apportionment. That same year Congress enacted the first income tax act under the amendment, and the income tax became a permanent feature of the U.S. tax system.

The passage of the Sixteenth Amendment marked the beginning of an era of significant expansion for the Bureau of Internal Revenue. The establishment of the Personal Income Tax Division greatly increased bureau staff, and many new taxes were imposed to finance WORLD WAR I, thus requiring new bureau divisions and programs. As the bureau's responsibilities continued to multiply, operations became more inefficient and disorganized. In the 1920s, for example, the national office of the bureau was housed in a dozen different buildings located all around the metropolitan Washington, D.C., area. Tax returns became backlogged, tax fraud and evasion were rampant, and an extensive patronage system enabled politically appointed collectors to operate unchecked, outraging their CIVIL SERVICE staffs. Beginning in 1945 Congress and the Treasury Department began efforts to overhaul the whole tax collection system. In 1952 the Bureau of Internal Revenue was reorganized and given a new name: the Internal Revenue Service. This new moniker was intended to emphasize the agency's focus on providing service to taxpayers. Patronage was eliminated, and power was decentralized, with the states being divided into seven regional districts through which all return processing, auditing, billing, and refunding would be administered.

Since 1952 the IRS has continued to undergo major changes and reorganizations. Advancements in technology have had a tremendous effect on IRS operations, beginning with the opening of the automatic data processing system in Martinsburg, West Virginia, in 1962. This system revolutionized the collection and audit process by enabling the IRS to maintain a master file of every taxpayer's account. More recent technological applications have changed the way taxpayers interact with the IRS. In 1995, for example, more than 14 million individuals and businesses used the IRS electronic filing program to submit their tax returns. Another approximately 685,000 taxpayers in ten states

filed their TAX RETURN using their touch-tone telephone. Taxes were also paid electronically, with more than 41,000 businesses making more than $232 billion in federal tax deposits by electronic funds transfer.

Over the years the IRS has faced continuing pressure from Congress and the public to adopt more reasonable enforcement policies, to provide better service to taxpayers, and to protect private information more carefully. In an attempt to protect taxpayers' rights, Congress in 1988 passed the TAXPAYER BILL OF RIGHTS (Pub. L. No. 100-647, tit. VI, §§ 6226–6247, 102 Stat. 3730–3752 [Nov. 10, 1988]), which outlines the rights and protections a taxpayer has when dealing with the IRS. Included are the right to have penalties waived if the taxpayer follows incorrect advice given by the IRS, the right to request relief when tax laws result in significant hardship, and the right to attorneys' fees in cases where IRS employees violate the Internal Revenue Code to the detriment of the taxpayer.

In 1995 the IRS administrative structure underwent a major reorganization. The seven regions that had been established in 1952 were reduced to four, and management was consolidated, decreasing the number of districts within those regions from 63 to 33.

The IRS came under close examination from Congress in the late 1990s following a series of allegations from taxpayers of improper behavior by IRS agents. In September 1997, over three days of televised hearings, the U.S. Senate Finance Committee heard a litany of horror stories: Taxpayers gave accounts of ruined lives, and IRS agents described a culture of lawlessness that included forgeries, spying, shakedowns, and cover-ups. The dramatic testimony capped a six-month committee probe into IRS misconduct.

The first to testify in the open hearings were taxpayers, from business owners to an elderly priest, who told the panel how unfair IRS audits had led to DIVORCE, BANKRUPTCY, and, in some cases, years of fighting inflexible rules to correct the agency's mistakes. Others said they paid the IRS large sums rather than fight and risk jeopardizing their businesses. Tom Savage, a 69-year-old Delaware construction company owner, told lawmakers that he paid $50,000 in fines despite the fact that the JUSTICE DEPARTMENT told the IRS that levying him was wrong. Another taxpayer, Nancy Jacobs of California, said that the IRS mistakenly assigned her husband a taxpayer identification number belonging to someone else but that she and her husband paid the agency $11,000 to stop enforcement actions in order to save her husband's optometrist practice.

IRS whistle-blowers also testified. Sitting behind screens with their voices garbled electronically to conceal their identities, they accused IRS management of several questionable practices: illegally snooping on private tax data, preying on vulnerable taxpayers, and unduly focusing collection efforts on lower- and middle-class taxpayers. Their chief allegation was that management evaluated employees based on their collection performance. Agents were pressured, they said, to seize as much taxpayer property and assets as possible, in violation of IRS policy and federal law. Jennifer Long, the only agent not to testify behind a curtain with a voice distortion mask, said that agents ignored cheating by friends and by those with resources to fight an audit. Statistics showed that the audit rate for people with annual incomes of more than $100,000 declined from 11.41 percent to 2.79 percent between 1988 and 1995. During that same period, the audit rate for people with annual incomes of less than $25,000 nearly doubled, from 1.03 percent to 1.96 percent.

In 1998 Congress passed the Internal Revenue Service Restructuring and Reform Act of 1998 (IRSRRA), Pub. L. No. 105-206, 112 Stat. 685 (codified in scattered sections of 26 U.S.C.A.), to overhaul operations within the IRS. Title I reorganized the structure and management of the IRS with three sections designed to improve taxpayer treatment. The act directed the commissioner to discard the IRS organizational structure, which had previously run operations through local, regional, and national offices. In its place the commissioner was required to substitute organizational units serving taxpayers with similar tax obligations, such as individuals, small businesses, large businesses, and nonprofit organizations.

The IRSRRA created the Internal Revenue Service Oversight Board, which operates within the DEPARTMENT OF THE TREASURY. The Oversight Board contains nine members, including the secretary of the treasury, the commissioners of the IRS, six civilians, and one federal government employee appointed by the president with the ADVICE AND CONSENT of the Senate. The

board's general responsibility is to oversee the IRS "in its administration, management, conduct, direction, and supervision of the execution and application of the internal revenue laws." Although the board may not view the tax returns of individual taxpayers and, therefore, cannot rectify individual taxpayer abuse, IRSRRA commands the board to ensure that the IRS treats taxpayers properly.

Under the IRSRRA, the commissioner of the IRS must terminate agency employees who engage in a list of forbidden conduct that includes the following: failing to obtain required signatures before seizing homes, personal belongings, and business assets to satisfy tax deficiencies; making a false statement under oath concerning a taxpayer's case; violating a taxpayer's constitutional or CIVIL RIGHTS; falsifying or destroying documents to conceal IRS mistakes; committing ASSAULT or BATTERY on a taxpayer; violating the tax laws or regulations for the purpose of retaliating against or harassing a taxpayer; and threatening to audit a taxpayer to extract a personal benefit. Although a LOOPHOLE allows the commissioner to take personnel action other than termination at his sole discretion, he may not delegate that authority to any other officer.

Title III of IRSRRA contains a Taxpayer BILL OF RIGHTS, also designed to reduce taxpayer abuse. Most notably, it shifts the BURDEN OF PROOF in most tax cases to the IRS. Previously, taxpayers sued by the IRS had the burden of proving that their tax calculation was correct. Under IRSRRA, if a taxpayer keeps the appropriate records, cooperates during IRS investigations, and presents "credible evidence" to support his or her tax calculation, the IRS has the burden of proving the calculation is wrong. The requirement that the taxpayer show credible evidence has proven difficult in some cases. For example, in *Higbee v. Commissioner*, 116 T.C. No. 28 (2001), the U.S. TAX COURT held that the testimony of the taxpayer and a document from a small-claims courts showing damages to a piece of property, which he alleged entitled him to a deduction, did not constitute credible evidence to shift the burden of proof to the IRS.

The Taxpayer Bill of Rights also regulates IRS collection efforts and helps specific groups of taxpayers who might lack power to protect themselves. Some evidence suggests that IRSRRA reduced taxpayer abuse shortly after its enactment. By March 1999, property seizures were down 98 percent from levels two years prior; GARNISHMENT of paychecks and bank accounts were down 75 percent; and liens, which ensure that a tax is paid when property is sold, were down 66 percent. Critics, however, contend that these figures reflect reduced, not better, enforcement efforts caused by IRS employees' fear of losing their jobs for violating the IRSRRA. Moreover, other evidence, addressed in a 2002 article in the *New York Times*, suggests that IRS agents are more likely to subject wage earners to heavy scrutiny over tax returns than they are businesses, trusts, and partnerships.

FURTHER READINGS

Burnham, David. 1989. *A Law unto Itself: Power, Politics, and the IRS.* New York: Random House.

Chommie, John C. 1970. *The Internal Revenue Service.* New York: International Thomson.

Ely, Mark H. 2003. "The 'New' IRS Audits." *The Tax Adviser* 34 (October).

Richardson, Margaret Milner. 1994. "Reinventing the Internal Revenue Service." *Federal Bar Association Section of Taxation Report* 1 (winter).

Treasury Department Web site. Internal Revenue Service Web site. Available online at http://www.irs.gov (accessed August 1, 2009).

U.S. Department of the Treasury. Internal Revenue Service. 1996. *Guide to the Internal Revenue Service.* Washington, D.C.: U.S. Government Printing Office.

Whitman, Donald R., ed. 1983. *Government Agencies.* Westport, CT: Greenwood.

CROSS REFERENCES

Civil Service; Customs Duties; Estate and Gift Taxes; Internal Revenue Code; *Pollock v. Farmers' Loan & Trust Co.*; Taxation; Tax Court; Tax Evasion; Sixteenth Amendment.

INTERNAL WATERS

See INLAND WATERS.

INTERNATIONAL COURT OF JUSTICE

The International Court of Justice (ICJ) is the main judicial tribunal of the UNITED NATIONS, to which all member states are parties. It is often informally referred to as the World Court. The ICJ was established in 1946 by the United Nations (Statute of the International Court of Justice [ICJ Statute], June 26, 1945, 59 Stat. 1055, 3 Bevans 1179). It replaced the former Permanent Court of International Justice, which had operated within The Hague, Netherlands, since 1922. Like its predecessor, the headquarters of the ICJ is also located in the Peace Palace at The Hague.

The function of the ICJ is to resolve disputes between sovereign states. Disputes may be placed before the court by parties upon conditions prescribed by the U.N. Security Council. No state, however, may be subject to the jurisdiction of the court without the state's consent. Consent may be given by express agreement at the time the dispute is presented to the court, by prior agreement to accept the jurisdiction of the court in particular categories of cases, or by treaty provisions with respect to disputes arising from matters covered by the treaty.

Article 36(2) of the court's statute, known as the Optional Clause, allows states to make a unilateral declaration recognizing "as compulsory IPSO FACTO and without special agreement, in relation to any other state accepting the same obligation, the jurisdiction of the Court in all legal disputes."

Many states have accepted the court's jurisdiction under the Optional Clause. A few states have done so with certain restrictions. The United States, for instance, has invoked the so-called self-judging reservation, or Connally Reservation. This reservation allows states to avoid the court's jurisdiction previously accepted under the Optional Clause if they decide not to respond to a particular suit. It is commonly exercised when a state determines that a particular dispute is of domestic rather than international character, and thus domestic jurisdiction applies. If a state invokes the self-judging reservation, another state may also invoke this reservation against that state, and thus a suit against the second state would be dismissed. This is called the rule of reciprocity, and stands for the principle that a state has to respond to a suit brought against it before the ICJ only if the state bringing the suit has also accepted the court's jurisdiction.

Under the ICJ Statute, the ICJ must decide cases in accordance with INTERNATIONAL LAW. This means that the ICJ must apply (1) any international conventions and treaties; (2) international custom; (3) general principles recognized as law by civilized nations; and (4) judicial decisions and the teachings of highly qualified publicists of the various nations.

One common type of conflict presented to the ICJ is treaty interpretation. In these cases the ICJ is asked to resolve disagreements over the meaning and application of terms in treaties

In April 1996, Bosnia went before the International Court of Justice seeking a verdict against Serbia, which it charged had violated the international convention against acts of genocide.

AP IMAGES

formed between two or more countries. Other cases range from nuclear testing and water boundary disputes to conflicts over the military presence of a foreign country.

The ICJ is made up of 15 jurists from different countries. No two judges at any given time may be from the same country. The court's composition is static but generally includes jurists from a variety of cultures.

Despite this diversity in structure, the ICJ has been criticized for favoring established powers. Under articles 3 and 9 of the ICJ Statute, the judges on the ICJ should represent "the main forms of civilization and … principal legal systems of the world." This definition suggests that the ICJ does not represent the interests of developing countries. Indeed, few Latin American countries have acquiesced to the jurisdiction of the ICJ. Conversely, most developed countries accept the compulsory jurisdiction of the ICJ.

The judgment of the ICJ is binding and (technically) cannot be appealed (arts. 59, 60) once the parties have consented to its jurisdiction and the court has rendered a decision. However, a state's failure to comply with the judgment violates the U.N. Charter, article 94(2). Noncompliance can be appealed to the U.N. Security Council, which may either make recommendations or authorize other measures by which the judgment shall be enforced. A decision by the Security Council to enforce compliance with a

judgment rendered by the court is subject to the veto power of permanent members, and thus depends on the members' willingness not only to resort to enforcement measures but also to support the original judgment.

The ICJ also may render advisory opinions on legal questions when requested to do so by the General Assembly, the Security Council, or other U.N. organs or agencies. For example, the World Health Organization and the General Assembly requested advisory opinions on the legality of NUCLEAR WEAPONS under international law. The World Court held hearings, in which 45 nations testified. It issued an ADVISORY OPINION in July 1996, which held that it was illegal for a nation to threaten nuclear war. The court is used infrequently, which suggests that most states prefer to handle their disputes by political means or by recourse to tribunals where the outcome may be more predictable or better controlled by the parties.

Since 2000 some of the contentious cases before the ICJ included a property dispute between Liechtenstein and Germany; a territorial and maritime dispute between Nicaragua and Colombia; a land, island, and frontier dispute between El Salvador and the Honduras (Nicaragua intervening); and a 2003 case by Mexico against the United States over alleged violations of consular communications with—and access to—several Mexican nationals sentenced to death in various U.S. states for crimes committed within. A 1993 case filed by Bosnia against the former Yugoslavia for violating the GENOCIDE Convention was still pending in 2003, as was a matter between the Republic of Congo and France over alleged crimes against humanity. Trials against individuals for alleged WAR CRIMES against humanity or genocides involving Bosnia, Croatia, Kosovo, Serbia, and the former Yugoslavia were being handled by the International Criminal Tribunal for the former Yugoslavia, a separate U.N. tribunal.

The ICJ has been maligned for the inconsistency of its decisions and its lack of real enforcement power. But its ambitious mission to resolve disputes between sovereign nations makes it a valuable source of support for many countries in their political interaction with other countries.

FURTHER READINGS

International Court of Justice. Available online at http://www.icj-cij.org (accessed August 1, 2009).

Kelly, Barbara. 1992. "The International Court of Justice: Its Role in a New World Legal Order." *Touro Journal of Transnational Law* 3.

Lelewer, Joanne K. 1989. "International Commercial Arbitration as a Model for Resolving Treaty Disputes." *New York Univ. Journal of International Law and Policy* 21.

Levarda, Daniela. 1995. "A Comparative Study of U.S. and British Approaches to Discovery Conflicts: Achieving a Uniform System of Extraterritorial Discovery." *Fordham International Law Journal* 18. Available online at http://members.cox.net/sbettwy/Comparative9assignedDiscoveryUK.htm; website home page: http://members.cox.net (accessed August 1, 2009).

CROSS REFERENCES

International Law; Ipso Facto; United Nations.

INTERNATIONAL CRIMINAL COURT

The International Criminal Court is a permanent tribunal empowered by the United Nations to prosecute individuals for acts of genocide, crimes against humanity, war crimes, and crimes of aggression.

The UNITED NATIONS established the International Criminal Court (ICC) with the signing of the Rome Treaty in 1998. The court is the first permanent international criminal tribunal, which came into force on July 1, 2002. As of December 2009, a total of 110 states have become members of the court. Another 38 states have signed the Romo Statute but have refused to ratify it. The United States signed the treaty on December 31, 2000, but later withdrew due to questions about the court's powers to PROSECUTE U.S. soldiers sent on peacekeeping missions.

International support for a permanent international tribunal to try WAR CRIMES and other atrocities began with the creation of war crimes courts at Nuremburg and Tokyo following WORLD WAR II. However, tensions during the COLD WAR prevented the development of the tribunal. Some courts were established for crimes in specific areas of the world, however. Such courts were created during the 1990s to try war crimes in the former Yugoslavia and Rwanda for crimes against humanity.

As the United Nations considered the establishment of an international criminal court, the general consensus among nations was that it should only have the power to hear cases involving major atrocities, such as GENOCIDE, war crimes, and crimes against humanity. Nations posed several questions, including those related to the powers the court should have and the

procedures by which the court should determine the cases that should be prosecuted. During the treaty's development, the United States proposed that the five permanent members of the U.N. Security Council should be permitted to veto any prosecution.

U.N. delegates in July 1998, without approval from the United States, approved the Rome Treaty by a vote of 120-7. The approval took place at the United Nations Diplomatic Conference of Plenipotentiaries on the Establishment of an International Criminal Court. Twenty-one nations abstained from signing the treaty.

Diplomats from the United States reiterated concerns that the court could be used to prosecute troops based on the political motivations of other nations. Many of the traditional allies of the United States, including Great Britain, Australia, and France, signed the treaty notwithstanding U.S. opposition. The United States garnered unusual support for such nations as Libya and China. The United States offered an amendment to the treaty that would have exempted members of peacekeeping forces and others from prosecution for actions during the engagement of their official duties, unless their home countries consented to trials. The vast majority of nations rejected the proposed amendment.

The treaty needed to be ratified by 60 nations for it to go into effect. The United States was one of 139 nations to sign the treaty by December 31, 2000, but several nations did not ratify the creation of the court until after that date. The 60th nation ratified the court on April 11, 2002, at a special event at the United Nations.

Former president BILL CLINTON approved the treaty even though members of Congress and members of his own administration had expressed concerns about the court's powers. Several conservative members of Congress, including former senator JESSE HELMS, vowed to fight the ratification of the treaty. The issue arose during confirmation hearings of the cabinet members of former president GEORGE W. BUSH.

In May 2002 the U.S. STATE DEPARTMENT submitted a letter to the secretary-general of the U.N. to inform the United Nations that the United States could not become a party to the treaty. U.S. ambassadors were instructed to explain the position of the United States to other nations. According to Bush, the court would not guarantee that U.S. citizens would enjoy rights guaranteed by the U.S. Constitution. Moreover, the court lacks a system of checks and balances, according to Bush's statements.

The three major categories of cases that the court can hear include genocide, crimes against humanity, and war crimes. Genocide includes intent by an individual or nation to destroy a national, ethnic, racial, or religious group. Crimes against humanity include MURDER, RAPE, sexual SLAVERY, and other acts of aggression. War crimes include any of a number of activities that violate generally accepted RULES OF WAR.

The ICC may sentence an individual to up to 30 years INCARCERATION or life imprisonment if the crime necessitates it. The court may also fine a convicted person and order the FORFEITURE of the property, proceeds, or assets that were received from the crime. In some instances, the court may order that the DEFENDANT pay reparations for damages and losses. The court cannot sentence a defendant to death.

The ICC is designated to complement national courts, rather than to impede their jurisdiction. The court only acts when a national court is unwilling or unable to prosecute an individual for a type of crime over which the court has jurisdiction. The prosecutor of the court, a party to the treaty, or the Security Council may initiate a prosecution. The court does not have jurisdiction to try cases involving crimes committee before July 1, 2002. Virtually anyone who is a citizen of a party to the treaty may be prosecuted by the ICC, which includes heads of state and soldiers who commit crimes, even if the soldier is acting under orders from a superior.

As of December 2009, three parties to the Rome Statute have referred situations occurring in their territories to the ICC. These parties include Uganda, the Democratic Republic of the Congo, and the Central African Republic. Moreover, the U.N. Security Council referred a situation occurring in Darfur, Sudan. The court has indicted a total of 14 people, though two of these individuals died after the indictment.

FURTHER READINGS

Feinstein, Lee. 2009. *Means to an End: U.S. Interest in the International Criminal Court.* Washington, D.C.: Brookings Institution Press.

Podgor, Ellen S. 2008. *Understanding International Criminal Law.* Newark, N.J.: LexisNexis.

Schiff, Benjamin N. 2008. *Building the International Criminal Court.* New York: Cambridge Univ. Press.

CROSS REFERENCES

Criminal Law; International Law

INTERNATIONAL LAW

The body of law that governs the legal relations between or among states or nations.

To qualify as a subject under the traditional definition of international law, a state had to be sovereign: It needed a territory, a population, a government, and the ability to engage in diplomatic or foreign relations. States within the United States, provinces, and cantons were not considered subjects of international law, because they lacked the legal authority to engage in foreign relations. In addition, individuals did not fall within the definition of subjects that enjoyed rights and obligations under international law.

A more contemporary definition expands the traditional notions of international law to confer rights and obligations on intergovernmental international organizations and even on individuals. The UNITED NATIONS, for example, is an international organization that has the capacity to engage in treaty relations governed by, and binding under, international law with states and other international organizations. Individual responsibility under international law is particularly significant in the context of prosecuting war criminals and the development of international HUMAN RIGHTS.

Sources of International Law

The INTERNATIONAL COURT OF JUSTICE (ICJ) was established in 1945 as the successor to the Permanent International Court of Justice (PICJ), which was created in 1920 under the supervision of the LEAGUE OF NATIONS (the precursor to the United Nations). The PICJ ceased to function during WORLD WAR II and was officially dissolved in 1946. The ICJ is a permanent international court located in the Hague, Netherlands, and it is the principal judicial organ of the United Nations (UN). It consists of 15 judges, each from a different state. The judges are elected by the UN General Assembly and the UN Security Council and must receive an absolute majority from both in order to take office.

The ICJ has jurisdiction only over states that have consented to it. It follows that the court cannot hear a dispute between two or more state parties when one of the parties has not accepted its jurisdiction. This can happen even where the non-consenting party adheres to the court's statute, for mere adherence to the statute does not imply consent to its tribunals. In addition, the court does not have jurisdiction over disputes between individuals or entities that are not states (I.C.J. Stat. art. 34(1)). It also lacks jurisdiction over matters that are governed by domestic law instead of international law (art. 38(1)).

Article 38(1) of the ICJ Statute enumerates the sources of international law and provides that international law has its basis in international custom, international conventions or treaties, and general principles of law. A rule must derive from one of these three sources in order to be considered international law.

In 2008 the U.S. Supreme Court rendered a controversial decision concluding that a U.S. court was not bound by an ICJ decision citing the United States for violation of the Vienna Convention rights of 51 Mexican nationals. *Medellin v. Texas*, 552 U.S. ___, 128 S.Ct. 1346 (2008). This was the second time the matter had come before the high court.

Medellin, a Mexican national, and six other members of the "Blacks and Whites" gang raped and murdered two young girls in Texas, then bragged about it to family members. One family member called the police, and all gang members were eventually arrested. Medellin was tried and convicted in a Texas state court and sentenced to death. The Texas Court of Criminal Appeals affirmed his CONVICTION and sentence on direct appeal, and the U.S. Supreme Court, after hearing oral arguments, denied CERTIORARI review as improvidently granted. *Medellin v. Dretke*, 544 U.S. 660 (2005).

Meanwhile, the Mexican government initiated proceedings against the United States in the ICJ, alleging violations of the Vienna Convention on behalf of more than 50 Mexican nationals facing the death penalty in the United States, including Medellin. *Case Concerning Avena and other Mexican Nationals (Mexico v. U.S.)*, 2004 I.C.J. No. 128 (later referred to as the Avena decision). Essentially, the petition argued that the Mexican nationals had been denied their right under Article 36 of the

Vienna Convention to contact their consulate after being detained for a crime. The ICJ determined that the Vienna Convention indeed guaranteed individually enforceable rights of access to the Mexican consulate. While denying Mexico's request that the convictions and sentences be nullified, the ICJ decision held that the United States must reconsider the convictions. Both MEXICO AND THE UNITED STATES voted with the majority in the 14-1 decision; Venezuela was the lone dissenting member.

President GEORGE W. BUSH had issued a memorandum stating that the United States would meet its international obligations under the *Avena* judgment by "having State Courts give effect to the [ICJ] decision in accordance with general principles of COMITY in cases filed by the 51 Mexican nationals addressed in that decision." It was his memorandum that became the focus in the second (2008) case. Ultimately, the Supreme Court held that the Texas courts were not bound by the ICJ because the signed Protocol of the Vienna Convention did not render the treaty SELF-EXECUTING. Until it was enacted into law by Congress, it was not binding on state courts. As to President Bush's memorandum, the Court characterized it as an attempt by the EXECUTIVE BRANCH to enforce a non-self-executing treaty without the necessary action by Congress.

Custom Customary international law is defined as a general practice of law under article 38(1)(b). States follow such a practice out of a sense of legal obligation. Rules or principles must be accepted by the states as legally binding in order to be considered rules of international law. Thus, the mere fact that a custom is widely followed does not make it a rule of international law. States also must view it as obligatory to follow the custom, and they must not believe that they are free to depart from it whenever they choose, or to observe it only as a matter of courtesy or moral obligation. This requirement is referred to as *opinio juris*.

Some criticism against customary international law is directed at its subjective character and its inconsistency. States vary greatly in their opinions and interpretations of issues regarding international law. Thus, it is almost impossible to find enough consistency among states to draw a customary international rule from general practice. In addition, even if one state or judge finds that a practice is a rule of customary international law, another decision maker might reach a different conclusion. Altogether, the process of establishing rules of customary international law is lengthy and impeded by today's fast-changing world.

Conventions and Treaties Conventional international law includes international agreements and legislative treaties that establish rules expressly recognized by consenting states. Only states that are parties to a treaty are bound by it. However, a very large number of states voluntarily adhere to treaties and accept their provisions as law, even without becoming parties to them. The most important treaties in this regard are the GENOCIDE Convention, the Vienna Conventions, and the provisions of the UN Charter.

UN Charter and United Nations

The UN Charter and the United Nations as an organization were established on October 26, 1945. The UN Charter is a multilateral treaty that serves as the organization's constitution. It contains a SUPREMACY CLAUSE that makes it the highest authority of international law. The clause states that the UN Charter shall prevail in the event of a conflict between the obligations of the members of the United Nations under the present charter and their obligations under any other international agreement (art. 103).

At its formation, the United Nations had 51 member states. Its membership had increased to 180 states in 1996, including almost all of the world's independent nations. The United Nations is designed to serve a multitude of purposes and is charged with a variety of responsibilities. Among these are peacekeeping; developing friendly relations among nations; achieving international cooperation in solving international problems of an economic, social, cultural, and humanitarian character; and promoting human rights and fundamental freedoms for all human beings without discrimination (UN Charter art. 1).

The United Nations comprises the Trusteeship Council, the General Assembly, the Security Council, the Economic and Social Council, and the ICJ. The Trusteeship Council's role is to supervise the administration of non-self-governing territories. Because all of these territories have now gained independence, the last one being Palau in 1993, the Trusteeship Council is no longer functional within the United Nations.

The General Assembly and the Security Council are the components of the organization that are most involved in lawmaking and legislative activities. Their respective authority varies greatly. Although the General Assembly lacks formal legislative authority to adopt resolutions that are binding on its members, it is highly active in the making and development of international law. This organ of the United Nations is required to initiate studies and to make recommendations that encourage the progressive development of international law and its CODIFICATION (UN Charter art. 13(1)(a)). Within this context, the General Assembly has originated much of the existing international legislation, and some of its resolutions are now accepted as customary international law, such as the Universal Declaration of Human Rights. Thus, resolutions adopted by the General Assembly, albeit formally considered non-binding, have legal character and contribute significantly to the development of international law.

The Security Council, on the other hand, has the authority to adopt binding decisions, and non-compliance with these decisions constitutes a violation of the UN Charter. However, this does not give the Security Council a general lawmaking authority, as its SUBJECT MATTER JURISDICTION is limited to concerns of international peace and security. According to the UN Charter, article 2(3), all nations are required to settle their disputes by peaceful means in such a manner that international peace, security, and justice are not endangered. Nations are advised to resort to peaceful dispute-settlement mechanisms (art. 33(1)) such as negotiation, mediation, and CONCILIATION. Where these measures fail, the parties must refer to the UN Security Council if their proposed measure would be a threat to peace and security. The Security Council then makes recommendations on further peaceful measures, and it resorts to the powers conferred on it under the UN Charter for its peacekeeping operations. The General Assembly's role in peacekeeping focuses mainly on providing a forum for public discussion of the issues. However, the assembly does have the power to bring issues that potentially endanger the peace before the Security Council.

In some cases, the Security Council fails to exercise its responsibility for maintaining international peace and security, and there is a threat to peace or an act of aggression. The General Assembly or Security Council may make appropriate recommendations and may authorize the threat of economic sanctions or the use of armed forces to maintain or restore international peace and security.

The UN Peacekeeping Forces are employed by the World Organization and may function either as unarmed observer forces, or armed military forces. Their presence in areas of conflict is intended as an incentive to either prevent or reduce the level of conflict. Both parties to a conflict must accept their presence.

However, the United Nations generally has not been very effective in *preventing* hostilities that involve the world's principal powers, either directly or indirectly. For example, in 1993 the second UN peace operation, UNOSOM II, was intended to assist in rebuilding Somalia and in disarming warring factions there. It met with stiff resistance, culminating in the public deaths of 18 U.S. troops serving with the operation. When the United States announced its withdrawal, the entire operation began to wind down, while the war continued unabated. Serious debate broke out within the UN over the scope and mission of peacekeeping functions, resulting in a general disengagement in such efforts. Sadly, even efforts to respond to the genocide in Rwanda subsequently failed.

Another area of intense UN deliberations has been the Middle East. In 1990 the UN Security Council imposed comprehensive economic sanctions against Iraq following its invasion of Kuwait. The efforts failed to deter Iraq's leader, Saddam Hussein. The following year, the United States led allied forces to expel Iraqi forces from Kuwait during the 1991 Persian Gulf War. Following that conflict, UN Security Council Resolution 687 required Iraq to destroy its arsenal of nuclear, chemical, and biological weapons, and to submit to UN inspection for compliance.

Over the next several years, despite Iraqi efforts to conceal them, such weapons were indeed found and destroyed by UN inspectors. However, the inspectors left in 1998, following U.S. and British air strikes bent on speeding up the process and destroying concealed weapons. When economic sanctions against Iraq failed to punish anyone but the Iraqi people, the UN began a humanitarian "Oil for Food" program, again with little impact. After 12 years of failed economic sanctions against Iraq, the United States petitioned the UN for international support and a coalition of military forces to oust the Hussein regime. The measure was vetoed by several superpowers, which favored the continuance of UN inspections. In early 2003 the United States and the United Kingdom, supported by several other smaller powers, conducted military strikes on Iraq and eliminated Saddam Hussein's regime. After the fact, the UN agreed to assist in peacekeeping while a new Iraqi government was organized and instituted.

UN peacekeepers have been increasingly charged with assisting electoral and political processes, reforming judicial decisions, disarming and reintegrating former combatants, and supporting the return of refugees. UN peacekeeping missions supported the election processes in several post-conflict countries such as Nepal, Afghanistan, Haiti, Liberia, and Iraq. As of 2009, there were almost 116,000 personnel serving on 17 peace operations. As of April 2009, 117 countries contributed military and police personnel to UN peacekeeping. The top providers of troops were Pakistan, Bangladesh, and India. The top providers of funds for the peacekeeping budget were the United States and Japan.

The UN Charter includes a general provision that concerns the human rights of the individual. On December 10, 1948, the United Nations adopted the Universal Declaration of Human Rights, which defines and enumerates specifically the human rights that the United Nations seeks to protect. Among those are freedom from systematic governmental acts and policies involving torture, SLAVERY, MURDER, prolonged arbitrary DETENTION, disappearance, and racial discrimination. The declaration guarantees the right to life; to EQUAL PROTECTION of the law; to free speech, assembly, and movement; to privacy; to work; to education; to health care; and to participation in the cultural life of the community. Although the Universal Declaration is not a binding instrument of international law, some of its provisions nonetheless have reached the status of customary international law. Under Articles 55 and 56 of the UN Charter, member states have an obligation to promote these rights. At the same time, the declaration acknowledges that states may limit these rights as they deem necessary, to ensure respect for the rights and freedoms of others.

In 1966 the UN General Assembly adopted three covenants that involve human rights: the International COVENANT on Civil and Political Rights; the International Covenant on Economic, Social, and Cultural Rights; and the Optional Protocol to the Civil and Political Covenant.

Unlike the Universal Declaration, these covenants are treaties that require ratification by member states. The United States is not a party to the covenants.

The human rights provisions of the UN Charter, the Universal Declaration of Human Rights, and the covenants constitute the International Bill of Human Rights. Other UN human rights instruments supplement this bill. The most important ones are the Genocide Convention (1948); the International Convention on the Elimination of All Forms of Racial Discrimination (1965); the Convention on the Political Rights of Women (1953); and the International Convention on the Suppression and Punishment of the Crime of Apartheid (1973). These conventions are legally binding on the parties that have ratified them. Most of the UN member states have ratified at least two: the Genocide Convention and the Racial Convention. The United States has ratified only the Women's Rights Convention and the Genocide Convention.

FURTHER READINGS

August, Ray. 1995. *Public International Law: Text, Cases, Readings.* Englewood Cliffs, N.J.: Prentice-Hall.

Janis, Mark W. 1988. *An Introduction to International Law.* Boston: Little, Brown.

"Size of UN Peacekeeping Forces: 1947–2001."; "Sanctions against Iraq"; "Weapons Inspection Program." 2002. Excerpted from *Iraq Crisis.* Available online at www.globalpolicy.org/security/peacekpg/data/pcekprs1.htm> (accessed November 20, 2003).

"United Nations Peacekeeping." Available online at www.una-uk.org/UN&UC/Peacekeeping.html (accessed November 20, 2003).

United Nations Peacekeeping. "Fact Sheet." Available online at home page and www.un.org/Depts/dpko/dpko/overview.shtml; website home page: www.un.org/Depts/dpko/dpko/ (accessed August 30, 2009)

CROSS REFERENCES

Ambassadors and Consuls; Arms Control and Disarmament; General Agreement on Tariffs and Trade; Geneva Conventions, 1949; Genocide; Hague Tribunal; International Court of Justice; Law of Nations; North American Free Trade Agreement; War

INTERNATIONAL MONETARY FUND

The International Monetary Fund (IMF) is a specialized agency of the UNITED NATIONS that seeks to promote international monetary cooperation and to stimulate international trade. The IMF, which had 186 nation-members as of 2009, has worked to stabilize world currencies and to develop programs of economic adjustment for nations that require economic reform.

The International Monetary Fund (IMF) was created in 1944 at the United Nations Monetary and Financial Conference held at Bretton Woods, New Hampshire. It first began operation in 1947 from its headquarters in Washington, D.C., with a fund of $9 billion in currency, of which the United States contributed almost a third. The creation of the IMF was seen as a way to prevent retaliatory currency devaluations and trade restrictions, which were seen as a major cause of the worldwide depression prior to WORLD WAR II.

Membership is open to countries willing to abide by terms established by the board of governors, which is composed of a representative from each member nation. General terms include obligations to avoid manipulating exchange rates, abstain from discriminatory currency practices, and refrain from imposing restrictions on the making of payments and currency transfers necessary to foreign trade.

The voting power of the governors is allocated according to the size of the quota of each member. The term *quota* refers to the IMF unit of account, which is based on each member's relative position in the world economy. This position is measured by the size of the country's economy, foreign trade, and relative importance in the international monetary system. Once a quota is set by the IMF, the country must deposit with the organization an amount equal to the size of the quota as a subscription. Up to three-fourths of a subscription may consist of the currency of the subscribing nation. Each subscription forms part of the reserve available to countries suffering from balance-of-payment problems.

When a member has a balance-of-payment problem, it may apply to the IMF for needed foreign currency from the reserve derived from its quota. The member may use this foreign exchange for up to five years to help solve its problems, and then return the currency to the IMF pool of resources. The IMF offers below-market rates of interest for using these funds. The member country whose currency is used receives most of the interest. A small amount goes to the IMF for operating expenses.

In its early years the IMF directed its major programs toward maintaining fixed exchange rates linked to the U.S. dollar, which in turn could be converted at a standard rate into gold. Present IMF policy emphasizes an orderly adjustment of currency exchange rates to reflect underlying economic forces. Special attention has been given to the needs of developing countries, in the form of programs to provide long-term assistance to cover foreign exchange demands necessitated by high import prices, declining export earnings, or development programs. In appropriate circumstances, the IMF may impose conditions on the use of IMF resources to encourage recipient countries to make needed economic reforms.

Since 1982 the IMF has concentrated on the problems of developing nations. It has gone beyond its own resources, encouraging additional lending from commercial banks. The IMF has also established new programs, using funds from its richer members, to provide money in larger amounts and for longer periods than those granted under the quota-driven lending procedures. It works closely with the WORLD BANK on these and other international monetary issues.

Starting in the 1990s, the IMF faced enormous economic challenges propelled by the increasing globalization of the world economy. Among the problems were the need to help a number of countries make the transition from a centrally-planned economic system to a market-oriented one, reducing turbulence in emerging financial markets such as Asia and Latin America, and promoting economic growth in the poorest nations. The IMF responded with a number of initiatives including creation of a loan fund to ensure sufficient funds to deal with major financial crises, a new approach to reducing poverty in low-income countries, and the Supplemental Reserve Facility created in 1997 specifically to help countries deal with large short-term financing needs resulting from a sudden reduction in capital outflows due to loss of market confidence.

Despite these moves, the IMF faced an increasing volume of worldwide criticism and protest against its fiscal policies in the late 1990s and early 2000s. A number of economists and other critics charged that IMF loan programs imposed on governments of developing countries resulted in severe economic pain for the populations of those countries, that IMF policies were poorly designed and often aggravated economic conditions in countries experiencing debt or currency crises, and that the IMF has forced

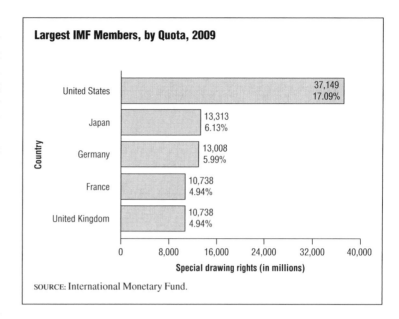

Largest IMF Members, by Quota, 2009

United States — 37,149 / 17.09%
Japan — 13,313 / 6.13%
Germany — 13,008 / 5.99%
France — 10,738 / 4.94%
United Kingdom — 10,738 / 4.94%

(x-axis: 0, 8,000, 16,000, 24,000, 32,000, 40,000)
Special drawing rights (in millions)
(y-axis: Country)

SOURCE: International Monetary Fund.

countries to borrow foreign capital in a manner that adversely affects them.

In 2000 the managing director and members of the IMF agreed on several governing principles including the promotion of sustained non-inflationary economic growth, encouraging the stability of the international finance system, focusing on core macroeconomic and financial areas and being an open institution that learns from experience and continually adapts to changing circumstances.

In 2008 the IMF revealed a new income and expenditure framework for the organization. Included in the new framework are various efforts designed to overcome its budget deficit, which is projected to be nearly $400 million by 2010. These efforts include an agreement to sell a portion of its gold holdings and implementation of sharp spending cuts totaling $100 million. The spending cuts include layoffs of up to 400 of the fund's employees, the highest percentage of job cuts since the organization's inception.

ILLUSTRATION BY GGS CREATIVE RESOURCES. REPRODUCED BY PERMISSION OF GALE, A PART OF CENGAGE LEARNING.

FURTHER READINGS

Davis, Bob. 2007. "IMF Plans to Cut Jobs, Lift Income." *Wall Street Journal* (December 7).

Humphreys, Norman K. 1999. *Historical Dictionary of the International Monetary Fund.* Lanham, MD: Scarecrow Press, Inc.

International Monetary Fund. Available online at http://www.imf.org (accessed June 10, 2009).

Landler, Mark. 2008. "Scandal Hinders I.M.F.'s Role in Global Lending." *New York Times* (October 21).

Rogoff, Kenneth. 2003. "The IMF Strikes Back." *Foreign Policy* January 1.

CROSS REFERENCES
International Law; United Nations; World Bank.

INTERNATIONAL TECHNOLOGY LAW ASSOCIATION

The International Technology Law Association, often referred to as ITechLaw, is one of the largest associations of legal professionals focused on technology and the law. It was founded in 1971 and incorporated in 1973 as the Computer Law Association. It was formed to fill the need for mutual education by lawyers concerned with the unique legal considerations related to the evolution, production, marketing, acquisition, and use of computer communications technology. It was originally open only to lawyers and law students. In 2006, it changed its name from the Computer Law Association to the International Technology Law Association to better reflect its international membership, global activities, and expanded focus. In 2008, it broadened its membership from lawyers and law students to include other professionals interested in technology law issues. The organization has over 1,000 members worldwide, representing six continents.

In addition to serving as a forum for members to discuss a wide range of legal issues and publishing the *ITechLaw eBulletin*, the association regularly organizes conferences that explore cutting-edge issues and trends in both information technology and intellectual PROPERTY LAW. Conferences take place in the United States, Europe, and Asia. It also sponsors webinars on technology-and-law issues that are open to both members and non-members, and runs a social networking site, called ITechLaw Connect, that allows members to participate in committee forums, access information, and take part in discussions.

The International Technology Law Association is headed by a president and an executive committee that reports to a board of directors. It also has an advisory board. Its mission is to "create unparalleled opportunities for international networking and exchanging knowledge and experience with experts and colleagues around the world."

Web site: www.itechlaw.org (accessed December 16, 2009).

CROSS REFERENCES
Computer Crime; Copyright.

INTERNATIONAL TRADE ORGANIZATION

Prior to WORLD WAR II, many countries employed "beggar thy neighbor" trade policies, raising tariffs and instituting non-tariff barriers that impede imports in an attempt to reduce unemployment and increase domestic output. However, other countries retaliated by raising their own barriers against imports. This resulted in reducing export markets, which then only worsened the already poor economic conditions. The problems created by such policies led United States to propose that a new international trade organization be established to regulate trade policies and settle disputes between trading partners. Under the U.S. proposal, the International Trade Organization (ITO) was to be a specialized agency of the UNITED NATIONS and was to have several broad functions: promoting the growth of trade by eliminating or reducing tariffs or other barriers to trade; regulating restrictive business practices hampering trade; regulating international COMMODITY agreements; assisting economic development and reconstruction; and settling disputes among member nations regarding harmful trade policies. Negotiations to establish the ITO began in Geneva, Switzerland, in 1947, with a more complete charter being drafted later in Havana, Cuba. Opposition to the charter of the ITO soon emerged, especially in the U.S. Congress. Subsequently, President HARRY TRUMAN's administration withdrew its support for the ITO, and interest in the ITO faded. The void left by the collapse of the ITO has been filled by other institutions, like the GENERAL AGREEMENT ON TARIFFS AND TRADE (GATT), the WORLD BANK, and the United Nations Conference on Trade and Development (UNCTAD).

INTERNATIONAL WATERWAYS

Narrow channels of marginal sea or inland waters through which international shipping has a right of passage.

In INTERNATIONAL LAW, INTERNATIONAL WATERWAYS are straits, canals, and rivers that connect two areas of the high seas or enable ocean shipping to reach interior ports on international seas, gulfs, or lakes that otherwise would be landlocked. International waterways also may be rivers that serve as international boundaries or traverse successively two or more states. Ships have a right of passage through international waterways. This right is based on customary international law and treaty arrangements.

Straits

Some straits are more important than others because they are the sole connecting links between oceans and interior waters. For example, the Strait of Gibraltar gives access from the Atlantic Ocean to the Mediterranean and Aegean Seas. Other straits are not as important. The availability of alternate routes does not in itself deprive a strait of its character as an international waterway. In the *Corfu Channel* case, 1949 I.C.J. 4, 1949 WL 1 (I.C.J.), the INTERNATIONAL COURT OF JUSTICE rejected the test of essentiality as the only route, ruling that "the decisive criterion is rather [the strait's] geographic situation as connecting two parts of the high seas and the fact of its being used for international navigation."

The 1958 Geneva Convention on the Territorial Sea and Contiguous Zone (516 U. N.T.S. 205, 15 U.S.T. 1606, T.I.A.S. No. 5639) does not deal comprehensively with international waterways, but does provide that "[t]here shall be no suspension of innocent passage of foreign ships through straits which are used for international navigation between one part of the high seas and another part of the high seas or the territorial sea of a foreign state" (art. 16, § 4). A territorial sea is the water that comes under the sovereign control of a state.

A coastal state has somewhat greater control of innocent passage through its territorial seas than of innocent passage through a strait joining two areas of high seas. Passage may be suspended through TERRITORIAL WATERS when essential for security. This means that warships are free to pass through straits but may be denied access to territorial seas.

Since the 1960s a great majority of coastal states have extended their claims on territorial seas from three miles to 12 miles from the low-water mark, some even farther. This change has been a matter of concern to the U.S. government, as a 12-mile limit converts 121 straits to territorial seas, some of which have strategic military importance.

Canals

With respect to international marine traffic, canals joining areas of the high seas or waters leading to them are geographically in the same position as straits. However, the significant canals have been constructed in accordance with international treaties or later placed under conventional legal regimes. The Suez Canal,

located in Egypt, and the Panama Canal are the two most important canals in international commerce.

The United States played the major role in the construction of the Panama Canal, which joins the Atlantic and Pacific Oceans across the Isthmus of Panama. The canal is more than 40 miles long and has a minimum width of three hundred feet.

In 1903, after several European-financed efforts to build a canal across the isthmus had failed, the U.S. government negotiated the Hay-Bunau-Varilla Treaty (T.S. No. 431, 33 Stat. 2234, 10 Bevans 663). Under this treaty the United States guaranteed the independence of Panama (which had just broken away from Colombia) and secured a perpetual lease on a ten-mile strip for the canal. Panama was to receive an initial payment of $10 million and an annuity of $250,000, beginning in 1913.

In 1906 President THEODORE ROOSEVELT directed construction of the canal to begin under the supervision of the U.S. Army Corps of Engineers. The Panama Canal was completed in 1914 and officially opened by President WOODROW WILSON on July 12, 1920.

The Hay-Bunau-Varilla Treaty stated that the canal was to be neutralized and free and open to vessels of commerce and war on terms of equality, and without discrimination as to tolls or conditions of passage. However, it did not mandate open access in times of war. The United States decided, in 1917, to close the canal and the territorial waters of the canal zone

Spanish King Juan Carlos and former President Jimmy Carter shake hands at a December 1999 ceremony transferring control of the Panama Canal to Panama. President Mireya Moscoso of Panama (sitting) looks on.

AP IMAGES

(the ten-mile-wide strip of land that contained the canal) to vessels of enemy states and their allies whenever the United States is a belligerent. This was done in World Wars I and II.

From the 1920s to the 1970s, the United States and Panama had many disputes concerning control of the Panama Canal Zone. Panamanians came to regard the zone as part of their country and believed that the 1903 treaty was unfairly favorable to the United States. In 1971 the two countries began negotiations for a new treaty to replace the 1903 agreement.

In 1977 Panama and the United States concluded the Treaty Governing the Permanent NEUTRALITY and Operation of the Panama Canal, and the Panama Canal Treaty (both Washington, D.C., 1977, in force 1979; *Digest of United States Practice in International Law,* 1978, at 1028–560). The treaties provided that the United States would relinquish control and administration of the canal to Panama by December 31, 1999, and stipulated an interim period for the training of, and progressive transfer of functions to, Panamanian personnel under the supervision of a mixed Panama Canal Commission.

The first treaty declared that the canal would be permanently neutralized (as would any other international waterway later constructed wholly or partly in Panamanian territory), with the object of securing it for peaceful transit in time of peace or of war for vessels of all nations on equal terms (arts. 1, 2). The right of passage extends not only to merchant ships but to vessels of war and auxiliary vessels in noncommercial service of all nations "at all times," irrespective of their internal operations, means of propulsion, origin, destination, or armament (art. 3, § 1[e]).

In early December 1999 a United States delegation, headed by former U.S. president JIMMY CARTER (who signed the original treaty in 1977), attended the official transfer of the canal into Panamanian hands. Other attendees included Spain's King Juan Carlos, and the presidents of Bolivia, Columbia, Ecuador, and Mexico. As of 2000, it was estimated that approximately 1,400 ships pass through the canal annually.

Rivers

Customary international law has never granted equal access and rights to countries that share navigable rivers either as boundaries between them or as waterways that traverse them successively. Freer use of international rivers has occurred in the nineteenth and twentieth centuries through the negotiation of treaties.

The St. Lawrence Seaway, opened for navigation by large ships in 1959, is an example of a legal and an administrative regime wholly devised and controlled by the two states (the United States and Canada) that share it. Based on a river in part, the seaway was developed with the construction of bypass canals, locks, and channel improvements, sometimes wholly within the territory of one state. In 1909 CANADA AND THE UNITED STATES consolidated and extended a number of earlier piecemeal arrangements in the Boundary Waters Treaty (36 Stat. 2448, 12 Bevans 359), to give both nations equal liberty of navigation in the St. Lawrence River, the Great Lakes, and the canals and waterways connecting the lakes. An international boundary line was drawn generally along the median line of the lakes (with some variation in Lake Michigan), but both nations were to exercise concurrent admiralty and criminal jurisdiction over the whole of the lakes and their connecting waterways. The admiralty jurisdiction reflected a disposition to treat the lakes as the high seas. This view was supported by the U.S. Supreme Court in *United States v. Rodgers,* 150 U.S. 249, 14 S. Ct. 109, 37 L. Ed. 1071 (1893), when it referred to the "high seas of the lakes."

The building of the St. Lawrence Seaway was complicated by the failure of Canada and the United States to negotiate an agreement for the creation of a joint international authority to supervise the project. Instead, each country established its own national agency to construct the canals, locks, and other works required for the 27-foot channel, making each agency responsible for work on its own side of the river. The agencies coordinated their work in a series of international agreements and informal arrangements. Where works extended over the international boundary, the two commissions allocated responsibility through the coordination of work at the technical level. They agreed on uniform rules of navigation, coordination of pilotage services, uniform tolls, and arrangements for collection.

Seagoing merchant vessels from other countries use the seaway regularly. Their right to do so rests not on any general principle of free navigation, but on national agreements and Article V of the GENERAL AGREEMENT ON TARIFFS AND TRADE, which mandates freedom of transit for merchant ships through the territories of signatories for traffic to or from the territory of other signatories. As the Great Lakes are inland waters and have been demilitarized since the Rush-Bagot Agreement of 1817 (T.S. No. 110 ½, 2 Miller 645, 12 Bevans 54), it is unlikely that foreign warships will request or receive permission to visit their ports.

FURTHER READINGS

International Water Law Project Web site. 2009. Available online at http://www.internationalwaterlaw.org/ (accessed September 5, 2009).

Nemecek, Sasha. 1999. "A Plan for Panama." *Scientific American* 281.

"Panama Takes Control of its Canal." 2000. *Hispanic* 13.

CROSS REFERENCES

Admiralty and Maritime Law; Territorial Waters.

INTERNET

The Internet is a worldwide telecommunications network of business, government, and personal computers.

The Internet is a network of computers linking countries around the world. Originally developed as a way for U.S. research scientists to communicate with each other, by the mid 1990s the Internet had become a popular form of telecommunication for personal computer users in the United States and in other countries. The dramatic growth in the number of persons using the network heralded the most important change in telecommunications since the introduction of television in the late 1940s. However, the sudden popularity of a new, unregulated communications technology raised many issues for U.S. law.

The Internet was created in 1969 for the U.S. DEFENSE DEPARTMENT. Funding from the Advanced Research Projects Agency (ARPA) allowed researchers to experiment with methods for computers to communicate with each other. Their creation, the Advanced Research Projects Agency Network (ARPANET), originally linked only four separate computer sites at U.S. universities and research institutes, where it was used primarily by scientists.

In the early 1970s other countries began to join ARPANET, and within a decade it was widely accessible to researchers, administrators, and students throughout the world. The National Science Foundation (NSF) assumed responsibility for linking these users of ARPANET, which was dismantled in 1990. The NSF Network (NSFNET) now serves as the technical backbone

---

Top Ten Activities of Adult Internet Users in 2008

1   Send or read e-mail
2   Use a search engine
3   Get news online
4   Check weather reports and forecasts
5   Look for news or information on politics
6   Engage in social networking
7   Conduct banking online
8   Watch a video on a video-sharing site
9   Look up information using Wikipedia
10 Send instant messages

SOURCE: Pew Internet and American Life Project Tracking surveys.

ILLUSTRATION BY GGS CREATIVE RESOURCES. REPRODUCED BY PERMISSION OF GALE, A PART OF CENGAGE LEARNING.

---

for all Internet communications in the United States.

The Internet grew at a fast pace in the 1990s as the general population discovered the power of the new medium. A significant portion of Internet content is written text, in the form of both electronic mail (e-mail) and articles posted in an electronic discussion forum known as the Usenet news groups. In the mid-1990s the appearance of the World Wide Web made the Internet even more popular. The World Wide Web is a multimedia interface that allows for the transmission of text, pictures, audio, and video together, known as Web pages, which commonly resemble pages in a magazine. Together, these various elements have made the Internet a medium for communication and for the retrieval of information on almost all topics.

The sudden growth of the Internet caught the legal system unprepared. Before 1996 Congress had passed little legislation on this form of telecommunication. In 1986 Congress passed the Electronic Communications Privacy Act (ECPA) (18 U.S.C.A. § 2701 et seq. [1996]), which made it illegal to read private e-mail. The ECPA extended most of the protection already granted to conventional mail to electronic mail. Just as workers in the post office may not read private letters, neither may the providers of private bulletin boards, online services, or Internet access. However, law enforcement agencies can SUBPOENA e-mail in a criminal investigation. The ECPA also permits employers to read their workers' e-mail. This provision was intended to protect companies against industrial spying, but it has generated lawsuits from employees who objected to the invasion of their privacy. Federal courts, however, have allowed employers to secretly monitor an employee's e-mail on a company-owned computer system, concluding that employees have no reasonable expectation of privacy when they use company e-mail.

Criminal activity on the Internet generally falls into the category of computer crime. It includes so-called hacking, or breaking into computer systems, stealing account passwords and credit-card numbers, and illegally copying INTELLECTUAL PROPERTY. Because personal computers can easily copy information, including everything from software to photographs and books, and the information can be sent anywhere in the world quickly, it has become much more difficult for COPYRIGHT owners to protect their property.

Public and legislative attention, especially in the mid to late 1990s, focused on Internet content, specifically sexually explicit material. The distribution of PORNOGRAPHY became a major concern in the 1990s, as private individuals and businesses found an unregulated means of giving away or selling pornographic images. As explicit and CHILD PORNOGRAPHY proliferated, Congress sought to impose restrictions on OBSCENE and indecent content on the Internet.

In 1996 Congress responded to concerns that indecent and obscene materials were freely distributed on the Internet by passing the Communications Decency Act (CDA) as part of the Telecommunications Act of 1996 (Pub. L. No. 104-104, 110 Stat. 56). This law forbade the knowing dissemination of obscene and indecent material to persons under the age of 18 through computer networks or other telecommunications media. The act included penalties for violations of up to five years imprisonment and fines of up to $250,000.

The AMERICAN CIVIL LIBERTIES UNION (ACLU) and online Internet services immediately challenged the CDA as an unconstitutional restriction on FREEDOM OF SPEECH. A special three-judge federal panel in Pennsylvania agreed with these groups, concluding that the law was overbroad because it could limit the speech of adults in its attempt to protect children (*American Civil Liberties Union v. Reno*, 929 F. Supp. 824 [E.D. Pa. 1996]).

The government appealed to the U.S. Supreme Court, but the Court affirmed the three-judge panel on a 7–2 vote, finding that the act violated the FIRST AMENDMENT (*Reno v.*

American Civil Liberties Union, 521 U.S. 844, 117 S. Ct. 2329, 136 L. Ed. 2d 236 [1997]). Though the Court recognized the "legitimacy and importance of the congressional goal of protecting children from the harmful materials" on the Internet, it ruled that the CDA abridged freedom of speech and that it, therefore, was unconstitutional.

Justice JOHN PAUL STEVENS, writing for the majority, acknowledged that the sexually explicit materials on the Internet range from the "modestly titillating to the hardest core." He concluded, however, that although this material is widely available, "users seldom encounter such content accidentally." In his view, a child would have to have "some sophistication and some ability to read to retrieve material and thereby to use the Internet unattended." He also pointed out that systems for personal computers have been developed to help parents limit access to objectionable material on the Internet and that many commercial Websites have age-verification systems in place.

Turning to the CDA, Stevens found that previous decisions of the Court that limited free speech out of concern for the protection of children were inapplicable. The CDA differed from the laws and orders upheld in the previous cases in significant ways. The CDA did not allow parents to consent to their children's use of restricted materials, and it was not limited to commercial transactions. In addition, the CDA failed to provide a definition of *indecent,* and its broad prohibitions were not limited to particular times of the day. Finally, the act's restrictions could not be analyzed as forms of time, place, and manner regulations because the act was a content-based blanket restriction on speech. Accordingly, it could not survive the First Amendment challenge.

In 1998 Congress responded to the decision by enacting the Child Online Protection Act (COPA), Pub. L. No. 105-277, 112 Stat. 2681. This act was narrower in its application than the CDA, applying only to commercial transactions and limited to content deemed to be "harmful to minors." The new statute was subject to immediate litigation. A federal district court placed a PRELIMINARY INJUNCTION on the application of the statute, and this decision was affirmed by the U.S. Court of Appeals for the Third Circuit (*American Civil Liberties Union v. Reno* (217 F.3d 162 [3d Cir. 2000]). Although the U.S. Supreme Court vacated the decision, it was due to procedural grounds rather than the merits of the challenge (*Ashcroft v. American Civil Liberties Union*, 535 U.S. 564, 122 S. Ct. 1700, 152 L. Ed. 2d 771 [2002]). On remand, the Third Circuit again affirmed the injunction, holding that the statute likely violated the First Amendment (*American Civil Liberties Union v. Ashcroft*, 322 F.3d 240 [3d Cir. 2003]).

The questions raised in *Reno* and subsequent decisions have also been raised in the debate over the use of Internet filters. Many schools and libraries, both public and private, have installed filters that prevent users from viewing vulgar, obscene, pornographic, or other types of materials deemed unsuitable by the institution installing the software.

The ACLU, library associations, and other organizations that promote greater access to information have objected to the use of these filters, especially in public libraries. The first reported case involving libraries and Internet filters occurred in *Mainstream Loudon v. Board of Trustees of the London County Library* (24 F. Supp. 2d 552 [E.D. Va. 1998]). A Virginia federal court judge in that case ruled that the use of screening software by a library was unconstitutional, as it restricted adults to materials that the software found suitable for children.

In 2000 Congress enacted the Children's Internet Protection Act (CIPA), Pub. L. No. 106-554, to address the issue of access to offensive content on the Internet using school and library computers. The statute imposes restrictions on any school or library that receives funding through what is known as the E-rate program, which makes technology more affordable for eligible institutions. The statute faced a legal challenge shortly after it was enacted in *United States v. American Library Ass'n* (539 U.S. 194 [2003]), wherein the plaintiffs alleged that it improperly required the restriction of the First Amendment rights of library patrons. In a 6–3 decision, the Supreme Court held that the use of filtering software at public libraries does not violate the First Amendment rights of library patrons and the CIPA is not unconstitutional. In doing so, the Court upheld the CIPA requirement that applicable institutions install filtering devices to prevent access to pornography and other content deemed inappropriate for children.

In addition to Internet filters used to screen content, another issue concerning the Internet that has been hotly debated is child pornography. The Internet resulted in substantially increased access to child pornography, causing federal and state taskforces designed to address the issue to expand aggressively in order to combat the growing problem. Though law enforcement has undertaken substantial efforts to eliminate child pornography on the Internet, data from the National Center for Missing and Exploited Children's CyberTipline suggests the problem is only increasing. In 2008 the CyberTipline had 85,301 reports relating to incidents of child pornography, a considerable increase from the 62,480 it reported in 2006.

Pornography is not the only concern of lawmakers and courts regarding potential crime on the Internet. The Internet has produced forms of terrorism that threaten the security of business, government, and private computers. Computer hackers have defeated computer network firewalls and have vandalized or stolen electronic data. Another form of terrorism is the propagation and distribution over the Internet of computer viruses that can corrupt computer software, hardware, and data files. Many companies now produce virus-checking software that seeks to screen and disable viruses when they arrive in the form of an e-mail or e-mail file attachment. However, computer hackers are constantly inventing new viruses, thus giving the viruses a window of time to wreak havoc before the virus checkers are updated. Moreover, the fear of viruses has led to hoaxes and panics.

One of the most infamous viruses, dubbed the Melissa virus, was created in 1999 by David Smith of New Jersey. It was sent through a Usenet newsgroup as an attachment to a message the purported to provide passwords for sex-related Websites. When the attachment was opened, it infected the user's computer. The program found the user's address book and sent a mass message with attachments containing the virus. Within a few days, it had infected computers across the globe and forced the shutdown of more than 300 computer networks from the heavy loads of e-mail that Melissa generated.

The Melissa virus represented one of the first instances in which law enforcement personnel were able to take advantage of new

SHOULD THE INTERNET BE POLICED?

Few observers could have predicted the fuss that the Internet began to generate in political and legal circles in the mid-1990s. After all, the global computer network linking 160 countries was hyped relentlessly in the media in the early 1990s. It spawned a multimillion-dollar industry in Internet services and a publishing empire devoted to the online experience—not to mention Hollywood movies, newspaper columns, and new jargon. But the honeymoon did not last. Like other communications media before it, the Internet provoked controversy about what was actually sent across it. Federal and state lawmakers proposed crackdowns on its content. Prosecutors took aim at its users. Civil liberties groups fought back. As the various factions engaged in a tug-of-war over the future of this sprawling medium, the debate became a question of freedom or control: Should the Internet be left alone as a marketplace of ideas, or should it be regulated, policed, and ultimately "cleaned up"? Although this question became heated during the early- to mid-1990s, it remained a debated issue into the early 2000s.

More than three decades after DEFENSE DEPARTMENT contractors put it up, the network remains free from official control. This system has no central governing authority for a very good reason: The general public was never intended to use it. Its designers in the late 1960s were scientists. Several years later, academics and students around the world got access to it. In the 1990s, millions of people in U.S. businesses and homes signed on. Before the public signed on, its predecessors had long since developed a kind of Internet culture—essentially a freewheeling, anything-goes setting. The opening of the Internet to everyone from citizens to corporations necessarily ruptured this formerly closed society, and conflicts appeared.

Speech rights quickly became a hot topic of debate. The Internet is a communications medium, and people have raised objections to speech online just as they have to speech in the real world. The Internet allows for a variety of media—text, pictures, movies, and sound—and PORNOGRAPHY is abundantly accessible online in all these forms. It is commonly "posted" as coded information to a part of the Internet called Usenet, a public issues forum that is used primarily for discussions. With over 10,000 topic areas, called news groups, Usenet literally caters to the world's panoply of interests and tastes. Certain news groups are devoted entirely to pornography. As the speed of the Internet increased dramatically with the development of broadband access in the late 1990s and early 2000s, not only has more of this type of information become more available, but also users have been able to access this information in greater quantity.

Several signs in 1994 predicted a legal crackdown on the Internet. Early on, U.S. attorney general JANET RENO said criminal investigators were exploring the originators of online CHILD PORNOGRAPHY. In July 1994 federal prosecutors won an OBSCENITY conviction in Tennessee against the operators of a computer bulletin board system (BBS) called the Amateur Action BBS, a private porn subscription service. Quickly becoming a cause célèbre in the online world, the case raised the question of how far off a general Internet crackdown could be.

In December 1994 a college student's FICTION raised a furor. Jake Baker, a sophomore in linguistics at the University of Michigan, published a story about sexual torture in the alt.sex.stories news group on Usenet. Its lurid detail was not unique in the news group, but something else was: Baker used the name of a female classmate for one of his fictional victims. Once the name was recognized, campus critics of pornography lashed out at Baker.

Baker's case demonstrated how seriously objections to Internet material

technologies to track the creator of the virus. On April 1, 1999, about a week after the virus first appeared on the Usenet newsgroups, police arrested Smith. He pleaded guilty to one count of computer fraud and abuse. He was sentenced to 20 months in prison and was fined $5,000.

Another area of legal concern is the issue of libel. In TORT LAW, LIBEL AND SLANDER occur when the communication of false information about a person injures the person's good name or reputation. Where the traditional media are concerned, it is well settled that libel suits provide both a means of redress for injury and a punitive corrective against sloppiness and malice. Regarding communication on the Internet, however, there is little CASE LAW, especially on the key issue of liability.

In suits against newspapers, courts traditionally held publishers liable, along with their reporters, because publishers were presumed to have reviewed the LIBELOUS material prior to

would be taken. In January 1995 the University of Michigan opened an investigation, and soon, FEDERAL BUREAU OF INVESTIGATION agents began reviewing Baker's E-MAIL. Baker insisted he meant no harm, suggesting that he wanted to be a creative writer. He even submitted to a psychological profile, which determined that he posed no danger to the student named in his story or to anyone else. But on February 9, 1995, federal authorities arrested him. He was charged with five counts of using interstate communications to make threats to injure—and kidnap— another person. Lacking any specific target for Baker's alleged threats, yet armed with allegedly incriminating e-mail, prosecutors charged that he was dangerous to other university students. The AMERICAN CIVIL LIBERTIES UNION (ACLU) came to his aid, arguing in an amicus brief that the accusations were baseless and moreover violated Baker's FIRST AMENDMENT rights. A U.S. district court judge threw out the case.

Congress had its own ideas about online speech. It enacted the Communications Decency Act of 1996 (47 U.S.C. A. § 223), which outlawed OBSCENE and other forms of indecent sexual material on the Internet. The act was challenged immediately. In *Reno v. American Civil Liberties Union* (521 U.S. 844, 117 S. Ct. 2329, 138 L. Ed. 2d 874 [1997]), the Supreme Court found that most of the statute's provisions violated the First Amendment. Congress subsequently sought to focus its attention on legislation that proscribes the transmission of child pornography, though the Supreme Court in a series of cases found that these statutes were likewise unconstitutional.

The central concern in *Reno* and the subsequent cases was that Congress has prohibited constitutionally protected speech in addition to speech that is not afforded First Amendment protection. Some members of Congress and supporters of such legislation suggested that restrictions on obscene and indecent information are necessary in order to protect children who use the Internet. But opponents of these restrictions noted that the Internet cannot be reduced to include only that information that is appropriate for children, and the Supreme Court reached this precise conclusion.

However, the Court did uphold the constitutionality of the Prosecutorial Remedies and Other Tools to End the Exploitation of Children Today Act of 2003 (117 Stat. 650). The law focused on the pandering of child pornography, which is the offering or soliciting of supposed pornographic images. The Supreme Court, in *U.S. v. Williams* (__U.S.__, 128 S. Ct. 1830, 170 L. Ed. 2d 650 [2008]), upheld the statute. The Court found that the law only "prohibits offers to provide and requests to obtain child pornography." The law did not require the "actual existence" of child pornography. Rather than focusing on the underlying material, the law targeted the "collateral speech that introduces such material into the child-pornography distribution network."

Although the debate about whether the government should regulate pornography and other obscene material continued, much of the focus about Internet policing shifted to other issues that involve the Internet. One important issue

has been how the government can protect COPYRIGHT and other INTELLECTUAL PROPERTY owners from piracy that is somewhat common on the medium. Another major issue is how the government can prevent the dissemination of unwanted advertising, usually sent through e-mail and commonly referred to as spam. Likewise, computer viruses have caused millions of dollars of damages to computer owners in the United States and worldwide, and most of these viruses have been distributed through the Internet.

Many Internet users, some of whom may otherwise object to government regulation of the medium, view governmental regulation that protects users from such problems as piracy, viruses, and spam more favorably than other forms of regulation. Nevertheless, even regulation of computer crime raises issues such as whether such regulation may violate users' First Amendment rights or how government regulation protecting against these harms can be effective. As the Internet continues to develop and even as the medium gradually becomes more standardized, these questions largely remain unanswered.

FURTHER READINGS

Crandall, Robert W., and James H. Alleman, eds. 2002. *Broadband: Should We Regulate High-Speed Internet Access?* Washington, D.C.: AEI-Brookings Joint Center for Regulatory Studies.

CROSS REFERENCE

E-mail.

publication. Because of this legal standard, publishers and editors are generally careful to review anything that they publish. However, the Internet is not a body of material that is carefully reviewed by a publisher, but an unrestricted flood of information. If a libelous or defamatory statement is posted on the Internet, which is owned by no one, the law is uncertain as to whether anyone other than the author can be held liable.

Some courts have held that online service providers, companies that connect their subscribers to the Internet, should be held liable if they allow their users to post libelous statements on their sites. An online provider is thus viewed like a traditional publisher.

Other courts have rejected the publisher analogy and instead have compared Internet service providers to bookstores. Like bookstores, providers are distributors of information and cannot reasonably be expected to review everything that they sell. U.S. libel law gives greater protection to bookstores because of this theory (*Smith v. California,* 361 U.S. 147, 80 S. Ct. 215, 4 L. Ed. 2d 205 [1959]), and some courts have applied it to online service providers.

Trademark infringement on the Internet has also led to controversy and legal disputes. One of the biggest concerns for registered trademark and SERVICE MARK holders is protection of the mark on the Internet. As Internet participants establish Websites, they must create domain names, which are names that designate the location of the Website. Besides providing a name to associate with the person or business that created the site, a domain name makes it easy for Internet users to find a particular home page or Website.

As individuals and businesses devised domain names in this medium, especially during the mid to late 1990s, they found that the names they created were similar to, or replicas of, registered TRADEMARKS and service marks. Several courts have considered complaints that use of a domain name violated the rights of a trademark or service mark holder, and early decisions did not favor these parties' rights.

In 1999 Congress enacted the Anticybersquatting CONSUMER PROTECTION Act (Pub. L. No. 106-113, 113 Stat. 1501). The act strengthened the rights of trademark holders by giving these owners a CAUSE OF ACTION against so-called "cybersquatters" or "cyberpirates," individuals who register a third-party's trademark as a domain name for the purpose of selling it back to the owner for a profit.

Prior to the enactment of this law, an individual could register a domain name using the trademark or service mark of a company, and the company would have to use a different domain name or pay the creator a sum of money for the right to use the name. Thus, for example, an individual could register the name www.ibm.com, which most Web users would have associated with International Business Machines (IBM), the universally recognized business. Because another individual used this domain name, IBM could not create a Website using www.ibm.com without paying the cybersquatter a fee for its use. The 1999 legislation eradicated this problem.

During the 1990s a number of companies were formed that operated completely on the Internet. Due to the overwhelming success of these companies, the media dubbed this phenomenon the "dot-com bubble." The success of these companies was relatively short-lived, as the "bubble" burst in early 2000. Many of these Internet companies went out of business, while those that remained had to consider new business strategies.

Despite these setbacks, the Internet has continued to develop and evolve. During the 1990s the vast majority of Internet users relied upon telephone systems to log on to the Internet. This trend changed drastically in the early 2000s, as many users subscribed to services that provide broadband access through such means as cable lines, satellite feeds, and other types of high-speed networks. These new methods for connecting to the Internet allow users to retrieve information at a much faster rate. They will likely continue to change the types of content that are available through this means of telecommunications.

FURTHER READINGS

"A Civil Liberties Ride on the Information Superhighway." 1994. *Civil Liberties: The National Newsletter of the ACLU* 380 (spring).

Blanke, Jordan M. 2003. "Minnesota Passes the Nation's First Internet Privacy Law." *Rutgers Computer & Technology Law Journal* 29 (summer).

Blakeslee, Melise R. 2010. *Internet Crimes, Torts and Scams: Investigation and Remedies.* New York: Oxford University Press.

"Can the Use of Cyberspace Be Governed?" 1995. *Congressional Quarterly Researcher* (June 30).

"Children's Internet Protection Act: FCC Consumer Facts." September 21, 2009. Federal Communications Commission Website. Available online at http://www.fcc.gov/cgb/consumerfacts/cipa.html> (accessed September 23, 2009).

"Constitutional Problems with the Communications Decency Amendment: A Legislative Analysis by the EFF." June 16, 1995. Electronic Frontier Foundation Website. Available online at www.eff.org> (accessed September 23, 2009).

"CyberTipline: Annual Report Totals by Incident Type." National Center for Missing and Exploited Children Website. Available online at www.missingkids.com> (accessed September 23, 2009).

Leiter, Richard A. 2003. "The Challenge of the Day: Permanent Public Access." *Legal Information Alert* 22 (February): 10.

Markon, Jerry. "Crackdown on Child Pornography: Federal Action, Focused on Internet, Sets Off a Debate." December 15, 2007. Washingtonpost.com. Available online at www.washingtonpost.com/wp-dyn/content/article/2007/12/14/AR2007121402257.html (accessed September 23, 2009).

Peck, Robert S. 2000. *Libraries, the First Amendment, and Cyberspace: What You Need to Know.* Chicago: American Library Association.

Peters, Robert. 2000. "'Marketplace of Ideas' or Anarchy: What Will Cyberspace Become?" *Mercer Law Review* 51 (spring): 909–17.

"Prodigy Stumbles as a Forum Again." Fall 1994. Electronic Frontier Foundation Website. Available online at www. eff.org> (accessed September 23, 2009).

Reed, Cynthia K., and Norman Solovay. 2003. *The Internet and Dispute Resolution: Untangling the Web.* Law Journal Press.

Riley, Gail Blasser. 2010. *Internet Piracy.* New York: Marshall Cavendish Benchmark.

Smith, Mark, ed. 2001. *Managing the Internet Controversy.* New York: Neal-Schuman.

Tsai, Daniel, and John Sullivan. 2003. "The Developing Law of Internet Jurisdiction." *The Advocate* 61 (July).

CROSS REFERENCES

First Amendment; Freedom of Speech; Internet Fraud; Telecommunications; Trademarks.

INTERNET FRAUD

A crime in which the perpetrator develops a scheme using one or more elements of the Internet to deprive a person of property or any interest, estate, or right by a false representation of a matter of fact, whether by providing misleading information or by concealment of information.

As increasing numbers of businesses and consumers rely on the Internet and other forms of electronic communication to conduct transactions, illegal activity using the very same media is similarly on the rise. FRAUDULENT schemes conducted via the Internet are generally difficult to trace and PROSECUTE, and they cost individuals and businesses millions of dollars each year.

From computer viruses to Web site hacking and financial fraud, Internet crime became a greater concern than ever in the 1990s and 2000s. In one sense, this situation was less a measure of growing pains than of the increasing importance of the Internet in daily life. More users surfing the Web, greater business reliance upon e-mail, and the tremendous upsurge in ELECTRONIC COMMERCE have raised financial stakes. A single virus outbreak in 1999 was blamed for more than $80 million in damage, while Web site hacking in early 2000 purportedly cost hundreds of millions more. Adding new wrinkles were complaints about rampant fraud on popular online auction sites. Together, the problems drew tough rhetoric from U.S. officials, who announced new initiatives, deployed cyber-crime units, made numerous arrests, and even pursued international manhunts.

According to a U.S. JUSTICE DEPARTMENT Web site devoted to the topic, Internet fraud refers to any type of scheme in which one or more Internet elements are employed in order to put forth "fraudulent solicitations to prospective victims, to conduct fraudulent transactions, or to transmit the proceeds of fraud to financial institutions or to others connected with the scheme." As pointed out in a report prepared by the National White Collar Crime Center and the FEDERAL BUREAU OF INVESTIGATION (FBI) in 2001, major categories of Internet fraud include, but are not limited to, auction or retail fraud, securities fraud, and IDENTITY THEFT.

Securities fraud, also called "investment fraud," involves the offer of bogus stocks or high-return investment opportunities, market manipulation schemes, pyramid and Ponzi schemes, or other "get-rich-quick" offerings. Identity theft, or identity fraud, is the wrongful obtaining and use of another person' personal data for one's own benefit; it usually involves economic or financial gain for the PERPETRATOR.

In its May 2002 issue, *Internet Scambusters* cited a study by GartnerG2 demonstrating that online merchants lost $700 million to Internet fraud in 2001. By comparison, the report showed that "online fraud losses were 19 times as high as offline fraud." In fact, the study pointed out that in the same year more than five percent of those making purchases via the Internet became victims of credit card fraud.

The IFCC, in its 2001 Internet fraud report, released statistics of complaints that had been received and then referred to law enforcement or regulatory agencies for action. For the 12-month period covered by the report, the IFCC received over 17 million inquiries to its Web site, with nearly 50,000 formal complaints lodged. It must be noted, however, that the number of complaints included reports of computer intrusions and unsolicited CHILD PORNOGRAPHY.

Significant findings in the report revealed that Internet auction fraud was the most reported offense, comprising 42.8 percent of referred complaints. Besides those mentioned above, top fraud complaints also involved non-delivery of merchandise or payment, credit/debit card fraud, and confidence fraud. While it

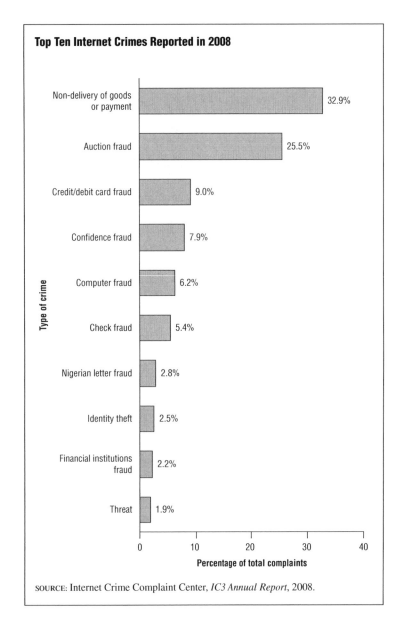

Top Ten Internet Crimes Reported in 2008

Type of crime

Non-delivery of goods or payment	32.9%
Auction fraud	25.5%
Credit/debit card fraud	9.0%
Confidence fraud	7.9%
Computer fraud	6.2%
Check fraud	5.4%
Nigerian letter fraud	2.8%
Identity theft	2.5%
Financial institutions fraud	2.2%
Threat	1.9%

Percentage of total complaints

0   10   20   30   40

SOURCE: Internet Crime Complaint Center, *IC3 Annual Report*, 2008.

may seem easy to dismiss these concerns as obvious, the schemes used to defraud customers of money or valuable information have become increasingly sophisticated and less discernible to the unsuspecting consumer.

The "IFCC 2001 Internet Report" revealed that 81 percent of those committing acts of fraud were believed to be male, and nearly 76 percent of those allegedly involved in acts of fraud were individuals. According to the report, California, Texas, Florida, New York, and Illinois were the states in which half of the perpetrators resided. The report also provided a shocking example of just how difficult a task tracking down those involved in Internet fraud can be. According to the report, out of

the more than 1,800 investigations initiated from complaints during 2001, only three arrests were made.

One example of the growing sophistication of Internet fraud cases can be seen in a 1997 case brought by the FEDERAL TRADE COMMISSION (FTC). *FTC v. Audiotex Connection, Inc.*, CV-970726 (E.D.N.Y.), dealt specifically with a scam in which Internet consumers were invited to view or to access free computer images. As reported in a February 10, 1998, FTC statement made before a Senate Subcommittee on Investigations of the Governmental Affairs Committee, when viewers attempted to access the images, their computer modems were surreptitiously disconnected from their local Internet Service Providers (ISPs) and were reconnected to the Internet through the defendants' expensive international modem connections. Exorbitantly priced long-distance telephone charges continued to accrue until the consumer turned off the computer, even if he or she had exited the defendant's Web site and moved elsewhere on the Internet. Approximately 38,000 consumers fell for this scam, losing $2.74 million.

The U.S. DEPARTMENT OF JUSTICE Web site that addresses the major types of Internet fraud reports the following recent examples of various types of illegal activity carried out using the medium.

Two separate Los Angeles cases demonstrate the intricacies of securities fraud and market manipulation. In the first case, defendants bought 130,000 shares of bogus stock in NEI Webworld, Inc., a bankrupt company whose assets had previously been liquidated. Defendants in the case then posted e-mail messages on various Internet bulletin boards, claiming that NEI was being acquired by a wireless telecommunications company. Within 45 minutes of the posting, shares increased from $8 to $15 each, during which time defendants "cashed out." The remaining stock was worth 25 cents per share within a 30-minute period. The second example involves a case in which an employee of PairGain Technologies set up a fraudulent Bloomberg news Web site and reported false information regarding the company's purchase by a foreign company. The employee then posted bogus e-mail messages on financial news bulletin boards that caused a 30 percent manipulation of PairGain stock prices within hours.

The Nigerian Scam

Anyone who uses email quickly realizes that there are thousands of people and organizations around the world that bombard email accounts with messages that offer cut-price goods, companionship for hire, and get-rich-quick plans. One particular Internet fraud has become known simply as the Nigerian Scam. It is based on a confidence trick called the Spanish Prisoner that was first tried in the 1920s. This history suggests some version of this scam will persist as part of Internet culture.

An advance-fee fraud is a very simple one: convince the target to give you money now and promise in return the prospect of gaining much greater wealth. The Nigerian Scam started in Nigeria in the 1980s. The scam messages were originally sent by letter or fax, but by the early 2000s email had become the preferred communication vehicle. The message supposedly comes from a bank employee or government officials, who asks the recipient for assistance out of embarrassment or regarding a legal problem. The recipient is asked to advance money and is told that she will be given a percentage of the funds that are currently tied up and unavailable. If the recipient sends money, the scammer will inform her that there have been problems and that more money is needed to bribe an official. The scam succeeds if the recipient is slowly separated from considerable sums of her money.

Most recipients hit their delete key when they read a Nigerian Scam message, but the few who do not are eager to advance money in hopes of an eventual windfall. In 1997 the U.S. Secret Service estimated that $100 million had been lost to the Nigerian Scam in a little more than one year. In 2008, an Oregon woman lost $400,000 to a Nigerian Scam scheme. Similar stories have been told around the world, which has led the Nigerian government bank to periodically issue advisories that it is not involved in these scams. However, Nigeria has many businesses that counterfeit documents, which are used to convince the target of the legitimacy of the transactions. Moreover, the Nigerian government has not been interested in aggressively ending the fraud.

The U.S. Secret Service asks that anyone who has been taken in by the scam should contact its Financial Crimes Division in Washington, D.C. However, the prospect of a victim recovering any money is dim at best.

In another example of investment fraud, perpetrators used the Internet, along with telemarketing techniques, to mislead more than 3,000 victims into investing almost $50 million in fraudulent "general partnerships involving purported high-tech investments, such as an Internet shopping mall and Internet access providers."

Internet-based identity theft emerged in the 2000s as a lucrative area for criminals. Computer hackers have broken into the databases of credit reporting companies, credit card companies, and government agencies and obtained personal information that could be used for financial fraud. As an example, over 100 U.S. military officers were involved in a case of identity theft. Defendants in the case illegally acquired the names and SOCIAL SECURITY numbers of the military personnel from a Web site and then used the Internet to apply for credit cards issued by a Delaware bank. In another case of identity theft and fraud, a DEFENDANT stole personal information from the Web site of a federal agency and then used the information to make applications for an online auto loan through Florida bank.

Hackers continue to find ways to take over personal computers and obtain social security numbers and other personal information. By 2009, however, identity thieves found ways of tricking individuals into providing information through a technique called "phishing." Phishing uses hijacked corporate logos and deceptive spam to convince the individual that a bank or credit card company needs them to visit a company Web site to take care of an urgent problem. When the link is clicked, the person is taken to a Web site that looks virtually identical to the legitimate company Web site. The fraudulent site asks the person to enter data, including credit card numbers, mother's maiden name, billing addresses, social security numbers, bank routing numbers, credit limits, personal identification numbers, and usernames and passwords. Armed with this information, the thief is able to plunder credit and debit card accounts and assume the person's identity online. In 2008, the FTC disclosed that 26 percent of complaints it received involved identity theft. It has established a resource page on its Web site, www.ftc.gov, that details the variations on this basic phishing scheme and provides information on how to combat it.

The Department of Justice Web site also gives an example of a widely reported version of credit card fraud. In the elaborate scheme, a perpetrator offers Internet consumers expensive electronics items, such as video cameras, at extremely low prices. As an incentive, they tell consumers that the item will ship before payment is finalized. When terms are agreed to, the perpetrator uses the consumer's name and address, but another party's illegally obtained credit card number, to purchase the item through a legitimate online vendor. Once the consumer has received the item, he or she authorizes credit card payment to the perpetrator. In the meantime, when the credit card holder, whose card number was used to purchase the item, stops payment on the unauthorized order, the vendor attempts to recollect the merchandise from the consumer. The defrauded consumer, the victim of the credit card theft, and the merchant usually have no simple means of redress, since by the time they "catch on," the perpetrator has usually transferred funds into untraceable accounts.

As Internet auction sites gained popularity, fraud also attracted federal attention. Complaints have soared since the late 1990s. By 2007 the Internet Crime Complaint Center (IC3), a partnership of the FBI and the National White Collar Crime Center, reported that almost 45 percent of the complaints it received involved Internet auctions. The leading Internet auction site eBay has worked with federal law enforcement to detect fraudulent activities.

FURTHER READINGS

Collins, Judith M. 2006 *Investigating Identity Theft: A Guide for Businesses, Law Enforcement, and Victims.* New York: Wiley.

Cullen, Terri. 2007 *The Wall Street Journal Complete Identity Theft Guidebook.* New York: Three Rivers Press.

Bureau of Justice Assistance. 2008. *2008 Internet Crime Report.* Washington, D.C. Available online at http://www.ic3.gov/media/annualreport/2008_IC3Report.pdf (accessed May 28, 2009).

Stickley, Jim. 2008. *The Truth about Identity Theft.* Upper Saddle River, New Jersey: FT Press.

CROSS REFERENCES

Antitrust Law; Computer Crime; Federal Trade Commission; Fraud; Intellectual Property; Privacy; Taxation; Trademarks.

INTERPLEADER

An equitable proceeding brought by a third person to have a court determine the ownership rights of rival claimants to the same money or property that is held by that third person.

Interpleader is a form of equitable relief. Equitable remedies are ways for courts to enforce rights other than by issuing a judgment for money damages. Interpleader is employed when two or more parties seek ownership of money or property that is held by a THIRD PARTY. The property in question is called the stake, and the third party who has custody of it is called the stakeholder. The stakeholder is faced with a legal dilemma: giving the property to either one of the parties will likely lead to a lawsuit by the other party against the stakeholder and the new property owner.

Interpleader enables the stakeholder to turn the controversy over to a court and to be dismissed from the legal action. It is designed to eliminate multiple lawsuits over the same stake and to protect the stakeholder from actual or potential multiple liability. Typically, interpleader will involve corporate securities or proceeds from insurance policies.

The stakeholder initiates an interpleader by filing an action that states that he or she has no claim to the money or property in controversy, and does not know to which claimant it should be lawfully delivered. The stakeholder must also establish the possibility of multiple lawsuits. The stakeholder then may be required to deposit the stake with the court, and notifies possible claimants that they can present their claims of ownership in court for determination.

The court must decide whether the interpleader is proper. It has discretion to allow the interpleader, and may deny the relief if the stakeholder is guilty of LACHES (unreasonable delay) or was responsible for the creation of the adverse claim. If the court grants the interpleader, the stakeholder is dismissed from the action. The rival claimants are given the right to litigate their claims, and they will be bound by the decision of the court.

Interpleader is primarily a device of federal CIVIL PROCEDURE. Two types of interpleader are available in federal courts: one under the Federal Rules of Civil Procedure and one under federal statute. When interpleader is sought through rule 22 of the Federal Rules of Civil Procedure, more than $10,000 must be at issue in the action, and the claimants must reside in the same state and must be citizens of a state other than the one in which the stakeholder is a citizen. The action can be tried where the stakeholder resides, where the CAUSE OF ACTION arose, or where the claimants reside. The stakeholder is not obligated to deposit the stake with the court, an important advantage when the property is used for purposes of investment and to generate income.

Interpleader authorized under 28 U.S.C.A. § 1335 differs in several respects from rule 22 interpleader. The dispute may involve as little as $500, at least two of the claimants must be from different states, and the citizenship of the stakeholder is immaterial. The venue, or place of trial, is anywhere that a claimant resides. At the time the suit is filed, the stakeholder must deposit the stake or post a bond in an amount equivalent to its value.

Claimants in an interpleader proceeding may be permitted to assert additional claims against each other or the stakeholder if they satisfy jurisdictional requirements and do not unreasonably complicate or delay the action. Courts must decide, on the particular facts of each case, whether such claims will be considered.

CROSS REFERENCE

Equity.

INTERPOL

Interpol is the acronym for the International Criminal Police Organization. It is an international organization of police forces from 176 countries designed to coordinate INTERNATIONAL LAW enforcement. Interpol furthers mutual aid and cooperation among the police forces of its national members in order to prevent and inhibit crime.

Interpol was established in 1923, with the General Secretariat—the international headquarters—located in Lyons, France. Delegates from member countries meet once per year to discuss police problems and admit new members. Each member nation maintains and staffs its own national central bureau. In the United States, the bureau is located in Washington, D.C. The U.S. bureau is under the direction and control of the Departments of Justice and of the Treasury, and is staffed by personnel from those departments.

The General Secretariat is supported by membership dues. Its budget is based on the Swiss franc, since that is a stable currency. Approximately five percent of the total budget is paid by the United States.

Interpol is forbidden by its constitution to undertake any intervention or activities of a political, military, religious, or racial character. Each national central bureau coordinates and responds to inquiries received from local and foreign law enforcement agencies. Each bureau also arranges for resolutions adopted by Interpol to be applied at the national level, and works to ensure that the basic principles laid down by Interpol's constitution are followed. National central bureaus are linked electronically to the Interpol General Secretariat's main database in Lyons.

The organization uses a system of international notices (circulars) to inform PEACE OFFICERS in the national bureaus of cases where known criminals abandon their usual residence and travel abroad surreptitiously. The color coded circulars are distributed by Interpol Headquarters to member countries within twenty days of their issue, or, in urgent cases, the same day. In the case of a fugitive whose arrest is requested and whose EXTRADITION is likely, a wanted notice containing details of the ARREST WARRANT and the offense committed is circulated.

In addition, Interpol conducts investigations of criminal activities, including drug trafficking, terrorism, COUNTERFEITING, SMUGGLING, ORGANIZED CRIME, and new forms of economic crime. It conducts criminal history checks for VISA and import permits and traces vehicle registration and ownership. Interpol also performs humanitarian services such as locating missing persons and providing notification of serious illness or death.

INTERPOLATION

The process of inserting additional words in a complete document or instrument in such manner as to alter its intended meaning; the addition of words to a complete document or instrument.

Interpolation is synonymous with INTER-LINEATION.

INTERPRETATION

The art or process of determining the intended meaning of a written document, such as a constitution, statute, contract, deed, or will.

The interpretation of written documents is fundamental to the process and practice of law. Interpretation takes place whenever the meaning of a legal document must be determined. Lawyers and judges search for meaning using various interpretive approaches and rules of construction. In constitutional and statutory law, legal interpretation can be a contentious issue.

Legal interpretation may be based on a literal reading of a document. For example, when John Doe signs a will that names his wife, Jane Doe, as his PERSONAL REPRESENTATIVE, his intent to name her the administrator of his estate can be determined solely from the specific language used in the will. There is no need to consider the surrounding facts and circumstances that went into his choice.

When the intended meaning of the words in a document is obscure and conjecture is needed to determine the sense in which they have been used, mixed interpretation occurs. In such a case, the words express an individual's intent only when they are correctly comprehended. If John Doe refers only to "my wife" in his will, a probate court will have to determine who his wife was at the time of his death. How a lawyer or judge ascertains intent when words are unclear is typically governed by rules of construction. For example, the general definition of a word will govern interpretation, unless through custom, usage, or legal precedent a special meaning has been attached to the term.

When a court interprets a statute, it is guided by rules of statutory construction. Judges are to first attempt to find the "plain meaning" of a law, based solely on the words of the statute. If the statute itself is not clear, a court then may look to EXTRINSIC EVIDENCE, in this case LEGISLATIVE HISTORY, to help interpret what the legislature meant when it enacted the statute. It is now common practice for statutes to contain "interpretation clauses," which include definitions of key words that occur frequently in the laws. These clauses are intended to promote the plain meaning of the law and to restrict courts from finding their own meaning.

Concern over whether courts apply strict or liberal methods of interpretation has generated the most controversy at the constitutional level. How the U.S. Supreme Court interprets the Constitution has been widely debated since the 1960s. Critics of the WARREN COURT, of the 1950s and 1960s, charged that the Court had usurped the lawmaking function by liberally interpreting constitutional provisions.

This criticism led to jurisprudence of "original intent," a philosophy that calls on the Supreme Court and other judges to seek the plain meaning of the Constitution. If plain textual meaning is lacking, the justices should attempt to determine the original intentions of the Framers. Those who advocate an ORIGINAL INTENT method of interpretation also emphasize the need for the justices to respect history, tradition, and legal precedent.

Opponents of original intent jurisprudence argue that discerning the intent of the Framers is impossible on many issues. Even if the original intent is knowable, some opponents believe that this intent should not govern contemporary decision making on constitutional issues. In their view the Constitution is a living document that should be interpreted according to the times. This interpretive philosophy would permit justices to read the Constitution as a dynamic document, with contemporary values assisting in the search for meaning.

CROSS REFERENCES

Judicial Review; Plain-Meaning Rule.

INTERROGATION, POLICE

See CUSTODIAL INTERROGATION; MIRANDA V. ARIZONA.

INTERROGATORIES

Written questions submitted to a party from his or her adversary to ascertain answers that are prepared in writing and signed under oath and that have relevance to the issues in a lawsuit.

Interrogatories

Small Claims Court _____ County, Colorado

Court Address:

PLAINTIFF(S): _____

Address: _____

City/State/Zip: _____

Phone: Home _____ Work _____

v.

DEFENDANT(S): _____

Address: _____

City/State/Zip: _____

Phone: Home _____ Work _____

▲ **COURT USE ONLY** ▲

_____

Case Number: _____

Division _____ Courtroom _____

MOTION AND ORDER FOR INTERROGATORIES – SHORT FORM

MOTION

Judgment was entered on: (date) _____, against the:

☐ Plaintiff   ☐ Defendant   By: ☐ Default   ☐ After trial

The judgment remains unsatisfied. Pursuant to Rule 518(a), C.R.C.P., the ☐ judgment creditor requests or the

☐ Court finds that the judgment debtor should be required to answer the following interrogatories.

Date: _____
Judgment Creditor's Signature

ORDER

☐ Pursuant to Rule 518(a), at the request of the judgment creditor. **OR**

On the Court's review of the above Motion **IT IS ORDERED:**

☐ That the judgment debtor shall answer the following questions and file the answers with the Court

☐ immediately   ☐ within ten days after service of these interrogatories upon the judgment debtor, or in lieu thereof, pay the judgment in full. **OR**

☐ That the judgment debtor answer the questions and appear in Court at (date)_____at (time)_____.

FAILURE TO TRUTHFULLY AND COMPLETELY ANSWER ALL OF THESE QUESTIONS AND RETURN THEM WITHIN TEN DAYS TO THE CLERK OF THE COURT, SMALL CLAIMS COURT, SHALL CAUSE A CITATION TO BE ISSUED FOR CONTEMPT OF COURT. A FINDING OF CONTEMPT BY THE COURT MAY RESULT IN A FINE OR JAIL SENTENCE.

Dated: _____   _____

☐ Judge   ☐ Magistrate

INTERROGATORIES

1. What is your full legal name: _____

   List any other names you have been known by: _____

   Home address: _____

   Home phone number: _____   Work phone number: _____

   Date of birth:_____   Social Security Number: _____

   Drivers license number: _____   State: _____

2. As to your employment, complete the following:

   The employer's/company's name: _____

   Address of employer: _____

   Phone number: _____   Supervisor's name: _____

   You are paid: ☐ hourly $ _____ ☐ monthly $ _____ ☐ or your annual rate of pay you

   earn $ _____ ☐ you are paid commissions, the manner in which commissions are calculated

   are: _____

   The days or days of the month on which you are paid: _____

JDF 252A R4/04 MOTION AND ORDER FOR INTERROGATORIES – SHORT FORM

[continued]

Sample interrogatories directed by a plaintiff to a corporation.

*Sample
interrogatories
directed by a plaintiff
to a corporation
(continued).*

Interrogatories

3. As to your bank accounts, complete the following: List the name and address and account number of every bank, saving and loan, credit union or other financial institution holding any funds that you have deposited or that you are allowed to withdraw without obtaining another person's signature.

Name of Bank Saving & Loan/Credit Union	Address/Location City/State	Account Number
Name of Bank Saving & Loan/Credit Union	Address/Location City/State	Account Number
Name of Bank Saving & Loan/Credit Union	Address/Location City/State	Account Number
Name of Bank Saving & Loan/Credit Union	Address/Location City/State	Account Number
Name of Bank Saving & Loan/Credit Union	Address/Location City/State	Account Number

4. State the full and correct address of all real estate you own or have an interest in:

Address	City/County State
Address	City/County State
Address	City/County State
Address	City/County State

5. As to debts owed to you, complete the following. List the name and address of every person who owes you money and the amount owed to you:

Name	Address City/State	$ Amount owed
Name	Address City/State	$ Amount owed
Name	Address City/State	$ Amount owed
Name	Address City/State	$ Amount owed

6. As to insurance coverage, complete the following: List the name and address of any insurance company providing liability coverage, including policy numbers with agent's name.

Name of Insurance Company – Name of Agent	Address/Location City/State	Policy Number
Name of Insurance Company – Name of Agent	Address/Location City/State	Policy Number
Name of Insurance Company – Name of Agent	Address/Location City/State	Policy Number

UNDER PENALTIES OF PERJURY, I DECLARE THAT THESE STATEMENTS ARE TRUE AND CORRECT.

Dated: _____

_____
Judgment debtor's signature

Subscribed and affirmed, or sworn to before me in the County of _____, State of

_____, this _____ day of _____, 20 _____.

My commission expires: _____

_____
Notary Public/Clerk of the Court/Deputy Clerk

[continued]

Interrogatories

Case Name _____ v. _____   Case Number: _____

AFFIDAVIT OF SERVICE
(Must be returned to Court)

I served a copy of the foregoing Interrogatories, on the following:

Name   **Date**   **Place**

If the person on whom service was made is not the named party to be served, I served the Interrogatories:

☐ At the regular place of abode of the person to be served, by leaving the Notice with a person over the age of 18 years who regularly resides at the place of abode. (Identify relationship to defendant _____.)

☐ At the regular place of business of the person to be served, by leaving the Notice with that person's secretary, bookkeeper, chief clerk, office receptionist/assistant or partner. (Circle title of person who was served.)

☐ By leaving the Notice with a partner, limited partner, associate, manager, elected official, receptionist/assistant, bookkeeper or general agent of the partnership, limited liability company, or other non-corporate entity, which was to be served. (Circle title of person who was served.)

☐ By leaving the Notice with an officer, manager, receptionist/assistant, legal assistant, paid legal advisor or general agent, registered agent for service of process, stockholder or principal employee of the corporation that was to be served. (Circle title of person who was served.)

I am over the age of 18 years, and I am not an interested party in this matter.

I have charged the following fees for my services in this matter:

☐ Private process server

☐ Sheriff, _____ County   _____
                                                     Signature of Process Server

Fee $ _____ Mileage $ _____

                                                     _____
                                                     Name (Print or type)

Subscribed and affirmed, or sworn to before me in the County of _____, State of _____,

this _____ day of _____, 20 _____.

My commission expires: _____   _____
                                                  Notary Public

CERTIFICATE OF SERVICE BY MAILING
(To be performed by Clerk within three days of filing)

I hereby certify that on (date)_____, I mailed a true and correct copy of the MOTION AND ORDER FOR INTERROGATORIES – SHORT FORM, by placing it in the United States Mail, postage pre-paid to the Defendant(s) at the address(es) listed above.

                                                  _____
                                                  Clerk of Court/Deputy Clerk

☐ (If applicable) Plaintiff notified of non-service on (date)_____. Clerk's Initials _____

JDF 252A 4/04 MOTION AND ORDER FOR INTERROGATORIES – SHORT FORM

Sample interrogatories directed by a plaintiff to a corporation (continued).
ILLUSTRATION BY GGS CREATIVE RESOURCES. REPRODUCED BY PERMISSION OF GALE, A PART OF CENGAGE LEARNING.

Interrogatories are a discovery device used by a party, usually a DEFENDANT, to enable the individual to learn the facts that are the basis for, or support, a pleading with which he or she has been served by the opposing party. They are used primarily to determine what issues are present in a case and how to frame a RESPONSIVE PLEADING or a DEPOSITION. Only parties to an action must respond to interrogatories, unlike depositions that question both parties and witnesses.

Interrogatories are used to obtain relevant information that a party has regarding a case, but they cannot be used to elicit privileged communications. The question must be stated precisely to evoke an answer relevant to the litigated issues. A party can seek information that is within the personal knowledge of the other or that might necessitate a review of his or her records in order to answer. The federal rules of CIVIL PROCEDURE and the rules governing state court proceedings provide that when interrogatories seek disclosure of information contained in corporate records, the party upon whom the request is served can designate the records that contain the answers, thereby making the requesting party find the answer for himself or herself. No party can be compelled to answer interrogatories that involve matters beyond the party's control. Objections to questions submitted can be raised and a party need not answer them until a court determines their validity.

Interrogatories are one of the most commonly used methods of discovery. They can be employed at any time and there is no limit on the number that can be served. Although they are not generally used for purposes of evidence in a trial, they might be admissible if they satisfy the rules of evidence, such as the BEST EVIDENCE rule or are an exception to the hearsay rule.

INTERSTATE COMMERCE ACT

The Interstate Commerce Act of 1887 (24 Stat. 379 [49 U.S.C.A. § 1 et seq.]) stands as a watershed in the history of the federal regulation of business. Originally designed to prevent unfair business practices in the railroad industry, the statute shifted responsibility for the regulation of economic affairs from the states to the federal government. It has been amended over the years to embrace new and different forms of interstate transportation, including pipelines, water transportation, and motor vehicle transportation. Among its many provisions, it established the INTERSTATE COMMERCE COMMISSION (ICC).

As part of its mission, the ICC heard complaints against the railroads and issued cease-and-desist orders to combat unfair practices. It later regulated many other forms of surface transportation, including motor vehicle and water transportation. The ICC was abolished in 1995, and many of its remaining functions were transferred to the TRANSPORTATION DEPARTMENT.

The Interstate Commerce Act was passed as a result of public concern with the growing power and wealth of corporations, particularly railroads, during the late nineteenth century. Railroads had become the principal form of transportation for people and goods, and the prices they charged and the practices they adopted greatly influenced individuals and businesses. In some cases, the railroads abused their power as a result of too little competition, as when they charged scandalously high fares in places where they exerted MONOPOLY control. Railroads also grouped together to form trusts that fixed rates at artificially high levels.

Too much competition also caused problems, as when railroads granted rebates to large businesses in order to secure exclusive access to their patronage. The rebates prevented other railroads from serving those businesses. Larger railroads sometimes lowered prices so much that they drove other carriers out of business, after which they raised prices dramatically. Railroads often charged more for short hauls than for long hauls, a scheme that effectively discriminated against smaller businesses. These schemes resulted in BANKRUPTCY for many rail carriers and their customers.

Responding to a widespread public outcry, states passed laws that were designed to curb railroad abuses. However, in an 1886 decision, *Wabash, St. Louis, & Pacific Railway Co. v. Illinois,* 118 U.S. 557, 7 S. Ct. 4, 30 L. Ed. 244, the U.S. Supreme Court ruled that state laws regulating interstate railroads were unconstitutional because they violated the COMMERCE CLAUSE, which gives Congress the exclusive power "to regulate Commerce with foreign nations, and among the several States, and with the Indian Tribes" (art. I, § 8). *Wabash* left a regulatory void that was soon filled by Congress. The following year, it passed the Interstate

Commerce Act, which President Grover Cleveland signed into law on February 4, 1887.

The law required that railroad rates be "reasonable and just," but it did not empower the federal government to fix specific rates. It prohibited trusts, rebates, and discriminatory fares. It also required carriers to publish their fares, and allowed them to change fares only after giving the public ten days' notice.

Now referred to as the Revised Interstate Commerce Act of 1978 (P.L. 95–473), the act was again revised in 1983 (P.L. 97–449) and 1994 (P.L.103–272). The latter revisions and recodifications simplified the language of the act and reorganized certain sections; no major substantive changes were made. The statute remains the bastion of regulatory guidance for the transportation and freight industries and for any other entity acting as a broker, shipper or shipper's exclusive agent, or carrier.

FURTHER READINGS

Augello, William J., and George Carl Pezold. 2009. *Freight Claims in Plain English.* 4th ed. Huntington, NY: Transportation & Logistics Council, Inc.

Interstate Commerce Act Web site. Available online at http://www.u-s-history.com/pages/h743.html; website home page: http://www.u-s-history.com (accessed September 5, 2009).

Interstate Commerce Commission. 1979. *Interstate Commerce Commission . . . in the Public Interest.*

Stone, Richard D. 1991. *The Interstate Commerce Commission and the Railroad Industry: A History of Regulatory Policy.* Santa Barbara, CA: Praeger.

CROSS REFERENCES

Railroad; Shipping Law.

INTERSTATE COMMERCE COMMISSION

The first independent regulatory agency created by the federal government, the Interstate Commerce Commission (ICC) regulated interstate surface transportation between 1887 and 1995. Over its 108-year history, the agency regulated and certified trains, trucks, buses, water carriers, freight forwarders, pipelines, and many other elements of interstate transportation.

The ICC was created by the INTERSTATE COMMERCE ACT of 1887 (24 Stat. 379 [49 U.S.C.A. § 1 et seq.]). The act created a five-person commission—later expanded to seven and then to 11—to be appointed by the president and confirmed by the Senate. Among the commission's first actions was the election of its first

president, THOMAS MCINTYRE COOLEY, a noted legal scholar who had been nominated by President Grover Cleveland.

Congress established the ICC to control the powerful railroad industry, then plagued by monopolistic and unfair pricing practices that often discriminated against smaller railroads and businesses as well as individual consumers. In its early years, the agency's regulatory effectiveness was severely limited by the courts, which in many cases retained the ability to review ICC rate rulings. The agency lost 15 of its first 16 lawsuits against the railroads, and the Supreme Court issued several decisions that hampered its regulatory powers.

Later laws gave the agency's rulings more teeth. The Elkins Act of 1903 (32 Stat. 847) allowed the ICC to punish shippers who practiced unfair competitive methods. The Hepburn Act of 1906 (34 Stat. 584) gave the agency wider powers to regulate railroad rates, making its rulings binding without a court order. The act also assigned to the ICC the oversight of all pipelines other than gas and water.

Over the years, Congress changed the focus and tasks of the ICC, gradually expanding its regulatory powers. In 1893 it entrusted the agency with the regulation of railroad safety. Later, the Motor Carrier Act of 1935 (49 Stat. 543) gave the ICC authority to regulate interstate trucking and other highway transportation. The agency even regulated telephone and telegraph communication from 1888 until 1934, when this task was transferred to the FEDERAL COMMUNICATIONS COMMISSION.

Other tasks performed by the ICC included conducting hearings to examine alleged abuses; authorizing mergers in the transportation industry; overseeing the movement of railroad traffic in certain areas; granting the right to operate railroads, trucking companies, bus lines, and water carriers; and maintaining CONSUMER PROTECTION programs that ensured fair, nondiscriminatory rates and services. At times, the agency participated in important social and political changes, as when it desegregated interstate buses and trains in the 1960s.

By the 1960s the ICC had reached a peak size of 2,400 employees, with field offices in 48 states. Its growth made it a target for those who sought to reduce the power and size of federal regulatory agencies. Critics claimed that ICC regulation created artificially high rates for many forms of transportation. Some charged the agency with corruption.

In 1976 the Railroad Revitalization and Regulatory Reform Act (90 Stat. 31 [45 U.S.C. A. § 801]) reduced the commission's powers to regulate carrier rates and practices except in a few areas where a single railroad or trucking firm monopolized a transportation route. This trend toward the deregulation of interstate commerce caused the ICC to gradually get smaller until December 29, 1995, when President BILL CLINTON signed The ICC Termination Act, Pub. L.No. 104-88, 109 Stat. 803 (1995), dissolving the ICC.

In its final year, the ICC employed 300 people and had a budget of $40 million. The legislation ending its existence moved 200 former ICC employees to the TRANSPORTATION DEPARTMENT, which assumed authority over former ICC functions deemed essential by Congress. These essential functions included approving railroad and bus mergers and handling railroad disputes. The new three-person Intermodal Surface Transportation Board within the DEPARTMENT OF TRANSPORTATION oversees many of the functions formerly conducted by the ICC.

FURTHER READINGS

"Commerce: ICC Elimination." 1996. *Congressional Quarterly's News* (January 8).

Interstate Commerce Commission. 1979. *Interstate Commerce Commission . . . in the Public Interest.*

U.S. Government Manual Website. Available online at http://www.gpoaccess.gov/gmanual (accessed July 21, 2009).

CROSS REFERENCES

Carriers; Highway; Railroad; Shipping Law.

INTERSTATE COMPACT

A voluntary arrangement between two or more states that is designed to solve their common problems and that becomes part of the laws of each state.

Interstate compacts in the United States were first used by the American colonies to settle boundary disputes. After the American Revolution, states continued to use interstate compacts to meet their various needs. Although these compacts were necessary for peaceful interaction between the states, they posed a threat to the future of the United States: If states were allowed to form powerful coalitions, they might be tempted to break away from the rest of the country and fracture the Union.

Under Article I, Section 10, Clause 3, of the U.S. Constitution, "No State shall, without the Consent of Congress . . . enter into any Agreement or Compact with another State." This clause, the Interstate Compact Clause, was adopted with no debate. Moreover, it received only cursory discussion in subsequent papers written by the Constitution's Framers, so its purpose and scope were not developed.

Most courts followed the lead of Justice JOSEPH STORY (1779–1845), of the Supreme Court, an influential legal commentator of the nineteenth century. According to Story, the clause was meant to protect the supremacy of the federal government. With this general principle as guidance, courts interpreted the clause to give Congress the power to nullify an interstate compact if it frustrated federal aims.

Over the years, four steps have evolved to guide courts in their review of interstate compact cases. First, there must be an agreement between two or more states. If no concerted effort is actually undertaken by two or more states, Congress has no power to review the state actions under the Interstate COMPACT CLAUSE. In determining whether there is an agreement, the court may ask whether the states have officially formed a joint organization, whether a state's action is conditioned on action by another state, and whether any state is free to modify its position without consulting other states.

If the court finds that there is an agreement, the court will examine the agreement to determine whether it infringes on federal sovereignty. Not all interstate compacts infringe on federal supremacy. The question the court asks is whether the agreement between the states interferes with federal statutes or initiatives. For example, consider the federal legislation that outlaws certain automatic and semiautomatic ASSAULT weapons: title XI of the Public Safety and Recreational Firearms Use Protection Act (Pub. L. No. 103-322, 108 Stat. 1807 [codified as amended in scattered sections of 42 U.S.C.A.]). The purpose of the legislation is to limit firearm ownership. An interstate compact that legalized the banned assault weapons, and thus expanded firearm ownership, would infringe on the federal statute, whereas an interstate compact that outlawed additional assault weapons, and thus further limited firearm ownership, would not infringe on the federal statute.

If an interstate compact is found to infringe on federal initiatives, the court will then determine whether Congress has given its approval for the compact. Congress may grant approval before or after a compact is formed. Congress may also give indirect approval to a compact. For example, Congress may give its tacit approval to a compact on state boundaries if it subsequently approves the federal elections, appointments, and tax schemes of the states.

Finally, Congress may seek to amend or change an interstate compact after it has been approved. Congress may amend a compact or completely revoke its approval of a compact. Congress may also grant its approval with conditions attached.

The most common interstate compacts concern agreements to share natural resources, such as water; build regional electric power sources; share parks and parkways; conserve fish and wildlife; protect air quality; manage radioactive and other hazardous wastes; control natural disasters, such as floods; share educational resources and facilities; share police and fire departments; and grant reciprocity for driver's licenses. Congress has passed statutes that require prior congressional approval for many such compacts.

If Congress has not asserted its authority over an interstate compact prior to its formation, the compact probably does not violate the Interstate Compact Clause. In *Northeast Bancorp v. Board of Governors,* 472 U.S. 159, 105 S. Ct. 2545, 86 L. Ed. 2d 112 (1985), Massachusetts and Connecticut passed statutes that allowed out-of-state holding companies in the New England region to acquire in-state banks. These statutes applied only if the state in which the out-of-state company was based also allowed out-of-state holding companies to acquire in-state banks. When the FEDERAL RESERVE BOARD (FRB) approved the interstate acquisition of banks in Massachusetts and Connecticut, three banking companies brought suit against the board.

The plaintiffs argued, in part, that the statutes constituted an interstate compact, and that the compact required congressional approval that had not been received. The U.S. Supreme Court disagreed. Assuming the statutes did create an interstate compact, they did not require congressional approval because they did not encroach on any asserted power of the federal government. In

An interstate compact between western states ultimately led to the construction of the Hoover Dam.

AP IMAGES

fact, Congress had authorized interstate bank acquisitions in an amendment to the Bank HOLDING COMPANY Act of 1956 (70 Stat. 133 [as amended, 12 U.S.C.A. § 1841, 1842(d)). The amendment prevented the FRB from approving interstate bank acquisitions unless the states had reciprocating statutes. Massachusetts and Connecticut had merely accomplished what was implicitly authorized by the amendment, and the High Court cleared the way for final approval of the acquisitions.

In practice, few interstate compacts are held to violate federal imperatives. Despite the freedom of states to form interstate compacts, the trend is toward increased federal participation and control. Congress has inserted itself into the negotiations over, administration of, and participation in interstate compacts. This level of control may decrease as the United States seeks to trim its budget. However, Congress will remain constitutionally required to prevent states from forming coalitions that wield powers challenging those of the federal government.

FURTHER READINGS

Darr, Frank P. 1993. "Electric Holding Company Regulation by Multistate Compact." *Energy Law Journal* 14.

Goble, Dale D. 1986. "The Council and the Constitution: An Article on the Constitutionality of the Northwest Power Planning Council." *Journal of Environmental Law and Litigation* 1.

Sundeen, Matt, and Janet B. Goehring. 1999. *IFTA Legislation and State Constitutional Provisions Project: Final Report.* Denver, CO: National Conference of State Legislatures.

CROSS REFERENCES

Federalism; Supremacy Clause.

INTERVENING CAUSE

A separate act or omission that breaks the direct connection between the defendant's actions and an injury or loss to another person, and may relieve the defendant of liability for the injury or loss.

Civil and criminal defendants alike may invoke the intervening cause doctrine to escape liability for their actions.

A DEFENDANT is held liable for an injury or loss to another person if the defendant's negligent or reckless conduct was the PROXIMATE CAUSE of the resulting injury or loss. This means that the defendant's conduct must have played a substantial part in bringing about or directly causing the injury or loss. However, the defendant may escape liability by showing that a subsequent act or event, or intervening cause, was the real cause of the injury.

Not all intervening causes relieve a defendant of liability. An intervening cause relieves a defendant of liability only if it would not have been foreseeable to a REASONABLE PERSON, and only if damage resulting from the defendant's own actions would not have been foreseeable to a reasonable person.

For example, assume that a farmer agrees to store a large, heavy sculpture for an artist. The sculpture is designed for outdoor display, so the farmer leaves it in her backyard. A tornado throws the sculpture several thousand feet, ruining it.

If the artist sues the farmer for damage to the sculpture, the farmer may argue that the tornado intervened between her negligent storage and the damage, relieving her from any liability. The farmer may claim that she could not have anticipated any detrimental effects of outdoor storage on the sculpture, because the sculpture was made for outdoor display.

At trial the issue of the farmer's liability is a QUESTION OF FACT to be determined by the judge or jury. The judge or jury asks whether a reasonable person would have anticipated a tornado. Generally, extraordinary weather conditions are deemed an unforeseeable intervening cause. However, if the farmer lives in Kansas, where tornadoes may be expected, and stored the sculpture outside without tethers during tornado season, the judge or jury may find that she should have anticipated the tornado and its damaging effects, and thus is liable for the damage.

Next, the fact-finder considers whether the farmer could have foreseen damage resulting from outdoor storage. Because the artist made the sculpture for outdoor display, damage to the sculpture from outdoor storage may be considered unforeseeable. Under these facts the tornado may be deemed an unforeseeable intervening cause of the damage to the sculpture, and the farmer may avoid liability.

Two types of intervening causes are considered: dependent and independent. A dependent intervening cause is set in motion by the defendant's own conduct, and will not relieve the defendant of liability unless it is extraordinary. For example, suppose the defendant poked an associate in the chest during a friendly discussion around a watercooler, and the associate subsequently jumped out a window. This unusual reaction may be deemed an extraordinary intervening cause that relieves the defendant of liability.

An independent intervening cause arises through NO FAULT of the defendant. It relieves a defendant of liability unless it was foreseeable by the defendant.

The most common intervening causes cited by defendants are natural forces and negligent human conduct. Natural forces include extraordinary weather, earthquakes, volcanic eruptions, and the conduct of animals. Negligent human conduct is conduct that exposes a person to abnormal risks. Criminal human conduct by a THIRD PARTY will not be considered an intervening cause relieving the defendant of liability if the defendant's NEGLIGENCE has contributed to the victim's loss. For example, assume that Martin borrows Tasha's vehicle, drives it to a neighborhood notorious for its high crime rate, and leaves it unlocked with the keys in the ignition. If the vehicle is stolen, Martin may be held liable to Tasha for her loss because a reasonable person would have anticipated the theft.

Cohen v. Petty, 62 App. D.C. 187, 65 F.2d 820 (D.C. Cir. 1933), illustrates how the doctrine of intervening cause works. In *Cohen,* Jeanette Cohen sued Joseph Petty for permanent injuries she suffered as a passenger in a vehicle when Petty drove it into an embankment.

At trial Petty argued that he had become sick without warning and had fainted while driving. The sudden sickness and fainting spell were, Petty claimed, an intervening cause that relieved him of liability. Petty testified that he had never fainted before and that he was feeling fine up to the point of the sudden illness. Petty's wife, Theresa Petty, who was sitting in the front passenger's seat, testified that just before the accident, Petty said, "Oh, Tree, I feel sick." Cohen herself testified that shortly before the accident, she heard Petty exclaim to his wife that he felt sick.

The trial court agreed with Petty and entered judgment in his favor. On appeal the Court of Appeals of the District of Columbia affirmed. According to the appeals court, the sudden illness was an intervening cause. Petty had had no reason to anticipate the illness, and because he had not been negligent in any way prior to the accident, the illness relieved him of all liability for Cohen's injuries.

Some jurisdictions use two terms to define the intervening cause doctrine: *intervening cause* and *superseding cause*. In these jurisdictions *intervening cause* describes any cause that comes between a defendant's conduct and the resulting injury, and an intervening cause that relieves a defendant of liability is called a superseding cause. Other jurisdictions do not use the term *superseding cause*. These jurisdictions simply ask whether the intervening cause is sufficient to relieve a defendant of liability. All jurisdictions differentiate between an intervening cause that relieves a defendant of liability and one that does not: the only difference is in the terminology.

FURTHER READINGS

Hodgson, Douglas. 2008. *The Law of Intervening Causation.* Aldershot, Hampshire, England: Ashgate.

Loehr, Cynthia. 2004. "The Doctrine of Independent Intervening Cause Does Not Apply in Cases of Multiple Acts of Negligence—Torres v. El Paso Electric Company." *New Mexico Law Review* 30 (spring).

Schlosser, William L. 1998. "Intervening-Cause Defense: Is It Still Viable under Comparative Fault?" *Res Gestae* 42 (July).

INTERVENOR

An individual who is not already a party to an existing lawsuit but who makes himself or herself a party either by joining with the plaintiff or uniting with the defendant in resistance of the plaintiff's claims.

INTERVENTION

A procedure used in a lawsuit by which the court allows a third person who was not originally a party to the suit to become a party, by joining with either the plaintiff or the defendant.

The federal rules of CIVIL PROCEDURE recognizes two types of intervention: *intervention of right* and *permissive intervention*.

Intervention of right arises when the INTERVENOR, the person who seeks to become a party to an existing lawsuit, can satisfactorily show that his or her interest is not adequately represented by the present parties, that the interest relates to the subject of the action, and that the disposition of the action might in some way impair his or her ability to protect such interest.

Permissive intervention is up to the discretion of the court. It arises when the intervenor's claim or defense and the instant suit have a QUESTION OF LAW or fact in common.

In deciding whether or not to permit intervention, the court ordinarily balances the needs and interest of the intervenor against the potential hardship on the existing parties if such intervention is allowed. The court will determine whether the intervenor and the parties to the suit share common issues. If the intervenor attempts to inject new causes of actions into the pending suit, his or her request will be denied, since to permit intervention would increase the potential for prejudice and delay in the original action. An intervenor need not argue that he or she will be prejudiced by the judgment if not joined, provided the intervenor is able to show that his or her interest will be impaired by the action if he or she is not involved.

INTESTACY

The state or condition of dying without having made a valid will or without having disposed by will of a segment of the property of the decedent.

INTESTATE

The description of a person who dies without making a valid will or the reference made to this condition.

INTESTATE SUCCESSION

The inheritance of an ancestor's property according to the laws of descent and distribution that are applied when the deceased has not executed a valid will.

INTOXICATION

A state in which a person's normal capacity to act or reason is inhibited by alcohol or drugs.

Generally, an intoxicated person is incapable of acting as an ordinary prudent and cautious person would act under similar conditions. In recognition of this factor, the law may allow intoxication to be used as a defense to certain crimes. In many jurisdictions, intoxication is a defense to specific-intent crimes. The underlying rationale is that the intoxicated individual cannot possess the requisite mental state necessary to establish the offense.

Other jurisdictions recognize it as a defense to general-intent crimes as well. For example, although RAPE is commonly considered a general-intent crime, there are states in which extreme intoxication may be alleged as a defense. It is unlikely, however, that the defense will be successful in such cases absent proof that the DEFENDANT was so intoxicated that he or she could not form the intent to have intercourse.

In HOMICIDE cases, intoxication is relevant to negate premeditation and deliberation necessary for first-degree MURDER. When the defense is successfully interposed, it will reduce a charge of first-degree murder to second-degree murder.

When a person is forced to consume an intoxicant against his or her will, the person is involuntarily intoxicated. In most jurisdictions, the defense of involuntary intoxication is treated similarly to the INSANITY DEFENSE. For example, an intoxicated person who cannot distinguish right from wrong at the time of committing the wrongful act would have a valid defense.

INTRINSIC EVIDENCE

Information necessary for the determination of an issue in a lawsuit that is gleaned from the provisions of a document itself, as opposed to testimony from a witness or the terms of other writings that have not been admitted by the court for consideration by the trier of fact.

INURE

To result; to take effect; to be of use, benefit, or advantage to an individual.

For example, when a will makes the provision that all PERSONAL PROPERTY is to inure to the benefit of a certain individual, such an individual is given the right to receive all the personal property owned by the TESTATOR upon his or her death.

INVALID

Null; void; without force or effect; lacking in authority.

For example, a will that has not been properly witnessed is invalid and unenforceable.

INVENTORY

An itemized list of property that contains a description of each specific article.

Inventory of a company, for example, is the annual account of stock taken in the business, or the quantity of goods or materials in stock. The term is also used to describe a list made by the executor or administrator of the estate of a deceased individual.

INVESTITURE

In ecclesiastical law, one of the formalities by which an archbishop confirms the election of a bishop. During the feudal ages, the rite by which an overlord granted a portion of his lands to his vassal.

The investiture ceremony, which took place in the presence of other vassals, consisted of the vassal taking an oath of fealty to the overlord who, in turn, gave him a clod of dirt or a twig, symbolic of the open and notorious transfer of possession of the land. The ritual, used at a time when writing and record keeping were not widely practiced, fixed the date of the vassal's acquisition of the land and, in cases of disputes over the land, provided a source of evidence in the form of testimony of the vassals who witnessed the proceedings.

CROSS REFERENCE

Feudalism.

INVESTMENT

The placement of a particular sum of money in business ventures, real estate, or securities of a permanent nature so that it will produce an income.

INVITATION

The act by which an owner or occupier of particular land or premises encourages or attracts others to enter, remain in, or otherwise make use of his or her property.

Common examples of those who extend invitations are the proprietors of stores, theaters, or banks, since they invite the general public to enter and utilize their facilities.

An individual who enters property as a result of an invitation is owed a higher duty of care than one who is a trespasser or licensee, one who enters another's property for his or her own purposes. The owner of property must exercise reasonable care toward an INVITEE to ascertain that the property is safe for his or her use.

INVITEE

An individual who enters another's premises as a result of an express or implied invitation of the owner or occupant for their mutual gain or benefit.

For example, a customer in a restaurant or a depositor entering a bank to cash a check are both invitees. The owner or occupier of the premises onto which an invitee goes has a duty to exercise reasonable care for such invitee's protection.

An invitee is distinguishable from a licensee, who enters another's premises with the occupier's CONSENT, but for his or her own purpose or benefit alone. A further distinction exists between an invitee and a trespasser, or one who intentionally enters another's property without consent or permission.

INVOICE

An itemized statement or written account of goods sent to a purchaser or consignee by a vendor that indicates the quantity and price of each piece of merchandise shipped.

A *consular invoice* is one used in foreign trade. It is signed by the consul of the nation to which the merchandise is shipped. Such an invoice facilitates the entry through the destination country, since the quality and value of the shipment are verified prior to its arrival.

INVOLUNTARY CONFESSION

An admission, especially by an individual who has been accused of a crime, that is not freely offered but rather is precipitated by a threat, fear, torture, or a promise.

The criminal justice system relies on confessions by defendants to help prove guilt at trial or to induce a guilty PLEA. Police interrogation of suspects has long been a controversial area of U.S. CRIMINAL PROCEDURE, as critics charge that COERCION and trickery have unfairly and unconstitutionally led to involuntary confessions. The FIFTH AMENDMENT grants a suspect the PRIVILEGE AGAINST SELF-INCRIMINATION, yet many suspects confess anyway. Because questioning of suspects takes place behind station house doors, little empirical evidence is available to document what usually occurs in a police interrogation.

The 1931 federal WICKERSHAM COMMISSION looked at police practices throughout the United States. This commission raised the issue of coercive interrogations, coining the term *the third degree* to describe physical and mental abuse inflicted on suspects during questioning. From 1936 to the early 1960s, the U.S. Supreme Court dealt with confessions admitted in state criminal proceedings in terms of the fundamental fairness required by the Fourteenth Amendment's Due Process Clause. The Court used a "voluntariness" test, which depended on the "totality of the circumstances," to determine whether a confession must be excluded from evidence. This approach became difficult to administer, as it called on courts to find and appraise all relevant facts for each case.

Legal debate over the validity of confessions gained momentum in the 1960s, as the U.S. Supreme Court took a hard look at the constitutionality of criminal procedure. In ESCOBEDO V. ILLINOIS, 378 U.S. 478, 84 S. Ct. 1758, 12 L. Ed. 2d 977 (1964), Justice ARTHUR J. GOLDBERG stated that "a system of CRIMINAL LAW enforcement which comes to depend on the 'confession' will, in the long run, be less reliable and more subject to abuses than a system which depends on EXTRINSIC EVIDENCE independently secured through skillful investigation." In *Escobedo* the defendant's confession was suppressed because it was obtained in violation of his RIGHT TO COUNSEL at the time of interrogation.

In 1966 the Supreme Court set out the *Miranda* warnings (MIRANDA V. ARIZONA, 384 U.S. 436, 86 S. Ct. 1602, 16 L. Ed. 2d 1694), which the police must communicate to a person who is placed in their custody. The warnings cover the right to remain silent, the fact that anything said can and will be used against the individual in court, the right to have a lawyer during interrogation, the right to have an attorney appointed if the individual cannot afford one, and the right to exercise the privilege against SELF-INCRIMINATION at any time during interrogation. These warnings provide basic avenues of inquiry for a court evaluating the "voluntariness" of a confession.

Miranda has been criticized by those who see it as an unfair restriction on law enforcement. Nevertheless, empirical studies conducted in the 1970s and 1980s have concluded that the *Miranda* warnings have not appreciably reduced the amount of talking by suspects, and police officers obtain about as many confessions now as they did before *Miranda.*

Yet the protection afforded to suspects by *Miranda* can be illusory. Police officers may sometimes give the required warnings but then engage in tactics that could make the confession involuntary. It is clear, however, that if police officers use interrogation practices that in the view of a court violate basic notions of human dignity, a confession produced from these practices will be judged involuntary. Physical violence, threats of violence, prolonged isolation, deceit, and trickery are some tactics that may render a confession involuntary, even when no danger exists that the confession is untrue. A defendant's age, state of health, mental condition, and intelligence are also relevant factors. The more vulnerable a DEFENDANT is, the more likely a court is to find certain interrogation practices abusive, leading to the conclusion that the confession was involuntary.

Each possibly relevant FACTOR must be evaluated in the context of each specific case. For example, no absolute rule exists that police trickery of a defendant will render a confession involuntary. However, if a defendant is particularly youthful and ignorant, such trickery may be an important factor inducing a court to find a confession involuntary.

FURTHER READINGS

Friedman, Lawrence M. 1994. *Crime and Punishment in American History.* New York: Basic.

O'Neill, Timothy. 2002. "Ruling Is Strong Shield on 'Involuntary' Confession." *Chicago Daily Law Bulletin* 148 (December 20). Available online at http://www.jmls.edu/facultypubs/oneill/Confessions62.pdf; website home page: http://www.jmls.edu (accessed September 14, 2009).

White, Welsh S. 1998. "What Is an Involuntary Confession Now?" *Rutgers Law Review* 50 (summer).

CROSS REFERENCES

Custodial Interrogation; Due Process of Law.

INVOLUNTARY MANSLAUGHTER

The act of unlawfully killing another human being unintentionally.

Most unintentional killings are not MURDER but involuntary manslaughter. The absence of the element of intent is the key distinguishing factor between voluntary and involuntary MANSLAUGHTER. In most states involuntary manslaughter results from an improper use of reasonable care or skill while performing a legal act, or while committing an act that is unlawful but not felonious.

Many states do not define involuntary manslaughter, or define it vaguely in common-law terms. Some jurisdictions describe the amount of NEGLIGENCE necessary to constitute manslaughter with terms such as CRIMINAL NEGLIGENCE, *gross negligence,* and *culpable negligence.* The only certainty that can be attached to these terms is that they require more than the ordinary negligence standard in a civil case. With this approach the state does not have to prove that the DEFENDANT was aware of the risk.

Other jurisdictions apply more subjective tests, such as "reckless" or "wanton," to describe the amount of negligence needed to constitute involuntary manslaughter. In this approach the defendant must have personally appreciated a risk and then chosen to take it anyway.

There are two types of involuntary manslaughter statutes: criminally negligent manslaughter and unlawful act manslaughter. Criminally negligent manslaughter occurs when death results from a high degree of negligence or recklessness. Modern criminal codes generally require a consciousness of risk and under some codes the absence of this element makes the offense a less serious HOMICIDE.

An omission to act or a failure to perform a duty constitutes criminally negligent manslaughter. The existence of the duty is essential. Since the law does not recognize that an ordinary person has a duty to aid or rescue another in distress, a death resulting from an ordinary person's failure to act is not manslaughter. On the other hand, an omission by someone who has a duty, such as a failure to attempt to save a drowning person by a lifeguard, might constitute involuntary manslaughter.

In many jurisdictions death that results from the operation of a vehicle in a criminally negligent manner is punishable as a separate offense. Usually it is considered a less severe offense than involuntary manslaughter. These jurisdictions usually call the offense reckless homicide, negligent homicide, or vehicular homicide. One reason for this lesser offense is the reluctance of juries to convict automobile drivers of manslaughter.

Unlawful act manslaughter occurs when someone causes a death while committing or attempting to commit an unlawful act, usually a MISDEMEANOR. Some states distinguish between conduct that is *malum in se* (bad in itself) and conduct that is *malum prohibitum* (bad because it is prohibited by law). Conduct that is *malum in se* is based on common-law definitions of crime; for example, an ASSAULT AND BATTERY could be classified as *malum in se*. Acts that are made illegal by legislation—for example, reckless driving— are *malum prohibitum*. In states that use this distinction, an act must be *malum in se* to constitute manslaughter. If an act is *malum prohibitum,* it is not manslaughter unless the person who committed it could have foreseen that death would be a direct result of the act.

In other states this distinction is not made. If death results from an unlawful act, the person who committed the act may be prosecuted for involuntary manslaughter even if the act was *malum prohibitum.* Courts will uphold unlawful act manslaughter where the statute was intended to prevent injury to another person.

CROSS REFERENCES

Criminal Negligence; Gross Negligence.

INVOLUNTARY SERVITUDE

Slavery; the condition of an individual who works for another individual against his or her will as a result of force, coercion, or imprisonment, regardless of whether the individual is paid for the labor.

The term *involuntary servitude* is used in reference to any type of SLAVERY, PEONAGE, or compulsory labor for the satisfaction of debts. Two essential elements of involuntary servitude are involuntariness, which is compulsion to act against one's will, and servitude, which is some form of labor for another. Imprisonment without forced labor is not involuntary servitude, nor is unpleasant labor when the only direct penalty for not performing it is the withholding of money or the loss of a job.

The importation of African slaves to the American colonies began in the seventeenth century. By the time of the American Revolution, the slave population had grown to over five hundred thousand people, most concentrated in the southern colonies. The Framers of the U.S. Constitution did not specifically refer to slavery in the document they drafted in 1787, but they did afford protection to southern slaveholding states. They included provisions prohibiting Congress from outlawing the slave trade until 1808 and requiring the return of fugitive slaves.

Between 1820 and 1860, political and legal tensions over slavery steadily escalated. The U.S. Supreme Court attempted to resolve the legal status of African Americans in DRED SCOTT V. SANDFORD, 60 U.S. (19 How.) 393, 15 L. Ed. 691 (1857). The Court concluded that Congress was powerless to extend the rights of U.S. citizenship to African Americans.

With the secession of southern states and the beginning of the Civil War in 1860 and 1861, the Union government was under almost complete control of free states. In 1865 Congress enacted the THIRTEENTH AMENDMENT, which the Union states ratified. Section 1 of the amendment provides that "[n]either slavery nor involuntary servitude, except as a punishment for crime whereof the party shall have been duly convicted, shall exist within the United States, or any place subject to their jurisdiction." Section 2 gives Congress the authority to enforce the provisions of section 1.

The Thirteenth Amendment makes involuntary servitude unlawful whether the compulsion is by a government or by a private person. The penalty for violation of the amendment must be prescribed by law. Although the principal purpose of the amendment was to abolish African slavery, it also abolished other forms of compulsory labor similar to slavery, no matter what they are called. For example, it abolished bond service and peonage, forms of compulsory service based on a servant's indebtedness to a master.

An individual has a right to refuse or discontinue employment. No state can make the quitting of work a crime, or establish criminal sanctions that hold unwilling persons to a particular labor. A state may, however, withhold unemployment or other benefits from those who, without JUST CAUSE, refuse to perform available gainful work.

A court has the authority to require a person to perform affirmative acts that the person has a legal duty to perform. It has generally been held, however, that this power does not extend to compelling the performance of labor or personal services, even in cases where the obligated party has been paid in advance. The remedy for failure to perform obligated labor is generally limited to monetary damages. A court may, without violating the Thirteenth Amendment, use its equity authority to enjoin, or prevent, a person from working at a particular task. Equity authority is the power of a court to issue injunctions that direct parties to do or refrain from doing something. A court also may prevent an artist or performer who has contracted to perform unique services for one person on a given date from performing such services for a competitor.

The Thirteenth Amendment does not interfere with the enforcement of duties a citizen owes to the state under the COMMON LAW. Government may require a person to serve on a petit or GRAND JURY, to work on public roads or instead pay taxes on those roads, or to serve in the MILITIA. Compulsory military service (the draft) is not a violation of the Thirteenth Amendment, nor is compulsory labor on work of national importance in lieu of military service, assigned to conscientious objectors.

Forced labor, with or without imprisonment, as a punishment upon conviction of a crime is a form of involuntary servitude allowed by the Thirteenth Amendment under its "punishment-for-crime" exception.

CROSS REFERENCES

Celia, a Slave; *Dred Scott v. Sandford*; Emancipation Proclamation; Fugitive Slave Act of 1850; Selective Service System.

IPSE DIXIT

[Latin, He himself said it.] *An unsupported statement that rests solely on the authority of the individual who makes it.*

A court decision, for example, that is in conflict with a particular statute might be said to have no legal support with the exception of the *ipse dixit* of the court.

IPSO FACTO

[Latin, By the fact itself; by the mere fact.]

IRA

See INDIVIDUAL RETIREMENT ACCOUNT.

IRAN-CONTRA AFFAIR

The Iran-Contra Affair involved a secret foreign policy operation directed by White House officials in the NATIONAL SECURITY COUNCIL (NSC) under President RONALD REAGAN. The operation had two goals: first, to sell arms to Iran in the hope of winning the release of U.S. hostages in Lebanon, and second, to illegally divert profits from these sales to the Contra rebels fighting to overthrow the Sandinista government of Nicaragua. Discovery of the secret operation, in 1986, triggered a legal and political uproar that rocked the Reagan administration. The numerous related investigations and indictments did not end until 1993 and even then questions remained about the roles of senior White House officials in this arms-for-hostages deal.

The affair came to public attention on November 3, 1986, when a Lebanese publication, *Al-Shiraa,* first reported that the United States had sold arms to Iran. The news was shocking because the Reagan administration had previously denounced Iran as a supporter of international terrorism. Shortly after the *Al-Shiraa* report Nicaraguan forces downed a U.S. plane and captured its pilot. The pilot's confession led to a second startling revelation: A private U.S. enterprise was supplying arms to Contra rebels.

The enterprise seemed designed to circumvent the will of Congress. In the early 1980s, after bitter debate, Congress had passed legislation barring the use of federal monies to overthrow the Nicaraguan government. Through a series of amendments to appropriations bills enacted between 1982 and 1986, known as the Boland amendments, this legislation blocked the Reagan administration's wish to go on supporting the Contras. Now it was revealed that private citizens and private monies were being used to this end. Moreover, the operation was being directed from within the White House by the NSC—the president's advisory cabinet on security affairs and covert operations. Directing the Iran-Contra enterprise were Vice Admiral John Poindexter, national security assistant, and his subordinate,

Lieutenant Colonel Oliver North, deputy director for political-military affairs.

Each branch of government quickly began a separate investigation into the affair. In December 1986, President Reagan issued an EXECUTIVE ORDER creating the Tower Commission, named after its chair, John Tower. The purpose of this three-member review board was to recommend changes in executive policy regarding the future roles and procedures of the NSC staff. Reagan's creation of the commission was a tacit disavowal of presidential knowledge or responsibility for the actions of Iran-Contra participants. Although admitting that his administration had negotiated secretly with Iran in order to free the hostages in Lebanon, he publicly denied knowing about the arms-supplying enterprise directed by his own NSC staff.

Simultaneously, the Senate and the House of Representatives each created a select Iran-Contra committee. These committees were charged with holding hearings to uncover facts and to recommend legislative action to prevent future illegal foreign policy operations. In their zeal to fully expose the affair, the committees granted limited forms of IMMUNITY to several key witnesses. This decision proved to be a mixed blessing. On the one hand, it provided Congress and the U.S. public with a wider understanding of the affair through televised hearings (which also made a public figure out of Lieutenant Colonel North). But it ultimately proved harmful to efforts to PROSECUTE North and Vice Admiral Poindexter.

The attorney general requested that an INDEPENDENT COUNSEL be appointed to investigate wrongdoing. An independent counsel is a special appointee who is given the authority to bring indictments and pursue convictions. For this important role, the U.S. Court of Appeals for the District of Columbia Circuit, Independent Counsel Division, selected Lawrence E. Walsh, a former AMERICAN BAR ASSOCIATION president and former federal judge. Legal authority for Walsh's appointment existed in provisions of the Ethics in Government Act (Pub. L. No. 95-521 [Oct. 26, 1978], 92 Stat. 1824 [28 U.S.C.A. § 592(c) (1) (1982)]).

The various Iran-Contra investigations soon uncovered a plethora of legal violations. The covert arms sales to Iran violated numerous statutes that restricted the transfer of arms to nations that support international terrorism, principally the Arms Export Control Act of 1976 (Pub. L. No. 90-629, 89 Stat. 1320 [22 U.S.C.A. §§ 2751–2796c (1989 Supp.)]). By failing to report the Iranian sales to Congress, the Reagan administration had ignored reporting provisions in the 1980 Intelligence Oversight Act (Pub. L. No. 96-450, tit. IV, 407(b) (1), 94 Stat. 1981 [50 U.S.C.A. § 413 (1982)]). That law required the president to notify Congress in a timely fashion of any "significant anticipated intelligence activity, and to make a formal written "finding" (declaration) that each covert operation was important to national security. Three findings were at issue in the Iran-Contra affair: (1) Not only had President Reagan failed to report the first arms sales, but he had also authorized them through Israeli intermediaries by "oral" findings that were not authorized by intelligence oversight statutes. (2) The CENTRAL INTELLIGENCE AGENCY (CIA) justified a second shipment of arms to the Iranians through a "retroactive" finding issued by the CIA's general counsel; Poindexter admitted destroying this finding. (3) President Reagan admitted signing a third written finding, in January 1986, but later claimed he had never read it.

The investigations took two turns. Congress and the Tower Commission completed their hearings and issued reports and independent counsel Walsh pursued wide-ranging indictments against several individuals, including Reagan administration officials. In 1987 Congress issued the 690-page *Report of the Congressional Committees Investigating the Iran-Contra Affair* (S. Rep. No. 216, H.R. Rep. No. 433, 100th Cong., 1st Sess. 423). The report charged the president with failing to execute his

Lieutenant Colonel Oliver North was convicted of obstructing Congress, destroying documents, and accepting an illegal gratuity, but the decision was later reversed by a higher court.

AP IMAGES

In December 1986 Lawrence E. Walsh was appointed independent counsel to investigate the Iran-Contra affair. The investigation of the scandal ended in August 1993.

AP IMAGES

constitutional duty to uphold the law. However, its conclusion did not support changes in legislation to prevent a future breakdown of legality in foreign policy affairs. Iran-Contra, the report said, reflected a failure of people rather than of laws. This assertion pointed to a central political disagreement about the affair: Although Democrats were harsh in their condemnation, Republican members of Congress tended to view the investigation itself as an effort by Democrats to interfere with a Republican president's foreign policy. In like fashion, the 1987 Tower Commission report downplayed any need for legislation to revise national security decision making. Instead, it criticized Reagan's lax management style.

After the reports, attention shifted to the independent counsel's investigation. In March 1988, GRAND JURY indictments were brought against North, Poindexter, Richard V. Secord, and Albert Hakim. The indictments included four distinct charges: conspiring to obstruct the U.S. government; diverting public funds from arms sales to Iran to aid the Contras in Nicaragua; stealing public funds for private ends; and lying to Congress and other government officials. With the exception of the routine criminal charge of

theft, the most serious points in the indictments essentially accused the defendants of conducting a private foreign policy in violation of constitutional norms.

Before independent counsel Walsh could begin his prosecutions, several pretrial delays took place. First, the law providing for an independent counsel was challenged. The Reagan administration, joining a number of its former officials who were subject to other independent counsel investigations, argued that the law unconstitutionally denied the president important executive power. In June 1988 the U.S. Supreme Court rejected this argument and upheld the law's constitutionality in *Morrison v. Olson*, 487 U.S. 654, 108 S. Ct. 2597, 101 L. Ed. 2d 569. Next, the first four Iran-Contra defendants—Poindexter, North, Secord, and Hakim—moved for dismissal of the charges brought by Walsh. They argued that their compelled testimony before the joint congressional committees had violated their FIFTH AMENDMENT rights against SELF-INCRIMINATION. In *United States v. Poindexter*, 698 F. Supp. 300 (D.D.C. 1988), U.S. district judge Gerhard Gesell denied the motion, clearing the way for the trials to begin.

Soon a more serious obstacle hampered Walsh's prosecution: The JUSTICE DEPARTMENT and the White House refused to release classified information crucial to the case on the grounds that it was vital to national security. Without this information, much of Walsh's case collapsed. He was forced to dismiss the broader charges of conspiracy and diversion—the crux of the Iran-Contra Affair's illegality—and to pursue instead the less serious charges remaining in the indictments.

Walsh won a conviction against Lieutenant Colonel North on May 4, 1989, for obstructing Congress, destroying documents, and accepting an illegal gratuity (*United States v. North*, 713 F. Supp. 1448 [D.D.C.]). The trial disclosed evidence that suggested that both Presidents Ronald Reagan and GEORGE H. W. BUSH had greater roles in the Iran-Contra Affair than either the Tower Commission or the congressional committees had concluded. During the trial, North's attorneys failed in an attempt to SUBPOENA Reagan, whom North would later squarely blame for complete knowledge of the affair, in his memoir *Under Fire: An American Story*. Subsequent to the conviction, Judge Gesell denied two motions for an ACQUITTAL and a MISTRIAL. Gesell sentenced North to two years' probation, 1,200 hours of COMMUNITY SERVICE, and a $150,000 fine.

North appealed. On July 20, 1990, the U.S. Court of Appeals for the District of Columbia, in *U.S. v. North*, 910 F.2d. 843 ((D.C. Cir. 1990), suspended all three of North's FELONY convictions and completely overturned his conviction for destroying classified documents. At issue was North's earlier testimony before Congress. The appellate ruling was based on the same reasoning as the contention made by North, Poindexter, Secord, and Hakim before their trials: Congress's decision to grant immunity to North had clashed with the Fifth Amendment protection of witnesses against self-incrimination. The appeals court directed the trial court to reexamine North's earlier testimony. Some critics argued that the appellate ruling, written by Judge Laurence Silberman, smacked of partisanship; Silberman had been, in 1980, cochair of the Reagan-Bush foreign policy advisory group. Walsh pressed on, but on September 16, 1991, Judge Gesell dropped all charges against North (*North*, 920 F. 2d 940 [D.C. Cir. 1990], *cert. denied*, 500 U.S. 941, 111 S. Ct. 2235, 114 L. Ed. 2d 477 [1991]).

Vice Admiral Poindexter's trial was similar to North's. After failing to win release of classified subpoenaed materials, Walsh narrowed his case to charges that Poindexter had provided false information and made false statements to Congress. Unlike North's attorneys, however, Poindexter's successfully subpoenaed former president Reagan, who became the first former president ordered to testify in a criminal trial regarding the conduct of affairs during his administration. Reagan provided an eight-hour videotaped DEPOSITION. However, Poindexter failed to win access to the former president's diaries, which his attorneys argued were crucial to Poindexter's defense.

Walsh's prosecution of Poindexter succeeded through a PREPONDERANCE OF EVIDENCE. In testimony for the prosecution, Lieutenant Colonel North said that he had seen Poindexter destroy a high-level secret document, signed by the president, which described the Iran arms sales as an exchange-for-hostages deal. North also claimed that he lied to members of Congress at Poindexter's direction. Other testimony revealed that Poindexter had erased some 5,000 computer files after the Iran-Contra story broke in the media in November 1986.

On April 7, 1990, jurors convicted Poindexter on all five of the counts in the indictment. Sentenced on June 11, 1990, to six months in prison, he became the first Iran-Contra DEFENDANT to receive a prison term, but remained free pending his appeal. Here, as in *North*, the conviction was overturned. The Court of Appeals for the District of Columbia ruled that Poindexter's testimony before Congress had been unfairly used against him in his trial (*Poindexter*, 951 F. 2d 369 [D.C. Cir. 1991]).

If the reversal of convictions against Poindexter and North represented a defeat to Walsh, so did several PLEA bargains that his office secured in the late 1980s. Critics had expected more serious convictions to result from his intense investigation. In March 1988 former national security adviser Robert McFarlane pleaded guilty to four MISDEMEANOR counts of withholding information from Congress and was fined a modest amount. Two private fundraisers, Carl Channell and Richard Miller, pleaded guilty to using a tax-exempt organization to raise money to purchase arms for the Contras. Channell was sentenced to probation only; Miller was ordered to do minimal public service. In November 1989 Secord, Hakim, and a corporation owned by Hakim all pleaded guilty to relatively minor counts. As Walsh's office persevered, it could show little in terms of prosecutions, and Republicans in Congress derided the multimillion-dollar investigation as a vindictive exercise in partisan politics.

Then in 1992 Walsh brought an indictment against the highest-ranking Reagan administration official to be charged in the Iran-Contra Affair: Caspar W. Weinberger, former defense secretary. Weinberger was indicted on June 16, 1992, on five felony counts: one count of obstructing the congressional committees' investigations; two counts of making false statements to investigators working for Walsh and Congress; and two counts of PERJURY related to his congressional testimony. Penalties for each count were a maximum of five years in prison and up to $250,000 in fines.

Walsh based the case on evidence gathered from notes that Weinberger had written while serving for six years in the Reagan administration. These nearly illegible notes, scrawled on 1,700 small scraps of paper, formed a personal diary. Weinberger had given them to the LIBRARY OF CONGRESS, with the requirement that no one could read them without his personal consent. Throughout Iran-Contra investigations, Weinberger had repeatedly testified to Congress and the Tower Commission that he had argued against the arms-for-hostages scheme when it was discussed by White House officials. Walsh did not make Weinberger's involvement an issue in the 1992 indictment. Instead, he zeroed in on Weinberger's testimony under oath that he had not kept notes or a personal diary during the arms sale period. The discovery of the notes in the Library of Congress suggested that Weinberger had presented false testimony.

On June 19, 1992, Weinberger pleaded not guilty to all five felony charges. Judge Thomas F. Hogan set a tentative trial date of November 2, 1992, one day before the presidential election. This timing raised the question of whether Weinberger's trial would cause political embarrassment for President George H. W. Bush, who was campaigning against BILL CLINTON. Four days before the election, Walsh announced a new indictment against Weinberger. It centered on a note that had been written by Weinberger about a 1986 White House meeting and that seemed to contradict Bush's claim that as VICE PRESIDENT he had not been involved in the arms-for-hostages decision making. Senate Republicans, angered by the indictment, asked the Justice Department to name an independent counsel to investigate whether the Clinton campaign had been behind the indictment. Attorney General WILLIAM P. BARR denied the request.

The case progressed no further. In a surprise reprieve on Christmas Eve, 1992, President Bush pardoned Weinberger and five others implicated in the Iran-Contra Affair. The pardon cited Weinberger's record of public and military service, his recent ill health, and a desire to put Iran-Contra to rest. Bush also pardoned former assistant secretary of state Elliot Abrams; former CIA officials Clair George, Duane Clarridge, and Alan Fiers; and former national security adviser McFarlane. Bush deemed all six men patriots and said their prosecution represented not law enforcement but the "criminalization of policy differences," essentially repeating his long-standing argument that Iran-Contra was really a case where Democrats had pursued a political witch-hunt to punish Republican officials over disagreements on foreign policy (Grant of Exec. CLEMENCY, Proclamation No. 6518, 57 Fed. Reg. 62,145).

Reaction to the pardons divided along party lines, with Republicans hailing Bush and Democrats criticizing him. Walsh accused Bush of furthering a cover-up and thwarting judicial process. He had long maintained that top Reagan administration officials had engaged in a cover-up to protect their president. Now, he promised, Bush would become the subject of his remaining investigation.

Bush's only testimony had taken place in a January 1988 videotaped deposition. An unsettled question was why Bush's personal diaries were withheld from prosecutors for six years; their existence was only disclosed to the independent counsel's office following the 1992 presidential election. Throughout 1993, Walsh sought to interview the former president but was blocked by Bush's attorneys. Bush consistently insisted on placing limits on any interview. Walsh refused those limits, complained that Bush was stalling the investigation, and ultimately abandoned the attempt to question Bush.

Walsh also chose, in 1993, not to indict another high-ranking Reagan administration official, former attorney general EDWIN MEESE III. In 1986 Meese said that Reagan did not know about the arms sales to Iran. Walsh contended that the statement was false, but admitted that building a criminal case against Meese would have been difficult: too much time had passed and could therefore have bolstered memory loss as a defense.

On August 6, 1992, after six-and-a-half years and $35.7 million, Walsh concluded the Iran-Contra investigation and submitted his final report to the special court that had appointed him. By 1993 the Iran-Contra Affair seemed over, in one sense. The STATUTE OF LIMITATIONS on crimes that may have been committed during it had expired, and no further prosecution would be forthcoming. However, additional revelations followed as historians sifted through emerging evidence, notably in the memoirs of key participants. The lessons of the affair continued to be debated. Some said that Iran-Contra exposed a pattern of zealous disregard, by the EXECUTIVE BRANCH, of legislative constraint on foreign policy, that dated back to the VIETNAM WAR. Others took the view held by the Reagan and Bush administrations: namely, that nothing terrible had happened.

FURTHER READINGS

Walsh, Lawrence E. 1993. *Final Report of the Independent Counsel for Iran/Contra Matters.* Washington, D.C.: Government Printing Office. Available online at http://www.fas.org/irp/offdocs/walsh/; website home page: http://www.fas.org (accessed August 2, 2009).

———. 1998. *Firewall: The Iran-Contra Conspiracy and Cover-Up.* New York: Norton.

Wolf, Julie. "The Iran-Contra Affair." *PBS People & Events.* Available online at http://www.pbs.org/wgbh/amex/reagan/peopleevents/pande08.html; website home page: http://www.pbs.org (accessed September 5, 2009).

IRAQ WAR

The Iraq War involved the invasion and subsequent occupation of Iraq by U.S. and U.N. forces beginning in March 2003.

The Iraq War, also known as Operation Iraqi Freedom, involved the invasion of Iraq by multinational forces along with the subsequent occupation of the country by U.S. and other UNITED NATIONS (UN) forces. In many ways, the conflict was a continuation of the first Gulf War, which took place in 1990 and 1991. The Iraq War resulted in the overthrow of Iraqi president Saddam Hussein, who was executed in 2006.

The hostilities in Iraq followed extensive efforts by the UN to disarm Iraq through diplomatic means. Efforts of the UN broke down, though, as U.S. and British military forces crossed into Iraq during March 2003. These military forces represented a coalition of nations seeking to enforce UN resolutions that required Iraq to disarm itself by destroying and accounting for its WEAPONS OF MASS DESTRUCTION (WMDs).

Diplomacy Gives Way to Force as a Means of Disarming Iraq

The original Persian Gulf War began when Iraq invaded Kuwait on August 2, 1990. In response, the UN Security Council passed Resolution 678, authorizing the UN to use force to remove Iraqi forces from Kuwait and restore peace to the region. The Resolution gave Iraq until January 15, 1991, to comply. When Saddam Hussein allowed the deadline to pass without removing his forces, the United States led an international coalition of more than 90 nations in a six-week war—dubbed "Operation Desert Storm" by President GEORGE H. W. BUSH—that liberated Kuwait from Iraqi occupation.

Fighting ended on March 1, 1991, and two days later, Iraq accepted UN Resolution 687, which set out the conditions of ceasefire. Specifically, Resolution 687 imposed continuing obligations on Iraq to eliminate its WMDs, which were defined to include all nuclear, chemical, and biological weapons. Resolution 687 suspended but did not terminate the authority to use force under Resolution 678. A material breach of Resolution 687 would revive the authority to use force under Resolution 678.

Working with the International Atomic Energy Agency (IAEA), the UN Security Council established the UN Special Commission (UNSCOM) in April 1991 to ensure that Iraq eliminated all of its WMDs and undertook no efforts to later develop or acquire such weapons. Iraq cooperated in part with UN inspections efforts until 1996, when Iraq began to block inspections at what it deemed "sensitive military sites," including certain presidential palaces. A year later, Iraq demanded that UN inspectors leave the country, claiming that some of the inspectors were U.S. and British spies. By 1998, all UNCOMS inspectors had been withdrawn from Iraq. In 1999, the UN created the United Nations Monitoring, Verification and Inspection Commission (UNMOVIC) to replace UNSCOM, but Iraq declined to allow inspections by the new body either.

For the next two and a half years, the ongoing problems with the Iraq weapons inspection took a backseat to the impeachment proceedings against President BILL CLINTON and the 2000 presidential election between GEORGE W. BUSH and AL GORE. However, the Iraq situation was revisited after September 11, 2001, when more than 3,000 people died in terrorist attacks on New York City and Washington, D.C.

Lacking proof that Iraq was connected with either the September 11 attacks or the al Qaeda terrorist network that was allegedly responsible for coordinating the attacks, Bush told Americans in November 2001 that force would be used to disarm Iraq and remove Saddam from power if the Iraqi president did not allow the UN to resume its inspections for WMDs. Anti-U.S. terrorists had proven their willingness to use WMDs to kill Americans, the president argued, and Saddam had proven his capacity to manufacture WMDs. So while there may have been no conclusive proof establishing a link between al Qaeda and Saddam, Bush said that his duties as president prevented him from waiting to protect Americans from "another September 11."

On January 29, 2002, Bush stepped up the rhetoric in his State of the Union address, identifying Iraq, Iran, and North Korea as members of the "axis of evil, arming to threaten the peace of the world." The president told Congress that he "would not wait on events while dangers gather," suggesting that he was contemplating pre-emptive strikes against those nations armed with WMDs. Secretary of State Colin Powell persuaded the president that if Saddam was to be disarmed, it was best to do so with the backing of the international community. The UN Security Council, Powell said, was ready to force Iraq to accept weapons inspectors for the first time since 1998. Bush pressed his case for resumed inspections before the UN on September 12, 2002.

Two months later, on November 8, the Security Council unanimously passed Resolution 1441, which declared that Iraq was in material noncompliance with Resolution 687, but gave Iraq a final opportunity to abide by its disarmament obligations. The resolution warned of "serious consequences" were Iraq again to be found in material breech of its disarmament obligations, but left undefined what that term meant. Iraq accepted the UN resolution and delivered a 12,000-page declaration of its weapons programs in December 2002. After reviewing the report, Hans Blix, executive chairman of UNMOVIC, told the Security Council that the declaration "is essentially a reorganized version" of information Iraq provided UNSCOM in 1997 and that it "is not enough to create confidence" that Iraq had destroyed its WMDs.

On January 27, 2003, Blix again appeared before the Security Council, this time to report that after 60 days of UN inspections Iraq "appears not to have come to a genuine acceptance, not even today" of demands that it disarm. In particular, Blix said that Iraq had failed to demonstrate it had destroyed 10,000 liters of anthrax, 40,000 liters of botulinum, hundreds of liters of ricin, hundreds of tons of mustard gas, and thousands of tons of the VX nerve agent, all of which Iraq possessed in 1998 kicked out the UN weapons inspectors.

A week later, Powell presented the Council with satellite photos and other so-called evidence demonstrating what he claimed were secret efforts at developing WMDs. However, any momentum Powell might have gained by his presentation was undercut when Blix reported on February 14 that Iraq had increased its cooperation with the UN. On March 1, Blix told the Security Council that Iraq had begun destroying 100 AI Samoud 2 missiles that violated the UN-established range for surface missiles.

Encouraged by what appeared to be heightened Iraqi cooperation, Russia and France, two permanent members of the Security Council, vowed to veto any new resolution that would expressly authorize the use of force to disarm Iraq. Germany, which in February had assumed the chairmanship of the Security Council in its role as a rotating, non-permanent member, opposed the use of military force. All three countries, along with peace activists around the world, urged the United States to allow the inspections to continue for several months before considering military action.

The United States, though, was not similarly encouraged. U.S. officials charged that Iraq's latest efforts were meaningless tokens of cooperation aimed at deceiving the UN and keeping Saddam in power. On March 17, Bush delivered a prime-time address in which he said that time had run out for Iraq. Bush said he was prepared to go to war with Iraq without a new UN resolution authorizing him to do so, suggesting that he already had UN authorization under Resolutions 1441, 687, and 678. Independent of UN authority, Bush stressed that he was authorized to use force by his constitutional powers and obligations to protect the American people as PRESIDENT OF THE UNITED STATES and commander in chief of the armed forces. Bush gave Saddam and his sons 48 hours to leave Iraq or face "the full force and might" of the U.S. military "at a time of our choosing."

In the pre-dawn hours of March 20, 2003, U.S. and British military forces commenced "Operation Iraqi Freedom," purporting to disarm Iraq of WMDs, removing Saddam from power, and liberating the people of Iraq. Approximately 40 countries supported the military campaign, according to White House sources. Three weeks later, U.S. troops reached the Iraqi capital of Baghdad.

The Demise of Saddam Hussein

By April 2003, much of the world watched live coverage via satellite of U.S. and coalition forces assisting Iraqi citizens to pull down a huge statue of Saddam Hussein that had dominated Baghdad's central square for decades. Photographs of the symbolic gesture appeared on the front pages of newspapers around the globe. By the end of the day, nearly every statue of Iraq's tyrannical leader had been removed, dismembered, defaced, or destroyed by a rowdy group of jubilant Iraqis. Thousands took to the streets cheering, while others burned and looted government buildings associated with Saddam's regime.

The jubilation seemed short-lived, quickly turning to anarchy. Downtown Baghdad was nearly gutted by looting and burning. Several Iraqis took advantage of the chaos to commit robberies and carry out revenge killings against fellow Iraqis. The MURDER rate in Baghdad jumped to 20 times its average. This took place in the presence of UN coalition troops who had taken over control of the capital.

One year later, in April 2004, the jury was still out as to how much life had actually improved for Iraqi citizens. Many polls indicated that the majority was satisfied to see the end of Saddam's control. But anti-coalition, anti-American sentiments were on the rise as frustration over on-and-off-again utilities, high unemployment, and warring among internal factions all took their toll. Moreover, violence from Iraqi insurgents had actually escalated as the June 30, 2004, deadline for transfer of governmental control from the United Nations' Coalition Provisional Authority (CPA) to the Iraqi people drew near. In addition to military casualties, there was a palpable increase in the use of suicide bombings and sniper attacks on civilian contractors or others perceived to be assisting the coalition. In May 2004 alone, the car bombing of the leader of the Iraqi Governing Council, as well as the beheading of an American contractor a few days earlier, served as somber reminders of the uncertain road ahead.

Almost a year earlier, on July 13, 2003, the 25-member Iraqi Governing Council, which had the power to appoint ministers and approve the budget for 2004, met for the first time to discuss the future of Iraq following the demise of Saddam's Baath regime. In the interim, the United Nations had designated the CPA as the lawful government of Iraq until such time as Iraq was politically and socially stable enough to accept sovereignty. All involved remained focused on the dual objectives of searching for weapons of mass destruction and rebuilding a strong and stable Iraq.

On July 22, 2003, Saddam's sons, Uday and Qusay, were shot and killed by coalition troops in a gun battle at their Mosul hideout. The hunt for Saddam himself seemed to dominate the news of the war. A $25 million reward and all of the CIA's finest intelligence failed to find him, but alleged sightings of Saddam were common throughout the country. Finally, in December 2003, an Iraqi official in U.S. custody buckled under interrogation and blurted out Saddam's whereabouts. Within twenty-four hours, U.S. Special Forces had closed in on a farmhouse south of Tikrit, Saddam's hometown, and began looking for a hidden bunker or underground facility. U.S. forces arrested Saddam after finding him hiding in a hole stocked with various supplies and $750,000 in U.S. currency. Saddam was removed to a cell in Baghdad for interrogation by the CENTRAL INTELLIGENCE AGENCY.

New Iraqi Government but Continued Hostilities

The official end of the occupation occurred on June 28, 2004, with the handover of governmental authority from the occupying forces to the new Iraqi interim government, headed by interim prime minister Iyad Allawi. The handover was conducted two days ahead of schedule and in a secret location, in order to deter insurgent attacks.

Insurgency continued to be a major problem for coalition forces. These insurgents were responsible for guerilla actions in the form of constant roadside and car bombings, assassinations of government officials, and SABOTAGE of infrastructure. They were also responsible for conventional military attacks and managed to seize police stations and entire towns. When coalition forces counterattacked, the insurgents were often able to melt into the population.

On September 15, 2004, U.N. secretary general Kofi Annan declared the war in Iraq illegal and in violation of the U.N. Charter. The United States, the United Kingdom, and Australia issued strong rebuttals to Annan's declaration, but much of the world's opinion was aligned with the U.N. By December 1, though, the Bush administration announced that it would increase troop levels to 150,000 by the middle of January 2005. The troop increase coincided with a rise in resistance from insurgents.

Saddam Tried and Executed

Saddam's trial for crimes against humanity began in October 2005. He had previously been formally charged by the Iraqi Special Tribunal.

SHOULD BUSH ADMINISTRATION OFFICIALS BE PROSECUTED FOR WAR CRIMES?

Few will ever forget the images of the aftermath of the terrorist attacks on September 11, 2001, which in many ways defined the first decade of the 2000s. One of the results of the attack was a major change in U.S. policy. The United States adopted a tough style that called for a significant increase in foreign engagement.

As the decade closed and President GEORGE W. BUSH left office, many remembered other appalling images and stories of atrocities committed by those ostensibly charged with protecting U.S. interests abroad. Some of these events involved random acts of violence, such as the RAPE and MURDER of 14-year-old Abeer Qassim al-Janabi in 2004 by five U.S. soldiers.

Other incidents appeared to be less random. Within a year of the invasion of Iraq, stories emerged about prisoner abuse occurring at the Abu Ghraib prison in Baghdad. Hundreds of images released to the public showed soldiers posing next to and mocking naked Iraqi detainees. Other pictures were more atrocious, showing what appeared to be gang rapes of Iraqi women held at the prison. U.S. soldiers were also accused of beating detainees to death.

The atrocities at Abu Ghraib were not without consequence. A total of eleven members of the military were charged for their roles in the incidents, though none was charged with murder. The highest ranking official charged with

a crime was Lieutenant Colonel Steven L. Jordan, who was accused of abusing detainees "by subjecting them to forced nudity and intimidation by military working dogs." He was also accused of lying about his knowledge of this abuse. In August 2007, though, Jordan was acquitted of most charges, though he was convicted of disobeying an order not to discuss an investigation into the allegations. Jordan later received a reprimand for this incident.

With Jordan's ACQUITTAL, no high-ranking officer faced any significant punishment for the atrocities at Abu Ghraig. Colonel Thomas M. Pappas, a military intelligence officer who ran the facility, received an administrative punishment and a fine for authorizing the use of dogs during interrogations. Former brigadier general Janis Karpinski, commander of the military police, also received administrative punishment and a demotion.

Democrats and even some Republicans were critical of the Bush administration's handling of the Abu Ghraib incident, with several officials calling for the resignation of then secretary of defense Donald Rumsfeld (who eventually resigned in December 2006). Rumsfeld took responsibility for what he referred to as acts of abuse and offered an apology to the people of Iraq. However, he refused to refer to the incidents as acts of torture.

The public became further outraged with news about the alleged torture of detainees at Guantanamo Bay in Cuba. Officials with the CENTRAL INTELLIGENCE AGENCY used a technique known as waterboarding to interrogate suspected terrorists at the facility. Waterboarding involves strapping a suspect down, placing a cloth over the suspect's face, and pouring water over the suspect's face. The technique, which dates back as far at the Spanish Inquisition, creates the sensation of drowning. Beginning in 2007, Congress held hearings regarding use of waterboarding, and several experts testified that the method is nothing short of torture. Members of the Bush administration, including former VICE PRESIDENT Dick Cheney, defended the use of the method, claiming that its use had led to a great deal of valuable information.

Although Bush attempted to distance himself with the atrocities committed at Abu Ghraib and Guantanamo Bay, members of his administration had provided the legal justification for the torture techniques. In the wake of the September 11, 2001, attacks, Bush administration officials wanted greater powers to investigate, capture, and interrogate suspected terrorists. Within two weeks of the attacks, attorneys with the Office of Legal Counsel began writing memoranda expressing opinions about certain courses of action. The first of

More specific charges related to crimes against the residents of Dujayl in 1982. In that incident, he allegedly ordered the murder of 148 people, the torture of women and children, and the illegal arrest of several hundred others. He was also accused of mass murders in Kurdistan-Iraq in 1987 and 1988 and in the Shi'I south in 1991. However, he was convicted of the Dujayl crimes before being tried for the latter crimes.

Saddam was found guilty on November 5, 2006, and was sentenced to be hanged. He appealed both convictions, but the convictions were affirmed, and he was executed on December 30, 2006.

Democrats Demand Policy Change

Democrats took control of Congress through the November 2006 elections, and immediately leaders in the DEMOCRATIC PARTY demanded

these memos concluded that a proposed amendment to the Foreign Intelligence Surveillance Act (50 U.S.C.A. §§ 1801 et seq.) would not violate the FOURTH AMENDMENT to the U.S. Constitution. One month later, another memo concluded that the president had authority under the Constitution and federal statutes to deploy the military to attack terrorists operating within the borders of the United States.

In 2002 and 2003, the Office of Legal Counsel wrote more memos focusing on the legality of detaining suspected terrorists. On February 7, 2002, Bush signed a memo declaring that the third Geneva Convention, which prescribes treatment of prisoners of war, did not apply to suspected members of the Taliban or the terrorist organization al-Qaeda. Another memo written in June 2002 concluded that the military could legally detain U.S. citizens, even though a federal statute specifically prohibits such DETENTION unless the detention is done pursuant to an act of Congress. This memo concluded that the president's authority as commander in chief was enough to provide legal justification for these detentions.

On March 14, 2003, a memo entitled "Military Interrogation of Alien Unlawful Combatants Held Outside the United States" concluded that neither the FIFTH AMENDMENT nor the EIGHTH AMENDMENT to the Constitution extended rights to ALIEN ENEMY combatants held outside the United States. The conclusions reached in this memo allegedly justified the use of waterboarding as an interrogation technique by the CIA.

Several of these memos were written by a staff member named John Yoo, who later became a law professor at the University of California at Berkeley. Another significant official involved with these memos was Jay Bybee, who later became a judge with the Ninth CIRCUIT COURT of Appeals. Bybee drafted what came to be known as the *Bybee Memo*, which described "enhanced interrogation techniques" that are widely considered to be methods of torture. Former attorney general and White House counsel Alberto Gonzalez drafted a memo that argued, in part, that the Geneva Convention was largely outdated.

As these memos became public knowledge in 2008 and 2009, some critics demanded punishment to those who authorized the torture techniques and other WAR CRIMES. Joe Klein of *Time Magazine* wrote that Bush's authorization of the February 2002 torture memo "was his single most callous and despicable act. It stands at the heart of the national embarrassment that was his presidency."

In April 2008 the JUSTICE DEPARTMENT began a probe into the background behind Yoo's memo of March 14, 2003. According to Senator Sheldon Whitehouse (D-RI), an outspoken critic of the interrogations, "The abject failure of legal scholarship in the Office of Legal Counsel's analysis of torture suggests that what mattered was not that the reasoning was sound, or that the research was comprehensive, but that it delivered what the Bush administration wanted."

Calls for prosecutions of Bush administration officials heated up in 2009, especially once President BARACK OBAMA decided to declassify the memos. In late April 2009, Obama said he was open to prosecuting those who provided the authority for the interrogation methods, saying that the U.S. lost "our moral bearings" in using the tactics.

Although some legal scholars suggested that the lawyers who drafted the opinions could be subject to prosecution, few believed that this would be a likely result. Prosecutors would have to show that these Justice Department officials had intentionally misstated the law against torture, which would be difficult to prove. Moreover, as Tom Malinowski, Washington director of HUMAN RIGHTS WATCH, told the *Los Angeles Times*, "Once you begin a serious discussion of criminal prosecution, the question quickly becomes: Why PROSECUTE those in the middle of the chain of command but not those who made the ultimate decisions at the top?"

Despite the likelihood that no official will be charged with a war crime, some officials may still pay the price for providing the reasoning that justified the torture. For instance, the Justice Department's Office of PROFESSIONAL RESPONSIBILITY has investigated Yoo, Bybee, and other lawyers involved in the memos. Moreover, members of Congress, including House Speaker Nancy Pelosi, have not ruled out the possibility that Bybee could be impeached from his position on the Ninth Circuit.

FURTHER READINGS

Klein, Joe. 2009. "The Bush Administration's Most Despicable Act." *Time*. January 8.

Savage, David G., and Josh Meyer. 2009. "Prosecuting 'Torture Memo' Authors Called a 'Real Stretch.'" *Los Angeles Times*. April 23.

changes in U.S. policy in Iraq. U.S. secretary of defense Donald Rumsfeld had long downplayed the magnitude of problems in Iraq, and critics charged the U.S. forces in Iraq were too small to accomplish the military's mission. Democrats and other critics began to demand for a timetable to withdraw forces.

Earlier in 2006, Congress had appointed a ten-member Iraq Study Group, which was charged with assessing the situation in Iraq and with making policy recommendations. The group was co-chaired by former secretary of state James Baker (a Republican) and former representative Lee H. Hamilton (a Democrat). The Iraq Study Group released its reports on December 6, 2006. Its conclusion, in part, was: "The Iraqi government should accelerate assuming responsibility for Iraqi security by increasing the number and quality of Iraqi Army brigades. While this process is under way, and to facilitate it, the United States should significantly increase the number of U.S. military personnel, including combat troops, imbedded in and supporting Iraqi Army units. As these actions proceed, U.S. combat forces could begin to move out of Iraq." Conservatives who supported the war effort were critical of the report upon its release.

Rumsfeld resigned at the end of 2006. Early in 2007 Bush announced that he was sending more than 21,000 additional troops to battle an increase in insurgency that had begun late in 2006. By the spring 2007, violence in Iraq had decreased significantly. In May 2007 Congress approved legislation that funded the war in Iraq but established deadlines for troop withdrawal. Bush vetoed this legislation.

By 2008 Bush announced that Iraq was returning to a normal, thanks in part to the U.S. military's efforts to increase security. In November 2008, following the election of President BARACK OBAMA, the Iraqi government approved a resolution calling for the United States to end its military presence in Iraq by 2011. In February 2009, Obama announced that the United States would withdraw combat forces within an 18-month window.

Failed Search for Weapons of Mass Destruction

On January 12, 2005, the Bush administration announced that the search for weapons of mass destruction in Iraq had ended, without any such weapons having been found. The announcement coincided with several reports calling into question the data on which Bush had based his allegations in 2002 about Iraq's attempts to obtain materials to create WMDs.

As Bush prepared to leave office in December 2008, he acknowledged that one of his biggest disappointments was the "intelligence failure in Iraq," referring specifically to the data used as the basis for the decision to go to war with Saddam.

FURTHER READINGS

Falk, Richard A. 2008. *The Costs of War: International Law, the U.N., and World Order after Iraq.* New York: Routledge.

Iraq Study Group. 2006. *Iraq Study Group Report.* Washington, D.C.: United States Institute of Peace.

Jaques, Richard B., ed. 2006. *Issues in International Law* Newport, R.I.: Naval War College.

CROSS REFERENCE

War on Terrorism.

❖ IREDELL, JAMES

James Iredell was one of the original U.S. Supreme Court justices appointed by GEORGE WASHINGTON.

Iredell was born October 5, 1751, in Lewes, England. At age 17 he began working in his family's MERCANTILE business in North Carolina and also undertook the study of law. He was licensed to practice law in 1771. In the next few years, he became active in the Revolutionary cause, arguing that the colonies not separate from England and advocating in his writings that the conflict be resolved through RECONCILIATION rather than war. In 1776 he was appointed to a commission to draft and revise the laws for the governance of North Carolina. A year later he served as a judge on the state superior court, and from 1779 to 1781 he was state attorney general. In 1787 he codified and revised the statutes of North Carolina, a process that resulted in the publication of *Iredell's Revisal* four years later.

A staunch supporter of the Constitutional Convention, Iredell led North Carolina in the movement for ratification through a series of

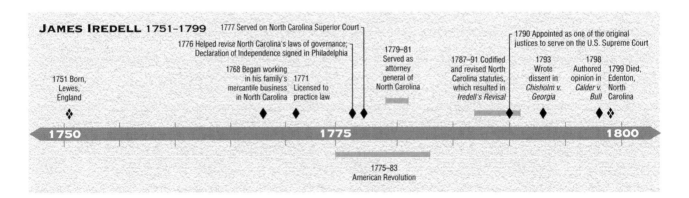

JAMES IREDELL 1751–1799

1777 Served on North Carolina Superior Court

1776 Helped revise North Carolina's laws of governance; Declaration of Independence signed in Philadelphia

1790 Appointed as one of the original justices to serve on the U.S. Supreme Court

1751 Born, Lewes, England

1768 Began working in his family's mercantile business in North Carolina

1771 Licensed to practice law

1779–81 Served as attorney general of North Carolina

1787–91 Codified and revised North Carolina statutes, which resulted in *Iredell's Revisal*

1793 Wrote dissent in *Chisholm v. Georgia*

1798 Authored opinion in *Calder v. Bull*

1799 Died, Edenton, North Carolina

1750   1775   1800

1775–83 American Revolution

acclaimed and well-publicized floor debates and speeches. In 1790 he drew the attention of President Washington, who appointed him to the newly formed U.S. Supreme Court. At age 38, Iredell was the youngest of the original justices.

In addition to hearing cases before the entire Supreme Court, the justices at that time presided over CIRCUIT COURT sessions throughout the United States, which required them to travel extensively to hear arguments. Iredell was assigned to the Southern Circuit and quickly developed a reputation as an exceptional jurist with respect to CONSTITUTIONAL LAW matters. He wrote a number of notable opinions, including a dissent in CHISHOLM V. GEORGIA, 2 U.S. (Dall.) 419, 1 L. Ed. 440 (1793), in which he argued that only a constitutional provision could SUPERSEDE the common-law principle that a state cannot be sued by a citizen from another state. Iredell maintained that the states were sovereign and did not owe their origins to the federal government. Iredell's view of states' rights would prevail in Congress's subsequent adoption of the ELEVENTH AMENDMENT.

Iredell also authored *Calder v. Bull,* 3 U.S. (Dall.) 386, 1 L. Ed. 648 (1798), in which he argued that a legislative act unauthorized by or in violation of the Constitution was void and that the courts were responsible for determining an act's status in that regard. This principle of JUDICIAL REVIEW would be amplified five years later in the landmark decision MARBURY V. MADISON, 5 U.S. (1 Cranch) 137, 2 L. Ed. 60 (1803), which held that the courts were indeed ultimately responsible for deciding the validity of laws passed by the legislative branch of government.

The strain of the travel required to cover his circuit, in addition to the heavy caseload of the Supreme Court, eventually took its toll on Iredell's health. He died at his home in North Carolina in 1799, less than ten years after ascending to the High Court.

❖ IRELAND, PATRICIA

Patricia Ireland is an attorney and social activist who became the ninth president of the NATIONAL ORGANIZATION FOR WOMEN (NOW) on December 15, 1991; she served as president for ten years, leaving in 2001 due to term limits. Ireland took over the presidency just as NOW was beginning

James Iredell.
ENGRAVING BY ALBERT ROSENTHAL. COLLECTION OF THE SUPREME COURT OF THE UNITED STATES

to feel a shift in its ranks and the United States was experiencing a renewed interest in the feminist movement.

Ireland was born October 19, 1945, in Oak Park, Illinois. She grew up on a farm in Valparaiso, Indiana, where her family raised honeybees. She is the younger of two daughters of James Ireland and Joan Filipek (older sister Kathy was killed in a horseback riding accident when Ireland was five years old). Ireland's father, a metallurgical engineer, taught her to be passionate about her profession. Her mother was a volunteer counselor with Planned Parenthood who became the first director of the local chapter. She was Ireland's social activist role model.

Ireland entered DePauw University when she was 16, but became pregnant and was forced to travel to Japan to obtain a legal ABORTION. She then married and transferred to the University of Tennessee, where she obtained a degree in German in 1966. Her first marriage lasted only a short time. She later began work as a graduate student and German teacher, but she quickly became bored with teaching. She and her second husband, artist James Humble, moved to Miami, where she became a flight attendant for Pan American World Airways.

Working as a flight attendant was a pivotal experience for Ireland. She discovered that her employee HEALTH INSURANCE plan would not cover her husband's dental expenses, even though it did pay such expenses for the wives of male employees. Ireland consulted Dade

A WRITTEN OPINION MUST FOR EVER AFTERWARDS SPEAK FOR ITSELF, AND COMMIT THE CHARACTER OF THE WRITER, IN LASTING COLORS, EITHER OF FAME OR INFAMY, OR NEUTRAL INSIGNIFICANCE, TO FUTURE AGES, AS WELL AS TO THE PRESENT.
—JAMES IREDELL

Patricia Ireland.
AP IMAGES

County NOW for advice. It referred her to the LABOR DEPARTMENT, the EQUAL EMPLOYMENT OPPORTUNITY COMMISSION (EEOC), and the flight attendants' union. As a result of Ireland's challenge, the insurance policy was amended. Her characteristic good humor is evident in her comments on the experience: "The vice-president of the labor task force at Dade County NOW is now the dean of women lawmakers in the Florida legislature. I am the president of NOW. And Pan am is bankrupt."

Taking on Pan Am's discriminatory insurance plan whet Ireland's appetite for more knowledge of the law. She enrolled in the law school at Florida State University while continuing to work as a flight attendant. Ireland began to notice that if she introduced herself

as a flight attendant, people had little to say to her, but if she introduced herself as a law student, they were eager to discuss complex legal issues and current events. The denigration of work traditionally done by women offended her growing feminist sensibilities. "My brain was the same, my ideas were just as worthy or unworthy, but there was a tremendous difference in the way that people perceived and treated me," she said. "I think traditional women's work is undervalued—teaching, health care, social work. That was part of the experience that made me want to be an activist."

Ireland earned her law degree from the University of Miami, where she had transferred from Florida State, in 1975. She both served on the school's LAW REVIEW and the *Lawyer of the Americas* (now the *University of Miami Inter-American Law Review*) and did PRO BONO work for Dade County NOW. After graduation, she practiced corporate law for 12 years, continued working for Dade County NOW, and helped corporate clients formulate AFFIRMATIVE ACTION programs.

Ireland's work in the women's rights movement expanded during her years as an attorney. In 1983, she became the chair of Florida NOW's lesbian rights task force. In 1985 she managed Eleanor C. Smeal's successful campaign for the presidency of NOW, and in 1987 she was elected NOW's executive VICE PRESIDENT, a post she held until May 1991, when she became acting president following the illness of Molly Yard. On December 15, 1991, Ireland was officially named NOW's ninth president.

As NOW's top officer, Ireland was charged with pursuing the group's four priority issues:

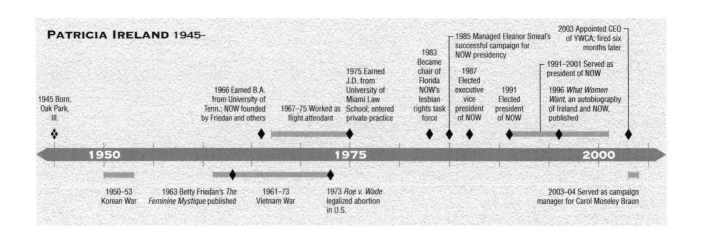

PATRICIA IRELAND 1945–

1945 Born, Oak Park, Ill.

1966 Earned B.A. from University of Tenn.; NOW founded by Friedan and others

1967–75 Worked as flight attendant

1975 Earned J.D. from University of Miami Law School; entered private practice

1983 Became chair of Florida NOW's lesbian rights task force

1985 Managed Eleanor Smeal's successful campaign for NOW presidency

1987 Elected executive vice president of NOW

1991 Elected president of NOW

1991–2001 Served as president of NOW

1996 *What Women Want*, an autobiography of Ireland and NOW, published

2003 Appointed CEO of YWCA; fired six months later

1950   **1975**   **2000**

1950–53 Korean War

1963 Betty Friedan's *The Feminine Mystique* published

1961–73 Vietnam War

1973 *Roe v. Wade* legalized abortion in U.S.

2003–04 Served as campaign manager for Carol Moseley Braun

protecting abortion rights; electing women to political leadership positions; forming coalitions with other CIVIL RIGHTS organizations; and advocating for international women's rights. She vowed to stir things up, and she did. During her years as president, Ireland developed and implemented a number of programs, including Project Stand Up for Women, an international program designed to protect women who seek abortion services and to combat anti-abortion clinic blockades; Elect Women for a Change, which provides experienced campaign support for feminist candidates; and the Global Feminist Program, which provides a forum for women around the world to discuss relevant women's issues. Ireland also served as legal counsel on several NOW landmark cases, and was a major organizer of such events as the 1993 March on Washington for Gay, Lesbian, and Bi Civil Rights.

Ireland's tenure, however, was not without detractors. Specifically, questions arose as to whether NOW, with Ireland at the helm, represented the majority of U.S. women, or whether its focus had become too narrow. Such questions were prompted when NOW announced that lesbian rights would be one of its top priorities. At about the same time, the *Advocate*, a gay and lesbian newspaper, revealed that Ireland, while maintaining her long-standing marriage to Humble, who lives in Florida, also had a female companion with whom she lived in Washington, D.C.

Even NOW's allies became concerned that the organization would be perceived as a fringe group that did not address the concerns of the majority, and that support for NOW causes would be eroded. BETTY N. FRIEDAN, the group's founding president, accused NOW of failing to address women's current concerns, such as juggling families and jobs. Ireland, however, maintained that NOW was on the right track for carrying on the fight for women's rights. "Someone has to raise the issues that make people uncomfortable, the issues that other people don't want to talk about.... [I]t's healthy to be angry at the situation women face. So, yes, we may be militant and angry but we're also thoughtful and intelligent."

In 2001, after ten years, Ireland stepped down as president of NOW. In 2003 she became the CEO of the YWCA of the USA. Some conservative critics raised eyebrows over the appointment. She spent six controversial months as president of the YWCA. Traditional Christian groups objected to her using a nominally Christian organization as a platform to advance feminist causes (the group's initials stand for "Young Women's Christian Association"), and the YWCA proved not to be as supportive of Ireland's controversial stands as she might have liked. "We have the deepest admiration for Ms. Ireland's dedication to women's issues and social justice, but the YWCA has proved to be the wrong platform for her to advocate for these issues," the YWCA's board said when they fired Ireland that October.

Ireland served as campaign manager for former Democratic senator Carol Moseley Braun's short-lived 2004 presidential campaign, from November of 2003 until Moseley Braun withdrew from the race two months later. Ireland's next stop was DontAmend.com, a web site and organization founded to lobby against a proposed CONSTITUTIONAL AMENDMENT to ban same-sex marriage. She joined that group in March of 2004 and was immediately sent to Capitol Hill to address the SENATE JUDICIARY COMMITTEE about the issue. "Equal marriage rights will be one of the most explosive issues of the 2004 elections," said Ireland when she joined forces with DontAmend.com. "This is also an incredible opportunity to make a quantum leap forward, and for me, it's an opportunity not to be missed."

In addition to her professional duties, Ireland is a frequent contributor to periodicals, newspapers, and journals, and, in 1996, she released her autobiography, *What Women Want.* Ireland is also a frequent guest speaker at universities and with HUMAN RIGHTS groups.

FURTHER READINGS

Ireland, Patricia. 1996. *What Women Want.* New York: Dutton.

Resnik, Judith. 2003. "Patricia Ireland: Women, Meeting (Again), in and beyond the United States." In *The Difference "Difference" Makes: Women and Leadership,* edited by Deborah L. Rhode. Palo Alto, Calif.: Stanford Univ. Press.

CROSS REFERENCES

Gay and Lesbian Rights; Sex Discrimination; Steinem, Gloria.

IRRECONCILABLE DIFFERENCES

The existence of significant differences between a married couple that are so great and beyond resolution as to make the marriage unworkable, and for which the law permits a divorce.

> FOR MOST WOMEN, EQUALITY IS A BREAD-AND-BUTTER ISSUE. WOMEN ARE STILL PAID LESS ON THE JOB AND CHARGED MORE FOR EVERYTHING FROM DRY CLEANING TO INSURANCE.
> —PATRICIA IRELAND

A DIVORCE premised on the ground of irreconcilable differences is considered a no-fault divorce since there is no need to establish that one party is more responsible or at fault for the end of the marriage than the other.

IRREGULARITY

A defect, failure, or mistake in a legal proceeding or lawsuit; a departure from a prescribed rule or regulation.

An irregularity is not an unlawful act, however, in certain instances, it is sufficiently serious to render a lawsuit invalid. For example, a number of states have statutes that require the appointment of a guardian to represent the interests of a child who is being sued. The failure to do so is an irregularity that can be used as a ground for invalidating and setting aside a judgment entered against the child.

In other cases, however, the flaw might be a simple HARMLESS ERROR that can be easily rectified, and, therefore, does not render the proceeding invalid.

IRRELEVANT

Unrelated or inapplicable to the matter in issue.

Irrelevant evidence has no tendency to prove or disprove any contested fact in a lawsuit.

IRREPARABLE INJURY

Any harm or loss that is not easily repaired, restored, or compensated by monetary damages. A serious wrong, generally of a repeated and continuing nature, that has an equitable remedy of injunctive relief.

IRRESISTIBLE IMPULSE

A test applied in a criminal prosecution to determine whether a person accused of a crime was compelled by a mental disease to commit it and therefore cannot be held criminally responsible for her or his actions; in a wrongful death case, a compulsion to commit suicide created by the defendant.

In most jurisdictions, a person may defend criminal charges on a ground of insanity. The INSANITY DEFENSE comes in two main forms. First, a DEFENDANT may argue that because of mental disease or defect, he or she lacked the capacity to distinguish right from wrong. This is cognitive insanity.

Second, a defendant may argue that because of mental disease or defect, she or he was unable to act in conformance with the law. This is volitional insanity, and it is known as the irresistible impulse defense. Under this defense, a defendant may be found not guilty by reason of insanity even though she or he was capable of distinguishing right from wrong at the time of the offense.

The success of an irresistible impulse defense depends on the facts of the case. For example, assume that a child has been molested. If the child's mother shoots and kills the suspected molester, the mother could argue that she was so enraged by the violation of her child that she was unable to control her actions. The mother need not have been diagnosed as mentally ill. Rather, she would need to show that she was mentally ill at the time of the shooting, and that the illness impaired her self-control.

Irresistible impulse emerged as a defense in the nineteenth century, when psychoanalysts formulated the concept of moral insanity to describe the temporary inability of otherwise sane persons to resist criminal behavior. Courts began to recognize the condition as one that rendered conduct involuntary and therefore not suitable for punishment. For the better part of a century, many states allowed both cognitive insanity and irresistible impulse insanity as defenses.

Congress and most states abolished the irresistible impulse defense after John Hinckley was acquitted on grounds of insanity for the attempted ASSASSINATION of President RONALD REAGAN in 1981. Only a handful of states currently allow irresistible impulse as a defense to criminal charges. These states permit it as a supplement to the cognitive insanity defense, which is the only insanity defense recognized in most jurisdictions. On the federal level, Congress abolished the irresistible impulse defense in the Insanity Defense Reform Act of 1984 (18 U.S.C.A. §§ 1 note, 17).

In some states, the irresistible impulse defense has never been adopted. In others, it has been adopted and subsequently withdrawn. Where it has been rejected, the reasons are generally the same: to prevent sane persons from escaping liability simply because they were unable to control their actions. In the words of one court, "There are many appetites and passions which by long indulgence acquire a mastery over men . . . but the law is far from excusing criminal acts committed under the impulse of such passions" (*State v. Brandon*, 53 N.C. 463 [1862]).

Under the MODEL PENAL CODE definition of irresistible impulse, a person may be found not guilty by reason of insanity if, at the time of the offense, he or she lacked "substantial capacity either to appreciate the criminality of [the] conduct or to conform [the] conduct to the requirements of law" (§ 4.01(1) [1962]). The "lacked substantial capacity" language creates a low threshold for the defendant: in some states, the defendant must allege complete impairment in order to invoke the defense.

Irresistible impulse is also a factor in civil actions. When a person commits suicide, survivors may sue for damages with a WRONGFUL DEATH claim or similar action if they can show that the suicide was caused by the actions of another person. In such a case, the plaintiffs must prove that the defendant caused a mental condition that caused the decedent to experience an irresistible impulse to commit suicide.

FURTHER READINGS

Falk, Patricia J. 1996. "Novel Theories of Criminal Defense Based upon the Toxicity of the Social Environment: Urban Psychosis, Television Intoxication, and Black Rage." *North Carolina Law Review* 74.

Gresham, Anne C. 1993. "The Insanity Plea: A Futile Defense for Serial Killers." *Law & Psychology Review* 17.

Kahan, Dan M. 1996. "Two Conceptions of Emotion in Criminal Law." *Columbia Law Review* 96. Available online at http://www.pennumbra.com/issues/pdfs/156-3/Kahan.pdf; website home page: http://www.pennumbra.com (accessed August 2, 2009).

IRRETRIEVABLE BREAKDOWN OF MARRIAGE

The situation that exists when either or both spouses no longer are able or willing to live with each other, thereby destroying their husband and wife relationship with no hope of resumption of spousal duties.

The irretrievable breakdown of a marriage provides the ground for a no-fault DIVORCE in many jurisdictions.

IRREVOCABLE

Unable to cancel or recall; that which is unalterable or irreversible.

IRS

See INTERNAL REVENUE SERVICE.

ISLAND

A land area surrounded by water and remaining above sea level during high tide.

Land areas exposed only during low tide are called low-tide elevations or drying rocks, reefs, or shoals. The existence of islands has generated numerous disputes, centering primarily on the size of the territorial sea surrounding an island and the determination of what state has sovereignty over a particular island. The size of the territorial sea has become an important question affecting fishing rights and the right of unrestricted passage for foreign vessels. Although the territorial sea of an island is usually determined by reference to its coastal baseline, some adjustments have been recognized in the cases of archipelagoes and islands located close to the mainland.

Determination of what state has title to an island has traditionally depended upon an open and continuous assertion of sovereignty over the island, which is usually, but not always, accompanied by physical presence of some representative of the state.

CROSS REFERENCE

Territorial Waters.

ISSUE

To promulgate or send out. In a lawsuit, a disputed point of law or QUESTION OF FACT, set forth in the pleadings, that is alleged by one party and denied by the other.

In the law governing the transfer or distribution of property, a child, children, and all individuals who descend from a common ancestor or descendents of any degree.

As applied to notes or bonds of a series, date of issue means the day fixed as the start of the period for which they run, with no reference to a specific date when the bonds or notes are to be sold and delivered. With regard to bonds only, bonds are issued to the purchaser when they are delivered.

When an issue of fact arises, the court or jury must consider and evaluate the weight of the evidence in order to reach a decision. An issue of law exists thereby providing a ground for a SUMMARY JUDGMENT sought by a party to the action when only one conclusion can be drawn by the court from the undisputed evidence, obviating the need for deliberation by a jury.

The term *issue* is frequently found in provisions of a deed. In TESTAMENTARY matters, the meaning of issue is derived from the intent of the TESTATOR, a maker of a will. The intent is determined from the provisions of the will.

ISSUE PRECLUSION

A concept that refers to the fact that a particular question of fact or law, one that has already been fully litigated by the parties in an action for which there has been a judgment on the merits, cannot be relitigated in any future action involving the same parties or their privies (persons who would be bound by the judgment rendered for the party).

The term *issue preclusion* is synonymous with COLLATERAL ESTOPPEL, a doctrine which bars the relitigation of the same issue that was the basis of a finding or VERDICT in an action by the same parties or their privies in subsequent lawsuits involving the same or different causes of action. It is not, however, the same as the doctrine of RES JUDICATA which bars the relitigation of an entire CAUSE OF ACTION, claim or demand, as opposed to an issue that makes up a cause of action, claim, or demand.

ITEMIZE

To individually state each item or article.

Frequently used in tax accounting, an itemized account or claim separately lists amounts that add up to the final sum of the total account on claim.

ITEMIZED DEDUCTION

See INCOME TAX.

A.	Atlantic Reporter	ACS	Agricultural Cooperative Service
A. 2d	Atlantic Reporter, Second Series	ACT	American College Test
AA	Alcoholics Anonymous	Act'g Legal Adv.	Acting Legal Advisor
AAA	American Arbitration Association; Agricultural Adjustment Act of 1933	ACUS	Administrative Conference of the United States
AALS	Association of American Law Schools	ACYF	Administration on Children, Youth, and Families
AAPRP	All African People's Revolutionary Party	A.D. 2d	Appellate Division, Second Series, N.Y.
AARP	American Association of Retired Persons	ADA	Americans with Disabilities Act of 1990
AAS	American Anti-Slavery Society	ADAMHA	Alcohol, Drug Abuse, and Mental Health Administration
ABA	American Bar Association; Architectural Barriers Act of 1968; American Bankers Association	ADC	Aid to Dependent Children
		ADD	Administration on Developmental Disabilities
ABC	American Broadcasting Companies, Inc. (formerly American Broadcasting Corporation)	ADEA	Age Discrimination in Employment Act of 1967
ABM	Antiballistic missile	ADL	Anti-Defamation League
ABM Treaty	Anti-Ballistic Missile Treaty of 1972	ADR	Alternative dispute resolution
ABVP	Anti-Biased Violence Project	AEC	Atomic Energy Commission
A/C	Account	AECB	Arms Export Control Board
A.C.	Appeal cases	AEDPA	Antiterrorism and Effective Death Penalty Act
ACAA	Air Carrier Access Act		
ACCA	Armed Career Criminal Act of 1984	A.E.R.	All England Law Reports
ACF	Administration for Children and Families	AFA	American Family Association; Alabama Freethought Association
ACLU	American Civil Liberties Union		
		AFB	American Farm Bureau
ACRS	Accelerated Cost Recovery System	AFBF	American Farm Bureau Federation

AFDC	Aid to Families with Dependent Children	Amer. St. Papers, For. Rels.	American State Papers, Legislative and Executive Documents of the Congress of the U.S., Class I, Foreign Relations, 1832–1859
aff'd per cur.	Affirmed by the court		
AFIS	Automated fingerprint identification system		
AFL	American Federation of Labor	AMS	Agricultural Marketing Service
AFL-CIO	American Federation of Labor and Congress of Industrial Organizations	AMVETS	American Veterans (of World War II)
AFRes	Air Force Reserve	ANA	Administration for Native Americans
AFSC	American Friends Service Committee	Ann. Dig.	Annual Digest of Public International Law Cases
AFSCME	American Federation of State, County, and Municipal Employees	ANPA	American Newspaper Publishers Association
AGRICOLA	Agricultural Online Access	ANSCA	Alaska Native Claims Act
		ANZUS	Australia-New Zealand-United States Security Treaty Organization
AIA	Association of Insurance Attorneys		
AIB	American Institute for Banking	AOA	Administration on Aging
		AOE	Arizonans for Official English
AID	Artificial insemination using a third-party donor's sperm; Agency for International Development	AOL	America Online
		AP	Associated Press
		APA	Administrative Procedure Act of 1946
AIDS	Acquired immune deficiency syndrome	APHIS	Animal and Plant Health Inspection Service
AIH	Artificial insemination using the husband's sperm	App. Div.	Appellate Division Reports, N.Y. Supreme Court
AIM	American Indian Movement	Arb. Trib., U.S.-British	Arbitration Tribunal, Claim Convention of 1853, United States and Great Britain Convention of 1853
AIPAC	American Israel Public Affairs Committee		
AIUSA	Amnesty International, U.S.A. Affiliate		
		Ardcor	American Roller Die Corporation
AJS	American Judicature Society	ARPA	Advanced Research Projects Agency
ALA	American Library Association	ARPANET	Advanced Research Projects Agency Network
Alcoa	Aluminum Company of America	ARS	Advanced Record System
ALEC	American Legislative Exchange Council	Art.	Article
ALF	Animal Liberation Front	ARU	American Railway Union
ALI	American Law Institute		
ALJ	Administrative law judge	ASCME	American Federation of State, County, and Municipal Employees
All E.R.	All England Law Reports		
ALO	Agency Liaison		
A.L.R.	American Law Reports	ASCS	Agriculture Stabilization and Conservation Service
ALY	American Law Yearbook		
AMA	American Medical Association	ASM	Available Seatmile
		ASPCA	American Society for the Prevention of Cruelty to Animals
AMAA	Agricultural Marketing Agreement Act		
Am. Dec.	American Decisions	Asst. Att. Gen.	Assistant Attorney General
amdt.	Amendment		

AT&T	American Telephone and Telegraph	BOCA	Building Officials and Code Administrators International
ATF	Alcohol, Tobacco, Firearms and Explosives Bureau	BOP	Bureau of Prisons
		BPP	Black Panther Party for Self-defense
ATLA	Association of Trial Lawyers of America	Brit. and For.	British and Foreign State Papers
ATO	Alpha Tau Omega	BSA	Boy Scouts of America
ATTD	Alcohol and Tobacco Tax Division	BTP	Beta Theta Pi
ATU	Alcohol Tax Unit	Burr.	James Burrows, *Report of Cases Argued and Determined in the Court of King's Bench during the Time of Lord Mansfield* (1766–1780)
AUAM	American Union against Militarism		
AUM	Animal Unit Month		
AZT	Azidothymidine		
BAC	Blood alcohol concentration	BVA	Board of Veterans Appeals
BALSA	Black-American Law Student Association	c.	Chapter
		C³I	Command, Control, Communications, and Intelligence
BATF	Bureau of Alcohol, Tobacco and Firearms		
BBS	Bulletin Board System	C.A.	Court of Appeals
BCCI	Bank of Credit and Commerce International	CAA	Clean Air Act
		CAB	Civil Aeronautics Board; Corporation for American Banking
BEA	Bureau of Economic Analysis		
Bell's Cr. C.	Bell's English Crown Cases	CAFE	Corporate average fuel economy
Bevans	United States Treaties, etc. *Treaties and Other International Agreements of the United States of America, 1776–1949* (compiled under the direction of Charles I. Bevans, 1968–76)	Cal. 2d	California Reports, Second Series
		Cal. 3d	California Reports, Third Series
		CALR	Computer-assisted legal research
		Cal. Rptr.	California Reporter
		CAP	Common Agricultural Policy
BFOQ	Bona fide occupational qualification	CARA	Classification and Ratings Administration
BI	Bureau of Investigation		
BIA	Bureau of Indian Affairs; Board of Immigration Appeals	CATV	Community antenna television
		CBO	Congressional Budget Office
BID	Business improvement district	CBS	Columbia Broadcasting System
BJS	Bureau of Justice Statistics	CBOEC	Chicago Board of Election Commissioners
Black.	Black's United States Supreme Court Reports	CCC	Commodity Credit Corporation
Blatchf.	Blatchford's United States Circuit Court Reports	CCDBG	Child Care and Development Block Grant of 1990
		C.C.D. Pa.	Circuit Court Decisions, Pennsylvania
BLM	Bureau of Land Management	C.C.D. Va.	Circuit Court Decisions, Virginia
BLS	Bureau of Labor Statistics		
BMD	Ballistic missile defense	CCEA	Cabinet Council on Economic Affairs
BNA	Bureau of National Affairs		

CCP	Chinese Communist Party	CHINS	Children in need of supervision
CCR	Center for Constitutional Rights	CHIPS	Child in need of protective services
C.C.R.I.	Circuit Court, Rhode Island	Ch.N.Y.	Chancery Reports, New York
CD	Certificate of deposit; compact disc	Chr. Rob.	Christopher Robinson, *Reports of Cases Argued and*
CDA	Communications Decency Act		*Determined in the High Court of Admiralty*
CDBG	Community Development Block Grant Program	CIA	*(1801–1808)* Central Intelligence Agency
CDC	Centers for Disease Control and Prevention; Community Development Corporation	CID	Commercial Item Descriptions
		C.I.F.	Cost, insurance, and freight
CDF	Children's Defense Fund	CINCNORAD	Commander in Chief,
CDL	Citizens for Decency through Law		North American Air Defense Command
CD-ROM	Compact disc read-only memory	C.I.O.	Congress of Industrial Organizations
CDS	Community Dispute Services	CIPE	Center for International Private Enterprise
CDW	Collision damage waiver	C.J.	Chief justice
CENTO	Central Treaty Organization	CJIS	Criminal Justice Information Services
CEO	Chief executive officer	C.J.S.	Corpus Juris Secundum
CEQ	Council on Environmental Quality	Claims Arb. under Spec. Conv.,	Frederick Kenelm Nielsen, *American and*
CERCLA	Comprehensive Environmental Response, Compensation, and Liability Act of 1980	Nielsen's Rept.	*British Claims Arbitration under the Special Agreement Concluded between the United States and Great*
cert.	*Certiorari*		*Britain, August 18, 1910*
CETA	Comprehensive Employment and Training Act		*(1926)*
		CLASP	Center for Law and Social Policy
C & F	Cost and freight	CLE	Center for Law and
CFC	Chlorofluorocarbon		Education; Continuing
CFE Treaty	Conventional Forces in Europe Treaty of 1990		Legal Education
		CLEO	Council on Legal
C.F. & I.	Cost, freight, and insurance		Education Opportunity; Chief Law Enforcement
C.F.R	Code of Federal Regulations		Officer
		CLP	Communist Labor Party
CFNP	Community Food and Nutrition Program		of America
		CLS	Christian Legal Society;
CFTA	Canadian Free Trade Agreement		critical legal studies (movement); Critical Legal
CFTC	Commodity Futures Trading Commission		Studies (membership organization)
Ch.	Chancery Division, English Law Reports	C.M.A.	Court of Military Appeals
CHAMPVA	Civilian Health and Medical Program at the Veterans Administration	CMEA	Council for Mutual Economic Assistance
		CMHS	Center for Mental Health Services
CHEP	Cuban/Haitian Entrant Program	C.M.R.	Court of Military Review

CNN	Cable News Network	CSA	Community Services Administration
CNO	Chief of Naval Operations	CSAP	Center for Substance Abuse Prevention
CNOL	Consolidated net operating loss	CSAT	Center for Substance Abuse Treatment
CNR	Chicago and Northwestern Railway	CSC	Civil Service Commission
CO	Conscientious Objector	CSCE	Conference on Security and Cooperation in Europe
C.O.D.	Cash on delivery		
COGP	Commission on Government Procurement		
COINTELPRO	Counterintelligence Program	CSG	Council of State Governments
Coke Rep.	Coke's English King's Bench Reports	CSO	Community Service Organization
COLA	Cost-of-living adjustment	CSP	Center for the Study of the Presidency
COMCEN	Federal Communications Center	C-SPAN	Cable-Satellite Public Affairs Network
Comp.	Compilation	CSRS	Cooperative State Research Service
Conn.	Connecticut Reports		
CONTU	National Commission on New Technological Uses of Copyrighted Works	CSWPL	Center on Social Welfare Policy and Law
		CTA	Cum testamento annexo (with the will attached)
Conv.	Convention		
COPA	Child Online Protection Act (1998)	Ct. Ap. D.C.	Court of Appeals, District of Columbia
COPS	Community Oriented Policing Services	Ct. App. No. Ireland	Court of Appeals, Northern Ireland
Corbin	Arthur L. Corbin, Corbin on Contracts: A Comprehensive Treatise on the Rules of Contract Law (1950)	Ct. Cl.	Court of Claims, United States
		Ct. Crim. Apps.	Court of Criminal Appeals (England)
		CTI	Consolidated taxable income
CORE	Congress on Racial Equality	Ct. of Sess., Scot.	Court of Sessions, Scotland
Cox's Crim. Cases	Cox's Criminal Cases (England)	CU	Credit union
COYOTE	Call Off Your Old Tired Ethics	CUNY	City University of New York
CPA	Certified public accountant	Cush.	Cushing's Massachusetts Reports
CPB	Corporation for Public Broadcasting, the	CWA	Civil Works Administration; Clean Water Act
CPI	Consumer Price Index		
CPPA	Child Pornography Prevention Act	DACORB	Department of the Army Conscientious Objector Review Board
CPSC	Consumer Product Safety Commission	Dall.	Dallas's Pennsylvania and United States Reports
Cranch	Cranch's United States Supreme Court Reports	DAR	Daughters of the American Revolution
CRF	Constitutional Rights Foundation	DARPA	Defense Advanced Research Projects Agency
CRR	Center for Constitutional Rights	DAVA	Defense Audiovisual Agency
CRS	Congressional Research Service; Community Relations Service	D.C.	United States District Court; District of Columbia
CRT	Critical race theory		

D.C. Del.	United States District Court, Delaware	DPT	Diphtheria, pertussis, and tetanus
D.C. Mass.	United States District Court, Massachusetts	DRI	Defense Research Institute
D.C. Md.	United States District Court, Maryland	DSAA	Defense Security Assistance Agency
D.C.N.D.Cal.	United States District Court, Northern District, California	DUI	Driving under the influence; driving under intoxication
D.C.N.Y.	United States District Court, New York	DVD	Digital versatile disc
D.C.Pa.	United States District Court, Pennsylvania	DWI	Driving while intoxicated
		EAHCA	Education for All Handicapped Children Act of 1975
DCS	Deputy Chiefs of Staff	EBT	Examination before trial
DCZ	District of the Canal Zone	E.coli	Escherichia coli
DDT	Dichlorodiphenyl-tricloroethane	ECPA	Electronic Communications Privacy Act of 1986
DEA	Drug Enforcement Administration	ECSC	Treaty of the European Coal and Steel Community
Decl. Lond.	Declaration of London, February 26, 1909	EDA	Economic Development Administration
Dev. & B.	Devereux & Battle's North Carolina Reports	EDF	Environmental Defense Fund
DFL	Minnesota Democratic-Farmer-Labor	E.D.N.Y.	Eastern District, New York
DFTA	Department for the Aging	EDP	Electronic data processing
DHS	Department of Homeland Security	E.D. Pa.	Eastern-District, Pennsylvania
Dig. U.S. Practice in Intl. Law	Digest of U.S. Practice in International Law	EDSC	Eastern District, South Carolina
Dist. Ct.	D.C. United States District Court, District of Columbia	EDT	Eastern daylight time
		E.D. Va.	Eastern District, Virginia
D.L.R.	Dominion Law Reports (Canada)	EEC	European Economic Community; European Economic Community Treaty
DMCA	Digital Millennium Copyright Act	EEOC	Equal Employment Opportunity Commission
DNA	Deoxyribonucleic acid		
Dnase	Deoxyribonuclease	EFF	Electronic Frontier Foundation
DNC	Democratic National Committee	EFT	Electronic funds transfer
DOC	Department of Commerce	Eliz.	Queen Elizabeth (Great Britain)
DOD	Department of Defense	Em. App.	Temporary Emergency Court of Appeals
DODEA	Department of Defense Education Activity	ENE	Early neutral evaluation
Dodson	Dodson's Reports, English Admiralty Courts	Eng. Rep.	English Reports
		EOP	Executive Office of the President
DOE	Department of Energy		
DOER	Department of Employee Relations	EPA	Environmental Protection Agency; Equal Pay Act of 1963
DOJ	Department of Justice		
DOL	Department of Labor	ERA	Equal Rights Amendment
DOMA	Defense of Marriage Act of 1996	ERDC	Energy Research and Development Commission
DOS	Disk operating system		
DOT	Department of Transportation	ERISA	Employee Retirement Income Security Act of 1974

ERS	Economic Research Service	FAS	Foreign Agricultural Service
ERTA	Economic Recovery Tax Act of 1981	FBA	Federal Bar Association
ESA	Endangered Species Act of 1973	FBI	Federal Bureau of Investigation
ESF	Emergency support function; Economic Support Fund	FCA	Farm Credit Administration
		F. Cas.	Federal Cases
ESRD	End-Stage Renal Disease Program	FCC	Federal Communications Commission
ETA	Employment and Training Administration	FCIA	Foreign Credit Insurance Association
ETS	Environmental tobacco smoke	FCIC	Federal Crop Insurance Corporation
et seq.	*Et sequentes* or *et sequentia* ("and the following")	FCLAA	Federal Cigarette Labeling and Advertising Act
EU	European Union	FCRA	Fair Credit Reporting Act
Euratom	European Atomic Energy Community	FCU	Federal credit unions
		FCUA	Federal Credit Union Act
Eur. Ct. H.R.	European Court of Human Rights	FCZ	Fishery Conservation Zone
Ex.	English Exchequer Reports, Welsby, Hurlstone & Gordon	FDA	Food and Drug Administration
Exch.	Exchequer Reports (Welsby, Hurlstone & Gordon)	FDIC	Federal Deposit Insurance Corporation
		FDPC	Federal Data Processing Center
Ex Com	Executive Committee of the National Security Council	FEC	Federal Election Commission
Eximbank	Export-Import Bank of the United States	FECA	Federal Election Campaign Act of 1971
F.	Federal Reporter	Fed. Cas.	Federal Cases
F. 2d	Federal Reporter, Second Series	FEHA	Fair Employment and Housing Act
FAA	Federal Aviation Administration; Federal Arbitration Act	FEHBA	Federal Employees Health Benefit Act
FAAA	Federal Alcohol Administration Act	FEMA	Federal Emergency Management Agency
FACE	Freedom of Access to Clinic Entrances Act of 1994	FERC	Federal Energy Regulatory Commission
		FFB	Federal Financing Bank
FACT	Feminist Anti-Censorship Task Force	FFDC	Federal Food, Drug, and Cosmetics Act
FAIRA	Federal Agriculture Improvement and Reform Act of 1996	FGIS	Federal Grain Inspection Service
		FHA	Federal Housing Administration
FAMLA	Family and Medical Leave Act of 1993	FHAA	Fair Housing Amendments Act of 1998
Fannie Mae	Federal National Mortgage Association	FHWA	Federal Highway Administration
FAO	Food and Agriculture Organization of the United Nations	FIA	Federal Insurance Administration
		FIC	Federal Information Centers; Federation of Insurance Counsel
FAR	Federal Acquisition Regulations		

FICA	Federal Insurance Contributions Act	FTA	U.S.-Canada Free Trade Agreement of 1988
FIFRA	Federal Insecticide, Fungicide, and Rodenticide Act	FTC	Federal Trade Commission
		FTCA	Federal Tort Claims Act
FIP	Forestry Incentives Program	FTS	Federal Telecommunications System
FIRREA	Financial Institutions Reform, Recovery, and Enforcement Act of 1989	FTS2000	Federal Telecommunications System 2000
FISA	Foreign Intelligence Surveillance Act of 1978	FUCA	Federal Unemployment Compensation Act of 1988
FISC	Foreign Intelligence Surveillance Court of Review	FUTA	Federal Unemployment Tax Act
FJC	Federal Judicial Center	FWPCA	Federal Water Pollution Control Act of 1948
FLSA	Fair Labor Standards Act		
FMC	Federal Maritime Commission	FWS	Fish and Wildlife Service
		GAL	Guardian ad litem
FMCS	Federal Mediation and Conciliation Service	GAO	General Accounting Office; Governmental Affairs Office
FmHA	Farmers Home Administration	GAOR	General Assembly Official Records, United Nations
FMLA	Family and Medical Leave Act of 1993		
FNMA	Federal National Mortgage Association, "Fannie Mae"	GAAP	Generally accepted accounting principles
		GA Res.	General Assembly Resolution (United Nations)
F.O.B.	Free on board		
FOIA	Freedom of Information Act	GATT	General Agreement on Tariffs and Trade
FOMC	Federal Open Market Committee	GCA	Gun Control Act
FPA	Federal Power Act of 1935	Gen. Cls. Comm.	General Claims Commission, United States and Panama; General Claims United States and Mexico
FPC	Federal Power Commission		
FPMR	Federal Property Management Regulations	Geo. II	King George II (Great Britain)
FPRS	Federal Property Resources Service	Geo. III	King George III (Great Britain)
FR	Federal Register		
FRA	Federal Railroad Administration	GHB	Gamma-hydroxybutrate
		GI	Government Issue
FRB	Federal Reserve Board	GID	General Intelligence Division
FRC	Federal Radio Commission		
		GM	General Motors
F.R.D.	Federal Rules Decisions	GNMA	Government National Mortgage Association, "Ginnie Mae"
FSA	Family Support Act		
FSB	Federal'naya Sluzhba Bezopasnosti (the Federal Security Service of Russia)	GNP	Gross national product
		GOP	Grand Old Party (Republican Party)
FSLIC	Federal Savings and Loan Insurance Corporation	GOPAC	Grand Old Party Action Committee
FSQS	Food Safety and Quality Service	GPA	Office of Governmental and Public Affairs
FSS	Federal Supply Service	GPO	Government Printing Office
F. Supp.	Federal Supplement		

GRAS	Generally recognized as safe	Hudson, Internatl. Legis.	Manley Ottmer Hudson, ed., *International Legislation: A Collection of the Texts of Multipartite International Instruments of General Interest Beginning with the Covenant of the League of Nations* (1931)
Gr. Br., Crim. Ct. App.	Great Britain, Court of Criminal Appeals		
GRNL	Gay Rights-National Lobby		
GSA	General Services Administration		
Hackworth	Green Haywood Hackworth, *Digest of International Law* (1940–1944)	Hudson, World Court Reps.	Manley Ottmer Hudson, ea., *World Court Reports* (1934–)
		Hun	Hun's New York Supreme Court Reports
Hay and Marriott	Great Britain. High Court of Admiralty, *Decisions in the High Court of Admiralty during the Time of Sir George Hay and of Sir James Marriott, Late Judges of That Court* (1801)	Hunt's Rept.	Bert L. Hunt, *Report of the American and Panamanian General Claims Arbitration* (1934)
		IAEA	International Atomic Energy Agency
		IALL	International Association of Law Libraries
H.B.	House Bill		
HBO	Home Box Office	IBA	International Bar Association
HCFA	Health Care Financing Administration	IBM	International Business Machines
H.Ct.	High Court	ICA	Interstate Commerce Act
HDS	Office of Human Development Services	ICBM	Intercontinental ballistic missile
Hen. & M.	Hening & Munford's Virginia Reports	ICC	Interstate Commerce Commission; International Criminal Court
HEW	Department of Health, Education, and Welfare		
HFCA	Health Care Financing Administration	ICJ	International Court of Justice
HGI	Handgun Control, Incorporated	ICM	Institute for Court Management
HHS	Department of Health and Human Services	IDEA	Individuals with Disabilities Education Act of 1975
Hill	Hill's New York Reports		
HIRE	Help through Industry Retraining and Employment	IDOP	International Dolphin Conservation Program
		IEP	Individualized educational program
HIV	Human immunodeficiency virus	IFC	International Finance Corporation
H.L.	House of Lords Cases (England)	IGRA	Indian Gaming Regulatory Act of 1988
H. Lords	House of Lords (England)	IJA	Institute of Judicial Administration
HMO	Health Maintenance Organization	IJC	International Joint Commission
HNIS	Human Nutrition Information Service	ILC	International Law Commission
Hong Kong L.R.	Hong Kong Law Reports	ILD	International Labor Defense
How.	Howard's United States Supreme Court Reports		
How. St. Trials	Howell's English State Trials	Ill. Dec.	Illinois Decisions
HUAC	House Un-American Activities Committee	ILO	International Labor Organization
HUD	Department of Housing and Urban Development	IMF	International Monetary Fund

INA	Immigration and Nationality Act	JCS	Joint Chiefs of Staff
IND	Investigational new drug	JDL	Jewish Defense League
INF Treaty	Intermediate-Range Nuclear Forces Treaty of 1987	JNOV	Judgment *non obstante veredicto* ("judgment nothing to recommend it" or "judgment notwithstanding the verdict")
INS	Immigration and Naturalization Service	JOBS	Jobs Opportunity and Basic Skills
INTELSAT	International Telecommunications Satellite Organization	John. Ch.	Johnson's New York Chancery Reports
Interpol	International Criminal Police Organization	Johns.	Johnson's Reports (New York)
Int'l. Law Reps.	International Law Reports	JP	Justice of the peace
Intl. Legal Mats.	International Legal Materials	K.B.	King's Bench Reports (England)
IOC	International Olympic Committee	KFC	Kentucky Fried Chicken
IPDC	International Program for the Development of Communication	KGB	Komitet Gosudarstvennoi Bezopasnosti (the State Security Committee for countries in the former Soviet Union)
IPO	Intellectual Property Owners	KKK	Ku Klux Klan
IPP	Independent power producer	KMT	Kuomintang (Chinese, "national people's party")
IQ	Intelligence quotient	LAD	Law Against Discrimination
I.R.	Irish Reports		
IRA	Individual retirement account; Irish Republican Army	LAPD	Los Angeles Police Department
IRC	Internal Revenue Code	LC	Library of Congress
IRCA	Immigration Reform and Control Act of 1986	LCHA	Longshoremen's and Harbor Workers Compensation Act of 1927
IRS	Internal Revenue Service	LD50	Lethal dose 50
ISO	Independent service organization	LDEF	Legal Defense and Education Fund (NOW)
ISP	Internet service provider	LDF	Legal Defense Fund, Legal Defense and Educational Fund of the NAACP
ISSN	International Standard Serial Numbers		
ITA	International Trade Administration	LEAA	Law Enforcement Assistance Administration
ITI	Information Technology Integration	L.Ed.	Lawyers' Edition Supreme Court Reports
ITO	International Trade Organization	LI	Letter of interpretation
ITS	Information Technology Service	LLC	Limited Liability Company
ITT	International Telephone and Telegraph Corporation	LLP	Limited Liability Partnership
ITU	International Telecommunication Union	LMSA	Labor-Management Services Administration
IUD	Intrauterine device	LNTS	League of Nations Treaty Series
IWC	International Whaling Commission	Lofft's Rep.	Lofft's English King's Bench Reports
IWW	Industrial Workers of the World	L.R.	Law Reports (English)
JAGC	Judge Advocate General's Corps	LSAC	Law School Admission Council

LSAS	Law School Admission Service	Miller	David Hunter Miller, ea., *Treaties and Other International Acts of the United States of America* (1931–1948)
LSAT	Law School Aptitude Test		
LSC	Legal Services Corporation; Legal Services for Children	Minn.	Minnesota Reports
		MINS	Minors in need of supervision
LSD	Lysergic acid diethylamide	MIRV	Multiple independently targetable reentry vehicle
LSDAS	Law School Data Assembly Service	MIRVed ICBM	Multiple independently targetable reentry vehicled intercontinental ballistic missile
LTBT	Limited Test Ban Treaty		
LTC	Long Term Care		
MAD	Mutual assured destruction	Misc.	Miscellaneous Reports, New York
MADD	Mothers against Drunk Driving	Mixed Claims Comm., Report of Decs	Mixed Claims Commission, United States and Germany, Report of Decisions
MALDEF	Mexican American Legal Defense and Educational Fund		
Malloy	William M. Malloy, ed., *Treaties, Conventions International Acts, Protocols, and Agreements between the United States of America and Other Powers* (1910–1938)	M.J.	Military Justice Reporter
		MLAP	Migrant Legal Action Program
		MLB	Major League Baseball
		MLDP	Mississippi Loyalist Democratic Party
		MMI	Moslem Mosque, Incorporated
Martens	Georg Friedrich von Martens, ea., *Noveau recueil général de traités et autres actes relatifs aux rapports de droit international* (Series I, 20 vols. [1843–1875]; Series II, 35 vols. [1876–1908]; Series III [1909–])	MMPA	Marine Mammal Protection Act of 1972
		Mo.	Missouri Reports
		MOD	Masters of Deception
		Mod.	Modern Reports, English King's Bench, etc.
		Moore, Dig. Intl. Law	John Bassett Moore, *A Digest of International Law*, 8 vols. (1906)
Mass.	Massachusetts Reports		
MCC	Metropolitan Correctional Center	Moore, Intl. Arbs.	John Bassett Moore, *History and Digest of the International Arbitrations to Which United States Has Been a Party*, 6 vols. (1898)
MCCA	Medicare Catastrophic Coverage Act of 1988		
MCH	Maternal and Child Health Bureau		
MCRA	Medical Care Recovery Act of 1962	Morison	William Maxwell Morison, *The Scots Revised Report: Morison's Dictionary of Decisions* (1908–09)
MDA	Medical Devices Amendments of 1976		
Md. App.	Maryland, Appeal Cases	M.P.	Member of Parliament
M.D. Ga.	Middle District, Georgia	MP3	MPEG Audio Layer 3
Mercy	Movement Ensuring the Right to Choose for Yourself	MPAA	Motion Picture Association of America
		MPAS	Michigan Protection and Advocacy Service
Metc.	Metcalf's Massachusetts Reports	MPEG	Motion Picture Experts Group
MFDP	Mississippi Freedom Democratic party	mpg	Miles per gallon
MGT	Management	MPPDA	Motion Picture Producers and Distributors of America
MHSS	Military Health Services System		

MPRSA	Marine Protection, Research, and Sanctuaries Act of 1972	NBS	National Bureau of Standards
M.R.	Master of the Rolls	NCA	Noise Control Act; National Command Authorities
MS-DOS	Microsoft Disk Operating System	NCAA	National Collegiate Athletic Association
MSHA	Mine Safety and Health Administration	NCAC	National Coalition against Censorship
MSPB	Merit Systems Protection Board	NCCB	National Consumer Cooperative Bank
MSSA	Military Selective Service Act	NCE	Northwest Community Exchange
N/A	Not Available	NCF	National Chamber Foundation
NAACP	National Association for the Advancement of Colored People	NCIP	National Crime Insurance Program
NAAQS	National Ambient Air Quality Standards	NCJA	National Criminal Justice Association
NAB	National Association of Broadcasters	NCLB	National Civil Liberties Bureau
NABSW	National Association of Black Social Workers	NCP	National contingency plan
NACDL	National Association of Criminal Defense Lawyers	NCSC	National Center for State Courts
NAFTA	North American Free Trade Agreement of 1993	NCUA	National Credit Union Administration
NAGHSR	National Association of Governors' Highway Safety Representatives	NDA	New drug application
		N.D. Ill.	Northern District, Illinois
NALA	National Association of Legal Assistants	NDU	National Defense University
NAM	National Association of Manufacturers	N.D. Wash.	Northern District, Washington
NAR	National Association of Realtors	N.E.	North Eastern Reporter
NARAL	National Abortion and Reproductive Rights Action League	N.E. 2d	North Eastern Reporter, Second Series
NARF	Native American Rights Fund	NEA	National Endowment for the Arts; National Education Association
NARS	National Archives and Record Service	NEH	National Endowment for the Humanities
NASA	National Aeronautics and Space Administration	NEPA	National Environmental Protection Act; National Endowment Policy Act
NASD	National Association of Securities Dealers		
NATO	North Atlantic Treaty Organization	NET Act	No Electronic Theft Act
NAVINFO	Navy Information Offices	NFIB	National Federation of Independent Businesses
NAWSA	National American Woman's Suffrage Association	NFIP	National Flood Insurance Program
		NFL	National Football League
NBA	National Bar Association; National Basketball Association	NFPA	National Federation of Paralegal Associations
		NGLTF	National Gay and Lesbian Task Force
NBC	National Broadcasting Company	NHL	National Hockey League
NBLSA	National Black Law Student Association	NHRA	Nursing Home Reform Act of 1987

NHTSA	National Highway Traffic Safety Administration	NPR	National Public Radio
		NPS	National Park Service
Nielsen's Rept.	Frederick Kenelm Nielsen, *American and British Claims Arbitration under the Special Agreement Concluded between the United States and Great Britain, August 18, 1910* (1926)	NPT	Nuclear Non-Proliferation Treaty of 1970
		NRA	National Rifle Association; National Recovery Act
		NRC	Nuclear Regulatory Commission
		NRLC	National Right to Life Committee
NIEO	New International Economic Order	NRTA	National Retired Teachers Association
NIGC	National Indian Gaming Commission	NSA	National Security Agency
NIH	National Institutes of Health	NSC	National Security Council
NIJ	National Institute of Justice	NSCLC	National Senior Citizens Law Center
NIRA	National Industrial Recovery Act of 1933; National Industrial Recovery Administration	NSF	National Science Foundation
		NSFNET	National Science Foundation Network
NIST	National Institute of Standards and Technology	NSI	Network Solutions, Inc.
N.J.	New Jersey Reports	NTIA	National Telecommunications and Information Administration
N.J. Super.	New Jersey Superior Court Reports		
NLEA	Nutrition Labeling and Education Act of 1990	NTID	National Technical Institute for the Deaf
NLRA	National Labor Relations Act	NTIS	National Technical Information Service
NLRB	National Labor Relations Board	NTS	Naval Telecommunications System
NMFS	National Marine Fisheries Service		
No.	Number	NTSB	National Transportation Safety Board
NOAA	National Oceanic and Atmospheric Administration	NVRA	National Voter Registration Act
NOC	National Olympic Committee	N.W.	North Western Reporter
		N.W. 2d	North Western Reporter, Second Series
NOI	Nation of Islam		
NOL	Net operating loss	NWSA	National Woman Suffrage Association
NORML	National Organization for the Reform of Marijuana Laws		
		N.Y.	New York Court of Appeals Reports
NOW	National Organization for Women	N.Y. 2d	New York Court of Appeals Reports, Second Series
NOW LDEF	National Organization for Women Legal Defense and Education Fund		
		N.Y.S.	New York Supplement Reporter
NOW/PAC	National Organization for Women Political Action Committee	N.Y.S. 2d	New York Supplement Reporter, Second Series
		NYSE	New York Stock Exchange
NPDES	National Pollutant Discharge Elimination System	NYSLA	New York State Liquor Authority
		N.Y. Sup.	New York Supreme Court Reports
NPL	National priorities list		

NYU	New York University	Ops. Comms.	Opinions of the Commissioners
OAAU	Organization of Afro American Unity	OPSP	Office of Product Standards Policy
OAP	Office of Administrative Procedure	O.R.	Ontario Reports
OAS	Organization of American States	OR	Official Records
OASDI	Old-age, Survivors, and Disability Insurance Benefits	OSHA	Occupational Safety and Health Act
OASHDS	Office of the Assistant Secretary for Human Development Services	OSHRC	Occupational Safety and Health Review Commission
OCC	Office of Comptroller of the Currency	OSM	Office of Surface Mining
		OSS	Office of Strategic Services
OCED	Office of Comprehensive Employment Development	OST	Office of the Secretary
OCHAMPUS	Office of Civilian Health and Medical Program of the Uniformed Services	OT	Office of Transportation
		OTA	Office of Technology Assessment
		OTC	Over-the-counter
OCSE	Office of Child Support Enforcement	OTS	Office of Thrift Supervisors
OEA	Organización de los Estados Americanos	OUI	Operating under the influence
		OVCI	Offshore Voluntary Compliance Initiative
OEM	Original Equipment Manufacturer	OWBPA	Older Workers Benefit Protection Act
OFCCP	Office of Federal Contract Compliance Programs	OWRT	Office of Water Research and Technology
		P.	Pacific Reporter
OFPP	Office of Federal Procurement Policy	P. 2d	Pacific Reporter, Second Series
OIC	Office of the Independent Counsel	PAC	Political action committee
OICD	Office of International Cooperation and Development	Pa. Oyer and Terminer	Pennsylvania Oyer and Terminer Reports
		PATCO	Professional Air Traffic Controllers Organization
OIG	Office of the Inspector General		
OJARS	Office of Justice Assistance, Research, and Statistics	PBGC	Pension Benefit Guaranty Corporation
OMB	Office of Management and Budget	PBS	Public Broadcasting Service; Public Buildings Service
OMPC	Office of Management, Planning, and Communications	P.C.	Privy Council (English Law Reports)
ONP	Office of National Programs	PC	Personal computer; politically correct
OPD	Office of Policy Development	PCBs	Polychlorinated biphenyls
OPEC	Organization of Petroleum Exporting Countries	PCIJ	Permanent Court of International Justice Series A-Judgments and Orders (1922–30)
OPIC	Overseas Private Investment Corporation		Series B-Advisory Opinions (1922–30)
Ops. Atts. Gen.	Opinions of the Attorneys-General of the United States		Series A/B-Judgments, Orders, and Advisory Opinions (1931–40)

	Series C-Pleadings, Oral Statements, and Documents relating to Judgments and Advisory Opinions (1923–42)	PLO	Palestine Liberation Organization
	Series D-Acts and Documents concerning the Organization of the World Court (1922 –47)	PLRA	Prison Litigation Reform Act of 1995
		PNET	Peaceful Nuclear Explosions Treaty
		PONY	Prostitutes of New York
	Series E-Annual Reports (1925–45)	POW-MIA	Prisoner of war-missing in action
PCP	Phencyclidine	Pratt	Frederic Thomas Pratt, *Law of Contraband of War, with a Selection of Cases from Papers of the Right Honourable Sir George Lee* (1856)
P.D.	Probate Division, English Law Reports (1876–1890)		
PDA	Pregnancy Discrimination Act of 1978	PRIDE	Prostitution to Independence, Dignity, and Equality
PD & R	Policy Development and Research	Proc.	Proceedings
Pepco	Potomac Electric Power Company	PRP	Potentially responsible party
Perm. Ct. of Arb.	Permanent Court of Arbitration	PSRO	Professional Standards Review Organization
PES	Post-Enumeration Survey	PTO	Patents and Trademark Office
Pet.	Peters' United States Supreme Court Reports	PURPA	Public Utilities Regulatory Policies Act
PETA	People for the Ethical Treatment of Animals	PUSH	People United to Serve Humanity
PGA	Professional Golfers Association	PUSH-Excel	PUSH for Excellence
PGM	Program	PWA	Public Works Administration
PHA	Public Housing Agency	PWSA	Ports and Waterways Safety Act of 1972
Phila. Ct. of Oyer and Terminer	Philadelphia Court of Oyer and Terminer	Q.B.	Queen's Bench (England)
PhRMA	Pharmaceutical Research and Manufacturers of America	QTIP	Qualified Terminable Interest Property
PHS	Public Health Service	Ralston's Rept.	Jackson Harvey Ralston, ed., *Venezuelan Arbitrations of 1903* (1904)
PIC	Private Industry Council		
PICJ	Permanent International Court of Justice	RC	Regional Commissioner
Pick.	Pickering's Massachusetts Reports	RCRA	Resource Conservation and Recovery Act
PIK	Payment in Kind	RCWP	Rural Clean Water Program
PINS	Persons in need of supervision	RDA	Rural Development Administration
PIRG	Public Interest Research Group	REA	Rural Electrification Administration
P.L.	Public Laws	Rec. des Decs. des Trib. Arb. Mixtes	G. Gidel, ed., *Recueil des décisions des tribunaux arbitraux mixtes, institués par les traités de paix* (1922–30)
PLAN	Pro-Life Action Network		
PLC	Plaintiffs' Legal Committee		
PLE	Product liability expenses		
PLI	Practicing Law Institute	Redmond	Vol. 3 of Charles I. Bevans, *Treaties and Other International Agreements of the United States of*
PLL	Product liability loss		
PLLP	Professional Limited Liability Partnership		

	America, 1776–1949 (compiled by C. F. Redmond) (1969)	Sandf.	Sandford's New York Superior Court Reports
RESPA	Real Estate Settlement Procedure Act of 1974	S and L	Savings and loan
		SARA	Superfund Amendment and Reauthorization Act
RFC	Reconstruction Finance Corporation	SAT	Scholastic Aptitude Test
RFRA	Religious Freedom Restoration Act of 1993	Sawy.	Sawyer's United States Circuit Court Reports
RIAA	Recording Industry Association of America	SBA	Small Business Administration
RICO	Racketeer Influenced and Corrupt Organizations	SBI	Small Business Institute
		SCCC	South Central Correctional Center
RLUIPA	Religious Land Use and Institutionalized Persons Act	SCLC	Southern Christian Leadership Conference
		Scott's Repts.	James Brown Scott, ed., *The Hague Court Reports*, 2 vols. (1916–32)
RNC	Republican National Committee		
Roscoe	Edward Stanley Roscoe, ed., *Reports of Prize Cases Determined in the High Court Admiralty before the Lords Commissioners of Appeals in Prize Causes and before the judicial Committee of the Privy Council from 1745 to 1859* (1905)	SCS	Soil Conservation Service; Social Conservative Service
		SCSEP	Senior Community Service Employment Program
		S.Ct.	Supreme Court Reporter
		S.D. Cal.	Southern District, California
		S.D. Fla.	Southern District, Florida
		S.D. Ga.	Southern District, Georgia
ROTC	Reserve Officers' Training Corps	SDI	Strategic Defense Initiative
RPP	Representative Payee Program	S.D. Me.	Southern District, Maine
R.S.	Revised Statutes	S.D.N.Y.	Southern District, New York
RTC	Resolution Trust Corp.		
RUDs	Reservations, understandings, and declarations	SDS	Students for a Democratic Society
		S.E.	South Eastern Reporter
Ryan White CARE Act	Ryan White Comprehensive AIDS Research Emergency Act of 1990	S.E. 2d	South Eastern Reporter, Second Series
		SEA	Science and Education Administration
SAC	Strategic Air Command	SEATO	Southeast Asia Treaty Organization
SACB	Subversive Activities Control Board	SEC	Securities and Exchange Commission
SADD	Students against Drunk Driving	Sec.	Section
SAF	Student Activities Fund	SEEK	Search for Elevation, Education and Knowledge
SAIF	Savings Association Insurance Fund	SEOO	State Economic Opportunity Office
SALT	Strategic Arms Limitation Talks	SEP	Simplified employee pension plan
SALT I	Strategic Arms Limitation Talks of 1969–72	Ser.	Series
		Sess.	Session
SALT II	Strategic Arms Limitation Talks of 1979	SGLI	Servicemen's Group Life Insurance
SAMHSA	Substance Abuse and Mental Health Services Administration	SIP	State implementation plan
		SLA	Symbionese Liberation Army

SLAPPs	Strategic Lawsuits Against Public Participation	TNT	Trinitrotoluene
SLBM	Submarine-launched ballistic missile	TOP	Targeted Outreach Program
SNCC	Student Nonviolent Coordinating Committee	TPUS	Transportation and Public Utilities Service
So.	Southern Reporter	TQM	Total Quality Management
So. 2d	Southern Reporter, Second Series	Tripartite Claims Comm., Decs. and Ops.	Tripartite Claims Commission (United States, Austria, and Hungary), Decisions and Opinions
SPA	Software Publisher's Association		
Spec. Sess.	Special Session		
SPLC	Southern Poverty Law Center	TRI-TAC	Joint Tactical Communications
SRA	Sentencing Reform Act of 1984	TRO	Temporary restraining order
SS	*Schutzstaffel* (German, "Protection Echelon")	TS	Treaty Series, United States
SSA	Social Security Administration	TSCA	Toxic Substance Control Act
SSI	Supplemental Security Income	TSDs	Transporters, storers, and disposers
START I	Strategic Arms Reduction Treaty of 1991	TSU	Texas Southern University
START II	Strategic Arms Reduction Treaty of 1993	TTBT	Threshold Test Ban Treaty
Stat.	United States Statutes at Large	TV	Television
STS	Space Transportation Systems	TVA	Tennessee Valley Authority
St. Tr.	State Trials, English	TWA	Trans World Airlines
STURAA	Surface Transportation and Uniform Relocation Assistance Act of 1987	UAW	United Auto Workers; United Automobile, Aerospace, and Agricultural Implements Workers of America
Sup. Ct. of Justice, Mexico	Supreme Court of Justice, Mexico	U.C.C.	Uniform Commercial Code; Universal Copyright Convention
Supp.	Supplement		
S.W.	South Western Reporter		
S.W. 2d	South Western Reporter, Second Series	U.C.C.C.	Uniform Consumer Credit Code
SWAPO	South-West Africa People's Organization	UCCJA	Uniform Child Custody Jurisdiction Act
SWAT	Special Weapons and Tactics	UCMJ	Uniform Code of Military Justice
SWP	Socialist Workers Party	UCPP	Urban Crime Prevention Program
TDP	Trade and Development Program	UCS	United Counseling Service
Tex. Sup.	Texas Supreme Court Reports	UDC	United Daughters of the Confederacy
THAAD	Theater High-Altitude Area Defense System	UFW	United Farm Workers
THC	Tetrahydrocannabinol	UHF	Ultrahigh frequency
TI	Tobacco Institute	UIFSA	Uniform Interstate Family Support Act
TIA	Trust Indenture Act of 1939	UIS	Unemployment Insurance Service
TIAS	Treaties and Other International Acts Series (United States)	UMDA	Uniform Marriage and Divorce Act

UMTA	Urban Mass Transportation Administration	USCMA	United States Court of Military Appeals
U.N.	United Nations	USDA	U.S. Department of Agriculture
UNCITRAL	United Nations Commission on International Trade Law	USES	United States Employment Service
UNCTAD	United Nations Conference on Trade and Development	USFA	United States Fire Administration
		USFS	U.S. Forest Service
UN Doc.	United Nations Documents	USGA	United States Golf Association
UNDP	United Nations Development Program	USICA	International Communication Agency, United States
UNEF	United Nations Emergency Force	USMS	U.S. Marshals Service
		USOC	U.S. Olympic Committee
UNESCO	United Nations Educational, Scientific, and Cultural Organization	USSC	U.S. Sentencing Commission
UNICEF	United Nations Children's Fund (formerly United Nations International Children's Emergency Fund)	USSG	United States Sentencing Guidelines
		U.S.S.R.	Union of Soviet Socialist Republics
UNIDO	United Nations Industrial and Development Organization	UST	United States Treaties
		USTS	United States Travel Service
Unif. L. Ann.	Uniform Laws Annotated	v.	*Versus*
UN Repts. Intl. Arb. Awards	United Nations Reports of International Arbitral Awards	VA	Department of Veterans Affairs
		VAR	Veterans Affairs and Rehabilitation Commission
UNTS	United Nations Treaty Series	VAWA	Violence against Women Act
UPI	United Press International	VFW	Veterans of Foreign Wars
URESA	Uniform Reciprocal Enforcement of Support Act	VGLI	Veterans Group Life Insurance
		Vict.	Queen Victoria (Great Britain)
U.S.	United States	VIN	Vehicle identification number
U.S.A.	United States of America		
USAF	United States Air Force	VISTA	Volunteers in Service to America
USA PATRIOT Act	Uniting and Strengthening America by Providing Appropriate Tools Required to Intercept and Obstruct Terrorism Act	VJRA	Veterans Judicial Review Act of 1988
		V.L.A.	Volunteer Lawyers for the Arts
		VMI	Virginia Military Institute
U.S. App. D.C.	United States Court of Appeals for the District of Columbia	VMLI	Veterans Mortgage Life Insurance
U.S.C.	United States Code; University of Southern California	VOCAL	Victims of Child Abuse Laws
		VRA	Voting Rights Act
U.S.C.A.	United States Code Annotated	WAC	Women's Army Corps
		Wall.	Wallace's United States Supreme Court Reports
U.S.C.C.A.N.	United States Code Congressional and Administrative News	Wash. 2d	Washington Reports, Second Series

WAVES	Women Accepted for Volunteer Service	WIC	Women, Infants, and Children program
WCTU	Women's Christian Temperance Union	Will. and Mar.	King William and Queen Mary (Great Britain)
W.D. Wash.	Western District, Washington	WIN	WESTLAW Is Natural; Whip Inflation Now; Work Incentive Program
W.D. Wis.	Western District, Wisconsin		
WEAL	*West's Encyclopedia of American Law,* Women's Equity Action League	WIPO	World Intellectual Property Organization
		WIU	Workers' Industrial Union
Wend.	Wendell's New York Reports	W.L.R.	Weekly Law Reports, England
WFSE	Washington Federation of State Employees	WPA	Works Progress Administration
Wheat.	Wheaton's United States Supreme Court Reports	WPPDA	Welfare and Pension Plans Disclosure Act
Wheel. Cr. Cases	Wheeler's New York Criminal Cases	WTO	World Trade Organization
WHISPER	Women Hurt in Systems of Prostitution Engaged in Revolt	WWI	World War I
		WWII	World War II
Whiteman	Marjorie Millace Whiteman, *Digest of International Law,* 15 vols. (1963–73)	Yates Sel. Cas.	Yates's New York Select Cases
		YMCA	Young Men's Christian Association
WHO	World Health Organization	YWCA	Young Women's Christian Association